TUDOR POETRY AND PROSE

Tudor
Poetry and Prose

SELECTED FROM EARLY EDITIONS AND
MANUSCRIPTS AND EDITED BY

J. William Hebel

LATE PROFESSOR OF ENGLISH
CORNELL UNIVERSITY

Hoyt H. Hudson

LATE PROFESSOR OF ENGLISH
STANFORD UNIVERSITY

Francis R. Johnson

PROFESSOR OF ENGLISH
STANFORD UNIVERSITY

A. Wigfall Green

PROFESSOR OF ENGLISH
UNIVERSITY OF MISSISSIPPI

Robert Hoopes

ASSISTANT PROFESSOR OF ENGLISH
STANFORD UNIVERSITY

APPLETON-CENTURY-CROFTS, Inc. New York

PRINTED IN THE UNITED STATES OF AMERICA

E 42885

PREFACE

Tudor Poetry and Prose is the result of bringing together in a single volume the material on sixteenth-century English writers that was included in two books already published: (1) Hebel and Hudson's *Poetry of the English Renaissance*, first issued by F. S. Crofts and Co. in 1929; and (2) Hebel, Hudson, Johnson, and Green's *Prose of the English Renaissance* (primarily the work of Professor Johnson), issued by Appleton-Century-Crofts, Inc. in 1952. The section of supplementary notes to the *Poetry* part of this volume, recording the principal modern editions and works of critical commentary that have appeared since 1929 was prepared by Professor Hoopes and checked by Professor Johnson.

In this combined volume, the relevant pages of the two antecedent volumes have not been reset; instead corrections and additions have been recorded in the section of supplementary notes, with the following exceptions:

(1) The text of Sir Thomas Wyatt's poems (pp. 13–27) has been revised by using the manuscripts more extensively than was done in 1929; for many of Wyatt's poems in which the text was previously based on Tottel's *Songs and Sonnets*, we have felt that a manuscript version (usually that of *Egerton Ms. 2711*) was sufficiently superior to require rejecting the printed volume as our copy text. The introduction and notes to Wyatt have also been revised.

(2) The scholarly work on Gascoigne since 1929 has caused the original introduction and notes for that writer to require such extensive revision that it has been simpler to rewrite it throughout.

This volume necessarily follows the principles of selection and of editorial policy that were set forth and explained in the prefaces to the two antecedent volumes. For the benefit of the reader we repeat here the most important of these:

1. In order that we might have sufficient space for the inclusion of a number of long poems, we have omitted Spenser and Shakespeare. We have been willing to do so because we believe all readers and students desire to have complete editions of these poets.

2. Our text is taken from original editions and manuscripts; if, in our opinion, a second or later edition more nearly represents the author's final intention, we have followed that edition in preference to

v

the first. The edition or manuscript used is always indicated at the beginning of the selection; the reasons for our choice of basic text is explained in the Introduction and Notes at the end of the volume.

3. With reluctance we have modernized the spelling. Although the original spelling, often the product of the printer's caprice or necessity, cannot be taken, in most cases, to represent the author's intent, yet some flavor departs when the Renaissance exuberance is curbed by standardization even in such a detail. In modernizing we had in mind the reader who is not a specialist and who may not be of antiquarian tastes. For the further convenience of the modern reader we have punctuated the text in accordance with the logical pointing of our day. Frequently the original punctuation has left the meaning ambiguous; we have been forced to settle upon the interpretation which seemed to us closest to the author's meaning. Exceptions to modernization of spelling will be found where rhythm or rhyme demands the original form of a word. When the suffix *ed* is to be pronounced as a syllable, we have marked it with a diaeresis except in the case of words, such as *yielded,* where the pronunciation is unmistakable. We have also indicated by a diaeresis, the dissyllabic *ion* where necessary for rhyme. We have sometimes indicated accentuation which varies from modern usage. Wherever necessary for rhythm both in the poetry and in the prose, we have retained the elision of the text, marking it with an apostrophe.

4. Our principle has been to include whole poems; but in order to represent such works as Surrey's Virgil, Warner's *Albion's England,* Daniel's *Musophilus,* Drayton's *Poly-Olbion,* and Chapman's *Homer,* we have given unified extracts. All omissions are indicated. By the saving of space so effected we have been able to give complete such notable longer poems as Sackville's *Induction,* Marlowe's *Hero and Leander,* Davies's *Orchestra,* and Drayton's *Nymphidia.* In the prose section, also, we have so far as possible included entire works, or unified major sections of works, at the sacrifice of the number of authors that could be represented. Wherever we have omitted any part of the original, the fact of this omission is clearly indicated—by hiatus periods for those of a page or less, and by asterisks for those of two pages or more. In the notes we have usually recorded the subjects discussed in the longer of the omitted passages so that the student may have a clear idea of the structure of the work as a whole.

5. We have supplied an introduction and notes to each author. These will be found at the end of the volume, so that the reader who desires to avoid any interruption need not be disturbed by them. The introductions give the minimum of biographical information necessary to the understanding of the writings; anecdotes which throw light upon the

character of the subject have been given preference over a recital of
dates and events. Critical comment has been directed toward showing a
given author's place with relation to the general course of Tudor-Stuart
poetry and prose. To each introduction we have appended a selected
bibliography of the best modern editions and critical comment, and a
statement of the location of the exemplar used as basic text. In order
fully to identify the edition used by us, we have given in parentheses
after the title the entry-number of the Bibliographical Society's *Short-
Title Catalogue . . . of English Books, 1475–1640,* compiled by Pollard and Redgrave.

6. In preparing the notes we have not thought it necessary to re-
place the desk dictionary; nor have we wished to rob the student of
the pleasure of finding for himself echoes of one poet in another or borrowings from well-known classics. Words and meanings of words now
unfamiliar but common in the sixteenth and seventeenth centuries we
have annotated once or twice, upon their first appearances in the volume.

7. Our Table of Contents for the Poetry section is by authors only. In
the Index at the end of the volume the authors, titles, and first lines
of all the poems are given in alphabetical arrangement. Inasmuch as our
Table of Contents for the Prose section is analytical, we have not attempted to supply an index to the Prose.

Determining which authors should be included in this volume of
Tudor Poetry and Prose has raised many questions, particularly when
considering writers whose literary careers began in the reign of Elizabeth and continued through the reign of King James. As long as we
retained the policy of representing the full range of the work of any
man included, to eliminate whatever he wrote or published after 1603
was a course we could not logically follow; it would lead only to confusion in any estimate of the quality of the poetry and prose of such
writers as Ralegh, Drayton, Bacon, Donne and even of Ben Jonson.
Consequently we have considered as a 'Tudor-Stuart' poet or prose
writer anyone who had written some of his important works before the
year 1603. That the greater part of his literary activity belonged to
the early seventeenth century we have not regarded as sufficient cause
to bar him from this anthology.

FRANCIS R. JOHNSON
ROBERT HOOPES

TABLE OF CONTENTS

TUDOR POETRY

TUDOR POETRY

JOHN SKELTON

The Introduction and Notes are at pages 1182 and 1271

FROM *Pithy, Pleasant, and Profitable Works*, 1568

Philip Sparrow

Pla ce bo,
Who is there? Who?
Di le xi,
Dame Margery.
Fa, re, mi, mi,
Wherefore and why, why?
For the soul of Philip Sparrow,
That was late slain at Carow
Among the Nunnës Blake,
For that sweet soul's sake   10
And for all sparrows' souls
Set in our beadrolls,
Pater noster qui
With an *Ave Mari*,
And with the corner of a Creed,
The more shall be your meed.

When I remember again
How my Philip was slain,
Never half the pain
Was between you twain,   20
Pyramus and Thisbe,
As then befell to me:
I wept and I wailed,
The tearës down hailed,—
But nothing it availed
To call Philip again,
Whom Gib, our cat, hath slain.

Gib, I say, our cat
Worrowëd her on that
Which I loved best.   30
It cannot be expressed—
My sorrowful heaviness,
But all without redress;

For within that stound,
Half slumb'ring, in a swound,
I fell down to the ground.
Unneth I cast mine eyes
Toward the cloudy skies,
But when I did behold
My sparrow dead and cold,   40
No creature but that wold
Have rued upon me,
To behold and see
What heaviness did me pang;
Wherewith my hands I wrang,
That my sinews cracked
As though I had been racked;
So pained and so strained
That no life well-nigh remained.

I sighed and I sobbed   50
For that I was robbed
Of my sparrow's life.
O maiden, widow, and wife,
Of what estate ye be,
Of high or low degree,
Great sorrow then ye might see,
And learn to weep at me!
Such pains did me fret
That mine heart did beat,
My visage pale and dead,   60
Wan and blue as lead,
The pangs of hateful death
Well-nigh stopped my breath.
Heu, heu, me,
That I am woe for thee!
*Ad Dominum, cum tribularer,
    clamavi:*
Of God nothing else crave I

3

But Philip's soul to keep
From the marees deep
Of Acheronte's well,   70
That is a flood of hell,
And from the great Pluto,
The prince of endless woe;
And from foul Alecto
With visage black and blo;
And from Medusa, that mare,
That like a fiend doth stare;
And from Megera's adders,
For ruffling of Philip's feathers,
And from her fiery sparklings   80
For burning of his wings;
And from the smokës sour
Of Proserpina's bower;
And from the dennës dark
Where Cerberus doth bark,
Whom Theseus did affray,
Whom Hercules did outray,
As famous poets say;
From that hell-hound
That lieth in chainës bound,   90
With ghastly headës three,
To Jupiter pray we
That Philip preserved may be!
Amen, say ye with me!
    Do mi nus,
Help now, sweet Jesus!

.   .   .   .   .

It was so pretty a fool,
It would sit on a stool
And learned after my school
For to keep his cut,   100
With, Philip, keep your cut!
    It had a velvet cap,
And would sit upon my lap
And seek after small worms
And sometime white bread
        crumbs;
And many times and oft
Between my brestës soft
It would lie and rest;
It was propre and prest.
    Sometime he would gasp   110

When he saw a wasp;
A fly or a gnat—
He would fly at that;
And prettily he would pant
When he saw an ant;
Lord, how he would pry
After the butterfly!
Lord, how he would hop
After the gressop!
And when I said, Phip! Phip!   120
Then he would leap and skip,
And take me by the lip.
Alas, it will me slo
That Philip is gone me fro!
    Si in i qui ta tes,
Alas, I was evil at ease!
    De pro fun dis cla ma vi,
When I saw my sparrow die!

.   .   .   .   .

    That vengeance I ask and cry,
By way of exclamation,   130
On all the whole nation
Of cattës wild and tame:
God send them sorrow and shame!
That cat specially
That slew so cruelly
My little pretty sparrow
That I brought up at Carow.
    O cat of churlish kind,
The fiend was in thy mind
When thou my bird un-
        twined,—   140
I would thou hadst been blind!
The leopardës savage,
The lions in their rage,
Might catch thee in their paws
And gnaw thee in their jaws!
These serpents of Lybany
Might sting thee venomously!
The dragons with their tongues
Might poison thy liver and lungs!
The mantycors of the moun-
        tains   150
Might feed them on thy brains!
    Melanchates, that hound

That plucked Acteon to the
    ground,
Gave him his mortal wound,
Changed to a deer;
The story doth appear
Was changed to an hart:
So thou, foul cat that thou art,
The self-same hound
Might thee confound   160
That his own lord bote,
Might bite asunder thy throat!
    Of Ind the greedy gripes
Might tear out all thy tripes!
Of Arcady the bears
Might pluck away thine ears!
The wild wolf Lycaon
Bite asunder thy back-bone!
Of Ætna the brenning hill
That day and night brenneth
    still,   170
Set in thy tail a blaze,
That all the world may gaze
And wonder upon thee,
From Ocean, the great sea,
Unto the isles of Orchady;
From Tilbury ferry
To the plain of Salisbury!
So traitorously my bird to kill,
That never ought thee evil will!
    Was never bird in cage   180
More gentle of corage
In doing his homage
Unto his soveraine.
Alas, I say again,
Death hath departed us twain!
The false cat hath thee slain,—
Farewell, Philip, adieu!
Our Lord thy soul rescue!
Farewell without restore,
Farewell for evermore!   190

.   .   .   .   .

Colin Clout

What can it avail
To drive forth a snail,
Or to make a sail

Of an herring's tail?
To rhyme or to rail,
To write or to indite,
Either for delight
Or else for despite?
Or books to compile
Of divers manner style,   10
Vice to revile
And sin to exile?
To teach or to preach
As reason will reach?
Say this, and say that:
His head is so fat
He wotteth never what
Nor whereof he speaketh;
He crieth and he creaketh,
He prieth and he peeketh,   20
He chides and he chatters,
He prates and he patters,
He clitters and he clatters,
He meddles and he smatters,
He glozes and he flatters!
Or if he speak plain,
Then he lacketh brain,
He is but a fool;
Let him go to school.
A three-footed stool!   30
That he may down sit,
For he lacketh wit!
And if that he hit
The nail on the head,
It standeth in no stead;
The devil, they say, is dead,
The devil is dead.
    It may well so be,
Or else they would see
Otherwise, and flee   40
From worldly vanity,
And foul covetousness
And other wretchedness,
Fickle falseness,
Variableness
With unstableness.
    And if ye stand in doubt
Who brought this rhyme about,
My name is Colin Clout.

I purpose to shake out   50
All my cunning bag
Like a clerkly hag;
For though my rhyme be ragged,
Tattered and jagged,
Rudely rain-beaten,
Rusty and moth-eaten,
If ye take well therewith
It hath in it some pith.
For, as far as I can see,
It is wrong with each degree: 60
For the temporalty
Accuseth the spiritualty;
The spiritual again
Doth grudge and complain
Upon temporal men;
Thus each of other blother,
The t'one against the t'other,—
Alas, they make me shudder!
For in hudder-mudder
The church is put in faute;   70
The prelates been so haut,
They say, and look so high
As though they would fly
Above the starry sky.
      Laymen say indeed
How they take no heed
Their seely sheep to feed,
But pluck away and pull
The fleeces of their wool;
Unnethes they leave a lock   80
Of wool amongst their flock;
And as for their cunning,
A glomming and a mumming,
And make thereof a jape;
They gasp and they gape
All to have promotion,
There is their whole devotion,
With money, if it will hap,
To catch the forkèd cap;
Forsooth, they are too lewd   90
To say so,—all beshrewed!

.   .

      Thus I, Colin Clout,
As I go about,

And wand'ring as I walk,
I hear the people talk.
Men say, for silver and gold
Mitres are bought and sold;
There shall no clergy appose
A mitre nor a crose,
But a full purse;   100
A straw for Goddës curse!
What are they the worse?
For a simoniac
Is but a harmoniac;
And no more ye make
Of simony, men say,
But a child's play.
      Over this, the foresaid lay
Report how the Pope may
A holy anker call   110
Out of the stony wall
And him a bishop make,
If he on him dare take
To keep so hard a rule—
To ride upon a mule
With gold all betrapped,
In purple and pall belapped;
Some hatted and some capped,
Richëly bewrapped,
God wot to their great pains,   120
In rotchets of fine Raynes,
White as morrow's milk;
Their tabards of fine silk,
Their stirrups of mixed gold be-
            garred;
There may no cost be spared;
Their mulës gold doth eat,
Their neighbors die for meat.
      What care they though Gil
            sweat,
Or Jack of the Noke?
The poor people they yoke   130
With summons and citations
And excommunications,
About churches and market;
The bishop on his carpet
At home full soft doth sit.
This is a fearful fit,
To hear the people jangle,

How warily they wrangle,—
Alas, why do ye not handle
And them all mangle?   140
Full falsely on you they lie,
And shamefully you ascry,
And say as untruly
As the butterfly
A man might say in mock
Were the weathercock
Of the steeple of Poules;
And thus they hurt their souls
In slandering you, for truth:
Alas, it is great ruth!   150

. . . . . .

To Mistress Isabel Pennell

By Saint Mary, my lady,
Your mammy and your dady
Brought forth a goodly baby!
   My maiden Isabel,
Reflaring rosabell,
The flagrant camamell,
   The ruddy rosary,
The sovereign rosemary,
The pretty strawberry,
   The columbine, the nepte,   10
The jeloffer well set,
The proper violet;
   Ennewëd your colowre
Is like the daisy flower
After the April shower;
   Star of the morrow gray,
The blossom on the spray,
The freshest flower of May:
   Maidenly demure,
Of womanhood the lure;   20
Wherefore I make you sure
   It were an heavenly health,
It were an endless wealth,
A life for God himself,
   To hear this nightingale

Among the birdës smale
Warbeling in the vale,—
Dug, dug, jug, jug,
Good year and good luck,   29
With chuck, chuck, chuck, chuck!

To Mistress Margaret Hussey

Merry Margaret,
As midsummer flower,
Gentil as falcon
Or hawk of the tower;
   With solace and gladness,
Much mirth and no madness,
All good and no badness,
So joyously,
So maidenly,
So womanly   10
Her demeaning
In every thing,—
Far, far passing
That I can endite
Or suffice to write
Of merry Margaret,
As midsummer flower,
Gentil as falcon
Or hawk of the tower.
   As patient and as still   20
And as full of good will
As fair Isiphill,
Coliander,
Sweet pomander,
Good Cassaunder;
Steadfast of thought,
Well made, well wrought;
Far may be sought
Erst that ye can find
So curteise, so kind   30
As merry Margaret,
This midsummer flower,
Gentil as falcon
Or hawk of the tower.

A prayer to the Father of heaven

O radiant luminary of light interminable,
Celestial Father, potential God of might,

Of heaven and earth O Lord incomparable,
  Of all perfections the essential most perfite!
O maker of mankind, that formëd day and night,
Whose power imperial comprehendeth every place:
  Mine heart, my mind, my thought, my whole delight
Is after this life to see thy glorious face.

Whose magnificence is incomprehensible,
  All arguments of reason which far doth exceed,   10
Whose deity doubtless is indivisible,
  From whom all goodness and virtue doth proceed;
  Of thy support all creätures have need:
Assist me, good Lord, and grant me of thy grace
  To live to thy pleasure in word, thought, and deed,
And after this life to see thy glorious face.

HENRY VIII

The Introduction and Notes are at page 1184

FROM *Additional Ms.* 31922

[*Pastime with good company*]

Pastime with good company
I love, and shall until I die.
Grutch who lust, but none deny,
So God be pleased, thus live will I.
For my pastance,
Hunt, sing, and dance,
My heart is set;
All goodly sport
For my comfort,
Who shall me let?   10

Youth must have some dalliance,
Of good or ill some pastance;
Company methinks then best,
All thoughts and fancies to digest.
For idleness is chief mistress
Of vices all; then who can say
But mirth and play
Is best of all?

Company with honesty
Is virtue, vices to flee;   20
Company is good and ill,
But every man hath his free will.
The best ensue,
The worst eschew;
My mind shall be,—
Virtue to use,
Vice to refuse,
Thus shall I use me.

[*Whereto should I express*]

Whereto should I express
My inward heaviness?
No mirth can make me fain
Till that we meet again.

Do 'way, dear heart, not so!
Let no thought you dismay;
Though ye now part me fro,
We shall meet when we may.

When I remember me
Of your most gentil mind,   10
It may in no wise agree
That I should be unkind.

The daisy delectable,
The violet wan and blo—
Ye are not variable,
I love you and no mo.

I make you fast and sure;
It is to me great pain
Thus longë to endure
Till that we meet again.   20

[Whoso that will]

Whoso that will for gracë sue
His intent must needs be true,
And lovë her in heart and deed,
Else it were pity that he should
    speed.
Many one saith that love is ill,
But those be they which can no
    skill.

Or else because they may not ob-
    tain,
They would that other should it
    disdain.
But love is a thing given by God,
In that therefore can be none
    odd;   10
But perfect indeed and between
    two,
Wherefore then should we it
    eschew?

[Green groweth the holly]

Green groweth the holly, so doth
        the ivy.
Though winter blasts blow never
        so high,
Green groweth the holly.

As the holly groweth green
    And never changeth hue,
So I am, and ever hath been,
    Unto my lady true.
        Green groweth . . . etc.

As the holly groweth green,
    With ivy all alone,   10
When flowerys cannot be seen
    And green-wood leaves be gone,
        ut supra

Now unto my lady
    Promise to her I make:
From all other only
    To her I me betake.
        ut supra

Adieu, mine own lady,
    Adieu, my spec''ial,   20
Who hath my heart truly,
    Be sure, and ever shall.

Green groweth the holly, so doth
        the ivy.
Though winter blasts blow never
        so high,
Green groweth the holly.

SIR THOMAS MORE

The Introduction and Notes are at pages 1185 and 1272

FROM Works, 1557

Childhood

I am called Childhood: in play is all my mind,
To cast a quoit, a cockstele, and a ball.

A top can I set, and drive it in his kind;
But would to God these hateful bookës all
Were in a fire brent to powder small!
Then might I lead my life always in play,
Which life God send me to mine ending day.

Manhood

Manhood I am: therefore I me delight
To hunt and hawk, to nourish up and feed
The greyhound to the course, the hawk to the flight,
And to bestride a good and lusty steed.
These things become a very man indeed.
Yet thinketh this boy his peevish game swetter,
But what! no force, his reason is no better.

Age

Old Age am I, with lockës thin and hoar:
Of our short life the last and best part,
Wise and discreet; the public weal therefore
I help to rule, to my labor and smart.
Therefore, Cupid, withdraw thy fiery dart,
Chargeable matters shall of love oppress
Thy childish game and idle business.

Two short ballettes . . .

Made for his pastime while he was prisoner in the Tower of London

Lewis, the lost lover

Eye-flattering fortune, look thou never so fair,
Or never so pleasantly begin to smile,
As though thou wouldst my ruin all repair;
During my life thou shalt me not beguile.
Trust shall I God, to enter in a while
His haven of heaven, sure and uniform;
Ever after thy calm look I for a storm.

Davy, the dicer

Long was I, Lady Luck, your serving-man,
And now have lost again all that I gat;
Wherefore, when I think on you now and than
And in my mind remember this and that,
Ye may not blame me though I beshrew your cat.
But, in faith, I bless you again, a thousand times,
For lending me now some leisure to make rhymes.

JOHN HEYWOOD

The Introduction and Notes are at pages 1185 and 1272

FROM RICHARD TOTTEL's *Songs and Sonnets*, 1557

A praise of his lady

Give place, you ladies, and be
    gone,
Boast not yourselves at all,
For here at hand approacheth one
    Whose face will stain you all.
    The virtue of her lively looks
Excels the precious stone,
I wish to have none other books
    To read or look upon!
    In each of her two crystal eyes
Smileth a naked boy;   10
It would you all in heart suffice
    To see that lamp of joy.
    I think nature hath lost the
    mould
Where she her shape did take,
Or else I doubt if nature could
    So fair a creature make.
    She may be well compared
Unto the phœnix kind,
Whose like was never seen nor
    heard,
That any man can find.   20
    In life she is Diana chast,
In truth, Penelope;
In word and eke in deed stead-
    fast—
What will you more we say?
    If all the world were sought so
    far,
Who could find such a wight?

Her beauty twinkleth like a star
    Within the frosty night.
    Her rosial color comes and goes
With such a comely grace,   30
More redier too than doth the
    rose
    Within her lively face.
    At Bacchus' feast none shall
    her meet,
Ne at no wanton play;
Nor gazing in an open street
    Nor gadding as a stray.
    The modest mirth that she doth
    use
Is mixed with shamefastness.
All vice she doth wholly refuse,
    And hateth idleness.   40
    O Lord, it is a world to see
How virtue can repair
And deck her in such honesty,
    Whom nature made so fair.
    Truly, she doth as far exceed
Our women nowadays
As doth the gillyflower a weed,
    And more, a thousand ways.
    How might I do to get a graff
Of this unspotted tree,   50
For all the rest are plain but chaff,
    Which seem good corn to be.
    This gift alone I shall her give
When death doth what he can:
Her honest fame shall ever live
    Within the mouth of man.

FROM *Works*, 1562

Jack and his father

Jack (quoth his father) how shall I ease take?
If I stand, my legs ache; and if I kneel

My knees ache; if I go, then my feet ache;
If I lie, my back ach'th; if I sit, I feel
My hips ache; and lean I never so weel,
My elbows ache. Sir (quoth Jack) pain to exile,
Since all these ease not, best ye hang awhile.

Of loving a dog

Love me, love my dog: by love to agree
I love thy dog as well as I love thee.

Of a sheep's eye

He cast a sheep's eye at her: a strange eye-spread
To see a sheep's eye look out of a calf's head.

Of enough and a feast

As good enough as a feast: yea, God save it!
Enough were even as good if we might have it.

Of late and never

Better late than never: yea, mate,
But as good never as too late.

Of a cat's look

A cat may look on a king: and what of that?
When a cat so looketh, a cat is but a cat.

Of Heywood

Art thou Heywood, with the mad merry wit?
Yea, forsooth, master! that same is even hit.
Art thou Heywood that applieth mirth more than thrift?
Yea, sir, I take merry mirth a golden gift.
Art thou Heywood that hath made many mad plays?
Yea, many plays; few good works in all my days.
Art thou Heywood that hath made men merry long?
Yea, and will, if I be made merry among.
Art thou Heywood that would be made merry now?
Yea, sir, help me to it now, I beseech yow.

SIR THOMAS WYATT

The Introduction and Notes are at page 1186

FROM *Egerton Ms.* 2711

[*The lover compareth his state to a ship in perilous storm tossed on the sea*]

My galley chargëd with forgetfulness
Thorrough sharp seas, in winter nights, doth pass
'Tween rock and rock; and eke mine enemy, alas,
That is my lord, steereth with cruelness;
And every oar a thought in readiness,
As though that death were light in such a case.
An endless wind doth tear the sail apace,
Of forcëd sighs and trusty fearfulness;
A rain of tears, a cloud of dark disdain,
Have done the wearied cords great hinderance;   10
Wreathëd with error and eke with ignorance,
The stars be hid that led me to this pain;
Drownëd is reason, that should me consort,
And I remain despairing of the port.

[*The lover's life compared to the Alps*]

Like to these unmeasurable mountains,
Is my painful life, the burden of ire,
For of great height be they, and high is my desire,
And I of tears, and they be full of fountains;
Under craggy rocks they have full barren plains,
Hard thoughts in me my woeful mind doth tire;
Small fruit and many leaves their toppës do attire,
Small effect with great trust in me remains.
The boistous windës oft their high boughs do blast,
Hot sighs from me continually be shed;   10
Cattle in them, and in me love is fed;
Immovable am I, and they are full steadfast.
Of the restless birds they have the tune and note,
And I always plaints that pass thorough my throat.

[*Description of the contrarious passions in a lover*]

I find no peace, and all my war is done;
I fear and hope; I burn, and freeze like ice;

I fly above the wind, yet can I not arise;
And nought I have, and all the world I season.
That looseth nor locketh holdeth me in prison,
And holdeth me not, yet can I 'scape no wise;
Nor letteth me live, nor die, at my devise,
And yet of death it giveth none occasion.
Without eyen, I see; and without tongue, I plain;
I desire to perish, and yet I askë health;
I love another, and thus I hate myself;
I feed me in sorrow, and laugh in all my pain.
Likewise displeaseth me both death and life,
And my delight is causer of this strife.

[*The lover for shamefastness hideth his desire within his faithful heart*]

The long love that in my thought doth harbor,
And in mine heart doth keep his residence,
Into my face presseth with bold pretense
And therein campeth, spreading his banner.
She that me learneth to love and suffer
And wills that my trust and lust's negligence
Be reined by reason, shame, and reverence,
With his hardiness taketh displeasure.
Wherewithall unto the heart's forest he fleeth,
Leaving his enterprise with pain and cry,
And there him hideth, and not appeareth:
What may I do when my master feareth
But in the field with him to live and die?
For good is the life ending faithfully.

[*A renouncing of love*]

Farewell, love, and all thy laws for ever,
Thy baited hooks shall tangle me no more;
Senec and Plato call me from thy lore
To perfect wealth, my wit for to endeavor;
In blindë error when I did perséver,
Thy sharp repulse that pricketh aye so sore
Hath taught me to set in trifles no store,
And scape forth, since liberty is lever.
Therefore, farewell! Go trouble younger hearts,
And in me claim no more authority;
With idle youth go use thy property,
And thereon spend thy many brittle darts.
For hitherto though I have lost all my time,
Me lusteth no longer rotten boughs to climb.

[*Whoso list to hunt*]

Whoso list to hunt, I know where is an hind,
But as for me—alas, I may no more.
The vain travail hath wearied me so sore,
I am of them that farthest cometh behind.
Yet may I, by no means, my wearied mind
Draw from the deer; but as she fleeth afore
Fainting I follow. I leave off therefore,
Since in a net I seek to hold the wind.
Who list her hunt, I put him out of doubt,
As well as I, may spend his time in vain.   10
And graven with diamonds in letters plain
There is written, her fair neck round about:
Noli me tangere, for Cæsar's I am,
And wild for to hold, though I seem tame.

FROM *Additional Ms.* 17492

[*Divers doth use*]

Divers doth use, as I have heard and know,
(When that to change their ladies do begin),
To mourn and wail, and never for to lin,
Hoping thereby to pease their painful woe.
And some there be, that when it chanceth so
That women change, and hate where love hath been,
They call them false, and think with words to win
The hearts of them which otherwhere doth grow.
But as for me, though that by chance indeed
Change hath outworn the favor that I had,   10
I will not wail, lament, nor yet be sad,
Nor call her false that falsely did me feed;
But let it pass, and think it is of kind
That often change doth please a woman's mind.

FROM RICHARD TOTTEL's *Songs and Sonnets*, 1557

Of his return from Spain

Tagus, farewell, that westward with thy streams
Turns up the grains of gold already tried;
For I with spur and sail go seek the Temes,
Gainward the sun, that showeth her wealthy pride;
And to the town that Brutus sought by dreams,
Like bended moon that leans her lusty side,

My king, my country, I seek, for whom I live—
O mighty Jove, the winds for this me give!

Of such as had forsaken him

Lux, my fair falcon, and thy fellows all,
How well pleasant it were, your liberty!
Ye not forsake me that fair might you fall;
But they that sometime liked my company
Like lice away from dead bodies they crawl—
Lo, what a proof in light adversity!
But ye, my birds, I swear by all your bells,
Ye be my friends, and very few else.

A description of such a one as he would love

A face that should content me wondrous well
Should not be fair, but lovely to behold,
Of lively look, all grief for to repel,
With right good grace, so would I that it should
Speak without word such words as none can tell;
The tress also should be of crispèd gold.
With wit, and these, perchance I might be tied,
And knit again with knot that should not slide.

That speaking or proffering brings alway speeding

Speak thou and speed, where will or power aught help'th,
Where power doth want, will must be won by wealth;
For need will speed where will works not his kind,
And gain, thy foes thy friends shall cause thee find:
For suit and gold—what do not they obtain?
Of good and bad the triers are these twain.

Description of a gun

Vulcan begat me; Minerva me taught;
Nature, my mother; craft nourished me year by year;
Three bodies are my food, my strength is in nought;
Anger, wrath, waste, and noise are my children dear:
Guess, friend, what I am and how I am wrought,
Monster of sea, or of land, or of elsewhere?
Know me, and use me, and I may thee defend,
And if I be thine enemy, I may thy life end.

FROM *Harleian Ms.* 78

[Wyatt being in prison, to Bryan]

Sighs are my food, drink are my tears;
Clinking of fetters such music would crave;

Stink and close air, away my life wears;
Innocency is all the hope I have.
Rain, wind, or weather I judge by mine ears;
Malice assaulted that righteousness should have.
Sure I am, Bryan, this wound shall heal again,
But yet, alas, the scar shall still remain.

From *Egerton Ms.* 2711

[*Of his love called Anna*]

What word is that, that changeth not
Though it be turned, and made in twain?
It is mine answer, God it wot,
And eke the causer of my pain.
A love rewardeth with disdain,
Yet is it loved—what would ye more?
It is my health, and eke my sore.

[*To a lady, to answer directly with yea or nay*]

Madam, withouten many words,
Once I am sure, ye will or no;
And if ye will, then leave your bordes,
And use your wit, and shew it so;
And with a beck ye shall me call.
And if of one that burneth alway
Ye have any pity at all,
Answer him fair, with yea or nay:
If it be yea, I shall be fain;
If it be nay, friends as before;   10
Ye shall another man obtain,
And I mine own, and yours no more.

From *Additional Ms.* 17492

[*The lover to his bed, with describing of his unquiet state*]

The restful place, reviver of my smart,
The labor's salve, increasing my sorrów,
The body's ease, and troubler of my heart,
Quieter of mind, and mine unquiet foe,
Forgetter of pain, remembering my woe,
The place of sleep wherein I do but wake,—
Besprent with tears, my bed, I thee forsake.
    The frost, the snow, may not redress my heat,
Nor yet no heat abate my fervent cold.
I know nothing to ease my painës meet;   10
Each care causeth increase by twenty fold,

Reviving cares upon my sorrows old;
Such overthwart affects they do me make,
Besprent with tears, my bed for to forsake.
Yet helpeth it not. I find no better ease
In bed, or out. This most causeth my pain,
Where most I seek how best that I may please,
My lost labor, alas, is all in vain.
Yet that I gave I cannot call again;
No place from me my grief away can take,   20
Wherefore with tears, my bed, I thee forsake.

FROM *Egerton Ms.* 2711

[*The lover showeth how he is forsaken of such as he
sometime enjoyed*]

They flee from me, that sometime did me seek,
With naked foot stalking in my chamber.
I have seen them gentle, tame, and meek,
That now are wild, and do not remember
That sometime they have put themselves in danger
To take bread at my hand; and now they range,
Busily seeking with a continual change.
Thanked be fortune it hath been otherwise,
Twenty times better; but once, in special,
In thin array, after a pleasant guise,   10
When her loose gown from her shoulders did fall,
And she me caught in her arms long and small;
Therewithal sweetly did me kiss
And softly said, 'Dear heart, how like you this?'
It was no dream; I lay broad waking.
But all is turned thorough my gentleness,
Into a strange fashion of forsaking;
And I have leave to go, of her goodëness,
And she also to use newfangleness.
But since that I so kindëly am served,
I would fain know what she hath deserved?

[*Help me to seek*]

Help me to seek—for I lost it there,
And if that ye have found it, ye that be here,
And seek to convey it secretly,
Handle it soft and treat it tenderly
Or else it will plain, and then appear.
But rather restore it mannerly,
Since that I do ask it thus honestly,
For to lese it, it sitteth me too near:
Help me to seek!

Alas, and is there no remedy? [10]
But have I thus lost it wilfully?
I wis it was a thing all too dear
To be bestowed, and wist not
    where:
It was mine heart! I pray you
    heartily
        Help me to seek.

FROM *Additional Ms.* 17492

[*Forget not yet*]

Forget not yet the tried intent
Of such a truth as I have meant,
My great travail, so gladly spent,
    Forget not yet.

Forget not yet when first began
The weary life ye know, since
    whan
The suit, the service none tell can,
    Forget not yet.

Forget not yet the great assays,
The cruel wrong, the scornful
    ways; [10]
The painful patience in denays,
    Forget not yet.

Forget not yet, forget not this,
How long ago hath been, and is,
The mind that never meant
    amiss,—
    Forget not yet.

Forget not, then, thine own ap-
    proved,
The which so long hath thee so
    loved,
Whose steadfast faith yet never
    moved,
    Forget not this. [20]

[*And wilt thou leave me
thus?*]

    And wilt thou leave me thus?
Say nay, say nay! For shame,

To save thee from the blame
Of all my grief and grame.
And wilt thou leave me thus?
Say nay, say nay.

    And wilt thou leave me thus,
That hath loved thee so long
In wealth and woe among?
And is thy heart so strong [10]
As for to leave me thus?
Say nay, say nay.

    And wilt thou leave me thus,
That hath given thee my heart,
Never for to depart
Neither for pain nor smart;
And wilt thou leave me thus?
Say nay, say nay.

    And wilt thou leave me thus,
And have no more pitý [20]
Of him that loveth thee?
Alas, thy cruelty!
And wilt thou leave me thus?
Say nay, say nay!

[*Blame not my lute*]

Blame not my lute, for he must
    sound
Of this or that as liketh me;
For lack of wit the lute is bound
To give such tunes as pleaseth
    me.
Though my songs be somewhat
    strange,
And speaks such words as touch
    thy change,
        Blame not my lute.

My lute, alas, doth not offend,
Though that perforce he must
    agree
To sound such tunes as I intend [10]
To sing to them that heareth me;
Then though my songs be some-
    what plain

And toucheth some that use to
    feign,
        Blame not my lute.

My lute and strings may not deny,
But as I strike they must obey;
Break not them, then, so wrong-
    fully,
But wreak thyself some wiser
    way;
And though the songs which I
    indite
Do quit thy change with right-
    ful spite,   20
        Blame not my lute.

Spite asketh spite, and changing
    change,
And falsèd faith must needs be
    known;
The fault so great, the case so
    strange,
Of right it must abroad be blown.
Then since that by thine own
    desart
My songs do tell how true thou
    art,
        Blame not my lute.

Blame but the self that hast mis-
    done
And well deservèd to have
    blame;   30
Charge thou thy way so evil be-
    gun
And then my lute shall sound
    that same;
But if till then my fingers play,
By thy desert, their wonted way,
        Blame not my lute.

Farewell, unknown, for though
    thou break
My strings in spite, with great dis-
    dain,
Yet have I found out for thy sake

Strings for to string my lute
    again.
And if perchance this foolish
    rhyme   40
Do make thee blush at any time,
        Blame not my lute.

[*Since you will needs*]

Since you will needs that I shall
    sing,
Take it in worth, such as I have,
Plenty of plaint, moan, and
    mourning
In deep despair and deadly pain,
Bootless for boot, crying to crave,
        To crave in vain.

Such hammers work within my
    head
That sound nought else unto my
    ears
But fast at board, and wake abed;
Such tune the temper to my song   10
To wail my wrong, that I want
    tears
        To wail my wrong.

Death and despair afore my face,
My days decays, my grief doth
    grow;
The cause thereof is in this place,
Whom cruelty doth still con-
    strain
For to rejoice, though it be woe
        To hear me plain.

A broken lute, untunèd strings
With such a song may well bear
    part,   20
That neither pleaseth him that
    sings
Nor them that hear, but her alone
That with her heart would strain
    my heart,
        To hear it groan.

If it grieve you to hear this same
That you do feel but in my voice,
Consider then what pleasant game
I do sustain in every part,
To cause me sing or to rejoice
      Within my heart. 30

[Tangled I was]

Tangled I was in love's snare,
Oppressed with pain, torment with
    care,
Of grief right sure, of joy full
    bare,
Clean in despair by cruelty,—
But ha! ha! ha! full well is me,
For I am now at liberty.

The woeful days so full of pain,
The weary night all spent in vain,
The labor lost for so small gain,
To write them all it will not
    be.   10
But ha! ha! ha! full well is me,
For I am now at liberty.

Everything that fair doth show,
When proof is made it proveth
    not so,
But turneth mirth to bitter woe;
Which in this case full well I see.
But ha! ha! ha! full well is me,
For I am now at liberty.

Too great desire was my guide
And wanton will went by my
    side;   20

Hope ruled still, and made me
    bide
Of love's craft th' extremity.
But ha! ha! ha! full well is me,
For I am now at liberty.

With feignëd words that were
    but wind
To long delays I was assigned;
Her wily looks my wits did blind;
Thus as she would I did agree.
But ha! ha! ha! full well is me,
For I am now at liberty.   30

Was never bird tangled in lime
That brake away in better time
Than I, that rotten boughs did
    climb,
And had no hurt, but scapëd free.
Now ha! ha! ha! full well is me,
For I am now at liberty.

[Hate whom ye list]

Hate whom ye list, for I care not,
Love whom ye list and spare not,
Do what ye list and dread not,
Think what ye list, I fear not,
For, as for me, I am not
But even as one that recks not
Whether ye hate or hate not;
For in your love I dote not,
Wherefore I pray you forget not,
But love whom ye list, for I care
    not.   10

From Richard Tottel's Songs and Sonnets, 1557

Of the mean and sure estate

Written to John Poins

My mother's maids when they do sew and spin,
They sing a song made of the fieldish mouse;
That forbecause her livelihood was but thin,
Would needs go see her townish sister's house.

She thought herself endured to grievous pain;
The stormy blasts her cave so sore did souse,
That when the furrows swimmëd with the rain,
She must lie cold and wet, in sorry plight.
And worse than that, bare meat there did remain
To comfort her when she her house had dight: 10
Sometime a barley corn, sometime a bean,
For which she labored hard both day and night
In harvest time, while she might go and glean.
And when her store was 'stroyëd with the flood,
Then wellaway, for she undone was clean.
Then was she fain to take instead of food
Sleep, if she might, her hunger to beguile.
My sister, quoth she, hath a living good,
And hence from me she dwelleth not a mile.
In cold and storm she lieth warm and dry   20
In bed of down, the dirt doth not defile
Her tender foot, she labors not as I;
Richly she feeds, and at the richman's cost,
And for her meat she needs not crave nor cry.
By sea, by land, of delicates the most
Her cater seeks, and spareth for no peril;
She feeds on boil meat, bake meat, and on roast,
And hath therefore no whit of charge nor travail.
And when she list, the liquor of the grape
Doth glad her heart, till that her belly swell.   30
And at this journey makes she but a jape;
So forth she goes, trusting of all this wealth
With her sister her part so for to shape
That if she might there keep herself in health,
To live a lady while her life doth last.
And to the door now is she come by stealth,
And with her foot anon she scrapes full fast.
T' other for fear durst not well scarce appear,
Of every noise so was the wretch aghast.
At last she askëd softly who was there.   40
And in her language as well as she could,
Peep, quoth the other, sister, I am here.
Peace, quoth the town mouse, why speakest thou so loud?
And by the hand she took her fair and well,
Welcome, quoth she, my sister, by the rood.
She feasted her that joy it was to tell
The fare they had, they drank the wine so clear;
And as to purpose, now and then it fell
She cheerëd her with, How, sister, what cheer?
Amid this joy befell a sorry chance,   50

That, wellaway, the stranger bought full dear
The fare she had. For as she looked askance,
Under a stool she spied two stemming eyes
In a round head, with sharp ears; in France
Was never mouse so feared, for the unwise
Had not yseën such a beast before;
Yet had nature taught her, after her guise,
To know her foe and dread him evermore.
The town mouse fled, she knew whither to go;
The other had no shift, but wonders sore,   60
Feared of her life; at home she wished her though!
And to the door, alas, as she did skip,
The heaven it would, lo, and eke her chance was so,
At the threshold her seely foot did trip,
And ere she might recover it again,
The traitor cat had caught her by the hip,
And made her there against her will remain,
That had forgot her power, surety, and rest,
For seeming wealth, wherein she thought to reign.
Alas, my Poins, how men do seek the best   70
And find the worst, by error as they stray.
And no marvel, when sight is so oppressed,
And blinds the guide; anon out of the way
Goeth guide and all in seeking quiet life.
O wretched minds, there is no gold that may
Grant that you seek, no war, no peace, no strife.
No, no, although thy head were hooped with gold,
Sergeant with mace, with hauberk, sword, nor knife,
Cannot repulse the care that follow should.
Each kind of life hath with him his disease.   80
Live in delight, even as thy lust would,
And thou shalt find when lust doth most thee please,
It irketh straight, and by itself doth fade.
A small thing is it that may thy mind appease;
None of you all there is that is so mad
To seek for grapes on brambles or on briars;
For none I trow that hath his wit so bad
To set his hay for conies over rivers,
Nor ye set not a dragnet for a hare;
And yet the thing that most is your desire   90
You do misseek with more travail and care.
Make plain thine heart, that it be not knotted
With hope of dread, and see thy will be bare
From all affects, whom vice hath ever spotted.
Thyself content with that is thee assigned,
And use it well that is to thee allotted.

Then seek no more out of thyself to find
The thing that thou hast sought so long before,
For thou shalt feel it sticking in thy mind,
Mad, if ye list to continue your sore,　　　　　100
Let present pass, and gape on time to come,
And deep yourself in travail more and more.
Henceforth, my Poins, this shall be all and sum;
These wretched fools shall have nought else of me;
But to the great God and to his high doom,
None other pain pray I for them to be,
But when the rage doth lead them from the right,
That looking backward, virtue they may see
Even as she is, so goodly fair and bright.
And whilst they clasp their lusts in arms across,　　　110
Grant them, good Lord, as thou mayst of thy might,
To fret inward for losing such a loss.

Of *the courtier's life*
Written to John Poins

Mine own John Poins, since ye delight to know
The causes why that homeward I me draw,
And flee the press of courts, whereso they go,
Rather than to live thrall, under the awe
Of lordly looks, wrappèd within my cloak,
To will and lust learning to set a law;
It is not for because I scorn or mock
The power of them, whom fortune here hath lent
Charge over us, of right to strike the stroke.
But true it is that I have always meant　　　　　10
Less to esteem them than the common sort,
Of outward things that judge in their intent
Without regard what doth inward resort.
I grant sometime that of glory the fire
Doth touch my heart. Me list not to report
Blame by honor, and honor to desire.
But how may I this honor now attain,
That cannot dye the color black a liar?
My Poins, I cannot frame my tune to feign,
To cloak the truth, for praise without desert,　　　20
Of them that list all vice for to retain.
I cannot honor them that set their part
With Venus and Bacchus all their life long;
Nor hold my peace of them, although I smart.
I cannot crouch nor kneel to such a wrong,
To worship them like God on earth alone,

That are as wolves these seely lambs among.
I cannot with my words complain and moan
And suffer nought, nor smart without complaint,
Nor turn the word that from my mouth is gone; 30
I cannot speak and look like as a saint,
Use wiles for wit, and make deceit a pleasure;
Call craft counsel, for lucre still to paint;
I cannot wrest the law to fill the coffer
With innocent blood to feed myself fat,
And do most hurt where that most help I offer.
I am not he that can allow the state
Of high Cæsar, and damn Cato to die;
That with his death did scape out of the gate
From Cæsar's hands, if Livy doth not lie, 40
And would not live where liberty was lost,
So did his heart the commonwealth apply.
I am not he, such eloquence to boast,
To make the crow in singing as the swan,
Nor call the lion of coward beasts the most,
That cannot take a mouse as the cat can;
And he that dieth for hunger of the gold,
Call him Alexander, and say that Pan
Passeth Apollo in music manifold;
Praise Sir Thopas for a noble tale, 50
And scorn the story that the Knight told;
Praise him for counsel that is drunk of ale;
Grin when he laughs that beareth all the sway,
Frown when he frowns, and groan when he is pale;
On others' lust to hang both night and day.
None of these points would ever frame in me;
My wit is nought, I cannot learn the way.
And much the less of things that greater be,
That asken help of colors of device
To join the mean with each extremity; 60
With nearest virtue aye to cloak the vice.
And as to purpose likewise it shall fall,
To press the virtue that it may not rise;
As drunkenness good fellowship to call;
The friendly foe, with his fair double face,
Say he is gentle and courteous therewithal;
Affirm that favel hath a goodly grace
In eloquence; and cruelty to name
Zeal of justice, and change in time and place;
And he that suff'reth offence without blame, 70
Call him pitiful, and him true and plain
That raileth reckless unto each man's shame;

Say he is rude that cannot lie and feign;
The lecher a lover, and tyranny
To be the right of a prince's reign.
I cannot, I; no, no, it will not be.
This is the cause that I could never yet
Hang on their sleeves, that weigh, as thou mayst see,
A chip of chance more than a pound of wit.
This maketh me at home to hunt and hawk, 80
And in foul weather at my book to sit,
In frost and snow then with my bow to stalk.
No man doth mark whereso I ride or go.
In lusty leas at liberty I walk,
And of these news I feel nor weal nor woe,
Save that a clog doth hang yet at my heel.
No force for that, for it is ordered so
That I may leap both hedge and dike full well;
I am not now in France, to judge the wine,
With sav'ry sauce those delicates to feel. 90
Nor yet in Spain where one must him incline,
Rather than to be, outwardly to seem.
I meddle not with wits that be so fine,
Nor Flanders' cheer lets not my sight to deem
Of black and white, nor takes my wit away
With beastliness; they beasts do so esteem.
Nor I am not where Christ is given in prey
For money, poison, and treason; at Rome
A common practice, usèd night and day.
But here I am in Kent and Christendom, 100
Among the Muses, where I read and rhyme;
Where if thou list, my Poins, for to come,
Thou shalt be judge how I do spend my time.

FROM *Egerton Ms.* 2711

[*The lover complaineth the unkindness of his love*]

My lute, awake, perform the last
Labor that thou and I shall waste,
And end that I have now begun;
For when this song is sung and
    past,
My lute, be still, for I have done.
    As to be heard where ear is none,
As lead to grave in marble stone,
My song may pierce her heart as
    soon.
Should we then sigh, or sing, or
    moan?

No, no, my lute, for I have done. 10
    The rocks do not so cruelly
Repulse the waves continually,
    As she my suit and affection;
So that I am past remedy,
    Whereby my lute and I have done.

    Proud of the spoil that thou hast
        got
Of simple hearts, thorough love's
    shot;
By whom, unkind, thou hast them
    won,

Think not he hath his bow forgot,
Although my lute and I have
    done.   20
Vengeance shall fall on thy dis-
    dain,
That makest but game on earnest
    pain;
Think not alone under the sun
Unquit to cause thy lovers plain,
Although my lute and I have done.
Perchance thee lie withered and
    old,
In winter nights that are so cold,
Plaining in vain unto the moon;
Thy wishes then dare not be told.
Care then who list, for I have
    done.   30

And then may chance thee to
    repent
The time that thou hast lost and
    spent
To cause thy lovers sigh and
    swoon;
Then shalt thou know beauty but
    lent,
And wish and want as I have done.
    Now cease, my lute, this is the
    last
Labor that thou and I shall waste,
And ended is that we begun.
Now is this song both sung and
    past,
My lute, be still, for I have done. 40

HENRY HOWARD, EARL OF SURREY

The Introduction and Notes are at pages 1189 and 1272

From Richard Tottel's *Songs and Sonnets*, 1557

Description of spring, wherein each thing renews save only the lover

The soote season that bud and bloom forth brings
With green hath clad the hill and eke the vale,
The nightingale with feathers new she sings,
The turtle to her make hath told her tale.
Summer is come, for every spray now springs,
The hart hath hung his old head on the pale,
The buck in brake his winter coat he flings,
The fishes float with new repairèd scale,
The adder all her slough away she slings,
The swift swallow pursueth the flyës smale,   10
The busy bee her honey now she mings,—
Winter is worn, that was the flowers' bale:
And thus I see, among these pleasant things
Each care decays—and yet my sorrow springs.

The frailty and hurtfulness of beauty

Brittle beauty that nature made so frail,
Whereof the gift is small, and short the season,

Flow'ring to-day, to-morrow apt to fail,
Tickle treasure, abhorred of reason,
Dangerous to deal with, vain, of none avail,
Costly in keeping, passed not worth two peason,
Slipper in sliding as is an eelë's tail,
Hard to attain, once gotten not geason,
Jewel of jeopardy that peril doth assail,
False and untrue, enticëd oft to treason,   10
En'my to youth (that most may I bewail!),
Ah, bitter sweet! infecting as the poison,
Thou farest as fruit that with the frost is taken:
To-day ready ripe, to-morrow all to-shaken.

Description and praise of his love Geraldine

From Tuscan came my lady's worthy race,
Fair Florence was sometime her ancient seat,
The western isle whose pleasant shore doth face
Wild Camber's cliffs did give her lively heat;
Fostered she was with milk of Irish breast,
Her sire an earl, her dame of princes' blood;
From tender years in Britain she doth rest
With king's child, where she tasteth costly food.
Hunsdon did first present her to mine eyne;
Bright is her hue, and Geraldine she hight;   10
Hampton me taught to wish her first for mine,
And Windsor, alas, doth chase me from her sight.
Her beauty, of kind; her virtues, from above;
Happy is he that can obtain her love.

A complaint by night of the lover not beloved

Alas, so all things now do hold their peace,
Heaven and earth disturbëd in nothing;
The beasts, the air, the birds their song do cease.
The nightë's chair the stars about doth bring;
Calm is the sea, the waves work less and less.
So am not I, whom love, alas, doth wring,
Bringing before my face the great increase
Of my desires, whereat I weep and sing
In joy and woe, as in a doubtful ease.
For my sweet thoughts sometime do pleasure bring,   10
But by and by the cause of my disease
Gives me a pang that inwardly doth sting,
When that I think what grief it is again
To live and lack the thing should rid my pain.

Complaint of a lover rebuked

Love that liveth and reigneth in my thought,
That built his seat within my captive breast,
Clad in the arms wherein with me he fought,
Oft in my face he doth his banner rest.
She that me taught to love and suffer pain,
My doubtful hope and eke my hot desire
With shamefast cloak to shadow and refrain,
Her smiling grace converteth straight to ire;
And coward love then to the heart apace
Taketh his flight, whereas he lurks and plains   10
His purpose lost, and dare not show his face.
For my lord's guilt thus faultless bide I pains;
Yet from my lord shall not my foot remove,—
Sweet is his death that takes his end by love.

Vow to love faithfully, howsoever he be rewarded

Set me whereas the sun doth parch the green,
Or where his beams do not dissolve the ice,
In temperate heat where he is felt and seen;
In presence prest of people, mad or wise;
Set me in high or yet in low degree,
In longest night or in the shortest day,
In clearest sky or where clouds thickest be,
In lusty youth or when my hairs are gray.
Set me in heaven, in earth, or else in hell;
In hill, or dale, or in the foaming flood;   10
Thrall or at large, alive whereso I dwell,
Sick or in health, in evil fame or good:
Hers will I be, and only with this thought
Content myself although my chance be nought.

The lover comforteth himself with the worthiness of his love

When raging love with extreme pain
Most cruelly distrains my heart,
When that my tears, as floods of rain,
Bear witness of my woeful smart;
When sighs have wasted so my breath
That I lie at the point of death,
    I call to mind the navy great
That the Greeks brought to Troyë town,
And how the boysteous winds did beat
Their ships, and rent their sails adown;   10

Till Agamemnon's daughter's blood
Appeased the gods that them withstood.
　　And how that in those ten years' war
Full many a bloody deed was done,
And many a lord that came full far
There caught his bane, alas, too soon;
And many a good knight overrun,
Before the Greeks had Helen won.
　　Then think I thus: sith such repair,
So long time war of valiant men,　　　　　20
Was all to win a lady fair,
Shall I not learn to suffer then,
And think my life well spent to be,
Serving a worthier wight than she?
　　Therefore I never will repent,
But pains contented still endure;
For like as when, rough winter spent,
The pleasant spring straight draweth in ure,
So, after raging storms of care,
Joyful at length may be my fare.　　　　　30

A praise of his love, wherein he reproveth them that compare their ladies with his

Give place, ye lovers here before
That spent your boasts and brags
　　in vain,
My lady's beauty passeth more
The best of yours, I dare well sayn,
Than doth the sun the candle-light,
Or brightest day the darkest night;
　　And thereto hath a troth as just
As had Penelope the fair;
For what she saith, ye may it trust
As it by writing sealèd were.　　10
And virtues hath she many mo
Than I with pen have skill to show.
　　I could rehearse, if that I wold,
The whole effect of nature's plaint
When she had lost the perfect
　　mould,
The like to whom she could not
　　paint;
With wringing hands how she did
　　cry,

And what she said, I know it, I.
　　I know she swore with raging
　　mind,
Her kingdom only set apart,　　20
There was no loss, by law of kind,
That could have gone so near her
　　heart.
And this was chiefly all her
　　pain,—
She could not make the like again.
　　Sith nature thus gave her the
　　praise,
To be the chiefest work she
　　wrought,
In faith, methink some better ways
On your behalf might well be
　　sought
Than to compare, as ye have
　　done,
To match the candle with the
　　sun.　　30

How no age is content with his own estate, and how the age
of children is the happiest, if they had skill to understand it

Laid in my quiet bed, in study as I were,
I saw within my troubled head a heap of thoughts appear,
And every thought did show so lively in mine eyes
That now I sighed, and then I smiled, as cause of thought did rise.
I saw the little boy, in thought, how oft that he
Did wish of God to scape the rod, a tall young man to be;
The young man eke that feels his bones with pains oppressed,
How he would be a rich old man, to live and lie at rest;
The rich old man that sees his end draw on so sore,
How he would be a boy again, to live so much the more.   10
Whereat full oft I smiled, to see how all these three,
From boy to man, from man to boy, would chop and change degree;
And musing thus, I think the case is very strange
That man from wealth to live in woe doth ever seek to change.
Thus thoughtful as I lay, I saw my withered skin,
How it doth show my dented jaws, the flesh was worn so thin;
And eke my toothless chaps, the gates of my right way,
That opes and shuts as I do speak, do thus unto me say:
Thy white and hoarish hairs, the messengers of age,
That show like lines of true belief that this life doth assuage,   20
Bids thee lay hand and feel them hanging on thy chin,
The which do write two ages past, the third now coming in.
Hang up, therefore, the bit of thy young wanton time,
And thou that therein beaten art, the happiest life define.
Whereat I sighed and said: Farewell, my wonted joy,
Truss up thy pack and trudge from me to every little boy,
And tell them thus from me, Their time most happy is,
If to their time they reason had to know the truth of this.

Of the death of Sir T. W. the elder

W. [yatt] resteth here, that quick could never rest;
Whose heavenly gifts increasèd by disdain,
And virtue sank the deeper in his breast,
Such profit he by envy could obtain.
A head where wisdom mysteries did frame,
Whose hammers beat still in that lively brain
As on a stithy, where that some work of fame
Was daily wrought, to turn to Britain's gain.
A visage stern and mild, where both did grow
Vice to contemn, in virtue to rejoice;   10
Amid great storms whom grace assurèd so
To live upright and smile at fortune's choice.

A hand that taught what might be said in rhyme,
That reft Chaucer the glory of his wit,
A mark the which (unparfited, for time)
Some may approach, but never none shall hit.
A tongue that served in foreign realms his king;
Whose courteous talk to virtue did inflame
Each noble heart; a worthy guide to bring
Our English youth by travail unto fame.   20
An eye whose judgment none affect could blind,
Friends to allure and foes to reconcile;
Whose piercing look did represent a mind
With virtue fraught, reposëd, void of guile.
A heart where dread was never so impressed,
To hide the thought that might the truth advance;
In neither fortune lost nor yet repressed,
To swell in wealth or yield unto mischance.
A valiant corps where force and beauty met,
Happy—alas, too happy, but for foes!   30
Lived, and ran the race that nature set,
Of manhood's shape where she the mould did lose.
But to the heavens that simple soul is fled,
Which left with such as covet Christ to know
Witness of faith that never shall be dead;
Sent for our health, but not receivëd so.
Thus for our guilt this jewel have we lost:
The earth, his bones; the heavens possess his ghost.

Prisoned in Windsor, he recounteth his pleasure there passed

So cruel prison how could betide, alas,
As proud Windsor? Where I in lust and joy
With a king's son my childish years did pass
In greater feast than Priam's sons of Troy;
Where each sweet place returns a taste full sour:
The large green courts where we were wont to hove
With eyes cast up into the maidens' tower,
And easy sighs, such as folk draw in love;
The stately seats, the ladies bright of hue,
The dances short, long tales of great delight;   10
With words and looks that tigers could but rue,
Where each of us did plead the other's right;
The palm play where, despoilëd for the game,
With dazëd eyes oft we by gleams of love
Have missed the ball and got sight of our dame,
To bait her eyes, which kept the leads above;

The gravel ground, with sleeves tied on the helm,
On foaming horse, with swords and friendly hearts,
With cheer, as though one should another whelm,
Where we have fought, and chasëd oft with darts; 20
With silver drops the mead yet spread for ruth,
In active games of nimbleness and strength,
Where we did strain, trainëd with swarms of youth,
Our tender limbs that yet shot up in length;
The secret groves which oft we made resound
Of pleasant plaint and of our ladies' praise,
Recording oft what grace each one had found,
What hope of speed, what dread of long delays;
The wild forest, the clothëd holts with green,
With reins avaled, and swift ybreathëd horse, 30
With cry of hounds and merry blasts between,
Where we did chase the fearful hart of force;
The wide vales eke that harbored us each night,
Wherewith, alas, reviveth in my breast
The sweet accord; such sleeps as yet delight,
The pleasant dreams, the quiet bed of rest;
The secret thoughts imparted with such trust,
The wanton talk, the divers change of play,
The friendship sworn, each promise kept so just,
Wherewith we passed the winter night away. 40
And with this thought the blood forsakes the face,
The tears berain my cheeks of deadly hue,
The which as soon as sobbing sighs, alas,
Upsuppëd have, thus I my plaint renew:
O place of bliss, renewer of my woes,
Give me account—where is my noble fere?
Whom in thy walls thou dost each night enclose,
To other lief, but unto me most dear!
Echo, alas, that doth my sorrow rue,
Returns thereto a hollow sound of plaint. 50
Thus I alone, where all my freedom grew,
In prison pine with bondage and restraint;
And with remembrance of the greater grief
To banish the less, I find my chief relief.

Exhortation to learn by others' trouble

My Ratcliffe, when thy reckless youth offends,
Receive thy scourge by others' chastisement;
For such calling, when it works none amends,
Then plagues are sent without advertisement.
Yet Solomon said, The wrongëd shall recure;
But Wyatt said true, The scar doth aye endure.

From William Baldwin's *Treatise of Moral Philosophy*, 1547

The things that cause a quiet life
Written by Martial

My friend, the things that do attain
The happy life be these, I find:
The riches left, not got with pain,
The fruitful ground, the quiet mind.

The equal friend—no grudge, no strife;
No charge of rule, nor governance;
Without disease, the healthy life,
The household of continuance;

The mean diet, no dainty fare;
Wisdom joined with simpleness; [10]
The night dischargèd of all care,
Where wine the wit may not oppress.

The faithful wife, without debate;
Such sleeps as may beguile the night:
Content thyself with thine estate,
Neither wish death, nor fear his might.

From *Additional Ms.* 36529

[*London, hast thou accusèd me?*]

London, hast thou accusèd me
Of breach of laws, the root of strife?
Within whose breast did boil to see,
So fervent hot, thy dissolute life,
That even the hate of sins that grow
Within thy wicked walls so rife,
For to break forth did convert so
That terror could not it repress.
The which, by words since preachers know
What hope is left for to redress, [10]
By unknown means it likèd me
My hidden burden to express,
Whereby it might appear to thee
That secret sin hath secret spite,
From justice' rod no fault is free;
But that all such as works unright
In most quiet are next ill rest.
In secret silence of the night
This made me, with a reckless breast,
To wake thy sluggards with my bow— [20]
A figure of the Lord's behest,
Whose scourge for sin the Scriptures show.
That, as the fearful thunder-clap
By sudden flame at hand we know,
Of pebble-stones the soundless rap
The dreadful plague might make thee see
Of God's wrath that doth thee enwrap;
That pride might know, from conscience free
How lofty works may her defend;
And envy find, as he hath sought [30]
How other seek him to offend;
And wrath taste of each cruel thought,
The just shapp higher in the end;
And idle sloth, that never wrought,
To heaven his spirit lift may begin;
And greedy lucre live in dread

To see what hate ill-got goods win;
The lechers, ye that lusts do feed,
Perceive what secrecy is in sin;
And gluttons' hearts for sorrow
 bleed,   40
Awakëd, when their fault they
 find:
In loathsome vice each drunken
 wight
To stir to God, this was my mind.
Thy windows had done me no spite,
But proud people that dread no
 fall,
Clothëd with falsehood and un-
 right,
Bred in the closures of thy wall;
But wrested to wrath in fervent
 zeal,
Thou haste to strife, my secret
 call.
Endurëd hearts no warning feel; 50
O shameless whore, is dread then
 gone
By such thy foes as meant thy weal?

O member of false Babylon!
The shop of craft, the den of ire!
Thy dreadful doom draws fast
 upon;
Thy martyrs' blood, by sword and
 fire,
In heaven and earth for justice
 call.
The Lord shall hear their just de-
 sire,
The flame of wrath shall on thee
 fall,
With famine and pest lamentably
Stricken shall be thy lechers all; 61
Thy proud towers and turrets high,
En'mies to God, beat stone from
 stone,
Thine idols burnt that wrought in-
 iquity;
When none thy ruin shall bemoan,
But render unto the right wise
 Lord
That so hath judgëd Babylon,
Immortal praise with one accord.

FROM *Certain Books of Virgil's Æneis*, 1557

Book II

They whisted all, with fixëd face attent,
When prince Æneas from the royal seat
Thus gan to speak: O Queen, it is thy will
I should renew a woe cannot be told!
How that the Greeks did spoil and overthrow
The Phrygian wealth and wailful realm of Troy.
Those ruthful things that I myself beheld
And whereof no small part fell to my share,
Which to express, who could refrain from tears?
What Myrmidon? or yet what Dolopes?
What stern Ulysses' wagëd soldïer?
And lo, moist night now from the welkin falls,
And stars, declining, counsel us to rest.
But since so great is thy delight to hear
Of our mishaps and Troyë's last decay,
Though to record the same my mind abhors
And plaint eschews, yet thus will I begin.
 The Greeks' chieftains, all irkëd with the war

Wherein they wasted had so many years,
And oft repulsed by fatal destiny,   20
A huge horse made, high raisëd like a hill,
By the divine science of Minerva,
(Of cloven fir compacted were his ribs)
For their return a feignëd sacrifice;
The fame whereof so wandered it at point.
In the dark bulk they closed bodies of men,
Chosen by lot, and did enstuff by stealth
The hollow womb with armëd soldïers.
    There stands in sight an isle hight Tenedon,
Rich and of fame while Priam's kingdom stood,   30
Now but a bay, and road unsure for ship.
Hither them secretly the Greeks withdrew,
Shrouding themselves under the desert shore.
And, weening we they had been fled and gone,
And with that wind had fet the land of Greece,
Troyë discharged her long-continued dole.
    The gates cast up, we issued out to play,
The Greekish camp desirous to behold,
The places void, and the forsaken coasts.
Here Pyrrhus' band, there fierce Achilles', pight;   40
Here rode their ships; there did their battles join.
Astonied, some the scatheful gift beheld,
Behight by vow unto the chaste Minerve,
All wond'ring at the hugeness of the horse.
    And first of all Timœtes gan advise
Within the walls to lead and draw the same,
And place it eke amid the palace court,—
Whether of guile or Troyë's fate it would.
Capys, with some of judgment more discreet,
Willed it to drown, or underset with flame,   50
The suspect present of the Greeks' deceit,
Or bore and gauge the hollow caves uncouth.
So diverse ran the giddy people's mind.
    Lo, foremost of a rout that followed him,
Kindled Laocoon hasted from the tower,
Crying far off, O wretched citizens,
What so great kind of frenzy fretteth you?
Deem ye the Greeks, our enemies, to be gone?
Or any Greekish gifts can you suppose
Devoid of guile? Is so Ulysses known?   60
Either the Greeks are in this timber hid
Or this an engine is to annoy our walls,
To view our towers and overwhelm our town.
Here lurks some craft. Good Trojans, give no trust

Unto this horse, for, whatsoever it be,
I dread the Greeks—yea, when they offer gifts!
And with that word with all his force a dart
He lancëd then into that crooked womb;
Which trembling stuck, and shook within the side,
Wherewith the caves gan hollowly resound. 70
And but for fates, and for our blind forecast,
The Greeks' device and guile had he descried,
Troy yet had stand, and Priam's towers so high.

.   .   .   .

Us caitiffs then a far more dreadful chance
Befell, that troubled our unarmëd breasts.
Whiles Laocoon, that chosen was by lot
Neptunus' priest, did sacrifice a bull
Before the holy altar, suddenly
From Tenedon, behold, in circles great
By the calm seas came fleeting adders twain, 80
Which plied towards the shore—I loathe to tell—
With rearëd breast lift up above the seas;
Whose bloody crests aloft the waves were seen.
The hinder part swam hidden in the flood,
Their grisly backs were linkëd manifold;
With sound of broken waves they gat the strand,
With glowing eyne, tainted with blood and fire;
Whose walt'ring tongues did lick their hissing mouths.
We fled away, our face the blood forsook;
But they, with gait direct, to Lacoon ran. 90
And first of all each serpent doth enwrap
The bodies small of his two tender sons,
Whose wretched limbs they bit, and fed thereon.
Then raught they him, who had his weapon caught
To rescue them. Twice winding him about,
With folded knots and circled tails his waist,
Their scalëd backs did compass twice his neck,
With rearëd heads aloft and stretchëd throats.
He with his hands strave to unloose the knots,
Whose sacred fillets all besprinkled were 100
With filth of gory blood and venom rank,
And to the stars such dreadful shouts he sent,
Like to the sound the roaring bull forth lows
Which from the altar wounded doth astart,
The swerving axe when he shakes from his neck.
The serpents twain with hasted trail they glide
To Pallas' temple and her towers of height;
Under the feet of which, the goddess stern,

Hidden behind her target's boss they crept.
New gripes of dread then pierce our trembling breasts.   110
They said Lacoon's deserts had dearly bought
His heinous deed, that piercèd had with steel
The sacred bulk, and thrown the wicked lance.
The people cried, with sundry greeing shouts,
To bring the horse to Pallas' temple blive,
In hope thereby the goddess' wrath t'appease.
We cleft the walls and closures of the town,
Whereto all help, and underset the feet
With sliding rolls and bound his neck with ropes.
This fatal gin thus overclamb our walls,   120
Stuffed with armed men; about the which there ran
Children and maids that holy carols sang,
And well were they whose hands might touch the cords.
With threatening cheer thus slided through our town
The subtle tree, to Pallas' temple-ward.
O native land! Ilion! And of the gods
The mansion place! O warlike walls of Troy!
Four times it stopped in th' entry of our gate;
Four times the harness clattered in the womb.
But we go on, unsound of memory,   130
And, blinded eke by rage, perséver still.
This fatal monster in the fane we place.

.   .   .   .

THOMAS, LORD VAUX

The Introduction and Notes are at pages 1192 and 1272

FROM RICHARD TOTTEL's *Songs and Sonnets,* 1557

The aged lover renounceth love

I loathe that I did love;
In youth that I thought sweet,
As time requires for my behove,
Me thinks they are not meet.
    My lusts they do me leave,
My fancies all be fled,
And tract of time begins to weave
Gray hairs upon my head.
    For age, with stealing steps,
Hath clawed me with his crutch;   10
And lusty life away she leaps
As there had been none such.
    My muse doth not delight
Me as she did before,
My hand and pen are not in plight
As they have been of yore.
    For reason me denies
This youthly idle rhyme,
And day by day to me she cries,

Leave off these toys in time! [20]
The wrinkles in my brow,
The furrows in my face,
Say limping age will hedge him
    now
Where youth must give him
    place.
The harbinger of death,
To me I see him ride;
The cough, the cold, the gasping
    breath,
Doth bid me to provide
A pickaxe and a spade,
And eke a shrouding sheet; [30]
A house of clay for to be made
For such a guest most meet.
Me thinks I hear the clerk
That knolls the careful knell,
And bids me leave my woeful
    work
Ere nature me compel.

My keepers knit the knot
That youth did laugh to scorn;
Of me that clean shall be forgot
As I had not been born. [40]
Thus must I youth give up,
Whose badge I long did wear;
To them I yield the wanton cup
That better may it bear.
Lo, here the barëd skull
By whose bald sign I know
That stooping age away shall pull
Which youthful years did sow.
For beauty, with her band,
These crooked cares hath
    wrought, [50]
And shippëd me into the land
From whence I first was brought.
And ye that bide behind,
Have ye none other trust;
As ye of clay were cast by kind,
So shall ye waste to dust.

FROM RICHARD EDWARDS's *Paradise of Dainty Devices*, 1576
A lover, disdained, complaineth

If ever man had love too dearly bought,
Lo, I am he, that plays within her maze,
And finds no way to get the same I sought;
But as the deer are driven unto the gaze.
And to augment the grief of my desire,
Myself to burn, I blow the fire.
But shall I come nigh you,
Of force I must fly you.

What death, alas, may be compared to this?
I play within the maze of my sweet foe, [10]
And when I would of her but crave a kiss,
Disdain enforceth her away to go.
Myself I check, yet do I twist the twine;
The pleasure hers, the pain is mine.
But shall I come nigh you,
Of force I must fly you.

You courtly wights that wants your pleasant choice,
Lend me a flood of tears to wail my chance!
Happy are they in love that can rejoice,

To their great pains, where fortune doth advance.   20
For sith my suit, alas, can not prevail,
Full fraught with care in grief still will I wail,
Sith you will needs fly me,
I may not come nigh you.

No pleasure without some pain

How can the tree but waste and wither away
That hath not some time comfort of the sun?
How can that flower but fade and soon decay
That always is with dark clouds over-run?
Is this a life? Nay, death you may it call,
That feels each pain and knoweth no joy at all.

What foodless beast can live long in good plight?
Or is it life where senses there be none?
Or what availeth eyes without their light?
Or else a tongue to him that is alone?   10
Is this a life? Nay, death you may it call,
That feels each pain and knows no joy at all.

Whereto serve ears if that there be no sound?
Or such a head where no device doth grow?
But all of plaints, since sorrow is the ground,
Whereby the heart doth pine in deadly woe.
Is this a life? Nay, death you may it call,
That feels each pain and knows no joy at all.

Of a contented mind

When all is done and said, in the end thus shall you find,
He most of all doth bathe in bliss that hath a quiet mind;
And, clear from worldly cares, to deem can be content
The sweetest time in all his life in thinking to be spent.

The body subject is to fickle fortune's power,
And to a million of mishaps is casual every hour.
And death in time doth change it to a clod of clay,
Whenas the mind, which is divine, runs never to decay.

Companion none is like unto the mind alone,
For many have been harmed by speech, through thinking few or
    none.   10
Few oftentimes restraineth words, but makes not thoughts to cease,
And he speaks best that hath the skill when for to hold his peace.

Our wealth leaves us at death, our kinsmen at the grave,
But virtues of the mind unto the heavens with us we have:
Wherefore, for virtue's sake, I can be well content
The sweetest time in all my life to deem in thinking spent.

MINOR 'COURTLY MAKERS' OF HENRY VIII'S REIGN

The Introduction and Notes are at page 1192

FROM *Additional Ms.* 5465

[*That was my woe*]

That was my woe is now my
  most gladness,
That was my pain is now my joyous chance;
That was my fear is now my sik-
  erness,
That was my grief is now my allegiance.
Thus hath now grace enrichëd
  my pleasance,
Wherefore I am, and shall be
  till I die,
Your true servant with thought,
  heart, and body.
        [*Robert Fairfax*]

FROM WYNKYN DE WORDE'S
Christmas Carols, 1521

*A carol, bringing in the boar's
        head*

Caput apri differo,
Reddens laudes domino.
The boar's head in hand bring I,
With garlands gay and rosemary;
I pray you all sing merrily,
  Qui estis in convivio.

The boar's head, I understand,
Is the chief service in this land;
Look wherever it be fand,
  Servite cum cantico.   10

Be glad, lords both more and less,
For this hath ordained our stew-
    ard
To cheer you all this Christmas,
The boar's head with mustard.

FROM *XX Songs,* 1530

[*In youth, in age*]

In youth, in age,
Both in wealth and woe,
Auxilium meum a domino.

Though poets feign that fortune,
  by her chance
And her free will, doth oppress
  and advance,
Fortune doth miss her will and
  liberty.
Then trust to virtue; let fortune
  go,
Auxilium meum a domino.

Of grace divine, with heavenly assistance,

If virtue do remain, virtue alway ¹⁰
When she list may call fortune's
   chance again.
What force I then though for-
   tune be my foe?
Auxilium meum a domino.
             [*Robert Cooper*]

[*Pleasure it is*]

Pleasure it is
To hear, I wis,
The birds sing;
The deer in the dale,
The sheep in the vale,
The corn springing;
God's purveyance
For sustenance
It is, for man.
Then we always   10
To him give praise
And thank him than,
And thank him than.
          [*William Cornish*]

FROM *Royal Ms. Appendix* 58

[*Ah! the sighs*]

Ah! the sighs that come from my
   heart,
   They grieve me passing sore;
Sith I must from my love depart,
   Farewell, my joy, for ever-
     more.

Oft to me with her goodly face
   She was wont to cast an eye,
And now absence to me in place—
   Alas, for woe I die, I die!

I was wont her to behold,
   And taken in armës twain;   10
And now with sighës manifold,
   Farewell, my joy, and wel-
    come, pain.

Ah! methink that I see her yet,
   As would to God that I might!
There might no joys compare with
   it
   Unto my heart, to make it
    light.
          [*William Cornish*]

[*Western wind*]

Western wind, when will thou
   blow?
The small rain down can rain,—
Christ, if my love were in my
   arms
And I in my bed again!

[*My little fool*]

My little fool
Is gone to play,
She will tarry no longer with me.
Hey ho, frisk-a jolly,
Under the greenwood tree!
Hey ho, frisk-a jolly,
Under the greenwood tree!
Hey ho, frisk-a jolly.

FROM *Additional Ms.* 31922

[*England, be glad*]

England, be glad, pluck up thy
   lusty heart!
Help now the king, the king, and
   take his part.

Against the Frenchmen in the
   field to fight
In the quarrel of the church, and
   in the right,
With spears and shields on goodly
   horses light,
Bows and arrows to put them all
   to flight,
To put them all to flight. Help
   now the king!

FROM *Harleian Ms.* 7578

[*These women all*]

These women all
Both great and small
    Are wavering to and fro,
Now here, now there,
Now everywhere,—
    But I will not say so.

So they love to range,
Their minds doth change
    And makes their friend their
        foe;
As lovers true   10
Each day they choose new,—
    But I will not say so.

They laugh, they smile,
They do beguile

As dice that men doth throw.
Who useth them much
Shall never be rich,—
    But I will not say so.

Some hot, some cold,
There is no hold   20
    But as the wind doth blow;
When all is done,
They change like the moon,—
    But I will not say so.

So thus one and other
Taketh after their mother
    As cock by kind doth crow.
My song is ended,
The best may be amended,—
    But I will not say so.   30
                        [*Heath*]

FROM *Additional Ms.* 26737

[*O death, rock me asleep*]

O death, O death, rock me
        asleep,
Bring me to quiet rest;
Let pass my weary guiltless ghost
Out of my careful breast.
    Toll on your passing bell,
    Ring out my doleful knell;
    Thy sound my death abroad will
        tell,
        For I must die,
        There is no remedy.

My pains, my pains, who can
        express?   10
Alas, they are so strong!
My dolors will not suffer strength
My life for to prolong.
    Toll on . . .

Alone, alone in prison strong
I wail my destiny.
Woe worth the cruel hap that I
Must taste this misery!
    Toll on . . .

Farewell, farewell, my pleas-
        ures past!   20
Welcome, my present pain!
I feel my torment so increase
That life can not remain.
    Cease now, then, passing bell,
    Ring out my doleful knoll;
    For thou my death dost tell.
    Lord, pity thou my soul!
        Death doth draw nigh,
        Sound dolefully!
        For now I die,   30
        I die, I die!

[*George Boleyn, Viscount Rochford?*]

From *Ashmole Ms.* 48

To his posterity
Written over a chamber door where he was wont to lie at Hallingbury

Never was I less alone than being alone
Here in this chamber. Evil thought had I none,
But always I thought to bring the mind to rest,
And that thought of all thoughts I judge it the best.
For if my coffers had been full of pearl and gold
And fortune had favored me even as that I wold,
The mind out of quiet, so sage Senec saith,
It had been no felicity, but a painful death.
Love then who love will to stand in high degree;
I blame him not a whit so that he follow me   10
And take his loss as quietly as when that he doth win.
Then fortune hath no mast'ry of that state he is in;
But rules, and is not ruled, and takes the better part.
Oh, that man is blessed that learns this gentle art!
This was my felicity, my pastime, and my game:
I wish all my posterity they would ensue the same.

[*Henry Parker, Lord Morley*]

From Richard Tottel's *Songs and Sonnets,* 1557

The poor estate to be holden for best

Experience now doth show what God us taught before,
Desired pomp is vain and seldom doth it last;
Who climbs to reign with kings may rue his fate full sore,—
Alas, the woeful end that comes with care full fast!
Reject him doth renown; his pomp full low is cast;
Deceivëd is the bird by sweetness of the call;
Expel that pleasant taste wherein is bitter gall.
Such as with oaten cakes in poor estate abides,
Of care have they no cure; the crab with mirth they roast.
More ease feel they than those that from their height down slides;   10
Excess doth breed their woe, they sail in Scylla's coast,
Remaining in the storms till ship and all be lost.
Serve God, therefore, thou poor; for lo, thou lives in rest;
Eschew the golden hall, thy thatchëd house is besT.

[*Edward Seymour, Duke of Somerset?*]

The lover showeth his woeful state and prayeth pity

Like as the lark within the marlian's foot
With piteous tunes doth chirp her yelden lay,

So sing I now, seeing none other boot,
My rendering song, and to your will obey.
Your virtue mounts above my force so high,
And with your beauty seized I am so sure,
That there avails resistance none in me,
But patiently your pleasure to endure.
For on your will my fancy shall attend;
My life, my death,—I put both in your choice;   10
And rather had this life by you to end,
Than live by other always to rejoice.
And if your cruelty do thirst my blood,
Then let it forth, if it may do you good.

Upon consideration of the state of this life he wisheth death

The longer life, the more of-
    fence;
The more offence, the greater
    pain;
The greater pain, the less de-
    fence;
The less defence, the lesser gain.
The loss of gain long ill doth try,
Wherefore come death, and let me
    die.
The shorter life, less count I
    find;
The less account, the sooner
    made;
The count soon made, the mer-
    rier mind;
The merry mind doth thought
    evade.   10
Short life in truth this thing doth
    try,
Wherefore come death, and let
    me die.
Come, gentle death, the ebb of
    care,
The ebb of care, the flood of life;
The flood of life, the joyful fare;
The joyful fare, the end of strife;

The end of strife, that thing wish
    I,
Wherefore come death, and let
    me die.

Of a new-married student

A student, at his book so placed
That wealth he might have won,
From book to wife did fleet in
    haste,
From wealth to woe to run.
Now, who hath played a feater
    cast
Since juggling first begun?
In knitting of himself so fast
Himself he hath undone.

*Harpalus' complaint of Phil-
lida's love bestowed on
Corin, who loved her not,
and denied him that
loved her*

Phillida was a fayer maid
And fresh as any flower,
Whom Harpalus, the herdman,
    prayed
To be his paramour.
Harpalus and eke Corin
Were herdmen both yfere:

And Phillida could twist and spin,
And thereto sing full clear.
　But Phillida was all too coy
For Harpalus to win;　　10
For Corin was her only joy,
Who forced her not a pin.
　How often would she flowers
　　twine,
How often garlands make
Of cowslips and of columbine,
And all for Corin's sake.
　But Corin he had hawks to
　　lure,
And forcëd more the field;
Of lovers' law he took no cure,
For once he was beguiled.　20
　Harpalus prevailëd nought,
His labor all was lost;
For he was farthest from her
　　thought,
And yet he loved her most.
　Therefore waxed he both pale
　　and lean,
And dry as clot of clay;
His flesh it was consumëd clean,
His color gone away.
　His beard it had not long be
　　shave,
His hair hung all unkempt;　30
A man most fit even for the grave,
Whom spiteful love had spent.
　His eyes were red and all for-
　　watched,
His face besprent with tears;
It seemed unhap had him long
　　hatched
In mids of his despairs.
　His clothes were black and also
　　bare,
As one forlorn was he;
Upon his head always he ware
A wreath of willow tree.　40
　His beasts he kept upon the hill,
And he sate in the dale;
And thus, with sighs and sorrows
　　shrill,

He gan to tell his tale:
　O Harpalus, thus would he say,
Unhappiest under sun,
The cause of thine unhappy day
By love was first begun;
　For thou wentest first by suit
　　to seek
A tiger to make tame,　　50
That sets not by thy love a leek,
But makes thy grief her game.
　As easy it were for to convert
The frost into the flame
As for to turn a froward heart
Whom thou so fain wouldst
　　frame.
　Corin he liveth carëless,
He leaps among the leaves;
He eats the fruits of thy redress;
Thou reaps, he takes the sheaves.　60
　My beasts, awhile your food re-
　　frain,
And hearken your herdman's
　　sound,
Whom spiteful love, alas, hath
　　slain,
Through-girt with many a wound.
　Oh, happy be ye, beastës wild,
That here your pasture takes;
I see that ye be not beguiled
Of these, your faithful makes.
　The hart he feedeth by the
　　hind,
The buck hard by the doe;　70
The turtle-dove is not unkind
To him that loves her so;
　The ewe she hath by her the
　　ram,
The young cow hath the bull;
The calf, with many a lusty lamb,
Do feed their hunger full.
　But, wellaway! that nature
　　wrought
Thee, Phillida, so fair;
For I may say that I have bought
Thy beauty all too dear.　80
　What reason is it that cruelty

With beauty should have part?
Or else that such great tyranny
Should dwell in woman's heart?
　I see therefore to shape my
　　death
She cruelly is prest;
To th' end that I may want my
　breath,
My days been at the best.
　O Cupid, grant this my request
And do not stop thine ears, 　90
That she may feel within her
　breast
The pains of my despairs;
Of Corin that is careless
That she may crave her fee
As I have done, in great distress,
That loved her faithfully.
　But since that I shall die her
　　slave,
Her slave and eke her thrall,
Write you, my friends, upon my
　grave
This chance that is befall: 　100
Here lieth unhappy Harpalus
Whom cruel love hath slain,
By Phillida unjustly thus
Murdered with false disdain.

From Richard Tottel's *Songs
and Sonnets*, 1557 (second
edition)

*Totus mundus in maligno
positus*

　Complain we may, much is
　　amiss:
Hope is nigh gone to have re-
　dress;
These days been ill, nothing sure
　is,
Kind heart is wrapped in heavi-
　ness.
　The stern is broke, the sail is
　　rent,

The ship is given to wind and
　wave,
All help is gone, the rock pres-
　ent;
That will be lost, what man can
　save?
Things hard therefore are now
　refused,
Labor in youth is thought but
　vain, 　10
Duty by 'will not' is excused;
Remove the stop, the way is plain.
　Learning is lewd and held a
　　fool,
Wisdom is shent, counted to rail,
Reason is banished out of school,
The blind is bold, and words pre-
　vail.
　Power, without care, sleepeth at
　　ease;
Will, without law, runn'th where
　he list;
Might, without mercy, cannot
　please. 　19
A wise man saith not, had I wist.
　When power lacks care and
　　forceth not,
When care is feeble and may
　not,
When might is slothful and will
　not,
Weeds may grow where good
　herbs cannot.
　Take wrong away, law needeth
　　not,
For law to wrong is bridle and
　pain;
Take fear away, law booteth not.
To strive 'gainst stream, it is but
　vain.
　Wily is witty, brainsick is wise,
Truth is folly, and might is
　right; 　30
Words are reason, and reason is
　lies,
The bad is good, darkness is light.

Wrong to redress, wisdom dare
   not.
Hardy is happy, and ruleth most;
Wilful is witless, and careth not
Which end go first, till all be
   lost.
   Few right do love and wrong
      refuse;
Pleasure is sought in every state;
Liking is lust; there is no choose;
The low give to the high check-
   mate.   40
   Order is broke in things of
      weight,—
Measure and mean, who doth not
   flee?
Two things prevail, money and
   sleight;
To seem is better than to be.
   The bowl is round and doth
      down slide;
Each one thrusteth, none doth up-
   hold.
A fall fails not where blind is
   guide;
The stay is gone,—who can him
   hold?
   Folly and falsehood prayeth
      apace;
Truth under bushel is fain to
   creep;   50
Flatt'ry is treble, pride sings the
   bass;
The mean the best part scant doth
   peep.
   This fiery plague the world in-
      fects;
To virtue and truth it gives no
   rest.
Men's hearts are burned with sun-
   dry sects,
And to each man his way is best.
   With floods and storms thus be
      we tossed,
Awake, good Lord, to thee we
   cry:

Our ship is almost sunk and lost,
Thy mercy help our misery!   60
   Man's strength is weak, man's
      wit is dull,
Man's reason is blind. These
   things t' amend,
Thy hand, O Lord, of might is
   full,
Awake betime and help us fend.
   In thee we trust, and in no
      wight.
Save us as chickens under the hen.
Our crookedness thou canst make
   right;
Glory to thee for aye! Amen.

An old lover to a young gentlewoman

Ye are too young to bring me in,
And I too old to gape for flies;
I have too long a lover been,
If such young babes should blear
   mine eyes.
But trill the ball before my face,
I am content to make you play;
I will not see, I hide my face,
And turn my back and run away.
   But if you follow on so fast,
And cross the ways where I should
   go,   10
Ye may wax weary at the last,
And then at length your self
   o'erthrow.
   I mean where you and all your
      flock
Devise to pen men in the pound,
I know a key can pick your lock
And make you run yourselves on
   ground.
   Some birds can eat the strawy
      corn
And flee the lime the fowlers set,
And some are 'feard of every
   thorn

And so thereby they scape the net. [20]
But some do light and never look
And seeth not who doth stand in wait,
As fish that swallow up the hook
And is beguilèd through the bait.
  But men can look before they leap
And be at price for every ware,
And pennyworths cast, to buy good cheap,
And in each thing hath eye and care;
But he that bluntly runs on head
And seeth not what the race shall be, [30]
Is like to bring a fool to bed,—
And thus ye get no more of me.

Of the vanity of man's life

Vain is the fleeting wealth
Whereon the world stays,

Sith stalking time by privy stealth
Encroacheth on our days.
  And eld, which creepeth fast
To taint us with her wound,
Will turn each bliss unto a blast,
Which lasteth but a stound.
  Of youth the lusty flower
Which whilom stood in price [10]
Shall vanish quite within an hour,
As fire consumes the ice.
  Where is become that wight
For whose sake Troy town
Withstood the Greeks till ten years' fight
Had razed the walls adown?
  Did not the worms consume
Her carrion to the dust?
Did dreadful death forbear his fume
For beauty, pride, or lust? [20]

NICHOLAS GRIMALD

The Introduction and Notes are at pages 1195 and 1272

From Richard Tottel's *Songs and Sonnets*, 1557

A true love

What sweet relief the showers to thirsty plants we see,
What dear delight the blooms to bees, my true love is to me.
  As fresh and lusty Ver foul winter doth exceed,
As morning bright, with scarlet sky, doth pass the evening's weed,
  As mellow pears above the crabs esteemèd be,
So doth my love surmount them all, whom yet I hap to see.
  The oak shall olives bear, the lamb the lion fray,
The owl shall match the nightingale in tuning of her lay,
  Or I my love let slip out of mine entire heart,
So deep reposèd in my breast is she, for her desert. [10]
  For many blessed gifts, O happy, happy land,
Where Mars and Pallas strive to make their glory most to stand,
  Yet, land, more is thy bliss that in this cruel age
A Venus' imp thou hast brought forth, so steadfast and so sage.

Among the Muses nine, a tenth, if Jove would make,
And to the Graces three, a fourth, her would Apollo take.
    Let some for honor hunt, and hoard the massy gold,
With her so I may live and die, my weal cannot be told.

Man's life, after Posidonius or Crates

What path list you to tread? what trade will you assay?
The courts of plea, by brawl and bate, drive gentle peace away.
In house, for wife and child, there is but cark and care;
With travail and with toil enough in fields we use to fare.
·Upon the seas lieth dread; the rich, in foreign land,
Do fear the loss; and there the poor like misers poorly stand.
Strife, with a wife; without, your thrift full hard to see;
Young brats a trouble; none at all, a maim it seems to be;
Youth, fond; age hath no heart, and pincheth all too nigh.
Choose then the liefer of these two: no life, or soon to die.

Metrodorus' mind to the contrary

What race of life run you? what trade will you assay?
In courts is glory got and wit increasëd, day by day.
At home we take our ease, and beek ourselves in rest;
The fields our nature do refresh with pleasures of the best.
On seas is gain to get; the stranger, he shall be
Esteemëd, having much; if not, none knoweth his lack but he.
A wife will trim thy house; no wife? then art thou free.
Brood is a lovely thing; without, thy life is loose to thee.
Young bloods be strong; old sires in double honor dwell.
Do 'way that choice, no life, or soon to die; for all is well.

Description of virtue

What one art thou, thus in torn weed yclad?
Virtue, in price whom ancient sages had.
Why poorly 'rayed? For fading goods past care.
Why double-faced? I mark each fortune's fare.
This bridle, what? Mind's rages to restrain.
Tools why bear you? I love to take great pain.
Why wings? I teach above the stars to fly.
Why tread you death? I only cannot die.

To his familiar friend

No image carved with cunning hand, no cloth of purple dye,
No precious weight of metal bright, no silver plate give I.
Such gear allures not heavenly hearts; such gifts no grace they bring;
I, lo, that know your mind, will send none such. What then? Nothing.

A funeral song, upon the decease of Annes, his mother

Yea, and a good cause why thus should I plain,
For what is he can quietly sustain
So great a grief with mouth as still as stone?
My love, my life, of joy my jewel, is gone.
This hearty zeal if any wight disprove
As woman's work, whom feeble mind doth move,
He neither knows the mighty nature's laws
Nor, touching elders' deeds, hath seen old saws.
Martius to vanquish Rome was set on fire,
But vanquished fell, at mother's boon, his ire.　　10
Into Hesperian land Sertorius, fled,
Of parent aye chief care had in his head.
Dear weight on shoulders Sicil brethren bore
While Ætna's giant spouted flames full sore.
Not more of Tyndar's imps hath Sparta spoke
Than Arge of chargëd necks with parent's yoke.
Nor only them thus did foretime entreat;
Then was the nurse also in honor great,
Caiet, the Phrygian, from amid fire-flame
Rescued, who gave to Latin strands the name;　　20
Acca, in double sense Lupa ycleped,
To Roman calendars a feast hath heaped.
His Capra Jove among the stars hath pight,
In welkin clear yet, lo, she shineth bright.
Hyades as gratefully Lyai did place,
Whom, in prime-tide, supports the Bull's fair face.
And should not I express my inward woe
When you, most loving dam, so soon hence go?
I, in your fruitful womb conceived, borne was
While wandering moon ten months did overpass.　　30
Me, brought to light, your tender arms sustained,
And with my lips your milky paps I strained.
You me embraced, in bosom soft you me
Cherished, as I your only child had be.
Of issue fair with numbers were you blest,
Yet I the best-beloved of all the rest.
Good luck certain fore-reading mothers have,
And you of me a special judgment gave.
Then, when firm pace I fixëd on the ground,
When tongue can cease to break the lisping sound,　　40
You me straightway did to the Muses send,
Ne suffered long a loitering life to spend;
What gain the wool, what gain the web had brought,

It was his meed that me there daily taught.
When with Minerve I had acquaintance won,
And Phœbus seemed to love me as his son,
Brownshold I bade, at parents' hest, farewell;
And gladly there in schools I gan to dwell
Where Granta gives the ladies nine such place
That they rejoice to see their blissful case.   50
With joys at heart in this Parnasse I bode
While through his signs five times great Titan glode;
And twice as long by that fair ford whereas
Swan-feeder Thames no further course can pass.
Oh, what desire had you, therewhile, of me!
Mid doubtful dreads what joys were wont to be!
Now linen clothes, wrought with those fingers fine,
Now other things of yours did you make mine;
Till your last threads gan Clotho to untwine,
And of your days the date extreme assign.   60
Hearing the chance, your neighbors made much moan;
A dear-worth dame, they thought, their comfort gone.
Kinswomen wept; your charge, the maidens, wept;
Your daughters wept, whom you so well had kept.
But my good sire gave, with soft words, relief,
And cloaks with outward cheer his inward grief,
Lest by his care your sickness should augment,
And on his case your thoughtful heart be bent.
You, not forgetting yet a mother's mood,
When at the door dart-thirling death there stood,   70
Did say: Adieu, dear spouse, my race is run;
Whereso he be, I have left you a son.
And Nicholas you named and named again,
With other speech, aspiring heavenly reign,
When into air your sprite departed fled
And left the corpse a-cold in lukewarm bed.
Ah, could you thus, dear mother, leave us all?
Now should you live, that yet, before your fall,
My songs you might have sung, have heard my voice,
And in commodities of your own rejoice.   80
My sisters, yet unwedded, who shall guide?
With whose good lessons shall they be applied?
Have, mother, monuments of our sore smart:
No costly tomb, areared with curious art,
Nor Mausolean mass, hung in the air,
Nor lofty steeples that will once appair;
But wailful verse and doleful song accept.
By verse the names of ancient peers be kept:

By verse lives Hercules; by verse, Achil;
Hector, Ene, by verse be famous still.
Such former years, such death hath chancëd thee,
Closed with good end good life is wont to be.
But now, my sacred parent, fare you well.
God shall cause us again together dwell,
What time this universal globe shall hear
Of the last trump the ringing voice, great fear
To some, to such as you a heavenly cheer.
Till then, reposed rest you in gentle sleep,
While He whom-to you are bequeathed, you keep.

Marcus Tullius Cicero's death

Now have I lived, O Rome, enough for me;
My passëd life nought suffereth me to doubt
Noisome oblivion of the loathsome death.
Slay me, yet all th' offspring to come shall know
And this decease shall bring eternal life.
Yea, and unless I fail and all in vain,
Rome, I sometime thy augur chosen was,
Not evermore shall friendly fortune thee
Favor, Antonius; once the day shall come
When her dear wights, by cruel spite thus slain,
Victorious Rome shall at thy hands require.
Me likes, therewhile, go see the hopëd heaven.
Speech had he left, and therewith he, good man,
His throat prepared, and held his head unmoved;
His hasting to those fates the very knights
Be loath to see, and rage rebated when
They his bare neck beheld, and his hoar hairs;
Scant could they hold the tears that forth gan burst,
And almost fell from bloody hands the swords.
Only the stern Herennius, with grim look,
Dastards, why stand you still, he saith, and straight
Swaps off the head with his presumptuous iron.
Ne with that slaughter yet is he not filled:
Foul shame on shame to heap is his delight.
Wherefore the hands also doth he off smite,
Which durst Antonius' life so lively paint.
Him, yielding strainëd ghost, from welkin high
With loathly cheer lord Phœbus gan behold,
And in black cloud, they say, long hid his head.

90

10

20

The Latin Muses, and the Grayes, they wept,
And for his fall eternally shall weep.
And lo, heart-piercing Pytho, strange to tell,
Who had to him sufficed both sense and words
When so he spake, and dressed with nectar soote
That flowing tongue; when his windpipe disclosed,
Fled with her fleeing friend, and, out alas,
Hath left the earth, ne will no more return.
Popilius flyeth, therewhile, and leaving there
The senseless stock, a grisly sight doth bear
Unto Antonius' board, with mischief fed.

ELIZABETH

The Introduction and Notes are at pages 1196 and 1272

FROM *Rawlinson Poetry Ms.* 85

[*When I was fair and young*]

When I was fair and young, and favor gracëd me,
    Of many was I sought, their mistress for to be;
But I did scorn them all, and answered them therefore,
    Go, go, go, seek some otherwhere,
      Impórtune me no more!

How many weeping eyes I made to pine with woe,
    How many sighing hearts, I have no skill to show;
Yet I the prouder grew, and answered them therefore,
    Go, go, go, seek some otherwhere,
      Impórtune me no more!   10

Then spake fair Venus' son, that proud victorious boy,
    And said: Fine dame, since that you be so coy,
I will so pluck your plumes that you shall say no more,
    Go, go, go, seek some otherwhere,
      Impórtune me no more!

When he had spake these words, such change grew in my breast
    That neither night nor day since that, I could take any rest.
Then lo! I did repent that I had said before,
    Go, go, go, seek some otherwhere,
      Impórtune me no more!   20

FROM *The Art of English Poesy,* 1589

[*The doubt of future foes*]

The doubt of future foes exiles my present joy,
And wit me warns to shun such snares as threaten mine annoy.
For falsehood now doth flow and subject faith doth ebb,
Which would not be if reason ruled or wisdom weaved the web.
But clouds of toys untried do cloak aspiring minds,
Which turn to rain of late repent by course of changëd winds.
The top of hope supposed, the root of ruth will be,
And fruitless all their graffëd guiles, as shortly ye shall see.
The dazzled eyes with pride, which great ambition blinds,
Shall be unseeled by worthy wights whose foresight falsehood finds. 10
The daughter of debate that eke discord doth sow
Shall reap no gain where former rule hath taught still peace to grow.
No foreign banished wight shall anchor in this port;
Our realm it brooks no stranger's force, let them elsewhere resort:
Our rusty sword with rest shall first his edge employ
To poll the tops that seek such change and gape for joy.

JOHN HARINGTON, THE ELDER

The Introduction and Notes are at page 1197

FROM *Nugæ Antiquæ,* 1769

*A sonnet made on Isabella Markham, when I first thought
her fair as she stood at the Princess's window in goodly
attire and talked to divers in the court-yard*

Whence comes my love? O heart, disclose!
'Twas from cheeks that shame the rose,
From lips that spoil the ruby's praise,
From eyes that mock the diamond's blaze.
Whence comes my woe? As freely own,
Ah me, 'twas from a heart like stone!

The blushing cheek speaks modest mind,
The lips, befitting words most kind;
The eye does tempt to love's desire,
And seems to say 'tis Cupid's fire. 10
Yet all so fair but speak my moan,
Since nought doth say the heart of stone.

Why thus, my love, so kind bespeak
Sweet lip, sweet eye, sweet blushing cheek,
Yet not a heart to save my pain?
O Venus, take thy gifts again;
Make not so fair to cause our moan,
Or make a heart that's like our own!

THOMAS SACKVILLE, EARL OF DORSET

The Introduction and Notes are at pages 1197 and 1272

FROM *A Mirror for Magistrates*, 1563

The induction

The wrathful winter, 'proaching on apace,
With blustering blasts had all ybared the treen,
And old Saturnus, with his frosty face,
With chilling cold had pierced the tender green;
The mantles rent, wherein enwrappèd been
　　The gladsome groves that now lay overthrown,
　　The tapets torn, and every bloom down blown.

The soil, that erst so seemly was to seen,
Was all despoilèd of her beauty's hue;
And soote fresh flowers, wherewith the summer's queen   10
Had clad the earth, now Boreas' blasts down blew;
And small fowls flocking, in their song did rue
　　The winter's wrath, wherewith each thing defaced
　　In woeful wise bewailed the summer past.

Hawthorn had lost his motley livery,
The naked twigs were shivering all for cold,
And dropping down the tears abundantly;
Each thing, methought, with weeping eye told
The cruel season, bidding me withhold
　　Myself within; for I was gotten out   21
　　Into the fields, whereas I walked about.

When lo, the night with misty mantles spread,
Gan dark the day and dim the azure skies;
And Venus in her message Hermes sped
To bloody Mars, to will him not to rise,
Which she herself approached in speedy wise;

And Virgo, hiding her disdainful breast,
With Thetis now had laid her down to rest.

Whiles Scorpio, dreading Sagittarius' dart,
Whose bow prest bent in fight, the string had slipped,   30
Down slid into the ocean flood apart;
The Bear, that in the Irish seas had dipped
His grisly feet, with speed from thence he whipped;
    For Thetis, hasting from the Virgin's bed,
    Pursued the Bear, that ere she came was fled.

And Phaethon now, near reaching to his race
With glist'ring beams, gold streaming where they bent,
Was prest to enter in his resting place;
Erythius, that in the cart first went,
Had even now attained his journey's stent;   40
    And, fast declining, hid away his head,
    While Titan couched him in his purple bed.

And pale Cynthia, with her borrowed light,
Beginning to supply her brother's place,
Was past the noonstead six degrees in sight,
When sparkling stars amid the heaven's face
With twinkling light shone on the earth apace,
    That, while they brought about the nightë's chair,
    The dark had dimmed the day ere I was ware.

And sorrowing I to see the summer flowers,   50
The lively green, the lusty leas forlorn,
The sturdy trees so shattered with the showers,
The fields so fade that flourished so beforn,
It taught me well all earthly things be born
    To die the death, for nought long time may last;
    The summer's beauty yields to winter's blast.

Then looking upward to the heaven's leams,
With nightë's stars thick powdered everywhere,
Which erst so glistened with the golden streams
That cheerful Phœbus spread down from his sphere,   60
Beholding dark oppressing day so near;
    The sudden sight reducëd to my mind
    The sundry changes that in earth we find.

That musing on this worldly wealth in thought,
Which comes and goes more faster than we see
The flickering flame that with the fire is wrought,

My busy mind presented unto me
Such fall of peers as in this realm had be,
   That oft I wished some would their woes descrive,
   To warn the rest whom fortune left alive.   70

And straight forth stalking with redoubled pace,
For that I saw the night drew on so fast,
In black all clad there fell before my face
A piteous wight, whom woe had all forwaste;
Forth from her eyne the crystal tears out brast,
   And sighing sore, her hands she wrung and fold,
   Tare all her hair, that ruth was to behold.

Her body small, forwithered and forspent,
As is the stalk that summer's drought oppressed;
Her welkèd face with woeful tears besprent,
Her color pale, ard, as it seemed her best,   80
In woe and plaint reposèd was her rest;
   And as the stone that drops of water wears,
   So dented were her cheeks with fall of tears.

Her eyes swollen with flowing streams afloat;
Wherewith, her looks thrown up full piteously,
Her forceless hands together oft she smote,
With doleful shrieks that echoed in the sky;
Whose plaint such sighs did straight accompany,
   That, in my doom, was never man did see   90
   A wight but half so woebegone as she.

I stood aghast, beholding all her plight,
'Tween dread and dolor, so distrained in heart
That, while my hairs upstarted with the sight,
The tears outstreamed for sorrow of her smart;
But when I saw no end that could apart
   The deadly deule which she so sore did make,
   With doleful voice then thus to her I spake:

Unwrap thy woes, whatever wight thou be,
And stint betime to spill thyself with plaint;   100
Tell what thou art, and whence, for well I see
Thou canst not dure, with sorrow thus attaint.
And with that word of sorrow, all forfaint
   She lookèd up, and prostrate as she lay,
   With piteous sound, lo, thus she gan to say:

Alas, I, wretch whom thus thou seest distrained
With wasting woes that never shall aslake,
Sorrow I am, in endless torments pained
Among the Furies in the infernal lake
Where Pluto, god of Hell, so grisly black,   110
   Doth hold his throne, and Lethe's deadly taste
   Doth reave remembrance of each thing forepast.

Whence come I am, the dreary destiny
And luckless lot for to bemoan of those
Whom fortune, in this maze of misery,
Of wretched chance, most woeful mirrors chose;
That when thou seest how lightly they did lose
   Their pomp, their power, and that they thought most sure,
   Thou mayst soon deem no earthly joy may dure.

Whose rueful voice no sooner had out brayed   120
Those woeful words wherewith she sorrowed so,
But out, alas, she shright and never stayed,
Fell down, and all to-dashed herself for woe;
The cold pale dread my limbs gan overgo,
   And I so sorrowed at her sorrows eft
   That, what with grief and fear, my wits were reft.

I stretched myself and straight my heart revives,
That dread and dolor erst did so appall;
Like him that with the fervent fever strives,
When sickness seeks his castle health to scale,   130
With gathered spirits so forced I fear to avale;
   And rearing her with anguish all fordone,
   My spirits returned and then I thus begun:

O Sorrow, alas, sith Sorrow is thy name,
And that to thee this drear doth well pertain,
In vain it were to seek to cease the same;
But as a man himself with sorrow slain,
So I, alas, do comfort thee in pain,
   That here in sorrow art forsunk so deep
   That at thy sight I can but sigh and weep.   140

I had no sooner spoken of a sike,
But that the storm so rumbled in her breast
As Æolus could never roar the like;
And showers down rainëd from her eyne so fast
That all bedrent the place, till at the last

Well easèd they the dolor of her mind,
As rage of rain doth swage the stormy wind.

For forth she pacèd in her fearful tale:
Come, come, quoth she, and see what I shall show;
Come hear the plaining and the bitter bale   150
Of worthy men by fortune overthrow;
Come thou and see them rueing all in row;
   They were but shades that erst in mind thou rolled;
   Come, come with me, thine eyes shall them behold.

What could these words but make me more aghast,
To hear her tell whereon I mused whilere?
So was I mazed therewith, till at the last,
Musing upon her words, and what they were,
All suddenly well-lessoned was my fear;
   For to my mind returnèd how she telled   160
   Both what she was and where her wone she held.

Whereby I knew that she a goddess was,
And therewithal resorted to my mind
My thought, that late presented me the glass
Of brittle state, of cares that here we find,
Of thousand woes to silly men assigned;
   And how she now bid me come and behold,
   To see with eye that erst in thought I rolled.

Flat down I fell, and with all reverence
Adored her, perceiving now that she,   170
A goddess sent by godly providence,
In earthly shape thus showed herself to me,
To wail and rue this world's uncertainty;
   And while I honored thus her godhead's might,
   With plaining voice these words to me she shright:

I shall guide thee first to the grisly lake
And thence unto the blissful place of rest
Where thou shalt see and hear the plaint they make
That whilom here bare swing among the best;
This shalt thou see, but great is the unrest   180
   That thou must bide before thou canst attain
   Unto the dreadful place where these remain.

And with these words, as I upraisèd stood,
And gan to follow her that straight forth paced,
Ere I was ware, into a desert wood

We now were come, where, hand in hand embraced,
She led the way and through the thick so traced
    As, but I had been guided by her might,
    It was no way for any mortal wight.

But lo, while thus amid the desert dark   190
We passëd on with steps and pace unmeet,
A rumbling roar, confused with howl and bark
Of dogs, shook all the ground under our feet,
And struck the din within our ears so deep
    As, half distraught, unto the ground I fell,
    Besought return, and not to visit hell.

But she, forthwith, uplifting me apace,
Removed my dread, and with a steadfast mind
Bade me come on; for here was now the place,
The place where we our travail end should find;   200
Wherewith I arose, and to the place assigned
    Astoined I stalk, when straight we approached near
    The dreadful place that you will dread to hear.

An hideous hole all vast, withouten shape,
Of endless depth, o'erwhelmed with ragged stone,
With ugly mouth and grisly jaws doth gape,
And to our sight confounds itself in one;
Here entered we, and yeding forth, anon
    An horrible loathly lake we might discern,
    As black as pitch, that clepëd is Avern.   210

A deadly gulf where nought but rubbish grows,
With foul black swelth in thickened lumps that lies,
Which up in the air such stinking vapors throws
That over there may fly no fowl but dies,
Choked with the pestilent savors that arise;
    Hither we come, whence forth we still did pace,
    In dreadful fear amid the dreadful place.

And first, within the porch and jaws of hell,
Sat deep Remorse of Conscience, all besprent
With tears, and to herself oft would she tell   220
Her wretchedness, and cursing never stent
To sob and sigh, but ever thus lament
    With thoughtful care as she that, all in vain,
    Would wear and waste continually in pain.

Her eyes unsteadfast, rolling here and there,
Whirled on each place, as place that vengeance brought,
So was her mind continually in fear,
Tossed and tormented with the tedious thought
Of those detested crimes which she had wrought;
   With dreadful cheer and looks thrown to the sky,   230
   Wishing for death, and yet she could not die.

Next saw we Dread, all trembling how he shook,
With foot uncertain, proffered here and there,
Benumbed of speech, and with a ghastly look,
Searched every place, all pale and dead for fear,
His cap borne up with staring of his hair,
   'Stoined and amazed at his own shade for dread,
   And fearing greater dangers than was need.

And next, within the entry of this lake,
Sat fell Revenge, gnashing her teeth for ire,   240
Devising means how she may vengeance take,
Never in rest till she have her desire;
But frets within so far forth with the fire
   Of wreaking flames, that now determines she
   To die by death, or venged by death to be.

When fell Revenge, with bloody foul pretense
Had showed herself as next in order set,
With trembling limbs we softly parted thence,
Till in our eyes another sight we met,
When from my heart a sigh forthwith I fet,   250
   Rueing, alas, upon the woeful plight
   Of Misery, that next appeared in sight.

His face was lean and somedeal pined away,
And eke his hands consumëd to the bone,
But what his body was I cannot say,
For on his carcass raiment had he none,
Save clouts and patches, piecëd one by one;
   With staff in hand and scrip on shoulders cast,
   His chief defence against the winter's blast.

His food, for most, was wild fruits of the tree,   260
Unless sometimes some crumbs fell to his share,
Which in his wallet long, God wot, kept he,
As on the which full daint'ly would he fare;
His drink, the running stream; his cup, the bare

Of his palm closed; his bed, the hard cold ground;
To this poor life was Misery ybound.

Whose wretched state when we had well beheld,
With tender ruth on him and on his fears,
In thoughtful cares forth then our pace we held;
And by and by another shape appears,   270
Of greedy Care, still brushing up the breres,
    His knuckles knobbed, his flesh deep dented in,
    With tawëd hands and hard ytannëd skin.

The morrow grey no sooner had begun
To spread his light, even peeping in our eyes,
When he is up and to his work yrun;
But let the night's black misty mantles rise,
And with foul dark never so much disguise
    The fair bright day, yet ceaseth he no while,   280
    But hath his candles to prolong his toil.

By him lay heavy Sleep, the cousin of Death,
Flat on the ground and still as any stone,
A very corpse, save yielding forth a breath;
Small keep took he whom fortune frownëd on
Or whom she lifted up into the throne
    Of high renown; but as a living death,
    So, dead alive, of life he drew the breath.

The body's rest, the quiet of the heart,
The travail's ease, the still night's fere was he,
And of our life in earth the better part;   290
Reaver of sight, and yet in whom we see
Things oft that tide, and oft that never be;
    Without respect, esteeming equally
    King Crœsus' pomp, and Irus' poverty.

And next in order sad Old Age we found,
His beard all hoar, his eyes hollow and blind,
With drooping cheer still poring on the ground,
As on the place where nature him assigned
To rest, when that the sisters had untwined
    His vital thread and ended with their knife   300
    The fleeting course of fast declining life.

There heard we him with broken and hollow plaint
Rue with himself his end approaching fast,
And all for nought his wretched mind torment

With sweet remembrance of his pleasures past,
And fresh delights of lusty youth forewaste;
 Recounting which, how would he sob and shriek,
 And to be young again of Jove beseek!

But, and the cruel fates so fixëd be
That time forepast cannot return again,   310
This one request of Jove yet prayëd he,
That in such withered plight and wretched pain
As eld, accompanied with his loathsome train,
 Had brought on him, all were it woe and grief,
 He might a while yet linger forth his life,

And not so soon descend into the pit
Where Death, when he the mortal corpse hath slain,
With reckless hand in grave doth cover it,
Thereafter never to enjoy again
The gladsome light, but in the ground ylain,   320
 In depth of darkness waste and wear to nought,
 As he had never into the world been brought.

But who had seen him sobbing, how he stood
Unto himself and how he would bemoan
His youth forepast, as though it wrought him good
To talk of youth, all were his youth foregone,
He would have mused and marvelled much, whereon
 This wretched Age should life desire so fain,
 And knows full well life doth but length his pain.

Crookbacked he was, tooth-shaken, and blear-eyed, 330
Went on three feet, and sometimes crept on four,
With old lame bones that rattled by his side,
His scalp all pilled and he with eld forlore;
His withered fist still knocking at Death's door,
 Fumbling and drivelling as he draws his breath;
 For brief, the shape and messenger of Death.

And fast by him pale Malady was placed,
Sore sick in bed, her color all foregone,
Bereft of stomach, savor, and of taste,
Ne could she brook no meat, but broths alone;   340
Her breath corrupt, her keepers every one
 Abhorring her, her sickness past recure,
 Detesting physic and all physic's cure.

But oh, the doleful sight that then we see!
We turned our look and on the other side
A grisly shape of Famine might we see,
With greedy looks and gaping mouth that cried
And roared for meat, as she should there have died;
    Her body thin and bare as any bone,
    Whereto was left nought but the case alone.   **350**

And that, alas, was gnawn on everywhere,
All full of holes that I ne mought refrain
From tears to see how she her arms could tear,
And with her teeth gnash on the bones in vain,
When all for nought, she fain would so sustain
    Her starven corpse, that rather seemed a shade
    Than any substance of a creature made.

Great was her force, whom stone wall could not stay,
Her tearing nails snatching at all she saw;
With gaping jaws that by no means ymay   **360**
Be satisfied from hunger of her maw,
But eats herself as she that hath no law;
    Gnawing, alas, her carcass all in vain,
    Where you may count each sinew, bone, and vein.

On her while we thus firmly fixed our eyes,
That bled for ruth of such a dreary sight,
Lo, suddenly she shrieked in so huge wise
As made hell gates to shiver with the might;
Wherewith a dart we saw, how it did light
    Right on her breast, and therewithal, pale Death   **370**
    Enthrilling it, to reave her of her breath.

And by and by a dumb dead corpse we saw,
Heavy and cold, the shape of Death aright,
That daunts all earthly creatures to his law;
Against whose force in vain it is to fight;
Ne peers, ne princes, nor no mortal wight,
    No towns, ne realms, cities, ne strongest tower,
    But all, perforce, must yield unto his power.

His dart, anon, out of the corpse he took,
And in his hand, a dreadful sight to see,   **380**
With great triumph eftsoons the same he shook,
That most of all my fears affrayèd me;
His body dight with nought but bones, perdy,
    The naked shape of man there saw I plain,
    All save the flesh, the sinew, and the vein.

Lastly, stood War, in glittering arms yclad,
With visage grim, stern looks, and blackly hued;
In his right hand a naked sword he had,
That to the hilts was all with blood imbrued;
And in his left, that kings and kingdoms rued,   390
    Famine and fire he held, and therewithal
    He razèd towns and threw down towers and all.

Cities he sacked and realms that whilom flowered
In honor, glory, and rule above the best,
He overwhelmed and all their fame devoured,
Consumed, destroyed, wasted, and never ceased
Till he their wealth, their name, and all oppressed;
    His face forhewed with wounds, and by his side
    There hung his targe, with gashes deep and wide.

In midst of which, depainted there, we found   400
Deadly Debate, all full of snaky hair,
That with a bloody fillet was ybound,
Out-breathing nought but discord everywhere,
And round about were portrayed, here and there,
    The hugy hosts, Darius and his power,
    His kings, princes, his peers, and all his flower.

Whom great Macedo vanquished there in sight
With deep slaughter, despoiling all his pride,
Pierced through his realms and daunted all his might;
Duke Hannibal beheld I there beside,   410
In Canna's field victor how he did ride,
    And woeful Romans that in vain withstood,
    And consul Paulus covered all in blood.

Yet saw I more: the fight at Thrasimene,
And Treby field, and eke when Hannibal
And worthy Scipio last in arms were seen
Before Carthago gate, to try for all
The world's empire, to whom it should befall;
    There saw I Pompey and Cæsar clad in arms,
    Their hosts allied and all their civil harms.   420

With conquerors' hands, forbathed in their own blood,
And Cæsar weeping over Pompey's head;
Yet saw I Sulla and Marius where they stood,
Their great cruelty and the deep bloodshed
Of friends; Cyrus I saw and his host dead,
    And how the queen with great despite hath flung
    His head in blood of them she overcome.

Xerxes, the Persian king, yet saw I there
With his huge host that drank the rivers dry,
Dismounted hills, and made the vales uprear,   430
His host and all yet saw I plain, perdy;
Thebes I saw, all razed how it did lie
   In heaps of stones, and Tyrus put to spoil,
   With walls and towers flat evened with the soil.

But Troy, alas, methought above them all,
It made mine eyes in very tears consume,
When I beheld the woeful word befall,
That by the wrathful will of gods was come;
And Jove's unmovëd sentence and foredoom
   On Priam king, and on his town so bent,   440
   I could not lin, but I must there lament.

And that the more, sith destiny was so stern
As, force perforce, there might no force avail,
But she must fall, and by her fall we learn
That cities, towers, wealth, world, and all shall quail;
No manhood, might, nor nothing mought prevail;
   All were there prest, full many a prince and peer,
   And many a knight that sold his death full dear.

Not worthy Hector, worthiest of them all,
Her hope, her joy, his force is now for nought;   450
O Troy, Troy, Troy, there is no boot but bale,
The hugy horse within thy walls is brought;
Thy turrets fall, thy knights, that whilom fought
   In arms amid the field, are slain in bed,
   Thy gods defiled and all thy honor dead.

The flames upspring and cruelly they creep
From wall to roof till all to cinders waste;
Some fire the houses where the wretches sleep,
Some rush in here, some run in there as fast;
In everywhere or sword or fire they taste;   460
   The walls are torn, the towers whirled to the ground;
   There is no mischief but may there be found.

Cassandra yet there saw I how they haled
From Pallas' house, with spercled tress undone,
Her wrists fast bound and with Greeks' rout empaled;
And Priam eke, in vain how did he run
To arms, whom Pyrrhus with despite hath done
   To cruel death, and bathed him in the baign
   Of his son's blood, before the altar slain.

But how can I descrive the doleful sight   470
That in the shield so livelike fair did shine?
Sith in this world I think was never wight
Could have set forth the half, not half so fine;
I can no more but tell how there is seen
    Fair Ilium fall in burning red gledes down,
    And from the soil great Troy, Neptunus' town.

Herefrom when scarce I could mine eyes withdraw,
That filled with tears as doth the springing well,
We passèd on so far forth till we saw
Rude Acheron, a loathsome lake to tell,   480
That boils and bubs up swelth as black as hell;
    Where grisly Charon, at their fixèd tide,
    Still ferries ghosts unto the farther side.

The aged god no sooner Sorrow spied,
But hasting straight unto the bank apace,
With hollow call unto the rout he cried
To swerve apart and give the goddess place;
Straight it was done, when to the shore we pace,
    Where, hand in hand as we then linkèd fast,
    Within the boat we are together placed.   490

And forth we launch full fraughted to the brink,
When with the unwonted weight, the rusty keel
Began to crack as if the same should sink;
We hoise up mast and sail, that in a while
We fetched the shore, where scarcely we had while
    For to arrive, but that we heard anon
    A three-sound bark confounded all in one.

We had not long forth passed but that we saw
Black Cerberus, the hideous hound of hell,
With bristles reared and with a three-mouthed jaw   500
Fordinning the air with his horrible yell,
Out of the deep dark cave where he did dwell;
    The goddess straight he knew, and by and by,
    He peased and couched while that we passèd by.

Thence come we to the horror and the hell,
The large great kingdoms and the dreadful reign
Of Pluto in his throne where he did dwell,
The wide waste places and the hugy plain,
The wailings, shrieks, and sundry sorts of pain,
    The sighs, the sobs, the deep and deadly groan,   510
    Earth, air, and all, resounding plaint and moan.

Here puled the babes, and here the maids unwed
With folded hands their sorry chance bewailed,
Here wept the guiltless slain, and lovers dead,
That slew themselves when nothing else availed;
A thousand sorts of sorrows here, that wailed
   With sighs and tears, sobs, shrieks, and all yfear,
   That oh, alas, it was a hell to hear.

We stayed us straight, and with a rueful fear,
Beheld this heavy sight, while from mine eyes   520
The vapored tears down stillëd here and there,
And Sorrow eke, in far more woeful wise,
Took on with plaint, upheaving to the skies
   Her wretched hands, that with her cry the rout
   Gan all in heaps to swarm us round about.

Lo here, quoth Sorrow, princes of renown,
That whilom sat on top of fortune's wheel,
Now laid full low, like wretches whirlëd down,
Even with one frown, that stayed but with a smile;
And now behold the thing that thou, erewhile,   530
   Saw only in thought, and what thou now shalt hear,
   Recount the same to kesar, king, and peer.

Then first came Henry, Duke of Buckingham,
His cloak of black all pilled and quite forworn,
Wringing his hands, and fortune oft doth blame,
Which of a duke hath made him now her scorn;
With ghastly looks, as one in manner lorn,
   Oft spread his arms, stretched hands he joins as fast
   With rueful cheer and vapored eyes upcast.

His cloak he rent, his manly breast he beat,   540
His hair all torn, about the place it lay;
My heart so molt to see his grief so great,
As feelingly methought it dropped away;
His eyes they whirled about withouten stay,
   With stormy sighs the place did so complain,
   As if his heart at each had burst in twain.

Thrice he began to tell his doleful tale,
And thrice with sighs did swallow up his voice,
At each of which he shriekëd so withal,
As though the heavens rivëd with the noise;   550
Till at the last, recovering his voice,
   Supping the tears that all his breast berained,
   On cruel fortune, weeping, thus he plained.

THOMAS TUSSER

The Introduction and Notes are at pages 1198 and 1273

FROM *Five Hundred Points of Good Husbandry*, 1580

A preface to the buyer of this book

What lookest thou herein to have?
    Fine verses thy fancy to please?
Of many my betters that crave;
    Look nothing but rudeness in
        these.

What other thing lookest thou
        then?
    Grave sentences many to find?
Such, poets have, twenty and ten—
    Yea, thousands—contenting thy
        mind.

What look ye, I pray you, show
        what?
    Terms painted with rhetoric
        fine?   10

Good husbandry seeketh   not
        that,
    Nor is't any meaning of mine.

What lookest thou? Speak at the
        last.
    Good lessons for thee and thy
        wife?
Then keep them in memory fast
    To help as a comfort to life.

What look ye for more in my book?
    Points needful and meet to be
        known?
Then daily be sure to look,
    To save, to be sure, thine own.   20

[*The praise of husbandry*]
As true as thy faith,
This riddle thus saith.

I seem but a drudge, yet I pass any king;
To such as can use me great wealth I do bring.
Since Adam first livëd I never did die,
When Noe was a shipman there also was I.
The earth to sustain me, the sea for my fish,
Be ready to pleasure me as I would wish.
What hath any life but I help to preserve?
What wight without me but is ready to starve?
In woodland, in champian, city, or town,
If long I be absent, what falleth not down?   10
If long I be present, what goodness can want?
Though things at my coming were never so scant.
So many as love me and use me aright
With treasure and pleasure I richly acquite.
Great kings I do succor, else wrong it would go;
The King of all kings hath appointed it so.

A description of the properties of winds at all times of the year

In winter	North winds send hail, South winds bring rain,
	East winds we bewail, West winds blow amain;
	North-east is too cold, South-east not too warm,
	North-west is too bold, South-west doth no harm.
At the spring	The North is a noyer to grass of all suits,
	The East a destroyer to herb and all fruits,
Summer	The South with his showers refresheth the corn,
	The West to all flowers may not be forborne.
Autumn	The West, as a father, all goodness doth bring,
	The East, a forbearer no manner of thing,
	The South, as unkind, draweth sickness too near,
	The North, as a friend, maketh all again clear.
God is the Governor of wind and weather	With temperate wind we be blessed of God,
	With tempest we find we are beat with his rod;
	All power, we know to remain in his hand,
	However wind blow, by sea or by land.

10

Christmas husbandly fare

Good husband and housewife now chiefly be glad
   Things handsome to have, as they ought to be had.
They both do provide, against Christmas do come,
   To welcome good neighbor, good cheer to have some.

Good bread and good drink, a good fire in the hall,
   Brawn, pudding, and souse, and good mustard withal.

Beef, mutton, and pork, shred pies of the best,
   Pig, veal, goose, and capon, and turkey well dressed,
Cheese, apples, and nuts; jolly carols to hear,
   As then in the country is counted good cheer.

10

What cost to good husband is any of this?
   Good household provision only it is.
Of other the like I leave out a many
   That costeth the husbandman never a penny.

A sonnet upon the author's first seven years service

Seven times hath Janus ta'en new year by hand,
Seven times hath blust'ring March blown forth his power,

To drive out April's buds, by sea and land,
For minion May to deck most trim with flower.
Seven times hath temperate Ver like pageant played,
And pleasant Æstas eke her flowers told,
Seven times Autumnë's heat hath been delayed
With Hiems' boisterous blasts and bitter cold.
Seven times the thirteen moons have changëd hue,
Seven times the sun his course hath gone about,   10
Seven times each bird her nest hath built anew,
Since first time you to serve I choosëd out.
Still yours am I, though thus the time hath passed,
And trust to be, as long as life shall last.

BARNABE GOOGE

The Introduction and Notes are at pages 1199 and 1273

FROM *Eclogues, Epitaphs, and Sonnets,* 1563

To the right worshipful M. William Lovelace, Esquire,
Reader of Gray's Inn, Barnabe Googe wisheth health.

*How loath I have been, being of long time earnestly required to
suffer these trifles of mine to come to light, it is not unknown to a
great number of my familiar acquaintance, who both daily and hourly
moved me thereunto, and little of long time prevailed therein. For
I both considered and weighed with myself the grossness of my style,
which thus committed to the gazing show of every eye should forthwith disclose the manifest folly of the writer, and also I feared and
mistrusted the disdainful minds of a number both scornful and carping correctors, whose heads are ever busied in taunting judgments,
lest they should otherwise interpret my doings than indeed I meant
them. These two so great mischiefs utterly dissuaded me from the
following of my friends' persuasions, and willed me rather to condemn them to continual darkness, whereby no inconvenience could
happen, than to endanger myself in giving them to light, to the disdainful doom of any offended mind. Notwithstanding, all the diligence
that I could use in the suppression thereof could not suffice; for I
myself being at that time out of the realm, little fearing any such
thing to happen, a very friend of mine, bearing, as it seemed, better
will to my doings than respecting the hazard of my name, committed
them altogether unpolished to the hands of the printer. In whose
hands, during his absence from the city till his return of late, they
remained. At which time he declared the matter wholly unto me,
showing me that being so far passed, and paper provided for the impression thereof, it could not without great hindrance of the poor
printer be now revoked. His sudden tale made me at the first utterly*

*amazed; and doubting a great while what was best to be done, at the
length agreeing both with necessity and his counsel, I said with Martial,* iam sed poteras tutior esse domi. *And calling to mind to whom I
might chiefly commit the fruits of my smiling muse, suddenly was
cast before my eyes the perfect view of your friendly mind, gentle
Master Lovelace; unto whom, for the numbered heaps of sundry
friendships accounting myself as bound, I have thought best to give
them, not doubting but that they shall be as well taken as I do
presently mean them.*

*Desiring you herein, as all such as shall read them, especially to bear
with the unpleasant form of my too hastily finished* Dream, *the greater
part whereof with little advice I lately ended, because the beginning
of it, as a senseless head separated from the body, was given with the
rest to be printed. And thus desiring but for recompense the friendly
receiving of my slender gift, I end; wishing unto you, good Master
Lovelace, in this life the happy enjoying of prosperous years, and
hereafter the blessed estate of never-ceasing joy.*

Yours assuredly,
Barnabe Googe.

Coming homeward out of Spain

O raging seas, and mighty Nep-
    tune's reign,
In monstrous hills that throwest
    thyself so high,
That with thy floods dost beat the
    shores of Spain,
And break the cliffs that dare thy
    force envý;
Cease now thy rage and lay thine
    ire aside.
And thou that hast the govern-
    ance of all,
O mighty God! grant weather,
    wind, and tide,
Till in my country coast our an-
    chor fall.

Out of sight, out of mind

The oftener seen, the more I lust,
The more I lust, the more I
    smart,

The more I smart, the more I
    trust,
The more I trust, the heavier
    heart;
The heavy heart breeds mine un-
    rest,
Thy absence, therefore, like I best.

The rarer seen, the less in mind,
The less in mind, the lesser pain,
The lesser pain, less grief I find,
The lesser grief, the greater
    gain,   10
The greater gain, the merrier I,
Therefore I wish thy sight to fly.

The further off, the more I joy,
The more I joy, the happier life,
The happier life, less hurts annoy,
The lesser hurts, pleasure most
    rife:
Such pleasures rife shall I obtain
When distance doth depart us
    twain.

[*Once musing as I sat*]

Once musing as I sat,
   and candle burning by,
When all were hushed, I might
   discern
   a simple silly fly,
That flew before mine eyes
   with free rejoicing heart,
And here and there with wings
   did play,
   as void of pain and smart.
Sometime by me she sat,
   when she had played her fill, 10
And ever when she rested had,
   about she flittered still.
When I perceived her well,
   rejoicing in her place,
O happy fly, quoth I, and eke

O worm in happy case,
   Which two of us is best?
I that have reason? No;
But thou that reason art without
   and therewith void of woe. 20
I live, and so dost thou,
   but I live all in pain,
And subject am to her, alas,
   that makes my grief her gain.
Thou livest, but feelst no grief,
   no love doth thee torment;
A happy thing for me it were,
   if God were so content,
That thou with pen wert placëd
   here
   and I sat in thy place, 30
Then I should joy, as thou dost
   now,
   and thou shouldst wail thy case.

To Doctor Bale

Good aged Bale, that with thy hoary hairs
Dost yet persist to turn the painful book,
O happy man, that hast obtained such years,
And leav'st not yet on papers pale to look,
Give over now to beat thy wearied brain,
And rest thy pen that long hath labored sore;
For aged men unfit sure is such pain,
And thee beseems to labor now no more.
But thou, I think, Don Plato's part will play,
With book in hand to have thy dying day.   10

An epitaph of the death of Nicholas Grimald

Behold this fleeting world, how all things fade,
How every thing doth pass and wear away;
Each state of life, by common course and trade,
Abides no time, but hath a passing day.
For look, as Life, that pleasant dame, hath brought
The pleasant years and days of lustiness,
So Death, our foe, consumeth all to nought;
Envýing thief, with dart doth us oppress.
And that which is the greatest grief of all,
The greedy gripe doth no estate respect,   10
But where he comes he makes them down to fall;

Nor stays he at the high sharp-witted sect.
For if that wit or worthy eloquence
Or learning deep could move him to forbear,
O Grimald, then thou hadst not yet gone hence,
But here hadst seen full many an aged year;
Nor had the Muses lost so fine a flower,
Nor had Minerva wept to leave thee so;
If wisdom might have fled the fatal hour,
Thou hadst not yet been suffered for to go.   20
A thousand doltish geese we might have spared,
A thousand witless heads death might have found,
And taken them for whom no man had cared,
And laid them low in deep oblivious ground:
But fortune favors fools, as old men say,
And lets them live, and takes the wise away.

GEORGE TURBERVILLE

The Introduction and Notes are at pages 1200 and 1273

FROM *Epitaphs, Epigrams, Songs and Sonnets,* 1567

To his love
That sent him a ring wherein was graved
'Let reason rule'

Shall reason rule where reason hath no right
Nor never had? Shall Cupid lose his lands?
His claim? his crown? his kingdom? name of might?
And yield himself to be in reason's bands?
No, friend, thy ring doth will me thus in vain.
Reason and love have ever yet been twain.
They are by kind of such contrary mould
As one mislikes the other's lewd device;
What reason wills, Cupido never would;
Love never yet thought reason to be wise.   10
To Cupid I my homage erst have done,
Let reason rule the hearts that she hath won.

Verse in praise of Lord Henry Howard, Earl of Surrey

What should I speak in praise of Surrey's skill
Unless I had a thousand tongues at will?
No one is able to depaint at full
The flowing fountain of his sacred skull,

Whose pen approved what wit he had in mew,
Where such a skill in making sonnets grew.
Each word in place with such a sleight is couched,
Each thing whereof he treats so firmly touched,
As Pallas seemed within his noble breast
To have sojourned and been a daily guest.   10
Our mother tongue by him hath got such light
As ruder speech thereby is banished quite.
Reprove him not for fancies that he wrought,
For fame thereby, and nothing else, he sought.
What though his verse with pleasant toys are fright?
Yet was his honor's life a lamp of light.
A mirror he, the simple sort to train,
That ever beat his brain for Britain's gain.
By him the nobles had their virtues blazed,
When spiteful death their honors' lives had razed;   20
Each that in life had well deservëd aught,
By Surrey's means an endless fame hath caught.
To quite his boon and aye well-meaning mind,
Whereby he did his sequel seem to bind,
Though want of skill to silence me procures,
I write of him whose fame for aye endures;
A worthy wight, a noble for his race,
A learned lord that had an earl's place.

Of drunkenness

At night when ale is in,
　　Like friends we part to bed;
In morrow grey, when ale is out,
　　Then hatred is in head.

The lover to his lady
That gazed much up to the skies

My girl, thou gazest much
　　Upon the golden skies:
Would I were heaven! I would behold
　　Thee then with all mine eyes.

From *Tragical Tales*, 1587

To a fair gentlewoman, false to her friend

Within the garden-plot of thy fair face
Doth grow a graff of divers qualities:
A matter rare, within so little space

A man to find such sundry properties;
For commonly the root in every tree,
Bark, body, boughs, bud, leaf, and fruit agree.
    First, for the root, is rigor in the breast,
Treason the tree that springeth of the same,
Beauty the bark that overspreads the rest,
The boughs are brave, and climbing up to fame;   10
Brawls be the buds that hang on every bough,
A blossom fit for such roots to allow.
    Love is the leaf that little time endures,
Flatt'ry the fruit which treason's tree doth bear;
Though beauty's bark at first the eye allure,
Yet at the last ill will, the worm, doth wear
Away the leaf, the blossoms, boughs, and all,
And rigor's root makes beauty's buds to fall.

He declares that albeit he were imprisoned in Russia, yet his mind was at liberty and did daily repair to his friend

    Now find I true that hath been often told,
No man may reave the freedom of the mind.
Though keeper's charge in chains the captive hold,
Yet can he not the soul in bondage bind;
That this is true, I find the proof in me,
Who captive am, and yet at liberty.
    Though at my heel a cruel clog they tie,
And ranging out by rigor be restrained,
Yet maugre might, my mind doth freely fly
Home to my friend,—it will not be enchained.   10
No churlë's check, no tyrant's threat can stay
A lover's heart that longs to be away.
    I do desire no aid of Dædalus,
By feat to forge such waxen wings anew
As erst he gave his son, young Icarus,
When they from Crete for fear of Minos flew;
Dame Fancy hath such feathers still in store
For me to fly, as I desire no more.

Unable by long and hard travel to banish love, returns her friend

    Wounded with love and piercing deep desire
Of your fair face, I left my native land
With Russia snow to slack mine English fire;
But well I see no cold can quench the brand
That Cupid's coals enkindle in the breast,

Frost hath no force where friendship is possessed.
The ocean sea, for all his fearful flood,
The perils great of passage, not prevail,
To banish love the rivers do no good,
The mountains high cause Cupid not to quail,   10
Wight are his wings, and fancy flies as fast
As any ship, for all his sails and mast.
The river Dwina cannot wash away
With all his waves the love I bear to thee,
Nor Suchan swift love's raging heat delay,—
Good will was graffed upon so sure a tree.
Sith travel then, nor frost, can cool this fire,
From Moscow I thy friend will home retire.

That he finds others as fair, but not so faithful as his friend

I sundry see, for beauty's gloss,
    That with my mistress may compare,
But few I find for true good will
    That to their friends so friendly are.
Look what she says, I may assure
    Myself thereof—she will not feign;
What others speak is hard to trust,
    They measure all their words by gain.
Her looks declare her loving mind,
    Her count'nance and her heart agree;   10
When others laugh they look as smooth
    But love not half so well as she.
The grief is hers when I am griped,
    My finger's ache is her disease;
With me though others mourn to sight,
    Yet are their hearts at quiet ease.
So that I mark, in Cupid's court
    Are many fair and fresh to see,
Each where is sown Dame Beauty's seed,
    But fair and faithful few there be.   20

To his friend, promising that though her beauty fade, yet his love shall last

I wot full well that beauty cannot last;
No rose that springs but lightly doth decay,
And feature like a lily leaf doth waste,
Or as the cowslip in the midst of May;
I know that tract of time doth conquer all,
And beauty's buds like fading flowers do fall.

That famous dame, fair Helen, lost her hue
When withered age with wrinkles changed her cheeks,
Her lovely looks did loathsomeness ensue
That was the *A per se* of all the Greeks.   10
And sundry mo that were as fair as she,
Yet Helen was as fresh as fresh might be.

No force for that, I price your beauty light
If so I find you steadfast in good will.
Though few there are that do in age delight,
I was your friend, and so do purpose still;
No change of looks shall breed my change of love,
Nor beauty's want my first good will remove.

THOMAS HOWELL

The Introduction and Notes are at page 1201

FROM *The Arbor of Amity*, 1568

When he thought himself contemned

O heart, why dost thou sigh, and wilt not break?
O doleful chance, thou hast a cause thereto;
For thy reward in love and kindness eke
Is recompensed by hate and deadly woe.

Have I so plight my heart and mind to thee?
Have I been bent so whole unto thy hand,
And others now obtain the fruit from me?
Thou art unkind, forsooth, such foe to stand.

O doleful heart, thus plunged in pinching pain,
Lament no more, but break, thy truth to try;   10
For where thy comfort was and joy did reign,
Now hate returns no news, O heart, now die!

Lo, thus the breeding birds their nests do build,
But others take the gains and fruits of them;
The crooked clown so ear'th the toiling field,
But oft the crop remains to other men.

Well, time may come wherein my fruitless part,
So ill bestowed, some others may bewail,
And wish they had received my yielding heart
Whose loving root took ground to small avail.   20

Of misery

Corpse, clad with carefulness,
Heart, heaped with heaviness,
Purse, poor and penniless,
Back, bare in bitterness,
Lips, laide with loathsomeness;
Oh, get my grave in readiness,
Fain would I die to end this stress,
Remédiless.

The rose

Whenas the mildest month
Of jolly June doth spring,
And gardens green with happy
    hue
    Their famous fruits do bring;
When eke the lustiest time
    Reviveth youthly blood,
Then springs the finest featured
    flower
    In border fair that stood;
Which moveth me to say,
    In time of pleasant year   10
Of all the pleasant flowers in
    June
    The red rose hath no peer.

To one who after death would leave his lively picture

To leave behind a picture, fine to see,
It may small time well stand in stead for thee;
But picture fair of noble acts of mind—
That far excels to learn to leave behind,
Which will maintain a noble name for aye
As Tully's tongue and Cæsar's acts can say;
As Chaucer shows, and eke our moral Gower,
With thousands more whose fame shall still endure.

Jack shows his qualities and great good will to Jone

Mine own zweet Jone, let me not
    moan,
    no more I thee require,
But as I crave, so let me have
    the thing I do desire.
And ich shall still even at thy will
    be ready at thy hand,
To fling, to spring, and run at ring
    whilst ich am able stand.
With cap and knee ich will serve
    thee,
    what should ich more de-
    clare?   10
Thy mind to please and body ease
    is only all my care.
Though ich am not zo seemly,
    'chwot,
    as been the courtnoles gay,
Yet 'ch'ave a flail that will not
    fail
    to thrash both night and
    day.
And vor manhood 'cham zure
    'cham good,
    vor all our town can zay
How stout ich stood with Robart
    Whood
    when Baldoone volk vetcht
    May;   20
And eke ich pass both more and lass

in dancing Downtoone's
round:
To trip, to skip, and handle a whip
'cham zure my peer's not
vound.
To clout a shoe, ich may tell you,
veow cunnigare there be;
And eke to thatch, where can ye
vetch
another like to me?
In husbandry ich am truly
ycounted to excel; 30
Yea, and ich can, if need be than,
wait at the table well.
For once ich went up into Kent
with the head man of our
town,
Where ich did wait at every bait,
chee vore the 'cham no
clown.
Why, for my manor, ich bear the
banner
before my Lord of May;
No country man there is that can
teach me, though I do zay. 40
And furthermore thou knowest
gay store
of good will fall to me;
Vor vather zed, when he is dead
that all mine own shall be:
Both calf and cow and our great
zow
that vifteen pigs did varrow
Even at one time, shall then be
mine,
and eke our new wheelbar-
row.
Beside all this, ich shall not miss
of red ones to have store, 50
That zaw no zun, nor yet the
moon,
of years 'cham zure a score.
And all, my Jone, shalt thou alone
at thy commandment have,
If thou wilt let me friscals vet
in place where ich do crave.

FROM *H. His Devices*, 1581

Of the golden world

The golden world is past, saith
some,
But now, say I, that world is
come:
Now all things may for gold be
had,
For gain of gold, both good and
bad.
Now honor high for gold is
bought,
That erst of greater price was
thought.
For gold the fool aloft doth
rise,
And oft is placed above the wise.
For gold the subtile show their
skill,
For gold the wicked win their
will. 10
For gold who shuns to wrest a
wrong,
And make it seem as right and
strong?
Who spares to plead as pleaseth
thee
If bring thou do a golden fee?
The fatherless is quite forgot
Where golden gifts do fall to
lot;
For gold the widow is oppressed,
And rightful heirs are dispossessed.
Poor Irus' cause at door doth
stand,
If Crœsus come with gold in
hand. 20
What mischief may almost be
thought
That now for gold not daily
wrought?
A heap of ills for gold are cloaked,
Yea, vice for gold hath virtue
choked.

For gain of gold the flatterer
    smiles
And on thee fawns with sundry
    wiles.
I will not, here, through golden
    traps
Say lovers light in ladies' laps.
But, brief to be, what can you
    crave
That now for gold you may not
    have?   30
Then truth to tell, and not to
    feign,
Right now the golden world doth
    reign.

To his lady, of her doubtful answer

'Twixt death and doubtfulness,
'Twixt pain and pensiveness,
'Twixt hell and heaviness,
Rests all my carefulness.

Oh, vain security,
That will not liberty,
Fie on that fantasy
That brings captivity!

My life is loathsomeness,
My pleasure pastimeless,   10
My end your doubtfulness
If you be merciless.

In doubt is jealousy,
Hope helpeth misery;
Most women commonly
Have answers readily.

THOMAS CHURCHYARD

The Introduction and Notes are at page 1201

FROM The First Part of Churchyard's Chips, 1575

The praise of our soldiers

Would God my pen might be your trump of fame,
To sound the praise that you deservëd there!
O martial men, that seeks but noble name,
Ye ought of right be honored ev'rywhere.
To you I speak, on whom the burthen lies
Of wars, and doth by sword and service rise,
Who spares no charge nor pain in prince's right,
When state must stand by stout and manly fight.

Your hearts are such you hate at home to bide
When any bruit or voice of wars is heard;   10

Ashamed in street on foot-cloth here to ride,
When forward minds in field should be preferred.
And scorning pomp and peevish pleasures vain
For true renown, ye trudge and toil amain
Where danger dwells and heaps of hazards are,
And hardness great you find, with hungry fare.

You ward the day and watch the winter's night,
In frost, in cold, in sun and heat also;
You are so bent that labor seemeth light
And in the stead of joy you welcome woe.   20
For wealth you take such want as doth befall,
Not shunning grief, but tasting sorrows all;
More glad to die than live with blame or blot,
Most ready still where least is to be got.

And least esteemed of all the men that lives
(Like hackney horse cast off when turn is served),
Yet are you those that greatest honor gives,
If world may judge what soldiers have deserved,
Unto your prince; for you are pale and park
To keep the deer, and lanterns in the dark   30
To show them light, that else at plain noon-day
Might stumble down, or slyly shrink away.

Who bides the brunt, or who bears off the blows
But you alone? Yea, who doth show his face
In time of need, among our foreign foes,
Or boldly saith, Let me supply your place?
Tush! that's a tale was never heard nor seen,—
That anyone, to serve a king or queen,
Did strive with you, or offered half so much
For fame as they who now these verses touch.   40

Wherefore step out, and bear a branch of bays
In sign of world the victors sure you are;
For this I know, in right respect of praise
And worthy laud, may none with you compare.
You may be called the awful martial band,
The jewels gay and garland of the land,
The buds of fame and blossoms of renown,
The country's hope, and beauty of the crown.

Now must you mark: I mean not hirelings here,
Nor summer birds and swallows for the time,   50
That wages takes and serves but once a year,
And sprouts a while as flowers do in their prime;
But those whose minds and noble manners shows
In peace or war, Lo! there a soldier goes,
Of life most clear, of deed and word full just,
In trial still a man of special trust.

FROM THOMAS PROCTER'S *Gorgeous Gallery of Gallant
Inventions*, 1578

*The lover deceived by his lady's unconstancy writeth unto her
as followeth*

The heat is past that did me fret,
The fire is out that nature wrought;
The plants of youth that I did set
Are dry and dead within my thought;
The frost hath slain the kindly sap
That kept the heart in lively state;
The sudden storm and thunder-clap
Hath turnëd love to mortal hate.

The mist is gone that bleared mine eyes,
The low'ring clouds I see appear;
Though that the blind eat many flies,   11
I would you knew my sight is clear.
Your sweet deceiving flatt'ring face
Did make me think that you were white;
I muse how you had such a grace
To seem a hawk, and be a kite.

Where precious ware is to be sold
They shall it have that giveth most;
All things we see are won with gold,
Few things is had where is no cost.   20
And so it fareth now by me,
Because I press to give no gifts
She takes my suit unthankfully,
And drives me off with many drifts.

Is this th' end of all my suit,
For my good will to have a scorn?
Is this of all my pains the fruit,
To have the chaff instead of corn?
Let them that list possess such dross,
For I deserve a better gain;   30
Yet had I rather leave with loss
Than serve and sue, and all in vain.

GEORGE GASCOIGNE

The Introduction and Notes are at page 1202

FROM *A Hundreth Sundry Flowers*, [1573]

Gascoigne's good morrow

You that have spent the silent
    night
In sleep and quiet rest,
And joy to see the cheerful light
    That riseth in the east,
Now clear your voice, now cheer
    your heart,
Come help me now to sing,
Each willing wight come bear a
    part,
    To praise the heavenly King.

And you whom care in prison
    keeps,
Or sickness doth suppress,   10
Or secret sorrow breaks your
    sleeps,
    Or dolors do distress,
Yet bear a part in doleful wise,
    Yea, think it good accord
And acceptáble sacrifice
    Each sprite to praise the Lord.

The dreadful night with dark-
    some storms
    Had overspread the light,
And sluggish sleep with drowsi-
    ness
Had over-pressed our might;   20
A glass wherein we may behold
    Each storm that stops our breath,
Our bed the grave, our clothes
    like mold,
    And sleep like dreadful death.

Yet, as this deadly night did
    last

But for a little space,
And heavenly day, now night is
    past,
Doth show his pleasant face,
So must we hope to see God's
    face
At last in heaven on high,   30
When we have changed this mor-
    tal place
    For immortality.

And of such haps and heavenly
    joys
As then we hope to hold,
All earthly sights, all worldly toys
    Are tokens to behold.
The day is like the day of doom,
    The sun, the Son of Man,
The skies the heavens, the earth
    the tomb
Wherein we rest till than.   40

The rainbow bending in the
    sky,
Bedecked with sundry hues,
Is like the seat of God on high
    And seems to tell these news:
That, as thereby he promisëd
    To drown the world no more,
So by the blood which Christ hath
    shed
    He will our health restore.

The misty clouds that fall some-
    time
And overcast the skies   50
Are like to troubles of our time,
    Which do but dim our eyes;

But as such dews are dried up
        quite
When Phœbus shows his face,
So are such fancies put to flight
Where God doth guide by grace.

The carrion crow, that loath-
        some beast,
Which cries against the rain,
Both for her hue and for the rest
The devil resembleth plain;   60
And as with guns we kill the
        crow
For spoiling our relief,
The devil so must we overthrow
With gunshot of belief.

The little birds which sing so
        sweet
Are like the angels' voice,
Which render God his praises
        meet
And teach us to rejoice;
And as they more esteem that
        mirth
Than dread the night's annoy, 70
So must we deem our days on
        earth
But hell to heavenly joy.

Unto which joys for to attain
God grant us all his grace,
And send us after worldly pain
In heaven to have a place,
Where we may still enjoy that
        light
Which never shall decay;
Lord, for thy mercy, lend us
        might
To see that joyful day!   80

Gascoigne's arraignment

At Beauty's bar as I did stand,
When False Suspect accusèd me,

George (quoth the judge), hold
        up thy hand.
Thou art arraigned of flattery;
Tell therefore how thou wilt be
        tried?
Whose judgment here wilt thou
        abide?

My lord (quoth I), this lady
        here,
Whom I esteem above the rest,
Doth know my guilt, if any were;
Wherefore her doom shall please
        me best.   10
Let her be judge and juror both,
To try me, guiltless by mine oath.

Quoth Beauty, No, it fitteth
        not,
A prince herself to judge the
        cause.
Here is our justice, well you wot,
Appointed to discuss our laws;
If you will guiltless seem to go,
God and your country quit you
        so.

Then Craft, the crier, called a
        quest,
Of whom was Falsehood fore-
        most fere;   20
A pack of pickthanks were the rest
Which came false witness for to
        bear.
The jury such, the judge unjust,
Sentence was said I should be
        trussed.

Jealous, the jailer, bound me
        fast,
To hear the verdict of the bill;
George (quoth the judge), now
        thou art cast,
Thou must go hence to Heavy
        Hill

And there be hanged, all but the
　　head:
God rest thy soul when thou art
　　dead.　　　　　30

Down fell I then upon my
　　knee,
All flat before Dame Beauty's
　　face,
And cried: Good lady, pardon
　　me,
Which here appeal unto your
　　grace!
You know if I have been untrue
It was in too much praising you.

And though this judge do make
　　such haste
To shed with shame my guiltless
　　blood,
Yet let your pity first be placed,
To save the man that meant you
　　good.　　　　　40
So shall you show yourself a
　　queen,
And I may be your servant seen.

Quoth Beauty, Well; because
　　I guess
What thou dost mean henceforth
　　to be.
Although thy faults deserve no
　　less
Than justice here hath judgëd
　　thee,
Wilt thou be bound to stint all
　　strife
And be true prisoner all thy life?

Yea, madam (quoth I), that I
　　shall.
Lo, Faith and Truth my sureties. 50
Why then (quoth she), come
　　when I call;
I ask no better warrantise.

Thus am I Beauty's bounden
　　thrall,
At her command when she doth
　　call.

Gascoigne's lullaby

Sing lullaby, as women do,
Wherewith they bring their babes
　　to rest,
And lullaby can I sing too
As womanly as can the best.
With lullaby they still the child,
And if I be not much beguiled,
Full many wanton babes have I
Which must be stilled with lul-
　　laby.

First, lullaby my youthful years,
It is now time to go to bed,　10
For crooked age and hoary hairs
Have won the haven within my
　　head;
With lullaby, then, youth be still,
With lullaby, content thy will,
Since courage quails and comes be-
　　hind,
Go sleep, and so beguile thy mind.

Next, lullaby my gazing eyes,
Which wonted were to glance
　　apace.
For every glass may now suf-
　　fice
To show the furrows in my face; 20
With lullaby, then, wink awhile,
With lullaby, your looks beguile,
Let no fair face nor beauty bright
Entice you eft with vain delight.

And lullaby, my wanton will,
Let reason's rule now reign thy
　　thought,
Since all too late I find by skill
How dear I have thy fancies
　　bought;

With lullaby, now take thine ease,
With lullaby, thy doubts appease;
For trust to this, if thou be still,   31
My body shall obey thy will.

Eke, lullaby my loving boy,
My little Robin, take thy rest;
Since age is cold and nothing coy,
Keep close thy coin, for so is best;
With lullaby, be thou content,
With lullaby, thy lusts relent,
Let others pay which have mo
    pence,
Thou art too poor for such ex-
    pense.   40

Thus lullaby, my youth, mine
    eyes,
My will, my ware, and all that
    was!
I can no mo delays devise,
But welcome pain, let pleasure
    pass;
With lullaby, now take your
    leave,
With lullaby, your dreams de-
    ceive,
And when you rise with waking
    eye,
Remember Gascoigne's lullaby.

Gascoigne's De profundis

*The occasion of the writing here-
of (as I have heard Master
Gascoigne say) was this: riding
alone between Chelmsford and
London, his mind mused upon
the days past, and therewithal
he gan accuse his own conscience of much time misspent,
when a great shower of rain
did overtake him; and he being
unprepared for the same, as in
a jerkin without a cloak, the
weather being very fair and un-*

*likely to have changed so, he
began to accuse himself of his
carelessness; and thereupon in
his good disposition compiled
first this sonnet, and afterwards
the translated Psalm of De
profundis. . . .*

The skies gan scowl, o'ercast
    with misty clouds,
When (as I rode alone by Lon-
    don way,
Cloakless, unclad) thus did I sing
    and say:
Behold, quoth I, bright Titan—
    how he shrouds
His head aback, and yields the
    rain his reach,
Till in his wrath Dan Jove have
    soused the soil
And washed me, wretch which in
    his travail toil.
But holla! here doth rudeness me
    apeach.
Since Jove is Lord and King of
    mighty power,
Which can command the sun to
    show his face,   10
And, when him list, to give the
    rain his place,
Why do not I my weary muses
    frame
(Although I be well soused in
    this shower)
To write some verse in honor of
    his name?

[Inscription in his garden]

If any flower that there is grown,
Or any herb, may ease your pain,
Take, and accompt it as your
    own,
But recompense the like again:
For some and some is honest play,
And so my wife taught me to say.

If here to walk you take de-
    light,
Why, come and welcome, when
    you will;
If I bid you sup here this night,
Bid me another time, and still   10
Think some and some is honest
    play,
For so my wife taught me to say.

Thus if you sup or dine with
    me,
If you walk here or sit at ease,
If you desire the thing you see,
And have the same, your mind to
    please,
Think some and some is honest
    play,
And so my wife taught me to say.

FROM *The Whole Works of George Gascoigne*, 1587

Deep Desire sung this song

Come, Muses, come, and help me to lament,
    Come woods, come waves, come hills, come doleful dales!
Since life and death are both against me bent,
    Come gods, come men, bear witness of my bales.
O heavenly nymphs, come help my heavy heart,
With sighs to see Dame Pleasure thus depart.

If death or dole could daunt a deep desire,
    If privy pangs could counterpeise my plaint,
If tract of time a true intent could tire,
    Or cramps of care a constant mind could taint;   10
Oh then might I at will here live and starve,
Although my deeds did more delight deserve.

But out, alas, no gripes of grief suffice
    To break in twain this harmless heart of mine;
For though delight be banished from mine eyes,
    Yet lives Desire, whom pains can never pine.
Oh strange affects! I live, which seem to die,
Yet die to see my dear delight go by.

Then farewell, sweet, for whom I taste such sour,
    Farewell, delight, for whom I dwell in dole!   20
Free will, farewell, farewell my fancy's flower,
    Farewell, content, whom cruel cares control.
Oh farewell, life; delightful death, farewell!
I die in heaven, yet live in darksome hell.

FROM *The Steel Glass*, [1576]

The steel glass

.   .   .   .

For whiles I mark this weak and wretched world,
Wherein I see how every kind of man

Can flatter still, and yet deceives himself,
I seem to muse, from whence such error springs,
Such gross conceits, such mists of dark mistake,
Such surquedry, such weening over-well
(And yet, indeed, such dealings too, too bad),
And as I stretch my weary wits, to weigh
The cause thereof, and whence it should proceed,
My battered brains (which now be shrewdly bruised   10
With cannon shot of much misgovernment)
Can spy no cause but only one conceit
Which makes me think the world goeth still awry.

I see and sigh (because it makes me sad)
That peevish pride doth all the world possess;
And every wight will have a looking-glass
To see himself, yet so he seeth him not.
Yea, shall I say, a glass of common glass,
Which glist'reth bright and shows a seemly show,
Is not enough: the days are past and gone   20
That beryl glass, with foils of lovely brown,
Might serve to show a seemly favored face.
That age is dead, and vanished long ago,
Which thought that steel both trusty was and true,
And needed not a foil of contraries,
But showed all things even as they were indeed.
Instead whereof, our curious years can find
The crystal glass, which glimpseth brave and bright,
And shows the thing much better than it is,
Beguiled with foils of sundry subtile sights,   30
So that they seem, and covet not to be.

This is the cause (believe me now, my lord)
That realms do rue from high prosperity,
That kings decline from princely government,
That lords do lack their ancestors' good will,
That knights consume their patrimony still,
That gentlemen do make the merchant rise,
That plowmen beg, and craftsmen cannot thrive,
That clergy quails and hath small reverence,
That laymen live by moving mischief still,   40
That courtiers thrive at latter Lammas Day,
That officers can scarce enrich their heirs,
That soldiers starve, or preach at Tyburn cross,
That lawyers buy, and purchase deadly hate,
That merchants climb, and fall again as fast,
That roisters brag above their betters' room,

That sycophants are counted jolly guests,
That Lais leads a lady's life aloft,
And Lucrece lurks with sober bashful grace.

This is the cause (or else my muse mistakes)   50
That things are thought which never yet were wrought,
And castles built above in lofty skies
Which never yet had good foundation.
And that the same may seem no feignëd dream,
But words of worth, and worthy to be weighed,
I have presumed my lord for to present
With this poor glass, which is of trusty steel,
And came to me by will and testament
Of one that was a glass-maker indeed.

Lucilius this worthy man was named,   60
Who at his death bequeathed the crystal glass
To such as love to seem but not to be;
And unto those that love to see themselves,
How foul or fair soever that they are,
He gan bequeath a glass of trusty steel,
Wherein they may be bold always to look,
Because it shows all things in their degree.
And since myself (now pride of youth is past)
Do love to be, and let all seeming pass;
Since I desire to see myself indeed—   70
Not what I would, but what I am, or should—
Therefore I like this trusty glass of steel.

.   .   .   .   .

But holla! here I see a wondrous sight,
I see a swarm of saints within my glass.
Behold, behold! I see a swarm indeed
Of holy saints, which walk in comely wise,
Not decked in robes nor garnishëd with gold,
But some unshod, yea, some full thinly clothed;
And yet they seem so heavenly for to see
As if their eyes were all of diamonds,   80
Their face of rubies, sapphires, and jacinths,
Their comely beards and hair of silver wires,—
And to be short, they seem angelical.
What should they be, my lord, what should they be?

O gracious God, I see now what they be.
These be my priests, which pray for ev'ry state;
These be my priests, divorcëd from the world,

And wedded yet to heaven and holiness;
Which are not proud nor covet to be rich,
Which go not gay nor feed on dainty food,   90
Which envy not nor know what malice means,
Which loathe all lust, disdaining drunkenness,
Which cannot feign, which hate hypocrisy,
Which never saw Sir Simony's deceits,
Which preach of peace, which carp contentions,
Which loiter not, but labor all the year,
Which thunder threats of God's most grievous wrath,
And yet do teach that mercy is in store.

Lo, these, my lord, be my good praying priests,
Descended from Melchizedek by line,   100
Cousins to Paul, to Peter, James, and John;
These be my priests, the seas'ning of the earth,
Which will not leese their sav'riness, I trow.

Not one of these, for twenty hundred groats,
Will teach the text that bids him take a wife,
And yet be cumbered with a concubine.

Not one of these will read the holy writ
Which doth forbid all greedy usury,
And yet receive a shilling for a pound.

Not one of these will preach of patience   110
And yet be found as angry as a wasp.

Not one of these can be content to sit
In taverns, inns, and alehouses all day,
But spends his time devoutly at his book.

Not one of these will rail at rulers' wrongs
And yet be blotted with extortion.

Not one of these will paint out worldly pride,
And he himself as gallant as he dare.

Not one of these rebuketh avarice
And yet procureth proud pluralities.   120

Not one of these reproveth vanity
Whiles he himself, with hawk upon his fist
And hounds at heel, doth quite forget his text.

Not one of these corrects contentions
For trifling things, and yet will sue for tithes.

Not one of these, not one of these, my lord,
Will be ashamed to do even as he teacheth.

My priests have learnt to pray unto the Lord,
And yet they trust not in their lip-labor.

My priests can fast, and use all abstinence   130
From vice and sin, and yet refuse no meats.

My priests can give in charitable wise
And love also to do good almës deeds,
Although they trust not in their own deserts.

My priests can place all penance in the heart
Without regard of outward ceremonies.

My priests can keep their temples undefiled
And yet defy all superstition.

Lo now, my lord, what think you by my priests,
Although they were the last that showed themselves?   140
I said at first their office was to pray;
And since the time is such, even nowadays,
As hath great need of prayers truly prayed,
Come forth, my priests, and I will bid your beads.
I will presume, although I be no priest,
To bid you pray as Paul and Peter prayed.

Then pray, my priests, yea, pray to God himself   *The Poet's*
That he vouchsafe, even for his Christë's sake,   *Beads:*
To give his word free passage here on earth,
And that his church, which now is militant,   150
May soon be seen triumphant over all;
And that he deign to end this wicked world
Which walloweth still in sinks of filthy sin.

Eke pray, my priests, for princes and for kings,   *For*
Emperors, monarchs, dukes, and all estates   *Princes;*
Which sway the sword of royal government
(Of whom our Queen, which lives without compare,
Must be the chief, in bidding of my beads,
Else I deserve to leese both beads and bones);
That God give light unto their noble minds,   160

To maintain truth, and therewith still to weigh
That here they reign not only for themselves,
And that they be but slaves to common wealth;
Since all their toils and all their broken sleeps
Shall scant suffice to hold it still upright.

Tell some (in Spain) how close they keep their closets,
How seld the wind doth blow upon their cheeks,
While as, meanwhile, their sunburnt suitors starve
And pine before their process be preferred.
Then pray, my priests, that God will give his grace   170
To such a prince, his fault in time to mend.

Tell some (in France) how much they love to dance,
While suitors dance—attendance at the door.
Yet pray, my priests, for prayers princes mend.

Tell some (in Portugal) how cold they be
In setting forth of right religion;
Which more esteem the present pleasures here
Than stablishing of God his holy word.
And pray, my priests, lest God such princes spit
And vomit them out of his angry mouth.   180

Tell some (Italian) princes how they wink
At stinking stews, and say they are, forsooth,
A remedy to quench foul, filthy lust;
Whenas in deed they be the sinks of sin.
And pray, my priests, that God will not impute
Such willful facts unto such princes' charge,
When he himself commandeth every man
To do none ill that good may grow thereby.

And pray likewise for all that rulers be   *For All*
By kings' commands, as their lieutenants here,   *Nobility* 190
All magistrates, all councillors, and all   *and Councillors;*
That sit in office or authority.
Pray, pray, my priests, that neither love nor meed
Do sway their minds from furthering of right,
That they be not too saintish nor too sour,
But bear the bridle evenly between both;
That still they stop one ear, to hear him speak
Which is accusèd, absent as he is;
That evermore they mark what mood doth move
The mouth which makes the information;   200
That faults forepast (so that they be not huge

Nor do exceed the bonds of loyalty)
Do never quench their charitable mind
Whenas they see repentance hold the reins
Of heady youth, which wont to run astray;
That malice make no mansion in their minds,
Nor envy fret to see how virtue climbs.
The greater birth the greater glory, sure,
If deeds maintain their ancestors' degree.

Eke pray, my priests, for them and for yourselves,   *For the*   210
For bishops, prelates, arch-deans, deans, and priests,   *Clergy;*
And all that preach, or otherwise profess
God's holy word, and take the cure of souls.
Pray, pray, that you, and every one of you,
May walk upright in your vocation;
And that you shine like lamps of perfect life,
To lend a light and lantern to our feet.

Say therewithal that some (I see them, I,
Whereas they fling in Flanders all afar,
For why my glass will show them as they be)   220
Do neither care for God nor yet for devil,
So liberty may launch about at large.

And some, again, (I see them well enough,
And note their names, in Liegeland where they lurk)
Under pretense of holy humble hearts,
Would pluck adown all princely diadem.
Pray, pray, my priests for these; they touch you near.

Shrink not to say that some do, Roman-like,
Esteem their pall and habit over-much.
And therefore pray, my priests, lest pride prevail.   230

Pray that the souls of sundry damnèd ghosts
Do not come in, and bring good evidence
Before the God which judgeth all men's thoughts
Of some whose wealth made them neglect their charge,
Till secret sins, untouched, infect their flocks
And bred a scab which brought the sheep to bane.

Some other ran before the greedy wolf,
And left the fold unfended from the fox,
Which durst nor bark nor bawl for both their ears.
Then pray, my priests, that such no more do so.   240

Pray for the nurses of our noble realm,
I mean the worthy Universities,
(And Cantabridge shall have the dignity,
Whereof I was unworthy member once)
That they bring up their babes in decent wise: *For All*
That Philosophy smell no secret smoke *Learned;*
Which Magic makes, in wicked mysteries;
That Logic leap not over every stile
Before he come a furlong near the hedge,
With curious *quids* to maintain argument; 250
That Sophistry do not deceive itself;
That Cosmography keep his compass well;
And such as be historiographers
Trust not too much in every tattling tongue,
Nor blinded be by partiality;
That Physic thrive not over-fast by murder;
That numb'ring men, in all their evens and odds,
Do not forget that only Unity
Unmeasurable, infinite, and one;
That Geometry measure not so long 260
Till all their measures out of measure be;
That Music with his heavenly harmony
Do not allure a heavenly mind from heaven,
Nor set men's thoughts in worldly melody
Till heavenly hierarchies be quite forgot;
That Rhetoric learn not to over-reach;
That Poetry presume not for to preach,
And bite men's faults with satire's corrosives,
Yet pamper up her own with poultices,
Or that she dote not upon Erato, 270
Which should invoke the good Calliope;
That Astrology look not over-high
And light, meanwhile, in every puddled pit;
That Grammar grudge not at our English tongue
Because it stands by *monosyllaba*
And cannot be declined, as others are.
Pray thus, my priests, for Universities.
And if I have forgotten any art
Which hath been taught or exercisèd there,
Pray you to God the good be not abused 280
With glorious show of overloading skill.

Now these be past, my priests, yet shall you pray *For the*
For common people, each in his degree, *Common-*
That God vouchsafe to grant them all his grace. *alty.*
Where should I now begin to bid my beads?

Or who shall first be put in common place?
My wits be weary and my eyes are dim,
I cannot see who best deserves the room;
Stand forth, good Piers, thou plowman, by thy name,—
Yet so, the sailor saith I do him wrong.   290
That one contends his pains are without peer;
That other saith that none be like to his;
Indeed they labor both exceedingly.
But since I see no shipman that can live
Without the plow, and yet I many see
Which live by land that never saw the seas,
Therefore I say, stand forth, Piers plowman, first;
Thou win'st the room by very worthiness.

Behold him, priests, and though he stink of sweat   *The*
Disdain him not. For, shall I tell you what?   *Plowman.* 300
Such climb to heaven before the shaven crowns.
But how? Forsooth, with true humility.
Not that they hoard their grain when it is cheap,
Nor that they kill the calf to have the milk,
Nor that they set debate between their lords
By earing up the balks that part their bounds;
Nor for because they can both crouch and creep
(The guileful'st men that ever God yet made)
Whenas they mean most mischief and deceit;
Nor that they can cry out on landlords loud,   310
And say they rack their rents an ace too high,
When they themselves do sell their landlord's lamb
For greater price than ewe was wont be worth.
(I see you, Piers; my glass was lately scoured.)
But for they feed with fruits of their great pains
Both king and knight, and priests in cloister pent,
Therefore, I say, that sooner some of them
Shall scale the walls which lead us up to heaven
Than corn-fed beasts whose belly is their god,
Although they preach of more perfection.   320

And yet, my priests, pray you to God for Piers,
As Piers can pinch it out for him and you.
And if you have a paternoster spare,
Then shall you pray for sailors (God them send
More mind of him whenas they come to land—
For toward shipwreck many men can pray),
That they once learn to speak without a lie,
And mean good faith without blaspheming oaths;
That they forget to steal from every freight,

And for to forge false cockets, free to pass;   330
That manners make them give their betters place,
And use good words, though deeds be nothing gay.

But here methinks my priests begin to frown
And say that thus they shall be overcharged,
To pray for all which seem to do amiss;
And one I hear, more saucy than the rest,
Which asketh me, When shall our prayers end?

I tell thee, priest: when shoemakers make shoes
That are well sewed, with never a stitch amiss,
And use no craft in utt'ring of the same;   340
When tailors steal no stuff from gentlemen;
When tanners are with curriers well agreed,
And both so dress their hides that we go dry;
When cutlers leave to sell old rusty blades,
And hide no cracks with solder nor deceit;
When tinkers make no more holes than they found,
When thatchers think their wages worth their work,
When colliers put no dust into their sacks,
When maltmen make us drink no firmentie,
When Davie Diker digs, and dallies not,   350
When smiths shoe horses as they would be shod,
When millers toll not with a golden thumb,
When bakers make not barm bear price of wheat,
When brewers put no baggage in their beer,
When butchers blow not over all their flesh,
When horse-coursers beguile no friends with jades,
When weavers' weight is found in housewives' web.
(But why dwell I so long among these louts?)

When mercers make more bones to swear and lie,
When vintners mix no water with their wine,   360
When printers pass none errors in their books,
When hatters use to buy none old cast robes,
When goldsmiths get no gain by soldered crowns,
When upholsters sell feathers without dust,
When pewterers infect no tin with lead,
When drapers draw no gains by giving day,
When parchmenters put in no ferret silk,
When surgeons heal all wounds without delay.
(Tush! these are toys, but yet my glass showeth all.)

When purveyors provide not for themselves,   370
When takers take no bribes nor use no brags,

When customers conceal no covin used,
When searchers see all corners in a ship
(And spy no pence by any sight they see),
When shrieves do serve all process as they ought,
When bailiffs strain none other thing but strays,
When auditors their counters cannot change,
When proud surveyors take no parting pence,
When silver sticks not on the teller's fingers,
And when receivers pay as they receive, 380
When all these folk have quite forgotten fraud.

(Again, my priests, a little, by your leave)
When sycophants can find no place in court
But are espied for echoes, as they are;
When roisters ruffle not above their rule,
Nor color craft by swearing precious coals;
When fencers' fees are like to apes' rewards—
A piece of bread, and therewithal a bob;
When Lais lives not like a lady's peer,
Nor useth art in dyeing of her hair: 390
When all these things are ordered as they ought,
And see themselves within my glass of steel,
Even then, my priests, may you make holiday
And pray no more but ordinary prayers.

And yet therein I pray you, my good priests,
Pray still for me, and for my glass of steel,
That it (nor I) do any mind offend
Because we show all colors in their kind.
And pray for me, that since my hap is such
To see men so, I may perceive myself. 400
Oh, worthy words to end my worthless verse—
Pray for me, priests, I pray you pray for me.

Tam Marti, quam Mercurio

GEORGE WHETSTONE

The Introduction and Notes are at pages 1204 and 1273

FROM *The Rock of Regard*, 1576

Description of cozeners

A lawyer's head to draw a crafty deed,
A harlot's look to witch with wanton sight,

A flatterer's tongue with sugared words to feed,
A tyrant's heart to wound the harmless wight,
To toll with cheer a greedy glutton's gorge,
A merchant's mouth of falsehood truth to forge,

A scrivener's fist by nimbleness to race,
To scrape, to forge, to counterfeit a name,
A lackey's leg to trudge in every place,
A desperate mind which dreads no kind of shame,—   10
These limbs, well linked, and set on cozener's soil,
A work were sure of all the devils the toil!

For each of them a fiend in force can bind;
Yet some, I grant, by virtue guides their place;
But seldom 'tis that kit ne follows kind,
If one be good, a score doth want the grace.
But all in league, their dealings lewd beware,
For then they do the devil and all off scare!

Epilogus

Lo, ladies, here (if you can use it well)
An arbor fenced from burning fire and frost;
A place it is where pride shall never dwell,
Nor fortune work a maze, do she her worst;
A place wherein the worthy dame should live,
Whom no extreme may change from virtuous thought:
Even such a place my muse, fair dames, doth give
To you, the which with double toil is wrought.
Here may you see, by lamps of others' lives,
A president to live in worthy name;   10
Here may you see, when death your days deprives,
In spite of death remembrance of your fame.

HUMPHREY GIFFORD

The Introduction and Notes are at page 1204

From *A Posy of Gillyflowers*, 1580

For soldiers

Ye buds of Brutus' land, courageous youths, now play your parts,
Unto your tackle stand, abide the brunt with valiant hearts!
For news is carried to and fro that we must forth to warfare go,
Men muster now in every place, and soldiers are pressed forth apace.

Faint not, spend blood, to do your Queen and country good!
Fair words, good pay, will make men cast all care away.

The time of war is come: prepare your corslet, spear, and shield.
Methinks I hear the drum strike doleful marches to the field,
Tantara, tantara! the trumpets sound, which makes our hearts with
    joy abound;
The roaring guns are heard afar, and every thing denounceth war.   10
Serve God, stand stout, bold courage brings this gear about;
Fear not, forth run, faint heart fair lady never won.

Ye curious carpet knights, that spend the time in sport and play,
Abroad, and see new sights! your country's cause calls you away.
Do not, to make your ladies game, bring blemish to your worthy name,
Away to field and win renown! with courage beat your enemies down!
Stout hearts gain praise when dastards sail in slander's seas.
Hap what hap shall, we sure shall die but once for all.

Alarm methinks they cry. Be packing, mates, be gone with speed!
Our foes are very nigh,—shame have that man that shrinks at need! 20
Unto it boldly let us stand, God will give right the upper hand;
Our cause is good, we need not doubt. In sign of courage give a
    shout!
March forth, be strong, good hap will come ere it be long;
Shrink not, fight well, for lusty lads must bear the bell.

All you that will shun evil must dwell in warfare every day,
The world, the flesh, and devil always do seek our souls' decay:
Strive with these foes with all your might, so shall you fight a worthy
    fight.
That conquest doth deserve most praise where vice do yield to virtue's
    ways.
Beat down foul sin! a worthy crown then shall ye win!
If we live well, in heaven with Christ our souls shall dwell.   30

A delectable dream

.   .   .   .   .

A woman's face is full of wiles,
  Her tears are like the crocodile;
With outward cheer on thee she
    smiles
  When in her heart she thinks
    thee ill.
Her tongue still chats of this and
    that,

Than aspen leaf it wags more
    fast;
And as she talks she knows not
    what,
There issues many a truthless
    blast.
Thou far dost take thy mark
    amiss

If thou think faith in them to
find.   10
The weathercock more constant is,
Which turns about with every
wind.
Oh, how in pity they abound!
Their heart is mild like marble
stone;
If in thyself no hope be found,
Be sure of them thou gettest
none.
I know some pepper-nosëd dame

Will term me fool and saucy
jack,
That dare their credit so defame
And lay such slanders on their
back.   20
What though on me they pour their
spite?
I may not use the glozer's trade:
I cannot say the crow is white,
But needs must call a spade a
spade.

. . . .

RICHARD STANYHURST

The Introduction and Notes are at pages 1205 and 1273

FROM *The First Four Books of Virgil*, 1582

A prayer to the Trinity

Trinity blessed, deity co-equal,
Unity sacred, God one eke in essence,
Yield to thy servant, pitifully calling,
    Merciful hearing.
Virtuous living did I long relinquish,
Thy will and precepts miserably scorning.
Grant to me, sinful, patïent repenting,
    Healthful amendment.
Blessed I judge him that in heart is healëd;
Cursëd I know him that in health is harmëd: 10
Thy physic therefore to me, wretch unhappy,
    Send, my redeemer!
Glory to God, the father, and his only
Son, the protector of us earthly sinners,
The sacred spirit, laborers refreshing,
    Still be renownëd!
                    Amen.

EDWARD DE VERE, EARL OF OXFORD

The Introduction and Notes are at page 1205

FROM RICHARD EDWARDS's *Paradise of Dainty Devices*, 1576

Of the mighty power of love

My meaning is to work what woundës love hath wrought,
Wherewith I muse why men of wit have love so dearly bought.

For love is worse than hate, and eke more harm hath done;
Record I take of those that rede of Paris, Priam's son.

It seemed the god of sleep had mazed so much his wits
When he refusëd wit for love, which cometh but by fits.
But why accuse I him whom earth hath covered long?
There be of his posterity alive; I do him wrong.

Whom I might well condemn, to be a cruel judge
Unto myself, who hath that crime in others that I grudge.   10

From *Rawlinson Poetry Ms.* 85

[*Who taught thee first to sigh?*]

Who taught thee first to sigh, alas, my heart?
Who taught thy tongue the woeful words of plaint?
Who filled your eyes with tears of bitter smart?
Who gave thee grief, and made thy joys to faint?

Who first did paint with colors pale thy face?
Who first did break thy sleeps of quiet rest?
Above the rest in court who gave thee grace?
Who made thee strive, in honor to be best?

In constant truth to bide so firm and sure?
To scorn the world, regarding but thy friends?   10
With patient mind each passion to endure?
In one desire to settle to the end?

Love then thy choice, wherein such choice thou bind
As nought but death may ever change thy mind.

[*If women could be fair*]

If women could be fair and yet not fond,
Or that their love were firm, not fickle, still,
I would not marvel that they make men bond,
By service long to purchase their good will.
    But when I see how frail those creatures are,
    I muse that men forget themselves so far.

To mark the choice they make and how they change,
How oft from Phœbus they do fly to Pan,
Unsettled still, like haggards wild they range,
These gentle birds that fly from man to man;   10

Who would not scorn, and shake them from the fist,
And let them fly, fair fools, which way they list?

Yet for disport we fawn and flatter both,
To pass the time when nothing else can please;
And train them to our lure with subtle oath
Till, weary of their wiles, ourselves we ease;
And then we say, when we their fancy try,
To play with fools, oh, what a fool was I!

From *Breton's Bower of Delights*, 1591

Of the birth and bringing up of Desire

When wert thou born, Desire? In pomp and prime of May.
By whom, sweet boy, wert thou begot? By Good Conceit, men say.
Tell me, who was thy nurse? Fresh Youth, in sugared joy.
What was thy meat and daily food? Sad sighs, with great annoy.
What had you then to drink? Unfeignèd lovers' tears.
What cradle were you rockèd in? In hope devoid of fears.
What brought you then asleep? Sweet Speech, which likes men best.
And where is now your dwelling-place? In gentle hearts I rest.
Doth company displease? It doth, in many one.
Where would Desire then choose to be? He likes to muse alone.   10
What feedeth most your sight? To gaze on favor still.
Who find you most to be your foe? Disdain of my good will.
Will ever age or death bring you unto decay?
No, no! Desire both lives and dies a thousand times a day.

From R. S.'s *Phœnix Nest*, 1593

[*What cunning can express?*]

What cunning can express
The favor of her face
To whom in this distress
I do appeal for grace?
  A thousand Cupids fly
  About her gentle eye.

From whence each throws a dart
That kindleth soft sweet fire
Within my sighing heart,
Possessèd by desire.   10
  No sweeter life I try
  Than in her love to die.

The lily in the field
That glories in his white,
For pureness now must yield
And render up his right.
  Heav'n pictured in her face
  Doth promise joy and grace.

Fair Cynthia's silver light
That beats on running streams   20
Compares not with her white,
Whose hairs are all sun-beams.
  Her virtues so do shine
  As day unto mine eyne.

With this there is a red
Exceeds the damask rose,
Which in her cheeks is spread,
Whence every favor grows.
  In sky there is no star
  That she surmounts not far. 30

When Phœbus from the bed
Of Thetis doth arise,
The morning blushing red

In fair carnation wise,
  He shows it in her face
  As queen of every grace.

This pleasant lily-white,
This taint of roseate red,
This Cynthia's silver light,
This sweet fair Dea spread, 40
These sun-beams in mine eye,
These beauties make me die!

SIR PHILIP SIDNEY

The Introduction and Notes are at pages 1206 and 1273

FROM *Sir P. S. his Astrophel and Stella,* 1591

To the worshipful and his very good friend, Ma. Francis Flower, Esquire, increase of all content.

It was my fortune (right worshipful) not many days since, to light upon the famous device of Astrophel and Stella, *which carrying the general commendation of all men of judgment, and being reported to be one of the rarest things that ever any Englishman set abroach, I have thought good to publish it under your name, both for I know the excellency of your worship's conceit, above all other to be such as is only fit to discern of all matters of wit, as also for the credit and countenance your patronage may give to such a work. Accept of it, I beseech you, as the first fruits of my affection, which desires to approve itself in all duty unto you; and though the argument perhaps may seem too light for your grave view, yet considering the worthiness of the author, I hope you will entertain it accordingly. For my part, I have been very careful in the printing of it, and whereas, being spread abroad in written copies it had gathered much corruption by ill writers, I have used their help and advice in correcting and restoring it to his first dignity, that I know were of skill and experience in those matters. And the rather was I moved to set it forth because I thought it pity anything proceeding from so rare a man should be obscured, or that his fame should not still be nourished in his works, whom the works with one united grief bewailed. Thus craving pardon for my bold attempt, and desiring the continuance of your worship's favor unto me, I end.*

Yours always to be commanded,
Tho. Newman.

FROM *The Countess of Pembroke's Arcadia,* 1598

To the reader.

The disfigured face, gentle reader, wherewith this work not long since appeared to the common view, moved that noble lady, to whose honor consecrated, to whose protection it was committed, to take in hand the wiping away those spots wherewith the beauties thereof were unworthily blemished. But as often in repairing a ruinous house, the mending of some old part occasioneth the making of some new, so here her honorable labor, begun in correcting the faults, ended in supplying the defects; by the view of what was ill done guided to the consideration of what was not done. Which part with what advice entered into, with what success it hath been passed through, most by her doing, all by her directing, if they may be entreated not to define, which are unfurnished of means to discern, the rest, it is hoped, will favorably censure. . . .

H. S.

Astrophel and Stella

Loving in truth, and fain in verse my love to show,
   That she, dear she, might take some pleasure of my pain,
   Pleasure might cause her read, reading might make her know,
   Knowledge might pity win, and pity grace obtain,—
I sought fit words to paint the blackest face of woe;
   Studying inventions fine, her wits to entertain,
   Oft turning others' leaves to see if thence would flow
   Some fresh and fruitful showers upon my sun-burned brain.
But words came halting forth, wanting invention's stay;
   Invention, nature's child, fled step-dame Study's blows,
   And others' feet still seemed but strangers in my way.
Thus, great with child to speak, and helpless in my throes,
   Biting my truant pen, beating myself for spite,
   Fool, said my muse to me, look in thy heart and write.

Not at the first sight, nor with a dribbed shot,
   Love gave the wound, which, while I breathe, will bleed;
   But known worth did in mine of time proceed,
   Till by degrees it had full conquest got.
I saw and liked; I liked but lovèd not;
   I loved, but straight did not what love decreed;
   At length to love's decrees I, forced, agreed,
   Yet with repining at so partial lot.
Now even that footstep of lost liberty
   Is gone, and now, like slave-born Muscovite,
   I call it praise to suffer tyranny;

And now employ the remnant of my wit
To make me self believe that all is well,
While, with a feeling skill, I paint my hell.

Let dainty wits cry on the sisters nine,
  That, bravely masked, their fancies may be told;
  Or Pindar's apes flaunt they in phrases fine,
  Enam'ling with pied flowers their thoughts of gold;
Or else let them in statelier glory shine,
  Ennobling new-found tropes with problems old;
  Or with strange similes enrich each line,
  Of herbs or beasts which Ind or Afric hold.
For me, in sooth, no Muse but one I know;
  Phrases and problems from my reach do grow,   10
  And strange things cost too dear for my poor sprites.
How then? even thus,—in Stella's face I read
  What love and beauty be, then all my deed
  But copying is, what in her Nature writes.

It is most true that eyes are formed to serve
  The inward light, and that the heavenly part
  Ought to be king, from whose rules who do swerve,
  Rebels to nature, strive for their own smart.
It is most true what we call Cupid's dart
  An image is which for ourselves we carve,
  And, fools, adore in temple of our heart
  Till that good god make church and churchman starve.
True, that true beauty virtue is indeed,
  Whereof this beauty can be but a shade,   10
  Which elements with mortal mixture breed.
True, that on earth we are but pilgrims made,
  And should in soul up to our country move;
  True, and yet true that I must Stella love.

Some lovers speak, when they their muses entertain,
  Of hopes begot by fear, of wot not what desires,
  Of force of heav'nly beams infusing hellish pain,
  Of living deaths, dear wounds, fair storms, and freezing fires;
Someone his song in Jove and Jove's strange tales attires,
  Bordered with bulls and swans, powdered with golden rain;
  Another humbler wit to shepherd's pipe retires,
  Yet hiding royal blood full oft in rural vein;

To some a sweetest plaint a sweetest style affords,
   While tears pour out his ink, and sighs breathe out his words,   10
   His paper pale despair, and pain his pen doth move.
I can speak what I feel, and feel as much as they,
   But think that all the map of my state I display
   When trembling voice brings forth that I do Stella love.

When nature made her chief work, Stella's eyes,
   In color black why wrapped she beams so bright?
   Would she in beamy black, like painter wise,
   Frame daintiest luster mixed of shades and light?
Or did she else that sober hue devise
   In object best to knit and strength our sight,
   Lest, if no veil these brave gleams did disguise,
   They, sunlike, should more dazzle than delight?
Or would she her miraculous power show,
   That, whereas black seems beauty's contrary,   10
   She even in black doth make all beauties flow?
Both so, and thus,—she, minding Love should be
   Placed ever there, gave him this mourning weed
   To honor all their deaths who for her bleed.

Alas, have I not pain enough, my friend,
   Upon whose breast a fiercer gripe doth tire
   Than did on him who first stole down the fire,
   While Love on me doth all his quiver spend,—
But with your rhubarb words ye must contend,
   To grieve me worse, in saying that desire
   Doth plunge my well-formed soul even in the mire
   Of sinful thoughts which do in ruin end?
If that be sin which doth the manners frame,
   Well stayed with truth in word and faith of deed,   10
   Ready of wit and fearing nought but shame;
If that be sin which in fixed hearts doth breed
   A loathing of all loose unchastity,
   Then love is sin, and let me sinful be.

You that do search for every purling spring
   Which from the ribs of old Parnassus flows,
   And every flower, not sweet perhaps, which grows
   Near thereabouts into your poesy wring;
You that do dictionary's method bring
   Into your rhymes, running in rattling rows;
   You that poor Petrarch's long-deceasèd woes
   With new-born sighs and denizened wit do sing;

You take wrong ways, those far-fet helps be such
　　As do bewray a want of inward touch,
　　And sure at length stol'n goods do come to light.
But if, both for your love and skill, your name
　　You seek to nurse at fullest breasts of Fame,
　　Stella behold, and then begin to endite.

———

Fly, fly, my friends, I have my death wound, fly;
　　See there that boy, that murth'ring boy, I say,
　　Who, like a thief, hid in dark bush doth lie
Till bloody bullet get him wrongful prey.
So tyrant he no fitter place could spy,
　　Nor so fair level in so secret stay,
　　As that sweet black which veils the heav'nly eye:
There himself with his shot he close doth lay.
Poor passenger, pass now thereby I did,
　　And stayed, pleased with the prospect of the place,
　　While that black hue from me the bad guest hid;
But straight I saw motions of lightning grace,
　　And then descried the glist'ring of his dart;
　　But ere I could fly thence, it pierced my heart.

———

Your words, my friend, (right healthful caustics) blame
　　My young mind marred, whom love doth windlass so
　　That mine own writings, like bad servants, show
My wits quick in vain thoughts, in virtue lame;
That Plato I read for nought but if he tame
　　Such coltish years; that to my birth I owe
　　Nobler desires, lest else that friendly foe,
Great expectation, wear a train of shame.
For since mad March great promise made of me,
　　If now the May of my years much decline,
　　What can be hoped my harvest time will be?
Sure, you say well, Your wisdom's golden mine
　　Dig deep with learning's spade. Now tell me this,
　　Hath this world aught so fair as Stella is?

———

Rich fools there be whose base and filthy heart
　　Lies hatching still the goods wherein they flow,
　　And damning their own selves to Tantal's smart,
Wealth breeding want, more blest, more wretched grow.
Yet to those fools heaven such wit doth impart,
　　As what their hands do hold, their heads do know;
　　And knowing, love; and loving, lay apart
As sacred things, far from all danger's show.

But that rich fool, who by blind fortune's lot
   The richest gem of love and life enjoys,   10
   And can with foul abuse such beauties blot,
Let him, deprived of sweet but unfelt joys,
   Exiled for aye from those high treasures which
   He knows not, grow in only folly rich!

You that with allegory's curious frame
   Of others' children changelings use to make,
   With me those pains, for God's sake, do not take;
   I list not dig so deep for brazen fame.
When I say Stella, I do mean the same
   Princess of beauty for whose only sake
   The reins of love I love, though never slake,
   And joy therein, though nations count it shame.
I beg no subject to use eloquence,
   Nor in hid ways do guide philosophy;   10
   Look at my hands for no such quintessence,
But know that I in pure simplicity
   Breathe out the flames which burn within my heart,
   Love only reading unto me this art.

Whether the Turkish new-moon minded be
   To fill his horns this year on Christian coast;
   How Poles' right king means without leave of host
   To warm with ill-made fire cold Muscovy;
If French can yet three parts in one agree;
   What now the Dutch in their full diets boast;
   How Holland hearts, now so good towns be lost,
   Trust in the shade of pleasing Orange-tree;
How Ulster likes of that same golden bit
   Wherewith my father once made it half tame;   10
   If in the Scotch Court be no welt'ring yet:
These questions busy wits to me do frame.
   I, cumbered with good manners, answer do,
   But know not how, for still I think of you.

With how sad steps, O moon, thou climb'st the skies!
   How silently, and with how wan a face!
   What! may it be that even in heav'nly place
   That busy archer his sharp arrows tries?
Sure, if that long-with-love-acquainted eyes
   Can judge of love, thou feel'st a lover's case;
   I read it in thy looks,—thy languished grace
   To me, that feel the like, thy state descries.

Then, ev'n of fellowship, O moon, tell me,
   Is constant love deemed there but want of wit?   10
   Are beauties there as proud as here they be?
Do they above love to be loved, and yet
   Those lovers scorn whom that love doth possess?
   Do they call virtue there ungratefulness?

I might—unhappy word!—oh me, I might,
   And then would not, or could not, see my bliss;
Till now, wrapped in a most infernal night,
   I find how heav'nly day, wretch, I did miss.
Heart, rent thyself, thou dost thyself but right;
   No lovely Paris made thy Helen his,
   No force, no fraud, robbed thee of thy delight,
   Nor fortune of thy fortune author is;
But to myself myself did give the blow,
   While too much wit, forsooth, so troubled me   10
   That I respects for both our sakes must show,
And yet could not by rising morn foresee
   How fair a day was near; oh, punished eyes,
   That I had been more foolish—or more wise!

Come, let me write. And to what end? To ease
   A burthened heart. How can words ease, which are
   The glasses of thy daily vexing care?
   Oft cruel fights well pictured forth do please.
Art not ashamed to publish thy disease?
   Nay, that may breed my fame, it is so rare.
   But will not wise men think thy words fond ware?
   Then be they close, and so none shall displease.
What idler thing than speak and not be heard?
   What harder thing than smart and not to speak?   10
   Peace, foolish wit! with wit my wit is marred.
Thus write I, while I doubt to write, and wreak
   My harms on ink's poor loss. Perhaps some find
   Stella's great powers, that so confuse my mind.

What may words say, or what may words not say,
   Where truth itself must speak like flattery?
   Within what bounds can one his liking stay,
   Where nature doth with infinite agree?
What Nestor's counsel can my flames allay,
   Since reason's self doth blow the coal in me?
   And ah, what hope that hope should once see day,
   Where Cupid is sworn page to chastity?

Honor is honored, that thou dost possess
Him as thy slave, and now long-needy Fame
Doth even grow rich, naming my Stella's name.
Wit learns in thee perfection to express,
Not thou by praise, but praise in thee is raised;
It is a praise to praise, when thou art praised.

My mouth doth water, and my breast doth swell,
My tongue doth itch, my thoughts in labor be;
Listen then, lordings, with good ear to me,
For of my life I must a riddle tell.
Toward Aurora's court a nymph doth dwell,
Rich in all beauties which man's eye can see;
Beauties so far from reach of words that we
Abase her praise saying she doth excel;
Rich in the treasure of deserved renown,
Rich in the riches of a royal heart,
Rich in those gifts which give th' eternal crown;
Who, though most rich in these and every part
Which make the patents of true worldly bliss,
Hath no misfortune but that Rich she is.

Come sleep! O sleep, the certain knot of peace,
The baiting place of wit, the balm of woe,
The poor man's wealth, the prisoner's release,
Th' indifferent judge between the high and low;
With shield of proof shield me from out the prease
Of those fierce darts despair at me doth throw;
O make in me those civil wars to cease;
I will good tribute pay, if thou do so.
Take thou of me smooth pillows, sweetest bed,
A chamber deaf to noise and blind to light,
A rosy garland and a weary head;
And if these things, as being thine by right,
Move not thy heavy grace, thou shalt in me,
Livelier than elsewhere, Stella's image see.

As good to write as for to lie and groan.
O Stella dear, how much thy power hath wrought,
That hast my mind, none of the basest, brought
My still-kept course, while other sleep, to moan;
Alas, if from the height of virtue's throne
Thou canst vouchsafe the influence of a thought
Upon a wretch that long thy grace hath sought,
Weigh then how I by thee am overthrown;

And then think thus—although thy beauty be
  Made manifest by such a victory,   10
  Yet noblest conquerors do wrecks avoid.
Since then thou hast so far subduèd me,
  That in my heart I offer still to thee,
  Oh, do not let thy temple be destroyed.

Having this day my horse, my hand, my lance
  Guided so well that I obtained the prize,
  Both by the judgment of the English eyes
  And of some sent from that sweet enemy, France;
Horsemen my skill in horsemanship advance,
  Town-folks my strength; a daintier judge applies
  His praise to sleight which from good use doth rise;
  Some lucky wits impute it but to chance;
Others, because of both sides I do take
  My blood from them who did excel in this,   10
  Think nature me a man of arms did make.
How far they shot awry! The true cause is,
  Stella looked on, and from her heav'nly face
  Sent forth the beams which made so fair my race.

Stella oft sees the very face of woe
  Painted in my beclouded stormy face,
  But cannot skill to pity my disgrace,
  Not though thereof the cause herself she know;
Yet hearing late a fable, which did show
  Of lovers never known a grievous case,
  Pity thereof gat in her breast such place
  That, from the sea derived, tears' spring did flow.
Alas, if fancy, drawn by imaged things
  Though false, yet with free scope, more grace doth breed   10
  Than servant's wrack, where new doubts honor brings;
Then think, my dear, that you in me do read
  Of lovers' ruin some sad tragedy.
  I am not I; pity the tale of me.

Because I breathe not love to every one,
  Nor do not use set colors for to wear,
  Nor nourish special locks of vowèd hair,
  Nor give each speech a full point of a groan,
The courtly nymphs, acquainted with the moan
  Of them who in their lips Love's standard bear,
  What, he! say they of me, Now I dare swear
  He cannot love; no, no, let him alone.

And think so still, so Stella know my mind;
   Profess indeed I do not Cupid's art;
But you, fair maids, at length this true shall find,
That his right badge is but worn in the heart;
   Dumb swans, not chatt'ring pies, do lovers prove;
   They love indeed who quake to say they love.

Muses, I oft invoked your holy aid,
   With choicest flowers my speech t' engarland so
   That it, despised in true but naked show,
Might win some grace in your sweet grace arrayed;
And oft whole troops of saddest words I stayed,
   Striving abroad a-foraging to go,
   Until by your inspiring I might know
How their black banner might be best displayed.
But now I mean no more your help to try,
   Nor other sug'ring of my speech to prove,
   But on her name incessantly to cry;
For let me but name her whom I do love,
   So sweet sounds straight mine ear and heart do hit,
   That I well find no eloquence like it.

O grammar-rules, O now your virtues show;
   So children still read you with awful eyes,
   As my young dove may, in your precepts wise,
Her grant to me by her own virtue know;
For late, with heart most high, with eyes most low,
   I craved the thing which ever she denies;
   She, lightning Love displaying Venus' skies,
Lest once should not be heard, twice said, No, No!
Sing then, my muse, now Io Pæan sing;
   Heav'ns envy not at my high triumphing,
   But grammar's force with sweet success confirm;
For grammar says,—oh this, dear Stella, weigh,—
   For grammar says,—to grammar who says nay?—
   That in one speech two negatives affirm!

First song

Doubt you to whom my muse these notes intendeth,
Which now my breast, o'ercharged, to music lendeth?
To you, to you, all song of praise is due;
Only in you my song begins and endeth.

Who hath the eyes which marry state with pleasure?
Who keeps the key of nature's chiefest treasure?

To you, to you, all song of praise is due;
Only for you the heaven forgat all measure.

Who hath the lips where wit in fairness reigneth?
Who womankind at once both decks and staineth?   10
To you, to you, all song of praise is due;
Only by you Cupid his crown maintaineth.

Who hath the feet whose step of sweetness planteth?
Who else, for whom fame worthy trumpets wanteth?
To you, to you, all song of praise is due;
Only to you her scepter Venus granteth.

Who hath the breast whose milk doth passions nourish?
Whose grace is such that when it chides doth cherish?
To you, to you, all song of praise is due;
Only through you the tree of life doth flourish.   20

Who hath the hand which without stroke subdueth?
Who long dead beauty with increase reneweth?
To you, to you, all song of praise is due;
Only at you all envy hopeless rueth.

Who hath the hair which, loosest, fastest tieth?
Who makes a man live then glad, when he dieth?
To you, to you, all song of praise is due;
Only of you the flatterer never lieth.

Who hath the voice which soul from senses sunders?
Whose force but yours the bolts of beauty thunders?   30
To you, to you, all song of praise is due;
Only with you not miracles are wonders.

Doubt you to whom my muse these notes intendeth,
Which now my breast, o'ercharged, to music lendeth?
To you, to you, all song of praise is due;
Only in you my song begins and endeth.

No more, my dear, no more these counsels try;
  Oh, give my passions leave to run their race;
  Let fortune lay on me her worst disgrace;
  Let folk o'ercharged with brain against me cry;
Let clouds bedim my face, break in mine eye;
  Let me no steps but of lost labor trace;
  Let all the earth with scorn recount my case,
But do not will me from my love to fly.

I do not envy Aristotle's wit,
  Nor do aspire to Cæsar's bleeding fame;
  Nor aught do care though some above me sit;
Nor hope nor wish another course to frame,
  But that which once may win thy cruel heart;
  Thou art my wit, and thou my virtue art.

10

Oh, joy too high for my low style to show!
  Oh, bliss fit for a nobler state than me!
  Envy, put out thine eyes, lest thou do see
What oceans of delight in me do flow!
My friend, that oft saw, through all masks, my woe,
  Come, come, and let me pour myself on thee.
Gone is the winter of my misery!
My spring appears, oh see what here doth grow;
For Stella hath, with words where faith doth shine,
  Of her high heart giv'n me the monarchy;
  I, I, oh I may say that she is mine!
And though she give but thus conditionly
  This realm of bliss, while virtuous course I take,
  No kings be crowned but they some covenants make.

I never drank of Aganippe well,
  Nor ever did in shade of Tempe sit,
  And Muses scorn with vulgar brains to dwell;
Poor layman I, for sacred rites unfit.
Some do I hear of poets' fury tell,
  But, God wot, wot not what they mean by it;
  And this I swear by blackest brook of hell,
I am no pick-purse of another's wit.
How falls it then, that with so smooth an ease
  My thoughts I speak, and what I speak doth flow
  In verse, and that my verse best wits doth please?

10

Guess we the cause? What, is it thus? Fie, no.
  Or so? Much less. How then? Sure thus it is:
  My lips are sweet, inspired with Stella's kiss.

Fourth song

Only joy, now here you are,	Night hath closed all in her cloak,
Fit to hear and ease my care;	Twinkling stars love-thoughts pro-
Let my whispering voice obtain	voke,
Sweet reward for sharpest pain;	Danger hence, good care doth
Take me to thee, and thee to me—	keep,
'No, no, no, no, my dear, let be.'	Jealousy itself doth sleep;

10

Take me to thee, and thee to me—
'No, no, no, no, my dear, let be.'

Better place no wit can find,
Cupid's yoke to loose or bind;
These sweet flowers on fine bed
   too,
Us in their best language woo;
Take me to thee, and thee to me—
'No, no, no, no, my dear, let be.'

This small light the moon bestows
Serves thy beams but to disclose;   20
So to raise my hap more high,
Fear not else, none can us spy;
Take me to thee, and thee to me—
'No, no, no, no, my dear, let be.'

That you heard was but a mouse,
Dumb sleep holdeth all the house;
Yet asleep, methinks they say,
Young folks, take time while you
   may;
Take me to thee, and thee to me—
'No, no, no, no, my dear, let be.'

Niggard time threats, if we miss
This large offer of our bliss,   32

Long stay ere he grant the same;
Sweet, then, while each thing doth
   frame,
Take me to thee, and thee to me—
'No, no, no, no, my dear, let be.'

Your fair mother is a-bed,
Candles out and curtains spread;
She thinks you do letters write;
Write, but let me first endite;   40
Take me to thee, and thee to me—
'No, no, no, no, my dear, let be.'

Sweet, alas, why strive you thus?
Concord better fitteth us;
Leave to Mars the force of hands,
Your power in your beauty stands;
Take thee to me, and me to thee—
'No, no, no, no, my dear, let be.'

Woe to me, and do you swear
Me to hate? but I forbear;   50
Cursèd be my destines all,
That brought me so high to fall;
Soon with my death I will please
   thee—
'No, no, no, no, my dear, let be.'

Stella, think not that I by verse seek fame,
  Who seek, who hope, who love, who live but thee;
  Thine eyes my pride, thy lips mine history;
If thou praise not, all other praise is shame.
Nor so ambitious am I as to frame
  A nest for my young praise in laurel tree;
  In truth, I swear I wish not there should be
Graved in mine epitaph a poet's name.
Ne, if I would, I could just title make,
  That any laud to me thereof should grow,   10
  Without my plumes from others' wings I take;
For nothing from my wit or will doth flow,
  Since all my words thy beauty doth endite,
  And love doth hold my hand and makes me write.

Envious wits, what hath been mine offence,
That with such poisonous care my looks you mark,
That to each word, nay sigh of mine, you hark,
As grudging me my sorrow's eloquence?
Ah, is it not enough that I am thence,
Thence, so far thence, that scarcely any spark
Of comfort dare come to this dungeon dark,
Where rigor's exile locks up all my sense?
But if I by a happy window pass,
If I but stars upon mine armor bear—   10
Sick, thirsty, glad, though but of empty glass—
Your moral notes straight my hid meaning tear
From out my ribs, and, puffing, proves that I
Do Stella love; fools, who doth it deny?

Eleventh song

Who is it that this dark night
Underneath my window plaineth?
It is one who from thy sight
Being, ah, exiled, disdaineth
Every other vulgar light.

Why, alas, and are you he?
Be not yet those fancies changëd?
Dear, when you find change
in me,
Though from me you be es-
trangëd,
Let my change to ruin be.   10

Well, in absence this will die;
Leave to see and leave to wonder.
Absence sure will help, if I
Can learn how myself to sunder
From what in my heart doth lie.

But time will these thoughts re-
move;
Time doth work what no man
knoweth.
Time doth as the subject prove;
With time still the affection
groweth
In the faithful turtle dove.   20

What if you new beauties see,
Will not they stir new affection?

I will think they pictures be,
Image-like, of saint's perfection,
Poorly counterfeiting thee.

But your reason's purest light
Bids you leave such minds to nour-
ish.
Dear, do reason no such spite;
Never doth thy beauty flourish
More than in my reason's sight.

But the wrongs love bears will
make   31
Love at length leave undertaking.
No, the more fools it do shake,
In a ground of so firm making
Deeper still they drive the stake.

Peace, I think that some give ear;
Come no more lest I get anger.
Bliss, I will my bliss forbear;
Fearing, sweet, you to endan-
ger;
But my soul shall harbor there.   40

Well, begone, begone, I say,
Lest that Argus' eyes perceive you.
Oh, unjust fortune's sway,
Which can make me thus to
leave you,
And from louts to run away.

CERTAIN SONNETS

[*The nightingale*]

The nightingale, as soon as April bringeth
Unto her rested sense a perfect waking,
While late bare earth, proud of new clothing, springeth,
    Sings out her woes, a thorn her song-book making,
    And mournfully bewailing,
    Her throat in tunes expresseth
    What grief her breast oppresseth
    For Tereus' force on her chaste will prevailing.
O Philomela fair, O take some gladness,
That here is juster cause of plaintful sadness: 10
Thine earth now springs, mine fadeth;
Thy thorn without, my thorn my heart invadeth.

Alas, she hath no other cause of anguish
But Tereus' love, on her by strong hand wroken,
Wherein she suffering, all her spirits languish;
    Full womanlike complains her will was broken.
    But I, who daily craving,
    Cannot have to content me,
    Have more cause to lament me,
    Since wanting is more woe than too much having.   20
O Philomela fair, O take some gladness,
That here is juster cause of plaintful sadness:
Thine earth now springs, mine fadeth;
Thy thorn without, my thorn my heart invadeth.

[*Ring out your bells*]

Ring out your bells, let mourning shows be spread;
For Love is dead—
    All Love is dead, infected
With plague of deep disdain;
    Worth, as nought worth, rejected,
And Faith fair scorn doth gain.
    From so ungrateful fancy,
    From such a female franzy,
    From them that use men thus,
    Good Lord, deliver us!   10

Weep, neighbors, weep; do you not hear it said
That Love is dead?
    His death-bed, peacock's folly;
His winding-sheet is shame;
    His will, false-seeming holy;
His sole exec'tor, blame.
    From so ungrateful, &c.

Let dirge be sung and trentals rightly read,
For Love is dead;   19

Sir Wrong his tomb ordaineth
My mistress Marble-heart,
  Which epitaph containeth,
  Her eyes were once his dart.
  From so ungrateful, &c.

Alas, I lie, rage hath this error
    bred;
Love is not dead;

Love is not dead, but sleepeth
In her unmatchëd mind,
  Where she his counsel keepeth,
  Till due desert she find.   30
Therefore from so vile fancy,
To call such wit a franzy,
  Who Love can temper thus,
  Good Lord, deliver us!

[*Thou blind man's mark*]

Thou blind man's mark, thou fool's self-chosen snare,
Fond fancy's scum, and dregs of scattered thought;
Band of all evils, cradle of causeless care;
Thou web of will, whose end is never wrought;
Desire, desire! I have too dearly bought,
With price of mangled mind, thy worthless ware;
Too long, too long, asleep thou hast me brought,
Who should my mind to higher things prepare.
But yet in vain thou hast my ruin sought;
In vain thou madest me to vain things aspire;   10
In vain thou kindlest all thy smoky fire;
For virtue hath this better lesson taught,—
Within myself to seek my only hire,
Desiring nought but how to kill desire.

[*Leave me, O love*]

Leave me, O love which reachest but to dust;
And thou, my mind, aspire to higher things;
Grow rich in that which never taketh rust,
Whatever fades but fading pleasure brings.
Draw in thy beams, and humble all thy might
To that sweet yoke where lasting freedoms be;
Which breaks the clouds and opens forth the light,
That doth both shine and give us sight to see.
O take fast hold; let that light be thy guide
In this small course which birth draws out to death,   10
And think how evil becometh him to slide,
Who seeketh heav'n, and comes of heav'nly breath.
  Then farewell, world; thy uttermost I see;
  Eternal Love, maintain thy life in me.

Splendidis longum valedico nugis.

From *The Countess of Pembroke's Arcadia*, 1593

[*O sweet woods*]

O sweet woods, the delight of solitariness!
Oh, how much I do like your solitariness!
Where man's mind hath a freed consideration,
Of goodness to receive lovely direction.
Where senses do behold th' order of heav'nly host,
And wise thoughts do behold what the creator is;
Contemplation here holdeth his only seat,
Bounded with no limits, born with a wing of hope,
Climbs even unto the stars, nature is under it.
Nought disturbs thy quiet, all to thy service yields,   10
Each sight draws on a thought (thought, mother of science)
Sweet birds kindly do grant harmony unto thee,
Fair trees' shade is enough fortification,
Nor danger to thyself if 't be not in thyself.

O sweet woods, the delight of solitariness!
Oh, how much I do like your solitariness!
Here nor treason is hid, veilèd in innocence,
Nor envy's snaky eye finds any harbor here,
Nor flatterers' venomous insinuations,
Nor coming humorists' puddled opinions,   20
Nor courteous ruin of proffered usury,
Nor time prattled away, cradle of ignorance,
Nor causeless duty, nor cumber of arrogance,
Nor trifling title of vanity dazzleth us,
Nor golden manacles stand for a paradise,
Here wrong's name is unheard, slander a monster is;
Keep thy sprite from abuse, here no abuse doth haunt.
What man grafts in a tree dissimulation?

O sweet woods, the delight of solitariness!
Oh, how well I do like your solitariness!   30
Yet, dear soil, if a soul closed in a mansion
As sweet as violets, fair as lily is,
Straight as cedar, a voice stains the canary birds,
Whose shade safety doth hold, danger avoideth her;
Such wisdom that in her lives speculation;
Such goodness that in her simplicity triumphs;
Where envy's snaky eye winketh or else dieth;

Slander wants a pretext, flattery gone beyond;
Oh! if such a one have bent to a lonely life,
Her steps glad we receive, glad we receive her eyes,   40
And think not she doth hurt our solitariness,
For such company decks such solitariness.

FROM FRANCIS DAVISON's *Poetical Rhapsody*, 1602

Two pastorals

*Made by Sir Philip Sidney, never yet published, upon his meeting with
his two worthy friends and fellow-poets, Sir Edward Dyer
and Master Fulke Greville*

Join mates in mirth to me,
  Grant pleasure to our meeting;
Let Pan, our good god, see
  How grateful is our greeting.
  *Join hearts and hands, so let
    it be,*
  *Make but one mind in bodies
    three.*

Ye hymns and singing skill
  Of god Apollo's giving,
Be prest our reeds to fill
  With sound of music living.   10
  Join hearts and hands, &c.

Sweet Orpheus' harp, whose sound
  The steadfast mountains movëd,
Let here thy skill abound
  To join sweet friends belovëd.
  Join hearts and hands, &c.

My two and I be met,
  A happy blessed trinity,
As three most jointly set
  In firmest band of unity.   20
  Join hands, &c.

Welcome, my two, to me,   E. D.
  The number best belovëd, F. G.
Within my heart you be   P. S.
  In friendship unremovëd.
  Join hands, &c.

Give leave your flocks to range,
  Let us the while be playing;
Within the elmy grange   29
  Your flocks will not be straying.
  Join hands, &c.

Cause all the mirth you can,
  Since I am now come hether,
Who never joy but when
  I am with you together.
  Join hands, &c.

Like lovers do their love,
  So joy I you in seeing;
Let nothing me remove
  From always with you being.   40
  Join hands, &c.

And as the turtle dove
  To mate with whom he liveth,
Such comfort fervent love
  Of you to my heart giveth.
  Join hands, &c.

Now joinëd be our hands,
  Let them be ne'er asunder,
But linked in binding bands
  By metamorphosed wonder.   50
  *So should our severed bodies
    three*
  As one for ever joinëd be.

SIR EDWARD DYER

The Introduction and Notes are at pages 1210 and 1273

FROM WILLIAM BYRD'S *Psalms, Sonnets, and Songs*, 1588

[*My mind to me a kingdom is*]

My mind to me a kingdom is;
　Such perfect joy therein I find
That it excels all other bliss
　Which God or nature hath as-
　　signed.
Though much I want that most
　would have,
Yet still my mind forbids to crave.

No princely port, nor wealthy
　store,
　No force to win a victory,
No wily wit to salve a sore,
　No shape to win a loving eye; [10]
To none of these I yield as thrall,—
For why? my mind despise them
　all.

I see that plenty surfeit oft,
　And hasty climbers soonest fall;
I see that such as are aloft
　Mishap doth threaten most of
　　all.
These get with toil and keep with
　fear;
Such cares my mind can never bear.

I press to bear no haughty sway,
　I wish no more than may suf-
　　fice, [20]
I do no more than well I may,
　Look, what I want my mind
　　supplies.
Lo! thus I triumph like a king,
My mind content with anything.

I laugh not at another's loss,
　Nor grudge not at another's
　　gain;
No worldly waves my mind can
　　toss;
　I brook that is another's bane.
I fear no foe, nor fawn on friend,
I loathe not life, nor dread mine
　　end. [30]

My wealth is health and perfect
　　ease,
　And conscience clear my chief
　　defence;
I never seek by bribes to please,
　Nor by desert to give offence.
Thus do I live, thus will I die,—
Would all did so as well as I!

FROM *Rawlinson Poetry Ms.* 85

[*The man whose thoughts*]

The man whose thoughts against him do conspire,
On whom mishap her story doth depaint,
The man of woe, the matter of mishap,
Free of the dead, that lives in endless pain,—
　His spirit am I, which in this desert lie,
　To rue his case whose cause I cannot fly.

Despair my name, who never finds relief,
Friended of none, but to myself a foe;
An idle care, maintained by firm belief
That praise of faith shall through my torments grow;   10
   And count those hopes that others' hearts do ease
   But base conceits the common sense to please.

For sure I am I never shall attain
The happy good from whence my joys arise;
Nor have I power my sorrows to refrain,
But wail the want, when nought else may suffice;
   Whereby my life the shape of death must bear,
   That death which feels the worst that life doth fear.

But what avails, with tragical complaint,
Not hoping help, the furies to awake?   20
Or why should I the happy minds acquaint
With doleful tunes, their settled peace to shake?
   All ye that here behold infortune's fare
   May judge no woe may with my grief compare.

FROM SIR PHILIP SIDNEY's *The Countess of Pembroke's
Arcadia*, 1598

[*Prometheus when first from heaven*]

Prometheus when first from heaven high
   He brought down fire, ere then on earth not seen,
Fond of delight, a satyr, standing by,
   Gave it a kiss, as it like sweet had been.

Feeling forthwith the other burning power,
   Wood with the smart, with shouts and shrieking shrill
He sought his ease in river, field, and bower,
   But for the time his grief went with him still.

So silly I, with that unwonted sight,
   In human shape an angel from above,
Feeding mine eyes, the impression there did light,   10
   That since I run and rest as pleaseth love.
   The difference is, the satyr's lips, my heart,
   He for a while, I evermore, have smart.

FULKE GREVILLE, LORD BROOKE

The Introduction and Notes are at pages 1211 and 1273

FROM R. S.'s *Phœnix Nest,* 1593

An epitaph upon the Right Honorable Sir Philip Sidney

Silence augmenteth grief, writing increaseth rage,
Staled are my thoughts, which loved and lost the wonder of our age;
Yet quickened now with fire, though dead with frost ere now,
Enraged I write I know not what; dead, quick, I know not how.

Hard-hearted minds relent and rigor's tears abound,
And envy strangely rues his end, in whom no fault was found.
Knowledge her light hath lost, valor hath slain her knight,
Sidney is dead, dead is my friend, dead is the world's delight.

Place, pensive, wails his fall whose presence was her pride;
Time crieth out, My ebb is come; his life was my spring tide. 10
Fame mourns in that she lost the ground of her reports;
Each living wight laments his lack, and all in sundry sorts.

He was (woe worth that word!) to each well-thinking mind
A spotless friend, a matchless man, whose virtue ever shined;
Declaring in his thoughts, his life, and that he writ,
Highest conceits, longest foresights, and deepest works of wit.

He, only like himself, was second unto none,
Whose death (though life) we rue, and wrong, and all in vain do
    moan;
Their loss, not him, wail they that fill the world with cries,
Death slew not him, but he made death his ladder to the skies. 20

Now sink of sorrow I who live—the more the wrong!
Who wishing death, whom death denies, whose thread is all too long;
Who tied to wretched life, who looks for no relief,
Must spend my ever dying days in never ending grief.

Heart's ease and only I, like parallels, run on,
Whose equal length keep equal breadth and never meet in one;
Yet for not wronging him, my thoughts, my sorrow's cell,
Shall not run out, though leak they will for liking him so well.

Farewell to you, my hopes, my wonted waking dreams,
Farewell, sometimes enjoyèd joy, eclipsèd are thy beams.   30
Farewell, self-pleasing thoughts which quietness brings forth,
And farewell, friendship's sacred league, uniting minds of worth.

And farewell, merry heart, the gift of guiltless minds,
And all sports which for life's restore variety assigns;
Let all that sweet is, void; in me no mirth may dwell:
Philip, the cause of all this woe, my life's content, farewell!

Now rhyme, the son of rage, which art no kin to skill,
And endless grief, which deads my life, yet knows not how to kill,
Go, seek that hapless tomb, which if ye hap to find
Salute the stones that keep the limbs that held so good a mind.   40

From John Bodenham's (?) *England's Helicon*, 1600

Another, of his Cynthia

Away with these self-loving lads,
Whom Cupid's arrow never glads.
Away, poor souls that sigh and
    weep,
In love of them that lie and sleep;
    For Cupid is a meadow god,
    And forceth none to kiss the
        rod.

God Cupid's shaft, like destiny,
Doth either good or ill decree.
Desert is born out of his bow,
Reward upon his feet doth go.   10
    What fools are they that have
        not known
    That Love likes no laws but his
        own?

My songs they be of Cynthia's
    praise,
I wear her rings on holy-days,
On every tree I write her name,
And every day I read the same.
    Where Honor, Cupid's rival, is,
    There miracles are seen of his.

If Cynthia crave her ring of me,
I blot her name out of the tree.
If doubt do darken things held
    dear,   21
Then welfare nothing once a year.
    For many run, but one must win;
    Fools only hedge the cuckoo in.

The worth that worthiness should
    move
Is love, which is the due of love.
And love as well the shepherd can
As can the mighty nobleman.
    Sweet nymph, 'tis true you
        worthy be,
    Yet without love, nought worth
        to me.   30

From *Mustapha*, 1609

Chorus sacerdotum

Oh, wearisome condition of humanity,
Born under one law, to another bound;

Vainly begot, and yet forbidden vanity,
Created sick, commanded to be sound.
What meaneth nature by these diverse laws?
Passion and reason self-division cause.
It is the mark or majesty of power
To make offences that it may forgive.
Nature herself doth her own self deflower,
To hate those errors she herself doth give. 10
For how should man think that he may not do,
If nature did not fail and punish too?
Tyrant to others, to herself unjust,
Only commands things difficult and hard,
Forbids us all things which it knows is lust,
Makes easy pains, unpossible reward.
If nature did not take delight in blood,
She would have made more easy ways to good.
We that are bound by vows and by promotion,
With pomp of holy sacrifice and rites, 20
To teach belief in God and still devotion,
To preach of heaven's wonders and delights,—
Yet when each of us in his own heart looks
He finds the God there far unlike his books.

FROM *Certain Learned and Elegant Works*, 1633

Cælica

You little stars that live in skies
And glory in Apollo's glory,
In whose aspects conjoinëd lies
The heaven's will and nature's story,
Joy to be likened to those eyes,
Which eyes make all eyes glad or sorry;
    For when you force thoughts from above,
    These overrule your force by love.

And thou, O love, which in these eyes
Hast married reason with affection, 10
And made them saints of beauty's skies,
Where joys are shadows of perfection,
Lend me thy wings that I may rise
Up, not by worth, but thy election;
    For I have vowed in strangest fashion,
    To love, and never seek compassion.

The world, that all contains, is ever moving;
The stars within their spheres for ever turned;

Nature, the queen of change, to change is loving,
And form to matter new is still adjourned.

Fortune, our fancy-god, to vary liketh;
Place is not bound to things within it placed;
The present time upon time passèd striketh;
With Phœbus' wand'ring course the earth is graced.

The air still moves, and by its moving cleareth;
The fire up ascends and planets feedeth;
The water passeth on and all lets weareth;
The earth stands still, yet change of changes breedeth.

Her plants, which summer ripes, in winter fade;
Each creature in unconstant mother lieth;
Man made of earth, and for whom earth is made,
Still dying lives and living ever dieth;
    Only, like fate, sweet Myra never varies,
    Yet in her eyes the doom of all change carries.

Cupid, thou naughty boy, when thou wert loathèd,
Naked and blind, for vagabonding noted,
Thy nakedness I in my reason clothèd,
Mine eyes I gave thee, so was I devoted.

Fie, wanton, fie! who would show children kindness?
No sooner he into mine eyes was gotten
But straight he clouds them with a seeing blindness,
Makes reason wish that reason were forgotten.

From thence to Myra's eyes the wanton strayeth,
Where while I charge him with ungrateful measure,
So with fair wonders he mine eyes betrayeth,
That my wounds and his wrongs become my pleasure;
    Till for more spite to Myra's heart he flyeth,
    Where living to the world, to me he dieth.

Fie, foolish earth, think you the heaven wants glory
Because your shadows do yourself benight?
All's dark unto the blind, let them be sorry;
The heavens in themselves are ever bright.

Fie, fond desire, think you that love wants glory
Because your shadows do yourself benight?
The hopes and fears of lust may make men sorry,
But love still in herself finds her delight.

Then earth, stand fast, the sky that you benight
Will turn again and so restore your glory; 10
Desire, be steady, hope is your delight,
An orb wherein no creature can be sorry,
  Love being placed above these middle regions
  Where every passion wars itself with legions.

Cælica, I overnight was finely used,
Lodged in the midst of paradise, your heart;
Kind thoughts had charge I might not be refused,
Of every fruit and flower I had part.

But curious knowledge, blown with busy flame,
The sweetest fruits had in down shadows hidden,
And for it found mine eyes had seen the same,
I from my paradise was straight forbidden.

Where that cur, rumor, runs in every place,
Barking with care, begotten out of fear; 10
And glassy honor, tender of disgrace,
Stand seraphim to see I come not there;
  While that fine soil which all these joys did yield,
  By broken fence is proved a common field.

Under a throne I saw a virgin sit,
The red and white rose quartered in her face;
Star of the north! and for true guards to it,
Princes, church, states, all pointing out her grace;
The homage done her was not born of wit;
Wisdom admired, zeal took ambition's place,
State in her eyes taught order how to fit
And fix confusion's unobserving race.
  Fortune can here claim nothing truly great,
  But that this princely creature is her seat. 10

The earth with thunder torn, with fire blasted,
With waters drowned, with windy palsy shaken,
Cannot for this with heaven be distasted,
Since thunder, rain, and winds from earth are taken;
Man torn with love, with inward furies blasted,
Drowned with despair, with fleshly lustings shaken,
Cannot for this with heaven be distasted;
Love, fury, lustings out of man are taken.
Then, man, endure thyself, those clouds will vanish;
Life is a top which whipping sorrow driveth; 10
Wisdom must bear what our flesh cannot banish.
The humble lead, the stubborn bootless striveth.

Or, man, forsake thyself, to heaven turn thee,
Her flames enlighten nature, never burn thee.

[Sion lies waste]

Sion lies waste, and thy Jerusalem,
O Lord, is fallen to utter desolation;
Against thy prophets and thy holy men
The sin hath wrought a fatal combination;
    Profaned thy name, thy worship overthrown,
    And made thee, living Lord, a God unknown.

Thy powerful laws, thy wonders of creation,
Thy word incarnate, glorious heaven, dark hell,
Lie shadowed under man's degeneration;
Thy Christ still crucified for doing well;   10
    Impiety, O Lord, sits on thy throne,
    Which makes thee, living light, a God unknown.

Man's superstition hath thy truths entombed,
His atheism again her pomps defaceth;
That sensual unsatiable vast womb
Of thy seen church thy unseen church disgraceth.
    There lives no truth with them that seem thine own,
    Which makes thee, living Lord, a God unknown.

Yet unto thee, Lord, mirror of transgression,
We who for earthly idols have forsaken   20
Thy heavenly image, sinless, pure impression,
And so in nets of vanity lie taken,
    All desolate implore that to thine own,
    Lord, thou no longer live a God unknown.

Yet, Lord, let Israel's plagues not be eternal,
Nor sin forever cloud thy sacred mountains,
Nor with false flames, spiritual but infernal,
Dry up thy mercy's ever springing fountains.
    Rather, sweet Jesus, fill up time and come
    To yield the sin her everlasting doom.   30

ROBERT DEVEREUX, EARL OF ESSEX

The Introduction and Notes are at page 1212
From Robert Dowland's *Musical Banquet*, 1610

[Change thy mind]

Change thy mind, since she doth change!
Let not fancy still abuse thee.

Thy untruth can not seem strange
When her falsehood doth excuse thee.
Love is dead and thou art free,
She doth live, but dead to thee.

Whilst she loved thee best a while,
See how she hath still delayed thee,
Using shows for to beguile
Those vain hopes that have deceived thee. 10
Now thou seest, although too late,
Love loves truth, which women hate.

Love no more, since she is gone—
She is gone, and loves another.
Being once deceived by one,
Leave her love, but love none other.
She was false—bid her adieu;
She was best, but yet untrue.

Love, farewell, more dear to me
Than my life, which thou preservest. 20
Life, all joys are gone from thee,
Others have what thou deservest.
Oh, my death doth spring from hence,
I must die for her offence.

Die, but yet before thou die,
Make her know what she hath gotten;
She, in whom my hopes did lie,
Now is changed—I, quite forgotten.
She is changed, but changëd base,
Baser in so vild a place. 30

[To plead my faith]

To plead my faith where faith had no reward,
To move remorse where favor is not borne,
To heap complaints where she doth not regard,—
Were fruitless, bootless, vain, and yield but scorn.

I lovëd her whom all the world admired,
I was refused of her that can love none;
And my vain hopes, which far too high aspired,
Is dead, and buried, and for ever gone.

Forget my name, since you have scorned my love,
And woman-like do not too late lament;   10
Since for your sake I do all mischief prove,
I none accuse nor nothing do repent.

I was as fond as ever she was fair,
Yet loved I not more than I now despair.

FROM *Chetham Ms.* 8012

A passion

Happy were he could finish forth his fate
In some unhaunted desert, more obscure
From all society, from love and hate
Of worldly folk; there might he sleep secure,
There wake again and give God ever praise;
Content with hips and haws and bramble-berry;
In contemplation passing still his days,
And change of holy thoughts to make him merry:
    That when he dies his tomb might be a bush
    Where harmless robin dwelleth with the thrush.   10

SIR WALTER RALEGH

The Introduction and Notes are at pages 1212 and 1274

FROM *Rawlinson Poetry Ms.* 160

To Queen Elizabeth

Our passions are most like to floods and streams,
    The shallow murmur, but the deep are dumb;
So, when affections yield discourse, it seems
    The bottom is but shallow whence they come.
They that are rich in words must needs discover
That they are poor in that which makes a lover.

Wrong not, dear empress of my heart,
    The merit of true passion
With thinking that he feels no smart
    That sues for no compassion;   10
Since, if my plaints serve not to prove
    The conquest of your beauty,
They come not from defect of love
    But from access of duty.

For knowing that I sue to serve
 A saint of such perfection
As all desire (yet none deserve)
 A place in her affection,
I rather choose to want relief
 Than venture the revealing;   20
When glory recommends the grief,
 Despair distrusts the healing.

Thus those desires that aim too high
 For any mortal lover,
When reason cannot make them die
 Discretion doth them cover.
Yet, when discretion doth bereave
 The plaints that they should utter,
Then your discretion may perceive
 That silence is a suitor.   30

Silence in love bewrays more woe
 Than words, though ne'er so witty;
A beggar that is dumb, you know,
 Deserveth double pity.
Then misconceive not, dearest heart,
 My true though secret passion;
He smarteth most that hides his smart
 And sues for no compassion.

From R. S.'s *Phœnix Nest*, 1593

[*Praised be Diana's fair and harmless light*]

Praised be Diana's fair and harmless light,
Praised be the dews wherewith she moists the ground;
Praised be her beams, the glory of the night;
Praised be her power, by which all powers abound.

Praised be her nymphs, with whom she decks the woods;
Praised be her knights, in whom true honor lives;
Praised be that force by which she moves the floods;
Let that Diana shine, which all these gives.

In heaven queen she is among the spheres;
In aye she mistress-like makes all things pure;   10
Eternity in her oft change she bears;
She beauty is; by her the fair endure.

Time wears her not—she doth his chariot guide;
Mortality below her orb is placed.
By her the virtue of the stars down slide,
In her is virtue's perfect image cast.

    A knowledge pure it is her worth to know;
    With Circes let them dwell that think not so.

[Like truthless dreams]

Like truthless dreams, so are my joys expired,
And past return are all my dandled days;
My love misled, and fancy quite retired—
Of all which passed the sorrow only stays.

My lost delights, now clean from sight of land,
Have left me all alone in unknown ways;
My mind to woe, my life in fortune's hand—
Of all which passed the sorrow only stays.

As in a country strange, without companion,
I only wail the wrong of death's delays,
Whose sweet spring spent, whose summer well-nigh done—
Of all which passed the sorrow only stays.

    Whom care forewarns, ere age and winter cold,
    To haste me hence to find my fortune's fold.

[Like to a hermit]

Like to a hermit poor in place obscure
I mean to spend my days of endless doubt,
To wail such woes as time cannot recure,
Where none but love shall ever find me out.

My food shall be of care and sorrow made,
My drink nought else but tears fall'n from mine eyes;
And for my light in such obscurèd shade
The flames shall serve which from my heart arise.

A gown of gray my body shall attire,
My staff of broken hope whereon I'll stay;
Of late repentance linked with long desire
The couch is framed whereon my limbs I'll lay;

    And at my gate despair shall linger still
    To let in death when love and fortune will.

A description of love

Now what is love? I pray thee,
   tell.
It is that fountain and that well
Where pleasure and repentance
   dwell.
It is perhaps that saucing bell
That tolls all into heaven or hell:
And this is love, as I hear tell.

Yet what is love? I pray thee say.
It is a work on holy-day;
It is December matched with
   May;   9
When lusty bloods, in fresh array,
Hear ten months after of the play:
And this is love, as I hear say.

Yet what is love? I pray thee sain.
It is a sunshine mixed with rain;
It is a tooth-ache, or like pain;

It is a game where none doth gain;
The lass saith no, and would full
   fain:
And this is love, as I hear sain.

Yet what is love? I pray thee say.
It is a yea, it is a nay,   20
A pretty kind of sporting fray;
It is a thing will soon away;
Then take the vantage while you
   may:
And this is love, as I hear say.

Yet what is love, I pray thee show.
A thing that creeps, it cannot go;
A prize that passeth to and fro;
A thing for one, a thing for mo;
And he that proves must find it so:
And this is love, sweet friend, I
   trow.   30

An epitaph upon the Right Honorable Sir Philip Sidney, Knight, Lord Governor of Flushing

To praise thy life or wail thy worthy death,
And want thy wit, thy wit high, pure, divine,
Is far beyond the power of mortal line;
Nor any one hath worth that draweth breath.

Yet rich in zeal, though poor in learning's lore,
And friendly care obscured in secret breast,
And love that envy in thy life suppressed,—
Thy dear life done, and death, hath doubled more.

And I, that in thy time and living state
Did only praise thy virtues in my thought,   10
As one that, seeled, the rising sun hath sought,
With words and tears now wail thy timeless fate.

Drawn was thy race aright from princely line,
Nor less than such, by gifts that nature gave
(The common mother that all creatures have),
Doth virtue show, and princely lineage shine.

A king gave thee thy name; a kingly mind,
That God thee gave, who found it now too dear
For this base world, and hath resumed it near
To sit in skies, and sort with powers divine.   20

Kent thy birth days, and Oxford held thy youth;
The heavens made haste and stayed nor years nor time;
The fruits of age grew ripe in thy first prime,
Thy will, thy words—thy words, the seals of truth.

Great gifts and wisdom rare employed thee thence
To treat from kings with those more great than kings,
Such hope men had to lay the highest things
On thy wise youth, to be transported hence.

Whence to sharp wars sweet honor did thee call,
Thy country's love, religion, and thy friends;   30
Of worthy men the marks, the lives, and ends,
And her defence for whom we labor all.

There didst thou vanquish shame and tedious age,
Grief, sorrow, sickness, and base fortune's might.
Thy rising day saw never woeful night,
But passed with praise from off this worldly stage.

Back to the camp by thee that day was brought
First, thine own death; and after, thy long fame;
Tears to the soldiers; the proud Castilian's shame;
Virtue expressed, and honor truly taught.   40

What hath he lost that such great grace hath won?
Young years for endless years, and hope unsure
Of fortune's gifts for wealth that still shall dure—
Oh, happy race, with so great praises run!

England doth hold thy limbs, that bred the same,
Flanders thy valor, where it last was tried,
The camp thy sorrow, where thy body died,
Thy friends thy want, the world thy virtue's fame.

Nations thy wit, our minds lay up thy love;
Letters thy learning; thy loss, years long to come;   50
In worthy hearts sorrow hath made thy tomb,
Thy soul and sprite enrich the heavens above.

Thy liberal heart embalmed in grateful tears,
Young sighs, sweet sighs, sage sighs bewail thy fall;
Envy her sting, and spite hath left her gall,
Malice herself a mourning garment wears.

That day their Hannibal died, our Scipio fell,
Scipio, Cicero, and Petrarch of our time,
Whose virtues, wounded by my worthless rhyme,
Let angels speak, and heavens thy praises tell.   60

From Edmund Spenser's *Fairy Queen*, 1590

A vision upon this conceit of the Fairy Queen

Methought I saw the grave where Laura lay,
Within that temple where the vestal flame
Was wont to burn; and passing by that way
To see that buried dust of living fame,
Whose tomb fair Love and fairer Virtue kept,
All suddenly I saw the Fairy Queen;
At whose approach the soul of Petrarch wept,
And from thenceforth those graces were not seen,
For they this Queen attended; in whose stead
Oblivion laid him down on Laura's hearse.   10
Hereat the hardest stones were seen to bleed,
And groans of buried ghosts the heavens did pierce;
    Where Homer's sprite did tremble all for grief,
    And cursed th' access of that celestial thief.

From John Bodenham's (?) *England's Helicon*, 1600

The nymph's reply to the shepherd

If all the world and love were young,
And truth in every shepherd's tongue,
These pretty pleasures might me move
To live with thee and be thy love.

Time drives the flocks from field to fold
When rivers rage and rocks grow cold,
And Philomel becometh dumb;
The rest complains of cares to come.

The flowers do fade, and wanton fields
To wayward winter reckoning yields;   10
A honey tongue, a heart of gall,
Is fancy's spring, but sorrow's fall.

Thy gowns, thy shoes, thy beds of roses,
Thy cap, thy kirtle, and thy posies
Soon break, soon wither, soon forgotten,—
In folly ripe, in reason rotten.

Thy belt of straw and ivy buds,
Thy coral clasps and amber studs,
All these in me no means can move
To come to thee and be thy love.   20

But could youth last and love still breed,
Had joys no date nor age no need,
Then these delights my mind might move
To live with thee and be thy love.

From *Malone Ms.* 19

To his son

Three things there be that prosper all apace
And flourish, while they are asunder far;
But on a day they meet all in a place,
And when they meet, they one another mar.
And they be these: the wood, the weed, the wag.
The wood is that that makes the gallows tree;
The weed is that that strings the hangman's bag;
The wag, my pretty knave, betokens thee.
Now mark, dear boy: while these assemble not,
Green springs the tree, hemp grows, the wag is wild;   10
But when they meet, it makes the timber rot,
It frets the halter, and it chokes the child.
        God bless the child!

From *Harleian Ms.* 6917

[*Nature, that washed her hands*]

Nature, that washed her hands in milk,
    And had forgot to dry them,
Instead of earth took snow and silk,
    At love's request to try them,
If she a mistress could compose
To please love's fancy out of those.

Her eyes he would should be of light,
    A violet breath, and lips of jelly;
Her hair not black, nor over-bright,
    And of the softest down her belly;   10
As for her inside he 'ld have it
Only of wantonness and wit.

At love's entreaty such a one
   Nature made, but with her
      beauty
She hath framed a heart of stone;
   So as love, by ill destiny,
Must die for her whom nature
      gave him,
Because her darling would not
     save him.

But time (which nature doth
     despise
   And rudely gives her love the
     lie,   20
Makes hope a fool, and sorrow
     wise)
   His hands do neither wash nor
     dry;
But being made of steel and rust,
Turns snow and silk and milk to
     dust.

The light, the belly, lips, and
     breath,
   He dims, discolors, and de-
     stroys;
With those he feeds but fills not
     death,
   Which sometimes were the food
     of joys.
Yea, time doth dull each lively
     wit,
And dries all wantonness with it. 30

Oh, cruel time! which takes in
     trust
   Our youth, our joys, and all
     we have,
And pays us but with age and
     dust;
   Who in the dark and silent
     grave
When we have wandered all our
     ways
Shuts up the story of our days.

FROM FRANCIS DAVISON'S
Poetical Rhapsody, 1608

The lie

Go, soul, the body's guest,
Upon a thankless arrant.
Fear not to touch the best;
The truth shall be thy warrant.
   Go, since I needs must die,
   And give the world the lie.

Say to the court, it glows
And shines like rotten wood;
Say to the church, it shows
What's good, and doth no good: 10
   If church and court reply,
   Then give them both the lie.

Tell potentates, they live
Acting by others' action,
Not loved unless they give,
Not strong but by affection:
   If potentates reply,
   Give potentates the lie.

Tell men of high condition
That manage the estate,   20
Their purpose is ambition,
Their practice only hate:
   And if they once reply,
   Then give them all the lie.

Tell them that brave it most,
They beg for more by spending,
Who, in their greatest cost,
Like nothing but commending:
   And if they make reply,
   Then give them all the lie. 30

Tell zeal it wants devotion;
Tell love it is but lust;
Tell time it meets but motion;
Tell flesh it is but dust:
   And wish them not reply,
   For thou must give the lie.

Tell age it daily wasteth;
Tell honor how it alters;
Tell beauty how she blasteth;
Tell favor how it falters: 40
    And as they shall reply,
    Give every one the lie.

Tell wit how much it wrangles
In tickle points of niceness;
Tell wisdom she entangles
Herself in over-wiseness:
    And when they do reply,
    Straight give them both the lie.

Tell physic of her boldness;
Tell skill it is prevention;   50
Tell charity of coldness;
Tell law it is contention:
    And as they do reply,
    So give them still the lie.

Tell fortune of her blindness;
Tell nature of decay;
Tell friendship of unkindness;

Tell justice of delay:
    And if they will reply,
    Then give them all the lie.   60

Tell arts they have no soundness,
But vary by esteeming;
Tell schools they want profound-
            ness,
And stand too much on seeming:
    If arts and schools reply,
    Give arts and schools the lie.

Tell faith it's fled the city;
Tell how the country erreth;
Tell, manhood shakes off pity,
Tell, virtue least preferrëd: 70
    And if they do reply,
    Spare not to give the lie.

So when thou hast, as I
Commanded thee, done blabbing,
Because to give the lie
Deserves no less than stabbing,
    Stab at thee he that will—
    No stab thy soul can kill.

FROM J. HANNAH's *Courtly Poets from Raleigh to Montrose*, 1870

The Ocean to Cynthia

Book XI

.   .   .   .

But stay, my thoughts, make end, give fortune way;
    Harsh is the voice of woe and sorrow's sound;
Complaints cure not, and tears do but allay
    Griefs for a time, which after more abound.

To seek for moisture in the Arabian sand
    Is but a loss of labor and of rest;
The links which time did break of hearty bands

Words cannot knit, or wailings make anew.
    Seek not the sun in clouds when it is set.
On highest mountains, where those cedars grew,   10
    Against whose banks the troubled ocean beat,

And were the marks to find thy hopëd port,
Into a soil far off themselves remove;
On Sestos' shore, Leander's late resort,
Hero hath left no lamp to guide her love.

Thou lookest for light in vain, and storms arise;
She sleeps thy death that erst thy danger sighed;
Strive then no more, bow down thy weary eyes,
Eyes which to all these woes thy heart have guided.

She is gone, she is lost, she is found, she is ever fair;   20
Sorrow draws weakly where love draws not too;
Woe's cries sound nothing, but only in love's ear.
Do then by dying what life cannot do.

Unfold thy flocks and leave them to the fields,
To feed on hills or dales, where likes them best,
Of what the summer or the springtime yields,
For love and time hath given thee leave to rest.

Thy heart which was their fold, now in decay
By often storms and winter's many blasts,
All torn and rent becomes misfortune's prey;   30
False hope, my shepherd's staff, now age hath brast.

My pipe, which love's own hand gave my desire
To sing her praises and my woe upon,
Despair hath often threatened to the fire,
As vain to keep now all the rest are gone.

Thus home I draw, as death's long night draws on;
Yet every foot, old thoughts turn back mine eyes;
Constraint me guides, as old age draws a stone
Against the hill, which over-weighty lies

For feeble arms or wasted strength to move;   40
My steps are backward, gazing on my loss,
My mind's affection and my soul's sole love,
Not mixed with fancy's chaff or fortune's dross.

To God I leave it, who first gave it me,
And I her gave, and she returned again,
As it was hers; so let His mercies be
Of my last comforts the essential mean.

But be it so or not, the effects are past;
Her love hath end, my woe must ever last.

From Anthony Scoloker's *Daiphantus*, 1604

The passionate man's pilgrimage, supposed to be written by one at the point of death

Give me my scallop-shell of quiet,
My staff of faith to walk upon,
My scrip of joy, immortal diet,
My bottle of salvatïon,
My gown of glory, hope's true gage,
And thus I'll take my pilgrimage.

Blood must be my body's balmer,
No other balm will there be given,
Whilst my soul like a white palmer
Travels to the land of heaven,   10
Over the silver mountains,
Where spring the nectar fountains;
And there I'll kiss
The bowl of bliss,
And drink my eternal fill
On every milken hill.
My soul will be a-dry before,
But after it will ne'er thirst more;
And by the happy blissful way
More peaceful pilgrims I shall see,   20
That have shook off their gowns of clay
And go appareled fresh like me.
I'll bring them first
To slake their thirst,
And then to taste those nectar suckets,
At the clear wells
Where sweetness dwells,
Drawn up by saints in crystal buckets.

And when our bottles and all we
Are filled with immortality,   30
Then the holy paths we'll travel,
Strewed with rubies thick as gravel,
Ceilings of diamonds, sapphire floors,
High walls of coral, and pearl bowers.

From thence to heaven's bribeless hall
Where no corrupted voices brawl,
No conscience molten into gold,
Nor forged accusers bought and sold,

No cause deferred, nor vain-spent journey,
For there Christ is the king's attorney,   40
Who pleads for all without degrees,
And he hath angels, but no fees.
When the grand twelve million jury
Of our sins and sinful fury,
'Gainst our souls black verdicts give,
Christ pleads his death, and then we live.
Be thou my speaker, taintless pleader,
Unblotted lawyer, true proceeder,
Thou movest salvation even for alms,
Not with a bribèd lawyer's palms.   50

And this is my eternal plea
To him that made heaven, earth, and sea,
Seeing my flesh must die so soon,
And want a head to dine next noon,
Just at the stroke when my veins start and spread,
Set on my soul an everlasting head.
Then am I ready, like a palmer fit,
To tread those blest paths which before I writ.

MARY HERBERT, COUNTESS OF PEMBROKE

The Introduction and Notes are at page 1215

FROM *Antonius*, 1592

Chorus

Alas, with what tormenting fire
Us martyreth this blind desire
  To stay our life from flying;
How ceaselessly our minds doth
    rack,
How heavy lies upon our back
  This dastard fear of dying!
Death rather healthful succor
    gives,
Death rather all mishaps relieves
  That life upon us throweth;
And ever to us doth unclose   10
The door whereby from cureless
    woes

Our weary soul out goeth.
What goddess else more mild than
    she
  To bury all our pain can be?
What remedy more pleasing?
Our painèd hearts, when dolor
    stings
And nothing rest or respite brings,
  What help have we more eas-
      ing?
Hope, which to us doth comfort
    give
And doth our fainting hearts re-
    vive,   20
  Hath not such force in anguish;
For, promising a vain relief,
She oft us fails in midst of grief

And helpless lets us languish.
But death, who call on her at
　　need,
Doth never with vain semblant
　　feed,
But, when them sorrow pain-
　　eth,
So rids their souls of all distress
Whose heavy weight did them op-
　　press,
That not one grief remain-
　　eth.　　　　　　　30

.　.　.　.

How abject him, how base! think
　　I,
Who, wanting courage, cannot
　　die
When need him thereto call-
　　eth;
From whom the dagger, drawn
　　to kill
The cureless griefs that vex him
　　still,
For fear and faintness fall-
　　eth.

O Antony, with thy dear mate,
Both in misfortunes fortunate,
　　Whose thoughts, to death aspir-
　　　　ing,
Shall you protect from victor's
　　rage,　　　　　　40
Who on each side doth you en-
　　cage,
　　To triumph much desiring.
That Cæsar may you not offend
Nought else but death can you de-
　　fend,
　　Which his weak force derid-
　　　　eth;
And all in this round earth con-
　　tained
Powerless on them whom, once
　　enchained,
　　Avernus' prison hideth
Where great Psammetic's ghost
　　doth rest,
Not with infernal pain possessed　50
　　But in sweet fields detainëd;
And old Amasis' soul likewise
And all our famous Ptolemies
　　That whilom on us reignëd.

WILLIAM WARNER

The Introduction and Notes are at page 1215

FROM *Albion's England*, 1592

Chapter XXXVIII

Eight Henry, heir indubitate of York and Lancaster,
Succeeded and with kingly rites his father did inter;
His mind, his words, his looks, his gait, his lineaments, and stature,
Were such for majesty as showed a king composed by nature.
All subjects now of civil strife, all counter-minds for reign,
All envious of his empire now were rid, were pleased, or slain.
Rich were his sundry triumphs, but his cost had foison then
When Terwin and strong Turnay in resisting France he won;
When Maximilian, emperor, did under Henry fight;
When English ships did often put the French sea-power to flight;　10

And that the French king was enforced to crave and buy his peace,
Who, wiving lovely Mary, so the wars for then did cease.
  This sister to our King, and then the French king's goodly queen,
Was welcomëd with triumphs such as erst in France unseen.
Jousts, barriers, tilts, and tourneys were proclaimed eachwhere for all;
Wherefore to Paris at the time flocked cavaliers full tall,
With princes brave and ladies fair of every realm about,
And hence, with mo, Charles Brandon, in fine chivalry most stout,
Whose body fitted to his mind, whose mind was puissant, and
Whose puissance yielded not to Mars; this Mars in France did land, 20
With whom encountered valiant knights, but none might him with-
        stand.
The English-French queen standing there, admired for beauty rare,
Beheld the triumphs, in the which high feats performëd were.
But Brandon, yet not duked, was the knight above the rest,
That in her eye (nor did she err) acquitted him the best.
For whether that he trots, or turns, or bounds his barded steed,
Did run at tilt at random, or did cast a spear with heed,
Or fight at barriers, he in all did most her fancy feed.
Weak on a couch her King lay there, whom though she lovëd well,
Yet liked she Brandon, and the same loved her ere this befell;   30
For chastely had they fancied long before she came to France,
Or that from mean estate to duke Henry did him advance.
  The days of triumph were expired and English peers with praise
Come home, and Louis, King of France, deceased within few days.
Charles Brandon, Duke of Suffolk then, with honor furnished hence,
Was sent to France for to return the widow queen from thence;
She had been wed scarce thrice three weeks unto a sickly king;
To her, a fair young queen, therefore small time might solace bring.
Yet less did time than brave Duke Charles assuage fair Mary's grief;
He chats, she cheers, he courts, she coys, he woos, she yields in brief. 40
No winds, thought she, assist those sails that seek no certain shore,
Nor find they constant lives that, but they live, respect no more.
Let each one's life aim some one end, as, if it be to marry,
Then see, hear, love, and soon conclude, it betters not to tarry.
To cast too many doubts, thought she, were oft to err no less
Than to be rash. And thus, no doubt, the gentle queen did guess,
That seeing this or that at first or last had likelihood,
A man so much a manly man were dastardly withstood.
Then kisses reveled on their lips to either's equal good,
And lest King Henry should dissent, they secretly did wed,   50
And then solicit his good will, and of their wishes speed.
The perjured valiant Scotch King James, slain at brave Flodden's
        slaughter,
Had also left in widowhood England's fair elder daughter.
She also weds a Scottish earl, unlicensed of her brother,

And was to her son's daughter's son, now sixth James, great-grand-
    mother.
A scruple, after twenty years, did enter Henry's mind,
For wedding of Queen Catherine, a lady fair and kind,
Spain's daughter, then the Emperor's aunt, and for her virtuous life
Well worthy Henry; but for she had been his brother's wife,
And also of their coiture surmise directed laws,   60
He seemed in conscience touched and sought to rid him of the cause.
Then was the matter of divorce through Christendom disputed,
The match of all adjudgëd void, and so the Queen non-suited;
Who, after tears to him from whom she was to be divorced,
Did humbly say, And am I not, my lord, to be remorsed,
That twenty years have been your wife and borne your children, and
Have loved and lived obediently, and unsuspected stand?
I am (ah, too too sweetly erred), I was, poor soul, the same
Whom once you did prefer, nor now of me you need to shame;
The blossoms of my beauty were your booty, nor my favor   70
Now alters so to alter so from me your late behavior.
But conscience is the color of this quarrel, well I wot;
I also have a conscience that in this accuseth not;
But as the same, perhaps, might say that me succeeds, say I
That for the pleasure of a prince go many things awry.
    Which her foredooms seemed to effect in her that her succeeded;
In Queen Anne Bullen, who, for she in Lutherism proceeded,
Was hated of the Papists and envied because preferred,
And through the King's too light belief (for kings have sometimes
    erred)
She lost her head, and might have said, some thought, ere she did die,   80
That for the pleasure of a prince go many things awry.
So died the gracious mother of our now most glorious Queen,
Whose zeal in reverent Foxe his works authentical is seen.
The King's four other queens (for why he died a sexamus)
Shall pass, though Jane did bear a son to him, a king to us,
Edward the sixth, and of the same we shall deliver thus.

THOMAS WATSON

The Introduction and Notes are at pages 1216 and 1274

From *Hecatompathia, or Passionate Century of Love,* [1582]

[Some that report]

    *The author still pursuing his invention upon the song of his mistress,
in the last staff of this sonnet he falleth into this fiction: that whilst he*

greedily laid open his ears to the hearing of his lady's voice, as one more than half in a doubt that Apollo himself had been at hand, Love, espying a time of advantage, transformed himself into the substance of air and so deceitfully entered into him with his own great good-will and desire, and now by main force still holdeth his possession.

Some that report great Alexander's life,
They say that harmony so moved his mind
That oft he rose from meat to warlike strife
At sound of trump or noise of battle kind;
 And then that music's force of softer vein
 Caused him return from strokes to meat again.
And as for me, I think it nothing strange
That music having birth from heav'ns above
By divers tunes can make the mind to change;
For I myself, in hearing my sweet love, 10
 By virtue of her song both tasted grief
 And such delight as yielded some relief.
When first I gan to give attentive ear,
Thinking Apollo's voice did haunt the place,
I little thought my lady had been there;
But whilst mine ears lay open in this case,
 Transformed to air love entered with my will
 And now perforce doth keep possession still.

[If Cupid were a child]

The author in this passion reproveth the usual description of love which old poets have so long time embraced, and proveth by probabilities that he neither is a child (as they say) nor blind nor winged like a bird nor armed archer-like with bow and arrows, neither frantic nor wise nor yet unclothed nor, to conclude, any god at all. And yet when he hath said all he can to this end, he crieth out upon the secret nature and quality of love as being that whereunto he can by no means attain, although he have spent a long and tedious course of time in his service.

If Cupid were a child, as poets feign,
How comes it then that Mars doth fear his might?
If blind, how chance so many to their pain
Whom he hath hit can witness of his sight?
 If he have wings to fly where thinks him best,
 How haps he lurketh still within my breast?
If bow and shafts should be his chiefest tools,
Why doth he set so many hearts on fire?
If he were mad, how could he further fools

To whet their wits as place and time require?
If wise, how could so many leese their wits
Or dote through love and die in frantic fits?
If naked still he wander to and fro,
How doth not sun or frost offend his skin?
If that a god he be, how falls it so
That all wants end which he doth once begin?
    Oh wondrous thing, that I whom love hath spent
    Can scarcely know himself or his intent.

My love is past

*The author feigneth here that Love, essaying with his brand to fire
the heart of some such lady on whom it would not work, immediately,
to try whether the old virtue of it were extinguished or no, applied it
unto his own breast and thereby foolishly consumed himself. His invention hath some relation unto the* Epitaph of Love *written by*
M. Girolimo Parabosco:

    In cenere giace qui sepolto Amore,
    Colpa di quella, che morir mi face, &c.

Resolved to dust, entombed here lieth Love
Through faults of her who here herself should lie;
He struck her breast, but all in vain did prove
To fire the ice; and doubting by and by
    His brand had lost his force, he gan to try
    Upon himself, which trial made him die.
In sooth, no force; let those lament that lust,
I'll sing a carol song for obsequy,
For towards me his dealings were unjust
And cause of all my passèd misery.
    The Fates, I think, seeing what I had passed,
    In my behalf wrought this revenge at last.
But somewhat more to pacify my mind
By illing him through whom I lived a slave,
I'll cast his ashes to the open wind
Or write this epitaph upon his grave:
    Here lieth Love, of Mars the bastard son,
    Whose foolish fault to death himself hath done.

FROM *The first set of Italian Madrigals Englished,* 1590

Vezzosi augelli

Ev'ry singing bird that in the wood rejoices,
Come and assist me with your charming voices.
Zephirus, come too, and make the leaves and the fountains

Gently to send a whisp'ring sound unto the mountains.
And from thence pleasant Echo sweetly replying,
Stay here playing, where my Phillis now is lying.
And lovely graces with wanton satyrs come and play,
Dancing and singing a horn-pipe or a roundelay.

Questo di verde

How long with vain complaining,
How long with dreary tears and joys refraining,
Shall we renew his dying?
Whose happy soul is flying
Not in a place of sadness,
But of eternal gladness.
Sweet Sidney lives in heav'n, oh, therefore let our weeping
Be turned to hymns and songs of pleasant greeting.

FROM *The Tears of Fancy*, 1593

I saw the object of my pining thought
Within a garden of sweet nature's placing,
Wherein an arbor, artificial wrought
By workman's wondrous skill, the garden gracing,
Did boast his glory, glory far renowned,
For in his shady boughs my mistress slept;
And with a garland of his branches crowned,
Her dainty forehead from the sun ykept.
Imperious love upon her eyelids tending,
Playing his wanton sports at every beck   10
And into every finest limb descending
From eyes to lips, from lips to ivory neck,
And every limb supplied, and t'every part
Had free access, but durst not touch her heart.

Each tree did boast the wishèd spring-time's pride
When solitary in the vale of love
I hid myself, so from the world to hide
The uncouth passions which my heart did prove.
No tree whose branches did not bravely spring,
No branch whereon a fine bird did not sit,
No bird but did her shrill notes sweetly sing,
No song but did contain a lovely dit.
Trees, branches, birds, and songs were framèd fair,
Fit to allure frail mind to careless ease;   10
But careful was my thought, yet in despair
I dwelt, for brittle hope me cannot please.

For when I view my love's fair eyes' reflecting
I entertain despair, vain hope rejecting.

In clouds she shines, and so obscurely shineth
That like a mastless ship at seas I wander,
For want of her to guide my heart that pineth,
Yet can I not entreat ne yet command her.
So am I tied in labyrinths of fancy,
In dark and obscure labyrinths of love,
That every one may plain behold that can see
How I am fettered and what pains I prove.
The lamp whose light should lead my ship about   10
Is placed upon my mistress' heavenly face;
Her hand doth hold the clew must lead me out
And free my heart from thraldom's loathèd place.
But clew to lead me out, or lamp to light me,
She scornfully denied—the more to spite me.

ROBERT GREENE

The Introduction and Notes are at pages 1217 and 1274

From *Menaphon*, 1589

Doron's description of Samela

Like to Diana in her summer weed,
Girt with a crimson robe of brightest dye,
          Goes fair Samela.
Whiter than be the flocks that straggling feed,
When washed by Arethusa faint they lie,
          Is fair Samela.
As fair Aurora in her morning-grey,
Decked with the ruddy glister of her love,
          Is fair Samela.
Like lovely Thetis on a calmèd day,   10
Whenas her brightness Neptune's fancy move,
          Shines fair Samela.
Her tresses gold, her eyes like glassy streams,
Her teeth are pearl, the breasts are ivory
          Of fair Samela;
Her cheeks, like rose and lily, yield forth gleams,
Her brows, bright arches framed of ebony.
          Thus fair Samela

Passeth fair Venus in her bravest hue,
And Juno in the show of majesty   20
        (For she's Samela),

Pallas in wit. All three, if you well view,
For beauty, wit, and matchless dignity,
        Yield to Samela.

Doron's jig

Through the shrubs as I can crack
  For my lambs' little ones,
'Mongst many pretty ones—
Nymphs, I mean,—whose hair
      was black
      As the crow,
      Like the snow
Her face and brows shined, I
    ween;
  I saw a little one,
  A bonny pretty one,
As bright, buxom, and as sheen[10]
    As was she
    On her knee
That lulled the god whose arrows
    warms
  Such merry little ones,

Such fair-faced pretty ones,
As dally in love's chiefest harms.
    Such was mine,
    Whose gay eyne
Made me love. I gan to woo
  This sweet little one,   20
  This bonny pretty one;
I wooed hard, a day or two,
    Till she bade,
    Be not sad,
Woo no more, I am thine own,
  Thy dearest little one,
  Thy truest pretty one.
Thus was faith and firm love
    shown
    As behoves
Shepherds' loves.   30

Sephestia's song to her child

Weep not, my wanton, smile upon my knee,
When thou art old there's grief enough for thee.
  Mother's wag, pretty boy,
  Father's sorrow, father's joy,
  When thy father first did see
  Such a boy by him and me,
  He was glad, I was woe;
  Fortune changed made him so,
  When he left his pretty boy,
  Last his sorrow, first his joy.   10

Weep not, my wanton, smile upon my knee,
When thou art old there's grief enough for thee.
  Streaming tears that never stint,
  Like pearl-drops from a flint,
  Fell by course from his eyes,

That one another's place supplies.
Thus he grieved in every part;
Tears of blood fell from his heart,
When he left his pretty boy,
Father's sorrow, father's joy.   20

Weep not, my wanton, smile upon my knee,
When thou art old there's grief enough for thee.
The wanton smiled, father wept,
Mother cried, baby leapt;
More he crowed, more we cried,
Nature could not sorrow hide.
He must go, he must kiss
Child and mother, baby bliss,
For he left his pretty boy,
Father's sorrow, father's joy.   30
Weep not, my wanton, smile upon my knee,
When thou art old there's grief enough for thee.

From *Greene's Mourning Garment*, 1590

The shepherd's wife's song

Ah, what is love? It is a pretty thing,
As sweet unto a shepherd as a king—
    And sweeter too,
For kings have cares that wait upon a crown,
And cares can make the sweetest love to frown.
        Ah then, ah then,
If country loves such sweet desires do gain,
What lady would not love a shepherd swain?

His flocks once folded, he comes home at night
As merry as a king in his delight—   10
    And merrier too,
For kings bethink them what the state require,
Where shepherds careless carol by the fire.
        Ah then, ah then,
If country loves such sweet desires gain,
What lady would not love a shepherd swain?

He kisseth first, then sits as blithe to eat
His cream and curds as doth the king his meat—
    And blither too,
For kings have often fears when they do sup,   20
Where shepherds dread no poison in their cup.
        Ah then, ah then,

If country loves such sweet desires gain,
What lady would not love a shepherd swain?

To bed he goes, as wanton then, I ween,
As is a king in dalliance with a queen—
    More wanton too,
For kings have many griefs, affects to move,
Where shepherds have no greater grief than love.
    Ah then, ah then,   30
If country loves such sweet desires gain,
What lady would not love a shepherd swain?

Upon his couch of straw he sleeps as sound
As doth the king upon his beds of down—
    More sounder too,
For cares cause kings full oft their sleep to spill,
Where weary shepherds lie and snort their fill.
    Ah then, ah then,
If country loves such sweet desires gain,
What lady would not love a shepherd swain?   40

Thus with his wife he spends the year, as blithe
As doth the king, at every tide or sithe—
    And blither too,
For kings have wars and broils to take in hand,
Where shepherds laugh and love upon the land.
    Ah then, ah then,
If country loves such sweet desires gain,
What lady would not love a shepherd swain?

Hexametra Alexis in laudem Rosamundi

Oft have I heard my lief Corydon report on a love-day,
When bonny maids do meet with the swains in the valley by Tempe,
How bright-eyed his Phillis was, how lovely they glancëd
When fro th'arches ebon black flew looks as a lightning
That set afire with piercing flames even hearts adamantine.
Face rose-hued, cherry-red, with a silver taint like a lily,
Venus' pride might abate, might abash with a blush to behold her.
Phœbus' wires, compared to her hairs, unworthy the praising;
Juno's state, and Pallas' wit, disgraced with the graces
That graced her whom poor Corydon did choose for a love-mate.   10
Ah! but had Corydon now seen the star that Alexis
Likes and loves so dear that he melts to sighs when he sees her;
Did Corydon but see those eyes, those amorous eyelids,
From whence fly holy flames of death or life in a moment;

Ah! did he see that face, those hairs that Venus, Apollo,
'Bashed to behold,—and both, disgraced, did grieve that a creature
Should exceed in hue, compare both a god and a goddess;
Ah! had he seen my sweet paramour, the saint of Alexis:
Then had he said, Phillis, sit down surpassèd in all points,
For there is one more fair than thou, beloved of Alexis.   20

FROM *Greene's Never too Late*, 1590

The palmer's ode

Old Menalcas on a day
As in field this shepherd lay,
Tuning of his oaten pipe,
Which he hit with many a stripe,
Said to Coridon that he
Once was young and full of glee.
Blithe and wanton was I then,—
Such desires follow men.
As I lay and kept my sheep,
Came the god that hateth sleep,   10
Clad in armor all of fire,
Hand in hand with queen desire;
And with a dart that wounded me
Pierced my heart as I did lie;
That when I woke I gan swear
Phillis' beauty palm did bear.
Up I start, forth went I
With her face to feed mine eye.
There I saw desire sit,
That my heart with love did hit,   20
Laying forth bright beauty's hooks
To entrap my gazing looks.
Love I did, and gan to woo,
Pray, and sigh; all would not do;
Women, when they take the toy,
Covet to be counted coy.
Coy was she that I gan court;
She thought love was but a sport;
Profound hell was in my thought,
Such a pain desire had wrought   30
That I sued with sighs and tears.
Still ingrate she stopped her ears
Till my youth I had spent.
Last, a passion of repent
Told me flat, that desire

Was a brand of love's fire,
Which consumeth men in thrall,
Virtue, youth, wit, and all.
At this saw, back I start,
Beat desire from my heart,   40
Shook off love, and made an oath
To be enemy to both.
Old I was when thus I fled
Such fond toys as cloyed my head;
But this I learned at virtue's gate,
The way to good is never late.

FROM *Greene's Farewell to Folly*, 1591

[*Sweet are the thoughts*]

Sweet are the thoughts that savor
    of content,
  The quiet mind is richer than
    a crown;
Sweet are the nights in careless
    slumber spent,
  The poor estate scorns fortune's
    angry frown:
Such sweet content, such minds,
    such sleep, such bliss,
Beggars enjoy, when princes oft
    do miss.

The homely house that harbors
    quiet rest,
  The cottage that affords no
    pride nor care,
The mean that grees with coun-
    try music best,
  The sweet consort of mirth and
    music's fare,   10

Obscurëd life sets down a type of
  bliss;
A mind content both crown and
  kingdom is.

FROM *Philomela, the Lady Fitzwater's Nightingale,* 1592

*Philomela's ode that she sung
  in her arbor*

Sitting by a river side
Where a silent stream did glide,
Muse I did of many things
That the mind in quiet brings.
I gan think how some men deem
Gold their god; and some esteem
Honor is the chief content
That to man in life is lent;
And some others do contend
Quiet none like to a friend;   10
Others hold there is no wealth
Compared to a perfect health;
Some man's mind in quiet stands
When he is lord of many lands:
But I did sigh, and said all this
Was but a shade of perfect bliss;

And in my thoughts I did approve
Nought so sweet as is true love.
Love 'twixt lovers passeth these,
When mouth kisseth and heart
  grees,   20
With folded arms and lippës meet-
  ing,
Each soul another sweetly greet-
  ing;
For by the breath the soul fleet-
  eth
And soul with soul in kissing
  meeteth.
If love be so sweet a thing,
That such happy bliss doth bring,
Happy is love's sugared thrall;
But unhappy maidens all,
Who esteem your virgin's blisses
Sweeter than a wife's sweet kisses.
No such quiet to the mind   31
As true love with kisses kind;
But if a kiss prove unchaste,
Then is true love quite disgraced.
Though love be sweet, learn this
  of me:
No love sweet but honesty.

FROM *Greene's Orpharion,* 1599

[*Cupid abroad was lated*]

Cupid abroad was lated in the night,
    His wings were wet with ranging in the rain;
  Harbor he sought, to me he took his flight
    To dry his plumes. I heard the boy complain;
      I oped the door and granted his desire,
      I rose myself, and made the wag a fire.

Looking more narrow by the fire's flame,
    I spied his quiver hanging by his back.
  Doubting the boy might my misfortune frame,
    I would have gone, for fear of further wrack;   10
      But what I drad did me, poor wretch, betide,
      For forth he drew an arrow from his side.

He pierced the quick, and I began to start,
    A pleasing wound but that it was too high;

His shaft procured a sharp yet sugared smart.
Away he flew, for why his wings were dry;
But left the arrow sticking in my breast,
That sore I grieved I welcomed such a guest.

THOMAS LODGE

The Introduction and Notes are at pages 1217 and 1274

FROM *Scilla's Metamorphosis*, 1589

Sonnet

The earth, late choked with
    showers,
Is now arrayed in green;
Her bosom springs with flowers,
The air dissolves her teen.
    The heavens laugh at her glory,
    Yet bide I sad and sorry.
The woods are decked with leaves
And trees are clothèd gay,
And Flora, crowned with sheaves,
With oaken boughs doth play; 10
    Where I am clad in black,
    The token of my wrack.

The birds upon the trees
Do sing with pleasant voices,
And chant in their degrees
Their loves and lucky choices;
    When I, whilst they are sing-
      ing,
    With sighs mine arms am
      wringing.
The thrushes seek the shade,
And I my fatal grave; 20
Their flight to heaven is made,
My walk on earth I have.
    They free, I thrall; they jolly,
    I sad and pensive wholly.

FROM *Rosalind*, 1592

Rosalind's madrigal

Love in my bosom like a bee
    Doth suck his sweet;
Now with his wings he plays with
    me,
    Now with his feet.
Within mine eyes he makes his
    nest,
His bed amidst my tender breast,
My kisses are his daily feast,
And yet he robs me of my rest—
    Ah, wanton, will ye?

And if I sleep, then percheth he 10
    With pretty flight,
And makes his pillow of my knee
    The livelong night.
Strike I my lute, he tunes the
    string,

He music plays if so I sing,
He lends me every lovely thing,
Yet cruel he my heart doth
    sting—
    Whist, wanton, still ye!

Else I with roses every day
    Will whip you hence, 20
And bind you, when you long to
    play,
    For your offence.
I'll shut mine eyes to keep you
    in,
I'll make you fast it for your
    sin,
I'll count your power not worth a
    pin;
    Alas! what hereby shall I win
    If he gainsay me?

What if I beat the wanton boy
With many a rod?
He will repay me with annoy, 30
Because a god.
Then sit thou safely on my knee,

And let thy bower my bosom be,
Lurk in mine eyes, I like of
thee.
O Cupid, so thou pity me,
Spare not, but play thee!

Montanus' sonnet

Phœbe sat,
Sweet she sat,
  Sweet sat Phœbe when I saw her;
White her brow,
Coy her eye,
  Brow and eye how much you please me!
Words I spent,
Sighs I sent,
  Sighs and words could never draw her.
O my love,   10
Thou art lost,
  Since no sight could ever ease thee.

Phœbe sat
By a fount,
  Sitting by a fount I spied her;
Sweet her touch,
Rare her voice,
  Touch and voice, what may distain you?
As she sang,
I did sigh,   20
  And by sighs whilst that I tried her,
O mine eyes,
You did lose
  Her first sight, whose want did pain you.

Phœbe's flocks
White as wool,
  Yet were Phœbe's locks more whiter;
Phœbe's eyes
Dovelike mild,
  Dovelike eyes, both mild and cruel;   30
Montan swears,
In your lamps
  He will die for to delight her.
Phœbe, yield,
Or I die—
  Shall true hearts be fancy's fuel?

Rosader's second sonetto

Turn I my looks unto the skies,
Love with his arrows wounds mine eyes;
If so I gaze upon the ground,
Love then in every flower is found;
Search I the shade, to fly my pain,
He meets me in the shade again;
Wend I to walk in secret grove,
Ev'n there I meet with sacred love;
If so I bain me in the spring,
Ev'n on the brink I hear him sing;   10
If so I meditate alone,
He will be partner of my moan;
If so I mourn, he weeps with me,
And where I am there will he be.
Whenas I talk of Rosalind
The god from coyness waxeth kind,
And seems in self-same flames to fry
Because he loves as well as I.
Sweet Rosalind, for pity rue!
For why than love I am more true.   20
He, if he speed, will quickly fly,
But in thy love I live and die.

FROM *The Life and Death of William Longbeard*, 1593

[*My mistress when she goes*]

My mistress when she goes
To pull the pink and rose
Along the river bounds,
And trippeth on the grounds,
And runs from rocks to rocks
With lovely scattered locks,
Whilst amorous wind doth play
With hairs so golden gay;
The water waxeth clear,
The fishes draw her near,   10
The sirens sing her praise,
Sweet flowers perfume her ways,
And Neptune, glad and fain,
Yields up to her his reign.

FROM R. S.'s *Phœnix Nest*, 1593

[*Strive no more*]

Strive no more,
Forspoken joys, to spring!
Since care hath clipt thy wing;
But stoop those lamps before
That nursed thee up at first with
        friendly smiles
And now through scorns thy trust
        beguiles.

Pine away,
That pining you may please,
For death betides you ease;

Oh, sweet and kind decay, [10]
To pine and die whilst love gives
    looking on
And pines to see your pining moan.

Dying joys,
Your shrine is constant heart

That glories in his smart,
    Your trophies are annoys;
And on your tomb by love these
    lines are placed,
Lo, here they lie whom scorn de-
    faced.

[The fatal star]

The fatal star that at my birthday shinëd,
  Were it of Jove, or Venus in her brightness,
All sad effects, sour fruits of love divinëd
        In my love's lightness.

Light was my love, that all too light believëd
  Heaven's ruth to dwell in fair alluring faces,
That love, that hope that damnëd and reprievëd
        To all disgraces!

Love that misled, hope that deceived my seeing;
  Love, hope no more, mocked with deluding object; [10]
Sight full of sorrow that denies the being
        Unto the subject.

Soul, leave the seat where thoughts with endless swelling
  Change into tears and words of no persuasion;
Tears, turn to tongues and spend your tunes in telling
        Sorrow's invasion.

Wonder, vain world, at beauty's proud refusal;
  Wonder in vain at love's unkind denial,
Why love thus lofty is, that doth abuse all
        And makes no trial. [20]

Tears, words, and tunes, all, signify my sadness!
  My speechless grief, look pale without dissembling.
Sorrow, sit mute and tell thy torment's madness
        With true heart's trembling.

And if pure vows, or hands heaved up to heaven,
  May move the gods to rue my wretched blindness,
My plaints shall make my joys in measure even
        With her unkindness.

That she whom my true heart hath found so cruel,
    Mourning all mirthless, may pursue the pleasure   30
That scorns her labors, poor in her joy's jewel
            And earthly treasure.

[*Like desert woods*]

Like desert woods with darksome shades obscured
Where dreadful beasts, where hateful horror reigneth,
Such is my wounded heart, whom sorrow paineth.

The trees are fatal shafts, to death inured,
That cruel love within my breast maintaineth
To whet my grief whenas my sorrow waneth.

The ghastly beasts, my thoughts in cares assured,
Which wage me war (whilst heart no succor gaineth)
With false suspect, and fear that still remaineth.

The horrors, burning sighs by cares procured,   10
Which forth I send whilst weeping eye complaineth,
To cool the heat the helpless heart containeth.

But shafts, but cares, sighs, horrors unrecured,
Were nought esteemed if, for these pains awarded,
My faithful love by you might be rewarded.

FROM *Phillis honored with Pastoral Sonnets, Elegies,*
        and Amorous Delights, 1593

O pleasing thoughts, apprentices of love,
Forerunners of desire, sweet mithridates
The poison of my sorrows to remove,
With whom my hopes and fear full oft debates,—
    Enrich yourselves and me by your self riches
Which are the thoughts you spend on heaven-bred beauty,
Rouse you my muse beyond our poets' pitches,
And working wonders, yet say all is duty;
    Use you no eaglets' eyes nor phœnix' feathers
To tower the heaven from whence heaven's wonder sallies,   10
For why, your sun sings sweetly to her weathers,
Making a spring of winter in the valleys.
    Show to the world, though poor and scant my skill is,
    How sweet thoughts be that are but thought on Phillis.

————

No stars her eyes, to clear the wandering night,
But shining suns of true divinity,

That make the soul conceive her perfect light;
No wanton beauties of humanity
   Her pretty brows, but beams that clear the sight
Of him that seeks the true philosophy;
No coral is her lip, no rose her fair,
But even that crimson that adorns the sun;
   No nymph is she, but mistress of the air,
By whom my glories are but new begun.   10
   But when I touch and taste as others do,
   I then shall write and you shall wonder too.

   Love guides the roses of thy lips
And flies about them like a bee;
   If I approach he forward skips,
And if I kiss he stingeth me.
   Love in thine eyes doth build his bower
And sleeps within their pretty shine;
   And if I look, the boy will lour
And from their orbs shoot shafts divine.
   Love works thy heart within his fire,   10
And in my tears doth firm the same;
   And if I tempt it will retire,
And of my plaints doth make a game.
   Love, let me cull her choicest flowers,
And pity me, and calm her eye,
   Make soft her heart, dissolve her lours,
Then will I praise thy deity.
   But if thou do not, Love, I'll truly serve her
   In spite of thee, and by firm faith deserve her.

My Phillis hath the morning sun
   At first to look upon her,
And Phillis hath morn-waking birds
   Her risings for to honor.
My Phillis hath prime-feathered flowers
   That smile when she treads on them,
And Phillis hath a gallant flock
   That leaps since she doth own them.
But Phillis hath so hard a heart
   (Alas, that she should have it!)   10
As yields no mercy to desert
   Nor grace to those that crave it.
Sweet sun, when thou lookest on,
   Pray her regard my moan;

Sweet birds, when you sing to her,
To yield some pity woo her;
Sweet flowers, whenas she treads on,
Tell her, her beauty deads one;
And if in life her love she nill agree me,
Pray her, before I die she will come see me.   20

I'll teach thee, lovely Phillis, what love is:
It is a vision, seeming such as thou,
That flies as fast as it assaults mine eyes;
It is affection that doth reason miss;
It is a shape of pleasure like to you,
Which meets the eye, and seen on sudden dies;
It is a doubled grief, a spark of pleasure
Begot by vain desire. And this is love,
Whom in our youth we count our chiefest treasure,
In age, for want of power, we do reprove.   10
Yea, such a power is love, whose loss is pain,
And having got him, we repent our gain.

An ode

Now I find thy looks were feignëd,
Quickly lost and quickly gainëd;
Soft thy skin like wool of wethers,
Heart unstable, light as feathers;
Tongue untrusty, subtle-sighted,
Wanton will, with change delighted.
  Siren pleasant, foe to reason,
  Cupid plague thee for this treason.

Feigned acceptance when I askëd,
Lovely words, with cunning maskëd;
Holy vows but heart unholy,—
Wretched man, my trust was folly;   20
Lily white, and pretty winking,
Solemn vows, but sorry thinking.
  Siren pleasant, foe to reason,
  Cupid plague thee for this treason.

Of thine eyes I made my mirror;
From thy beauty came mine error;   10
All thy words I counted witty;
All thy smiles I deemëd pity;
Thy false tears that me aggrievëd
First of all my trust deceivëd.
  Siren pleasant, foe to reason,
  Cupid plague thee for this treason.

Now I see (O seemly cruel!)
Others warm them at my fuel.
Wit shall guide me in this durance,
Since in love is no assurance.
Change thy pasture, take thy pleasure;
Beauty is a fading treasure.   30
  Siren pleasant, foe to reason,
  Cupid plague thee for this treason.

Prime youth lasts not, age will follow,
And make white these tresses yellow;
Wrinkled face for looks delightful
Shall acquaint the dame despiteful;

And when time shall eat thy glory,
Then too late thou wilt be sorry.
Siren pleasant, foe to reason,
Cupid plague thee for this treason.

NICHOLAS BRETON

The Introduction and Notes are at pages 1218 and 1274

FROM *The Arbor of Amorous Devices*, 1597

A pastoral of Phillis and Coridon

On a hill there grows a flower,
  Fair befall the dainty sweet!
By that flower there is a bower
  Where the heavenly Muses meet.

In that bower there is a chair
  Fringëd all about with gold,
Where doth sit the fairest fair
  That did ever eye behold.

It is Phillis fair and bright,
  She that is the shepherds' joy, 10
She that Venus did despite
  And did blind her little boy.

This is she, the wise, the rich,
  And the world desires to see;
This is *ipsa quæ* the which
  There is none but only she.

Who would not this face admire?
  Who would not this saint adore?
Who would not this sight desire,
  Though he thought to see no more? 20

O fair eyes, yet let me see!
  One good look, and I am gone,

Look on me, for I am he—
  Thy poor silly Coridon.

Thou that art the shepherds' queen,
  Look upon thy silly swain;
By thy comfort have been seen
  Dead men brought to life again.

A sweet lullaby

Come, little babe; come, silly soul,
Thy father's shame, thy mother's grief,
Born, as I doubt, to all our dole
And to thyself unhappy chief:
  Sing lullaby, and lap it warm,
  Poor soul that thinks no creature harm.

Thou little think'st and less dost know
The cause of this thy mother's moan,
Thou want'st the wit to wail her woe,
And I myself am all alone. 10
  Why dost thou weep? why dost thou wail?
  And knowest not yet what thou dost ail.

Come, little wretch—ah, silly
    heart,
Mine only joy, what can I more?
If there be any wrong thy smart,
That may the destinies implore,
    'Twas I, I say, against my
        will;
    I wail the time, but be thou
        still.

And dost thou smile? Oh, thy
    sweet face,
Would God himself he might
    thee see;   20
No doubt thou wouldst soon pur-
    chase grace,
I know right well, for thee and
    me.
    But come to mother, babe, and
        play,
    For father false is fled away.

Sweet boy, if it by fortune chance
Thy father home again to send,
If death do strike me with his
    lance,
Yet mayst thou me to him com-
    mend;
    If any ask thy mother's name,
    Tell how by love she purchased
        blame.   30

Then will his gentle heart soon
    yield;
I know him of a noble mind.
Although a lion in the field,
A lamb in town thou shalt him
    find.
    Ask blessing, babe, be not
        afraid;
    His sugared words hath me be-
        trayed.

Then mayst thou joy and be right
    glad,
Although in woe I seem to moan.
Thy father is no rascal lad,

A noble youth of blood and
    bone;   40
His glancing looks, if he once
    smile,
Right honest women may be-
    guile.

Come, little boy, and rock asleep,
Sing lullaby, and be thou still;
I that can do nought else but
    weep
Will sit by thee and wail my fill.
    God bless my babe, and lul-
        laby,
    From this thy father's quality.

From John Bodenham's (?)
    England's Helicon, 1600

[*Say that I should say*]

Say that I should say I love ye,
    Would you say 'tis but a say-
        ing?
But if love in prayers move ye,
    Will you not be moved with
        praying?

Think I think that love should
    know ye,
    Will you think 'tis but a think-
        ing?
But if love the thought do show
    ye,
    Will ye lose your eyes with
        winking?

Write that I do write you blessed,
    Will you write 'tis but a writ-
        ing?   10
But if truth and love confess it,
    Will ye doubt the true indit-
        ing?

No: I say, and think, and write
    it,—

Write, and think, and say your
    pleasure.
Love and truth and I indite it,
    You are blessed out of measure.

Phillida and Coridon

In the merry month of May,
In a morn by break of day
Forth I walked by the wood-side,
Whenas May was in his pride.
There I spiëd, all alone,
Phillida and Coridon.
Much ado there was, God wot,
He would love and she would
    not.
She said, Never man was true;
He said, None was false to you.   10
He said he had loved her long.
She said, Love should have no
    wrong.
Coridon would kiss her then;
She said maids must kiss no men
Till they did for good and all.
Then she made the shepherd call
All the heavens to witness truth,
Never loved a truer youth.
Thus, with many a pretty oath,
Yea and nay, and faith and
    troth,   20
Such as silly shepherds use
When they will not love abuse,
Love which had been long de-
    luded
Was with kisses sweet concluded.
And Phillida with garlands gay
Was made the lady of the May.

Song of Phillida and Coridon

Fair in a morn (O fairest morn,
    Was never morn so fair)
There shone a sun, though not the
    sun
    That shineth in the air.
For the earth and from the earth,
    (Was never such a creature)

Did come this face; (was never
    face
    That carried such a feature).
Upon a hill (O blessed hill,
    Was never hill so blessed)   10
There stood a man; (was never
    man
    For woman so distressëd).
This man beheld a heavenly view
    Which did such virtue give
As clears the blind and helps the
    lame,
    And makes the dead man live.
This man had hap (O happy
    man,
    More happy none than he),
For he had hap to see the hap
    That none had hap to see.   20
This silly swain (and silly swains
    Are men of meanest grace)
Had yet the grace (O gracious
    guest)
    To hap on such a face.
He pity cried, and pity came,
    And pitied so his pain,
As dying, would not let him die,
    But gave him life again.
For joy whereof he made such
    mirth
    As all the woods did ring;   30
And Pan with all his swains came
    forth
    To hear the shepherd sing.
But such a song sung never was,
    Nor shall be sung again,
Of Phillida, the shepherds' queen,
    And Coridon, the swain.
Fair Phillis is the shepherds'
    queen
    (Was never such a queen as
    she),
And Coridon her only swain
    (Was never such a swain as
    he).   40
Fair Phillis hath the fairest face
    That ever eye did yet behold,

And Coridon the constants' faith
  That ever yet kept flock in fold.
Sweet Phillis is the sweetest sweet
  That ever yet the earth did
    yield,
And Coridon the kindest swain
  That ever yet kept lambs in
    field.
Sweet Philomel is Phillis' bird,
  Though Coridon be he that
    caught her;   50
And Coridon doth hear her sing,
  Though Phillida be she that
    taught her.
Poor Coridon doth keep the fields,
  Though Phillida be she that
    owes them;
And Phillida doth walk the
    meads,
  Though Coridon be he that
    mows them.
The little lambs are Phillis' love,
  Though Coridon is he that
    feeds them;
The gardens fair are Phillis'
    ground,
  Though Coridon be he that
    weeds them.   60
Since then that Phillis only is
  The only shepherd's only queen,
And Coridon the only swain
  That only hath her shepherd
    been;
Though Phillis keep her bower of
    state,
  Shall Coridon consume away?
No, shepherd, no, work out the
    week,
  And Sunday shall be holy-day.

FROM *Melancholic Humors*, 1600

An odd conceit

Lovely kind, and kindly loving,
Such a mind were worth the mov-
    ing;

Truly fair, and fairly true,
Where are all these but in you?

Wisely kind, and kindly wise—
Blessed life, where such love lies!
Wise, and kind, and fair, and
    true,
Lovely live all these in you.

Sweetly dear, and dearly sweet—
Blessed, where these blessings
    meet!   10
Sweet, fair, wise, kind, blessed,
    true,
Blessed be all these in you!

FROM *The Passionate Shepherd*,
  1604

Pastoral [1]

Flora hath been all about
And hath brought her wardrobe
    out,
With her fairest, sweetest flowers,
All to trim up all your bowers.
Bid the shepherds and their
    swains
See the beauty of their plains,
And command them, with their
    flocks,
To do reverence on the rocks,
Where they may so happy be
As her shadow but to see.   10
Bid the birds in every bush
Not a bird to be at hush,
But to sit, chirrup, and sing
To the beauty of the spring.
Call the sylvan nymphs together,
Bid them bring their music
    hither.
Trees their barky silence break,
Crack, yet though they cannot
    speak.
Bid the purest, whitest swan
Of her feathers make her fan.   20
Let the hound the hare go chase,

Lambs and rabbits run at base,
Flies be dancing in the sun,
While the silk-worm's webs are
    spun;
Hang a fish on every hook
As she goes along the brook:
So with all your sweetest powers
Entertain her in your bowers,
Where her ear may joy to hear
How ye make your sweetest
    choir; 30
And in all your sweetest vein,
Still, Aglaia! strike the strain.
But when she her walk doth turn,
Then begin as fast to mourn,
All your flowers and garlands
    wither,
Put up all your pipes together;
Never strike a pleasing strain
Till she come abroad again!

Pastoral [2]

Who can live in heart so glad
As the merry country lad?
Who upon a fair green balk
May at pleasure sit and walk,
And amid the azure skies
See the morning sun arise;
While he hears in every spring
How the birds do chirp and sing;
Or before the hounds in cry
See the hare go stealing by; 10
Or along the shallow brook
Angling with a baited hook,
See the fishes leap and play
In a blessed sunny day;
Or to hear the partridge call
Till she have her covey all;
Or to see the subtle fox,
How the villain plies the box,
After feeding on his prey
How he closely sneaks away 20
Through the hedge and down the
    furrow,
Till he gets into his burrow;

Then the bee to gather honey,
And the little black-haired coney
On a bank for sunny place
With her forefeet wash her face:
Are not these, with thousands
    mo
Than the courts of kings do
    know,
The true pleasing-spirits sights
That may breed true love's de-
    lights? 30
But with all this happiness
To behold that shepherdess
To whose eyes all shepherds yield,
All the fairest of the field,
Fair Aglaia, in whose face
Lives the shepherds' highest
    grace,
In whose worthy-wonder praise
See what her true shepherd says:
She is neither proud nor fine,
But in spirit more divine; 40
She can neither lour nor leer,
But a sweeter smiling cheer;
She had never painted face,
But a sweeter smiling grace;
She can never love dissemble,
Truth doth so her thoughts as-
    semble
That where wisdom guides her
    will
She is kind and constant still.
All in sum, she is that creature
Of that truest comfort's nature, 50
That doth show (but in exceed-
    ings)
How their praises had their breed-
    ings.
Let, then, poets feign their pleas-
    ure
In their fictions of love's treasure,
Proud high spirits seek their
    graces
In their idol-painted faces;
My love's spirit's lowliness
In affection's humbleness

Under heav'n no happiness
Seeks but in this shepherdess.   60
For whose sake I say and swear
By the passions that I bear,
Had I got a kingly grace
I would leave my kingly place
And in heart be truly glad
To become a country lad,

Hard to lie, and go full bare,
And to feed on hungry fare,
So I might but live to be
Where I might but sit to see   70
Once a day, or all day long,
The sweet subject of my song—
In Aglaia's only eyes
All my worldly paradise.

CHRISTOPHER MARLOWE

The Introduction and Notes are at pages 1219 and 1275

From John Bodenham's (?) *England's Helicon*, 1600

The passionate shepherd to his love

Come live with me and be my love,
And we will all the pleasures prove
That valleys, groves, hills, and
      fields,
Woods, or steepy mountain yields.

And we will sit upon the rocks,
Seeing the shepherds feed their
      flocks,
By shallow rivers to whose falls
Melodious birds sings madrigals.

And I will make thee beds of roses
And a thousand fragrant posies,[10]
A cap of flowers, and a kirtle
Embroidered all with leaves of
      myrtle;

A gown made of the finest wool
Which from our pretty lambs we
      pull;
Fair linëd slippers for the cold,
With buckles of the purest gold;

A belt of straw and ivy buds,
With coral clasps and amber studs:
And if these pleasures may thee
      move,
Come live with me, and be my
      love.   20

The shepherds' swains shall dance
      and sing
For thy delight each May morning:
If these delights thy mind may
      move,
Then live with me and be my love.

From *Hero and Leander . . . for Edward Blunt*, 1598

To the Right Worshipful Sir Thomas Walsingham, Knight.

*Sir, we think not ourselves discharged of the duty we owe to our
friend when we have brought the breathless body to the earth; for
albeit the eye there taketh his ever farewell of that beloved object, yet
the impression of the man that hath been dear unto us, living an after
life in our memory, there putteth us in mind of farther obsequies due*

unto the deceased. And namely of the performance of whatsoever we may judge shall make to his living credit, and to the effecting of his determinations prevented by the stroke of death. By these meditations, as by an intellectual will, I suppose myself executor to the unhappily deceased author of this poem, upon whom knowing that in his life-time you bestowed many kind favors, entertaining the parts of reckon-ing and worth which you found in him, with good countenance and liberal affection, I cannot but see so far into the will of him dead, that whatsoever issue of his brain should chance to come abroad, that the first breath it should take might be the gentle air of your liking; for since his self had been accustomed thereunto, it would prove more agreeable and thriving to his right children than any other foster countenance whatsoever. At this time seeing that this unfinished tragedy happens under my hands to be imprinted, of a double duty, the one to yourself, the other to the deceased, I present the same to your most favorable allowance, offering my utmost self now and ever to be ready at your Worship's disposing.

Edward Blunt.

Hero and Leander

[First sestiad]

On Hellespont, guilty of true love's blood,
In view, and opposite, two cities stood,
Sea-borderers, disjoined by Neptune's might;
The one Abydos, the other Sestos hight.
At Sestos, Hero dwelt; Hero the fair,
Whom young Apollo courted for her hair,
And offered as a dower his burning throne,
Where she should sit for men to gaze upon.
The outside of her garments were of lawn,
The lining purple silk, with gilt stars drawn;   10
Her wide sleeves green, and bordered with a grove
Where Venus in her naked glory strove
To please the careless and disdainful eyes
Of proud Adonis, that before her lies;
Her kirtle blue, whereon was many a stain,
Made with the blood of wretched lovers slain.
Upon her head she ware a myrtle wreath,
From whence her veil reached to the ground beneath.
Her veil was artificial flowers and leaves,
Whose workmanship both man and beast deceives;   20
Many would praise the sweet smell as she passed,
When 'twas the odor which her breath forth cast;
And there for honey bees have sought in vain,

And, beat from thence, have lighted there again.
About her neck hung chains of pebble-stone,
Which, lightened by her neck, like diamonds shone.
She ware no gloves, for neither sun nor wind
Would burn or parch her hands, but to her mind,
Or warm or cool them, for they took delight
To play upon those hands, they were so white.   10
Buskins of shells all silvered, usèd she,
And branched with blushing coral to the knee,
Where sparrows perched, of hollow pearl and gold,
Such as the world would wonder to behold;
Those with sweet water oft her handmaid fills,
Which, as she went, would chirrup through the bills.
Some say, for her the fairest Cupid pined,
And, looking in her face, was strooken blind.
But this is true: so like was one the other,
As he imagined Hero was his mother;   40
And oftentimes into her bosom flew,
About her naked neck his bare arms threw,
And laid his childish head upon her breast,
And with still panting rocked, there took his rest.
So lovely fair was Hero, Venus' nun,
As nature wept, thinking she was undone,
Because she took more from her than she left
And of such wondrous beauty her bereft;
Therefore, in sign her treasure suffered wrack,
Since Hero's time hath half the world been black.   50
Amorous Leander, beautiful and young,
(Whose tragedy divine Musæus sung)
Dwelt at Abydos; since him dwelt there none
For whom succeeding times make greater moan.
His dangling tresses that were never shorn,
Had they been cut and unto Colchis borne,
Would have allured the vent'rous youth of Greece
To hazard more than for the Golden Fleece.
Fair Cynthia wished his arms might be her sphere;
Grief makes her pale, because she moves not there.   60
His body was as straight as Circe's wand;
Jove might have sipped out nectar from his hand.
Even as delicious meat is to the taste,
So was his neck in touching, and surpassed
The white of Pelops' shoulder. I could tell ye
How smooth his breast was, and how white his belly,
And whose immortal fingers did imprint
That heavenly path, with many a curious dint,
That runs along his back; but my rude pen

Can hardly blazon forth the loves of men,
Much less of powerful gods; let it suffice
That my slack muse sings of Leander's eyes,
Those orient cheeks and lips, exceeding his
That leapt into the water for a kiss
Of his own shadow, and despising many,
Died ere he could enjoy the love of any.
Had wild Hippolytus Leander seen,
Enamoured of his beauty had he been;
His presence made the rudest peasant melt,
That in the vast uplandish country dwelt;
The barbarous Thracian soldier, moved with nought,
Was moved with him, and for his favor sought.
Some swore he was a maid in man's attire,
For in his looks were all that men desire:
A pleasant smiling cheek, a speaking eye,
A brow for love to banquet royally;
And such as knew he was a man, would say,
Leander, thou art made for amorous play;
Why art thou not in love, and loved of all?
Though thou be fair, yet be not thine own thrall.

    The men of wealthy Sestos every year,
For his sake whom their goddess held so dear,
Rose-cheeked Adonis, kept a solemn feast.
Thither resorted many a wand'ring guest
To meet their loves; such as had none at all,
Came lovers home from this great festival.
For every street, like to a firmament,
Glistered with breathing stars, who, where they went,
Frighted the melancholy earth, which deemed
Eternal heaven to burn, for so it seemed
As if another Phaeton had got
The guidance of the sun's rich chariot.
But, far above the loveliest, Hero shined,
And stole away th' enchanted gazer's mind;
For like sea-nymphs' inveigling harmony,
So was her beauty to the standers by.
Nor that night-wand'ring pale and wat'ry star
(When yawning dragons draw her thirling car
From Latmos' mount up to the gloomy sky,
Where, crowned with blazing light and majesty,
She proudly sits) more over-rules the flood,
Than she the hearts of those that near her stood.
Even as when gaudy nymphs pursue the chase,
Wretched Ixion's shaggy-footed race,
Incensed with savage heat, gallop amain

From steep pine-bearing mountains to the plain,
So ran the people forth to gaze upon her,
And all that viewed her were enamoured on her.
And as in fury of a dreadful fight,
Their fellows being slain or put to flight,   120
Poor soldiers stand with fear of death dead-strooken,
So at her presence all, surprised and tooken,
Await the sentence of her scornful eyes;
He whom she favors lives, the other dies.
There might you see one sigh, another rage,
And some, their violent passions to assuage,
Compile sharp satires; but alas, too late,
For faithful love will never turn to hate.
And many, seeing great princes were denied,
Pined as they went, and thinking on her, died.   130
On this feast day, oh, cursed day and hour!
Went Hero thorough Sestos, from her tower
To Venus' temple, where unhappily,
As after chanced, they did each other spy.
So fair a church as this had Venus none;
The walls were of discolored jasper stone,
Wherein was Proteus carvëd, and o'erhead
A lively vine of green sea-agate spread,
Where by one hand light-headed Bacchus hung,
And with the other wine from grapes out-wrung.   140
Of crystal shining fair the pavement was;
The town of Sestos called it Venus' glass;
There might you see the gods in sundry shapes,
Committing heady riots, incest, rapes;
For know that underneath this radiant floor
Was Danaë's statue in a brazen tower;
Jove slyly stealing from his sister's bed
To dally with Idalian Ganymed,
And for his love Europa bellowing loud,
And tumbling with the rainbow in a cloud;   150
Blood-quaffing Mars heaving the iron net
Which limping Vulcan and his Cyclops set;
Love kindling fire to burn such towns as Troy;
Silvanus weeping for the lovely boy
That now is turned into a cypress tree,
Under whose shade the wood-gods love to be.
And in the midst a silver altar stood;
There Hero sacrificing turtles' blood,
Veiled to the ground, veiling her eyelids close,
And modestly they opened as she rose;   160
Thence flew love's arrow with the golden head,

And thus Leander was enamourëd.
Stone still he stood, and evermore he gazed,
Till with the fire that from his count'nance blazed,
Relenting Hero's gentle heart was strook;
Such force and virtue hath an amorous look.
   It lies not in our power to love or hate,
For will in us is over-ruled by fate.
When two are stripped, long ere the course begin
We wish that one should lose, the other win;   170
And one especially do we affect
Of two gold ingots, like in each respect.
The reason no man knows, let it suffice,
What we behold is censured by our eyes.
Where both deliberate, the love is slight;
Who ever loved, that loved not at first sight?
   He kneeled, but unto her devoutly prayed;
Chaste Hero to herself thus softly said:
Were I the saint he worships, I would hear him;
And as she spake these words, came somewhat near him.   180
He started up; she blushed as one ashamed;
Wherewith Leander much more was inflamed.
He touched her hand; in touching it she trembled;
Love deeply grounded hardly is dissembled.
These lovers parlëd by the touch of hands;
True love is mute, and oft amazëd stands.
Thus while dumb signs their yielding hearts entangled,
The air with sparks of living fire was spangled,
And night, deep drenched in misty Acheron,
Heaved up her head, and half the world upon   190
Breathed darkness forth (dark night is Cupid's day).
And now begins Leander to display
Love's holy fire with words, with sighs, and tears,
Which like sweet music entered Hero's ears;
And yet at every word she turned aside,
And always cut him off as he replied.
At last, like to a bold sharp sophister,
With cheerful hope thus he accosted her:
   Fair creature, let me speak without offence;
I would my rude words had the influence   200
To lead thy thoughts as thy fair looks do mine!
Then shouldst thou be his prisoner who is thine.
Be not unkind and fair; misshapen stuff
Are of behavior boisterous and rough.
Oh, shun me not, but hear me ere you go,
God knows I cannot force love, as you do.
My words shall be as spotless as my youth,

Full of simplicity and naked truth.
This sacrifice, whose sweet perfume descending
From Venus' altar to your footsteps bending,   210
Doth testify that you exceed her far,
To whom you offer, and whose nun you are.
Why should you worship her? her you surpass
As much as sparkling diamonds flaring glass.
A diamond set in lead his worth retains;
A heavenly nymph, beloved of human swains,
Receives no blemish, but ofttimes more grace;
Which makes me hope, although I am but base,
Base in respect of thee, divine and pure,
Dutiful service may thy love procure,   220
And I in duty will excel all other,
As thou in beauty dost exceed Love's mother.
Nor heaven, nor thou, were made to gaze upon;
As heaven preserves all things, so save thou one.
A stately builded ship, well rigged and tall,
The ocean maketh more majestical;
Why vowest thou then to live in Sestos here,
Who on love's seas more glorious would appear?
Like untuned golden strings all women are,
Which long time lie untouched, will harshly jar.   230
Vessels of brass, oft handled, brightly shine;
What difference betwixt the richest mine
And basest mold, but use? for both, not used,
Are of like worth. Then treasure is abused,
When misers keep it; being put to loan,
In time it will return us two for one.
Rich robes themselves and others do adorn;
Neither themselves nor others, if not worn.
Who builds a palace, and rams up the gate,
Shall see it ruinous and desolate.   240
Ah, simple Hero, learn thyself to cherish!
Lone women, like to empty houses, perish.
Less sins the poor rich man that starves himself
In heaping up a mass of drossy pelf,
Than such as you; his golden earth remains,
Which after his decease some other gains;
But this fair gem, sweet in the loss alone,
When you fleet hence, can be bequeathed to none.
Or if it could, down from th' enamelled sky
All heaven would come to claim this legacy,   250
And with intestine broils the world destroy,
And quite confound nature's sweet harmony.
Well therefore by the gods decreed it is

We human creatures should enjoy that bliss.
One is no number; maids are nothing, then,
Without the sweet society of men.
Wilt thou live single still? one shalt thou be
Though never-singling Hymen couple thee.
Wild savages, that drink of running springs,
Think water far excels all earthly things,   260
But they that daily taste neat wine, despise it;
Virginity, albeit some highly prize it,
Compared with marriage, had you tried them both,
Differs as much as wine and water doth.
Base bullion for the stamp's sake we allow;
Even so for men's impression do we you,
By which alone, our reverend fathers say,
Women receive perfection every way.
This idol which you term virginity
Is neither essence subject to the eye,   270
No, nor to any one exterior sense,
Nor hath it any place of residence,
Nor is 't of earth or mould celestial,
Or capable of any form at all.
Of that which hath no being, do not boast;
Things that are not at all, are never lost.
Men foolishly do call it virtuous;
What virtue is it, that is born with us?
Much less can honor be ascribed thereto;
Honor is purchased by the deeds we do.   280
Believe me, Hero, honor is not won
Until some honorable deed be done.
Seek you, for chastity, immortal fame,
And know that some have wronged Diana's name?
Whose name is it, if she be false or not,
So she be fair, but some vile tongues will blot?
But you are fair, ay me, so wondrous fair,
So young, so gentle, and so debonair,
As Greece will think, if thus you live alone,
Some one or other keeps you as his own.   290
Then, Hero, hate me not, nor from me fly
To follow swiftly blasting infamy.
Perhaps thy sacred priesthood makes thee loath;
Tell me, to whom mad'st thou that heedless oath?
    To Venus, answered she, and as she spake,
Forth from those two tralucent cisterns brake
A stream of liquid pearl, which down her face
Made milk-white paths, whereon the gods might trace
To Jove's high court. He thus replied: The rites

In which love's beauteous empress most delights   300
Are banquets, Doric music, midnight revel,
Plays, masks, and all that stern age counteth evil.
Thee as a holy idiot doth she scorn,
For thou, in vowing chastity, hast sworn
To rob her name and honor, and thereby
Commit'st a sin far worse than perjury,
Even sacrilege against her deity,
Through regular and formal purity.
To expiate which sin, kiss and shake hands;
Such sacrifice as this Venus demands.   310
    Thereat she smiled, and did deny him so
As, put thereby, yet might he hope for mo.
Which makes him quickly reinforce his speech,
And her in humble manner thus beseech:
    Though neither gods nor men may thee deserve,
Yet for her sake whom you have vowed to serve,
Abandon fruitless cold virginity,
The gentle queen of love's sole enemy.
Then shall you most resemble Venus' nun,
When Venus' sweet rites are performed and done.   320
Flint-breasted Pallas joys in single life,
But Pallas and your mistress are at strife.
Love, Hero, then, and be not tyrannous,
But heal the heart that thou hast wounded thus;
Nor stain thy youthful years with avarice;
Fair fools delight to be accounted nice.
The richest corn dies if it be not reaped;
Beauty alone is lost, too warily kept.
These arguments he used, and many more,
Wherewith she yielded, that was won before.   330
Hero's looks yielded, but her words made war;
Women are won when they begin to jar.
Thus having swallowed Cupid's golden hook,
The more she strived, the deeper was she strook;
Yet, evilly feigning anger, strove she still,
And would be thought to grant against her will.
So having paused a while, at last she said:
Who taught thee rhetoric to deceive a maid?
Ay me! such words as these should I abhor,
And yet I like them for the orator.   340
    With that Leander stooped to have embraced her,
But from his spreading arms away she cast her,
And thus bespake him: Gentle youth, forbear
To touch the sacred garments which I wear.
    Upon a rock, and underneath a hill,

Far from the town, where all is whist and still
Save that the sea playing on yellow sand
Sends forth a rattling murmur to the land,
Whose sound allures the golden Morpheus
In silence of the night to visit us, 350
My turret stands; and there, God knows, I play
With Venus' swans and sparrows all the day.
A dwarfish beldame bears me company,
That hops about the chamber where I lie,
And spends the night, that might be better spent,
In vain discourse and apish merriment.
Come thither. As she spake this, her tongue tripped,
For unawares, Come thither, from her slipped;
And suddenly her former color changed,
And here and there her eyes through anger ranged. 360
And like a planet moving several ways
At one self instant, she, poor soul, assays,
Loving, not to love at all, and every part
Strove to resist the motions of her heart;
And hands so pure, so innocent, nay such
As might have made heaven stoop to have a touch,
Did she uphold to Venus, and again
Vowed spotless chastity, but all in vain.
Cupid beats down her prayers with his wings;
Her vows above the empty air he flings; 370
All deep enraged, his sinewy bow he bent,
And shot a shaft that burning from him went;
Wherewith she, strooken, looked so dolefully,
As made Love sigh to see his tyranny.
And as she wept, her tears to pearl he turned,
And wound them on his arm, and for her mourned.
Then towards the palace of the Destinies,
Laden with languishment and grief, he flies,
And to those stern nymphs humbly made request,
Both might enjoy each other, and be blest. 380
But with a ghastly dreadful countenance,
Threat'ning a thousand deaths at every glance,
They answered Love, nor would vouchsafe so much
As one poor word, their hate to him was such.
Hearken awhile, and I will tell you why:
Heaven's wingèd herald, Jove-born Mercury,
The self-same day that he asleep had laid
Enchanted Argus, spied a country maid,
Whose careless hair, instead of pearl t' adorn it,
Glistered with dew, as one that seemed to scorn it; 390
Her breath as fragrant as the morning rose,

Her mind pure, and her tongue untaught to gloze;
Yet proud she was, for lofty pride that dwells
In towered courts is oft in shepherds' cells,
And too too well the fair vermilion knew,
And silver tincture of her cheeks, that drew
The love of every swain. On her this god
Enamoured was, and with his snaky rod
Did charm her nimble feet, and made her stay,
The while upon a hillock down he lay,   400
And sweetly on his pipe began to play,
And with smooth speech her fancy to assay;
Till in his twining arms he locked her fast,
And then he wooed with kisses, and at last,
As shepherds do, her on the ground he laid,
And tumbling in the grass, he often strayed
Beyond the bounds of shame, in being bold
To eye those parts which no eye should behold.
And like an insolent commanding lover,
Boasting his parentage, would needs discover   410
The way to new Elysium; but she,
Whose only dower was her chastity,
Having striv'n in vain, was now about to cry,
And crave the help of shepherds that were nigh.
Herewith he stayed his fury, and began
To give her leave to rise; away she ran;
After went Mercury, who used such cunning,
As she, to hear his tale, left off her running;
Maids are not won by brutish force and might,
But speeches full of pleasure and delight;   420
And knowing Hermes courted her, was glad
That she such loveliness and beauty had
As could provoke his liking, yet was mute,
And neither would deny nor grant his suit.
Still vowed he love, she wanting no excuse
To feed him with delays, as women use,
Or thirsting after immortality—
All women are ambitious naturally—
Imposed upon her lover such a task
As he ought not perform, nor yet she ask.   430
A draught of flowing nectar she requested,
Wherewith the king of gods and men is feasted.
He, ready to accomplish what she willed,
Stole some from Hebe (Hebe Jove's cup filled)
And gave it to his simple rustic love;
Which being known (as what is hid from Jove?)

He inly stormed, and waxed more furious
Than for the fire filched by Prometheus,
And thrusts him down from heaven; he wand'ring here
In mournful terms, with sad and heavy cheer,   440
Complained to Cupid. Cupid, for his sake,
To be revenged on Jove did undertake;
And those on whom heaven, earth, and hell relies,
I mean the adamantine Destinies,
He wounds with love, and forced them equally
To dote upon deceitful Mercury.
They offered him the deadly fatal knife
That shears the slender threads of human life;
At his fair-feathered feet the engines laid
Which th' earth from ugly Chaos' den upweighed;   450
These he regarded not, but did entreat
That Jove, usurper of his father's seat,
Might presently be banished into hell,
And aged Saturn in Olympus dwell.
They granted what he craved, and once again
Saturn and Ops began their golden reign.
Murder, rape, war, lust, and treachery
Were with Jove closed in Stygian empery.
But long this blessed time continued not;
As soon as he his wishèd purpose got,   460
He, reckless of his promise, did despise
The love of th' everlasting Destinies.
They seeing it, both Love and him abhorred,
And Jupiter unto his place restored.
And but that Learning, in despite of Fate,
Will mount aloft, and enter heaven gate,
And to the seat of Jove itself advance,
Hermes had slept in hell with Ignorance;
Yet as a punishment they added this,
That he and Poverty should always kiss.   470
And to this day is every scholar poor;
Gross gold from them runs headlong to the boor.
Likewise, the angry sisters thus deluded,
To venge themselves on Hermes, have concluded
That Midas' brood shall sit in Honor's chair,
To which the Muses' sons are only heir;
And fruitful wits that inaspiring are,
Shall, discontent, run into regions far;
And few great lords in virtuous deeds shall joy,
But be surprised with every garish toy;   480
And still enrich the lofty servile clown,

Who with encroaching guile keeps learning down.
Then muse not Cupid's suit no better sped,
Seeing in their loves the Fates were injurëd.

[Second sestiad]

By this, sad Hero, with love unacquainted,
Viewing Leander's face, fell down and fainted.
He kissed her and breathed life into her lips,
Wherewith, as one displeased, away she trips.
Yet as she went, full often looked behind,
And many poor excuses did she find
To linger by the way, and once she stayed
And would have turned again, but was afraid,
In off'ring parley, to be counted light.
So on she goes, and in her idle flight,   10
Her painted fan of curlëd plumes let fall,
Thinking to train Leander therewithal.
He, being a novice, knew not what she meant,
But stayed, and after her a letter sent,
Which joyful Hero answered in such sort
As he had hope to scale the beauteous fort
Wherein the liberal graces locked their wealth,
And therefore to her tower he got by stealth.
Wide open stood the door, he need not climb;
And she herself, before the 'pointed time,   20
Had spread the board, with roses strewed the room,
And oft looked out, and mused he did not come.
At last he came; oh, who can tell the greeting
These greedy lovers had at their first meeting.
He asked, she gave, and nothing was denied;
Both to each other quickly were affied.
Look how their hands, so were their hearts united,
And what he did she willingly requited.
Sweet are the kisses, the embracements sweet,
When like desires and affections meet;   30
For from the earth to heaven is Cupid raised,
Where fancy is in equal balance peised.
Yet she this rashness suddenly repented,
And turned aside, and to herself lamented,
As if her name and honor had been wronged
By being possessed of him for whom she longed;
Ay, and she wished, albeit not from her heart,
That he would leave her turret and depart.
The mirthful god of amorous pleasure smiled
To see how he this captive nymph beguiled;   40

For hitherto he did but fan the fire,
And kept it down that it might mount the higher.
Now waxed she jealous lest his love abated,
Fearing her own thoughts made her to be hated.
Therefore unto him hastily she goes,
And like light Salmacis, her body throws
Upon his bosom, where with yielding eyes
She offers up herself, a sacrifice
To slake his anger if he were displeased.
Oh, what god would not therewith be appeased?   50
Like Æsop's cock, this jewel he enjoyed,
And as a brother with his sister toyed,
Supposing nothing else was to be done,
Now he her favor and goodwill had won.
But know you not that creatures wanting sense
By nature have a mutual appetence,
And wanting organs to advance a step,
Moved by love's force, unto each other lep?
Much more in subjects having intellect,
Some hidden influence breeds like effect.   60
Albeit Leander, rude in love and raw,
Long dallying with Hero, nothing saw
That might delight him more, yet he suspected
Some amorous rites or other were neglected.
Therefore unto his body hers he clung;
She, fearing on the rushes to be flung,
Strived with redoubled strength; the more she strived,
The more a gentle pleasing heat revived,
Which taught him all that elder lovers know;
And now the same gan so to scorch and glow,   70
As in plain terms, yet cunningly, he craved it;
Love always makes those eloquent that have it.
She, with a kind of granting, put him by it,
And ever as he thought himself most nigh it,
Like to the tree of Tantalus she fled,
And, seeming lavish, saved her maidenhead.
Ne'er king more sought to keep his diadem,
Than Hero this inestimable gem.
Above our life we love a steadfast friend,
Yet when a token of great worth we send,   80
We often kiss it, often look thereon,
And stay the messenger that would be gone;
No marvel then though Hero would not yield
So soon to part from that she dearly held;
Jewels being lost are found again, this never;
'Tis lost but once, and once lost, lost forever.

Now had the morn espied her lover's steeds,
Whereat she starts, puts on her purple weeds,
And, red for anger that he stayed so long,
All headlong throws herself the clouds among.   90
And now Leander, fearing to be missed,
Embraced her suddenly, took leave, and kissed.
Long was he taking leave, and loath to go,
And kissed again, as lovers use to do.
Sad Hero wrung him by the hand and wept,
Saying, Let your vows and promises be kept.
Then, standing at the door, she turned about,
As loath to see Leander going out.
And now the sun that through th' horizon peeps,
As pitying these lovers, downward creeps,   100
So that in silence of the cloudy night,
Though it was morning, did he take his flight.
But what the secret trusty night concealed,
Leander's amorous habit soon revealed;
With Cupid's myrtle was his bonnet crowned,
About his arms the purple riband wound
Wherewith she wreathed her largely-spreading hair;
Nor could the youth abstain, but he must wear
The sacred ring wherewith she was endowed,
When first religious chastity she vowed;   110
Which made his love through Sestos to be known,
And thence unto Abydos sooner blown
Than he could sail, for incorporeal Fame,
Whose weight consists in nothing but her name,
Is swifter than the wind, whose tardy plumes
Are reeking water and dull earthly fumes.
Home, when he came, he seemed not to be there,
But like exilèd air thrust from his sphere,
Set in a foreign place; and straight from thence,
Alcides like, by mighty violence   120
He would have chased away the swelling main
That him from her unjustly did detain.
Like as the sun in a diameter
Fires and inflames objects removèd far,
And heateth kindly, shining lat'rally,
So beauty sweetly quickens when 'tis nigh,
But being separated and removed,
Burns where it cherished, murders where it loved.
Therefore even as an index to a book,
So to his mind was young Leander's look.   130
Oh, none but gods have power their love to hide;
Affection by the count'nance is descried.

The light of hidden fire itself discovers,
And love that is concealed betrays poor lovers.
His secret flame apparently was seen;
Leander's father knew where he had been,
And for the same mildly rebuked his son,
Thinking to quench the sparkles new begun.
But love, resisted once, grows passionate,
And nothing more than counsel lovers hate;   140
For as a hot proud horse highly disdains
To have his head controlled, but breaks the reins,
Spits forth the ringled bit, and with his hooves
Checks the submissive ground, so he that loves,
The more he is restrained, the worse he fares.
What is it now but mad Leander dares?
O Hero, Hero! thus he cried full oft,
And then he got him to a rock aloft,
Where having spied her tower, long stared he on 't,
And prayed the narrow toiling Hellespont   150
To part in twain, that he might come and go;
But still the rising billows answered no.
With that he stripped him to the iv'ry skin,
And crying, Love, I come, leaped lively in.
Whereat the sapphire-visaged god grew proud,
And made his cap'ring Triton sound aloud,
Imagining that Ganymede, displeased,
Had left the heavens; therefore on him he seized.
Leander strived; the waves about him wound,
And pulled him to the bottom, where the ground   160
Was strewed with pearl, and in low coral groves
Sweet singing mermaids sported with their loves
On heaps of heavy gold, and took great pleasure
To spurn in careless sort the shipwreck treasure.
For here the stately azure palace stood,
Where kingly Neptune and his train abode.
The lusty god embraced him, called him love,
And swore he never should return to Jove.
But when he knew it was not Ganymed,
For under water he was almost dead,   170
He heaved him up, and looking on his face,
Beat down the bold waves with his triple mace,
Which mounted up, intending to have kissed him,
And fell in drops like tears, because they missed him.
Leander, being up, began to swim,
And looking back, saw Neptune follow him;
Whereat aghast, the poor soul gan to cry:
Oh, let me visit Hero ere I die!

The god put Helle's bracelet on his arm,   180
And swore the sea should never do him harm.
He clapped his plump cheeks, with his tresses played,
And smiling wantonly, his love bewrayed.
He watched his arms, and as they opened wide,
At every stroke betwixt them would he slide,
And steal a kiss, and then run out and dance,
And as he turned, cast many a lustful glance,
And threw him gaudy toys to please his eye,
And dive into the water, and there pry
Upon his breast, his thighs, and every limb,
And up again, and close beside him swim,   190
And talk of love. Leander made reply:
You are deceived, I am no woman, I.
Thereat smiled Neptune, and then told a tale
How that a shepherd, sitting in a vale,
Played with a boy so fair and kind,
As for his love both earth and heaven pined;
That of the cooling river durst not drink
Lest water-nymphs should pull him from the brink;
And when he sported in the fragrant lawns,
Goat-footed satyrs and up-staring fauns   200
Would steal him thence. Ere half this tale was done,
Ay me, Leander cried, th' enamoured sun,
That now should shine on Thetis' glassy bower,
Descends upon my radiant Hero's tower.
Oh, that these tardy arms of mine were wings!
And as he spake, upon the waves he springs.
Neptune was angry that he gave no ear,
And in his heart revenging malice bear;
He flung at him his mace, but as it went
He called it in, for love made him repent.   210
The mace returning back, his own hand hit,
As meaning to be venged for darting it.
When this fresh bleeding wound Leander viewed,
His color went and came, as if he rued
The grief which Neptune felt. In gentle breasts
Relenting thoughts, remorse, and pity rests;
And who have hard hearts and obdurate minds
But vicious, hare-brained, and illit'rate hinds?
The god, seeing him with pity to be moved,
Thereon concluded that he was beloved.   220
(Love is too full of faith, too credulous,
With folly and false hope deluding us.)
Wherefore, Leander's fancy to surprise,
To the rich oceän for gifts he flies.

'Tis wisdom to give much; a gift prevails
When deep persuading oratory fails.
By this, Leander being near the land,
Cast down his weary feet, and felt the sand.
Breathless albeit he were, he rested not
Till to the solitary tower he got,   230
And knocked and called, at which celestial noise
The longing heart of Hero much more joys
Than nymphs or shepherds when the timbrel rings,
Or crooked dolphin when the sailor sings;
She stayed not for her robes, but straight arose,
And drunk with gladness, to the door she goes;
Where seeing a naked man, she screeched for fear,
(Such sights as this to tender maids are rare)
And ran into the dark herself to hide.
Rich jewels in the dark are soonest spied;   240
Unto her was he led, or rather drawn,
By those white limbs which sparkled through the lawn.
The nearer that he came, the more she fled,
And seeking refuge, slipped into her bed.
Whereon Leander sitting, thus began,
Through numbing cold all feeble, faint, and wan:
   If not for love, yet, love, for pity sake,
Me in thy bed and maiden bosom take;
At least vouchsafe these arms some little room,
Who, hoping to embrace thee, cheerly swoom;   250
This head was beat with many a churlish billow,
And therefore let it rest upon thy pillow.
Herewith affrighted Hero shrunk away,
And in her lukewarm place Leander lay,
Whose lively heat like fire from heaven fet,
Would animate gross clay, and higher set
The drooping thoughts of base declining souls,
Than dreary Mars carousing nectar bowls.
His hands he cast upon her like a snare;
She, overcome with shame and sallow fear,   260
Like chaste Diana, when Actæon spied her,
Being suddenly betrayed, dived down to hide her;
And as her silver body downward went,
With both her hands she made the bed a tent,
And in her own mind thought herself secure,
O'ercast with dim and darksome coverture.
And now she lets him whisper in her ear,
Flatter, entreat, promise, protest, and swear;
Yet ever as he greedily assayed
To touch those dainties, she the harpy played,   270

And every limb did, as a soldier stout,
Defend the fort and keep the foeman out;
For though the rising iv'ry mount he scaled,
Which is with azure circling lines empaled,
Much like a globe (a globe may I term this,
By which love sails to regions full of bliss)
Yet there with Sisyphus he toiled in vain,
Till gentle parley did the truce obtain.
Wherein Leander on her quivering breast,
Breathless spoke something, and sighed out the rest;   280
Which so prevailed, as he with small ado
Enclosed her in his arms and kissed her too.
And every kiss to her was as a charm,
And to Leander as a fresh alarm,
So that the truce was broke, and she, alas,
Poor silly maiden, at his mercy was.
Love is not full of pity, as men say,
But deaf and cruel where he means to prey.
Even as a bird, which in our hands we wring,
Forth plunges and oft flutters with her wing,   290
She trembling strove; this strife of hers, like that
Which made the world, another world begat
Of unknown joy. Treason was in her thought,
And cunningly to yield herself she sought.
Seeming not won, yet won she was at length;
In such wars women use but half their strength.
Leander now, like Theban Hercules,
Entered the orchard of th' Hesperides,
Whose fruit none rightly can describe but he
That pulls or shakes it from the golden tree.   300
And now she wished this night were never done,
And sighed to think upon th' approaching sun;
For much it grieved her that the bright daylight
Should know the pleasure of this blessed night,
And them like Mars and Erycine displayed,
Both in each other's arms chained as they laid.
Again she knew not how to frame her look,
Or speak to him who in a moment took
That which so long so charily she kept;
And fain by stealth away she would have crept,   310
And to some corner secretly have gone,
Leaving Leander in the bed alone.
But as her naked feet were whipping out,
He on the sudden clinged her so about,
That mermaid-like unto the floor she slid,
One half appeared, the other half was hid.

Thus near the bed she blushing stood upright,
And from her countenance behold ye might
A kind of twilight break, which through the hair,
As from an orient cloud, glimpse here and there;   320
And round about the chamber this false morn
Brought forth the day before the day was born.
So Hero's ruddy cheek Hero betrayed,
And her all naked to his sight displayed;
Whence his admiring eyes more pleasure took
Than Dis on heaps of gold fixing his look.
By this, Apollo's golden harp began
To sound forth music to the oceän;
Which watchful Hesperus no sooner heard,
But he the day-bright-bearing car prepared,   330
And ran before, as harbinger of light,
And with his flaring beams mocked ugly night
Till she, o'ercome with anguish, shame, and rage,
Danged down to hell her loathsome carriage.
> *Desunt nonnulla.*

ELIZABETHAN MISCELLANIES

The Introduction and Notes are at pages 1221 and 1275

FROM GEORGE GASCOIGNE'S *Hundreth Sundry Flowers*, [1573]

A strange passion of a lover

Amid my bale I bathe in bliss,
I swim in heaven, I sink in hell;
I find amends for every miss,
And yet my moan no tongue can tell.
I live and love (what would you more?)
As never lover lived before.

I laugh sometimes with little lust;
So jest I oft and feel no joy;
Mine ease is builded all on trust,
And yet mistrust breeds mine annoy.   10
I live and lack, I lack and have,
I have and miss the thing I crave.

These things seem strange, yet are they true.

Believe me, sweet, my state is such,
One pleasure which I would eschew
Both slakes my grief and breeds my grutch.
So doth one pain which I would shun
Renew my joys where grief begun.

Then like the lark, that passed the night
In heavy sleep, with cares oppressed,   20
Yet when she spies the pleasant light,
She sends sweet notes from out her breast,
So sing I now because I think

How joys approach when sorrows shrink.

And as fair Philomene, again,
Can watch and sing when other sleep,
And taketh pleasure in her pain,
To wray the woe that makes her weep,

So sing I now for to bewray
The loathsome life I lead alway. [30]

The which to thee, dear wench, I write,
That know'st my mirth but not my moan.
I pray God grant thee deep delight
To live in joys when I am gone.
I cannot live—it will not be:
I die to think to part from thee.

The lover declareth his affection, together with the cause thereof

When first I thee beheld, in colors black and white,
Thy face in form well framed, with favor blooming still,
My burning breast in cares did choose his chief delight
With pen to paint thy praise, contrary to my skill;
Whose worthiness compared with this my rude devise,
I blush, and am abashed this work to enterprise.

But when I call to mind thy sundry gifts of grace,
Full fraught with manners meek, in happy quiet mind,
My hasty hand forthwith doth scribble on apace,
Lest willing heart might think it meant to come behind.   10
Thus do both hand and heart these careful meters use,
'Twixt hope and trembling fear, my duty to excuse.

Wherefore accept these lines, and banish dark disdain.
Be sure they come from one that loveth thee in chief;
And guerdon me, thy friend, in like with love again.
So shalt thou well be sure to yield me such relief
As only may redress my sorrows and my smart.
For proof whereof I pledge, dear dame, to thee my heart.

FROM RICHARD EDWARDS's *Paradise of Dainty Devices,* 1576

Amantium iræ amoris redintegratio est

In going to my naked bed as one that would have slept,
I heard a wife sing to her child, that long before had wept.
She sighèd sore and sang full sweet to bring the babe to rest,
That would not rest, but criëd still, in sucking at her breast.
She was full weary of her watch and grievèd with her child,
She rockèd it and rated it until on her it smiled.
Then did she say, Now have I found the proverb true to prove,
The falling out of faithful friends is the renewing of love.

Then took I paper, pen, and ink, this proverb for to write,
In register for to remain of such a worthy wight.   10
As she proceeded thus in song unto her little brat,
Much matter uttered she of weight, in place whereas she sat;
And provëd plain there was no beast, nor creature bearing life,
Could well be known to live in love without discord and strife.
Then kissëd she her little babe and sware, by God above,
The falling out of faithful friends is the renewing of love.

She said that neither king, ne prince, ne lord could live aright
Until their puissance they did prove, their manhood, and their might;
When manhood shall be matchëd so that fear can take no place,
Then weary works makes warriors each other to embrace,   20
And leave their force that failëd them, which did consume the rout,
That might before have lived their time and nature out.
Then did she sing as one that thought no man could her reprove,
The falling out of faithful friends is the renewing of love.

She said she saw no fish, ne fowl, nor beast within her haunt
That met a stranger in their kind, but could give it a taunt.
Since flesh might not endure, but rest must wrath succeed,
And force the fight to fall to play in pasture where they feed,
So noble nature can well end the works she hath begun,
And bridle well that will not cease her tragedy in some.   30
Thus in her song she oft rehearsed, as did her well behove,
The falling out of faithful friends is the renewing of love.

I marvel much, perdy, (quoth she) for to behold the rout,
To see man, woman, boy, and beast, to toss the world about.
Some kneel, some crouch, some beck, some check, and some can
        smoothly smile,
And some embrace others in arms, and there think many a wile.
Some stand aloof at cap and knee, some humble and some stout,
Yet are they never friends indeed until they once fall out!
Thus ended she her song, and said, before she did remove,
The falling out of faithful friends is the renewing of love.

                                           [*Richard Edwards*]

M. Edwards' May

When May is in his prime, then may each heart rejoice;
When May bedecks each branch with green, each bird strains forth
        his voice.
The lively sap creeps up into the blooming thorn;
The flowers which cold in prison kept now laughs the frost to scorn.
All nature's imps triumphs whiles joyful May doth last;
When May is gone, of all the year the pleasant time is past.

May makes the cheerful hue, May breeds and brings new blood;
May marcheth throughout every limb, May makes the merry mood.
May pricketh tender hearts their warbling notes to tune,—
Full strange it is, yet some we see do make their May in June.   10
Thus things are strangely wrought whiles joyful May doth last;
Take May in time, when May is gone the pleasant time is past.

All ye that live on earth, and have your May at will,
Rejoice in May, as I do now, and use your May with skill.
Use May while that you may, for May hath but his time,
When all the fruit is gone, it is too late the tree to climb.
Your liking and your lust is fresh whiles May doth last;
When May is gone, of all the year the pleasant time is past.

[*Richard Edwards*]

Being importunate, at the length he obtaineth

A. Shall I no way win you to grant my desire?
B. What woman will grant you the thing you require?
A. You only to love me is all that I crave.
B. You only to leave me is all I would have.
A. My dear, alas, now say not so!
B. To love you best I must say no.
A. Yet will I not flit. *B.* Then play on the bit.
A. I will. *B.* Do still. *A.* Yet kill not. *B.* I will not.
A. Make me your man! *B.* Beshrew me than!

A. The swifter I follow, then you fly away.   10
B. Swift hawks in their flying oft times miss their prey.
A. Yet some killeth deadly that fly to the mark.
B. You shall touch no feather thereof, take no cark!
A. Yet hope shall further my desire.
B. You blow the coals and raise no fire.
A. Yet will I not flit. *B.* Then play on the bit.
A. I will. *B.* Do still. *A.* Yet kill not. *B.* I will not.
A. Make me your man! *B.* Beshrew me than!

A. To love is no danger where true love is meant.
B. I will love no ranger lest that I repent.   20
A. My love is no ranger, I make God a vow.
B. To trust your smooth sayings I sure know not how.
A. Most truth I mean, as time shall well try.
B. No truth in men I oft espy.
A. Yet will I not flit. *B.* Then play on the bit.
A. I will. *B.* Do still. *A.* Yet kill not. *B.* I will not.
A. Make me your man! *B.* Beshrew me than!

A. Some women may say nay, and mean love most true.
B. Some women can make fools of as wise men as you.
A. In time I shall catch you, I know when and where.   30
B. I will soon dispatch you, you shall not come there.
A. Some speeds at length that oft have missed.
B. I am well armed, come when you list.
A. Yet will I not flit. *B.* Then play on the bit.
A. I will. *B.* Do still. *A.* Yet kill not. *B.* I will not.
A. Make me your man! *B.* Beshrew me than!

A. Yet work your kind kindly, grant me love for love.
B. I will use you friendly, as I shall you prove.
A. Most close you shall find me, I this do protest.
B. Then sure you shall bind me to grant your request.   40
A. Oh, happy thread now have I spun!
B. You sing before the conquest won!
A. Why, then, will you swerve? *B.* Even as you deserve.
A. Love still. *B.* I will. *A.* Yet kill not. *B.* I will not.
A. Make me your man! *B.* Come to me than!

                                        [*Richard Edwards?*]

No pains comparable to his attempt

What watch, what woe, what want, what wrack,
Is due to those that toil the seas!
Life led with loss, of pains no lack,
In storms to win much restless ease;
A bedless board in sea's unrest
May hap to him that chanceth best.

How sundry sounds with lead and line
Unto the deep the shipman throws;
'No foot to spare,' he cries oft times,
'No near!' when 'How?' the master blows.   10
If Neptune frown, all be undone,
Straightway the ship the wrack hath won.

These dangers great do oft befall
On those that sheer upon the sand,—
Judge of their lives, the best who shall?
How vile it is, few understand.
Alack, who then may judge their game?
Not they which have not felt the same.

But they that fall in storms and wind,
And days and years have spent therein,   20

Such well may judge, since proof they find,
In rage no rest till calm begin.
No more, then, those that love do feign
Give judgment of true lovers' pain.

[*William Hunnis*]

Look or you leap

If thou in surety safe wilt sit,
If thou delight at rest to dwell,
Spend no more words than shall
    seem fit,
Let tongue in silence talk expel;
In all things that thou seest men
    bent,
See all, say nought, hold thee con-
    tent.

In worldly works degrees are
    three,
Makers, doers, and lookers-on:
The lookers-on have liberty
Both the others to judge upon; ¹⁰
Wherefore, in all, as men are bent,
See all, say nought, hold thee con-
    tent.

The makers oft are in fault
    found,

The doers doubt of praise or
    shame;
The lookers-on find surest ground,
They have the fruit, yet free from
    blame:
This doth persuade in all here
    meant,
See all, say nought, hold thee con-
    tent.

The proverb is not south and
    west
Which hath been said long time
    ago: ²⁰
Of little meddling cometh rest,
The busy man ne'er wanted
    woe.
The best way is in all worlds
    sent,
See all, say nought, hold thee con-
    tent.

[*Jasper Heywood*]

FROM THOMAS PROCTER'S *Gorgeous Gallery of Gallant Inventions,*
1578

Respice finem

Lo, here the state of every mortal wight,
See here the fine of all their gallant joys;
Behold their pomp, their beauty, and delight,
Whereof they vaunt as safe from all annoys.
To earth the stout, the proud, the rich shall yield,
The weak, the meek, the poor shall shrouded lie
In dampish mold; the stout with spear and shield
Cannot defend himself when he shall die.
The proudest wight, for all his lively shows,
Shall leave his pomp, cut off by dreadful death;   ¹⁰
The rich, whose hutch with golden ruddocks flows,

At length shall rest uncoined in dampish earth.
By nature's law we all are born to die,
But where or when, the best uncertain be;
No time prefixed, no goods our life shall buy,
Of dreadful death no friends shall set us free.
We subject be a thousand ways to death:
Small sickness moves the valiant's heart to fear;
A little push bereaves your breathing breath
Of brave delights, whereto you subject are.   20
Your world is vain; no trust in earth you find;
Your valiant'st prime is but a brittle glass;
Your pleasures vade, your thoughts a puff of wind;
Your ancient years are but a withered grass.

[Thomas Procter]

A proper sonnet, how time consumeth all earthly things

Ay me, ay me, I sigh to see the scythe afield,
Down goeth the grass, soon wrought to withered hay.
Ay me, alas! ay me, alas, that beauty needs must yield,
And princes pass, as grass doth fade away.

Ay me, ay me, that life cannot have lasting leave,
Nor gold take hold of everlasting joy.
Ay me, alas! ay me, alas, that time hath talents to receive,
And yet no time can make a sure stay.

Ay me, ay me, that wit cannot have wishëd choice,
Nor wish can win that will desires to see.   10
Ay me, alas! ay me, alas, that mirth can promise no rejoice,
Nor study tell what afterward shall be.

Ay me, ay me, that no sure staff is given to age,
Nor age can give sure wit that youth will take.
Ay me, alas! ay me, alas, that no counsel wise and sage
Will shun the show that all doth mar and make.

Ay me, ay me, come time, shear on and shake thy hay,
It is no boot to balk thy bitter blows.
Ay me, alas! ay me, alas, come time, take every thing away,
For all is thine, be it good or bad that grows.   20

A true description of love

Ask what love is? It is a passïon
Begun with rest and pampered up in play,
Planted on sight, and nourished day by day,
With talk at large, for hope to graze upon.
It is a short joy, long sought and soon gone;
An endless maze wherein our wills do stray;

A guileful gain, repentance is the pay;
A great fire bred of small occasïon;
A plague to make our frailty to us known,
Where we thereby are subject to their lay   10
Whose frailty ought to lean until our stay,
In case ourselves this custom had not known,
Of hope and health, such creatures for to pray
Whose glory resteth chiefly on denay.

The lover in the praise of his beloved and comparison of her beauty

Not she for whom proud Troy did fall and burn,
The Greeks eke slain, that bloody race did run;
Nor she for spite that did Acteon turn
Into an hart her beauty coy did shun;
Nor she whose blood upon Achilles' tomb,
Whose face would tame a tiger's heart;
Nor she that won by wise of Paris' doom
Th' apple of gold for beauty to her part;
Nor she whose eyes did pierce true Troilus' breast,
And made him yield that knew in love no law,—   10
Might be compared to the fairest and the best,
Whom nature made to keep the rest in awe,
For beauty's sake sent down from Jove above.
Thrice happy is he that can attain her love!

The lover exhorteth his lady to be constant
To the tune of, *Attend thee, go play thee*

Not light of love, lady!
Though fancy do prick thee,
Let constancy possess thy heart.
Well worthy of blaming
They be, and defaming,
From plighted troth which back do
    start.
  Dear dame,
Then fickleness banish
And folly extinguish,
Be skillful in guiding   10
    And stay thee from sliding,
    And stay thee, &c.

The constant are praisëd,
Their fame high is raisëd,

Their worthiness doth pierce the
    sky.
The fickle are blamëd,
Their lightilove shamëd,
Their foolishness doth make them
    die.
    As well
Can Cressid bear witness,   20
Forge of her own distress,
Whom leprosy painted
    And penury tainted,
    And penury, &c.

Still muses are busy
To tell us of Thisbe,

Whom steadfastness doth much
　　commend.
And Camma is placëd
To blame the defacëd,
That light of love do send.　30
　　Phedra
Is checked most duly
Because that untruly,
Forced thereto by love light,
She slayeth Hippolite,
She slayeth, &c.

A spring of annoyance
And well of disturbance
New-fangleness in love hath been:
It killeth the master,　40
It poisons the taster,
No worldly wight by it doth win.
　　Therefore,
Good lady, be constant,
So shall you not be shent
But worthily praisëd
As you have deservëd,
As you have, &c.

From H. C.'s *Forest of Fancy*, 1579

A plain description of perfect friendship

True friendship unfeignëd
Doth rest unrestrainëd,
　No terror can tame it.
Not gaining nor losing
Nor gallant gay glozing
　Can ever reclaim it.

In pain and in pleasure
The most truest measure
　That may be desirëd
Is loyal love deemëd,　10
Of wisdom esteemëd,
　And chiefly requirëd.

The strange pangs of a poor passionate lover

Not as I am, nor as I wish to be,
But as false fortune frames my froward fate,
Even so I am not bound nor fully free,
Not quite forlorn, nor yet in quiet state.
I wish for death, and yet the death I hate,
This life lead I, which life is wondrous strange,
Yet for no life would I my life exchange.
I seek the sight of that I sigh to see,
I joy in that which breeds my great unrest,—
Such contraries do daily cumber me　10
As in one thing I find both joy and rest,
Which gain he gets that is Cupido's guest;
For whom he catcheth in his cursed snare
He gives great hope, yet kills his heart with care.

From *Chetham Ms.* 8012

Epigram

Were I a king, I could command content;
Were I obscure, hidden should be my cares;
Or were I dead, no cares should me torment,

Nor hopes, nor hates, nor loves, nor griefs, nor fears.
A doubtful choice, of these three which to crave—
A kingdom, or a cottage, or a grave.

[*Edward de Vere, Earl of Oxford*]

Answered thus by Sir P. S.

Wert thou a king, yet not command content,
Sith empire none thy mind could yet suffice;
Wert thou obscure, still cares would thee torment;
But wert thou dead, all care and sorrow dies.
An easy choice, of these three which to crave:
No kingdom, nor a cottage, but a grave.

[*Sir Philip Sidney*]

Another, of another mind [1]

A king, oh boon for my aspiring mind!
A cottage makes a country swad rejoice;
And as for death, I like him in his kind,
But God forbid that he should be my choice!
A kingdom or a cottage or a grave,—
Nor last, nor next, but first and best I crave;
The rest I can whenas I list enjoy,
Till then salute me thus, *Vive le Roy!*

[*F. M.*]

Another, of another mind [2]

The greatest kings do least command content,
For greatest cares do still attend a crown;
A grave all happy fortunes do prevent,
Making the noble equal with the clown;
A quiet country life to lead I crave,—
A cottage then; no kingdom nor a grave.

FROM *Verses of Praise and Joy written upon Her Majesty's
Preservation,* 1586

Tichborne's elegy, written with his own hand in the Tower before his execution

My prime of youth is but a frost of cares,
My feast of joy is but a dish of pain,
My crop of corn is but a field of tares,
And all my good is but vain hope of gain;
The day is past, and yet I saw no sun,
And now I live, and now my life is done.

My tale was heard and yet it was not told,
My fruit is fall'n and yet my leaves are green,
My youth is spent and yet I am not old,
I saw the world and yet I was not seen;   10
My thread is cut and yet it is not spun,
And now I live, and now my life is done.

I sought my death and found it in my womb,
I looked for life and saw it was a shade,
I trod the earth and knew it was my tomb,
And now I die, and now I was but made;
My glass is full, and now my glass is run,
And now I live, and now my life is done.

[*Chidiock Tichborne*]

FROM R. S.'s *Phœnix Nest*, 1593

[*The time when first*]

The time when first I fell in love,
   Which now I must lament;
The year wherein I lost such time
   To compass my content;

The day wherein I saw too late
   The follies of a lover;
The hour wherein I found such loss
   As care cannot recover;

And last, the minute of mishap,   9
   Which makes me thus to plain
The doleful fruits of lovers' suits,
   Which labor lose in vain:

Doth make me solemnly protest,
   As I with pain do prove,
There is no time, year, day, nor hour,
   Nor minute, good to love.

[*O night, O jealous night*]

O night, O jealous night, repugnant to my pleasures,
   O night so long desired yet cross to my content,
There's none but only thou that can perform my pleasures,
   Yet none but only thou that hindereth my intent.

Thy beams, thy spiteful beams, thy lamps that burn too brightly,
   Discover all my trains, and naked lay my drifts;
That night by night I hope, yet fail my purpose nightly,
   Thy envious glaring gleam defeateth so my shifts.

Sweet night, withhold thy beams, withhold them till to-morrow,
   Whose joys, in lack so long, a hell of torments breeds;   10
Sweet night, sweet gentle night, do not prolong my sorrow,
   Desire is guide to me, and love no lode-star needs.

Let sailors gaze on stars and moon so freshly shining,
    Let them that miss the way be guided by the light;
I know my lady's bower, there needs no more divining,
    Affection sees in dark, and love hath eyes by night.

Dame Cynthia, couch awhile, hold in thy horns for shining,
    And glad not low'ring night with thy too glorious rays;
But be she dim and dark, tempestuous and repining,
    That in her spite my sport may work thy endless praise.   20

And when my will is wrought, then, Cynthia, shine, good lady,
    All other nights and days in honor of that night,
That happy, heavenly night, that night so dark and shady,
    Wherein my love had eyes that lighted my delight.

[*Set me where Phœbus' heat*]

Set me where Phœbus' heat the flowers slayeth
Or where continual snow withstands his forces;
Set me where he his temp'rate rays displayeth,
Or where he comes, or where he never courses;

Set me in fortune's grace, or else dischargëd,
In sweet and pleasant air, or dark and glooming,
Where days and nights are lesser or enlargëd,
In years of strength, in failing age or blooming;

Set me in heaven or earth, or in the center;
Low in a vale, or on a mountain placëd;   10
Set me to danger, peril, and adventure,
Gracëd by fame, or infamy disgracëd:
    Set me to these, or any other trial,
    Except my mistress' anger and denial.

[*Sought by the world*]

Sought by the world, and hath the world disdained,
    Is she, my heart, for whom thou dost endure;
Unto whose grace, sith kings have not obtained,
    Sweet is thy choice, though loss of life be sour;
        Yet to the man whose youth such pains must prove
        No better end than that which comes by love.

Steer then thy course unto the port of death
    (Sith thy hard hap no better hap may find)
Where, when thou shalt unlade thy latest breath,
    Envy herself shall swim, to save thy mind   10
        Whose body sunk in search to gain that shore
        Where many a prince had perishëd before.

And yet, my heart, it might have been foreseen,
  Sith skillful med'cines mends each kind of grief,
Then in my breast full safely hadst thou been;
  But thou, my heart, wouldst never me believe
Who told thee true when first thou didst aspire,
Death was the end of every such desire.

FROM JOHN BODENHAM'S (?) *England's Helicon,* 1600

A nymph's disdain of love

Hey down, a down, did Dian sing,
  Amongst her virgins sitting,
Than love there is no vainer thing,
  For maidens most unfitting.
And so think I, with a down, down, derry.

When women knew no woe,
  But lived themselves to please,
Men's feigning guiles they did not know,
  The ground of their disease.
Unborn was false suspect,   10
  No thought of jealousy;
From wanton toys and fond affect
  The virgin's life was free.
    Hey down, a down, did Dian sing, &c.

At length men usëd charms;
  To which what maids gave ear,
Embracing gladly endless harms,
  Anon enthrallëd were.
Thus women welcomed woe
  Disguised in name of love;   20
A jealous hell, a painted show,
  So shall they find that prove.

Hey down, a down, did Dian sing,
  Amongst her virgins sitting,
Than love there is no vainer thing,
  For virgins most unfitting.
And so think I, with a down, down, derry.

Phillida's love-call to her Corydon, and his replying

Phil. Corydon, arise my Corydon,
    Titan shineth clear.
Cor. Who is it that calleth Corydon?
    Who is it that I hear?

Phil. Phillida, thy true love, calleth thee.
    Arise then, arise then,
      Arise and keep thy flock with me.
Cor. Phillida, my true love, is it she?
    I come then, I come then,
      I come and keep my flock with thee.   10

Phil. Here are cherries ripe, my Corydon,
    Eat them for my sake.
Cor. Here's my oaten pipe, my lovely one,
    Sport for thee to make.
Phil. Here are threads, my true love, fine as silk,
    To knit thee, to knit thee
      A pair of stockings white as milk.
Cor. Here are reeds, my true love, fine and neat,
    To make thee, to make thee
      A bonnet to withstand the heat.   20

Phil. I will gather flowers, my Corydon,
    To set in thy cap.
Cor. I will gather pears, my lovely one,
    To put in thy lap.
Phil. I will buy my true love garters gay
    For Sundays, for Sundays,
      To wear about his legs so tall.
Cor. I will buy my true love yellow say
    For Sundays, for Sundays,
      To wear about her middle small.   30

Phil. When my Corydon sits on a hill,
    Making melody,—
Cor. When my lovely one goes to her wheel,
    Singing cheerily,—
Phil. Sure methinks my true love doth excel
    For sweetness, for sweetness,
      Our Pan, that old Arcadian knight.
Cor. And methinks my true love bears the bell
    For clearness, for clearness,
      Beyond the nymphs that be so bright.   40

Phil. Had my Corydon, my Corydon,
    Been, alack, my swain,—
Cor. Had my lovely one, my lovely one,
    Been in Ida plain,—
Phil. Cynthia Endymion had refused,
    Preferring, preferring
      My Corydon to play withal;

Cor. The queen of love had been excused,
    Bequeathing, bequeathing
      My Phillida the golden ball.   50

Phil. Yonder comes my mother, Corydon,
    Whither shall I fly?
Cor. Under yonder beech, my lovely one,
    While she passeth by.
Phil. Say to her thy true love was not here.
    Remember, remember,
      To-morrow is another day.
Cor. Doubt me not, my true love. Do not fear.
    Farewell then, farewell then,
      Heaven keep our loves alway.   60

The nymph Selvagia, her song

Shepherd, who can pass such wrong,
    And a life in woes so deep?
Which to live is too too long,
    As it is too short to weep.

Grievous sighs in vain I waste,
    Leesing my affiance, and
I perceive my hope at last
    With a candle in the hand.

What time then to hope among
    Bitter hopes that never sleep?   10

When this life is too too long,
    As it is too short to weep.

This grief which I feel so rife,
    Wretch, I do deserve as hire,
Since I came to put my life
    In the hands of my desire.

Then cease not my complaints so strong,
    For, though life her course doth keep,
It is not to live so long,
    As it is too short to weep.   20

            [*Bartholomew Young*]

Melisea, her song in scorn of her shepherd Narcissus

Young shepherd, turn aside and move
    Me not to follow thee;
For I will neither kill with love,
    Nor love shall not kill me.

Since I will live and never show,
    Then die not, for my love I will not give,
For I will never have thee love me so,
    As I do mean to hate thee while I live.

That since the lover so doth prove
His death, as thou dost see,   10
Be bold, I will not kill with love,
Nor love shall not kill me.

[*Bartholomew Young*]

A palinode

As withereth the primrose by the river,
As fadeth summer's sun from gliding fountains,
As vanisheth the light-blown bubble ever,
As melteth snow upon the mossy mountains:
So melts, so vanisheth, so fades, so withers
The rose, the shine, the bubble, and the snow,
Of praise, pomp, glory, joy, which short life gathers,
Fair praise, vain pomp, sweet glory, brittle joy.
The withered primrose by the mourning river,
The faded summer's sun from weeping fountains,   10
The light-blown bubble, vanishëd for ever,
The molten snow upon the naked mountains,
    Are emblems that the treasures we uplay
    Soon wither, vanish, fade, and melt away.

For as the snow, whose lawn did overspread
Th' ambitious hills which giant-like did threat
To pierce the heaven with their aspiring head,
Naked and bare doth leave their craggy seat;
Whenas the bubble, which did empty fly
The dalliance of the undiscernëd wind   20
On whose calm rolling waves it did rely,
Hath shipwreck made where it did dalliance find;
And when the sunshine which dissolved the snow,
Colored the bubble with a pleasant vary,
And made the rathe and timely primrose grow,
Swarth clouds withdrawn, which longer time do tarry:
    Oh, what is praise, pomp, glory, joy, but so
    As shine by fountains, bubbles, flowers, or snow?

[*Edmund Bolton*]

A canzon pastoral in honor of Her Majesty

Alas, what pleasure, now the pleasant spring
    Hath given place
To harsh black frosts the sad ground covering,
    Can we, poor we, embrace?
When every bird on every branch can sing

Nought but this note of woe, alas!
Alas, this note of woe why should we sound?
With us, as May, September hath a prime;
Then, birds and branches, your *alas* is fond,
Which call upon the absent summer-time.   10
    For did flowers make our May
    Or the sun-beams your day,
When night and winter did the world embrace,
Well might you wail your ill, and sing, alas!

Lo, matron-like the earth herself attires
    In habit grave;
Naked the fields are, bloomless are the briers,
    Yet we a summer have,
Who in our clime kindleth these living fires,
    Which blooms can on the briers save.   20
No ice doth crystallize the running brook,
No blast deflowers the flower-adornëd field;
Crystal is clear, but clearer is the look
Which to our climes these living fires doth yield;
    Winter, though everywhere,
    Hath no abiding here,
On brooks and briers she doth rule alone,—
The sun which lights our world is always one.

                     [Edmund Bolton]

To Colin Clout

Beauty sat bathing by a spring
    Where fairest shades did hide
        her;
The winds blew calm, the birds
        did sing,
    The cool streams ran beside her.
My wanton thoughts enticed mine
        eye
    To see what was forbidden,
But better memory said fie!
    So vain desire was chidden.
    Hey nonny, nonny, &c.

Into a slumber then I fell,   10
    When fond imagination
Seemed to see, but could not tell
    Her feature or her fashion.
But even as babes in dreams do
    smile
    And sometime fall a-weep-
        ing,
So I awaked, as wise this while
    As when I fell a-sleeping.
    Hey nonny, nonny, &c.
        [Anthony Munday]

FROM FRANCIS DAVISON's *Poetical Rhapsody*, 1602

Ode

Absence, hear thou my protestation
    Against thy strength,
    Distance, and length;

Do what thou canst for alteration,
   For hearts of truest mettle
   Absence doth join, and time doth settle.

Who loves a mistress of such quality,
   He soon hath found
   Affection's ground
Beyond time, place, and all mortality.   10
   To hearts that cannot vary
   Absence is present, time doth tarry.

My senses want their outward motions,
   Which now within
   Reason doth win,
Redoubled in her secret notions;
   Like rich men that take pleasure
   In hiding, more than handling, treasure.

By absence this good means I gain,
   That I can catch her   20
   Where none can watch her,
In some close corner of my brain;
   There I embrace and kiss her,
   And so I both enjoy and miss her.

                    [*John Hoskins?*]

Madrigal

My love in her attire doth show her wit,
   It doth so well become her;
For every season she hath dressings fit,
   For winter, spring, and summer.
   No beauty she doth miss
   When all her robes are on;
   But beauty's self she is
   When all her robes are gone.

To time

Eternal time, that wastest without waste,
   That art and art not, diest and livest still;
Most slow of all and yet of greatest haste,
   Both ill and good, and neither good nor ill:
   How can I justly praise thee or dispraise?
   Dark are thy nights, but bright and clear thy days.

Both free and scarce, thou giv'st and tak'st again;
  Thy womb, that all doth breed, is tomb to all;
What so by thee hath life by thee is slain;
  From thee do all things rise, by thee they fall;   10
    Constant, inconstant, moving, standing still.
  Was, Is, Shall be, do thee both breed and kill.

I lose thee while I seek to find thee out.
  The farther off, the more I follow thee;
The faster hold, the greater cause of doubt;
  Was, Is, I know; but *Shall* I cannot see.
    All things by thee are measured; thou, by none;
    All are in thee; thou, in thyself alone.

[A. W.]

Upon visiting his lady by moonlight

The night, say all, was made for rest;
  And so say I, but not for all:
To them the darkest nights are best,
  Which give them leave asleep to fall;
    But I that seek my rest by light
    Hate sleep, and praise the clearest night.

Bright was the moon, as bright as day,
  And Venus glistered in the west,
Whose light did lead the ready way
  That brought me to my wishèd rest;   10
    Then each of them increased their light
    While I enjoyed her heavenly sight.

Say, gentle dames, what moved your mind
  To shine so bright above your wont?
Would Phœbe fair Endymion find?
  Would Venus see Adonis hunt?
    No, no, you fearèd by her sight
    To lose the praise of beauty bright.

At last for shame you shrunk away,
  And thought to reave the world of light;   20
Then shone my dame with brighter ray
  Than that which comes from Phœbus' sight:
    None other light but hers I praise
    Whose nights are clearer than the days.

[A. W.]

A fiction

How Cupid made a nymph wound herself with his arrows

It chanced of late, a shepherd's swain,
That went to seek a strayëd sheep,
Within a thicket on the plain
Espied a dainty nymph asleep.

Her golden hair o'erspread her face,
Her careless arms abroad were cast,
Her quiver had her pillow's place,
Her breast lay bare to every blast.

The shepherd stood and gazed his fill;
Nought durst he do, nought durst he say,   10
When chance, or else perhaps his will,
Did guide the god of love that way.

The crafty boy that sees her sleep—
Whom, if she waked, he durst not see—
Behind her closely seeks to creep,
Before her nap should ended be.

There come, he steals her shafts away
And puts his own into their place;
Ne dares he any longer stay,
But ere she wakes hies thence apace.   20

Scarce was he gone when she awakes
And spies the shepherd standing by.
Her bended bow in haste she takes,
And at the simple swain let fly.

Forth flew the shaft and pierced his heart,
That to the ground he fell with pain;
Yet up again forthwith he start,
And to the nymph he ran amain.

Amazed to see so strange a sight,
She shot, and shot, but all in vain;   30
The more his wounds, the more his might;
Love yieldeth strength in midst of pain.

Her angry eyes are great with tears;
She blames her hands, she blames her skill;

The bluntness of her shafts she fears,
And try them on herself she will.

Take heed, sweet nymph, try not the shaft,
Each little touch will prick the heart.
Alas, thou knowest not Cupid's craft,—
Revenge is joy, the end is smart.   40

Yet try she will, and prick some bare;
Her hands were gloved, and next to hand
Was that fair breast, that breast so rare,
That made the shepherd senseless stand.

That breast she pricked, and through that breast
Love finds an entry to her heart;
At feeling of this new-come guest,
Lord, how the gentle nymph doth start!

She runs not now, she shoots no more.
Away she throws both shafts and bow;   50
She seeks for that she shunned before,
She thinks the shepherd's haste too slow.

Though mountains meet not, lovers may;
So others do, and so do they.
The god of love sits on a tree
And laughs that pleasant sight to see.

                                        [*A. W.*]

Sonnet

Were I as base as is the lowly plain,
And you, my love, as high as heav'n above,
Yet should the thoughts of me, your humble swain,
Ascend to heaven in honor of my love.
Were I as high as heav'n above the plain,
And you, my love, as humble and as low
As are the deepest bottoms of the main,
Wheresoe'er you were, with you my love should go.
Were you the earth, dear love, and I the skies,
My love should shine on you like to the sun,   10
And look upon you with ten thousand eyes,
Till heaven waxed blind and till the world were dun.
    Wheresoe'er I am, below, or else above you,
    Wheresoe'er you are, my heart shall truly love you.
                                        [*Joshua Sylvester?*]

Commendation of her beauty, stature, behavior, and wit

Some there are as fair to see to,
But by art and not by nature;
Some as tall and goodly be, too,
But want beauty to their stature;
Some have gracious kind behavior,
But are foul or simple creatures;
Some have wit, but want sweet favor,
Or are proud of their good features.
  Only you in court or city
  Are both fair, tall, kind, and witty. 10

          [Francis Davison]

Upon his timorous silence in her presence

Are lovers full of fire?
How comes it then my verses are so cold?
  And how, when I am nigh her,
And fit occasion wills me to be bold,
The more I burn, the more I do desire,
  The less I dare require.
Ah, love, this is thy wondrous art,
To freeze the tongue, and fire the heart.

          [Francis Davison]

To Cupid

Love, if a god thou art,
Then evermore thou must
Be merciful and just.
If thou be just, oh, wherefore doth thy dart
Wound mine alone, and not my lady's heart?

If merciful, then why
Am I to pain reserved
Who have thee truly served?
While she that by thy power sets not a fly
Laughs thee to scorn and lives in liberty? 10

Then if a god thou wouldst accounted be,
Heal me like her, or else wound her like me.

          [Francis Davison]

FROM FRANCIS DAVISON's *Poetical Rhapsody*, 1608

[*The sound of thy sweet name*]

The sound of thy sweet name, my dearest treasure,
   Delights me more than sight of other faces;
A glimpse of thy sweet face breeds me more pleasure
   Than any other's kindest words and graces.

One gracious word that from thy lips proceedeth
   I value more than others' dove-like kisses,
And thy chaste kiss in my conceit exceedeth
   Others' embraces, and love's chiefest blisses.

                            [*Francis Davison*]

A sonnet of the moon

Look how the pale queen of the silent night
Doth cause the ocean to attend upon her,
And he, as long as she is in his sight,
With her full tide is ready her to honor.
But when the silver waggon of the moon
Is mounted up so high he cannot follow,
The sea calls home his crystal waves to moan,
And with low ebb doth manifest his sorrow.
So you that are the sovereign of my heart
Have all my joys attending on your will;   10
My joys low-ebbing when you do depart,
When you return their tide my heart doth fill.
   So as you come and as you do depart,
   Joys ebb and flow within my tender heart.

                            [*Charles Best*]

SONNET-SEQUENCES

The Introduction and Notes are at pages 1226 and 1275

FROM GILES FLETCHER's *Licia*, [1593]

To the Reader.

*I had thought, courteous and gentle reader, not to have troubled
thy patience with these lines; but that, in the neglect thereof, I should
either scorn thee, as careless of thine opinion, a thing savoring of a*

*proud humor; or despair to obtain thy favor, which I am loath to
conceive of thy good nature.*

*If I were known, I would entreat in the best manner; and speak
for him whom thou knewest. But being not known, thou speakest not
against me; and therefore I much care not. For this kind of poetry
wherein I wrote, I did it only to try my humor. And for the matter
of love, it may be I am so devoted to some one into whose hands these
may light by chance that she may say (which thou now sayest) that
surely he is in love; which if she do, then have I the full recompense of
my labor, and the poems have dealt sufficiently for the discharge of
their own duty. . . .*

*If thou muse what my Licia is: take her to be some Diana, at the
least chaste; or some Minerva; no Venus—fairer far. It may be she
is learning's image, or some heavenly wonder, which the precisest may
not mislike. Perhaps under that name I have shadowed Discipline. It
may be I mean that kind courtesy which I found at the patroness of
these poems; it may be some college. It may be my conceit, and portend
nothing. . . .*

Licia

Sad, all alone, not long I musing sat,
But that my thoughts compelled me to aspire;
A laurel garland in my hand I gat,
So the Muses I approached the nigher.
My suit was this, a poet to become,
To drink with them, and from the heavens be fed.
Phœbus denied, and sware there was no room,
Such to be poets as fond fancy led.
With that I mourned and sat me down to weep;
Venus she smiled, and smiling to me said,   10
Come drink with me, and sit thee still, and sleep.
This voice I heard; and Venus I obeyed.
That poison sweet hath done me all this wrong,
For now of love must needs be all my song.

First did I fear, when first my love began,
Possessed in fits by watchful jealousy;
I sought to keep what I by favor wan,
And brooked no partner in my love to be.
But tyrant sickness fed upon my love,
And spread his ensigns, dyed with color white;'
Then was suspicion glad for to remove,
And, loving much, did fear to lose her quite.
Erect, fair sweet, the colors thou didst wear;
Dislodge thy griefs, the short'ners of content;   10

For now of life, not love, is all my fear,
Lest life and love be both together spent.
     Live but, fair love, and banish thy disease,
     And love, kind heart, both when and whom thou please.

Seven are the lights that wander in the skies,
And at these seven I wonder in my love:
So see the moon, how pale she doth arise,
Standing amazed as though she durst not move;
So is my sweet much paler than the snow,
Constant her looks, those looks that cannot change.
Mercury the next, a god sweet-tongued we know,
But her sweet voice doth wonders speak more strange.
The rising sun doth boast him of his pride,
And yet my love is far more fair than he.
The warlike Mars can wieldless weapons guide,
But yet that god is far more weak than she.
The lovely Venus seemeth to be fair,
But at her best, my love is far more bright.
Saturn for age with groans doth dim the air,
Whereas my love with smiles doth give it light.
     Gaze at her brows, where heaven ingrafted is;
     Then sigh, and swear, there is no heaven but this.

I live, sweet love, whereas the gentle wind
Murmurs with sport in midst of thickest boughs,
Where loving woodbine doth the harbor bind,
And chirping birds do echo forth my vows;
Where strongest elm can scarce support the vine,
And sweetest flowers enameled have the ground;
Where Muses dwell; and yet hereat repine
That on the earth so rare a place was found.
But winds delight, I wish to be content;
I praise the woodbine, but I take no joy;
I moan the birds that music thus have spent;
As for the rest, they breed but mine annoy.
     Live then, fair Licia, in this place alone;
     Then shall I joy though all of these were gone.

In time the strong and stately turrets fall,
In time the rose and silver lilies die,
In time the monarchs captive are, and thrall,
In time the sea and rivers are made dry;
The hardest flint in time doth melt asunder;
Still-living fame in time doth fade away;
The mountains proud we see in time come under;

And earth, for age, we see in time decay.
The sun in time forgets for to retire
From out the east where he was wont to rise;
The basest thoughts we see in time aspire,
And greedy minds in time do wealth despise.
   Thus all, sweet fair, in time must have an end,
   Except thy beauty, virtues, and thy friend.

10

Whenas her lute is tunëd to her voice,
The air grows proud for honor of that sound,
And rocks do leap to show how they rejoice
That in the earth such music should be found.
Whenas her hair, more worth, more pale, than gold,
Like silver thread lies wafting in the air,
Diana-like she looks, but yet more bold,
Cruel in chase, more chaste and yet more fair.
Whenas she smiles, the clouds for envy breaks;
She Jove, in pride, encounters with a check;
The sun doth shine for joy whenas she speaks;
Thus heaven and earth do homage at her beck.
   Yet all these graces blots, not graces, are,
   If you, my love, of love do take no care.

10

Like Memnon's rock, touched with the rising sun,
Which yields a sound and echoes forth a voice;
But when it's drowned in western seas is done,
And drowsy-like leaves off to make a noise;
So I, my love, enlightened with your shine,
A poet's skill within my soul I shroud—
Not rude, like that which finer wits decline,
But such as Muses to the best allowed.
But when your figure and your shape is gone,
I speechless am, like as I was before;
Or if I write, my verse is filled with moan,
And blurred with tears by falling in such store;
   Then muse not, Licia, if my muse be slack,
   For when I wrote I did thy beauty lack.

10

If sad complaint would show a lover's pain,
Or tears express the torments of my heart,
If melting sighs would ruth and pity gain,
Or true laments but ease a lover's smart;

Then should my plaints the thunder's noise surmount,
And tears like seas should flow from out my eyes;

Then sighs like air should far exceed all count,
And true laments with sorrow dim the skies.

But plaints and tears, laments and sighs I spend,
Yet greater torments do my heart destroy;   10
I could all these from out my heart still send,
If after these I might my love enjoy.

But heavens conspire, and heavens I must obey,
That seeking love I still must want my ease;
For greatest joys are tempered with delay,
Things soon obtained do least of all us please.

My thoughts repine and think the time too long;
My love, impatient, wisheth to obtain;
I blame the heavens that do me all this wrong,
To make me loved, and will not ease my pain.   20

No pain like this, to love and not enjoy;
No grief like this, to mourn and not be heard;
No time so long as that which breeds annoy;
No hell like this, to love and be deferred.

But heaven shall stand, and earth inconstant fly,
The sun shall freeze, and ice inconstant burn,
The mountains flow and all the earth be dry,
Ere time shall force my loving thoughts to turn.

Do you resolve, sweet love, to do the same;
Say that you do, and seal it with a kiss.   30
Then shall our truths the heavens' unkindness blame,
That can not hurt, yet shows their spite in this.

The silly prentice, bound for many years,
Doth hope that time his service will release;
The town besieged that lives in midst of fears
Doth hope in time the cruel wars will cease.

The toiling plowman sings in hope to reap,
The tossèd bark expecteth for a shore;
The boy at school to be at play doth leap
And straight forgets the fear he had before.   40

If those by hope do joy in their distress,
And constant are in hope to conquer time,

Then let not hope in us, sweet friend, be less,
And cause our love to wither in the prime.

Let me conspire, and time will have an end,
So both of us in time shall have a friend.

From Barnabe Barnes's *Parthenophil and Parthenophe*, [1593]

Mistress, behold in this true-speaking glass
  Thy beauty's graces, of all women rarest,
  Where thou mayst find how largely they surpass
And stain in glorious loveliness the fairest.
But read, sweet mistress, and behold it nearer,
  Pond'ring my sorrow's outrage with some pity;
  Then shalt thou find no worldly creature dearer
Than thou to me, thyself in each love ditty.
But in this mirror equally compare
  Thy matchless beauty with mine endless grief;   10
  There like thyself none can be found so fair,
Of chiefest pains there, are my pains the chief.
  Betwixt these both, this one doubt shalt thou find:
  Whether are here extremest in their kind?

Madrigal

Once in an arbor was my mistress sleeping,
  With rose and woodbine woven,
Whose person thousand graces had in keeping;
Where for mine heart her heart's hard flint was cloven
To keep him safe. Behind stood, pertly peeping,
  Poor Cupid, softly creeping,
And drave small birds out of the myrtle bushes,
  Scared with his arrows; who sate cheeping
On every sprig; whom Cupid calls and hushes
From branch to branch; whiles I, poor soul, sate weeping   16
  To see her breathe (not knowing)
Incense into the clouds, and bless with breath
The winds and air; whiles Cupid underneath
With birds, with songs, nor any posies throwing,
  Could her awake—
Each noise sweet lullaby was, for her sake.

————

Ah, sweet content, where is thy mild abode?
  Is it with shepherds and light-hearted swains
Which sing upon the downs and pipe abroad,
  Tending their flocks and cattle on the plains?
Ah, sweet content, where dost thou safely rest?

In heaven, with angels? which the praises sing
  Of him that made, and rules at his behest,
The minds and hearts of every living thing.
Ah, sweet content, where doth thine harbor hold?
  Is it in churches, with religious men
                                              10
  Which please the gods with prayers manifold,
And in their studies meditate it then?
Whether thou dost in heaven or earth appear,
  Be where thou wilt, thou wilt not harbor here!

Burn on, sweet fire, for I live by that fuel
  Whose smoke is as an incense to my soul.
Each sigh prolongs my smart. Be fierce and cruel,
  My fair Parthenophe. Frown and control,
Vex, torture, scald, disgrace me. Do thy will!
Stop up thine ears; with flint immure thine heart,
And kill me with thy looks, if they would kill.
Thine eyes, those crystal phials which impart
The perfect balm to my dead-wounded breast,
Thine eyes, the quivers whence those darts were drawn   10
Which me to thy love's bondage have addressed;
  Thy smile and frown, night-star and daylight's dawn,
Burn on, frown on, vex, stop thine ears, torment me!
  More, for thy beauty borne, would not repent me.

This careful head, with divers thoughts distressed,
  My fancy's chronicler, my sorrow's muse;
  These watchful eyes, whose heedless aim I curse,
  Love's sentinels, and fountains of unrest;
This tongue still trembling, herald fit addressed
  To my love's grief (than any torment worse);
  This heart, true fortress of my spotless love,
  And rageous furnace of my long desire:
Of these, by nature, am I not possessed,
  Though nature their first means in me did move.   10
  But thou, dear sweet, with thy love's holy fire,
  My head grief's anvil made, with cares oppressed;
Mine eyes, a spring; my tongue, a leaf, wind-shaken;
  My heart, a wasteful wilderness forsaken.

Ode

When I walk forth into the
    woods,
With heavy passion to complain,
I view the trees with blushing buds

Ashamed, or grievéd at my pain.
There amaranth, with rosy stain,
Me pitying, doth his leaves in-
    grain.

When I pass pensive to the
  shore,
The water-birds about me fly,
As if they mourned; when rivers
  roar,
Chiding thy wrathful cruelty,   10
Halcyon watcheth warily
To chide thee when thou comest
  by.

If to the city I repair,
Mine eyes thy cruelty betray;
And those which view me find my
  care—
Swoll'n eyes and sorrows it betray,
Whose figures in my forehead are.
These curse the cause of mine ill
  fare.

When I go forth to feed my
  flocks,

As I, so they, hang down their
  heads.   20
If I complain to ruthless rocks,
(For that it seems hard rocks her
  bred)
Rocks' ruth in rivers may be
  read,
Which from those rocks down
  tricklëd.

When shepherds would know
  how I fare,
And ask, How doth Parthenophil?
Ill, Echo answers in void air,
And with these news each place
  doth fill.
Poor herd-grooms from each cottage will
Sing my complaints on every
  hill.   30

FROM BARNABE BARNES's *Divine Century of Spiritual Sonnets*, 1595

No more lewd lays of lighter loves I sing,
  Nor teach my lustful muse abused to fly
  With sparrows' plumes, and for compassion cry
To mortal beauties which no succor bring.
But my muse, feathered with an angel's wing,
  Divinely mounts aloft unto the sky,
  Where her love's subjects, with my hopes, do lie.
For Cupid's darts prefigurate hell's sting;
His quenchless torch foreshows hell's quenchless fire,   10
  Kindling men's wits with lustful lays of sin—
Thy wounds my cure, dear Savior! I desire,
  To pierce my thoughts, thy fiery cherubin,
  By kindling my desires true zeal t'infuse,
  Thy love my theme, and Holy Ghost my muse!

Fortress of hope, anchor of faithful zeal,
  Rock of affiance, bulwark of sure trust,
  In whom all nations for salvation must
Put certain confidence of their souls' weal:
Those sacred mysteries, dear Lord, reveal
  Of that large volume, righteous and just.
  From me, though blinded with this earthly dust,

Do not those gracious mysteries conceal;
That I by them, as from some beamsome lamp,
May find the bright and right direction 10
To my soul, blinded, marching to that camp
Of sacred soldiers whose protection
He that victorious on a white horse rideth
Taketh, and evermore triumphant guideth.

A blast of wind, a momentary breath,
A wat'ry bubble symbolized with air,
A sun-blown rose, but for a season fair,
A ghostly glance, a skeleton of death;
A morning dew, pearling the grass beneath,
Whose moisture sun's appearance doth impair;
A lightning glimpse, a muse of thought and care,
A planet's shot, a shade which followeth,
A voice which vanisheth so soon as heard,
The thriftless heir of time, a rolling wave, 10
A show, no more in action than regard,
A mass of dust, world's momentary slave,—
Is man, in state of our old Adam made,
Soon born to die, soon flourishing to fade.

FROM WILLIAM PERCY'S *Cœlia*, 1594

Judged by my goddess' doom to endless pain,
Lo, here I ope my sorrow's passion,
That every silly eye may view most plain
A sentence given on no occasion.
If that by chance they fall (most fortunate)
Within those cruel hands that did enact it,
Say but, Alas, he was too passionate,
My doom is passed, nor can be now unactit.
So mayst thou see I was a spotless lover,
And grieve withal that e'er thou dealt so sore; 10
Unto remorse who goes about to move her,
Pursues the wingëd winds, and tills the shore.
  Lovely is her semblance, hard is her heart,
  Wavering is her mind, sure is her dart.

Relent, my dear yet unkind Cœlia,
At length relent, and give my sorrows end.
So shall I keep my long-wished holiday,
And set a trophy on a froward friend.
  Nor tributes, nor imposts, nor other duties
Demand I will, as lawful conqueror;

Duties, tributes, imposts unto thy beauties
Myself will pay as yielded servitor.
   Then quick relent, thyself surrender us.
Brave sir, and why (quoth she) must I relent?   **10**
Relent (cried I), thyself doth conquer us.
When eftsoons with my proper instrument
   She cut me off, ay me, and answerëd,
   You cannot conquer, and be conquerëd.

It shall be said I died for Cœlia;
Then quick, thou grisly man of Erebus,
Transport me hence unto Proserpina,
To be adjudged as—wilful amorous;
   To be hung up within the liquid air,
For all the sighs which I in vain have wasted;
To be through Lethe's waters cleansëd fair,
For those dark clouds which have my looks o'ercasted;
   To be condemned to everlasting fire,
Because at Cupid's fire I wilful brent me;   **10**
And to be clad for deadly dumps in mire.
Among so many plagues which shall torment me
   One solace I shall find, when I am over,—
   It will be known I died a constant lover.

FROM *Zepheria*, 1594

Alli veri figlioli delle Muse

Ye modern laureates, famoused for your writ,
Who for your pregnance may in Delos dwell,
On your sweet lines eternity doth sit,
Their brows ennobling with applause and laurel.
Triumph and honor aye invest your writ!
Ye fet your pens from wing of singing swan,
When (sweetly warbling to herself) she floats
Adown Meander streams, and like to organ
Imparts into her quills melodious notes.
Ye from the father of delicious phrases   **10**
Borrow such hymns as make your mistress live
When time is dead; nay, Hermes tunes the praises
Which ye in sonnets to your mistress give.
Report throughout our western isle doth ring
The sweet-tuned accents of your Delian sonnetry,
Which to Apollo's violin ye sing,—
Oh then, your high strains drown his melody.
From forth dead sleep of everlasting dark.

Fame, with her trump's shrill summon, hath awaked
The Roman Naso and the Tuscan Petrarch,   20
Your spirit-ravishing lines to wonder at.
  Oh, theme befitting high-mused Astrophil,
He to your silvery songs lent sweetest touch,
Your songs, the immortal spirit of your quill!
Oh pardon, for my artless pen too much
Doth dim your glories through his infant skill.
  Though may I not with you the spoils divide
(Ye sacred offspring of Mnemosyne)
Of endless praise, which have your pens achieved
(Your pens the trumps to immortality);   30
Yet be it lawful that like maims I bide,
Like brunts and scars in your love's warfare,
And here, though in my homespun verse, of them declare.

Proud in thy love, how many have I cited
Impartial thee to view, whose eyes have lavished
Sweet beauteous objects oft have men delighted;
But thou above delight their sense hast ravished.
  They, amorous artists, thee pronounced love's queen,
And unto thy supremacy did swear;
(Venus, at Paphos keep, no more be seen!)
Now Cupid after thee his shafts shall bear.
  How have I spent my spirit of invention
In penning amorous stanzas to thy beauty,   10
But heavenly graces may not brook dimension;
Nor more may thine, for infinite they be.
  But now in harsh tune I of amours sing,
  My pipe for them grows hoarse, but shrill to plaining.

When we, in kind embracements, had agreed
To keep a royal banquet on our lips,
How soon have we another feast decreed,
And how, at parting, have we mourned by fits!
  Eftsoons, in absence have we wailed much more
Till those void hours of intermission
Were spent, that we might revel as before.
How have we bribèd time for expedition!
  And when remitted to our former love-plays,
How have we, overweening in delight,   10
Accused the father sexton of the days
That then with eagle's wings he took his flight.
  But now, old man, fly on as swift as thought,
  Sith eyes from love, and hope from heart, is wrought.

What? Shall I ne'er more see those halcyon days,
Those sunny Sabbaths, days of jubilee,
Wherein I caroled merry roundelays,
Odes, and love songs? which, being viewed by thee,
    Received allowance worthy better writ.
When we on shepherds' holy-days have hied
Down to the flow'ry pastures (flowers for thy treading fit)
Holy the day, when thou it sanctified!
    When thou, Zepheria, wouldst but deign to bless it,
How have I, jealous over Phœbus' rays,   10
Clouded thy fair; then, fearing he would guess it
By thy white brow, it have I cinct with bays.
    But woe is me, that I have fenced thy beauty,
    Sith other must enjoy it, and not I!

From E. C.'s *Emaricdulfe*, 1595

Within her hair Venus and Cupid sport them;
    Some time they twist it, amber-like, in gold,
To which the whistling winds do oft resort them,
    As if they strove to have the knots unrolled;
Some time they let their golden tresses dangle,
    And therewith nets and amorous gins they make
Wherewith the hearts of lovers to entangle,
    Which once enthralled, no ransom they will take.
But as two tyrants sitting in their thrones
    Look on their slaves with tyrannizing eyes;   10
So they, no whit regarding lovers' moans,
    Doom worlds of hearts to endless slaveries
Unless they subject-like swear to adore
And serve Emaricdulfe forevermore.

I am enchanted with thy snow-white hands
    That maze me with their quaint dexterity,
And with their touch tie in a thousand bands
    My yielding heart ever to honor thee;
Thought of thy dainty fingers long and small,
    For pretty action that exceed compare,
Sufficient is to bless me, and withal
    To free my chainèd thoughts from sorrow's snare.
But that which crowns my soul with heavenly bliss,
    And gives my heart fruition of all joys,   10
Their dainty concord and sweet music is,
    That poisons grief and cureth all annoys.

Those eyes that see, those ears are blest that hear
These heavenly gifts of nature in my dear.

My heart is like a ship on Neptune's back;
   Thy beauty is the sea where my ship saileth;
Thy frowns the surges are that threat my wrack,
   Thy smiles the winds that on my sails soft galeth.
Long tossed betwixt fair hope and foul despair,
   My sea-sick heart, arrivèd on thy shore—
Thy love, I mean—begs that he may repair
   His broken vessel with thy bounteous store.
Dido relieved Æneas in distress,
   And lent him love, and gave to him her heart;   10
If half such bounty thou to me express,
   From thy fair shore I never will depart,
But thank kind fortune that my course did sort
To suffer shipwreck on so sweet a port.

From Richard Lynche's *Diella*, 1596

Soon as the azure-colored gates of th' east
   Were set wide open by the watchful morn,
I walked abroad, as having took no rest
   (For nights are tedious to a man forlorn);
And viewing well each pearl-bedewèd flower,
   Then waxing dry by splendor of the sun,
All scarlet-hued I saw him 'gin to lour
   And blush, as though some heinous act were done.
At this amazed, I hied me home amain,
   Thinking that I his anger causèd had.   10
And at his set, abroad I walked again;
   When lo, the moon looked wondrous pale and sad:
Anger the one, and envy moved the other,
To see my love more fair than Love's fair mother.

What sugared terms, what all-persuading art,
   What sweet mellifluous words, what wounding looks
Love used for his admittance to my heart!
   Such eloquence was never read in books.
He promised pleasure, rest, and endless joy,
   Fruition of the fairest she alive.
His pleasure, pain; rest, trouble; joy, annoy,
   Have I since found, which me of bliss deprive.
The Trojan horse thus have I now let in,
   Wherein enclosed these armèd men were placed—   10
Bright eyes, fair cheeks, sweet lips, and milk-white skin;

These foes my life have overthrown and razed.
Fair outward shows prove inwardly the worst,
Love looketh fair, but lovers are accurst.

Weary with serving where I nought could get,
   I thought to cross great Neptune's greatest seas,
To live in exile; but my drift was let
   By cruel fortune, spiteful of such ease.
The ship I had to pass in was my mind,
   Greedy desire was topsail of the same,
My tears were surges, sighs did serve for wind,
   Of all my ship despair was chiefest frame;
Sorrow was master; care, the cable rope;
   Grief was the mainmast; love, the captain of it;   10
He that did rule the helm was foolish hope;
   But beauty was the rock that my ship split,
Which since hath made such shipwreck of my joy
That still I swim in th' ocean of annoy.

End this enchantment, love, of my desires,
   Let me no longer languish for thy love.
Joy not to see me thus consume in fires,
   But let my cruel pains thy hard heart move.
And now, at last with pitiful regard
   Eye me, thy lover, lorn for lack of thee,
Which, dying, lives in hope of sweet reward
   Which hate hath hitherto withheld from me.
Constant have I been, still in fancy fast,
   Ordained by heavens to dote upon thy fair;   10
Nor will I e'er, so long as life shall last,
   Say any's fairer, breathing vital air.
But when the ocean sands shall lie unwet,
Then shall my soul to love thee, dear, forget.

FROM WILLIAM SMITH's *Chloris*, 1596

To the most excellent and learned shepherd, Colin Clout

Colin, my dear and most entire beloved,
   My muse audacious stoops her pitch to thee,
Desiring that thy patience be not moved
   By these rude lines, written here you see;
Fain would my muse, whom cruel love hath wronged,
   Shroud her love-labors under thy protection,
And I myself with ardent zeal have longed
   That thou mightst know to thee my true affection.

Therefore, good Colin, graciously accept
  A few sad sonnets which my muse hath framed;   10
Though they but newly from the shell are crept,
  Suffer them not by envy to be blamed.
But underneath the shadow of thy wings
Give warmth to these young-hatchèd orphan things.

Feed, silly sheep, although your keeper pineth,
  Yet like to Tantalus doth see his food.
  Skip you and leap, no bright Apollo shineth,
  Whilst I bewail my sorrows in yon wood
Where woeful Philomela doth record,
  And sings with notes of sad and dire lament
  The tragedy wrought by her sister's lord;
  I'll bear a part in her black discontent.
That pipe which erst was wont to make you glee,
  Upon these downs whereon you careless graze,   10
  Shall to her mournful music tunèd be.
  Let not my plaints, poor lambkins, you amaze;
There underneath that dark and dusky bower
Whole showers of tears to Chloris I will pour.

Whole showers of tears to Chloris I will pour
  As true oblations of my sincere love;
  If that will not suffice, most fairest flower,
  Then shall my sighs thee unto pity move.
If neither tears nor sighs can aught prevail,
  My streaming blood thine anger shall appease;
  This hand of mine by vigor shall assail
  To tear my heart asunder thee to please.
Celestial powers, on you I invocate:
  You know the chaste affections of my mind,   10
  I never did my faith yet violate,
  Why should my Chloris then be so unkind?
That neither tears, nor sighs, nor streaming blood
Can unto mercy move her cruel mood.

When I more large thy praises forth shall show,
  That all the world thy beauty shall admire,
  Desiring that most sacred nymph to know
  Which hath the shepherd's fancy set on fire;
Till then, my dear, let these thine eyes content;
  Till then, fair love, think if I merit favor;
  Till then, oh, let thy merciful assent
  Relish my hopes with some comforting savor.
So shall you add such courage to my muse

That she shall climb the steep Parnassus hill,   10
That learned poets shall my deeds peruse
When I from thence obtainëd have more skill.
And what I sing shall always be of thee
As long as life or breath remains in me!

FROM BARTHOLOMEW GRIFFIN'S *Fidessa, More Chaste than Kind,* 1596

Arraigned, poor captive at the bar I stand,
    The bar of beauty, bar to all my joys;
And up I hold my ever-trembling hand,
    Wishing or life or death to end annoys.
And when the judge doth question of the guilt
    And bids me speak, then sorrow shuts up words.
Yea, though he say, Speak boldly what thou wilt,
    Yet my confused affects no speech affords.
For why, alas, my passions have no bound,
    For fear of death that penetrates so near;   10
And still one grief another doth confound,
    Yet doth at length a way to speech appear.
Then, for I speak too late, the judge doth give
His sentence that in prison I shall live.

———

Compare me to the child that plays with fire,
    Or to the fly that dieth in the flame,
Or to the foolish boy that did aspire
    To touch the glory of high heaven's frame;
Compare me to Leander struggling in the waves,
    Not able to attain his safety's shore,
Or to the sick that do expect their graves,
    Or to the captive crying evermore;
Compare me to the weeping wounded hart,
    Moaning with tears the period of his life,   10
Or to the boar that will not feel his smart
    When he is stricken with the butcher's knife:
No man to these can fitly me compare;
These live to die, I die to live in care.

———

Care-charmer sleep, sweet ease in restless misery,
    The captive's liberty, and his freedom's song,
Balm of the bruisëd heart, man's chief felicity,
    Brother of quiet death, when life is too, too long!
A comedy it is, and now an history—
    What is not sleep unto the feeble mind!
It easeth him that toils and him that's sorry,
    It makes the deaf to hear, to see the blind.

Ungentle sleep, thou helpest all but me,
  For when I sleep my soul is vexëd most.   10
It is Fidessa that doth master thee;
  If she approach, alas, thy power is lost.
But here she is. See, how he runs amain!
I fear at night he will not come again.

Fly to her heart, hover about her heart,
  With dainty kisses mollify her heart,
Pierce with thy arrows her obdurate heart,
  With sweet allurements ever move her heart,
At mid-day and at midnight touch her heart,
  Be lurking closely, nestle about her heart,
With power (thou art a god) command her heart,
  Kindle thy coals of love about her heart,
Yea, even into thyself transform her heart.
Ah, she must love! Be sure thou have her heart,   10
  And I must die if thou have not her heart,
Thy bed, if thou rest well, must be her heart,
  He hath the best part sure that hath the heart.
What have I not, if I have but her heart!

I have not spent the April of my time,
  The sweet of youth, in plotting in the air,
But do at first adventure seek to climb,
  Whilst flowers of blooming years are green and fair.
I am no leaving of all-withering age,
  I have not suffered many winter lours;
I feel no storm unless my love do rage,
  And then in grief I spend both days and hours.
This yet doth comfort, that my flower lasted
  Until it did approach my sun too near,   10
And then, alas, untimely was it blasted,
  So soon as once thy beauty did appear.
But after all, my comfort rests in this,
That for thy sake my youth decayëd is.

Fair is my love that feeds among the lilies,
  The lilies growing in that pleasant garden
Where Cupid's mount, that well belovëd hill is,
  And where that little god himself is warden.
See where my love sits in the beds of spices,
  Beset all round with camphor, myrrh, and roses,
And interlaced with curious devices,
  Which her from all the world apart incloses.

There doth she tune her lute for her delight,
    And with sweet music makes the ground to move,
    Whilst I, poor I, do sit in heavy plight,
    Wailing alone my unrespected love;
Not daring rush into so rare a place,
That gives to her, and she to it, a grace.

Tell me of love, sweet Love, who is thy sire?
    Or if thou mortal or immortal be?
    Some say thou art begotten by desire,
    Nourished with hope, and fed with fantasy,
Engendered by a heavenly goddess' eye,
    Lurking most sweetly in an angel's face;
    Others, that beauty thee doth deify—
    O sovereign beauty, full of power and grace!
But I must be absurd all this denying,
    Because the fairest fair alive ne'er knew thee.
    Now, Cupid, comes thy godhead to the trying:
    'Twas she alone (such is her power) that slew me.
She shall be love, and thou a foolish boy,
Whose virtue proves thy power but a toy.

Work, work apace, you blessed sisters three,
    In restless twining of my fatal thread.
    O let your nimble hands at once agree
    To weave it out and cut it off with speed.
Then shall my vexèd and tormented ghost
    Have quiet passage to the Elysian rest,
    And sweetly over death and fortune boast
    In everlasting triumphs with the blest.
But ah, too well I know you have conspired
    A lingering death for him that loatheth life,
    As if with woes he never could be tired;
    For this you hide your all-dividing knife.
One comfort yet the heavens have assigned me,
That I must die and leave my griefs behind me.

If great Apollo offered as a dower
    His burning throne to beauty's excellence;
    If Jove himself came in a golden shower
    Down to the earth, to fetch fair Io thence;
If Venus in the curlèd locks were tied
    Of proud Adonis not of gentle kind;
    If Tellus for a shepherd's favor died,
    The favor cruel love to her assigned;

If heaven's wingëd herald, Hermes, had
  His heart enchanted with a country maid;
  If poor Pygmalion were for beauty mad;
  If gods and men have all for beauty strayed:
I am not then ashamed to be included
'Mongst those that love, and be with love deluded.

From Robert Tofte's *Laura*, 1597

Unto thy favor, which when nature formed
She went beyond herself with cunning hand,
I may compare what is in world adorned
With beauty most and with most grace doth stand.
But every mortal whiteness ne'er so white
The ivory white of thy white hand exceeds,
So that my soul, which doth fair whiteness like,
Rests on fair whiteness and on whiteness feeds.
  For this is thought and hopëd of from thee:
  White as thy hands, so white thy faith shall be.

When she was born she came with smiling eye
Laughing into the world, a sign of glee;
When I was born, to her quite contrary,
Wailing I came into the world to see.
  Then mark this wonder strange: what nature gave,
  From first to th' last this fashion kept we have.
She in my sad laments doth take great joy;
I through her laughing die, and languish must
Unless that love, to save me from this 'noy,
Do unto me, unworthy, show so just
  As for to change her laughter into pain,
  And my complaints into her joy again.

In love his kingdom great, two fools there be:
My lady's one, myself the other am.
The fond behavior of both which to see,
Whoso but nicely marks will say the same.
Foolish our thoughts are; foolish our desire;
Foolish our hearts in fancy's flame to fry;
Foolish to burn in love's hot scorching fire,—
But what! Fools are we none. My tongue doth lie.
  For who most foolish is and fond, in love,
  More wiser far than others oft doth prove.

Strange is this thing! My horse I cannot make
With spur, with speech, nor yet with rod in hand
Force him to go, although great pains I take.

Do what I can, he still as tired doth stand.
No doubt he feels an heavy weight of me,
Which is the cause he standeth still as stone;
Nor is he ware that now he carrieth three—
He thinks, poor jade, I am on's back alone.
  But three we are: with mine own self, I prove,
  Laura is in my heart, in soul is love.   10

FROM HENRY LOK's *Sonnets of Christian Passions*,
published with *Ecclesiastes*, 1597

It is not, Lord, the sound of many words,
  The bowëd knee, or abstinence of man,
  The filëd phrase that eloquence affords,
  Or poet's pen, that heavens do pierce, or can;
By heavy cheer of color pale and wan,
  By pinëd body of the Pharisay,
  A mortal eye repentance oft doth scan,
  Whose judgment doth on outward shadows stay.
But thou, O God, dost heart's intent bewray
  For from thy sight, Lord, nothing is concealed,   10
  Thou formedst the frame fro out the very clay,
  To thee the thoughts of hearts are all revealed.
    To thee, therefore, with heart and mind prostrate,
    With tears I thus deplore my sinful state.

Words may well want, both ink and paper fail,
  Wits may grow dull, and will may weary grow,
  And world's affairs may make my pen more slow,
  But yet my heart and courage shall not quail.
Though cares and troubles do my peace assail
  And drive me to delay thy praise awhile,
  Yet all the world shall not from thoughts exile
  Thy mercies, Lord, by which my plaints prevail.
And though the world with face should grateful smile
  And me her peddler's pack of pleasures show,   10
  No hearty love on her I would bestow,
  Because I know she seeks me to beguile;
    Ne will defile my happy peace of mind
    For all the solace I in earth may find.

FROM ALEXANDER CRAIG's *Amorous Songs, Sonnets, and
Elegies*, 1606

To Pandora

Go you, O winds that blow from north to south,
Convey my secret sighs unto my sweet;

Deliver them from mine unto her mouth,
And make my commendations till we meet.
But if perhaps her proud aspiring sprite
Will not accept nor yet receive the same,
The breast and bulwark of her bosom beat,
Knock at her heart, and tell from whence you came;
Importune her, nor cease nor shrink for shame.
Sport with her curls of amber-colored hair,   10
And when she sighs, immix yourselves with thame,
Give her her own, and thus beguile the fair.
   Blow winds, fly sighs, whereas my heart doth haunt,
   And secretly commend me to my saunt.

To his Pandora, from England

Now, while amid those dainty downs and dales
With shepherd swains I sit, unknown to me,
We sweetly sing and tell pastoral tales,
But my discourse and song's theme is of thee.
For otherways, alas, how can it be?
Let Venus leave her blest abode above
To tempt my love, yet thou, sweet soul, shalt see
That I thy man and thou shalt die my love.
No tract of time nor sad eclipse of place
Nor absence long, which sometime were due cures   10
To my disease, shall make thy slave to cease
From serving thee till life or breath endures;
   And till we meet, my rustic mates and I
   Through woods and plains Pandora's praise shall cry.

HENRY CONSTABLE

The Introduction and Notes are at pages 1232 and 1275

From *Diana*, 1592

Mine eye with all the deadly sins is fraught.
   First *proud*, sith it presumed to look so high;
   A watchman being made, stood gazing by,
And *idle*, took no heed till I was caught;
And *envious* bears envy that my thought
   Should in his absence be to her so nigh;
   To kill my heart, mine eye let in her eye,
And so consent gave to a *murder* wrought;
   And *covetous*, it never would remove

From her fair hair, gold so doth please his sight;
  Unchaste, a bawd between my heart and love;
A glutton eye, with tears drunk every night:
  These sins procurèd have a goddess' ire,
  Wherefore my heart is damned in love's sweet fire.   10

FROM Diana, [1594]

Dear to my soul, then leave me not forsaken!
  Fly not, my heart within thy bosom sleepeth.
Even from myself and sense I have betaken
  Me unto thee for whom my spirit weepeth,
And on the shore of that salt teary sea,
  Couched in a bed of unseen seeming pleasure,
  Where in imaginary thoughts thy fair self lay;
  But being waked, robbed of my life's best treasure,
I call the heavens, air, earth, and seas to hear
My love, my truth, and black disdained estate;   10
  Beating the rocks with bellowings of despair,
  Which still with plaints my words reverberate;
Sighing, Alas, what shall become of me?
Whilst echo cries, What shall become of me?

Whilst echo cries, What shall become of me?
  And desolate, my desolations pity,
  Thou in thy beauty's carrack sit'st to see
  My tragic downfall, and my funeral ditty.
No timbrel, but my heart thou play'st upon,
  Whose strings are stretched unto the highest key;
  The diapason, love; love is the unison;
  In love my life and labors waste away.
Only regardless to the world thou leav'st me,
  Whilst slain hopes, turning from the feast of sorrow   10
  Unto despair, their king which ne'er deceives me,
  Captives my heart, whose black night hates the morrow;
And he in ruth of my distressèd cry
Plants me a weeping star within my eye.

To live in hell and heaven to behold;
  To welcome life and die a living death;
  To sweat with heat, and yet be freezing cold;
  To grasp at stars and lie the earth beneath;
To tread a maze that never shall have end;
  To burn in sighs and starve in daily tears;
  To climb a hill and never to descend;
  Giants to kill, and quake at childish fears;

To pine for food, and watch th' Hesperian tree;
  To thirst for drink, and nectar still to draw;   10
  To live accursed, whom men hold blest to be,
  And weep those wrongs which never creature saw:
If this be love, if love in these be founded,
My heart is love, for these in it are grounded.

Fair grace of graces, muse of muses all,
  Thou paradise, thou only heaven I know,
  What influence hath bred my hateful woe,
That I from thee and them am forced to fall?
Thou fall'n from me, from thee I never shall;
  Although my fortunes thou hast brought so low,
  Yet shall my faith and service with thee go,
For live I do on heaven and thee to call.
Banished all grace, no graces with me dwell;
  Compelled to muse, my muses from me fly;   10
  Excluded heaven, what can remain but hell?
  Exiled from paradise, in hate I lie
Cursing my stars; albeit I find it true,
I lost all these when I lost love and you.

FROM THOMAS PARK'S *Harleian Miscellany*, vol. ix, 1812
To his mistress
*Upon occasion of a Petrarch he gave her, showing her the reason why
the Italian commenters dissent so much in the exposition
thereof*

Miracle of the world, I never will deny
That former poets praise the beauty of their days,
But all those beauties were but figures of thy praise
And all those poets did of thee but prophesy.

Thy coming to the world hath taught us to descry
What Petrarch's Laura meant, for truth the lip bewrays.
Lo, why th' Italians, yet which never saw thy rays,
To find out Petrarch's sense such forgëd glosses try:

The beauties which he in a veil enclosed beheld
But revelations were within his secret heart,   10
By which in parables thy coming he foretold.
His songs were hymns of thee, which only now before
  Thy image should be sung; for thou that goddess art
  Which only we without idolatry adore.

FROM *Harleian Ms.* 7553

To St. Peter and St. Paul

He that for fear his Master did deny,
   And at a maiden's voice amazëd stood,
   The mightiest monarch of the earth withstood,
And on his Master's cross rejoiced to die.
He whose blind zeal did rage with cruelty
   And helped to shed the first of martyrs' blood,
   By light from heaven his blindness understood,
And with the chief apostle slain doth lie.
O three times happy two! O golden pair!
   Who with your blood did lay the church's ground   10
   Within the fatal town which twins did found,
And settled there the Hebrew fisher's chair
   Where first the Latin shepherd raised his throne,
   And since, the world and church were ruled by one.

To St. Mary Magdalen

Such as, retired from sight of men, like thee
   By penance seek the joys of heaven to win,
   In deserts make their paradise begin
And even among wild beasts do angels see.
In such a place my soul doth seem to be,
   When in my body she laments her sin
   And none but brutal passions finds therein,
Except they be sent down from heaven to me.
Yet if those graces God to me impart
   Which he inspired thy blessed breast withal,   10
   I may find heaven in my retired heart;
And if thou change the object of my love,
   The winged affection which men Cupid call
   May get his sight, and like an angel prove.

FROM JOHN BODENHAM'S (?) *England's Helicon,* 1600

Damelus' song to his Diaphenia

Diaphenia, like the daffadown-
      dilly,
White as the sun, fair as the lily,
   Heigh ho, how I do love
      thee!
I do love thee as my lambs
Are belovëd of their dams—

How blest were I if thou
   wouldst prove me!

Diaphenia, like the spreading roses,
That in thy sweets all sweets in-
      closes,
   Fair sweet, how I do love thee!

I do love thee as each flower 10
Loves the sun's life-giving power,
For, dead, thy breath to life
    might move me.

Diaphenia, like to all things
    blessed,

When all thy praises are ex-
    pressëd,
Dear joy, how I do love
    thee!
As the birds do love the spring,
Or the bees their careful king,—
Then in requite, sweet virgin,
    love me!

The shepherd's song of Venus and Adonis

Venus fair did ride,
    Silver doves they drew her
By the pleasant lawns,
    Ere the sun did rise;
Vesta's beauty rich
    Opened wide to view her,
Philomel records
    Pleasing harmonies;
Every bird of spring
    Cheerfully did sing,   10
        Paphos' goddess they sa-
        lute.
Now love's queen so fair
    Had of mirth no care,
        For her son had made her
        mute.
In her breast so tender
He a shaft did enter,
    When her eyes beheld a
    boy,
Adonis was he named,
By his mother shamed,
    Yet he now is Venus'
    joy.   20

Him alone she met,
    Ready bound for hunting;
Him she kindly greets,
    And his journey stays;
Him she seeks to kiss,
    No devices wanting,
Him her eyes still woo,
    Him her tongue still prays.
He with blushing red
    Hangeth down the head,   30
        Not a kiss can he afford;

His face is turned away,
Silence said her nay,
    Still she wooed him for a
    word.
Speak, she said, thou fairest,
Beauty thou impairest;
    See me, I am pale and wan;
Lovers all adore me,
I for love implore thee.
    Crystal tears with that ran
    down.   40

Him herewith she forced
    To come sit down by her;
She his neck embraced,
    Gazing in his face;
He, like one transformed,
    Stirred no look to eye her.
Every herb did woo him,
    Growing in that place;
        Each bird with a ditty
        Prayëd him for pity   50
        In behalf of beauty's
        queen;
Waters' gentle murmur
    Cravëd him to love her,
        Yet no liking could be
        seen.
Boy, she said, look on me,
Still I gaze upon thee,
    Speak, I pray thee, my de-
    light.
Coldly he replied,
And, in brief, denied
    To bestow on her a sight. 60

I am now too young
  To be won by beauty;
Tender are my years,
  I am yet a bud.
Fair thou art, she said,
  Then it is thy duty,
Wert thou but a blossom,
  To effect my good.
    Every beauteous flower
      Boasteth in my power, 70
    Birds and beasts my laws ef-
      fect.
Myrrha, thy fair mother,
  Most of any other
    Did my lovely hests re-
      spect.
Be with me delighted,
Thou shalt be requited,
    Every nymph on thee shall
      tend;
All the gods shall love thee,
Man shall not reprove thee,
    Love himself shall be thy
      friend. 80

Wend thee from me, Venus,
  I am not disposed;
Thou wring'st me too hard,
  Prithee, let me go;
Fie, what a pain it is
  Thus to be enclosed;
If love begin with labor,
  It will end in woe.
    Kiss me, I will leave.
      Here a kiss receive. 90
        A short kiss I do it find,
        Wilt thou leave me so?
          Yet thou shalt not go;
            Breathe once more thy
              balmy wind,
It smelleth of the myrrh tree
That to the world did bring
  thee,
    Never was perfume so
      sweet.
When she had thus spoken,

She gave him a token,
  And their naked bosoms
    meet. 100

Now, he said, let's go,
  Hark, the hounds are crying,
Grisly boar is up,
  Huntsmen follow fast.
At the name of boar
  Venus seemèd dying,
Deadly-colored pale,
  Roses overcast.
    Speak, said she, no more
      Of following the boar; 110
        Thou, unfit for such a
          chase,
          Course the fearful hare,
          Venison do not spare,
            If thou wilt yield Venus
              grace.
Shun the boar, I pray thee,
Else I still will stay thee.
    Herein he vowed to
      please her mind;
Then her arms enlarged,
Loath she him discharged,
    Forth he went as swift
      as wind. 120

Thetis Phœbus' steeds
  In the west retained;
Hunting sport was past,
  Love her love did seek;
Sight of him too soon,
  Gentle queen she gained.
On the ground he lay;
  Blood had left his cheek,
    For an orpèd swine
      Smit him in the groin, 130
        Deadly wound his death
          did bring.
Which when Venus found
  She fell in a swound,
    And awaked, her hands
      did wring.

Nymphs and satyrs skipping
  Came together tripping,
    Echo every cry ex-
      pressed.

Venus by her power
  Turned him to a flower,
    Which she weareth in her
      crest.   140

ROBERT SOUTHWELL

The Introduction and Notes are at pages 1233 and 1275

FROM *Mœoniæ*, 1595

Upon the image of death

Before my face the picture hangs
  That daily should put me in
    mind
Of those cold names and bitter
    pangs
  That shortly I am like to find;
But yet, alas, full little I
  Do think hereon that I must
    die.
I often look upon a face
  Most ugly, grisly, bare, and
    thin;
I often view the hollow place
  Where eyes and nose had some-
    times been;   10
I see the bones across that lie,
  Yet little think that I must die.
I read the label underneath,
  That telleth me whereto I
    must;
I see the sentence eke that saith
  *Remember, man, that thou art
    dust!*
But yet, alas, but seldom I
  Do think indeed that I must
    die.
Continually at my bed's head
  A hearse doth hang, which doth
    me tell   20
That I ere morning may be dead,
  Though now I feel myself full
    well;
But yet, alas, for all this, I

Have little mind that I must
    die.
The gown which I do use to wear,
  The knife wherewith I cut my
    meat,
And eke that old and ancient chair
  Which is my only usual seat,—
All those do tell me I must die,
  And yet my life amend not I.   30
My ancestors are turned to clay,
  And many of my mates are
    gone;
My youngers daily drop away,
  And can I think to 'scape
    alone?
No, no, I know that I must die,
  And yet my life amend not I.
Not Solomon for all his wit,
  Nor Samson, though he were so
    strong,
No king nor person ever yet
  Could 'scape but death laid him
    along;   40
Wherefore I know that I must
    die,
  And yet my life amend not I.
Though all the East did quake to
    hear
  Of Alexander's dreadful name,
And all the West did likewise fear
  To hear of Julius Cæsar's fame,
Yet both by death in dust now lie;

Who then can 'scape but he
    must die?
If none can 'scape death's dread-
    ful dart,
If rich and poor his beck obey,   50
If strong, if wise, if all do smart,

Then I to 'scape shall have no
    way.
Oh, grant me grace, O God, that
    I
My life may mend, sith I must
    die.

FROM *St. Peter's Complaint . . . for J. Wolfe,* 1595

Look home

Retirëd thoughts enjoy their own delights,
As beauty doth in self-beholding eye;
Man's mind a mirror is of heavenly sights,
A brief wherein all marvels summëd lie,
Of fairest forms and sweetest shapes the store,
Most graceful all, yet thought may grace them more.

The mind a creature is, yet can create,
To nature's patterns adding higher skill;
Of finest works wit better could the state
If force of wit had equal power of will.   10
Device of man in working hath no end,
What thought can think, another thought can mend.

Man's soul of endless beauty image is,
Drawn by the work of endless skill and might;
This skillful might gave many sparks of bliss
And, to discern this bliss, a native light;
To frame God's image as his worths required
His might, his skill, his word and will conspired.

All that he had his image should present,
All that it should present it could afford,   20
To that he could afford his will was bent,
His will was followed with performing word.
Let this suffice, by this conceive the rest,—
He should, he could, he would, he did, the best.

Love's servile lot

Love mistress is of many minds
    Yet few know whom they
      serve;
They reckon least how little love
    Their service doth deserve.

The will she robbeth from the wit,

    The sense from reason's lore;
She is delightful in the rind,
    Corrupted in the core.

She shroudeth vice in virtue's
    veil,
    Pretending much good will,   10

She off'reth joy, affordeth grief,
  A kiss where she doth kill.

A honey-shower rains from her
    lips,
  Sweet lights shine in her face;
She hath the blush of virgin mild,
  The mind of viper's race.

She makes thee seek yet fear to
    find,
  To find but not enjoy;
In many frowns some gliding
    smiles
  She yields—to more annoy. 20

She woos thee to come near the
    fire
  Yet doth she draw it from
    thee;
Far off she makes thy heart to
    fry
  And yet to freeze within thee.

She letteth fall some luring baits
  For fools to gather up;
To sweet, to sour, to every taste,
  She tempereth her cup.

Soft souls she binds in tender
    twist,
  Small flies in spinner's web; 30
She sets afloat some luring streams
  But makes them soon to ebb.

Her watery eyes have burning
    force,
  Her floods and flames conspire;
Tears kindle sparks, sobs fuel are,
  And sighs do blow her fire.

May never was the month of love
  For May is full of flowers,
But rather April, wet by kind,
  For love is full of showers. 40

Like tyrant cruel wounds she
    gives,
  Like surgeon salve she lends,
But salve and sore have equal
    force,
  For death is both their ends.

With soothing words enthrallëd
    souls
  She chains in servile bands;
Her eye in silence hath a speech
  Which eye best understands.

Her little sweet hath many sours;
  Short hap, immortal harms; 50
Her loving looks are murd'ring
    darts,
  Her songs, bewitching charms.

Like winter rose and summer ice
  Her joys are still untimely;
Before her, hope; behind, re-
    morse;
  Fair first, in fine unseemly.

Moods, passions, fancies, jealous
    fits
  Attend upon her train;
She yieldeth rest without repose,
  A heaven in hellish pain. 60

Her house is sloth, her door de-
    ceit,
  And slippery hope her stairs;
Unbashful boldness bids her
    guests
  And every vice repairs.

Her diet is of such delights
  As please till they be past,
But then the poison kills the heart
  That did entice the taste.

Her sleep in sin doth end in
    wrath,
  Remorse rings her awake; 70
Death calls her up, shame drives
    her out,
  Despairs her upshot make.

Plow not the seas, sow not the
        sands,
Leave off your idle pain;

Seek other mistress for your
        minds,
Love's service is in vain.

FROM *St. Peter's Complaint, newly augmented*, [c. 1605]

New prince, new pomp

Behold, a seely tender babe
    In freezing winter night
In homely manger trembling
        lies,—
    Alas, a piteous sight!
The inns are full, no man will
        yield
    This little pilgrim bed,
But forced he is with seely beasts
    In crib to shroud his head.
Despise him not for lying there,
    First, what he is enquire,   10
An orient pearl is often found
    In depth of dirty mire.
Weigh not his crib, his wooden
        dish,
    Nor beasts that by him feed;

Weigh not his mother's poor at-
        tire,
    Nor Joseph's simple weed.
This stable is a prince's court,
    This crib his chair of state,
The beasts are parcel of his pomp,
    The wooden dish his plate.   20
The persons in that poor attire
    His royal liveries wear;
The prince himself is come from
        heaven—
    This pomp is prizèd there.
With joy approach, O Christian
        wight,
    Do homage to thy king;
And highly prize his humble
        pomp
    Which he from heaven doth
        bring.

The burning babe

As I in hoary winter's night stood shivering in the snow,
Surprised I was with sudden heat which made my heart to glow;
And lifting up a fearful eye to view what fire was near,
A pretty babe all burning bright did in the air appear;
Who, scorchèd with excessive heat, such floods of tears did shed
As though his floods should quench his flames which with his tears were
        fed.
Alas, quoth he, but newly born in fiery heats I fry,
Yet none approach to warm their hearts or feel my fire but I!
My faultless breast the furnace is, the fuel wounding thorns,
Love is the fire, and sighs the smoke, the ashes shame and scorns;   10
The fuel justice layeth on, and mercy blows the coals,
The metal in this furnace wrought are men's defilèd souls,
For which, as now on fire I am to work them to their good,
So will I melt into a bath to wash them in my blood.
With this he vanished out of sight and swiftly shrunk away,
And straight I callèd unto mind that it was Christmas day.

RICHARD BARNFIELD

The Introduction and Notes are at page 1233

FROM *Cynthia*, 1595

To his mistress

Bright star of beauty, fairest fair alive,
Rare president of peerless chastity,
(In whom the Muses and the Graces strive,
Which shall possess the chiefest part of thee)
O let these simple lines accepted be,
    Which here I offer at thy sacred shrine,
    Sacred, because sweet beauty is divine.

And though I cannot please each curious ear
With sugared notes of heavenly harmony,
Yet if my love shall to thy self appear,   10
No other muse I will invoke but thee;
And if thou wilt my fair Thalia be,
    I'll sing sweet hymns and praises to thy name
    In that clear temple of eternal fame.

But ah, alas, how can mine infant muse,
That never heard of Helicon before,
Perform my promise past, when they refuse
Poor shepherds' plaints? Yet will I still adore
Thy sacred name, although I write no more;
    Yet hope I shall, if this accepted be,   20
    If not, in silence sleep eternally.

FROM *Poems in Divers Humors*, published with *The Encomion of
Lady Pecunia*, 1598

To his friend Master R. L., in praise of music and poetry

If music and sweet poetry agree,
As they must needs (the sister and the brother),
Then must the love be great 'twixt thee and me,
    Because thou lov'st the one, and I the other.
    Dowland to thee is dear, whose heavenly touch
Upon the lute doth ravish human sense;
Spenser to me, whose deep conceit is such
    As, passing all conceit, needs no defence.
    Thou lov'st to hear the sweet melodious sound

That Phœbus' lute (the queen of music) makes;
And I in deep delight am chiefly drowned
    Whenas himself to singing he betakes.
      One god is god of both (as poets feign),
      One knight loves both, and both in thee remain.

        10

Against the dispraisers of poetry

  Chaucer is dead; and Gower lies in grave;
The Earl of Surrey long ago is gone;
Sir Philip Sidney's soul the heavens have;
George Gascoigne him before was tombed in stone.
  Yet, though their bodies lie full low in ground,
As every thing must die that erst was born,
Their living fame no fortune can confound,
Nor ever shall their labors be forlorn.
  And you, that discommend sweet poetry,
(So that the subject of the same be good)
Here may you see your fond simplicity,
Sith kings have favored it, of royal blood.
  The King of Scots (now living) is a poet,
As his *Lepanto* and his *Furies* show it.

        10

A remembrance of some English poets

Live, Spenser, ever in thy *Fairy Queen*,
Whose like, for deep conceit, was never seen.
Crowned mayst thou be, unto thy more renown,
As king of poets, with a laurel crown.

And Daniel, praisëd for thy sweet-chaste verse,
Whose fame is graved on Rosamond's black hearse,
Still mayst thou live; and still be honorëd
For that rare work, *The White Rose and the Red*.

And Drayton, whose well-written tragedies
And sweet epistles soar thy fame to skies,
Thy learned name is equal with the rest,
Whose stately numbers are so well addressed.

        10

And Shakespeare, thou whose honey-flowing vein,
Pleasing the world, thy praises doth obtain;
Whose *Venus* and whose *Lucrece*, sweet and chaste,
Thy name in fame's immortal book have placed:
    Live ever you, at least in fame live ever;
    Well may the body die, but fame dies never.

An ode

As it fell upon a day
In the merry month of May,
Sitting in a pleasant shade
Which a grove of myrtles made,
Beasts did leap and birds did sing,
Trees did grow and plants did spring;
Every thing did banish moan,
Save the nightingale alone.
She, poor bird, as all forlorn,
Leaned her breast up-till a thorn   10
And there sung the doleful'st ditty,
That to hear it was great pity.
Fie, fie, fie, now would she cry,
Teru, teru, by and by;
That to hear her so complain,
Scarce I could from tears refrain;
For her griefs so lively shown
Made me think upon mine own.
Ah, thought I, thou mourn'st in vain;
None takes pity on thy pain;   20
Senseless trees, they cannot hear thee;
Ruthless bears, they will not cheer thee.
King Pandion, he is dead,
All thy friends are lapped in lead.
All thy fellow birds do sing,
Careless of thy sorrowing.

Whilst as fickle fortune smiled,
Thou and I were both beguiled.
Every one that flatters thee
Is no friend in misery: 30
Words are easy, like the wind,
Faithful friends are hard to find;
Every man will be thy friend
Whilst thou hast wherewith to spend,
But if store of crowns be scant,
No man will supply thy want.
If that one be prodigal,
Bountiful they will him call;
And with such-like flattering
Pity but he were a king.   40
If he be addict to vice,
Quickly him they will entice;
If to women he be bent,
They have at commandëment;
But if fortune once do frown,
Then farewell his great renown;
They that fawned on him before
Use his company no more.
He that is thy friend indeed
He will help thee in thy need: 50
If thou sorrow, he will weep;
If thou wake, he cannot sleep;
Thus of every grief, in heart,
He with thee doth bear a part.
These are certain signs to know
Faithful friend from flatt'ring foe.

FROM JOHN BODENHAM'S (?) *England's Helicon,* 1600
The unknown shepherd's complaint

My flocks feed not, my ewes breed not,
My rams speed not, all is amiss;
Love is denying, faith is defying,
Heart's renying, causer of this.
All my merry jigs are quite forgot,
All my lady's love is lost, God wot;
Where her faith was firmly fixed in love,
There a nay is placed without remove.

One silly cross wrought all my loss, 10
O frowning fortune, cursed fickle dame,
For now I see inconstancy
More in women than in men remain.

In black mourn I, all fears scorn I,
Love hath forlorn me, living in thrall;
Heart is bleeding, all help needing,
Oh, cruel speeding, fraughted with gall.
My shepherd's pipe can sound no deal,
My wether's bell rings doleful knell.
My curtail dog that wont to have played
Plays not at all, but seems afraid; 20
 With sighs so deep, procures to weep
 In howling wise to see my doleful plight:
 How sighs resound through heartless ground
 Like a thousand vanquished men in bloody fight.

Clear wells spring not, sweet birds sing not,
Green plants bring not forth their dye;
Herds stand weeping, flocks all sleeping,
Nymphs back peeping fearfully.
All our pleasure known to us poor swains,
All our merry meeting on the plains, 30
All our evening sports from us are fled,
All our love is lost, for love is dead.
 Farewell, sweet love, thy like ne'er was
 For sweet content, the cause of all my moan.
 Poor Coridon must live alone,—
 Other help for him I see that there is none.

SAMUEL DANIEL

The Introduction and Notes are at pages 1234 and 1275

FROM *Delia*, 1594

To the Right Honorable, the Lady Mary, Countess of Pembroke

Wonder of these! glory of other times!
 O thou whom envy ev'n is forced t' admire!
Great patroness of these my humble rhymes,
 Which thou from out thy greatness dost inspire!
Sith only thou hast deigned to raise them higher,

Vouchsafe now to accept them as thine own,
Begotten by thy hand and my desire,
Wherein my zeal and thy great might is shown;
And seeing this unto the world is known,
O leave not still to grace thy work in me.   10
Let not the quick'ning seed be overthrown,
Of that which may be born to honor thee;
Whereof the travail I may challenge mine,
But yet the glory, madam, must be thine.

FROM *The Whole Works,* 1623

To Delia

Fair is my love, and cruel as she's fair:
Her brow shades frowns, although her eyes are sunny,
Her smiles are lightning, though her pride despair,
And her disdains are gall, her favors honey.
A modest maid, decked with a blush of honor,
Whose feet do tread green paths of youth and love;
The wonder of all eyes that look upon her,
Sacred on earth, designed a saint above.
Chastity and beauty, which were deadly foes,
Live reconcilëd friends within her brow;   10
And had she pity to conjoin with those,
Then who had heard the plaints I utter now?
For had she not been fair and thus unkind,
My muse had slept, and none had known my mind.

Why should I sing in verse, why should I frame
These sad neglected notes for her dear sake?
Why should I offer up unto her name
The sweetest sacrifice my youth can make?
Why should I strive to make her live forever,
That never deigns to give me joy to live?
Why should m' afflicted muse so much endeavor
Such honor unto cruelty to give?
If her defects have purchased her this fame,
What should her virtues do, her smiles, her love?   10
If this her worst, how should her best inflame?
What passions would her milder favors move?
Favors, I think, would sense quite overcome,
And that makes happy lovers ever dumb.

Look, Delia, how w' esteem the half-blown rose,
The image of thy blush and summer's honor,
Whilst yet her tender bud doth undisclose

That full of beauty time bestows upon her.
No sooner spreads her glory in the air
    But straight her wide-blown pomp comes to decline;
    She then is scorned that late adorned the fair;
    So fade the roses of those cheeks of thine.
No April can revive thy withered flowers,
    Whose springing grace adorns the glory now;   10
    Swift speedy time, feathered with flying hours,
    Dissolves the beauty of the fairest brow.
Then do not thou such treasure waste in vain,
But love now whilst thou mayst be loved again.

But love whilst that thou mayst be loved again,
    Now whilst thy May hath filled thy lap with flowers,
    Now whilst thy beauty bears without a stain;
    Now use the summer smiles ere winter lours.
And whilst thou spread'st unto the rising sun
    The fairest flower that ever saw the light,
    Now joy thy time before thy sweet be done;
    And, Delia, think thy morning must have night,
And that thy brightness sets at length to west,
    When thou wilt close up that which now thou show'st,   10
    And think the same becomes thy fading best,
    Which then shall most inveil and shadow most.
Men do not weigh the stalk for that it was,
When once they find her flower, her glory, pass.

When men shall find thy flower, thy glory, pass,
    And thou with careful brow sitting alone,
    Receivèd hast this message from thy glass,
    That tells the truth and says that all is gone;
Fresh shalt thou see in me the wounds thou mad'st,
    Though spent thy flame, in me the heat remaining;
    I that have loved thee thus before thou fad'st,
    My faith shall wax when thou art in thy waning.
The world shall find this miracle in me,
    That fire can burn when all the matter's spent;   10
    Then what my faith hath been, thyself shall see,
    And that thou wast unkind, thou mayst repent.
Thou mayst repent that thou hast scorned my tears,
When winter snows upon thy sable hairs.

When winter snows upon thy sable hairs,
    And frost of age hath nipped thy beauties near,
    When dark shall seem thy day that never clears,
    And all lies withered that was held so dear,

Then take this picture which I here present thee,
　　Limned with a pencil not all unworthy;
　　Here see the gifts that God and nature lent thee,
　　Here read thyself and what I suffered for thee.
This may remain thy lasting monument,
　　Which happily posterity may cherish;
　　These colors with thy fading are not spent,
　　These may remain when thou and I shall perish.
If they remain, then thou shalt live thereby;
They will remain, and so thou canst not die.

Thou canst not die whilst any zeal abound
　　In feeling hearts that can conceive these lines;
　　Though thou, a Laura, hast no Petrarch found,
　　In base attire yet clearly beauty shines.
And I, though born within a colder clime,
　　Do feel mine inward heat as great (I know it),
　　He never had more faith, although more rhyme;
　　I love as well, though he could better show it.
But I may add one feather to thy fame,
　　To help her flight throughout the fairest isle,
　　And if my pen could more enlarge thy name,
　　Then shouldst thou live in an immortal style.
For though that Laura better limnèd be,
Suffice, thou shalt be loved as well as she.

Most fair and lovely maid, look from the shore,
　　See thy Leander striving in these waves,
　　Poor soul, quite spent, whose force can do no more;
　　Now send forth hope, for now calm pity saves,
And waft him to thee with these lovely eyes,
　　A happy convoy to a holy land.
　　Now show thy power and where thy virtue lies;
　　To save thine own, stretch out the fairest hand.
Stretch out the fairest hand, a pledge of peace,
　　That hand that darts so right and never misses;
　　I shall forget old wrongs, my griefs shall cease;
　　And that which gave me wounds, I'll give it kisses,
Once let the ocean of my cares find shore,
That thou be pleased, and I may sigh no more.

Beauty, sweet love, is like the morning dew,
　　Whose short refresh upon the tender green
　　Cheers for a time, but till the sun doth shew,
　　And straight 'tis gone as it had never been.
Soon doth it fade that makes the fairest flourish,

Short is the glory of the blushing rose;
The hue which thou so carefully dost nourish,
Yet which at length thou must be forced to lose,
When thou, surcharged with the burthen of thy years,
Shalt bend thy wrinkles homeward to the earth,
And that in beauty's iease expired appears
The date of age, the kalends of our death.
But ah! no more, this must not be foretold,
For women grieve to think they must be old.

Care-charmer sleep, son of the sable night,
Brother to death, in silent darkness born,
Relieve my languish and restore the light;
With dark forgetting of my care, return.
And let the day be time enough to mourn
The shipwreck of my ill-adventured youth;
Let waking eyes suffice to wail their scorn
Without the torment of the night's untruth.
Cease, dreams, th' images of day-desires,
To model forth the passions of the morrow;
Never let rising sun approve you liars,
To add more grief to aggravate my sorrow.
Still let me sleep, embracing clouds in vain,
And never wake to feel the day's disdain.

Let others sing of knights and paladins
In agëd accents and untimely words,
Paint shadows in imaginary lines
Which well the reach of their high wits records;
But I must sing of thee, and those fair eyes
Authentic shall my verse in time to come,
When yet th' unborn shall say, Lo where she lies,
Whose beauty made him speak that else was dumb.
These are the arks, the trophies I erect,
That fortify thy name against old age;
And these thy sacred virtues must protect
Against the dark and time's consuming rage.
Though th' error of my youth in them appear,
Suffice, they show I lived and loved thee dear.

None other fame mine unambitious muse
Affected ever but t' eternize thee;
All other honors do my hopes refuse,
Which meaner prized and momentary be.
For God forbid I should my papers blot
With mercenary lines, with servile pen,

Praising virtues in them that have them not,
 Basely attending on the hopes of men.
No, no, my verse respects nor Thames nor theaters,
 Nor seeks it to be known unto the great;
 But Avon, poor in fame and poor in waters,
 Shall have my song, where Delia hath her seat.
Avon shall be my Thames and she my song;
No other prouder brooks shall hear my wrong.

Lo, here the impost of a faith entire,
 Which love doth pay and her disdain extorts;
Behold the message of a chaste desire
 Which tells the world how much my grief imports.
These tributary passions, beauty's due,
 I send those eyes, the cabinets of love,
That cruelty herself might grieve to view
 Th' affliction her unkind disdain doth move,
And how I live, cast down from off all mirth,
 Pensive, alone, only but with despair;
My joys, abortive, perish in their birth;
 My griefs long lived, and care succeeding care.
This is my state, and Delia's heart is such;
I say no more, I fear I said too much.

An ode

Now each creature joys the other,
 Passing happy days and hours;
One bird reports unto another
 In the fall of silver showers,
Whilst the earth, our common
    mother,
 Hath her bosom decked with
    flowers.

Whilst the greatest torch of heaven
 With bright rays warms Flora's
    lap,
Making nights and days both even,
 Cheering plants with fresher
    sap;
My field of flowers quite bereaven
 Wants refresh of better hap.

Echo, daughter of the air,
 Babbling guest of rocks and
    hills,
Knows the name of my fierce fair,
 And sounds the accents of my
    ills.
Each thing pities my despair,
 Whilst that she her lover kills;

Whilst that she, oh, cruel maid!
 Doth me and my love de-
    spise;
My life's flourish is decayed,
 That depended on her eyes.
But her will must be obeyed,
 And well he ends for love who
    dies.

The complaint of Rosamond

Out from the horror of infernal deeps
My poor afflicted ghost comes here to plain it,

Attended with my shame that never sleeps,
The spot wherewith my kind and youth did stain it;
My body found a grave where to contain it,
    A sheet could hide my face, but not my sin,
    For fame finds never tomb t' inclose it in.

And which is worse, my soul is now denied
Her transport to the sweet Elysian rest,
The joyful bliss for ghosts repurified,
The ever-springing gardens of the blest;
Charon denies me waftage with the rest,
    And says my soul can never pass the river,
    Till lovers' sighs on earth shall it deliver.

So shall I never pass, for how should I
Procure this sacrifice amongst the living?
Time hath long since worn out the memory
Both of my life and life's unjust depriving;
Sorrow for me is dead for aye reviving.
    Rosamond hath little left her but her name,
    And that disgraced, for time hath wronged the same.

No muse suggests the pity of my case;
Each pen doth overpass my just complaint,
Whilst others are preferred, though far more base;
Shore's wife is graced, and passes for a saint;
Her legend justifies her foul attaint.
    Her well-told tale did such compassion find
    That she is passed, and I am left behind.

Which seen with grief, my miserable ghost
(Whilom invested in so fair a veil,
Which whilst it lived was honored of the most,
And being dead, gives matter to bewail)
Comes to solicit thee, whilst others fail,
    To take this task and in thy woeful song
    To form my case and register my wrong.

Although I know thy just lamenting muse,
Toiled in th' affection of thine own distress,
In others' cares hath little time to use,
And therefore mayst esteem of mine the less;
Yet as thy hopes attend happy redress,
    The joys depending on a woman's grace,
    So move thy mind a woeful woman's case.

Delia may hap to deign to read our story,
And offer up her sighs among the rest,
Whose merit would suffice for both our glory,
Whereby thou mightst be graced and I be blest;
That indulgence would profit me the best.
   Such power she hath by whom thy youth is led,
   To joy the living and to bless the dead.

So I, through beauty made the woeful'st wight,   50
By beauty might have comfort after death;
That dying fairest, by the fairest might
Find life above on earth, and rest beneath.
She that can bless us with one happy breath,
   Give comfort to thy muse to do her best,
   That thereby thou mayst joy and I might rest.

Thus said, forthwith moved with a tender care
And pity, which myself could never find,
What she desired my muse deigned to declare,
And therefore willed her boldly tell her mind;   60
And I, more willing, took this charge assigned
   Because her griefs were worthy to be known,
   And telling hers, might hap forget mine own.

Then write, quoth she, the ruin of my youth,
Report the downfall of my slipp'ry state;
Of all my life reveal the simple truth,
To teach to others what I learnt too late.
Exemplify my frailty, tell how fate
   Keeps in eternal dark our fortunes hidden,
   And ere they come, to know them 'tis forbidden.   70

For whilst the sunshine of my fortune lasted,
I joyed the happiest warmth, the sweetest heat
That ever yet imperious beauty tasted;
I had what glory ever flesh could get,
But this fair morning had a shameful set.
   Disgrace darked honor, sin did cloud my brow,
   As note the sequel, and I'll tell thee how.

The blood I stained was good and of the best,
My birth had honor and my beauty fame;
Nature and fortune joined to make me blest,   80
Had I had grace t' have known to use the same.
My education showed from whence I came,
   And all concurred to make me happy first,
   That so great hope might make me more accursed.

Happy lived I whilst parents' eye did guide
The indiscretion of my feeble ways,
And country home kept me from being eyed,
Where best unknown I spent my sweetest days;
Till that my friends mine honor sought to raise
    To higher place, which greater credit yields,   90
    Deeming such beauty was unfit for fields.

From country then to court I was preferred,
From calm to storms, from shore into the deeps;
There where I perished, where my youth first erred;
There where I lost the flower which honor keeps;
There where the worser thrives, the better weeps.
    Ah me, poor wench, on this unhappy shelf
    I grounded me and cast away myself.

There whereas frail and tender beauty stands
With all assaulting powers environèd;   100
Having but prayers and weak feeble hands
To hold their honor's fort unvanquishèd;
There where to stand and be unconquerèd
    Is to b' above the nature of our kind,
    That cannot long for pity be unkind.

For thither comed (when years had armed my youth
With rarest proof of beauty ever seen,
When my reviving eye had learnt the truth
That it had power to make the winter green,
And flower affections whereas none had been),   110
    Soon could I teach my brow to tyrannize,
    And make the world do homage to mine eyes.

For age, I saw (though years with cold conceit
Congealed their thoughts against a warm desire)
Yet sigh their want, and look at such a bait;
I saw how youth was wax before the fire;
I saw by stealth, I framed my look a liar,
    Yet well perceived how fortune made me then
    The envy of my sex, and wonder unto men.

Look how a comet at the first appearing   120
Draws all men's eyes with wonder to behold it;
Or as the saddest tale at sudden hearing
Makes silent list'ning unto him that told it;
So did my speech when rubies did unfold it,
    So did the blazing of my blush appear
    T' amaze the world, that holds such sights so dear.

Ah, beauty! siren! fair enchanting good!
Sweet silent rhetoric of persuading eyes!
Dumb eloquence, whose power doth move the blood
More than the words or wisdom of the wise!   130
Still harmony, whose diapason lies
   Within a brow, the key which passions move
   To ravish sense and play a world in love!

What might I then not do whose power was such?
What cannot women do that know their power?
What woman knows it not (I fear too much)
How bliss or bale lies in their laugh or lour,
Whilst they enjoy their happy blooming flower,
   Whilst nature decks them in their best attires
   Of youth and beauty, which the world admires?   140

Such one was I, my beauty was mine own,
No borrowed blush which bankrupt beauties seek;
That new-found shame, a sin to us unknown,
Th' adulterate beauty of a falsèd cheek,
Vile stain to honor and to women eke,
   Seeing that time our fading must detect,
   Thus with defect to cover our defect.

Impiety of times, chastity's abater,
Falsehood, wherein thyself thyself deniest,
Treason to counterfeit the seal of nature,   150
The stamp of heaven, impressed by the highest,
Disgrace unto the world, to whom thou liest,
   Idol unto thyself, shame to the wise,
   And all that honor thee idolatrize.

Far was that sin from us whose age was pure,
When simple beauty was accounted best,
The time when women had no other lure
But modesty, pure cheeks, a virtuous breast,
This was the pomp wherewith my youth was blest;
   These were the weapons which mine honor won   160
   In all the conflicts which my eyes begun;

Which were not small—I wrought on no mean object;
A crown was at my feet, scepters obeyed me;
Whom fortune made my king, love made my subject;
Who did command the land most humbly prayed me;
Henry the second, that so highly weighed me,
   Found well, by proof, the privilege of beauty,
   That it had power to countermand all duty.

For after all his victories in France,
And all the triumphs of his honor won,   170
Unmatched by sword, was vanquished by a glance,
And hotter wars within his breast begun—
Wars whom whole legions of desires drew on,
   Against all which my chastity contends
   With force of honor, which my shame defends.

     .   .   .   .   .   .

And safe mine honor stood, till that in truth
One of my sex, of place and nature bad,
Was set in ambush to entrap my youth,
One in the habit of like frailty clad,
One who the liv'ry of like weakness had,   180
   A seeming matron, yet a sinful monster,
   As by her words the chaster sort may conster.

She set upon me with the smoothest speech
That court and age could cunningly devise;
Th' one authentic made her fit to teach,
The other learned her how to subtilize.
Both were enough to circumvent the wise,
   A document that well might teach the sage
   That there's no trust in youth, nor hope in age.

     .   .   .   .   .   .

So well the golden balls cast down before me   190
Could entertain my course, hinder my way;
Whereat my wretchless youth, stooping to store me,
Lost me the goal, the glory, and the day.
Pleasure had set my well-schooled thoughts to play,
   And bade me use the virtue of mine eyes,
   For sweetly it fits the fair to wantonize.

Thus wrought to sin, soon was I trained from court
T' a solitary grange, there to attend
The time the king should thither make resort,
Where he love's long-desirëd work should end.   200
Thither he daily messages doth send,
   With costly jewels, orators of love,
   Which (ah, too well men know) do women move.

The day before the night of my defeature
He greets me with a casket richly wrought,
So rare that art did seem to strive with nature
T' express the cunning workman's curious thought;
The mystery whereof I prying sought,

And found engraven on the lid above
Amymone, how she with Neptune strove.   210

Amymone, old Danaus' fairest daughter,
As she was fetching water all alone
At Lerna, whereas Neptune came and caught her,
From whom she strived and struggled to be gone,
Bathing the air with cries and piteous moan;
 But all in vain, with him she's forced to go.
 'Tis shame that men should use poor maidens so.

There might I see describèd how she lay,
At those proud feet not satisfied with prayer;
Wailing her heavy hap, cursing the day,   220
In act so piteous to express despair.
And by how much more grieved, so much more fair;
 Her tears upon her cheeks, poor careful girl,
 Did seem, against the sun, crystal and pearl;

Whose pure clear streams, which lo, so fair appears,
Wrought hotter flames (oh, miracle of love)
That kindles fire in water, heat in tears,
And makes neglected beauty mightier prove,
Teaching afflicted eyes affects to move;
 To show that nothing ill becomes the fair,   230
 But cruelty, which yields unto no prayer.

This having viewed, and therewith something moved,
Figured I find within the other squares
Transformèd Io, Jovè's dearly loved;
In her affliction how she strangely fares,
Strangely distressed (oh beauty, born to cares),
 Turned to a heifer, kept with jealous eyes,
 Always in danger of her hateful spies.

These precedents presented to my view,
Wherein the presage of my fall was shown,   240
Might have forewarned me well what would ensue,
And others' harms have made me shun mine own;
But fate is not prevented, though foreknown,
 For that must hap, decreed by heavenly powers
 Who work our fall yet make the fault still ours.

Witness the world, wherein is nothing rifer
Than miseries unkenned before they come.
Who can the characters of chance decipher,

Written in clouds of our concealèd dome?
Which though perhaps have been revealed to some, 250
  Yet that so doubtful (as success did prove them)
  That men must know they have the heav'ns above them.

I saw the sin wherein my foot was ent'ring,
I saw how that dishonor did attend it,
I saw the shame whereon my flesh was vent'ring,
Yet had I not the power for to defend it.
So weak is sense, when error hath condemned it;
  We see what's good, and thereto we consent,
  But yet we choose the worst, and soon repent.

   .   .   .   .

What greater torment ever could have been, 260
Than to enforce the fair to live retired?
For what is beauty if it be not seen?
Or what is 't to be seen if not admired,
And though admired, unless in love desired?
  Never were cheeks of roses, locks of amber,
  Ordained to live imprisoned in a chamber.

Nature created beauty for the view,
Like as the fire for heat, the sun for light;
The fair do hold this privilege as due
By ancient charter, to live most in sight, 270
And she that is debarred it, hath not right.
  In vain our friends from this do us dehort,
  For beauty will be where is most resort.

Witness the fairest streets that Thames doth visit,
The wondrous concourse of the glitt'ring fair;
For what rare woman decked with beauty is it
That thither covets not to make repair?
The solitary country may not stay her;
  Here is the center of all beauties best,
  Excepting Delia, left t' adorn the west. 280

Here doth the curious with judicial eyes
Contemplate beauty gloriously attired;
And herein all our chiefest glory lies,
To live where we are praised and most desired.
Oh, how we joy to see ourselves admired,
  Whilst niggardly our favors we discover;
  We love to be beloved, yet scorn the lover.

Yet would to God my foot had never moved
From country safety, from the fields of rest,
To know the danger to be highly loved,   290
And live in pomp to brave among the best;
Happy for me, better had I been blest,
  If I unluckily had never strayed,
  But lived at home a happy country maid,

Whose unaffected innocency thinks
No guileful fraud, as doth the courtly liver;
She's decked with truth; the river where she drinks
Doth serve her for her glass, her counsel-giver;
She loves sincerely, and is lovèd ever;
  Her days are peace, and so she ends her breath—   300
  True life, that knows not what's to die till death.

So should I never have been regist'red
In the black book of the unfortunate,
Nor had my name enrolled with maids misled,
Which bought their pleasures at so high a rate;
Nor had I taught, through my unhappy fate,
  This lesson, which myself learnt with expense,
  How most it hurts that most delights the sense.

Shame follows sin, disgrace is duly given,
Impiety will out, never so closely done;   310
No walls can hide us from the eye of heaven,
For shame must end what wickedness begun;
Forth breaks reproach when we least think thereon,
  And this is ever proper unto courts,
  That nothing can be done but fame reports.

Fame doth explore what lies most secret hidden,
Ent'ring the closet of the palace dweller,
Abroad revealing what is most forbidden;
Of truth and falsehood both an equal teller,
'Tis not a guard can serve for to expel her.   320
  The sword of justice cannot cut her wings,
  Nor stop her mouth from utt'ring secret things.

And this our stealth she could not long conceal
From her whom such a forfeit most concerned,
The wrongèd queen, who could so closely deal
That she the whole of all our practice learned,
And watched a time when least it was discerned,

In absence of the king, to wreak her wrong
With such revenge as she desirëd long.

The labyrinth she entered by that thread 330
That served a conduct to my absent lord,
Left there by chance, reserved for such a deed,
Where she surprised me whom she so abhorred.
Enraged with madness, scarce she speaks a word,
But flies with eager fury to my face,
Off'ring me most unwomanly disgrace.

Look how a tigress that hath lost her whelp
Runs fiercely ranging through the woods astray,
And seeing herself deprived of hope or help,
Furiously assaults what's in her way, 340
To satisfy her wrath, not for a prey;
So fell she on me in outrageous wise,
As could disdain and jealousy devise.

And after all her vile reproaches used,
She forced me take the poison she had brought
To end the life that had her so abused,
And free her fears and ease her jealous thought.
No cruelty her wrath could leave unwrought,
No spiteful act that to revenge is common,
No beast being fiercer than a jealous woman. 350

Here take, saith she, thou impudent, unclean,
Base, graceless strumpet, take this next your heart;
Your love-sick heart, that overcharged hath been
With pleasure's surfeit, must be purged with art.
This potion hath a power that will convert
To nought those humors that oppress you so;
And, girl, I'll see you take it ere I go.

What, stand you now amazed, retire you back?
Tremble you, minion? Come, dispatch with speed;
There is no help, your champion now you lack, 360
And all these tears you shed will nothing stead;
Those dainty fingers needs must do the deed.
Take it, or I will drench you else by force,
And trifle not, lest that I use you worse.

Having this bloody doom from hellish breath,
My woeful eyes on every side I cast,
Rigor about me, in my hand my death,

Presenting me the horror of my last,
All hope of pity and of comfort past.
No means, no power, no forces to contend, 370
My trembling hands must give myself my end.

Those hands that beauty's ministers had been,
They must give death, that me adorned of late;
That mouth that newly gave consent to sin,
Must now receive destruction in thereat;
That body which my lust did violate,
    Must sacrifice itself t' appease the wrong:
    So short is pleasure, glory lasts not long.

And she no sooner saw I had it taken,
But forth she rushes, proud with victory, 380
And leaves m' alone, of all the world forsaken,
Except of death, which she had left with me;
Death and myself alone together be,
    To whom she did her full revenge refer;
    Oh, poor weak conquest, both for him and her.

Then straight my conscience summons up my sin
T' appear before me in a hideous face;
Now doth the terror of my soul begin,
When ev'ry corner of that hateful place
Dictates mine error and reveals disgrace; 390
    Whilst I remain oppressed in every part,
    Death in my body, horror at my heart.

Down on my bed my loathsome self I cast,
The bed that likewise gives in evidence
Against my soul, and tells I was unchaste,
Tells I was wanton, tells I followed sense;
And therefore cast by guilt of mine offence,
    Must here the right of heaven needs satisfy,
    And where I wanton lay, must wretched die.

Here I began to wail my hard mishap, 400
My sudden, strange, unlooked-for misery;
Accusing them that did my youth entrap,
To give me such a fall of infamy.
And, Poor distressèd Rosamond, said I,
    Is this thy glory got, to die forlorn
    In deserts where no ear can hear thee mourn?

Nor any eye of pity to behold
The woeful end of my sad tragedy?
But that thy wrongs unseen, thy tale untold,
Must here in secret silence buried lie,   410
And with thee thine excuse together die.
  Thy sin revealed, but thy repentance hid,
  Thy shame alive, but dead what thy death did.

．　　．　　．　　．　　．

This, and much more, I would have uttered then,
A testament to be recorded still,
Signed with my blood, subscribed with conscience' pen,
To warn the fair and beautiful from ill.
Though I could wish, by th' example of my will,
  I had not left this note unto the fair,
  But died intestate to have had no heir.   420

But now the poison spread through all my veins
Gan dispossess my living senses quite,
And nought-respecting death, the last of pains,
Placed his pale colors, th' ensign of his might,
Upon his new-got spoil before his right;
  Thence chased my soul, setting my day ere noon,
  When I least thought my joys could end so soon.

And as conveyed t' untimely funerals,
My scarce-cold corpse not suffered longer stay,
Behold, the king, by chance returning, falls   430
T' encounter with the same upon the way,
As he repaired to see his dearest joy;
  Not thinking such a meeting could have been,
  To see his love, and seeing been unseen.

Judge those whom chance deprives of sweetest treasure,
What 'tis to lose a thing we hold so dear,
The best delight wherein our soul takes pleasure,
The sweet of life, that penetrates so near.
What passions feels that heart, enforced to bear
  The deep impression of so strange a sight   440
  That overwhelms us, or confounds us quite?

Amazed he stands, nor voice nor body steers,
Words had no passage, tears no issue found,
For sorrow shut up words, wrath kept in tears;
Confused affects each other do confound,
Oppressed with grief his passions had no bound.

Striving to tell his woes, words would not come,
For light cares speak, when mighty griefs are dumb.

At length extremity breaks out a way,
Through which th' imprisoned voice with tears attended   450
Wails out a sound that sorrows do bewray,
With arms a-cross and eyes to heaven bended,
Vaporing out sighs that to the skies ascended—
    Sighs, the poor ease calamity affords,
    Which serve for speech when sorrow wanteth words.

O heavens, quoth he, why do mine eyes behold
The hateful rays of this unhappy sun?
Why have I light to see my sins controlled,
With blood of mine own shame thus vilely done?
How can my sight endure to look thereon?   460
    Why doth not black eternal darkness hide
    That from mine eyes my heart cannot abide?

What saw my life wherein my soul might joy?
What had my days, whom troubles still afflicted,
But only this to counterpoise annoy?
This joy, this hope, which death hath interdicted;
This sweet, whose loss hath all distress inflicted;
    This, that did season all my sour of life,
    Vexed still at home with broils, abroad in strife.

Vexed still at home with broils, abroad in strife,   470
Dissension in my blood, jars in my bed,
Distrust at board, suspecting still my life,
Spending the night in horror, days in dread:
Such life hath tyrants, and this life I led.
    These miseries go masked in glittering shows,
    Which wise men see, the vulgar little knows.

Thus as these passions do him overwhelm,
He draws him near my body to behold it;
And as the vine married unto the elm
With strict embraces, so doth he enfold it;   480
And as he in his careful arms doth hold it,
    Viewing the face that even death commends,
    On senseless lips millions of kisses spends.

Pitiful mouth, saith he, that living gavest
The sweetest comfort that my soul could wish,
Oh, be it lawful now, that dead thou havest

This sorrowful farewell of a dying kiss;
And you, fair eyes, containers of my bliss,
   Motives of love, born to be matchëd never,
   Entombed in your sweet circles, sleep forever.   490

Ah, how methinks I see death dallying seeks
To entertain itself in love's sweet place;
Decayëd roses of discolored cheeks
Do yet retain dear notes of former grace,
And ugly death sits fair within her face;
   Sweet remnants resting of vermilion red,
   That death itself doubts whether she be dead.

Wonder of beauty, O receive these plaints,
These obsequies, the last that I shall make thee;
For lo, my soul that now already faints,   500
That loved thee living, dead will not forsake thee,
Hastens her speedy course to overtake thee.
   I'll meet my death, and free myself thereby,
   For, ah, what can he do that cannot die?

Yet ere I die, this much my soul doth vow,
Revenge shall sweeten death with ease of mind,
And I will cause posterity shall know
How fair thou wert above all women-kind,
And after-ages monuments shall find
   Showing thy beauty's title, not thy name,   510
   Rose of the world, that sweetened so the same.

This said, though more desirous yet to say,
For sorrow is unwilling to give over,
He doth repress what grief would else bewray,
Lest he too much his passions should discover;
And yet respect scarce bridles such a lover,
   So far transported that he knows not whither,
   For love and majesty dwell ill together.

Then were my funerals not long deferred,
But done with all the rites pomp could devise,   520
At Godstow, where my body was interred,
And richly tombed in honorable wise,
Where yet as now scarce any note descries
   Unto these times the memory of me,
   Marble and brass so little lasting be.

    .   .   .   .   .   .

But here an end, I may no longer stay,
I must return t' attend at Stygian flood;
Yet ere I go, this one word more I pray,
Tell Delia now her sigh may do me good,
And will her note the frailty of our blood;   530
   And if I pass unto those happy banks,
   Then she must have her praise, thy pen her thanks.

So vanished she, and left me to return
To prosecute the tenor of my woes,
Eternal matter for my muse to mourn;
But yet the world hath heard too much of those,
My youth such errors must no more disclose.
   I'll hide the rest, and grieve for what hath been;
   Who made me known must make me live unseen.

To the Lady Margaret, Countess of Cumberland

He that of such a height hath built his mind,
And reared the dwelling of his thoughts so strong
As neither fear nor hope can shake the frame
Of his resolvèd powers, nor all the wind
Of vanity or malice pierce to wrong
His settled peace, or to disturb the same,
   What a fair seat hath he, from whence he may
   The boundless wastes and wilds of man survey.

And with how free an eye doth he look down
Upon these lower regions of turmoil   10
Where all the storms of passions mainly beat
On flesh and blood; where honor, power, renown,
Are only gay afflictions, golden toil,
Where greatness stands upon as feeble feet
   As frailty doth, and only great doth seem
   To little minds, who do it so esteem.

He looks upon the mightiest monarchs' wars
But only as on stately robberies,
Where evermore the fortune that prevails
Must be the right, the ill-succeeding mars   20
The fairest and the best-faced enterprise;
The great pirate, Pompey, lesser pirates quails.
   Justice, he sees, as if seducèd, still
   Conspires with power, whose cause must not be ill.

He sees the face of right t' appear as manifold
As are the passions of uncertain man,

Who puts it in all colors, all attires,
To serve his ends and make his courses hold;
He sees that let deceit work what it can,
Plot and contrive base ways to high desires,   30
That the all-guiding Providence doth yet
All disappoint, and mocks this smoke of wit.

Nor is he moved with all the thunder-cracks
Of tyrants' threats, or with the surly brow
Of power, that proudly sits on others' crimes,
Charged with more crying sins than those he checks;
The storms of sad confusion that may grow
Up in the present, for the coming times,
Appal not him, that hath no side at all
But of himself, and knows the worst can fall.   40

Although his heart, so near allied to earth,
Cannot but pity the perplexëd state
Of troublous and distressed mortality,
That thus make way unto the ugly birth
Of their own sorrows, and do still beget
Affliction upon imbecility;
Yet seeing thus the course of things must run,
He looks thereon, not strange, but as foredone.

And whilst distraught ambition compasses
And is encompassed, whilst as craft deceives   50
And is deceived, whilst man doth ransack man,
And builds on blood, and rises by distress,
And th' inheritance of desolation leaves
To great-expecting hopes, he looks thereon
As from the shore of peace with unwet eye,
And bears no venture in impiety.

Thus, madam, fares that man that hath prepared
A rest for his desires, and sees all things
Beneath him, and hath learned this book of man,
Full of the notes of frailty, and compared   60
The best of glory with her sufferings,
By whom I see you labor all you can
To plant your heart, and set your thoughts as near
His glorious mansion as your powers can bear;

Which, madam, are so soundly fashionëd
By that clear judgment that hath carried you
Beyond the feeble limits of your kind,

As they can stand against the strongest head
Passion can make, inured to any hue
The world can cast, that cannot cast that mind   70
Out of her form of goodness, that doth see
Both what the best and worst of earth can be.

Which makes that, whatsoever here befalls,
You in the region of yourself remain,
Where no vain breath of th' impudent molests;
That hath secured within the brazen walls
Of a clear conscience that without all stain
Rises in peace, in innocency rests,
Whilst all what malice from without procures
Shows her own ugly heart, but hurts not yours.   80

And whereas none rejoice more in revenge
Than women use to do, yet you well know
That wrong is better checked by being contemned
Than being pursued, leaving to him t' avenge
To whom it appertains; wherein you show
How worthily your clearness hath condemned
Base malediction, living in the dark,
That at the rays of goodness still doth bark.

Knowing the heart of man is set to be
The center of this world, about the which   90
These revolutions of disturbances
Still roll, where all th' aspects of misery
Predominate, whose strong effects are such
As he must bear, being powerless to redress;
And that unless above himself he can
Erect himself, how poor a thing is man!

And how turmoiled they are that level lie
With earth, and cannot lift themselves from thence;
That never are at peace with their desires,
But work beyond their years, and even deny   100
Dotage her rest, and hardly will dispense
With death; that when ability expires,
Desire lives still, so much delight they have
To carry toil and travail to the grave.

Whose ends you see, and what can be the best
They reach unto, when they have cast the sum
And reckonings of their glory, and you know
This floating life hath but this port of rest—

A heart prepared, that fears no ill to come.
And that man's greatness rests but in his show,   110
The best of all whose days consumèd are
Either in war, or peace conceiving war.

This concord, madam, of a well-tuned mind
Hath been so set by that all-working hand
Of heaven, that though the world hath done his worst
To put it out by discords most unkind,
Yet doth it still in perfect union stand
With God and man, nor ever will be forced
From that most sweet accord, but still agree,
Equal in fortunes in equality.   120

And this note, madam, of your worthiness
Remains recorded in so many hearts,
As time nor malice cannot wrong your right
In th' inheritance of fame you must possess;
You that have built you by your great deserts,
Out of small means, a far more exquisite
And glorious dwelling for your honored name
Than all the gold that leaden minds can frame.

To the Lady Lucy, Countess of Bedford

Though virtue be the same when low she stands
    In th' humble shadows of obscurity,
    As when she either sweats in martial bands
Or sits in court clad with authority,
    Yet, madam, doth the strictness of her room
    Greatly detract from her ability;
For, as in-walled within a living tomb
    Her hands and arms of action labor not,
    Her thoughts, as if abortive from the womb,
Come never born, though happily begot.   10
But where she hath mounted in open sight,
    An eminent and spacious dwelling got,
    Where she may stir at will and use her might,
There is she more herself, and more her own;
    There in the fair attire of honor dight
    She sits at ease and makes her glory known;
Applause attends her hands, her deeds have grace;
    Her worth, new-born, is straight as if full grown.
    With such a godly and respected face
Doth virtue look, that's set to look from high,   20
    And such a fair advantage by her place

Hath state and greatness to do worthily.
And therefore well did your high fortunes meet
  With her, that gracing you, comes graced thereby;
  And well was let into a house so sweet,
So good, so fair, so fair, so good a guest,
  Who now remains as blessed in her seat,
  As you are with her residency blest.
And this fair course of knowledge whereunto
  Your studies, learned lady, are addressed,   30
  Is th' only certain way that you can go
Unto true glory, to true happiness;
  All passages on earth besides are so
  Encumbered with such vain disturbances
As still we lose our rest in seeking it,
  Being but deluded with appearances;
  And no key had you else that was so fit
T' unlock that prison of your sex as this,
  To let you out of weakness, and admit
  Your powers into the freedom of that bliss   40
That sets you there where you may oversee
  This rolling world, and view it as it is,
  And apprehend how th' outsides do agree
With th' inward, being of the things we deem
  And hold in our ill-cast accounts to be
  Of highest value and of best esteem;
Since all the good we have rests in the mind,
  By whose proportions only we redeem
  Our thoughts from out confusion, and do find
The measure of ourselves and of our powers;   50
  And that all happiness remains confined
  Within the kingdom of this breast of ours,
Without whose bounds all that we look on lies
  In others' jurisdictions, others' powers,
  Out of the circuit of our liberties.
All glory, honor, fame, applause, renown,
  Are not belonging to our royalties,
  But t' others' wills, wherein they're only grown;
And that unless we find us all within,
  We never can without us be our own,   60
  Nor call it right our life that we live in,
But a possession held for others' use,
  That seem to have most interest therein;
  Which we do so dissever, part, traduce,
Let out to custom, fashion, and to show,
  As we enjoy but only the abuse
  And have no other deed at all to show.

How oft are we constrainëd to appear
  With other countenance than that we owe,
  And be ourselves far off, when we are near!   70
How oft are we forced on a cloudy heart
  To set a shining face and make it clear,
  Seeming content to put ourselves apart
To bear a part of others' weaknesses!
  As if we only were composed by art,
  Not nature, and did all our deeds address
T' opinion, not t' a conscience, what is right;
  As framed b' example, not advisedness,
  Into those forms that entertain our sight.
And though books, madam, cannot make this mind   80
  Which we must bring apt to be set aright,
  Yet do they rectify it in that kind,
And touch it so as that it turns that way
  Where judgment lies; and though we cannot find
  The certain place of truth, yet do they stay
And entertain us near about the same,
  And give the soul the best delight that may
  Encheer it most, and most our spirits inflame
To thoughts of glory, and to worthy ends;
  And therefore in a course that best became   90
  The clearness of your heart, and best commends
Your worthy powers, you run the rightest way
  That is on earth, that can true glory give,
  By which, when all consumes, your fame shall live.

Musophilus
Containing a general defence of all learning

Philocosmus.

Fond man, Musophilus, that thus dost spend
In an ungainful art thy dearest days,
Tiring thy wits and toiling to no end
But to attain that idle smoke of praise,
Now when this busy world cannot attend
Th' untimely music of neglected lays:
  Other delights than these, other desires,
  This wiser profit-seeking age requires.

Musophilus.

Friend Philocosmus, I confess indeed
I love this sacred art thou set'st so light,
And though it never stand my life in steed,   10

It is enough it gives myself delight
  The whiles my unafflicted mind doth feed
  On no unholy thoughts for benefit.
Be it that my unseasonable song
  Come out of time, that fault is in the time,
  And I must not do virtue so much wrong
  As love her aught the worse for other's crime;
  And yet I find some blessed spirits among
  That cherish me, and like and grace my rhyme.   20
Again, that I do more in soul esteem
  Than all the gain of dust the world doth crave;
  And if I may attain but to redeem
  My name from dissolution and the grave,
  I shall have done enough, and better deem
  T' have lived to be, than to have died to have.
Short-breathed mortality would yet extend
  That span of life so far forth as it may,
  And rob her fate, seek to beguile her end
  Of some few ling'ring days of after-stay,   30
  That all this little all might not descend
  Into the dark a universal prey;
  And give our labors yet this poor delight,
  That when our days do end they are not done;
  And though we die, we shall not perish quite,
  But live two lives, where other have but one.

Philocosmus.

Silly desires of self-abusing man,
  Striving to gain th' inheritance of air,
  That having done the uttermost he can,
  Leaves yet, perhaps, but beggary to his heir.   40
  All that great purchase of the breath he wan
  Feeds not his race or makes his house more fair.
And what art thou the better, thus to leave
  A multitude of words to small effect,
  Which other times may scorn, and so deceive
  Thy promised name of what thou dost expect?
  Besides, some viperous critic may bereave
  Th' opinion of thy worth for some defect,
And get more reputation of his wit
  By but controlling of some word or sense,   50
  Than thou shalt honor for contriving it,
  With all thy travail, care, and diligence,
  Being learning now enough to contradict
  And censure others with bold insolence.

Besides, so many so confusedly sing,
  Whose diverse discords have the music marred,
  And in contempt that mystery doth bring,
  That he must sing aloud that will be heard;
  And the received opinion of the thing,
  For some unhallowed string that vilely jarred, 60
Hath so unseasoned now the ears of men
  That who doth touch the tenor of that vein
  Is held but vain, and his unreckoned pen
  The title but of levity doth gain—
  A poor, light gain, to recompense their toil
  That thought to get eternity the while.
And therefore, leave the left and outworn course
  Of unregarded ways, and labor how
  To fit the times with what is most in force;
  Be new with men's affections that are new; 70
  Strive not to run an idle counter-course
  Out from the scent of humors men allow.
For, not discreetly to compose our parts
  Unto the frame of men, which we must be,
  Is to put off ourselves, and make our arts
  Rebels to nature and society;
  Whereby we come to bury our deserts
  In th' obscure grave of singularity.

Musophilus.

Do not profane the work of doing well, 80
  Seducëd man, that canst not look so high
  From out that mist of earth, as thou canst tell
  The ways of right which virtue doth descry,
  That overlooks the base contemptibly,
  And low-laid follies of mortality;
Nor mete out truth and right-discerning praise
  By that wrong measure of confusion,
  The vulgar foot that never takes his ways
  By reason, but by imitation,
  Rolling on with the rest, and never weighs 90
  The course which he should go, but what is gone.
Well were it with mankind if what the most
  Did like were best; but ignorance will live
  By others' square, as by example lost,
  And man to man must th' hand of error give
  That none can fall alone, at their own cost,
  And all because men judge not, but believe.
For what poor bounds have they whom but th' earth bounds?

What is their end whereto their care attains,
When the thing got relieves not, but confounds,
Having but travail to succeed their pains? 100
What joy hath he of living, that propounds
Affliction but his end, and grief his gains?
Gath'ring, encroaching, wresting, joining to,
Destroying, building, decking, furnishing,
Repairing, alt'ring, and so much ado
To his soul's toil and body's travailing,—
And all this doth he, little knowing who
Fortune ordains to have th' inheriting.
And his fair house raised high in envy's eye,
Whose pillars reared, perhaps, on blood and wrong, 110
The spoils and pillage of iniquity,
Who can assure it to continue long?
If rage spared not the walls of piety,
Shall the profanest piles of sin keep strong?
How many proud aspiring palaces
Have we known made the prey of wrath and pride,
Leveled with th' earth, left to forgetfulness
Whilst titlers their pretended rights decide,
Or civil tumults, or an orderless
Order, pretending change of some strong side? 120
Then where is that proud title of thy name?
Written in ice of melting vanity.
Where is thine heir left to possess the same?
Perhaps not so well as in beggary.
Something may rise to be beyond the shame
Of vile and unregarded poverty,
Which I confess, although I often strive
To clothe in the best habit of my skill,
In all the fairest colors I can give,
Yet for all that methinks she looks but ill; 130
I cannot brook that face, which dead-alive
Shows a quick body but a buried will.
Yet oft we see the bars of this restraint
Holds goodness in, which loose wealth would let fly,
And fruitless riches, barrener than want,
Brings forth small worth from idle liberty,
Which when disorders shall again make scant,
It must refetch her state from poverty.
But yet in all this interchange of all,
Virtue, we see, with her fair grace stands fast; 140
For what high races hath there come to fall
With low disgrace, quite vanishëd and past,
Since Chaucer lived, who yet lives, and yet shall,

Though (which I grieve to say) but in his last.
Yet what a time hath he wrested from time
  And won upon the mighty waste of days,
  Unto th' immortal honor of our clime
  That by his means came first adorned with bays;
  Unto the sacred relics of whose rhyme
  We yet are bound in zeal to offer praise.   150
And could our lines, begotten in this age,
  Obtain but such a blessed hand of years,
  And scape the fury of that threat'ning rage
  Which in confusèd clouds ghastly appears,
  Who would not strain his travails to engage
  When such true glory should succeed his cares?
But whereas he came planted in the spring,
  And had the sun before him of respect,
  We, set in th' autumn, in the withering
  And sullen season of a cold defect,   160
  Must taste those sour distastes the times do bring
  Upon the fullness of a cloyed neglect;
Although the stronger constitutions shall
  Wear out th' infection of distempered days,
  And come with glory to outlive this fall,
  Recov'ring of another springing of praise,
  Cleared from th' oppressing humors wherewithal
  The idle multitude surcharge their lays.
Whenas, perhaps, the words thou scornest now
  May live, the speaking picture of the mind,   170
  The extract of the soul that labored how
  To leave the image of herself behind,
  Wherein posterity, that love to know,
  The just proportion of our spirits may find.
For these lines are the veins, the arteries,
  And undecaying life-strings of those hearts
  That still shall pant, and still shall exercise
  The motion, spirit and nature both imparts;
  And shall with those alive so sympathize
  As, nourished with their powers, enjoy their parts.   180
O blessed letters, that combine in one
  All ages past, and make one live with all,
  By you we do confer with who are gone,
  And the dead-living unto council call;
  By you th' unborn shall have communïon
  Of what we feel and what doth us befall.
Soul of the world, knowledge, without thee
  What hath the earth that truly glorious is?
  Why should our pride make such a stir to be,

To be forgot? What good is like to this, 190
To do worthy the writing, and to write
Worthy the reading, and the world's delight?
And let th' unnatural and wayward race,
Born of one womb with us, but to our shame,
That never read t' observe, but to disgrace,
Raise all the tempest of their power to blame;
That puff of folly never can deface
The work a happy genius took to frame.
Yet why should civil learning seek to wound
And mangle her own members with despite? 200
Prodigious wits that study to confound
The life of wit, to seem to know aright,
As if themselves had fortunately found
Some stand from off the earth beyond our sight,
Whence, overlooking all as from above,
Their grace is not to work, but to reprove—
But how came they placed in so high degree,
Above the reach and compass of the rest?
Who hath admitted them only to be
Free denizens of skill, to judge the best? 210
From whom the world as yet could never see
The warrant of their wit soundly expressed.
T' acquaint our times with that perfectïon
Of high conceit, which only they possess,
That we might have things exquisitely done,
Measured with all their strict observances,
Such would, I know, scorn a translation,
Or bring but others' labors to the press;
Yet, oft these monster-breeding mountains will
Bring forth small mice of great expected skill. 220
Presumption, ever fullest of defects,
Fails in the doing to perform her part;
And I have known proud words and poor effects
Of such indeed as do condemn this art;
But let them rest, it ever hath been known,
They others' virtues scorn that doubt their own.
And for the divers disagreeing chords
Of inter-jangling ignorance that fill
The dainty ears and leave no room for words,
The worthier minds neglect, or pardon will; 230
Knowing the best he hath, he frankly 'fords,
And scorns to be a niggard of his skill.
And that the rather, since this short-lived race,
Being fatally the sons of but one day,
That now with all their power ply it apace,

To hold out with the greatest might they may
Against confusion, that hath all in chase,
To make of all an universal prey.
For now great nature hath laid down at last
That mighty birth wherewith so long she went,   240
And overwent the times of ages past,
Here to lie in, upon our soft content,
Where fruitful she hath multiplied so fast
That all she hath on these times seemed t' have spent.
All that which might have many ages graced
Is born in one, to make one cloyed with all,
Where plenty hath impressed a deep distaste
Of best and worst, and all in general,
That goodness seems goodness to have defaced,
And virtue hath to virtue given the fall.   250
For emulation, that proud nurse of wit,
Scorning to stay below or come behind,
Labors upon that narrow top to sit
Of sole perfection in the highest kind;
Envy and wonder, looking after it,
Thrust likewise on the selfsame bliss to find,
And so, long striving till they can no more,
Do stuff the place, or others' hopes shut out,
Who, doubting to overtake those gone before,
Give up their care and cast no more about;   260
And so in scorn leave all as fore-possessed,
And will be none where they may not be best.
Ev'n like some empty creek that long hath lain
Left or neglected of the river by,
Whose searching sides, pleased with a wand'ring vein,
Finding some little way that close did lie,
Steal in at first, then other streams again
Second the first, then more than all supply,
Till all the mighty main hath borne, at last,
The glory of his chiefest power that way,   270
Plying this new-found pleasant room so fast,
Till all be full, and all be at a stay;
And then about and back again doth cast,
Leaving that, full, to fall another way:
So fares this hum'rous world, that evermore
Rapt with the current of a present course,
Runs into that which lay contemned before,
Then, glutted, leaves the same and falls t' a worse.
Now zeal holds all, no life but to adore,
Then cold in spirit, and faith is of no force;   280
Straight, all that holy was unhallowed lies,

The scattered carcasses of ruined vows;
Then truth is false, and now hath blindness eyes,
Then zeal trusts all, now scarcely what it knows,
That evermore, too foolish or too wise,
It fatal is to be seduced with shows.
Sacred religion, mother of form and fear,
How gorgeously sometimes dost thou sit decked!
What pompous vestures do we make thee wear!
What stately piles we prodigal erect!   290
How sweet perfumed thou art, how shining clear!
How solemnly observed, with what respect!
Another time, all plain, all quite threadbare,
Thou must have all within and nought without,
Sit poorly without light, disrobed, no care
Of outward grace to amuse the poor devout,
Powerless, unfollowed, scarcely men can spare
The necessary rites to set thee out.
Either truth, goodness, virtue, are not still
The selfsame which they are, and always one,   300
But alter to the project of our will;
Or we our actions make them wait upon,
Putting them in the livery of our skill,
And cast them off again when we have done.
You mighty lords that with respected grace
Do at the stern of fair example stand,
And all the body of this populace
Guide with the turning of your hand,
Keep a right course, bear up from all disgrace,
Observe the point of glory to our land,   310
Hold up disgracèd knowledge from the ground,
Keep virtue in request, give worth her due,
Let not neglect with barbarous means confound
So fair a good to bring in night anew:
Be not, oh, be not accessory found
Unto her death, that must give life to you.
Where will you have your virtuous name safe laid?
In gorgeous tombs, in sacred cells secure?
Do you not see those prostrate heaps betrayed
Your fathers' bones, and could not keep them sure?   320
And will you trust deceitful stones fair laid,
And think they will be to your honor truer?
No, no, unsparing time will proudly send
A warrant unto wrath, that with one frown
Will all these mock'ries of vain glory rend,
And make them as before, ungraced, unknown,
Poor idle honors that can ill defend

Your memories that cannot keep their own.
And whereto serve that wondrous trophy now,
  That on the goodly plain near Wilton stands?   330
  That huge dumb heap that cannot tell us how,
  Nor what, nor whence it is, nor with whose hands,
  Nor for whose glory, it was set to show
  How much our pride mocks that of other lands.
Whereon, when as the gazing passenger
  Hath greedy looked with admiration,
  And fain would know his birth, and what he were,
  How there erected, and how long agone,
  Inquires, and asks his fellow traveller
  What he hath heard, and his opinïon,   340
And he knows nothing; then he turns again
  And looks, and sighs, and then admires afresh,
  And in himself with sorrow doth complain
  The misery of dark forgetfulness,
  Angry with time that nothing should remain
  Our greatest wonder's wonder to express.
Then ignorance, with fabulous discourse,
  Robbing fair art and cunning of their right,
  Tells how those stones were by the devil's force
  From Afric brought to Ireland in a night,   350
  And thence to Britainy by magic course,
  From giants' hands redeemed by Merlin's sleight,
And then near Ambri placed, in memory
  Of all those noble Britons murthered there
  By Hengist and his Saxon treachery,
  Coming to parle in peace at unaware.
  With this old legend then credulity
  Holds her content, and closes up her care.
But is antiquity so great a liar?
  Or do her younger sons her age abuse,   360
  Seeing after-comers still so apt t' admire
  The grave authority that she doth use,
  That reverence and respect dares not require
  Proof of her deeds, or once her words refuse?
Yet wrong they did us to presume so far
  Upon our easy credit and delight;
  For, once found false, they straight became to mar
  Our faith and their own reputation quite,
  That now her truths hardly believëd are,
  And though sh' avouch the right, she scarce hath right.   370
And as for thee, thou huge and mighty frame
  That stands corrupted so with time's despite,
  And giv'st false evidence against their fame

That set thee there to testify their right,
And art become a traitor to their name
That trusted thee with all the best they might,
Thou shalt stand still belied and slanderëd,
The only gazing-stock of ignorance,
And by thy guile the wise, admonishëd,
Shall never more desire such heaps t' advance, 380
Nor trust their living glory with the dead
That cannot speak; but leave their fame to chance,
Considering in how small a room do lie,
And yet lie safe, as fresh as if alive,
All those great worthies of antiquity
Which long forelived thee and shall long survive,
Who stronger tombs found for eternity
Than could the powers of all the earth contrive;
Where they remain these trifles to upbraid,
Out of the reach of spoil and way of rage, 390
Though time with all his power of years hath laid
Long battery, backed with undermining age;
Yet they make head only with their own aid,
And war with his all-conquering forces wage,
Pleading the heav'ns prescription to be free,
And t' have a grant t' endure as long as he.

Philocosmus.

Behold how every man, drawn with delight
Of what he doth, flatters him in his way,
Striving to make his course seem only right,
Doth his own rest and his own thoughts betray; 400
Imagination bringing, bravely dight,
Her pleasing images in best array,
With flattering glasses that must show him fair
And others foul; his skill and wit best,
Others seduced, deceived, and wrong in their;
His knowledge right, all ignorant the rest;
Not feeling how these minions in the air
Present a face of things falsely expressed,
And that the glimmering of these errors shown
Are but a light to let him see his own. 410
Alas, poor fame, in what a narrow room,
As an encagëd parrot, art thou pent
Here amongst us, where even as good be dumb
As speak and to be heard with no attent!
How can you promise of the time to come,
Whenas the present are so negligent?

Is this the walk of all your wide renown,
  This little point, this scarce-discernëd isle,
  Thrust from the world, with whom our speech unknown
  Made never any traffic of our style?   420
  And in this all, where all this care is shown,
  T' enchant your fame to last so long a while,
  And for that happier tongues have won so much,
  Think you to make your barbarous language such?

Poor narrow limits for so mighty pains,
  That cannot promise any foreign vent;
  And yet if here to all your wondrous veins
  Were generally known, it might content;
  But lo, how many reads not, or disdains,
  The labor of the chief and excellent?   430

How many thousands never heard the name
  Of Sidney, or of Spenser, or of their books?
  And yet brave fellows, and presume of fame,
  And seem to bear down all the world with looks.
  What then shall they expect of meaner frame,
  On whose endeavors few or none scarce looks?

Do you not see these pamphlets, libels, and rhymes,
  These strange confusëd tumults of the mind,
  Are grown to be the sickness of these times,
  The great disease inflicted on mankind?   440
  Your virtues, by your follies made your crimes,
  Have issue with your indiscretion joined.

Schools, arts, professions, all in so great store,
  Pass the proportion of the present state,
  Where, being as great a number as before,
  And fewer rooms them to accommodate,
  It cannot be but they must throng the more,
  And kick, and thrust, and shoulder with debate.

For when the greater wits cannot attain
  Th' expected good which they account their right,   450
  And yet perceive others to reap that gain
  Of far inferior virtues in their sight,
  They, present with the sharp of envy, strain
  To wound them with reproaches and despite;
  And for these cannot have as well as they,
  They scorn their faith should deign to look that way.

Hence discontented sects and schisms arise,
  Hence interwounding controversies spring,
  That feed the simple and offend the wise,
  Who know the consequence of cavilling   460
  Disgrace, that these to others do devise.
  Contempt and scorn on all in th' end doth bring,

Like scolding wives, reck'ning each other's fault,
Make standers-by imagine both are naught.
For when to these rare dainties time admits
    All comers, all complexions, all that will,
    Where none should be let in but choicest wits,
    Whose mild discretion could comport with skill,
    For when the place their humor neither fits,
    Nor they the place, who can expect but ill?   470
For being unapt for what they took in hand,
    And for aught else whereto they shall b' addressed,
    They ev'n become th' encumbrance of the land,
    As out of rank, disord'ring all the rest.
    This grace of theirs, to seem to understand,
    Mars all their grace to do without their rest.
Men find that action is another thing
    Than what they in discoursing papers read:
    The world's affairs require in managing
    More arts than those wherein you clerks proceed;   480
    Whilst timorous knowledge stands considering,
    Audacious ignorance hath done the deed;
    For who knows most, the more he knows to doubt,
    The least discourse is commonly most stout.
This sweet enchanting knowledge turns you clean
    Out from the fields of natural delight,
    And makes you hide, unwilling to be seen
    In th' open concourse of a public sight;
    This skill, wherewith you have so cunning been,
    Unsinews all your powers, unmans you quite.   490
Public society and commerce of men
    Requires another grace, another port;
    This eloquence, these rhymes, these phrases then,
    Begot in shades, do serve us in no sort;
    Th' unmaterial swelling of your pen
    Touch not the spirit that action doth import.
A manly style, fitted to manly ears,
    Best grees with wit, not that which goes so gay,
    And commonly the gaudy liv'ry wears
    Of nice corruptions, which the times do sway,   500
    And waits on th' humor of his pulse that bears
    His passions set to such a pleasing kay.
    Such dainties serve only for stomachs weak,
    For men do foulest when they finest speak.
Yet do I not dislike that in some wise
    Be sung the great heroical deserts
    Of brave renownèd spirits, whose exercise
    Of worthy deeds may call up others' hearts,

And serve a model for posterities,
To fashion them fit for like glorious parts;   510
But so that all our spirits may tend hereto,
To make it not our grace to say, but do.

Musophilus.

Much thou hast said, and willingly I hear,
    As one that am not so possessed with love
    Of what I do, but that I rather bear
    An ear to learn than a tongue to disprove;
    I know men must, as carried in their sphere,
    According to their proper motions, move,
    And that course likes them best which they are on,
    Yet truth hath certain bounds, but falsehood none.   520
I do confess our limits are but small,
    Compared with all the whole vast earth beside,
    All which, again rated to that great all,
    Is likewise as a point, scarcely descried;
    So that in these respects we may this call
    A point but of a point, where we abide.
But if we shall descend from that high stand
    Of over-looking contemplation,
    And cast our thoughts but to, and not beyond
    This spacious circuit which we tread upon,   530
    We then may estimate our mighty land
    A world within a world, standing alone;
Where if our fame, confined, cannot get out,
    What, shall we imagine it is penned
    That hath so great a world to walk about,
    Whose bounds with her reports have both one end?
    Why shall we not rather esteem her stout
    That farther than her own scorn to extend?
Where being so large a room, both to do well
    And eke to hear th' applause of things well done,   540
    That farther, if men shall our virtues tell,
    We have more mouths but not more merit won;
    It doth not greater make that which is laudable,
    The flame is bigger blown, the fire all one.
And for the few that only lend their ear,
    That few is all the world, which with a few
    Do ever live, and move, and work, and stir.
This is the heart doth feel and only know;
    The rest of all that only bodies bear,
    Roll up and down, and fill up but the row,   550
And serves as others' members, not their own,

The instruments of those that do direct.
Then, what disgrace is this, not to be known
To those know not to give themselves respect?
And though they swell, with pomp of folly blown,
They live ungraced and die but in neglect.
And for my part, if only one allow
The care my laboring spirits take in this,
He is to me a theater large enow,
And his applause only sufficient is,   560
All my respect is bent but to his brow;
That is my all, and all I am is his.
And if some worthy spirits be pleasëd too,
It shall more comfort breed, but not more will.
But what if none? It cannot yet undo
The love I bear unto this holy skill;
This is the thing that I was born to do,
This is my scene, this part must I fulfil.

. . . .

Power above powers, O heavenly eloquence,
That with the strong rein of commanding words   570
Dost manage, guide, and master th' eminence
Of men's affections more than all their swords,—
Shall we not offer to thy excellence
The richest treasure that our wit affords?
Thou that canst do much more with one poor pen
Than all the powers of princes can effect,
And draw, divert, dispose, and fashion men
Better than force or rigor can direct,—
Should we this ornament of glory then,
As th' unmaterial fruits of shades, neglect?   580
Or should we, careless, come behind the rest
In power of words, that go before in worth?
Whenas our accents, equal to the best,
Is able greater wonders to bring forth;
When all that ever hotter spirits expressed,
Comes bettered by the patience of the north.
And who, in time, knows whither we may vent
The treasure of our tongue, to what strange shores
This gain of our best glory shall be sent
T' enrich unknowing nations with our stores?   590
What worlds in th' yet unformëd occident
May come refined with th' accents that are ours?
Or who can tell for what great work in hand
The greatness of our style is now ordained?
What powers it shall bring in, what spirits command,

What thoughts let out, what humors keep restrained,
What mischief it may powerfully withstand,
And what fair ends may thereby be attained?

. . . . .

[*Love is a sickness*]

Love is a sickness full of woes,
  All remedies refusing;
A plant that with most cutting
    grows,
  Most barren with best using.
      Why so?
  More we enjoy it, more it dies;
If not enjoyed it sighing cries,
      Hey ho.

Love is a torment of the mind,
  A tempest everlasting;   10
And Jove hath made it of a kind,
  Not well, nor full, nor fasting.
      Why so?
  More we enjoy it, more it dies;
If not enjoyed it sighing cries,
      Hey ho.
      From *Hymen's Triumph*

FROM *Certain Small Poems*, 1605

Ulysses and the Siren

Sir. Come, worthy Greek, Ulys-
    ses, come,
Possess these shores with me;
The winds and seas are trouble-
    some,
  And here we may be free.
    Here may we sit and view
      their toil
  That travail on the deep,
And joy the day in mirth the
    while,
  And spend the night in sleep.

Ulys. Fair nymph, if fame or
    honor were
  To be attained with ease,   10
Then would I come and rest
    with thee,
  And leave such toils as these.
    But here it dwells, and here
      must I
  With danger seek it forth;
To spend the time luxuriously
  Becomes not men of worth.

Sir. Ulysses, O be not deceived
  With that unreal name;
This honor is a thing conceived,

And rests on others' fame.   20
  Begotten only to molest
Our peace, and to beguile
The best thing of our life, our
    rest,
  And give us up to toil.

Ulys. Delicious nymph, suppose
    there were
Nor honor nor report,
Yet manliness would scorn to
    wear
  The time in idle sport.
    For toil doth give a better
      touch,
  To make us feel our joy;   30
And ease finds tediousness, as
    much
  As labor, yields annoy.

Sir. Then pleasure likewise seems
    the shore
Whereto tends all your toil,
Which you forgo to make it
    more,
  And perish oft the while.
    Who may disport them di-
      versly,
  Find never tedious day,

And ease may have variety
As well as action may.   40

Ulys. But natures of the noblest
frame
These toils and dangers please,
And they take comfort in the
same
As much as you in ease,
    And with the thoughts of ac-
tions past
Are recreated still;
When pleasure leaves a touch at
last
To show that it was ill.

Sir. That doth opinion only cause
That's out of custom bred,   50
Which makes us many other
laws
Than ever nature did.
    No widows wail for our de-
lights,
Our sports are without blood;
The world, we see, by warlike
wights

Receives more hurt than good.

Ulys. But yet the state of things
require
These motions of unrest,
And these great spirits of high
desire
Seem born to turn them best,   60
    To purge the mischiefs that
increase
And all good order mar;
For oft we see a wicked peace
To be well changed for war.

Sir. Well, well, Ulysses, then I
see
I shall not have thee here,
And therefore I will come to
thee,
And take my fortunes there.
    I must be won that cannot
win,
Yet lost were I not won: 70
For beauty hath created been
T' undo, or be undone.

FROM *Tethys' Festival*, 1610

[*Are they shadows?*]

Are they shadows that we see?
And can shadows pleasure give?
Pleasures only shadows be
Cast by bodies we conceive,
And are made the things we
deem
In those figures which they
seem.
But these pleasures vanish fast,
Which by shadows are expressed.
Pleasures are not, if they last;

In their passing is their best.   10
Glory is most bright and gay
In a flash, and so away.
Feed apace then, greedy eyes,
On the wonder you behold.
Take it sudden as it flies,
Though you take it not to hold;
When your eyes have done their
part,
Thought must length it in the
heart.

MICHAEL DRAYTON

The Introduction and Notes are at pages 1236 and 1276

FROM *Idea, the Shepherd's Garland*, 1593

The eighth eclogue

.   .   .   .

Far in the country of Arden
There wonned a knight hight
     Cassemen,
   As bold as Isenbras;
Fell was he and eager bent
In battle and in tournament,
   As was the good Sir Thopas.
He had, as antique stories tell,
A daughter clepëd Dowsabell,
   A maiden fair and free;
And for she was her father's
     heir,   10
Full well she was yconned the
     lere
   Of mickle courtesy.
The silk well couth she twist and
     twine,
And make the fine marchpine,
   And with the needle work;
And she couth help the priest to
     say
His matins on a holy-day,
   And sing a psalm in kirk.
She ware a frock of frolic green
Might well beseem a maiden
     queen,   20
   Which seemly was to see;
A hood to that so neat and fine,
In color like the columbine,
   Ywrought full featously.
Her feature all as fresh above
As is the grass that grows by
     Dove,
   As lithe as lass of Kent;
Her skin as soft as Lemster wool,
As white as snow on Peakish
     hull,

Or swan that swims in
     Trent.   30
This maiden in a morn betime
Went forth when May was in her
     prime
   To get sweet cetywall,
The honeysuckle, the harlock,
The lily, and the lady-smock,
   To deck her summer hall.
Thus as she wandered here and
     there,
Ypicking of the bloomëd breer,
   She chancëd to espy
A shepherd sitting on a bank;   40
Like chanticleer he crowëd crank,
   And piped with merry glee.
He leared his sheep as he him
     list,
When he would whistle in his
     fist,
   To feed about him round,
Whilst he full many a carol
     sung,
Until the fields and meadows
     rung,
   And that the woods did sound.
In favor this same shepherd's
     swain
Was like the bedlam Tambur-
     laine,   50
   Which held proud kings in
     awe.
But meek he was as lamb mought
     be,
Ylike that gentle Abel he,
   Whom his lewd brother slaw.
This shepherd ware a sheep-grey
     cloak,
Which was of the finest loke

That could be cut with shear;
His mittens were of bauzens' skin,
His cockers were of cordiwin,
His hood of meniveere; 60
His awl and lingel in a thong,
His tar-box on his broad belt
hung,
His breech of cointrie blue.
Full crisp and curlèd were his
locks,
His brows as white as Albion
rocks,
So like a lover true.
And piping still he spent the day,
So merry as the popinjay;
Which likèd Dowsabell,
That would she aught or would
she nought, 70
This lad would never from her
thought,
She in love-longing fell.
At length she tuckèd up her
frock,
White as the lily was her smock,
She drew the shepherd nigh.
But then the shepherd piped a
good
That all his sheep forsook their
food
To hear his melody.
Thy sheep, quoth she, cannot be
lean,
That have a jolly shepherd's
swain 80
The which can pipe so well.
Yea but, saith he, their shepherd
may,
If piping thus he pine away
In love of Dowsabell.
Of love, fond boy, take thou no
keep,
Quoth she, look well unto thy
sheep
Lest they should hap to stray.
Quoth he, So had I done full
well,

Had I not seen fair Dowsabell
Come forth to gather May. 90
With that she gan to vail her
head;
Her cheeks were like the roses
red,
But not a word she said.
With that the shepherd gan to
frown;
He threw his pretty pipes adown,
And on the ground him laid.
Saith she, I may not stay till
night
And leave my summer hall un-
dight,
And all for long of thee.
My cote, saith he, nor yet my
fold, 100
Shall neither sheep nor shepherd
hold,
Except thou favor me.
Saith she, Yet liefer I were
dead,
Than I should lose my maiden-
head,
And all for love of men.
Saith he, Yet are you too un-
kind,
If in your heart you cannot find
To love us now and then;
And I to thee will be as kind
As Colin was to Rosalind, 110
Of courtesy the flower.
Then will I be as true, quoth she,
As ever maiden yet might be
Unto her paramour.
With that she bent her snow-
white knee;
Down by the shepherd kneelèd
she,
And him she sweetly kissed.
With that the shepherd whooped
for joy;
Quoth he, There's never shep-
herd's boy
That ever was so blist. 120

FROM *Idea's Mirror*, 1594

To the dear child of the Muses, and his ever kind Mæcenas, Ma. Anthony Cooke, Esquire

Vouchsafe to grace these rude unpolished rhymes,
  Which long, dear friend, have slept in sable night,
And come abroad now in these glorious times,
  Can hardly brook the pureness of the light.
But sith you see their destiny is such
  That in the world their fortune they must try,
Perhaps they better shall abide the touch
  Wearing your name, their gracious livery.
Yet these mine own, I wrong not other men,   10
  Nor traffic further than this happy clime,
Nor filch from Portes' nor from Petrarch's pen,
  A fault too common in this latter time.
Divine Sir Philip, I avouch thy writ,
I am no pickpurse of another's wit.

Black pitchy night, companion of my woe,
  The inn of care, the nurse of dreary sorrow,
Why length'nest thou thy darkest hours so,
  Still to prolong my long-time-looked-for morrow?
Thou sable shadow, image of despair,
  Portrait of hell, the air's black mourning weed,
Recorder of revenge, remembrancer of care,
  The shadow and the veil of every sinful deed,
Death like to thee, so live thou still in death,
  The grave of joy, prison of day's delight.   10
Let heavens withdraw their sweet ambrosian breath,
  Nor moon nor stars lend thee their shining light,
For thou alone renew'st that old desire
Which still torments me in day's burning fire.

FROM *England's Heroical Epistles*, 1599

Many there be excelling in this kind,
Whose well-tricked rhymes with all invention swell;
Let each commend as best shall like his mind,
Some Sidney, Constable, some Daniel.
That thus their names familiarly I sing,
Let none think them disparagèd to be;
Poor men with reverence may speak of a king,
And so may these be spoken of by me.
My wanton verse ne'er keeps one certain stay,

But now at hand, then seeks invention far,
And with each little motion runs astray,
Wild, madding, jocund, and irregular;
    Like me that lust, my honest merry rhymes
    Nor care for critic, nor regard the times.

From *Poems*, 1619

Idea

To the reader of these sonnets

Into these loves who but for passion looks,
At this first sight here let him lay them by,
And seek elsewhere, in turning other books
Which better may his labor satisfy.
No far-fetched sigh shall ever wound my breast,
Love from mine eye a tear shall never wring,
Nor in *Ah me's* my whining sonnets dressed.
A libertine, fantastically I sing;
My verse is the true image of my mind,
Ever in motion, still desiring change.
And as thus to variety inclined,
So in all humors sportively I range;
    My muse is rightly of the English strain,
    That cannot long one fashion entertain.

Like an adventurous seafarer am I,
Who hath some long and dang'rous voyage been,
And called to tell of his discovery,
How far he sailed, what countries he had seen;
Proceeding from the port whence he put forth,
Shows by his compass how his course he steered,
When east, when west, when south, and when by north,
As how the pole to ev'ry place was reared,
What capes he doubled, of what continent,
The gulfs and straits that strangely he had passed,
Where most becalmed, where with foul weather spent,
And on what rocks in peril to be cast:
    Thus in my love, time calls me to relate
    My tedious travels and oft-varying fate.

How many paltry, foolish, painted things,
That now in coaches trouble ev'ry street,
Shall be forgotten, whom no poet sings,
Ere they be well wrapped in their winding sheet!
Where I to thee eternity shall give,

When nothing else remaineth of these days,
And queens hereafter shall be glad to live
Upon the alms of thy superfluous praise;
Virgins and matrons reading these my rhymes
Shall be so much delighted with thy story   10
That they shall grieve they lived not in these times,
To have seen thee, their sex's only glory.
 So shalt thou fly above the vulgar throng,
 Still to survive in my immortal song.

As other men, so I myself do muse
Why in this sort I wrest invention so,
And why these giddy metaphors I use,
Leaving the path the greater part do go.
I will resolve you: I am lunatic,
And ever this in madmen you shall find—
What they last thought of, when the brain grew sick,
In most distraction they keep that in mind.
Thus talking idly in this bedlam fit,
Reason and I, you must conceive, are twain;   10
'Tis nine years now since first I lost my wit,
Bear with me, then, though troubled be my brain.
 With diet and correction, men distraught
 (Not too far past) may to their wits be brought.

To nothing fitter can I thee compare
Than to the son of some rich penny-father,
Who having now brought on his end with care,
Leaves to his son all he had heaped together;
This new-rich novice, lavish of his chest,
To one man gives, doth on another spend,
Then here he riots; yet amongst the rest
Haps to lend some to one true honest friend.
Thy gifts thou in obscurity dost waste,
False friends thy kindness, born but to deceive thee;   10
Thy love, that is on the unworthy placed;
Time hath thy beauty, which with age will leave thee;
 Only that little which to me was lent,
 I give thee back, when all the rest is spent.

An evil spirit, your beauty, haunts me still,
Wherewith, alas, I have been long possessed,
Which ceaseth not to tempt me to each ill,
Nor gives me once but one poor minute's rest;
In me it speaks, whether I sleep or wake,
And when by means to drive it out I try,

With greater torments then it me doth take,
And tortures me in most extremity;
Before my face it lays down my despairs,
And hastes me on unto a sudden death,   10
Now tempting me to drown myself in tears,
And then in sighing to give up my breath.
    Thus am I still provoked to every evil
    By this good wicked spirit, sweet angel devil.

A witless gallant, a young wench that wooed
(Yet his dull spirit her not one jot could move),
Entreated me, as e'er I wished his good
To write him but one sonnet to his love;
When I, as fast as e'er my pen could trot,
Poured out what first from quick invention came,
Nor never stood one word thereof to blot,
Much like his wit, that was to use the same;
But with my verses he his mistress won,
Who doted on the dolt beyond all measure.   10
But see, for you to heav'n for phrase I run,
And ransack all Apollo's golden treasure;
    Yet by my froth this fool his love obtains,
    And I lose you for all my wit and pains.

Methinks I see some crooked mimic jeer,
And tax my muse with this fantastic grace;
Turning my papers, asks, What have we here?
Making withal some filthy antic face.
I fear no censure, nor what thou canst say,
Nor shall my spirit one jot of vigor lose.
Think'st thou my wit shall keep the pack-horse way
That ev'ry dudgeon low invention goes?
Since sonnets thus in bundles are impressed,
And ev'ry drudge doth dull our satiate ear,   10
Think'st thou my love shall in those rags be dressed
That ev'ry dowdy, ev'ry trull doth wear?
    Up to my pitch no common judgment flies,
    I scorn all earthly dung-bred scarabies.

Our floods' queen, Thames, for ships and swans is crowned,
And stately Severn for her shore is praised;
The crystal Trent for fords and fish renowned,
And Avon's fame to Albion's cliffs is raised;
Carlegion Chester vaunts her holy Dee;
York many wonders of her Ouse can tell,
The Peak her Dove, whose banks so fertile be,

And Kent will say her Medway doth excel;
Cotswold commends her Isis to the Tame;
Our northern borders boast of Tweed's fair flood;   10
Our western parts extol their Wylye's fame,
And the old Lea brags of the Danish blood;
　　Arden's sweet Anker, let thy glory be
　　That fair Idea only lives by thee.

———

Some misbelieving and profane in love,
When I do speak of miracles by thee,
May say that thou art flatterëd by me
Who only write my skill in verse to prove;
See miracles, ye unbelieving, see
A dumb-born muse made to express the mind,
A cripple hand to write, yet lame by kind,
One by thy name, the other touching thee;
Blind were mine eyes till they were seen of thine,
And mine ears deaf by thy fame healëd be,   10
My vices cured by virtues sprung from thee,
My hopes revived, which long in grave had lyne;
　　All unclean thoughts foul spirits cast out in me
　　Only by virtue that proceeds from thee.

———

Dear, why should you command me to my rest,
When now the night doth summon all to sleep?
Methinks this time becometh lovers best;
Night was ordained together friends to keep.
How happy are all other living things,
Which though the day disjoin by sev'ral flight,
The quiet evening yet together brings,
And each returns unto his love at night!
O thou that art so courteous else to all,
Why shouldst thou, Night, abuse me only thus,   10
That ev'ry creature to his kind dost call,
And yet 'tis thou dost only sever us?
　　Well could I wish it would be ever day,
　　If when night comes you bid me go away.

———

Some men there be which like my method well,
And much commend the strangeness of my vein;
Some say I have a passing pleasing strain,
Some say that in my humor I excel;
Some, who not kindly relish my conceit,
They say, as poets do, I use to feign,
And in bare words paint out my passion's pain.
Thus sundry men their sundry minds repeat.

I pass not, I, how men affected be,
Nor who commends or discommends my verse;   10
It pleaseth me if I my woes rehearse,
And in my lines if she my love may see.
  Only my comfort still consists in this,
  Writing her praise I cannot write amiss.

Whilst thus my pen strives to eternize thee,
Age rules my lines with wrinkles in my face,
Where, in the map of all my misery,
Is modeled out the world of my disgrace;
Whilst in despite of tyrannizing times,
Medea-like I make thee young again.
Proudly thou scorn'st my world-outwearing rhymes,
And murther'st virtue with thy coy disdain;
And though in youth my youth untimely perish
To keep thee from oblivion and the grave,   10
Ensuing ages yet my rhymes shall cherish,
Where I, entombed, my better part shall save;
  And though this earthly body fade and die,
  My name shall mount upon eternity.

In pride of wit, when high desire of fame
Gave life and courage to my lab'ring pen,
And first the sound and virtue of my name
Won grace and credit in the ears of men;
With those the throngèd theaters that press
I in the circuit for the laurel strove,
Where the full praise, I freely must confess,
In heat of blood, a modest mind might move.
With shouts and claps at ev'ry little pause,
When the proud round on ev'ry side hath rung,   10
Sadly I sit, unmoved with the applause,
As though to me it nothing did belong.
  No public glory vainly I pursue,
  All that I seek is to eternize you.

Clear Anker, on whose silver-sanded shore
My soul-shrined saint, my fair Idea lies,
O blessed brook, whose milk-white swans adore
Thy crystal stream, refinèd by her eyes,
Where sweet myrrh-breathing Zephyr in the spring
Gently distils his nectar-dropping showers,
Where nightingales in Arden sit and sing
Amongst the dainty dew-empearlèd flowers;
Say thus, fair brook, when thou shalt see thy queen:

Lo, here thy shepherd spent his wand'ring years,
And in these shades, dear nymph, he oft hath been,
And here to thee he sacrificed his tears.
　　Fair Arden, thou my Tempe art alone,
　　And thou, sweet Anker, art my Helicon.

Since there's no help, come let us kiss and part;
Nay, I have done, you get no more of me,
And I am glad, yea glad with all my heart
That thus so cleanly I myself can free;
Shake hands forever, cancel all our vows,
And when we meet at any time again,
Be it not seen in either of our brows
That we one jot of former love retain.
Now at the last gasp of love's latest breath,
When, his pulse failing, passion speechless lies,
When faith is kneeling by his bed of death,
And innocence is closing up his eyes,
　　Now if thou wouldst, when all have given him over,
　　From death to life thou mightst him yet recover.

Truce, gentle love, a parley now I crave;
Methinks 'tis long since first these wars begun,
Nor thou, nor I, the better yet can have;
Bad is the match where neither party won.
I offer free conditions of fair peace,
My heart for hostage that it shall remain;
Discharge our forces, here let malice cease,
So for my pledge thou give me pledge again;
Or if no thing but death will serve thy turn,
Still thirsting for subversion of my state,
Do what thou canst, raze, massacre, and burn,
Let the world see the utmost of thy hate;
　　I send defiance, since if overthrown,
　　Thou vanquishing, the conquest is mine own.

England's Heroical Epistles

Henry Howard, Earl of Surrey, to the Lady Geraldine

THE ARGUMENT

The Earl of Surrey, that renownëd lord,
Th' old English glory bravely that restored,
That prince and poet (a name more divine),
Falling in love with beauteous Geraldine

Of the Geraldi, which derive their name
From Florence, whither, to advance her fame,
He travels, and in public jousts maintained
Her beauty peerless, which by arms he gained;
But staying long, fair Italy to see,
To let her know him constant still to be,
From Tuscany this letter to her writes,
Which her rescription instantly invites.

From learned Florence, long time rich in fame,
From whence thy race, thy noble grandsires, came
To famous England, that kind nurse of mine,
Thy Surrey sends to heav'nly Geraldine;
Yet let not Tuscan think I do it wrong,
That I from thence write in my native tongue,
That in these harsh-tuned cadences I sing,
Sitting so near the Muses' sacred spring;
But rather think itself adorned thereby,
That England reads the praise of Italy.   10
Though to the Tuscans I the smoothness grant,
Our dialect no majesty doth want
To set thy praises in as high a key
As France, or Spain, or Germany, or they.
  What day I quit the foreland of fair Kent,
And that my ship her course for Flanders bent,
Yet think I with how many a heavy look
My leave of England and of thee I took,
And did entreat the tide, if it might be,
But to convey me one sigh back to thee.   20
Up to the deck a billow lightly skips,
Taking my sigh, and down again it slips;
Into the gulf itself it headlong throws,
And as a post to England-ward it goes.
As I sat wond'ring how the rough seas stirred,
I might far off perceive a little bird,
Which, as she fain from shore to shore would fly,
Had lost herself in the broad vasty sky,
Her feeble wing beginning to deceive her,
The seas of life still gaping to bereave her;   30
Unto the ship she makes, which she discovers,
And there, poor fool, a while for refuge hovers.
And when at length her flagging pinion fails,
Panting she hangs upon the rattling sails,
And being forced to loose her hold with pain,
Yet beaten off, she straight lights on again,
And tossed with flaws, with storms, with wind, with weather,

Yet still departing thence, still turneth thither;
Now with the poop, now with the prow doth bear,
Now on this side, now that, now here, now there.   40
Methinks these storms should be my sad depart,
The silly helpless bird is my poor heart,
The ship to which for succor it repairs,
That is yourself, regardless of my cares.
Of every surge doth fall, or waves doth rise,
To some one thing I sit and moralize.

When for thy love I left the Belgic shore,
Divine Erasmus and our famous More,
Whose happy presence gave me such delight
As made a minute of a winter's night,   50
With whom a while I stayed at Rotterdam,
Now so renownëd by Erasmus' name;
Yet every hour did seem a world of time
Till I had seen that soul-reviving clime,
And thought the foggy Netherlands unfit,
A wat'ry soil to clog a fiery wit.
And as that wealthy Germany I passed,
Coming unto the Emperor's court at last,
Great learn'd Agrippa, so profound in art,
Who the infernal secrets doth impart,   60
When of thy health I did desire to know,
Me in a glass my Geraldine did show,
Sick in thy bed and, for thou couldst not sleep,
By a wax taper set the light to keep;
I do remember thou didst read that ode
Sent back whilst I in Thanet made abode,
Where when thou cam'st unto that word of love,
Even in thine eyes I saw how passion strove;
That snowy lawn which coverëd thy bed,
Methought looked white, to see thy cheek so red,   70
Thy rosy cheek, oft changing in my sight,
Yet still was red, to see the lawn so white;
The little taper which should give thee light,
Methought waxed dim to see thine eye so bright;
Thine eye again supplied the taper's turn,
And with his beams more brightly made it burn;
The shrugging air about thy temples hurls
And wrapped thy breath in little clouded curls,
And as it did ascend, it straight did seize it,
And as it sunk, it presently did raise it.   80
Canst thou by sickness banish beauty so?
Which if put from thee knows not where to go,
To make her shift and for her succor seek

To every riveled face, each bankrupt cheek.
If health preserved, thou beauty still dost cherish,
If that neglected, beauty soon doth perish.
Care draws on care, woe comforts woe again,
Sorrow breeds sorrow, one grief brings forth twain;
If live or die, as thou dost so do I,
If live, I live, and if thou die, I die: 90
One heart, one love, one joy, one grief, one troth,
One good, one ill, one life, one death to both.
　　If Howard's blood thou hold'st as but too vile,
Or not esteem'st of Norfolk's princely style,
If Scotland's coat no mark of fame can lend,
That lion placed in our bright silver bend,
(Which as a trophy beautifies our shield
Since Scottish blood discolored Flodden field,
When the proud Cheviot our brave ensign bare
As a rich jewel in a lady's hair,   100
And did fair Bramston's neighboring valleys choke
With clouds of cannons, fire-disgorgèd smoke),
Or Surrey's earldom insufficient be
And not a dower so well contenting thee,
Yet am I one of great Apollo's heirs,
The sacred Muses challenge me for theirs.
By princes my immortal lines are sung,
My flowing verses graced with ev'ry tongue;
The little children, when they learn to go,
By painful mothers daded to and fro,   110
Are taught my sugared numbers to rehearse,
And have their sweet lips seasoned with my verse.
　　When heav'n would strive to do the best it can,
And put an angel's spirit into a man,
The utmost power it hath it then doth spend
When to the world a poet it doth intend;
That little diff'rence 'twixt the gods and us,
By them confirmed, distinguished only thus:
Whom they, in birth, ordain to happy days,
The gods commit their glory to our praise;   120
T' eternal life when they dissolve their breath,
We likewise share a second power by death.
　　When time shall turn those amber locks to gray,
My verse again shall gild and make them gay,
And trick them up in knotted curls anew,
And to thy autumn give a summer's hue;
That sacred power that in my ink remains,
Shall put fresh blood into thy withered veins,
And on thy red decayed, thy whiteness dead,

Shall set a white more white, a red more red;   130
When thy dim sight thy glass cannot descry,
Nor thy crazed mirror can discern thine eye,
My verse, to tell th' one what the other was,
Shall represent them both, thine eye and glass,
Where both thy mirror and thine eye shall see
What once thou saw'st in that, that saw in thee,
And to them both shall tell the simple truth,
What that in pureness was, what thou in youth.
    If Florence once should lose her old renown,
As famous Athens, now a fisher town,   140
My lines for thee a Florence shall erect
Which great Apollo ever shall protect,
And with the numbers from my pen that falls
Bring marble mines to re-erect those walls.
Nor beauteous Stanhope, whom all tongues report
To be the glory of the English court,
Shall by our nation be so much admired,
If ever Surrey truly were inspired.
And famous Wyatt, who in numbers sings
To that enchanting Thracian harper's strings,   150
To whom Phœbus, the poets' god, did drink
A bowl of nectar filled up to the brink,
And sweet-tongued Bryan, whom the Muses kept
And in his cradle rocked him whilst he slept,
In sacred verses most divinely penned,
Upon thy praises ever shall attend.
    What time I came into this famous town
And made the cause of my arrival known,
Great Medici a list for triumphs built;
Within the which, upon a tree of gilt,   160
Which was with sundry rare devices set,
I did erect thy lovely counterfeit
To answer those Italian dames' desire,
Which daily came thy beauty to admire;
By which my lion, in his gaping jaws,
Held up my lance, and in his dreadful paws
Reacheth my gauntlet unto him that dare
A beauty with my Geraldine's compare.
Which, when each manly valiant arm assays,
After so many brave triumphant days   170
The glorious prize upon my lance I bare,
By herald's voice proclaimed to be thy share.
The shivered staves, here for thy beauty broke,
With fierce encounters passed at ev'ry shock,
When stormy courses answered cuff for cuff,

Denting proud beavers with the counter-buff,
Upon an altar, burnt with holy flame,
I sacrificed as incense to thy fame;
Where, as the phœnix from her spicëd fume
Renews herself in that she doth consume,   180
So from these sacred ashes live we both,
Ev'n as that one Arabian wonder doth.

When to my chamber I myself retire,
Burnt with the sparks that kindled all this fire,
Thinking of England, which my hope contains,
The happy isle where Geraldine remains,
Of Hunsdon, where those sweet celestial eyne
At first did pierce this tender breast of mine,
Of Hampton Court and Windsor, where abound
All pleasures that in paradise were found;   190
Near that fair castle is a little grove,
With hanging rocks all covered from above,
Which on the bank of goodly Thames doth stand,
Clipped by the water from the other land,
Whose bushy top doth bid the sun forbear
And checks his proud beams that would enter there;
Whose leaves still mutt'ring as the air doth breathe,
With the sweet bubbling of the stream beneath,
Doth rock the senses, whilst the small birds sing,
Lullëd asleep with gentle murmuring;   200
Where light-foot fairies sport at prison-base
(No doubt there is some power frequents the place),
There the soft poplar and smooth beech do bear
Our names together carvëd ev'rywhere,
And Gordian knots do curiously entwine
The names of Henry and of Geraldine.
Oh, let this grove in happy times to come
Be called the lovers' blest Elysium;
Whither my mistress wonted to resort,
In summer's heat in those sweet shades to sport; 210
A thousand sundry names I have it given,
And called it Wonder-hider, Cover-heaven,
The roof where beauty her rich court doth keep,
Under whose compass all the stars do sleep.
There is one tree which now I call to mind,
Doth bear these verses carvëd in his rind:
When Geraldine shall sit in thy fair shade,
Fan her sweet tresses with perfumëd air,
Let thy large boughs a canopy be made
To keep the sun from gazing on my fair;   220
And when thy spreading branchëd arms be sunk,

And thou no sap nor pith shalt more retain,
Ev'n from the dust of thy unwieldy trunk
I will renew thee, phœnix-like, again,
And from thy dry decayèd root will bring
A new-born stem, another Æson's spring.

 I find no cause, nor judge I reason why
My country should give place to Lombardy;
As goodly flowers on Thamesis do grow
As beautify the banks of wanton Po;   230
As many nymphs as haunt rich Arno's strand,
By silver Severn tripping hand in hand;
Our shade's as sweet, though not to us so dear,
Because the sun hath greater power there;
This distant place doth give me greater woe,
Far off, my sighs the farther have to go.
Ah absence! why shouldst thou seem so long?
Or wherefore shouldst thou offer time such wrong,
Summer so soon to steal on winter's cold,
Or winter's blasts so soon make summer old?   240
Love did us both with one self arrow strike,
Our wound's both one, our cure should be the like,
Except thou hast found out some mean by art,
Some powerful med'cine to withdraw the dart;
But mine is fixed, and absence being proved,
It sticks too fast, it cannot be removed.
 Adieu, adieu, from Florence when I go
By my next letters Geraldine shall know,
Which if good fortune shall by course direct,
From Venice by some messenger expect;   250
Till when, I leave thee to thy heart's desire:
By him that lives thy virtues to admire.

ODES

To the Virginian voyage

You brave heroic minds
Worthy your country's name,
 That honor still pursue,
 Go, and subdue,
Whilst loit'ring hinds
Lurk here at home, with shame.

Britons, you stay too long;
Quickly aboard bestow you,
 And with a merry gale

Swell your stretched sail,   10
 With vows as strong
As the winds that blow you.

Your course securely steer,
West and by south forth keep,
 Rocks, lee-shores, nor shoals,
 When Æolus scowls,
You need not fear,
So absolute the deep.

And cheerfully at sea,
Success you still entice,   20

To get the pearl and gold,
And ours to hold,
Virginia,
Earth's only paradise,

Where nature hath in store
Fowl, venison, and fish,
   And the fruitful'st soil
   Without your toil
Three harvests more,
All greater than your wish.   30

And the ambitious vine
Crowns with his purple mass,
   The cedar reaching high
   To kiss the sky,
The cypress, pine,
And useful sassafras.

To whose the golden age
Still nature's laws doth give,
   No other cares that tend,
   But them to defend   40
From winter's age,
That long there doth not live.

Whenas the luscious smell
Of that delicious land,
   Above the seas that flows,
   The clear wind throws,
Your hearts to swell
Approaching the dear strand,

In kenning of the shore,
Thanks to God first given,   50
   O you, the happi'st men,
   Be frolic then,
Let cannons roar,
Frighting the wide heaven.

And in regions far
Such heroes bring ye forth
   As those from whom we came,
   And plant our name
Under that star
Not known unto our north.   60

And as there plenty grows
Of laurel everywhere,
   Apollo's sacred tree,
   You it may see
A poet's brows
To crown, that may sing there.

Thy voyages attend,
Industrious Hakluÿt,
   Whose reading shall enflame
   Men to seek fame,   70
And much commend
To after times thy wit.

The crier

Good folk, for gold or hire,
But help me to a crier;
For my poor heart is run astray
After two eyes that passed this
      way.
   Oyes, oyes, oyes,
   If there be any man
   In town or country can
Bring me my heart again,
I'll please him for his pain;
And by these marks I will you
      show   10
That only I this heart do owe.
   It is a wounded heart,
   Wherein yet sticks the dart;
Ev'ry piece sore hurt throughout
      it,
Faith and troth writ round about
      it;
It was a tame heart, and a dear,
   And never used to roam;
   But having got this haunt, I
      fear
'Twill hardly stay at home.
For God's sake, walking by the
      way,   20
   If you my heart do see,
Either impound it for a stray,
   Or send it back to me.

To the Cambro-Britons and their harp, his ballad of Agincourt

Fair stood the wind for France,
When we our sails advance,
Nor now to prove our chance,
    Longer will tarry;
But putting to the main
At Kaux, the mouth of Seine,
With all his martial train,
    Landed King Harry.

And taking many a fort,
Furnished in warlike sort,   10
Marcheth towards Agincourt,
    In happy hour;
Skirmishing day by day
With those that stopped his way,
Where the French gen'ral lay
    With all his power.

Which in his height of pride,
King Henry to deride,
His ransom to provide
    To the King sending;   20
Which he neglects the while
As from a nation vile,
Yet with an angry smile
    Their fall portending.

And turning to his men,
Quoth our brave Henry then:
Though they to one be ten,
    Be not amazèd.
Yet have we well begun,
Battles so bravely won   30
Have ever to the sun
    By fame been raisèd.

And for myself, quoth he,
This my full rest shall be,
England ne'er mourn for me,
    Nor more esteem me;
Victor I will remain,
Or on this earth lie slain,

Never shall she sustain
    Loss to redeem me.   40

Poitiers and Crécy tell,
When most their pride did swell,
Under our swords they fell;
    No less our skill is
Than when our grandsire great,
Claiming the regal seat
By many a warlike feat,
    Lopped the French lilies.

The Duke of York so dread
The eager vaward led;   50
With the main Henry sped
    Amongst his henchmen.
Excester had the rear,
A braver man not there,
O Lord, how hot they were
    On the false Frenchmen!

They now to fight are gone,
Armor on armor shone,
Drum now to drum did groan,
    To hear was wonder,   60
That with cries they make
The very earth did shake,
Trumpet to trumpet spake,
    Thunder to thunder.

Well it thine age became,
O noble Erpingham,
Which didst the signal aim
    To our hid forces;
When from a meadow by,
Like a storm suddenly,   70
The English archery
    Stuck the French horses.

With Spanish yew so strong,
Arrows a cloth-yard long,
That like to serpents stung,
    Piercing the weather;
None from his fellow starts,
But playing manly parts,

And like true English hearts,
Stuck close together.   80

When down their bows they
    threw,
And forth their bilboes drew,
And on the French they flew,
  Not one was tardy;
Arms were from shoulders sent,
Scalps to the teeth were rent,
Down the French peasants went;
  Our men were hardy.

This while our noble King,
His broad sword brandishing,   90
Down the French host did ding,
  As to o'erwhelm it;
And many a deep wound lent,
His arms with blood besprent,
And many a cruel dent
  Bruisèd his helmet.

Gloster, that Duke so good,
Next of the royal blood,

For famous England stood
  With his brave brother;   100
Clarence, in steel so bright,
Though but a maiden knight,
Yet in that furious fight,
  Scarce such another.

Warwick in blood did wade,
Oxford the foe invade,
And cruel slaughter made,
  Still as they ran up;
Suffolk his axe did ply,
Beaumont and Willoughby   110
Bare them right doughtily,
  Ferrers and Fanhope.

Upon Saint Crispin's day
Fought was this noble fray,
Which fame did not delay
  To England to carry;
Oh, when shall English men
With such acts fill a pen,
Or England breed again
  Such a King Harry?   120

ECLOGUES

The ninth eclogue

Batt. Gorbo, as thou cam'st this
    way
  By yonder little hill,
Or as thou through the fields
    didst stray,
  Saw'st thou my Daffodil?

She's in a frock of Lincoln
    green,
  Which color likes her sight,
And never hath her beauty seen
  But through a veil of white;

Than roses, richer to behold,
  That trim up lovers' bowers,   10
The pansy and the marigold,
  Though Phœbus' paramours.

Gorbo. Thou well describ'st the
    daffodil;

It is not full an hour
Since by the spring, near yonder
    hill,
  I saw that lovely flower.

Batt. Yet my fair flower thou
    didst not meet,
  Nor news of her didst bring,
And yet my Daffodil's more
    sweet
  Than that by yonder spring.   20

Gorbo. I saw a shepherd that doth
    keep
  In yonder field of lilies,
Was making, as he fed his sheep,
  A wreath of daffodillies.

Batt. Yet, Gorbo, thou delud'st
  me still,

My flower thou didst not see,
For know, my pretty Daffodil
Is worn of none but me.

To show itself but near her seat
No lily is so bold,   30
Except to shade her from the
    heat,
Or keep her from the cold.

Gorbo. Through yonder vale as I
    did pass,
Descending from the hill,
I met a smirking bonny lass,
They call her Daffodil;

Whose presence, as along she
    went,

The pretty flowers did greet,
As though their heads they
    downward bent
With homage to her feet.   40

And all the shepherds that were
    nigh,
From top of every hill,
Unto the valleys loud did cry,
There goes sweet Daffodil.

Batt. Ay, gentle shepherd, now
    with joy
Thou all my flocks dost fill,
That's she alone, kind shep-
    herd's boy,
Let us to Daffodil.

.   .   .   .   .

FROM *Poly-Olbion,* [1612]

The thirteenth song

Upon the midlands now th' industrious muse doth fall,
That shire which we the heart of England well may call,
As she herself extends (the midst which is decreed)
Betwixt St. Michael's Mount and Berwick-bord'ring Tweed,
Brave Warwick, that abroad so long advanced her bear,
By her illustrious earls renownèd everywhere,
Above her neighboring shires which always bore her head.
    My native country then, which so brave spirits hast bred,
If there be virtue yet remaining in thy earth,
Or any good of thine thou breath'dst into my birth,   10
Accept it as thine own whilst now I sing of thee,
Of all thy later brood th' unworthiest though I be.
    Muse, first of Arden tell, whose footsteps yet are found
In her rough woodlands, more than any other ground
That mighty Arden held even in her height of pride,
Her one hand touching Trent, the other Severn's side.
    The very sound of these the wood-nymphs doth awake,
When thus of her own self the ancient forest spake:
    My many goodly sites when first I came to show,
Here opened I the way to mine own overthrow;   20
For when the world found out the fitness of my soil,
The gripple wretch began immediately to spoil
My tall and goodly woods, and did my grounds inclose,
By which in little time my bounds I came to lose.
    When Britain first her fields with villages had filled,

Her people waxing still and wanting where to build,
They oft dislodged the hart and set their houses where
He in the broom and brakes had long time made his lair.
Of all the forests here within this mighty isle,
If those old Britons then me sovereign did instyle,   30
I needs must be the great'st, for greatness 'tis alone
That gives our kind the place, else were there many a one
For pleasantness of shade that far doth me excel.
But of our forests' kind the quality to tell,
We equally partake with woodland as with plain,
Alike with hill and dale, and every day maintain
The sundry kinds of beasts upon our copious wastes
That men for profit breed, as well as those of chase.
  Here Arden of herself ceased any more to show,
And with her sylvan joys the muse along doth go.   40
  When Phœbus lifts his head out of the winter's wave,
No sooner doth the earth her flowery bosom brave,
At such time as the year brings on the pleasant spring,
But Hunts-up to the morn the feathered sylvans sing,
And in the lower grove, as on the rising knoll,
Upon the highest spray of every mounting pole,
Those quiristers are perched with many a speckled breast.
Then from her burnished gate the goodly glitt'ring east
Gilds every lofty top, which late the humorous night
Bespangled had with pearl to please the morning's sight;   50
On which the mirthful choirs with their clear open throats
Unto the joyful morn so strain their warbling notes
That hills and valleys ring, and even the echoing air
Seems all composed of sounds, about them everywhere.
The throstle, with shrill sharps, as purposely he song
T' awake the lustless sun, or chiding that so long
He was in coming forth that should the thickets thrill;
The woosell near at hand, that hath a golden bill,
As nature him had marked of purpose t' let us see
That from all other birds his tunes should different be;   60
For with their vocal sounds they sing to pleasant May.
Upon his dulcet pipe the merle doth only play;
When in the lower brake the nightingale hard by
In such lamenting strains the joyful hours doth ply,
As though the other birds she to her tunes would draw;
And but that nature, by her all-constraining law,
Each bird to her own kind this season doth invite,
They else, alone to hear that charmer of the night
(The more to use their ears) their voices sure would spare,
That moduleth her tunes so admirably rare,   70
As man to set in parts at first had learned of her.

To Philomel the next the linnet we prefer,
And by that warbling bird the wood-lark place we then,
The red sparrow, the nope, the redbreast, and the wren,
The yellowpate, which though she hurt the blooming tree,
Yet scarce hath any bird a finer pipe than she;
And of these chanting fowls the goldfinch not behind,
That hath so many sorts descending from her kind.
The tydie for her notes as delicate as they,
The laughing hecco, then the counterfeiting jay,   80
The softer with the shrill (some hid among the leaves,
Some in the taller trees, some in the lower greaves),
Thus sing away the morn, until the mounting sun
Through thick exhalèd fogs his golden head hath run,
And through the twisted tops of our close covert creeps
To kiss the gentle shade, this while that sweetly sleeps.
   And near to these our thicks, the wild and frightful herds,
Not hearing other noise but this of chattering birds,
Feed fairly on the lands; both sorts of seasoned deer,
Here walk the stately red, the freckled fallow there;   90
The bucks and lusty stags amongst the rascals strewed,
As sometime gallant spirits amongst the multitude.

.   .   .   .

   To forests that belongs, but yet this is not all:
With solitude what sorts that here's not wondrous rife?
Whereas the hermit leads a sweet retirèd life,
From villages replete with ragg'd and sweating clowns,
And from the loathsome airs of smoky citied towns.
Suppose 'twixt noon and night the sun his halfway wrought,
The shadows to be large by his descending brought,
Who with a fervent eye looks through the twiring glades   100
And his dispersèd rays commixeth with the shades,
Exhaling the milch dew, which there had tarried long
And on the ranker grass till past the noon-stead hong,
Whenas the hermit comes out of his homely cell,
Where from all rude resort he happily doth dwell;
Who in the strength of youth a man-at-arms hath been,
Or one who of this world the vileness having seen,
Retires him from it quite, and with a constant mind
Man's beastliness so loathes, that flying human kind,
The black and darksome nights, the bright and gladsome days 110
Indifferent are to him, his hope on God that stays.
Each little village yields his short and homely fare;
To gather wind-fall'n sticks his great'st and only care,
Which every aged tree still yieldeth to his fire.
   This man that is alone a king in his desire,

By no proud ignorant lord is basely overawed,
Nor his false praise affects who, grossly being clawed,
Stands like an itchy moil; nor of a pin he weighs
What fools abusëd kings and humorous ladies raise.
His free and noble thought ne'er envies at the grace   120
That oftentimes is given unto a bawd most base,
Nor stirs it him to think on the impostor vile
Who seeming what he's not, doth sensually beguile
The sottish purblind world; but absolutely free,
His happy time he spends the works of God to see
In those so sundry herbs which there in plenty grow,
Whose sundry strange effects he only seeks to know.
And in a little maund, being made of osiers small,
Which serveth him to do full many a thing withal,
He very choicely sorts his simples got abroad.   130

. . . .

But from our hermit here the muse we must enforce,
And zealously proceed in our intended course:
How Arden of her rills and riverets doth dispose;
By Alcester how Alne to Arrow eas'ly flows,
And mildly being mixed, to Avon hold their way;
And likewise toward the north, how lovely tripping Rhea
T' attend the lustier Tame is from her fountain sent;
So little Cole and Blythe go on with him to Trent;
His Tamworth at the last he in his way doth win,
There playing him awhile till Anker should come in,   140
Which trifleth 'twixt her banks, observing state, so slow
As though into his arms she scorned herself to throw;
Yet Arden willed her Tame to serve her on his knee,
For by that nymph alone they both should honored be.
The forest so much fall'n from what she was before,
That to her former height fate could her not restore,
Though oft in her behalf the genius of the land
Importunëd the heavens with an auspicious hand.
Yet granted at the last, the aged nymph to grace,
They by a lady's birth would more renown that place   150
Than if her woods their heads above the hills should seat;
And for that purpose first made Coventry so great,
(A poor thatched village then, or scarcely none at all,
That could not once have dreamed of her now stately wall)
And thither wisely brought that goodly virgin band,
Th' eleven thousand maids, chaste Ursula's command,
Whom then the Briton kings gave her full power to press,
For matches to their friends in Brittany the less.
At whose departure thence, each by her just bequest

Some special virtue gave, ordaining it to rest   160
With one of their own sex, that there her birth should have,
Till fullness of the time which fate did choicely save
Until the Saxons' reign, when Coventry at length
From her small mean regard recovered state and strength,
By Leofric, her lord, yet in base bondage held,
The people from her marts by tollage who expelled;
Whose duchess, which desired this tribute to release,
Their freedom often begged. The duke, to make her cease,
Told her that if she would his loss so far enforce,
His will was she should ride stark nak'd upon a horse   170
By daylight through the street; which certainly he thought
In her heroic breast so deeply would have wrought,
That in her former suit she would have left to deal.
But that most princely dame, as one devoured with zeal,
Went on, and by that mean the city clearly freed.

                    .   .   .   .   .   .

But whilst about this tale smooth Anker trifling stays,
Unto the lustier Tame as loath to come her ways,
The flood entreats her thus: Dear brook, why dost thou wrong
Our mutual love so much, and tediously prolong
Our mirthful marriage hour, for which I still prepare?   180
Haste to my broader banks, my joy and only care.
For as of all my floods thou art the first in fame,
When frankly thou shalt yield thine honor to my name,
I will protect thy state; then do not wrong thy kind.
What pleasure hath the world that here thou mayst not find?

                    .   .   .   .   .   .

FROM *The Battle of Agincourt*, 1627

To my most dearly loved friend, Henry Reynolds, Esquire Of poets and poesy

My dearly lovèd friend, how oft have we
In winter evenings, meaning to be free,
To some well-chosen place used to retire,
And there with moderate meat, and wine, and fire,
Have passed the hours contentedly with chat;
Now talked of this, and then discoursed of that,
Spoke our own verses 'twixt ourselves; if not,
Other men's lines which we by chance had got,
Or some stage pieces famous long before,
Of which your happy memory had store;   10
And I remember you much pleasèd were
Of those who livèd long ago to hear,

As well as of those of these latter times
Who have enriched our language with their rhymes,
And in succession how still up they grew,
Which is the subject that I now pursue.
For from my cradle you must know that I
Was still inclined to noble poesy,
And when that once *Pueriles* I had read,
And newly had my Cato construëd,
In my small self I greatly marveled then,
Amongst all other, what strange kind of men
These poets were; and pleasëd with the name,
To my mild tutor merrily I came,
(For I was then a proper goodly page,
Much like a pigmy, scarce ten years of age)
Clasping my slender arms about his thigh,
O my dear master! cannot you, quoth I,
Make me a poet? Do it if you can,
And you shall see I'll quickly be a man.
Who me thus answered smiling: Boy, quoth he,
If you'll not play the wag, but I may see
You ply your learning, I will shortly read
Some poets to you. Phœbus be my speed,
To 't hard went I, when shortly he began
And first read to me honest Mantuan,
Then Virgil's *Eclogues*; being entered thus,
Methought I straight had mounted Pegasus,
And in his full career could make him stop
And bound upon Parnassus' bi-clift top.
I scorned your ballad then, though it were done
And had for finis, William Elderton.
But soft, in sporting with this childish jest
I from my subject have too long digressed;
Then to the matter that we took in hand,
Jove and Apollo for the Muses stand.
   Then noble Chaucer, in those former times
The first enriched our English with his rhymes,
And was the first of ours that ever brake
Into the Muses' treasure, and first spake
In weighty numbers, delving in the mine
Of perfect knowledge, which he could refine
And coin for current; and as much as then
The English language could express to men,
He made it do, and by his wondrous skill,
Gave us much light from his abundant quill.
   And honest Gower, who in respect of him
Had only sipped at Aganippe's brim,

20

30

40

50

And though in years this last was him before,
Yet fell he far short of the other's store.   60
　　When after those, four ages very near,
They with the Muses which conversëd were:
That princely Surrey, early in the time
Of the eight Henry, who was then the prime
Of England's noble youth; with him there came
Wyatt, with reverence whom we still do name
Amongst our poets; Bryan had a share
With the two former, which accompted are
That time's best makers, and the authors were
Of those small poems which the title bear   70
Of *Songs and Sonnets,* wherein oft they hit
On many dainty passages of wit.
　　Gascoigne and Churchyard after them again
In the beginning of Eliza's reign,
Accompted were great meterers many a day,
But not inspirëd with brave fire; had they
Lived but a little longer they had seen
Their works before them to have buried been.
　　Grave moral Spenser after these came on,
Than whom I am persuaded there was none   80
Since the blind bard his *Iliads* up did make
Fitter a task like that to undertake,
To set down boldly, bravely to invent,
In all high knowledge surely excellent.
　　The noble Sidney with this last arose,
That heroë for numbers and for prose,
That throughly paced our language as to show
The plenteous English hand in hand might go
With Greek or Latin; and did first reduce
Our tongue from Lyly's writing, then in use: 90
Talking of stones, stars, plants, of fishes, flies,
Playing with words and idle similes;
As th' English apes and very zanies be,
Of everything that they do hear and see,
So imitating his ridiculous tricks,
They spake and writ all like mere lunatics.
　　Then Warner, though his lines were not so trimmed,
Nor yet his poem so exactly limned
And neatly jointed, but the critic may
Easily reprove him, yet thus let me say   100
For my old friend: some passages there be
In him which I protest have taken me
With almost wonder, so fine, clear, and new
As yet they have been equallëd by few.

Neat Marlowe, bathëd in the Thespian springs,
Had in him those brave translunary things
That the first poets had; his raptures were
All air and fire, which made his verses clear,
For that fine madness still he did retain
Which rightly should possess a poet's brain.   110
   And surely Nashe, though he a proser were,
A branch of laurel yet deserves to bear;
Sharply satiric was he, and that way
He went, since that his being to this day
Few have attempted, and I surely think
Those words shall hardly be set down with ink,
Shall scorch and blast so as his could, where he
Would inflict vengeance. And be it said of thee,
Shakespeare, thou hadst as smooth a comic vein,
Fitting the sock, and in thy natural brain   120
As strong conception and as clear a rage
As anyone that trafficked with the stage.
   Amongst these, Samuel Daniel, whom if I
May speak of, but to censure do deny,
Only have heard some wise men him rehearse
To be too much historian in verse;
His rhymes were smooth, his meters well did close,
But yet his manner better fitted prose.
Next these, learn'd Jonson in this list I bring,
Who had drunk deep of the Pierian spring,   130
Whose knowledge did him worthily prefer,
And long was lord here of the theater;
Who in opinion made our learn'st to stick,
Whether in poems rightly dramatic,
Strong Seneca or Plautus, he or they
Should bear the buskin or the sock away.
Others again here livëd in my days
That have of us deservëd no less praise
For their translations than the daintiest wit
That on Parnassus thinks he high'st doth sit,   140
And for a chair may 'mongst the muses call
As the most curious maker of them all;
As reverent Chapman, who hath brought to us
Musæus, Homer, and Hesiodus
Out of the Greek, and by his skill hath reared
Them to that height, and to our tongues endeared,
That were those poets at this day alive
To see their books thus with us to survive,
They would think, having neglected them so long,
They had been written in the English tongue.   150

And Sylvester, who from the French more weak
Made Bartas of his six days' labor speak
In natural English; who, had he there stayed
He had done well, and never had bewrayed
His own invention to have been so poor,
Who still wrote less in striving to write more.

   Then dainty Sandys, that hath to English done
Smooth sliding Ovid, and hath made him run
With so much sweetness and unusual grace,
As though the neatness of the English pace   160
Should tell the jetting Latin that it came
But slowly after, as though stiff and lame.

   So Scotland sent us hither, for our own,
That man whose name I ever would have known
To stand by mine, that most ingenious knight,
My Alexander, to whom in his right
I want extremely, yet in speaking thus
I do but show the love that was 'twixt us,
And not his numbers which were brave and high,
So like his mind was his clear poesy;   170
And my dear Drummond, to whom much I owe
For his much love, and proud I was to know
His poesy; for which two worthy men,
I Menstry still shall love, and Hawthornden.

   Then the two Beaumonts and my Browne arose,
My dear companions whom I freely chose
My bosom friends, and in their several ways
Rightly born poets, and in these last days
Men of much note and no less nobler parts,
Such as have freely told to me their hearts,   180
As I have mine to them; but if you shall
Say in your knowledge that these be not all
Have writ in numbers, be informed that I
Only myself to these few men do tie,
Whose works oft printed, set on every post,
To public censure subject have been most;
For such whose poems, be they ne'er so rare,
In private chambers that encloistered are,
And by transcription daintily must go,
As though the world unworthy were to know   190
Their rich composures, let those men that keep
These wonderous relics in their judgment deep,
And cry them up so, let such pieces be
Spoke of by those that shall come after me;
I pass not for them, nor do mean to run
In quest of these that them applause have won

Upon our stages in these latter days,
That are so many—let them have their bays
That do deserve it; let those wits that haunt
Those public circuits, let them freely chant 200
Their fine composures, and their praise pursue;
And so, my dear friend, for this time, adieu.

Nymphidia, the court of fairy

Old Chaucer doth of Thopas tell,
Mad Rab'lais of Pantagruel,
A latter third of Dowsabell,
    With such poor trifles playing;
Others the like have labored at,
Some of this thing and some of
        that,
And many of they know not
        what,
    But that they must be saying.

Another sort there be that will
Be talking of the fairies still, 10
Nor never can they have their
        fill,
    As they were wedded to them;
No tales of them their thirst can
        slake,
So much delight therein they take,
And some strange thing they fain
        would make,
    Knew they the way to do them.

Then since no muse hath been so
        bold,
Or of the later, or the old,
Those elvish secrets to unfold,
    Which lie from others' read-
        ing, 20
My active muse to light shall
        bring
The court of that proud fairy
        king,
And tell there of the reveling;
    Jove prosper my proceeding.

And thou, Nymphidia, gentle fay,
Which meeting me upon the way
These secrets didst to me bewray,
    Which now I am in telling,
My pretty light fantastic maid,
I here invoke thee to my aid 30
That I may speak what thou hast
        said,
    In numbers smoothly swelling.

This palace standeth in the air,
By necromancy placëd there,
That it no tempests needs to fear,
    Which way soe'er it blow it.
And somewhat southward toward
        the noon,
Whence lies a way up to the
        moon,
And thence the fairy can as soon
    Pass to the earth below it. 40

The walls of spiders' legs are
        made,
Well mortisëd and finely laid;
He was the master of his trade,
    It curiously that builded;
The windows of the eyes of cats,
And for the roof, instead of slats,
Is covered with the skins of bats,
    With moonshine that are
        gilded.

Hence Oberon him sport to make,
Their rest when weary mortals
        take, 50
And none but only fairies wake,
    Descendeth for his pleasure.

And Mab, his merry queen, by
    night
Bestrides young folks that lie up-
    right,
(In elder times the Mare that
    hight)
    Which plagues them out of
        measure.

Hence shadows, seeming idle
    shapes,
Of little frisking elves and apes,
To earth do make their wanton
    scapes,
    As hope of pastime hastes
        them;   60
Which maids think on the hearth
    they see
When fires well ne'er consumèd
    be,
There dancing hays by two and
    three,
    Just as their fancy casts them.

These make our girls their slut-
    tery rue
By pinching them both black and
    blue,
And put a penny in their shoe,
    The house for cleanly sweep-
        ing;
And in their courses make that
    round,
In meadows and in marshes
    found,   70
Of them so called the fairy
    ground,
    Of which they have the keep-
        ing.

These, when a child haps to be
    got
Which after proves an idiot,
When folk perceive it thriveth
    not,
    The fault therein to smother,

Some silly doting brainless calf
That understands things by the
    half,
Say that the fairy left this auf
    And took away the other.   80

But listen and I shall you tell
A chance in fairy that befell,
Which certainly may please some
    well,
    In love and arms delighting:
Of Oberon that jealous grew
Of one of his own fairy crew,
Too well, he feared, his queen
    that knew,
    His love but ill requiting.

Pigwiggen was this fairy knight,
One wondrous gracious in the
    sight   90
Of fair Queen Mab, which day
    and night
    He amorously observèd;
Which made King Oberon sus-
    pect
His service took too good effect,
His sauciness and often checked,
    And could have wished him
        starvèd.

Pigwiggen gladly would com-
    mend
Some token to Queen Mab to
    send,
If sea or land him aught could
    lend,
    Were worthy of her wear-
        ing;   100
At length this lover doth devise
A bracelet made of emmets' eyes,
A thing he thought that she
    would prize,
    No whit her state impairing.

And to the queen a letter writes,
Which he most curiously indites,

Conjuring her by all the rites
  Of love, she would be pleasëd
To meet him, her true servant,
    where
They might without suspect or
    fear   110
Themselves to one another clear,
  And have their poor hearts
    easëd.

At midnight the appointed hour,
And for the queen a fitting bower,
Quoth he, is that fair cowslip
    flower
  On Hipcut hill that groweth;
In all your train there's not a fay
That ever went to gather May
But she hath made it in her way,
  The tallest there that grow-
    eth.   120

When by Tom Thumb, a fairy
    page,
He sent it, and doth him engage,
By promise of a mighty wage,
  It secretly to carry;
Which done, the queen her maids
    doth call,
And bids them to be ready all;
She would go see her summer
    hall,
  She could no longer tarry.

Her chariot ready straight is
    made,
Each thing therein is fitting
    laid   130
That she by nothing might be
    stayed,
  For nought must her be let-
    ting;
Four nimble gnats the horses
    were,
Their harnesses of gossamer,
Fly Cranion, her charioteer,
  Upon the coach-box getting.

Her chariot of a snail's fine shell,
Which for the colors did excel,
The fair Queen Mab becoming
    well,
  So lively was the limning;   140
The seat the soft wool of the bee;
The cover, gallantly to see,
The wing of a pied butterflee,
  I trow, 'twas simple trimming.

The wheels composed of crickets'
    bones,
And daintily made for the nonce;
For fear of rattling on the stones
  With thistle-down they shod
    it;
For all her maidens much did
    fear,
If Oberon had chanced to hear 150
That Mab his queen should have
    been there,
  He would not have abode it.

She mounts her chariot with a
    trice,
Nor would she stay for no advice,
Until her maids, that were so
    nice,
  To wait on her were fitted,
But ran herself away alone;
Which when they heard, there
    was not one
But hasted after to be gone,
  As she had been diswitted.   160

Hop and Mop and Drop so clear,
Pip and Trip and Skip that were
To Mab, their sovereign, ever
    dear,
  Her special maids of honor;
Fib and Tib and Pink and Pin,
Tick and Quick and Jill and Jin,
Tit and Nit and Wap and Win,
  The train that wait upon her.

Upon a grasshopper they got,
And what with amble and with
    trot,   170
For hedge nor ditch they sparëd
    not,
    But after her they hie them.
A cobweb over them they throw,
To shield the wind if it should
    blow;
Themselves they wisely could be-
    stow,
    Lest any should espy them.

But let us leave Queen Mab a
    while,
Through many a gate, o'er many
    a stile,
That now had gotten by this
    wile,
    Her dear Pigwiggen kissing, 180
And tell how Oberon doth fare,
Who grew as mad as any hare,
When he had sought each place
    with care
    And found his queen was miss-
    ing.

By grisly Pluto he doth swear,
He rent his clothes and tore his
    hair,
And as he runneth here and there
    An acorn cup he greeteth;
Which soon he taketh by the
    stalk,
About his head he lets it walk, 190
Nor doth he any creature balk,
    But lays on all he meeteth.

The Tuscan poet doth advance
The frantic Paladin of France,
And those more ancient do en-
    hance
    Alcides in his fury;
And others, Ajax, Telamon;
But to this time there hath been
    none

So bedlam as our Oberon,
    Of which I dare assure you. 200

And first encount'ring with a
    wasp,
He in his arms the fly doth clasp
As though his breath he forth
    would grasp,
    Him for Pigwiggen taking.
Where is my wife, thou rogue?
    quoth he,
Pigwiggen, she is come to thee,
Restore her or thou di'st by me.
    Whereat the poor wasp quak-
    ing,

Cries, Oberon, great Fairy King,
Content thee I am no such
    thing;   210
I am a wasp, behold my sting.
    At which the fairy started;
When soon away the wasp doth
    go,
Poor wretch was never frighted
    so,
He thought his wings were much
    too slow,
    O'erjoyed they so were parted.

He next upon a glow-worm light,
(You must suppose it now was
    night),
Which for her hinder part was
    bright,
    He took to be a devil.   220
And furiously doth her assail
For carrying fire in her tail;
He thrashed her rough coat with
    his flail,
    The mad king feared no evil.

O, quoth the glow-worm, hold
    thy hand,
Thou puissant King of Fairyland,
Thy mighty strokes who may
    withstand;

Hold, or of life despair I!
Together then herself doth roll,
And tumbling down into a hole, 230
She seemed as black as any coal,
Which vexed away the fairy.

From thence he ran into a hive,
Amongst the bees he letteth drive,
And down their combs begins to rive,
All likely to have spoilëd;
Which with their wax his face be-smeared,
And with their honey daubed his beard;
It would have made a man afeard
To see how he was moilëd. 240

A new adventure him betides,
He met an ant, which he be-strides,
And post thereon away he rides,
Which with his haste doth stumble
And came full over on her snout,
Her heels so threw the dirt about,
For she by no means could get out,
But over him doth tumble.

And being in this piteous case,
And all beslurried, head and face, 250
On runs he in this wild-goose chase;
As here and there he rambles
Half blind, against a molehill hit,
And for a mountain taking it,
For all he was out of his wit,
Yet to the top he scrambles.

And being gotten to the top,
Yet there himself he could not stop,

But down on th' other side doth chop,
And to the foot came rum-bling, 260
So that the grubs therein that bred,
Hearing such turmoil overhead,
Thought surely they had all been dead,
So fearful was the jumbling.

And falling down into a lake,
Which him up to the neck doth take,
His fury somewhat it doth slake,
He calleth for a ferry;
Where you may some recovery note,
What was his club he made his boat, 270
And in his oaken cup doth float
As safe as in a wherry.

Men talk of the adventures strange
Of Don Quishott, and of their change
Through which he armëd oft did range,
Of Sancho Pancha's travel;
But should a man tell everything
Done by this frantic fairy king,
And them in lofty numbers sing,
It well his wits might gravel. 280

Scarce set on shore, but there-withal
He meeteth Puck, which most men call
Hobgoblin, and on him doth fall
With words from frenzy spoken.
Ho, ho, quoth Hob, God save thy grace,

Who dressed thee in this piteous
    case?
He thus that spoiled my sover-
    eign's face
    I would his neck were broken.

This Puck seems but a dreaming
    dolt,
Still walking like a ragged colt, 290
And oft out of a bush doth bolt,
    Of purpose to deceive us.
And leading us, makes us to stray,
Long winter's nights, out of the
    way,
And when we stick in mire and
    clay,
    Hob doth with laughter leave
      us.

Dear Puck, quoth he, my wife is
    gone;
As e'er thou lov'st King Oberon,
Let everything but this alone,
    With vengeance and pursue
      her; 300
Bring her to me alive or dead,
Or that vile thief Pigwiggen's
    head.
That villain hath defiled my bed,
    He to this folly drew her.

Quoth Puck, My liege, I'll never
    lin,
But I will thorough thick and
    thin
Until at length I bring her in,
    My dearest lord, ne'er doubt it.
Thorough brake, thorough brier,
Thorough muck, thorough mire,
Thorough water, thorough fire, 311
    And thus goes Puck about it.

This thing Nymphidia overheard,
That on this mad king had a
    guard,
Not doubting of a great reward

For first this business broach-
    ing;
And through the air away doth
    go,
Swift as an arrow from the bow,
To let her sovereign Mab to
    know
    What peril was approach-
      ing. 320

The queen, bound with love's
    powerful'st charm,
Sat with Pigwiggen, arm in arm;
Her merry maids that thought no
    harm
    About the room were skipping.
A humble-bee, their minstrel,
    played
Upon his hautboy; ev'ry maid
Fit for this revels was arrayed,
    The hornpipe neatly tripping.

In comes Nymphidia and doth
    cry:
My sovereign, for your safety
    fly, 330
For there is danger but too nigh,
    I posted to forewarn you;
The king hath sent Hobgoblin
    out
To seek you all the fields about,
And of your safety you may
    doubt,
    If he but once discern you.

When like an uproar in a town,
Before them everything went
    down;
Some tore a ruff and some a
    gown,
    'Gainst one another just-
      ling. 340
They flew about like chaff i' th'
    wind,
For haste some left their masks
    behind,

Some could not stay their gloves
    to find,
  There never was such bustling.

Forth ran they by a secret way
Into a brake that near them lay,
Yet much they doubted there to
    stay
  Lest Hob should hap to find
    them;
He had a sharp and piercing sight,
All one to him the day and night,
And therefore were resolved by
    flight   351
  To leave this place behind
    them.

At length one chanced to find a
    nut
In th' end of which a hole was
    cut,
Which lay upon a hazel root,
  There scattered by a squirrel
Which out the kernel gotten had;
When quoth this fay, Dear
    Queen, be glad,
Let Oberon be ne'er so mad,
  I'll set you safe from peril. 360

Come all into this nut, quoth she,
Come closely in, be ruled by me,
Each one may here a chooser be,
  For room ye need not wrastle,
Nor need ye be together heaped.
So one by one therein they crept,
And lying down they soundly
    slept,
  As safe as in a castle.

Nymphidia, that this while doth
    watch,
Perceived if Puck the queen should
    catch,   370
That he would be her over-match,
  Of which she well bethought
    her.

Found it must be some powerful
    charm,
The queen against him that must
    arm,
Or surely he would do her harm,
  For throughly he had sought
    her.

And list'ning if she aught could
    hear
That her might hinder, or might
    fear,
But finding still the coast was
    clear,   379
  Nor creature had descried her;
Each circumstance and having
    scanned,
She came thereby to understand
Puck would be with them out of
    hand,
  When to her charms she hied
    her.

And first her fern seed doth be-
    stow,
The kernel of the mistletoe,
And here and there as Puck should
    go,
  With terror to affright him,
She nightshade straws to work
    him ill,
Therewith her vervain and her
    dill,   390
That hind'reth witches of their
    will,
  Of purpose to despite him.

Then sprinkles she the juice of
    rue
That groweth underneath the
    yew,
With nine drops of the midnight
    dew,
  From lunary distilling;
The molewarp's brain mixed
    therewithal,

And with the same the pismire's
  gall,
For she in nothing short would
  fall,
  The fairy was so willing.   400

Then thrice under a brier doth
  creep,
Which at both ends was rooted
  deep,
And over it three times she leap,
  Her magic much availing;
Then on Proserpina doth call,
And so upon her spell doth fall,
Which here to you repeat I shall,
  Not in one tittle failing:

By the croaking of the frog,
By the howling of the dog,   410
By the crying of the hog,
  Against the storm arising;
By the evening curfew bell,
By the doleful dying knell,
Oh, let this my direful spell,
  Hob, hinder thy surprising.

By the mandrake's dreadful
  groans,
By the lubrican's sad moans,
By the noise of dead men's bones
  In charnel houses rattling;   420
By the hissing of the snake,
The rustling of the fire-drake,
I charge thee thou this place for-
  sake,
  Nor of Queen Mab be prat-
  tling.

By the whirlwind's hollow sound,
By the thunder's dreadful stound,
Yells of spirits under ground,
  I charge thee not to fear us;
By the screech-owl's dismal note,
By the black night-raven's throat,
I charge thee, Hob, to tear thy
  coat   431

With thorns, if thou come near
  us.

Her spell thus spoke, she stepped
  aside,
And in a chink herself doth hide
To see thereof what would betide,
  For she doth only mind him;
When presently she Puck espies,
And well she marked his gloating
  eyes,
How under every leaf he pries,
  In seeking still to find them.   440

But once the circle got within,
The charms to work do straight
  begin,
And he was caught as in a gin;
  For as he thus was busy,
A pain he in his head-piece feels,
Against a stubbëd tree he reels,
And up went poor Hobgoblin's
  heels,
  Alas, his brain was dizzy.

At length upon his feet he gets,
Hobgoblin fumes, Hobgoblin
  frets,   450
And as again he forward sets,
  And through the bushes scram-
  bles,
A stump doth trip him in his pace,
Down comes poor Hob upon his
  face,
And lamentably tore his case
  Amongst the briers and bram-
  bles.

A plague upon Queen Mab, quoth
  he,
And all her maids, where'er they
  be,
I think the devil guided me
  To seek her so provokëd.   460
Where stumbling at a piece of
  wood

He fell into a ditch of mud,
Where to the very chin he stood
In danger to be chokëd.

Now worse than e'er he was be-
    fore,
Poor Puck doth yell, poor Puck
    doth roar,
That waked Queen Mab, what
    doubted sore
Some treason had been wrought
    her,
Until Nymphidia told the queen
What she had done, what she had
    seen,   470
Who then had well-near cracked
    her spleen
With very extreme laughter.

But leave we Hob to clamber out,
Queen Mab and all her fairy
    rout,
And come again to have about
With Oberon, yet madding;
And with Pigwiggen now dis-
    traught,
Who much was troubled in his
    thought,
That he so long the queen had
    sought,
And through the fields was gad-
    ding.   480

And as he runs he still doth cry:
King Oberon, I thee defy,
And dare thee here in arms to try
    For my dear lady's honor;
For that she is a queen right good,
In whose defence I'll shed my
    blood,
And that thou in this jealous mood
    Hast laid this slander on her.

And quickly arms him for the
    field,
A little cockle-shell his shield, 490

Which he could very bravely
    wield,
    Yet could it not be piercëd;
His spear, a bent both stiff and
    strong,
And well near of two inches long;
The pile was of a horsefly's
    tongue,
    Whose sharpness nought re-
    versëd.

And puts him on a coat of mail,
Which was of a fish's scale,
That when his foe should him as-
    sail,
    No point should be prevail-
    ing;   500
His rapier was a hornet's sting,
It was a very dangerous thing,
For if he chanced to hurt the king
    It would be long in healing.

His helmet was a beetle's head,
Most horrible and full of dread,
That able was to strike one dead,
    Yet did it well become him;
And for a plume a horse's hair,
Which being tossëd with the air
Had force to strike his foe with
    fear,   511
    And turn his weapon from
    him.

Himself he on an earwig set,
Yet scarce he on his back could
    get,
So oft and high he did curvet
    Ere he himself could settle;
He made him turn, and stop, and
    bound,
To gallop, and to trot the round,
He scarce could stand on any
    ground,
    He was so full of mettle. 520

When soon he met with Tomalin,
One that a valiant knight had
    been,
And to King Oberon of kin;
    Quoth he, Thou manly fairy,
Tell Oberon I come prepared,
Then bid him stand upon his
    guard,
This hand his baseness shall re-
    ward,
    Let him be ne'er so wary.

Say to him thus, that I defy
His slanders and his infamy,   530
And as a mortal enemy
    Do publicly proclaim him;
Withal, that if I had mine own
He should not wear the fairy
    crown,
But with a vengeance should come
    down,
    Nor we a king should name
        him.

This Tomalin could not abide
To hear his sovereign vilified,
But to the fairy court him hied,
    Full furiously he posted,   540
With ev'rything Pigwiggen said:
How title to the crown he laid,
And in what arms he was arrayed,
    And how himself he boasted.

'Twixt head and foot, from point
    to point,
He told th' arming of each joint,
In every piece how neat and
    quaint,
    For Tomalin could do it;
How fair he sat, how sure he rid,
As of the courser he bestrid,   550
How managed, and how well he
    did.
    The king which listened to it,

Quoth he, Go, Tomalin, with
    speed,
Provide me arms, provide my
    steed,
And everything that I shall need,
    By thee I will be guided.
To strait account call thou thy
    wit,
See there be wanting not a whit,
In everything see thou me fit,
    Just as my foe's provided.   560

Soon flew this news through fairy-
    land,
Which gave Queen Mab to under-
    stand
The combat that was then in hand
    Betwixt those men so mighty;
Which greatly she began to rue,
Perceiving that all fairy knew
The first occasion from her grew,
    Of these affairs so weighty.

Wherefore, attended with her
    maids,
Through fogs and mists and
    damps she wades,   570
To Proserpine, the Queen of
    Shades,
    To treat that it would please
        her
The cause into her hands to take,
For ancient love and friendship's
    sake,
And soon thereof an end to make,
    Which of much care would ease
        her.

A while there let we Mab alone,
And come we to King Oberon,
Who armed to meet his foe is
    gone,   579
    For proud Pigwiggen crying;
Who sought the fairy king as fast,
And had so well his journeys cast
That he arrivèd at the last,
    His puissant foe espying.

Stout Tomalin came with the king,
Tom Thumb doth on Pigwiggen bring,
That perfect were in everything
  To single fights belonging.
And therefore they themselves engage
To see them exercise their rage 590
With fair and comely equipage,
  Not one the other wronging.

So like in arms these champions were
As they had been a very pair,
So that a man would almost swear
  That either had been either;
Their furious steeds began to neigh,
That they were heard a mighty way;
Their staves upon their rests they lay,
  Yet ere they flew together 600

Their seconds minister an oath,
Which was indifferent to them both,
That on their knightly faith and troth
  No magic them supplièd;
And sought them that they had no charms
Wherewith to work each other's harms,
But came with simple open arms
  To have their causes trièd.

Together furiously they ran,
That to the ground came horse and man, 610
The blood out of their helmets span,
  So sharp were their encounters;
And though they to the earth were thrown

Yet quickly they regained their own,
Such nimbleness was never shown,
  They were two gallant mounters.

When in a second course again
They forward came with might and main,
Yet which had better of the twain
  The seconds could not judge yet; 620
Their shields were into pieces cleft,
Their helmets from their heads were reft,
And to defend them nothing left,
  These champions would not budge yet.

Away from them their staves they threw,
Their cruel swords they quickly drew,
And freshly they the fight renew,
  They every stroke redoubled;
Which made Proserpina take heed,
And make to them the greater speed, 630
For fear lest they too much should bleed,
  Which wondrously her troubled.

When to th' infernal Styx she goes,
She takes the fogs from thence that rose
And in a bag doth them enclose;
  When well she had them blended,
She hies her then to Lethe spring,
A bottle and thereof doth bring,
Wherewith she meant to work the thing
  Which only she intended. 640

Now Proserpine with Mab is gone
Unto the place where Oberon
And proud Pigwiggen, one to one,
   Both to be slain were likely;
And there themselves they closely
   hide,
Because they would not be espied,
For Proserpine meant to decide
   The matter very quickly.

And suddenly unties the poke,
Which out of it sent such a smoke
As ready was them all to choke, 651
   So grievous was the pother;
So that the knights each other
   lost,
And stood as still as any post,
Tom Thumb nor Tomalin could
   boast
   Themselves of any other.

But when the mist gan somewhat
   cease,
Proserpina commandeth peace,
And that awhile they should re-
   lease
   Each other of their peril; 660
Which here, quoth she, I do pro-
   claim
To all, in dreadful Pluto's name,
That as ye will eschew his blame,
   You let me hear the quarrel.

But here yourselves you must en-
   gage,
Somewhat to cool your spleenish
   rage,
Your grievous thirst and to as-
   suage,
   That first you drink this liquor,
Which shall your understanding
   clear,
As plainly shall to you appear, 670
Those things from me that you
   shall hear
   Conceiving much the quicker.

This Lethe water, you must know,
The memory destroyeth so,
That of our weal or of our woe
   It all remembrance blotted;
Of it nor can you ever think,
For they no sooner took this drink,
But nought into their brains could
   sink
   Of what had them besotted. 680

King Oberon forgotten had
That he for jealousy ran mad;
But of his queen was wondrous
   glad,
   And asked how they came
   thither.
Pigwiggen likewise doth forget
That he Queen Mab had ever
   met,
Or that they were so hard beset
   When they were found to-
   gether.

Nor neither of them both had
   thought
That e'er they had each other
   sought, 690
Much less that they a combat
   fought,
   But such a dream were loathing.
Tom Thumb had got a little sup,
And Tomalin scarce kissed the
   cup,
Yet had their brains so sure locked
   up
   That they remembered nothing.

Queen Mab and her light maids
   the while
Amongst themselves do closely
   smile
To see the king caught with this
   wile,
   With one another jesting. 700

And to the fairy court they
 went,
With mickle joy and merriment,

Which thing was done with good
 intent,
And thus I left them feasting.

The Shepherd's Sirena

. . . .

Near to the silver Trent
 Sirena dwelleth,
She to whom nature lent
 All that excelleth;
By which the Muses late,
 And the neat Graces,
Have for their greater state
 Taken their places;
Twisting an anadem,
 Wherewith to crown her, 10
As it belonged to them
 Most to renown her.
  On thy bank,
  In a rank,
Let the swans sing her,
 And with their music
Along let them bring her.

Tagus and Pactolus
 Are to thee debtor,
Nor for their gold to us 20
 Are they the better;
Henceforth of all the rest
 Be thou the river,
Which as the daintiest
 Puts them down ever.
For as my precious one
 O'er thee doth travel,
She to pearl paragon
 Turneth thy gravel.
  On thy bank, 30
  In a rank,
Let thy swans sing her,
 And with their music
Along let them bring her.

Our mournful Philomel,
 That rarest tuner,
Henceforth in Aperil

Shall wake the sooner,
And to her shall complain
 From the thick cover, 40
Redoubling every strain
 Over and over;
For when my love too long
 Her chamber keepeth,
As though it suffered wrong
 The morning weepeth.
  On thy bank,
  In a rank,
Let thy swans sing her,
 And with their music 50
Along let them bring her.

Oft have I seen the sun,
 To do her honor,
Fix himself at his noon
 To look upon her;
And hath gilt every grove,
 Every hill near her,
With his flames from above
 Striving to cheer her,
And when she from his sight 60
 Hath herself turnëd,
He, as it had been night,
 In clouds hath mournëd.
  On thy bank,
  In a rank,
Let thy swans sing her,
 And with their music
Along let them bring her.

The verdant meads are seen,
 When she doth view them, 70
In fresh and gallant green
 Straight to renew them;
And every little grass
 Broad itself spreadeth,
Proud that this bonny lass
 Upon it treadeth;

Nor flower is so sweet
  In this large cincture,
But it upon her feet
  Leaveth some tincture.   80
    On thy bank,
    In a rank,
  Let thy swans sing her,
  And with their music
Along let them bring her.

The fishes in the flood,
  When she doth angle,
For the hook strive a good
  Them to entangle,
And leaping on the land   90
  From the clear water,
Their scales upon the sand
  Lavishly scatter;
Therewith to pave the mold
  Whereon she passes,
So herself to behold
  As in her glasses.
    On thy bank,
    In a rank,
  Let thy swans sing her,   100
  And with their music
Along let them bring her.

When she looks out by night
  The stars stand gazing,
Like comets to our sight
  Fearfully blazing,
As wond'ring at her eyes
  With their much brightness,
Which to amaze the skies,
  Dimming their lightness;   110
The raging tempests are calm
  When she speaketh,
Such most delightsome balm
  From her lips breaketh.
    On thy bank,
    In a rank,
  Let thy swans sing her
  And with their music
Along let them bring her.

In all our Britainy   120
  There's not a fairer,
Nor can you fit any
  Should you compare her.
Angels her eyelids keep,
  All hearts surprising,
Which look whilst she doth sleep
  Like the sun's rising;
She alone of her kind
  Knoweth true measure,
And her unmatchèd mind   130
  Is heaven's treasure.
    On thy bank,
    In a rank,
  Let thy swans sing her,
  And with their music
Along let them bring her.

Fair Dove and Darwin clear,
  Boast ye your beauties,
To Trent, your mistress, here
  Yet pay your duties;   140
My love was higher born
  Towards the full fountains,
Yet she doth moorland scorn
  And the Peak mountains;
Nor would she none should dream
  Where she abideth,
Humble as is the stream
  Which by her slideth.
    On thy bank,
    In a rank,   150
  Let thy swans sing her,
  And with their music
Along let them bring her.

Yet my poor rustic muse
  Nothing can move her,
Nor the means I can use,
  Though her true lover;
Many a long winter's night
  Have I waked for her,
Yet this my piteous plight   160
  Nothing can stir her.
All thy sands, silver Trent,
  Down to the Humber,

The sighs that I have spent
    Never can number.
        On thy bank,
        In a rank,

Let thy swans sing her,
    And with their music
Along let them bring her.   170

FROM *The Muses' Elysium*, 1630

The description of Elysium

A paradise on earth is found,
Though far from vulgar sight,
Which with those pleasures doth
        abound
That it Elysium hight.

Where in delights that never fade
The Muses lullëd be,
And sit at pleasure in the shade
Of many a stately tree,

Which no rough tempest makes to
        reel
Nor their straight bodies bows;   10
Their lofty tops do never feel
The weight of winter's snows.

In groves that evermore are green,
No falling leaf is there,
But Philomel, of birds the queen,
In music spends the year.

The merle upon her myrtle perch,
There to the mavis sings,
Who from the top of some curled
        birch
Those notes redoubled rings.   20

There daisies damask every place,
Nor once their beauties lose,
That when proud Phœbus hides
        his face
Themselves they scorn to close.

The pansy and the violet here,
As seeming to descend
Both from one root, a very pair,
For sweetness yet contend.

And pointing to a pink, to tell
Which bears it, it is loath   30
To judge it; but replies, for smell
That it excels them both.

Wherewith displeased they hang
        their heads,
So angry soon they grow,
And from their odoriferous beds
Their sweets at it they throw.

The winter here a summer is,
No waste is made by time,
Nor doth the autumn ever miss
The blossoms of the prime.   40

The flower that July forth doth
        bring,
In April here is seen;
The primrose that puts on the
        spring,
In July decks each green.

The sweets for sovereignty con-
        tend,
And so abundant be
That to the very earth they lend
And bark of every tree.

Rills rising out of every bank
In wild meanders strain,   50
And playing many a wanton prank
Upon the speckled plain,

In gambols and lascivious gyres
Their time they still bestow,
Nor to their fountains none retires,
Nor on their course will go.

Those brooks with lilies bravely
   decked,
So proud and wanton made
That they their courses quite neg-
   lect,
And seem as though they stayed [60]

Fair Flora in her state to view,
Which through those lilies looks;
Or as those lilies leaned to shew
Their beauties to the brooks,

That Phœbus in his lofty race
Oft lays aside his beams
And comes to cool his glowing face
In these delicious streams.

Oft spreading vines climb up the
   clives,
Whose ripened clusters there   [70]
Their liquid purple drop, which
   drives
A vintage through the year,

Those clives whose craggy sides
   are clad
With trees of sundry suits,
Which make continual summer
   glad,
Even bending with their fruits,

Some ripening, ready some to fall,
Some blossomed, some to bloom,
Like gorgeous hangings on the
   wall
Of some rich princely room.   [80]

Pomegranates, lemons, citrons, so
Their laded branches bow,
Their leaves in number that outgo
Nor roomth will them allow.

There in perpetual summer's shade
Apollo's prophets sit
Among the flowers that never fade,
But flourish like their wit;

To whom the nymphs upon their
   lyres
Tune many a curious lay,   [90]
And with their most melodious
   choirs
Make short the longest day.

The thrice three virgins heavenly
   clear
Their trembling timbrels sound,
Whilst the three comely Graces
   there
Dance many a dainty round.

Decay nor age there nothing
   knows,
There is continual youth,
As time on plant or creatures
   grows,
So still their strength renew'th.   [100]

The poets' paradise this is,
To which but few can come,
The Muses' only bower of bliss,
Their dear Elysium;

Here happy souls, their blessed
   bowers
Free from the rude resort
Of beastly people, spend the hours
In harmless mirth and sport.

Then on to the Elysian plains
Apollo doth invite you,   [110]
Where he provides with pastoral
   strains
In nymphals to delight you.

The sixth nymphal

Silvius, Halcius, Melanthus.

A woodman, fisher, and a swain
This nymphal through with mirth maintain,
Whose pleadings so the nymphs do please
That presently they give them bays.

Clear had the day been from the dawn,
All checkered was the sky,
Thin clouds like scarfs of cobweb lawn
Veiled heaven's most glorious eye.
The wind had no more strength than this,
That leisurely it blew
To make one leaf the next to kiss
That closely by it grew.
The rills that on the pebbles played
Might now be heard at will;   10
This world they only music made,
Else everything was still.
The flowers like brave embroidered girls
Looked as they much desired
To see whose head with orient pearls
Most curiously was tired;
And to itself the subtle air
Such sovereignty assumes,
That it received too large a share
From nature's rich perfumes.   20
When the Elysian youth were met
That were of most account,
And to disport themselves were set
Upon an easy mount;
Near which of stately fir and pine
There grew abundant store,
The tree that weepeth turpentine,
And shady sycamore.
Amongst this merry youthful train
A forester they had,   30
A fisher, and a shepherd's swain,
A lively country lad;
Betwixt which three a question grew
Who should the worthiest be,
Which violently they pursue
Nor stickled would they be;
That it the company doth please

This civil strife to stay,
Freely to hear what each of these
For his brave self could say.   40
When first this forester of all,
That Silvius had to name,
To whom the lot being cast doth fall,
Doth thus begin the game.

Silvius. For my profession, then, and for the life I lead,
All others to excel, thus for myself I plead:
I am the prince of sports, the forest is my fee,
He's not upon the earth for pleasure lives like me;
The morn no sooner puts her rosy mantle on,
But from my quiet lodge I instantly am gone,   50
When the melodious birds from every bush and brier
Of the wild spacious wastes make a continual choir;
The motlied meadows then, new varnished with the sun,
Shut up their spicy sweets upon the winds that run
In eas'ly ambling gales, and softly seem to pace,
That it the longer might their lusciousness embrace.
I am clad in youthful green, I other color scorn;
My silken baldrick bears my bugle or my horn,
Which setting to my lips I wind so loud and shrill,
As makes the echoes shout from every neighboring hill.   60
My doghook at my belt, to which my lyam's tied,
My sheaf of arrows by, my woodknife at my side,
My crossbow in my hand, my gaffle, or my rack
To bend it when I please or it I list to slack;
My hound then in my lyam, I by the woodman's art
Forecast where I may lodge the goodly high-palmed hart;
To view the grazing herds, so sundry times I use,
Where by the loftiest head I know my deer to choose,
And to unherd him then I gallop o'er the ground
Upon my well-breathed nag to cheer my earning hound.   70
Sometime I pitch my toils the deer alive to take,
Sometime I like the cry the deep-mouthed kennel make;
Then underneath my horse I stalk my game to strike,
And with a single dog to hunt him, hurt, I like.
The sylvans are to me true subjects, I their king;
The stately hart his hind doth to my presence bring,
The buck his lovèd doe, the roe his tripping mate,
Before me to my bower, whereas I sit in state.
The dryads, hamadryads, the satyrs and the fauns
Oft play at hide and seek before me on the lawns;   80
The frisking fairy oft when hornèd Cynthia shines
Before me as I walk dance wanton matachines;

The numerous feathered flocks that the wild forests haunt
Their sylvan songs to me in cheerful ditties chaunt;
The shades, like ample shields, defend me from the sun,
Through which me to refresh the gentle rivulets run;
No little bubbling brook from any spring that falls
But on the pebbles plays me pretty madrigals.
I' th' morn I climb the hills, where wholesome winds do blow,
At noontide to the vales and shady groves below,   90
Towards evening I again the crystal floods frequent,
In pleasure thus my life continually is spent.
As princes and great lords have palaces, so I
Have in the forests here my hall and gallery;
The tall and stately woods, which underneath are plain,
The groves my gardens are; the heath and downs again
My wide and spacious walks; then say all what ye can,
The forester is still your only gallant man.

He of his speech scarce made an end
But him they load with praise;   100
The nymphs most highly him commend,
And vow to give him bays.
He's now cried up of everyone,
And who but only he?
The forester's the man alone,
The worthiest of the three.
When some, than th' other far more staid,
Willed them a while to pause,
For there was more yet to be said
That might deserve applause.   110
When Halcius his turn next plies,
And silence having won,
Room for the fisherman, he cries,
And thus his plea begun.

Halcius. No, forester, it so must not be borne away,
But hear what for himself the fisher first can say:
The crystal-current streams continually I keep,
Where every pearl-paved ford, and every blue-eyed deep,
With me familiar are; when in my boat being set
My oar I take in hand, my angle and my net   120
About me; like a prince myself in state I steer,
Now up, now down the stream, now am I here, now there;
The pilot and the fraught myself, and at my ease
Can land me when I list, or in what place I please;
The silver-scalèd shoals about me in the streams,
As thick as ye discern the atoms in the beams,

Near to the shady bank where slender sallows grow
And willows their shag'd tops down towards the waters bow,
I shove in with my boat to shield me from the heat,
Where choosing from my bag some proved especial bait,   130
The goodly well-grown trout I with my angle strike,
And with my bearded wire I take the ravenous pike,
Of whom when I have hold he seldom breaks away,
Though at my line's full length so long I let him play
Till by my hand I find he well-near wearied be,
When softly by degrees I draw him up to me.
The lusty salmon too I oft with angling take,
Which me above the rest most lordly sport doth make,
Who feeling he is caught, such frisks and bounds doth fetch,
And by his very strength my line so far doth stretch   140
As draws my floating cork down to the very ground,
And wresting of my rod doth make my boat turn round.
I never idle am: sometime I bait my weels,
With which by night I take the dainty silver eels,
And with my draught-net then I sweep the streaming flood;
And to my trammel next and cast-net, from the mud
I beat the scaly brood; no hour I idly spend,
But wearied with my work I bring the day to end.
The naiades and nymphs that in the rivers keep,
Which take into their care the store of every deep,   150
Amongst the flowery flags, the bulrushes and reed,
That of the spawn have charge, abundantly to breed,
Well mounted upon swans, their naked bodies lend
To my discerning eye, and on my boat attend;
And dance upon the waves before me, for my sake,
To th' music the soft wind upon the reeds doth make;
And for my pleasure more, the rougher gods of seas
From Neptune's court send in the blue Nereides,
Which from his bracky realm upon the billows ride
And bear the rivers back with every streaming tide;   160
Those billows 'gainst my boat, borne with delightful gales,
Oft seeming as I row to tell me pretty tales,
Whilst ropes of liquid pearl still load my laboring oars,
As stretched upon the stream they strike me to the shores;
The silent meadows seem delighted with my lays,
As sitting in my boat I sing my lass's praise;
Then let them that like the forester up-cry,
Your noble fisher is your only man, say I.

This speech of Halcius turned the tide,
And brought it so about   170

That all upon the fisher cried
That he would bear it out;
Him for the speech he made, to clap
Who lent him not a hand,
And said 'twould be the water's hap
Quite to put down the land?
This while Melanthus silent sits,
For so the shepherd hight,
And having heard these dainty wits
Each pleading for his right,   180
To hear them honored in this wise
His patience doth provoke;
When, For a shepherd, room, he cries,
And for himself thus spoke.

Melanthus. Well, fisher, you have done, and forester, for you,
Your tale is neatly told—s' are both's, to give you due,
And now my turn comes next, then hear a shepherd speak:
My watchfulness and care gives day scarce leave to break
But to the fields I haste, my folded flock to see,
Where, when I find nor wolf nor fox hath injured me,   190
I to my bottle straight, and soundly baste my throat;
Which done, some country song or roundelay I rote
So merrily that to the music that I make
I force the lark to sing ere she be well awake;
Then Baull, my cut-tailed cur, and I begin to play,
He o'er my sheephook leaps, now th' one, now th' other way,
Then on his hinder feet he doth himself advance,
I tune, and to my note my lively dog doth dance;
Then whistle in my fist, my fellow swains to call,
Down go our hooks and scrips, and we to nine-holes fall,   200
At dust-point or at quoits else are we at it hard,
All false and cheating games we shepherds are debarred.
Surveying of my sheep, if ewe or wether look
As though it were amiss, or with my cur or crook
I take it, and when once I find what it doth ail,
It hardly hath that hurt but that my skill can heal;
And when my careful eye I cast upon my sheep,
I sort them in my pens, and sorted so I keep;
Those that are big'st of bone I still reserve for breed,
My cullings I put off, or for the chapman feed.   210
When the evening doth approach I to my bagpipe take,
And to my grazing flocks such music then I make
That they forbear to feed; then me a king you see,

I playing go before, my subjects follow me.
My bell-wether most brave before the rest doth stalk,
The father of the flock, and after him doth walk
My writhen-headed ram with posies crowned in pride,
Fast to his crooked horns with ribands neatly tied.
And at our shepherds' board that's cut out of the ground,
My fellow swains and I together at it round,   220
With green-cheese, clouted cream, with flawns and custards stored,
Whig, cider, and with whey, I domineer, a lord.
When shearing time is come I to the river drive
My goodly well-fleeced flocks (by pleasure thus I thrive)
Which being washed at will, upon the shearing day
My wool I forth in lokes fit for the winder lay,
Which upon lusty heaps into my cote I heave,
That in the handling feels as soft as any sleave;
When every ewe two lambs that yeanëd hath that year,
About her new-shorn neck a chaplet then doth wear.   230
My tarbox and my scrip, my bagpipe at my back,
My sheephook in my hand, what can I say I lack?
He that a scepter swayed, a sheephook in his hand
Hath not disdained to have, for shepherds then I stand;
Then forester, and you, my fisher, cease your strife,
I say your shepherd leads your only merry life.

They had not cried the forester
And fisher up before
So much, but now the nymphs prefer
The shepherd ten times more,   240
And all the ging goes on his side,
Their minion him they make,
To him themselves they all apply,
And all his party take;
Till some in their discretion cast,
Since first the strife begun,
In all that from them there had passed,
None absolutely won;
That equal honor they should share
And their deserts to show,   250
For each a garland they prepare,
Which they on them bestow,
Of all the choicest flowers that were,
Which purposely they gather,
With which they crown them, parting there
As they came first together.

SIR JOHN DAVIES

The Introduction and Notes are at pages 1239 and 1276

FROM *Epigrams and Elegies*, [*c.* 1595]

Of a gull

Oft in my laughing rhymes I name a gull,
But this new term will many questions breed;
Therefore at first I will express at full
Who is a true and perfect gull indeed:
A gull is he who fears a velvet gown,
And when a wench is brave dares not speak to her;
A gull is he which traverseth the town,
And is for marriage known a common wooer;
A gull is he which while he proudly wears
A silver-hilted rapier by his side   10
Endures the lies and knocks about the ears,
Whilst in his sheath his sleeping sword doth bide;
A gull is he which wears good handsome clothes,
And stands in presence stroking up his hair,
And fills up his unperfect speech with oaths,
But speaks not one wise word throughout the year.
    But to define a gull in terms precise,
    A gull is he which seems, and is not, wise.

In Ciprium

The fine youth Ciprius is more terse and neat
Than the new garden of the Old Temple is,
And still the newest fashion he doth get
And with the time doth change from that to this.
He wears a hat now of the flat-crown block,
The treble ruffs, long cloak, and doublet French;
He takes tobacco, and doth wear a lock,
And wastes more time in dressing than a wench:
    Yet this new-fangled youth, made for these times,
    Doth above all praise old Gascoigne's rhymes!   10

In Haywodum

Heywood, which did in epigrams excel,
Is now put down since my light muse arose—
As buckets are put down into a well
Or as a school-boy putteth down his hose.

In Dacum

Dacus, with some good color and pretense,
Terms his love's beauty *silent eloquence*,—
   For she doth lay more colors on her face
   Than ever Tully used his speech to grace.

In Titum

Titus, the brave and valorous young gallant,
Three years together in this town hath been;
Yet my Lord Chancellor's tomb he hath not seen,
Nor the new water-work, nor the elephant.
   I cannot tell the cause without a smile,—
   He hath been in the Counter all this while.

In Flaccum

The false knave Flaccus once a bribe I gave;
The more fool I to bribe so false a knave.
But he gave back my bribe; the more fool he
That for my folly did not cozen me.

In Decium

Audacious painters have nine worthies made,
But poet Decius, more audacious far,
Making his mistress march with men of war,
With title of Tenth Worthy doth her lade.
   Methinks that gull did use his terms as fit
   Which termed his love *a giant for her wit*.

From *Chetham Ms.* 8012

To his good friend, Sir Anthony Cooke

Here my chameleon muse herself doth change
To divers shapes of gross absurdities,
And like an antic mocks with fashion strange
The fond admirers of lewd gulleries.
Your judgment sees with pity and with scorn
The bastard sonnets of these rhymers base,
Which in this whisking age are daily born,
To their own shames and poetry's disgrace.
Yet some praise those—and some perhaps will praise
Even these of mine; and therefore these I send
To you, that pass in court your glorious days;   10

That if some rich rash gull these rhymes commend,
Thus you may set this formal wit to school,
Use your own grace, and beg him for a fool.

Gulling Sonnets

The lover, under burthen of his mistress' love
Which like to Ætna did his heart oppress,
Did give such piteous groans that he did move
The heav'ns at length to pity his distress.
But for the Fates, in their high court above,
Forbade to make the grievous burthen less,
The gracious powers did all conspire to prove
If miracle this mischief might redress.
Therefore, regarding that the load was such
As no man might with one man's might sustain,   10
And that mild patïence imported much
To him that should endure an endless pain,
By their decree he soon transformëd was
Into a patient burden-bearing ass.

The hardness of her heart and truth of mine
When the all-seeing eyes of heaven did see,
They straight concluded that by power divine
To other forms our hearts should turnëd be.
Then hers, as hard as flint, a flint became,
And mine, as true as steel, to steel was turned;
And then between our hearts sprang forth the flame
Of kindest love, which unextinguished burned.
And long the sacred lamp of mutual love
Incessantly did burn in glory bright,   10
Until my folly did her fury move
To recompense my service with despite;
And to put out with snuffers of her pride
The lamp of love which else had never died.

The sacred muse that first made love divine
Hath made him naked and without attire;
But I will clothe him with this pen of mine,
That all the world his fashion shall admire:
His hat of hope, his band of beauty fine,
His cloak of craft, his doublet of desire,
Grief, for a girdle, shall about him twine,
His points of pride, his eyelet-holes of ire,
His hose of hate, his codpiece of conceit,
His stockings of stern strife, his shirt of shame, 10

His garters of vain-glory gay and slight,
His pantofles of passions I will frame;
Pumps of presumption shall adorn his feet,
And socks of sullenness exceeding sweet.

My case is this: I love Zepheria bright;
Of her I hold my heart by fealty,
Which I discharge to her perpetually;
Yet she thereof will never me acquite.
For now, supposing I withhold her right,
She hath distrained my heart to satisfy
The duty which I never did deny,
And far away impounds it with despite.
I labor therefore justly to repleve
My heart, which she unjustly doth impound;   10
But quick conceit, which now is love's high shrieve
Returns; it is esloigned, not to be found.
Then, which the law affords, I only crave
Her heart for mine in withernam to have.

FROM *Orchestra*, 1596

Orchestra, or a poem of dancing

Where lives the man that never yet did hear
Of chaste Penelope, Ulysses' queen?
Who kept her faith unspotted twenty year,
Till he returned, that far away had been,
And many men and many towns had seen;
 Ten year at siege of Troy he lingering lay,
 And ten year in the midland sea did stray.

Homer, to whom the Muses did carouse
A great deep cup with heavenly nectar filled;
The greatest deepest cup in Jove's great house,   10
(For Jove himself had so expressly willed),
He drank of all, ne let one drop be spilled;
 Since when his brain, that had before been dry,
 Became the wellspring of all poetry,—

Homer doth tell, in his abundant verse,
The long laborious travails of the man,
And of his lady too he doth rehearse,
How she illudes, with all the art she can,
Th' ungrateful love which other lords began;
 For of her lord false fame long since had sworn   20
 That Neptune's monsters had his carcass torn.

All this he tells, but one thing he forgot,
One thing most worthy his eternal song;
But he was old and blind and saw it not,
Or else he thought he should Ulysses wrong,
To mingle it his tragic acts among;
 Yet was there not, in all the world of things,
 A sweeter burden for his muse's wings.

The courtly love Antinous did make,
Antinous, that fresh and jolly knight,   30
Which of the gallants that did undertake
To win the widow, had most wealth and might,
Wit to persuade, and beauty to delight;
 The courtly love he made unto the queen,
 Homer forgot, as if it had not been.

Sing then, Terpsichore, my light Muse, sing
His gentle art and cunning courtesy!
You, lady, can remember everything,
For you are daughter of queen Memory;
But sing a plain and easy melody,   40
 For the soft mean that warbleth but the ground
 To my rude ear doth yield the sweetest sound.

Only one night's discourse I can report:
When the great torchbearer of heaven was gone
Down, in a mask, unto the Ocean's court,
To revel it with Tethys, all alone
Antinous, disguisèd and unknown,
 Like to the spring in gaudy ornament,
 Unto the castle of the princess went.

The sovereign castle of the rocky isle,   50
Wherein Penelope the princess lay,
Shone with a thousand lamps, which did exile
The dim dark shades, and turned the night to day.
Not Jove's blue tent, what time the sunny ray
 Behind the bulwark of the earth retires,
 Is seen to sparkle with more twinkling fires.

That night the queen came forth from far within,
And in the presence of her court was seen.
For the sweet singer Phœmius did begin
To praise the worthies that at Troy had been;   60
Somewhat of her Ulysses she did ween
 In his grave hymn the heav'nly man would sing,
 Or of his wars, or of his wandering.

Pallas that hour, with her sweet breath divine,
Inspired immortal beauty in her eyes,
That with celestial glory she did shine
Brighter than Venus, when she doth arise
Out of the waters to adorn the skies.
 The wooers, all amazëd, do admire
 And check their own presumptuous desire. 70

Only Antinous, when at first he viewed
Her star-bright eyes that with new honor shined,
Was not dismayed; but therewithal renewed
The noblesse and the splendor of his mind;
And as he did fit circumstances find,
 Unto the throne he boldly gan advance,
 And with fair manners, wooed the queen to dance:

Goddess of women! sith your heav'nliness
Hath now vouchsafed itself to represent
To our dim eyes, which though they see the less, 80
Yet are they blest in their astonishment;
Imitate heav'n, whose beauties excellent
 Are in continual motion day and night,
 And move thereby more wonder and delight.

Let me the mover be, to turn about
Those glorious ornaments that youth and love
Have fixëd in you, every part throughout;
Which if you will in timely measure move,
Not all those precious gems in heaven above
 Shall yield a sight more pleasing to behold 90
 With all their turns and tracings manifold.

With this the modest princess blushed and smiled
Like to a clear and rosy eventide,
And softly did return this answer mild:
Fair sir! you needs must fairly be denied,
Where your demand cannot be satisfied.
 My feet, which only nature taught to go,
 Did never yet the art of footing know.

But why persuade you me to this new rage? 100
For all disorder and misrule is new,
For such misgovernment in former age
Our old divine forefathers never knew;
Who if they lived, and did the follies view
 Which their fond nephews make their chief affairs,
 Would hate themselves, that had begot such heirs.

Sole heir of virtue, and of beauty both!
Whence cometh it, Antinous replies,
That your imperious virtue is so loath
To grant your beauty her chief exercise?
Or from what spring doth your opinion rise   110
    That dancing is a frenzy and a rage,
    First known and used in this new-fangled age?

Dancing, bright lady, then began to be
When the first seeds whereof the world did spring,
The fire, air, earth, and water did agree
By Love's persuasion, nature's mighty king,
To leave their first disordered combating,
    And in a dance such measure to observe
    As all the world their motion should preserve.

Since when they still are carried in a round,   120
And changing come one in another's place;
Yet do they neither mingle nor confound,
But every one doth keep the bounded space
Wherein the dance doth bid it turn or trace.
    This wondrous miracle did Love devise,
    For dancing is love's proper exercise.

Like this he framed the gods' eternal bower,
And of a shapeless and confusëd mass,
By his through-piercing and digesting power,
The turning vault of heaven formëd was,   130
Whose starry wheels he hath so made to pass
    As that their movings do a music frame,
    And they themselves still dance unto the same.

Or if this all, which round about we see,
As idle Morpheus some sick brains hath taught,
Of undivided motes compacted be,
How was this goodly architecture wrought?
Or by what means were they together brought?
    They err that say they did concur by chance;
    Love made them meet in a well-ordered dance!   140

As when Amphion with his charming lyre
Begot so sweet a siren of the air,
That, with her rhetoric, made the stones conspire
The ruins of a city to repair,
A work of wit and reason's wise affair;
    So Love's smooth tongue the motes such measure taught
    That they joined hands, and so the world was wrought!

How justly then is dancing termëd new,
Which with the world in point of time began?
Yea, Time itself, whose birth Jove never knew,   150
And which is far more ancient than the sun,
Had not one moment of his age outrun,
    When out leaped Dancing from the heap of things
    And lightly rode upon his nimble wings.

Reason hath both their pictures in her treasure:
Where Time the measure of all moving is,
And Dancing is a moving all in measure.
Now, if you do resemble that to this,
And think both one, I think you think amiss;
    But if you judge them twins, together got,   160
    And Time first born, your judgment erreth not.

Thus doth it equal age with Age enjoy,
And yet in lusty youth forever flowers;
Like Love, his sire, whom painters make a boy,
Yet is he eldest of the heav'nly powers;
Or like his brother Time, whose wingëd hours,
    Going and coming, will not let him die,
    But still preserve him in his infancy.

This said, the queen, with her sweet lips divine,
Gently began to move the subtle air,   170
Which gladly yielding, did itself incline
To take a shape between those rubies fair;
And being formed, softly did repair,
    With twenty doublings in the empty way,
    Unto Antinous' ears, and thus did say:

What eye doth see the heav'n, but doth admire
When it the movings of the heav'ns doth see?
Myself, if I to heav'n may once aspire,
If that be dancing, will a dancer be;
But as for this, your frantic jollity,   180
    How it began, or whence you did it learn,
    I never could with reason's eye discern.

Antinous answered: Jewel of the earth!
Worthy you are that heav'nly dance to lead;
But for you think our Dancing base of birth,
And newly born but of a brain-sick head,
I will forthwith his antique gentry read,
    And, for I love him, will his herald be,
    And blaze his arms, and draw his pedigree.

When Love had shaped this world, this great fair wight,   190
That all wights else in this wide womb contains,
And had instructed it to dance aright
A thousand measures, with a thousand strains,
Which it should practise with delightful pains
    Until that fatal instant should revolve,
    When all to nothing should again resolve;

The comely order and proportion fair
On every side did please his wand'ring eye;
Till, glancing through the thin transparent air,
A rude disordered rout he did espy   200
Of men and women, that most spitefully
    Did one another throng and crowd so sore
    That his kind eye, in pity, wept therefor.

And swifter than the lightning down he came,
Another shapeless chaos to digest;
He will begin another world to frame,
For Love, till all be well, will never rest.
Then with such words as cannot be expressed
    He cuts the troops, that all asunder fling,
    And ere they wist he casts them in a ring.   210

Then did he rarefy the element,
And in the center of the ring appear;
The beams that from his forehead shining went
Begot a horror and religious fear
In all the souls that round about him were,
    Which in their ears attentiveness procures,
    While he, with such like sounds, their minds allures:

How doth Confusion's mother, headlong Chance,
Put Reason's noble squadron to the rout?
Or how should you, that have the governance   220
Of Nature's children, heaven and earth throughout,
Prescribe them rules, and live yourselves without?
    Why should your fellowship a trouble be,
    Since man's chief pleasure is society?

If sense hath not yet taught you, learn of me
A comely moderation and discreet,
That your assemblies may well ordered be;
When my uniting power shall make you meet,
With heav'nly tunes it shall be tempered sweet,
    And be the model of the world's great frame,   230
    And you, earth's children, dancing shall it name.

Behold the world, how it is whirlèd round!
And for it is so whirled, is namèd so;
In whose large volume many rules are found
Of this new art, which it doth fairly show.
For your quick eyes in wand'ring to and fro,
    From east to west, on no one thing can glance,
    But, if you mark it well, it seems to dance.

First you see fixed in this huge mirror blue
Of trembling lights a number numberless;   240
Fixed, they are named, but with a name untrue;
For they are moved and in a dance express
The great long year that doth contain no less
    Than threescore hundreds of those years in all,
    Which the sun makes with his course natural.

What if to you these sparks disordered seem,
As if by chance they had been scattered there?
The gods a solemn measure do it deem
And see a just proportion everywhere,
And know the points whence first their movings were,   250
    To which first points, when all return again,
    The axletree of heav'n shall break in twain.

Under that spangled sky five wand'ring flames,
Besides the king of day and queen of night,
Are wheeled around, all in their sundry frames,
And all in sundry measures do delight;
Yet altogether keep no measure right;
    For by itself each doth itself advance,
    And by itself each doth a galliard dance.

Venus, the mother of that bastard Love,   260
Which doth usurp the world's great marshal's name,
Just with the sun her dainty feet doth move;
And unto him doth all her gestures frame,
Now after, now afore, the flattering dame
    With divers cunning passages doth err,
    Still him respecting that respects not her.

For that brave sun, the father of the day,
Doth love this earth, the mother of the night;
And, like a reveler in rich array,
Doth dance his galliard in his leman's sight,   270
Both back and forth and sideways passing light.
    His gallant grace doth so the gods amaze
    That all stand still and at his beauty gaze.

But see the earth when she approacheth near,
How she for joy doth spring and sweetly smile;
But see again her sad and heavy cheer,
When changing places, he retires a while;
But those black clouds he shortly will exile,
 And make them all before his presence fly,
 As mists consumed before his cheerful eye.   280

Who doth not see the measure of the moon?
Which thirteen times she danceth every year,
And ends her pavan thirteen times as soon
As doth her brother, of whose golden hair
She borroweth part, and proudly doth it wear.
 Then doth she coyly turn her face aside
 That half her cheek is scarce sometimes descried.

Next her, the pure, subtile, and cleansing fire
Is swiftly carried in a circle even,
Though Vulcan be pronounced by many a liar   290
The only halting god that dwells in heaven;
But that foul name may be more fitly given
 To your false fire, that far from heaven is fall,
 And doth consume, waste, spoil, disorder all.

And now behold your tender nurse, the air,
And common neighbor that aye runs around;
How many pictures and impressions fair
Within her empty regions are there found,
Which to your senses dancing do propound?
 For what are breath, speech, echoes, music, winds,   300
 But dancings of the air, in sundry kinds?

For when you breathe the air in order moves,
Now in, now out, in time and measure true,
And when you speak, so well the dancing loves
That doubling oft and oft redoubling new,
With thousand forms she doth herself endue.
 For all the words that from your lips repair
 Are nought but tricks and turnings of the air.

Hence is her prattling daughter, Echo, born,
That dances to all voices she can hear.   310
There is no sound so harsh that she doth scorn,
Nor any time wherein she will forbear
The airy pavement with her feet to wear;
 And yet her hearing sense is nothing quick,
 For after time she endeth every trick.

And thou, sweet music, dancing's only life,
The ear's sole happiness, the air's best speech,
Lodestone of fellowship, charming rod of strife,
The soft mind's paradise, the sick mind's leech,
With thine own tongue thou trees and stones canst teach,   320
    That when the air doth dance her finest measure,
    Then art thou born, the gods' and men's sweet pleasure.

Lastly, where keep the winds their revelry,
Their violent turnings and wild whirling hays,
But in the air's tralucent gallery?
Where she herself is turned a hundred ways,
While with those maskers wantonly she plays.
    Yet in this misrule they such rule embrace
    As two, at once, encumber not the place.

If then fire, air, wand'ring and fixëd lights,   330
In every province of th' imperial sky,
Yield perfect forms of dancing to your sights,
In vain I teach the ear that which the eye,
With certain view, already doth descry;
    But for your eyes perceive not all they see,
    In this I will your senses' master be.

For lo, the sea that fleets about the land,
And like a girdle clips her solid waist,
Music and measure both doth understand;
For his great crystal eye is always cast   340
Up to the moon, and on her fixëd fast;
    And as she danceth in her pallid sphere,
    So danceth he about the center here.

Sometimes his proud green waves in order set,
One after other, flow unto the shore;
Which when they have with many kisses wet,
They ebb away in order, as before;
And to make known his courtly love the more,
    He oft doth lay aside his three-forked mace,
    And with his arms the timorous earth embrace.   350

Only the earth doth stand forever still:
Her rocks remove not, nor her mountains meet,
Although some wits enriched with learning's skill
Say heav'n stands firm and that the earth doth fleet,
And swiftly turneth underneath their feet;
    Yet, though the earth is ever steadfast seen,
    On her broad breast hath dancing ever been.

For those blue veins that through her body spread,
Those sapphire streams which from great hills do spring,
The earth's great dugs, for every wight is fed   360
With sweet fresh moisture from them issuing,
Observe a dance in their wild wandering;
    And still their dance begets a murmur sweet,
    And still the murmur with the dance doth meet.

Of all their ways, I love Meander's path,
Which, to the tunes of dying swans, doth dance
Such winding sleights. Such turns and tricks he hath,
Such creeks, such wrenches, and such dalliance
That, whether it be hap or heedless chance,
    In his indented course and wringling play,   370
    He seems to dance a perfect cunning hay.

But wherefore do these streams forever run?
To keep themselves forever sweet and clear;
For let their everlasting course be done,
They straight corrupt and foul with mud appear.
O ye sweet nymphs, that beauty's loss do fear,
    Contemn the drugs that physic doth devise,
    And learn of Love this dainty exercise.

See how those flowers, that have sweet beauty too,
The only jewels that the earth doth wear   380
When the young sun in bravery her doth woo,
As oft as they the whistling wind do hear,
Do wave their tender bodies here and there;
    And though their dance no perfect measure is,
    Yet oftentimes their music makes them kiss.

What makes the vine about the elm to dance
With turnings, windings, and embracements round?
What makes the lodestone to the north advance
His subtile point, as if from thence he found
His chief attractive virtue to redound?   390
    Kind nature first doth cause all things to love;
    Love makes them dance, and in just order move.

Hark how the birds do sing! and mark then how,
Jump with the modulation of their lays,
They lightly leap and skip from bough to bough;
Yet do the cranes deserve a greater praise,
Which keep such measure in their airy ways,
    As when they all in order rankèd are,
    They make a perfect form triangular.

In the chief angle flies the watchful guide;   40
And all the followers their heads do lay
On their foregoers' backs, on either side;
But, for the captain hath no rest to stay
His head, forwearied with the windy way,
 He back retires; and then the next behind,
 As his lieutenant, leads them through the wind.

But why relate I every singular?
Since all the world's great fortunes and affairs
Forward and backward rapt and whirlëd are,
According to the music of the spheres;   41(
And Chance herself her nimble feet upbears
 On a round slippery wheel, that rolleth aye,
 And turns all states with her impetuous sway;

Learn then to dance, you that are princes born,
And lawful lords of earthly creatures all;
Imitate them, and thereof take no scorn,
For this new art to them is natural.
And imitate the stars celestïal;
 For when pale death your vital twist shall sever,
 Your better parts must dance with them forever.   420

Thus Love persuades, and all the crowd of men
That stands around, doth make a murmuring,
As when the wind, loosed from his hollow den,
Among the trees a gentle bass doth sing,
Or as a brook, through pebbles wandering;
 But in their looks they uttered this plain speech:
 That they would learn to dance, if Love would teach.

Then, first of all, he doth demonstrate plain
The motions seven that are in nature found;
Upward and downward, forth and back again,   430
To this side and to that, and turning round;
Whereof a thousand brawls he doth compound,
 Which he doth teach unto the multitude,
 And ever with a turn they must conclude.

As when a nymph arising from the land,
Leadeth a dance with her long watery train,
Down to the sea she wries to every hand,
And every way doth cross the fertile plain;
But when, at last, she falls into the main,
 Then all her traverses concluded are,   440
 And with the sea her course is circular.

Thus when at first Love had them marshallëd,
As erst he did the shapeless mass of things,
He taught them rounds and winding hays to tread,
And about trees to cast themselves in rings;
As the two Bears, whom the first mover flings
   With a short turn about heaven's axletree,
   In a round dance forever wheeling be.

But after these, as men more civil grew,
He did more grave and solemn measures frame;   450
With such fair order and proportion true,
And correspondence every way the same,
That no fault-finding eye did ever blame;
   For every eye was movëd at the sight
   With sober wond'ring and with sweet delight.

Not those old students of the heavenly book,
Atlas the great, Prometheus the wise,
Which on the stars did all their lifetime look,
Could ever find such measures in the skies,
So full of change and rare varieties;   460
   Yet all the feet whereon these measures go
   Are only spondees, solemn, grave, and slow.

But for more divers and more pleasing show,
A swift and wand'ring dance she did invent,
With passages uncertain, to and fro,
Yet with a certain answer and consent
To the quick music of the instrument.
   Five was the number of the music's feet,
   Which still the dance did with five paces meet.

A gallant dance! that lively doth bewray   470
A spirit and a virtue masculine;
Impatient that her house on earth should stay,
Since she herself is fiery and divine.
Oft doth she make her body upward flyne
   With lofty turns and caprioles in the air,
   Which with the lusty tunes accordeth fair.

What shall I name those current traverses,
That on a triple dactyl foot do run,
Close by the ground, with sliding passages?
Wherein that dancer greatest praise hath won,   480
Which with best order can all orders shun;
   For everywhere he wantonly must range,
   And turn, and wind, with unexpected change.

Yet is there one, the most delightful kind,
A lofty jumping, or a leaping round,
When, arm in arm, two dancers are entwined,
And whirl themselves with strict embracements bound,
And still their feet an anapest do sound;
 An anapest is all their music's song,
 Whose first two feet are short, and third is long. 490

As the victorious twins of Leda and Jove,
That taught the Spartans dancing on the sands
Of swift Eurotas, dance in heav'n above,
Knit and united with eternal bands,
Among the stars their double image stands,
 Where both are carried with an equal pace,
 Together jumping in their turning race.

This is the net wherein the sun's bright eye
Venus and Mars entangled did behold;
For in this dance their arms they so imply, 500
As each doth seem the other to enfold.
What if lewd wits another tale have told,
 Of jealous Vulcan, and of iron chains?
 Yet this true sense that forgèd lie contains.

These various forms of dancing Love did frame,
And besides these, a hundred million mo;
And as he did invent, he taught the same,
With goodly gesture and with comely show,
Now keeping state, now humbly honoring low.
 And ever for the persons and the place, 510
 He taught most fit, and best according grace.

For Love, within his fertile working brain,
Did then conceive those gracious virgins three,
Whose civil moderation did maintain
All decent order and conveniency,
And fair respect, and seemly modesty;
 And then he thought it fit they should be born,
 That their sweet presence dancing might adorn.

Hence is it that these Graces painted are
With hand in hand, dancing an endless round; 520
And with regarding eyes, that still beware
That there be no disgrace amongst them found,
With equal foot they beat the flow'ry ground,
 Laughing or singing, as their passions will;
 Yet nothing that they do becomes them ill.

Thus Love taught men! and men thus learned of Love
Sweet music's sound with feet to counterfeit;
Which was long time before high-thundering Jove
Was lifted up to heav'n's imperial seat.
For though by birth he were the prince of Crete, 530
   Nor Crete nor heav'n should that young prince have seen,
   If dancers with their timbrels had not been.

Since when all ceremonious mysteries,
All sacred orgies and religious rites,
All pomps and triumphs and solemnities,
All funerals, nuptials, and like public sights,
All parliaments of peace, and warlike fights,
   All learned arts, and every great affair,
   A lively shape of dancing seems to bear.

For what did he, who with his ten-tongued lute 540
Gave beasts and blocks an understanding ear,
Or rather into bestial minds and brutes
Shed and infused the beams of reason clear?
Doubtless, for men that rude and savage were,
   A civil form of dancing he devised,
   Wherewith unto their gods they sacrificed.

So did Musæus, so Amphion did,
And Linus with his sweet enchanting song,
And he whose hand the earth of monsters rid,
And had men's ears fast chainëd to his tongue, 550
And Theseus to his wood-born slaves among,
   Used dancing as the finest policy
   To plant religion and society.

And therefore, now, the Thracian Orpheus' lyre
And Hercules himself are stellified,
And in high heaven, amidst the starry choir,
Dancing their parts, continually do slide;
So, on the zodiac, Ganymede doth ride,
   And so is Hebe with the Muses nine,
   For pleasing Jove with dancing, made divine. 560

Wherefore was Proteus said himself to change
Into a stream, a lion, and a tree,
And many other forms fantastic strange,
As in his fickle thought he wished to be?
But that he danced with such facility,
   As like a lion he could pace with pride,
   Ply like a plant, and like a river slide.

And how was Cæneus made at first a man,
And then a woman, then a man again,
But in a dance? which when he first began, 570
He the man's part in measure did sustain;
But when he changed into a second strain,
   He danced the woman's part another space,
   And then returned unto his former place.

Hence sprang the fable of Tiresias,
That he the pleasure of both sexes tried;
For in a dance he man and woman was,
By often change of place, from side to side;
But for the woman easily did slide,
   And smoothly swim with cunning hidden art, 580
   He took more pleasure in a woman's part.

So to a fish Venus herself did change,
And swimming through the soft and yielding wave,
With gentle motions did so smoothly range
As none might see where she the water drave;
But this plain truth that falsëd fable gave,
   That she did dance with sliding easiness,
   Pliant and quick in wand'ring passages.

And merry Bacchus practised dancing too,
And to the Lydian numbers rounds did make; 590
The like he did in th' eastern India do,
And taught them all, when Phœbus did awake,
And when at night he did his coach forsake,
   To honor heav'n, and heav'n's great rolling eye,
   With turning dances and with melody.

Thus they who first did found a commonweal,
And they who first religion did ordain,
By dancing first the people's hearts did steal;
Of whom we now a thousand tales do feign.
Yet do we now their perfect rules retain, 600
   And use them still in such devices new,
   As in the world, long since, their withering grew.

For after towns and kingdoms founded were,
Between great states arose well-ordered war,
Wherein most perfect measure doth appear;
Whether their well-set ranks respected are
In quadrant forms or semicircular,
   Or else the march, when all the troops advance
   And to the drum in gallant order dance.

And after wars, when white-winged victory
Is with a glorious triumph beautified,
And everyone doth Io, Io! cry,
While all in gold the conqueror doth ride,
The solemn pomp that fills the city wide
  Observes such rank and measure everywhere,
  As if they all together dancing were.

The like just order mourners do observe,
But with unlike affection and attire,
When some great man that nobly did deserve,
And whom his friends impatiently desire,
Is brought with honor to his latest fire.
  The dead corpse too in that sad dance is moved,
  As if both dead and living, dancing loved.

A diverse cause, but like solemnity,
Unto the temple leads the bashful bride,
Which blusheth like the Indian ivory
Which is with dip of Tyrian purple dyed;
A golden troop doth pass on every side
  Of flourishing young men and virgins gay,
  Which keep fair measure all the flow'ry way.

And not alone the general multitude,
But those choice Nestors, which in council grave
Of cities and of kingdoms do conclude,
Most comely order in their sessions have;
Wherefore the wise Thessalians ever gave
  The name of leader of their country's dance
  To him that had their country's governance.

And those great masters of the liberal arts
In all their several schools do dancing teach;
For humble grammar first doth set the parts
Of congruent and well-according speech,
Which rhetoric, whose state the clouds doth reach,
  And heavenly poetry do forward lead,
  And divers measures diversly do tread.

For rhetoric, clothing speech in rich array,
The looser numbers teacheth her to range
With twenty tropes, and turnings every way,
And various figures, and licentious change;
But poetry, with rule and order strange,
  So curiously doth move each single pace
  As all is marred if she one foot misplace.

610

620

630

640

650

These arts of speech the guides and marshals are,
But logic leadeth reason in a dance,
Reason, the cynosure and bright lodestar
In this world's sea, t' avoid the rocks of chance,
For with close following and continuance,
    One reason doth another so ensue
    As, in conclusion, still the dance is true.

So music to her own sweet tunes doth trip,
With tricks of 3, 5, 8, 15, and more;   660
So doth the art of numb'ring seem to skip
From ev'n to odd, in her proportioned score;
So do those skills, whose quick eyes do explore
    The just dimension both of earth and heav'n,
    In all their rules observe a measure ev'n.

Lo, this is Dancing's true nobility:
Dancing, the child of Music and of Love;
Dancing itself, both love and harmony,
Where all agree and all in order move;
Dancing, the art that all arts do approve;   670
    The fair cháracter of the world's consent,
    The heav'n's true figure, and th' earth's ornament.

The queen, whose dainty ears had borne too long
The tedious praise of that she did despise,
Adding once more the music of the tongue
To the sweet speech of her alluring eyes,
Began to answer in such winning wise
    As that forthwith Antinous' tongue was tied,
    His eyes fast fixed, his ears were open wide.

Forsooth, quoth she, great glory you have won   680
To your trim minion, Dancing, all this while,
By blazing him Love's first begotten son,
Of every ill the hateful father vile,
That doth the world with sorceries beguile,
    Cunningly mad, religiously profane,
    Wit's monster, reason's canker, sense's bane.

Love taught the mother that unkind desire
To wash her hands in her own infant's blood;
Love taught the daughter to betray her sire
Into most base unworthy servitude;   690
Love taught the brother to prepare such food
    To feast his brothers that the all-seeing sun,
    Wrapped in a cloud, the wicked sight did shun.

And even this self-same Love hath dancing taught,
An art that showeth th' idea of his mind
With vainness, frenzy, and misorder fraught;
Sometimes with blood and cruelties unkind,
For in a dance Tereus' mad wife did find
　　Fit time and place, by murdering her son,
　　T' avenge the wrong his traitorous sire had done.　　　700

What mean the mermaids when they dance and sing,
But certain death unto the mariner?
What tidings do the dancing dolphins bring,
But that some dangerous storm approacheth near?
Then sith both Love and Dancing liveries bear
　　Of such ill hap, unhappy may they prove
　　That, sitting free, will either dance or love!

Yet once again Antinous did reply:
Great Queen! condemn not Love the innocent,
For this mischievous Lust, which traitorously　　　710
Usurps his name and steals his ornament;
For that true Love, which dancing did invent,
　　Is he that tuned the world's whole harmony,
　　And linked all men in sweet society.

He first extracted from th' earth-mingled mind
That heav'nly fire, or quintessence divine,
Which doth such sympathy in beauty find
As is between the elm and fruitful vine,
And so to beauty ever doth incline;
　　Life's life it is, and cordial to the heart,　　　720
　　And of our better part the better part.

This is true Love, by that true Cupid got,
Which danceth galliards in your amorous eyes,
But to your frozen heart approacheth not;
Only your heart he dares not enterprise,
And yet through every other part he flies,
　　And everywhere he nimbly danceth now,
　　That in yourself yourself perceive not how.

For your sweet beauty daintily transfused
With due proportion throughout every part,　　　730
What is it but a dance where Love hath used
His finer cunning and more curious art?
Where all the elements themselves impart,
　　And turn, and wind, and mingle with such measure
　　That th' eye that sees it surfeits with the pleasure.

Love in the twinkling of your eyelids danceth,
Love danceth in your pulses and your veins,
Love, when you sew, your needle's point advanceth,
And makes it dance a thousand curious strains
Of winding rounds, whereof the form remains   740
    To show that your fair hands can dance the hay,
    Which your fine feet would learn as well as they.

And when your ivory fingers touch the strings
Of any silver-sounding instrument,
Love makes them dance to those sweet murmurings
With busy skill and cunning excellent.
Oh, that your feet those tunes would represent
    With artificial motions to and fro,
    That Love this art in ev'ry part might show!

Yet your fair soul, which came from heav'n above   750
To rule this house (another heav'n below)
With divers powers in harmony doth move;
And all the virtues that from her do flow
In a round measure, hand in hand do go;
    Could I now see, as I conceive this dance,
    Wonder and love would cast me in a trance.

The richest jewel in all the heav'nly treasure,
That ever yet unto the earth was shown,
Is perfect concord, th' only perfect pleasure
That wretched earth-born men have ever known;   760
For many hearts it doth compound in one,
    That whatso one doth will, or speak, or do,
    With one consent they all agree thereto.

Concord's true picture shineth in this art,
Where divers men and women rankëd be,
And everyone doth dance a several part,
Yet all as one in measure do agree,
Observing perfect uniformity;
    All turn together, all together trace,
    And all together honor and embrace.   770

If they whom sacred Love hath linked in one
Do as they dance, in all their course of life,
Never shall burning grief nor bitter moan
Nor factious difference nor unkind strife
Arise between the husband and the wife;
    For whether forth, or back, or round he go,
    As doth the man, so must the woman do.

What if by often interchange of place
Sometime the woman gets the upper hand?
That is but done for more delightful grace,   780
For on that part she doth not ever stand;
But as the measure's law doth her command,
    She wheels about, and ere the dance doth end,
    Into her former place she doth transcend.

But not alone this correspondence meet
And uniform consent doth dancing praise;
For Comeliness, the child of Order sweet,
Enamels it with her eye-pleasing rays;
Fair Comeliness ten hundred thousand ways   790
    Through dancing sheds itself, and makes it shine
    With glorious beauty and with grace divine.

For comeliness is a disposing fair
Of things and actions in fit time and place,
Which doth in dancing show itself most clear
When troops confused, which here and there do trace
Without distinguishment or bounded space,
    By dancing rule into such ranks are brought
    As glads the eye and ravisheth the thought.

Then why should reason judge that reasonless
Which is wit's offspring, and the work of art,   800
Image of concord and of comeliness?
Who sees a clock moving in every part,
A sailing pinnace, or a wheeling cart,
    But thinks that reason, ere it came to pass,
    The first impulsive cause and mover was?

Who sees an army all in rank advance,
But deems a wise commander is in place,
Which leadeth on that brave victorious dance?
Much more in dancing's art, in dancing's grace,
Blindness itself may reason's footsteps trace;   810
    For of love's maze it is the curious plot,
    And of man's fellowship the true-love knot.

But if these eyes of yours, lodestars of love,
Showing the world's great dance to your mind's eye,
Cannot, with all their demonstrations, move
Kind apprehension in your fantasy
Of dancing's virtue and nobility,
    How can my barbarous tongue win you thereto,
    Which heav'n and earth's fair speech could never do?

O Love, my king! if all my wit and power   820
Have done you all the service that they can,
O be you present in this present hour
And help your servant and your true liegeman!
End that persuasion which I erst began!
    For who in praise of dancing can persuade
    With such sweet force as Love, which dancing made?

Love heard his prayer, and swifter than the wind,
Like to a page in habit, face, and speech,
He came, and stood Antinous behind,
And many secrets of his thoughts did teach.   830
At last a crystal mirror he did reach
    Unto his hands, that he with one rash view
    All forms therein by Love's revealing knew.

And humbly honoring, gave it to the queen
With this fair speech: See, fairest queen, quoth he,
The fairest sight that ever shall be seen,
And th' only wonder of posterity!
The richest work in nature's treasury!
    Which she disdains to show on this world's stage,
    And thinks it far too good for our rude age.   840

But in another world, divided far,
In the great fortunate triangled isle,
Thrice twelve degrees removed from the North Star,
She will this glorious workmanship compile,
Which she hath been conceiving all this while
    Since the world's birth; and will bring forth at last,
    When six and twenty hundred years are past.

Penelope the queen, when she had viewed
The strange eye-dazzling admirable sight,
Fain would have praised the state and pulchritude;   850
But she was stroken dumb with wonder quite,
Yet her sweet mind retained her thinking might.
    Her ravished mind in heav'nly thoughts did dwell;
    But what she thought no mortal tongue can tell.

You, lady Muse, whom Jove the counsellor
Begot of Memory, Wisdom's treasuress,
To your divining tongue is given a power
Of uttering secrets, large and limitless;
You can Penelope's strange thoughts express,
    Which she conceived, and then would fain have told,   860
    When she the wondrous crystal did behold.

Her wingèd thoughts bore up her mind so high
As that she weened she saw the glorious throne
Where the bright moon doth sit in majesty;
A thousand sparkling stars about her shone,
But she herself did sparkle more alone
    Than all those thousand beauties would have done
    If they had been confounded all in one.

And yet she thought those stars moved in such measure
To do their sovereign honor and delight,   870
As soothed her mind with sweet enchanting pleasure,
Although the various change amazed her sight,
And her weak judgment did entangle quite;
    Beside, their moving made them shine more clear,
    As diamonds moved more sparkling do appear.

This was the picture of her wondrous thought!
But who can wonder that her thought was so,
Sith Vulcan, king of fire, that mirror wrought,
Which things to come, present, and past doth know,
And there did represent in lively show   880
    Our glorious English court's divine imáge,
    As it should be in this our golden age?

Away, Terpsichore, light Muse, away!
And come, Urania, prophetess divine!
Come, Muse of heav'n, my burning thirst allay!
Even now for want of sacred drink I tine;
In heav'nly moisture dip this pen of mine,
    And let my mouth with nectar overflow,
    For I must more than mortal glory show!

Oh, that I had Homer's abundant vein,   890
I would hereof another *Ilias* make!
Or else the man of Mantua's charmèd brain,
In whose large throat great Jove the thunder spake!
Oh, that I could old Geoffrey's muse awake,
    Or borrow Colin's fair heroic style,
    Or smooth my rhymes with Delia's servant's file!

Oh, could I, sweet companion, sing like you,
Which of a shadow, under a shadow sing!
Or like fair Salve's sad lover true!
Or like the bay, the marigold's darling,   900
Whose sudden verse Love covers with his wing!
    Oh, that your brains were mingled all with mine,
    T' enlarge my wit for this great work divine!

Yet Astrophel might one for all suffice,
Whose supple muse chameleon-like doth change
Into all forms of excellent device;
So might the swallow, whose swift muse doth range
Through rare Idæas and inventions strange,
  And ever doth enjoy her joyful spring,
  And sweeter than the nightingale doth sing.   910

Oh, that I might that singing swallow hear,
To whom I owe my service and my love!
His sugared tunes would so enchant mine ear,
And in my mind such sacred fury move,
As I should knock at heav'n's great gate above
  With my proud rhymes; while of this heav'nly state
  I do aspire the shadow to relate.

FROM *Hymns of Astræa*, 1599

Of Astræa

E arly before the day doth spring
L et us awake, my muse, and sing,
I t is no time to slumber;
S o many joys this time doth bring
A s time will fail to number.

B ut whereto shall we bend our lays?
E ven up to heaven, again to raise
T he maid which thence descended,
H ath brought again the golden days
A nd all the world amended.   10

R udeness itself she doth refine,
E ven like an alchemist divine,
G ross times of iron turning
I nto the purest form of gold,
N ot to corrupt till heaven wax old,
A nd be refined with burning.

To the spring

E arth now is green and heaven is blue,
L ively spring which makes all new,
I olly spring, doth enter;
S weet young sun-beams do subdue
A ngry, aged winter.

B lasts are mild and seas are calm,
E very meadow flows with balm,
T he earth wears all her riches;
H armonious birds sing such a psalm
A s ear and heart bewitches.   10

R eserve, sweet spring, this nymph of ours
E ternal garlands of thy flowers,
G reen garlands never wasting;
I n her shall last our state's fair spring
N ow and forever flourishing
A s long as heaven is lasting.

To the rose

E ye of the garden, queen of flowers,
L ove's cup wherein he nectar pours,
I ngendered first of nectar;
S weet nurse-child of the spring's young hours,
A nd beauty's fair chárácter.

B lest jewel that the earth doth wear
E ven when the brave young sun draws near,
T o her hot love pretending,
H imself likewise like form doth bear
A t rising and descending.   10

R ose of the queen of love beloved,—
E ngland's great kings, divinely moved,
G ave roses in their banner;
I t showed that beauty's rose indeed
N ow in this age should them succeed,
A nd reign in more sweet manner.

FROM *Nosce Teipsum*, 1599

Of human knowledge

Why did my parents send me to the schools
  That I with knowledge might enrich my mind?
Since the desire to know first made men fools,
  And did corrupt the root of all mankind.

For when God's hand had written in the hearts
  Of the first parents all the rules of good,
So that their skill infused did pass all arts
  That ever were, before or since the flood,

And when their reason's eye was sharp and clear,
   And, as an eagle can behold the sun,   10
   Could have approached th' eternal light as near
   As the intellectual angels could have done,

Even then to them the spirit of lies suggests
   That they were blind, because they saw not ill,
   And breathes into their incorrupted breasts
   A curious wish, which did corrupt their will.

For that same ill they straight desired to know;
   Which ill, being nought but a defect of good,
   And all God's works the devil could not show
   While man their lord in his perfection stood.   20

So that themselves were first to do the ill,
   Ere they thereof the knowledge could attain;
   Like him that knew not poison's power to kill,
   Until, by tasting it, himself was slain.

Even so by tasting of that fruit forbid,
   Where they sought knowledge, they did error find;
   Ill they desired to know, and ill they did,
   And to give passion eyes, made reason blind.

For then their minds did first in passion see
   Those wretched shapes of misery and woe,   30
   Of nakedness, of shame, of poverty,
   Which then their own experience made them know.

But then grew reason dark, that she no more
   Could the fair forms of good and truth discern;
   Bats they became, that eagles were before,
   And this they got by their desire to learn.

But we, their wretched offspring, what do we?
   Do not we still taste of the fruit forbid,
   Whiles with fond fruitless curiosity
   In books profane we seek for knowledge hid?   40

What is this knowledge but the sky-stolen fire
   For which the thief still chained in ice doth sit,
   And which the poor rude satyr did admire,
   And needs would kiss, but burnt his lips with it.

What is it but the cloud of empty rain,
    Which when Jove's guest embraced, he monsters got?
    Or the false pails which oft being filled with pain,
    Received the water, but retained it not?

Shortly, what is it but the fiery coach
    Which the youth sought, and sought his death withal?   50
    Or the boy's wings, which when he did approach
    The sun's hot beams, did melt and let him fall?

And yet, alas, when all our lamps are burned,
    Our bodies wasted, and our spirits spent,
    When we have all the learned volumes turned,
    Which yield men's wits both help and ornament,

What can we know, or what can we discern,
    When error chokes the windows of the mind,
    The diverse forms of things, how can we learn,
    That have been ever from our birthday blind?   60

When reason's lamp, which like the sun in sky,
    Throughout man's little world her beams did spread,
    Is now become a sparkle which doth lie
    Under the ashes, half extinct and dead;

How can we hope that through the eye and ear
    This dying sparkle, in this cloudy place,
    Can recollect these beams of knowledge clear,
    Which were infused in the first minds by grace?

So might the heir whose father hath in play
    Wasted a thousand pound of ancient rent,   70
    By painful earning of a groat a day
    Hope to restore the patrimony spent.

The wits that dived most deep and soared most high,
    Seeking man's powers, have found his weakness such;
    Skill comes so slow and life so fast doth fly,
    We learn so little and forget so much.

For this the wisest of all mortal men
    Said, He knew nought but that he nought did know;
    And the great mocking master mocked not then,
    When he said, Truth was buried deep below.   80

For how may we to others' things attain,
    When none of us his own soul understands?
For which the devil mocks our curious brain,
    When, Know thyself, his oracle commands.

For why should we the busy soul believe,
    When boldly she concludes of that and this;
When of herself she can no judgment give,
    Nor how, nor whence, nor where, nor what she is?

All things without, which round about we see,
    We seek to know, and how therewith to do;   90
But that whereby we reason, live, and be,
    Within ourselves we strangers are thereto.

We seek to know the moving of each sphere,
    And the strange cause of th' ebbs and floods of Nile;
But of that clock within our breasts we bear,
    The subtle motions we forget the while.

We that acquaint ourselves with every zone,
    And pass both tropics and behold the poles,
When we come home, are to ourselves unknown,
    And unacquainted still with our own souls.   100

We study speech, but others we persuade;
    We leech-craft learn, but others cure with it;
We interpret laws, which other men have made,
    But read not those which in our hearts are writ.

Is it because the mind is like the eye,
    Through which it gathers knowledge by degrees—
Whose rays reflect not, but spread outwardly—
    Not seeing itself when other things it sees?

No, doubtless, for the mind can backward cast
    Upon herself her understanding light;   110
But she is so corrupt and so defaced,
    As her own image doth herself affright.

As in the fable of the lady fair,
    Which for her lust was turned into a cow:
When thirsty to a stream she did repair,
    And saw herself transformed, she wist not how,

At first she startles, then she stands amazed,
   At last with terror she from thence doth fly,
   And loathes the wat'ry glass wherein she gazed,
   And shuns it still, though she for thirst do die.   120

Even so man's soul, which did God's image bear,
   And was at first fair, good, and spotless pure,
   Since with her sins her beauties blotted were,
   Doth of all sights her own sight least endure.

For even at first reflection she espies
   Such strange chimeras and such monsters there,
   Such toys, such antics, and such vanities,
   As she retires and shrinks for shame and fear.

And as the man loves least at home to be,
   That hath a sluttish house haunted with sprites,   130
   So she, impatient her own faults to see,
   Turns from herself and in strange things delights.

For this, few know themselves; for merchants broke
   View their estate with discontent and pain,
   And seas are troubled when they do revoke
   Their flowing waves into themselves again.

And while the face of outward things we find
   Pleasing and fair, agreeable and sweet,
   These things transport and carry out the mind,
   That with herself herself can never meet.   140

Yet if affliction once her wars begin,
   And threat the feebler sense with sword and fire,
   The mind contracts herself and shrinketh in,
   And to herself she gladly doth retire,

As spiders touched seek their webs' inmost part,
   As bees in storms unto their hives return,
   As blood in danger gathers to the heart,
   As men seek towns when foes the country burn.

If aught can teach us aught, affliction's looks,
   Making us look into ourselves so near,   150
   Teach us to know ourselves beyond all books,
   Or all the learned schools that ever were.

This mistress lately plucked me by the ear,
  And many a golden lesson hath me taught;
  Hath made my senses quick and reason clear,
  Reformed my will and rectified my thought.

So do the winds and thunders cleanse the air;
  So working lees settle and purge the wine;
  So lopped and prunëd trees do flourish fair;   160
  So doth the fire the drossy gold refine.

Neither Minerva nor the learned muse,
  Nor rules of art, nor precepts of the wise,
  Could in my brain those beams of skill infuse,
  As but the glance of this dame's angry eyes.

She within lists my ranging mind hath brought,
  That now beyond myself I list not go;
  Myself am center of my circling thought,
  Only myself I study, learn, and know.

I know my body's of so frail a kind
  As force without, fevers within, can kill;   170
  I know the heavenly nature of my mind,
  But 'tis corrupted both in wit and will;

I know my soul hath power to know all things,
  Yet is she blind and ignorant in all;
  I know I am one of nature's little kings,
  Yet to the least and vilest things am thrall.

I know my life's a pain and but a span,
  I know my sense is mocked with everything;
  And to conclude, I know myself a man,
  Which is a proud and yet a wretched thing.   180

That the soul is immortal, and cannot die

Nor hath He given these blessings for a day,
  Nor made them on the body's life depend;
  The soul, though made in time, survives for aye,
  And though it hath beginning, sees no end.

Her only end is never-ending bliss,
  Which is, th' eternal face of God to see,
  Who last of ends and first of causes is;
  And to do this she must eternal be.

How senseless, then, and dead a soul hath he   10
   Which thinks his soul doth with his body die!
Or thinks not so, but so would have it be,
   That he might sin with more security.

For though these light and vicious persons say,
   Our soul is but a smoke or airy blast,
Which during life doth in our nostrils play,
   And when we die doth turn to wind at last;

Although they say, Come, let us eat and drink,
   Our life is but a spark which quickly dies;
Though thus they say, they know not what to think,
   But in their minds ten thousand doubts arise.   20

Therefore no heretics desire to spread
   Their light opinions like these Epicures;
For so the staggering thoughts are comforted,
   And other men's assent their doubt assures.

Yet though these men against their conscience strive,
   There are some sparkles in their flinty breasts
Which cannot be extinct, but still revive,
   That though they would, they cannot quite be beasts.

But whoso makes a mirror of his mind
   And doth with patience view himself therein,   30
His soul's eternity shall clearly find,
   Though th' other beauties be defaced with sin.

An acclamation

O ignorant poor man, what dost thou bear
   Locked up within the casket of thy breast?
What jewels and what riches hast thou there?
   What heavenly treasure in so weak a chest?

Look in thy soul and thou shalt beauties find
   Like those which drowned Narcissus in the flood;
Honor and pleasure both are in thy mind,
   And all that in the world is counted good.

Think of her worth, and think that God did mean
   This worthy mind should worthy things embrace;   10
Blot not her beauties with thy thoughts unclean,
   Nor her dishonor with thy passions base.

Kill not her quick'ning power with surfeitings,
  Mar not her sense with sensuality,
  Cast not her serious wit on idle things,
  Make not her free-will slave to vanity.

And when thou think'st of her eternity,
  Think not that death against her nature is;
  Think it a birth, and when thou goest to die,
  Sing like a swan, as if thou went'st to bliss.   20

And if thou, like a child, didst fear before,
  Being in the dark where thou didst nothing see,
  Now I have brought the torchlight, fear no more,
  Now when thou diest, thou canst not hoodwinked be.

And thou, my soul, which turn'st thy curious eye
  To view the beams of thine own form divine,
  Know that thou canst know nothing perfectly
  While thou art clouded with this flesh of mine.

Take heed of overweening, and compare
  Thy peacock's feet with thy gay peacock's train;   30
  Study the best and highest things that are,
  But of thyself an humble thought retain.

Cast down thyself, and only strive to raise
  The glory of thy maker's sacred name;
  Use all thy powers that blessed power to praise,
  Which gives thee power to be, and use the same.

JOSEPH HALL, BISHOP OF NORWICH

The Introduction and Notes are at pages 1242 and 1276

From *Virgidemiarum,* 1597

Satire I

Nor lady's wanton love, nor wand'ring knight
Legend I out in rhymes all richly dight;
Nor fright the reader with the pagan vaunt
Of mighty Mahound and great Termagaunt.
Nor list I sonnet of my mistress' face,
To paint some blowess with a borrowed grace;
Nor can I bide to pen some hungry scene

For thick-skin ears, and undiscerning eyne.
Nor ever could my scornful muse abide
With tragic shoes her ankles for to hide.   10
Nor can I crouch, and writhe my fawning tail
To some great patron, for my best avail.
Such hunger-starven trencher-poetry,
Or let it never live, or timely die;
Nor under every bank and every tree,
Speak rhymes unto my oaten minstrelsy;
Nor carol out so pleasing lively lays
As mought the Graces move my mirth to praise.
Trumpet, and reeds, and socks, and buskins fine,
I them bequeath whose statues wand'ring twine   20
Of ivy, mixed with bays, circlen around,
Their living temples likewise laurel-bound.
Rather had I, albe in careless rhymes,
Check the mis-ordered world and lawless times;
Nor need I crave the muse's midwifery
To bring to light so worthless poetry.
Or, if we list, what baser muse can bide
To sit and sing by Granta's naked side?
They haunt the tided Thames and salt Medway
E'er since the fame of their late bridal day.   30
Nought have we here but willow-shaded shore
To tell our Grant his banks are left forlore.

Satire VI

Another scorns the homespun thread of rhymes
Matched with the lofty feet of elder times.
Give me the numbered verse that Virgil sung
And Virgil self shall speak the English tongue:
Manhood and garboils shall he chant, with changèd feet,
And headstrong dactyls making music meet;
The nimble dactyls striving to outgo
The drawling spondees pacing it below;
The ling'ring spondees, laboring to delay
The breathless dactyls with a sudden stay.   10
Whoever saw a colt, wanton and wild,
Yoked with a slow-foot ox on fallow field,
Can right areed how handsomely besets
Dull spondees with the English dactylets.
If Jove speak English in a thund'ring cloud,
Thwick thwack, and riff raff, roars he out aloud.
Fie on the forgèd mint that did create
New coin of words never articulate!

Satire VI (Book II)

A gentle squire would gladly entertain
Into his house some trencher-chaplain,
Some willing man that might instruct his sons
And that would stand to good conditïons.
First, that he lie upon the truckle-bed
Whiles his young master lieth o'er his head.
Second, that he do on no default
Ever presume to sit above the salt.
Third, that he never change his trencher twice.
Fourth, that he use all common courtesies,   10
Sit bare at meals, and one half rise and wait.
Last, that he never his young master beat
But he must ask his mother to define
How many jerks she would his breech should line.
All these observed, he could contented be
To give five marks and winter livery.

JOHN MARSTON

The Introduction and Notes are at pages 1243 and 1276

FROM *The Scourge of Villainy*, 1598

To Detraction I present my poesy

Foul canker of fair virtuous action,
Vile blaster of the freshest blooms on earth,
Envy's abhorrèd child, Detraction,
I here expose to thy all-tainting breath
    The issue of my brain; snarl, rail, bark, bite,
    Know that my spirit scorns Detraction's spite.

Know that the genius which attendeth on
And guides my powers intellectual,
Holds in all vile repute Detractïon;
My soul, an essence metaphysical   10
    That in the basest sort scorns critics' rage,
    Because he knows his sacred parentage.

My spirit is not huffed up with fat fume
Of slimy ale, nor Bacchus' heating grape.
My mind disdains the dungy muddy scum

Of abject thoughts, and envy's raging hate.
  True judgment slight regards opinïon;
  A sprightly wit disdains Detraction.

A partial praise shall never elevate
My settled censure of mine own esteem.   20
A cankered verdict of malignant hate
Shall ne'er provoke me worse myself to deem.
  Spite of despite and rancor's villainy,
  I am myself, so is my poesy.

Satire X

Humors

Sleep, grim reproof, my jocund muse doth sing
In other keys, to nimbler fingering.
Dull-sprited Melancholy, leave my brain!
To hell, Cimmerian night! in lively vein
I strive to paint; then hence, all dark intent
And sullen frowns! Come, sporting merriment,
Cheek-dimpling laughter, crown my very soul
With jouissance, whilst mirthful jests control
The gouty humors of these pride-swollen days,
Which I do long until my pen displays.   10
Oh, I am great with mirth; some midwifery,
Or I shall break my sides at vanity!
  Room for a capering mouth, whose lips ne'er stir
But in discoursing of the graceful slur;
Who ever heard spruce skipping Curio
E'er prate of aught but of the whirl on toe,
The turn above ground, Robrus' sprawling kicks,
Fabius' caper, Harry's tossing tricks?
Did ever any ear e'er hear him speak
Unless his tongue of cross-points did entreat?   20
His teeth do caper whilst he eats his meat,
His heels do caper whilst he takes his seat,
His very soul, his intellectual,
Is nothing but a mincing capreal.
He dreams of toe-turns, each gallant he doth meet
He fronts him with a traverse in the street;
Praise but *Orchestra* and the skipping art,
You shall command him; faith, you have his heart
Even cap'ring in your fist. A hall, a hall,
Room for the spheres, the orbs celestial   30
Will dance Kemp's jig. They'll revel with neat jumps;
A worthy poet hath put on their pumps! . . .

Luscus, what's played to-day? Faith, now I know
I set thy lips abroach, from whence doth flow
Nought but pure Juliet and Romeo.
Say, who acts best, Drusus or Roscio?
Now I have him, that ne'er of aught did speak
But when of plays or players he did treat.
H' hath made a commonplace book out of plays
And speaks in print; at least, whate'er he says   40
Is warranted by Curtain plaudities;
If e'er you heard him courting Lesbia's eyes,
Say, courteous sir, speaks he not movingly
From out some new pathetic tragedy?
He writes, he rails, he jests, he courts, what not,
And all from out his huge, long-scrapéd stock
Of well-penned plays. . . .
      But room for Tuscus, that jest-monging youth,
Who ne'er did ope his apish gerning mouth
But to retail and broke another's wit.   50
Discourse of what you will, he straight can fit
Your present talk with, Sir, I'll tell a jest,
(Of some sweet lady or grand lord, at least)
Then on he goes; and ne'er his tongue shall lie
Till his engrosséd jests are all drawn dry;
But then as dumb as Maurus, when at play
H' hath lost his crowns and pawned his trim array.
He doth nought but retail jests; break but one,
Out flies his table-book, let him alone,
He'll have 't, i' faith. Lad, hast an epigram,   60
Wilt have it put into the chaps of fame?
Give Tuscus copies; sooth, as his own wit,
His proper issue he will father it.
Oh, that this echo, that doth speak, spit, write,
Nought but the excrements of others' sprite,
This ill-stuffed trunk of jests, whose very soul
Is but a heap of gibes, should once enroll
His name 'mong creatures terméd rational,
Whose chief repute, whose sense, whose soul and all
Are fed with offal scraps that sometimes fall   70
From liberal wits, in their large festival.

To everlasting Oblivion

Thou mighty gulf, insatiate cormorant,
Deride me not, though I seem petulant
To fall into thy chops. Let others pray
Forever their fair poems flourish may;
But as for me, hungry Oblivion,

Devour me quick, accept my orison,
My earnest prayers, which do impórtune thee
With gloomy shade of thy still empery,
To veil both me and my rude poesy.

Far worthier lines in silence of thy state   10
Do sleep securely, free from love or hate,
From which this, living, ne'er can be exempt,
But whilst it breathes will hate and fury tempt.
Then close his eyes with thy all-dimming hand,
Which not right glorious actions can withstand.
Peace, hateful tongues, I now in silence pace;
Unless some hound do wake me from my place,
I with this sharp, yet well-meant poesy,
Will sleep secure, right free from injury
Of cankered hate or rankest villainy.   20

FROM *The Dutch Courtezan*, 1605

[*O love, how strangely sweet*]

O love, how strangely sweet
    Are thy weak passions,
That love and joy should meet
    In self-same fashions.
Oh, who can tell
    The cause why this should move?
But only this:
    No reason ask of love.

GEORGE CHAPMAN

The Introduction and Notes are at pages 1244 and 1276

FROM *The Shadow of Night*, 1594

Hymnus in Noctem

.   .   .   .

All you possessed with indepressed spiríts,
Indued with nimble and aspiring wits,
Come consecrate with me to sacred night
Your whole endeavors, and detest the light.
Sweet peace's richest crown is made of stars,
Most certain guides of honored marinars.
No pen can anything eternal write

That is not steeped in humor of the night.
  Hence, beasts and birds, to caves and bushes, then,
And welcome night, ye noblest heirs of men.   10
Hence, Phœbus, to thy glassy strumpet's bed
And nevermore let Themis' daughters spread
Thy golden harness on thy rosy horse,
But in close thickets run thy oblique course.
  See, now ascends the glorious bride of brides,
Nuptials and triumphs glitt'ring by her sides;
Juno and Hymen do her train adorn,
Ten thousand torches round about them borne.
Dumb Silence, mounted on the Cyprian star,
With becks rebukes the winds before his car,   20
Where she, advanced, beats down with cloudy mace
The feeble light to black Saturnius' paláce.
Behind her, with a brace of silver hinds,
In ivory chariot swifter than the winds,
Is great Hyperion's horned daughter drawn,
Enchantress-like, decked in disparent lawn,
Circled with charms and incantations
That ride huge spirits and outrageous passions.
Music and mood she loves, but love she hates
(As curious ladies do their public cates).   30
This train, with meteors, comets, lightenings,
The dreadful presence of our empress sings:
Which grant for ever, O eternal night,
Till virtue flourish in the light of light!

FROM *Ovid's Banquet of Sense*, 1595

A coronet for his mistress Philosophy

Muses that sing love's sensual empery,
    And lovers kindling your enragèd fires
  At Cupid's bonfires burning in the eye,
    Blown with the empty breath of vain desires;
You that prefer the painted cabinet
    Before the wealthy jewels it doth store ye,
  That all your joys in dying figures set,
    And stain the living substance of your glory:
Abjure those joys, abhor their memory,
    And let my love the honored subject be   10
  Of love, and honor's complete history;
    Your eyes were never yet let in to see
The majesty and riches of the mind,
But dwell in darkness; for your god is blind.

FROM *The Mask of the Middle Temple and Lincoln's Inn,* 1613

[*Descend, fair sun*]

One alone.

Descend, fair sun, and sweetly rest
  In Tethys' crystal arms thy toil.
Fall burning on her marble breast
  And make with love her billows boil.

Another alone.

Blow, blow, sweet winds. Oh, blow away
  All vapors from the finëd air,
That to this golden head no ray
  May languish with the least impair.

Cho.

Dance, Tethys, and thy love's red beams
  Embrace with joy; he now descends,   10
Burns, burns with love to drink thy streams,
  And on him endless youth attends.

[*Now, sleep, bind fast*]

Now, sleep, bind fast the flood of air,
  Strike all things dumb and deaf,
And to disturb our nuptial pair
  Let stir no aspen leaf.
Send flocks of golden dreams
  That all true joys presage,
Bring, in thy oily streams,
  The milk and honey age.
Now close the world-round sphere of bliss
And fill it with a heavenly kiss.   10

FROM *The Whole Works of Homer,* [*c.* 1616]

Iliad

Book XVIII

. . . .

This said, he left her there, and forth did to his bellows go,
Apposed them to the fire again, commanding them to blow.
Through twenty holes made to his hearth at once blew twenty pair
That fired his coals, sometimes with soft, sometimes with vehement
  air,

As he willed and his work required. Amids the flame he cast
Tin, silver, precious gold, and brass; and in the stock he placed
A mighty anvil; his right hand a weighty hammer held,
His left his tongs. And first he forged a strong and spacious shield,
Adorned with twenty several hues; about whose verge he beat
A ring, three-fold and radiant, and on the back he set   10
A silver handle. Five-fold were the equal lines he drew
About the whole circumference, in which his hand did shew
(Directed with a knowing mind) a rare variety:
For in it he presented earth; in it the sea and sky;
In it the never-wearied sun, the moon exactly round,
And all those stars with which the brows of ample heaven are crowned,
Orion, all the Pleiades, and those sev'n Atlas got,
The close-beamed Hyades, the Bear, surnamed the Chariot,
That turns about heav'n's axle-tree, holds ope a constant eye
Upon Orion; and, of all the cressets in the sky,   20
His golden forehead never bows to th' ocean empery.
    Two cities in the spacious shield he built, with goodly state
Of divers-languaged men. The one did nuptials celebrate,
Observing at them solemn feasts, the brides from forth their bowers
With torches ushered through the streets, a world of paramours
Excited by them; youths and maids in lovely circles danced,
To whom the merry pipe and harp the spritely sounds advanced,
The matrons standing in the doors admiring. Otherwhere
A solemn court of law was kept, where throngs of people were.

.   .   .   .

    The other city other wars employed as busily: 30
Two armies glittering in arms of one confederacy
Besieged it; and a parley had with those within the town.
Two ways they stood resolved,—to see the city overthrown,
Or that the citizens should heap in two parts all their wealth
And give them half. They neither liked, but armed themselves by
        stealth,
Left all their old men, wives, and boys behind to man their walls,
And stole out to their enemy's town. The queen of martials
And Mars himself conducted them,—both which being forged of gold
Must needs have golden furniture, and men might so behold
They were presented deities; the people Vulcan forged   40
Of meaner metal. When they came where that was to be urged
For which they went, within a vale close to a flood whose stream
Used to give all their cattle drink, they were enambushed them;
And sent two scouts out to descry when th' enemy's herds and sheep
Were setting out. They straight came forth, with two that used to
        keep
Their passage always, both which piped and went on merrily,

Nor dreamed of ambuscadoes there. The ambush then let fly,
Slew all their white-fleeced sheep, and neat, and by them laid their
    guard.
When those in siege before the town so strange an uproar heard
Behind, amongst their flocks and herds—being then in council set— 50
They then start up, took horse, and soon their subtle enemy met,
Fought with them on the river's shore, where both gave mutual blows
With well-piled darts. Amongst them all perverse Contention rose,
Amongst them Tumult was enraged, amongst them ruinous Fate
Had her red finger; some they took in an unhurt estate,
Some hurt, yet living; some quite slain, and those they tugged to them
By both the feet, stripped off and took their weeds, with all the stream
Of blood upon them that their steels had manfully let out;
They fared as men alive indeed drew dead indeed about.

    To these the fiery artisan did add a new-eared field, 60
Larged and thrice plowed, the soil being soft and of a wealthy yield;
And many men at plow he made, that drave earth here and there,
And turned up stitches orderly,—at whose end when they were
A fellow ever gave their hands full cups of luscious wine,
Which emptied, for another stitch the earth they undermine,
And long till th' utmost bound be reached of all the ample close.
The soil turned up behind the plow all black like earth arose,
Though forged of nothing else but gold; and lay in show as light
As if it had been plowed indeed, miraculous to sight.

    There grew by this a field of corn, high, ripe, where reapers
    wrought, 70
And let thick handfuls fall to earth, for which some other brought
Bands and made sheaves. Three binders stood and took the handfuls
    reaped
From boys that gathered quickly up, and by them armfuls heaped.
Amongst these, at a furrow's end, the king stood pleased at heart,
Said no word, but his scepter showed. And from him much apart
His harvest-bailiffs underneath an oak a feast prepared,
And having killed a mighty ox, stood there to see him shared,
Which women for their harvest-folks (then come to sup) had dressed,
And many white wheat-cakes bestowed, to make it up a feast.

    He set near this a vine of gold that cracked beneath the weight 80
Of bunches black with being ripe, to keep which at the height
A silver rail ran all along, and round about it flowed
An azure moat, and to this guard a quick-set was bestowed,
Of tin,—one only path to all, by which the pressmen came
In time of vintage. Youths, and maids that bore not yet the flame
Of manly Hymen, baskets bore of grapes and mellow fruit.
A lad that sweetly touched a harp to which his voice did suit
Centered the circles of that youth, all whose skill could not do
The wantons' pleasure to their minds, that danced, sung, whistled too.

A herd of oxen then he carved, with high raised heads, forged all 9°
Of gold and tin for color mixed, and bellowing from their stall
Rushed to their pastures at a flood, that echoed all their throats,
Exceeding swift and full of reeds; and all in yellow coats
Four herdsmen followed; after whom nine mastiffs went. In head
Of all the herd, upon a bull that deadly bellowëd
Two horrid lions ramped and seized and tugged off, bellowing still.
Both men and dogs came; yet they tore the hide, and lapped their fill
Of black blood, and the entrails ate. In vain the men assayed
To set their dogs on; none durst pinch, but cur-like stood and bayed
In both the faces of their kings, and all their onsets fled.   100
Then in a passing pleasant vale the famous artsman fed
Upon a goodly pasture-ground rich flocks of white-fleeced sheep,
Built stables, cottages, and cotes, that did the shepherds keep
From wind and weather. Next to these he cut a dancing-place
All full of turnings, that was like the admirable maze
For fair-haired Ariadne made by cunning Dædalus;
And in it youths and virgins danced, all young and beauteous,
And gluëd in another's palms. Weeds that the wind did toss
The virgins wore; the youths, woven coats that cast a faint dim gloss
Like that of oil. Fresh garlands, too, the virgins' temples crowned.   110
The youths gilt swords wore at their thighs, with silver baldrics bound.
Sometimes all wound close in a ring, to which as fast they spun
As any wheel a turner makes, being tried how it will run,
While he is set; and out again as full of speed they wound,
Not one left fast, or breaking hands. A multitude stood round,
Delighted with their nimble sport; to end which, two begun
Mids all a song, and turning sung the sport's conclusïon.
All this he circled in the shield, with pouring round about
In all his rage the ocëan, that it might never out.

FROM *Homer's Odysseys,* [*c.* 1614]

Odyssey

Book XII

In mean time flew our ships, and straight we fetched
The sirens' isle; a spleenless wind so stretched
Her wings to waft us, and so urged our keel.
But having reached this isle, we could not feel
The least gasp of it; it was stricken dead,
And all the sea in prostrate slumber spread,—
The sirens' devil charmed all. Up then flew
My friends to work, struck sail, together drew

And under hatches stowed them, sat, and plied
Their polished oars; and did in curls divide   10
The white-head waters. My part then came on:
A mighty waxen cake I set upon,
Chopped it in fragments with my sword, and wrought
With strong hand every piece till all were soft;
The great power of the sun, in such a beam
As then flew burning from his diadem,
To liquefaction helped us. Orderly
I stopped their ears; and they as fair did ply
My feet and hands with cords, and to the mast   20
With other halsers made me soundly fast.
   Then took they seat, and forth our passage strook;
The foamy sea beneath their labor shook.
   Rowed on, in reach of an erected voice,
The sirens soon took note, without our noise,
Tuned those sweet accents that made charms so strong,
And these learn'd numbers made the sirens' song:
   Come here, thou, worthy of a world of praise,
That dost so high the Grecian glory raise!
Ulysses, stay thy ship! and that song hear
That none passed ever but it bent his ear,   30
But left him ravished, and instructed more
By us than any ever heard before.
For we know all things whatsoever were
In wide Troy labored; whatsoever there
The Grecians and the Trojans both sustained
By those high issues that the gods ordained.
And whatsoever all the earth can show
T' inform a knowledge of desert, we know.
   This they gave accent in the sweetest strain
That ever opened an enamoured vein.

       .   .   .   .

EDWARD FAIRFAX

The Introduction and Notes are at pages 1245 and 1277

From *Godfrey of Bulloigne*, 1600

Book XVI

       .   .   .   .   .   .

When they had passëd all those troubled ways,
The garden sweet spread forth her green to show,
The moving crystal from the fountains plays,

Fair trees, high plants, strange herbs and flowerets new,
Sunshiny hills, dales hid from Phœbus' rays,
Groves, arbors, mossy caves, at once they view,
    And that which beauty most, most wonder brought,
    Nowhere appeared the art which all this wrought.

So with the rude the polished mingled was
That natural seemed all and every part,
Nature would craft in counterfeiting pass,
And imitate her imitator art;
Mild was the air, the skies were clear as glass,
The trees no whirlwind felt, nor tempest smart;
    But ere their fruit drop off, the blossom comes,
    This springs, that falls, that ripeneth and this blooms.

The leaves upon the self-same bough did hide
Beside the young the old and ripened fig,
Here fruit was green, there ripe with vermeil side,
The apples new and old grew on one twig,
The fruitful vine her arms spread high and wide
That bended underneath their clusters big,
    The grapes were tender here, hard, young, and sour,
    There purple ripe, and nectar sweet forth pour.

The joyous birds, hid under greenwood shade,
Sung merry notes on every branch and bough,
The wind that in the leaves and waters played
With murmur sweet, now sung, and whistled now;
Ceasëd the birds, the wind loud answer made,
And while they sung, it rumbled soft and low;
    Thus were it hap or cunning, chance or art,
    The wind in this strange music bore his part.

With parti-colored plumes and purple bill,
A wondrous bird among the rest there flew,
That in plain speech sung love-lays loud and shrill,
Her leden was like human language true;
So much she talked, and with such wit and skill,
That strange it seemëd how much good she knew,
    Her feathered fellows all stood hush to hear,
    Dumb was the wind, the waters silent were.

The gently budding rose, quoth she, behold,
That first scant peeping forth with virgin beams,
Half ope, half shut, her beauties doth upfold
In their dear leaves, and less seen, fairer seems,

And after spreads them forth more broad and bold,
Then languisheth and dies in last extremes;
    Nor seems the same that deckëd bed and bower
    Of many a lady late, and paramour;

So, in the passing of a day, doth pass
The bud and blossom of the life of man,   50
Nor e'er doth flourish more, but like the grass
Cut down, becometh withered, pale and wan.
Oh, gather then the rose while time thou hast,
Short is the day, done when it scant began,
    Gather the rose of love, while yet thou mayest,
    Loving, be loved; embracing, be embraced.

He ceased, and as approving all he spoke,
The choir of birds their heavenly tunes renew,
The turtles sighed, and sighs with kisses broke,
The fowls to shades unseen by pairs withdrew;   60
It seemed the laurel chaste, and stubborn oak,
And all the gentle trees on earth that grew,
    It seemed the land, the sea, and heaven above,
    All breathed out fancy sweet, and sighed out love.

  ·   ·   ·   ·   ·   ·   ·

SONGS FROM PLAYS

The Introduction and Notes are at pages 1246 and 1277

FROM JOHN BALE's *King John, Devonshire Ms.,* [*c.* 1538]

    Wassail, wassail, out of the milk-pail,
    Wassail, wassail, as white as my nail,
    Wassail, wassail, in snow, frost, and hail,
    Wassail, wassail, with partridge and rail,
    Wassail, wassail, that much doth avail,
    Wassail, wassail, that never will fail.

FROM R. WEVER's *Lusty Juventus,* [*c.* 1560]

    In a herber green, asleep whereas I lay,
    The birds sang sweet in the middës of the day;
    I dreamëd fast of mirth and play,
        In youth is pleasure, in youth is pleasure.

    Methought as I walked still to and fro,
    And from her company I could not go;

But when I waked it was not so,
 In youth is pleasure, in youth is pleasure.

Therefore my heart is surely pight
Of her alone to have a sight,   10
Which is my joy and heart's delight,
 In youth is pleasure, in youth is pleasure.

FROM WILLIAM STEVENSON'S *Gammer Gurton's Needle*, 1575

Back and side go bare, go bare,
 Both foot and hand go cold;
But, belly, God send thee good ale
  enough,
 Whether it be new or old.

I cannot eat but little meat,
 My stomach is not good;
But sure I think that I can drink
 With him that wears a hood.
Though I go bare, take ye no care,
 I am nothing a-cold;   10
I stuff my skin so full within
 Of jolly good ale and old.

Back and side go bare, go bare,
 Both foot and hand go cold;
But, belly, God send thee good ale
  enough,
 Whether it be new or old.

I love no roast but a nutbrown
  toast,
 And a crab laid in the fire;
A little bread shall do me stead,
 Much bread I not desire. 20
No frost nor snow, no wind, I
  trow,
 Can hurt me if I would,

I am so wrapped, and throughly
  lapped
 Of jolly good ale and old.

Back and side go bare, &c.

And Tib my wife, that as her life
 Loveth well good ale to seek,
Full oft drinks she, till ye may see
 The tears run down her cheeks.
Then doth she troll to me the bowl,
 Even as a maltworm should, 31
And saith, Sweetheart, I took my
  part
 Of this jolly good ale and old.

Back and side go bare, &c.

Now let them drink, till they nod
  and wink,
 Even as good fellows should do;
They shall not miss to have the
  bliss
 Good ale doth bring men to;
And all poor souls that have
  scoured bowls
 Or have them lustily trolled, 40
God save the lives of them and
  their wives,
 Whether they be young or old.

Back and side go bare, &c.

FROM *Tom Tyler and His Wife*, 1661

The proverb reporteth, no man can deny,
 That wedding and hanging is destiny.

I am a poor tiler in simple array,
And get a poor living, but eightpence a day,

My wife as I get it, doth spend it away;
　　And I cannot help it, she saith; wot ye why?
　　For wedding and hanging is destiny.

I thought when I wed her, she had been a sheep,
At board to be friendly, to sleep when I sleep.
She loves so unkindly, she makes me to weep;   10
　　But I dare say nothing, God wot, wot ye why?
　　For wedding and hanging is destiny.

Besides this unkindness whereof my grief grows,
I think few tilers are matched with such shrows;
Before she leaves brawling, she falls to deal blows
　　　Which early and late doth cause me cry
　　　That wedding and hanging is destiny.

The more that I please her, the worse she doth like me,
The more I forbear her, the more she doth strike me,
The more that I get her, the more she doth glike me;   20
　　　Woe worth this ill fortune that maketh me cry
　　　That wedding and hanging is destiny.

If I had been hangëd when I had been married,
My torments had ended, though I had miscarried;
If I had been warnëd, then would I have tarried;
　　　But now all too lately I feel and cry
　　　That wedding and hanging is destiny.

FROM *Misogonus, Devonshire Ms.,* [1560–1577]

A song to the tune of Heart's Ease

Sing care away with sport and play,
　　Pastime is all our pleasure;
If well we fare for nought we care,
　　In mirth consist our treasure.

Let snudges lurk and drudges work,
　　We do defy their slavery;
He is but a fool that goes to school,
　　All we delight in bravery.

What doth avail far hence to sail
　　And lead our life in toiling;   10
Or to what end should we here spend
　　Our days in irksome moiling?

It is the best to live at rest,
　　And take 't as God doth send it,
To haunt each wake and mirth to make,
　　And with good fellows spend it.

Nothing is worse than a full purse
　　To niggards and to pinchers;
They always spare and live in care,
　　There's no man loves such flinchers.   20

The merry man with cup and can
　　Lives longer than doth twenty;
The miser's wealth doth hurt his health,
　　Examples we have plenty.

'Tis a beastly thing to lie mus-
    ing
With pensiveness and sorrow,
For who can tell that he shall
    well
    Live here until the morrow?

We will therefore for evermore,
    While this our life is lasting,   30
Eat, drink, and sleep, and lemans
    keep;
    It's popery to use fasting.

In cards and dice our comfort lies,
    In sporting and in dancing,
Our minds to please and live at
    ease,
    And sometimes to use prancing.

With Bess and Nell we love to
    dwell,
    In kissing and in haking;
But whoop ho holly, with trolly
    lolly,
    To them we'll now be walk-
    ing.   40

FROM JOHN PHILLIPS's *Comedy of Patient and Meek Grissell*
[*c.* 1566]

Lulla by baby, lulla by baby,
Thy nurse will tend thee, as duly as may be.

Be still, my sweet sweeting, no longer do cry,
    Sing lulla by baby, lulla by baby.
Let dolors be fleeting, I fancy thee, I,
    To rock and to lull thee, I will not delay me.
    Lulla by baby, &c.

What creature now living would hasten thy woe?
    Sing lulla by, lulla by, lulla by baby.
See for thy relieving, the time I bestow,   10
    To dance, and to prance thee, as prett'ly as may be.
    Lulla by baby, &c.

The gods be thy shield and comfort in need,
    Sing lulla by, lulla by, lulla by baby;
They give thee good fortune and well for to speed,
    And this to desire, I will not delay me.

FROM JOHN PICKERING's *New Interlude of Vice, containing the
History of Horestes*, 1567

Farewell, adieu, that courtly life,
To war we tend to go;
It is good sport to see the strife
Of soldiers in a row.
    How merrily they forward
    march

These enemies to slay,
With hey, trim, and trixie too,
Their banners they display.

Now shall we have the golden
    cheats,

When others want the same;   10
And soldiers have full many
    feats
Their enemies to tame;
   With cocking here, and boom-
    ing there,
  They break their foe's array;
  And lusty lads amid the
    fields
Their ensigns do display.

The drum and flute play lustily,
The trumpet blows amain,
And venturous knights coura-
    geously
Do march before their train   20
  With spears in rest, so lively
    dressed
  In armor bright and gay;
  With hey, trim, and trixie too,
  Their banners they display.

From *The Trial of Treasure*, 1567

Hey ho, care away, let the world pass,
For I am as lusty as ever I was,
In flowers I flourish as blossoms in May,
Hey ho, care away; hey ho, care away.

Am not I in blessed case,
Treasure and pleasure to possess?
I would not wish no better place,
If I may still have wealthiness,
And to enjoy in perfect peace
    My lady, lady.
My pleasant pleasure shall increase,
    My dear lady.

Helen may not comparèd be,
Nor Cressida that was so bright,   10
These cannot stain the shine of thee,
Nor yet Minerva of great might.
Thou passest Venus far away,
    Lady, lady;
Love thee I will both night and day,
    My dear lady.

My mouse, my nobs, my coney sweet,
My hope and joy, my whole delight,
Dame Nature may fall at thy feet,
And may yield to thee her crown of right.   20
I will thy body now embrace,
    Lady, lady,
And kiss thy sweet and pleasant face,
    My dear lady.

FROM *The Marriage of Wit and Science*, [*c.* 1570]

Idleness singeth

Come, come, lie down, and thou shalt see
None like to me to entertain
Thy bones and thee oppressed with pain.
Come, come and ease thee in my lap,
And if it please thee, take a nap;
A nap that shall delight thee so
That fancies all will thee forgo.
By musing still, what canst thou find
But wants of will and restless mind?
A mind that mars and mangles all,   10
And breedeth jars to work thy fall;
Come, gentle Wit, I thee require,
And thou shalt hit thy chief desire,
Thy chief desire, thy hopëd prey,
First ease thee here, and then away!

FROM *Common Conditions*, [*c.* 1576]

Lustily, lustily, lustily let us sail forth,
The wind trim doth serve us, it blows at the north.

All things we have ready, and nothing we want,
To furnish our ship that rideth hereby:
Victuals and weapons, they be nothing scant,
Like worthy mariners ourselves we will try.
    Lustily, lustily, &c.

Her flags be new trimmed set flaunting aloft,
Our ship for swift swimming, oh, she doth excel;
We fear no enemies, we have escaped them oft;   10
Of all ships that swimmeth, she beareth the bell.
    Lustily, lustily, &c.

And here is a master excelleth in skill,
And our master's mate, he is not to seek;
And here is a boatswain will do his good will,
And here is a shipboy, we never had his leek.
    Lustily, lustily, &c.

If fortune then fail not, and our next voyage prove,
We will return merrily, and make good cheer,
And hold all together as friends linked in love;   20
The cans shall be filled with wine, ale, and beer.
    Lustily, lustily, &c.

FROM *Fedele and Fortunio, or the Two Italian Gentlemen,* 1585

If love be like the flower that in the night,
When darkness drowns the glory of the skies,
Smells sweet, and glitters in the gazer's sight,
But when the gladsome sun begins to rise,
　And he that views it would the same embrace,
　It withereth and loseth all his grace;

Why do I love and like the cursed tree,
Whose buds appear, but fruit will not be seen?
Why do I languish for the flower I see,
Whose root is rot, when all the leaves be green?　　10
　In such a case it is a point of skill
　To follow chance, and love against my will.

FROM JOHN LYLY'S *Six Court Comedies,* 1632

Cupid and my Campaspe played
At cards for kisses; Cupid paid.
He stakes his quiver, bow, and arrows,
His mother's doves and team of sparrows,
Loses them too; then down he throws
The coral of his lip, the rose
Growing on's cheek (but none knows how),
With these the crystal of his brow,
And then the dimple of his chin:
All these did my Campaspe win.　　10
At last he set her both his eyes;
She won, and Cupid blind did rise.
　O Love! has she done this to thee?
　What shall, alas, become of me?

From *Alexander and Campaspe*

What bird so sings, yet so does wail?
Oh, 'tis the ravished nightingale.
Jug, jug, jug, jug, tereu, she cries,
And still her woes at midnight rise.
Brave prick-song! who is't now we hear?
None but the lark so shrill and clear;
How at heaven's gates she claps her wings,
The morn not waking till she sings.
Hark, hark, with what a pretty throat
Poor robin redbreast tunes his note;　　10
Hark how the jolly cuckoos sing
Cuckoo, to welcome in the spring,
Cuckoo, to welcome in the spring.

From *Alexander and Campaspe*

A song in making of the arrows

My shag-hair Cyclops, come, let's
    ply
Our Lemnian hammers lustily.
By my wife's sparrows,
I swear these arrows
Shall singing fly
Through many a wanton's eye.
These headed are with golden
    blisses,
These silver ones feathered with
    kisses;

But this of lead   10
Strikes a clown dead,
When in a dance
He falls in a trance,
To see his black-brow lass not buss
    him,
And then whines out for death t'
    untruss him.
So, so, our work being done, let's
    play,
Holiday, boys, cry holiday.

From *Sapho and Phao*

Song by fairies

Omnes. Pinch him, pinch him, black and blue,
        Saucy mortals must not view
        What the queen of stars is doing,
        Nor pry into our fairy wooing.
1 *Fairy.*   Pinch him blue.
2 *Fairy.*   And pinch him black.
3 *Fairy.*   Let him not lack
        Sharp nails to pinch him blue and red,
        Till sleep has rocked his addlehead.
4 *Fairy.* For the trespass he hath done,   10
        Spots o'er all his flesh shall run.
        Kiss Endymion, kiss his eyes,
        Then to our midnight haydegyes.

From *Endymion*

FROM GEORGE PEELE's *Arraignment of Paris*, 1584

Œnone. Fair and fair and twice
    so fair,
    As fair as any may be;
The fairest shepherd on our
    green,
A love for any lady.

Paris. Fair and fair and twice so
    fair,
    As fair as any may be;
Thy love is fair for thee alone,
    And for no other lady.

Œnone. My love is fair, my love
    is gay,
    As fresh as been the flowers in
    May,   10
    And of my love my rounde-
    lay,
My merry, merry, merry
    roundelay
Concludes with Cupid's curse:
They that do change old love
    for new,
Pray gods they change for worse.

Ambo simul. They that do change,
    &c.
Œnone. Fair and fair, &c.
Paris. Fair and fair, &c. Thy love
    is fair, &c.
Œnone. My love can pipe, my
    love can sing,

My love can many a pretty
    thing,   20
And of his lovely praises ring
My merry, merry roundelays.
    Amen to Cupid's curse:
They that do change, &c.
Paris. They that do change, &c.
Ambo. Fair and fair, &c.

From George Peele's *Polyhymnia*, 1590

His golden locks time hath to silver turned;
    Oh, time too swift, oh, swiftness never ceasing!
His youth 'gainst time and age hath ever spurned,
    But spurned in vain; youth waneth by increasing.
Beauty, strength, youth, are flowers but fading seen;
Duty, faith, love, are roots, and ever green.

His helmet now shall make a hive for bees,
    And lover's sonnets turned to holy psalms,
A man-at-arms must now serve on his knees,
    And feed on prayers, which are age his alms;   10
But though from court to cottage he depart,
His saint is sure of his unspotted heart.

And when he saddest sits in homely cell,
    He'll teach his swains this carol for a song:
Blest be the hearts that wish my sovereign well,
    Cursed be the souls that think her any wrong!
Goddess, allow this aged man his right,
To be your beadsman now, that was your knight.

From George Peele's *Hunting of Cupid*, [c. 1591]

What thing is love? for, well I wot, love is a thing.
It is a prick, it is a sting,
It is a pretty, pretty thing;
It is a fire, it is a coal,
Whose flame creeps in at ev'ry hole;
And as my wit doth best devise,
Love's dwelling is in ladies' eyes,
From whence do glance love's piercing darts
That make such holes into our hearts;
And all the world herein accord   10
Love is a great and mighty lord;
And when he list to mount so high,
With Venus he in heaven doth lie,

And evermore hath been a god
Since Mars and she played even and odd.

Coridon and Melampus' song

Cor. Melampus, when will love be void of fears?
Mel. When jealousy hath neither eyes nor ears.
Cor. Melampus, when will love be thoroughly shrieved?
Mel. When it is hard to speak, and not believed.
Cor. Melampus, when is love most malcontent?
Mel. When lovers range and bear their bows unbent.
Cor. Melampus, tell me when love takes least harm?
Mel. When swains' sweet pipes are puffed, and trulls are warm.
Cor. Melampus, tell me when is love best fed?
Mel. When it hath sucked the sweet that ease hath bred.   10
Cor. Melampus, when is time in love ill-spent?
Mel. When it earns meed and yet receives no rent.
Cor. Melampus, when is time well-spent in love?
Mel. When deeds win meeds, and words love's works do prove.

FROM GEORGE PEELE'S *Old Wive's Tale*, 1595

Whenas the rye reach to the chin,
And chopcherry, chopcherry ripe within,
Strawberries swimming in the cream,
And schoolboys playing in the stream;
Then oh, then oh, then oh, my true love said,
Till that time come again,
She could not live a maid.

FROM GEORGE PEELE'S *Love of King David and Fair Bethsabe*, 1599

Hot sun, cool fire, tempered with sweet air,
Black shade, fair nurse, shadow my white hair.
Shine, sun; burn, fire; breathe, air, and ease me;
Black shade, fair nurse, shroud me and please me;
Shadow, my sweet nurse, keep me from burning,
Make not my glad cause cause of mourning.
    Let not my beauty's fire
    Inflame unstaid desire,
    Nor pierce any bright eye
    That wand'reth lightly.   10

FROM *The Lamentable Tragedy of Locrine,* 1595

Strumbo, Dorothy, Trumpart, cobbling shoes

Trum.	We cobblers lead a merry life,
All.	Dan, dan, dan, dan;
Strum.	Void of all envy and of strife,
All.	Dan diddle dan.
Dor.	Our ease is great, our labor small,
All.	Dan, dan, dan, dan;
Strum.	And yet our gains be much withal,
All.	Dan diddle dan.
Dor.	With this art so fine and fair,
All.	Dan, dan, dan, dan,
Trum.	No occupation may compare,
All.	Dan diddle dan.
Strum.	For merry pastime and joyful glee,
	Dan, dan, dan, dan,
Dor.	Most happy men we cobblers be,
	Dan diddle dan.
Trum.	The can stands full of nappy ale,
	Dan, dan, dan, dan,
Strum.	In our shop still withouten fail,
	Dan diddle dan.
Dor.	This is our meat, this is our food,
	Dan, dan, dan, dan;
Trum.	This brings us to a merry mood,
	Dan diddle dan;
Strum.	This makes us work for company,
	Dan, dan, dan, dan,
Dor.	To pull the tankards cheerfully,
	Dan diddle dan.
Trum.	Drink to thy husband, Dorothy,
	Dan, dan, dan, dan.
Dor.	Why, then, my Strumbo, there's to thee,
	Dan diddle dan.
Strum.	Drink thou the rest, Trumpart, amain,
	Dan, dan, dan, dan.
Dor.	When that is gone, we'll fill 't again,
	Dan diddle dan.

10

20

30

FROM *The Maid's Metamorphosis,* 1600

By the moon we sport and play,
With the night begins our day,
As we dance the dew doth fall;

Trip it, little urchins all,
Lightly as the little bee,
Two by two, and three by three;
And about go we, and about go we.

FROM *Wily Beguiled*, 1606

Old Tithon must forsake his dear,
The lark doth chant her cheerful lay;
Aurora smiles with merry cheer,
To welcome in a happy day.

The beasts do skip,
The sweet birds sing,
The wood nymphs dance,
The echoes ring.

The hollow caves with joy resounds,
And pleasure everywhere abounds;   10
The Graces, linking hand in hand,
In love have knit a glorious band.

FROM *The Thracian Wonder*, 1661

Love is a law, a discord of such force
That 'twixt our sense and reason makes divorce.
Love's a desire that to obtain betime,
We lose an age of tears plucked from our prime.
Love is a thing to which we soon consent,
As soon refuse, but sooner far repent.

Then what must women be that are the cause,
That love hath life, that lovers feel such laws?
They're like the winds upon Lapanthæ's shore,
That still are changing. Oh, then love no more.   10
A woman's love is like that Syrian flower
That buds and spreads, and withers in an hour.

FROM THOMAS NASHE's *Summer's Last Will and Testament*, 1600

Adieu, farewell earth's bliss,
This world uncertain is;
Fond are life's lustful joys,
Death proves them all but toys,
None from his darts can fly.
I am sick, I must die.
　　Lord, have mercy on us!

Rich men, trust not in wealth,
Gold cannot buy you health;
Physic himself must fade,   10
All things to end are made.
The plague full swift goes by;
I am sick, I must die.
　　Lord, have mercy on us!

Beauty is but a flower
Which wrinkles will devour:
Brightness falls from the air,
Queens have died young and fair,
Dust hath closed Helen's eye.
I am sick, I must die.   20
    Lord, have mercy on us!

Wit with his wantonness
Tasteth death's bitterness;   30
Hell's executioner
Hath no ears for to hear
What vain art can reply.
I am sick, I must die.
    Lord, have mercy on us!

Strength stoops unto the grave,
Worms feed on Hector brave,
Swords may not fight with fate.
Earth still holds ope her gate;
Come! come! the bells do cry.
I am sick, I must die.
    Lord, have mercy on us!

Haste, therefore, each degree,
To welcome destiny.
Heaven is our heritage,
Earth but a player's stage;
Mount we unto the sky.   40
I am sick, I must die.
    Lord, have mercy on us!

Spring, the sweet spring, is the year's pleasant king;
Then blooms each thing, then maids dance in a ring,
Cold doth not sting, the pretty birds do sing:
    Cuckoo, jug-jug, pu-we, to-witta-woo!

The palm and may make country houses gay,
Lambs frisk and play, the shepherds pipe all day,
And we hear aye birds tune this merry lay:
    Cuckoo, jug-jug, pu-we, to-witta-woo!

The fields breathe sweet, the daisies kiss our feet,
Young lovers meet, old wives a-sunning sit,   1t
In every street these tunes our ears do greet:
    Cuckoo, jug-jug, pu-we, to-witta-woo!
        Spring, the sweet spring!

Fair summer droops, droop men and beasts therefor;
So fair a summer look for never more.
All good things vanish less than in a day,
Peace, plenty, pleasure, suddenly decay.
    Go not yet away, bright soul of the sad year,
    The earth is hell when thou leav'st to appear.

What, shall those flowers that decked thy garland erst,
Upon thy grave be wastefully dispersed?
O trees, consume your sap in sorrow's source;
Streams, turn to tears your tributary course.   10
    Go not yet hence, bright soul of the sad year,
    The earth is hell when thou leav'st to appear.

Autumn hath all the summer's fruitful treasure;
Gone is our sport, fled is poor Croydon's pleasure.
Short days, sharp days, long nights come on apace,—
Ah, who shall hide us from the winter's face?
Cold doth increase, the sickness will not cease,
And here we lie, God knows, with little ease.
　　From winter, plague, and pestilence, good Lord deliver us!

London doth mourn, Lambeth is quite forlorn;
Trades cry, Woe worth that ever they were born.
The want of term is town and city's harm;　　　　　　10
Close chambers we do want to keep us warm.
Long banished must we live from our friends;
This low-built house will bring us to our ends.
　　From winter, plague, and pestilence, good Lord deliver us!

FROM THOMAS DEKKER'S *Shoemaker's Holiday, or the Gentle Craft*, 1600

Cold's the wind, and wet's the rain,
　　Saint Hugh be our good speed;
Ill is the weather that bringeth no gain,
　　Nor helps good hearts in need.

Troll the bowl, the jolly nut-brown bowl,
　　And here, kind mate, to thee;
Let's sing a dirge for Saint Hugh's soul,
　　And down it merrily.

Down-a-down, hey, down-a-down,
　　Hey derry derry down-a-down,　　　　　　　　　　10
Close with the tenor, boy;
Ho! well done, to me let come,
　　Ring compass, gentle joy.

Troll the bowl, the nut-brown bowl,
　　And here, kind, &c. (*As often as there be men to drink.*)

　　(*At last, when all have drunk, this verse.*)

Cold's the wind, and wet's the rain,
　　Saint Hugh be our good speed;
Ill is the weather that bringeth no gain,
　　Nor helps good hearts in need.　　　　　　　　　20

FROM THOMAS DEKKER's *Pleasant Comedy of Patient Grissill*, 1603

Art thou poor, yet hast thou golden slumbers?
    Oh, sweet content!
Art thou rich, yet is thy mind perplexed?
    Oh, punishment!
Dost thou laugh to see how fools are vexed
To add to golden numbers golden numbers?
    Oh, sweet content, oh, sweet, &c.

Work apace, apace, apace, apace;
Honest labor bears a lovely face,
Then hey noney, noney, hey noney, noney.   10

Canst drink the waters of the crispëd spring?
    Oh, sweet content!
Swim'st thou in wealth, yet sink'st in thine own tears?
    Oh, punishment!
Then he that patiently want's burden bears,
No burden bears, but is a king, a king.
    Oh, sweet content, &c.
Work apace, apace, &c.

———

Golden slumbers kiss your eyes,
Smiles awake you when you rise;
Sleep, pretty wantons, do not cry,
And I will sing a lullaby,
Rock them, rock them, lullaby.

Care is heavy, therefore sleep you,
You are care, and care must keep you;
Sleep, pretty wantons, do not cry,
And I will sing a lullaby,
Rock them, rock them, lullaby.   10

———

Beauty arise, show forth thy glorious shining,
Thine eyes feed love, for them he standeth pining;
Honor and youth attend to do their duty
To thee, their only sovereign, Beauty.
Beauty arise, whilst we, thy servants, sing
Io to Hymen, wedlock's jocund king.
    Io to Hymen, Io, Io, sing;
    Of wedlock, love, and youth is Hymen king.

Beauty arise, Beauty arise, thy glorious lights display,
Whilst we sing Io, glad to see this day.   10

Io, Io, to Hymen, Io, Io, sing;
Of wedlock, love, and youth is Hymen king.

FROM THOMAS DEKKER'S *London's Tempe*, [1629]

Brave iron! brave hammer! from your sound
The art of music has her ground;
On the anvil thou keep'st time,
Thy knick-a-knock is a smith's best chime.
    Yet thwick-a-thwack,
      Thwick, thwack-a-thwack, thwack,
    Make our brawny sinews crack,
    Then pit-a-pat, pat, pit-a-pat, pat,
    Till thickest bars be beaten flat.

We shoe the horses of the sun,
Harness the dragons of the moon,
Forge Cupid's quiver, bow, and arrows,
And our dame's coach that's drawn with sparrows.
    Till thwick-a-thwack, &c.

Jove's roaring cannons, and his rammers
We beat out with our Lemnian hammers;
Mars his gauntlet, helm, and spear,
And Gorgon shield, are all made here.
    Till thwick-a-thwack, &c.

The grate which, shut, the day outbars,   20
Those golden studs which nail the stars,
The globe's case, and the axle-tree,
Who can hammer these but we?
    Till thwick-a-thwack, &c.

A warming-pan to heat earth's bed,
Lying i' th' frozen zone half-dead;
Hob-nails to serve the man i' th' moon,
And sparrowbills to clout Pan's shoon,
    Whose work but ours?
    Till thick-a-thwack, &c.   30

Venus' kettles, pots, and pans
We make, or else she brawls and bans;
Tongs, shovels, andirons have their places,
Else she scratches all our faces.
    Till thwick-a-thwack, &c.

FROM THOMAS DEKKER and JOHN FORD'S *Sun's Darling*, 1656

Cast away care, he that loves sorrow
Lengthens not a day, nor can buy to-morrow;
　　Money is trash, and he that will spend it,
　　Let him drink merrily, fortune will send it.
Merrily, merrily, merrily, oh, ho!
Play it off stiffly, we may not part so.

Wine is a charm, it heats the blood too,
Cowards it will arm, if the wine be good too;
　　Quickens the wit, and makes the back able,
　　Scorns to submit to the watch or constable.　　　10
Merrily, &c.

Pots fly about, give us more liquor,
Brothers of a rout, our brains will flow quicker;
　　Empty the cask, score up, we care not;
　　Fill all the pots again, drink on, and spare not.
Merrily, &c.

FROM JOHN WEBSTER'S *White Devil*, 1612

Call for the robin redbreast and the wren,
Since o'er shady groves they hover,
And with leaves and flowers do cover
The friendless bodies of unburied men.
Call unto his funeral dole
The ant, the field-mouse, and the mole,
To rear him hillocks that shall keep him warm,
And, when gay tombs are robbed, sustain no harm;
But keep the wolf far thence, that's foe to men,
For with his nails he'll dig them up again.　　　10

FROM JOHN WEBSTER'S *Duchess of Malfi*, 1623

Hark, now everything is still;
The screech-owl and the whistler shrill
Call upon our dame aloud,
And bid her quickly don her shroud;
Much you had of land and rent,
Your length in clay's now competent.
A long war disturbed your mind;
Here your perfect peace is signed.
Of what is 't fools make such vain keeping?
Sin their conception, their birth weeping,　　　10

Their life a general mist of error,
Their death a hideous storm of terror.
Strew your hair with powders sweet,
Don clean linen, bathe your feet,
And, the foul fiend more to check,
A crucifix let bless your neck;
'Tis now full tide, 'tween night and day,
End your groan and come away.

FROM FRANCIS BEAUMONT and JOHN FLETCHER'S *Knight of the Burning Pestle*, 1613

Come, you whose loves are dead,
  And whiles I sing,
    Weep, and wring
Every hand, and every head
Bind with cypress and sad yew;
Ribands black and candles blue
For him that was of men most true.

Come with heavy mourning,
  And on his grave
    Let him have
Sacrifice of sighs and groaning;
Let him have fair flowers enow,
White and purple, green and yellow,
For him that was of men most true.

10

Better music ne'er was known
Than a choir of hearts in one.
Let each other that hath been
Troubled with the gall or spleen,
Learn of us to keep his brow
Smooth and plain as ours are now.
Sing though before the hour of dying,
He shall rise, and then be crying
Hey ho! 'Tis nought but mirth
That keeps the body from the earth.

10

FROM FRANCIS BEAUMONT and JOHN FLETCHER'S *The Maid's Tragedy*, 1619

Cynthia, to thy power and thee
  We obey.
Joy to this great company;
  And no day
Come to steal this night away,

Till the rites of love are ended,
And the lusty bridegroom say,
Welcome, light, of all befriended.

Pace out, you watery powers below;
   Let your feet,
Like the galleys when they row,
   Even beat.
Let your unknown measures, set
To the still winds, tell to all
That gods are come, immortal, great,
To honor this great nuptïal.

From *The Maid's Tragedy*, 1622

Lay a garland on my hearse of the dismal yew,
Maidens, willow branches bear, say I dïed true.
My love was false, but I was firm from my hour of birth;
Upon my buried body lay lightly, gently, earth.

I could never have the power
To love one above an hour,
But my head would prompt mine eye
On some other man to fly.
Venus, fix mine eyes fast,
Or, if not, give me all that I shall see at last.

From John Fletcher's *Faithful Shepherdess*, [c. 1610]

Do not fear to put thy feet
Naked in the river, sweet;
Think not leech, or newt, or toad
Will bite thy foot when thou hast trod;
Nor let the water rising high,
As thou wad'st in, make thee cry
And sob; but ever live with me,
And not a wave shall trouble thee.

From John Fletcher's *Bloody Brother*, 1639

The drinking song

Drink to-day, and drown all sorrow,
You shall perhaps not do it to-morrow.
Best, while you have it, use your breath;
There is no drinking after death.

Wine works the heart up, wakes the wit;
There is no cure 'gainst age but it.

It helps the headache, cough, and tisic,
And is for all diseases physic.

Then let us swill, boys, for our health;
Who drinks well, loves the commonwealth.   10
And he that will to bed go sober,
Falls with the leaf still in October.

Take, oh, take those lips away
    That so sweetly were forsworn,
And those eyes, like break of day,
    Lights that do mislead the morn;
But my kisses bring again,
    Seals of love, though sealed in vain.

Hide, oh, hide those hills of snow,
    Which thy frozen bosom bears,
On whose tops the pinks that grow
    Are of those that April wears.   10
But first set my poor heart free,
    Bound in those icy chains by thee.

From Francis Beaumont and John Fletcher's *Comedies and Tragedies*, 1647

Care-charming Sleep, thou easer of all woes,
Brother to Death, sweetly thyself dispose
On this afflicted prince; fall like a cloud
In gentle showers; give nothing that is loud
Or painful to his slumbers; easy, sweet,
And as a purling stream, thou son of Night,
Pass by his troubled senses; sing his pain,
Like hollow murmuring wind or silver rain;
Into this prince gently, oh, gently slide,
And kiss him into slumbers like a bride.   10
                        From John Fletcher's *Valentinian*

God Lyæus, ever young,
    Ever honored, ever sung;
Stained with blood of lusty grapes,
    In a thousand lusty shapes,
Dance upon the mazer's brim,
    In the crimson liquor swim;
From thy plenteous hand divine,
    Let a river run with wine.

God of youth, let this day here
Enter neither care nor fear.   10
> From John Fletcher's *Valentinian*

Cast our caps and cares away,
This is beggars' holiday.
At the crowning of our king,
Thus we ever dance and sing.
In the world look out and see,
Where so happy a prince as he?
Where the nation live so free,
And so merry as do we?
Be it peace, or be it war,
Here at liberty we are,   10
And enjoy our ease and rest;
To the field we are not pressed;
Nor are called into the town
To be troubled with the gown.
Hang all officers, we cry,
And the magistrate too, by.
When the subsidy's increased,
We are not a penny cessed;
Nor will any go to law
With the beggar for a straw.   20
All which happiness, he brags,
He doth owe unto his rags.
> From John Fletcher's *Beggars' Bush*

Hence, all you vain delights,
As short as are the nights
  Wherein you spend your folly,
There's nought in this life sweet,
If man were wise to see't,
  But only melancholy,
  Oh, sweetest melancholy.
Welcome, folded arms and fixëd eyes,
A sigh that piercing mortifies,
A look that's fastened to the ground,
A tongue chained up without a sound.   10
Fountain-heads, and pathless groves,
Places which pale passion loves,
Moonlight walks, when all the fowls
Are warmly housed, save bats and owls,
  A midnight bell, a parting groan,
    These are the sounds we feed upon;

Then stretch our bones in a still gloomy valley,
Nothing's so dainty sweet as lovely melancholy.

From John Fletcher's Nice Valor

From Francis Beaumont and John Fletcher's *Fifty Comedies and Tragedies*, 1679

Let the bells ring, and let the boys sing,
  The young lasses skip and play,
Let the cups go round, till round goes the ground,
  Our learned old vicar will stay.

Let the pig turn merrily, merrily, ah,
  And let the fat goose swim,
For verily, verily, verily, ah,
  Our vicar this day shall be trim.

The stewed cock shall crow, cock-a-loodle-loo,
  A loud cock-a-loodle shall he crow;   10
The duck and the drake shall swim in a lake
  Of onions and claret below.

Our wives shall be neat, to bring in our meat
  To thee, our most noble adviser;
Our pains shall be great, and bottles shall sweat,
  And we ourselves will be wiser.

We'll labor and swink, we'll kiss and we'll drink,
  And tithes shall come thicker and thicker;
We'll fall to our plow, and get children enow,
  And thou shalt be learned old vicar.   20

From John Fletcher's Spanish Curate

Weep no more, nor sigh, nor groan,
Sorrow calls no time that's gone;
Violets plucked, the sweetest rain
Makes not fresh nor grow again;
Trim thy locks, look cheerfully;
Fate's hid ends eyes cannot see.
Joys as wingèd dreams fly fast,
Why should sadness longer last?
Grief is but a wound to woe;
Gentlest fair, mourn, mourn no mo.

From John Fletcher's Queen of Corinth

FROM *Mr. William Shakespeare's Comedies, Histories, and Tragedies,*
1623

Orpheus with his lute made trees,
And the mountain-tops that freeze,
Bow themselves when he did sing;
To his music plants and flowers
Ever sprung, as sun and showers
There had made a lasting spring.
Everything that heard him play,
Even the billows of the sea,
Hung their heads, and then lay by.
In sweet music is such art,   10
Killing care and grief of heart
Fall asleep or, hearing, die.
From Shakespeare and Fletcher's *King Henry VIII*

FROM THOMAS MIDDLETON'S *Chaste Maid in Cheapside,* 1630

Weep eyes, break heart!
My love and I must part.
Cruel fates true love do soonest sever;
Oh, I shall see thee never, never, never.
Oh, happy is the maid whose life takes end
Ere it knows parent's frown or loss of friend.
Weep eyes, break heart!
My love and I must part.

FROM THOMAS MIDDLETON'S *The Widow,* 1652

Give me fortune, give me health,
Give me freedom, I'll get wealth.
Who complains his fate's amiss,
When he has the wide world his?
He that has the devil in fee,
Can have but all, and so have we.
Give us fortune, give us health,
Give us freedom, we'll get wealth.
In every hamlet, town, and city,
He has lands that was born witty.

FROM THOMAS MIDDLETON'S *More Dissemblers Besides Women,*
1657

Captain. Come, my dainty doxies,
My dells, my dells most dear,
We have neither house nor land,
Yet never want good cheer.

All. We never want good
cheer.
Captain. We take no care for
candle rents.

2 *Gipsy.* We lie. *3 Gipsy.* We
    snort.
Captain. We sport in tents,
    Then rouse betimes and steal
        our dinners.
    Our store is never taken   10
    Without pigs, hens, or ba-
        con,
    And that's good meat for sin-
        ners.
    At wakes and fairs we cozen
    Poor country folks by dozen;
    If one have money, he disburses;
    Whilst some tell fortunes, some
        pick purses;
    Rather than be out of use,

We'll steal garters, hose or
        shoes,
    Boots, or spurs with jingling
        rowels,
    Shirts or napkins, smocks or
        towels.   20
    Come live with us, come live
        with us,
    All you that love your eases;
        He that's a gipsy
        May be drunk or tipsy
    At any hour he pleases.
All. We laugh, we quaff, we roar,
        we scuffle,
    We cheat, we drab, we filch, we
        shuffle.

From Philip Massinger's *Emperor of the East,* 1632

Why art thou slow, thou rest of trouble, Death,
    To stop a wretch's breath,
That calls on thee and offers her sad heart
    A prey unto thy dart?
I am nor young nor fair; be, therefore, bold;
    Sorrow hath made me old,
Deformed, and wrinkled; all that I can crave
    Is quiet in my grave.
Such as live happy, hold long life a jewel,
    But to me thou art cruel   10
If thou end not my tedious misery,
    And I soon cease to be.
Strike, and strike home, then; pity unto me,
    In one short hour's delay, is tyranny.

From Nathan Field's *Amends for Ladies,* 1618

Rise, lady mistress, rise,
    The night hath tedious been;
No sleep hath fallen into my
        eyes,
    Nor slumbers made me sin.
Is not she a saint, then, say,
Thought of whom keeps sin
        away?

Rise, madam, rise and give me
        light,
    Whom darkness still will cover,
And ignorance darker than night,
    Till thou smile on thy lover.   10
All want day till thy beauty rise,
For the grey morn breaks from
        thine eyes.

FROM BARTEN HOLIDAY'S *Technogamia or the Marriage of the Arts,*
1618

Tobacco's a musician,
And in a pipe delighteth;
  It descends in a close,
  Through the organ of the nose,
With a relish that inviteth.
  This makes me sing, So ho ho,
    so ho ho, boys,
  Ho boys, sound I loudly;
    Earth ne'er did breed
    Such a jovial weed,
  Whereof to boast so proudly. 10

Tobacco is a lawyer,
His pipes do love long cases;
  When our brains it enters,
  Our feet do make indentures,
Which we seal with stamping
    paces.
  This makes me sing, So ho, &c.

Tobacco's a physician,
Good both for sound and sickly;
  'Tis a hot perfume
  That expels cold rheum,   20
And makes it flow down quickly.
  This makes me sing, &c.

Tobacco is a traveler,
Come from the Indies hither;
  It passed sea and land

Ere it came to my hand,
And scaped the wind and weather.
  This makes me sing, &c.

Tobacco is a critic,
That still old paper turneth;   30
  Whose labor and care
  Is as smoke in the air
That ascends from a rag when it
    burneth.
  This makes me sing, &c.

Tobacco's an *ignis fatuus,*
A fat and fiery vapor;
  That leads men about
  Till the fire be out,
Consuming like a taper.
  This makes me sing, &c.   40

Tobacco is a whiffler
And cries, Huff snuff, with fury;
  His pipe's his club and link,
  He's the visor that does drink,
Thus armed I fear not a jury.
  This makes me sing, So ho ho,
    so ho ho, boys,
  Ho boys, sound I loudly;
    Earth ne'er did breed
    Such a jovial weed,
  Whereof to boast so proudly. 50

FROM PETER HAUSTED'S *Rival Friends,* 1632

Have pity, grief, I cannot pay
  The tribute which I owe thee, tears;
    Alas, those fountains are grown dry,
    And 'tis in vain to hope supply
  From others' eyes; for each man bears
    Enough about him of his own
    To spend his stock of tears upon.

Woo then the heavens, gentle love,
  To melt a cloud for my relief;

10

Or woo the deep, or woo the grave;
Woo what thou wilt, so I may have
Wherewith to pay my debt, for grief
Has vowed, unless I quickly pay,
To take both life and love away.

Have you a desire to see
The glorious heaven's epitome?
Or an abstract of the spring?
Adonis' garden? or a thing
Fuller of wonder, nature's shop displayed,
Hung with the choicest pieces she has made?
Here behold it open laid.

Or else would you bless your eyes
With a type of paradise?
Or behold how poets feign
Jove to sit amidst his train?
Or see what made Actæon rue,
Diana 'mongst her virgin crew?
Lift up your eyes and view.

FROM JOHN FORD's *The Broken Heart*, 1633

Can you paint a thought, or number
Every fancy in a slumber?
Can you count soft minutes roving
From a dial's point by moving?
Can you grasp a sigh, or lastly,
Rob a virgin's honor chastely?
No, oh no; yet you may
Sooner do both that and this,
This and that, and never miss,
Than by any praise display
Beauty's beauty; such a glory
As (beyond all fate, all story)
All arms, all arts,
All loves, all hearts,
Greater than those or they,
Do, shall, and must obey.

Oh, no more, no more, too late
Sighs are spent; the burning tapers
Of a life as chaste as fate,
Pure as are unwritten papers,
Are burnt out; no heat, no light

Now remains, 'tis ever night.
Love is dead, let lovers' eyes,
   Locked in endless dreams,
   Th' extremes of all extremes,
Ope no more, for now love dies,   10
   Now love dies, implying
Love's martyrs must be ever, ever dying.

All. Glories, pleasures, pomps, delights, and ease
         Can but please
    Outward senses, when the mind
    Is not untroubled, or by peace refined.
 1. Crowns may flourish and decay,
    Beauties shine, but fade away.
 2. Youth may revel, yet it must
    Lie down in a bed of dust.
 3. Earthly honors flow and waste,
    Time alone doth change and last.   10
All. Sorrows mingled with contents, prepare
      Rest for care;
    Love only reigns in death; though art
    Can find no comfort for a broken heart.

FROM JASPER FISHER'S *Fuimus Troes*, 1633

So the silver-feathered swan,
Both by death and color wan,
Loves to sing before she die,
Leaving life so willingly.
But how can I sing a note
When dead hoarseness stops my throat?
Or how can I play a stroke
When my heartstrings are all broke?

A morisco

The sky is glad that stars above
   Do give a brighter splendor;
The stars unfold their flaming gold
   To make the ground more tender;
The ground doth send a fragrant smell
   That air may be the sweeter;
The air doth charm the swelling seas
   With pretty chirping meter;
The sea with rivers water doth
   The plants and flowers dainty;   10
The plants do yield their fruitful seed

That beasts may live in plenty;
The beasts do give both food and cloth
That man high Jove may honor;
And so the world runs merrily round,
When peace doth smile upon her.
Oh then, then oh; oh then, then oh;
This jubilee last forever,
That foreign spite or civil fight
Our quiet trouble never!   20

FROM THOMAS GOFFE's *Tragedy of Orestes*, 1633

Lullaby, lullaby baby,
Great Argos' joy,
The King of Greece thou art born
     to be,
In despite of Troy.
Rest ever wait upon thy head,
Sleep close thine eyes;
The blessed guard tend on thy bed
     Of deities.
Oh, how his brow will beseem a
     crown!
How these locks will shine!   10
Like the rays of the sun on the
     ground,
These locks of thine.
The nurse of heaven still send
     thee milk;
Mayst thou suck a queen.
Thy drink, Jove's nectar, and
     clothes of silk;
A god mayst thou seem.
Cupid sit on this rosean cheek,
     On these ruby lips.
May thy mind like a lamb be
     meek,
In the vale which trips.   20
Lullaby, lullaby baby.

FROM WILLIAM SAMPSON's *Vow Breaker*, 1636

When from the wars I do return,
And at a cup of good ale mourn,

I'll tell how towns without fire
     we did burn,
     And is not that a wonder?

I'll tell how that my general
Entered the breach, and scaled the
     wall,
And made the foremost battery of
     all,
     And is not that a wonder?

How that we went to take a fort,
And took it too in warlike sort;   10
I'll swear that a lie is a true report,
     And is not that a wonder?

How that we soldiers had true pay,
And cloth, and victuals every day,
And never a captain ran away,
     And is not that a wonder?

FROM JOHN JONES's *Adrasta*, 1635

Come, lovers, bring your cares,
Bring sigh-perfumèd sweets,
Bedew the grave with tears,
Where death and virtue meets;
Sigh for the hapless hour
That knit two hearts in one,
And only gave love power
To die when 'twas begun.

FROM THOMAS MAY's *Tragedy of Cleopatra*, 1639

Not he that knows how to acquire,
     But to enjoy, is blest.

Nor does our happiness consist
  In motion, but in rest.

The gods pass man in bliss, because
  They toil not for more height;
But can enjoy, and in their own
  Eternal rest delight.

Then, princes, do not toil nor care; 10
  Enjoy what you possess.
Which whilst you do, you equalize
  The gods in happiness.

FROM THOMAS MAY's *Old Couple*, 1658

Dear, do not your fair beauty
  wrong,
In thinking still you are too young.
The roses and lilies in your cheek
Flourish, and no more ripening
  seek.
Your cherry lip, red, soft, and
  sweet,
Proclaims such fruit for taste most
  meet;
Then lose no time, for love has
  wings,
And flies away from aged things.

FROM THOMAS NABBES's *Hannibal and Scipio*, 1637

Beauty no more the subject be
Of wanton art to flatter thee;
Or in dull figures call thee spring,
Lily, or rose, or other thing;
All which beneath thee are, and
  grow
Into contempt when thou dost
  show
The unmatched glory of thy brow.
Behold a sphere of virgins move,
None 'mongst them less than queen
  of love;
And yet their queen so far excels, 10
Beauty and she are only parallels.

FROM JAMES SHIRLEY's *Changes, or Love in a Maze*, 1632

Melancholy, hence! go get
Some piece of earth to be thy seat;
Here the air and nimble fire
Would shoot up to meet desire;
Sullen humor, leave her blood,
Mix not with the purer flood,
But let pleasures swelling there
Make a springtide all the year.

FROM JAMES SHIRLEY's *Triumph of Peace*, 1633

Come away, away, away,
See the dawning of the day,
Risen from the murmuring
  streams;
Some stars show with sickly beams
What stock of flame they are al-
  lowed,
Each retiring to a cloud;
Bid your active sports adieu,
The morning else will blush for
  you.

Ye feathered-footed hours, run
To dress the chariot of the sun; 10
Harness the steeds, it quickly will
Be time to mount the eastern hill.

The lights grow pale with modest
  fears,
Lest you offend those sacred ears
And eyes, that lent you all this
  grace;
Retire, retire, to your own place.

And as you move from that blest
  pair,
Let each heart kneel and think a
  prayer,
That all, that can make up the
  glory,
Of good and great may fill their
  story. 20

FROM JAMES SHIRLEY's *Triumph of Beauty*, 1646

Cease, warring thoughts, and let his brain
No more discord entertain,
But be smooth and calm again.

Ye crystal rivers that are nigh,
As your streams are passing by,
Teach your murmurs harmony.

Ye winds that wait upon the spring,
And perfumes to flowers do bring,
Let your amorous whispers here
Breathe soft music to his ear.   10

Ye warbling nightingales repair
From every wood to charm this air,
And with the wonders of your breast,
Each striving to excel the rest.
    When it is time to wake him, close your parts,
    And drop down from the trees with broken hearts.

FROM JAMES SHIRLEY's *Cupid and Death*, 1653

Victorious men of earth, no more
    Proclaim how wide your empires are;
Though you bind in every shore,
    And your triumphs reach as far
        As night or day,
Yet you, proud monarchs, must obey
And mingle with forgotten ashes when
Death calls ye to the crowd of common men.

Devouring famine, plague, and war,

Each able to undo mankind,   10
Death's servile emissaries are;
    Nor to these alone confined,
        He hath at will
    More quaint and subtle ways to kill;
A smile or kiss, as he will use the art,
Shall have the cunning skill to break a heart.

FROM JAMES SHIRLEY's *Contention of Ajax and Ulysses*, 1659

The glories of our blood and state
    Are shadows, not substantial things;
There is no armor against fate;
    Death lays his icy hand on kings.
        Scepter and crown
        Must tumble down,
And in the dust be equal made
With the poor crooked scythe and spade.

Some men with swords may reap the field,
    And plant fresh laurels where they kill;   10
But their strong nerves at last must yield,
    They tame but one another still.
        Early or late,
        They stoop to fate,
And must give up their murmuring breath,
When they, pale captives, creep to death.

The garlands wither on your brow,
    Then boast no more your mighty deeds;
Upon death's purple altar now,
    See where the victor-victim bleeds.   20
        Your heads must come

To the cold tomb;
Only the actions of the just
Smell sweet and blossom in their
    dust.

FROM HENRY SHIRLEY's *Martyred Soldier*, 1638

What are earthly honors
But sin's glorious banners?
Let not golden gifts delight
    thee,
Let not death nor torments fright
    thee,
From thy place thy captain gives
    thee;
When thou faintest, he relieves
    thee.
Hark how the lark
Is to the morning singing;
Hark how the bells are ring-
    ing;
It is for joy that thou to heaven art
    flying;   10
This is not life, true life is got by
    dying.

FROM RICHARD BROME's *Northern Lass*, 1632

A bonny, bonny bird I had,
    A bird that was my marrow;
A bird whose pastime made me
    glad,
    And Philip, 'twas my sparrow.
A pretty play-fere, chirp it would,
    And hop, and fly to fist,
Keep cut, as 'twere a usurer's gold,
    And bill me when I list.
    Philip, Philip, Philip, it cries,
      But he is fled, and my joy
        dies.   10

But were my Philip come again,
    I would not change my love
For Juno's bird with gaudy train,
    Nor yet for Venus' dove.
Nay, would my Philip come again,
    I would not change my state,
For his great namesake's wealth of
    Spain,
    To be another's mate.
    Philip, Philip, Philip, it cries,
      But he is fled, and my joy
        dies.   20

FROM RICHARD BROME's *Jovial Crew or the Merry Beggars*, 1652

A round, a round, a round, boys, a round,
Let mirth fly aloft and sorrow be drowned.
Old sack and old songs and a merry old crew
Can charm away cares when the ground looks blue.

FROM SIR WILLIAM BERKELEY's *Lost Lady*, 1639

Where did you borrow that last
    sigh,
    And that relenting groan?
For those that sigh, and not for
    love,
    Usurp what's not their own.
Love's arrows sooner armor pierce
    Than your soft snowy skin;
Your eyes can only teach us love,
    But cannot take it in.

FROM ROBERT CHAMBERLAIN's *Swaggering Damsel*, 1640

Farewell this company
If you love sadness,
For melancholy is
Nothing but madness;
Hang up proud costly clothes,
Peddlers and pack-toys;
Let us make the hogs-head
    weep
Claret and sack, boys.

FROM ROBERT DAVENPORT'S
King John and Matilda, 1655

Matilda, now go take thy bed
In the dark dwellings of the
dead,

And rise in the great waking day,
Sweet as incense, fresh as May.

Rest thou, chaste soul, fixed in thy
proper sphere,
Amongst heaven's fair ones, all are
fair ones there.

Rest there, chaste soul, whilst
we here troubled say,
Time gives us griefs, death takes
our joys away.

BROADSIDE BALLADS

The Introduction and Notes are at pages 1250 and 1277

The king's hunt is up

The hunt is up, the hunt is up,
And it is well nigh day;
And Harry our king is gone hunt-
ing,
To bring his deer to bay.

The east is bright with morning
light,
And darkness it is fled;
And the merry horn wakes up the
morn
To leave his idle bed.

Behold the skies with golden dyes
Are glowing all around;   10
The grass is green, and so are the
treen,
All laughing with the sound.

The horses snort to be at the sport,
The dogs are running free;
The woods rejoice at the merry
noise
Of hey tantara tee ree!

The sun is glad to see us clad
All in our lusty green,
And smiles in the sky as he riseth
high
To see and to be seen.   20

Awake all men, I say again,
Be merry as you may;

For Harry our king is gone hunting
To bring his deer to bay.
              [*Gray of Reading*]

A song between the Queen's Majesty and England

E [*ngland*]. Come over the bourn,
Bessy,
    Come over the bourn, Bessy,
Sweet Bessy, come over to me;
    And I shall thee take
    And my dear lady make,
Before all other that ever I see.

B [*essy*]. Methink I hear a voice
    At whom I do rejoice,
And answer thee now I shall:
    Tell me, I say,   10
    What art thou that bids me
    come away,
And so earnestly dost me call?

E.   I am thy lover fair,
    Hath chose thee to mine heir,
And my name is merry England;
    Therefore come away,
    And make no more delay,
Sweet Bessy, give me thy hand!

B.   Here is my hand,
    My dear lover, England;   20
I am thine both with mind and
    heart,

Forever to endure,
Thou mayest be sure,
Until death us two depart.

E. Lady, this long space
Have I loved thy grace,
More than I durst well say;
Hoping at the last,
When all storms were past,
For to see this joyful day.   30

B. Yet, my lover England,
Ye shall understand
How fortune on me did lour;
I was tumbled and tossed
From pillar to post,
And prisoner in the Tower.

E. Dear Lady, we do know
How tyrants, not a few,
Went about for to seek thy blood;
And contrary to right   40
They did what they might,
That now bear two faces in one
hood.

B. Then was I carried to
Woodstock,
And kept close under lock,
That no man might with me
speak;
And against all reason
They accused me of treason,
And terribly they did me threat.

E. Oh, my lover fair!
My darling and mine heir!   50
Full sore for thee I did lament;
But no man durst speak,
But they would him threat
And quickly make him repent.

B. Then was I delivered their
hands,
But was fain to put in bands
And good sureties for my forth
coming;

Not from my house to de-
part,
Nor nowhere else to start,
As though I had been away running.   60

E. Why, dear Lady, I trow,
Those madmen did not
know
That ye were daughter unto King
Harry,
And a princess of birth,
One of the noblest on earth,
And sister unto Queen Mary.

B. Yes, yet I must forgive
All such as do live,
If they will hereafter amend;   69
And for those that are gone,
God forgive them every one,
And his mercy on them extend.

E. Yet, my lover dear,
Tell me now here,
For what cause had ye this pun-
ishment?
For the commons did not
know,
Nor no man would them
show,
The chief cause of your imprison-
ment.

B. No, nor they themself,
That would have decayed my
wealth,   80
But only by power and abusion,
They could not detect me,
But that they did suspect me,
That I was not of their religion.

E. Oh, cruel tyrants,
And also monstrous giants,
That would such a sweet blossom
devour!
But the Lord, of his might,
Defended thee in right,

And shortened their arm and
    power.   90

B. Yet, my lover dear,
    Mark me well here,
Though they were men of the
    devil,
    The Scripture plainly saith,
    All they that be of faith
Must needs do good against evil.

E. O sweet virgin pure!
    Long may ye endure
To reign over us in this land;
    For your works do ac-
        cord,   100
    Ye are the handmaid of the
        Lord,
For he hath blessed you with his
    hand.

B. My sweet realm, be obedient
    To God's holy command-
        ment,
And my proceedings embrace;
    And for that that is abused,
    Shall be better used,
And that within short space.

E. Dear Lady and Queen,
    I trust it shall be seen   110
Ye shall reign quietly without
    strife;
    And if any traitors there be,
    Of any kind or degree,
I pray God send them short life.

B. I trust all faithful hearts
    Will play true subjects' parts,
Knowing me their Queen and
    true heir by right;
    And that much the rather
    For the love of my father,
That worthy prince, King Henry
    th' Eight.   120

E. Therefore let us pray
    To God both night and day,

Continually and never to cease,
    That he will preserve your
        grace
    To reign over us long space
In tranquility, wealth, and peace.

Both. All honor, laud, and praise
    Be to the Lord God always,
Who hath all princes' hearts in
    his hands;
    That by his power and
        might,   130
    He may guide them right,
For the wealth of all Christian
    lands.
    Finis, quod WILLIAM BIRCHE.
    God save the Queen.

*A proper song, entitled: Fain
would I have a pretty thing to
give unto my lady*

To the tune of Lusty Gallant

Fain would I have a pretty thing
    To give unto my lady;
I name no thing, nor I mean no
    thing,
    But as pretty a thing as may
    be.

Twenty journeys would I make,
    And twenty ways would hie
    me,
To make adventure for her sake,
    To set some matter by me.

But I would fain have a pretty
    thing, &c.,
I name no thing, nor I mean no
    thing, &c.   10

Some do long for pretty knacks,
    And some for strange devices;
God send me that my lady lacks,
    I care not what the price is.
    Thus fain, &c.

Some go here, and some go there,
  Where gazes be not geason;
And I go gaping everywhere,
  But still come out of season.
    Yet fain, &c.   20

I walk the town and tread the
    street,
  In every corner seeking
The pretty thing I cannot meet,
  That's for my lady's liking.
    Fain, &c.

The mercers pull me going by,
  The silky-wives say, What lack
    ye?
The thing you have not, then say
    I,
  Ye foolish fools, go pack ye.
    But fain, &c.   30

It is not all the silk in Cheap,
  Nor all the golden treasure,
Nor twenty bushels on a heap,
  Can do my lady pleasure.
    But fain, &c.

The gravers of the golden shows
  With jewels do beset me;
The seamsters in the shops that
    sews,
  They do nothing but let me.
    But fain, &c.   40

But were it in the wit of man
  By any means to make it,
I could for money buy it than,
  And say, Fair lady, take it.
    Thus fain, &c.

O lady, what a luck is this,
  That my good willing miss-
    eth
To find what pretty thing it is
  That my good lady wisheth.

Thus fain would I have had this
    pretty thing   50

To give unto my lady;
I said no harm, nor I meant no
    harm,
  But as pretty a thing as may
    be.

A new courtly sonnet, of the Lady Greensleeves

To the new tune of *Greensleeves*

Greensleeves was all my joy,
  Greensleeves was my delight;
Greensleeves was my heart of
    gold,
  And who but Lady Green-
    sleeves?

Alas, my love, ye do me wrong
  To cast me off discourteously;
And I have lovëd you so long,
  Delighting in your company.

Greensleeves was all my joy,
  Greensleeves was my delight;
Greensleeves was my heart of
    gold,   11
  And who but Lady Green-
    sleeves?

I have been ready at your hand
  To grant whatever you would
    crave;
I have both wagëd life and land,
  Your love and good will for
    to have.

Greensleeves was all my joy, &c.

I bought thee kerchiefs to thy
    head,
  That were wrought fine and
    gallantly;
I kept thee both at board and
    bed,   20
  Which cost my purse well
    favoredly.

Greensleeves was all my joy, &c.

I bought thee petticoats of the
  best,
　The cloth so fine as fine might
  be;
I gave thee jewels for thy chest,
　And all this cost I spent on
  thee.

Greensleeves was all my joy, &c.

Thy smock of silk both fair and
  white,
　With gold embroidered gor-
  geously;
Thy petticoat of sendal right, 30
　And thus I bought thee gladly.

Greensleeves was all my joy, &c.

Thy girdle of gold so red,
　With pearls bedeckëd sumptu-
  ously;
The like no other lasses had,
　And yet thou wouldst not love
  me.

Greensleeves was all my joy, &c.

Thy purse and eke thy gay gilt
  knives,
　Thy pin-case, gallant to the
  eye,
No better wore the burgess'
  wives,   40
　And yet thou wouldst not love
  me.

Greensleeves was all my joy, &c.

Thy crimson stockings all of silk,
　With gold all wrought above
  the knee,
Thy pumps as white as was the
  milk,
　And yet thou wouldst not love
  me.

Greensleeves was all my joy, &c.

Thy gown was of the grossy
  green,
　Thy sleeves of satin hanging
  by,
Which made thee be our harvest
  queen,   50
　And yet thou wouldst not love
  me.

Greensleeves was all my joy, &c.

Thy garters fringëd with the
  gold,
　And silver aglets hanging by,
Which made thee blithe for to behold,
　And yet thou wouldst not love
  me.

Greensleeves was all my joy, &c.

My gayest gelding I thee gave,
　To ride wherever liked thee;
No lady ever was so brave,   60
　And yet thou wouldst not love
  me.

Greensleeves was all my joy, &c.

My men were clothëd all in
  green,
　And they did ever wait on
  thee;
All this was gallant to be seen,
　And yet thou wouldst not love
  me.

Greensleeves was all my joy, &c.

They set thee up, they took thee
  down,
　They served thee with humility;

Thy foot might not once touch
 the ground,   70
And yet thou wouldst not love
 me.

Greensleeves was all my joy, &c.

For every morning when thou
 rose
 I sent thee dainties orderly,
To cheer thy stomach from all
 woes,
 And yet thou wouldst not love
 me.

Greensleeves was all my joy, &c.

Thou couldst desire no earthly
 thing,
 But still thou hadst it readily;
Thy music still to play and sing, 80
And yet thou wouldst not love
 me.

Greensleeves was all my joy, &c.

And who did pay for all this gear
 That thou didst spend when
 pleased thee?
Even I that am rejected here,
 And thou disdain'st to love me.

Greensleeves was all my joy, &c.

Well, I will pray to God on high
 That thou my constancy mayest
 see;
And that yet once before I die 90
 Thou wilt vouchsafe to love
 me.

Greensleeves was all my joy, &c.

Greensleeves, now farewell, adieu,
 God I pray to prosper thee;
For I am still thy lover true,
 Come once again and love me.

Greensleeves was all my joy, &c.

A proper new song made by a student in Cambridge

To the tune of *I wish to see those happy days*

I which was once a happy wight
 and high in fortune's grace,
And which did spend my golden
 prime
 in running pleasure's race,
  Am now enforced of late
  contrariwise to mourn,
  Since fortune joys into annoys
  my former state to turn.

The toiling ox, the horse, the ass
 have time to take their rest; 10
Yea, all things else which nature
 wrought
 sometimes have joys in breast,
  Save only I, and such
  which vexëd are with
  pain;
  For still in tears my life it
  wears,
  and so I must remain.

How oft have I in folded arms
 enjoyëd my delight!
How oft have I excuses made,
 of her to have a sight! 20
  But now to fortune's will
  I causëd am to bow,
  And for to reap a hugy heap
  which youthful years did
  sow.

Wherefore all ye which do as yet
 remain and bide behind,
Whose eyes Dame Beauty's blazing beams
 as yet did never blind,
  Example let me be
  to you and other more 30

Whose heavy heart hath felt
the smart,
subdued by Cupid's lore.

Take heed of gazing over-much
on damsels fair unknown,
For oftentimes the snake doth lie
with roses overgrown;
And under fairest flowers
do noisome adders lurk,
Of whom take heed, I thee
areed,
lest that thy cares they
work.   40

What though that she doth smile
on thee?
perchance she doth not love;
And though she smack thee once
or twice,
she thinks thee so to prove;
And when that thou dost
think
she loveth none but thee,
She hath in store perhaps
some more
which so deceivëd be.

Trust not therefore the outward
show,
beware in any case: 50
For good conditions do not lie
where is a pleasant face.
But if it be thy chance
a lover true to have,
Be sure of this, thou shalt
not miss
each thing that thou wilt
crave.

And whenas thou, good reader,
shalt
peruse this scroll of mine,
Let this a warning be to thee,
and say a friend of thine   60
Did write thee this of love
and of a zealous mind,

Because that he sufficiently
hath tried the female kind.

Here, Cambridge, now I bid farewell!
adieu to students all!
Adieu unto the colleges
and unto Gonville Hall!
And you, my fellows once,
pray unto Jove that I   70
May have relief for this my
grief,
and speedy remedy.

And that he shield you everyone
from beauty's luring looks,
Whose bait hath brought me to
my bane
and caught me from my books.
Wherefore, for you my
prayer shall be
to send you better grace,
That modesty with honesty
may guide your youthful
race.   80
Finis, quod THOMAS RICHARD-
SON, *sometime student in
Cambridge.*

*As you came from the holy
land of Walsingham*

As you came from the holy land
Of Walsingham,
Met you not with my true love,
By the way as you came?
How should I know your true
love,
That have met many a one,
As I came from the holy land,
That have come, that have
gone?

She is neither white nor brown,
But as the heavens fair: 10

There is none hath her form so
    divine,
On the earth, in the air.
Such a one did I meet, good sir,
    With angel-like face,
Who like a nymph, like a queen
    did appear
    In her gait, in her grace.

She hath left me here alone,
    All alone unknown,
Who sometime loved me as her
    life,
    And callèd me her own.   20
What is the cause she hath left
    thee alone,
And a new way doth take,
That sometime did thee love as
    herself,
    And her joy did thee make?

I have loved her all my youth,
    But now am old as you see;

Love liketh not the falling fruit,
    Nor the withered tree.
For love is a careless child,
    And forgets promise past;   30
He is blind, he is deaf, when he
    list,
    And in faith never fast.

His desire is fickle found,
    And a trustless joy;
He is won with a world of de-
    spair,
    And is lost with a toy.
Such is the love of women-kind,
    Or the word, love, abused,
Under which many childish de-
    sires
    And conceits are excused.   40

But love, it is a durable fire
    In the mind ever burning,
Never sick, never dead, never
    cold,
    From itself never turning.

The valorous acts performed at Gaunt by the brave bonny lass,
Mary Ambree, who in revenge of her lover's death,
did play her part most gallantly

The tune is *The blind beggar*

When Captain Courageous, whom death could not daunt,
Had roundly besiegèd the city of Gaunt,
And manly they marched by two and by three,
And foremost in battle was Mary Ambree.

Thus being enforced to fight with her foes,
On each side most fiercely they seemed to close;
Each one sought for honor in every degree,
But none so much won it as Mary Ambree.

When brave Sergeant Major was slain in the fight,
Who was her own true love, her joy and delight,   10
She swore unrevenged his blood should not be;
Was not this a brave bonny lass, Mary Ambree?

She clothed herself from the top to the toe
With buff of the bravest and seemly to show;
A fair shirt of mail over that striped she;
Was not this a brave bonny lass, Mary Ambree?

A helmet of proof she put on her head,
A strong armed sword she girt on her side,
A fair goodly gauntlet on her hand wore she;
Was not this a brave bonny lass, Mary Ambree? 20

Then took she her sword and her target in hand,
And called all those that would be of her band,—
To wait on her person there came thousands three;
Was not this a brave bonny lass, Mary Ambree?

Before you shall perish, the worst of you all,
Or come to any danger of enemy's thrall,
This hand and this life of mine shall set you free;
Was not this a brave bonny lass, Mary Ambree?

The drums and the trumpets did sound out alarm,
And many a hundred did lose leg and arm, 30
And many a thousand she brought on their knee;
Was not this a brave bonny lass, Mary Ambree?

The sky then she filled with smoke of her shot,
And her enemies' bodies with bullets so hot,
For one of her own men, a score killed she;
Was not this a brave bonny lass, Mary Ambree?

And then her false gunner did spoil her intent,
Her powder and bullets away he had spent,
And then with her weapon she slashed them in three;
Was not this a brave bonny lass, Mary Ambree? 40

Then took she her castle where she did abide,
Her enemies besieged her on every side;
To beat down her castle walls they did agree,
And all for to overcome Mary Ambree.

Then took she her sword and her target in hand,
And on her castle walls stoutly did stand,
So daring the captains to match any three;
Oh, what a brave captain was Mary Ambree!

At her then they smiled, not thinking in heart
That she could have performed so valorous a part; 50
The one said to the other, we shortly shall see
This gallant brave captain before us to flee.

Why, what do you think or take me to be?
Unto these brave soldiers so valiant spoke she.
A knight, sir, of England, and captain, quoth they,
Whom shortly we mean to take prisoner away.

No captain of England behold in your sight,
Two breasts in my bosom, and therefore no knight;
No knight, sir, of England, nor captain, quoth she,
But even a poor bonny lass, Mary Ambree. 60

But art thou a woman as thou dost declare,
That hath made us thus spend our armor in war?
The like in our lives we never did see,
And therefore we'll honor brave Mary Ambree.

The Prince of great Parma heard of her renown,
Who long had advanced for England's fair crown;
In token he sent a glove and a ring,
And said she should be his bride at his wedding.

Why, what do you think or take me to be?
Though he be a prince of great dignity, 70
It shall never be said in England so free
That a stranger did marry with Mary Ambree.

Then unto fair England she back did return,
Still holding the foes of brave England in scorn;
In valor no man was ever like she;
Was not this a brave bonny lass, Mary Ambree?

In this woman's praises I'll here end my song,
Whose heart was approved in valor most strong;
Let all sorts of people, whatever they be,
Sing forth the brave valors of Mary Ambree. 80

Lord Willoughby

To the tune of *Lord Willoughby*

The fifteen day of July,
  With glistering spear and
    shield,

A famous fight in Flanders
  Was foughten in the field;
The most courageous officers
  Was English captains three,
But the bravest man in battle
  Was brave Lord Willoughby.

The next was Captain Norris,
    A valiant man was he;   10
The other, Captain Turner,
    That from field would never
        flee.
With fifteen hundred fighting
        men,
    Alas, there was no more,
They fought with forty thousand
        then,
    Upon the bloody shore.

Stand to it, noble pike-men,
    And look you round about;
And shoot you right, you bow-
        men,
    And we will keep them out;   20
You musket and caliver men,
    Do you prove true to me,
I'll be the foremost man in fight,
    Says brave Lord Willoughby.

And then the bloody enemy
    They fiercely did assail,
And fought it out most valiantly,
    Not doubting to prevail;
The wounded men on both sides
        fell,
    Most piteous for to see,   30
Yet nothing could the courage
        quell
    Of brave Lord Willoughby.

For seven hours to all men's view
    This fight endurèd sore,
Until our men so feeble grew
    That they could fight no more;
And then upon dead horses
    Full savorly they eat,
And drank the puddle water,
    For no better they could get.   40

When they had fed so freely,
    They kneelèd on the ground,
And praisèd God devoutly
    For the favor they had found;

And bearing up their colors
    The fight they did renew,
And turning toward the Spaniard,
    Five thousand more they slew.

The sharp steel-pointed arrows
    And bullets thick did fly;   50
Then did our valiant soldiers
    Charge on most furiously;
Which made the Spaniards waver,
    They thought it best to flee,
They feared the stout behavior
    Of brave Lord Willoughby.

Then quoth the Spanish general,
    Come, let us march away,
I fear we shall be spoilèd all,
    If that we longer stay;   60
For yonder comes Lord Wil-
        loughby
    With courage fierce and fell,
He will not give one inch of
        ground
    For all the devils in hell.

And then the fearful enemy
    Was quickly put to flight;
Our men pursued courageously,
    And rout their forces quite.
And at last they gave a shout,
    Which echoed through the
        sky,   70
God and Saint George for Eng-
        land!
    The conquerors did cry.

This news was brought to Eng-
        land
    With all the speed might be,
And told unto our gracious
        Queen,
    Of this same victory;
Oh, this is brave Lord Willough-
        by,
    My love hath ever won;

Of all the lords of honor,
  'Tis he great deeds hath
    done.   80

For soldiers that were maimed
  And wounded in the fray,
The Queen allowed a pension
  Of eighteen pence a day;
Besides, all costs and charges
  She quit and set them free,
And this she did all for the sake
  Of brave Lord Willoughby.

Then courage, noble Englishmen,
  And never be dismayed,   90
If that we be but one to ten,
  We will not be afraid
To fight with foreign enemies,
  And set our country free;
And thus I end this bloody bout
  Of brave Lord Willoughby.

A sonnet upon the pitiful burning of the Globe Playhouse in London

Now sit thee down, Melpomene,
Wrapped in a sea-coal robe,
And tell the doleful tragedy
That late was played at Globe;
For no man that can sing and
  say
Was scared on St. Peter's Day.
Oh sorrow, pitiful sorrow, and
  yet all this is true.

All you that please to understand,
Come listen to my story,
To see Death with his raking
  brand   10
'Mongst such an auditory;
Regarding neither Cardinal's
  might,
Nor yet the rugged face of Henry
  the eight.—Oh sorrow, &c.

This fearful fire began above,
A wonder strange and true,
And to the stage-house did re-
  move,
As round as tailor's clew;
And burnt down both beam and
  snag,
And did not spare the silken flag.
  —Oh sorrow, &c.

Out run the knights, out run the
  lords,   20
And there was great ado;
Some lost their hats and some their
  swords,
Then out run Burbage too;
The reprobates, though drunk on
  Monday,
Prayed for the fool and Henry
  Condye.—Oh sorrow, &c.

The periwigs and drum-heads fry,
Like to a butter firkin;
A woeful burning did betide
To many a good buff jerkin.
Then with swollen eyes, like
  drunken Flemings,   30
Distressëd stood old stuttering
  Hemings.—Oh sorrow, &c.

No shower his rain did there down
  force,
In all that sunshine weather,
To save that great renownëd
  house,
Nor thou, O ale-house, neither.
Had it begun below, *sans doute*,
Their wives for fear. . .—Oh
  sorrow, &c.

Be warned, you stage strutters all,
Lest you again be catched,
And such a burning do befall   40
As to them whose house was
  thatched;

Forbear your whoring, breeding
    biles,
And lay up that expense for tiles.
    —Oh sorrow, &c.

Go draw you a petition,
And do you not abhor it,
And get, with low submission,
A license to beg for it
In churches, *sans* churchwardens'
    checks,
In Surrey and in Middlesex.
Oh sorrow, pitiful sorrow, and yet
    all this is true.   50

The shepherd's wooing Dulcina

Tune is *Dulcina*

As at noon Dulcina rested
    In her sweet and shady bower,
Came a shepherd and requested
    In her arms to sleep an hour;
But from her look a wound he
    took,
So far that for a farther boon
The nymph he prays; wherefore
    she says,
    Forgo me now, come to me
        soon!

But in vain she did conjure him
    For to leave her presence so, 10
Having thousand means to allure
    him,
    And but one to let him go;
Where lips invite, and eyes de-
    light,
And cheeks as fresh as rose in
    June,
Persuade to stay, what boots to
    say,
    Forgo me now, come to me
        soon?

Words whose hopes have now
    enjoined
    Him to let Dulcina sleep,
Could a man's love be confined,
    Or a maid her promise keep? 20
No, for her waist he held as fast
As she was constant to her tune;
And still she spake, For Cupid's
    sake,
    Forgo me now, come to me
        soon!

He demands, What time or lei-
    sure
    Can there be more fit than
        now?
She says, Night gives love that
    pleasure
    That the day doth not allow.
The sun's kind light forgives de-
    light,
Quoth he, more easily than the
    moon;   30
In Venus' plays be bold. She says,
    Forgo me now, come to me
        soon!

But no promise nor profession
    From his hands could purchase
        scope;
Who would sell the sweet pos-
    session
    Of such a beauty for a hope?
Or for the sight of ling'ring night
Forgo the present joys of noon?
Though none so fair, her speeches
    were,
    Forgo me now, come to me
        soon!   40

How at last agreed these lovers?
    She was fair and he was young;
Tongue may tell what eye dis-
    covers,
    Joys unseen are never sung.
He said, My dear, my love not
    fear!

Bright Phœbus' beams outshine
  the moon.
Dulcina prays, and to him says,
  Forgo me now, come to me
    soon!

*Truth's integrity; or a curious
northern ditty called, Love
will find out the way*

To a pleasant new tune

Over the mountains
  And under the waves,
Over the fountains
  And under the graves,
Over floods which are the deep-
    est
  Which do Neptune obey,
Over rocks which are steepest,
  Love will find out the way.

Where there is no place
  For the glow-worm to lie; 10
Where there is no space
  For receipt of a fly;
Where the gnat she dares not
    venter,
  Lest herself fast she lay;
But if Love come, he will enter,
  And will find out the way.

You may esteem him
  A child by his force,
Or you may deem him
  A coward, which is worse; 20
But if he whom Love doth honor
  Be concealed from the day,
Set a thousand guards upon him,
  Love will find out the way.

Some think to lose him,
  Which is too unkind;
And some do suppose him,
  Poor heart, to be blind;
If that he were hidden,
  Do the best that you may, 30

Blind Love, if so you call him,
  Will find out the way.

Well may the eagle
  Stoop down to the fist;
Or you may inveigle
  The phœnix of the east;
With fear the tiger's movëd
  To give over his prey,
But never stop a lover,
  He will post on his way. 40

From Dover to Berwick,
  And nations throughout,
Brave Guy of Warwick,
  That champion so stout,
With his warlike behavior,
  Through the world he did
    stray
To win his Phyllis' favor—
  Love will find out the way.

In order next enters
  Bevis so brave; 50
After adventures,
  And policy grave,
To see whom he desired,
  His Josian so gay,
For whom his heart was fired,
  Love found out the way.

The Gordian knot
  Which true lovers knit,
Undo you cannot,
  Nor yet break it; 60
Make use of your inventions
  Their fancies to betray,
To frustrate your intentions
  Love will find out the way.

From court to the cottage,
  In bower and in hall,
From the king unto the beggar,
  Love conquers all;
Though ne'er so stout and lordly,
  Strive, do what you may, 70

Yet, be you ne'er so hardy,
Love will find out the way.

Love hath power over princes
And greatest emperor;
In any provinces,
Such is Love's power,
There is no resisting,
But him to obey;
In spite of all contesting,
Love will find out the way. 80

If that he were hidden,
And all men that are,
Were strictly forbidden
That place to declare,
Winds that have no abidings,
Pitying their delay,
Will come and bring him tidings,
And direct him the way.

If the earth should part him
He would gallop it o'er; 90
If the seas should o'erthwart him,
He would swim to the shore;
Should his love become a swallow,
Through the air to stray,
Love would lend wings to follow,
And will find out the way.

There is no striving
To cross his intent,
There is no contriving
His plots to prevent; 100
But if once the message greet him
That his true love doth stay,
If death should come and meet him,
Love will find out the way.

The milkmaid's life

To a curious new tune called
The milkmaid's dumps

You rural goddesses
That woods and fields possess,
Assist me with your skill,

That may direct my quill
More jocundly to express
The mirth and delight,
Both morning and night,
On mountain or in dale,
Of them who choose
This trade to use, 10
And through cold dews
Do never refuse
To carry the milking pail.

The bravest lasses gay
Live not so merry as they;
In honest civil sort
They make each other sport,
As they trudge on their way;
Come fair or foul weather,
They're fearful of neither, 20
Their courages never quail;
In wet and dry,
Though winds be high,
And dark's the sky,
They ne'er deny
To carry the milking pail.

Their hearts are free from care,
They never will despair
Whatever them befall;
They bravely bear out all, 30
And fortune's frowns out-dare.
They pleasantly sing
To welcome the spring,
'Gainst heaven they never rail.
If grass well grow,
Their thanks they show;
And, frost or snow,
They merrily go
Along with the milking pail.

Base idleness they do scorn; 40
They rise very early i' th' morn,
And walk into the field,
Where pretty birds do yield
Brave music on every thorn;
The linnet and thrush

Do sing on each bush,
  And the dulcet nightingale
Her note doth strain
In a jocund vein,
To entertain   50
That worthy train
  Which carry the milking pail.

Their labor doth health preserve;
  No doctors' rules they observe,
While others, too nice
In taking their advice,
  Look always as though they
    would starve.
Their meat is digested,
They ne'er are molested,
  No sickness doth them assail; 60
Their time is spent
In merriment;
While limbs are lent,
They are content
  To carry the milking pail.

Those lasses, nice and strange,
  That keep shops in the ex-
    change,
Sit pricking of clouts
And giving of flouts,
  They seldom abroad do range;
Then comes the green sickness 71
And changeth their likeness,
  All this is for want of good
    sale;
But 'tis not so,
As proof doth show,
By them that go
In frost and snow
  To carry the milking pail.

If they any sweethearts have,
  That do their affections crave,
Their privilege is this,   81
Which many others miss,
  They can give them welcome
    brave.
With them they may walk,

And pleasantly talk,
  With a bottle of wine or ale;
The gentle cow
Doth them allow,
As they know how.
God speed the plow,   90
  And bless the milking pail!

Upon the first of May,
  With garlands fresh and gay,
With mirth and music sweet,
For such a season meet,
  They pass their time away;
They dance away sorrow,
And all the day thorough
  Their legs do never fail;
They nimbly   100
Their feet do ply,
And bravely try
The victory,
  In honor o' th' milking pail.

If any think that I
  Do practise flattery,
In seeking thus to raise
The merry milkmaids' praise,
  I'll to them thus reply:
It is their desert   110
Inviteth my art
  To study this pleasant tale
In their defence,
Whose innocence
And providence
Gets honest pence
  Out of the milking pail.
    [*Martin Parker*]

The four wonders

The four wonders of this land,
  Which unto you we will de-
    clare.
The Lord's great mercy, it is
    great;
  God give us grace to stand in
    fear,

*And watch and pray both night
        and day
That God may give us all his
        grace,
To repent our sins then every
        one,—
Our time is going on apace.*

Tune of *Dear love, regard my
        grief*

Sweet England, call for grace!
    With speed leave off thy sin,
And with a contrite heart
    To prayers now begin.

For sure the time is come
    That Christ our Savior told;
Towards the latter day
    We wonders shall behold.

And now strange wonders rare
    The Lord from heaven doth
        send,   10
In earth and in the air,
    Because we should amend.

Great lights within the sky
    Hath oft been seen, we hear,
To many people's view,
    In countries far and near.

But what it doth presage
    No man on earth does know;
None but the living God
    Such wonders strange can
        show.   20

But to the subject now
    Which I do mean to write,
The strangest news I'll tell
    Which time has brought to
        light.

In London now doth live
    One Mr. Clark by name,

A tailor by his trade,
    Of good report and fame.

His wife, being with child,
    Unto her grief and woe   30
She with a neighbor's wife
    Fell out,—the truth is so.

And after many words,
    To fighting then they go;
This woman, being with child,
    Received a grievous blow

Upon her belly; then,
    Which makes my heart to
        bleed,
That she went home and sent 39
    For midwife's help, with speed.

In haste the midwife came,
    And other women store,
When, by the help of God,
    She seven children bore!

Seven dainty boys she had,
    All which were born in sight,
All framed with perfect shape,
    With joints and limbs aright.

But they were all still-born,
    Which grieved their parents
        sore;   50
But of the works of God
    In this they do deplore.

The woman now doth mend,
    Whereby God's works are
        known;
And now this wondrous news
    Both far and near is shown.

The second news I tell
    Comes from brave Yorkshire;
A monster there was born,
    The like you ne'er did hear. 60

Three miles from Pomfret lived
 A woman of great worth,
In travail fell, and brought
 To light a monstrous birth,

Just the shape of a colt,
 To all the people's sight;
Which bred amazement great,
 With tears and with fright,

To see this woman's grief,
 And trouble of her mind,   70
In bringing forth a colt,
 Contrary unto kind.

Long legs, round feet, long nose,
 And headed like a horse;
Which filled these women's hearts
 With pity and remorse.

This woman now doth mend,
 Whereby God's works are known;
And now this wondrous news
 Both far and near is shown. 80

And the third news most rare,
 The which I have to tell,
London can witness true
 That there a monster fell.

In Christ-Church parish lived
 A woman known full well,
Of honest carriage, which
 Her neighbors all can tell.

This woman being with child,
 Which grief and sorrow bred, 90
Into the world she bore
 A child without a head!

The face was in the breast,
 To all the people's view;
But it died suddenly,
 This is approvëd true.

It is for certain true,
 And is approvëd plain;
From earth, I say, it came,
 And to earth it turned again. 100

These women now all three
 Are on the mending hand;
But three such monstrous births
 Was ne'er in fair England.

The fourth news most rare,
 The which I have to tell:
In famous Gloucestershire
 A wondrous shower fell.

Not far from Gloucester Town,
 A place is called Brand-wood;   110
Upon a hedge of cloths,
 For truth, it rainëd blood!

A maid being starching there,
 As reason doth require,
She went to fetch in wood
 Wherewith to make a fire;

And having on such cuffs
 As starchers oft do use,
Upon them fell some drops
 Of blood, which made her muse. 120

And holding up her head,
 Which made her wonder more,
She saw the hedge of cloths
 With blood besprinkled o'er.

Then she throwed down the wood,
 And, with amazement great,
She went into the house
 And this news did repeat.

The people then came forth
 And found the news was true, 130

They saw the hedge of cloths
  With blood besprinkled, to their
      view.

Then they took in the cloths,
  And washed them that same
      day;
But water, lees, nor soap,
  Could take the blood away.

We are so wicked grown
  The heavens do for us bleed,
And wonders strange are shown,
  All this is true indeed!   140

Sodom was warned afore,
  So was Jerusalem,
And many places more
  Whom God did plague for sin.

But we are like the Jews,
  Our hearts are now so hard
That we will not believe,
  Nor yet God's word regard.

Now think upon each sin,
  Pride, whoredom, drunken-
      ness,   150
Swearing, deceit, and lies,
  And vile covetousness.

Then we shall see our God
  Will take us for his own,
If we believe these signs
  And tokens God hath shown.

Concluding thus my news,
  The God of truth and peace
Grant that the gospel may
  Continually increase.   160

Sailors for my money

To the tune of *The jovial cobbler*

Country men of England,
  Who live at home with ease,
And little think what dangers
  Are incident o' th' seas,

Give ear unto the sailor
  Who unto you will show
His case, his case,
  Howe'er the wind doth blow.

He that is a sailor
  Must have a valiant heart,   10
For when he is upon the sea
  He is not like to start,
But must, with noble courage,
  All dangers undergo;
Resolve, resolve,
  Howe'er the wind doth blow.

Our calling is laborious
  And subject to much woe,
But we must still contented be
  With what falls to our share.   20
We must not be faint-hearted,
  Come tempest, rain, or snow,
Nor shrink, nor shrink,
  Howe'er the wind doth blow.

Sometimes on Neptune's bosom
  Our ship is tossed with waves,
And every minute we expect
  The sea must be our graves.
Sometimes on high she mounteth,
  Then falls again as low,   30
With waves, with waves,
  When stormy winds do blow.

Then with unfeignëd prayers,
  As Christian duty binds,
We turn unto the Lord of Hosts,
  With all our hearts and minds;
To him we fly for succor,
  For he, we surely know,
Can save, can save,
  Howe'er the wind doth blow.   40

Then he who breaks the rage,
  The rough and blusterous seas,
When his disciples were afraid,
  Will straight the storms ap-
      pease;

And give us cause to thank,
　On bended knees full low,
Who saves, who saves,
　Howe'er the wind doth blow.

Our enemies approaching,
　When we on sea espy,　　　　50
We must resolve incontinent
　To fight although we die;
With noble resolution
　We must oppose our foe,
In fight, in fight,
　Howe'er the wind does blow.

And when by God's assistance
　Our foes are put to th' foil,
To animate our courages
　We all have share o' th'
　　　spoil.　　　　60
Our foes into the ocean
　We back to back do throw,
To sink, or swim,
　Howe'er the wind doth blow.

Thus we gallant seamen,
　In midst of greatest dangers,
Do always prove our valor,
　We never are no changers;
But whatsoe'er betide us
　We stoutly undergo,　　　　70
Resolved, resolved,
　Howe'er the wind doth blow.

If fortune do befriend us,
　In what we take in hand,
We prove ourselves still generous
　Whene'er we come to land;
There's few that shall out-brave
　　　us,
　Though ne'er so great in show,
We spend, and lend,
　Howe'er the wind doth blow.　80

We travel to the Indies,
　From them we bring some
　　　spice;

Here we buy rich merchandise
　At very little price.
And many wealthy prizes
　We conquer from the foe,
In fight, in fight,
　Howe'er the wind doth blow.

Into our native country
　With wealth we do return,　90
And cheer our wives and chil-
　　　dren,
　Who for our absence mourn.
Then do we bravely flourish,
　And wheresoe'er we go,
We roar, we roar,
　Howe'er the wind doth blow.

For when we have received
　Our wages for our pains,
The vintners and the tapsters
　By us have golden gains.　100
We call for liquor roundly,
　And pay before we go;
And sing, and drink,
　Howe'er the wind doth blow.

We bravely are respected
　When we walk up and down,
For if we meet good company
　We care not for a crown;
There's none more free than sail-
　　　ors,
　Where'er he come or go,　110
Though he'll roar o' th' shore,
　Howe'er the wind doth blow.

Then who would live in England
　And nourish vice with ease,
When he that is in poverty
　May riches get o' th' seas?
Let's sail unto the Indies,
　Where golden grass doth grow;
To sea, to sea,　　　　119
　Howe'er the wind doth blow.

[*Martin Parker*]

When the King enjoys his own again

To be joyfully sung with its own proper tune

What Booker can prognosticate
Concerning king's or kingdom's fate?
I think myself to be as wise
As he that gazeth on the skies.
My skill goes beyond the depth of a pond,
   Or rivers in the greatest rain;
Whereby I can tell, all things will be well,
   When the King enjoys his own again.

There's neither swallow, dove, nor dade,
Can soar more high, or deeper wade,
Nor show a reason from the stars
Which causeth peace or civil wars;
The man in the moon may wear out his shoon,
   By running after Charles his wain;
But all's to no end, for the times will not mend
   Till the King enjoys his own again.

Though for a time we see Whitehall
With cobwebs hanging on the wall,
Instead of silk and silver brave
Which formerly it used to have,
With rich perfume in every room,
   Delightful to that princely train;
Which again you shall see, when the time it shall be,
   That the King enjoys his own again.

Full forty years the royal crown
Hath been his father's and his own;
And is there anyone but he
That in the same should sharer be?
For who better may the scepter sway
   Than he that hath such right to reign?
Then let's hope for a peace, for the wars will not cease
   Till the King enjoys his own again.

Till then upon Ararat's hill
My hope shall cast her anchor still,
Until I see some peaceful dove
Bring home the branch she dearly love;

10

20

30

Then will I wait till the waters abate
Which now disturb my troubled brain,
Else never rejoice till I hear the voice,
That the King enjoys his own again. 40

[*Martin Parker*]

LYRICS FROM SONG-BOOKS

The Introduction and Notes are at pages 1254 and 1277

From William Byrd's *Psalms, Sonnets, and Songs of Sadness and Piety,* 1588

Reasons briefly set down by the author to persuade everyone to
learn to sing.

*First, it is a knowledge easily taught and quickly learned, where there
is a good master and an apt scholar.*

2. *The exercise of singing is delightful to nature, and good to preserve
the health of man.*

3. *It doth strengthen all the parts of the breast, and doth open the
pipes.*

4. *It is a singular good remedy for a stutting and stammering in the
speech.*

5. *It is the best means to procure a perfect pronunciation, and to make
a good orator.*

6. *It is the only way to know where nature hath bestowed the benefit of
a good voice; which gift is so rare as there is not one among a thousand that hath it, and in many that excellent gift is lost because they
want art to express nature.*

7. *There is not any music of instruments whatsoever comparable to that
which is made of the voices of men, where the voices are good, and
the same well sorted and ordered.*

8. *The better the voice is, the meeter it is to honor and serve God
therewith; and the voice of man is chiefly to be employed to that end.*

Omnis spiritus laudet Dominum.

Since singing is so good a thing,
I wish all men would learn to sing.

[*Lulla, my sweet little baby*]

Lulla, la lulla, lulla lullaby.
My sweet little baby, what meanest thou to cry?
Be still, my blessed babe, though cause thou hast to mourn,

Whose blood most innocent to shed the cruel king hath sworn.
And lo, alas, behold what slaughter he doth make,
Shedding the blood of infants all, sweet Savior, for thy sake.
A King is born, they say, which King this king would kill.
Oh woe, and woeful heavy day, when wretches have their will!

    Lulla, la lulla, lulla lullaby.
    My sweet little baby, what meanest thou to cry?   10
Three kings this King of kings to see are come from far,
To each unknown, with offerings great, by guiding of a star.
And shepherds heard the song which angels bright did sing,
Giving all glory unto God for coming of this King,
Which must be made away, King Herod would him kill.
Oh woe, and woeful heavy day, when wretches have their will!

    Lulla, la lulla, lulla lullaby.
    My sweet little baby, what meanest thou to cry?
Lo, my little babe, be still, lament no more;
From fury thou shalt step aside, help have we still in store.   20
We heavenly warning have some other soil to seek,
From death must fly the Lord of life, as lamb both mild and meek.
Thus must my babe obey the king that would him kill.
Oh woe, and woeful heavy day, when wretches have their will!

    Lulla, la lulla, lulla lullaby.
    My sweet little baby, what meanest thou to cry?
But thou shalt live and reign as Sibyls have foresaid,
As all the prophets prophesy, whose mother, yet a maid
And perfect virgin pure, with her breasts shall upbreed
Both God and man, that all hath made, the Son of heavenly seed,   30
Whom caitiffs none can 'tray, whom tyrants none can kill.
Oh joy, and joyful happy day, when wretches want their will!

From William Byrd's *Songs of Sundry Natures*, 1589

A carol for Christmas Day

    An earthly tree a heavenly fruit it bare;
      A case of clay contained a crown immortal,
    A crown of crowns, a King, whose cost and care
      Redeemed poor man—whose race before was thrall
    To death, to doom, to pains of everlasting—
    By his sweet death, scorns, stripes, and often fasting.
        Cast off all doubtful care,
          Exile and banish tears,
        To joyful news divine
          Lend us your listening ears.   10

A star above the stars, a sun of light,
  Whose blessed beams this wretched earth bespread
With hope of heaven and of God's Son the sight,
  Which in our flesh and sinful soul lay dead.
O faith, O hope, O joys renowned forever,
O lively life that deathless shall perséver!
      Cast off all our doubtful care,
        Exile and banish tears,
      To joyful news divine
        Lend us your listening ears.   20

Then let us sing the lullabies of sleep
  To this sweet babe, born to awake us all
From drowsy sin, that made old Adam weep,
  And by his fault gave to mankind the fall.
For lo, this day, the birthday, day of days,
Summons our songs to give him laud and praise.
      Cast off all doubtful care,
        Exile and banish tears,
      To joyful news divine
        Lend us your listening ears.   30

FROM THOMAS MORLEY'S *Canzonets*, 1593

[*Arise, get up, my dear love*]

Arise, get up, my dear love, rise, make haste, begone thee!
Lo, where the bride, fair Daphne bright, still stays on thee!
Hark! O hark! Yon merry wanton maidens squealing!
Spice cake, sops in wine, spice cakes, are a-dealing!
      Run then, run apace,
      Get a bride lace
And a gilt rosemary branch while yet there is catching,
  And then hold fast for fear of old snatching.
      Alas, my love, why weep ye?
      O fear not that, dear love, the next day keep we.   10
List, hark yon minstrels! How fine they firk it!
  And see how the maids jerk it!
      With Kate and Will,
      Tom and Jill,
      Hey ho brave,
      Now a skip,
      There a trip,
      Finely set aloft,
      On a fine wedding day,
All for fair Daphne's wedding day!   20

FROM JOHN MUNDY'S *Songs and Psalms,* 1594

[*In midst of woods*]

In midst of woods or pleasant grove
   Where all sweet birds do sing,
Methought I heard so rare a sound
   Which made the heavens to
     ring.
The charm was good, the noise
     full sweet,
   Each bird did play his part;
And I admired to hear the same,
   Joy sprung into my heart.

The blackbird made the sweetest
     sound,
   Whose tunes did far excel,   10
Full pleasantly and most profound
   Was all things placëd well.

Thy pretty tunes, mine own sweet
     bird,
   Done with so good a grace,
Extols thy name, prefers the same
   Abroad in every place.

Thy music grave, bedeckëd well
   With sundry points of skill,
Bewrays thy knowledge excellent,
   Engrafted in thy will.   20
My tongue shall speak, my pen
     shall write,
   In praise of thee to tell.
The sweetest bird that ever was,
   In friendly sort, farewell.

FROM JOHN DOWLAND'S *Second Book of Songs or Airs,* 1600

[*Fine knacks for ladies*]

Fine knacks for ladies, cheap, choice, brave, and new!
   Good pennyworths! but money cannot move.
I keep a fair but for the fair to view;
   A beggar may be liberal of love.
Though all my wares be trash, the heart is true.

Great gifts are guiles and look for gifts again;
   My trifles come as treasures from my mind.
It is a precious jewel to be plain;
   Sometimes in shell th' orient'st pearls we find.
Of others take a sheaf, of me a grain.   10

Within this pack, pins, points, laces, and gloves,
   And divers toys fitting a country fair;
But my heart lives where duty serves and loves,
   Turtles and twins, court's brood, a heavenly pair.
Happy the heart that thinks of no removes!

[*Now cease, my wandering eyes*]

Now cease, my wandering eyes,
   Strange beauties to admire.

In change least comfort lies;
 Long joys yield long desire.
   One faith, one love
Makes our frail pleasures eternal, and in sweetness prove
   New hopes, new joys
Are still with sorrow declining unto deep annoys.

   One man hath but one soul,
     Which art cannot divide;   10
   If all one soul must love,
     Two loves must be denied.
       One soul, one love,
By faith and merit united, cannot remove.
     Distracted sprites
Are ever changing and hapless in their delights.

   Nature two eyes hath given
     All beauty to impart,
   As well in earth as heaven;
     But she hath given one heart,   20
       That though we see
Ten thousand beauties, yet in us one should be
     One steadfast love,
Because our hearts stand fixed, although our eyes do move.

FROM JOHN DOWLAND's *Third and Last Book of Songs or Airs*, 1603

[*Weep you no more, sad fountains*]

Weep you no more, sad fountains;
 What need you flow so fast?
Look how the snowy mountains
 Heaven's sun doth gently waste.
But my sun's heavenly eyes
 View not your weeping,
 That now lie sleeping
Softly, now softly lies
 Sleeping.

Sleep is a reconciling,   10
 A rest that peace begets.
Doth not the sun rise smiling
 When fair at even he sets?
Rest you then, rest, sad eyes,
 Melt not in weeping
 While she lies sleeping
Softly, now softly lies
 Sleeping.

FROM THOMAS BATESON's *First Set of English Madrigals*, 1604

[*Beauty is a lovely sweet*]

Beauty is a lovely sweet
Where pure white and crimson
 meet,
Joined with favor of the face,

Chiefest flower of female race.
But if virtue might be seen,
It would more delight the
 eyne.

[*Your shining eyes*]

Your shining eyes and golden
hair,
Your lily-rosëd lips most fair,
Your other beauties that excel,

Men cannot choose but like them
well;
But when for them they say they'll
die,
Believe them not, they do but lie.

FROM TOBIAS HUME'S *Musical Humors. The first part of Airs*, 1605

The soldier's song

I sing the praise of honored
wars,
The glory of well-gotten
scars,
The bravery of glittering
shields,
Of lusty hearts and famous
fields;
For that is music worth the ear of
Jove,
A sight for kings, and still the
soldier's love.

Look! Oh, methinks I see
The grace of chivalry;

The colors are displayed,   9
The captains bright ar-
rayed.
See now the battle's ranged,
Bullets now thick are
changed.
Hark! shots and wounds
abound,
The drums alarum sound.
The captains cry: Za-za!
The trumpets sound ta-ra!
Oh, this is music worth the ear of
Jove,
A sight for kings, and still the
soldier's love.

[*Tobacco, tobacco*]

Tobacco, tobacco, sing sweetly for tobacco!
Tobacco is like love, oh love it;
For you see, I will prove it.
Love maketh lean the fat men's tumor,
So doth tobacco.
Love still dries up the wanton humor,
So doth tobacco.
Love makes men sail from shore to shore,
So doth tobacco.
'Tis fond love often makes men poor,   10
So doth tobacco.
Love makes men scorn all coward fears,
So doth tobacco.
Love often sets men by the ears,
So doth tobacco.
Tobacco, tobacco,
Sing sweetly for tobacco.
Tobacco is like love, oh love it;
For you see I have proved it.

[*Fain would I change that note*]

Fain would I change that note
  To which fond love hath
    charmed me,
Long, long to sing by rote,
  Fancying that that harmed me.
Yet when this thought doth come,
Love is the perfect sum
  Of all delight,
I have no other choice
Either for pen or voice,
  To sing or write.   10

O love, they wrong thee much
  That say thy sweet is bit-
    ter;
When thy ripe fruit is such
  As nothing can be sweeter.
Fair house of joy and bliss
Where truest pleasure is,
  I do adore thee.
I know thee what thou art,
I serve thee with my heart
  And fall before thee.   20

From Michael East's *Second Set of Madrigals*, 1606

[*O metaphysical tobacco*]

O metaphysical tobacco,
Fetched as far as from Morocco,
  Thy searching fume
  Exhales the rheum,
O metaphysical tobacco.

From John Cooper's *Funeral Tears, for the death of the Right Honorable the Earl of Devonshire*, 1606

[*Oft thou hast*]

Oft thou hast with greedy ear
  Drunk my notes and words of
    pleasure;
  In affection's equal measure
Now my songs of sorrow hear,
  Since from thee my griefs do
    grow,
  Whom alive I prized so dear:
  The more my joy, the more my
    woe.

Music, though it sweetens pain,
  Yet no whit impairs lament-
    ing,
  But in passions like consenting 10
Makes them constant that com-
    plain,
  And enchants their fancies so
That all comforts they disdain,
  And fly from joy to dwell with
    woe.

From Tobias Hume's *Poetical Music*, 1607

The hunting song

Come, come my hearts, a-hunting let us wend,
That echoing cries the hills and heavens may rend
  With shouts and sounds
  Of horns and hounds.

Why then, my lads, uncouple
Kill-buck, keen Ringwood and Roler,
  Chanter and Joler,
  Trouncer and Drummer,
  Bowman and Gunner.
Actæon's hounds were ne'er like these, I ween.   10

The stag is now roused, the game is on foot.
 Hark! hark! beauty Dainty prates.
The cry is full. Hark! how they hold the cry;
  But soft, the huntsmen rates!
  Clowder hunts counter
  And so doth Mounter,
  They're all at fault.
  Hark! Ringwood spends
  And makes amends.
    List of Joler,   20
    That's he, ho! ho!
    Joler crossed it,
    Else we had lost it.
  The buck is quite spent,
  Since to soil he went.

Why, heavenlier sport than this there cannot be.
  See, Plowman hath pinched,
  And Joler ne'er flinched.
Now with full cry they all come, frowling, trowling to the fall.
   Wind the morte!   30
   O well done there, boys!
 All other sports to these are but toys.

FROM ROBERT JONES's *Ultimum Vale*, 1608

[*Think'st thou, Kate?*]

Think'st thou, Kate, to put me
 down
With a no or with a frown?
Since love holds my heart in bands,
I must do as love commands.

Love commands the hands to dare
When the tongue of speech is
 spare;
Chiefest lesson in love's school,
Put it in adventure, fool.

Fools are they that fainting flinch
For a squeak, a scratch, a pinch. 10
Women's words have double sense,
Stand away, a simple fence.

If thy mistress swears she'll cry,
Fear her not; she'll swear and lie.
Such sweet oaths no sorrow bring
Till the prick of conscience
  sting.

FROM THOMAS WEELKES'S *Airs or Fantastic Spirits*, 1608

[*Though my carriage*]

Though my carriage be but careless,
    Though my looks be of the sternest,
Yet my passions are compareless;
    When I love, I love in earnest.

No, my wits are not so wild,
    But a gentle soul may yoke me;
Nor my heart so hard compiled,
    But it melts if love provoke me.

FROM JOHN WILBYE'S *Second Set of Madrigals*, 1609

[*Ye that do live in pleasures*]

Ye that do live in pleasures plenty,
    And dwell in music's sweetest airs,
Whose eyes are quick, whose ears are dainty,
    Not clogged with earth or worldly cares,
Come sing this song made in Amphion's praise,
Who now is dead, yet you his fame can raise.

Call him again, let him not die,
    But live in music's sweetest breath.
Place him in fairest memory,
    And let him triumph over death.   10
Oh, sweetly sung! his living wish attend ye.
These were his words: The mirth of heaven God send ye.

[*Draw on, sweet night*]

Draw on, sweet night, best friend unto those cares
    That do arise from painful melancholy.
My life so ill through want of comfort fares,
    That unto thee I consecrate it wholly.

Sweet night, draw on! my griefs, when they be told
    To shades and darkness, find some ease from paining;
And while thou all in silence dost enfold,
    I then shall have best time for my complaining.

FROM ROBERT JONES'S *Muses' Garden for Delights*, 1610

[*The sea hath many thousands sands*]

The sea hath many thousands
    sands,
  The sun hath motes as many,
The sky is full of stars, and love
  As full of woes as any.
Believe me, that do know the elf,
And make no trial by thyself.

It is in truth a pretty toy
  For babes to play withal;
But oh, the honeys of our youth
  Are oft our age's gall.   10

Self proof in time will make thee
    know
He was a prophet told thee so,

A prophet that Cassandra-like
  Tells truth without belief,
For headstrong youth will run his
    race
  Although his goal be grief.
Love's martyr, when his heat is
    past,
Proves care's confessor at the last.

[*Once did my thoughts*]

Once did my thoughts both ebb
    and flow,
  As passion did them move;
Once did I hope, straight fear
    again,
  And then I was in love.

Once did I waking spend the night,
  And told how many minutes
    move,
Once did I wishing waste the day,
  And then I was in love.

Once by my carving true love's
    knot,
  The weeping trees did prove   10
That wounds and tears were both
    our lots,
  And then I was in love.

Once did I breathe another's
    breath,
  And in my mistress move;
Once was I not mine own at all,
  And then I was in love.

Once wore I bracelets made of hair,
  And collars did approve,
Once were my clothes made out of
    wax,
  And then I was in love.   20

Once did I sonnet to my saint,
  My soul in number moved,
Once did I tell a thousand lies,
  And then in truth I loved.

Once in my ear did dangling hang
  A little turtle-dove,
Once, in a word, I was a fool,
  And then I was in love.

FROM ORLANDO GIBBONS'S *First Set of Madrigals and Motets*, 1612

[*The silver swan*]

The silver swan, who living had no note,
  When death approached, unlocked her silent throat;

Leaning her breast against the reedy shore,
Thus sung her first and last, and sung no more.
Farewell, all joys; O death, come close mine eyes;
More geese than swans now live, more fools than wise.

[*Dainty fine bird*]

Dainty fine bird that art encagèd there,
Alas, how like thine and my fortunes are.
Both prisoners be; and both singing, thus
Strive to please her that hath imprisoned us.
Only thus we differ, thou and I:
Thou liv'st singing, but I sing and die.

[*Ah, dear heart*]

Ah, dear heart, why do you rise?
The light that shines comes from your eyes.
The day breaks not, it is my heart,
To think that you and I must part.
O stay, or else my joys will die
And perish in their infancy.

From John Dowland's *Pilgrim's Solace*, 1612

[*In this trembling shadow*]

In this trembling shadow cast
    From those boughs which thy wings shake,
Far from human troubles placed,
    Songs to the Lord would I make.
    Darkness from my mind then take;
For thy rites none may begin
Till they feel thy light within.

As I sing, sweet flowers I'll strow
    From the fruitful valleys brought;
Praising him by whom they grow,
    Him that heaven and earth hath wrought,
    Him that all things framed of nought,
Him that all for man did make,
But made man for his own sake.

Music, all thy sweetness lend
    While of his high power I speak,

On whom all powers else depend;
   But my breast is now too weak,
   Trumpets shrill the air should break.
All in vain my sounds I raise,   20
Boundless power asks boundless praise.

From Thomas Bateson's *Second Set of Madrigals*, 1618

[*I heard a noise*]

I heard a noise and wishëd for a sight;
   I looked aside and did a shadow see
Whose substance was the sum of my delight;
   It came unseen and so it went from me.
But yet conceit persuaded my intent
There was a substance where the shadow went.
I did not play Narcissus in conceit,
   I did not see my shadow in a spring;
I knew my eyes were dimmed with no deceit,
   For as I saw the shadow passing by,   10
I had a glance of something in my eye.
Shadow, or she, or both, or choose you whether,
Blest be the thing that brought the shadow hither.

From Martin Peerson's *Private Music*, 1620

[*Can a maid that is well bred*]

Can a maid that is well bred,
Hath a blush so lovely red,
Modest looks, wise, mild, discreet,
And a nature passing sweet,
Break her promise, untrue prove,
On a sudden change her love,
Or be won e'er to neglect
Him to whom she vowed respect?

Such a maid, alas, I know.
Oh, that weeds 'mongst corn
   should grow,   10
Or a rose should prickles have,

Wounding where she ought to
   save!
I that did her parts extol,
Will my lavish tongue control.
Outward parts do blind the eyes,
Gall in golden pills oft lies.

Reason, wake, and sleep no more,
Land upon some safer shore;
Think on her and be afraid
Of a faithless fickle maid.   20
Of a faithless fickle maid
Thus true love is still betrayed.
Yet it is some ease to sing
That a maid is light of wing.

From Thomas Tomkins's *Songs of three, four, five, and six parts*, 1622

[*Our hasty life*]

Our hasty life away doth post
Before we know what we have lost.

Hours into days, days into years are gone,
Years make a life, which straight is none.
Thus soon is man's short story told,
We scarce are young, when we are waxëd old.

FROM JOHN ATTEY's *First Book of Airs,* 1622

[*On a time*]

On a time the amorous Silvy
Said to her shepherd, Sweet, how do you?
Kiss me this once, and then God b' wi' you,
    My sweetest dear!
Kiss me this once, and then God b' wi' you,
For now the morning draweth near.

With that, her fairest bosom showing,
Opening her lips, rich perfumes blowing,
She said, Now kiss me and be going,
    My sweetest dear!   10
Kiss me this once and then be going,
For now the morning draweth near.

With that the shepherd waked from sleeping,
And spying where the day was peeping,
He said, Now take my soul in keeping,
    My sweetest dear!
Kiss me, and take my soul in keeping,
Since I must go, now day is near.

FROM *Christ Church Ms.* K 3

[*Yet if his majesty*]

Yet if his majesty, our sovereign lord,
Should of his own accord
Friendly himself invite,
And say, I'll be your guest to-morrow night,
How should we stir ourselves, call and command
All hands to work! Let no man idle stand!
Set me fine Spanish tables in the hall;
See they be fitted all;
Let there be room to eat,
And order taken that there want no meat. 10
See every sconce and candlestick made bright,
That without tapers they may give a light.
Look to the presence; are the carpets spread,

The dais o'er the head,
The cushions in the chairs,
And all the candles lighted on the stairs?
Perfume the chambers, and in any case
Let each man give attendance in his place.
Thus if the king were coming would we do,
And 'twere good reason too;   20
For 'tis a duteous thing
To show all honor to an earthly king,
And after all our travail and our cost,
So he be pleased, to think no labor lost.
But at the coming of the King of Heaven
All's set at six and seven;
We wallow in our sin;
Christ cannot find a chamber in the inn.
We entertain him always like a stranger,
And as at first still lodge him in the manger.   30

FROM JOHN PLAYFORD's *Select Musical Airs and Dialogues*, 1653

[*When, Celia, I intend*]

When, Celia, I intend to flatter you,
And tell you lies to make you true,
            I swear
            There's none so fair—
            And you believe it too.

Oft have I matched you with the rose, and said
No twins so like hath nature made;
            But 'tis
            Only in this—
            You prick my hand, and fade.   10

Oft have I said there is no precious stone
But may be found in you alone;
            Though I
            No stone espy—
            Unless your heart be one.

When I praise your skin, I quote the wool
That silkworms from their entrails pull,
            And show
            That new-fall'n snow
            Is not more beautiful.   20

Yet grow not proud by such hyperboles;
Were you as excellent as these,
Whilst I
Before you lie,
They might be had with ease.

FROM HENRY LAWES's *Airs and Dialogues*, 1653

Love above beauty

Lovely Chloris, though thine eyes
Far outshine the jewels of the skies,
That grace which all admire in
thee,
No, nor the beauties of thy breast,
Which far outblaze the rest,
  Might e'er comparëd be
  To my fidelity.

Those alluring smiles that place
An eternal April on thy face,
Such as no sun did ever see,   10
No, nor the treasures of thy breast,
Which far outblaze the rest,
  Might e'er comparëd be
  To my fidelity.
                      [*Henry Reynolds*]

FROM HENRY LAWES's *Airs and Dialogues*, 1655

[*Was it a form?*]

Was it a form, a gait, a grace,
  Was it their sweetness merely?
Was it the heaven of a bright face,
  That made me love so dearly?

Was it a skin of silk and snow,
  That soul and senses wounded?
Was 't any of these, or all of these,
  Whereon my faith was founded?

Ah, no! 'Twas a far deeper part
  Than all the rest that won me;   10
'Twas a fair-clothed but feigning heart
  I loved, and has undone me.
                      [*Henry Reynolds*]

FROM JOHN WILSON's *Cheerful Airs or Ballads*, 1660

[*Greedy lover, pause awhile*]

Greedy lover, pause awhile,
And remember that a smile
Heretofore

Would have made thy hopes a
  feast;
Which is more,

Since thy diet was increased,
    Than both looks and language too,
    Or the face itself can do.

Such a province is my hand
As, if thou couldst command   10
    Heretofore,
There thy lips would seem to dwell;
    Which is more,
Ever since they sped so well,
    Than they can be brought to do
By my neck and bosom too.

If the center of my breast,
A dominion unpossessed
    Heretofore,
May thy wand'ring thoughts suffice,   20
    Seek no more,
And my heart shall be thy prize;

So thou keep above the line,
All the hemisphere is thine.

If the flames of love were pure,
Which by oath thou didst assure
    Heretofore,
Gold that goes into the clear
    Shines the more
When it leaves again the fire;   30
    Let not then those looks of thine
Blemish what they should refine.

I have cast into the fire
Almost all thou couldst desire
    Heretofore,
But I see thou art to crave
    More and more.
Should I cast in all I have,
    So that were I ne'er so free,
    Thou wouldst burn, though not
        for me.   40
            [Sir Albertus Morton]

THOMAS CAMPION

The Introduction and Notes are at pages 1257 and 1277

FROM *A Book of Airs*, 1601

To the Reader.

What epigrams are in poetry, the same are airs in music: then in their chief perfection when they are short and well seasoned. But to clog a light song with a long præludium *is to corrupt the nature of it. Many rests in music were invented either for necessity of the fugue, or granted as an harmonical license in songs of many parts; but in airs I find no use they have, unless it be to make a vulgar and trivial modulation seem to the ignorant strange, and to the judicial tedious. A naked air without guide, or prop, or color but his own, is easily censured of every ear, and requires so much the more invention to make it please. And as Martial speaks in defence of his short epigrams, so may I say in th' apology of airs, that where there is a full volume there can be no imputation of shortness. The lyric poets among the Greeks and Latins were first inventors of airs, tying themselves strictly to the number and value of their syllables, of which sort you shall find*

*here only one song in Sapphic verse; the rest are after the fashion
of the time, ear-pleasing rhymes without art. The subject of them is,
for the most part, amorous; and why not amorous songs as well as
amorous attires? Or why not new airs as well as new fashions? . . .*

FROM *Two Books of Airs,* [*c.* 1613]

To the Reader.

*. . . These airs were for the most part framed at first for one voice
with the lute, or viol, but upon occasion they have since been filled
with more parts, which whoso please may use, who like not may leave.
Yet do we daily observe that when any shall sing a treble to an instrument, the standers-by will be offering at an inward part out of
their own nature; and, true or false, out it must, though to the per-
verting of the whole harmony. Also, if we consider well, the treble
tunes (which are with us commonly called airs) are but tenors mounted
eight notes higher, and therefore an inward part must needs well become them, such as may take up the whole distance of the diapason, and
fill up the gaping between the two extreme parts; whereby though they
are not three parts in perfection, yet they yield a sweetness and content both to the ear and mind, which is the aim and perfection of music.
Short airs, if they be skillfully framed and naturally expressed, are like
quick and good epigrams in poesy, many of them showing as much
artifice, and breeding as great difficulty as a larger poem. Non omnia
possumus omnes, said the Roman epic poet. But some there are who
admit only French or Italian airs, as if every country had not his
proper air, which the people thereof naturally usurp in their music.
Others taste nothing that comes forth in print, as if Catullus' or
Martial's epigrams were the worse for being published. In these English airs, I have chiefly aimed to couple my words and notes lovingly
together, which will be much for him to do that hath not power over
both. The light of this will best appear to him who hath peised our
monosyllables and syllables combined, both of which are so loaded
with consonants as that they will hardly keep company with swift notes,
or give the vowel convenient liberty. To conclude; mine own opinion
of these songs I deliver thus:*

> Omnia nec nostris bona sunt, sed nec mala libris;
> Si placet hac cantes, hac quoque lege legas.

Farewell.

FROM ROBERT JONES'S *Second Book of Songs and Airs,* 1601

[*My love bound me*]

My love bound me with a kiss
　That I should no longer stay;
When I felt so sweet a bliss

I had less power to pass away.
Alas! that women do not know
Kisses make men loath to go.

Yet she knows it but too well,
 For I heard when Venus' dove
In her ear did softly tell
 That kisses were the seals of
  love.   10
Oh, muse not then though it be so,
Kisses make men loath to go.

Wherefore did she thus inflame
 My desires, heat my blood,
Instantly to quench the same
 And starve whom she had given
  food?

I the common sense can show:
Kisses make men loath to go.

Had she bid me go at first
 It would ne'er have grieved my
  heart;   20
Hope delayed had been the worst.
 But ah! to kiss and then to
  part!
How deep it struck; speak, gods,
 you know
Kisses make men loath to go.

FROM RICHARD ALISON'S *An Hour's Recreation in Music,* 1606

[What if a day]

What if a day, or a month, or a year
Crown thy delights with a thousand sweet contentings?
Cannot a chance of a night or an hour
Cross thy desires with as many sad tormentings?
  Fortune, honor, beauty, youth
  Are but blossoms dying;
  Wanton pleasure, doting love
  Are but shadows flying.
  All our joys are but toys,
  Idle thoughts deceiving;   10
  None have power of an hour
  In their lives' bereaving.

Earth's but a point to the world, and a man
Is but a point to the world's compared centure;
Shall then the point of a point be so vain
As to triumph in a seely point's adventure?
  All is hazard that we have,
  There is nothing biding;
  Days of pleasure are like streams
  Through fair meadows gliding.   20
  Weal and woe, time doth go,
  Time is never turning;
  Secret fates guide our states,
  Both in mirth and mourning.

FROM *A Book of Airs*, 1601

[*My sweetest Lesbia*]

My sweetest Lesbia, let us live and love,
And though the sager sort our deeds reprove,
Let us not weigh them. Heav'n's great lamps do dive
Into their west, and straight again revive,
But soon as once set is our little light,
Then must we sleep one ever-during night.

If all would lead their lives in love like me,
Then bloody swords and armor should not be;
No drum nor trumpet peaceful sleeps should move,
Unless alarm came from the camp of love.   10
But fools do live, and waste their little light,
And seek with pain their ever-during night.

When timely death my life and fortune ends,
Let not my hearse be vexed with mourning friends,
But let all lovers, rich in triumph, come
And with sweet pastimes grace my happy tomb;
And Lesbia, close up thou my little light,
And crown with love my ever-during night.

[*When to her lute Corinna sings*]

When to her lute Corinna sings,
Her voice revives the leaden strings,
And doth in highest notes appear
As any challenged echo clear;
But when she doth of mourning speak,
Ev'n with her sighs the strings do break.

And as her lute doth live or die,
Led by her passion, so must I:
For when of pleasure she doth sing,
My thoughts enjoy a sudden spring,   10
But if she doth of sorrow speak,
Ev'n from my heart the strings do break.

[*Follow your saint*]

Follow your saint, follow with accents sweet;
Haste you, sad notes, fall at her flying feet.
There, wrapped in cloud of sorrow, pity move,
And tell the ravisher of my soul I perish for her love.

But if she scorns my never-ceasing pain,
Then burst with sighing in her sight and ne'er return again.

All that I sung still to her praise did tend,
Still she was first, still she my songs did end.
Yet she my love and music both doth fly,
The music that her echo is and beauty's sympathy.   10
Then let my notes pursue her scornful flight:
It shall suffice that they were breathed and died for her delight.

[*Thou art not fair*]

Thou art not fair for all thy red and white,
    For all those rosy ornaments in thee;
Thou art not sweet, though made of mere delight,
    Nor fair nor sweet, unless you pity me.
I will not soothe thy fancies; thou shalt prove
That beauty is no beauty without love.

Yet love not me, nor seek thou to allure
    My thoughts with beauty, were it more divine;
Thy smiles and kisses I cannot endure,
    I'll not be wrapped up in those arms of thine.   10
Now show it, if thou be a woman right,—
Embrace, and kiss, and love me in despite.

[*The man of life upright*]

The man of life upright,
    Whose guiltless heart is free
From all dishonest deeds,
    Or thought of vanity;

The man whose silent days
    In harmless joys are spent,
Whom hopes cannot delude,
    Nor sorrow discontent;

That man needs neither towers
    Nor armor for defence,   10
Nor secret vaults to fly
    From thunder's violence.

He only can behold
    With unaffrighted eyes
The horrors of the deep
    And terrors of the skies.

Thus, scorning all the cares
    That fate or fortune brings,
He makes the heav'n his book,
    His wisdom heav'nly things,   20

Good thoughts his only friends,
    His wealth a well-spent age,
The earth his sober inn
    And quiet pilgrimage.

[*Hark, all you ladies*]

Hark, all you ladies that do sleep!
    The fairy queen Proserpina
Bids you awake and pity them that
        weep.

You may do in the dark
    What the day doth forbid;
Fear not the dogs that bark,
    Night will have all hid.

But if you let your lovers moan,
  The fairy queen Proserpina
Will send abroad her fairies ev'ry
    one,   10
That shall pinch black and blue
  Your white hands and fair
    arms
That did not kindly rue
  Your paramours' harms.

In myrtle arbors on the downs
  The fairy queen Proserpina,
This night by moonshine leading
  merry rounds,
Holds a watch with sweet love,
  Down the dale, up the hill;
No plaints or groans may move
  Their holy vigil.   21

All you that will hold watch with
  love,
  The fairy queen Proserpina
Will make you fairer than Dione's
  dove;
Roses red, lilies white,
  And the clear damask hue,
Shall on your cheeks alight;
  Love will adorn you.

All you that love, or loved before,
  The fairy queen Proserpina 30
Bids you increase that loving
  humor more;
They that yet have not fed
  On delight amorous,
She vows that they shall lead
  Apes in Avernus.

[When thou must home]

When thou must home to shades of underground,
  And there arrived, a new admirëd guest,
The beauteous spirits do engirt thee round,
  White Iope, blithe Helen, and the rest,
To hear the stories of thy finished love
From that smooth tongue whose music hell can move,

Then wilt thou speak of banqueting delights,
  Of masks and revels which sweet youth did make,
Of tourneys and great challenges of knights,
  And all these triumphs for thy beauty's sake;   10
When thou hast told these honors done to thee,
Then tell, O tell, how thou didst murder me.

FROM *Observations in the Art of English Poesy*, 1602

[Rose-cheeked Laura]

Rose-cheeked Laura, come,
Sing thou smoothly with thy
  beauty's
Silent music, either other
  Sweetly gracing.

Lovely forms do flow
From concent divinely framëd;
Heav'n is music, and thy beau-
  ty's
  Birth is heavenly.

These dull notes we sing
Discords need for helps to grace
    them;   10
Only beauty purely loving
    Knows no discord,

But still moves delight,
Like clear springs renewed by
    flowing,
Ever perfect, ever in them-
    Selves eternal.

FROM *Two Books of Airs*, [*c.* 1613]

[*To music bent*]

To music bent is my retirèd mind,
    And fain would I some song of pleasure sing,
But in vain joys no comfort now I find;
    From heav'nly thoughts all true delight doth spring.
Thy power, O God, thy mercies, to record,
Will sweeten ev'ry note and ev'ry word.

All earthly pomp or beauty to express,
    Is but to carve in snow, on waves to write.
Celestial things, though men conceive them less,
    Yet fullest are they in themselves of light;   10
Such beams they yield as know no means to die,
Such heat they cast as lifts the spirit high.

[*Never weather-beaten sail*]

Never weather-beaten sail more willing bent to shore,
Never tired pilgrim's limbs affected slumber more
Than my wearied sprite now longs to fly out of my troubled breast.
O come quickly, sweetest Lord, and take my soul to rest.

Ever-blooming are the joys of heav'n's high paradise,
Cold age deafs not there our ears, nor vapor dims our eyes;
Glory there the sun outshines, whose beams the blessed only see;
O come quickly, glorious Lord, and raise my sprite to thee.

[*Jack and Joan*]

Jack and Joan they think no ill,
But loving live, and merry still;
Do their week-days' work and
    pray
Devoutly on the holy day;
Skip and trip it on the green,
And help to choose the summer
    queen;
Lash out, at a country feast,
Their silver penny with the best.

Well can they judge of nappy ale,
And tell at large a winter tale;   10
Climb up to the apple loft,
And turn the crabs till they be
    soft.
Tib is all the father's joy,
And little Tom the mother's boy.
All their pleasure is content,
And care, to pay their yearly
    rent.

Joan can call by name her cows,
And deck her windows with green
   boughs;
She can wreaths and tutties make,
And trim with plums a bridal
   cake.   20
Jack knows what brings gain or
   loss,
And his long flail can stoutly toss;
Make the hedge, which others
   break,
And ever thinks what he doth
   speak.

Now, you courtly dames and
   knights,
That study only strange de-
   lights,
Though you scorn the home-spun
   gray,
And revel in your rich array;
Though your tongues dissemble
   deep,
And can your heads from danger
   keep;   30
Yet for all your pomp and train,
Securer lives the silly swain.

[Give beauty all her right]

Give beauty all her right,
She's not to one form tied;
Each shape yields fair delight,
Where her perfections bide.
Helen, I grant, might pleasing
   be,
And Ros'mond was as sweet as she.

Some the quick eye commends;
Some swelling lips and red;
Pale looks have many friends,
Through sacred sweetness
   bred.   10

Meadows have flowers that pleasure move,
Though roses are the flowers of
   love.

Free beauty is not bound
To one unmovèd clime;
She visits ev'ry ground,
And favors ev'ry time.
Let the old loves with mine com-
   pare,
My sov'reign is as sweet and
   fair.

FROM *The Late Royal Entertainment . . . at Cawsome House,* 1613

[Night as well as brightest day]

Night as well as brightest day hath her delight.
Let us then with mirth and music deck the night;
   Never did glad day such store
      Of joy to night bequeath;
   Her stars then adore,
   Both in heav'n, and here beneath.

Love and beauty, mirth and music yield true joys,
Though the cynics in their folly count them toys;
   Raise your spirits ne'er so high,
      They will be apt to fall;   10
   None brave thoughts envý
   Who had e'er brave thought at all.

Joy is the sweet friend of life, the nurse of blood,
Patron of all health, and fountain of all good.
      Never may joy hence depart,
            But all your thoughts attend;
      Nought can hurt the heart,
            That retains so sweet a friend.

FROM *The Third and Fourth Book of Airs*, [*c.* 1617]

To the Reader.

The apothecaries have books of gold whose leaves, being opened,
are so light as that they are subject to be shaken with the least breath,
yet rightly handled, they serve both for ornament and use; such are
light airs. But if any squeamish stomachs shall check at two or three
vain ditties in the end of this book, let them pour off the clearest and
leave those as dregs in the bottom. Howsoever, if they be but conferred
with the Canterbury *Tales of that venerable poet,* Chaucer, *they will*
then appear toothsome enough. Some words are in these books which
have been clothed in music by others, and I am content they then
served their turn; yet give me now leave to make use of mine own.
Likewise you may find here some three or four songs that have been
published before, but for them, I refer you to the players' bill, that is
styled, newly revived, with additions, *for you shall find all of them re-*
formed, either in words or notes. To be brief, all these songs are mine,
if you express them well, otherwise they are your own. Farewell.

                    Yours, as you are his,
                              Thomas Campion.

[*Maids are simple*]

Maids are simple, some men say,
They, forsooth, will trust no men.
But should they men's wills obey,
Maids were very simple then.

Truth a rare flower now is grown,
Few men wear it in their hearts;
Lovers are more easily known
By their follies than deserts.

Safer may we credit give
To a faithless wand'ring Jew,   10
Than a young man's vows believe
When he swears his love is true.

Love they make a poor blind child,
But let none trust such as he;
Rather than to be beguiled,
Ever let me simple be.

[*Now winter nights enlarge*]

Now winter nights enlarge
   The number of their hours,
And clouds their storms discharge
   Upon the airy towers.

Let now the chimneys blaze
   And cups o'erflow with wine;
Let well-tuned words amaze
   With harmony divine.

Now yellow waxen lights
  Shall wait on honey love,   10
While youthful revels, masks, and
    courtly sights
Sleep's leaden spells remove.

This time doth well dispense
  With lovers' long discourse;
Much speech hath some defence,
  Though beauty no remorse.

All do not all things well:
  Some measures comely tread;
Some knotted riddles tell;
  Some poems smoothly read.   20
The summer hath his joys,
  And winter his delights;
Though love and all his pleasures
    are but toys,
They shorten tedious nights.

[*Thrice toss these oaken ashes*]

Thrice toss these oaken ashes in the air,
Thrice sit thou mute in this enchanted chair,
Then thrice three times tie up this true love's knot,
And murmur soft, She will, or she will not.

Go burn these pois'nous weeds in yon blue fire,
These screech-owl's feathers and this prickling brier,
This cypress gathered at a dead man's grave,
That all thy fears and cares an end may have.

Then come, you fairies, dance with me a round;
Melt her hard heart with your melodious sound.   10
In vain are all the charms I can devise:
She hath an art to break them with her eyes.

[*Never love unless you can*]

Never love unless you can
Bear with all the faults of man;
Men sometimes will jealous be,
Though but little cause they see,
  And hang the head, as discontent,
  And speak what straight they will repent.

Men that but one saint adore
Make a show of love to more;
Beauty must be scorned in none,
Though but truly served in one;   10
  For what is courtship but disguise?
  True hearts may have dissembling eyes.

Men when their affairs require
Must a while themselves retire,
Sometimes hunt, and sometimes hawk,

And not ever sit and talk.
If these and such like you can bear,
Then like, and love, and never fear.

[Respect my faith]

Respect my faith, regard my service past;
The hope you winged call home to you at last.
Great prize it is that I in you shall gain,
So great for you hath been my loss and pain.
My wits I spent and time for you alone,
Observing you and losing all for one.

Some raised to rich estates in this time are,
That held their hopes to mine inferior far;
Such, scoffing me, or pitying me, say thus,
Had he not loved, he might have lived like us.   10
O then, dear sweet, for love and pity's sake
My faith reward, and from me scandal take.

[There is a garden]

There is a garden in her face,
Where roses and white lilies grow;
A heav'nly paradise is that place,
Wherein all pleasant fruits do flow.
There cherries grow which none may buy
Till cherry-ripe themselves do cry.

Those cherries fairly do enclose
Of orient pearl a double row,
Which when her lovely laughter shows,
They look like rosebuds filled with snow.   10
Yet them nor peer nor prince can buy,
Till cherry-ripe themselves do cry.

Her eyes like angels watch them still;
Her brows like bended bows do stand,
Threat'ning with piercing frowns to kill
All that attempt with eye or hand
Those sacred cherries to come nigh,
Till cherry-ripe themselves do cry.

[Young and simple though I am]

Young and simple though I am,
I have heard of Cupid's name;
Guess I can what thing it is

Men desire when they do kiss.
Smoke can never burn, they say,
But the flames that follow may.

I am not so foul or fair
To be proud, nor to despair;
Yet my lips have oft observed,
Men that kiss them press them
    hard,   10
  As glad lovers use to do
  When their new-met loves they
    woo.

Faith, 'tis but a foolish mind,
Yet methinks a heat I find,
Like thirst-longing, that doth bide
Ever on my weaker side,
  Where they say my heart doth
    move.
  Venus, grant it be not love.

If it be, alas, what then?
Were not women made for men?
As good 'twere a thing were
  past,   21
That must needs be done at last.
  Roses that are over-blown
  Grow less sweet, then fall alone.

Yet nor churl nor silken gull
Shall my maiden blossom pull;
Who shall not I soon can tell,
Who shall, would I could as
  well;
  This I know, whoe'er he be,
  Love he must, or flatter me. 30

[Fain would I wed]

Fain would I wed a fair young man that night and day could
  please me,
When my mind or body grieved that had the power to ease me.
Maids are full of longing thoughts that breed a bloodless sickness,
And that, oft I hear men say, is only cured by quickness.
Oft I have been wooed and praised, but never could be movèd;
Many for a day or so I have most dearly lovèd,
But this foolish mind of mine straight loathes the thing resolvèd;
If to love be sin in me, that sin is soon absolvèd.
Sure I think I shall at last fly to some holy order;
When I once am settled there, then can I fly no farther.   10
Yet I would not die a maid, because I had a mother,
As I was by one brought forth, I would bring forth another.

JOHN DONNE

The Introduction and Notes are at pages 1259 and 1278

FROM *Poems,* 1633

SONGS AND SONNETS

Love's deity

I long to talk with some old lover's ghost,
  Who died before the god of love was born:
I cannot think that he, who then loved most,
  Sunk so low as to love one which did scorn.
But since this god produced a destiny,

And that vice-nature, custom, lets it be,
　I must love her that loves not me.

Sure, they which made him god meant not so much,
　Nor he in his young godhead practised it;
But when an even flame two hearts did touch,　　　　　10
　His office was indulgently to fit
Actives to passives. Correspondency
Only his subject was; it cannot be
　Love, till I love her that loves me.

But every modern god will now extend
　His vast prerogative as far as Jove.
To rage, to lust, to write to, to commend,
　All is the purlieu of the god of love.
Oh, were we wakened by this tyranny
To ungod this child again, it could not be　　　　　20
　I should love her, who loves not me.

Rebel and atheist too, why murmur I,
　As though I felt the worst that love could do?
Love may make me leave loving, or might try
　A deeper plague, to make her love me too,
Which, since she loves before, I'am loath to see;
Falsehood is worse than hate; and that must be,
　If she whom I love, should love me.

Song

Go and catch a falling star,
　Get with child a mandrake root,
Tell me where all past years are,
　Or who cleft the devil's foot,
Teach me to hear mermaids singing,
　Or to keep off envy's stinging,
　　　　And find
　　　　What wind
Serves to advance an honest mind.

If thou beest born to strange sights,　　　　　10
　Things invisible to see,
Ride ten thousand days and nights,
　Till age snow white hairs on thee,
Thou, when thou return'st, wilt tell me
All strange wonders that befell thee,
　　　　And swear
　　　　No where
Lives a woman true, and fair.

If thou find'st one, let me know,
    Such a pilgrimage were sweet;   20
Yet do not, I would not go,
    Though at next door we might meet;
Though she were true when you met her,
And last till you write your letter,
        Yet she
        Will be
False, ere I come, to two or three.

Woman's constancy

Now thou hast loved me one whole day,
To-morrow when thou leav'st, what wilt thou say?
Wilt thou then antedate some new-made vow?
    Or say that now
We are not just those persons which we were?
Or, that oaths made in reverential fear
Of love, and his wrath, any may forswear?
Or, as true deaths true marriages untie,
So lovers' contracts, images of those,
Bind but till sleep, death's image, them unloose?   10
    Or, your own end to justify,
For having purposed change and falsehood, you
Can have no way but falsehood to be true?
Vain lunatic, against these scapes I could
    Dispute and conquer, if I would;
        Which I abstain to do,
For by to-morrow, I may think so too.

The indifferent

I can love both fair and brown,
Her whom abundance melts, and her whom want betrays,
Her who loves loneness best, and her who masks and plays,
Her whom the country formed, and whom the town,
Her who believes, and her who tries,
Her who still weeps with spongy eyes,
And her who is dry cork, and never cries;
I can love her and her, and you and you,
I can love any, so she be not true.

Will no other vice content you?   10
Will it not serve your turn to do as did your mothers?
Or have you all old vices spent, and now would find out others?
Or doth a fear that men are true, torment you?
Oh, we are not, be not you so,

Let me, and do you, twenty know.
Rob me, but bind me not, and let me go.
Must I, who came to travail thorough you,
Grow your fixed subject, because you are true?

Venus heard me sigh this song,
And by love's sweetest part, variety, she swore,   20
She heard not this till now; and that it should be so no more.
She went, examined, and returned ere long,
And said, Alas, some two or three
Poor heretics in love there be,
Which think to 'stablish dangerous constancy.
But I have told them, Since you will be true,
You shall be true to them who'are false to you.

The flea

Mark but this flea, and mark in this,
How little that which thou deny'st me is;
It sucked me first, and now sucks thee,
And in this flea our two bloods mingled be;
Thou know'st that this cannot be said
A sin, nor shame, nor loss of maidenhead;
    Yet this enjoys before it woo,
    And pampered swells with one blood made of two,
    And this, alas, is more than we would do.

Oh stay, three lives in one flea spare,   10
Where we almost, yea, more than married are.
This flea is you and I, and this
Our marriage bed, and marriage temple is;
Though parents grudge, and you, w' are met,
And cloistered in these living walls of jet.
    Though use make you apt to kill me,
    Let not to that, self-murder added be,
    And sacrilege, three sins in killing three.

Cruel and sudden, hast thou since
Purpled thy nail in blood of innocence?   20
Wherein could this flea guilty be,
Except in that drop which it sucked from thee?
Yet thou triumph'st and say'st that thou
Find'st not thyself, nor me the weaker now;
    'Tis true, then learn how false fears be:
    Just so much honor, when thou yield'st to me,
    Will waste, as this flea's death took life from thee.

The message

Send home my long strayed eyes to me,
Which, oh, too long have dwelt on thee;
Yet since there they have learned such ill,
    Such forced fashions,
    And false passions,
      That they be
      Made by thee
Fit for no good sight, keep them still.

Send home my harmless heart again,
Which no unworthy thought could stain;   10
Which if it be taught by thine
    To make jestings
    Of protestings,
      And break both
      Word and oath,
Keep it, for then 'tis none of mine.

Yet send me back my heart and eyes
That I may know and see thy lies,
And may laugh and joy, when thou
    Art in anguish   20
    And dost languish
      For some one
      That will none,
Or prove as false as thou art now.

The bait

Come live with me, and be my love,
And we will some new pleasures prove,
Of golden sands, and crystal brooks,
With silken lines, and silver hooks.

There will the river whispering run,
Warmed by thy eyes more than the sun.
And there the'enamoured fish will stay,
Begging themselves they may betray.

When thou wilt swim in that live bath,
Each fish, which every channel hath,   10
Will amorously to thee swim,
Gladder to catch thee, than thou him.

If thou, to be so seen, beest loath,
By sun or moon, thou dark'nest both;
And if myself have leave to see,
I need not their light, having thee.

Let others freeze with angling reeds,
And cut their legs with shells and weeds,
Or treacherously poor fish beset
With strangling snare, or windowy net.　　20

Let coarse bold hands from slimy nest
The bedded fish in banks out-wrest,
Or curious traitors, sleave-silk flies,
Bewitch poor fishes' wand'ring eyes.

For thee, thou need'st no such deceit,
For thou thyself art thine own bait;
That fish that is not catched thereby,
Alas, is wiser far than I.

The will

Before I sigh my last gasp, let me breathe,
Great Love, some legacies: here I bequeath
Mine eyes to Argus, if mine eyes can see;
If they be blind, then Love, I give them thee;
My tongue to Fame; to'ambassadors mine ears;
　　To women or the sea, my tears.
　　Thou, Love, hast taught me heretofore
By making me serve her who'had twenty more,
That I should give to none but such as had too much before.

My constancy I to the planets give;　　10
My truth to them who at the court do live;
Mine ingenuity and openness
To Jesuits; to buffoons my pensiveness;
My silence to'any who abroad hath been;
　　My money to a Capuchin.
　　Thou, Love, taught'st me, by appointing me
To love there where no love received can be,
Only to give to such as have an incapacity.

My faith I give to Roman Catholics;　　20
All my good works unto the schismatics
Of Amsterdam; my best civility
And courtship to an University;

My modesty I give to soldiers bare;
 My patience let gamesters share.
 Thou, Love, taught'st me, by making me
Love her that holds my love disparity,
Only to give to those that count my gifts indignity.

I give my reputation to those
Which were my friends; mine industry to foes;
To schoolmen I bequeath my doubtfulness;   30
My sickness to physicians, or excess;
To nature, all that I in rhyme have writ;
 And to my company my wit.
 Thou, Love, by making me adore
Her who begot this love in me before,
Taught'st me to make as though I gave, when I did but restore.

To him for whom the passing bell next tolls,
I give my physic books; my written rolls
Of moral counsels, I to Bedlam give;
My brazen medals unto them which live   40
In want of bread; to them which pass among
 All foreigners, mine English tongue.
 Thou, Love, by making me love one
Who thinks her friendship a fit portïon
For younger lovers, dost my gifts thus disproportïon.

Therefore I'll give no more, but I'll undo
The world by dying, because love dies too.
Then all your beauties will be no more worth
Than gold in mines, where none doth draw it forth;
And all your graces no more use shall have   50
 Than a sun-dial in a grave.
 Thou, Love, taught'st me, by making me
Love her who doth neglect both me and thee,
To'invent, and practise this one way, to'annihilate all three.

The sun rising

 Busy old fool, unruly sun,
  Why dost thou thus
Through windows and through curtains call on us?
Must to thy motions lovers' seasons run?
  Saucy pedantic wretch, go chide
  Late schoolboys and sour prentices,
 Go tell court-huntsmen that the King will ride,
 Call country ants to harvest offices;

Love, all alike, no season knows, nor clime,
Nor hours, days, months, which are the rags of time. 10

Thy beams, so reverend and strong
Why shouldst thou think?
I could eclipse and cloud them with a wink,
But that I would not lose her sight so long;
If her eyes have not blinded thine,
Look, and to-morrow late tell me
Whether both the'Indias of spice and mine
Be where thou left'st them, or lie here with me.
Ask for those kings whom thou saw'st yesterday,
And thou shalt hear, all here in one bed lay. 20

She'is all states, and all princes I;
Nothing else is.
Princes do but play us; compared to this,
All honor's mimic, all wealth alchemy.
Thou, sun, art half as happy'as we,
In that the world's contracted thus;
Thine age asks ease, and since thy duties be
To warm the world, that's done in warming us.
Shine here to us, and thou art everywhere;
This bed thy center is, these walls thy sphere. 30

Break of day

'Tis true, 'tis day; what though it be?
Oh, wilt thou therefore rise from me?
Why should we rise because 'tis light?
Did we lie down because 'twas night?
Love which in spite of darkness brought us hither,
Should in despite of light keep us together.

Light hath no tongue, but is all eye;
If it could speak as well as spy,
This were the worst that it could say,
That being well I fain would stay,
And that I loved my heart and honor so
That I would not from him, that had them, go. 10

Must business thee from hence remove?
Oh, that's the worst disease of love,
The poor, the foul, the false, love can
Admit, but not the busied man.
He which hath business, and makes love, doth do
Such wrong as when a married man doth woo.

The computation

For the first twenty years, since yesterday,
I scarce believed thou couldst be gone away;
For forty more I fed on favors past,
And forty'on hopes, that thou wouldst they might last.
Tears drowned one hundred, and sighs blew out two;
A thousand, I did neither think nor do,
Or not divide, all being one thought of you;
Or in a thousand more, forgot that too.
Yet call not this long life, but think that I
Am, by being dead, immortal; can ghosts die?   11

Confined love

Some man unworthy to be possessor
Of old or new love, himself being false or weak,
Thought his pain and shame would be lesser
If on womankind he might his anger wreak,
    And thence a law did grow,
    One might but one man know;
    But are other creatures so?

Are sun, moon, or stars by law forbidden
To smile where they list, or lend away their light?
Are birds divorced, or are they chidden   10
If they leave their mate, or lie abroad a night?
    Beasts do no jointures lose
    Though they new lovers choose,
    But we are made worse than those.

Whoe'er rigged fair ship to lie in harbors,
And not to seek new lands, or not to deal with all?
Or built fair houses, set trees and arbors,
Only to lock up, or else to let them fall?
    Good is not good, unless
    A thousand it possess,   20
    But doth waste with greediness.

The broken heart

He is stark mad, whoever says
    That he hath been in love an hour;
Yet not that love so soon decays,
    But that it can ten in less space devour.
Who will believe me if I swear

That I have had the plague a year?
  Who would not laugh at me if I should say
I saw a flask of powder burn a day?

Ah, what a trifle is a heart,
  If once into love's hands it come!   10
All other griefs allow a part
  To other griefs, and ask themselves but some;
They come to us, but us love draws,
He swallows us, and never chaws;
  By him, as by chained shot, whole ranks do die,
  He is the tyrant pike, our hearts the fry.

If 'twere not so, what did become
  Of my heart when I first saw thee?
I brought a heart into the room,
  But from the room I carried none with me;   20
If it had gone to thee, I know
Mine would have taught thine heart to show
  More pity unto me, but love, alas,
  At one first blow did shiver it as glass.

Yet nothing can to nothing fall,
  Nor any place be empty quite;
Therefore I think my breast hath all
  Those pieces still, though they be not unite;
And now as broken glasses show
A hundred lesser faces, so   30
  My rags of heart can like, wish, and adore,
  But after one such love, can love no more.

A lecture upon the shadow

Stand still, and I will read to thee
A lecture, love, in love's philosophy.
  These three hours that we have spent
  Walking here, two shadows went
Along with us, which we ourselves produced;
  But, now the sun is just above our head,
  We do those shadows tread,
And to brave clearness all things are reduced.
  So whilst our infant loves did grow,
  Disguises did, and shadows, flow   10
  From us and our cares, but now 'tis not so.

That love hath not attained the high'st degree,
Which is still diligent lest others see.

Except our loves at this noon stay,
We shall new shadows make the other way.
  As the first were made to blind
  Others, these which come behind
Will work upon ourselves, and blind our eyes.
  If our loves faint, and westwardly decline,
  To me thou falsely thine,   20
And I to thee, mine actions shall disguise.
  The morning shadows wear away,
  But these grow longer all the day;
But oh, love's day is short, if love decay.

Love is a growing, or full constant light,
And his short minute after noon, is night.

Love's alchemy

Some that have deeper digged love's mine than I,
Say where his centric happiness doth lie;
    I have loved, and got, and told,
But should I love, get, tell, till I were old,
I should not find that hidden mystery.
    Oh, 'tis imposture all,
And as no chemic yet th' elixir got,
    But glorifies his pregnant pot
    If by the way to him befall
Some odoriferous thing, or medicinal,   10
    So lovers dream a rich and long delight,
    But get a winter-seeming summer's night.

Our ease, our thrift, our honor, and our day,
Shall we for this vain bubble's shadow pay?
    Ends love in this, that my man
Can be as happy'as I can, if he can
Endure the short scorn of a bridegroom's play?
    That loving wretch that swears
'Tis not the bodies marry, but the minds,
    Which he in her angelic finds,   20
    Would swear as justly that he hears,
In that day's rude hoarse minstrelsy, the spheres.
    Hope not for mind in women: at their best,
    Sweetness and wit, they'are but mummy possessed.

The ecstasy

Where, like a pillow on a bed,
    A pregnant bank swelled up to rest

The violet's reclining head,
   Sat we two, one another's best.
Our hands were firmly cémented
   With a fast balm, which thence did spring;
Our eye-beams twisted, and did thread
   Our eyes upon one double string;
So to'entergraft our hands, as yet
   Was all the means to make us one,   10
And pictures in our eyes to get
   Was all our propagatïon.
As 'twixt two equal armies fate
   Suspends uncertain victory,
Our souls, which to advance their state
   Were gone out, hung 'twixt her and me.
And whilst our souls negotiate there,
   We like sepulchral statues lay;
All day, the same our postures were,
   And we said nothing, all the day.   20
If any, so by love refined
   That he soul's language understood,
And by good love were grown all mind,
   Within convenient distance stood,
He, though he knew not which soul spake,
   Because both meant, both spake the same,
Might thence a new concoction take
   And part far purer than he came.
This ecstasy doth unperplex,
   We said, and tell us what we love: 30
We see by this it was not sex,
   We see we saw not what did move;
But as all several souls contain
   Mixture of things, they know not what,
Love these mixed souls doth mix again
   And makes both one, each this and that.
A single violet transplant,
   The strength, the color, and the size,
All which before was poor and scant,
   Redoubles still, and multiplies.   40
When love with one another so
   Interinanimates two souls,
That abler soul, which thence doth flow,
   Defects of loneliness controls.
We then, who are this new soul, know
   Of what we are composed and made,
For th' atomies of which we grow
   Are souls, whom no change can invade.

But oh, alas, so long, so far,
    Our bodies why do we forbear? 50
They are ours, though not we; we are
    The intelligences, they the sphere.
We owe them thanks, because they thus
    Did us to us at first convey,
Yielded their forces, sense, to us,
    Nor are dross to us, but allay.
On man heaven's influence works not so,
    But that it first imprints the air;
For soul into the soul may flow,
    Though it to body first repair. 60
As our blood labors to beget
    Spirits, as like souls as it can,
Because such fingers need to knit
    That subtle knot which makes us man,
So must pure lovers' souls descend
    T' affections, and to faculties,
Which sense may reach and apprehend,
    Else a great prince in prison lies.
To'our bodies turn we then, that so
    Weak men on love revealed may look; 70
Love's mysteries in souls do grow,
    But yet the body is his book.
And if some lover, such as we,
    Have heard this dialogue of one,
Let him still mark us, he shall see
    Small change when we'are to bodies gone.

The good-morrow

I wonder by my troth, what thou and I
Did, till we loved? Were we not weaned till then,
But sucked on country pleasures, childishly?
Or snorted we in the seven sleepers' den?
'Twas so; but this, all pleasures fancies be.
If ever any beauty I did see,
Which I desired, and got, 'twas but a dream of thee.

And now good morrow to our waking souls,
Which watch not one another out of fear;
For love all love of other sights controls, 10
And makes one little room an everywhere.
Let sea-discoverers to new worlds have gone,
Let maps to other, worlds on worlds have shown;
Let us possess one world, each hath one, and is one.

My face in thine eye, thine in mine appears,
And true plain hearts do in the faces rest;
Where can we find two better hemispheres
Without sharp north, without declining west?
Whatever dies was not mixed equally;   20
If our two loves be one, or thou and I
Love so alike that none do slacken, none can die.

Air and angels

Twice or thrice had I loved thee,
Before I knew thy face or name;
So in a voice, so in a shapeless flame,
Angels affect us oft, and worshipped be;
    Still when, to where thou wert, I came,
Some lovely glorious nothing I did see.
    But since my soul, whose child love is,
Takes limbs of flesh, and else could nothing do,
    More subtle than the parent is
Love must not be, but take a body too;   19
    And therefore what thou wert, and who,
        I bid love ask, and now
That it assume thy body I allow,
And fix itself in thy lip, eye, and brow.

Whilst thus to ballast love I thought,
And so more steadily to have gone,
With wares which would sink admiration,
I saw I had love's pinnace overfraught;
    Ev'ry thy hair for love to work upon
Is much too much, some fitter must be sought;   20
    For, nor in nothing, nor in things
Extreme and scatt'ring bright, can love inhere;
    Then as an angel, face and wings
Of air, not pure as it, yet pure doth wear,
    So thy love may be my love's sphere;
        Just such disparity
As is 'twixt air and angels' purity,
'Twixt women's love and men's will ever be.

The prohibition

    Take heed of loving me;
At least remember, I forbade it thee;
Not that I shall repair my'unthrifty waste
Of breath and blood, upon thy sighs and tears,
By being to thee then what to me thou wast;

But so great joy our life at once outwears;
Then, lest thy love by my death frustrate be,
If thou love me, take heed of loving me.

Take heed of hating me,
Or too much triumph in the victory. 10
Not that I shall be mine own officer,
And hate with hate again retaliate;
But thou wilt lose the style of conqueror,
If I, thy conquest, perish by thy hate.
Then, lest my being nothing lessen thee,
If thou hate me, take heed of hating me.

Yet love and hate me too,
So these extremes shall ne'er their office do:
Love me, that I may die the gentler way,
Hate me, because thy love is too great for me, 20
Or let these two, themselves not me decay;
So shall I live, thy stage not triumph be;
Lest thou thy love and hate and me undo,
To let me live, O love and hate me too.

The undertaking

I have done one braver thing
  Than all the worthies did,
And yet a braver thence doth
    spring,
  Which is, to keep that hid.

It were but madness now t' impart
  The skill of specular stone,
When he which can have learned
    the art
  To cut it, can find none.

So if I now should utter this,
  Others, because no more 10
Such stuff to work upon there is,
  Would love but as before.

But he who loveliness within
  Hath found, all outward loathes,

For he who color loves, and skin,
  Loves but their oldest clothes.

If, as I have, you also do
  Virtue'attired in woman see,
And dare love that, and say so too,
  And forget the he and she; 20

And if this love, though placëd so,
  From profane men you hide,
Which will no faith on this be-
    stow,
  Or, if they do, deride,

Then you have done a braver thing
  Than all the worthies did;
And a braver thence will spring,
  Which is, to keep that hid.

Lovers' infiniteness

If yet I have not all thy love,
  Dear, I shall never have it all;

I cannot breathe one other sigh to move,
Nor can entreat one other tear to fall,
And all my treasure, which should purchase thee,
Sighs, tears, and oaths, and letters, I have spent.
Yet no more can be due to me
Than at the bargain made was meant;
If then thy gift of love were partïal,
That some to me, some should to others fall,   10
  Dear, I shall never have thee all.

Or if then thou gavest me all,
All was but all, which thou hadst then;
But if in thy heart since there be, or shall
New love created be, by other men
Which have their stocks entire, and can in tears,
In sighs, in oaths, and letters outbid me,
This new love may beget new fears,
For this love was not vowed by thee.
And yet it was, thy gift being general;   20
The ground, thy heart, is mine; whatever shall
  Grow there, dear, I should have it all.

Yet I would not have all yet;
He that hath all can have no more,
And since my love doth every day admit
New growth, thou shouldst have new rewards in store;
Thou canst not every day give me thy heart,
If thou canst give it, then thou never gavest it;
Love's riddles are, that though thy heart depart,
It stays at home, and thou with losing savest it;   30
But we will have a way more liberal
Than changing hearts to join them, so we shall
  Be one, and one another's all.

Love's growth

I scarce believe my love to be so pure
    As I had thought it was,
    Because it doth endure
Vicissitude, and season, as the grass;
Methinks I lied all winter, when I swore
My love was infinite, if spring make it more.
But if this medicine, love, which cures all sorrow
With more, not only be no quintessénce,
But mixed of all stuffs, paining soul or sense,
And of the sun his working vigor borrow,   10

Love's not so pure and abstract as they use
To say, which have no mistress but their muse;
But as all else, being elemented too,
Love sometimes would contemplate, sometimes do.

And yet no greater, but more eminent,
    Love by the spring is grown;
      As in the firmament,
Stars by the sun are not enlarged, but shown.
Gentle love-deeds, as blossoms on a bough,
From love's awakened root do bud out now.   20
If, as in water stirred more circles be
Produced by one, love such additions take,
Those like so many spheres but one heaven make,
For they are all concentric unto thee.
And though each spring do add to love new heat,
As princes do in times of action get
New taxes, and remit them not in peace,
No winter shall abate the spring's increase.

The anniversary

All kings, and all their favorites,
    All glory of honors, beauties, wits,
The sun itself, which makes times as they pass,
Is elder by a year now, than it was
When thou and I first one another saw;
All other things to their destruction draw,
    Only our love hath no decay;
This no to-morrow hath, nor yesterday,
Running, it never runs from us away,
But truly keeps his first, last, everlasting day.   10

    Two graves must hide thine and my corse;
    If one might, death were no divorce.
Alas, as well as other princes, we,
Who prince enough in one another be,
Must leave at last in death these eyes and ears,
Oft fed with true oaths, and with sweet salt tears;
    But souls where nothing dwells but love,
All other thoughts being inmates, then shall prove
This, or a love increasèd there above,
When bodies to their graves, souls from their graves, remove.   20

    And then we shall be throughly blest,
    But we no more than all the rest;

Here upon earth we'are kings, and none but we
Can be such kings, nor of such subjects be.
Who is so safe as we, where none can do
Treason to us, except one of us two?
  True and false fears let us refrain;
Let us love nobly, and live, and add again
Years and years unto years, till we attain
To write threescore; this is the second of our reign.   30

The canonization

For God's sake hold your tongue, and let me love,
  Or chide my palsy, or my gout,
My five gray hairs, or ruined fortune flout;
  With wealth your state, your mind with arts improve,
    Take you a course, get you a place,
    Observe his honor, or his grace;
Or the king's real, or his stampèd face
  Contemplate; what you will, approve,
  So you will let me love.

Alas, alas, who's injured by my love?   10
  What merchants' ships have my sighs drowned?
Who says my tears have overflowed his ground?
  When did my colds a forward spring remove?
    When did the heats which my veins fill
    Add one more to the plaguy bill?
Soldiers find wars, and lawyers find out still
  Litigious men, which quarrels move,
  Though she and I do love.

Call us what you will, we are made such by love;
  Call her one, me another fly,   20
We'are tapers too, and at our own cost die,
  And we in us find the'eagle and the dove.
    The phœnix ridále hath more wit
    By us; we two being one, are it.
So to one neutral thing both sexes fit,
  We die and rise the same, and prove
  Mysterious by this love.

We can die by it, if not live by love,
  And if unfit for tombs and hearse
Our legend be, it will be fit for verse;   30
  And if no piece of chronicle we prove,
    We'll build in sonnets pretty rooms;

As well a well-wrought urn becomes
The greatest ashes, as half-acre tombs,
    And by these hymns, all shall approve
    Us canonized for love,

And thus invoke us: You whom reverend love
    Made one another's hermitage;
You, to whom love was peace, that now is rage;
    Who did the whole world's soul contract, and drove   40
    Into the glasses of your eyes—
    So made such mirrors and such spies
That they did all to you epitomize,—
    Countries, towns, courts; beg from above
    A pattern of your love!

A valediction of weeping

    Let me pour forth
My tears before thy face whilst I stay here,
For thy face coins them, and thy stamp they bear,
And by this mintage they are something worth,
    For thus they be
    Pregnant of thee;
Fruits of much grief they are, emblems of more—
When a tear falls, that thou fallst which it bore,
So thou and I are nothing then, when on a diverse shore.

    On a round ball   10
A workman that hath copies by, can lay
An Europe, Afric, and an Asïa,
And quickly make that which was nothing, all;
    So doth each tear
    Which thee doth wear,
A globe, yea world, by that impression grow,
Till thy tears mixed with mine do overflow
This world; by waters sent from thee, my heaven dissolvëd so.

    O more than moon,
Draw not up seas to drown me in thy sphere;   20
Weep me not dead, in thine arms, but forbear
To teach the sea what it may do too soon;
    Let not the wind
    Example find,
To do me more harm than it purposeth;
Since thou and I sigh one another's breath,
Whoe'er sighs most is cruellest, and hastes the other's death.

Song

Sweetest love, I do not go
   For weariness of thee,
Nor in hope the world can show
   A fitter love for me;
     But since that I
  Must die at last, 'tis best,
   To use myself in jest
    Thus by feigned deaths to die.

Yesternight the sun went hence,
   And yet is here to-day;   10
He hath no desire nor sense,
   Nor half so short a way;
     Then fear not me,
But believe that I shall make
Speedier journeys, since I take
   More wings and spurs than he.

Oh, how feeble is man's power,
   That if good fortune fall,
Cannot add another hour,
   Nor a lost hour recall!   20
     But come bad chance,

And we join to'it our strength,
And we teach it art and length,
   Itself o'er us to'advance.

When thou sigh'st, thou sigh'st not
        wind,
   But sigh'st my soul away;
When thou weep'st, unkindly kind,
   My life's blood doth decay.
     It cannot be
That thou lov'st me, as thou
        say'st,   30
If in thine my life thou waste;
   Thou art the best of me.

Let not thy divining heart
   Forethink me any ill,
Destiny may take thy part,
   And may thy fears fulfil;
     But think that we
Are but turned aside to sleep;
They who one another keep
   Alive, ne'er parted be.   40

A valediction forbidding mourning

As virtuous men pass mildly away,
   And whisper to their souls to go,
Whilst some of their sad friends do
     say,
   The breath goes now, and some
     say, No;

So let us melt, and make no noise,
   No tear-floods, nor sigh-tempests
     move;
'Twere profanation of our joys
   To tell the laity our love.

Moving of th' earth brings harms
     and fears,
   Men reckon what it did and
     meant;   10
But trepidation of the spheres,
   Though greater far, is innocent.

Dull sublunary lovers' love,
   Whose soul is sense, cannot
     admit
Absence, because it doth remove
   Those things which elemented
     it.

But we by a love so much refined
   That ourselves know not what it
     is,
Inter-assurèd of the mind,
   Care less eyes, lips, hands to
     miss.   20

Our two souls therefore, which are
     one,
   Though I must go, endure not
     yet

A breach, but an expansion,
    Like gold to airy thinness beat.

If they be two, they are two so
    As stiff twin compasses are two;
Thy soul, the fixed foot, makes no show
    To move, but doth if the'other do.

And though it in the center sit,
    Yet when the other far doth roam,   ³⁰

It leans, and hearkens after it,
    And grows erect as that comes home.

Such wilt thou be to me who must,
    Like th' other foot, obliquely run;
Thy firmness makes my circle just,
    And makes me end where I begun.

The funeral

Whoever comes to shroud me, do not harm
    Nor question much
That subtile wreath of hair which crowns my arm;
The mystery, the sign you must not touch,
    For 'tis my outward soul,
Viceroy to that, which unto heaven being gone,
    Will leave this to control
And keep these limbs, her provinces, from dissolution.

For if the sinewy thread my brain lets fall
    Through every part,   10
Can tie those parts, and make me one of all,
Those hairs, which upward grew, and strength and art
    Have from a better brain,
Can better do'it; except she meant that I
    By this should know my pain,
As prisoners then are manacled, when they'are condemned to die.

Whate'er she meant by'it, bury it with me,
    For since I am
Love's martyr, it might breed idolatry
If into others' hands these relics came;   20
    As 'twas humility
To afford to it all that a soul can do,
    So 'tis some bravery,
That since you would have none of me, I bury some of you.

The relic

    When my grave is broke up again
    Some second guest to entertain,—
    For graves have learned that woman-head,

To be to more than one a bed—
    And he that digs it, spies
A bracelet of bright hair about the bone,
    Will he not let'us alone,
And think that there a loving couple lies,
Who thought that this device might be some way
To make their souls, at the last busy day,   10
Meet at this grave, and make a little stay?

If this fall in a time or land
    Where mis-devotion doth command,
    Then he that digs us up will bring
    Us to the bishop and the king,
        To make us relics; then
Thou shalt be a Mary Magdalen, and I
    A something else thereby;
All women shall adore us, and some men;
And since at such time miracles are sought,   20
I would have that age by this paper taught
What miracles we harmless lovers wrought.

First, we loved well and faithfully,
    Yet knew not what we loved, nor why,
    Difference of sex no more we knew
    Than our guardian angels do;
        Coming and going, we
Perchance might kiss, but not between those meals;
    Our hands ne'er touched the seals,
Which nature, injured by late law, sets free;   30
These miracles we did, but now alas,
All measure and all language I should pass,
Should I tell what a miracle she was.

Twicknam garden

Blasted with sighs, and surrounded with tears,
    Hither I come to seek the spring,
    And at mine eyes, and at mine ears,
Receive such balms as else cure everything;
    But oh, self traitor, I do bring
The spider love, which transubstantiates all,
    And can convert manna to gall;
And that this place may thoroughly be thought
    True paradise, I have the serpent brought.

'Twere wholesomer for me that winter did   10
    Benight the glory of this place,
    And that a grave frost did forbid
These trees to laugh and mock me to my face;
    But that I may not this disgrace
Endure, nor yet leave loving, Love, let me
    Some senseless piece of this place be;
Make me a mandrake, so I may groan here,
    Or a stone fountain weeping out my year.

Hither with crystal vials, lovers, come
    And take my tears, which are love's wine,   20
    And try your mistress' tears at home,
For all are false that taste not just like mine;
    Alas, hearts do not in eyes shine,
Nor can you more judge woman's thoughts by tears,
    Than by her shadow what she wears.
O perverse sex, where none is true but she,
    Who's therefore true, because her truth kills me.

A nocturnal upon Saint Lucy's Day, being the shortest day

'Tis the year's midnight, and it is the day's,
Lucy's, who scarce seven hours herself unmasks;
    The sun is spent, and now his flasks
    Send forth light squibs, no constant rays;
      The world's whole sap is sunk;
The general balm th' hydroptic earth hath drunk,
Whither, as to the bed's feet, life is shrunk,
Dead and interred; yet all these seem to laugh,
Compared with me, who am their epitaph.

Study me then, you who shall lovers be   10
At the next world, that is, at the next spring;
    For I am every dead thing,
    In whom Love wrought new alchemy.
      For his art did express
A quintessence even from nothingness,
From dull privations, and lean emptiness;
He ruined me, and I am re-begot
Of absence, darkness, death—things which are not.

All others from all things draw all that's good,
Life, soul, form, spirit, whence they being have;   20
    I, by Love's limbec, am the grave

Of all that's nothing. Oft a flood
   Have we two wept, and so
Drowned the whole world, us two; oft did we grow
To be two chaoses, when we did show
Care to aught else; and often absences
Withdrew our souls, and made us carcasses.

But I am by her death, which word wrongs her,
Of the first nothing the elixir grown;
   Were I a man, that I were one
    I needs must know; I should prefer,   30
     If I were any beast,
Some ends, some means; yea plants, yea stones detest
And love; all, all some properties invest;
If I an ordinary nothing were,
As shadow, a light and body must be here.

But I am none; nor will my sun renew.
You lovers, for whose sake the lesser sun
   At this time to the Goat is run
    To fetch new lust, and give it you,   40
     Enjoy your summer all;
Since she enjoys her long night's festival,
Let me prepare towards her, and let me call
This hour her vigil, and her eve, since this
Both the year's and the day's deep midnight is.

ELEGIES

On his mistress

By our first strange and fatal interview,
By all desires which thereof did ensue,
By our long starving hopes, by that remorse
Which my words' masculine persuasive force
Begot in thee, and by the memory
Of hurts which spies and rivals threatened me,
I calmly beg; but by thy father's wrath,
By all pains, which want and divorcement hath,
I conjure thee; and all the oaths which I
And thou have sworn to seal joint constancy,   10
Here I unswear, and overswear them thus:
Thou shalt not love by ways so dangerous.
Temper, O fair love, love's impetuous rage,
Be my true mistress still, not my feigned page;
I'll go, and by thy kind leave, leave behind

Thee, only worthy to nurse in my mind
Thirst to come back; oh, if thou die before,
My soul from other lands to thee shall soar.
Thy else almighty beauty cannot move
Rage from the seas, nor thy love teach them love,   20
Nor tame wild Boreas' harshness; thou hast read
How roughly he in pieces shiverëd
Fair Orithea, whom he swore he loved.
Fall ill or good, 'tis madness to have proved
Dangers unurged; feed on this flattery,
That absent lovers one in th' other be.
Dissemble nothing, not a boy, nor change
Thy body's habit, nor mind's; be not strange
To thyself only; all will spy in thy face
A blushing womanly discovering grace.   30
Richly clothed apes are called apes; and as soon
Eclipsed as bright, we call the moon the moon.
Men of France, changeable chameleons,
Spitals of diseases, shops of fashions,
Love's fuellers, and the rightest company
Of players which upon the world's stage be,
Will quickly know thee, and no less, alas!
Th' indifferent Italian, as we pass
His warm land, well content to think thee page,
Will hunt thee with such lust and hideous rage   40
As Lot's fair guests were vexed. But none of these,
Nor spongy hydroptic Dutch shall thee displease,
If thou stay here. Oh, stay here! for, for thee,
England is only a worthy gallery
To walk in expectation, till from thence
Our greatest King call thee to his presénce.
When I am gone, dream me some happiness,
Nor let thy looks our long hid love confess,
Nor praise, nor dispraise me, nor bless nor curse
Openly love's force, nor in bed fright thy nurse   50
With midnight's startings, crying out, Oh, oh,
Nurse, oh, my love is slain, I saw him go
O'er the white Alps alone; I saw him, I,
Assailed, fight, taken, stabbed, bleed, fall, and die.
Augur me better chance, except dread Jove
Think it enough for me to'have had thy love.

The autumnal

No spring nor summer beauty hath such grace
As I have seen in one autumnal face.

Young beauties force our love, and that's a rape,
   This doth but counsel, yet you cannot scape.
If 'twere a shame to love, here 'twere no shame;
   Affection here takes reverence's name.
Were her first years the golden age? That's true,
   But now they'are gold oft tried and ever new.
That was her torrid and inflaming time,
   This is her tolerable tropic clime.   10
Fair eyes! who asks more heat than comes from hence,
   He in a fever wishes pestilence.
Call not these wrinkles, graves; if graves they were,
   They were Love's graves, for else he is no where.
Yet lies not Love dead here, but here doth sit
   Vowed to this trench, like an anachorit;
And here till hers, which must be his death, come,
   He doth not dig a grave, but build a tomb.
Here dwells he; though he sojourn ev'rywhere
   In progress, yet his standing house is here—   20
Here where still evening is, not noon nor night,
   Where no voluptuousness, yet all delight.
In all her words, unto all hearers fit,
   You may at revels, you at council, sit.
This is Love's timber, youth his underwood;
   There he, as wine in June, enrages blood,
Which then comes seasonabliest when our taste
   And appetite to other things is past.
Xerxes' strange Lydian love, the platan tree,
   Was loved for age, none being so large as she,   30
Or else because, being young, nature did bless
   Her youth with age's glory, barrenness.
If we love things long sought, age is a thing
   Which we are fifty years in compassing;
If transitory things, which soon decay,
   Age must be loveliest at the latest day.
But name not winter faces, whose skin's slack,
   Lank as an unthrift's purse, but a soul's sack;
Whose eyes seek light within, for all here's shade;
   Whose mouths are holes, rather worn out than made;   40
Whose every tooth to a several place is gone,
   To vex their souls at resurrection:
Name not these living death's-heads unto me,
   For these, not ancient, but antique be.
I hate extremes, yet I had rather stay
   With tombs than cradles, to wear out a day.
Since such love's motion natural is, may still
   My love descend, and journey down the hill,

Not panting after growing beauties; so
I shall ebb out with them who homeward go. 50

SATIRES

Satire III

Kind pity chokes my spleen; brave scorn forbids
Those tears to issue which swell my eyelids;
I must not laugh, nor weep sins and be wise;
Can railing then cure these worn maladies?
Is not our mistress, fair religïon,
As worthy of all our souls' devotïon
As virtue was in the first blinded age?
Are not heaven's joys as valiant to assuage
Lusts as earth's honor was to them? Alas,
As we do them in means, shall they surpass 10
Us in the end? and shall thy father's spirit
Meet blind philosophers in heaven, whose merit
Of strict life may be imputed faith, and hear
Thee, whom he taught so easy ways and near
To follow, damned? Oh, if thou dar'st, fear this;
This fear great courage and high valor is.
Dar'st thou aid mutinous Dutch, and dar'st thou lay
Thee in ships, wooden sepulchers, a prey
To leaders' rage, to storms, to shot, to dearth?
Dar'st thou dive seas, and dungeons of the earth? 20
Hast thou courageous fire to thaw the ice
Of frozen North discoveries? and thrice
Colder than salamanders, like divine
Children in th' oven, fires of Spain and the Line,
Whose countries limbecs to our bodies be,
Canst thou for gain bear? and must every he
Which cries not, Goddess, to thy mistress, draw
Or eat thy poisonous words? Courage of straw!
O desperate coward, wilt thou seem bold and
To thy foes and His, who made thee to stand 30
Sentinel in his world's garrison, thus yield,
And for forbidden wars leave th' appointed field?
Know thy foes: the foul devil, whom thou
Strivest to please, for hate, not love, would allow
Thee fain his whole realm to be quit; and as
The world's all parts wither away and pass,
So the world's self, thy other loved foe, is
In her decrepit wane, and thou, loving this,
Dost love a withered and worn strumpet; last,

Flesh, itself death, and joys which flesh can taste   40
Thou lovest, and thy fair goodly soul, which doth
Give this flesh power to taste joy, thou dost loathe.
Seek true religion. Oh, where? Mirreus,
Thinking her unhoused here and fled from us,
Seeks her at Rome; there, because he doth know
That she was there a thousand years ago;
He loves her rags so, as we here obey
The statecloth where the prince sat yesterday.
Crantz to such brave loves will not be enthralled,   50
But loves her only, who at Geneva is called
Religion, plain, simple, sullen, young,
Contemptuous, yet unhandsome; as among
Lecherous humors, there is one that judges
No wenches wholesome, but coarse country drudges.
Graius stays still at home here, and because
Some preachers, vile ambitious bawds, and laws,
Still new like fashions, bid him think that she
Which dwells with us is only perfect, he
Embraceth her whom his godfathers will   60
Tender to him, being tender; as wards still
Take such wives as their guardians offer, or
Pay values. Careless Phrygius doth abhor
All, because all cannot be good; as one,
Knowing some women whores, dares marry none.
Gracchus loves all as one, and thinks that so
As women do in divers countries go
In divers habits, yet are still one kind,
So doth, so is religion; and this blind-
Ness too much light breeds; but unmovëd, thou   70
Of force must one, and forced but one allow,
And the right; ask thy father which is she,
Let him ask his; though truth and falsehood be
Near twins, yet truth a little elder is;
Be busy to seek her; believe me this,
He's not of none, nor worst, that seeks the best.
To adore, or scorn an image, or protest,
May all be bad. Doubt wisely; in strange way
To stand inquiring right, is not to stray;
To sleep, or run wrong, is. On a huge hill,   80
Cragged and steep, Truth stands, and he that will
Reach her, about must and about must go,
And what the hill's suddenness resists, win so.
Yet strive so that before age, death's twilight,
Thy soul rest, for none can work in that night.
To will implies delay, therefore now do

Hard deeds, the body's pains; hard knowledge too
The mind's endeavors reach, and mysteries
Are like the sun, dazzling, yet plain to all eyes.
Keep the truth which thou hast found; men do not stand
In so ill case, that God hath with his hand　　　　　90
Signed kings blank charters to kill whom they hate;
Nor are they vicars, but hangmen, to fate.
Fool and wretch, wilt thou let thy soul be tied
To man's laws, by which she shall not be tried
At the last day? Will it then boot thee
To say a Philip or a Gregory,
A Harry or a Martin, taught thee this?
Is not this excuse for mere contraries
Equally strong? Cannot both sides say so?
That thou mayest rightly obey power, her bounds know;　　100
Those past, her nature and name is changed; to be
Then humble to her is idolatry.
As streams are, power is; those blest flowers that dwell
At the rough stream's calm head, thrive and do well,
But having left their roots, and themselves given
To the stream's tyrannous rage, alas, are driven
Through mills and rocks and woods, and at last, almost
Consumed in going, in the sea are lost.
So perish souls, which more choose men's unjust
Power from God claimed, than God himself to trust.　　110

EPIGRAMS

A lame beggar

I am unable, yonder beggar cries,
To stand or move; if he say true, he lies.

Antiquary

If in his study he hath so much care
To'hang all old strange things, let his wife beware.

Phryne

Thy flattering picture, Phryne, is like thee—
Only in this, that you both painted be.

LETTERS

The calm

[To Mr. Christopher Brooke]

Our storm is past, and that storm's tyrannous rage
A stupid calm, but nothing it, doth suage.

The fable is inverted, and far more
A block afflicts now, than a stork before.
Storms chafe, and soon wear out themselves, or us;
In calms, heaven laughs to see us languish thus.
As steady'as I can wish that my thoughts were,
Smooth as thy mistress' glass, or what shines there,
The sea is now; and as the isles which we
Seek, when we can move, our ships rooted be.   10
As water did in storms, now pitch runs out,
As lead, when a fired church becomes one spout;
And all our beauty, and our trim, decays
Like courts removing, or like ended plays.
The fighting place now seamen's rags supply,
And all the tackling is a frippery.
No use of lanthorns; and in one place lay
Feathers and dust, to-day and yesterday.
Earth's hollownesses, which the world's lungs are,
Have no more wind than the upper vault of air.   20
We can nor lost friends nor sought foes recover,
But meteor-like, save that we move not, hover.
Only the calenture together draws
Dear friends, which meet dead in great fishes' jaws;
And on the hatches, as on altars, lies
Each one, his own priest and own sacrifice;
Who live, that miracle do multiply
Where walkers in hot ovens do not die.
If in despite of these we swim, that hath
No more refreshing than our brimstone bath;   30
But from the sea into the ship we turn,
Like parboiled wretches, on the coals to burn.
Like Bajazet encaged, the shepherd's scoff,
Or like slack-sinewed Samson, his hair off,
Languish our ships. Now as a myriad
Of ants durst th' emperor's loved snake invade,
The crawling galleys, sea-gaols, finny chips,
Might brave our pinnaces, now bed-rid ships.
Whether a rotten state, and hope of gain,
Or to disuse me from the queasy pain   40
Of being beloved, and loving, or the thirst
Of honor, or fair death, out-pushed me first,
I lose my end; for here as well as I,
A desperate may live, and a coward die.
Stag, dog, and all which from or towards flies,
Is paid with life or prey, or doing, dies.
Fate grudges us all, and doth subtly lay
A scourge, 'gainst which we all forget to pray;

He that at sea prays for more wind, as well
Under the poles may beg cold, heat in hell.
What are we then? How little more, alas,
Is man now, than before he was! He was
Nothing; for us, we are for nothing fit;
Chance, or ourselves, still disproportion it.
We have no power, no will, no sense; I lie,
I should not then thus feel this misery.

To Sir Henry Wotton

Here's no more news than virtue:'I may as well
Tell you Cales' or Saint Michael's tale for news, as tell
That vice doth here habitually dwell.

Yet, as to'get stomachs we walk up and down,
And toil to sweeten rest, so, may God frown
If, but to loathe both, I haunt court or town.

For here no one is from the'extremity
Of vice by any other reason free,
But that the next to'him still is worse than he.

In this world's warfare, they whom rugged Fate,
God's commissary, doth so throughly hate
As in'the court's squadron to marshal their state;

If they stand armed with seely honesty,
With wishing prayers, and neat integrity,
Like Indians 'gainst Spanish hosts they be.

Suspicious boldness to this place belongs,
And to'have as many ears as all have tongues;
Tender to know, tough to ackowledge wrongs.

Believe me, Sir, in my youth's giddiest days,
When to be like the court was a play's praise,
Plays were not so like courts as courts'are like plays.

Then let us at these mimic antics jest,
Whose deepest projects and egregious gests
Are but dull morals of a game at chests.

But now 'tis incongruity to smile,
Therefore I end, and bid farewell awhile;
At court; though *From court* were the better style.

[*THE ANNIVERSARIES*]

An Anatomy of the World

The first anniversary

So did the world from the first hour decay,
That evening was beginning of the day;
And now the springs and summers which we see,
Like sons of women after fifty be.
And new philosophy calls all in doubt;
The element of fire is quite put out;
The sun is lost, and th' earth, and no man's wit
Can well direct him where to look for it.
And freely men confess that this world's spent,
When in the planets and the firmament   10
They seek so many new; they see that this
Is crumbled out again to his atomies.
'Tis all in pieces, all coherence gone,
All just supply, and all relation;
Prince, subject, father, son, are things forgot,
For every man alone thinks he hath got
To be a phœnix, and that then can be
None of that kind of which he is, but he.
This is the world's condition now, and now
She that should all parts to reunion bow,   20
She that had all magnetic force alone
To draw and fasten sundered parts in one,
She whom wise nature had invented then
When she observed that every sort of men
Did in their voyage in this world's sea stray,
And needed a new compass for their way,
She that was best, and first original
Of all fair copies, and the general
Steward to fate, she whose rich eyes and breast
Gilt the West Indies, and perfumed the East,   30
Whose having breathed in this world did bestow
Spice on those isles, and bade them still smell so,
And that rich Indie which doth gold inter
Is but as single money, coined from her,
She to whom this world must itself refer
As suburbs or the microcosm of her,
She, she is dead, she's dead; when thou know'st this,
Thou know'st how lame a cripple this world is.

Of the Progress of the Soul
The second anniversary

. . . .

She of whose soul, if we may say 'twas gold,
Her body was th' electrum, and did hold
Many degrees of that; we understood
Her by her sight; her pure and eloquent blood
Spoke in her cheeks, and so distinctly wrought
That one might almost say her body thought;
She, she, thus richly and largely housed, is gone,
And chides us slow-paced snails who crawl upon
Our prison's prison, earth, nor think us well
Longer than whilst we bear our brittle shell.   10
But 'twere but little to have changed our room,
If, as we were in this our living tomb
Oppressed with ignorance, we still were so.
Poor soul, in this thy flesh what dost thou know?
Thou know'st thyself so little, as thou know'st not
How thou didst die, nor how thou wast begot.
Thou neither know'st how thou at first cam'st in,
Nor how thou took'st the poison of man's sin.
Nor dost thou, though thou know'st that thou art so,
By what way thou art made immortal, know.   20
Thou art too narrow, wretch, to comprehend
Even thyself; yea, though thou wouldst but bend
To know thy body. Have not all souls thought
For many ages that our body'is wrought
Of air, and fire, and other elements?
And now they think of new ingredients,
And one soul thinks one, and another way
Another thinks, and 'tis an even lay.
Know'st thou but how the stone doth enter in
The bladder's cave, and never break the skin?   30
Know'st thou how blood, which to the heart doth flow,
Doth from one ventricle to th' other go?
And for the putrid stuff which thou dost spit,
Know'st thou how thy lungs have attracted it?
There are no passages, so that there is,
For aught thou know'st, piercing of substances.
And of those many opinions which men raise
Of nails and hairs, dost thou know which to praise?
What hope have we to know ourselves, when we
Know not the least things which for our use be?   40
We see in authors, too stiff to recant,

A hundred controversies of an ant;
And yet one watches, starves, freezes, and sweats,
To know but catechisms and alphabets
Of unconcerning things, matters of fact—
How others on our stage their parts did act,
What Cæsar did, yea, and what Cicero said.
Why grass is green, or why our blood is red,
Are mysteries which none have reached unto.
In this low form, poor soul, what wilt thou do?   50
When wilt thou shake off this pedantery
Of being taught by sense, and fantasy?
Thou look'st through spectacles; small things seem great
Below; but up unto the watch-tower get,
And see all things despoiled of fallacies;
Thou shalt not peep through lattices of eyes,
Nor hear through labyrinths of ears, nor learn
By circuit or collections to discern.
In heaven thou straight know'st all concerning it,
And what concerns it not, shalt straight forget.   60

. . . .

DIVINE POEMS

Show me, dear Christ, thy spouse so bright and clear.
What! is it she which on the other shore
Goes richly painted? or which, robbed and tore,
Laments and mourns in Germany and here?
Sleeps she a thousand, then peeps up one year?
Is she self-truth, and errs? now new, now outwore?
Doth she, and did she, and shall she evermore
On one, on seven, or on no hill appear?
Dwells she with us, or like adventuring knights
First travel we to seek, and then make love?   10
Betray, kind husband, thy spouse to our sights,
And let mine amorous soul court thy mild dove,
Who is most true and pleasing to thee then
When she'is embraced and open to most men.

———

Batter my heart, three-personed God, for you
As yet but knock, breathe, shine, and seek to mend;
That I may rise and stand, o'erthrow me;'and bend
Your force to break, blow, burn, and make me new.
I, like an usurped town to'another due,
Labor to'admit you, but oh, to no end.
Reason, your viceroy in me, me should defend,
But is captived, and proves weak or untrue.

Yet dearly'I love you,'and would be lovëd fain,
But am betrothed unto your enemy;
Divorce me,'untie or break that knot again;
Take me to you, imprison me, for I,
Except you'enthrall me, never shall be free,
Nor ever chaste, except you ravish me.

Why are we by all creatures waited on?
Why do the prodigal elements supply
Life and food to me, being more pure than I,
Simple and further from corruptïon?
Why brook'st thou, ignorant horse, subjectïon?
Why dost thou, bull and boar, so seelily
Dissemble weakness, and by'one man's stroke die,
Whose whole kind you might swallow and feed upon?
Weaker I am, woe is me, and worse than you;
You have not sinned, nor need be timorous.
But wonder at a greater wonder, for to us
Created nature doth these things subdue;
But their Creator, whom sin nor nature tied,
For us, his creatures and his foes, hath died.

If poisonous minerals, and if that tree
Whose fruit threw death on else immortal us,
If lecherous goats, if serpents envious
Cannot be damned, alas! why should I be?
Why should intent or reason, born in me,
Make sins else equal, in me more heinous?
And mercy being easy and glorious
To God, in his stern wrath why threatens he?
But who am I, that dare dispute with thee,
O God? Oh, of thine only worthy blood
And my tears, make a heavenly Lethean flood,
And drown in it my sins' black memory.
That thou remember them, some claim as debt;
I think it mercy, if thou wilt forget.

This is my play's last scene; here heavens appoint
My pilgrimage's last mile; and my race,
Idly yet quickly run, hath this last pace;
My span's last inch, my minutes' latest point;
And gluttonous death will instantly unjoint
My body and my soul, and I shall sleep a space;
But my'ever-waking part shall see that face
Whose fear already shakes my every joint.
Then as my soul to'heaven, her first seat, takes flight,

And earth-born body in the earth shall dwell,
So fall my sins, that all may have their right,
To where they'are bred, and would press me,—to hell.
Impute me righteous, thus purged of evil,
For thus I leave the world, the flesh, the devil.

What if this present were the world's last night?
Mark in my heart, O soul, where thou dost dwell,
The picture of Christ crucified, and tell
Whether his countenance can thee affright:
Tears in his eyes quench the amazing light,
Blood fills his frowns, which from his pierced head fell.
And can that tongue adjudge thee unto hell,
Which prayed forgiveness for his foes' fierce spite?
No, no; but as in my idolatry
I said to all my profane mistresses,
Beauty, of pity, foulness only is
A sign of rigor; so I say to thee:
To wicked spirits are horrid shapes assigned;
This beauteous form assumes a piteous mind.

At the round earth's imagined corners, blow
Your trumpets, angels; and arise, arise
From death, you numberless infinities
Of souls, and to your scattered bodies go;
All whom the flood did, and fire shall o'erthrow,
All whom war, dearth, age, agues, tyrannies,
Despair, law, chance hath slain, and you whose eyes
Shall behold God and never taste death's woe.
But let them sleep, Lord, and me mourn a space,
For if above all these my sins abound,
'Tis late to ask abundance of thy grace
When we are there; here on this lowly ground
Teach me how to repent; for that's as good
As if thou'hadst sealed my pardon with thy blood.

Death, be not proud, though some have callèd thee
Mighty and dreadful, for thou art not so;
For those whom thou think'st thou dost overthrow
Die not, poor Death, nor yet canst thou kill me.
From rest and sleep, which but thy pictures be,
Much pleasure; then from thee much more must flow,
And soonest our best men with thee do go,
Rest of their bones, and soul's delivery.
Thou art slave to fate, chance, kings, and desperate men,
And dost with poison, war, and sickness dwell,

And poppy or charms can make us sleep as well
And better than thy stroke; why swell'st thou then?
One short sleep past, we wake eternally,
And death shall be no more; Death, thou shalt die.

Good Friday, 1613. Riding westward

Let man's soul be a sphere, and then in this
The intelligence that moves, devotion is;
And as the other spheres, by being grown
Subject to foreign motion, lose their own,
And being by others hurried every day
Scarce in a year their natural form obey,
Pleasure or business, so, our souls admit
For their first mover, and are whirled by it.
Hence is 't that I am carried towards the west
This day, when my soul's form bends towards the east.   10
There I should see a sun, by rising set,
And by that setting, endless day beget;
But that Christ on this cross did rise and fall,
Sin had eternally benighted all.
Yet dare I'almost be glad I do not see
That spectacle of too much weight for me.
Who sees God's face, that is self life, must die;
What a death were it then to see God die!
It made his own lieutenant, nature, shrink;
It made his footstool crack, and the sun wink.   20
Could I behold those hands which span the poles
And tune all spheres at once, pierced with those holes?
Could I behold that endless height, which is
Zenith to us and our antipodes,
Humbled below us? or that blood which is
The seat of all our souls, if not of his,
Made dirt of dust, or that flesh which was worn
By God for his apparel, ragg'd and torn?
If on these things I durst not look, durst I
Upon his miserable mother cast mine eye,   30
Who was God's partner here, and furnished thus
Half of that sacrifice which ransomed us?
Though these things, as I ride, be from mine eye,
They'are present yet unto my memory,
For that looks towards them; and thou look'st towards me,
O Savior, as thou hang'st upon the tree;
I turn my back to thee but to receive
Corrections, till thy mercies bid thee leave.
Oh, think me worth thine anger, punish me,

Burn off my rusts, and my deformity;   40
Restore thine image, so much, by thy grace,
That thou mayst know me, and I'll turn my face.

A hymn to Christ, at the author's last going into Germany

In what torn ship soever I embark,
That ship shall be my emblem of thy ark;
What sea soever swallow me, that flood
Shall be to me an emblem of thy blood;
Though thou with clouds of anger do disguise
Thy face, yet through that mask I know those eyes,
    Which, though they turn away sometimes,
       They never will despise.

I sacrifice this island unto thee,
And all whom I loved there, and who loved me;   10
When I have put our seas 'twixt them and me,
Put thou thy seas betwixt my sins and thee.
As the tree's sap doth seek the root below
In winter, in my winter now I go
    Where none but thee, th' eternal root
       Of true love, I may know.

Nor thou nor thy religion dost control
The amorousness of an harmonious soul,
But thou wouldst have that love thyself; as thou
Art jealous, Lord, so I am jealous now;   20
Thou lov'st not, till from loving more thou free
My soul; whoever gives, takes liberty;
    Oh, if thou car'st not whom I love,
       Alas, thou lov'st not me.

Seal then this bill of my divorce to all
On whom those fainter beams of love did fall;
Marry those loves, which in youth scattered be
On fame, wit, hopes (false mistresses), to thee.
Churches are best for prayer that have least light:
To see God only, I go out of sight;   30
    And to scape stormy days, I choose
       An everlasting night.

A hymn to God the Father

Wilt thou forgive that sin where I begun,
    Which was my sin, though it were done before?

Wilt thou forgive that sin through which I run,
　　And do run still, though still I do deplore?
　　When thou hast done, thou has not done,
　　　　For I have more.

Wilt thou forgive that sin which I have won
　　Others to sin, and made my sin their door?
　　Wilt thou forgive that sin which I did shun
　　A year or two, but wallowed in a score?　　　　　　10
　　　　When thou hast done, thou hast not done,
　　　　　　For I have more.

I have a sin of fear, that when I have spun
　　My last thread, I shall perish on the shore;
But swear by thyself, that at my death thy Son
　　Shall shine as he shines now, and heretofore;
　　　　And having done that, thou hast done;
　　　　　　I fear no more.

Hymn to God, my God, in my sickness

Since I am coming to that holy room
　　Where, with thy choir of saints for evermore,
I shall be made thy music, as I come
　　I tune the instrument here at the door,
　　And what I must do then, think here before.

Whilst my physicians by their love are grown
　　Cosmographers, and I their map, who lie
Flat on this bed, that by them may be shown
　　That this is my south-west discovery,
　　Per fretum febris, by these straits to die,　　　　　15

I joy, that in these straits I see my west;
　　For though their currents yield return to none,
What shall my west hurt me? As west and east
　　In all flat maps, and I am one, are one,
　　So death doth touch the resurrection.

Is the Pacific sea my home? or are
　　The eastern riches? is Jerusalem?
Anyan and Magellan and Gibraltar,
　　All straits, and none but straits, are ways to them,
　　Whether where Japhet dwelt, or Cham, or Shem.　　20

We think that Paradise and Calvary,
　　Christ's cross and Adam's tree, stood in one place;

Look, Lord, and find both Adams met in me:
    As the first Adam's sweat surrounds my face,
    May the last Adam's blood my soul embrace.

So, in his purple wrapped, receive me, Lord;
    By these, his thorns, give me his other crown;
And as to others' souls I preached thy word,
    Be this my text, my sermon to mine own:
Therefore that he may raise, the Lord throws down.   30

BEN JONSON

The Introduction and Notes are at pages 1263 and 1278

FROM *The Works of Benjamin Jonson*, 1616

EPIGRAMS

To the reader

Pray thee, take care, that tak'st my book in hand,
    To read it well—that is, to understand.

To my book

It will be looked for, book, when some but see
    Thy title, *Epigrams*, and named of me,
Thou shouldst be bold, licentious, full of gall,
    Wormwood and sulphur, sharp, and toothed withal;
Become a petulant thing, hurl ink and wit
    As madmen stones, not caring whom they hit.
Deceive their malice, who could wish it so.
    And by thy wiser temper, let men know
Thou art not covetous of least self-fame
    Made from the hazard of another's shame;   10
Much less, with lewd, profane, and beastly phrase,
    To catch the world's loose laughter, or vain gaze.
He that departs with his own honesty
    For vulgar praise, doth it too dearly buy.

To my bookseller

Thou that mak'st gain thy end, and wisely well
    Call'st a book good or bad as it doth sell,
Use mine so too, I give thee leave; but crave,
    For the luck's sake, it thus much favor have,

To lie upon thy stall till it be sought,
  Not offered, as it made suit to be bought;
Nor have my title-leaf on posts or walls,
  Or in cleft-sticks, advancëd to make calls
For termers, or some clerk-like servingman
  Who scarce can spell th' hard names, whose knight less can.   10
If, without these vile arts, it will not sell,
  Send it to Bucklersbury, there 'twill well.

To my mere English censurer

To thee my way in epigrams seems new,
  When both it is the old way and the true.
Thou sayst that cannot be, for thou hast seen
  Davies and Weever, and the best have been,
And mine come nothing like. I hope so; yet
  As theirs did with thee, mine might credit get,
If thou'dst but use thy faith, as thou didst then
  When thou wert wont t' admire, not censure men.
Prithee believe still, and not judge so fast,
  Thy faith is all the knowledge that thou hast.   10

On something that walks somewhere

At court I met it, in clothes brave enough
  To be a courtier, and looks grave enough
To seem a statesman; as I near it came,
  It made me a great face; I asked the name.
A Lord, it cried, buried in flesh and blood,
  And such from whom let no man hope least good,
For I will do none; and as little ill,
  For I will dare none. Good Lord, walk dead still.

To Doctor Empiric

When men a dangerous disease did 'scape
  Of old, they gave a cock to Æsculape;
Let me give two, that doubly am got free:
  From my disease's danger, and from thee.

To William Camden

Camden, most reverend head, to whom I owe
  All that I am in arts, all that I know
(How nothing's that); to whom my country owes
  The great renown and name wherewith she goes;
Than thee the age sees not that thing more grave,

More high, more holy, that she more would crave.
What name, what skill, what faith hast thou in things!
What sight in searching the most antique springs!
What weight and what authority in thy speech!
Man scarce can make that doubt, but thou canst teach. 10
Pardon free truth and let thy modesty,
Which conquers all, be once overcome by thee.
Many of thine this better could than I,
But for their powers, accept my piety.

To Francis Beaumont

How I do love thee, Beaumont, and thy muse,
That unto me dost such religion use!
How I do fear myself, that am not worth
The least indulgent thought thy pen drops forth!
At once thou mak'st me happy, and unmak'st;
And giving largely to me, more thou tak'st.
What fate is mine, that so itself bereaves?
What art is thine, that so thy friend deceives?
When even there where most thou praisest me,
For writing better, I must envy thee. 10

To John Donne

Who shall doubt, Donne, where I a poet be,
When I dare send my *Epigrams* to thee?
That so alone canst judge, so alone dost make;
And, in thy censures, evenly dost take
As free simplicity to disavow
As thou hast best authority t' allow.
Read all I send; and if I find but one
Marked by thy hand, and with the better stone,
My title's sealed. Those that for claps do write,
Let pui'nes', porters', players' praise delight, 10
And till they burst their backs, like asses load;
A man should seek great glory, and not broad.

On Lucy, Countess of Bedford

This morning, timely rapt with holy fire,
I thought to form unto my zealous muse
What kind of creature I could most desire
To honor, serve, and love, as poets use.
I meant to make her fair, and free, and wise,
Of greatest blood, and yet more good than great;

I meant the day-star should not brighter rise,
　　Nor lend like influence from his lucent seat;
I meant she should be courteous, facile, sweet,
　　Hating that solemn vice of greatness, pride; 　　　10
I meant each softest virtue there should meet,
　　Fit in that softer bosom to reside.
Only a learned, and a manly soul
　　I purposed her; that should, with even powers,
The rock, the spindle, and the shears control
　　Of destiny, and spin her own free hours.
Such when I meant to feign, and wished to see,
　　My muse bade, Bedford write, and that was she.

To Lucy, Countess of Bedford, with Mr. Donne's satires

Lucy, you brightness of our sphere, who are
　　Life of the Muses' day, their morning star!
If works, not th' author's, their own grace should look,
　　Whose poems would not wish to be your book?
But these, desired by you, the maker's ends
　　Crown with their own; rare poems ask rare friends.
Yet satires, since the most of mankind be
　　Their unavoided subject, fewest see;
For none e'er took that pleasure in sin's sense,
　　But, when they heard it taxed, took more offence. 　　10
They, then, that living where the matter is bred,
　　Dare for these poems, yet, both ask and read
And like them too, must needfully, though few,
　　Be of the best, and 'mongst those best are you,
Lucy, you brightness of our sphere, who are
　　The Muses' evening, as their morning star.

Inviting a friend to supper

To-night, grave sir, both my poor house and I
　　Do equally desire your company;
Not that we think us worthy such a guest,
　　But that your worth will dignify our feast
With those that come, whose grace may make that seem
　　Something, which else could hope for no esteem.
It is the fair acceptance, sir, creates
　　The entertainment perfect, not the cates.
Yet shall you have, to rectify your palate,
　　An olive, capers, or some better salad 　　　10
Ush'ring the mutton; with a short-legged hen,
　　If we can get her, full of eggs, and then

Lemons and wine for sauce; to these, a coney
   Is not to be despaired of, for our money;
And though fowl now be scarce, yet there are clerks,
   The sky not falling, think we may have larks.
I'll tell you of more, and lie, so you will come,
   Of partridge, pheasant, woodcock, of which some
May yet be there; and godwit, if we can,
   Gnat, rail, and ruff too. Howsoe'er, my man   20
Shall read a piece of Virgil, Tacitus,
   Livy, or of some better book to us,
Of which we'll speak our minds amidst our meat;
   And I'll profess no verses to repeat;
To this, if aught appear which I know not of,
   That will the pastry, not my paper, show of.
Digestive cheese, and fruit there sure will be;
   But that which most doth take my muse, and me,
Is a pure cup of rich Canary wine,
   Which is the Mermaid's now, but shall be mine;   30
Of which had Horace or Anacreon tasted,
   Their lives, as do their lines, till now had lasted.
Tobacco, nectar, or the Thespian springs
   Are all but Luther's beer to this I sing.
Of this we will sup free, but moderately,
   And we will have no polly, or parrot by;
Nor shall our cups make any guilty men,
   But at our parting we will be as when
We innocently met. No simple word
   That shall be uttered at our mirthful board
Shall make us sad next morning, or affright
   The liberty that we'll enjoy to-night.

On my first son

Farewell, thou child of my right hand, and joy;
   My sin was too much hope of thee, loved boy.
Seven years thou wert lent to me, and I thee pay,
   Exacted by thy fate, on the just day.
Oh, could I lose all father now! For why
   Will man lament the state he should envý?
To have so soon 'scaped world's and flesh's rage,
   And if no other misery, yet age!
Rest in soft peace, and asked, say, Here doth lie
   Ben Jonson his best piece of poetry.   10
For whose sake henceforth all his vows be such
   As what he loves may never like too much.

An epitaph on S[alomon] P[avy], a child of Q[ueen]
El[izabeth's] Chapel

Weep with me, all you that read
    This little story;
And know, for whom a tear you shed
    Death's self is sorry.
'Twas a child that so did thrive
    In grace and feature,
As heaven and nature seemed to strive
    Which owned the creature.
Years he numbered scarce thirteen
    When fates turned cruel,   10
Yet three filled zodiacs had he been
    The stage's jewel;
And did act, what now we moan,
    Old men so duly,
As, sooth, the Parcæ thought him one,
    He played so truly.
So by error, to his fate
    They all consented;
But viewing him since, alas too late,
    They have repented,   20
And have sought, to give new birth,
    In baths to steep him;
But being so much too good for earth,
    Heaven vows to keep him.

Epitaph on Elizabeth, L. H.

Wouldst thou hear what man can say
    In a little? Reader, stay.
Underneath this stone doth lie
    As much beauty as could die;
Which in life did harbor give
    To more virtue than doth live.
If at all she had a fault,
    Leave it buried in this vault.
One name was Elizabeth,
    Th' other let it sleep with death;   10
Fitter, where it died to tell,
    Than that it lived at all. Farewell.

THE FOREST

Why I write not of Love

Some act of Love's bound to rehearse,
I thought to bind him in my verse;
Which when he felt, Away, quoth he,
Can poets hope to fetter me?
It is enough they once did get
Mars and my mother in their net;
I wear not these my wings in vain.
With which he fled me, and again
Into my rhymes could ne'er be got
By any art. Then wonder not   10
That since my numbers are so cold,
When Love is fled, and I grow old.

To Penshurst

Thou art not, Penshurst, built to envious show
    Of touch or marble, nor canst boast a row
Of polished pillars, or a roof of gold;
    Thou hast no lantern whereof tales are told,
Or stairs or courts; but stand'st an ancient pile,
    And these, grudged at, art reverenced the while.
Thou joy'st in better marks, of soil, of air,
    Of wood, of water; therein thou art fair.
Thou hast thy walks for health as well as sport;
    Thy mount, to which the Dryads do resort,   10
Where Pan and Bacchus their high feasts have made
    Beneath the broad beech, and the chestnut shade,
That taller tree, which of a nut was set
    At his great birth, where all the Muses met.
There in the writhèd bark are cut the names
    Of many a sylvan, taken with his flames;
And thence the ruddy satyrs oft provoke
    The lighter fauns to reach thy Lady's oak.
Thy copse too, named of Gamage, thou hast there,
    That never fails to serve thee seasoned deer   20
When thou wouldst feast, or exercise thy friends.
    The lower land, that to the river bends,
Thy sheep, thy bullocks, kine, and calves do feed;
    The middle grounds thy mares and horses breed.
Each bank doth yield thee conies; and the tops,
    Fertile of wood, Ashore and Sidney's copse,
To crown thy open table, doth provide

The purpled pheasant with the speckled side;
The painted partridge lies in every field,
    And, for thy mess, is willing to be killed.   30
And if the high-swollen Medway fail thy dish,
    Thou hast thy ponds that pay thee tribute fish,
Fat aged carps that run into thy net,
    And pikes, now weary their own kind to eat,
As loath the second draught or cast to stay,
    Officiously at first themselves betray;
Bright eels that emulate them, and leap on land
    Before the fisher, or into his hand.
Then hath thy orchard fruit, thy garden flowers
    Fresh as the air, and new as are the hours.   40
The early cherry, with the later plum,
    Fig, grape, and quince, each in his time doth come;
The blushing apricot and woolly peach
    Hang on thy walls, that every child may reach.
And though thy walls be of the country stone,
    They'are reared with no man's ruin, no man's groan;
There's none that dwell about them wish them down,
    But all come in, the farmer and the clown,
And no one empty handed, to salute
    Thy lord and lady, though they have no suit.   50
Some bring a capon, some a rural cake,
    Some nuts, some apples; some that think they make
The better cheeses bring 'em, or else send
    By their ripe daughters whom they would commend
This way to husbands, and whose baskets bear
    An emblem of themselves in plum or pear.
But what can this, more than express their love,
    Add to thy free provisions, far above
The need of such, whose liberal board doth flow
    With all that hospitality doth know?   60
Where comes no guest but is allowed to eat,
    Without his fear, and of thy lord's own meat;
Where the same beer and bread, and self-same wine
    That is his lordship's shall be also mine.
And I not fain to sit, as some this day
    At great men's tables, and yet dine away.
Here no man tells my cups, nor, standing by,
    A waiter doth my gluttony envý,
But gives me what I call and lets me eat;
    He knows below he shall find plenty of meat.   70
Thy tables hoard not up for the next day,
    Nor when I take my lodging need I pray
For fire or lights or livery; all is there

As if thou then wert mine, or I reigned here;
　There's nothing I can wish, for which I stay.
That found King James, when hunting late this way
　With his brave son, the prince, they saw thy fires
　Shine bright on every hearth as the desires
Of thy Penates had been set on flame
　To entertain them, or the country came
With all their zeal to warm their welcome here.
　What great I will not say, but sudden cheer
Didst thou then make 'em! and what praise was heaped
　On thy good lady then! who therein reaped
The just reward of her high huswifery;
　To have her linen, plate, and all things nigh
When she was far, and not a room but dressed
　As if it had expected such a guest!
These, Penshurst, are thy praise, and yet not all.
　Thy lady's noble, fruitful, chaste withal;
His children thy great lord may call his own,
　A fortune in this age but rarely known.
They are and have been taught religion; thence
　Their gentler spirits have sucked innocence.
Each morn and even they are taught to pray
　With the whole household, and may every day
Read, in their virtuous parents' noble parts,
　The mysteries of manners, arms, and arts.
Now, Penshurst, they that will proportion thee
　With other edifices when they see
Those proud, ambitious heaps and nothing else,
　May say, their lords have built, but thy lord dwells.

80

90

100

Song, to Celia [*1*]

Come, my Celia, let us prove
While we may the sports of love;
Time will not be ours forever,
He at length our good will sever.
Spend not then his gifts in vain;
Suns that set may rise again,
But if once we lose this light,
'Tis with us perpetual night.
Why should we defer our joys?

Fame and rumor are but toys.
Cannot we delude the eyes
Of a few poor household spies?
Or his easier ears beguile,
So removèd by our wile?
'Tis no sin love's fruit to steal;
But the sweet theft to reveal,
To be taken, to be seen,
These have crimes accounted been.

10

Song, to Celia [*2*]

Drink to me only with thine
　　eyes,
And I will pledge with mine;
Or leave a kiss but in the cup,

And I'll not look for wine.
The thirst that from the soul doth
　　rise
Doth ask a drink divine;

But might I of Jove's nectar sup,
  I would not change for thine.
I sent thee late a rosy wreath,
  Not so much honoring thee,   10
As giving it a hope that there
  It could not withered be.

But thou thereon didst only
  breathe,
  And sent'st it back to me,
Since when it grows and smells, I
  swear,
  Not of itself, but thee.

FROM *The Works of Benjamin Jonson,* 1641

UNDERWOODS

A celebration of Charis in ten lyric pieces

His excuse for loving

Let it not your wonder move,
Less your laughter, that I love.
Though I now write fifty years,
I have had, and have, my peers;
Poets though divine are men,
Some have loved as old again.
And it is not always face,
Clothes, or fortune, gives the grace,
Or the feature, or the youth;
But the language and the truth,   10
With the ardor and the passion,
Gives the lover weight and fash-
    ion.

If you then will read the story,
First prepare you to be sorry
That you never knew till now
Either whom to love, or how;
But be glad, as soon with me,
When you know that this is she
Of whose beauty it was sung:
She shall make the old man
  young,   20
Keep the middle age at stay,
And let nothing high decay;
Till she be the reason why
All the world for love may die.

Her triumph

See the chariot at hand here of love,
  Wherein my lady rideth!
Each that draws is a swan or a dove,
  And well the car love guideth.
As she goes all hearts do duty
    Unto her beauty,
And enamoured do wish so they might
    But enjoy such a sight,
That they still were to run by her side,
Through swords, through seas, whither she would ride.   10

Do but look on her eyes; they do light
  All that love's world compriseth!
Do but look on her hair; it is bright
  As love's star when it riseth!
Do but mark, her forehead's smoother
    Than words that soothe her;

And from her arched brows, such a grace
   Sheds itself through the face,
As alone there triumphs to the life
All the gain, all the good of the elements' strife.   20

Have you seen but a bright lily grow
   Before rude hands have touched it?
Ha' you marked but the fall o' the snow
   Before the soil hath smutched it?
Ha' you felt the wool of beaver,
   Or swan's down ever?
Or have smelt o' the bud o' the briar?
   Or the nard in the fire?
Or have tasted the bag of the bee?
O so white! O so soft! O so sweet is she!   30

Begging another [kiss], on color of mending the former

For love's sake, kiss me once again;
  I long, and should not beg in vain,
    Here's none to spy or see;
     Why do you doubt or stay?
  I'll taste as lightly as the bee
That doth but touch his flower and flies away.
  Once more, and faith I will be gone;
  Can he that loves ask less than one?
    Nay, you may err in this
     And all your bounty wrong;   10
    This could be called but half a kiss,
What we're but once to do, we should do long.
  I will but mend the last, and tell
  Where, how it would have relished well;
    Join lip to lip, and try,
     Each suck other's breath.
  And whilst our tongues perplexëd lie,
Let who will, think us dead or wish our death.

An ode to himself

Where dost thou careless lie,
  Buried in ease and sloth?
Knowledge that sleeps doth
    die;
And this security,
  It is the common moth
That eats on wits and arts, and
    destroys them both.

Are all th' Aonian springs
  Dried up? Lies Thespia
    waste?
Doth Clarius' harp want
    strings,
That not a nymph now
    sings?   10
Or droop they as disgraced,

To see their seats and bowers by
    chatt'ring pies de-
    faced?

If hence thy silence be,
    As 'tis too just a cause,
Let this thought quicken thee:
Minds that are great and free
Should not on fortune
    pause;
'Tis crown enough to virtue still,
    her own applause.

What though the greedy fry
Be taken with false baits   20
Of worded balladry,
And think it poesy?
    They die with their con-
    ceits,

And only piteous scorn upon their
    folly waits.

Then take in hand thy lyre,
    Strike in thy proper strain,
With Japhet's line aspire
Sol's chariot for new fire
    To give the world again;
Who aided him, will thee, the issue
    of Jove's brain.   30

And since our dainty age
    Cannot endure reproof,
Make not thyself a page
To that strumpet, the stage,
    But sing high and aloof,
Safe from the wolf's black jaw,
    and the dull ass's
    hoof.

A fit of rhyme against rhyme

Rhyme, the rack of finest wits,
That expresseth but by fits
    True conceit,
Spoiling senses of their treasure,
Cozening judgment with a meas-
    ure,
    But false weight;
Wresting words from their true
    calling,
Propping verse for fear of falling
    To the ground;
Jointing syllabes, drowning let-
    ters,   10
Fast'ning vowels as with fetters
    They were bound!
Soon as lazy thou wert known,
All good poetry hence was
    flown,
    And are banished.
For a thousand years together
All Parnassus' green did wither,
    And wit vanished.
Pegasus did fly away,
At the wells no Muse did stay,   20
    But bewailed
So to see the fountain dry,

And Apollo's music die,
    All light failed!
Starveling rhymes did fill the
    stage;
Not a poet in an age
    Worth crowning;
Not a work deserving bays,
Not a line deserving praise,
    Pallas frowning;   30
Greek was free from rhyme's in-
    fection,
Happy Greek by this protection
    Was not spoiled.
Whilst the Latin, queen of tongues,
Is not yet free from rhyme's
    wrongs,
    But rests foiled.
Scarce the hill again doth flourish,
Scarce the world a wit doth nourish
    To restore
Phœbus to his crown again,   40
And the Muses to their brain,
    As before.
Vulgar languages that want
Words and sweetness, and be scant
    Of true measure,

Tyrant rhyme hath so abusëd,
That they long since have refusëd
Other cæsure.
He that first invented thee,
May his joints tormented be,   50
Cramped forever.
Still may syllabes jar with time,

Still may reason war with rhyme,
Resting never.
May his sense when it would meet
The cold tumor in his feet,
Grow unsounder;
And his title be long fool,
That in rearing such a school
Was the founder.   60

To the immortal memory and friendship of that noble pair, Sir Lucius Cary and Sir H. Morison

THE TURN

Brave infant of Saguntum, clear
Thy coming forth in that great year
When the prodigious Hannibal did crown
His rage with razing your immortal town.
Thou, looking then about,
Ere thou wert half got out,
Wise child, didst hastily return
And mad'st thy mother's womb thine urn.
How summed a circle didst thou leave mankind,
Of deepest lore, could we the center find!   10

THE COUNTER-TURN

Did wiser nature draw thee back
From out the horror of that sack,
Where shame, faith, honor, and regard of right
Lay trampled on? The deeds of death and night
Urged, hurried forth, and hurled
Upon th' affrighted world;
Sword, fire, and famine with fell fury met,
And all on utmost ruin set;
As, could they but life's miseries foresee,
No doubt all infants would return like thee.   20

THE STAND

For what is life, if measured by the space,
Not by the act?
Or maskëd man, if valued by his face,
Above his fact?
Here's one outlived his peers,
And told forth fourscore years;
He vexëd time, and busied the whole state,
Troubled both foes and friends,

But ever to no ends;
What did this stirrer but die late?　　　　　30
How well at twenty had he fallen or stood!
For three of his fourscore he did no good.

THE TURN

He entered well, by virtuous parts
Got up, and thrived with honest arts;
He purchased friends and fame, and honors then,
And had his noble name advanced with men.
But weary of that flight,
He stooped in all men's sight
To sordid flatteries, acts of strife,
And sunk in that dead sea of life　　　　　40
So deep as he did then death's waters sup,
But that the cork of title buoyed him up.

THE COUNTER-TURN

Alas, but Morison fell young!
He never fell,—thou fall'st, my tongue.
He stood, a soldier to the last right end,
A perfect patriot and a noble friend,
But most, a virtuous son.
All offices were done
By him so ample, full, and round,
In weight, in measure, number, sound,　　　　　50
As, though his age imperfect might appear,
His life was of humanity the sphere.

THE STAND

Go now, and tell out days summed up with fears,
And make them years;
Produce thy mass of miseries on the stage,
To swell thine age;
Repeat of things a throng,
To show thou hast been long,
Not lived, for life doth her great actions spell
By what was done and wrought　　　　　60
In season, and so brought
To light; her measures are, how well
Each syllabe answered, and was formed how fair;
These make the lines of life, and that's her air.

THE TURN

It is not growing like a tree
In bulk, doth make man better be;

Or standing long an oak, three hundred year,
To fall a log at last, dry, bald, and sere;
A lily of a day
Is fairer far in May,   70
Although it fall and die that night,
It was the plant and flower of light.
In small proportions we just beauties see;
And in short measures, life may perfect be.

THE COUNTER-TURN

Call, noble Lucius, then for wine,
And let thy looks with gladness shine;
Accept this garland, plant it on thy head,
And think, nay know, thy Morison's not dead.
He leaped the present age,
Possessed with holy rage,   80
To see that bright eternal day
Of which we priests and poets say
Such truths as we expect for happy men,
And there he lives with memory, and Ben

THE STAND

Jonson, who sung this of him, ere he went
Himself to rest,
Or taste a part of that full joy he meant
To have expressed
In this bright asterism,
Where it were friendship's schism,   90
Were not his Lucius long with us to tarry,
To separate these twi-
Lights, the Dioscuri,
And keep the one half from his Harry.
But fate doth so alternate the design,
Whilst that in heav'n, this light on earth must shine.

THE TURN

And shine as you exalted are,
Two names of friendship, but one star;
Of hearts the union, and those not by chance
Made, or indenture, or leased out t' advance   100
The profits for a time.
No pleasures vain did chime
Of rhymes, or riots at your feasts,
Orgies of drink, or feigned protests;

But simple love of greatness and of good,
That knits brave minds and manners more than blood.

THE COUNTER-TURN

This made you first to know the why
You liked, then after to apply
That liking; and approach so one the t' other
Till either grew a portion of the other;   110
Each stylëd by his end
The copy of his friend.
You lived to be the great surnames
And titles by which all made claims
Unto the virtue; nothing perfect done
But as a Cary, or a Morison.

THE STAND

And such a force the fair example had,
As they that saw
The good, and durst not practise it, were glad
That such a law   120
Was left yet to mankind,
Where they might read and find
Friendship in deed was written, not in words;
And with the heart, not pen,
Of two so early men,
Whose lines her rolls were, and recórds;
Who, ere the first down bloomëd on the chin,
Had sowed these fruits, and got the harvest in.

An epistle answering to one that asked to be sealed of the Tribe of Ben

Men that are safe and sure in all they do,
    Care not what trials they are put unto;
They meet the fire, the test, as martyrs would,
    And though opinion stamp them not, are gold.
I could say more of such, but that I fly
    To speak myself out too ambitiously,
And showing so weak an act to vulgar eyes
    Put conscience and my right to compromise.
Let those that merely talk and never think,
    That live in the wild anarchy of drink,   10
Subject to quarrel only, or else such
    As make it their proficiency how much
They've glutted in and lechered out that week,

That never yet did friend or friendship seek
But for a sealing—let these men protest.
    Or th' other on their borders, that will jest
On all souls that are absent, even the dead,
    Like flies or worms, which man's corrupt parts fed;
That to speak well, think it above all sin,
    Of any company but that they are in,   20
Call every night to supper in these fits
    And are received for the covey of wits;
That censure all the town and all th' affairs,
    And know whose ignorance is more than theirs,—
Let these men have their ways, and take their times
    To vent their libels and to issue rhymes;
I have no portion in them, nor their deal
    Of news they get to strew out the long meal;
I study other friendships, and more one
    Than these can ever be, or else with none.   30
What is 't to me whether the French design
    Be, or be not, to get the Valteline?
Or the States' ships sent forth belike to meet
    Some hopes of Spain in their West Indian fleet?
Whether the dispensation yet be sent,
    Or that the match from Spain was ever meant?
I wish all well, and pray high heaven conspire
    My prince's safety and my king's desire;
But if for honor we must draw the sword,
    And force back that which will not be restored,   40
I have a body yet that spirit draws
    To live, or fall a carcass, in the cause.
So far without enquiries what the States,
    Brunsfield, and Mansfield do this year, my fates
Shall carry me at call, and I'll be well,
    Though I do neither hear these news, nor tell
Of Spain or France, or were not pricked down one
    Of the late mystery of reception,
Although my fame to his not under-hears,
    That guides the motions and directs the bears.   50
But that's a blow by which in time I may
    Lose all my credit with my Christmas clay,
And animated porcelain of the court;
    Ay, and for this neglect, the coarser sort
Of earthen jars there may molest me too.
    Well, with mine own frail pitcher, what to do
I have decreed; keep it from waves and press,
    Lest it be jostled, cracked, made nought or less;
Live to that point I will for which I am man,

And dwell as in my center as I can,
Still looking to and ever loving heaven,
  With reverence using all the gifts then given;
'Mongst which, if I have any friendships sent
  Such as are square, well-tagged, and permanent,
Not built with canvas, paper, and false lights
  As are the glorious scenes at the great sights,
And that there be no fev'ry heats nor colds,
  Oily expansions, or shrunk dirty folds,
But all so clear, and led by reason's flame,
  As but to stumble in her sight were shame,—
These I will honor, love, embrace, and serve,
  And free it from all question to preserve.
So short you read my character, and theirs
  I would call mine, to which not many stairs
Are asked to climb. First give me faith, who know
  Myself a little; I will take you so
As you have writ yourself. Now stand; and then,
  Sir, you are sealed of the Tribe of Ben.

FROM *Mr. William Shakespeare's Comedies, Histories, and
Tragedies,* 1623

*To the memory of my beloved the author,
Mr. William Shakespeare, and what he hath left us*

To draw no envy, Shakespeare, on thy name,
  Am I thus ample to thy book and fame,
While I confess thy writings to be such
  As neither man nor Muse can praise too much;
'Tis true, and all men's suffrage. But these ways
  Were not the paths I meant unto thy praise,
For seeliest ignorance on these may light,
  Which when it sounds at best but echoes right;
Or blind affection which doth ne'er advance
  The truth, but gropes and urgeth all by chance;
Or crafty malice might pretend this praise,
  And think to ruin where it seemed to raise.
These are as some infamous bawd or whore
  Should praise a matron; what could hurt her more?
But thou art proof against them, and indeed
  Above th' ill fortune of them, or the need.
I, therefore, will begin. Soul of the age!
  The applause, delight, the wonder of our stage!
My Shakespeare, rise; I will not lodge thee by

Chaucer, or Spenser, or bid Beaumont lie   20
  A little further to make thee a room;
    Thou art a monument, without a tomb,
  And art alive still, while thy book doth live
    And we have wits to read and praise to give.
That I not mix thee so, my brain excuses—
  I mean with great but disproportioned muses,—
For if I thought my judgment were of years
  I should commit thee surely with thy peers,
And tell how far thou didst our Lyly outshine,
  Or sporting Kyd, or Marlowe's mighty line.   30
And though thou hadst small Latin and less Greek,
  From thence to honor thee I would not seek
For names, but call forth thund'ring Æschylus,
  Euripides, and Sophocles to us,
Pacuvius, Accius, him of Cordova dead,
  To life again, to hear thy buskin tread
And shake a stage; or, when thy socks were on,
  Leave thee alone for the comparison
Of all that insolent Greece or haughty Rome
  Sent forth, or since did from their ashes come.   40
Triumph, my Britain, thou hast one to show
  To whom all scenes of Europe homage owe.
He was not of an age, but for all time!
  And all the Muses still were in their prime,
When like Apollo he came forth to warm
  Our ears, or like a Mercury to charm!
Nature herself was proud of his designs,
  And joyed to wear the dressing of his lines
Which were so richly spun, and woven so fit,
  As since, she will vouchsafe no other wit;   50
The merry Greek, tart Aristophanes,
  Neat Terence, witty Plautus, now not please,
But antiquated and deserted lie
  As they were not of nature's family.
Yet must I not give nature all; thy art,
  My gentle Shakespeare, must enjoy a part;
For though the poet's matter nature be,
  His art doth give the fashion; and that he
Who casts to write a living line, must sweat,
  Such as thine are, and strike the second heat   60
Upon the Muses' anvil, turn the same,
  And himself with it, that he thinks to frame;
Or for the laurel he may gain a scorn,
  For a good poet's made, as well as born;
And such wert thou. Look how the father's face

Lives in his issue; even so the race
Of Shakespeare's mind and manners brightly shines
　In his well-turnëd and true-filëd lines,
In each of which he seems to shake a lance,
　As brandished at the eyes of ignorance.　　　70
Sweet swan of Avon! what a sight it were
　To see thee in our waters yet appear,
And make those flights upon the banks of Thames
　That so did take Eliza, and our James!
But stay, I see thee in the hemisphere
　Advanced, and made a constellation there!
Shine forth, thou star of poets, and with rage
　Or influence chide or cheer the drooping stage;
Which since thy flight from hence, hath mourned like night,
　And despairs day, but for thy volume's light.　　80

FROM ALEXANDER BROME'S *Songs and other Poems*, 1661

Ben Jonson's Sociable Rules for the Apollo

[A translation of Jonson's *Leges Convivales*]

Let none but guests or clubbers hither come,
Let dunces, fools, sad sordid men, keep home;
Let learned, civil, merry men b'invited,
And modest too; nor the choice ladies slighted.
Let nothing in the treat offend the guests;
More for delight than cost prepare the feasts.
The cook and purveyor must our palates know;
And none contend who shall sit high or low.
Our waiters must quick-sighted be and dumb,
And let the drawers hear and come.　　　10
Let not our wine be mixed, but brisk and neat,
Or else the drinkers may the vintners beat.
And let our only emulation be,
Not drinking much, but talking wittily.
Let it be voted lawful to stir up
Each other with a moderate chirping cup.
Let not our company be, or talk, too much;
On serious things or sacred let's not touch
With sated heads and bellies. Neither may
Fiddlers unasked obtrude themselves to play;　　20
With laughing, leaping, dancing, jests and songs,
And whate'er else to grateful mirth belongs,
Let's celebrate our feasts; and let us see
That all our jests without reflection be.
Insipid poems let no man rehearse,

Nor any be compelled to write a verse.
All noise of vain disputes must be forborne,
And let no lover in a corner mourn.
To fight and brawl, like Hectors, let none dare,
Glasses or windows break, or hangings tear.   30
Whoe'er shall publish what's here done or said
From our society must be banishëd.
Let none by drinking do or suffer harm,
And while we stay, let us be always warm.

[SONGS FROM THE PLAYS AND MASKS]

From *The Works of Benjamin Jonson*, 1616

[Slow, slow, fresh fount]

Slow, slow, fresh fount, keep time with my salt tears;
   Yet slower yet, oh faintly, gentle springs;
List to the heavy part the music bears,
   Woe weeps out her division when she sings.
     Droop herbs and flowers,
     Fall grief in showers;
     Our beauties are not ours;
      Oh, I could still,
Like melting snow upon some craggy hill,
    Drop, drop, drop, drop,   10
Since nature's pride is now a withered daffodil.

From Cynthia's Revels

[Oh, that joy so soon should waste]

Oh, that joy so soon should waste!
   Or so sweet a bliss
   As a kiss
Might not forever last!
So sugared, so melting, so soft, so delicious!
   The dew that lies on roses
When morn herself discloses,
   Is not so precious.
Oh, rather than I would it smother,
Were I to taste such another,   10
   It should be my wishing
   That I might die kissing.

From Cynthia's Revels

[Queen and huntress]

Queen and huntress, chaste and fair,
Now the sun is laid to sleep,

Seated in thy silver chair
State in wonted manner keep;
 Hesperus entreats thy light,
 Goddess excellently bright.

Earth, let not thy envious shade
Dare itself to interpose;
Cynthia's shining orb was made
Heaven to clear, when day did close;
 Bless us then with wishèd sight,
 Goddess excellently bright.

Lay thy bow of pearl apart,
And thy crystal shining quiver;
Give unto the flying hart
Space to breathe, how short soever,
 Thou that mak'st a day of night,
 Goddess excellently bright.

From Cynthia's Revels

[*If I freely may discover*]

If I freely may discover
What would please me in my lover:
 I would have her fair and witty,
 Savoring more of court than city;
 A little proud, but full of pity;
 Light and humorous in her toying,
 Oft building hopes and soon destroying;
 Long, but sweet, in the enjoying;
Neither too easy, nor too hard,
All extremes I would have barred.

She should be allowed her passions,
So they were but used as fashions;
 Sometimes froward, and then frowning,
 Sometimes sickish, and then swowning,
 Every fit with change still crowning.
 Purely jealous I would have her;
 Then only constant when I crave her,
 'Tis a virtue should not save her.
Thus, nor her delicates would cloy me,
Neither her peevishness annoy me.

From The Poetaster

[*Swell me a bowl*]

Swell me a bowl with lusty wine,
Till I may see the plump Lyæus swim
　　Above the brim;
I drink as I would write,
In flowing measure, filled with flame and sprite.

From The Poetaster

[*Fools*]

Fools, they are the only nation
Worth men's envy or admiration,
Free from care or sorrow-taking,
Selves and others merry making;
All they speak or do is sterling.
Your fool he is your great man's darling,
And your lady's sport and pleasure;
Tongue and babble are his treasure,
E'en his face begetteth laughter,
And he speaks truth free from slaughter;　　　10
He's the grace of every feast,
And sometimes the chiefest guest
Hath his trencher and his stool,
When wit waits upon the fool.
　　Oh, who would not be
　　He, he, he?

From Volpone, or the Fox

[*Still to be neat*]

Still to be neat, still to be dressed
As you were going to a feast;
Still to be powdered, still perfumed:
Lady, it is to be presumed,
Though art's hid causes are not found,
All is not sweet, all is not sound.

Give me a look, give me a face
That makes simplicity a grace;
Robes loosely flowing, hair as free:
Such sweet neglect more taketh me　　　10
Than all th' adulteries of art;
They strike mine eyes, but not my heart.

From Epicœne, or the Silent Woman

[*Had those that dwell in error foul*]

Had those that dwell in error foul
And hold that women have no soul,
But seen these move, they would have then
Said, Women were the souls of men.
　So they do move each heart and eye
　With the world's soul, true harmony.

From *The Second Mask, which was of Beauty*

[*Beauties, have ye seen*]

1 Grace.　Beauties, have ye seen
　　　this toy
Called Love, a little boy,
Almost naked, wanton, blind,
Cruel now, and then as kind?
If he be amongst ye, say;
He is Venus' runaway.

2 Grace.　She that will but now
　　　discover
Where the wingèd wag doth
　　　hover,
Shall to-night receive a kiss
How or where herself would
　　　wish;　　　　　　10
But who brings him to his
　　　mother,
Shall have that kiss and
　　　another.

3 Grace.　H' hath of marks about
　　　him plenty;
You shall know him among
　　　twenty.
All his body is a fire,
And his breath a flame entire,
That being shot like light-
　　　ning in,
Wounds the heart, but not
　　　the skin.

1 Grace.　At his sight the sun
　　　hath turned,
Neptune in the waters
　　　burned,　　　　　　20

Hell hath felt a greater heat,
Jove himself forsook his seat;
From the center to the sky
Are his trophies rearèd high.

2 Grace.　Wings he hath, which
　　　though ye clip,
He will leap from lip to lip,
Over liver, lights, and heart,
But not stay in any part;
And if chance his arrow
　　　misses,
He will shoot himself in
　　　kisses.　　　　　　30

3 Grace.　He doth bear a golden
　　　bow,
And a quiver, hanging low,
Full of arrows that out-brave
Dian's shafts; where if he
　　　have
Any head more sharp than
　　　other,
With that first he strikes his
　　　mother.

1 Grace.　Still the fairest are his
　　　fuel.
When his days are to be cruel,
Lovers' hearts are all his food,
And his baths their warmest
　　　blood;　　　　　　40
Nought but wounds his hand
　　　doth season,
And he hates none like to
　　　reason.

2 Grace. Trust him not; his
    words, though sweet,
Seldom with his heart do
    meet.
All his practice is deceit;
Every gift it is a bait;
Not a kiss but poison bears,
And most treason in his tears.

3 Grace. Idle minutes are his
    reign,
Then the straggler makes his
    gain   50
By presenting maids with
    toys,
And would have ye think 'em
    joys;

'Tis the ambition of the elf
To have all childish as him-
    self.

1 Grace. If by these ye please to
    know him,
Beauties, be not nice, but
    show him.

2 Grace. Though ye had a will
    to hide him,
Now, we hope, ye'll not abide
    him.

3 Grace. Since ye hear his falser
    play,
And that he is Venus' run-
    away.   60

From *The Description of the Mask . . . at
the Lord Viscount Hadington's Marriage*

[*Buz, quoth the blue fly*]

Buz, quoth the blue fly,
    Hum, quoth the bee;
Buz and hum they cry,
    And so do we.
In his ear, in his nose,
    Thus, do you see?
He eat the dormouse,
    Else it was he.

From *Oberon, the Fairy Prince*

FROM *The Works of Benjamin Jonson,* 1641

[*The fairy beam upon you*]

The fairy beam upon you,
The stars to glister on you;
    A moon of light
    In the noon of night,
Till the fire-drake hath o'ergone you.
The wheel of fortune guide you,
The boy with the bow beside you;
    Run aye in the way
    Till the bird of day,
And the luckier lot betide you.

From *The Gypsies Metamorphosed*

[*Thus, thus begin*]

1 Nymph. Thus, thus begin the yearly rites
Are due to Pan on these bright nights;
His morn now riseth, and invites
To sports, to dances, and delights;
    All envious and profane away,
    This is the shepherds' holy-day.

2 Nymph. Strew, strew the glad and smiling ground
With every flower, yet not confound
The primrose-drop, the spring's own spouse,
Bright daisies, and the lips of cows,   10
    The garden-star, the queen of May,
    The rose, to crown the holy-day.

3 Nymph. Drop, drop, you violets, change your hues,
Now red, now pale, as lovers use,
And in your death go out as well
As when you lived unto the smell;
    That from your odor all may say,
    This is the shepherds' holy-day.

From *Pan's Anniversary*

[*Here she was wont to go*]

Here she was wont to go, and here! and here!
Just where those daisies, pinks, and violets grow;
The world may find the spring by following her,
For other print her airy steps ne'er left;
Her treading would not bend a blade of grass!
Or shake the downy blow-ball from his stalk!
But like the soft west-wind she shot along,
And where she went the flowers took thickest root,
As she had sowed 'em with her odorous foot.

From *The Sad Shepherd*

[*Though I am young*]

Though I am young and cannot tell
  Either what death or love is well,
Yet I have heard they both bear darts,
  And both do aim at human hearts.
And then again I have been told
  Love wounds with heat, as death with cold;
So that I fear they do but bring
  Extremes to touch, and mean one thing.

As in a ruin we it call
   One thing to be blown up, or fall;   10
Or to our end, like way may have
   By a flash of lightning or a wave;
So love's inflaměd shaft or brand
   May kill as soon as death's cold hand;
Except love's fires the virtue have
   To fright the frost out of the grave.

                From *The Sad Shepherd*

EPIGRAMS

The Introduction and Notes are at pages 1267 and 1279

FROM TIMOTHE KENDALL'S *Flowers of Epigrams,* 1577

To Sabidius

I love thee not, Sabidius,
   I can not tell thee why;
I can say nought but this alone,—
   I do not love thee, I.

To Fidentinus

The book which thou dost read, it is,
   Friend Fidentinus, mine;
But when thou ill dost read it, then
   Begins it to be thine.

To a married couple that could not agree

Sith that you both are like in life—
   A naughty man, a wicked wife,—
I muse ye live not void of strife.

Of Fuscus, a drunkard

A certain man in physic skilled
   To F. spake in this wise:
F., drink not overmuch; take heed!
   For drink will lose your eyes.
He paused upon this sentence given,
   And pondered what was spoke,
And when he had bethought him, thus
   At last his mind he broke:
I will by drinking lose mine eyes!

Quoth he, 'tis better so
Than for to keep them for the worms
To gnaw them out below.

Of Alphus

No egg on Friday Alph will eat,
　　But drunken he will be
On Friday still. Oh, what a pure
　　Religious man is he!

To the reader

Take in good part these trifling toys,
　　Good reader, which I write;
Whenas I was a boy with boys
　　These toys I did indite.
Tush, tush, they foolish are! thou sayst.
　　I grant they are indeed:
But where are thy wise wondrous works?
　　Now where are they to read?

From Sir John Harington's *Elegant and Witty Epigrams*, 1618

Comparison of the sonnet and the epigram

Once by mishap two poets fell a-squaring,
The sonnet and our epigram comparing;
And Faustus, having long demurred upon it,
Yet at the last gave sentence for the sonnet.
Now for such censure this his chief defence is,
Their sugared taste best likes his lick'rous senses.
　　Well, though I grant sugar may please the taste,
　　Yet let my verse have salt to make it last.

Against writers that carp at other men's books

The readers and the hearers like my books,
But yet some writers cannot them digest.
But what care I? For when I make a feast,
I would my guests should praise it, not the cooks.

Of Faustus, a stealer of verses

I heard that Faustus oftentimes rehearses
To his chaste mistress certain of my verses,
In which, with use, so perfect he is grown
That she, poor fool, now thinks they are his own.

I would esteem it (trust me) grace, not shame,
If Davies, or if Daniel, did the same,—
For would I thank, or would I quarrel pick?
I, when I list, could do to them the like.
But who can wish a man a fouler spite
Than have a blind man take away his light?　　　10
    A begging thief is dangerous to my purse;
    A baggage poet to my verse is worse.

Of treason

Treason doth never prosper; what's the reason?
For if it prosper, none dare call it treason.

To Sextus, an ill reader

That epigram that last you did rehearse
Was sharp, and in the making neat and terse;
But thou dost read so harsh, point so perverse,
It seemed now neither witty nor a verse.
    For shame point better and pronounce it clearer,
    Or be no reader, Sextus—be a hearer.

From *Additional Ms.* 12049

Of clergymen and their livings

In ancient time old men observëd that
The clergymen were lean, their livings fat;
But in these days the case is altered clean,
The clergymen are fat, their livings lean.
    I, searching, find this cause that change to breed,—
    Now they feed fast; then they did fast and feed.

                  [*Sir John Harington*]

To Mr. John Davies

My dear friend Davies, some against us partial
Have found we steal some good conceits from Martial;
So, though they grant our verse hath some acumen,
Yet make they fools suspect we scant are true men.
But Surrey did the same, and worthy Wyatt,
And they had praise and reputation by it;
And Heywood, whom your putting down hath raised,
Did use the same, and with the same is praised.
Wherefore, if they had wit that so did trace us,
They must again for their own credits grace us;　　　10

Or else to our more honor, and their grieves,
Match us, at least, with honorable thieves.

[*Sir John Harington*]

FROM EVERARD GUILPIN'S *Skialetheia*, 1598

Of Titus

Titus oft vaunts his gentry everywhere,
Blazoning his coat, deriving's pedigree.
What needest thou daily, Titus, jade mine ear?
I will believe thy house's ancestry:
If that be ancient which we do forget,
Thy gentry is so—none can remember it.

Of Cornelius

See you him yonder who sits o'er the stage
With the tobacco-pipe now at his mouth?
It is Cornelius, that brave gallant youth,
Who is new printed to this fangled age.
He wears a jerkin cudgeled with gold lace,
A profound slop, a hat scarce pipkin-high;
For boots a pair of dagge cases; his face
Furred with cad's-beard, his poniard on his thigh.
He wallows in his walk, his slop to grace;
Swears by the Lord, deigns no salutation   10
But to some jade that's sick of his own fashion,
As, Farewell, sweet captain, or, Boy, come apace.
Yet this Sir Bevis or the fairy knight
Put up the lie because he durst not fight.

Satyra quinta

Let me alone, I prithee, in this cell;
Entice me not into the city's hell;
Tempt me not forth this Eden of content
To taste of that which I shall soon repent.
Prithee, excuse me; I am not alone,
Accompanied with meditation
And calm content, whose taste more pleaseth me
Than all the city's luscious vanity.
I had rather be encoffined in this chest
Amongst these books and papers, I protest,   10
Than free-booting abroad purchase offence,
And scandal my calm thoughts with discontents.
Here I converse with those diviner spirits

Whose knowledge and admire the world inherits:
Here doth the famous profound Stagirite
With nature's mystic harmony delight
My ravished contemplation; I here see
The now-old world's youth in an history;
Here I may be grave Plato's auditor,
And learning of that moral lecturer   20
To temper mine affections, gallantly
Get of myself a glorious victory.
And then for change, as we delight in change
(For this my study is indeed m'Exchange),
Here may I sit, yet walk to Westminster
And hear Fitzherbert, Plowden, Brooke, and Dyer
Canvass a law-case; or, if my dispose
Persuade me to a play, I'll to the Rose
Or Curtain—one of Plautus' comedies
Or the pathetic Spaniard's tragedies.   30
If my desire doth rather with the fields,
Some speaking painter, some poet, straightway yields
A flower-bespangled walk, where I may hear
Some amorous swain his passïons declare
To his sun-burnt love. Thus my books' little case,
My study, is mine all, mine every place.

. . . .

FROM THOMAS BASTARD'S *Chrestoleros*, 1598

Ad lectorem

How quickly doth the reader pass away
My pen's long task and travail of the day!
Four lines which hold me tug an hour or twain
He sups up with a breath, and takes no pain.
Yet use me well, reader, which to procure
Thy one short pleasure two long pains endure:
   The one of writing, when it is begun,
   Th'other of shame if't please not when 'tis done.

_____

       The first and riper world of men and skill
       Yields to our later time for three inventions:
       Miraculously we write, we sail, we kill,
       As neither ancient scroll nor story mentions.
Print   The first hath opened learnings old concealed,
       And obscured arts restorëd to the light;
Lodestone The second hidden countries hath revealed,
       And sent Christ's gospel to each living wight.

These we commend, but oh, what needed more
Guns   To teach death more skill than it had before!   10

Lætus did in his mistress' quarrel die,
Quintus was slain defending of the lie,
Germanus in his friend's defence did fall,
Sakellus died striving for the wall,
Merus did spend his life upon a jest,
Sannius lost it at a drunken feast,
Mirus at Sunday's wake revenged the wrong
Of his bull-dog, until he lay along:
What sayst thou now, contemned religion?
Vice hath her saints and martyrs,—thou hast none.   10

De piscatione

Fishing, if I, a fisher, may protest,
Of pleasures is the sweet'st, of sports the best,
Of exercises the most excellent,
Of recreations the most innocent.
But now the sport is marred, and wot ye why?
Fishes decrease, and fishers multiply.

FROM JOHN WEEVER's *Epigrams in the Oldest Cut and Newest Fashion*, 1599

In Nigellum

If I should choose, yea, for my life,
To be thy hawk, Nigell, or wife,
I would the hawk choose of the one,—
She wears a hood, thy wife wears none.

De se

Some men marriage do commend
And all their life in wiving spend,
But if that I should wives have three
(God keep me from polygamy!)
   I'll give the devil two for pay
   If he will fetch the third away.

Translat. ex Martial

Sabidi, I love thee not, nor why I wot,
But this I wot, Sabidi: I love thee not.

In Rudionem

Yon goes a gallant which will get repute,
From head to heel in his carnation suit,
Slops, doublet, stockings, shoes, hat, band, and feather,
Red yard-long ribbon,—see, the youth comes hither;
Who, lest his Dutchman hose should be unseen,
Above his mid-thigh he his cloak doth pin.
   Oh, that he had to his carnation hose—
I wish him well—a fair, rich, crimson nose.

In tumulum Abrahami Simple

Within this place lies Abraham the Civil,
Who never did good, who never did evil,—
Too ill then for God, too good for the devil.

Ad Io. Marston & Ben. Ionson

Marston, thy muse enharbors Horace' vein,
Then some Augustus give thee Horace' merit;
And thine, embuskined Jonson, doth retain
So rich a style and wondrous gallant spirit
That, if to praise your muses I desired,
My muse would muse. Such wits must be admired.

Ad Gulielmum Shakespeare

Honey-tongued Shakespeare, when I saw thine issue,
I swore Apollo got them, and none other;
Their rosy-tainted features, clothed in tissue,
Some heaven-born goddess said to be their mother:
Rose-cheeked Adonis, with his amber tresses,
Fair fire-hot Venus charming him to love her;
Chaste Lucretia, virgin-like her dresses,
Proud lust-stung Tarquin, seeking still to prove her;
Romeo, Richard,—more, whose names I know not—
Their sugared tongues and power-attractive beauty
Say they are saints, although that saints they show not,
For thousands vows to them subjective duty;
They burn in love; thy children, Shakespeare, het them.
Go, woo thy muse, more nymphish brood beget them.

10

FROM SAMUEL ROWLANDS'S *Letting of Humor's Blood*, 1600

Severus is extreme in eloquence,
In perfumed words plunged over head and ears;

He doth create rare phrase, but rarer sense;
Fragments of Latin all about he bears.
Unto his serving-man, *alias* his boy,
He utters speech exceeding quaint and coy:
Diminutive, and my defective slave,
Reach my corps' coverture immediately.
My pleasure's pleasure is the same to have,
T'ensconce my person from frigidity.   10
His man believes all's Welsh his master spoke,
Till he rails English, Rogue, go fetch my cloak!

From Samuel Rowlands's *Humor's Looking-Glass*, 1608

A scholar newly entered marriage life,
Following his studies, did offend his wife;
Because when she his company expected
By bookish business she was still neglected.
Coming unto his study, Lord (quoth she),
Can papers cause you love them more than me?
I would I were transformed into a book,
That your affection might upon me look;
But in my wish withal be it decreed
I would be such a book you love to read.   10
Husband (quoth she), which book's form should I take?
Marry (said he), t'were best an almanake.
The reason wherefore I do wish thee so
Is, every year we have a new, you know.

From *Chetham Ms.* 8012

An epitaph on a bellows-maker

Here lies John Goddard, maker of bellows,
His craft's master, and king of good fellows;
But for all that, he came to his death,
For he that made bellows could not make breath.

[John Hoskins]

Of a cozener

And was not death a lusty struggler
In overthrowing James the Juggler?
His life so little truth did use
That here he lies—it is no news.

[John Hoskins]

An epitaph on a man for doing nothing

Here lies the man was born, and cried,
Told three-score years, fell sick, and died.

[*John Hoskins*]

FROM *Reliquiæ Wottonianæ*, 1672

John Hoskins to his little child Benjamin, from the Tower

Sweet Benjamin, since thou art young
And hast not yet the use of tongue,
Make it thy slave, while thou art free,—
Imprison it, lest it do thee.

[*John Hoskins*]

FROM *Chetham Ms.* 8012

In Chus

Chus doth so often to the doctor go,
To know whether he be in health or no,
That shortly if his friend chance to pass by
And ask him how he doth, in courtesy,
He will not answer him a point so nice
Until he hath had his doctor's advice.

In Norgum

Mistaking brains praise Norgus' wit for great,
Because great store of jests he can repeat;
When 'tis his memory deserveth most
For hoarding up what witty men have lost.
And who knows not that these two always hit—
A great memory and a little wit?

FROM HENRY PARROT'S *Mouse-Trap*, 1606

Peter hath lost his purse, but will conceal it,
Lest she that stole it to his shame reveal it.

———

Paulus a pamphlet doth in prose present
   Unto his lord,—the fruits of idle time—
Who, far more careless than therewith content,
   Wishèd he would convert it into rhyme.
Which done, and brought him at another season,
Said, Now 'tis rhyme—before nor rhyme nor reason.

———

Magus would needs, forsooth, this other day
Upon an idle humor see a play;
When asking him at door that held the box,
What might you call the play? Quoth he, *The Fox.*
In goes my gen-man (who could judge of wit),
And being askèd how he likèd it,
Said, All was ill—both fox and him that played it.
But was not he, think you, a goose that said it?

From Henry Parrot's *Epigrams,* 1608

Ortus novus urbe Britannus

Who braves it now as doth young Histrie
Walking in Paul's like to some potentate,
Richly replenished from the top to th' toe
As if he were derived from high estate?
Alas, there's not a man but may descry
His begging trade and bastard faculty.

Impar impares odit

Sotus hates wise men, for himself is none;
And fools he hates, because himself is one.

From Henry Parrot's *Laquei Ridiculosi,* 1613

Suum cuique pulchrum

Posthumus, not the last of many more,
Asks why I writ in such an idle vein,
Seeing there are of epigrams such store.
Oh, give me leave to tell thee once again
    That epigrams are fitted to the season
    Of such as best know how to make rhyme reason.

From Henry Parrot's *Mastive,* 1615

Nuptiæ post nummos

There was a time when men for love did marry
And not for lucre sake, as now we see;
Which from that former age so much doth vary
As all's for—what you'll give? or nought must be.
So that this ancient word called *matrimony*
Is wholly made *a matter now of money.*

Ebrius dissimulans

Battus, though bound from drinking wine of late,
Can thus far with his oath equivocate;
He will not drink, and yet be drunk ere noon—
His manner is to eat it with a spoon.

FROM JOHN HEATH'S *Two Centuries of Epigrams*, 1610

Ad modernos epigrammatistas

Heywood, th' old English epigrammatist,
Had wit at will, and art was all he missed;
But nowadays, we of the modern fry
Have art, and labor with wit's penury.
Wit is the substance, art the polishment;
Art does adorn, and wit it does invent;
Since, then, they are so jointly linked that neither
Can well subsist without the help of either,
I gladly could have wished, with all my heart,
That we had had his wit, or he our art.   10

Ad Zoilum

I might be better busied; I grant so.
Could I be better idle? Surely, no.
Then hold your idle chat, for I profess
These are the fruits but of my idleness.

In Porcum

Porcus, that foul unsociable hog,
Grunts me out this still: Love me, love my dog.
And reason is there why we should so do,
Since that his dog's the lovelier of the two.

Ad Tho. Bastardum epigrammatistam

Thy epigrams are of no bastard race,
For they dare gaze the world's eye in the face.

In Beatricem præpropere defunctam

In Beatrice did all perfections grow
That she could wish or nature could bestow;
When death, enamoured with that excellence,
Straight grew in love with her, and took her hence.

Ad Collegium Wintoniensem

If in this book dullness do chance to lurk,
I'll father it, 'tis mine own handiwork;
If in this book there be one witty line,
I utterly disclaim't; 'tis wholly thine.

FROM THOMAS FREEMAN'S *Rub and a Great Cast*, 1614

Me quoque vatem

Why am I not an epigrammatist?
I write in covert, and conceal their names
Whose lives I burden with some bitter jest;
Themselves I cloak, and yet uncloud their shames.
Again, methinks I am not shallow-sprited,
Nor seems my wit so insufficient;
Although not like to others, deep-conceited,
It can indite, although not excellent.
  The reader laughs, this reason he rehearses:
  The ape likes her own whelps, and I my verses.   10

To the stationer

I tell thee, stationer,—why, never fear!
They'll sell, i' faith, and 't be but for their title.
Thou canst not lose. Nay, I dare warrant clear
They'll get thee twenty nobles—not so little!
Why, read this epigram, or that, or any;
Do they not make thee itch, and move thy blood?
Of all thou hast had (and thou hast had many)
Hast e'er read better? Nay, hast read so good?
Dost laugh? They'll make the rigid'st Cato do it;
Besides, smooth verse, quaint phrase,—come, what wilt give?   10
No more but so! Ah, what shall I say to it?
  I pity poetry, but curse the time
  When none will bid us reason for our rhyme.

In epitaphium pingui minerva compositum

When Crassus died, his friends, to grace his hearse,
Requested one to make his funeral verse.
Of whom they did procure it in the end,
A ruthful one, and pitifully penned;
That sure the man who made it made great moan—
His epitaph was such a sorry one.

Aliud

I must needs say, were thou mine own brother,
This epitaph of thine deserveth another;
Such sorrow would make the learned to laugh,
To read: *Here lies a dead epitaph.*

In Phædram

Now, by her troth, she hath been, Phædra says,
At a play far better edified
Than at a sermon ever in her days.
Phædra, 'tis true, it cannot be denied;
  For stage-plays thou has given ear to many,
  But sermons, Phædra, never heardst thou any.

Of Spenser's Fairy Queen

Virgil from Homer, th' Italian from him,
Spenser from all; and all of these, I ween,
Were born when Helicon was full to th' brim;
Witness their works, witness our *Fairy Queen!*
  That lasting monument of Spenser's wit
  Was ne'er come near to, much less equalled, yet.

———————

Pity, oh pity! death had power
Over Chaucer, Lydgate, Gower:
They that equalled all the sages
Of these, their own, of former ages,
And did their learned lights advance
In times of darkest ignorance;
When palpable impurity
Kept knowledge in obscurity,
And all went hood-winked in this isle,
They could see and shine the while.   10
Nor Greece nor Rome could reckon us
As then among the barbarous,
Since these three knew to turn, perdy,
The screw-pin of philosophy
As well as they; and left behind
As rich memorials of the mind;
By which they live, though they are dead;
As all may see that will but read,
And on good works will spend good hours
In Chaucers, Lydgates, and in Gowers.   20

TUDOR PROSE

SIR THOMAS MORE

The Introduction and Notes are at page 1284

FROM *A fruteful and pleasaunt worke of the beste state of a publyque weale, and of the newe yle called Utopia: written in Latine by Syr Thomas More, knyght, and translated into Englyshe by Raphe Robynson,* 1551

[The first Latin edition was published in 1516]

Utopia

The first book of the communication of Raphael Hythloday concerning the best state of a commonwealth.

THE MOST victorious and triumphant king of England, Henry, the eighth of that name, in all royal virtues prince most peerless, had of late in controversy with the right high and mighty king of Castile weighty matters, and of great importance, for the debatement and final determination whereof the King's Majesty sent me ambassador into Flanders, joined in commission with Cuthbert Tunstall, a man doubtless out of comparison, and whom the King's Majesty of late, to the great rejoicing of all men, did prefer to the office of Master of the Rolls, but of this man's praises I will say nothing; not because I do fear that small credence shall be given to the testimony that cometh out of a friend's mouth; but because his virtue and learning be greater and of more excellency than that I am able to praise them: and also in all places so famous, and so perfectly well known, that they need not nor ought not of me to be praised, unless I would seem to shew and set forth the brightness of the sun with a candle, as the proverb saith.

There met us at Bruges (for thus it was before agreed) they whom their prince had for that matter appointed commissioners, excellent men all. The chief and the head of them was the margrave (as they call him) of Bruges, a right honorable man; but the wisest and the best spoken of them was George Temsice, provost of Cassel, a man not only by learning but also by nature of singular eloquence, and in the laws profoundly learned: but in reasoning, and debating of matters, what by his natural wit, and what by daily exercise, surely he had few fellows. After that we had once or twice met, and upon certain points or articles could not fully and thoroughly agree, they for a certain space took their leave of us, and

535

departed to Brussels, there to know their prince's pleasure. I, in the mean-time (for so my business lay), went straight thence to Antwerp.

Whiles I was there abiding, oftentimes among other, but which to me was more welcome than any other, did visit me one Peter Giles, a citizen of Antwerp, a man there in his country of honest reputation, and also preferred to high promotions, worthy truly of the highest. For it is hard to say whether the young man be in learning or in honesty more excellent. For he is both of wonderful virtuous conditions, and also singularly well learned, and towards all sorts of people exceeding gentle; but towards his
10 friends so kind-hearted, so loving, so faithful, so trusty, and of so earnest affection, that it were very hard in any place to find a man that with him in all points of friendship may be compared. No man can be more lowly or courteous. No man useth less simulation or dissimulation, in no man is more prudent simplicity. Besides this, he is in his talk and communication so merry and pleasant, yea, and that without harm, that, through his gentle entertainment and his sweet and delectable communication, in me was greatly abated and diminished the fervent desire that I had to see my native country, my wife and my children; whom then I did much long and covet to see, because that at that time I had been more than four
20 months from them.

Upon a certain day as I was hearing the divine service in Our Lady's Church, which is the fairest, the most gorgeous and curious church of building in all the city, and also most frequented of people, and when the divine was done, was ready to go home to my lodging, I chanced to espy this foresaid Peter talking with a certain stranger, a man well stricken in age, with a black sunburned face, a long beard, and a cloak cast homely about his shoulders, whom by his favor and apparel forthwith I judged to be a mariner. But when this Peter saw me, he cometh to me and saluteth me. And as I was about to answer him: "See you this man?"
30 saith he (and therewith he pointed to the man that I saw him talking with before). "I was minded," quod he, "to bring him straight home to you."

"He should have been very welcome to me," said I, "for your sake."

"Nay," quod he, "for his own sake, if you knew him, for there is no man this day living that can tell you of so many strange and unknown peoples and countries as this man can. And I know well that you be very desirous to hear of such news."

"Then I conjectured not far amiss," quod I, "for even at the first sight I judged him to be a mariner."

"Nay," quod he "there ye were greatly deceived: he hath sailed indeed,
40 not as the mariner Palynure, but as the expert and prudent prince Ulysses: Yea, rather as the ancient and sage philosopher Plato. For this same Raphael Hythloday (for this is his name) is very well learned in the

Latin tongue; but profound and excellent in the Greek tongue: wherein he ever bestowed more study than in the Latin, because he had given himself wholly to the study of philosophy. Whereof he knew that there is nothing extant in the Latin tongue that is to any purpose, saving a few of Seneca's and Cicero's doings. His patrimony that he was born unto he left to his brethren (for he is a Portugal born) and for the desire that he had to see and know the far countries of the world, he joined himself in company with Amerigo Vespucci, and in the three last voyages of those four, that be now in print and abroad in every man's hands, he continued still in his company, saving that in the last voyage he came not home again 10 with him. For he made such means and shift, what by entreatance and what by importune suit, that he got license of Master Amerigo (though it were sore against his will) to be one of the twenty-four which in the end of the last voyage were left [in the country of Gulike] in the fort. He was therefore left behind for his mind's sake, as one that took more thought and care for traveling than dying: having customably in his mouth these sayings. He that hath no grave is covered with the sky, and, The way to heaven out of all places is of like length and distance. Which fantasy of his (if God had not been his better friend) he had surely bought full dear.   20

"But after the departing of Master Vespucci, when he had traveled through and about many countries, with five of his companions [Guli-kians] of the fort, at the last by marvelous chance he arrived in Tapro-bane, from whence he went to Calicut, where he chanced to find certain of his country ships, wherein he returned again into his country, nothing less than looked for."

All this when Peter had told me: I thanked him for his gentle kindness, that he had vouchsafed to bring me to the speech of that man whose communication he thought should be to me pleasant and acceptable. And therewith I turned me to Raphael, and when we had hailsed the one the 30 other, and had spoken these common words that be customably spoken at the first meeting and acquaintance of strangers, we went thence to my house, and there in my garden, upon a bench covered with green turves, we sat down talking together.

There he told us how that, after the departing of Vespucci, he and his fellows, that tarried behind in Gulike, began by little and little, through fair and gentle speech, to win the love and favor of the people of that country, insomuch that, within short space, they did dwell amongst them not only harmless, but also occupied with them very familiarly. He told us also that they were in high reputation and favor with a certain great 40 man (whose name and country is now quite out of my remembrance), which of his mere liberality did bear the costs and charges of him and his

five companions, and besides that gave them a trusty guide to conduct
them in their journey (which by water was in boats and by land in
wagons) and to bring them to other princes with very friendly commendations. Thus after many days' journeys, he said they found towns
and cities, and weal publics full of people, governed by good and wholesome laws. For under the line equinoctial and of both sides of the same,
as far as the sun doth extend his course, lieth (quod he) great and wide
deserts and wildernesses, parched, burned, and dried up with continual
and intolerable heat. All things be hideous, terrible, loathsome, and un-
10 pleasant to behold: all things out of fashion and comeliness, inhabited with
wild beasts and serpents, or at the leastwise with people that be no less
savage, wild, and noisome than the very beasts themselves be. But a little
farther beyond that, all things begin by little and little to wax pleasant.
The air soft, temperate, and gentle. The ground covered with green
grass. Less wildness in the beasts. At the last shall ye come again to
people, cities, and towns wherein is continual intercourse and occupying
of merchandise and chaffer, not only among themselves and with their
borders, but also with merchants of far countries both by land and water.
There I had occasion (said he) to go to many countries of every side. For
20 there was no ship ready to any voyage or journey, but I and my fellows
were into it very gladly received. The ships that they found first were
made plain, flat, and broad in the bottom, troughwise. The sails were
made of great rushes, or of wickers, and in some places of leather. Afterward they found ships with ridged keels, and sails of canvas; yea, and
shortly after, having all things like ours. The shipmen also very expert
and cunning both in the sea and in the weather.

But he said that he found great favor and friendship among them for
teaching them the feat and use of the loadstone, which to them before
that time was unknown; and therefore they were wont to be very timor-
30 ous and fearful upon the sea, nor to venture upon it, but only in the
summertime. But now they have such a confidence in that stone that they
fear not stormy winter; in so doing farther from care than jeopardy.
Insomuch that it is greatly to be doubted lest that thing, through their
own foolish hardiness, shall turn them to evil and harm, which at the
first was supposed should be to them good and commodious.

But what he told us that he saw, in every country where he came, it
were very long to declare. Neither is it my purpose at this time to make
rehearsal thereof. But peradventure in another place, I will speak of it,
chiefly such things as shall be profitable to be known; as in special be those
40 decrees and ordinances that he marked to be well and wisely provided
and enacted among such peoples as do live together in a civil policy and
good order. For of such things did we busily inquire and demand of him,

and he likewise very willingly told us of the same. But as for monsters, because they be no news, of them we were nothing inquisitive. For nothing is more easy to be found than be barking Scyllas, ravening Celaenos, and Laestrygons, devourers of people, and such like great and uncredible monsters, but to find citizens ruled by good and wholesome laws, that is an exceeding rare and hard thing.

But as he marked many fond and foolish laws in those new-found lands, so he rehearsed many acts and constitutions whereby these our cities, nations, countries, and kingdoms may take example, to amend their faults, enormities, and errors, whereof in another place, as I said, I will entreat. Now at this time I am determined to rehearse only that he told us of the manners, customs, laws, and ordinances of the Utopians. But first I will repeat our former communication, by the occasion, and, as I might say, the drift whereof he was brought into the mention of that weal public.

For when Raphael had very prudently touched divers things that be amiss some here and some there, yea very many of both parts, and again had spoken of such wise and prudent laws and decrees as be established and used both here among us and also there among them, as a man so cunning and expert in the laws and customs of every several country, as though into what place soever he came guestwise, there he had led all his life: then Peter much marvelling at the man: "Surely Master Raphael," quod he, "I wonder greatly why you get you not into some king's court, for I am sure there is no prince living that would not be very glad of you, as a man not only able highly to delight him with your profound learning, and this your knowledge of countries and peoples, but also are meet to instruct him with examples and help him with counsel. And thus doing you shall bring yourself in a very good case, and also be in ability to help all your friends and kinsfolk."

"As concerning my friends and kinsfolk," quod he, "I pass not greatly for them. For I think I have sufficiently done my part towards them already. For these things that other men do not depart from until they be old and sick, yea which they be then very loath to leave when they can no longer keep, those very same things did I being not only lusty, and in good health, but also in the flower of my youth, divide among my friends and kinsfolks, which I think with this my liberality ought to hold them contented and not to require nor to look that besides this I should for their sakes give myself in bondage to kings."

"Nay God forbid," quod Peter. "It is not my mind that you should be in bondage to kings, but as a retainer to them at your pleasure, which surely I think is the nearest way that you can devise how to bestow your time fruitfully, not only for the private commodity of your friends and for the general profit of all sorts of people, but also for the advancement of yourself to a much wealthier state and condition than you be now in."

"To a wealthier condition," quod Raphael, "by that means—that my mind standeth clean against! Now I live at liberty after mine own mind and pleasure, which I think very few of these great states and peers of realms can say. Yea, and there be enough of them that seek for great men's friendships: and therefore think it no great hurt if they have not me nor two or three such other as I am."

"Well I perceive plainly friend Raphael," quod I, "that you be desirous neither of riches, nor of power. And truly I have in no less reverence
10 and estimation a man that is of your mind, than any of them all that be so high in power and authority. But you shall do as it becometh you, yea and according to this wisdom and this high and free courage of yours, if you can find in your heart so to appoint and dispose yourself that you may apply your wit and diligence to the profit of the weal public, though it be somewhat to your own pain and hindrance. And this shall you never so well do, nor with so great profit perform, as if you be of some great prince's counsel, and put in his head (as I doubt not but you will) honest opinions, and virtuous persuasions. For from the prince, as from a perpetual wellspring, cometh among the people the flood of all that is good or evil. But
20 in you is so perfect learning that without any experience, and again so great experience that, without any learning, you may well be any king's counsellor."

"You be twice deceived Master More," quod he, "first in me, and again in the thing itself. For neither is in me that ability that you force upon me, and if it were never so much, yet in disquieting mine own quietness I should nothing further the weal public, for first of all the most part of all princes have more delight in warlike matters and feats of chivalry (the knowledge whereof I neither have nor desire) than in the good feats of peace, and employ much more study how by right or by wrong to en-
30 large their dominions, than how well and peaceably to rule and govern that they have already. Moreover they that be counsellors to kings, every one of them either is of himself so wise in deed that he need not or else he thinketh himself so wise, that he will not allow another man's counsel: saving that they do shamefully and flatteringly give assent to the fond and foolish sayings of certain great men. Whose favors, because they be in high authority with their prince, by assentation and flattering they labor to obtain. And verily it is naturally given to all men to esteem their own inventions best. So both the raven and the ape think their own young ones fairest.

40 "Then if a man in such a company, where some disdain and have despite at other men's inventions, and some count their own best—if among

such men, I say, a man should bring forth anything that he hath read
done in times past, or that he hath seen done in other places, there the
hearers fare as though the whole existimation of their wisdom were in
jeopardy to be overthrown, and that ever after they should be counted
for very dizzards, unless they could in other men's inventions pick out
matter to reprehend and find fault at. If all other poor helps fail: then
this is their extreme refuge. These things (say they) pleased our forefathers and ancestors: would God we could be so wise as they were: and
as though they had wittily concluded the matter and with this answer
stopped every man's mouth, they sit down again. As who should say it 10
were very dangerous matter, if a man in any point should be found wiser
than his forefathers were. And yet be we content to suffer the best and
wittiest of their decrees to lie unexecuted: but if in anything a better order
might have been taken, than by them was, there we take fast hold and
find many faults. Many times have I chanced upon such proud, lewd,
overthwart, and wayward Judgments; yea, and ones in England.

"I pray you, Sir," quod I, "have you been in our country?"

"Yea forsooth," quod he, "and there I tarried for the space of four or
five months together, not long after the insurrection that the western
Englishmen made against their king; which by their own miserable and 20
pitiful slaughter was suppressed and ended. In the mean season, I was
much bound and beholden to the right reverend father, John Morton,
archbishop and cardinal of Canterbury, and at that time also lord chancellor of England, a man, Master Peter (for Master More knoweth already
that I will say), not more honorable for his authority than for his prudence
and virtue. He was of a mean stature and stricken in age, though yet bare
he his body upright. In his face did shine such an amiable reverence as
was pleasant to behold. Gentle in communication, yet earnest and sage.
He had great delight many times with rough speech to his suitors to prove,
but without harm, what prompt wit and what bold sprite were in every 30
man. In the which, as in a virtue much agreeing with his nature, so that
therewith were not joined impudency, he took great delectation. And the
same person, as apt and meet to have an administration in the weal public,
he did lovingly embrace. In his speech he was fine, eloquent, and pithy.
In the law he had profound knowledge, in wit he was incomparable, and
in memory wonderful excellent. These qualities, which in him were by
nature singular, he by learning and use had made perfect.

"The king put much trust in his counsel, the weal public also in a
manner leaned unto him when I was there. For even in the chief of his
youth he was taken from school into the court, and there passed all his 40
time in much trouble and business, and was continually troubled and

tossed with divers misfortunes and adversities. And so by many and great dangers he learned the experience of the world, which so being learned cannot easily be forgotten.

"It chanced on a certain day when I sat at his table, there was also a certain layman, cunning in the laws of your realm. Which, I cannot tell whereof taking occasion, began diligently and busily to praise that strait and rigorous justice which at that time was there executed upon felons, who, as he said, were for the most part twenty hanged together upon one gallows. And, seeing so few escaped punishment, he said he could not
10 choose but greatly wonder and marvel how and by what evil luck it should so come to pass that thieves nevertheless in every place so rife and rank.

" 'Nay, Sir,' quod I (for I durst boldly speak my mind before the cardinal), 'marvel nothing hereat, for this punishment of thieves passeth of the limits justice, and is also very hurtful to the weal public. For it is too extreme and cruel a punishment for theft, and yet not sufficient to refrain men from theft. For simple theft is not so great an offense that it ought to be punished with death. Neither there is any punishment so horrible that it can keep them from stealing which have no other craft
20 whereby to get their living. Therefore in this point, not you only, but also the most part of the world, be like evil schoolmasters, which be readier to beat than to teach their scholars. For great and horrible punishments be appointed for thieves, whereas much rather provision should have been made that there were some means whereby they might get their living, so that no man should be driven to this extreme necessity, first to steal, and then to die.'

" 'Yes,' quod he, 'this matter is well enough provided for already. There be handicrafts, there is husbandry, to get their living by, if they would not willingly be nought.'

30 " 'Nay,' quod I, 'you shall not 'scape so, for, first of all, I will speak nothing of them that come home out of war maimed and lame, as not long ago out of Blackheath field, and a little before that out of the wars in France: such (I say) as put their lives in jeopardy for the weal public's or the king's sake, and by the reason of weakness and lameness be not able to occupy their old crafts, and be too aged to learn new: of them I will speak nothing, because war, like the tide, ebbeth and floweth. But let us consider those things that chance daily before our eyes.

" 'First, there is a great number of gentlemen which cannot be content to live idle themselves, like dors, of that which other have labored for:
40 their tenants, I mean, whom they poll and shave to the quick by raising their rents (for this only point of frugality do they use, men else through their lavish and prodigal spending able to bring themselves to very beg-

gary), these gentlemen (I say) do not only live in idleness themselves,
but also carry about with them at their tails a great flock or train of idle
and loitering servingmen, which never learned any craft whereby to get
their livings. These men, as soon as their master is dead, or be sick themselves, be incontinent thrust out of doors. For gentlemen had rather keep
idle persons than sick men, and many times the dead man's heir is not
able to maintain so great a house, and keep so many servingmen as his
father did. Then, in the mean season, they that be thus destitute of service
other starve for hunger, or manfully play the thieves. For what would
you have them to do? When they have wandered abroad so long until 10
they have worn threadbare their apparel and also appaired their health,
then gentlemen, because of their pale and sick faces and patched coats,
will not take them into service. And husbandmen dare not set them a-
work, knowing well enough that he is nothing meet to do true and faithful service to a poor man with a spade and a mattock, for small wages
and hard fare, which, being daintily and tenderly pampered up in idleness
and pleasure, was wont with a sword and a buckler by his side to jet
through the street with a bragging look, and to think himself too good to
be any man's mate.'

" 'Nay, by St. Mary, Sir,' quod the lawyer, 'not so, for this kind of men 20
must we make most of. For in them, as men of stouter stomachs, bolder
spirits, and manlier courages, than handicraftsmen and plowmen be, doth
consist the whole power, strength, and puissance of our host, when we
must fight in battle.'

" 'Forsooth, sir, as well you might say,' quod I, 'that for wars' sake you
must cherish thieves. For surely you shall never lack thieves whiles you
have them. No, nor thieves be not the most false and faint-hearted soldiers,
nor soldiers be not the cowardliest thieves, so well these two crafts agree
together. But this fault, though it be much used among you, yet is it not
peculiar to you only, but common also almost to all nations. Yet France, 30
besides this, is troubled and infected with a much sorer plague. The whole
realm is filled and besieged with hired soldiers in peace time, if that be
peace which be brought in under the same color and pretense that hath
persuaded you to keep these idle servingmen. For these wise fools and
very archdolts thought the wealth of the whole country herein to consist,
if there were ever in a readiness a strong and a sure garrison, specially of
old practised soldiers, for they put no trust at all in men unexercised. And
therefore they must be fain to seek for war, to the end they may ever have
practised soldiers and cunning manslayers: lest that (as it is prettily said
of Sallust) their hands and their minds through idleness or lack of exercise 40
should wax dull. But how pernicious and pestilent a thing it is to maintain such beasts, the Frenchmen by their own harms have learned, and

the examples of the Romans, Carthaginians, Syrians, and of many other countries, do manifestly declare. For not only the empire, but also the fields and cities of all these, by divers occasions have been overrunned and destroyed of their own armies beforehand had in a readiness. Now how unnecessary a thing this is, hereby it may appear: that the French soldiers, which from their youth have been practised and ured in feats of arms, do not crack nor advance themselves to have very often got the upper hand mastery of your new-made and unpractised soldiers. But in this point I will not use many words, lest perchance I may seem to flatter you.
10 No, nor those same handicraftmen of yours in cities, nor yet the rude and uplandish plowmen of the country, are not supposed to be greatly afraid of your gentlemen's idle servingmen, unless it be such as be not of body or stature correspondent to their strength and courage, or else whose bold stomachs be discouraged through poverty. Thus you may see that it is not to be feared lest they should be effeminated if they were brought up in good crafts and laborsome works, whereby to get their living, whose stout and sturdy bodies (for gentlemen vouchsafe to corrupt and spill none but picked and chosen men) now, other by reason of rest and idleness be brought to weakness, or else by too easy and womanly exercises
20 be made feeble and unable to endure hardiness. Truly, howsoever the case standeth, this me thinketh is nothing available to the weal public for war sake, which you never have but when you will yourselves, to keep and maintain an unnumerable flock of that sort of men that be so troublesome and noyous in peace, whereof you ought to have a thousand times more regard than of war.

" 'But yet this is not only the necessary cause of stealing. There is another which, as I suppose, is proper and peculiar to you Englishmen alone.'

" 'What is that?' quod the cardinal.

" 'Forsooth,' quod I, 'your sheep, that were wont to be so meek and
30 tame, and so small eaters, now, as I hear say, be become so great devourers, and so wild, that they eat up and swallow down the very men themselves. They consume, destroy, and devour whole fields, houses, and cities. For look in what parts of the realm doth grow the finest, and therefore dearest, wool, there noblemen and gentlemen, yea, and certain abbots, holy men, God wot, not contenting themselves with the yearly revenues and profits that were wont to grow to their forefathers and predecessors of their lands, nor being content that they live in rest and pleasure, nothing profiting, yea, much noying the weal public, leave no ground for tillage: they enclose all in pastures; they throw down houses; they pluck
40 down towns, and leave nothing standing but only the church, to make of it a sheephouse. And, as though you lost no small quantity of ground by

forests, chases, lands, and parks, those good holy men turn all dwellings, places, and all glebe-land into desolation and wilderness.

" 'Therefore, that one covetous and unsatiable cormorant and very plague of his native country may compass about and enclose many thousand acres of ground together within one pale or hedge, the husbandmen be thrust out of their own, or else other by covin or fraud, or by violent oppression, they be put besides it, or by wrongs and injuries they be so worried that they be compelled to sell all: by one means, therefore, or by other, other by hook or crook, they must needs depart away, poor, silly, wretched souls, men, women, husbands, wives, fatherless children, wid- 10 ows, woeful mothers with their young babes, and their whole household small in substance, and much in number, as husbandry requireth many hands. Away they trudge, I say, out of their known and accustomed houses, finding no places to rest in. All their household stuff, which is very little worth, though it might well abide the sale: yet, being suddenly thrust out, they be constrained to sell it for a thing of naught. And when they have, wandering about, soon spent that, what can they else do but steal, and then justly, God wot, be hanged, or else go about a-begging? And yet then also they be cast in prison as vagabonds, because they go about and work not; whom no man will set a-work, though they never so will- 20 ingly offer themselves thereto. For one shepherd or herdman is enough to eat up that ground with cattle, to the occupying whereof about husbandry many hands were requisite. And this is also the cause that victuals be now in many places dearer.

" 'Yea, besides this, the price of wool is so risen that poor folks, which were wont to work it and make cloth of it, be now able to buy none at all. And, by this means, very many be fain to forsake work, and to give themselves to idleness. For, after that so much ground was enclosed for pasture, an infinite multitude of sheep died of the rot, such vengeaunce God took of their inordinate and unsatiable covetousness, sending among 30 the sheep that pestiferous murrain, which much more justly should have fallen on the sheepmasters' own heads. And though the number of sheep increase never so fast, yet the price falleth not one mite, because there be so few sellers. For they be almost all come into a few rich men's hands, whom no need driveth to sell before they lust, and they lust not before they may sell as dear as they lust. Now the same cause bringeth in like dearth of the other kinds of cattle, yea, and that so much the more, because that after farms plucked down, and husbandry decayed, there is no man that passeth for the breeding of young store. For these rich men bring not up the young ones of great cattle as they do lambs. But first 40 they buy them abroad very cheap, and afterward, when they be fatted

in their pastures, they sell them again exceeding dear. And therefore (as I suppose) the whole incommodity hereof is not yet felt. For yet they make dearth only in those places where they sell. But when they shall fetch them away from thence where they be bred, faster than they can be brought up, then shall there also be felt great dearth, when store beginneth to fail there where the ware is bought. Thus the unreasonable covetousness of a few hath turned that thing to the utter undoing of your island, in the which thing the chief felicity of your realm did consist. For this great dearth of victuals causeth every man to keep as little houses
10 and as small hospitality as he possibly may. And to put away their servants: whither, I pray you, but a-begging? or else, which these gentle bloods and stout stomachs will sooner set their minds unto, a-stealing?

" 'Now, to amend the matters, to this wretched beggary and miserable poverty is joined great wantonness, importunate superfluity, and excessive riot. For not only gentlemen's servants, but also handicraftmen, yea, and almost the plowmen of the country, with all other sorts of people, use much strange and proud newfangleness in their apparel, and too much prodigal riot and sumptuous fare at their table. Now bawds, queans, whores, harlots, strumpets, brothelhouses, stews, and yet another stews:
20 wine taverns, alehouses, and tippling houses, with so many naughty, lewd, and unlawful games, as dice, cards, tables, tennis, bowls, quoits, do not all these send the haunters of them straight a-stealing when their money is gone?

" 'Cast out these pernicious abominations, make a law that they which plucked down farms and towns of husbandry shall build them up again, or else yield and uprender the possession of them to such as will go to the cost of building them anew. Suffer not these rich men to buy up all, to engross and forestall, and with their monopoly to keep the market alone as please them. Let not so many be brought up in idleness, let husbandry
30 and tillage be restored again, let cloth-working be renewed, that there may be honest labors for this idle sort to pass their time in profitably, which hitherto other poverty hath caused to be thieves, or else now be other vagabonds or idle servingmen, and shortly will be thieves. Doubtless, unless you find a remedy for these enormities, you shall be in vain advance yourselves of executing justice upon felons. For this justice is more beautiful than just or profitable. For by suffering your youth wantonly and viciously to be brought up, and to be infected even from their tender age, by little and little, with vice, then, a God's name, to be punished when they commit the same faults after they be come to man's state
40 which from their youth they were ever like to do: in this point, I pray you, what other thing do you than make thieves and then punish them?' "

*　　*　　*　　*　　*

"Suppose that some king and his council were together, whetting their wits and devising what subtle craft they might invent to enrich the king with great treasures of money. First one counselleth to raise and enhance the valuation of money when the king must pay any: and again to call down the value of coin to less than it is worth when he must receive or gather any. For thus great sums shall be paid with a little money, and where little is due much shall be received. Another counselleth to feign war, that when, under this color and pretense, the king hath gathered great abundance of money, he may, when it shall please him, make peace with great solemnity and holy ceremonies, to blind the eyes of the poor ₁₀ commonalty, as taking pity and compassion, God wot, upon man's blood, like a loving and a merciful prince. Another putteth the king in remembrance of certain old and moth-eaten laws that of long time have not been put in execution, which, because no man can remember that they were made, every man hath transgressed. The fines of these laws he counselleth the king to require: for there is no way so profitable nor more honorable as the which hath a shew and color of justice. Another adviseth him to forbid many things under great penalties and fines, specially such things as is for the people's profit not be used, and afterward to dispense for money with them which by this prohibition sustain loss and damage. For, ₂₀ by this means, the favor of the people is won and profit riseth two ways. First by taking forfeits of them whom covetousness of gains hath brought in danger of this statute, and also by selling privileges and licenses, which the better that the prince is, forsooth, the dearer he selleth them: as one that is loath to grant to any private person anything that is against the profit of his people. And therefore may sell none but at an exceeding dear price.

"Another giveth the king counsel to endanger unto his grace the judges of the realm, that he may have them ever on his side, which must, in every matter, dispute and reason for the king's right. And they must be called ₃₀ into the king's palace, and be desired to argue and discuss his matters in his own presence. So there shall be no matter of his so openly wrong and unjust wherein one or other of them, either because he will have something to allege and object, or that he is ashamed to say that which is said already, or else to pick a thank with his prince, will not find some hole open to set a snare in, wherewith to take the contrary part in a trip. Thus while the judges cannot agree amongst themselves, reasoning and arguing of that which is plain enough, and bringing the manifest truth in doubt: in the mean season, the king may take a fit occasion to understand the law as shall most make for his advantage, whereunto all, other for ₄₀ shame or for fear, will agree. Then the judges may be bold to pronounce of the king's side. For he that giveth sentence for the king cannot be with-

out a good excuse. For it shall be sufficient for him to have equity of his part, or the bare words of the law, or a writhen and wrested understanding of the same, or else, which with good and just judges is of greater force than all laws be, the king's indisputable prerogative. To conclude, all the counsellors agree and consent together with the rich Crassus, that no abundance of gold can be sufficient for a prince, which must keep and maintain an army: furthermore, that a king, though he would, can do nothing unjustly. For all that all men have, yea, also the men themselves, be all his. And that every man hath so much of his own as the king's
10 gentleness hath not taken from him. And that it shall be most for the king's advantage that his subjects have very little or nothing in their possession, as whose safeguard doth herein consist, that his people do not wax wanton and wealthy through riches and liberty, because where these things be, there men be not wont patiently to obey hard, unjust, and unlawful commandments. Whereas, on the other part, need and poverty doth hold down and keep under stout courages, and maketh them patient perforce, taking from them bold and rebelling stomachs.

"Here again, if I should rise up and boldly affirm that all these counsels be to the king dishonor and reproach, whose honor and safety is more and
20 rather supported and upholden by the wealth and riches of his people than by his own treasures; and if I should declare that the commonalty chooseth their king for their own sake and not for his sake: for this intent that through his labor and study they might all live wealthily, safe from wrongs and injuries: and that, therefore, the king ought to take more care for the wealth of his people than for his own wealth, even as the office and duty of a shepherd is, in that he is a shepherd, to feed his sheep rather than himself. For, as touching this, that they think the defense and maintenance of peace to consist in the poverty of the people, the thing itself sheweth that they be far out of the way. For where shall a man find more wran-
30 gling, quarreling, brawling, and chiding than among beggars? Who be more desirous of new mutations and alterations than they that be not content with the present state of their life? Or, finally, who be bolder stomached to bring all in hurly-burly (thereby trusting to get some windfall) than they that have now nothing to lose? And if so be that there were any king that were so smally regarded or so behated of his subjects that other ways he could not keep them in awe but only by open wrongs, by polling and shaving, and by bringing them to beggary, surely it were better for him to forsake his kingdom than to hold it by this means: whereby, though the name of a king be kept, yet the majesty is lost. For
40 it is against the dignity of a king to have rule over beggars, but rather over rich and wealthy men. Of this mind was the hardy and courageous Fabrice, when he said that he had rather be a ruler of rich men than be rich

himself. And verily one man to live in pleasure and wealth, whiles all other weep and smart for it, that is the part not of a king but of a jailer.

"To be short, as he is a foolish physician that cannot cure his patient's disease unless he cast him in another sickness, so he that cannot amend the lives of his subjects but by taking from them the wealth and commodity of life, he must needs grant that he knoweth not the feat how to govern free men. But let him rather amend his own life, renounce unhonest pleasures, and forsake pride. For these be the chief vices that cause him to run in the contempt or hatred of his people. Let him live of his own, hurting no man. Let him do cost not above his power. Let him restrain wickedness. Let him prevent vices and take away the occasions of offenses by well ordering his subjects, and not by suffering wickedness to increase, afterward to be punished. Let him not be too hasty in calling again laws which a custom hath abrogated: specially such as have been long forgotten and never lacked nor needed. And let him never, under the cloak and pretense of transgression, take such fines and forfeits as no judge will suffer a private person to take, as unjust and full of guile.

"Here, if I should bring forth before them the law of the Macariens, which be not far distant from Utopia: whose king the day of his coronation is bound by a solemn oath that he shall never at any time have in his treasure above a thousand pound of gold or silver. They say a very good king, which took more care for the wealth and commodity of his country than for the enriching of himself, made this law to be a stop and a bar to kings for heaping and hoarding up so much money as might impoverish their people. For he foresaw that this sum of treasure would suffice to support the king in battle against his own people, if they should chance to rebel: and also to maintain his wars against the invasions of his foreign enemies. Again he perceived the same stock of money to be too little and unsufficient to encourage and enable him wrongfully to take away other men's goods, which was the chief cause why the law was made. Another cause was this. He thought that by this provision his people should not lack money wherewith to maintain their daily occupying and chaffer. And, seeing the king could not choose but lay out and bestow all that came in above the prescript sum of his stock, he thought he would seek no occasions to do his subjects injury. Such a king shall be feared of evil men and loved of good men. These and such other informations if I should use among men wholly inclined and given to the contrary part, how deaf hearers, think you, should I have?"

"Deaf hearers, doubtless," quod I. "And, in good faith, no marvel. And to speak as I think, truly I cannot allow that such communication shall be used or such counsel given as you be sure shall never be regarded nor received. For how can so strange informations be profitable, or how

can they be beaten into their heads whose minds be already prevented
with clean contrary persuasions? This school philosophy is not unpleasant
among friends in familiar communication, but in the councils of kings,
where great matters be debated and reasoned with great authority, these
things have no place."

"That is it which I meant," quod he, "when I said philosophy had no
place among kings."

"Indeed," quod I, "this school philosophy hath not: which thinketh all
things meet for every place. But there is another philosophy more civil,
which knoweth, as ye would say, her own stage, and thereafter ordering
and behaving herself in the play that she hath in hand, playeth her part
accordingly with comeliness, uttering nothing out of due order and fashion. And this is the philosophy that you must use. Or else, whiles a comedy
of Plautus is playing and the vile bondmen scoffing and trifling among
themselves, if you should suddenly come upon the stage in a philosopher's
apparel and rehearse out of *Octavia* the place wherein Seneca disputeth
with Nero: had it not been better for you to have played the dumb person
than by rehearsing that which served neither for the time nor place to have
made such a tragical comedy or gallimaufry? For, by bringing in other
stuff that nothing appertaineth to the present matter, you must needs mar
and pervert the play that is in hand, though the stuff that you bring be
much better. What part soever you have taken upon you, play that as well
as you can and make the best of it: and do not, therefore, disturb and
bring out of order the whole matter, because that another which is merrier
and better cometh to your remembrance.

"So the case standeth in a commonwealth, and so it is in the consultations of kings and princes. If evil opinions and naughty persuasions cannot
be utterly and quite plucked out of their hearts, if you cannot even as you
would, remedy vices which use and custom hath confirmed: yet, for this
cause, you must not leave and forsake the commonwealth: you must not
forsake the ship in a tempest because you cannot rule and keep down the
winds. No, nor you must not labor to drive into their heads new and
strange informations, which you know well shall be nothing regarded
with them that be of clean contrary minds. But you must with a crafty
wile and a subtle train, study and endeavor yourself, as much as in you
lieth, to handle the matter wittily and handsomely for the purpose, and
that which you cannot turn to good, so to order it that it be not very bad.
For it is not possible for all things to be well unless all men were good.
Which I think will not be yet this good many years."

"By this means," quod he, "nothing else will be brought to pass, but,
whiles that I go about to remedy the madness of others, I should be even
as mad as they. For if I would speak things that be true, I must needs

speak such things: but as for to speak false things, whether that be a philosopher's part or no, I cannot tell, truly it is not my part. Howbeit, this communication of mine, though peradventure it may seem unpleasant to them, yet can I not see why it should seem strange or foolishly new-fangled. If so be that I should speak those things that Plato feigneth in his weal public, or that the Utopians do in theirs, these things, though they were (as they be indeed) better, yet they might seem spoken out of place. Forasmuch as here amongst us every man hath his possessions several to himself, and there all things be common.

"But what was in my communication contained that might not and ought not in any place to be spoken? Saving that to them which have thoroughly decreed and determined with themselves to roam headlong the contrary way, it cannot be acceptable and pleasant, because it calleth them back and sheweth them the jeopardies. Verily, if all things that evil and vicious manners have caused to seem inconvenient and naught should be refused, as things unmeet and reproachful, then we must among Christian people wink at the most part of all those things which Christ taught us, and so straitly forbade them to be winked at that those things also which He whispered in the ears of his disciples, He commanded to be proclaimed in open houses. And yet the most part of them is more dissident from the manners of the world nowadays than my communication was. But preachers, sly and wily men, following your counsel (as I suppose) because they saw men evil willing to frame their manners to Christ's rule, they have wrested and wried his doctrine, and, like a rule of lead, have applied it to men's manners: that, by some means, at the least way, they might agree together. Whereby I cannot see what good they have done, but that men may more sickerly be evil. And I truly should prevail even as much in kings' councils. For other I must say otherways than they say, and then I were as good to say nothing, or else I must say the same that they say, and (as Mitio saith in Terence) help to further their madness. For that crafty wile and subtle train of yours, I cannot perceive to what purpose it serveth, wherewith you would have me to study and endeavor myself, if all things cannot be made good, yet to handle them wittily and handsomely for the purpose, that, as farforth as is possible, they may not be very evil. For there is no place to dissemble in nor to wink in. Naughty counsels must be openly allowed and very pestilent decrees must be approved. He shall be counted worse than a spy, yea, almost as evil as a traitor, that with a faint heart doth praise evil and noisome decrees.

"Moreover, a man can have no occasion to do good, chancing into the company of them which will sooner make naught a good man than be made good themselves: through whose evil company he shall be marred,

or else if he remain good and innocent, yet the wickedness and foolishness
of others shall be imputed to him and laid in his neck. So that it is impossible with that crafty wile and subtle train to turn anything to better.
Wherefore Plato by a goodly similitude declareth why wise men refrain
to meddle in the commonwealth. For when they see the people swarm
into the streets, and daily wet to the skin with rain, and yet cannot persuade them to go out of the rain and take to their houses, knowing well
that if they should go out to them, they should nothing prevail, nor win
aught by it, but be wet also in the rain, they do keep themselves within
heir houses, being content that they be safe themselves, seeing they cannot remedy the folly of the people.

"Howbeit, doubtless, Master More (to speak truly as my mind giveth
me) wheresoever possessions be private, where money beareth all the
stroke, it is hard and almost impossible that there the weal public may
justly be governed and prosperously flourish. Unless you think thus: that
justice is there executed where all things come into the hands of evil men,
or that prosperity there flourisheth where all is divided among a few;
which few, nevertheless, do not lead their lives very wealthily, and the
residue live miserably, wretchedly, and beggarly. Wherefore when I
consider with myself and weigh in my mind the wise and godly ordinances of the Utopians, among whom with very few laws all things be
so well and wealthily ordered that virtue is had in price and estimation,
and yet all things being there common, every man hath abundance of
everything. Again, on the other part, when I compare with them so
many nations ever making new laws, yet none of them all well and sufficiently furnished with laws: where every man calleth that he hath gotten
his own proper and private goods, where so many new laws daily made
be not sufficient for every man to enjoy, defend, and know from another
man's that which he calleth his own: which thing the infinite controversies in the law, that daily rise never to be ended, plainly declare to be
true. These things (I say) when I consider with myself, I hold well with
Plato, and do nothing marvel that he would make no laws for them that
refused those laws, whereby all men should have and enjoy equal portions
of wealths and commodities. For the wise man did easily foresee that this
is the one and only way to the wealth of a commonalty, if equality of all
things should be brought in and stablished. Which I think is not possible
to be observed, where every man's goods be proper and peculiar to himself. For where every man under certain titles and pretenses draweth
and plucketh to himself as much as he can, and so a few divide among
themselves all the riches that there is, be there never so much abundance
and store, there to the residue is left lack and poverty. And, for the most
part, it chanceth that this latter sort is more worthy to enjoy that state of

wealth than the other be, because the rich men be covetous, crafty, and unprofitable. On the other part, the poor be lowly, simple, and by their daily labor more profitable to the commonwealth than to themselves.

"Thus I do fully persuade myself that no equal and just distribution of things can be made, nor that perfect wealth shall ever be among men, unless this propriety be exiled and banished. But so long as it shall continue, so long shall remain among the most and best part of men the heavy and inevitable burden of poverty and wretchedness. Which, as I grant that it may be somewhat eased, so I utterly deny that it can wholly be taken away. For if there were a statute made that no man should possess above a certain measure of ground, and that no man should have in his stock above a prescript and appointed sum of money: if it were by certain laws decreed that nother the king should be of too great power, nother the people too proud and wealthy: and that offices should not be obtained by inordinate suit or by bribes and gifts: that they should nother be bought nor sold, nor that it should be needful for the officers to be at any cost or charge in their offices: for so occasion is given to the officers by fraud and ravin to gather up their money again, and by reason of gifts and bribes the offices be given to rich men, which should rather have been executed of wise men: by such laws, I say, like as sick bodies that be desperate and past cure be wont with continual good cherishing to be kept up: so these evils also might be lightened and mitigated. But that they may be perfectly cured and brought to a good and upright state, it is not to be hoped for whiles every man is master of his own to himself. Yea, and whiles you go about to do your cure of one part, you shall make bigger the sore of another part, so the help of one causeth another's harm. Forasmuch as nothing can be given to any man unless it be taken from another."

"But I am of a contrary opinion," quod I, "for methinketh that men shall never there live wealthily where all things be common. For how can there be abundance of goods, or of anything, where every man withdraweth his hand from labor? Whom the regard of his own gains driveth not to work? and the hope that he hath in other men's travails maketh him slothful. Then when they be pricked with poverty and yet no man can by any law or right defend that for his own which he hath gotten with the labor of his own hands, shall not there of necessity be continual sedition and bloodshed? Specially the authority and reverend of magistrates being taken away, which, what place it may have with such men among whom is no difference, I cannot devise."

"I marvel not," quod he, "that you be of this opinion. For you conceive in your mind either none at all, or else a very false image and similitude of this thing. But if you had been with me in Utopia and had presently seen their fashions and laws, as I did, which lived there five years and more, and would never have come thence but only to make that new land known here: then doubtless you would grant that you never saw people well ordered but only there."

"Surely," quod Master Peter, "it shall be hard for you to make me believe that there is better order in that new land than is here in these countries that we know. For good wits be as well here as there; and I think our commonwealths be ancienter than theirs: wherein long use and experience hath found out many things commodious for man's life, besides that many things here among us have been found by chance, 10 which no wit could ever have devised."

"As touching the ancientness," quod he, "of commonwealths, then you might better judge if you had read the histories and chronicles of that land, which if we may believe, cities were there before there were men here. Now what thing soever hitherto by wit hath been devised, or found by chance, that might be as well there as here. But I think verily, though it were so that we did pass them in wit, yet in study and laborsome endeavor they far pass us. For (as their chronicles testify) before our arrival there, they never heard anything of us, whom they call the ultraequinoctials; saving that once, about twelve hundred years ago, a certain ship was lost 20 by the Isle of Utopia which was driven thither by tempest. Certain Romans and Egyptians were cast on land, which after that never went thence.

"Mark now what profit they took of this one occasion, through diligence and earnest travail. There was no craft nor science within the empery of Rome whereof any profit could rise, but they other learned it of these strangers, or else, of them taking occasion to search for it, found it out. So great profit was it to them that ever any went thither from hence. But if any like chance before this hath brought any man from thence hither, that is as quite out of remembrance as this also perchance 30 in time to come shall be forgotten that ever I was there. And like as they quickly, almost at the first meeting, made their own whatsoever is among us wealthily devised, so I suppose it would be long before we would receive anything that among them is better instituted than among us. And this I suppose is the chief cause why their commonwealths be wiselier governed and do flourish in more wealth than ours, though we neither in wit nor in riches be their inferiors."

"Therefore, gentle Master Raphael," quod I, "I pray you and beseech you describe unto us the island. And study not to be short; but declare largely in order their grounds, their rivers, their cities, their people, their 40 manners, their ordinances, their laws, and, to be short, all things that you shall think us desirous to know. And you shall think us desirous to know whatsoever we know not yet."

"There is nothing," quod he, "that I will do gladlier. For all these things I have fresh in mind. But the matter requireth leisure."

"Let us go in, therefore," quod I, "to dinner: afterward we will bestow the time at our pleasure."

"Content," quod he; "be it."

So we went in and dined. When dinner was done, we came into the same place again, and sat us down upon the same bench, commanding our servants that no man should trouble us. Then I and Master Peter Giles desired Master Raphael to perform his promise. He, therefore, seeing us desirous and willing to hearken to him, when he had sit still and paused a little while, musing and bethinking himself, thus he began to speak.

The end of the first book.

The second book of the communication of Raphael Hythloday, concerning the best state of a commonwealth: containing the description of Utopia, with a large declaration of the godly government, and of all the good laws and orders of the same island.

The island of Utopia containeth in breadth in the middle part of it (for there it is broadest) two hundred miles. Which breadth continueth through the most part of the land, saving that, by little and little, it cometh in, and waxeth narrower towards both the ends. Which fetching about a circuit or compass of five hundred miles, do fashion the whole island like to the new moon. Between these two corners the sea runneth in, dividing them asunder by the distance of eleven miles or thereabouts, and there surmounteth into a large and wide sea, which, by reason that the land of every side compasseth it about and sheltereth it from the winds, is not rough, nor mounteth not with great waves, but almost floweth quietly, not much unlike a great standing pool: and maketh almost all the space within the belly of the land in manner of a haven: and to the great commodity of the inhabitants receiveth in ships towards every part of the land. The forefronts or frontiers of the two corners, what with fords and shelves and what with rocks, be very jeopardous and dangerous. In the middle distance between them both standeth up above the water a great rock, which therefore is nothing perilous because it is in sight. Upon the top of this rock is a fair and a strong tower builded, which they hold with a garrison of men. Other rocks there be, that lie hid under the water, and therefor be dangerous. The channels be known only to themselves. And therefor it seldom chanceth that any stranger, unless he be guided by a Utopian, can come into this haven. Insomuch that they themselves could scarcely enter without jeopardy, but that their way is directed and ruled by certain landmarks standing on the shore. By turning, translating, and removing these marks into other places, they may destroy their enemies' navies, be they never so many. The outside of the land is also full of havens, but the landing is so surely defensed, what by nature and what by workmanship of man's hand, that a few defenders may drive back many armies.

* * * * *

Of the religions in Utopia

There be divers kinds of religion not only in sundry parts of the island but also in divers places of every city. Some worship for god the sun; some the moon; some, some other of the planets. There be that give worship to a man that was once of excellent virtue or of famous glory, not only as god but also as the chiefest and highest god. But the most and the wisest part (rejecting all these) believe that there is a certain godly power unknown, everlasting, incomprehensible, inexplicable, far above the capacity and reach of man's wit, dispersed throughout all the world, not in bigness but in virtue and power. Him they call the father of all. To him alone they attribute the beginnings, the increasings, the proceedings, the changes, and the ends of all things. Nother they give divine honors to any other than to him.

* * * * *

For king Utopus, even at the first beginning, hearing that the inhabitants of the land were before his coming thither at continual dissension and strife among themselves for their religions: perceiving also that this common dissension, whiles every several sect took several parts in fighting for their country, was the only occasion of his conquest over them all; as soon as he had gotten the victory, first of all he made a decree that it should be lawfull for every man to favor and follow what religion he would, and that he might do the best he could to bring other to his opinion; so that he did it peaceably, gently, quietly, and soberly, without hasty and contentious rebuking and inveighing against other. If he could not by fair and gentle speech induce them unto his opinion, yet he should use no kind of violence, and refrain from displeasant and seditious words. To him that would vehemently and fervently in this cause strive and contend, was decreed banishment or bondage. This law did king Utopus make not only for the maintenance of peace which he saw through continual contention and mortal hatred utterly extinguished, but also because he thought this decree should make for the furtherance of religion. Whereof he durst define and determine nothing unadvisedly, as doubt-

ing whether God desiring manifold and divers sorts of honor, would inspire sundry men with sundry kinds of religion. And this surely he thought
a very unmeet and foolish thing, and a point of arrogant presumption to
compel all other by violence and threatenings to agree to the same that
thou believest to be true.

Furthermore, though there be one religion which alone is true, and all
other vain and superstitious, yet did he well foresee (so that the matter
were handled with reason and sober modesty), that the truth of the own
power would at the last issue out and come to light. But if contention
and debate in that behalf should continually be used, as the worst men be 10
most obstinate and stubborn, and in their evil opinion most constant, he
perceived that then the best and holiest religion would be trodden under
foot and destroyed by most vain superstitions, even as good corn is by
thorns and weeds overgrown and choked.

Therefore all this matter he left undiscussed, and gave to every man
free liberty and choice to believe what he would; saving that he earnestly
and straightly charged them, that no man should conceive so vile and
base an opinion of the dignity of man's nature as to think that the souls
do die and perish with the body; or that the world runneth at all adventures, governed by no divine providence. And therefore they believe 20
that after this life vices be extremely punished, and virtues bountifully
rewarded. Him that is of a contrary opinion they count not in the number
of men, as one that hath avaled the high nature of his soul to the vileness
of brute beasts' bodies; much less in the number of their citizens, whose
laws and ordinances, if it were not for fear, he would nothing at all esteem. For you may be sure that he will study other with craft privily to
mock, or else violently to break, the common laws of his country, in
whom remaineth no further fear than of the laws, nor no further hope
than of the body. Wherefore he that is thus minded is deprived of all
honors, excluded from all offices, and reject from all common adminis- 30
trations in the weal public. And thus he is of all sort despised as of an
unprofitable, and of a base and vile nature. Howbeit they put him to no
punishment, because they be persuaded that it is in no man's power to
believe what he list. No, nor they constrained him not with threatenings
to dissemble his mind, and shew countenance contrary to his thought.
For deceit, and falshood, and all manner of lies, as next unto fraud, they
do marvelously detest and abhor. But they suffer him not to dispute in
his opinion and that only among the common people. For else apart among
the priests and men of gravity they do not only suffer but also exhort him
to dispute and argue, hoping that at the last that madness will give place 40
to reason.

*　　*　　*　　*　　*

Thus when Raphael had made an end of his tale, though many things came to my mind which in the manners and laws of that people seemed to be instituted and founded of no good reason, not only in the fashion of their chivalry and in their sacrifices and religions, and in other of their laws, but also, yea, and chiefly, in that which is the principal foundation of all their ordinances, that is to say in the community of their life and living, without any occupying of money, by the which thing only all nobility, magnificence, worship, honor and majesty, the true ornaments and honors, as the common opinion is, of a commonwealth, utterly be 10 overthrown and destroyed: yet because I knew that he was weary of talking, and was not sure whether he could abide that anything should be said against his mind: specially because I remembered that he had reprehended this fault in other, which be afraid lest they should seem not to be wise enough unless they could find some fault in other men's inventions: therefore I, praising both their institutions and his communication, took him by the hand and led him in to supper, saying that we would choose another time to weigh and examine the same matters, and to talk with him more at large therein. Which would to God it might once come to pass. In the meantime, as I cannot agree and consent to all things that 20 he said, being else without doubt a man singularly well learned, and also in all worldly matters exactly and profoundly experienced, so must I needs confess and grant that many things be in the Utopian weal public which in our cities I may rather wish for than hope for.

Thus endeth the afternoon's talk of Raphael Hythloday concerning the laws and institutions of the island of Utopia.

JOHN BOURCHIER, LORD BERNERS

The Introduction and Notes are at page 1288

FROM *Sir John Froyssart: of the cronycles of Englande, Fraunce, Spayne,* etc., 1523

The Chronicles of Froissart

The Preface of John Bourchier, knight, Lord Berners, translator of this present chronicle

40 WHAT condign graces and thanks ought men to give to the writers of histories, who with their great labors have done so much profit to the human life! They shew, open, manifest and declare to the reader, by

example of old antiquity, what we should inquire, desire, and follow. And also what we should eschew, avoid, and utterly flee. For when we (being unexpert of chances) see, behold, and read the ancient acts, gestes, and deeds, how, and with what labors, dangers, and perils they were gested and done, they right greatly admonish, ensign, and teach us how we may lead forth our lives. And farther, he that hath the perfect knowledge of others' joy, wealth, and high prosperity, and also, trouble, sorrow, and great adversity, hath the expert doctrine of all perils. And, albeit that mortal folk are marvelously separated, both by land and water, and right wondrously situate, yet are they and their acts (done peradventure by the space of a thousand years) compact together by the historiographer, as it were the deeds of one self city, and in one man's life. Wherefore I say that history may well be called a Divine Providence. For as the celestial bodies above complect all and at every time the universal world, the creatures therein contained, and all their deeds, semblably so doth history. Is it not a right noble thing for us, by the faults and errors of other, to amend and erect our life into better? We should not seek and acquire that other did, but what thing was most best, most laudable, and worthily done, we should put before our eyes to follow. Be not the sage counsels of two or three old fathers in a city, town, or country, whom long age hath made wise, discreet, and prudent, far more praised, lauded, and dearly loved than of the young men? How much more then ought histories to be commended, praised, and loved, in whom is included so many sage counsels, great reasons, and high wisdoms: of so innumerable persons, of sundry nations, and of every age: and that in so long space as four or five hundred year. The most profitable thing in this world, for the institution of the human life, is history. Once, the continual reading thereof maketh young men equal in prudence to old men: and to old fathers stricken in age, it ministereth experience of things. More, it yieldeth private persons worthy of dignity, rule, and governance. It compelleth the emperors, high rulers, and governors to do noble deeds: to the end they may obtain immortal glory. It exciteth, moveth, and stirreth the strong, hardy warriors, for the great laud that they have after they been dead, promptly to go in hand with great and hard perils in defense of their country. And it prohibiteth reprovable persons to do mischievous deeds, for fear of infamy and shame. So thus, through the monuments of writing, which is the testimony unto virtue, many men have been moved, some to build cities, some to devise and establish laws right profitable, necessary, and behoveful for the human life, some other to find new arts, crafts, and sciences, very requisite to the use of mankind. But above all things, whereby man's wealth riseth, special laud and cause ought to be given to history. It is the keeper of such things as have been virtuously done, and

the witness of evil deeds. And, by the benefit of history, all noble, high,
and virtuous acts be immortal. What moved the strong and fierce Hercules to enterprise in his life so many great, incomparable labors and
perils? Certainly naught else but that for his merits immortality might
be given to him of all folk. In semblable wise did his imitator, noble Duke
Theseus, and many other innumerable worthy princes and famous men,
whose virtues been redeemed from oblivion, and shine by history. And
whereas other monuments in process of time, by variable chances, are
confused and lost, the virtue of history, diffused and spread through the
10 universal world, hath to her custos and keeper it (that is to say, time)
which consumeth the other writings. And albeit that those men are right
worthy of great laud and praise who by their writings shew and lead us
the way to virtue: yet nevertheless the poems, laws, and other arts that
they found, devised, and writ been mixed with some damage. And sometime for the truth, they ensign a man to lie. But only history, truly with
words representing the acts, gestes, and deeds done, complecteth all
profit. It moveth, stirreth, and compelleth to honesty; detesteth, irketh,
and abhorreth vices. It extolleth, enhanceth, and lifteth up such as been
noble and virtuous: depresseth, poistereth, and thrusteth down such as
20 been wicked, evil, and reprovable. What knowledge should we have of
ancient things past, and history were not? Which is the testimony thereof,
the light of truth, the mistress of the life human, the president of remembrance, and the messenger of antiquity. Why moved and stirred Phalerius
the King Ptolemy oft and diligently to read books? Forsooth, for none
other cause but that those things are found written in books that the
friends dare not shew to the prince. Much more I would fain write of
the incomparable profit of history, but I fear me that I should too sore
torment the reader of this, my preface. And also I doubt not but that the
great utility thereof is better known than I could declare; wherefore,
30 I shall briefly come to a point. Thus, when I advertised and remembered
the manifold commodities of history, how beneficial it is to mortal folk,
and eke how laudable and meritorious a deed it is to write histories, fixed
my mind to do something therein. And ever when this imagination came
to me, I volved, turned, and read many volumes and books containing
famous histories. And among all other, I read diligently the four volumes
or books of Sir John Froissart of the country of Hainault, written in the
French tongue: which I judged commodious, necessary, and profitable to
be had in English, sith they treat of the famous acts done in our parts.
That is to say: in England, France, Spain, Portugal, Scotland, Bretagne,
40 Flanders, and other places adjoining: and specially, they redound to the
honor of Englishmen. What pleasure shall it be to the noble gentlemen
of England to see, behold, and read the high enterprises, famous acts,

and glorious deeds, done and achieved by their valiant ancestors! Forsooth
and God: this hath moved me at the high commandment of my most
redoubted sovereign lord, King Henry the Eighth, king of England and
of France, and high defender of the Christian faith, etc., under his gracious
supportation, to do my devoir to translate out of French into our maternal
English tongue, the said volumes of Sir John Froissart, which chronicle
beginneth at the reign of the most noble and valiant King Edward the
Third, the year of our Lord, a thousand three hundred and sixteen, and
continueth to the beginning of the reign of King Henry the Fourth, the
year of our Lord God a thousand and four hundred (the space between 10
is threescore and fourteen years), requiring all the readers and hearers
thereof to take this, my rude translation, in gree. And in that I have not
followed mine author word by word, yet I trust I have ensued the true
report of the sentence of the matter. And as for the true naming of all
manner of personages, countries, cities, towns, rivers, or fields: whereas
I could not name them properly nor aptly in English, I have written them
according as I found them in French. And though I have not given every
lord, knight, or squire his true addition, yet I trust I have not swerved from
the true sentence of the matter. And thereas I have named the distance
between places by miles and leagues, they must be understood according 20
to the custom of the countries whereas they be named, for in some place
they be longer than in some other. In England a league or mile is well
known, in France a league is two miles, and in some place three; and in
other countries more or less; every nation hath sundry customs. And if
any fault be in this my rude translation, I remit the correction thereof to
them that discreetly shall find any reasonable default. And in their so
doing, I shall pray God to send them the bliss of heaven. Amen.

* * * *

VOL. I, CHAP. 146   30

How the town of Calais was given up to the king of England.

After that the French king was thus departed from Sangate, they within
Calais saw well how their succor failed them, for the which they were
in great sorrow. Then they desired so much their captain Sir John of
Vienne that he went to the walls of the town and made a sign to speak
with some person of the host. When the king heard thereof, he sent thither
Sir Gaultier of Manny and Sir Basset; then Sir John of Vienne said to
them: "Sirs, ye be right valiant knights in deeds of arms and ye know well
how the king my master hath sent me and other to this town, and com- 40
manded us to keep it to his behalf: in such wise that we take no blame nor
to him no damage, and we have done all that lieth in our power. Now

our succours hath failed us and we be so sore strained that we have naught
to live withal but that we must all die or else enrage for famine: without
the noble and gentle king of yours will take mercy on us, the which to
do we require you to desire him to have pity on us and to let us go and
depart as we be and let him take the town and castle and all the goods
that be therein, the which is great abundance."

Then Sir Gaultier of Manny said: "Sir we know somewhat of the intention of the king our master, for he hath shewed it unto us. Surely know
for truth it is not his mind that ye nor they within the town should depart
10 so, for it is his will that ye all should put yourselves into his pure will to
ransom all such as pleaseth him and to put to death such as he list, for they
of Calais hath done him such contraries and dispights and hath caused
him to dispend so much good and lost many of his men that he is sore
grieved against them."

Then the captain said: "Sir, this is too hard a matter to us. We are here
within a small sort of knights and squires who hath truly served the king
our master as well as ye serve yours. In like case and we have endured
much pain and unease but we shall yet endure as much pain as ever knights
did rather than to consent that the worst lad in the town should have any
20 more evil than the greatest of us all. Therefore, sir, we pray you that of
your humility, yet that ye will go and speak to the king of England: and
desire him to have pity of us for we trust in him so much gentleness that
by the grace of God his purpose shall change."

Sir Gaultier of Manny and Sir Basset returned to the king and declared
to him all that had been said; the king said he would none otherwise but
that they should yield them up simply to his pleasure. Then Sir Gaultier
said: "Sir, saving your displeasure in this, ye may be in the wrong, for ye
shall give by this an evil example; if ye send any of us your servants into
any fortress, we will not be very glad to go, if ye put any of them in the
30 town to death after they be yielded. For in like wise they will deal with
us, if the case fell like." The which words diverse other lords that were
there present sustained and maintained.

Then the king said: "Sirs, I will not be alone against you all; therefore,
Sir Gaultier of Manny, ye shall go and say to the captain, that all the
grace that he shall find now in me is, that they let six of the chief burgesses
of the town come out bareheaded, barefooted, and barelegged, and in
their shirts with halters about their necks, with the keys of the town and
castle in their hands, and let them six yield themselves purely to my will,
and the residue I will take to mercy."

40 Then Sir Gaultier returned and found Sir John of Vienne still on the
wall, abiding for an answer. Then Sir Gaultier shewed him all the grace
that he could get of the king. "Well," quod Sir John, "Sir, I require you

tarry here a certain space till I go in to the town and shew this to the commons of the town, who sent me hither."

Then Sir John went unto the market place and sounded the common bell. Then incontinent men and women assembled there; then the captain made report of all that he had done, and said: "Sirs, it will be none otherwise; therefore now take advice and make a short answer."

Then all the people began to weep and to make such sorrow that there was not so hard a heart if they had seen them, but that would have had great pity of them. The captain himself wept piteously. At last the most rich burgess of all the town, called Eustace of St. Peters, rose up and said openly: "Sirs great and small, great mischief it should be to suffer to die such people as be in this town, other by famine or otherwise, when there is a mean to save them. I think he or they should have great merit of our Lord God that might keep them from such mischief; as for my part, I have so good trust in our Lord God that if I die in the quarrel to save the residue, that God would pardon me. Wherefore to save them I will be the first to put my life in jeopardy."

When he had thus said, every man worshipped him, and divers kneeled down at his feet with sore weeping and sore sighs. Then another honest burgess rose and said: "I will keep company with my gossip Eustace." He was called John Dayre. Then rose up Jaques of Wyssant, who was rich in goods and heritage. He said also that he would hold company with his two cousins in like wise; so did Peter of Wyssant his brother; and then rose two other, they said they would do the same. Then they went and apparelled them as the king desired.

Then the captain went with them to the gate; there was great lamentation made of men, women, and children at their departing; then the gate was opened and he issued out with the six burgesses and closed the gate again, so that they were between the gate and the barriers. Then he said to Sir Gaultier of Manny: "Sir, I deliver here to you as captain of Calais, by the whole consent of all the people of the town, these six burgesses, and I swear to you truly that they be, or were, today most honorable, rich, and most notable burgesses of all the town of Calais; wherefore, gentle knight, I require you, pray the king to have mercy on them that they die not."

Quod Sir Gaultier: "I cannot say what the king will do, but I shall do for them the best I can."

Then the barriers were opened, the six burgesses went towards the king, and the captain entered again into the town. When Sir Gaultier presented these burgesses to the king they kneeled down and held up their hands and said: "Gentle king, behold here we six who were burgesses of Calais and great merchants. We have brought to you the keys of the town and of the castle, and we submit ourselves clearly into your will and pleasure, to save the residue of the people of Calais, who have suffered great pain. Sir, we beseech your grace to have mercy and pity on us through your high noblesse." Then all the earls and barons, and other that were there, wept for pity.

The king looked felly on them, for greatly he hated the people of Calais for the great damages and displeasures they had done him on the sea before. Then he commanded their heads to be stricken off; then every man required the king for mercy, but he would hear no man in that behalf; then Sir Gaultier of Manny said: "Ah, noble king, for God's sake refrain
10 your courage. Ye have the name of sovereign noblesse; therefore now do not a thing that should blemish your renown nor to give cause to some to speak of your villainy. Every man will say it is a great cruelty to put to death such honest persons who by their own wills put themselves into your grace to save their company."

Then the king wryed away from him and commanded to send for the hangman and said they of Calais hath caused many of my men to be slain; wherefore these shall die in like wise.

Then the queen, being great with child, kneeled down afore weeping said: "O gentle sir, since I passed the sea in great peril I have desired noth-
20 ing of you; therefore now I humbly require you in the honor of the Son of the Virgin Mary, and for the love of me, that ye will take mercy of these six burgesses."

The king beheld the queen and stood still in a study a space and then said: "O dame, I would ye had been as now in some other place. Ye make such request to me that I cannot deny you; wherefore I give them to you to do your pleasure with them."

Then the queen caused them to be brought into her chamber and made the halters to be taken from their necks and caused them to be new clothed and gave them their dinner at their leisure. And then she gave each of
30 them six nobles and made them to be brought out of the host in safeguard and set at their liberty.

SIMON FISH

The Introduction and Notes are at page 1289

FROM *A supplicacyon for the Beggars*, [1529]

A Supplication for the Beggars

To the King, our sovereign lord   10

MOST lamentably complaineth their woeful misery unto Your Highness your poor daily bedemen, the wretched, hideous monsters (on whom scarcely for horror any eye dare look), the foul, unhappy sort of lepers and other sore people, needy, impotent, blind, lame, and sick, that live only by alms, how that their number is daily so sore increased that all the alms of all the well-disposed people of this your realm is not half enough for to sustain them, but that for very constraint they die for hunger. And this most pestilent mischief is comen upon your said poor bedemen by the reason that there is, in the times of your noble predecessors past, craftily crept into this 20 your realm another sort, not of impotent but of strong, puissant, and counterfeit-holy, and idle beggars and vagabonds, which, since the time of their first entry, by all the craft and wiliness of Satan are now increased under your sight not only into a great number, but also into a kingdom. These are (not the herds, but the ravenous wolves going in herds' clothing, devouring the flock) the bishops, abbots, priors, deacons, archdeacons, suffragans, priests, monks, canons, friars, pardoners, and summoners.

And who is able to number this idle, ravenous sort which (setting all labor aside) have begged so importunately that they have gotten into their hands more than the third part of all your realm. The goodliest lordships, 30 manors, lands, and territories are theirs. Besides this, they have the tenth part of all the corn, meadow, pasture, grass, wool, colts, calves, lambs, pigs, geese, and chickens. Over and besides the tenth part of every servant's wages, the tenth part of the wool, milk, honey, wax, cheese, and butter. Yea, and they look so narrowly upon their profits that the poor wives must be countable to them of every tenth egg or else she getteth not her rights at Easter, shall be taken as an heretic. Hereto have they their four offering days. What money pull they in by probates of testaments, privy tithes, and by men's offerings to their pilgrimages, and at their first masses? Every man and child that is buried must pay somewhat for masses and dirges to be 40 sung for him, or else they will accuse the dead's friends and executors of heresy. What money get they by mortuaries, by hearing of confessions (and yet they will keep thereof no counsel), by hallowing of churches, altars, superaltars, chapels, and bells, by cursing of men and absolving them again for money? What a multitude of money gather the pardoners in a year? How much money get the summoners by extortion in a year by acciting the people to the commissaries' court and afterward releasing th'appearance for money? Finally, the infinite number of begging friars, what get they in a year?

Here, if it please Your Grace to mark, ye shall see a thing far out of joint. There are within your realm of England fifty-two thousand parish
10 churches. And this standing that there be but ten households in every parish, yet are there five hundred thousand and twenty thousand households. And of every of these households hath every of the five orders of friars a penny a quarter for every order, that is, for all the five orders, five pence a quarter for every house. That is, for all the five orders, twenty pence a year of every house. *Summa,* five hundred thousand and twenty thousand quarters of angels. That is, two hundred sixty thousand half angels. *Summa,* one hundred thirty thousand angels. *Summa totalis,* forty-three thousand pounds and three hundred thirty-three pounds, six shillings, and eight pence sterling, whereof not four hundred years past they had not one penny. Oh,
20 grievous and painful exactions thus yearly to be paid! from the which the people of your noble predecessors, the kings of the ancient Britons, ever stood free. And this will they have or else they will procure him that will not give it them to be taken as an heretic.

What tyrant ever oppressed the people like this cruel and vengeable generation? What subjects shall be able to help their prince that be after this fashion yearly polled? What good Christian people can be able to succor us poor lepers, blind, sore, and lame, that be thus yearly oppressed? Is it any marvel that your people so complain of poverty? Is it any marvel that the taxes, fifteens, and subsidies that Your Grace most tenderly, of
30 great compassion, hath taken among your people to defend them from the threatened ruin of their commonwealth have been so slothfully, yea painfully, levied? Seeing that almost the utmost penny that might have been levied hath been gathered before yearly by this ravenous, cruel, and insatiable generation. The Danes, neither the Saxons, in the time of the ancient Britons should never have been able to have brought their armies from so far hither into your land to have conquered it if they had had at that time such a sort of idle gluttons to find at home. The noble King Arthur had never been able to have carried his army to the foot of the mountains to resist the coming down of Lucius the emperor, if such yearly
40 exactions had been taken of his people. The Greeks had never been able to have so long continued at the siege of Troy if they had had at home such an idle sort of cormorants to find. The ancient Romans had never been

able to have put all the whole world under their obeisance if their people had been thus yearly oppressed. The Turk now, in your time, should never be able to get so much ground of Christendom if he had in his empire such a sort of locusts to devour his substance. Lay then these sums to the foresaid third part of the possessions of the realm that ye may see whether it draw nigh unto the half of the whole substance of the realm or not, so shall ye find that it draweth far above. Now let us then compare the number of this unkind, idle sort unto the number of the lay people, and we shall see whether it be indifferently shifted or not that they should have half. Compare them to the number of men; so are they not the hundredth person. Compare them to men, women, and children, then are they not the four hundredth person in number. One part, therefore, in four hundred parts divided were too much for them except they did labor. What an unequal burthen is it that they have half with the multitude and are not the four hundredth person of their number? What tongue is able to tell that ever there was any commonwealth so sore oppressed since the world first began?

And what do all these greedy sort of sturdy, idle, holy thieves with these yearly exactions that they take of the people? Truly nothing but exempt themselves from th'obedience of Your Grace. Nothing but translate all rule, power, lordship, authority, obedience, and dignity from Your Grace unto them. Nothing but that all your subjects should fall into disobedience and rebellion against Your Grace and be under them. As they did unto your noble predecessor, King John: which, forbecause that he would have punished certain traitors that had conspired with the French king to have deposed him from his crown and dignity (among the which a clerk called Stephen, whom afterward, against the king's will, the pope made bishop of Canterbury, was one), interdicted his land. For the which matter your most noble realm wrongfully (alas, for shame) hath stood tributary (not unto any kind temporal prince, but unto a cruel, devilish bloodsupper, drunken in the blood of the saints and martyrs of Christ) ever since.

Here were an holy sort of prelates that thus cruelly could punish such a righteous king, all his realm, and succession, for doing right! Here were a charitable sort of holy men that could thus interdict an whole realm, and pluck away the obedience of the people from their natural liege lord and king, for none other cause but for his righteousness. Here were a blessed sort, not of meek herds but of bloodsuppers, that could set the French king upon such a righteous prince to cause him to lose his crown and dignity, to make effusion of the blood of his people, unless this good and blessed king of great compassion, more fearing and lamenting the shedding of the blood of his people than the loss of his crown and dignity, against all right and conscience had submitted himself unto them. Oh case most horrible that ever so noble a king, realm, and succession should thus be made to stoop to such a sort of bloodsuppers! Where was his sword, power, crown, and dignity become whereby he might have done justice in this manner? Where was their obedience become that should have been subject under his high power in this matter? Yea, where was the obedience of all his subjects become that, for maintenance of the commonwealth, should have holpen him manfully to have resisted these bloodsuppers to the shedding of their blood? Was not all together by their policy translated from this good king unto them?

Yea, and what do they more? Truly, nothing but apply themselves, by
10 all the sleights they may, to have to do with every man's wife, every man's daughter, and every man's maid, that cuckoldry and bawdry should reign over all among your subjects, that no man should know his own child, that their bastards might inherit the possessions of every man, to put the right-begotten children clear beside their inheritance in subversion of all estates and godly order. These be they that, by their abstaining from marriage, do let the generation of the people whereby all the realm at length, if it should be continued, shall be made desert and inhabitable. These be they that have made an hundred thousand idle whores in your realm, which would have gotten their living honestly, in the sweat of their faces, had not their super-
20 fluous riches illected them to unclean lust and idleness. These be they that corrupt the whole generation of mankind in your realm, that catch the pox of one woman and bear them to another, that be brent with one woman and bear it to another, that catch the lepry of one woman and bear it to another. Yea, some one of them shall boast among his fellows that he hath meddled with an hundred women. These be they that, when they have once drawn men's wives to such incontinency, spend away their husbands' goods, make the women to run away from their husbands, yea, run away themselves both with wife and goods, bring both man, wife, and children to idleness, theft, and beggary.

30 Yea, who is able to number the great and broad bottomless ocean-seaful of evils that this mischievous and sinful generation may lawfully bring upon us unpunished? Where is your sword, power, crown, and dignity become, that should punish (by punishment of death, even as other men are punished) the felonies, rapes, murders, and treasons committed by this sinful generation? Where is their obedience become that should be under your high power in this matter? Is not all together translated and exempt from Your Grace unto them? Yes, truly. What an infinite number of people might have been increased to have peopled the realm if these sort of folk had been married like other men? What breach of matrimony
40 is there brought in by them? Such truly as was never since the world began among the whole multitude of the heathen.

Who is she that will set her hands to work to get three pence a day, and may have at least twenty pence a day to sleep an hour with a friar, a monk, or a priest? What is he that would labor for a groat a day, and may have at least twelve pence a day to be bawd to a priest, a monk, or a friar? What a sort are there of them that marry priests' sovereign ladies but to cloak the priests' incontinency, and that they may have a living of the priest themselves for their labor? How many thousands doth such lubricity bring to beggary, theft, and idleness which should have kept their good name and have set themselves to work had not been this excess treasure of the spiritualty? What honest man dare take any man or woman in his service that hath been at such a school with a spiritual man? Oh the grievous shipwrack of the commonwealth, which in ancient time, before the coming in of these ravenous wolves, was so prosperous that then there were but few thieves; yea, theft was at that time so rare that Caesar was not compelled to make penalty of death upon felony, as Your Grace may well perceive in his *Institutes*. There was also at that time but few poor people, and yet they did not beg, but there was given them enough unasked, for there was at that time none of these ravenous wolves to ask it from them, as it appeareth in the Acts of the Apostles. Is it any marvel though there be now so many beggars, thieves, and idle people? Nay, truly.

What remedy? Make laws against them? I am in doubt whether ye be able. Are they not stronger in your own parliament house than yourself? What a number of bishops, abbots, and priors are lords of your parliament? Are not all the learned men in your realm in fee with them to speak in your parliament house for them against your crown, dignity, and commonwealth of your realm, a few of your own learned counsel only excepted? What law can be made against them that may be available? Who is he (though he be grieved never so sore), for the murder of his ancestor, ravishment of his wife, of his daughter, robbery, trespass, mayhem, debt, or any other offense, dare lay it to their charge by any way of action; and if he do, then is he, by and by, by their wiliness accused of heresy. Yea, they will so handle him or he pass that, except he will bear a faggot for their pleasure, he shall be excommunicate, and then be all his actions dashed. So captive are your laws unto them that no man that they list to excommunicate may be admitted to sue any action in any of your courts. If any man in your sessions dare be so hardy to indict a priest of any such crime, he hath, or the year go out, such a yoke of heresy laid in his neck that it maketh him wish that he had not done it. Your Grace may see what a work there is in London, how the bishop rageth for indicting of certain curates of extortion and incontinency the last year in the warmoll quest. Had not Richard Hunne commenced action of praemunire against a priest, he had been yet alive and none heretic at all, but an honest man.

Did not divers of your noble progenitors, seeing their crown and dignity run into ruin and to be thus craftily translated into the hands of this mischievous generation, make divers statutes for the reformation thereof, among which the statute of mortmain was one, to the intent that after that time they should have no more given unto them?

But what availed it? Have they not gotten into their hands more lands since than any duke in England hath, the statute notwithstanding? Yea, have they not, for all that, translated into their hands from Your Grace half your kingdom thoroughly? The whole name, as reason is, for the ancienty of your kingdom, which was before theirs and out of the which theirs is grown, only abiding with Your Grace? and of one kingdom made twain: the spiritual kingdom (as they call it) for they will be named first, and your temporal kingdom. And which of these two kingdoms, suppose ye, is like to overgrow the other, yea, to put the other clear out of memory? Truly the kingdom of the bloodsuppers, for to them is given daily out of your kingdom. And that that is once given them cometh never from them again. Such laws have they that none of them may neither give nor sell nothing.

What law can be made so strong against them that they other with money or else with other policy will not break and set at naught? What kingdom can endure that ever giveth thus from him and receiveth nothing again? O, how all the substance of your realm forthwith, your sword, power, crown, dignity, and obedience of your people, runneth headlong into the insatiable whirlpool of these greedy goulafres, to be swallowed and devoured!

Neither have they any other color to gather these yearly exactions into their hands but that they say they pray for us to God to deliver our souls out of the pains of purgatory, without whose prayer, they say, or at least without the pope's pardon, we could never be delivered thence; which, if it be true, then is it good reason that we give them all these things, all were it one hundred times as much; but there be many men of great literature and judgment that, for the love they have unto the truth and unto the commonwealth, have not feared to put themself into the greatest infamy that may be, in abjection of all the world, yea, in peril of death, to declare their opinion in this matter, which is that there is no purgatory, but that it is a thing invented by the covetousness of the spiritualty only to translate all kingdoms from other princes unto them, and that there is not one word spoken of it in all Holy Scripture. They say also that, if there were a purgatory, and also if that the pope with his pardons for money may deliver one soul thence, he may deliver him as well without money; if he may deliver one, he may deliver a thousand; if he may deliver a thousand, he may deliver them all, and so destroy purgatory. And

then is he a cruel tyrant, without all charity, if he keep them there in
prison and in pain till men will give him money.

Likewise say they of all the whole sort of the spiritualty, that, if they
will not pray for no man but for them that give them money, they are
tyrants and lack charity, and suffer those souls to be punished and pained
uncharitably for lack of their prayers. These sort of folks they call heretics, these they burn, these they rage against, put to open shame, and
make them bear faggots. But whether they be heretics or no, well I wot
that this purgatory and the pope's pardons is all the cause of translation
of your kingdom so fast into their hands; wherefore it is manifest it can- 10
not be of Christ, for He gave more to the temporal kingdom, He himself paid tribute to Caesar. He took nothing from him, but taught that
the high powers should be always obeyed; yea, He himself (although
He were most free lord of all and innocent) was obedient unto the high
powers unto death. This is the great scab why they will not let the New
Testament go abroad in your mother tongue lest men should espy that
they, by their cloaked hypocrisy, do translate thus fast your kingdom into
their hands; that they are not obedient unto your high power; that they
are cruel, unclean, unmerciful, and hypocrites, that they seek not the
honor of Christ but their own; that remission of sins are not given by the 20
pope's pardon, but by Christ, for the sure faith and trust that we have in
Him. Here may Your Grace well perceive that, except ye suffer their
hypocrisy to be disclosed, all is like to run into their hands, and, as long
as it is covered, so long shall it seem to every man to be a great impiety not
to give them. For this I am sure Your Grace thinketh (as the truth is):
I am as good a man as my father; why may I not as well give them as
much as my father did? And of this mind I am sure are all the lords,
knights, squires, gentlemen, and yeomen in England, yea, and until it
be disclosed, all your people will think that your statute of mortmain was
never made with no good conscience, seeing that it taketh away the 30
liberty of your people, in that they may not as lawfully buy their souls out
of purgatory by giving to the spiritualty as their predecessors did in times
past.

Wherefore, if ye will eschew the ruin of your crown and dignity, let
their hypocrisy be uttered, and that shall be more speedful in this matter
than all the laws that may be made, be they never so strong. For to make
a law for to punish any offender, except it were more for to give other men
an ensample to beware to commit such like offense, what should it avail?
Did not Dr. Allen most presumptuously, now in your time, against all
his allegiance, all that ever he could to pull from you the knowledge of 40
such pleas as long unto your high courts unto another court, in derogation of your crown and dignity? Did not also Dr. Horsey and his com-

plices most heinously, as all the world knoweth, murder in prison that honest merchant, Richard Hunne, for that he sued your writ of praemunire against a priest that wrongfully held him in plea in a spiritual court for a matter whereof the knowledge belonged unto your high courts? And what punishment was there done that any man may take example of to beware of like offense? Truly none, but that the one paid five hundred pounds (as it is said to the building of your Star Chamber), and, when that payment was once past, the captains of his kingdom (because he fought so manfully against your crown and dignity) have heaped to
10 him benefice upon benefice, so that he is rewarded ten times as much. The other, as it is said, paid six hundred pounds for him and his complices, which, forbecause that he had likewise fought so manfully against your crown and dignity, was immediately (as he had obtained your most gracious pardon) promoted by the captains of his kingdom with benefice upon benefice to the value of four times as much. Who can take example of this punishment to beware of such like offense? Who is he of their kingdom that will not rather take courage to commit like offense, seeing the promotions that fell to these men for their so offending. So weak and blunt is your sword to strike at one of the offenders of this crooked and
20 perverse generation. And this is by the reason that the chief instrument of your law, yea, the chief of your counsel, and he which hath your sword in his hand, to whom also all the other instruments are obedient, is always a spiritual man which hath ever such an inordinate love unto his own kingdom that he will maintain that, though all the temporal kingdoms and commonwealth of the world should therefor utterly be undone.

Here leave we out the greatest matter of all, lest that we, declaring such an horrible carrion of evil against the ministers of iniquity, should seem to declare the one only fault, or rather the ignorance, of our best beloved minister of righteousness, which is to be hid till he may be learned
30 by these small enormities that we have spoken of, to know it plainly himself. But what remedy to relieve us, your poor, sick, lame, and sore bedemen? To make many hospitals for the relief of the poor people? Nay, truly. The more the worse, for ever the fat of the whole foundation hangeth on the priests' beards. Divers of your noble predecessors, kings of this realm, have given lands to monasteries to give a certain sum of money yearly to the poor people, whereof, for the anciency of the time, they give never one penny. They have likewise given to them to have a certain masses said daily for them, whereof they say never one. If the abbot of Westminster should sing every day as many masses for his found-
40 ers as he is bound to do by his foundation, one thousand monks were too few. Wherefore, if Your Grace will build a sure hospital that never shall fail to relieve us all, your poor bedemen, so take from them all these

things. Set these sturdy loobies abroad in the world to get them wives of their own, to get their living with their labor in the sweat of their faces, according to the commandment of God (Gen. iii.), to give other idle people by their example occasion to go to labor. Tie these holy, idle thieves to the carts to be whipped naked about every market town till they will fall to labor, that they, by their importunate begging, take not away the alms that the good Christian people would give unto us sore, impotent, miserable people, your bedemen.

Then shall as well the number of our foresaid monstrous sort, as of the bawds, whores, thieves, and idle people decrease. Then shall these ₁₀ great yearly exactions cease. Then shall not your sword, power, crown, dignity, and obedience of your people be translated from you. Then shall you have full obedience of your people. Then shall the idle people be set to work. Then shall matrimony be much better kept. Then shall the generation of your people be increased. Then shall your commons increase in riches. Then shall the Gospel be preached. Then shall none beg our alms from us. Then shall we have enough and more than shall suffice us, which shall be the best hospital that ever was founded for us. Then shall we daily pray to God for your most noble estate long to endure.

Domine salvum fac regem.   ₂₀

SIR THOMAS ELYOT

The Introduction and Notes are at page 1291

From *The boke named the Gouernour,* 1531

The Governour   ₃₀

The proem of Thomas Elyot, knight, unto the most noble and victorious prince, King Henry the Eight, king of England and France, defender of the true faith, and lord of Ireland.

I, LATE considering (most excellent Prince and mine only redoubted Sovereign Lord) my duty that I owe to my natural country, with my faith also of allegiance and oath, wherewith I am double bounden unto Your Majesty, moreover the accompt that I have to render for that one little talent delivered to me, to employ (as I suppose) to the increase of virtue, I am (as God judge me) violently stirred to divulgate or set ₄₀ forth some part of my study, trusting thereby t' acquit me of my duties to God, Your Highness, and this my country. Wherefore, taking com-

fort and boldness partly of Your Grace's most benevolent inclination
toward the universal weal of your subjects, partly inflamed with zeal, I
have now enterprised to describe in our vulgar tongue the form of a just
public weal: which matter I have gathered as well of the sayings of most
noble authors (Greeks and Latins) as by mine own experience: I being
continually trained in some daily affairs of the public weal of this, your
most noble realm, almost from my childhood. Which attemptate is not
of presumption to teach any person, I myself having most need of teaching; but only to the intent that men which will be studious about the weal
public may find the thing thereto expedient compendiously written. And
forasmuch as this present book treateth of the education of them that
hereafter may be deemed worthy to be governors of the public weal under
Your Highness (which Plato affirmeth to be the first and chief part of a
public weal, Solomon saying also where governors be not, the people
shall fall into ruin) I therefore have named it *The Governor,* and do now
dedicate it unto Your Highness as the first fruits of my study: verily
trusting that your most excellent wisdom will therein esteem my loyal
heart and diligent endeavor by the example of Artaxerxes, the noble king
of Persia, who rejected not the poor husbandman which offered to him
his homely hands full of clean water, but most graciously received it with
thanks, esteeming the present not after the value but rather to the will
of the giver. Semblably, King Alexander retained with him the poet
Cherilus honorably for writing his history, although that the poet was but
of a small estimation: which that prince did, not for lack of judgment, he
being of excellent learning as disciple to Aristotle; but to th'intent that
his liberality employed on Cherilus should animate or give courage to
others, much better learned, to contend with him in a semblable enterprise. And if, most virtuous Prince, I may perceive Your Highness to be
herewith pleased, I shall soon after (God giving me quietness) present
Your Grace with the residue of my study and labors. Wherein Your
Highness shall well perceive that I nothing esteem so much in this world
as your royal estate (my most dear Sovereign Lord) and the public weal
of my country, protesting unto Your Excellent Majesty that where I
commend herein any one virtue or dispraise any one vice, I mean the general description of th'one and th'other, without any other particular meaning to the reproach of any one person: to the which protestation I am now
driven through the malignity of this present time, all disposed to malicious
detraction. Wherefore I most humbly beseech Your Highness to deign
to be patron and defender of this little work again the assaults of malign
interpreters, which fail not to rent and deface the renown of writers,
they themselves being in nothing to the public weal profitable: which is

by no man sooner perceived than by Your Highness, being both in wisdom
and very nobility equal to the most excellent princes, whom, I beseech
God, ye may surmount in long life and perfect felicity. Amen.

*   *   *   *   *

THE FIRST BOOK

*   *   *   *   *

The education or form of bringing up of the child of a gentleman   10
which is to have authority in a public weal. Cap. iiii.

Forasmuch as all noble authors do conclude, and also common experience proveth, that where the governors of realms and cities be founden
adorned with virtues, and do employ their study and mind to the public
weal, as well to the augmentation thereof as to the establishing and long
continuance of the same: there a public weal must needs be both honorable and wealthy. To the intent that I will declare how such personages
may be prepared, I will use the policy of a wise and cunning gardener,
who, purposing to have in his garden a fine and precious herb, that should
be to him and all other repairing thereto excellently commodious or 20
pleasant, he will first search throughout his garden where he can find
the most mellow and fertile earth, and therein will he put the seed of the
herb to grow and be nourished: and in most diligent wise attend that no
weed be suffered to grow or approach nigh unto it: and, to the intent it
may thrive the faster, as soon as the form of an herb once appeareth, he
will set a vessel of water by it in such wise that it may continually distil
on the root sweet drops: and, as it springeth in stalk, underset it with
something, that it break not, and alway keep it clean from weeds. Semblable order will I ensue in the forming the gentle wits of noblemen's
children, who, from the wombs of their mother, shall be made propice 30
or apt to the governance of a public weal.

First, they unto whom the bringing up of such children appertaineth
ought, again the time that their mother shall be of them delivered, to be
sure of a nurse, which should be of no servile condition or vice notable.
For, as some ancient writers do suppose, oftentimes the child sucketh the
vice of his nurse with the milk of her pap. And also observe that she be
of mature or ripe age, not under twenty years or above thirty, her body
also being clean from all sickness or deformity, and having her complexion
most of the right and pure sanguine. Forasmuch as the milk thereof
coming excelleth all other, both in sweetness and substance. Moreover, 40
to the nurse should be appointed another woman of approved virtue, dis-

cretion, and gravity, who shall not suffer, in the child's presence, to be
shewed any act or tache dishonest, or any wanton or unclean word to be
spoken; and for that cause all men, except physicians only, should be excluded and kept out of the nursery. Perchance some will scorn me for
that I am so serious, saying that there is no such damage to be feared in
an infant, who, for tenderness of years, hath not the understanding to
discern good from evil. And yet no man will deny but, in that innocency,
he will discern milk from butter, and bread from pap, and, ere he can
speak, he will with his hand or countenance signify which he desireth.
10 And I verily do suppose that in the brains and hearts of children, which
be members spiritual whiles they be tender, and the little slips of reason
begin in them to burgeon, there may hap, by evil custom, some pestiferous
dew of vice to pierce the said members and infect and corrupt the soft and
tender buds, whereby the fruit may grow wild and sometime contain in
it fervent and mortal poison, to the utter destruction of a realm.

And we have in daily experience that little infants assayeth to follow
not only the words but also the faictes and gesture of them that be provecte
in years. For we daily hear, to our great heaviness, children swear great
oaths and speak lascivious and unclean words by the example of other
20 whom they hear, whereat the lewd parents do rejoice, soon after, or in
this world or elsewhere, to their great pain and torment. Contrariwise,
we behold some children, kneeling in their game before images and holding up their little white hands, do move their pretty mouths as they were
praying: other going and singing as it were in procession. Whereby they
do express their disposition to the imitation of those things, be they good
or evil, which they usually do see or hear. Wherefore not only princes,
but also all other children, from their nurses' paps, are to be kept diligently from the hearing or seeing of any vice or evil tache. And incontinent as soon as they can speak, it behooveth, with most pleasant allurings,
30 to instil in them sweet manners and virtuous custom. Also to provide for
them such companions and playfellows which shall not do in his presence
any reproachable act or speak any unclean word or oath, ne to advaunt
him with flattery, remembering his nobility or any other like thing wherein
he might glory: unless it be to persuade him to virtue: or to withdraw him
from vice: in the remembering to him the danger of his evil example.
For noblemen more grievously offend by their example than by their
deed. Yet often remembrance to them of their estate may happen to
radicate in their hearts intolerable pride, the most dangerous poison to
nobleness. Wherefore there is required to be therein much cautel and
40 soberness.

*   *   *   *   *

At what age a tutor should be provided and what shall appertain to his office to do. Cap. vi.

After that a child is come to seven years of age, I hold it expedient that he be taken from the company of women: saving that he may have, one year or two at the most, an ancient and sad matron attending on him in his chamber, which shall not have any young woman in her company: for though there be no peril of offense in that tender and innocent age, yet in some children nature is more prone to vice than to virtue, and in the tender wits be sparks of voluptuosity: which, nourished by any occasion or object, increase oftentimes in so terrible a fire that therewith all virtue and reason is consumed. Wherefore, to eschew that danger, the most sure counsel is to withdraw him from all company of women, and to assign unto him a tutor, which should be an ancient and worshipful man, in whom is approved to be much gentleness mixed with gravity, and, as nigh as can be, such one as the child, by imitation following, may grow to be excellent. And if he be also learned, he is the more commendable. Peleus, the father of Achilles, committed the governance of his son to Phaenix, which was a stranger born: who, as well in speaking elegantly as in doing valiantly, was master to Achilles (as Homer saith). How much profited it to King Philip, father to the great Alexander, that he was delivered in hostage to the Thebans? where he was kept and brought up under the governance of Epaminondas, a noble and valiant captain, of whom he received such learning, as well in acts martial as in other liberal sciences, that he excelled all other kings that were before his time in Greece: and finally, as well by wisdom as prowess, subdued all that country.

Semblably he ordained for his son Alexander a noble tutor called Leonidas, unto whom, for his wisdom, humanity, and learning, he committed the rule and preëminence over all the masters and servants of Alexander. In whom, notwithstanding, was such a familiar vice which Alexander, apprehending in childhood, could never abandon, some suppose it to be fury and hastiness, other superfluous drinking of wine; which of them it were, it is a good warning for gentlemen to be the more serious, ensearching not only for the virtues but also for the vices of them unto whose tuition and governance they will commit their children.

The office of a tutor is first to know the nature of his pupil, that is to say, whereto he is most inclined or disposed, and in what thing he setteth his most delectation or appetite. If he be of nature courteous, piteous, and of a free and liberal heart, it is a principal token of grace (as it is by all Scripture determined). Then shall a wise tutor purposely commend those

virtues, extolling also his pupil for having of them: and therewith he shall
declare them to be of all men most fortunate which shall happen to have
such a master. And, moreover, shall declare to him what honor, what
love, what commodity shall happen to him by these virtues. And if any
have been of disposition contrary, then to express the enormities of their
vice with as much detestation as may be. And if any danger have thereby
ensued, misfortune, or punishment, to aggrieve it in such wise, with so
vehement words, as the child may abhor it and fear the semblable adventure.

*In what wise music may be to a nobleman necessary: and what
modesty ought to be therein.* Cap. vii.

The discretion of a tutor consisteth in temperance: that is to say, that
he suffer not the child to be fatigate with continual study or learning,
wherewith the delicate and tender wit may be dulled or oppressed; but
that there may be therewith interlaced and mixed some pleasant learning
and exercise, as playing on instruments of music, which, moderately used
and without diminution of honor, that is to say, without wanton countenance and dissolute gesture, is not to be contemned.

* * * * *

*That it is commendable in a gentleman to paint and carve exactly,
if nature thereto doth induce him.* Cap. viii.

If the child be of nature inclined (as many have been) to paint with
a pen or to form images in stone or tree: he should not be therefrom withdrawn, or nature be rebuked, which is to him benevolent: but putting one
to him which is in that craft wherein he delighteth most excellent, in
vacant times from other more serious learning, he should be in the most
pure wise instructed in painting or carving.

* * * * *

*What order should be in learning, and which authors should be
first read.* Cap. x.

Now let us return to the order of learning apt for a gentleman.
Wherein I am of the opinion of Quintilian that I would have him learn
Greek and Latin authors both at one time: or else to begin with Greek,
forasmuch as that it is hardest to come by, by reason of the diversity of
tongues, which be five in number: and all must be known or else uneth
any poet can be well understande. And if a child do begin therein at

seven years of age, he may continually learn Greek authors three years and, in the meantime, use the Latin tongue as a familiar language: which, in a nobleman's son, may well come to pass, having none other persons to serve him or keeping him company but such as can speak Latin elegantly. And what doubt is there but so may he as soon speak good Latin as he may do pure French, which now is brought into as many rules and figures and as long a grammar as is Latin or Greek? I will not contend who among them that do write grammars of Greek (which now almost be innumerable) is the best: but that I refer to the discretion of a wise master. Alway I would advise him not to detain the child too long in that tedious labors either in the Greek or Latin grammar. For a gentle wit is therewith soon fatigate.

Grammar being but an introduction to the understanding of authors, if it be made too long or exquisite to the learner, it in a manner mortifieth his corage: and by that time he cometh to the most sweet and pleasant reading of old authors, the sparks of fervent desire of learning is extinct with the burden of grammar, like as a little fire is soon quenched with a great heap of small sticks: so that it can never come to the principal logs, where it should long burn in a great, pleasant fire. Now to follow my purpose: after a few and quick rules of grammar, immediately, or interlacing it therewith, would be read to the child Æsop's fables in Greek: in which argument children much do delight. And surely it is a much pleasant lesson and also profitable, as well for that it is elegant and brief (and, notwithstanding, it hath much variety in words, and therewith much helpeth to the understanding of Greek) as also in those fables is included much moral and politic wisdom. Wherefore, in the teaching of them, the master diligently must gather together those fables which may be most accommodate to the advancement of some virtue whereto he perceiveth the child inclined: or to the rebuke of some vice whereto he findeth his nature disposed. And therein the master ought to exercise his wit as well to make the child plainly to understand the fable as also declaring the signification thereof compendiously and to the purpose. Foreseen alway that as well this lesson as all other authors which the child shall learn, either Greek or Latin, verse or prose, be perfectly had without the book: whereby he shall not only attain plenty of the tongues called Copie but also increase and nourish remembrance wonderfully. The next lesson would be some quick and merry dialogues elect out of Lucian which be without ribaldry or too much scorning, for either of them is exactly to be eschewed, specially for a nobleman, the one annoying the soul, the other his estimation concerning his gravity. The comedies of Aristophanes may be in the place of Lucian, and, by reason that they be in meter, they be the sooner learned by heart, I dare make none other comparison between them, for offending the friends of them both: but thus much dare I say, that it were better that a child should never read any part of Lucian than all Lucian.

　　I could rehearse divers other poets which, for matter and eloquence, be very necessary, but I fear me to be too long from noble Homer, from whom, as from a fountain, proceeded all eloquence and learning. For in his books be contained, and most perfectly expressed, not only the documents martial and discipline of arms but also incomparable wisdoms and instructions for politic governance of people: with the worthy com-
10 mendation and laud of noble princes: wherewith the readers shall be so all-inflamed that they most fervently shall desire and covet, by the imitation of their virtues, to acquire semblable glory. For the which occasion, Aristotle, most sharpest witted and excellent-learned philosopher, as soon as he had received Alexander from King Philip, his father: he, before any other thing, taught him the most noble works of Homer. Wherein Alexander found such sweetness and fruit that, ever after, he had Homer not only with him in all his journeys but also laid him under his pillow when he went to rest: and oftentimes would purposely wake some hours of the night to take, as it were, his pastime with that most noble poet. For by
20 the reading of his work called *Iliados*, where the assembly of the most noble Greeks again Troy is recited with their affairs, he gathered courage and strength again his enemies, wisdom and eloquence for consultations and persuasions to his people and army. And by the other work called *Odissea*, which recounteth the sundry adventures of the wise Ulysses, he, by the example of Ulysses, apprehended many noble virtues; and also learned to escape the fraud and deceitful imaginations of sundry and subtle crafty wits. Also there shall he learn to ensearch and perceive the manners and conditions of them that be his familiars, sifting out (as I might say) the best from the worst, whereby he may surely commit his
30 affairs and trust to every person after his virtues.

　　Therefore, I now conclude that there is no lesson for a young gentleman to be compared with Homer, if he be plainly and substantially expouned and declared by the master.

　　Notwithstanding forasmuch as the said works be very long and do require therefor a great time to be all learned and conned: some Latin author would be therewith mixed, and specially Virgil: which, in his work called *Eneidos*, is most like to Homer, and almost the same Homer in Latin. Also, by the joining together of those authors, the one shall be the better understande by the other. And verily (as I before said),
40 none one author serveth to so divers wits as doth Virgil. For there is not that affect or desire, whereto any child's fantasy is disposed, but in some of Virgil's works may be founden matter thereto apt and propice.

For what thing can be more familiar than his *Bucolics?* nor no work so nigh approacheth to the common dalliance and manners of children, and the pretty controversies of the simple shepherds therein contained wonderfully rejoiceth the child that heareth it well declared, as I know by mine own experience. In his *Georgics,* Lord, what pleasant variety there is: the divers grains, herbs, and flowers that be there described, that, reading therein, it seemeth to a man to be in a delectable garden or paradise. What plowman knoweth so much of husbandry as there is expressed? who delighting in good horses shall not be thereto more inflamed, reading thereof the breeding, choosing, and keeping of them? In the declara- 10 tion whereof Virgil leaveth far behind him all breeders, hackneymen, and skosers. Is there any astronomer that more exactly setteth out the order and course of the celestial bodies: or that more truly doth divine in his prognostications of the times of the year, in their qualities, with the future estate of all things provided by husbandry, than Virgil doth recite in that work?

If the child have a delight in hunting, what pleasure shall he take of the fable of Aristaeus! Semblably in the hunting of Dido and Æneas, which is described most elegantly in his book of *Eneidos.*

If he have pleasure in wrastling, running, or other like exercise, where 20 shall he see any more pleasant esbatements than that which was done by Eurealus and other Trojans which accompanied Æneas!

If he take solace in hearing minstrels, what minstrel may be compared to Iopas, which sang before Dido and Æneas! Or to blind Demodocus, that played or sang most sweetly at the dinner that the king Alcinous made to Ulysses, whose ditties and melody excelled as far the songs of our minstrels as Homer and Virgil excel all other poets.

If he be more desirous (as the most part of children be) to hear things marvelous and exquisite which hath in it a visage of some things incredible, whereat shall he more wonder than when he shall behold Æneas 30 follow Sibyl into hell! What shall he more dread than the terrible visages of Cerberus, Gorgon, Megaera, and other furies and monsters! How shall he abhor tyranny, fraud, and avarice when he doth see the pains of Duke Theseus, Prometheus, Sisyphus, and such other tormented for their dissolute and vicious living! How glad soon after shall he be when he shall behold in the pleasant fields of Elysius the souls of noble princes and captains, which, for their virtue and labors in advancing the public weals of their countries, do live eternally in pleasure inexplicable! And in the last books of *Eneidos* shall he find matter to minister to him audacity, valiant courage, and policy to take and sustain noble enterprises, 40 if any shall be needful for the assailing of his enemies. Finally (as I have said) this noble Virgil, like to a good nurse, giveth to a child, if he will take it, everything apt for his wit and capacity. Wherefore he is in the order of learning to be preferred before any other author Latin.

I would set next unto him two books of Ovid, the one called *Metamorphosios*, which is as much to say as changing of men into other figure or form; the other is entitled *De fastis*, where the ceremonies of the Gentiles, and specially the Romans, be expressed: both right necessary for the understanding of other poets. But, because there is little other learning in them, concerning either virtuous manners or policy, I suppose it were better that, as fables and ceremonies happen to come in a lesson, 10 it were declared abundantly by the master than that in the said two books a long time should be spent and almost lost: which might be better employed on such authors that do minister both eloquence, civil policy, and exhortation to virtue. Wherefore in his place let us bring in Horace, in whom is contained much variety of learning and quickness of sentence. This poet may be interlaced with the lesson of *Odissea* of Homer, wherein is declared the wonderful prudence and fortitude of Ulisses in his passage from Troy. And if the child were induced to make verses by the imitation of Virgil and Homer, it should minister to him much delectation and courage to study: nay, the making of verses is not discommended in a 20 noble man, since the noble Augustus and almost all the old emperors made books in verses.

The two noble poets Silius and Lucane be very expedient to be learned: for the one setteth out the emulation in qualities and prowess of two noble and valiant captains, one enemy to the other, that is to say, Silius writeth of Scipio the Roman, and Haniball duke of Cartaginensis: Lucane declareth a semblable matter, but much more lamentable, for as much as the wars were civile, and, as it were, in the bowels of the Romans, that is to say, under the standards of Julius Cesar and Pompey.

Hesiodus, in Greek, is more brief than Virgil, where he writeth of 30 husbandry, and doth not rise so high in philosophy, but is fuller of fables: and therefore is more illecebrous.

And here I conclude to speak any more of poets necessary for the childhood of a gentleman: for as much as these, I doubt not, will suffice until he pass the age of thirteen years. In which time childhood declineth, and reason waxeth ripe, and deprehendeth things with a more constant judgment. Here I would should be remembered that I require not that all these works should be thoroughly read of a child in this time, which were almost impossible. But I only desire that they have, in every of the said books, so much instruction that they may take thereby some profit. Then 40 the child's courage, inflamed by the frequent reading of noble poets, daily more and more desireth to have experience in those things that they so vehemently do commend in them that they write of.

Leonidas, the noble king of Spartanes, being once demanded, of what estimation in poetry Tirtæus (as he supposed) was, it is written that he answering said, that, for stirring the minds of young men he was excellent, for as much as they, being moved with his verses, do run into the battle, regarding no peril, as men all inflamed in martial courage.

And when a man is comen to mature years, and that reason in him is confirmed with serious learning and long experience, then shall he, in reading tragedies, execrate and abhor the intollerable life of tyrants: and shall condemn the folly and dotage expressed by poets lascivious.

Here will I leave to speak of the first part of a noble man's study: and now will I write of the second part, which is more serious, and containeth in it sundry manners of learning.

The most commodious and necessary studies succeeding ordinatly the lesson of poets. Cap. xi.

After that fourteen years be passed of a child's age, his master, if he can, or some other studiously exercised in the art of an orator, shall first read to him somewhat of that part of logic that is called *Topica,* either of Cicero, or else of that noble clerk of Almaine, which late flowered, called Agricola: whose work prepareth invention, telling the places from whence an argument for the proof of any matter may be taken with little study; and that lesson, with much and diligent learning, having mixed therewith none other exercise, will in the space of half a year be perfectly known.

Immediately after that, the art of Rhetoric would be semblably taught, either in Greek, out of Hermogenes, or of Quintilian in Latin, beginning at the third book, and instructing diligently the child in that part of Rhetoric, principally, which concerneth persuasion, for as much as it is most apt for consultations. There can be no shorter instruction of Rhetoric than the treatise that Tully wrote unto his son, which book is named *The Partition of Rhetoric.* And in good faith, to speak boldly that I think: for him that needeth not, or doth not desire to be an exquisite orator, the little book made by the famous Erasmus (whom all gentle wits are bounden to thank and support), which he calleth *Copiam Verborum et Rerum,* that is to say, plenty of words and matters, shall be sufficient.

Isocrates concerning the lesson of orators is everywhere wonderful profitable, having almost as many wise sentences as he hath words: and with that is so sweet and delectable to read, that, after him, almost all other seem unsavory and tedious: and in persuading as well a prince as a private person to virtue, in two very little and compendious works, whereof he made the one to King Nicocles, the other to his friend Demonicus, would be perfectly conned, and had in continual memory.

Demosthenes and Tully, by the consent of all learned men, have preeminence and sovereignty over all orators: the one reigning in wonderful eloquence in the public weal of the Romans, who had the empire and dominion of all the world: the other of no less estimation in the city of Athens, which of long time was accounted the mother of Sapience, and the palace of muses and all liberal sciences. . . . .

The utility that a noble man shall have by reading these orators is, that when he shall happen to reason in council, or shall speak in a great audience, or to strange ambassadors of great princes, he shall not be constrained to speak words sudden and disordered, but shall bestow them aptly and in their places. Wherefore the most noble emperor Octavius is highly commended, for that he never spake in the Senate, or to the people of Rome, but in an oration prepared and purposely made.

Also to prepare the child to understanding of histories, which, being replenished with the names of countries and towns unknown to the reader, do make the history tedious or else the less pleasant; so if they be in any wise known, it increaseth an inexplicable delectation. It shall be therefore, and also for refreshing the wit, a convenient lesson to behold the old tables of Ptolemy, where in all the world is painted, having first some introduction into the sphere, whereof now of late be made very good treatises, and more plain and easy to learn than was wont to be.

Albeit there is none so good learning as the demonstration of cosmography by material figures and instruments, having a good instructor. And surely this lesson is both pleasant and necessary. For what pleasure is it, in one hour, to behold those realms, cities, seas, rivers, and mountains, that uneth in an old man's life can not be journeyed and pursued: what incredible delight is taken in beholding the diversities of people, beasts, fowls, fishes, trees, fruits, and herbs: to know the sundry manners and conditions of people, and the variety of their natures, and that in a warm study or parlor, without peril of the sea, or danger of long and painful journeys. I can not tell what more pleasure should happen to a gentle wit, than to behold in his own house every thing that within all the world is contained. The commodity thereof knew the great king Alexander, as some writers do remember. For he caused the countries whereunto he proposed any enterprise diligently and cunningly to be described and painted, that, beholding the picture, he might perceive which places were most dangerous, and where he and his host might have most easy and covenable passage. . . . . . .

Cosmography being substantially perceived, it is then time to induce a child to the reading of histories: but first to set him in a fervent courage, the master in the most pleasant and elegant wise expressing what incomparable delectation, utility, and commodity shall happen to emperors, kings, princes, and all other gentlemen by reading of histories: showing to him that Demetrius Phalareus, a man of excellent wisdom and learning, and which in Athens had been long exercised in the public weal, exhorted Ptolemy, king of Egypt, chiefly above all other studies to haunt and embrace histories and such other books wherein were contained precepts made to kings and princes: saying that in them he should read those things which no man durst report unto his person. Also Cicero, father of the Latin eloquence, calleth an history the witness of times, mistress of life, the life of remembrance, of truth the light, and messenger of antiquity. Moreover, the sweet Isocrates exhorteth the king Nicocles, whom he instructeth to leave behind him statues and images that shall represent rather the figure and similitude of his mind than the features of his body, signifying thereby the remembrance of his acts written in histories.

By semblable advertisements shall a noble heart be trained to delight in histories. And then, according to the counsel of Quintilian, it is best that he begin with Titus Livius, not only for his elegance of writing, which floweth in him like a fountain of sweet milk; but also for as much as by reading that author he may know how the most noble city of Rome, of a small and poor beginning, by prowess and virtue, little and little came to the empire and dominion of all the world.

Also in that city he may behold the form of a public weal: which, if the insolency and pride of Tarquine had not excluded kings out of the city, it had been the most noble and perfect of all other.

Xenophon, being both a philosopher and an excellent captain, so invented and ordered his work named *Pædia Cyri*, which may be interpreted the Childhood or discipline of Cyrus, that he leaveth to the readers thereof an incomparable sweetness and example of living, specially for the conducting and well ordering of hosts or armies. And therefore the noble Scipio, who was called Africanus, as well in peace as in war was never seen without this book of Xenophon. . . . .

Surely if a noble man do thus seriously and diligently read histories, I dare affirm there is no study or science for him of equal commodity and pleasure, having regard to every time and age.

By the time that the child do come to seventeen years of age, to the intent his courage be bridled with reason, it were needful to read unto him some works of philosophy, specially that part that may inform him unto virtuous manners, which part of philosophy is called moral. Wherefore there would be read to him, for an introduction, two the first books of the work of Aristotle called *Ethicae*, wherein is contained the definitions and proper significations of every virtue; and that to be learned in Greek;

for the translations that we yet have be but a rude and gross shadow of the eloquence and wisdom of Aristotle. Forthwith would follow the work of Cicero called in Latin *De officiis,* whereunto yet is no proper English word to be given; but to provide for it some manner of exposition, it may be said in this form: Of the duties and manners appertaining to men. But above all other, the works of Plato would be most studiously read when the judgment of a man is come to perfection, and by the other studies is instructed in the form of speaking that philosophers used. Lord God, what incomparable sweetness of words and matter shall he find in
10 the said works of Plato and Cicero; wherein is joined gravity with delectation, excellent wisdom with divine eloquence, absolute virtue with pleasure incredible, and every place is so enforced with profitable counsel, joined with honesty, that those three books be almost sufficient to make a perfect and excellent governor.

The proverbs of Salomon with the books of *Ecclesiastes* and *Ecclesiasticus* be very good lessons. All the historial parts of the Bible be right necessary for to be read of a noble man, after that he is mature in years. And the residue (with the New Testament) is to be reverently touched, as a celestial jewell or relic, having the chief interpreter of those books
20 true and constant faith, and dreadfully to set hands thereon, remembering that Oza, for putting his hand to the holy shrine that was called *Archa federis,* when it was brought by king David from the city of Gaba, though it were wavering and in danger to fall, yet was he stricken of God, and fell dead immediately. It would not be forgotten that the little book of the most excellent doctor Erasmus Roterodamus (which he wrote to Charles, now being emperor and then prince of Castile), which book is entitled the *Institution of a Christian Prince,* would be as familiar always with gentlemen, at all times, and in every age, as was Homer with the great king Alexander, or Xenophon with Scipio; for as all men may
30 judge that have read the work of Erasmus, that there was never book written in Latin that, in so little a portion, contained of sentence, eloquence, and virtuous exhortation, a more compendious abundance. And here I make an end of the learning and study whereby noble men may attain to be worthy to have authority in a public weal. Always I shall exhort tutors and governors of noble children, that they suffer them not to use ingurgitations of meat or drink, ne to sleep much, that is to say, above eight hours at the most. For undoubtedly both repletion and superfluous sleep be capital enemies to study, as they be semblably to health of body and soul. Aulus Gellius sayeth that children, if they use of meat and
40 sleep over much, be made therewith dull to learn, and we see that thereof slowness is taken, and the children's personages do wax uncomely, and less grow in stature. Galen will not permit that pure wine, without allay

of water, should in any wise be given to children, for as much as it
humecteth the body, or maketh it moister and hotter than is convenient;
also it filleth the head with fume, in them specially which be like as children, of hot and moist temperature. These be well nigh the words of the
noble Galen.

*   *   *   *   *

10

EDWARD HALLE

The Introduction and Notes are at page 1295

FROM *The Union of the two noble and illustre famelies of Lancastre &*
Yorke, 1548

To the most mighty, virtuous, and excellent prince, Edward
the Sixth, by the grace of God king of England, France, and
Ireland, defender of the Catholic faith, and under God supreme head of the churches of England and Ireland. Your   20
most humble subject Edward Halle wisheth health, honor,
and felicity.

OBLIVION, the cankered enemy to fame and renown, the sucking serpent
of ancient memory, the deadly dart to the glory of princes, and the de-
facer of all conquests and notable acts, so much bare rule in the first and
second age of the world that nothing was set out to men's knowledge,
either how the world was made, either how man and beasts were created,
or how the world was destroyed by water till father Moses had, by divine
inspiration in the third age, invented letters, the treasure of memory,
and set forth five notable books to the great comfort of all people living at 30
this day. Likewise Mercury in Egypt invented letters and writing, which
Cadmus after brought into Greece. So every nation was desirous to enhance Lady Fame and to suppress that deadly beast Oblivion. For what
diversity is between a noble prince and a poor beggar, yea, a reasonable
man and a brute beast if, after their death, there be left of them no remembrance or token. So that evidently it appeareth that fame is the
triumph of glory, and memory by literature is the very dilator and setter
forth of fame. How much, therefore, are princes, governors, and noblemen bound to them which have so lively set forth the lives and acts of
their parents that, although they be dead by mortal death, yet they, by 40
writing and fame, live and be continually present. If no man had written
the goodness of noble Augustus, nor the pity of merciful Trajan, how

should their successors have followed their steps in virtue and princely qualities: on the contrary part, if the cruelty of Nero, the ungracious life of Caligula, had not been put in remembrance, young princes and frail governors might likewise have fallen in a like pit, but, by reading their vices and seeing their mischievous end, they be compelled to leave their evil ways and embrace the good qualities of notable princes and prudent governors: thus, writing is the key to induce virtue and repress vice. Thus memory maketh men dead many a thousand year still to live as though they were present: thus fame triumpheth upon death, and renown upon 10 oblivion, and all by reason of writing and history.

Alas, my sovereign lord, my heart lamenteth to know and remember what rule this tyrant Oblivion bare in this realm in the time of the Britons. For from the first habitation of this land, no man of the Britons either set forth history of their beginning or wrote the whole lives of their princes and kings, except Gildas, which inveighed against the evil doings of a few tyrants and evil governors. Insomuch that Caesar writeth that when he was in this realm the people could not tell their lineage nor their beginning. But one Geoffrey of Monmouth, a thousand year and more after Julius Caesar, translated a certain British or Welsh book containing 20 the coming of Brute, with the sequel of his lineage till the time of Cad- walader, which British book, if it had slept a little longer, Brute, with all his posterity, had been buried in the poke of Oblivion for lack of writing.

The strong Saxons, after they had gained this land, set up the banner of fame, and had their lives notably written by divers and sundry famous clerks, even from their first entry into this land till the first monarchy, and so successively. In the Normans' time, many notable works hath been set forth, some of one prince particularly and some of mo: so that, in fine, all the stories of kings, from King William the First to King Edward the Third, be set forth at length by divers authors in the Latin 30 tongue, as by Matthew of Paris, sometime religious in Saint Albans and other. After whom John Froissart wrote the lives of King Edward the Third and King Richard the Second so compendiously and so largely that, if there were not so many things spoken of in his long works, I might believe all written in his great volumes to be as true as the Gospel. But I have read an old proverb, which saith that in many words a lie or twain soon may scape. Sith the end of Froissart, which endeth at the beginning of King Henry the Fourth, no man in the English tongue hath either set forth their honors according to their deserts, nor yet declared many notable acts worthy of memory done in the time of seven kings 40 which after King Richard succeeded, except Robert Fabyan and one without name, which wrote the common English chronicle—men worthy to be praised for their diligence, but far shooting wide from the butt of an history.

Wherefore, most dread and benign Sovereign Lord, lest cankered Oblivion should deface the glory of these seven princes, to whom you be of all sides lineal heir and very inheritor, I have compiled and gathered (and not made) out of divers writers, as well foreign as English, this simple treatise, which I have named *The Union of the Noble Houses of Lancaster and York,* conjoined together by the godly marriage of your most noble grandfather and your virtuous grandmother. For, as King Henry the Fourth was the beginning and root of the great discord and division: 10 so was the godly matrimony the final end of all dissensions, titles, and debates.

Beseeching Your High Majesty to take this, my simple and rude work, according to your accustomed goodness, in good part, not regarding the thing, but my good will to my native country, whose fame, for lack of writing, may much be darkened and defaced, and thus I pray to the celestial Lord to send you victory over your enemies, peace with your confederates, love of your subjects: and, in conclusion, perpetual joy and eternal felicity.

* * * * *   20

The xxi. year [of King Henry the VIII].

* * * * *

The twenty and three day of October the king came to his manor of Greenwich, and there much consulted with his council for a meet man to be his chancellor, so that in no wise he were no man of the spiritualty, and so, after long debate, the king resoluted himself upon Sir Thomas More, knight, chancellor of the duchy of Lancaster, a man well learned in the tongues and also in the common law, whose wit was fine and full 30 of imaginations, by reason whereof he was too much given to mocking, which was to his gravity a great blemish. And then on the Sunday, the twenty and four day of the same month, the king made him his chancellor and delivered him the great seal, which lord chancellor, the next morrow after, was led into the chancery by the two dukes of Norfolk and Suffolk, and there sworn, and then the mace was borne before him.

Here is to be remembered that, at this present time, William Tyndale had newly translated and imprinted the New Testament in English, and the bishop of London, not pleased with the translation thereof, debated with himself how he might compass and devise to destroy that false and 40 erroneous translation (as he said). And so it happened that one Augustine

Packington, a mercer and merchant of London, and of a great honesty, the same time was in Antwerp, where the bishop then was, and this Packington was a man that highly favored William Tyndale, but to the bishop utterly shewed himself to the contrary. The bishop, desirous to have his purpose brought to pass, commoned of the New Testaments, and how gladly he would buy them. Packington, then hearing that he wished for, said unto the bishop, "My Lord, if it be your pleasure, I can, in this matter, do more, I daresay, than most of the merchants of England that are here, for I know the Dutchmen and strangers that have 10 bought them of Tyndale and have them here to sell, so that, if it be Your Lordship's pleasure to pay for them, for otherwise I cannot come by them, but I must disburse money for them, I will then assure you to have every book of them that is imprinted and is here unsold."

The bishop, thinking that he had God by the toe when, indeed, he had (as after he thought) the devil by the fist, said, "Gentle Master Packington, do your diligence and get them, and with all my heart I will pay for them whatsoever they cost you, for the books are erroneous and naughts, and I intend surely to destroy them all, and to burn them at Paul's Cross."

20   Augustine Packington came to William Tyndale and said, "William, I know thou art a poor man, and hast a heap of New Testaments and books by thee, for the which thou hast both endangered thy friends and beggared thyself, and I have now gotten thee a merchant which, with ready money, shall dispatch thee of all that thou hast, if you think it so profitable for yourself."

"Who is the merchant?" said Tyndale.

"The bishop of London," said Packington.

"Oh, that is because he will burn them," said Tyndale.

"Yea, Mary," quoth Packington.

30   "I am the gladder," said Tyndale, "for these two benefits shall come thereof: I shall get money of him for these books to bring myself out of debt (and the whole world shall cry out upon the burning of God's word). And the overplus of the money that shall remain to me shall make me more studious to correct the said New Testament and so newly to imprint the same once again, and I trust the second will much better like you than ever did the first."

And so forward went the bargain; the bishop had the books, Packington had the thanks, and Tyndale had the money.

Afterward, when mo New Testaments were imprinted, they came 40 thick and threefold into England, the bishop of London, hearing that still there were so many New Testaments abroad, sent for Augustine Packington and said unto him: "Sir, how cometh this, that there are so many New Testaments abroad, and you promised and assured me that you had bought all?"

Then said Packington, "I promise you I bought all that then was to be had: but I perceive they have made more since, and it will never be better as long as they have the letters and stamps; therefore it were best for Your Lordship to buy the stamps too, and then are you sure." The bishop smiled at him and said, "Well, Packington, well." And so ended this matter.

*   *   *   *   *

The xxv. year.   10

The receiving, conveying, and coronation of Queen Anne, wife to the high and mighty prince, King Henry the Eight.

After that the King's Highness had addressed his gracious letters to the mayor and commonalty of the city, signifying to them that his pleasure was to solemnize and celebrate the coronation of his most dear and well-beloved wife, Queen Anne, at Westminster, the Whitsunday next ensuing, willing them to make preparation as well to fetch Her Grace from Greenwich to the Tower by water as to see the city ordered and 20 garnished with pageants in places accustomed, for the honor of Her Grace. When she should be conveyed from the Tower to Westminster, there was a common council called, and commandment was given to the Haberdashers (of which craft the mayor, Sir Stephen Pecock, then was) that they should prepare a barge for the bachelors, with a wafter and a foist garnished with banners and streamers likewise as they use to do when the mayor is presented at Westminster on the morrow after Simon and Jude. Also all the other crafts were commanded to prepare barges and to garnish them not alonely with their banners accustomed, but also to deck them with targets by the sides of the barges, and so set up all such 30 seemly banners and bannerettes as they had in their halls or could get, meet to furnish their said barges, and every barge to have minstrelsy, according to which commandments great preparation was made for all things necessary for such a noble triumph.

The coming by water from Greenwich the Thursday.

The xix. day of May, the mayor and his brethren, all in scarlet, and such as were knights had Collars of Esses (and the remnant having good chains), and the council of the city with them, assembled at St. Mary Hill, and at one of the clock descended to the Newstair to their barge, 40 which was garnished with many goodly banners and streamers and richly covered, in which barge were shalms, shagbushes, and divers other instruments which continually made a goodly [h]armony. After that the mayor and his brethren were in their barge, seeing that all the companies, to the number of fifty barges, were ready to wait upon them. They gave commandment to the companies that no barge should row nearer to another than twice the length of the barge, upon a great pain. And to see the order kept, there were three light wherries prepared, and in every one of them two officers to call on them to keep their order, after which commandment given, they set forth in order as hereafter is described.

First before the mayor's barge was a foist or wafter full of ordnance,
10 in which foist was a great dragon continually moving and casting wildfire, and round about the said foist stood terrible monsters and wild men casting fire and making hideous noises. Next after the foist, a good distance, came the mayor's barge, on whose right hand was the bachelors' barge, in the which were trumpets and divers other melodious instruments. The decks of the said barge and the sailyards and the topcastles were hanged with rich cloth of gold and silk. At the foreship and the stern were two great banners rich beaten with the arms of the king and the queen, and on the topcastle also was a long streamer newly beaten with the said arms. The sides of the barge was set full of flags and ban-
20 ners of the devices of the Company of Haberdashers and Merchants Adventurers, and the cords were hanged with innumerable pensels, having little bells at the ends, which made a goodly noise and a goodly sight wavering in the wind. On the outside of the barge were three dozen scutcheons in metal of arms of the king and the queen, which were beaten upon square buckram, divided so that the right side had the king's colors and the left side the queen's, which scutcheons were fastened on the cloths of gold and silver hanging on the decks on the left hand. On the left hand of the mayor was another foist, in the which was a mount, and on the same stood a white falcon crowned upon a root of gold environed with
30 white roses and red, which was the queen's device: about which mount sat virgins singing and playing sweetly. Next after the mayor followed his fellowship the Haberdashers, next after them the Mercers, then the Grocers, and so every company in his order, and last of all the mayors' and sheriffs' officers, every company having melody in his barge by himself, and goodly garnished with banners and some garnished with silk and some with arras and rich carpets, which was a goodly sight to behold, and in this order they rowed to Greenwich to the point next beyond Greenwich, and there they turned backward in another order, that is to wit, the mayor and sheriffs officers first, and the meanest craft next,
40 and so ascending to the uttermost crafts in order, and the mayor last, as they go to Paul's at Christmas, and in that order they rowed downward to Greenwich town and there cast anchor, making great melody.

At three of the clock the queen appeared in rich cloth of gold, entered into her barge accompanied with divers ladies and gentlewomen, and incontinent the citizens set forwards in their order, their minstrels continually playing, and the bachelors' barge going on the queen's right hand, which she took great pleasure to behold. About the queen's barge were many noblemen, as the Duke of Suffolk, the Marquess Dorset, the Earl of Wiltshire her father, the Earls of Arundel, Derby, Rutland, Worcester, Huntington, Sussex, Oxford, and many bishops and noblemen, every one in his barge, which was a goodly sight to behold. She, thus being accompanied, rowed toward the Tower, and, in the mean way, the ships which were commanded to lie on the shore for letting of barges, shot divers peals of guns, and, or she landed, there was a marvelous shot out of the Tower as ever was heard there. And at her landing, there met with her the lord chamberlain with the officers of arms and brought her to the king, which received her with loving countenance at the postern by the water side and kissed her, and then she turned back again and thanked the mayor and the citizens with many goodly words, and so entered into the Tower. After which entry the citizens all this while hoved before the Tower, making great melody, and went not aland, for none were assigned to land but the mayor, the recorder, and two aldermen. But for to speak of the people that stood on every shore to behold the sight, he that saw it not would not believe it.

On Friday at dinner served the king all such as were appointed by His Highness to be Knights of the Bath, which after dinner were brought to their chambers, and that night were bathed and shriven according to the old usage of England, and the next day in the morning the king dubbed them according to the ceremonies thereto belonging, whose names ensueth.

The Marquis Dorset	Sir William Windsor
The Earl of Derby	Sir Francis Weston
The Lord Clifford	Sir Thomas Arundel
The Lord Fitzwater	Sir John Hulstone
The Lord Hastings	Sir Thomas Pownings
The Lord Mounteagle	Sir Henry Savell
Sir John Mordant	Sir George Fitzwilliam
The Lord Vaux	Sir John Tyndall
Sir Henry Parker	Sir Thomas Jermey

Saturday, the xxxi. day. The receiving and conveying of the queen through London.

* * * *

Sunday being Whitsunday, the first day of June and the day of her coronation.

On Sunday the mayor, clad in crimson velvet and with his collar, and
10 all the aldermen and sheriffs in scarlet, and the council of the city, took
their barge at the Crane by seven of the clock and came to Westminster,
where they were welcomed and brought into the hall by Master Treasurer
and other of the king's house, and so gave their attendance till the queen
should come forth. Between eight and nine she came into the hall and
stood under the cloth of estate, and then came in the king's chapel and the
monks of Westminster all in rich copes, and many bishops and abbots in
copes and miters, which went into the midst of the hall and there stood a
season.

Then was there a ray cloth spread from the queen's standing in the
20 hall through the palace and sanctuary, which was railed on both sides to
the high altar of Westminster. After that the ray cloth was cast, the officers
of arms appointed the order accustomed. First went gentlemen, then
esquires, then knights, then the aldermen of the city in their cloaks of
scarlet; after them the judges in their mantles of scarlet and coifs. Then
followed the Knights of the Bath being no lords, every man having a white
lace on his left sleeve. Then followed barons and viscounts in their parliament robes of scarlet. After them came earls, marquises, and dukes in their
robes of estate of crimson velvet furred with ermine, powdered according
to their degrees. After them came the Lord Chancellor in a robe of scarlet,
30 open before, bordered with lettice; after him came the king's chapel and
the monks solemnly singing with procession; then came abbots and bishops
mitered; then sergeants and officers of arms; then after them went the
mayor of London with his mace, and garter in his coat of arms; then went
the Marquis Dorset in a robe of estate which bare the scepter of gold, and
the Earl of Arundel, which bare the rod of ivory with the dove, both together. Then went alone the Earl of Oxford, High Chamberlain of England, which bare the crown; after him went the Duke of Suffolk in his
robe of estate also, for that day being High Steward of England, having a
long white rod in his hand; and the Lord William Howard with the rod
40 of the marshalship; and every Knight of the Garter had on his collar of
the order.

Then proceeded forth the queen in a surcoat and robe of purple velvet furred with ermine; in her hair, coif and circlet as she had the Saturday; and over her was borne the canopy by four of the five Ports, all crimson with points of blue and red hanging on their sleeves; and the bishops of London and Winchester bare up the laps of the queen's robe. The queen's train, which was very long, was borne by the old Duchess of Norfolk; after her followed ladies, being lords' wives, which had surcoats of scarlet with narrow sleeves, the breast all lettice with bars of borders according to their degrees. And over that they had mantles of scarlet furred, and every mantle had lettice about the neck like a neckercher likewise powdered, so that, by the powderings, their degree was known. Then followed ladies, 10 being knights' wives, in gowns of scarlet with narrow sleeves without trains, only edged with lettice; and likewise had all the queen's gentlewomen.

When she was thus brought to the high place made in the midst of the church, between the choir and the high altar, she was set in a rich chair. And after that she had rested a while, she descended down to the high altar, and there prostrate herself while the archbishop of Canterbury said certain collects. Then she rose and the bishop anointed her on the head and on the breast, and then she was led up again, where, after divers orisons said, the archbishop set the crown of Saint Edward on her head, 20 and then delivered her the scepter of gold in her right hand, and the rod of ivory with the dove in the left hand, and then all the choir sang *Te Deum, etc.* Which done, the bishop took off the crown of Saint Edward, being heavy, and set on the crown made for her, and so went to mass. And when the offertory was begun, she descended down and offered, being crowned, and so ascended up again and sate in her chair till *Agnus,* and then she went down and kneeled before the altar, where she received of the archbishop the holy sacrament, and then went up to her place again. After that mass was done, she went to Saint Edward's shrine and there offered, after which offering done, she withdrew her into a little 30 place made for the nonce on the one side of the choir. Now, in the mean season, every duchess had put on their bonnets a coronal of gold, wrought with flowers, and every marquess put on a demi-coronal of gold, every countess a plain circlet of gold without flowers, and every king of arms put on a crown of copper and gilt, all which were worn till night.

When the queen had a little reposed her, the company returned in the same order that they set forth, and the queen went crowned, and so did the ladies aforesaid. Her right hand was sustained by the Earl of Wiltshire her father, and her left hand by the Lord Talbot, deputy for the Earl of Shrewsbury, and Lord Forinfall, his father. And when she was out of 40 the sanctuary and appeared within the palace, the trumpets played marvelous freshly, and so she was brought to Westminster Hall, and so to her withdrawing chamber, during which time the lords, judges, mayor, and aldermen put off their robes, mantles, and cloaks, and took their hoods from their necks and cast them about their shoulders; and the lords sat only in the surcoats, and the judges and aldermen in their gowns. And all the lords that served that day served in their surcoats and their hoods about their shoulders. Also divers officers of the king's house, being no lords, had surcoats and hoods of scarlet edged with miniver, as the treasurer, controller, and master of the jewel house, but their surcoats were not gilt.

10   *   *   *   *   *

The vii. day of September, being Sunday, between three and four of the clock at afternoon, the queen was delivered of a fair lady, which day the Duke of Norfolk came home to the christening, and, for the queen's good deliverance, *Te Deum* was sung incontinently, and great preparation was made for the christening. And the mayor and his brethren and forty of the chief of the citizens were commanded to be at the christening the Wednesday following, upon which day the mayor, Sir Stephen Pecock, in a gown of crimson velvet, with his collar of *s.s.*, and all the 20 aldermen in scarlet, with collars and chains, and all the council of the city with them, took their barge after dinner at one of the clock, and the citizens had another barge, and so rowed to Greenwich, where were many lords, knights, and gentlemen assembled. All the walls between the king's place and the Friars' were hanged with arras, and all the way strawed with green rushes: the Friars' church was also hanged with arras. The font was of silver, and stood in the midst of the church, three steps high, which was covered with a fine cloth, and divers gentlemen with aprons, and towels about their necks, gave attendance about it, that no filth should come in the font. Over it hung a square canopy of crimson satin, fringed 30 with gold; about it was a rail covered with red say. Between the choir and the body of the church was a close place with a pan of fire, to make the child ready in. When all these things were ordered, the child was brought to the hall, and then every man set forward: first, the citizens two and two; then gentlemen, esquires, and chaplains; next after them the aldermen, and the mayor alone; next the mayor the king's council; the king's chapel in copes; then barons, bishops, earls; then came the Earl of Essex bearing the covered basins gilt; after him the Marquess of Exeter with the taper of virgin wax; next him the Marquess Dorset, bearing the salt; behind him the Lady Mary of Norfolk, bearing the 40 chrysm, which was very rich of pearl and stone. The old Duchess of Norfolk bare the child, in a mantle of purple velvet, with a long train furred with ermine. The Duke of Norfolk, with his marshal rod, went on the right hand of the said duchess, and the Duke of Suffolk on the left hand, and before them went the officers of arms. The Countess of Kent bare the long train of the child's mantle, and between the Countess of Kent and the child went the Earl of Wiltshire on the right hand, and the Earl of Derby on the left hand, supporting the said train in the midst. Over the said child was borne a canopy by the Lord Rocheford, the Lord Husey, the Lord William Howard, and by the Lord Thomas Howard the elder; after the child followed many ladies and gentlewomen.

When the child was come to the church door, the Bishop of London met it with divers bishops and abbots mitered, and began the observances 10 of the sacrament. The godfather was the Lord Archbishop of Canterbury; the godmothers were the old Duchess of Norfolk and the old Marchioness of Dorset, widows. And the child was named Elizabeth. And after that all thing was done, at the church door the child was brought to the font and christened, and, this done, garter chief king of arms cried aloud, "God of His infinite goodness send prosperous life and long to the high and mighty princess of England, Elizabeth!" And then the trumpets blew.

Then the child was brought up to the altar and the Gospel said over it; and after that immediately the Archbishop of Canterbury confirmed it, 20 the Marchioness of Exeter being godmother. Then the Archbishop of Canterbury gave to the princess a standing cup of gold; the Duchess of Norfolk gave to her a standing cup of gold, fretted with pearl; the Marchioness of Dorset gave three gilt bowls, pounced with a cover; and the Marchioness of Exeter gave three standing bowls graven, all gilt, with a cover. Then was brought in wafers, comfits, and hippocras in such plenty that every man had as much as he would desire.

Then they set forwards, the trumpets going before in the same order, toward the king's place, as they did when they came thitherward, saving that the gifts that the godfather and the godmothers gave were borne 30 before the child by four persons, that is to say: first, Sir John Dudley bare the gift of the lady of Exeter; the Lord Thomas Howard the younger bare the gift of the lady of Dorset; the Lord Fitzwater bare the gift of the lady of Norfolk; and the Earl of Worcester bare the gift of the Archbishop of Canterbury. And all the one side as they went was full of staff torches, to the number of five hundred, borne by the guard and other of the king's servants. And about the child were borne many other proper torches borne by gentlemen. And in this order they brought the princess to the queen's chamber, and tarried there a while with his brethren the aldermen. And at the last the Dukes of Norfolk and Suffolk 40 came out from the king, thanking them heartily, and [said the king] commanded them to give them thanks in his name. And from thence they were had to the cellar to drink, and so went to their barges.

* * * * *

The xxvii year.

. . . Also the vi. day of July was Sir Thomas More beheaded for the
like treason before rehearsed, which, as you have heard, was for the denying of the King's Majesty's supremacy. This man was also counted
learned, and, as you have heard before, he was Lord Chancellor of
England, and in that time a great persecutor of such as detested the
10 supremacy of the bishop of Rome, which he himself so highly favored
that he stood to it till he was brought to the scaffold on the Tower Hill,
where on a block his head was stricken from his shoulders and had no
more harm.

I cannot tell whether I should call him a foolish wise man or a wise
foolish man, for undoubtedly he, beside his learning, had a great wit, but
it was so mingled with taunting and mocking that it seemed to them that
best knew him that he thought nothing to be well spoken except he had
ministered some mock in the communication, insomuch as, at his coming
to the Tower, one of the officers demanded his upper garment for his
20 fee, meaning his gown, and he answered he should have it, and took him
his cap, saying it was the uppermost garment that he had. Likewise, even
going to his death, at the Tower gate a poor woman called unto him and
besought him to declare that he had certain evidences of hers in the time
that he was in office (which after he was apprehended she could not come
by), and that he would entreat she might have them again, or else she
was undone. He answered, "Good woman, have patience a little while,
for the king is so good unto me that even within this half hour he will
discharge me of all businesses and help thee himself."

Also when he went up the stair on the scaffold, he desired one of the
30 sheriff's officers to give him his hand to help him up, and said, "When
I come down again, let me shift for myself as well as I can." Also the
hangman kneeled down to him asking him forgiveness of his death (as
the manner is), to whom he said, "I forgive thee, but I promise thee
that thou shalt never have honesty of the striking off my head, my neck
is so short." Also, even when he should lay down his head on the block,
he, having a great grey beard, striked out his beard and said to the hangman, "I pray you let me lay my beard over the block lest ye should cut it."
Thus with a mock he ended his life. . . .

HUGH LATIMER

The Introduction and Notes are at page 1298

FROM *The fyrste Sermon of Mayster Hughe Latimer, whiche he preached before the Kinges Maiestie,* 1549

The argument of the sermon   10

IN THIS first sermon is declared and taught the godly election of a king, and a rule of godly living as touching his own person. Where he proveth our most excellent King Edward to be our most lawful king, both by nativity and country, yea, and now appointed in these our days to deliver us from the danger and captivity of Egypt and wicked Pharaoh, that is, from error and ignorance and the devilish Antichrist, the pope of Rome. The form of his godly rule, also, he divided here in this sermon in three parts. First, that he should not trust too much upon his own strength and policy, but only to walk ordinately with God and to make Him his lodesman and chief guide. Secondarily, that he live not lasciviously and wan- 20 tonly, following venereal affections, but to live chastely. And, when time shall require, to lead a pure life under the yoke of matrimony, admonishing both His Grace and all other magistrates to be circumspect in choosing a wife, either for themselves or for their children, having this always in mind, that she be of a faithful house, godly brought up, and of a pure life. Thirdly, he admonished the King's Grace that he should not desire gold and silver too much, proving by many arguments that kind of vice, with the other foresaid, to be destruction not only unto the King's Grace: but also unto the whole realm and people. In these things consisteth the whole sum of this sermon.   30

Quecunque scripta sunt: ad nostram doctrinam scripta sunt. Whatsoever things are written aforetime, are written for our learning, that we through patience and comfort of scriptures might have hope. In taking this part of scripture (most noble audience) I play as a truant, which when he is at school will choose a lesson wherein he is perfect, because he is loth to take pain in studying a new lesson, or else feareth stripes for his slothfulness. In like manner, I might seem now in my old age to some men to take this part of scripture because I would wade easily away therewith, and drive my matter at my pleasure and not to be bound unto a certain theme. But ye shall consider that the foresaid words of Paul are 40 not to be understande of all scriptures, but only of those which are of God, written in God's book, and all things which are therein are written for our learning. The excellency of this word is so great, and of high dignity, that there is no earthly thing to be compared unto it. The author thereof is great; that is, God himself, eternal, almighty, everlasting. The scripture, because of Him, is also great, eternal, most mighty, and holy.

There is no king, emperor, magistrate, and ruler, of what state soever they be, but are bound to obey this God, and to give credence unto His holy word in directing their steps ordinately according unto the same word. Yea, truly, they are not only bound to obey God's book, but also the minister of the same, for the word's sake, so far as he speaketh sitting in
10 Moses' chair; that is, if His doctrine be taken out of Moses' law. For in this world God hath two swords; the one is a temporal sword, the other a spiritual. The temporal sword resteth in the hands of kings, magistrates, and rulers under him, whereunto all subjects, as well the clergy as the laity, be subject, and punishable for any offense contrary to the same book.

The spiritual sword is in the hands of the ministers and preachers, whereunto all kings, magistrates, and rulers ought to be obedient; that is, to hear and follow so long as the ministers sit in Christ's chair—that is, speaking out of Christ's book.

The king correcteth transgressors with the temporal sword; yea, and
20 the preacher also, if he be an offender. But the preacher can not correct the king, if he be a transgressor of God's word, with the temporal sword. But he must correct and reprove him with the spiritual sword, fearing no man, setting God only before his eyes, under whom he is a minister to supplant and root up all vice and mischief by God's word, whereunto all men ought to be obedient, as is mentioned in many places of scripture, and amongst many, this is one:

Quecunque jusserint vos servare, servate, et facite.

Whatsoever they bid you observe, that observe and do. Therefore let the preacher teach, improve, amend, and instruct in righteousness with
30 the spiritual sword, fearing no man though death should ensue. Thus Moses, fearing no man, with this sword did reprove King Pharaoh at God's commandment.

*   *   *   *   *

I have thought it good to intreat upon these words following which are written in the xvii. Chapter of Deuteronomy: *Cum veneris in terram quam Dominus Deus dat tibi possederisque, et cetera.* That is: when thou art come unto the land which the Lord thy God giveth thee, and enjoyest it, and dwellest therein, if thou shalt say, I will set a king over me, like
40 unto all the nations that are about me: then thou shalt make him king over thee whom the Lord thy God shall choose.

One of thy brethren must thou make king over thee, and mayst not set a stranger over thee which is not of thy brethren. But in any wise, let him not hold too many horses, that he bring not the people again to Egypt, through the multitude of horses, for as much as the Lord hath said unto you: ye shall henceforth go no more again that way. Also he shall not have too many wives, lest his heart turn away; neither shall he gather him silver and gold too much.

As in divers other places of scriptures is meet matter for all estates, so in this foresaid place is described chiefly the doctrine fit for a king. 10

* * * * *

God is great grandmaster of the king's house, and will take account of every one that beareth rule therein, for the executing of their offices: whether they have justly and truly served the king in their offices or no. Yea, God looketh upon the king himself if he worketh well or not. Every king is subject unto God, and all other men are subjects unto the king. In a king God requireth faith, not excess of horses. Horses for a king be good and necessary, if they be well used. But horses are not to be preferred above poor men. I was once offended with the king's horses, and therefore took occasion to speak in the presence of the King's Majesty that dead 20 is, when abbeys stood. Abbeys were ordained for the comfort of the poor. Wherefore I said it was not decent that the king's horses should be kept in them (as many were at that time), the living of poor men thereby minished and taken away. But afterward a certain nobleman said to me, "What hast thou to do with the king's horses?"

I answered and said, "I speak my conscience as God's word directeth me."

He said: "Horses be the maintenances and part of a king's honor, and also of his realm, wherefore, in speaking against them, ye are against the king's honor." 30

I answered: "God teacheth what honor is decent for the king and for all other men according unto their vocations. God appointeth every king a sufficient living for his state and degree, both by lands and other customs. And it is lawful for every king to enjoy the same goods and possessions; but to extort and take away the right of the poor is against the honor of the king. And you do move the king to do after that manner; then you speak against the honor of the king. For I full certify you extortioners, violent oppressors, engrossers of tenements and lands, through whose covetousness villages decay and fall down, the king's liege people, for lack of sustenance, are famished and decayed. They be those which 40 speak against the honor of the king. God requireth in the king and all

magistrates a good heart, to walk directly in His ways. And, in all subjects, an obedience due unto a king. Therefore, I pray God both the king
and also we, his people, may endeavor diligently to walk in His ways, to
His great honor and our profit."

* * * * *

He shall not multiply unto himself too much gold and silver. Is there
too much, think you, for a king? God doth allow much unto a king, and
it is expedient that he should have much, for he hath great expenses and
10 many occasions to spend much for the defense and surety of his realm and
subjects.

And necessary it is that a king have a treasure always in a readiness for
that and such other affairs as be daily in his hands. The which treasure,
if it be not sufficient, he may lawfully, and with a salve conscience, take
taxes of his subjects. For it were not meet the treasure should be in the
subjects' purses when the money should be occupied, nor it were not best
for themselves: for the lack thereof, it might cause both it and all the rest
that they have should not long be theirs. And so, for a necessary and
expedient occasion, it is warranted by God's word to take of the subjects.
20 But if there be sufficient treasures and the burdening of subjects be for
a vain thing, so that he will require thus much or so much of his subjects
(which perchance are in great necessity and penury), then this covetous
intent, and the request thereof is too much, which God forbiddeth the
king, here in this place of Scripture, to have.

But who shall see this too much, or tell the king of this too much. Think
you any of the king's privy chamber? No. For fear of loss of favor. Shall
any of his sworn chaplains? No. They be of the closet and keep close
such matters. But the king himself must see this too much, and that shall
he do by no means with the corporal eyes. Wherefore, he must have a
30 pair of spectacles, which shall have two clear sights in them; that is, that
one is faith, not a seasonable faith, which shall last but a while, but a faith
which is continuing in GOD. The second clear sight is charity, which is
fervent towards his Christian brother. By them two must the king see
ever when he hath too much. But few there be that useth these spectacles, the more is their damnation. Not without cause Chrysostom with
admiration saith, *Miror si aliquis rectorum potest salvari.* I marvel if any
ruler can be saved. Which words he speaketh not of an impossibility but of
a great difficulty, for that their charge is marvelous great, and that none
about them dare shew them the truth of the thing how it goeth.
40 Well, then, if God will not allow a king too much, whether will he
allow a subject too much? No, that he will not. Whether hath any man
here in England too much? I doubt most rich men have too much, for,

without too much, we can get nothing. As for example, the physician. If the poor man be diseased, he can have no help without too much. And of the lawyer the poor man can get no counsel, expedition, nor help in his matter except he give him too much. At merchants' hands, no kind of wares can be had except we give for it too much. You landlords, you rent-raisers, I may say you steplords, you unnatural lords, you have for your possessions yearly too much. For that herebefore went for twenty or forty pound by year, which is an honest portion to be had gratis in one lordship of another man's sweat and labor: now is it let for fifty or a hundred pound by year. Of this too much cometh this monstrous and 10 portentous dearths made by man, notwithstanding GOD doth send us plentifully the fruits of the earth, mercifully, contrary unto our deserts. Notwithstanding, too much, which these rich men have, causeth such dearth that poor men (which live of their labor) cannot, with the sweat of their face have a living, all kind of victuals is so dear. Pigs, geese, capons, chickens, eggs, *etc.*: these things, with other, are so unreasonably enhanced. And I think verily that if yet this continue, we shall at length be constrained to pay for a pig a pound. I will tell you, my lords and masters, this is not for the king's honor.

Yet some will say, knowest thou what belongeth unto the king's honor 20 better than we? I answer that the true honor of a king is most perfectly mentioned and painted forth in the Scriptures, of which, if ye be ignorant, for lack of time, that ye cannot read it, albeit that your counsels be never so politic, yet is it not for the king's honor. What his honor meaneth ye cannot tell. It is the king's honor that his subjects be led in the true religion. That all his prelates and clergy be set about their work in preaching and studying and not to be interrupted from their charge. Also it is the king's honor that the commonwealth be advanced, that the dearth of these foresaid things be provided for, and the commodities of this realm so employed as it may be to the setting his subjects on work and keeping them 30 from idleness. And herein resteth the king's honor and his office. So doing, his account before God shall be allowed and rewarded.

Furthermore, if the king's honor (as some men say) standeth in the great multitude of people, then these graziers, enclosers, and rent-rearers are hinderers of the king's honor. For whereas have been a great many of householders and inhabitants, there is now but a shepherd and his dog, so they hinder the king's honor most of all. My lords and masters, I say also that all such proceedings which are against the king's honor (as I have a part declared before), and as far as I can perceive, do intend plainly to make the yeomanry slavery and the clergy shavery. For such 40 works are all singular, private wealth and commodity. We of the clergy had too much, but that is taken away, and now we have too little. But for mine own part, I have no cause to complain, for I thank God and the king I have sufficient, and God is my judge I came not to crave of any man anything. But I know them that have too little. There lieth a great matter by these appropriations, great reformations is to be had in them. I know where is a great market town with divers hamlets and inhabitants, where do rise yearly of their labors to the value of fifty pound, and the vicar that serveth (being so great a cure) hath but twelve or fourteen marks by year, so that, of this pension, he is not able to buy him books nor give his neighbor drink, all the great gain goeth another way.

10 My father was a yeoman and had no lands of his own, only he had a farm of three or four pound by year at the uttermost, and hereupon he tilled so much as kept half a dozen men. He had walk for a hundred sheep, and my mother milked thirty kine. He was able and did find the king a harness, with himself and his horse, while he came to the place that he should receive the king's wages. I can remember that I buckled his harness when he went unto Blackheath field. He kept me to school, or else I had not been able to have preached before the King's Majesty now. He married my sisters with five pound or twenty nobles apiece, so that he brought them up in godliness and fear of God. He kept hospitality for his poor 20 neighbors, and some alms he gave to the poor. And all this did he of the said farm, where he that now hath it payeth sixteen pound by year or more, and is not able to do anything for his prince, for himself, nor for his children, or give a cup of drink to the poor.

Thus all the enhancing and rearing goeth to your private commodity and wealth. So that, where ye had a single too much, you have that; and since the same, ye have enhanced the rent, and so have increased another too much. So now ye have double too much, which is too, too much. But let the preacher preach till his tongue be worn to the stomps, nothing is amended. We have good statutes made for the commonwealth as touch- 30 ing commoners, enclosers; many meetings and sessions; but, in the end of the matter, there cometh nothing forth.

Well, well, this is one thing I will say unto you, from whence it cometh I know—even from the devil. I know his intent in it. For if ye bring it to pass that the yeomanry be not able to put their sons to school (as indeed universities do wondrously decay already) and that they be not able to marry their daughters to the avoiding of whoredom, I say ye pluck salvation from the people and utterly destroy the realm. For by yeomen's sons the faith of Christ is, and hath been, maintained chiefly. Is this realm taught by rich men's sons? No, no, read the chronicles. Ye 40 shall find sometime noblemen's sons which have been unpreaching bishops and prelates, but ye shall find none of them learned men. But, verily, they that should look to the redress of these things be the greatest against them.

In this realm are a great many of folks, and, amongst many, I know but one of tender zeal, at the motion of his poor tenants, hath let down his lands to the old rents for their relief. For God's love, let not him be a phoenix, let him not be alone, let him not be an hermit closed in a wall! Some good man follow him and do as he giveth example. Surveyors there be that greedily gorge up their covetous guts; handmakers, I mean (honest men I touch not), but all such as survey; they make up their mouths, but the commons be utterly undone by them. Whose bitter cry ascending up to the ears of the God of Sabaoth, the greedy pit of hell burning fire (without great repentance) to tarry and look for them.   10

A redress God grant. For surely, surely, but that two things do comfort me, I would despair of the redress in these matters. One is that the King's Majesty, when he cometh to age, will see a redress of these things so out of frame, giving example by letting down his own lands first, and then enjoin his subjects to follow him. The second hope I have is I believe that the general accounting day is at hand, the dreadful day of judgment, I mean, which shall make an end of all these calamities and miseries. For as the Scriptures be, *Cum dixerint pax pax,* When they shall say, peace, peace: *Omnia tuta,* All things are sure: then is the day at hand. A merry day, I say, for all such as do in this world study to serve and please 20 God and continue in His faith, fear, and love; and a dreadful, horrible day for them that decline from God, walking in their own ways, to whom, as it is written in the xxv. of Matthew, is said: *Ite maledicti in ignem eternum.* Go, ye cursed, into everlasting punishment. Where shall be wailing and gnashing of teeth. But unto the other he shall say: *Venite benedicti,* Come, ye blessed children of my Father, possess ye the kingdom prepared for you from the beginning of the world, of the which God make us all partakers. Amen.

ROGER ASCHAM

The Introduction and Notes are at page 1299

FROM *Toxophilus, the schole of shootinge,* 1545

Toxophilus

To the most gracious and our most dread sovereign lord, King Henry the VIII, by the grace of God, King of England, France, and Ireland, Defender of the faith, and of the Church of England, and also of Ireland, in earth supreme head, next under Christ, be all health, victory, and felicity.

WHAT time as, Most Gracious Prince, Your Highness this last year past took that your most honorable and victorious journey into France, accompanied with such a port of the nobility and yeomanry of England as neither hath been like known by experience, nor yet read of in history:
20 accompanied also with the daily prayers, good hearts, and wills of all and every one Your Grace's subjects left behind you here at home in England: the same time I being at my book in Cambridge, sorry that my little ability could stretch out no better to help forward so noble an enterprise, yet with my good will, prayer, and heart, nothing behind him that was foremost of all, conceived a wonderful desire by the prayer, wishing, talking, and communication that was in every man's mouth for Your Grace's most victorious return, to offer up something at your homecoming to Your Highness which should both be a token of my love and duty toward Your Majesty and also a sign of my good mind and zeal toward my
30 country.

This occasion given to me at that time caused me to take in hand again this little purpose of shooting, begun of me before, yet not ended then, for other studies more meet for that trade of living which God and my friends had set me unto. But when Your Grace's most joyful and happy victory prevented my daily and speedy diligency to perform this matter, I was compelled to wait another time to prepare and offer up this little book unto Your Majesty. And when it hath pleased Your Highness of your infinite goodness, and also your most honorable counsel to know and peruse over the contents and some part of this book, and so to allow it,
40 that other men might read it, through the furtherance and setting forth of the right worshipful and my singular good master, Sir William Paget, knight, most worthy secretary to Your Highness, and most open and

ready succor to all poor, honest, learned men's suits, I most humbly beseech Your Grace to take in good worth this little treatise purposed, began and ended of me only for this intent: that labor, honest pastime, and
virtue might recover again that place and right, that idleness, unthrifty
gaming and vice hath put them fro.

And although to have written this book either in Latin or Greek (which
thing I would be very glad yet to do if I might surely know Your Grace's
pleasure therein) had been more easier and fit for my trade in study, yet
nevertheless, I, supposing it no point of honesty that my commodity should
stop and hinder any part either of the pleasure or profit of many, have 10
written this English matter in the English tongue for Englishmen:
wherein this I trust: that Your Grace (if it shall please Your Highness to
read it) shall perceive it to be a thing honest for me to write, pleasant for
some to read, and profitable for many to follow, containing a pastime
honest for the mind, wholesome for the body, fit for every man, vile for
no man, using the day and open place for honesty to rule it, not lurking
in corners for misorder to abuse it. Therefore, I trust it shall appear to
be both a sure token of my zeal to set forward shooting and some sign of
my mind towards honesty and learning.

Thus I will trouble Your Grace no longer, but with my daily prayer 20
I will beseech God to preserve Your Grace in all health and felicity, to
the fear and overthrow of all your enemies; to the pleasure, joyfulness,
and succor of all your subjects; to the utter destruction of papistry and
heresy; to the continual setting forth of God's word and His glory.

Your Grace's most bounden scholar.

ROGER ASCHAM.

To all Gentlemen and Yeomen of England.

Bias, the wise man, came to Croesus, the rich king, on a time when he
was making new ships, purposing to have subdued by water the out isles 30
lying betwixt Greece and Asia Minor. "What news now in Greece?"
saith the king to Bias.

"None other news but these," saith Bias; "that the isles of Greece have
prepared a wonderful company of horsemen to overrun Lydia withal."

"There is nothing under heaven," saith the king, "that I would so soon
wish as that they durst be so bold to meet us on the land with horse."

"And think you," saith Bias, "that there is anything which they would
sooner wish than that you should be so fond to meet them on the water
with ships?"

And so Croesus, hearing not the true news, but perceiving the wise 40
man's mind and counsel, both gave then over making of his ships and
left also behind him a wonderful example for all commonwealths to fol-

low: that is evermore to regard and set most by that thing whereunto nature hath made them most apt and use hath made them most fit.

By this matter I mean the shooting in the long-bow for Englishmen: which thing with all my heart I do wish, and if I were of authority I would counsel all the gentlemen and yeomen of England not to change it with any other thing, how good soever it seem to be: but that still, according to the old wont of England, youth should use it for the most honest pastime in peace, that men might handle it as a most sure weapon in war. Other strong weapons which both experience doth prove to be good and the wisdom of the King's Majesty and his council provides to be had, are not ordained to take away shooting: but that both, not compared together, whether should be better than the other, but so joined together that the one should be always an aid and help for the other, might so strengthen the realm on all sides that no kind of enemy in any kind of weapon might pass and go beyond us.

For this purpose, I, partly provoked by the counsel of some gentlemen, partly moved by the love which I have always borne toward shooting, have written this little treatise, wherein if I have not satisfied any man, I trust he will the rather be content with my doing, because I am (I suppose) the first which hath said anything in this matter (and few beginnings be perfect, saith wise men), and also because if I have said amiss, I am content that any man amend it, or if I have said too little, any man that will to add what him pleaseth to it.

My mind is, in profiting and pleasing every man, to hurt or displease no man, intending none other purpose but that youth might be stirred to labor, honest pastime, and virtue, and as much as lay in me, plucked from idleness, unthrifty games, and vice: which thing I have labored only in this book, shewing how fit shooting is for all kinds of men, how honest a pastime for the mind, how wholesome an exercise for the body, not vile for great men to use, not costly for poor men to sustain, not lurking in holes and corners for ill men at their pleasure to misuse it, but abiding in the open sight and face of the world, for good men, if it fault, by their wisdom to correct it.

And here I would desire all gentlemen and yeomen to use this pastime in such a mean that the outrageousness of great gaming should not hurt the honesty of shooting, which of his own nature is always joined with honesty, yet for men's faults oftentimes blamed unworthily, as all good things have been and evermore shall be.

If any man would blame me either for taking such a matter in hand or else for writing it in the English tongue, this answer I may make him, that when the best of the realm think it honest for them to use, I, one of the meanest sort, ought not to suppose it vile for me to write. And though to have written it in another tongue had been more profitable for my study, and also more honest for my name, yet I can think my labor well bestowed if, with a little hindrance of my profit and name, may come any furtherance to the pleasure or commodity of the gentlemen and yeomen of England, for whose sake I took this matter in hand. And as for the Latin or Greek tongue, everything is so excellently done in them that none can do better; in the English tongue, contrary, everything in a manner so meanly, both for the matter and handling, that no man can do worse. For therein the least learned for the most part have been always most ready to write. And they which had least hope in Latin have been 10 most bold in English, when surely every man that is most ready to talk is not most able to write. He that will write well in any tongue must follow this counsel of Aristotle: to speak as the common people do, to think as wise men do; and so should every man understand him, and the judgment of wise men allow him. Many English writers have not done so, but using strange words as Latin, French, and Italian do make all things dark and hard. Once I communed with a man which reasoned the English tongue to be enriched and increased thereby, saying: "Who will not praise that feast, where a man shall drink at a dinner both wine, ale, and beer?"

"Truly," quod I, "they be all good, every one taken by himself alone, 20 but if you put malvesy and sack, red wine and white, ale and beer, and all in one pot, you shall make a drink neither easy to be known nor yet wholesome for the body. Cicero, in following Isocrates, Plato, and Demosthenes, increased the Latin tongue after another sort. This way, because divers men that write do not know, they can neither follow it, because of their ignorancy, nor yet will praise it, for very arrogancy, two faults seldom the one out of the other's company.

English writers, by diversity of time, have taken divers matters in hand. In our fathers' time nothing was read but books of feigned chivalry, wherein a man by reading should be led to none other end but only to 30 manslaughter and bawdry. If any man suppose they were good enough to pass the time withal, he is deceived. For surely vain words do work no small thing in vain, ignorant, and young minds, specially if they be given anything thereunto of their own nature. These books (as I have heard say) were made the most part in abbeys and monasteries, a very likely and fit fruit of such an idle and blind kind of living.

In our time now, when every man is given to know much rather than to live well, very many do write, but after such a fashion as very many do shoot. Some shooters take in hand stronger bows than they be able to maintain. This thing maketh them sometime to outshoot the mark, sometime to 40 shoot far wide, and perchance hurt some that look on. Other that never learned to shoot, nor yet knoweth good shaft nor bow, will be as busy as the best; but such one commonly plucketh down a side, and crafty archers which be against him will be both glad of him and also ever ready to lay and bet with him. It were better for such one to sit down than shoot. Other there be which have very good bow and shafts and good knowledge in shooting, but they have been brought up in such evil-favored shooting that they can neither shoot fair nor yet near. If any man will apply these things together, shall not see the one far differ from the other.

And I also, amongst all other, in writing this little treatise have followed some young shooters, which both will begin to shoot for a little money 10 and also will use to shoot once or twice about the mark for naught afore they begin agood. And therefore did I take this little matter in hand to assay myself, and hereafter, by the grace of God, if the judgment of wise men that look on think that I can do any good, I may, perchance, cast my shaft among other for better game.

Yet in writing this book, some man will marvel, perchance, why that I, being an unperfect shooter, should take in hand to write of making a perfect archer. The same man, peradventure, will marvel how a whetstone which is blunt can make the edge of a knife sharp. I would the same man should consider also that in going about any matter there be 20 four things to be considered: doing, saying, thinking, and perfectness. First, there is no man that doth so well but he can say better, or else some men which be now stark naught should be too good; again, no man can utter with his tongue so well as he is able to imagine with his mind; and yet perfectness itself is far above all thinking. Then seeing that saying is one step nearer perfectness than doing, let every man leave marveling why my word shall rather express, than my deed shall perform, perfect shooting.

I trust no man will be offended with this little book, except it be some fletchers and bowyers, thinking hereby that many that love shooting shall 30 be taught to refuse such naughty wares as they would utter. Honest fletchers and bowyers do not so, and they that be unhonest ought rather to amend themselves for doing ill than be angry with me for saying well. A fletcher hath even as good a quarrel to be angry with an archer that refuseth an ill shaft as a bladesmith hath to a fletcher that forsaketh to buy of him a naughty knife. For as an archer must be content that a fletcher know a good shaft in every point for the perfecter making of it, so an honest fletcher will also be content that a shooter know a good shaft in every point for the perfecter using of it; because the one knoweth, like a fletcher, how to make it, the other knoweth, like an archer, how to use it. 40 And seeing the knowledge is one in them both, yet the end diverse, surely that fletcher is an enemy to archers and artillery which cannot be content that an archer know a shaft as well for his use in shooting as he himself should know a shaft for his advantage in selling. And the rather because shafts be not made so much to be sold, but chiefly to be used. And seeing that use and occupying is the end why a shaft is made, the making, as it were, a mean for occupying, surely the knowledge in every point of a good shaft is more to be required in a shooter than a fletcher.

Yet, as I said before, no honest fletcher will be angry with me, seeing I do not teach how to make a shaft, which belongeth only to a good fletcher, but to know and handle a shaft, which belongeth to an archer. And this little book, I trust, shall please and profit both parts; for good bows and shafts shall be better known to the commodity of all shooters, 10 and good shooting may, perchance, be the more occupied to the profit of all bowyers and fletchers. And thus I pray God that all fletchers getting their living truly and all archers using shooting honestly, and all manner of men that favor artillery may live continually in health and merriness, obeying their prince as they should and loving God as they ought, to whom for all things be all honor and glory forever. Amen.

FROM *The Scholemaster*, 1570

The Schoolmaster 20

To the honorable Sir William Cecil, knight, principal secretary to the Queen's most excellent Majesty.

SUNDRY and reasonable be the causes why learned men have used to offer and dedicate such works as they put abroad to some such personage as they think fittest, either in respect of ability of defense, or skill for judgment, or private regard of kindness and duty. Every one of those considerations, sir, move me of right to offer this, my late husband's, Mr. Ascham's, work unto you. For well remembering how much all good learning oweth unto you for defense thereof, as the University of Cambridge, of which my said late husband was a member, have in choosing you their worthy 30 chancellor acknowledged; and how happily you have spent your time in such studies and carried the use thereof to the right end, to the good service of the Queen's Majesty and your country, to all our benefits; thirdly, how much my said husband was many ways bound unto you, and how gladly and comfortably he used, in his life, to recognize and report your goodness toward him, leaving with me, then his poor widow, and a great sort of orphans a good comfort in the hope of your good continuance, which I have truly found to me and mine, and therefore do duly and daily pray for you and yours: I could not find any man for whose name this book was more agreeable for hope of protection, more meet for sub- 40 mission to judgment, nor more due for respect of worthiness of your part and thankfulness of my husband's and mine. Good I trust it shall do, as

I am put in great hope by many very well learned that can well judge thereof. Meet, therefore, I compt it that such good as my husband was able to do and leave to the commonweal, it should be received under your name, and that the world should owe thank thereof to you, to whom my husband, the author of it, was for good received of you, most dutifully bounden. And so beseeching you to take on you the defense of this book, to advance the good that may come of it by your allowance and further-ance to public use and benefit, and to accept the thankful recognition of me and my poor children, trusting of the continuance of your good
10 memory of Mr. Ascham and his, and daily commending the prosperous estate of you and yours to God, whom you serve and whose you are, I rest to trouble you.

Your humble, MARGARET
ASCHAM.

*A Preface to the
Reader*

WHEN the great plague was at London the year 1563, the Queen's Majesty, Queen Elizabeth, lay at her Castle of Windsor: Where, upon
20 the 10 day of December, it fortuned that, in Sir William Cecil's cham-ber, Her Highness' principal secretary, there dined together these per-sonages: Mr. Secretary himself, Sir William Peter, Sir J. Mason, D. Wot-ton, Sir Richard Sackville, treasurer of the exchequer, Sir Walter Mild-may, chancellor of the exchequer, Mr. Haddon, master of requests, Mr. John Astley, master of the jewel house, Mr. Bernard Hampton, Mr. Nicasius, and I. Of which number, the most part were of Her Majesty's most honorable privy council, and the rest serving her in very good place. I was glad then, and do rejoice yet to remember, that my chance was so happy to be there that day, in the company of so many wise and good
30 men together, as hardly then could have been picked out again, out of all England beside.

Mr. Secretary hath this accustomed manner: though his head be never so full of most weighty affairs of the realm, yet at dinner time he doth seem to lay them always aside, and findeth ever fit occasion to talk pleasantly of other matters; but most gladly of some matter of learning, wherein he will courteously hear the mind of the meanest at his table.

Not long after our sitting down, "I have strange news brought me," saith Mr. Secretary, "this morning, that divers scholars of Eton be run away from the school for fear of beating." Whereupon Mr. Secretary
40 took occasion to wish that some more discretion were in many school-masters in using correction than commonly there is, who many times punish rather the weakness of nature than the fault of the scholar.

Whereby many scholars, that might else prove well, be driven to hate learning before they know what learning meaneth, and so are made willing to forsake their book and be glad to be put to any other kind of living.

Mr. Peter, as one somewhat severe of nature, said plainly that the rod only was the sword that must keep the school in obedience and the scholar in good order. Mr. Wotton, a man mild of nature, with soft voice and few words, inclined to Mr. Secretary's judgment, and said, "In mine opinion, the schoolhouse should be in deed, as it is called by name, the house of play and pleasure, and not of fear and bondage; and, as I do remember, so saith Socrates in one place of Plato. And therefore if a rod 10 carry the fear of a sword, it is no marvel if those that be fearful of nature choose rather to forsake the play than to stand always within the fear of a sword in a fond man's handling."

Mr. Mason, after his manner, was very merry with both parties, pleasantly playing both with the shrewd touches of many curst boys and with the small discretion of many lewd schoolmasters. Mr. Haddon was fully of Mr. Peter's opinion, and said that the best schoolmaster of our time was the greatest beater, and named the person. "Though," quoth I, "it was his good fortune to send from his school unto the university one of the best scholars indeed of all our time, yet wise men do think that that 20 came so to pass rather by the great towardness of the scholar than by the great beating of the master; and whether this be true or no, you yourself are best witness." I said somewhat farther in the matter, how and why young children were sooner allured by love than driven by beating to attain good learning, wherein I was the bolder to say my mind because Mr. Secretary courteously provoked me thereunto; or else, in such a company, and namely in his presence, my wont is to be more willing to use mine ears than to occupy my tongue.

Sir Walter Mildmay, Mr. Astley, and the rest said very little; only Sir Richard Sackville said nothing at all. After dinner I went up to read 30 with the Queen's Majesty. We read then together in the Greek tongue, as I well remember, that noble oration of Demosthenes against Æschines for his false dealing in his embassage to King Philip of Macedonia. Sir Richard Sackville came up soon after; and, finding me in Her Majesty's privy chamber, he took me by the hand, and, carrying me to a window, said, "Mr. Ascham, I would not for a good deal of money have been this day absent from dinner, where, though I said nothing, yet I gave as good ear, and do consider as well the talk that passed as any one did there. Mr. Secretary said very wisely, and most truly, that many young wits be driven to hate learning before they know what learning is. I can be good 40 witness to this myself; for a fond schoolmaster, before I was fully fourteen year old, drave me so, with fear of beating, from all love of learning

as now, when I know what difference it is to have learning and to have little or none at all, I feel it my greatest grief, and find it my greatest hurt that ever came to me, that it was my so ill chance to light upon so lewd a schoolmaster. But seeing it is but in vain to lament things past, and also wisdom to look to things to come, surely, God willing, if God lend me life, I will make this my mishap some occasion of good hap to little Robert Sackville, my son's son, for whose bringing up, I would gladly, if it so please you, use specially your good advice. I hear say you have a son much of his age. We will deal thus together. Point you out a schoolmaster who,
10 by your order, shall teach my son and yours, and for all the rest I will provide, yea, though they three do cost me a couple of hundred pounds by year; and, beside, you shall find me as fast a friend to you and yours as perchance any you have." Which promise the worthy gentleman surely kept with me until his dying day.

We had then farther talk together of bringing up of children: of the nature of quick and hard wits; of the right choice of a good wit; of fear and love in teaching children. We passed from children and came to young men, namely gentlemen. We talked of their too much liberty to live as they lust; of their letting loose too soon, to overmuch experience of
20 ill, contrary to the good order of many good old commonwealths of the Persians and Greeks; of wit gathered and good fortune gotten by some only by experience, without learning. And, lastly, he required of me very earnestly to shew what I thought of the common going of Englishmen into Italy. "But," saith he, "because this place and this time will not suffer so long talk as these good matters require, therefore, I pray you, at my request and at your leisure, put in some order of writing the chief points of this our talk concerning the right order of teaching and honesty of living for the good bringing up of children and young men. And surely, beside contenting me, you shall both please and profit very many others."
30 I made some excuse by lack of ability and weakness of body: "Well," saith he, "I am not now to learn what you can do. Our dear friend, good Mr. Goodricke, whose judgment I could well believe, did once for all satisfy me fully therein. Again, I heard you say, not long ago, that you may thank Sir John Cheke for all the learning you have; and I know very well myself that you did teach the queen. And therefore, seeing God did so bless you to make you the scholar of the best master and also the schoolmaster of the best scholar that ever were in our time, surely you should please God, benefit your country, and honest your own name if you would take the pains to impart to others what you learned of such a mas-
40 ter, and how ye taught such a scholar. And, in uttering the stuff ye received of the one, in declaring the order ye took with the other, ye shall

never lack neither matter nor manner what to write, nor how to write,
in this kind of argument."

I, beginning some farther excuse, suddenly was called to come to the
queen. The night following I slept little, my head was so full of this our
former talk, and I so mindful somewhat to satisfy the honest request of
so dear a friend. I thought to prepare some little treatise for a New Year's
gift that Christmas; but, as it chanceth to busy builders, so, in building
this my poor schoolhouse (the rather because the form of it is somewhat
new and differing from others), the work rose daily higher and wider
than I thought it would at the beginning.   10

And though it appear now, and be in very deed, but a small cottage,
poor for the stuff and rude for the workmanship, yet, in going forward,
I found the site so good as I was loath to give it over; but the making so
costly, outreaching my ability, as many times I wished that some one of
those three, my dear friends with full purses, Sir Thomas Smith, Mr.
Haddon, or Mr. Watson, had had the doing of it. Yet, nevertheless, I
myself spending gladly that little that I gat at home by good Sir John
Cheke and that that I borrowed abroad of my friend Sturmius, beside
somewhat that was left me in reversion by my old masters, Plato, Aristotle, and Cicero, I have at last patched it up as I could, and as you see. 20
If the matter be mean and meanly handled, I pray you bear both with
me and it; for never work went up in worse weather, with mo lets and
stops, than this poor schoolhouse of mine. Westminster Hall can bear
some witness, beside much weakness of body, but more trouble of mind,
by some such sores as grieve me to touch them myself, and therefore I
purpose not to open them to others. And, in midst of outward injuries and
inward cares, to increase them withal good Sir Richard Sackville dieth,
that worthy gentleman; that earnest favorer and furtherer of God's true
religion; that faithful servitor to his prince and country; a lover of learning and all learned men; wise in all doings; courteous to all persons, shew- 30
ing spite to none, doing good to many; and, as I well found, to me so
fast a friend as I never lost the like before. When he was gone, my heart
was dead. There was not one that wore a black gown for him who carried
a heavier heart for him than I. When he was gone, I cast this book away;
I could not look upon it but with weeping eyes, in remembering him who
was the only setter on to do it, and would have been not only a glad com-
mender of it but also a sure and certain comfort to me and mine for it.
Almost two years together this book lay scattered and neglected, and had
been quite given over of me if the goodness of one had not given me some
life and spirit again. God, the mover of goodness, prosper always him and 40
his as he hath many times comforted me and mine, and, I trust to God,

shall comfort more and more. Of whom most justly I may say, and very oft, and always gladly, I am wont to say that sweet verse of Sophocles spoken by Oedipus to worthy Theseus:

$$\text{ἔχω, γὰρ ἄχω δἳὰ σὲ, κοὔκ ἄλλον βροτῶν.}$$

This hope hath helped me to end this book: which, if he allow, I shall think my labors well employed, and shall not much esteem the misliking of any others. And I trust he shall think the better of it because he shall find the best part thereof to come out of his school whom he of all men loved and liked best.

¹⁰ Yet some men, friendly enough of nature but of small judgment in learning, do think I take too much pains and spend too much time in setting forth these children's affairs. But those good men were never brought up in Socrates' school, who saith plainly that no man goeth about a more godly purpose than he that is mindful of the good bringing up both of his own and other men's children.

Therefore, I trust good and wise men will think well of this my doing. And of other that think otherwise, I will think myself they are but men to be pardoned for their folly and pitied for their ignorance.

In writing this book, I have had earnest respect to three special points: ²⁰ truth of religion, honesty in living, right order in learning. In which three ways I pray God my poor children may diligently walk; for whose sake, as nature moved, and reason required, and necessity also somewhat compelled, I was the willinger to take these pains.

For, seeing at my death I am not like to leave them any great store of living, therefore in my lifetime I thought good to bequeath unto them, in this little book, as in my will and testament, the right way to good learning; which, if they follow with the fear of God, they shall very well come to sufficiency of living.

I wish also, with all my heart, that young Mr. Robert Sackville may ³⁰ take that fruit of this labor that his worthy grandfather purposed he should have done; and if any other do take either profit or pleasure hereby, they have cause to thank Mr. Robert Sackville, for whom specially this my schoolmaster was provided.

And one thing I would have the reader consider in reading this book, that, because no schoolmaster hath charge of any child before he enter into his school, therefore I, leaving all former care of their good bringing up to wise and good parents as a matter not belonging to the schoolmaster, I do appoint this my schoolmaster then and there to begin where his office and charge beginneth. Which charge lasteth not long, but until ⁴⁰ the scholar be made able to go to the university, to proceed in logic, rhetoric, and other kinds of learning.

Yet if my schoolmaster, for love he beareth to his scholar, shall teach him somewhat for his furtherance and better judgment in learning that may serve him seven year after in the university, he doth his scholar no more wrong, nor deserveth no worse name thereby, than he doth in London who, selling silk or cloth unto his friend, doth give him better measure than either his promise or bargain was.

Farewell in Christ.

The first book for the youth

After the child hath learned perfectly the eight parts of speech, let him then learn the right joining together of substantives with adjectives, the noun with the verb, the relative with the antecedent. And in learning farther his syntaxis, by mine advice he shall not use the common order in common schools for making of Latins; whereby the child commonly learneth, first, an evil choice of words (and right choice of words, saith *Caesar*, is the foundation of eloquence); then, a wrong placing of words; and lastly, an ill framing of the sentence, with a perverse judgment both of words and sentences. These faults, taking once root in youth, be never, or hardly, plucked away in age. Moreover, there is no one thing that hath more either dulled the wits or taken away the will of children from learning than the care they have to satisfy their masters in making of Latins.

For the scholar is commonly beat for the making when the master were more worthy to be beat for the mending, or rather marring, of the same: the master many times being as ignorant as the child what to say properly and fitly to the matter.

Two schoolmasters have set forth in print, either of them, a book of such kind of Latins, Horman and Whittington. A child shall learn of the better of them that which another day, if he be wise and come to judgment, he must be fain to unlearn again.

There is a way, touched in the first book of *Cicero de Oratore*, which, wisely brought into schools, truly taught, and constantly used, would not only take wholly away this butcherly fear in making of Latins, but would also with ease and pleasure, and in short time, as I know by good experience, work a true choice and placing of words, a right ordering of sentences, an easy understanding of the tongue, a readiness to speak, a facility to write, a true judgment both of his own and other men's doings, what tongue soever he doth use.

The way is this. After the three concordances learned, as I touched before, let the master read unto him the epistles of Cicero, gathered together and chosen out by Sturmius for the capacity of children.

First, let him teach the child cheerfully and plainly the cause and matter of the letter; then let him construe it into English so oft as the child may easily carry away the understanding of it; lastly, parse it over perfectly. This done thus, let the child, by and by, both construe and parse it over again, so that it may appear that the child doubteth in nothing that his master taught him before. After this, the child must take a paper book and, sitting in some place where no man shall prompt him, by himself let him translate into English his former lesson. Then, shewing it to his master, let the master take from him his Latin book and, pausing an hour at the least, then let the child translate his own English into Latin again in another paper book. When the child bringeth it turned into Latin, the master must compare it with Tully's book and lay them both together; and where the child doth well, either in choosing or true placing of Tully's words, let the master praise him and say, "Here you do well." For I assure you, there is no such whetstone to sharpen a good wit and encourage a will to learning as is praise.

But if the child miss, either in forgetting a word or in changing a good with a worse, or misordering the sentence, I would not have the master either frown or chide with him if the child have done his diligence and used no truantship therein. For I know by good experience that a child shall take more profit of two faults gently warned of than of four things rightly hit. For then the master shall have good occasion to say unto him, "N., Tully would have used such a word, not this; Tully would have placed this word here, not there; would have used this case, this number, this person, this degree, this gender; he would have used this mood, this tense, this simple rather than this compound, this adverb here, not there; he would have ended the sentence with this verb, not with that noun or participle, etc."

In these few lines, I have wrapped up the most tedious part of grammar; and also the ground of almost all the rules that are so busily taught by the master and so hardly learned by the scholar in all common schools, which, after this sort, the master shall teach without all error, and the scholar shall learn without great pain: the master being led by so sure a guide, and the scholar being brought into so plain and easy a way. And therefore we do not contemn rules, but we gladly teach rules; and teach them more plainly, sensibly, and orderly than they be commonly taught in common schools. For when the master shall compare Tully's book with the scholar's translation, let the master at the first lead and teach his scholar to join the rules of his grammar book with the examples of his present lesson, until the scholar, by himself, be able to fetch out of his grammar every rule for every example: so as the grammar book be ever in the scholar's hand, and also used of him as a dictionary for every present use. This is a lively and perfect way of teaching of rules: where the common way, used in common schools, to read the grammar alone by itself is tedious for the master, hard for the scholar, cold and uncomfortable for them both.

Let your scholar be never afraid to ask you any doubt, but use discreetly the best allurements ye can to encourage him to the same, lest his over-much fearing of you drive him to seek some misorderly shift: as to seek to be helped by some other book or to be prompted by some other scholar, and so go about to beguile you much and himself more.

With this way of good understanding the matter, plain construing, diligent parsing, daily translating, cheerful admonishing, and heedful amending of faults, never leaving behind just praise for well doing, I 10 would have the scholar brought up withal till he had read and translated over the first book of epistles chosen out by Sturmius, with a good piece of a comedy of Terence also.

All this while, by mine advice, the child shall use to speak no Latin for as Cicero saith in like matter, with like words, *Loquendo, male loqui discunt.* And that excellent learned man G. Budaeus, in his Greek commentaries, sore complaineth that when he began to learn the Latin tongue, use of speaking Latin at the table and elsewhere unadvisedly did bring him to such an evil choice of words, to such a crooked framing of sentences, that no one thing did hurt or hinder him more all the days of his life after- 20 ward, both for readiness in speaking and also good judgment in writing.

In very deed, if children were brought up in such a house or such a school, where the Latin tongue were properly and perfectly spoken, as Tiberius and Caius Gracchi were brought up in their mother Cornelia's house, surely then the daily use of speaking were the best and readiest way to learn the Latin tongue. But now commonly in the best schools in England, for words, right choice is smally regarded, true propriety wholly neglected, confusion is brought in, barbarousness is bred up so in young wits as afterward they be not only marred for speaking but also cor-rupted in judgment: as with much ado, or never at all, they be brought to 30 right frame again.

Yet all men covet to have their children speak Latin; and so do I very earnestly too. We both have one purpose; we agree in desire, we wish one end; but we differ somewhat in order and way that leadeth rightly to that end. Other would have them speak at all adventures; and, so they be speaking, to speak, the master careth not, the scholar knoweth not, what. This is to seem and not to be, except it be to be bold without shame, rash without skill, full of words without wit. I wish to have them speak so as it may well appear that the brain doth govern the tongue, and that reason leadeth forth the talk. Socrates' doctrine is true in Plato, and well 40 marked and truly uttered by Horace in *Arte Poetica,* that, wheresoever

knowledge doth accompany the wit, there best utterance doth always
await upon the tongue. For good understanding must first be bred in the
child, which, being nourished with skill and use of writing (as I will
teach more largely hereafter), is the only way to bring him to judgment
and readiness in speaking; and that in far shorter time (if he follow constantly the trade of this little lesson) than he shall do by common teaching
of the common schools in England.

But to go forward, as you perceive your scholar to go better and better
on away, first, with understanding his lesson more quickly, with parsing
10 more readily, with translating more speedily and perfectly than he was
wont, after, give him longer lessons to translate: and withal begin to
teach him, both in nouns and verbs, what is *proprium*, and what is *translatum*; what *synonymum*, what *diversum*; which be *contraria*, and
which be most notable *phrases* in all his lecture.

As:

Proprium.	*Rex sepultus est magnificè.*
Translatum.	*Cum illo principe, sepulta est et gloria et salus republicae.*
Synonyma.	*Ensis, gladius; Laudare, praedicare.*
Diversa.	*Diligere, amare; Calere, exardescere; Inimicus, hostis.*
Contraria.	*Acerbum et luctuosum bellum. Dulcis et laeta pax.*
Phrases.	*Dare verba; Abjicere obedientiam.*

Your scholar then must have the third paper book: in the which, after
he hath done his double translation, let him write, after this sort, four
of these forenamed six, diligently marked out of every lesson:

Quatuor.	*Propria. Translata. Synonyma. Diversa. Contraria. Phrases.*

Or else three, or two, if there be no moe: and if there be none of these at all in some lecture, yet not omit the order, but write these:

$$\begin{cases} Diversa\ nulla, \\ Contraria\ nulla,\ etc. \end{cases}$$

This diligent translating, joined with his heedful marking in the foresaid epistles, and afterward in some plain oration of Tully, as, *pro lege Manilia, pro Archia Poeta,* or in those three *ad C. Caesarem,* shall work such a right choice of words, so straight a framing of sentences, such a true judgment, both to write skilfully and speak wittily, as wise men shall both praise and marvel at.

If your scholar do miss sometimes in marking rightly these foresaid six things, chide not hastily, for that shall both dull his wit and discourage his diligence; but monish him gently, which shall make him both willing to amend and glad to go forward in love and hope of learning.

I have now wished, twice or thrice, this gentle nature to be in a schoolmaster. And that I have done so neither by chance nor without some reason, I will now declare at large why, in mine opinion, love is fitter than fear, gentleness better than beating, to bring up a child rightly in learning.

With the common use of teaching and beating in common schools of England, I will not greatly contend: which, if I did, it were but a small grammatical controversy, neither belonging to heresy nor treason, nor greatly touching God nor the prince; although, in very deed, in the end the good or ill bringing up of children doth as much serve to the good or ill service of God, our prince, and our whole country, as any one thing doth beside.

I do gladly agree with all good schoolmasters in these points: to have children brought to good perfectness in learning, to all honesty in manners, to have all faults rightly amended, to have every vice severely corrected; but for the order and way that leadeth rightly to these points, we somewhat differ. For commonly many schoolmasters, some as I have seen, moe as I have heard tell, be of so crooked a nature as, when they meet with a hard-witted scholar, they rather break him than bow him, rather mar him than mend him. For when the schoolmaster is angry with some other matter, then will he soonest fall to beat his scholar; and though he himself should be punished for his folly, yet must he beat some scholar for his pleasure, though there be no cause for him to do so, nor yet fault in the scholar to deserve so. These, ye will say, be fond schoolmasters, and few they be that be found to be such. They be fond indeed, but surely overmany such be found everywhere. But this will I say, that even the wisest of your great beaters do as oft punish nature as they do correct faults. Yea, many times the better nature is sorer punished. For if one, by quickness of wit, take his lesson readily, another, by hardness of wit, taketh it not so speedily, the first is always commended, the other is commonly punished: when a wise schoolmaster should rather discreetly consider the right disposition of both their natures, and not so much weigh what either of them is able to do now as what either of them is likely to do hereafter. For this I know, not only by reading of books in my study but also by experience of life abroad in the world, that those which be commonly the wisest, the best learned, and best men also, when they be 10 old, were never commonly the quickest of wit when they were young. The causes why, amongst other, which be many, that move me thus to think, be these few which I will reckon.

Quick wits commonly be apt to take, unapt to keep; soon hot and desirous of this and that; as cold and soon weary of the same again; more quick to enter speedily than able to pierce far: even like oversharp tools, whose edges be very soon turned. Such wits delight themselves in easy and pleasant studies, and never pass far forward in high and hard sciences. And therefore the quickest wits commonly may prove the best poets but not the wisest orators; ready of tongue to speak boldly, not deep of judg-20 ment, either for good counsel or wise writing. Also, for manners and life, quick wits commonly be, in desire, newfangle, in purpose, unconstant; light to promise anything, ready to forget everything, both benefit and injury: and thereby neither fast to friend nor fearful to foe; inquisitive of every trifle, not secret in greatest affairs; bold with any person; busy in every matter; soothing such as be present, nipping any that is absent; of nature also always flattering their betters, envying their equals, despising their inferiors; and, by quickness of wit, very quick and ready to like none so well as themselves.

Moreover, commonly men very quick of wit be also very light of con-30 ditions; and thereby very ready of disposition to be carried overquickly, by any light company, to any riot and unthriftiness when they be young; and therefore seldom either honest of life or rich in living when they be old. For quick in wit and light in manners be either seldom troubled or very soon weary in carrying a very heavy purse. Quick wits also be, in most part of all their doings, overquick, hasty, rash, heady, and brainsick. These two last words, "heady" and "brainsick," be fit and proper words, rising naturally of the matter and termed aptly by the condition of overmuch quickness of wit. In youth also they be ready scoffers, privy mockers, and ever overlight and merry: in age, soon testy, very waspish, and always 40 overmiserable. And yet few of them come to any great age, by reason of their misordered life when they were young; but a great deal fewer of them come to shew any great countenance or bear any great authority abroad in the world, but either live obscurely, men know not how, or die obscurely, men mark not when. They be like trees that shew forth fair blossoms and broad leaves in springtime, but bring out small and not long-lasting fruit in harvest time, and that only such as fall and rot before they be ripe, and so never, or seldom, come to any good at all. For this ye shall find most true by experience: that, amongst a number of quick wits in youth, few be found, in the end, either very fortunate for themselves or very profitable to serve the commonwealth, but decay and vanish, men know not which way; except a very few, to whom peradventure blood and happy parentage may perchance purchase a long standing upon the 10 stage. The which felicity, because it cometh by others' procuring, not by their own deserving, and stand by other men's feet and not by their own, what outward brag soever is borne by them is indeed of itself, and in wise men's eyes, of no great estimation.

Some wits, moderate enough by nature, be many times marred by overmuch study and use of some sciences, namely music, arithmetic, and geometry. These sciences, as they sharpen men's wits overmuch, so they change men's manners oversore if they be not moderately mingled and wisely applied to some good use of life. Mark all mathematical heads which be only and wholly bent to those sciences, how solitary they be 20 themselves, how unfit to live with others, and how unapt to serve in the world. This is not only known now by common experience, but uttered long before by wise men's judgment and sentence. Galen saith much music marreth men's manners; and Plato hath a notable place of the same thing in his books *de Rep.*, well marked also and excellently trans-lated by Tully himself. Of this matter I wrote once more at large, twenty year ago, in my book of shooting; now I thought but to touch it to prove that overmuch quickness of wit, either given by nature or sharpened by study, doth not commonly bring forth either greatest learning, best man-ners, or happiest life in the end.   30

Contrariwise, a wit in youth that is not overdull, heavy, knotty, and lumpish, but hard, rough, and, though somewhat staffish (as Tully wisheth, *otium quietum, non languidum:* and *negotium cum labore, non cum periculo*), such a wit, I say, if it be at the first well handled by the mother, and rightly smoothed and wrought as it should, not overthwartly and against the wood, by the schoolmaster, both for learning and whole course of living proveth always the best. In wood and stone, not the soft-est, but hardest be always aptest for portraiture, both fairest for pleasure and most durable for profit. Hard wits be hard to receive but sure to keep; painful without weariness, heedful without wavering, constant 40 without newfangleness; bearing heavy things, though not lightly yet will-ingly; entering hard things, though not easily yet deeply; and so come to that perfectness of learning in the end that quick wits seem in hope but do not indeed, or else very seldom, ever attain unto. Also, for manners and life, hard wits commonly are hardly carried either to desire every new thing or else to marvel at every strange thing; and therefore they be careful and diligent in their own matters, not curious and busy in other men's affairs; and so they become wise themselves, and also are counted honest by others. They be grave, steadfast, silent of tongue, secret of heart; not hasty in making, but constant in keeping any promise; not rash in uttering, but ware in considering every matter; and thereby not quick

10 in speaking, but deep of judgment, whether they write or give counsel, in all weighty affairs. And these be the men that become, in the end, both most happy for themselves and always best esteemed abroad in the world.

I have been longer in describing the nature, the good or ill success, of the quick and hard wit than perchance some will think this place and matter doth require. But my purpose was hereby plainly to utter what injury is offered to all learning and to the commonwealth also, first, by the fond father in choosing, but chiefly by the lewd schoolmaster in beating and driving away the best natures from learning. A child that is still, silent, constant, and somewhat hard of wit is either never chosen by the

20 father to be made a scholar, or else, when he cometh to the school, he is smally regarded, little looked unto; he lacketh teaching, he lacketh couraging, he lacketh all things, only he never lacketh beating, nor any word that may move him to hate learning, nor any deed that may drive him from learning to any other kind of living.

And when this sad-natured and hard-witted child is beat from his book and becometh after either student of the common law, or page in the court, or servingman, or bound prentice to a merchant, or to some handicraft, he proveth in the end wiser, happier, and many times honester, too, than many of these quick wits do by their learning.

30 Learning is both hindered and injured, too, by the ill choice of them that send young scholars to the universities, of whom must needs come all our divines, lawyers, and physicians.

These young scholars be chosen commonly as young apples be chosen by children in a fair garden about St. James's tide. A child will choose a sweeting because it is presently fair and pleasant, and refuse a rennet because it is then green, hard, and sour; when the one, if it be eaten, doth breed both worms and ill humors; the other, if it stand his time, be ordered and kept as it should, is wholesome of itself and helpeth to the good digestion of other meats. Sweetings will receive worms, rot, and die

40 on the tree, and never, or seldom, come to the gathering for good and lasting store.

For very grief of heart I will not apply the similitude: but hereby is plainly seen how learning is robbed of her best wits, first, by the great beating, and after, by the ill choosing of scholars to go to the universities. Whereof cometh partly that lewd and spiteful proverb, sounding to the great hurt of learning and shame of learned men, that "the greatest clerks be not the wisest men."

And though I, in all this discourse, seem plainly to prefer hard and rough wits before quick and light wits, both for learning and manners, yet am I not ignorant that some quickness of wit is a singular gift of God, and so most rare amongst men; and namely such a wit as is quick without lightness, sharp without brittleness, desirous of good things without new- 10 fangleness, diligent in painful things without wearisomeness, and constant in good will to do all things well, as I know was in Sir John Cheke, and is in some that yet live, in whom all these fair qualities of wit are fully met together.

But it is notable and true that Socrates saith in Plato to his friend Crito. That that number of men is fewest which far exceed either in good or ill, in wisdom or folly, but the mean betwixt both be the greatest number. Which he proveth true in divers other things: as in greyhounds, amongst which few are found exceeding great or exceeding little, exceeding swift or exceeding slow; and therefore I speaking of quick and hard wits, I 20 meant the common number of quick and hard wits, amongst the which, for the most part, the hard wit proveth many times the better learned, wiser, and honester man. And therefore do I the more lament that such wits commonly be either kept from learning by fond fathers or beat from learning by lewd schoolmasters.

And speaking thus much of the wits of children for learning, the opportunity of the place and goodness of the matter might require to have here declared the most special notes of a good wit for learning in a child, after the manner and custom of a good horseman who is skilful to know, and able to tell others, how by certain sure signs a man may choose a colt 30 that is like to prove another day excellent for the saddle. And it is pity that commonly more care is had, yea, and that amongst very wise men, to find out rather a cunning man for their horse than a cunning man for their children. They say nay in word, but they do so in deed. For, to the one, they will gladly give a stipend of 200 crowns by year, and loathe to offer to the other 200 shillings. God that sitteth in heaven laugheth their choice to scorn, and rewardeth their liberality as it should; for he suffereth them to have tame and well-ordered horse, but wild and unfortunate children; and therefore in the end they find more pleasure in their horse than comfort in their children. 40

But concerning the true notes of the best wits for learning in a child, I will report not mine own opinion but the very judgment of him that was counted the best teacher and wisest man that learning maketh mention of, and that is Socrates in Plato, who expresseth orderly these seven plain notes to choose a good wit in a child for learning.

1. Εὐφυής.
2. Μνήμων.
3. φιλομαθής.
4. φιλόπονος.
5. φιλήκοος.
10   6. Ζητητικός.
7. φιλέπαινος.

And because I write English and to Englishmen, I will plainly declare in English both what these words of Plato mean, and how aptly they be linked, and how orderly they follow one another.

1. Εὐφυής.

Is he that is apt by goodness of wit, and appliable by readiness of will, to learning, having all other qualities of the mind and parts of the body that must another day serve learning; not troubled, mangled, and halved, 20 but sound, whole, full, and able to do their office. As, a tongue not stammering or overhardly drawing forth words, but plain and ready to deliver the meaning of the mind; a voice not soft, weak, piping, womanish, but audible, strong, and manlike; a countenance not wearish and crabbed, but fair and comely; a personage not wretched and deformed, but tall and goodly; for surely a comely countenance with a goodly stature giveth credit to learning and authority to the person; otherwise, commonly, either open contempt or privy disfavor doth hurt or hinder both person and learning. And even as a fair stone requireth to be set in the finest gold with the best workmanship, or else it loseth much of the grace and price; 30 even so, excellency in learning, and namely divinity, joined with a comely personage, is a marvelous jewel in the world. And how can a comely body be better employed than to serve the fairest exercise of God's greatest gift, and that is learning. But commonly the fairest bodies are bestowed on the foulest purposes. I would it were not so, and with examples herein I will not meddle; yet I wish that those should both mind it and meddle with it which have most occasion to look to it, as good and wise fathers should do, and greatest authority to amend it, as good and wise magistrates ought to do. And yet I will not let openly to lament the unfortunate case of learning herein.

40   For if a father have four sons, three fair and well formed both mind and body, the fourth, wretched, lame, and deformed, his choice shall be to put the worst to learning, as one good enough to become a scholar. I

have spent the most part of my life in the university, and therefore I can bear good witness that many fathers commonly do thus; whereof I have heard many wise, learned, and as good men as ever I knew, make great and oft complaint. A good horseman will choose no such colt, neither for his own nor yet for his master's saddle. And thus much of the first note.

2. Μνήμων.

Good of memory. A special part of the first note εὐφυής, and a mere benefit of nature. Yet it is so necessary for learning, as Plato maketh it a separate and perfect note of itself, and that so principal a note as, without it, all other gifts of nature do small service to learning. Afranius, that old Latin poet, maketh memory the mother of learning and wisdom, saying thus, *Usus me genuit, mater peperit memoria.* And though it be the mere gift of nature, yet is memory well preserved by use and much increased by order, as our scholar must learn another day in the university. But, in a child, a good memory is well known by three properties: that is, if it be quick in receiving, sure in keeping, and ready in delivering forth again.

3. φιλομαθής.

Given to love learning. For though a child have all the gifts of nature at wish, and perfection of memory at will, yet if he have not a special love to learning he shall never attain to much learning. And therefore Isocrates, one of the noblest schoolmasters that is in memory of learning, who taught kings and princes, as Halicarnassaeus writeth, and out of whose school, as Tully saith, came forth mo noble captains, mo wise counselors, than did out of Epeius' horse at Troy—this Isocrates, I say, did cause to be written at the entry of his school in golden letters this golden sentence ἐὰν ἧς φιλομαθής, ἔσῃ πολυμαθής, which, excellently said in Greek, is thus rudely in English: "if thou lovest learning, thou shalt attain to much learning."

4. φιλόπονος.

Is he that hath a lust to labor and a will to take pains. For if a child have all the benefits of nature, with perfection of memory, love, like, and praise learning never so much, yet if he be not of himself painful he shall never attain unto it. And yet where love is present, labor is seldom absent, and namely in study of learning and matters of the mind; and therefore did Isocrates rightly judge that if his scholar were φιλομαθής, he cared for no more. Aristotle, varying from Isocrates in private affairs of life but agreeing with Isocrates in common judgment of learning, for love and labor in learning is of the same opinion, uttered in these words in his rhetoric *ad Theodecten:* "Liberty kindleth love: love refuseth no labor:

and labor obtaineth whatsoever it seeketh." And yet, nevertheless, goodness of nature may do little good; perfection of memory may serve to
small use; all love may be employed in vain; any labor may be soon
graveled if a man trust always to his own singular wit and will not be glad
sometime to hear, take advice, and learn of another. And therefore doth
Socrates very notably add the fifth note.

5. φιλήκοος.

He that is glad to hear and learn of another. For otherwise he shall
10 stick with great trouble, where he might go easily forward; and also
catch hardly a very little by his own toil, when he might gather quickly a
good deal by another man's teaching. But now there be some that have
great love to learning, good lust to labor, be willing to learn of others,
yet, either of a fond shamefastness, or else of a proud folly, they dare
not, or will not, go to learn of another. And therefore doth Socrates
wisely add the sixth note of a good wit in a child for learning, and that is.

6. Ζητητικός.

He that is naturally bold to ask any question, desirous to search out any
20 doubt, not ashamed to learn of the meanest, not afraid to go to the greatest, until he be perfectly taught and fully satisfied. The seventh and last
point is.

7. φιλέπαινος.

He that loveth to be praised for well doing at his father['s] or master's
hand. A child of this nature will earnestly love learning, gladly labor for
learning, willingly learn of other, boldly ask any doubt. And thus, by
Socrates' judgment, a good father and a wise schoolmaster should choose
a child to make a scholar of that hath by nature the foresaid perfect quali-
30 ties and comely furniture, both of mind and body; hath memory, quick
to receive, sure to keep, and ready to deliver; hath love to learning; hath
lust to labor; hath desire to learn of others; hath boldness to ask any
question; hath mind wholly bent to win praise by well doing.

The two first points be special benefits of nature; which, nevertheless,
be well preserved and much increased by good order. But as for the five
last—love, labor, gladness to learn of others, boldness to ask doubts, and
will to win praise—be won and maintained by the only wisdom and discretion of the schoolmaster. Which five points, whether a schoolmaster
shall work sooner in a child by fearful beating or courteous handling, you
40 that be wise, judge.

Yet some men, wise indeed, but in this matter more by severity of
nature than any wisdom at all, do laugh at us when we thus wish and

reason that young children should rather be allured to learning by gentleness and love than compelled to learning by beating and fear. They say our reasons serve only to breed forth talk and pass away time; but we never saw good schoolmaster do so, nor never read of wise man that thought so.

Yes, forsooth; as wise as they be, either in other men's opinion or in their own conceit, I will bring the contrary judgment of him who they themselves shall confess was as wise as they are, or else they may be justly thought to have small wit at all; and that is Socrates, whose judgment in Plato is plainly this in these words: which, because they be very notable, I will recite them in his own tongue, οὐδὲν μάθημα μετὰ δουλείας χρὴ μανθάνειν: οἱ μὲν γὰρ τοῦ σώματος πόνοι βίᾳ πονούμενοι χεῖρον οὐδὲν τὸ σῶμα ἀπεργάζονται; ψυχῇ δέ, βίαιον οὐδὲν ἔμμονον μάθημα: in English thus. "No learning ought to be learned with bondage; for bodily labors, wrought by compulsion, hurt not the body: but any learning learned by compulsion tarrieth not long in the mind." And why? For whatsoever the mind doth learn unwillingly with fear, the same it doth quickly forget without care. And lest proud wits, that love not to be contraried but have lust to wrangle or trifle away troth, will say that Socrates meaneth not this of children's teaching but of some other higher learning, hear what Socrates in the same place doth more plainly say: μὴ τοίνυν βίᾳ; ὦ ἄριστε, τοὺς παῖδας ἐν τοῖς μαθήμασιν, ἀλλὰ παίζοντας τρέφε, that is to say, "and therefore, my dear friend, bring not up your children in learning by compulsion and fear, but by playing and pleasure." And you that do read Plato as ye should, do well perceive that these be no questions asked by Socrates as doubts, but they be sentences first affirmed by Socrates as mere truths, and after given forth by Socrates as right rules, most necessary to be marked and fit to be followed of all them that would have children taught as they should. And in this counsel, judgment, and authority of Socrates, I will repose myself until I meet with a man of the contrary mind whom I may justly take to be wiser than I think Socrates was. Fond schoolmasters neither can understand nor will follow this good counsel of Socrates, but wise riders, in their office, can and will do both. Which is the only cause that commonly the young gentlemen of England go so unwillingly to school, and run so fast to the stable; for, in very deed, fond schoolmasters by fear do beat into them the hatred of learning, and wise riders, by gentle allurements, do breed up in them the love of riding. They find fear and bondage in schools. They feel liberty and freedom in stables. Which causeth them utterly to abhor the one and most gladly to haunt the other. And I do not write this that, in exhorting to the one, I would dissuade young gentlemen from the other; yea, I am sorry with all my heart that they be given no more to riding than they be.

For, of all outward qualities, to ride fair is most comely for himself, most necessary for his country; and the greater he is in blood, the greater is his praise the more he doth exceed all other therein. It was one of the three excellent praises amongst the noble gentlemen the old Persians: always to say truth, to ride fair, and shoot well; and so it was engraven upon Darius' tomb, as Strabo beareth witness.

> Darius the king lieth buried here,
> Who in riding and shooting had never peer.

₁₀ But to our purpose. Young men by any means losing the love of learning, when by time they come to their own rule, they carry commonly from the school with them a perpetual hatred of their master and a continual contempt of learning. If ten gentlemen be asked why they forget so soon in court that which they were learning so long in school, eight of them, or let me [be] blamed, will lay the fault on their ill handling by their schoolmasters. Cuspinian doth report that that noble emperor Maximilian would lament very oft his misfortune herein.

Yet some will say that children of nature love pastime and mislike learning; because, in their kind, the one is easy and pleasant, the other hard ₂₀ and wearisome. Which is an opinion not so true as some men ween; for the matter lieth not so much in the disposition of them that be young as in the order and manner of bringing up by them that be old, nor yet in the difference of learning and pastime. For beat a child if he dance not well, and cherish him though he learn not well, ye shall have him unwilling to go to dance and glad to go to his book. Knock him always when he draweth his shaft ill, and favor him again though he fault at his book, ye shall have him very loath to be in the field and very willing to be in the school. Yea, I say more, and not of myself but by the judgment of those from whom few wise men will gladly dissent, that if ever the nature of ₃₀ man be given at any time more than other to receive goodness, it is in innocency of young years, before that experience of evil have taken root in him. For the pure clean wit of a sweet young babe is like the newest wax, most able to receive the best and fairest printing; and like a new, bright silver dish never occupied, to receive and keep clean any good thing that is put into it.

And thus, will in children, wisely wrought withal, may easily be won to be very well willing to learn. And wit in children, by nature, namely memory, the only key and keeper of all learning, is readiest to receive and surest to keep any manner of thing that is learned in youth. This, lewd ₄₀ and learned, by common experience, know to be most true. For we remember nothing so well when we be old as those things which we learned when we were young. And this is not strange, but common in all nature's works. Every man sees (as I said before) new wax is best for printing, new clay fittest for working, new-shorn wool aptest for soon and surest dyeing, new-fresh flesh for good and durable salting. And this similitude is not rude, nor borrowed of the larder house, but out of his schoolhouse of whom the wisest of England need not be ashamed to learn. Young grafts grow not only soonest but also fairest, and bring always forth the best and sweetest fruit; young whelps learn easily to carry; young popin-jays learn quickly to speak; and so, to be short, if in all other things, though they lack reason, sense, and life, the similitude of youth is fittest to all goodness, surely nature in mankind is most beneficial and effectual 10 in this behalf.

Therefore, if to the goodness of nature be joined the wisdom of the teacher in leading young wits into a right and plain way of learning, surely children kept up in God's fear and governed by His grace may most easily be brought well to serve God and country, both by virtue and wisdom.

But if will and wit, by farther age, be once allured from innocency, de-lighted in vain sights, filled with foul talk, crooked with wilfulness, hard-ened with stubbornness, and let loose to disobedience, surely it is hard with gentleness, but unpossible with severe cruelty, to call them back to good frame again. For where the one perchance may bend it, the other 20 shall surely break it; and so, instead of some hope, leave an assured desper-ation and shameless contempt of all goodness, the farthest point in all mischief, as Xenophon doth most truly and most wittily mark.

Therefore, to love or to hate, to like or contemn, to ply this way or that way to good or to bad, ye shall have as ye use a child in his youth.

And one example whether love or fear doth work more in a child for virtue and learning, I will gladly report; which may be heard with some pleasure and followed with more profit. Before I went into Germany, I came to Broadgate in Leicestershire to take my leave of that noble lady, Jane Grey, to whom I was exceeding much beholding. Her parents, 30 the duke and the duchess, with all the household, gentlemen and gentle-women, were hunting in the park. I found her in her chamber reading *Phaedon Platonis* in Greek, and that with as much delight as some gentle-man would read a merry tale in Bocace. After salutation and duty done, with some other talk, I asked her why she would lose such pastime in the park? Smiling, she answered me: "I wis, all their sport in the park is but a shadow to that pleasure that I find in Plato. Alas! good folk, they never felt what true pleasure meant."

"And how came you, madam," quoth I, "to this deep knowledge of pleasure, and what did chiefly allure you unto it, seeing not many women, 40 but very few men, have attained thereunto?"

"I will tell you," quoth she, "and tell you a truth which perchance ye

will marvel at. One of the greatest benefits that ever God gave me is that he sent me so sharp and severe parents and so gentle a schoolmaster. For when I am in presence either of father or mother, whether I speak, keep silence, sit, stand, or go, eat, drink, be merry, or sad, be sewing, playing, dancing, or doing anything else, I must do it, as it were, in such weight, measure, and number, even so perfectly as God made the world, or else I am so sharply taunted, so cruelly threatened, yea, presently sometimes with pinches, nips, and bobs, and other ways which I will not name for the honor I bear them, so without measure misordered that I
10 think myself in hell till time come that I must go to Mr. Elmer; who teacheth me so gently, so pleasantly, with such fair allurements to learning that I think all the time nothing whiles I am with him. And when I am called from him, I fall on weeping, because whatsoever I do else but learning is full of grief, trouble, fear, and whole misliking unto me. And thus my book hath been so much my pleasure, and bringeth daily to me more pleasure and more, that in respect of it all other pleasures, in very deed, be but trifles and troubles unto me."

I remember this talk gladly, both because it is so worthy of memory and because also it was the last talk that ever I had, and the last time that ever
20 I saw that noble and worthy lady.

I could be overlong, both in shewing just causes and in reciting true examples why learning should be taught rather by love than fear. He that would see a perfect discourse of it, let him read that learned treatise which my friend John Sturmius wrote, *De Institutione Principis*, to the Duke of Cleves.

The godly counsels of Solomon, and Jesus the son of Sirach, for sharp keeping in and bridling of youth, are meant rather for fatherly correction than masterly beating, rather for manners than for learning; for other places than for schools. For God forbid but all evil touches, wantonness,
30 lying, picking, sloth, will, stubbornness, and disobedience should be with sharp chastisement daily cut away.

This discipline was well known and diligently used among the Grecians and old Romans, as doth appear in Aristophanes, Isocrates, and Plato, and also in the comedies of Plautus, where we see that children were under the rule of three persons: *praeceptore, paedagogo, parente*. The schoolmaster taught him learning with all gentleness; the governor corrected his manners with much sharpness; the father held the stern of his whole obedience. And so, he that used to teach did not commonly use to beat, but remitted that over to another man's charge. But what shall we
40 say when now, in our days, the schoolmaster is used both for *praeceptor* in learning and *paedagogus* in manners? Surely I would he should not confound their offices, but discreetly use the duty of both so that neither

ill touches should be left unpunished nor gentleness in teaching any wise omitted. And he shall well do both if wisely he do appoint diversity of time and separate place for either purpose, using always such discreet moderation as the schoolhouse should be counted a sanctuary against fear, and very well learning a common pardon for ill doing, if the fault of itself be not overheinous.

And thus the children, kept up in God's fear and preserved by His grace, finding pain in ill doing and pleasure in well studying, should easily be brought to honesty of life and perfectness of learning, the only mark that good and wise fathers do wish and labor that their children should most busily and carefully shoot at.

There is another discommodity, besides cruelty in schoolmasters in beating away the love of learning from children, which hindereth learning and virtue and good bringing up of youth, and namely young gentlemen, very much in England. This fault is clean contrary to the first. I wished before to have love of learning bred up in children; I wish as much now to have young men brought up in good order of living and in some more severe discipline than commonly they be. We have lack in England of such good order as the old noble Persians so carefully used, whose children, to the age of twenty-one year, were brought up in learning and exercises of labor, and that in such place where they should neither see that was uncomely nor hear that was unhonest. Yea, a young gentleman was never free to go where he would and do what he list himself, but under the keep and by the counsel of some grave governor until he was either married or called to bear some office in the commonwealth.

And see the great obedience that was used in old time to fathers and governors. No son, were he never so old of years, never so great of birth, though he were a king's son, might not marry but by his father, and mother's also, consent. Cyrus the Great, after he had conquered Babylon and subdued rich King Croesus with whole Asia Minor, coming triumphantly home, his uncle, Cyaxeris, offered him his daughter to wife. Cyrus thanked his uncle and praised the maid, but, for marriage, he answered him with these wise and sweet words, as they be uttered by Xenophon, ὦ κναξάρη, τὸ τε γένος ἐπαινῶ καὶ τὴν παῖδα, καὶ τὰ δῶρα. βούλομαι δέ, ἔφη, σὺν τῇ τοῦ πατρὸς γνώμῃ καὶ [τῇ] τῆς μητρὸς ταῦτά σοι συναινέσαί, etc.; that is to say: "Uncle Cyaxeris, I commend the stock, I like the maid, and I allow well the dowry; but," saith he, "by the counsel and consent of my father and mother, I will determine farther of these matters."

Strong Samson also, in Scripture, saw a maid that liked him, but he spake not to her but went home to his father and his mother and desired both father and mother to make the marriage for him. Doth this modesty,

doth this obedience, that was in great King Cyrus and stout Samson remain in our young men at this day? No, surely. For we live not longer
after them by time than we live far different from them by good order.
Our time is so far from that old discipline and obedience as now not only
young gentlemen, but even very girls, dare, without all fear though not
without open shame, where they list, and how they list, marry themselves
in spite of father, mother, God, good order, and all. The cause of this
evil is that youth is least looked unto when they stand in most need of
good keep and regard. It availeth not to see them well taught in young
10 years, and after, when they come to lust and youthful days, to give them
license to live as they lust themselves. For if ye suffer the eye of a young
gentleman once to be entangled with vain sights and the ear to be corrupted with fond or filthy talk, the mind shall quickly fall sick, and soon
vomit and cast up all the wholesome doctrine that he received in childhood, though he were never so well brought up before. And being once
englutted with vanity, he will straightway loathe all learning and all
good counsel to the same. And the parents, for all their great cost and
charge, reap only in the end the fruit of grief and care.

   This evil is not common to poor men, as God will have it, but proper to
20 rich and great men's children, as they deserve it. Indeed, from seven to
seventeen, young gentlemen commonly be carefully enough brought up.
But from seventeen to seven and twenty (the most dangerous time of all
a man's life, and most slippery to stay well in), they have commonly the
rein of all license in their own hand, and specially such as do live in the
court. And that which is most to be marveled at, commonly the wisest
and also best men be found the fondest fathers in this behalf. And if some
good father will seek some remedy herein, yet the mother (if the house
hold of our lady) had rather, yea and will, too, have her son cunning
and bold, in making him to live trimly when he is young, than by learn-
30 ing and travel to be able to serve his prince and his country, both wisely
in peace and stoutly in war, when he is old.

   The fault is in yourselves, ye noblemen's sons, and therefore ye deserve
the greater blame, that commonly the meaner men's children come to be
the wisest counselors and greatest doers in the weighty affairs of this
realm. And why? For God will have it so, of His providence; because ye
will have it no other wise, by your negligence.

   And God is a good God, and wisest in all His doings, that will place
virtue and displace vice in those kingdoms where he doth govern. For he
knoweth that nobility, without virtue and wisdom, is blood indeed, but
40 blood truly without bones and sinews; and so of itself, without the other,
very weak to bear the burden of weighty affairs.

   The greatest ship, indeed, commonly carrieth the greatest burden, but yet always with the greatest jeopardy, not only for the persons and goods committed unto it but even for the ship itself, except it be governed with the greater wisdom.

But nobility, governed by learning and wisdom, is indeed most like a fair ship having tide and wind at will, under the rule of a skilful master. When, contrariwise, a ship carried, yea, with the highest tide and greatest wind, lacking a skilful master, most commonly doth either sink itself upon sands or break itself upon rocks. And even so, how many have been either drowned in vain pleasure or overwhelmed by stout wilfulness the histories of England be able to afford overmany examples unto us. There- 10 fore, ye great and noble men's children, if ye will have rightfully that praise, and enjoy surely that place which your fathers have, and elders had, and left unto you, ye must keep it as they gat it; and that is by the only way of virtue, wisdom, and worthiness.

For wisdom and virtue, there be many fair examples in this court for young gentlemen to follow. But they be, like fair marks in the field, out of a man's reach, too far off to shoot at well. The best and worthiest men, indeed, be sometimes seen but seldom talked withal. A young gentleman may sometime kneel to their person, smally use their company for their better instruction.
20

But young gentlemen are fain commonly to do in the court as young archers do in the field; that is, take such marks as be nigh them, although they be never so foul to shoot at. I mean they be driven to keep company with the worst; and what force ill company hath to corrupt good wits, the wisest men know best.

And not ill company only, but the ill opinion also of the most part, doth much harm, and namely of those which should be wise in the true deciphering of the good disposition of nature, of comeliness in courtly manners, and all right doings of men.

But error and fantasy do commonly occupy the place of truth and 30 judgment. For, if a young gentleman be demure and still of nature, they say he is simple and lacketh wit; if he be bashful and will soon blush, they call him a babyish and ill brought up thing, when Xenophon doth precisely note in Cyrus that his bashfulness in youth was the very true sign of his virtue and stoutness after; if he be innocent and ignorant of ill, they say he is rude and hath no grace, so ungraciously do some graceless men misuse the fair and godly word GRACE.

But if ye would know what grace they mean, go and look and learn amongst them, and ye shall see that it is: first, to blush at nothing. And blushing in youth, saith Aristotle, is nothing else but fear to do ill; which 40 fear being once lustily frayed away from youth, then followeth to dare do any mischief, to contemn stoutly any goodness, to be busy in every matter, to be skilful in everything, to acknowledge no ignorance at all. To do thus in court is counted of some the chief and greatest grace of all, and termed by the name of a virtue called courage and boldness, when Crassus in Cicero teacheth the clean contrary, and that most wittily, saying thus: *Audere, cum bonis etiam rebus coniunctum, per seipsum est magnopere fugiendum.* Which is to say, "To be bold, yea, in a good matter, is for itself greatly to be eschewed."

Moreover, where the swing goeth, there to follow, fawn, flatter, laugh, and lie lustily at other men's liking. To face, stand foremost, shove back;
10 and to the meaner man or unknown in the court, to seem somewhat solemn, coy, big, and dangerous of look, talk, and answer. To think well of himself, to be lusty in contemning of others, to have some trim grace in a privy mock. And, in greater presence, to bear a brave look; to be warlike, though he never looked enemy in the face in war; yet some war-like sign must be used, either a slovenly busking, or an overstaring frounced head, as though out of every hair's top should suddenly start out a good big oath when need requireth; yet, praised be God, England hath at this time many worthy captains and good soldiers which be indeed so honest of behavior, so comely of conditions, so mild of manners, as
20 they may be examples of good order to a good sort of others which never came in war. But to return where I left. In place also to be able to raise talk and make discourse of every rishe; to have a very good will to hear himself speak; to be seen in palmistry, whereby to convey to chaste ears some fond or filthy talk.

And if some Smithfield ruffian take up some strange going, some new mowing with the mouth, some wrenching with the shoulder, some brave proverb, some fresh new oath that is not stale but will run round in the mouth, some new disguised garment or desperate hat, fond in fashion or garish in color: whatsoever it cost, how small soever his living be, by what
30 shift soever it be gotten, gotten must it be and used with the first, or else the grace of it is stale and gone. Some part of this graceless grace was described by me in a little rude verse long ago,

> To laugh, to lie, to flatter, to face:
> Four ways in court to win men grace,
> If thou be thrall to none of these,
> Away, good Peek Goose, hence John Cheese:
> Mark well my word, and mark their deed,
> And think this verse part of thy creed.

40 Would to God this talk were not true, and that some men's doings were not thus. I write not to hurt any, but to profit some; to accuse none, but to monish such who, allured by ill counsel and following ill example,

contrary to their good bringing up, and against their own good nature, yield overmuch to these follies and faults. I know many servingmen of good order and well staid; and again, I hear say there be some serving-men do but ill service to their young masters. Yea, read Terence and Plautus advisedly over, and ye shall find in those two wise writers, al-most in every comedy, no unthrifty young man that is not brought there-unto by the subtle enticement of some lewd servant. And even now, in our days, Getae and Davi, Gnatos and many bold, bawdy Phormios too, be pressing in to prattle on every stage, to meddle in every matter, when honest Parmenos shall not be heard, but bear small swing with their mas- 10 ters. Their company, their talk, their overgreat experience in mischief, doth easily corrupt the best natures and best brought up wits.

But I marvel the less that these misorders be amongst some in the court, for commonly in the country, also everywhere, innocency is gone; bashfulness is banished; much presumption in youth; small authority in age; reverence is neglected; duties be confounded; and, to be short, dis-obedience doth overflow the banks of good order, almost in every place, almost in every degree of man.

Mean men have eyes to see, and cause to lament, and occasion to com-plain of these miseries; but other have authority to remedy them, and 20 will do so too when God shall think time fit. For all these misorders be God's just plagues, by His sufferance brought justly upon us for our sins, which be infinite in number and horrible in deed, but namely for the great abominable sin of unkindness. But what unkindness? Even such unkind-ness as was in the Jews in contemning God's voice, in shrinking from His word, in wishing back again for Egypt, in committing adultery and whoredom, not with the women but with the doctrine of Babylon, did bring all the plagues, destructions, and captivities that fell so oft and horribly upon Israel.

We have cause also in England to beware of unkindness, who have 30 had, in so few years, the candle of God's word so oft lightened, so oft put out, and yet will venture by our unthankfulness in doctrine and sin-ful life to lose again light, candle, candlestick, and all.

God keep us in His fear, God graft in us the true knowledge of His word, with a forward will to follow it, and so to bring forth the sweet fruits of it, and then shall He preserve us by His grace from all manner of terrible days.

The remedy of this doth not stand only in making good common laws for the whole realm, but also (and perchance chiefly) in observing private discipline every man carefully in his own house; and namely if special 40 regard be had to youth, and that not so much in teaching them what is good as in keeping them from that that is ill.

Therefore, if wise fathers be not as well ware in weeding from their children ill things and ill company as they were before in grafting in them learning and providing for them good schoolmasters, what fruit they shall reap of all their cost and care, common experience doth tell.

Here is the place, in youth is the time, when some ignorance is as necessary as much knowledge, and not in matters of our duty towards God, as some wilful wits, willingly against their own knowledge, perniciously against their own conscience, have of late openly taught. Indeed St. Chrysostom, that noble and eloquent doctor, in a sermon *contra fatum* and the curious searching of nativities, doth wisely say that ignorance therein is better than knowledge. But to wring this sentence, to wrest thereby out of men's hands the knowledge of God's doctrine is without all reason, against common sense, contrary to the judgment also of them which be the discreetest men and best learned on their own side. I know Julianus Apostata did so, but I never heard or read that any ancient father of the primitive church either thought or wrote so.

But this ignorance in youth which I spake on, or rather this simplicity, or, most truly, this innocency, is that which the noble Persians, as wise Xenophon doth testify, were so careful to breed up their youth in. But Christian fathers commonly do not so. And I will tell you a tale as much to be misliked as the Persians' example is to be followed.

This last summer I was in a gentleman's house, where a young child somewhat past four year old could in no wise frame his tongue to say a little, short grace; and yet he could roundly rap out so many ugly oaths, and those of the newest fashion, as some good man of fourscore year old hath never heard named before. And that which was most detestable of all, his father and mother would laugh at it. I much doubt what comfort another day this child shall bring unto them. This child, using much the company of servingmen and giving good ear to their talk, did easily learn which he shall hardly forget all days of his life hereafter. So likewise in the court, if a young gentleman will venture himself into the company of ruffians, it is overgreat a jeopardy lest their fashions, manners, thoughts, talk, and deeds, will very soon be ever like. The confounding of companies breedeth confusion of good manners both in the court and everywhere else.

And it may be a great wonder, but a greater shame, to us Christian men to understand what a heathen writer, Isocrates, doth leave in memory of writing concerning the care that the noble city of Athens had to bring up their youth in honest company and virtuous discipline, whose talk in Greek is to this effect in English.

"The city was not more careful to see their children well taught than to see their young men well governed, which they brought to pass not so much by common law as by private discipline. For they had more regard that their youth, by good order, should not offend than how, by law, they might be punished. And if offense were committed, there was neither way to hide it, neither hope of pardon for it. Good natures were not so much openly praised as they were secretly marked and watchfully regarded, lest they should lose the goodness they had. Therefore, in schools of singing and dancing and other honest exercises, governors were appointed, more diligent to oversee their good manners than their masters were to teach them any learning. It was some shame to a young man to be seen in the open market; and if, for business, he passed through it, he did it with a marvelous modesty and bashful fashion. To eat or drink in a tavern was not only a shame but also punishable in a young man. To contrary or to stand in terms with an old man was more heinous than, in some place, to rebuke and scold with his own father." With many other mo good orders and fair disciplines which I refer to their reading that have lust to look upon the description of such a worthy commonwealth.

And to know what worthy fruit did spring of such worthy seed, I will tell you the most marvel of all, and yet such a truth as no man shall deny it, except such as be ignorant in knowledge of the best stories.

Athens, by this discipline and good ordering of youth, did breed up, within the circuit of that one city, within the compass of one hundred year, within the memory of one man's life, so many notable captains in war for worthiness, wisdom, and learning as be scarce matchable; no, not in the state of Rome, in the compass of those seven hundred years when it flourished most.

And because I will not only say it, but also prove it, the names of them be these. Miltiades, Themistocles, Xanthippus, Pericles, Cimon, Alcibiades, Thrasybulus, Conon, Iphicrates, Xenophon, Timotheus, Theopompus, Demetrius, and divers other mo: of which every one may justly be spoken that worthy praise which was given to Scipio Africanus, who Cicero doubteth whether he were more noble captain in war or more eloquent and wise counselor in peace. And if ye believe not me, read diligently Æmilius Probus in Latin and Plutarch in Greek, which two had no cause either to flatter or lie upon any of those which I have recited.

And beside nobility in war, for excellent and matchless masters in all manner of learning in that one city, in memory of one age, were mo learned men, and that in a manner altogether, than all time doth remember, than all place doth afford, than all other tongues do contain. And I do not mean of those authors which, by injury of time, by negligence of men, by cruelty of fire and sword, be lost, but even of those which, by God's grace, are left yet unto us: of which, I thank God, even my poor study lacketh not one. As in philosophy, Plato, Aristotle, Xenophon,

Euclid, and Theophrastus; in eloquence and civil law, Demosthenes, Æschines, Lycurgus, Dinarchus, Demades, Isocrates, Isaeus, Lysias, Antisthenes, Andocides; in histories, Herodotus, Thucydides, Xenophon, and, which we lack to our great loss, Theopompus and Ephorus; in poetry, Æschylus, Sophocles, Euripides, Aristophanes, and somewhat of Menander, Demosthenes' sister son.

Now let Italian, and Latin itself, Spanish, French, Dutch, and English bring forth their learning and recite their authors, Cicero only excepted and one or two more in Latin, they be all patched clouts and rags in com-
10 parison of fair woven broadcloths. And truly, if there be any good in them, it is either learned, borrowed, or stolen from some one of those worthy wits of Athens.

The remembrance of such a commonwealth, using such discipline and order for youth and thereby bringing forth to their praise and leaving to us for our example such captains for war, such counselors for peace, and matchless masters for all kinds of learning, is pleasant for me to recite, and not irksome, I trust, for other to hear, except it be such as make neither count of virtue nor learning.

And whether there be any such or no, I cannot well tell; yet I hear say
20 some young gentlemen of ours count it their shame to be counted learned; and perchance they count it their shame to be counted honest also, for I hear say they meddle as little with the one as with the other. A marvelous case that gentlemen should so be ashamed of good learning and never a whit ashamed of ill manners. Such do say for them that the gentlemen of France do so; which is a lie, as God will have it: Langaeus, and Bellaeus, that be dead, and the noble Vidam of Chartres, that is alive, and infinite mo in France which I hear tell of prove this to be most false. And though some in France which will needs be gentlemen, whether men will or no, and have more gentleship in their hat than in their head, be
30 at deadly feud with both learning and honesty, yet I believe, if that noble prince King Francis the First were alive, they should have neither place in his court nor pension in his wars, if he had knowledge of them. This opinion is not French, but plain Turkish; from whence some French fetch mo faults than this: which, I pray God, keep out of England, and send also those of ours better minds, which bend themselves against virtue and learning, to the contempt of God, dishonor of their country, to the hurt of many others, and at length to the greatest harm and utter destruction of themselves.

Some other, having better nature but less wit (for ill commonly have
40 overmuch wit), do not utterly dispraise learning, but they say that, without learning, common experience, knowledge of all fashions, and haunting all companies shall work in youth both wisdom and ability to execute

any weighty affair. Surely long experience doth profit much, but most, and almost only, to him (if we mean honest affairs) that is diligently before instructed with precepts of well doing. For good precepts of learning be the eyes of the mind, to look wisely before a man which way to go right and which not.

Learning teacheth more in one year than experience in twenty. And learning teacheth safely when experience maketh mo miserable than wise. He hazardeth sore that waxeth wise by experience. An unhappy master he is that is made cunning by many shipwrecks; a miserable merchant that is neither rich nor wise but after some bankrouts. It is costly wisdom 10 that is bought by experience. We know by experience itself that it is a marvelous pain to find out but a short way by long wandering. And surely he that would prove wise by experience, he may be witty indeed, but even like a swift runner that runneth fast out of his way, and upon the night, he knoweth not whither. And verily they be fewest of number that be happy or wise by unlearned experience. And look well upon the former life of those few, whether your example be old or young, who without learning have gathered, by long experience, a little wisdom and some happiness; and when you do consider what mischief they have committed, what dangers they have escaped (and yet twenty for one do perish in the 20 adventure), then think well with yourself whether ye would that your own son should come to wisdom and happiness by the way of such experience or no.

It is a notable tale that old Sir Roger Chamloe, sometime chief justice, would tell of himself. When he was ancient in Inn of Court, certain young gentlemen were brought before him to be corrected for certain misorders; and one of the lustiest said: "Sir, we be young gentlemen, and wise men before us have proved all fashions, and yet those have done full well." This they said because it was well known that Sir Roger had been a good fellow in his youth. But he answered them very wisely: "Indeed," 30 saith he, "in youth I was as you are now; and I had twelve fellows like unto myself, but not one of them came to a good end. And therefore follow not my example in youth, but follow my counsel in age if ever ye think to come to this place or to these years that I am come unto, lest ye meet either with poverty or Tyburn in the way."

Thus, experience of all fashions in youth being in proof always dangerous, in issue seldom lucky, is a way indeed to overmuch knowledge, yet used commonly of such men which be either carried by some curious affection of mind, or driven by some hard necessity of life, to hazard the trial of overmany perilous adventures. 40

Erasmus, the honor of learning of all our time, said wisely that experience is the common schoolhouse of fools and ill men. Men of wit and honesty be otherwise instructed. For there be that keep them out of fire, and yet was never burned; that beware of water and yet was never nigh drowning; that hate harlots and was never at the stews; that abhor false-hood and never brake promise themselves.

But will ye see a fit similitude of this adventured experience. A father that doth let loose his son to all experiences is most like a fond hunter that letteth slip a whelp to the whole herd. Twenty to one, he shall fall upon a rascal and let go the fair game. Men that hunt so be either ignorant persons, privy stealers, or night walkers.

10 Learning, therefore, ye wise fathers, and good bringing up, and not blind and dangerous experience, is the next and readiest way that must lead your children, first to wisdom, and then to worthiness, if ever ye purpose they shall come there.

And to say all in short, though I lack authority to give counsel, yet I lack not good will to wish, that the youth in England, specially gentle-men, and namely nobility, should be, by good bringing up, so grounded in judgment of learning, so founded in love of honesty, as, when they should be called forth to the execution of great affairs in service of their prince and country, they might be able to use and to order all experiences, 20 were they good, were they bad, and that according to the square, rule, and line, of wisdom, learning, and virtue.

And I do not mean by all this, my talk, that young gentlemen should always be poring on a book, and, by using good studies, should leave honest pleasure and haunt no good pastime. I mean nothing less. For it is well known that I both like and love, and have always, and do yet still use, all exercises and pastimes that be fit for my nature and ability. And beside natural disposition, in judgment also I was never either Stoic in doctrine or Anabaptist in religion to mislike a merry, pleasant, and play-ful nature, if no outrage be committed against law, measure, and good 30 order.

Therefore, I would wish that, beside some good time fitly appointed and constantly kept to increase by reading the knowledge of the tongues and learning, young gentlemen should use and delight in all courtly exercises and gentlemanlike pastimes. And good cause why; for the self-same noble city of Athens, justly commended of me before, did wisely and upon great consideration appoint the Muses, Apollo, and Pallas, to be patrons of learning to their youth. For the Muses, besides learning, were also ladies of dancing, mirth, and minstrelsy; Apollo was god of shooting and author of cunning playing upon instruments; Pallas also was lady 40 mistress in wars. Whereby was nothing else meant but that learning should be always mingled with honest mirth and comely exercises; and that war also should be governed by learning and moderated by wisdom, as did well appear in those captains of Athens named by me before, and also in Scipio and Caesar, the two diamonds of Rome. And Pallas was no more feared in wearing *ægida* than she was praised for choosing *oliva;* whereby shineth the glory of learning, which thus was governor and mistress in the noble city of Athens, both of war and peace.

Therefore, to ride comely; to run fair at the tilt or ring; to play at all weapons; to shoot fair in bow, or surely in gun; to vault lustily; to run; to leap; to wrestle; to swim; to dance comely; to sing and play of instruments cunningly; to hawk; to hunt; to play at tennis and all pastimes generally which be joined with labor, used in open place, and on the 10 daylight, containing either some fit exercise for war or some pleasant pastime for peace, be not only comely and decent, but also very necessary for a courtly gentleman to use.

But of all kind of pastimes fit for a gentleman, I will, God willing, in fitter place more at large declare fully in my book of the cockpit: which I do write to satisfy some, I trust with some reason, that be more curious in marking other men's doings than careful in mending their own faults. And some also will needs busy themselves in marveling and adding thereunto unfriendly talk why I, a man of good years and of no ill place, I thank God and my prince, do make choice to spend such time in writing 20 of trifles as the *School of shooting,* the *Cockpit,* and this book of the first principles of grammar, rather than to take some weighty matter in hand, either of religion or civil discipline.

Wise men, I know, will well allow of my choice herein; and as for such who have not wit of themselves, but must learn of others to judge right of men's doings, let them read that wise poet Horace in his *Arte Poetica,* who willeth wise men to beware of high and lofty titles. For great ships require costly tackling and also afterward dangerous government. Small boats be neither very chargeable in making nor very oft in great jeopardy; and yet they carry many times as good and costly ware 30 as greater vessels do. A mean argument may easily bear the light burden of a small fault and have always at hand a ready excuse for ill handling; and some praise it is if it so chance to be better indeed than a man dare venture to seem. A high title doth charge a man with the heavy burden of too great a promise; and therefore saith Horace very wittily that that poet was a very fool that began his book with a goodly verse indeed but overproud a promise:

Fortunam Priami cantabo et nobile bellum.

And after, as wisely: 40

Quantò rectius hic, qui nil molitur ineptè, etc.

Meaning Homer, who, within the compass of a small argument of one harlot and of one good wife, did utter so much learning in all kind of sciences as, by the judgment of Quintilian, he deserveth so high a praise that no man yet deserved to sit in the second degree beneath him. And thus much out of my way, concerning my purpose in spending pen, and paper, and time upon trifles; and namely to answer some that have neither wit nor learning to do anything themselves, neither will nor honesty to say well of other.

To join learning with comely exercises, Conto Baldassare Castiglione, 10 in his book *Cortegiano*, doth trimly teach; which book, advisedly read and diligently followed but one year at home in England, would do a young gentleman more good, I wis, than three years' travel abroad spent in Italy. And I marvel this book is no more read in the court than it is, seeing it is so well translated into English by a worthy gentleman, Sir Thomas Hoby, who was many ways well furnished with learning and very expert in knowledge of divers tongues.

And beside good precepts in books in all kind of tongues, this court also never lacked many fair examples for young gentlemen to follow: and surely one example is more valuable, both to good and ill, than twenty 20 precepts written in books; and so Plato, not in one or two but divers places, doth plainly teach.

If King Edward had lived a little longer, his only example had bred such a race of worthy learned gentlemen as this realm never yet did afford.

And, in the second degree, two noble primroses of nobility, the young Duke of Suffolk and Lord Henry Matrevers were such two examples to the court for learning as our time may rather wish than look for again.

At Cambridge also, in St. John's College, in my time, I do know that not so much the good statutes as two gentlemen of worthy memory, Sir 30 John Cheke and Dr. Readman, by their only example of excellency in learning, of godliness in living, of diligence in studying, of counsel in exhorting, of good order in all thing, did breed up so many learned men in that one college of St. John's at one time as I believe the whole University of Louvain in many years was never able to afford.

Present examples of this present time I list not to touch; yet there is one example for all the gentlemen of this court to follow that may well satisfy them, or nothing will serve them, nor no example move them to goodness and learning.

It is your shame (I speak to you all, you young gentlemen of England) 40 that one maid should go beyond you all in excellency of learning and knowledge of divers tongues. Point forth six of the best given gentlemen of this court, and all they together shew not so much good will, spend not so much time, bestow not so many hours, daily, orderly, and constantly, for the increase of learning and knowledge, as doth the Queen's Majesty herself. Yea, I believe that beside her perfect readiness in Latin, Italian, French, and Spanish, she readeth here now at Windsor more Greek every day than some prebendary of this church doth read Latin in a whole week. And that which is most praiseworthy of all, within the walls of her privy chamber she hath obtained that excellency of learning to understand, speak, and write, both wittily with head and fair with hand, as scarce one or two rare wits in both the universities have in many years reached unto. Amongst all the benefits that God hath blessed me 10 withal, next the knowledge of Christ's true religion, I count this the greatest: that it pleased God to call me to be one poor minister in setting forward these excellent gifts of learning in this most excellent prince, whose only example, if the rest of our nobility would follow, then might England be for learning and wisdom in nobility a spectacle to all the world beside. But see the mishap of men. The best examples have never such force to move to any goodness as the bad, vain, light, and fond have to all illness.

And one example, though out of the compass of learning, yet not out of the order of good manners, was notable in this court not fully twenty- 20 four years ago, when all the acts of Parliament, many good proclamations, divers strait commandments, sore punishment openly, special regard privately, could not do so much to take away one misorder as the example of one big one of this court did, still to keep up the same: the memory whereof doth yet remain in a common proverb of Birching Lane.

Take heed, therefore, ye great ones in the court, yea, though ye be the greatest of all, take heed what ye do, take heed how ye live. For as you great ones use to do, so all mean men love to do. You be indeed makers or marrers of all men's manners within the realm. For though God hath placed you to be chief in making of laws, to bear greatest authority, to 30 command all others, yet God doth order that all your laws, all your authority, all your commandments do not half so much with mean men as doth your example and manner of living. And, for example even in the greatest matter, if you yourselves do serve God gladly and orderly for conscience' sake, not coldly, and sometime for manner sake, you carry all the court with you, and the whole realm beside, earnestly and orderly to do the same. If you do otherwise, you be the only authors of all misorders in religion, not only to the court, but to all England beside. Infinite shall be made cold in religion by your example that never were hurt by reading of books. 40

And, in meaner matters, if three or four great ones in court will needs outrage in apparel, in huge hose, in monstrous hats, in garish colors, let

the prince proclaim, make laws, order, punish, command every gate in
London daily to be watched, let all good men beside do everywhere what
they can; surely the misorder of apparel in mean men abroad shall never
be amended except the greatest in court will order and mend themselves
first. I know some great and good ones in court were authors that honest
citizens of London should watch at every gate to take misordered persons
in apparel. I know that honest Londoners did so. And I saw, which I saw
then and report now with some grief, that some courtly men were offended with these good men of London. And that which grieved me most
10 of all, I saw the very same time, for all these good orders commanded
from the court and executed in London—I saw, I say, come out of London, even unto the presence of the prince, a great rabble of mean and
light persons, in apparel, for matter, against law, for making, against
order, for fashion, namely hose, so without all order as he thought himself most brave that durst do most in breaking order and was most
monstrous in misorder. And for all the great commandments that came
out of the court, yet this bold misorder was winked at and borne withal in
the court. I thought it was not well that some great ones of the court
durst declare themselves offended with good men of London for doing
20 their duty, and the good ones of the court would not shew themselves
offended with ill men of London for breaking good order. I found thereby
a saying of Socrates to be most true, that ill men be more hasty than good
men be forward to prosecute their purposes, even as Christ himself saith
of the children of light and darkness.

Beside apparel, in all other things too, not so much good laws and
strait commandments as the example and manner of living of great men
doth carry all mean men everywhere to like, and love, and do as they do.
For if but two or three noblemen in the court would but begin to shoot,
all young gentlemen, the whole court, all London, the whole realm,
30 would straightway exercise shooting.

What praise should they win to themselves, what commodity should
they bring to their country, that would thus deserve to be pointed at:
"Behold, there goeth the author of good order, the guide of good men!"
I could say more, and yet not overmuch. But perchance some will say
I have stepped too far out of my school into the commonwealth, from
teaching a young scholar to monish great and noble men; yet I trust
good and wise men will think and judge of me that my mind was not
so much to be busy and bold with them that be great now as to give
true advice to them that may be great hereafter. Who, if they do as I
40 wish them to do, how great soever they be now by blood and other men's
means, they shall become a great deal greater hereafter by learning,
virtue, and their own deserts; which is true praise, right worthiness, and

very nobility indeed. Yet, if some will needs press me that I am too bold
with great men, and stray too far from my matter, I will answer them
with St. Paul, *sive per contentionem, sive quocunque modo, modò Christus
praedicetur, etc.*, even so, whether in place or out of place, with my matter, or beside my matter, if I can hereby either provoke the good or stay
the ill, I shall think my writing herein well employed.

But to come down from great men and higher matters to my little
children and poor schoolhouse again; I will, God willing, go forward
orderly, as I purposed, to instruct children and young men both for learning and manners.   10

Hitherto I have shewed what harm overmuch fear bringeth to children,
and what hurt ill company and overmuch liberty breedeth in youth, meaning thereby that from seven year old to seventeen, love is the best allurement to learning; from seventeen to seven and twenty, that wise men
should carefully see the steps of youth surely stayed by good order in
that most slippery time; and specially in the court, a place most dangerous for youth to live in without great grace, good regard, and diligent
looking to.

Sir Richard Sackville, that worthy gentleman of worthy memory, as
I said in the beginning, in the queen's privy chamber at Windsor, after he 20
had talked with me for the right choice of a good wit in a child for learning and of the true difference betwixt quick and hard wits, of alluring
young children by gentleness to love learning, and of the special care that
was to be had to keep young men from licentious living, he was most
earnest with me to have me say my mind, also what I thought, concerning
the fancy that many young gentlemen of England have to travel abroad,
and namely to lead a long life in Italy. His request, both for his authority
and good will toward me, was a sufficient commandment unto me to
satisfy his pleasure with uttering plainly my opinion in that matter. "Sir,"
quoth I, "I take going thither and living there, for a young gentleman 30
that doth not go under the keep and guard of such a man as both by
wisdom can, and authority dare, rule him, to be marvelous dangerous."

And why I said so then I will declare at large now, which I said then
privately and write now openly; not because I do contemn either the
knowledge of strange and divers tongues, and namely the Italian tongue,
which, next the Greek and Latin tongue, I like and love above all other,
or else because I do despise the learning that is gotten or the experience
that is gathered in strange countries; or for any private malice that I
bear to Italy; which country, and in it namely Rome, I have always
specially honored; because time was when Italy and Rome have been, to 40
the great good of us that now live, the best breeders and bringers up of
the worthiest men, not only for wise speaking, but also for well doing, in

all civil affairs, that ever was in the world. But now that time is gone; and though the place remain, yet the old and present manners do differ as far as black and white, as virtue and vice. Virtue once made that country mistress over all the world; vice now maketh that country slave to them that before were glad to serve it. All men seeth it; they themselves confess it, namely such as be best and wisest amongst them. For sin, by lust and vanity, hath and doth breed up everywhere common contempt of God's word, private contention in many families, open factions in every city; and so, making themselves bond to vanity and vice at home, they are content to bear the yoke of serving strangers abroad. Italy now is not that Italy that it was wont to be; and therefore now not so fit a place as some do count it, for young men to fetch either wisdom or honesty from thence. For surely they will make others but bad scholars that be so ill masters to themselves. Yet, if a gentleman will needs travel into Italy, he shall do well to look on the life of the wisest traveler that ever traveled thither, set out by the wisest writer that ever spake with tongue, God's doctrine only excepted; and that is Ulysses in Homer.

Ulysses and his travel I wish our travelers to look upon, not so much to fear them with the great dangers that he many times suffered, as to instruct them with his excellent wisdom, which he always and everywhere used. Yea, even those that be learned and witty travelers, when they be disposed to praise traveling, as a great commendation, and the best scripture they have for it, they gladly recite the third verse of Homer, in his first book of *Odyssea*, containing a great praise of Ulysses for the wit he gathered and wisdom he used in his traveling.

Which verse, because in mine opinion it was not made at the first more naturally in Greek by Homer, nor after turned more aptly into Latin by Horace, than it was a good while ago in Cambridge translated into English, both plainly for the sense and roundly for the verse, by one of the best scholars that ever St. John's College bred, Mr. Watson, mine old friend, sometime Bishop of Lincoln. Therefore for their sake that have lust to see how our English tongue in avoiding barbarous rhyming may as well receive rich quantity of syllables and true order of versifying (of which matter more at large hereafter) as either Greek or Latin, if a cunning man have it in handling, I will set forth that one verse in all three tongues, for an example to good wits that shall delight in like learned exercise.

HOMERUS.—πολλῶν δ'ανθρώπων 'ἴδεν ἄστεα καὶ νόον ἔγνω
HORATIUS.—*Qui mores hominum multorum vidit, et urbes.*
MR. WATSON:

All travelers do gladly report great praise of Ulysses,
For that he knew many men's manners, and saw many cities.

And yet is not Ulysses commended so much, nor so oft in Homer, because he was πολύτροπος, that is, skillful in many men's manners and fashions; as because he was πολύμητις, that is, wise in all purposes, and ware in all places. Which wisdom and wareness will not serve neither a traveler, except Pallas be always at his elbow, that is, God's special grace from heaven, to keep him in God's fear in all his doings, in all his journey. For he shall not always, in his absence out of England, light upon a gentle Alcinous, and walk in his fair gardens full of all harmless pleasures; but he shall sometimes fall either into the hands of some cruel Cyclops, or into the lap of some wanton and dallying dame Calypso; and so suffer the danger of many a deadly den, not so full of perils to destroy the body as full of vain pleasures to poison the mind. Some Siren shall sing him a song, sweet in tune, but sounding in the end to his utter destruction. If Scylla drown him not, Charybdis may fortune to swallow him. Some Circe shall make him of a plain Englishman a right Italian. And at length to hell, or to some hellish place, is he likely to go, from whence is hard returning, although one Ulysses, and that by Pallas's aid, and good counsel of Tiresias, once escaped that horrible den of deadly darkness.

Therefore, if wise men will needs send their sons into Italy, let them do it wisely, under the keep and guard of him who, by his wisdom and honesty, by his example and authority, may be able to keep them safe and sound in the fear of God, in Christ's true religion, in good order and honesty of living; except they will have them run headlong into over-many jeopardies, as Ulysses had done many times if Pallas had not always governed him; if he had not used to stop his ears with wax, to bind himself to the mast of his ship, to feed daily upon that sweet herb Moly, with the black root and white flower, given unto him by Mercury to avoid all the enchantments of Circe. Whereby the divine poet Homer meant covertly (as wise and godly men do judge) that love of honesty and hatred of ill which David more plainly doth call the fear of God, the only remedy against all enchantments of sin.

I know divers noble personages, and many worthy gentlemen of England, whom all the siren songs of Italy could never untwine from the mast of God's Word, nor no enchantment of vanity overturn them from the fear of God and love of honesty.

But I know as many, or more, and some sometime my dear friends, for whose sake I hate going into that country the more, who, parting out of England fervent in the love of Christ's doctrine and well furnished with the fear of God, returned out of Italy worse transformed than ever was any in Circe's court. I know divers that went out of England men of innocent life, men of excellent learning, who returned out of Italy not only with worse manners but also with less learning; neither so willing to live orderly, nor yet so able to speak learnedly, as they were at home, before they went abroad. And why? Plato, that wise writer, and worthy traveler himself, telleth the cause why. He went into Sicilia, a country no nigher Italy by site of place than Italy that is now is like Sicilia that was then in all corrupt manners and licentiousness of life. Plato found in Sicilia every city full of vanity, full of factions, even as Italy is now. And as Homer, like a learned poet, doth feign that Circe by pleasant enchantments did turn men into beasts, some into swine, some into asses, some into foxes, some into wolves, etc., even so Plato, like a wise philosopher, doth plainly declare that pleasure, by licentious vanity, that sweet and perilous poison of all youth, doth engender in all those that yield themselves to her, four notorious properties,

$$
\left\{
\begin{array}{l}
\text{1. } \lambda\acute{\eta}\theta\eta\nu \\
\text{2. } \delta\upsilon\sigma\mu\alpha\theta\acute{\iota}\alpha\nu \\
\text{3. } \acute{\alpha}\phi\rho\sigma\acute{\upsilon}\nu\eta\nu \\
\text{4. } \acute{\upsilon}\beta\rho\iota\nu.
\end{array}
\right.
$$

The first, forgetfulness of all good things learned before; the second, dullness to receive either learning or honesty ever after; the third, a mind embracing lightly the worse opinion, and barren of discretion to make true difference betwixt good and ill, betwixt truth and vanity; the fourth, a proud disdainfulness of other good men in all honest matters.

Homer and Plato have both one meaning, look both to one end. For if a man inglut himself with vanity, or welter in filthiness like a swine, all learning, all goodness, is soon forgotten. Then quickly shall he become a dull ass to understand either learning or honesty; and yet shall he be as subtle as a fox in breeding of mischief, in bringing in misorder, with a busy head, a discoursing tongue, and a factious heart, in every private affair, in all matters of state; with this pretty property, always glad to commend the worse party, and ever ready to defend the falser opinion. And why? For where will is given from goodness to vanity, the mind is soon carried from right judgment to any fond opinion in religion, in philosophy, or any other kind of learning. The fourth fruit of vain pleasure, by Homer and Plato's judgment, is pride in themselves, contempt of others, the very badge of all those that serve in Circe's court. The true meaning of both Homer and Plato is plainly declared in one short sentence of the holy prophet of God, Hieremy, crying out of the vain and vicious life of the Israelites: "This people," saith he, "be fools and dull-heads to all goodness, but subtle, cunning, and bold in any mischief," etc.

The true medicine against the enchantments of Circe, the vanity of licentious pleasure, the enticements of all sin, is in Homer the herb Moly, with the black root and white flower, sour at first, but sweet in the end; which Hesiodus termeth the study of virtue, hard and irksome in the beginning, but in the end easy and pleasant. And that which is most to be marvelled at, the divine poet Homer saith plainly that this medicine against sin and vanity is not found out by man, but given and taught by God. And for someone's sake that will delight to read that sweet and godly verse, I will recite the very words of Homer, and also turn them into rude English meter:

χαλεπὸν δέ τ' ὀρύσσειν
ἀνδράσι γε θνητοῖσι, θεοὶ δέ τε πάντα δύνανται.

In English thus: 10

No mortal man, with sweat of brow or toil of mind,
But only God, who can do all, that herb doth find.

Plato also, that divine philosopher, hath many godly medicines against the poison of vain pleasure, in many places, but specially in his epistles to Dionysius, the tyrant of Sicily. Yet against those that will needs become beasts with serving of Circe, the prophet David crieth most loud: *Nolite fieri sicut equus et mulus;* and by and by giveth the right medicine, the true herb Moly, *In camo et freno maxillas eorum constringe;* that is to say, let God's grace be the bit, let God's fear be the bridle, to stay them 20 from running headlong into vice, and to turn them into the right way again. David, in the second psalm after, giveth the same medicine, but in these plainer words, *Diverte a malo, et fac bonum.*

But I am afraid that overmany of our travelers into Italy do not eschew the way to Circe's court, but go, and ride, and run, and fly thither; they make great haste to come to her; they make great suit to serve her; yea, I could point out some with my finger that never had gone out of England but only to serve Circe in Italy. Vanity and vice and any license to ill living in England was counted stale and rude unto them. And so, being mules and horses before they went, returned very swine and asses 30 home again; yet everywhere very foxes with subtle and busy heads; and, where they may, very wolves with cruel, malicious hearts. A marvelous monster which, for filthiness of living, for dulness to learning himself, for wiliness in dealing with others, for malice in hurting without cause, should carry at once in one body the belly of a swine, the head of an ass, the brain of a fox, the womb of a wolf. If you think we judge amiss and write too sore against you, hear what the Italian saith of the Englishman, what the master reporteth of the scholar, who uttereth plainly what is taught by him and what is learned by you, saying, *Englese Italianato, e un diabolo incarnato;* that is to say, you remain men in shape and fashion 40 but become devils in life and condition.

This is not the opinion of one for some private spite, but the judgment

of all, in a common proverb which riseth of that learning and those manners which you gather in Italy. A good schoolhouse of wholesome doctrine, and worthy masters of commendable scholars, where the master
had rather defame himself for his teaching than not shame his scholar
for his learning! A good nature of the master and fair conditions of the
scholars! And now choose you, you Italian Englishmen, whether you
will be angry with us for calling you monsters, or with the Italians for
calling you devils, or else with your own selves that take so much pains and
go so far to make yourselves both. If some yet do not well understand
what is an Englishman Italianated, I will plainly tell him: he that by
living and traveling in Italy bringeth home into England out of Italy the
religion, the learning, the policy, the experience, the manners of Italy.
That is to say, for religion, papistry or worse: for learning, less, commonly,
than they carried out with them; for policy, a factious heart, a discoursing
head, a mind to meddle in all men's matters; for experience, plenty of new
mischiefs never known in England before; for manners, variety of vanities, and change of filthy living.

These be the enchantments of Circe, brought out of Italy to mar
men's manners in England; much by example of ill life, but more by
precepts of fond books of late translated out of Italian into English, sold
in every shop in London; commended by honest titles, the sooner to corrupt honest manners; dedicated overboldly to virtuous and honorable
personages, the easilier to beguile simple and innocent wits. It is pity that
those which have authority and charge to allow and disallow books to be
printed be no more circumspect herein than they are. Ten sermons at
Paul's Cross do not so much good for moving men to true doctrine as
one of those books do harm with enticing men to ill living. Yea, I say
farther, those books tend not so much to corrupt honest living as they do
to subvert true religion. Mo papists be made by your merry books of Italy
than by your earnest books of Louvain. And because our great physicians
do wink at the matter and make no count of this sore, I, though not admitted one of their fellowship, yet having been many years a prentice to
God's true religion, and trust to continue a poor journeymen therein all
days of my life for the duty I owe and love I bear both to true doctrine and
honest living, though I have no authority to amend the sore myself, yet I
will declare my good will to discover the sore to others.

St. Paul saith that sects and ill opinions be the works of the flesh and
fruits of sin. This is spoken no more truly for the doctrine than sensibly for
the reason. And why? For ill doings breed ill thinkings. And of corrupted
manners spring perverted judgments. And how? There be in man two
special things: man's will, man's mind. Where will inclineth to goodness,
the mind is bent to truth; where will is carried from goodness to vanity,

the mind is soon drawn from truth to false opinion. And so the readiest way to entangle the mind with false doctrine is first to entice the will to wanton living. Therefore, when the busy and open papists abroad could not, by their contentious books, turn men in England fast enough from truth and right judgment in doctrine, then the subtle and secret papists at home procured bawdy books to be translated out of the Italian tongue, whereby overmany young wills and wits allured to wantonness do now boldly contemn all severe books that sound to honesty and godliness. In our forefathers' time, when papistry, as a standing pool, covered and overflowed all England, few books were read in our tongue, saving cer- tain books of chivalry, as they said, for pastime and pleasure, which, as some say, were made in monasteries by idle monks or wanton canons. As one, for example, *Morte Arthure;* the whole pleasure of which book standeth in two special points, in open manslaughter and bold bawdry. In which book those be counted the noblest knights that do kill most men without any quarrel and commit foulest adulteries by subtlest shifts; as Sir Launcelot with the wife of King Arthur, his master; Sir Tristram with the wife of King Mark, his uncle; Sir Lamerock with the wife of King Lot, that was his own aunt. This is good stuff for wise men to laugh at or honest men to take pleasure at. Yet I know when God's Bible was banished the court and *Morte Arthure* received into the prince's chamber.

What toys the daily reading of such a book may work in the will of a young gentleman or a young maid that liveth wealthily and idly, wise men can judge, and honest men do pity. And yet ten *Morte Arthures* do not the tenth part so much harm as one of these books made in Italy and trans- lated in England. They open not fond and common ways to vice, but such subtle, cunning, new, and divers shifts to carry young wills to vanity and young wits to mischief, to teach old bawds new school points as the simple head of an Englishman is not able to invent, nor never was heard of in England before, yea, when papistry overflowed all. Suffer these books to be read, and they shall soon displace all books of godly learning. For they, carrying the will to vanity, and marring good manners, shall easily corrupt the mind with ill opinions and false judgment in doctrine; first, to think ill of all true religion, and at last to think nothing of God Himself, one special point that is to be learned in Italy and Italian books. And that which is most to be lamented, and therefore more needful to be looked to, there be mo of these ungracious books set out in print within these few months than have been seen in England many score year before. And be- cause our Englishmen made Italians cannot hurt but certain persons and in certain places, therefore these Italian books are made English, to bring mischief enough openly and boldly to all states, great and mean, young and old, everywhere.

And thus you see how will enticed to wantonness doth easily allure the mind to false opinions; and how corrupt manners in living breed false judgment in doctrine; how sin and fleshliness bring forth sects and heresies: and therefore suffer not vain books to breed vanity in men's wills if you would have God's truth take root in men's minds.

That Italian that first invented the Italian proverb against our Englishmen Italianated meant no more their vanity in living than their lewd opinion in religion; for, in calling them devils, he carrieth them clean from God; and yet he carrieth them no farther than they willingly go them-
10 selves; that is, where they may freely say their minds to the open contempt of God and all godliness, both in living and doctrine.

And how? I will express how: not by a fable of Homer nor by the philosophy of Plato, but by a plain truth of God's word, sensibly uttered by David thus: these men, *abhominabiles facti in studüs suis*, think verily and sing gladly the verse before, *Dixit insipiens in corde suo, non est Deus*; that is to say, they, giving themselves up to vanity, shaking off the motions of grace, driving from them the fear of God, and running headlong into all sin, first lustily contemn God, then scornfully mock His word, and also spitefully hate and hurt all wellwillers thereof. Then they have in more
20 reverence the *Triumphs* of Petrarch than the *Genesis* of Moses. They make more account of Tully's *Offices* than St. Paul's *Epistles*; of a tale in Bocace than a story of the Bible. Then they count as fables the holy mysteries of Christian religion. They make Christ and His Gospel only serve civil policy. Then neither religion cometh amiss to them; in time they be promoters of both openly; in place again mockers of both privily, as I wrote once in a rude rhyme.

> Now new, now old, now both, now neither,
> To serve the world's course, they care not with whether.

30 For where they dare, in company where they like, they boldly laugh to scorn both Protestant and papist. They care for no Scripture. They make no count of general councils; they contemn the consent of the church. They pass for no doctors. They mock the Pope; they rail on Luther. They allow neither side; they like none, but only themselves. The mark they shoot at, the end they look for, the heaven they desire is only their own present pleasure and private profit; whereby they plainly declare of whose school, of what religion, they be; that is, epicures in living and ἄθεοι in doctrine. This last word is no more unknown now to plain Englishmen than the person was unknown some time in England,
40 until some Englishman took pains to fetch that devilish opinion out of Italy. These men, thus Italianated abroad, cannot abide our godly Italian church at home; they be not of that parish, they be not of that fellowship;

they like not that preacher; they hear not his sermons, except sometimes for company they come thither to hear the Italian tongue naturally spoken, not to hear God's doctrine truly preached.

And yet these men, in matters of divinity, openly pretend a great knowledge, and have privately to themselves a very compendious understanding of all; which nevertheless they will utter when and where they list. And that is this: all the mysteries of Moses, the whole law and ceremonies, the Psalms and prophets, Christ and His Gospel, GOD and the devil, heaven and hell, faith, conscience, sin, death, and all, they shortly wrap up, they quickly expound, with this one-half verse of Horace: *Credat Iudaeus* 10 *Appella.*

Yet though in Italy they may freely be of no religion, as they are in England in very deed too; nevertheless, returning home into England, they must countenance the profession of the one or the other, howsoever inwardly they laugh to scorn both. And though, for their private matters, they can follow, fawn, and flatter noble personages contrary to them in all respects; yet commonly they ally themselves with the worst papists, to whom they be wedded, and do well agree together in three proper opinions: in open contempt of God's word; in a secret security of sin; and in a bloody desire to have all taken away, by sword or burning, that be not 20 of their faction. They that do read with indifferent judgment Pygius and Machiavelli, two indifferent patriarchs of these two religions, do know full well that I say true.

Ye see what manners and doctrine our Englishmen fetch out of Italy; for finding no other there, they can bring no other hither. And therefore many godly and excellent learned Englishmen, not many years ago, did make a better choice, when open cruelty drave them out of this country, to place themselves there where Christ's doctrine, the fear of God, punishment of sin, and discipline of honesty were had in special regard.

I was once in Italy myself; but, I thank God, my abode there was but 30 nine days. And yet I saw, in that little time, in one city, more liberty to sin than ever I heard tell of in our noble city of London in nine year. I saw it was there as free to sin, not only without all punishment but also without any man's marking, as it is free in the city of London to choose, without all blame, whether a man lust to wear shoe or pantocle. And good cause why; for, being unlike in truth of religion, they must needs be unlike in honesty of living. For, blessed be Christ, in our city of London commonly the commandments of God be more diligently taught and the service of God more reverently used, and that daily in many private men's houses, than they be in Italy once a week in their common churches; 40 where masking ceremonies to delight the eye and vain sounds to please the ear do quite thrust out of the churches all service of God in spirit and

truth. Yea, the lord mayor of London, being but a civil officer, is commonly for his time more diligent in punishing sin, the bent enemy against God and good order, than all the bloody inquisitors in Italy be in seven year. For their care and charge is not to punish sin, not to amend manners, not to purge doctrine, but only to watch and oversee that Christ's true religion set no sure footing where the pope hath any jurisdiction. I learned, when I was at Venice, that there it is counted good policy, when there be four or five brethren of one family, one only to marry: and all the rest to welter with as little shame in open lechery as swine do here in the com-
10 mon mire. Yea, there be as fair houses of religion, as great provision, as diligent officers to keep up this misorder, as Bridewell is, and all the masters there, to keep down misorder. And therefore if the pope himself do not only grant pardons to further these wicked purposes abroad in Italy, but also (although this present pope in the beginning made some shew of misliking thereof) assign both meed and merit to the maintenance of stews and brothel houses at home in Rome, then let wise men think Italy a safe place for wholesome doctrine and godly manners, and a fit school for young gentlemen of England to be brought up in.

Our Italians bring home with them other faults from Italy, though not
20 so great as this of religion, yet a great deal greater than many good men can well bear. For commonly they come home common contemners of marriage and ready persuaders of all other to the same; not because they love virginity, nor yet because they hate pretty young virgins, but, being free in Italy to go whithersoever lust will carry them, they do not like that law and honesty should be such a bar to their like liberty at home in England. And yet they be the greatest makers of love, the daily dalliers, with such pleasant words, with such smiling and secret countenances, with such signs, tokens, wagers, purposed to be lost before they were purposed to be made, with bargains of wearing colors, flowers, and herbs to breed
30 occasion of ofter meeting of him and her, and bolder talking of this and that, etc. And although I have seen some, innocent of all ill and staid in all honesty, that have used these things without all harm, without all suspicion of harm, yet these knacks were brought first into England by them that learned them before in Italy in Circe's court; and how courtly courtesies soever they be counted now, yet if the meaning and manners of some that do use them were somewhat amended, it were no great hurt, neither to themselves nor to others.

Another property of this our English Italians is to be marvelous singular in all their matters: singular in knowledge, ignorant of nothing; so
40 singular in wisdom (in their own opinion) as scarce they count the best counselor the prince hath comparable with them; common discoursers of all matters; busy searchers of most secret affairs; open flatterers of great men; privy mislikers of good men; fair speakers with smiling counte-

nances, and much courtesy openly to all men; ready backbiters, sore nippers, and spiteful reporters privily of good men. And being brought up in Italy in some free city, as all cities be there, where a man may freely discourse against what he will, against whom he lust, against any prince, against any government, yea, against God himself and his whole religion; where he must be either Guelph or Ghibelline, either French or Spanish; and always compelled to be of some party, of some faction, he shall never be compelled to be of any religion. And if he meddle not overmuch with Christ's true religion, he shall have free liberty to embrace all religions, and become, if he lust, at once, without any let or punishment, Jewish, 10 Turkish, papish, and devilish.

A young gentleman thus bred up in this goodly school to learn the next and ready way to sin, to have a busy head, a factious heart, a talkative tongue, fed with discoursing of factions, led to contemn God and His religion, shall come home into England but very ill taught, either to be an honest man himself, a quiet subject to his prince, or willing to serve God under the obedience of true doctrine or within the order of honest living.

I know none will be offended with this my general writing, but only such as find themselves guilty privately therein; who shall have good leave to be offended with me until they begin to amend themselves. I touch 20 not them that be good, and I say too little of them that be naught. And so, though not enough for their deserving, yet sufficiently for this time, and more else when if occasion so require.

And thus far have I wandered from my first purpose of teaching a child, yet not altogether out of the way, because this whole talk hath tended to the only advancement of truth in religion and honesty of living, and hath been wholly within the compass of learning and good manners, the special points belonging in the right bringing up of youth.

But to my matter. As I began plainly and simply with my young scholar, so will I not leave him, God willing, until I have brought him a 30 perfect scholar out of the school and placed him in the university, to become a fit student for logic and rhetoric; and so after to physic, law, or divinity, as aptness of nature, advice of friends, and God's disposition shall lead him.

The end of the first book.

The second book

*   *   *   *   *

Imitatio

40

Imitation is a faculty to express lively and perfectly that example which ye go about to follow. And of itself, it is large and wide; for all the works of nature, in a manner, be examples for art to follow.

But to our purpose. All languages, both learned and mother tongues, be gotten, and gotten only, by Imitation. For as ye use to hear, so ye learn to speak; if ye hear no other, ye speak not yourself; and whom ye only hear, of them ye only learn.

And therefore, if ye would speak as the best and wisest do, ye must be conversant where the best and wisest are; but if you be born or brought up in a rude country, you shall not chose but speak rudely: the rudest man of all knoweth this to be true.

Yet nevertheless, the rudeness of common and mother tongues is no
10 bar for wise speaking. For in the rudest country, and most barbarous mother language, many be found can speak very wisely; but in the Greek and Latin tongue, the two only learned tongues, which be kept, not in common talk, but in private books, we find always wisdom and eloquence, good matter and good utterance never or seldom asunder. For all such authors as be fullest of good matter and right judgment in doctrine, be likewise always most proper in words, most apt in sentence, most plain and pure in uttering the same.

And contrariwise, in those two tongues all writers, either in Religion or any sect of Philosophy, who so ever be found fond in judgment of
20 matter, be commonly found as rude in uttering their mind. For Stoics, Anabaptists, and Friars, with Epicures, Libertines and Monks, being most like in learning and life, are no fonder and pernicious in their opinions than they be rude and barbarous in their writings. They be not wise, therefore, that say, "What care I for a man's words and utterance, if his matter and reasons be good?" Such men say so, not so much of ignorance as either of some singular pride in themselves, or some special malice of other, or for some private or partial matter either in Religion or other kind of learning. For good and choice meats be no more requisite for healthy bodies than proper and apt words be for good matters, and
30 also plain and sensible utterance for the best and deepest reasons; in which two points standeth perfect eloquence, one of the fairest and rarest gifts that God doth give to man.

You know not what hurt you do to learning that care not for words but for matter, and so make a divorce betwixt the tongue and the heart. For mark all ages, look upon the whole course of both the Greek and Latin tongue, and you shall surely find that when apt and good words began to be neglected, and properties of those two tongues to be confounded, then also began ill deeds to spring; strange manners to oppress good orders; new and fond opinions to strive with old and true doctrine,
40 first in Philosophy, and after in Religion: right judgment of all things to be perverted; and so virtue with learning is condemned, and study left off; of ill thoughts cometh perverse judgment; of ill deeds spring-

eth lewd talk. Which four misorders, as they mar man's life, so destroy they good learning withal.

But behold the goodness of God's providence for learning: all old authors and sects of Philosophy which were fondest in opinion and rudest in utterance, as Stoics and Epicures, first condemned of wise men and after forgotten of all men, be so consumed by times as they be now not only out of use, but also out of memory of man; which thing, I surely think, will shortly chance to the whole doctrine and all the books of phantastical Anabaptists and Friars, and of the beastly Libertines and Monks.

Again behold, on the other side, how God's wisdom hath wrought that of *Academici* and *Peripatetici*, those that were wisest in judgment of matters and purest in uttering their minds, the first and chiefest that wrote most and best in either tongue, as Plato and Aristotle in Greek, Tully in Latin, be so either wholly or sufficiently left on to us as I never knew yet scholar that gave himself to like, and love, and follow chiefly those three authors but he proved both learned, wise, and also an honest man, if he joined with all the true doctrine of God's holy Bible, without the which the other three be but fine edge tools in a fool or mad-man's hand.

But to return to Imitation again. There be three kinds of it in matters of learning.

The whole doctrine of Comedies and Tragedies is a perfect imitation, or fair lively painted picture of the life of every degree of man. Of this Imitation writeth Plato at large in 3. *de Rep.*, but it doth not much belong at this time to our purpose.

The second kind of Imitation is to follow for learning of tongues and sciences the best authors. Here riseth among proud and envious wits a great controversy, whether one or many are to be followed; and if one, who is that one: Seneca, or Cicero; Sallust or Caesar; and so forth in Greek and Latin.

The third kind of Imitation belongeth to the second, as when you be determined whether you will follow one or mo, to know perfectly, and which way, to follow that one; in what place; by what means and order; by what tools and instruments you shall do it; by what skill and judgment you shall truly discern whether you follow rightly or no.

This *Imitatio* is *dissimilis materei similis tractatio:* and also, *similis materei dissimilis tractatio*. As Virgil followed Homer, but the Argument to the one was Ulysses, to the other Aeneas; Tully persecuted Antony with the same weapons of eloquence that Demosthenes used before against Philip.

Horace followeth Pindar, but either of them his own Argument and

Person; as the one, Hiero king of Sicily, the other Augustus the Emperor; and yet both for like respects, that is for their courageous stoutness in war and just government in peace.

One of the best examples for right Imitation we lack, and that is Menander, whom our Terence (as the matter required), in like argument, in the same Persons, with equal eloquence, foot by foot did follow. Some pieces remain, like broken Jewels, whereby men may rightly esteem, and justly lament, the loss of the whole.

Erasmus, the ornament of learning in our time, doth wish that some man of learning and diligence would take the like pains in Demosthenes and Tully that Macrobius hath done in Homer and Virgil; that is, to write out and join together where the one doth imitate the other. Erasmus' wish is good, but surely it is not good enough; for Macrobius' gatherings for the *Æneidos* out of Homer, and Eobanus Hessus' more diligent gatherings for the *Bucolics* out of Theocritus, as they be not fully taken out of the whole heap, as they should be, but even as though they had not sought for them of purpose but found them scattered here and there by chance in their way; even so, only to point out and nakedly to join together their sentences, with no farther declaring the manner and way how the one doth follow the other were but a cold help to the increase of learning.

But if a man would take this pain also, when he hath laid two places of Homer and Virgil, or of Demosthenes and Tully together, to teach plainly withal after this sort.

1. Tully retaineth thus much of the matter, these sentences, these words.

2. This and that he leaveth out, which he doth wittily to this end and purpose.

3. This he addeth here.

4. This he diminisheth there.

5. This he ordereth thus, with placing that here, not there.

6. This he altereth and changeth, either in property of words, in form of sentence, in substance of the matter, or in one or other convenient circumstance of the author's present purpose. In these few rude English wordes are wrapt up all the necessary tools and instruments wherewith true Imitation is rightly wrought withal in any tongue. Which tools, I openly confess, be not of mine own forging, but partly left unto me by the cunningest Master and one of the worthiest Gentlemen that ever England bred, Sir John Cheke: partly borrowed by me out of the shop of the dearest friend I have out of England, Joannes Sturmius. And therefore I am the bolder to borrow of him, and here to leave them to other, and namely, to my Children. Which tools, if it please God that another

day they may be able to use rightly, as I do wish and daily pray they may do, I shall be more glad than if I were able to leave them a great quantity of land.

This foresaid order and doctrine of Imitation would bring forth more learning, and breed by truer judgment, than any other exercise that can be used; but not for young beginners, because they shall not be able to consider duly thereof. And truly, it may be a shame to good students who, having so fair examples to follow as Plato and Tully, do not use so wise ways in following them for the obtaining of wisdom and learning as rude ignorant Artificers do for gaining a small commodity. For surely the meanest painter useth more wit, better art, greater diligence in his shop, in following the picture of any mean man's face, than commonly the best students do, even in the university, for the attaining of learning itself.

Some ignorant, unlearned, and idle students, or some busy looker upon this little poor book, that hath neither will to do good himself nor skill to judge right of others, but can lustily condemn by pride and ignorance all painful diligence and right order in study, will perchance say that I am too precise, too curious, in marking and piddling thus about the imitation of others; and that the old worthy authors did never busy their heads and wits in following so precisely either the matter what other men wrote, or else the manner how other men wrote. They will say, it were a plain slavery, and injury too, to shackle and tie a good wit, and hinder the course of a man's good nature with such bonds of servitude in following other.

Except such men think themselves wiser than Cicero for teaching of eloquence, they must be content to turn a new leaf.

The best book that ever Tully wrote, by all men's judgment, and by his own testimony too, in writing whereof he employed most care, study, learning and judgment, is his book *de Oratore ad Q.F.* Now let us see what he did for the matter and also for the manner of writing thereof. For the whole book consisteth in these two points only: in good matter, and good handling of the matter. And first for the matter, it is whole Aristotle's, whatsoever Antony in the second, and Crassus in the third doth teach. Trust not me, but believe Tully himself, who writeth so, first, in that goodly long *Epistle ad P. Lentulum,* and after in diverse places *ad Atticum.* And in the very book itself Tully will not have it hidden, but both Catullus and Crassus do oft and pleasantly lay that stealth to Antony's charge. Now, for the handling of the matter, was Tully so precise and curious rather to follow another man's pattern than to invent some new shape himself, namely in that book wherein he purposed to leave to posterity the glory of his wit? Yea forsooth, that he did. And this is not my guessing and gathering, nor only performed by Tully in very deed, but uttered also by Tully in plain words, to teach other men, thereby, what they should do in taking like matter in hand.

And that which is specially to be marked, Tully doth utter plainly his conceit and purpose therein by the mouth of the wisest man in all that company: for saith Scaevola himself, *Cur non imitamur, Crasse, Socratem illum, quis est in Phaedro Platonis, etc.*

And further to understand that Tully did not *obiter* and by chance, but purposely and mindfully bend himself to a precise and curious Imitation of Plato concerning the shape and form of those books, mark, I pray
10 you, how curious Tully is to utter his purpose and doing therein, writing thus to Atticus:

"While praising those books, you miss the character of Scaevola from the scene. It was not without good reason that I removed him. Our god Plato did the same in his *Republic*. When Socrates called on that wealthy and cheery old soul Cephalus in the Piraeus, the old man takes part in the discussion during the introductory conversation; but after a very neat speech, he pleads that he wants to go to a divine service, and does not come back again. I fancy Plato thought it would have been inartistic to keep a man of that age any longer in so lengthy a discussion. I thought there was
20 still more reason to be careful in the case of Scaevola, who was at the age and in the state of health in which you must remember he was, and was crowned with such honours that it would hardly have been proper for him to spend several days with Crassus at his villa at Tusculum. Besides, the talk in the first book was not unconnected with Scaevola's pursuits: while the remaining books contained a technical discussion, as you know. In such I did not like the merry old man, you remember, to take a part."

If Cicero had not opened himself and declared his own thought and doings herein, men that be idle, and ignorant, and envious of other men's diligence and well doings would have sworn that Tully had never minded
30 any such things, but that of a precise curiosity, we fain and forge and father such things of Tully as he never meant in deed. I write this, not for nought; for I have heard some both well learned and otherways very wise, that by their lusty misliking of such diligence have drawen back the forwardness of very good wits. But even as such men themselves do sometimes stumble upon doing well by chance and benefit of good wit, so would I have our scholar always able to do well by order of learning and right skill of judgment.

Concerning Imitation, many learned men have written, with much diversity for the matter, and therefore with great contrariety and some
40 stomach amongst themselves. I have read as many as I could get diligently, and what I think of everyone of them I will freely say my mind. With

which freedom I trust good men will bear, because it shall tend to neither spiteful nor harmful controversy. . . .

Others have written also, as Cortesius to Politian, and that very well; Bembus *ad Picum* a great deal better, but Joan. Sturmius *de Nobilitate literata* and *de Amissa dicendi ratione* far best of all, in mine opinion, that ever took this matter in hand. For all the rest declare chiefly this point: whether one, or many, or all, are to be followed; but Sturmius only hath most learnedly declared who is to be followed, what is to be followed, and, the best point of all, by what way and order true Imitation is rightly to be exercised. And although Sturmius herein doth far pass all other, yet 10 hath he not so fully and perfectly done it as I do wish he had and as I know he could. For though he hath done it perfectly for precept, yet hath he not done it perfectly enough for example; which he did neither for lack of skill nor by negligence, but of purpose, contented with one or two examples, because he was minded in those two books to write of it both shortly and also had to touch other matters.

Barthol. Riccius Ferrariensis also hath written learnedly diligently and very largely of this matter even as he did before very well *de Apparatu linguae Latinae*. He writeth the better in mine opinion because his whole doctrine, judgment, and order, seemeth to be borrowed out of Joannes 20 Sturmius' books. He addeth also examples, the best kind of teaching, wherein he doth well, but not well enough; indeed, he commiteth no fault, but yet deserveth small praise. He is content with the mean, and followeth not the best: as a man that would feed upon acorns, when he may eat as good cheap the finest wheat bread. He teacheth, for example, where and how two or three late Italian poets do follow Virgil; and how Virgil himself in the story of Dido doth wholly imitate Catullus in the like matter of Ariadne. Wherein I like better his diligence and order of teaching than his judgment in choice of examples for Imitation. But, if he had done thus: if he had declared where and how, how oft and how 30 many ways, Virgil doth follow Homer; as for example the coming of Ulysses to Alcinous and Calypso, with the coming of Aeneas to Carthage and Dido; likewise the games, running, wrestling, and shooting that Achilles maketh in Homer, with the selfsame games that Aeneas maketh in Virgil; the harness of Achilles, with the harness of Aeneas, and the manner of making of them both by Vulcan; the notable combat betwixt Achilles and Hector, with as notable a combat betwixt Aeneas and Turnus; the going down to hell of Ulysses in Homer, with the going down to hell of Aeneas in Virgil; and other places infinite more, as similitudes, narrations, messages, descriptions of persons, places, battles, tempests, ship- 40 wrecks, and commonplaces for diverse purposes, which be as precisely taken out of Homer, as ever did painter in London follow the picture of any fair personage. And when these places had been gathered together by this way of diligence, then to have conferred them together by this order of teaching: as, diligently to mark what is kept and used in either author, in words, in sentences, in matter; what is added; what is left out; what ordered otherwise, either *praeponendo, interponendo,* or *postponendo;* and what is altered for any respect, in word, phrase, sentence, figure, reasons, argument, or by any way of circumstance. If Riccius had done this, he had not only been well liked for his diligence in teaching, but also

10 justly commended for his right judgment in right choice of examples for the best Imitation.

*　　*　　*　　*　　*

ROBERT RECORDE

The Introduction and Notes are at page 1303

FROM *The Castle of Knowledge,* 1556

SCHOLAR: Since my last talk with you about the knowledge of the world and the parts of it, I have read divers books that entreat of that matter, as namely Proclus' *Sphere,* Joannes de Sacrobosco, Orontius' *Cosmography,* and divers other, whose words in many things I remember, but of the matter I have sundry doubts, and therefore desire much your help therein. For, although I have consulted with divers men therein, yet methinketh they tell me but the same words in like sort as I read them before, or little other ways altered, but light of understanding I have gotten little yet.

30 MASTER: Then prove again; peradventure your chance may be better; that which at the first seemeth hard may at length become easy, for use maketh mastery, all men confess. And the best things are not most easiest to attain. Begin in that order as your authors do.

SCHOLAR: Their orders be as divers as their names be, so that I know not whose order is best. For Proclus in treating of the sphere, defineth first the Axe tree of the world, before he had shewed other what the world is, or what he calleth a sphere, or what need the world hath of any Axe tree. Therefore I turned to Joannes de Sacrobosco our countryman, which beginneth first with the definition of a sphere, but nothing like to that

40 sphere which I before had bought as an apt instrument to learn by. Then see I Orontius disagree from them both, and generally everyone from other, so that I know not where to begin.

MASTER: As touching those writers, I will say no more now, but although everyone of them have some things that exactly scanned may be misliked, yet he that hath done worst is worthy of thanks for his studious pains in furthering of knowledge. And seeing you doubt of their order, let the thing itself minister order. What is it that you desire to know?

SCHOLAR: I see in the heaven marvelous motions, and in the rest of the world strange transmutations, and therefore desire much to know what the world is, and what are the principal parts of it, and also how all these strange sights do come.

MASTER: Then is the world the thing that you would know first, since 10 all these other things are incident to it. What do your authors call the world?

SCHOLAR: Orontius defineth the world to be the perfect and entire composition of all things, a divine work, infinite and wonderful, adorned with all kinds and forms of bodies that nature could make.

MASTER: This definition doth much agree with those that be written by ancient authors, and namely Aristotle which defineth it thus: . . . The world is an apt frame of heaven and earth and all other natural things contained in them. The like words hath Cleomedes and others. So that the world is that entire body, which containeth all things that ever 20 God made and man can see; nothing excepted but God himself only, which is not comprehensible by any worldly means. This work is so pure and wonderful in beauty, that it beareth the name of cleanness both in Greek and Latin; that is κόσμος in Greek, and *Mundus* in Latin, and thereto alludeth Sibyll in her verses, speaking of the dissolution of the world, saying: . . . The world shall be unclean, or lose his beauty, when all men shall perish.

SCHOLAR: And so doth that sentence lose his beauty by the translation, for there can be no such allusion of words in the English of that sentence as there is in the other tongues.   30

MASTER: You say truth, except a man would rather allude at the words than express the sentence, for so might it be translated thus: It shall be an unworldly world, when all men shall perish. But here the sense is lost; for this name world, hath not the like derivation of cleanness in English, as the Latin and Greek names have in their tongues. Neither can I well tell whereof this English name is derived, although I remember some other significations of this word, as first it is used in Scripture for a name of long continuance of time, when we say: "world without end," and, "through world of worlds," which signifieth forever. Also this name doth signify sometimes a great wonder, as when we say: "It is a world 40 to see the craft that some men use under color of simplicity." Now if any man will contend that this word world doth principally betoken a wonder,

and that the world for the wonderful shape of it took that name, as the chief wonder of all wonders, I will not greatly repine, but then must I needs wonder to see the chief worldly men to wonder so little at this wonderful wonder, and to bend all their study to the center of the world, I mean the Earth, which in comparison to the whole world is not only a part without all notable quantity but also least adorned with marvelous works, and most subject to all frail transmutation and change, still replenished with continuall corruption. And yet on it only doth the greatest number set all their study. For it they sustain great travail and toil; for it
10 they chide, quarrel and fight; to get it they venture life and limb; and when they think most assuredly that they have gotten the Earth, then indeed the earth hath gotten them, and most commonly then doth the earth consume them, when they think themselves full masters of it.

SCHOLAR: By these men's travail (I think) it came to pass that the Earth doth usurp the name of the World, as though it were all, and that besides it were nothing.

MASTER: Thereof cometh that common proverb of a covetous man: "All the world is too little for him, where he indeed seeketh nothing but the earth." Which earth in comparison to the whole World beareth no
20 greater view than a mustard corn on Malborne hills, or a drop of water in the ocean sea; for of all the parts of the World, the Earth is the least, and that without comparison, as hereafter I shall not only tell you but also prove it by invincible reason. And therefore to proceed in our matter, I think it best not only to make discourse lightly of the principal parts of the world, but to do it in such a brief sort, as the mind may conceive it soonest, and the memory also retain it longest. And therefore will I omit all proofs till we have once generally drawn the image of the whole World, so shall not your memory be troubled with sundry things at once, as in learning a science which seemeth something strange, and in conceiving
30 the reasons of it, which in declaring, seem much more strange.

SCHOLAR: Indeed I have felt the discommodity of such hasty desires, for where I have sought reason before I understood whereto that reason tended, I have troubled my mind and hindered my knowledge. Wherefore it may please you in your order to proceed.

MASTER: I have already said that of all the parts of the World the Earth is the least; whereby you may conceive that within it is nothing, for so should that (whatsoever it were) be lesser than the Earth. But without the Earth, doth the Water lie, which covereth a great part of the same; about them both doth the Air run, and occupieth (as we may
40 easily consider) much more room than both the sea and the land; above the Air and round about it (after the agreement of most wise men), doth the Fire occupy his place. And these four, that is, Earth, Water, Air and

Fire, are named the four elements, that is to say, the first simple and original matters, whereof all mixt and compound bodies be made, and into which all shall turn again.

SCHOLAR: Oftentimes have I heard it, that both man and beasts are made of earth, and into earth shall return again; but I thought not that they had been made of water, and much less of air or fire.

MASTER: Of earth only, nothing is made but earth; for an herb or tree can not grow (as all men confess) except it be helped and nourished with air convenient, and due watering, and also have the heat of the sun. And generally, since all thing is maintained by his like, and is destroyed by 10 his contrary, then if man cannot be maintained without fire, air, and water, it must needs appear, that he is made of them, as well as of earth, and so likewise all other things that be compound.

SCHOLAR: This talk delighteth me marvelously, so that I cannot be weary of it, as long as it shall please you to continue it.

MASTER: This talk is not for this place, partly for that it is more physical than astronomical, and partly because I determined, in this first part, to omit the causes and reasons of all things, and briefly to declare the parts of the World, whereof these four elements, being uncompound of themselves, that is simple and unmixt, are accounted as one part of the World, 20 which therefore is called the Elementary part. And because those elements do daily increase and decrease in some parts of them (though not in all parts at once) and are subject to continual corruption, they are distinct from the rest of the World, which hath no such alteration nor corruption. Which part is above all the four elements, and compasseth them about, and is called the Sky, or Welkin, & also the Heavens. This part hath in it divers lesser or special parts, named commonly Spheres: as the sphere of the Moon which is lowest, and next unto the elements; then above it, the sphere of Mercury; and next to it the sphere of Venus; then followeth the Sun with his sphere; and then Mars in his order; above 30 him is Jupiter; and above him is Saturn. These seven, are named the seven planets, every one having his sphere by himself severally, and his motion also several, and unlike in time to any other. But above these seven planets is there another heaven or sky, which commonly is named the Firmament, and hath in it an infinite number of stars, whereof it is called the starry sky. And because it is the eighth in order of the heavens or spheres, it is named also the Eighth Sphere. This heaven is manifest enough to all men's eyes, so that no man needeth to doubt of it; for it is that sky wherein are all those stars that we see, except the five lesser planets, which I did name before; that is Saturn, Jupiter, Mars, Venus, and Mercury. 40

SCHOLAR: The Sun and Moon also must be except out of that number, for they have their spheres by themselves, as well as the other planets.

MASTER: Truth it is, but because no man doth account them as stars, therefore they need none exception where mention is made of stars only; whereas the other five smaller planets (which I named before) are so like to other stars that no man, but such as are of good experience in astronomy, can discern them from the other stars, although many men do make a difference of them by twinkling, affirming that the fixed stars do twinkle and not the planets, with other differences difficult to observe and scarce certain in distinction. But this is their most certain difference: that all those stars which be in the firmament do stand and continue in
10 one form of distance each from other, and change not their places in their sphere. And therefore be they called fixed stars; for although they go around about the world in 24 hours, that is every day once, yet they keep their places in their sphere, and turn only with their sphere, or (as Aratus saith) they be drawn with their heaven; whereas the seven planets are not only carried round about the earth with the like motion of heaven every day, but they do move of themselves, and do change their places in their own spheres; and for that cause are they called planets, that is to say, wandering stars.

SCHOLAR: Oftentimes have I heard this, but yet can I not tell how to
20 perceive it.

MASTER: That shall be referred to the fourth treatise, where I will shew you the proof of all that you shall think doubtful.

SCHOLAR: Yet I beseech you let me know this: Why are those heavens called Spheres? For (in my phantasy) they are nothing like that instrument of sundry circles which is commonly called the sphere, since neither can I see in them such circles as are in that material sphere; neither is there in the material sphere any such representation of such divers heavens; neither of such variety of stars.

MASTER: This doubt was moved before now by Joachim Ringelbergh
30 in a treatise that he wrote of the sphere, but it shall be answered easily by yourself, after a little declaration of the celestial spheres. And for that cause I will omit it till anon, and will first declare certain other accidents of the heavens, and of the other parts of the world.

Hitherto you have heard only the names of the parts of the world, and of their situation, how they be placed in order. Now for the form and shape of them, you shall understand that the whole world is round exactly as any ball or globe, and so are all the principal parts of it, every sphere severally and jointly, as well of the planets as of the fixed stars, and so are all the four elements. And they are aptly placed together, not as a number
40 of round balls in a net, but every sphere includeth other as they be in order of greatness, beginning at the eighth sphere or firmament, and so descending to the last and lowest sphere, is the Sphere of the Moon, under

which the four elements succeed: first the fire, then the air; next followeth the water, which with the earth jointly annexed, maketh, as it were,
one sphere only.

SCHOLAR: This I do well understand in words, and the easier by this
picture which I find in every book of the sphere; but that I see there more
spheres than you speak of; for in some books mention is made of nine
spheres, and in other are ten spheres named, where you set forth but eight.

MASTER: The cause of this diversity will I in the fourth treatise declare.
In the mean season, I think it best to tell you of no more spheres than
are perceptible by sight, for so many are we certain of. And therefore
understand you thus: that as the Eighth Sphere is the greatest, and hath
none other without him that may be seen, so the Earth is the least, and
hath none other within him, but it standeth in the middle and in the center
of the whole world, and of every one of these spheres, and therefore it is
called the center of the world. So that although the Earth in itself have a
great and notable quantity, yet in comparison to the firmament it is to be
esteemed but as a center or little prick, yea indeed much less than any
notable star that you see. And if I shall speak boldly that which I intend
hereafter to prove certainly, the earth is lesser than the least star in the
firmament which is commonly seen, but yet is it greater than Venus or
Mercury, yea greater than the Moon.

SCHOLAR: This affirmation seemeth to me impossible, or at the least
contrary to sense, for the Moon seemeth bigger much than any star, yea
somewhat bigger than the Sun.

MASTER: Content yourself to credit me till time serve for the proof of
my words; and in the mean season, to proceed as I began. You must
think that the earth and the water annexed together in one globe are of
no notable quantity in comparison to the firmament, and that it standeth
as the center of the world and hath no motion out of his place, nor yet
circular moving about his own center, but resteth (as we may say) quiet
without all such moving. Like ways must you think of the other elements,
which of their own nature have none other motion than a stone or a light
feather, so that they may be accounted all four to be without natural
motion.

SCHOLAR: Yet in the water and in the air we see every day notable
moving. And sometime I have heard of moving of the earth, by earth-
quakes; and as for the fire that we see, it always moveth and flickereth in
burning.

MASTER: And so you have seen a stone move swiftly when it fell from
any high place, but these motions have an end quickly, except they be continued with violence, as hereafter I will sufficiently declare. But as the
stone, although it will move in falling, yet in his place lieth quiet without

motion, so the earth of itself, and the other elements, must be accounted quiet by nature, and without motion.

The heavens contrariwise have such a natural motion that never resteth night nor day, neither can be stayed by any violence. This motion we see in the heavens daily by their moving from the east to the west, and from the west to the east again, about the earth once every 24 hours; and therefore is this motion named the daily motion, for it is the measure of a natural day, commonly accounted. And this motion is likewise called of ancient writers the motion of the first firmament, according to which motion you 10 see the Sun in the daytime, and the stars in the night time, and the Moon both in the day and the night, to pass from the east into the south, and so into the west, and at the end of 24 hours to come again into the east. Whereby you may easily understand that this motion is common to all the spheres of heaven.

SCHOLAR: This may all men see that can see anything. Yet have I heard of some so grossly witted that they doubted which way the Sun and the Moon did come into the east again, as though they did not think that the sky did move about the earth.

MASTER: Such gross ignorance happened sometimes to famous men for 20 lack of due consideration of that which all men may see, as I will in place convenient more largely note.

SCHOLAR: Yet one doubt I have of which I would gladly be rid, and that is of the Moon; for as you say, and by sight we perceive, all the stars with the Sun and Moon go round about the earth in 24 hours, save that the Moon is slacker than all the rest, for she is every day later in rising by an hour than she was the day before; but how that cometh to pass I do not understand.

MASTER: This doubt is well moved, and in good time; for by it will I take occasion to instruct you not only in the true knowledge of it, but also 30 of other sundry motions in all the heavens; for in every one of them doth there appear a like motion, contrary to the daily moving of the firmament, which in the Moon is most swiftest, and therefore may be perceived daily of all men; but in the Sun it is not so swift, and therefore not so easily perceived; yet all men see a great alteration in the moving of the Sun in one year. For sometimes he is higher and nearer over our heads, and sometime farther from our heads, and lower in the south; yea sometime he shineth with us almost 18 hours (as in the middle of the summer), and in the middle of winter he shineth but 6 hours or little more. This every child doth see, although they know not the reason thereof.

40 SCHOLAR: Yet the reason of that is easy enough to be conceived, for when the day is at the longest, the Sun must needs shine the more time,

and so must it needs shine the lesser time when the day is at the shortest; this reason I have heard many men declare.

MASTER: That may well be called a crabbed reason, for it goeth backward like a crab. The day maketh not the sun to shine, but the Sun shining maketh the day. And so the length of the day maketh not the Sun to shine long, nor the shortness of the day causeth not the Sun to shine the lesser time, but contrariwise the long shining of the Sun maketh the long day, and the short shining of the Sun maketh the lesser day; else answer me, what maketh the days long or short?

SCHOLAR: I have heard wise men say, that summer maketh the long 10 days, and winter maketh the long nights.

MASTER: They might have said more wisely, that long days make summer, and short days make winter.

SCHOLAR: Why all that seemeth one thing to me.

MASTER: Is it all one to say: God made the Earth, and the Earth made God? Covetousness overcometh all men, and all men overcome covetousness?

SCHOLAR: No not so, for here the effect is turned to be the cause, and the agent is made the patient.

MASTER: So is it to say, summer maketh long days, where you should 20 say, long days make summer.

SCHOLAR: I perceive it now, but I was so blinded with the vulgar error that if you had demanded of me farther what did make the summer, I had been like to have answered that green leaves do make summer; and the sooner by remembrance of an old saying: that a year should come in which the summer should not be known but by the green leaves.

MASTER: Yet this saying doth not import that green leaves do make summer, but they betoken summer; so are they the sign and not the cause of summer.

SCHOLAR: So I perceive now that the long shining of the Sun doth make 30 the days long. But now can I not tell what causeth the Sun to shine longer one time of the year than another.

MASTER: That is it that drove wise men to search and mark the motions of the Sun, whereby at length they found that the Sun hath another course, contrary to the daily motion of the sky. And as the Moon doth accomplish her proper course (which is from the west into the east, contrary to the daily motion) every month in the year, so the Sun doth end his course, in his proper motion, but once in the year. And to express it aptly, I must say that the true term of a year is nothing else but the very time of the course of the Sun from a certain point in heaven till his return 40 to the same point again. And a month is the just time of the proper course of the Moon, from change to change; and every quarter of the Moon maketh a week; of which I will speak more in the next treatise, with the declaration of the diversity for the beginning of months and years. But now to continue our principal matter the more orderly, I would have you repeat the chief articles of our talk hitherto.

SCHOLAR: This is the sum of all your doctrine hitherto.

1. That the world is that entire body which containeth in it all the heavens and the elements, with all that in them is.

2. The parts of the world are two especial, the heavens which are eight in number, and the elements which are 4 in kind.

3. The order and situation of all these parts, as well elements as heavenly spheres, beginning at the highest, and proceeding to the lowest, is this: the Firmament, Saturn, Jupiter, Mars, the Sun, Venus, Mercury, and the Moon.

THE FOUR ELEMENTS

Fire, Air, Water, and Earth and ever the higher encloseth all that is under it.

4. The world and all his principal parts are round in form and shape, as a globe or ball.

5. The earth is in the middle of the world, as the center of it, and beareth no view of quantity in comparison to the world.

6. The earth hath no motion of itself, no more than a stone, but restest quietly; and so the other elements do, except they be forceably moved.

7. The heavens do move continually from the east to the west, and that motion is called the daily motion, and is the measure of the common day.

8. The Moon hath a several motion from the west toward the east, contrary to that moving of the daily course, and that motion is the just measure of a month, and every quarter doth make a week.

9. The Sun also hath a peculiar motion from the west toward the east, which he accomplisheth in a year, and of that course the year taketh his measure and quantity.

GEORGE CAVENDISH

The Introduction and Notes are at page 1304

FROM *Egerton Ms. 2402*

The Life of Cardinal Wolsey

Prologue   10

.. . . Forsooth this cardinal was my lord and master, whom in his life
I served, and so remained with him, after his fall, continually, during the
term of all his trouble, until he died; as well in the south as in the north
parts, and noted all his demeanor and usage in all that time; as also in his
wealthy triumph and glorious estate. And since his death I have heard
diverse sundry surmises and imagined tales made of his proceedings and
doings, which I myself have perfectly known to be most untrue; unto the
which I could have sufficiently answered according to the truth, but, as
me seemeth, then it was much better for me to suffer and dissemble the 20
matter, and the same to remain still as lies, than to reply against their
untruth, of whom I might, for my boldness, sooner have kindled a great
flame of displeasure than to quench one spark of their malicious untruth.
Therefore I commit the truth to Him that knoweth all truth. For,
whatsoever any man hath conceived in him when he lived, or since his
death, thus much I dare be bold to say without displeasure to any person,
or of affection, that in my judgment I never saw this realm in better order,
quietness, and obedience than it was in the time of his authority and rule,
nor justice better ministered with indifferency; as I could evidently prove
if I should not be accused of too much affection, or else that I set forth 30
more than truth. I will therefore here desist to speak any more in his
commendation, and proceed first to his original beginning, ascending by
fortune's favour to high honours, dignities, promotions, and riches.

Truth it is, Cardinal Wolsey, sometime Archbishop of York, was an
honest poor man's son, born in Ipswich, within the county of Suffolk;
and being but a child, was very apt to learning; by means whereof his
parents, or his good friends and masters, conveyed him to the University
of Oxford, where he prospered so in learning that, as he told me [in] his
own person, he was called the boy-bachelor, forasmuch as he was made 40
Bachelor of Arts at fifteen years of age, which was a rare thing, and
seldom seen.

Thus prospering and increasing in learning, [he] was made Fellow of Magdalen College, and after appointed, for his learning, to be schoolmaster there; at which time the Lord Marquess Dorset had three of his sons at school there with him, committing as well unto him their virtuous education as their instruction and learning. It pleased the said marquess against a Christmas season, to send as well for the schoolmaster as for his children home to his house for their recreation in that pleasant and honourable feast. They being then there, my lord their father perceived them to be right well employed in learning for their time, which con-
10 tented him so well that he, having a benefice in his gift being at that time void, gave the same to the schoolmaster, in reward for his diligence, at his departing after Christmas upon his return to the University. And having the presentation thereof, [he] repaired to the ordinary for his institution and induction; then being fully furnished of all necessary instruments at the ordinary's hands for his preferment, made speed without any farther delay to the said benefice to take thereof possession. And being there for that intent, one Sir Amyas Pawlet, knight, dwelling in the country thereabout, took an occasion of displeasure against him, upon what ground I know not: but, sir, by your leave, he was so bold to
20 set the schoolmaster by the feet during his pleasure; the which was afterward neither forgotten nor forgiven. For when the schoolmaster mounted the dignity to be Chancellor of England, he was not oblivious of the old displeasure ministered unto him by master Pawlet, but sent for him, and after many sharp and heinous words, enjoined him to attend upon the council until he were by them dismissed, and not to depart without license, upon an urgent pain and forfeiture: so that he continued within the Middle Temple, the space of five or six years, or more; whose lodging there was in the gate-house next the street, which he reedified very sumptuously, garnishing the same, on the outside thereof, with cardinals' hats
30 and arms, badges and cognisances of the cardinal's, with divers other devices, in so glorious a sort that he thought thereby to appease his old unkind displeasure.

Now may this be a good example and precedent to men in authority, which will sometimes work their will without wit, to remember in their authority, how authority may decay; and [those] whom they punish of will more than of justice may after be advanced in the public weal to high dignities and governance, and they based as low, who will then seek the means to be revenged of old wrongs sustained wrongfully before. Who would have thought then, that when Sir Amyas Pawlet punished this poor
40 scholar, that ever he should have attained to be Chancellor of England, considering his baseness in every condition. These be wonderful works of God, and fortune. Therefore I would wish all men in authority and

dignity to know and fear God in all their triumphs and glory; considering in all their doings that authorities be not permanent, but may slide and vanish, as princes' pleasures do alter and change.

Then as all living things must of very necessity pay the due debt of nature, which no earthly creature can resist, it chanced the Lord Marquess to depart out of this present life. After whose death this schoolmaster, considering then with himself to be but a small beneficed man, and to have lost his fellowship in the College (for, as I understand, if a fellow of that college be once promoted to a benefice he shall by the rules of the house be dismissed of his fellowship), and perceiving himself also to be destitute of his singular good lord, thought not to be long unprovided of some other succour or staff to defend him from all such harms as he lately sustained.

* * * *

And the next day he took his journey with Master Kingston and the guard. And as soon as they espied their old master in such a lamentable estate, lamented him with weeping eyes. Whom my lord took by the hands, and divers times, by the way as he rode, he would talk with them, sometime with one and sometime with another. At night he was lodged at a house of the Earl of Shrewsbury's, called Hardwick Hall, very evil at ease. The next day he rode to Nottingham, and there lodged that night, more sicker; and the next day we rode to Leicester Abbey, and by the way he waxed so sick that he was divers times likely to have fallen from his mule; and being night ere we came to the abbey aforesaid, where at his coming in at the gates the abbot of the place with all his convent met him with the light of many torches; whom they right honourably received with great reverence. To whom my lord said, "Father Abbot, I am come hither to leave my bones among you"; whom they brought on his mule to the stair's foot of his chamber, and there lighted, and Master Kingston then took him by the arm, and led him up the stairs; who told me afterwards that he never carried so heavy a burden in all his life. And as soon as he was in his chamber, he went incontinent to his bed, very sick. This was upon Saturday at night; and there he continued sicker and sicker.

Upon Monday in the morning, as I stood by his bedside, about eight of the clock, the windows being close shut, having wax lights burning upon the cupboard, I beheld him, as me seemed, drawing fast to his end. He perceived my shadow upon the wall by his bedside; asked who was there?

"Sir, I am here," quoth I.

"How do you?" quoth he to me.

"Very well, sir," quoth I, "if I might see your grace well."

"What is it of the clock?" quoth he to me.

"Forsooth, sir," quoth I, "it is past eight of the clock in the morning."

"Eight of the clock?" quoth he, "that cannot be," rehearsing divers times, "eight of the clock, eight of the clock, nay, nay," quoth he at the last, "it cannot be eight of the clock: for by eight of the clock ye shall lose your master; for my time draweth near that I must depart out of this world."

With that Master Doctor Palmes, a worshipful gentleman, being his chaplain and ghostly father, standing by, bade me secretly to demand of him if he would be shriven, and to be in a readiness towards God, whatsoever should chance. At whose desire I asked him that question.

"What have you to do," quoth he, "to ask me any such question?" and began to be very angry with me for my presumption; until at the last Master Doctor took my part, and talked with him in Latin, and so pacified him.

*   *   *   *   *

Howbeit my lord waxed very sick, most likeliest to die that night, and often swooned, and as me thought drew fast toward his end, until it was four of the clock in the morning, at which time I asked him how he did.

"Well," quoth he, "if I had any meat; I pray you give me some."

"Sir, there is none ready."

"I wis, ye be the more to blame, for you should have always some meat for me in a readiness, to eat when my stomach serveth me; therefore I pray you get me some; for I intend this day, God willing, to make me strong, to the intent I may occupy myself in confession, and make me ready to God."

"Then, sir," quoth I, "I will call up the cook to provide some meat for you; and will also, if it be your pleasure, call for Master Palmes, that ye may commune with him until your meat be ready."

"With a good will," quoth he.

And therewith I went first, and called up the cook, commanding him to prepare some meat for my lord; and then I went to Master Palmes and told him what case my lord was in, willing him to rise, and to resort to him with speed. And then I went to Master Kingston, and gave him warning that, as I thought, he would not live; advertising him that if he had anything to say to him, that he should make haste, for he was in great danger.

"In good faith," quoth Master Kingston, "ye be to blame; for ye make him believe that he is sicker, and in more danger than he is."

"Well, sir," quoth I, "ye shall not say another day but that I gave you warning, as I am bound to do, in discharge of my duty. Therefore, I pray you, whatsoever shall chance, let no negligence be ascribed to me herein; for I assure you his life is very short. Do therefore now as ye think best."

Yet nevertheless he arose, and made him ready, and came to him. After he had eaten of a cullis made of a chicken, a spoonful or two, at the last quoth he, "Whereof was this cullis made?"

"Forsooth, sir," quoth I, "of a chicken."

"Why," quoth he, "it is fasting day, and St. Andrew's Eve."

"What though [it be], sir?" quoth Doctor Palmes. "Ye be excused by reason of your sickness."

"Yea," quoth he, "what though? I will eat no more."

Then was he in confession the space of an hour. And when he had ended his confession, Master Kingston bade him good-morrow (for it was about seven of the clock in the morning), and asked him how he did.

"Sir," quoth he, "I tarry but the will and pleasure of God, to render unto him my simple soul into his divine hands."

"Not yet so, sir," quoth Master Kingston. "With the grace of God, ye shall live, and do very well, if ye will be of good cheer."

"Master Kingston, my disease is such that I cannot live; I have had some experience in my disease, and thus it is: I have a flux with a continual fever, the nature whereof is this: that if there be no alteration with me of the same within eight days, then must either ensue excoriation of the entrails, or frenzy, or else present death; and the best thereof is death. And as I suppose, this is the eighth day; and if ye see in me no alteration, then is there no remedy (although I may live a day or twaine) but death, which is the best remedy of the three."

"Nay, sir, in good faith," quoth Master Kingston, "you be in such dolor and pensiveness, doubting that thing that indeed ye need not to fear, which maketh you much worse than ye should be."

"Well, well, Master Kingston," quoth he, "I see the matter against me, how it is framed; but if I had served God as diligently as I have done the king, he would not have given me over in my grey hairs. Howbeit this is the just reward that I must receive for my worldly diligence and pains that I have had to do him service; only to satisfy his vain pleasures, not regarding my godly duty. Wherefore I pray you, with all my heart, to have me most humbly commended unto his royal majesty, beseeching him in my behalf to call to his most gracious remembrance all matters proceeding between him and me from the beginning of the world unto this day, and the progress of the same; and most chiefly in the weighty matter yet depending (meaning the matter newly begun between him and good Queen Katherine); then shall his conscience declare whether I have offended him or no. He is sure a prince of a royal courage, and

hath a princely heart; and rather than he will either miss or want any part
of his will or appetite, he will put the loss of one half of his realm in danger.
For I assure you I have often kneeled before him in his privy chamber on
my knees the space of an hour or two, to persuade him from his will and
appetite; but I could never bring to pass to dissuade him therefrom. Therefore, Master Kingston, if it chance hereafter you to be one of his privy
council, as for your wisdom and other qualities ye are meet to be, I warn
you to be well advised and assured what matter ye put in his head, for ye
shall never put it out again.

10   "And say furthermore, that I require his grace, in God's name, that
he have a vigilant eye to depress this new pernicious sect of the Lutherans,
that it do not increase within his dominions through his negligence, in
such a sort as that he shall be fain at length to put harness upon his back
to subdue them; as the king of Bohemia did, who had good game to see
his rude commons (then infected with Wycliffe's heresies) to spoil and
murder the spiritual men and religious persons of his realm; the which
fled to the king and his nobles for succour against their frantic rage; of
whom they could get no help of defence or refuge, but [they] laughed
them to scorn, having good game at their spoil and consumption, not re-
20 garding their duties nor their own defence. And when these erroneous
heretics had subdued all the clergy and spiritual persons, taking the spoil
of their riches, both of churches, monasteries, and all other spiritual things,
having no more to spoil, [they] caught such a courage of their former
liberty that then they disdained their prince and sovereign lord with all
other noble personages, and the head governors of the country, and began to fall in hand with the temporal lords to slay and spoil them, without pity or mercy, most cruelly. Insomuch that the king and other his
nobles were constrained to put harness upon their backs, to resist the ungodly powers of those traitorous heretics, and to defend their lives and
30 liberties, who pitched a field royal against them; in which field these traitors so stoutly encountered, that the party of them was so cruel and vehement, that in fine they were victors, and slew the king, the lords, and all
the gentlemen of the realm, leaving not one person that bare the name or
port of a gentleman alive, or of any person that had any rule or authority
in the common weal. By means of which slaughter they have lived ever
since in great misery and poverty without a head or governor, but lived
all in common like wild beasts abhorred of all Christian nations. Let this
be to him an evident example to avoid the like danger, I pray you, good
Master Kingston. There is no trust in routs, or unlawful assemblies of the
40 common people; for when the riotous multitude be assembled, there is
among them no mercy or consideration of their bounden duty; as in the
history of King Richard the Second, one of his noble progenitors, which

[lived] in that same time of Wycliffe's seditious opinions, did not the commons, I pray you, rise against the king and the nobles of the realm of England; whereof some they apprehended, whom they without mercy or justice put to death? And did they not fall to spoiling and robbery, to th'intent they might bring all things in common; and at the last, without discretion or reverence, spared not in their rage to take the king's most royal person out of the Tower of London, and carried him about the city most presumptuously, causing him, for the preservation of his life, to be agreeable to their lewd proclamations? Did not also that traitorous heretic, Sir John Oldcastle, pitch a field against King Harry the Fifth, against whom the king was constrained to encounter in his royal person, to whom God gave the victory? Alas! Master Kingston, if these be not plain precedents, and sufficient persuasions to admonish a prince to be circumspect against the semblable mischief; and if he be negligent, then will God strike and take from him his power, and diminish his regality, taking from him his prudent counsellors and valiant captains, and leave us in our own hands without his help and aid; and then will ensue mischief upon mischief, inconvenience upon inconvenience, barrenness and scarcity of all things for lack of good order in the commonwealth, to the utter destruction and desolation of this noble realm; from the which mischief God of his tender mercy defend us.

"Master Kingston, farewell, I can no more, but wish all things to have good success. My time draweth on fast. I may not tarry with you. And forget not, I pray you, what I have said and charged you withal: for when I am dead, ye shall peradventure remember my words much better."

And even with these words he began to draw his speech at length, and his tongue to fail; his eyes being set in his head, whose sight failed him. Then we began to put him in remembrance of Christ's passion; and sent for the abbot of the place to anele him, who came with all speed, and ministered unto him all the service to the same belonging; and caused also the guard to stand by, both to hear him talk before his death, and also to be witness of the same; and incontinent the clock struck eight, at which time he gave up the ghost, and thus departed he this present life. And calling to our remembrance his words, the day before, how he said that at eight of the clock we should lose our master, one of us looking upon another, supposing that he prophesied of his departure.

Here is the end and fall of pride and arrogancy of such men, exalted by fortune to honours and high dignities: for I assure you, in his time of authority and glory, he was the haughtiest man in all his proceedings that then lived, having more respect to the worldly honour of his person than he had to his spiritual profession; wherein should be all meekness, humil-

ity, and charity; the process whereof I leave to them that be learned and
seen in divine laws.

SIR JOHN CHEKE

The Introduction and Notes are at page 1306
FROM SIR THOMAS HOBY's translation of CASTIGLIONE's
The Courtyer, 1561; the letter was printed at the end of the volume

A Letter of syr J. Cheekes.

To his loving frind Mayster Thomas Hoby

FOR YOUR opinion of my gud will unto you as you wriit, you can not be
deceived: for submitting your doinges to mi judgement, I thanke you: for
taking this pain of your translation, you worthilie deserv great thankes of
all sortes. I have taken sum pain at your request cheflie in your preface,
20 iot in the reading of it for that was pleasaunt unto me boath for the round-
nes of your saienges and welspeakinges of the saam, but in changing certein
wordes which might verie well be let aloan, but that I am verie curious in
mi freendes matters, not to determiin, but to debaat what is best. Whearin,
I seek not the bestnes haplie bi truth, but bi miin own phansie, and shew of
goodnes.

I am of this opinion that our own tung shold be written cleane and pure,
unmixt and unmangeled with borowing of other tunges, wherin if we
take not heed by tiim, ever borowing and never payeng, she shall be fain
to keep her house as bankrupt. For then doth our tung naturallie and
30 praisablie utter her meaning, when she bouroweth no counterfeitness of
other tunges to attire her self withall, but useth plainlie her own, with
such shift, as nature, craft, experiens and folowing of other excellent doth
lead her unto, and if she want at ani tiim (as being unperfight she must)
yet let her borow with suche bashfulnes, that it mai appeer, that if either
the mould of our own tung could serve us to fascion a woord of our own,
or if the old denisoned wordes could content and ease this neede, we
wold not boldly venture of unknowen wordes. This I say not for reproof
of you, who have scarslie and necessarily used whear occasion serveth a
strange word so, as it seemeth to grow out of the matter and not to be
40 sought for: but for miin own defens, who might be counted overstraight
a deemer of thinges, if I gave not thys accompt to you, mi freend and wiis,
of mi marring this your handiwork. But I am called awai, I prai you

pardon mi shortnes, the rest of mi saienges should be but praise and ex-
hortacion in this your doinges, which at moar leisor I shold do better.
From my house in Woodstreete the 16. of July, 1557.

Yours assured

JOAN. CHEEK.

SIR THOMAS HOBY

The Introduction and Notes are at page 1307

FROM *The Courtyer*, 1561, HOBY's translation of *Il Cortegiano* by
COUNT BALDASSARE CASTIGLIONE, first published in 1528

The Courtier

The First Book of the Courtier of Count Baldassare Castiglione, unto Master Alphonsus Ariosto.

I HAVE a long time doubted with myself (most loving M Alphonsus) 20
which of the two were harder for me, either to deny you the thing that
you have with such instance many times required of me, or to take it in
hand; because, on the one side, methought it a very hard matter to deny
anything, especially, the request being honest, to the person whom I love
dearly, and of whom I perceive myself dearly beloved. Again, on the
other side, to undertake an enterprise which I do not know myself able
to bring to an end, I judged it uncomely for him that weigheth due re-
proofs so much as they ought to be weighed. At length, after much debating, I have determined to prove in this behalf what aid that affection
and great desire to please can bring unto my diligence, which, in other 30
things, is wont to increase the labor of men. You then require me to write
what is (to my thinking) the trade and manner of courtiers which is
most fitting for a gentleman that liveth in the court of princes, by the
which he may have the knowledge how to serve them perfectly in every
reasonable matter, and obtain thereby favor of them and praise of other
men. Finally, of what sort he ought to be that deserveth to be called so
perfect a courtier that there be no want in him?

Wherefore I, considering this kind of request, say that, in case it should
not appear to myself a greater blame to have you esteem me to be of small
friendship than all other men of little wisdom, I would have rid my hands 40
of this labor, for fear lest I should be counted rash of all such as know what
a hard matter it is, among such diversity of manners that are used in the

courts of Christendom, to pick out the perfectest trade and way, and (as it were) the flower of this courtiership. Because use maketh us many times to delight in, and to set little by, the self-same things: whereby sometime it proceedeth that manners, garments, customs, and fashions which at some time have been in price become not regarded, and, contrariwise, the not regarded, become of price. Therefore, it is manifestly to be discerned that use hath greater force than reason to bring up new inventions among us, and to abolish the old, of the which whoso goeth about to judge the perfection is oftentimes deceived. For which consideration, perceiving this
10 and many other lets in the matter propounded for me to write upon, I am constrained to make a piece of an excuse, and to open plainly that this error (if it may be termed an error) is common to us both, that if any blame happen to me about it, it may be also partened with you. For it ought to be reckoned a no less offense in you to lay upon me a burden that passeth my strength than in me to take it upon me.

Let us, therefore, at length settle ourselves to begin that is our purpose and drift, and (if it be possible) let us fashion such a courtier as the prince that shall be worthy to have him in his service, although his state be but small, may, notwithstanding, be called a mighty lord. We will not in
20 these books follow any certain order or rule of appointed precepts, the which, for the most part, is wont to be observed in the teaching of anything, whatsoever it be: but, after the manner of men of old time, renewing a grateful memory, we will repeat certain reasonings that were debated in times past between men very excellent for that purpose. And although I was not there present, but, at the time when they were debated, it was my chance to be in England, yet soon after my return I heard them of a person that faithfully reported them unto me. And I will endeavor myself, for so much as my memory will serve me, to call them particularly to remembrance, that you may see what men worthy great
30 commendation, and unto whose judgment a man may in every point give an undoubted credit, have judged and believed in this matter. Neither shall we swerve from the purpose to arrive in good order at the end unto the which all our communication is directed, if we disclose the cause of the reasonings that hereafter follow.

As every man knoweth, the little city of Urbin is situated upon the side of the Apennine (in a manner) in the midst of Italy, towards the Gulf of Venice. The which for all it is placed among hills, and those not so pleasant as perhaps some other that we behold in many places, yet, in this point, the element hath been favorable unto it, that, all about, the country is
40 very plentiful and full of fruits; so that beside the wholesomeness of air, it is very abundant and stored with all things necessary for the life of man. But among the greatest felicities that men can reckon it to have, I count

this the chief: that now a long time it hath always been governed with very good princes, although, in the common calamities of the wars of Italy, it remained also a season without any at all. But, without searching further of this, we may make a good proof with the famous memory of Duke Frederick, who in his days was the light of Italy. Neither do we want true and very large testimonies yet remaining of his wisdom, courtesy, justice, liberality, of his invincible courage and policy of war. And of this, do his so many victories make proof, chiefly his conquering of places impregnable, his sudden readiness in setting forward to give battle, his putting to flight sundry times, with a small number, very great and puissant armies, and never sustained loss in any conflict; so that we may, not without cause, compare him to many famous men of old time. This man, among his other deeds praiseworthy, in the hard and sharp situation of Urbin built a palace, to the opinion of many men the fairest that was to be found in all Italy, and so furnished it with every necessary implement belonging thereto that it appeared not a palace but a city in form of a palace, and that not only with ordinary matters, as silver plate, hangings for chambers of very rich cloth of gold, of silk, and other like, but also for sightliness; and, to deck it out withal, placed there a wondrous number of ancient images of marble and metal, very excellent paintings and instruments of music of all sorts, and nothing would he have there but what was most rare and excellent. To this, with very great charges, he gathered together a great number of most excellent and rare books, in Greek, Latin, and Hebrew, the which all he garnished with gold and silver, esteeming this to be the chiefest ornament of his great palace. This duke then, following the course of nature when he was sixty-five years of age, as he had lived so did he end his life with glory. And left duke after him a child of ten years, having no more male, and without mother, who hight Guidubaldo.

This child, as of the state, so did it appear also that he was heir of all his father's virtues; and suddenly, with a marvelous towardness, began to promise so much of himself as a man would not have thought possible to be hoped of a man mortal. So that the opinion of men was that, of all Duke Frederick's notable deeds, there was none greater than that he begat such a son. But fortune, envying this so great virtue, with all her might gainstood this so glorious a beginning, in such wise that before Duke Guidubaldo was twenty years of age, he fell sick of the gout, the which increasing upon him with most bitter pains, in a short time so numbed him of all his members that he could neither stand on foot nor move himself. And in this manner was one of the best favored and towardliest personages in the world deformed and marred in his green age. And beside, not satisfied with this, fortune was so contrary to him in all his purposes that

very seldom he brought to pass anything to his mind. And for all he had in
him most wise counsel and an invincible courage, yet it seemed that whatsoever he took in hand, both in feats of arms and in every other thing,
small or great, it came always to ill success. And of this make proof his
many and divers calamities, which he always bore out with such stoutness
of courage that virtue never yielded to fortune. But, with a bold stomach
despising her storms, lived with great dignity and estimation among all
men: in sickness, as one that was sound, and in adversity, as one that was
most fortunate. So that, for all he was thus diseased in his body, he served
10 in time of war with most honorable entertainment under the most famous
kings of Naples, Alphonsus and Ferdinand the younger; afterward with
Pope Alexander the VI. with the lords of Venice and Florence. And
when Julius the II. was created pope, he was then made general captain
of the church; at which time, proceeding in his accustomed usage, he set
his delight above all things to have his house furnished with most noble
and valiant gentlemen, with whom he lived very familiarly, enjoying their
conversation; wherein the pleasure which he gave unto other men was
no less than that he received of other, because he was very well seen in
both tongues, and, together with a loving behavior and pleasantness, he
20 had also accompanied the knowledge of infinite things. And beside this,
the greatness of his courage so quickened him that where he was not in
case with his person to practise the feats of chivalry as he had done long
before, yet did he take very great delight to behold them in other men; and
with his words sometime correcting, and other while praising, every man
according to his deserts, he declared evidently how great a judgment he
had in those matters. And upon this, at tilt, at tourney, in riding, in playing at all sorts of weapon, also in inventing devices, in pastimes, in music,
finally in all exercises meet for noble gentlemen, every man strived to
show himself such a one as might deserve to be judged worthy of so noble
30 an assembly. Therefore were all the hours of the day divided into honorable and pleasant exercises, as well of the body as of the mind.

But because the duke used continually, by reason of his infirmity, soon
after supper to go to his rest, every man ordinarily at that hour drew
where the duchess was, the Lady Elizabeth Gonzaga. Where also continually was the Lady Emilia Pia, who, for that she was endowed with so
lively a wit and judgment, as you know, seemed the mistress and ring-
leader of all the company, and that every man at her received understanding and courage. There was then to be heard pleasant communication and
merry conceits, and in every man's countenance a man might perceive
40 painted a loving jocundness. So that this house truly might well be called
the very mansion place of mirth and joy. And I believe it was never so
tasted in other place, what manner a thing the sweet conversation [is]

that is occasioned of an amiable and loving company, as it was once there. For, leaving apart what honor it was to all us to serve such a lord as he whom I declared unto you right now, every man conceived in his mind an high contentation every time we came into the duchess' sight. And it appeared that this was a chain that kept all linked together in love, in such wise that there was never agreement of will or hearty love greater between brethren than was there between us all. The like was between the women, with whom we had such free and honest conversation that every man might commune, sit, dally, and laugh with whom he had lusted. But such was the respect which we bore to the duchess' will that the self-same liberty was a very great bridle. Neither was there any that thought it not the greatest pleasure he could have in the world to please her, and the greatest grief to offend her. For this respect were there most honest conditions coupled with wondrous great liberty, and devices of pastimes and laughing matters tempered in her sight, beside most witty jests with so comely and grave a majesty, that the very sober mood and greatness that did knit together all the acts, words, and gestures of the duchess in jesting and laughing made them also, that had never seen her in their life before, to count her a very great lady. And all that came in her presence having this respect fixed in their breast, it seemed she had made them to her beck; so that every man enforced himself to follow this trade, taking (as it were) a rule and example of fair conditions at the presence of so great and so virtuous a lady. Whose most excellent qualities I intend not now to express, for it is neither my purpose, and again they are well enough known to the world, and much better than I am able, either with tongue or with pen, to indite. And such as would perhaps have lien hid a space, fortune, as she that wondereth at so rare virtues, hath thought good, with many adversities and temptations of miseries, to disclose them, to make trial thereby that in the tender breast of a woman, in company with singular beauty, there can dwell wisdom, and stoutness of courage, and all other virtues that in grave men themselves are most seldom.

But leaving this apart, I say that the manner of all the gentlemen in the house was immediately after supper to assemble together where the duchess was. Where, among other recreations, music and dancing, which they used continually, sometime they propounded feat questions, other while they invented certain witty sports and pastimes, at the device sometime of one, sometime of another, in the which, under sundry coverts, oftentimes the standers-by opened subtlely their imaginations unto whom they thought best. At other times there arose other disputations of divers matters, or else jestings with prompt inventions. Many times they fell into purposes, as we nowadays term them, where, in this kind of talk and debating of matters, there was wondrous great pleasure on all sides, because (as I have said) the house was replenished with most noble wits. Among which (as you know) were most famous the Lord Octavian Fregoso, Sir Frederick, his brother, the Lord Julian de Medici, M. Peter Bembo, the Lord Cesare Gonzaga, Count Lewis of Canossa, the Lord Gaspar Pallavicin, the Lord Lodovicus Pius, M. Morello of Ortona, Peter of Naples, M. Robert of Bari, and infinite other most worthy knights and gentlemen. Beside these there were many that for all ordinarily they dwelled not there, yet spent they most of their time there, as M. Bernard Bibiena, Unico Aretino, Johnchristopher Romano, Peter Mount, Therpander, M. Nicholas Phrisio, so that thither ran continually poets, musicians, and all kind of men of skill, and the excellentest in every faculty that were in all Italy.

After Pope Julius the II. had with his own presence, by the aid of the Frenchmen, brought Bologna to the obedience of the apostolic see again, in the year 1506, in his return toward Rome, he took Urbin in his way, where he was received as honorably as was possible, and with as sumptuous and costly preparation as could have been in any other city of Italy, whatsoever it be. So that, beside the pope, all the cardinals and other courtiers thought themselves thoroughly satisfied. And some there were that, provoked with the sweetness of this company, after the pope and the court was departed, continued many days together in Urbin. At which time they did not only proceed in their accustomed trade of disporting and ordinary recreations, but also every man set to his helping hand to augment them somewhat, and especially in pastimes, which they had up almost every night. And the order thereof was such that, as soon as they were assembled where the duchess was, every man sat him down at his will or as it fell to his lot, in a circle together, and, in sitting, were divided a man and a woman, as long as there were women, for always (lightly) the number of men was far the greater. Then were they governed as the duchess thought best, which many times gave this charge unto the Lady Emilia.

So the day after the pope was departed, the company being gathered to the accustomed place, after much pleasant talk, the duchess' pleasure was that the Lady Emilia should begin these pastimes. And she, after a little refusing of that charge, said in this manner: "Sith it is your pleasure (madam), I shall be she that must give the onset in our pastimes this night, because I ought not of reason disobey you, I think meet to propound a pastime whereof I suppose shall ensue little blame and less travail. And that shall be to have every man, as nigh as he can, propound a device not yet heard of, then shall we choose out such a one as shall be thought meet to be taken in hand in this company."

And after she had thus spoken, she turned her unto the Lord Gaspar

Pallavicin, willing him to propound his; who immediately made answer: "But first (madam) you must begin to propound yours."

Then said the Lady Emilia: "I have already done. But Your Grace must command him (madam) to be obedient."

Then the duchess laughing, "To the intent," quoth she, "every man shall obey you, I make you my deputy, and give unto you all mine authority."

"It is surely a great matter," answered the Lord Gaspar, "that it is always lawful for women to have this privilege, to be exempt and free from painstaking, and truly reason would we should in any wise know 10 why. But because I will not be he that shall give example to disobey, I shall leave this until another time, and will speak of that I am now charged withal, and thus I begin. Mine opinion is that our minds, as in other things, so also in loving, are diverse in judgment, and therefore it chanceth oftentimes that the thing which is most acceptable unto one is most abhorred of another. Yet, for all that, they always agree in that every man counteth most dear the wight beloved. So that many times the overmuch affection in lovers doth so deceive their judgment that they ween the person whom they love to be so garnished with all excellent virtues and without fault that he hath no peer in the world. But because the nature of man 20 doth not admit such full perfections, and there is no man that hath not some default or want in him, it cannot be said that such as these be are not deceived, and that the lover doth not become blind as touching the beloved. I would, therefore, our pastime should be this night to have every man open what virtues he would principally the person he loveth should be endowed withal. And seeing it is so necessarily that we all have some spot, what vice he would also have in him: to see who can find out most praiseworthy and manly virtues and most tolerable vices that should be least hurtful both to him that loveth and to the wight beloved."

After the Lord Gaspar had thus spoken, the Lady Emilia made a sign 30 unto the Lady Constance Fregosa, because she was next in order to follow; who was now about to speak, when the duchess suddenly said: "Seeing the Lady Emilia will not take the pain to find out some pastime, reason willeth that the other ladies should be partakers of the same privilege, and be also free from this burden for this night, especially seeing there are so many men in place; for assure yourself we shall want no pastimes."

"So shall we do," answered the Lady Emilia, and, putting the Lady Constance to silence, turned her to the Lord Cesare Gonzaga, that sat next her, commanding him to speak, and thus he began: "Whoso will 40 diligently consider all our doings, he shall find always in them sundry imperfections. And that happeneth because nature doth vary as well in this

as in all other things. Unto one she hath given the light of reason in one thing, and unto another in another thing. Therefore it cometh to pass where one man knoweth that another knoweth not, and is ignorant in the thing that the other hath understanding in; each man doth easily perceive the error of his fellow, and not his own, and we all think ourselves to be very wise, and peradventure in that point most wherein we are most foolish. So that we have seen by experience in this house many men which at the beginning were counted most wise, in process of time were known to be most foolish. Which hath proceeded of no other thing
10 but of our own diligence, like as it is said to be in Pulia of them that are bitten with a tarantula, about whom men occupy many instruments of music, and with sundry sounds go searching out, until the humor that maketh this disease, by a certain concordance it hath with some of those sounds, feeling it, doth suddenly move, and so stirreth the patient, that, by that stirring, he recovereth his health again. In like manner, we, when we have felt some privy operation of folly, we provoke it so subtlely and with such sundry persuasions, and so divers ways that at length we understand whither it tended. Afterward, the humor known, we so stir it that always it is brought to the perfection of open folly. And some is waxed
20 foolish in verses, some in music, some in love, some in dancing, some in making antiques, some in riding, some in playing at fence, every man according to the moine of his metal; whereby hath ensued (as you know) marvelous great pastime. I hold therefore for certain that in every one of us there is some seed of folly, the which being stirred may multiply (in a manner) infinite. Therefore, I would this night our pastime were to dispute upon this matter: and that every man might say his mind, seeing I must be openly foolish in what sort of folly I am foolish, and over what matter, judging it the issue for the sparkles of folly that are daily seen to proceed from me. And let the like be said of all the rest, keeping the order
30 of our devices, and let every man do his best to ground his opinion upon some sure sign and argument, and so, by this our pastime, shall every one of us get profit, in that we shall know our defaults and then shall we the better take heed. And in case the vein of folly which we shall discover be so rank that it shall appear to us past remedy, we will set thereto our helping hand, and, according to the doctrine of Friar Marion, we shall gain a soul, which shall be no small gain."

At this device there was much laughing, and none could refrain from speaking. One said, I should be found foolish in imagining; another, in viewing; another said he was already become foolish for love; and such
40 like matters. . . .

Every man looked what the Lady Emilia would make answer to this, but, without any word speaking to Bembo, she turned her and made a sign

to Sir Frederick Fregoso to shew his device. And he incontinently began
thus: "Madam, I would it were lawful for me, as the manner is many
times, to remit me to the judgment of another, for I, for my part, would,
with all my heart, allow some of the pastimes that have been already
propounded by these lords, because, indeed, methink they would be worth
the hearing. Yet, lest I should break the order, this I say: whoso would
take in hand to praise our court, leaving apart the deserts of the duchess,
which ghostly spirit, with her influence, is sufficient to draw from the
earth up into heaven the simplest wits in the world, he might well do it
without suspicion of flattery. For peradventure in all Italy a man shall .o
have much ado to find out so many gentlemen and noble personages that
are so worthy and, beside the principal profession of chivalry, so excellent
in sundry things, as are presently here. Therefore, if, in any place, men
may be found that deserve the name of good courtiers and can judge what
belongeth to the perfection of courtiership, by reason a man may believe
them to be here. To disgrace, therefore, many untowardly assheads that
through malapertness think to purchase them the name of a good courtier,
I would have such a pastime for this night that one of the company might
be picked out who should take in hand to shape in words a good courtier,
specifying all such conditions and particular qualities as of necessity must 20
be in him that deserveth this name. And in such things as shall not appear
necessary, that it may be lawful for every man to reply against them, as
the manner of philosophers' schools is against him that keepeth disputations."

Sir Frederick proceeded still forward in his talk when the Lady Emilia,
interrupting him, said: "If it be My Lady the Duchess pleases, this shall
be our pastime for this once."

The duchess answered: "I am well pleased."

Then (in manner) all the company began to say both to the Duchess
and among themselves that this was the trimmest pastime they could have, 30
and, without looking for answer the one of the other, they craved upon
the Lady Emilia to appoint who should first begin. Who, turning her
toward the duchess, said: "Command you (madam) whom shall please
you to take this enterprise in hand, for I will not, by choosing more one
than another, declare myself to judge in this behalf, whom I think to be
better skilled than the rest, and so do wrong to some."

The Duchess answered: "Make you this choice yourself, and take heed
that in disobeying you be not a precedent to the rest to be disobedient."

Then the Lady Emilia said, laughing, unto Lewis, Count of Canossa:
"Therefore, for losing any more time, you (Count) shall be he that shall 40
take this enterprise upon him in form and manner as Sir Frederick hath
declared. Not for that we know ye are so good a courtier that you have at

your fingers' ends that belongeth thereto; but because, in repeating everything arsyversy, as we hope ye will, we shall have so much the more pastime, and every one shall be able to answer you, where, if another more
skilful than you should take it in hand, there should be nothing said against
him for telling the truth, and so should we have but a cold pastime."

The count answered by and by: "We need not fear (madam) that
we shall want contrarying in words against him that telleth the truth as
long as you be here." And after they had laughed a while at this answer,
he proceeded on: "But truly I would, with all my heart, be rid of this
10 burden, for it is too hard for me. And I know that to be most true in me
which you have spoken in jest; namely, that I have no understanding in
that belongeth to a good courtier. And this do I not seek to prove with any
other trial, for, seeing I do not the deeds, a man may judge I understand
it not, and I believe I am the less to be blamed. For out of doubt it is a
worse matter not to do well than not to understand how to do it. Yet,
seeing your pleasure is that I shall take this charge upon me, I cannot,
nor will, refuse it, for withstanding your order and judgment, the which
I know is much better than mine."

Then the Lord Cesare Gonzaga: "Because it is now," quoth he, "well
20 forward in night and have here ready for us other sorts of pastimes,
peradventure it should not be amiss to defer this reasoning until to-morrow, and the count shall have leisure to think better upon that he hath
to say: for, in very deed, to entreat upon such a matter at the first sight,
it is a hard thing."

Then answered the count: "I will not do as he did that stripped himself into his doublet and leaped less ground than he did before in his coat.
And methink my luck is good that it is late, because the shortness of time
shall make me use few words, and the suddenness of the matter shall so
excuse me that it shall be lawful for me to speak without blame whatso-
30 ever cometh first to mind. Because I will not, therefore, carry this burden
of duty any longer upon my shoulders, this I say: in everything it is so
hard a matter to know the true perfection that it is almost unpossible, and
that by reason of the variety of judgments. Therefore, many there are
that delight in a man of much talk, and him they call a pleasant fellow.
Some will delight more in modesty, some other will fancy a man that is
active and always doing; other, one that sheweth a quietness and a respect
in everything. And thus doth every man praise or dispraise according to
his fancy, always covering a vice with the name of the next virtue to it, and
a virtue with the name of the next vice: as in calling him that is saucy,
40 bold; him that is sober, dry; him that is seely, good; him that is unhappy,
witty; and likewise in the rest. Yet do I think that each thing hath his
perfection, although it be hid, and, with reasonable discourses, might be

judged of him that hath knowledge in the matter. And forasmuch as the truth (as I have said) is oftentimes hid, and I take not upon me to have this knowledge, I cannot praise but that kind of courtiers which I set most by, and allow that which seemeth unto me most nigh the truth, in my small judgment. The which you shall follow if ye think it good, or else stick to your own, if it shall vary from mine. Neither will I (for all that) stand stiff that mine is better than yours, for not only one thing may seem unto you and another to me, but also unto myself it may appear sometime one thing, sometime another.

"I will have this, our courtier, therefore, to be a gentleman born and of 10 a good house. For it is a great deal less dispraise for him that is not born a gentleman to fail in the acts of virtue than for a gentleman. If he swerve from the steps of his ancestors, he staineth the name of his family, and doth not only not get, but loseth, that is already gotten. For nobleness of birth is (as it were) a clear lamp that sheweth forth and bringeth into light works both good and bad, and inflameth and provoketh unto virtue, as well with the fear of slander as also with the hope of praise. And whereas this brightness of nobleness doth not discover the works of the unnoble, they have a want of provocation and of fear of slander, and they reckon not themselves bound to wade any further than their ancestors did before 20 them, whereas the noble of birth count it a shame not to arrive, at the least, at the bounds of their predecessors set forth unto them. Therefore, it chanceth always (in a manner), both in arms and in all other virtuous acts, that the most famous men are gentlemen. Because nature in everything hath deeply sowed that privy seed which giveth a certain force and property of her beginning unto whatsoever springeth of it and maketh it like unto herself. As we see by example not only in the race of horses and other beasts, but also in trees, whose slips and grafts always, for the most part, are like unto the stock of the tree they came from; and if at any time they grow out of kind, the fault is in the husbandman. And the 30 like is in men, if they be trained up in good nurture, most commonly they resemble them from whom they come and oftentimes pass them, but if they have not one that can well train them up, they grow (as it were) wild, and never come to their ripeness. Truth it is, whether it be through the favor of the stars or of nature, some there are born endowed with such graces that they seem not to have been born, but rather fashioned with the very hand of some god, and abound in all goodness both of body and mind. As again we see some so unapt and dull that a man will not believe but nature hath brought them into the world for a spite and mockery. And like as these, with continual diligence and good bringing up, for the most 40 part can bring small fruit; even so, the other, with little attendance, climb to the full perfection of all excellency. Mark me, the Lord Hippolitus da

Este, Cardinal of Ferrara, he hath had so happy a birth that his person, his countenance, his words, and all his gestures are so fashioned and compact with this grace that, among the most ancient prelates (for all he is but young), he doth represent so grave an authority that a man would ween he were more meet to teach than needful to learn. Likewise, in company with men and women of all degrees, in sporting, in laughing, and in jesting he hath in him a certain sweetness and so comely demeanors that whoso speaketh with him or yet beholdeth him must needs bear him an affection forever.

10 "But, returning to our purpose, I say that, between this excellent grace and that fond foolishness, there is yet a mean, and they that are not by nature so perfectly furnished, with study and diligence may polish and correct a great part of the defaults of nature. The courtier, therefore, beside nobleness of birth, I will have him to be fortunate in this behalf, and by nature to have not only a wit and a comely shape of person and countenance, but also a certain grace, and (as they say) a hue that shall make him, at the first sight, acceptable and loving unto whoso beholdeth him. And let this be an ornament to frame and accompany all his acts, and to assure men in his look such a one to be worthy the company and favor of 20 every great man."

* * * *

[From the Fourth Book]

Then the Lord Gaspar: "I remember," quoth he, "that these lords yesternight, reasoning of the Courtier's qualities, did allow him to be a lover, and in making rehearsal of as much as hitherto hath been spoken, a man may pick out a conclusion that the Courtier (which with his worthiness and credit must incline his Prince to virtue) must in manner of ne- 30 cessity be aged, for knowledge cometh very seldom times before years, and specially in matters that be learned with experience. I cannot see, when he is well drawn in years, how it will stand well with him to be a lover, considering (as it hath been said the other night) love frameth not with old men, and the tricks that in young men be gallantness, courtesy and preciseness so acceptable to women, in them are mere follies and fondness to be laughed at, and purchase him that useth them hatred of women and mocks of others. Therefore in case this your Aristotle (an old Courtier) were a lover, and practiced the feats that young lovers do (as some that we have seen in our days), I fear me he would forget to 40 teach his Prince; and paraventure boys would mock him behind his back, and women would have none other delight in him but to make him a jesting stock."

Then said the Lord Octavian: "Since all the other qualities appointed to the Courtier are meet for him, although he be old, me think we should not then bar him from this happiness to love."

"Nay rather," quoth the Lord Gaspar, "to take this love from him, is a perfection over and above, and a making him to live happily out of misery and wretchedness."

M[aster]. Peter Bembo said: "Remember you not (my Lord Gaspar) that the Lord Octavian declared the other night in his device of pastimes, although he be not skilful in love, to know yet that there be some lovers which reckon the disdains, the angers, the debates and torments which they receive of their ladies, sweet? Whereupon he required to be taught the cause of this sweetness. Therefore in case our Courtier (though he be old) were kindled with those loves that be sweet without any bitter smack, he should feel no misery nor wretchedness at all. And being wise, as we set case he is, he should not be deceived in thinking to be meet for him whatsoever were meet for young men, but in loving should perhaps love after a sort that might not only not bring him in slander but to much praise and great happiness, without any loathsomeness at all, the which very seldom or (in manner) never happeneth to young men; so should he neither lay aside the teaching of his Prince, nor yet commit anything that should deserve the mocking of boys."

Then spake the Duchess: "I am glad (M. Peter) that you have not been much troubled, in our reasonings this night, for now we may be the bolder to give you in charge to speak, and to teach the Courtier this so happy a love, which bringeth with it neither slander, nor any inconvenience; for perhaps it shall be one of the necessariest and profitablest qualities that hitherto hath been given him; therefore speak of good fellowship as much as you know therein."

M. Peter laughed and said: "I would be loath (madam) where I say that it is lawful for old men to love, it should be an occasion for these ladies to think me old; therefore hardly give you this enterprise to another."

The Duchess answered: "You ought not to refuse to be counted old in knowledge, though ye be young in years. Therefore say on, and excuse yourself no more."

M. Peter said: "Surely (madam) if I must entreat upon this matter, I must first go ask counsel of my hermit Lavinello."

The Lady Emilia said then, half in anger: "There is never a one in all the company so disobedient as you be (M. Peter); therefore should the Duchess do well to chastise you somewhat for it."

M. Peter said smiling: "For love of God (madam) be not angry with me, for I will say whatever you will have me."

"Go to, say on then," answered the Lady Emilia.

Then M. Peter, after a while's silence, somewhat settling himself as though he should entreat upon a weighty matter, said thus: "My Lords, to show that old men may love not only without slander, but otherwhile more happily than young men, I must be enforced to make a little discourse to declare what love is, and wherein consisteth the happiness that lovers may have. Therefore I beseech ye give the hearing with heedfulness, for I hope to make you understand that it were not unfitting for any man here to be a lover, in case he were fifteen or twenty years older than M. Morello."

And here, after they had laughed a while, M. Peter proceeded: "I say therefore that according as it is defined of the wise men of old time, Love is nothing else but a certain coveting to enjoy beauty; and forsomuch as coveting longeth for nothing but for things known, it is requisite that knowledge go evermore before coveting, which of his own nature willeth the good, but of himself is blind and knoweth it not. Therefore hath nature so ordained that to every virtue of knowledge there is annexed a virtue of longing. And because in our soul there be three manner ways to know; namely, by sense, reason, and understanding: of sense, there ariseth appetite or longing, which is common to us with brute beasts; of reason ariseth election or choice, which is proper to man; of understanding, by the which man may be partner with angels, ariseth will. Even as therefore the sense knoweth not but sensible matters and that which may be felt, so the appetite or coveting only desireth the same; and even as the understanding is bent but to behold things that may be understood, so is that will only fed with spiritual goods.

"Man of nature endowed with reason, placed (as it were) in the middle between these two extremities, may through his choice inclining to sense, or reaching to understanding, come nigh to the coveting sometime of the one sometime of the other part. In these sorts therefore may beauty be coveted, the general name whereof may be applied to all things, either natural or artificial, that are framed in good proportion, and due temper, as their nature beareth.

"But speaking of the beauty that we mean, which is only it that appeareth in bodies, and especially in the face of man, and moveth this fervent coveting which we call love, we will term it an influence of the heavenly bountifulness, the which for all it stretcheth over all things that be created (like the light of the sun) yet when it findeth out a face well proportioned, and framed with a certain lively agreement of several colors, and set forth with lights and shadows, and with an orderly distance and limits of lines, thereinto it distilleth itself and appeareth most well favored, and decketh out and lighteneth the subject where it shineth with a marvelous

grace and glistering (like the sunbeams that strike against beautiful plate
of fine gold wrought and set with precious jewels) so that it draweth
unto it men's eyes with pleasure, and piercing through them imprinteth
himself in the soul, and with an unwonted sweetness all to stirreth her
and delighteth, and, setting her on fire, maketh her to covet him. When
the soul then is taken with coveting to enjoy this beauty as a good thing,
in case she suffer herself to be guided with the judgment of sense, she
falleth into most deep errors, and judgeth the body in which beauty is
discerned to be the principal cause thereof; whereupon, to enjoy it, she
reckoneth it necessary to join as inwardly as she can with that body, which 10
is false; and therefore whoso thinketh in possessing the body to enjoy
beauty, he is far deceived, and is moved to it, not with true knowledge by
the choice of reason, but with false opinion by the longing of sense. Whereupon the pleasure that followeth it, is also false and of necessity full of
errors.

"And therefore into one of the two vices run all those lovers that satisfy
their unhonest lusts with the women whom they love; for either as soon
as they be come to the coveted end, they not only feel a fullness and loathsomeness, but also conceive a hatred against the wight beloved, as though
longing repented him of his offense and acknowledged the deceit wrought 20
him by the false judgment of sense, that made him believe the ill to be
good; or else they continue in the very same coveting and greediness, as
though they were not indeed come to the end which they sought for. And
albeit through the blind opinion that hath made them drunken (to their
seeming) in that instant they feel a contentment, as the diseased otherwhile, that dream they drink of some clear spring; yet be they not satisfied, nor leave off so. And because of possessing coveted goodness there
ariseth always quietness and satisfaction in the possessor's mind, in case
this were the true and right end of their coveting, when they possess it
they would be at quietness and thoroughly satisfied. Which they be not; 30
but rather deceived through that likeness, they forthwith return again to
unbridled coveting, and with the very same trouble which they felt at the
first they fall again into the raging and most burning thirst of the thing
that they hope in vain to possess perfectly.

"These kind of lovers therefore love most unluckily, for either they
never come by their covetings, which is a great unluckiness, or else if they
do come by them, they find they come by their hurt, and end their miseries
with other greater miseries; for both in the beginning and middle of this
love there is never other thing felt but afflictions, torments, griefs, pining,
travail, so that to be wan, vexed with continual tears and sighs, to live 40
with a discontented mind, to be always dumb, or to lament, to covet death,
in conclusion to be most unlucky, are the properties which (they say) be-

long to lovers. The cause therefore of this wretchedness in men's minds, is principally sense, which in youthful age beareth most sway, because the lustiness of the flesh and of the blood, in that season addeth unto him even so much force as it withdraweth from reason. Therefore doth it easily train the soul to follow appetite or longing, for when she seeth herself drowned in the earthly prison, because she is set in the office to govern the body, she cannot of herself understand plainly at the first the truth of spiritual beholding. Wherefore, to compass the understanding of things, she must go beg the beginning at the senses, and therefore she believeth
10 them, and giveth ear to them, and is contented to be led by them, especially when they have so much courage, that (in a manner) they enforce her and because they be deceitful they fill her with errors and false opinions. Whereupon most commonly it happeneth that young men be wrapped in this sensual love, which is a very rebel against reason; and therefore they make themselves unworthy to enjoy the favors and benefits which love bestoweth upon his true subjects; neither in love feel they any other pleasures than what beasts without reason do, but much more grievous afflictions.

"Setting case therefore this to be so, which is most true, I say that the
20 contrary chanceth to them of a more ripe age. For in case they, when the soul is not now so much weighed down with the bodily burden, and when the natural burning assuageth and draweth to a warmth, if they be inflamed with beauty and to it bend their coveting guided by reasonable choice, they be not deceived, and possess beauty perfectly, and therefore through the possessing of it, always goodness ensueth to them. Because beauty is good, and consequently the true love of it is most good and holy, and evermore bringeth forth good fruites in the souls of them that with the bridle of reason restrain the ill disposition of sense, the which old men can much sooner do than young. It is not therefore out of reason to say
30 that old men may also love without slander and more happily than young men, taking notwithstanding this name old not for the age at the pit's brink, nor when the canals of the body be so feeble that the soul cannot through them work her feats, but when knowledge in us is in his right strength.

"And I will not also hide this from you; namely, that I suppose where sensual love in every age is naught, yet in young men it deserveth excuse, and perhaps in some case lawfull. For although it putteth them in afflictions, dangers, travails, and the unfortunateness that is said, yet are there many that to win them the good will of their ladies practice virtuous
40 things, which for all they be not bent to a good end, yet are they good of themselves; and so of that much bitterness they pick out a little sweetness,

and through the adversities which they sustain, in the end they acknowledge their error. As I judge therefore those young men that bridle their
appetites, and love with reason, to be godly; so do I hold excused such as
yield to sensual love, whereunto they be so inclined through the weakness
and frailty of man, so they show therein meekness, courtesy, and prowess,
and the other worthy conditions that these Lords have spoken of, and
when those youthful years be gone and past, leave it off clean, keeping
aloof from this sensual coveting as from the lowermost step of the stairs
by the which a man may ascend to true love. But in case after they draw
in years once, they reserve still in their cold heart the fire of appetites, 10
and bring stout reason in subjection to feeble sense, it cannot be said how
much they are to be blamed; for like men without sense they deserve with
an everlasting shame to be put in the number of unreasonable living creatures, because the thoughts and ways of sensual love be far unfitting for
ripe age."

Here Bembo paused a while as though he would breathe him, and when
all things were whist M. Morello of Ortona said: "And in case there
were some old man more fresh and lusty and of a better complexion than
many young men, why would you not have it lawful for him to love with
the love that young men love?" 20

The Duchess laughed and said: "If the love of young men be so unlucky, why would you (M. Morello) that old men should also love with
this unluckiness? But in case you were old (as these men say you be)
you would not thus procure the hurt of old men."

M. Morello answered: "The hurt of old men (meseemeth) M. Peter
Bembo procureth, who will have them to love after a sort that I for my
part understand not; and (methink) the possessing of this beauty, which
he praiseth so much, without the body, is a dream."

"Do you believe, M. Morello," quoth then Count Lewis, "that beauty
is always so good a thing as M. Peter Bembo speaketh of?" 30

"Not I in good sooth," answered M. Morello. "But I remember
rather that I have seen many beautiful women of a most ill inclination,
cruel, and spiteful, and it seemeth that (in a manner) it happeneth always
so, for beauty maketh them proud; and pride, cruel."

Count Lewis said smiling: "To you perhaps they seem cruel, because
they content you not with it that you would have. But cause M. Peter
Bembo to teach you in what sort old men ought to covet beauty, and what
to seek at their ladies' hands, and what to content themselves withal; and
in not passing out of these bounds, you shall see that they shall be neither
proud nor cruel, and will satisfy you with what you shall require." 40

M. Morello seemed then somewhat out of patience, and said: "I will

not know the thing that toucheth me not. But cause you to be taught how
the young men ought to covet this beauty, that are not so fresh and lusty
as old men be."

Here Sir Frederick, to pacify M. Morello and to break their talk, would
not suffer Count Lewis to make answer, but interrupting him said: "Perhaps M. Morello is not altogether out of the way in saying that beauty
is not always good, for the beauty of women is many times cause of infinite evils in the world: hatred, war, mortality, and destruction, whereof
the razing of Troy can be a good witness. And beautiful women for the
¹⁰ most part be either proud and cruel (as is said) or unchaste, but M.
Morello would find no fault with that. There be also many wicked men
that have the comeliness of a beautiful countenance, and it seemeth that
nature hath so shaped them, because they may be the readier to deceive,
and that this amiable look were like a bait that covereth the hook."

Then M. Peter Bembo: "Believe not," quoth he, "but beauty is always good."

Here Count Lewis, because he would return again to his former purpose, interrupted him and said: "Since M. Morello passeth not to understand that which is so necessary for him, teach it me, and show me how old
²⁰ men may come by this happiness of love, for I will not care to be counted
old, so it may profit me."

M. Peter Bembo laughed and said: "First will I take the error out of
these gentlemen's minds, and afterward will I satisfy you also." So, beginning afresh, "My Lords," quoth he, "I would not that with speaking ill
of beauty, which is a holy thing, any of us, as profane and wicked, should
purchase him the wrath of God. Therefore to give M. Morello and Sir
Frederick warning that they lose not their sight, as Stesichorus did, a pain
most meet for whoso dispraiseth beauty, I say that beauty cometh of God,
and is like a circle, the goodness whereof is the center. And therefore, as
³⁰ there can be no circle without a center, no more can beauty be without
goodness. Whereupon doth very seldom an ill soul dwell in a beautiful
body. And therefore is the outward beauty a true sign of the inward
goodness, and in bodies this comeliness is imprinted more or less (as it
were) for a mark of the soul, whereby she is outwardly known; as in
trees, in which the beauty of the buds giveth a testimony of the goodness
of the fruit. And the very same happeneth in bodies, as it is seen that
palmisters by the visage know many times the conditions, and otherwhile
the thoughts of men. And which is more, in beasts also a man may discern
by the face the quality of the courage which in the body declareth itself
⁴⁰ as much as it can. Judge you how plainly in the face of a lion, a horse, and
an eagle, a man shall discern anger, fierceness, and stoutness; in lambs
and doves simpleness and very innocence; the crafty subtlety in foxes and

wolves, and the like (in a manner) in all other living creatures. The foul therefore for the most part be also evil, and the beautiful, good. Therefore it may be said that beauty is a face pleasant, merry, comely, and to be desired for goodness; and foulness a face dark, uglysome, unpleasant and to be shunned for ill. And in case you will consider all things, ye shall find that whatsoever is good and profitable hath also evermore the comeliness of beauty.

"Behold the state of this great engine of the world, which God created for the health and preservation of everything that was made. The heaven round beset with so many heavenly lights; and in the middle, the Earth 10 environed with the Elements, and upheld with the very weight of itself. The sun that, compassing about, giveth light to the whole, and in winter season draweth to the lowermost sign; afterward by little and little climbeth again to the other part. The moon, that of him taketh her light, according as she draweth nigh, or goeth farther from him. And the other five stars, that diversely keep the very same course. These things among themselves have such force by the knitting together of an order so necessarily framed that, with altering them any one jot, they should be all loosed, and the world would decay. They have also such beauty and comeliness, that all the wits men have can not imagine a more beauti- 20 ful matter.

"Think now of the shape of man, which may be called a little world; in whom every parcel of his body is seen to be necessarily framed by art and not by hap, and then the form all together most beautiful, so that it were a hard matter to judge whether the members, as the eyes, the nose, the mouth, the ears, the arms, the breast, and in like manner the other parts give either more profit to the countenance and the rest of the body, or comeliness. The like may be said of all other living creatures. Behold the feathers of fowls, the leaves and boughs of trees, which be given them of nature to keep them in their being, and yet have they withal a very great 30 sightliness. Leave nature, and come to art. What thing is so necessary in sailing vessels as the forepart, the sides, the main yards, the mast, the sails, the stern, oars, anchors, and tacklings; all these things notwithstanding are so well-favored in the eye that unto whoso beholdeth them they seem to have been found out as well for pleasure as for profit. Pillars and great beams uphold high buildings and palaces, and yet are they no less pleasureful unto the eyes of the beholders than profitable to the buildings. When men began first to build, in the middle of temples and houses they reared the ridge of the roof, not to make the works to have a better show, but because the water might the more commodiously avoid on both sides; yet 40 unto profit there was forthwith adjoined a fair sightliness, so that if under the sky where there falleth neither hail nor rain a man should build a temple, without a reared ridge, it is to be thought that it could have neither a sightly show nor any beauty. Beside other things, therefore, it giveth a great praise to the world in saying that it is beautiful. It is praised in saying the beautiful heaven, beautiful earth, beautiful sea, beautiful rivers, beautiful woods, trees, gardens, beautiful cities, beautiful churches, houses, armies. In conclusion this comely and holy beauty is a wonderous setting out of everything.

"And it may be said that good and beautiful be after a sort one self thing, especially in the bodies of men; of the beauty whereof the highest
10 cause (I suppose) is the beauty of the soul, the which, as a partner of the right and heavenly beauty, maketh sightly and beautiful whatever she toucheth; and most of all, if the body where she dwelleth, be not of so vile a matter that she cannot imprint in it her property. Therefore beauty is the true monument and spoil of the victory of the soul, when she with heavenly influence beareth rule over material and gross nature, and with her light overcometh the darkness of the body. It is not then to be spoken that beauty maketh women proud or cruel, although it seems so to M. Morello. Neither yet ought beautiful women to bear the blame of that hatred, mortality, and destruction which the unbridled appetites of men
20 are the cause of. I will not now deny but it is possible also to find in the world beautiful women unchaste, yet not because beauty inclineth them to unchaste living; for it rather plucketh them from it, and leadeth them into the way of vertuous conditions, through the affinity that beauty hath with goodness. But otherwhile ill bringing up, the continual provocations of lovers, tokens, poverty, hope, deceits, fear, and a thousand other matters overcome the steadfastness, yea of beautiful and good women, and for these and like causes may also beautiful men become wicked."

Then said the Lord Cesare: "In case the Lord Gaspar's saying be true of yesternight, there is no doubt but the fair women be more chaste than
30 the foul."

"And what was my saying?" quoth the Lord Gaspar.

The Lord Cesare answered: "If I do well bear in mind, your saying was that 'The women that are sued to, always refuse to satisfy him that sueth to them, but those that are not sued to, sue to others.' There is no doubt but the beautiful women have always more suitors, and be more instantly laid at in love than the foul. Therefore the beautiful always deny and consequently be more chaste than the foul, which, not being sued to, sue unto others."

M. Peter Bembo laughed and said: "This argument cannot be an-
40 swered to." Afterward he proceeded: "It chanceth also oftentimes that as the other senses, so the sight is deceived, and judgeth a face beautiful which indeed is not beautiful. And because in the eyes and in the whole

countenance of some women a man beholdeth otherwhile a certain lavish wantonness painted with dishonest flickerings, many—whom that manner delighteth because it promiseth them an easiness to come by the thing that they covet—call it beauty, but indeed it is a cloaked unshamefastness, unworthy of so honorable and holy a name."

M. Peter Bembo held his peace, and those lords still were earnest upon him to speak somewhat of this love and of the way to enjoy beauty aright, and at the last: "Methink," quoth he, "I have showed plainly enough that old men may love more happily than young, which was my drift; therefore it belongeth not me to enter any farther."

Count Lewis answered: "You have better declared the unluckiness of young men than the happiness of old men, whom you have not as yet taught what way they must follow in this love of theirs; only you have said that they must suffer themselves to be guided by reason, and the opinion of many is that it is impossible for love to stand with reason."

Bembo notwithstanding sought to make an end of reasoning, but the Duchess desired him to say on, and he began thus afresh: "Too unlucky were the nature of man, if our soul (in the which this so fervent coveting may lightly arise) should be driven to nourish it with that only which is common to her with beasts, and could not turn it to the other noble part which is proper to her. Therefore, since it is to your pleasure, I will not refuse to reason upon this noble matter. And because I know myself unworthy to talk of the most holy mysteries of love, I beseech him to lead my thought and my tongue so that I may show this excellent Courtier how to love contrary to the wonted manner of the common ignorant sort. And even as from my childhood I have dedicated all my whole life unto him, so also now that my words may be answerable to the same intent and to the praise of him, I say therefore that since the nature of man in youthful age is so much inclined to sense, it may be granted the Courtier, while he is young, to love sensually. But in case afterward also in his riper years, he chance to be set on fire with this coveting of love, he ought to be good and circumspect, and heedful that he beguile not himself to be led willfully into the wretchedness that in young men deserveth more to be pitied than blamed, and contrariwise in old men, more to be blamed than pitied. Therefore, when an amiable countenance of a beautiful woman cometh in his sight, that is accompanied with noble conditions and honest behaviors, so that, as one practiced in love, he wotteth well that his hue hath an agreement with hers, as soon as he is aware that his eyes snatch that image and carry it to the heart, and that the soul beginneth to behold it with pleasure and feeleth within herself the influence that stirreth her and by little and little setteth her in heat, and that those lively spirits that twinkle out through the eyes put continually fresh nourishment to the fire: he ought in this beginning to seek a speedy remedy and to raise up reason, and with her to fence the fortress of his heart, and to shut in such wise the passages against sense and appetites that they may enter neither with force nor subtle practice. Thus if the flame be quenched, the jeopardy is also quenched.

"But in case it continue or increase, then must the courtier determine (when he preceiveth he is taken) to shun throughly all filthiness of common love, and so enter into the holy way of love with the guide of reason, and first consider that the body, where that beauty shineth, is not the fountain from whence beauty springeth, but rather because beauty is bodiless and (as we have said) an heavenly shining beam, she loseth much of her honor when she is coupled with that vile subject and full of corruption, because the less she is partner thereof, the more perfect she is, and clean sundered from it, is most perfect. And as a man heareth not with his mouth, nor smelleth with his ears, no more can he also in any manner wise enjoy beauty, nor satisfy the desire that she stirreth up in our minds with feeling, but with the sense unto whom beauty is the very butt to level at; namely, the virtue of seeing. Let him lay aside therefore the blind judgment of the sense, and enjoy with his eyes the brightness, the comeliness, the loving sparkles, laughters, gestures, and all the other pleasant furnitures of beauty; especially with hearing the sweetness of her voice, the tunableness of her words, the melody of her singing and playing on instruments (in case the woman beloved be a musician); and so shall he with most dainty food feed the soul through the means of these two senses which have little bodily substance in them, and be the ministers of reason, without entering farther toward the body with coveting unto any longing otherwise than honest.

"Afterward let him obey, please, and honor with all reverence his woman, and reckon her more dear to him than his own life, and prefer all her commodities and pleasures before his own, and love no less in her the beauty of the mind, than of the body. Therefore let him have a care not to suffer her to run into any error, but with lessons and good exhortations seek always to frame her to modesty, to temperance, to true honesty, and so to work that there may never take place in her other than pure thoughts and far wide from all filthiness of vices. And thus in sowing of virtue in the garden of that mind, he shall also gather the fruits of most beautiful conditions, and savor them with a marvelous good relish. And this shall be the right engendering and imprinting of beauty in beauty, the which some hold opinion to be the end of love. In this manner shall our courtier be most acceptable to his lady, and she will always show herself toward him tractable, lowly, and sweet in language, and as willing to please him as to be beloved of him; and the wills of them both shall be most honest and agreeable, and they consequently shall be most happy."

Here M. Morello: "The engendering," quoth he, "of beauty in beauty aright were the engendering of a beautiful child in a beautiful woman. And I would think it a more manifest token a great deal that she loved her lover, if she pleased him with this than with the sweetness of language that you speak of."

Peter Bembo laughed and said: "You must not, M. Morello, pass your bounds. I may tell you, it is not a small token that a woman loveth when she giveth unto her lover her beauty, which is so precious a matter, and by the ways that be a passage to the soul (that is to say, the sight and the 10 hearing) sendeth the looks of her eyes, the image of her countenance, and the voice of her words, that pierce into the lover's heart, and give a witness of her love."

M. Morello said: "Looks and words may be, and oftentimes are, false witnesses. Therefore whoso hath not a better pledge of love (in my judgment) he is in an ill assurance. And surely I looked still that you would have made this woman of yours somewhat more courteous and free toward the courtier than my Lord Julian hath made his; but (meseemeth) ye be both of the property of those judges that (to appear wise) give sentence against their own." 20

Bembo said: "I am well pleased to have this woman much more courteous toward my Courtier not young than the Lord Julian's is to the young, and that with good reason, because mine coveteth but honest matters; and therefore may the woman grant him them all without blame. But my Lord Julian's woman, that is not so assured of the modesty of the young man, ought to grant him the honest matters only and deny him the dishonest. Therefore more happy is mine, that hath granted him whatsoever he requireth, than the other, that hath part granted and part denied.

"And because you may, moreover, the better understand that reason- 30 able love is more happy than sensual, I say unto you that selfsame things in sensual ought to be denied otherwhile, and in reasonable, granted; because in the one, they be honest, and in the other dishonest. Therefore the woman to please her good lover, beside the granting him merry countenances, familiar and secret talk, jesting, dallying, hand in hand, may also lawfully and without blame come to kissing, which in sensual love, according to Lord Julian's rules, is not lawful. For since a kiss is a knitting together both of body and soul, it is to be feared lest the sensual lover will be more inclined to the part of the body than of the soul; but the reasonable lover woteth well that although the mouth be a parcel of the body, 40 yet is it an issue for the words that be the interpreters of the soul, and for the inward breath which is also called the soul; and therefore hath a delight to join his mouth with the woman's beloved with a kiss, not to stir him to any unhonest desire, but because he feeleth that that bond is the opening of an entry to the souls which, drawn with a coveting the one of the other, pour themselves by turn, the one into the other's body, and be so mingled together that each of them hath two souls, and one alone so framed of them both ruleth (in a manner) two bodies.

"Whereupon a kiss may be said to be rather a coupling together of the soul than of the body, because it hath such force in her that it draweth her unto it, and (as it were) separateth her from the body. For this do all chaste lovers covet a kiss as a coupling of souls together. And therefore Plato the divine lover saith that in kissing his soul came as far as his lips to depart out of the body. And because the separating of the soul from the matters of the sense and the thorough coupling her with matters of understanding may be betokened by a kiss, Solomon saith in his heavenly book of ballads: 'Oh that he would kiss me with a kiss of his mouth,' to express the desire he had that his soul might be ravished through heavenly love to the beholding of heavenly beauty in such manner that coupling herself inwardly with it, she might forsake the body."

They stood all hearkening heedfully to Bembo's reasoning, and after he had stayed a while and saw that none spake, he said: "Since you have made me to begin to show our not young Courtier this happy love, I will lead him yet somewhat farther forward, because to stand still at this stay were somewhat perilous for him, considering (as we have oftentimes said) the soul is most inclined to the senses, and for all reason with discourse chooseth well, and knoweth that beauty not to spring of the body, and therefore setteth a bridle to the unhonest desires, yet to behold it always in that body doth oftentimes corrupt the right judgment. And where no other inconvenience ensueth upon it, one's absence from the wight beloved carryeth a great passion with it, because the influence of that beauty when it is present giveth a wondrous delight to the lover, and setting his heart on fire, quickeneth and melteth certain virtues in a trance and congealed in the soul, the which, nourished with the heat of love, flow about and go bubbling nigh the heart and thrust out through the eyes those spirits which be most fine vapors made of the purest and clearest part of the blood, which receive the image of beauty and deck it with a thousand sundry furnitures. Whereupon the soul taketh a delight, and with a certain wonder is aghast, and yet enjoyeth she it, and (as it were) astonied together with the pleasure, feeleth the fear and reverence that men accustomably have toward holy matters and thinketh herself to be in paradise.

"The lover therefore that considereth only the beauty in the body loseth this treasure and happiness as soon as the woman beloved with her

departure leaveth the eyes without their brightness, and consequently the
soul, as a widow, without her joy. For since beauty is far off, that influence of love setteth not the heart on fire, as it did in presence. Whereupon
the pores be dried up and withered, and yet doth the remembrance of
beauty somewhat stir those virtues of the soul in such wise that they seek
to scatter abroad the spirits, and they, finding the ways closed up, have
no issue, and still they seek to get out and so, with those shootings inclosed,
prick the soul and torment her bitterly, as young children when in their
tender gums they begin to breed teeth. And hence come the tears, sighs,
vexations, and torments of lovers, because the soul is always in affliction ₁₀
and travail and (in a manner) waxeth wode, until the beloved beauty
cometh before her once again; and then is she immediately pacified and
taketh breath, and throughly bent to it, is nourished with most dainty
food, and by her will would never depart from so sweet a sight. To avoid,
therefore, the torment of this absence, and to enjoy beauty without passion, the Courtier, by the help of reason, must full and wholly call back
again the coveting of the body to beauty alone, and (in what he can)
behold it in itself simple and pure, and frame it within in his imagination
sundered from all matter, and so make it friendly and loving to his soul,
and there enjoy it, and have it with him day and night, in every time and ₂₀
place, without mistrust ever to lose it, keeping always fast in mind that
the body is a most diverse thing from beauty, and not only not increaseth,
but diminisheth the perfection of it. In this wise shall our not young
Courtier be out of all bitterness and wretchedness that young men feel
(in a manner) continually, as jealousies, suspicions, disdains, angers,
desperations, and certain rages full of madness; whereby many times they
be led into so great error that some do not only beat the women whom
they love but rid themselves out of their life. He shall do no wrong to the
husband, father, brethren or kinsfolk of the woman beloved. He shall
not bring her in slander. He shall not be in case with much ado otherwhile ₃₀
to refrain his eyes and tongue from discovering his desires to others. He
shall not take thought at departure or in absence, because he shall evermore carry his precious treasure about with him shut fast within his heart.
And beside, through the virtue of imagination he shall fashion within
himself that beauty much more fair than it is indeed.

"But among these commodities the lover shall find another yet far
greater, in case he will take this love for a stair (as it were) to climb up
to another part higher than it. The which he shall bring to pass, if he
will go and consider with himself what a strict bond it is to be always in
the trouble to behold the beauty of one body alone. And therefore, to ₄₀
come out of this so narrow a room, he shall gather in his thought by little
and little so many ornaments that, meddling all beauties together, he

shall make an universal concept and bring the multitude of them to the
unity of one alone, that is generally spread over all the nature of man. And
thus shall he behold no more the particular beauty of one woman, but an
universal that decketh out all bodies. Whereupon, being made dim with
this greater light, he shall not pass upon the lesser, and burning in a more
excellent flame, he shall little esteem it that he set great store by at the first.
This stair of love, though it be very noble and such as few arrive at it, yet
is it not in this sort to be called perfect, for so much as where the imagination is of force to make conveyance and hath no knowledge but through
10 those beginnings that the senses help her withal, she is not clean purged
from gross darkness: and therefore, though she do consider that universal
beauty in sunder and in itself alone, yet doth she not well and clearly discern it, nor without some doubtfulness, by reason of the agreement that
the fancies have with the body. Wherefore such as come to this love are
like young birds almost flush, which for all they flutter a little their tender
wings, yet dare not stray far from the nest, nor commit themselves to
the wind and open weather.

"When our Courtier therefore shall be come to this point, although he
may be called a good and happy lover in respect of them that be drowned
20 in the misery of sensual love, yet will I not have him to set his heart at
rest, but boldly proceed farther, following the high way after his guide,
that leadeth him to the point of true happiness. And thus instead of going
out of his wit with thought, as he must do that will consider the bodily
beauty, he may come into his wit, to behold the beauty that is seen with
the eyes of the mind, which then begin to be sharp and through-seeing
when the eyes of the body lose the flower of their sightliness. Therefore
the soul rid of vices, purged with the studies of true philosophy, occupied
in spiritual, and exercised in matters of understanding, turning her to
the beholding of her own substance, as it were raised out of a most deep
30 sleep, openeth the eyes that all men have, and few occupy, and seeth in
herself a shining beam of that light which is the true image of the angelic
beauty partened with her, whereof she also partneth with the body a feeble
shadow. Therefore waxed blind about earthly matters, [she] is made
most quick of sight about heavenly. And otherwhile when the stirring
virtues of the body are withdrawn alone through earnest beholding, either
fast bound through sleep, when she is not hindered by them, she feeleth a
certain privy smell of the right angelic beauty; and, ravished with the
shining of that light, beginneth to be inflamed, and so greedily followeth
after, that (in a manner) she waxeth drunken and beside herself for
40 coveting to couple herself with it, having found (to her weening) the
footsteps of God, in the beholding of whom (as in her happy end) she
seeketh to settle herself. And therefore, burning in this most happy flame,

she ariseth to the noblest part of her (which is the understanding) and there, no more shadowed with the dark night of earthly matters, seeth the heavenly beauty.

"But yet doth she not for all that enjoy it altogether perfectly, because she beholdeth it only in her particular understanding, which cannot conceive the passing great universal beauty; whereupon, not throughly satisfied with this benefit, love giveth unto the soul a greater happiness. For like as through the particular beauty of one body he guideth her to the universal beauty of all bodies, even so in the last degree of perfection, through particular understanding he guideth her to the universal under- 10 standing. Thus the soul, kindled in the most holy fire of true heavenly love, fleeth to couple herself with the nature of angels, and not only clean forsaketh sense, but hath no more need of the discourse of reason; for, being changed into an angel, she understandeth all things that may be understood; and without any veil or cloud, she seeth the main sea of the pure heavenly beauty and receiveth it into her, and enjoyeth that sovereign happiness that cannot be comprehended of the senses.

"Since, therefore, the beauties which we daily see with these our dim eyes in bodies subject to corruption, that nevertheless be nothing else but dreams and most thin shadows of beauty, seem unto us so well favored 20 and comely that oftentimes they kindle in us a most burning fire, and with such delight that we reckon no happiness may be compared to it that we feel otherwhile through the only look which the beloved countenance of a woman casteth at us; what happy wonder, what blessed abashment may we reckon that to be that taketh the souls which come to have a sight of the heavenly beauty? What sweet flame? What sweet incense may a man believe that to be which ariseth of the fountain of the sovereign and right beauty? Which is the origin of all other beauty; which never increaseth nor diminisheth, always beautiful, and of itself, as well on the one part as on the other, most simple, only like itself, and partner of none 30 other, but in such wise beautiful that all other beautiful things be beautiful because they be partners of the beauty of it.

"This is the beauty inseparable from the high bounty which with her voice calleth and draweth to her all things; and not only to the endowed with understanding giveth understanding; to the reasonable reason, to the sensual sense and appetite to live, but also partaketh with plants and stones (as a print of herself) stirring, and the natural provocation of their properties. So much therefore is this love greater and happier than others as the cause that stirreth it is more excellent. And therefore, as common fire trieth gold and maketh it fine, so this most holy fire in souls destroyeth 40 and consumeth whatsoever there is mortal in them, and relieveth and maketh beautiful the heavenly part, which at the first by reason of the

sense was dead and buried in them. This is the great fire in the which (the
poets write) that Hercules was burned on the top of the mountain Oeta,
and through that consuming with fire, after his death was holy and immortal. This is the fiery bush of Moses; the divided tongues of fire; the
inflamed chariot of Helias, which doubleth grace and happiness in their
souls that be worthy to see it when they forsake this earthly baseness and
flee up unto heaven. Let us therefore bend all our force and thoughts of
soul to this most holy light that showeth us the way which leadeth to
heaven; and after it, putting off the affections we were clad withal at our
10 coming down, let us climb up the stairs, which at the lowermost step have
the shadow of sensual beauty, to the high mansion place where the heavenly, amiable, and right beauty dwelleth, which lieth hid in the innermost secrets of God, lest unhallowed eyes should come to the sight of it;
and there shall we find a most happy end for our desires, true rest for our
travails, certain remedy for miseries, a most healthful medicine for sickness, a most sure haven in the troublesome storms of the tempestuous sea
of this life.

   "What tongue mortal is there then (O most holy love), that can sufficiently praise thy worthiness? Thou most beautiful, most good, most wise,
20 art derived of the unity of heavenly beauty, goodness and wisdom, and
therein dost thou abide, and unto it, through it (as in a circle) turnest
about. Thou the most sweet bond of the world, a mean betwixt heavenly
and earthly things, with a bountiful temper bindest the high virtues to the
government of the lower, and turning back the minds of mortal men to
their beginning, couplest them with it. Thou with agreement bringest the
Elements in one, stirrest nature to bring forth, and that which ariseth
and is born for the succession of the life. Thou bringest severed matters
into one, to the imperfect givest perfection, to the unlike likeness, to enmity amity, to the earth fruits, to the sea calmness, to the heaven lively
30 light. Thou art the father of true pleasures, of grace, peace, lowliness,
and good will; enemy to rude wildness and sluggishness—to be short,
the beginning and end of all goodness. And forsomuch as thou delightest
to dwell in the flower of beautiful bodies and beautiful souls, I suppose
that thy abiding place is now here among us, and from above otherwhile
showest thyself a little to the eyes and minds of them that be worthy to
see thee.

   "Therefore vouchsafe (Lord) to harken to our prayers, pour thyself
into our hearts, and with the brightness of thy most holy fire lighten our
darkness, and like a trusty guide in this blind maze, show us the right
40 way; reform the falsehood of the senses, and after long wandering in
vanity give us the right and sound joy. Make us to smell those spiritual

savors that relieve the virtues of the understanding, and to hear the heavenly harmony so tunable that no discord of passion take place any more in us. Make us drunken with the bottomless fountain of contentation that always doth delight, and never giveth fill, and that giveth a smack of the right bliss unto whoso drinketh of the running and clear water thereof. Purge with the shining beams of thy light our eyes from misty ignorance, that they may no more set by mortal beauty, and well perceive that the things which at the first they thought themselves to see, be not indeed, and those that they saw not, to be in effect. Accept our souls that be offered unto thee for a sacrifice. Burn them in the lively flame that wasteth all gross filthiness, that, after they be clean sundered from the body, they may be coupled with an everlasting and most sweet bond to the heavenly beauty. And we, severed from ourselves, may be changed like right lovers into the beloved, and after we be drawn from the earth, admitted to the feast of the angels; where fed with immortal ambrosia and nectar, in the end we may die a most happy and lively death, as in times past died the fathers of old time, whose souls with most fervent zeal of beholding thou didst hale from the body and coupledst them with God."

When Bembo had hitherto spoken with such vehemency that a man would have thought him (as it were) ravished and beside himself, he stood still without once moving, holding his eyes toward heaven as astonied, when the Lady Emilia, which together with the rest gave most diligent ear to this talk, took him by the pleat of his garment and plucking him a little, said: "Take heed (M. Peter) that these thoughts make not your soul also to forsake the body."

"Madam," answered M. Peter, "it should not be the first miracle that love hath wrought in me."

Then the Duchess and all the rest began afresh to be instant upon M. Bembo that he would proceed once more in his talk, and everyone thought he felt in his mind (as it were) a certain sparkle of that godly love that pricked him, and they all coveted to hear further; but M. Bembo: "My Lords," quoth he, "I have spoken what the holy fury of love hath (unsought for) indited to me. Now that (it seemeth) he inspireth me no more, I wot not what to say. And I think verily that love will not have his secrets discovered any farther, nor that the Courtier should pass the degree that his pleasure is I should show him, and therefore it is not perhaps lawful to speak any more in this matter."

"Surely," quoth the Duchess, "if the not young Courtier be such a one that he can follow this way which you have showed him, of right he ought to be satisfied with so great a happiness, and not to envy the younger."

Then the Lord Cesare Gonzaga: "The way," quoth he, "that leadeth to this happiness is so steep (in my mind) that I believe it will be much ado to get to it."

The Lord Gaspar said: "I believe it be hard to get up for men, but impossible for women."

The Lady Emilia laughed and said: "If ye fall so often to offend us, I promise you ye shall be no more forgiven."

The Lord Gaspar answered: "It is no offence to you in saying that women's souls be not so purged from passions as men's be, nor accustomed
10 in beholdings, as M. Peter hath said is necessary for them to be that will taste of the heavenly love. Therefore it is not read that ever woman hath had this grace; but many men have had it, as Plato, Socrates, Plotinus, and many other; and a number of our holy fathers, as Saint Francis, in whom a fervent spirit of love imprinted the most holy seal of the five wounds. And nothing but the virtue of love could hale up Saint Paul the Apostle to the sight of those secrets which is not lawful for man to speak of, nor show Saint Stephen the heavens open."

Here answered the Lord Julian: "In this point men shall nothing pass women, for Socrates himself doth confess that all the mysteries of love
20 which he knew were opened unto him by a woman, which was Diotima. And the Angel that with the fire of love imprinted the five wounds in Saint Francis hath also made some women worthy of the same print in our age. You must remember, moreover, that Saint Mary Magdalen had many faults forgiven her because she loved much, and perhaps with no less grace than Saint Paul was she many times through angelic love haled up to the third heaven. And many other (as I showed you yesterday more at large) that for love of the name of Christ have not passed upon life, nor feared torments, nor any other kind of death how terrible and cruel ever it were. And they were not (as M. Peter will have his Courtier to
30 be) aged, but soft and tender maidens, and in the age when he saith that sensual love ought to be borne withal in men."

The Lord Gaspar began to prepare himself to speak, but the Duchess: "Of this," quoth she, "let M. Peter be judge, and the matter shall stand to his verdict, whether women be not as meet for heavenly love as men. But because the plead between you may happen be too long, it shall not be amiss to defer it until tomorrow."

"Nay, tonight," quoth the Lord Cesare Gonzaga.

"And how can it be tonight?" quoth the Duchess.

The Lord Cesare answered: "Because it is day already"; and showed
40 her the light that began to enter in at the clefts of the windows.

Then every man arose upon his feet with much wonder, because they had not thought that the reasonings had lasted longer than the accustomed

wont, saving only that they were begun much later, and with their pleasantness had deceived so the Lords' minds that they wist not of the going
away of the hours. And not one of them felt any heaviness of sleep in his
eyes, the which often happeneth when a man is up after his accustomed
hour to go to bed. When the windows then were opened on the side of
the palace that hath his prospect toward the high top of Mount Catri,
they saw already risen in the east a fair morning like unto the color of
roses, and all stars voided, saving only the sweet governess of the heaven,
Venus, which keepeth the bounds of the night and the day; from which
appeared to blow a sweet blast, that, filling the air with a biting cold, be- 10
gan to quicken the tunable notes of the pretty birds among the hushing
woods of the hills at hand. Whereupon they all, taking their leave with
reverence of the Duchess, departed toward their lodgings without torch,
the light of the day sufficing. And as they were now passing out at the
great chamber door, the Lord General turned him to the Duchess, and
said: "Madam, to take up the variance between the Lord Gaspar and
the Lord Julian, we will assemble this night with the judge sooner than
we did yesterday."

The Lady Emilia answered, "Upon condition that in case my Lord
Gaspar will accuse women, and give them (as his wont is) some false 20
report, he will also put us in surety to stand to trial, for I reckon him a
wavering starter."

*　　*　　*　　*　　*

A brief rehearsal of the chief conditions and qualities in a Courtier.

To be well born and of a good stock.

To be of a mean stature, rather with the least than too high, and well
made to his proportion.

To be portly and amiable in countenance unto whoso beholdeth him. 30

Not to be womanish in his sayings or doings.

Not to praise himself unshamefully and out of reason.

Not to crake and boast of his acts and good qualities.

To shun affectation or curiosity about all thing in all things.

To do his feats with a slight, as though they were rather naturally in
him than learned with study; and use a recklessness to cover art, without minding greatly what he hath in hand, to a man's seeming.

Not to carry about tales and trifling news.

Not to be overseen in speaking words otherwhile that may offend where
he meant it not. 40

Not to be stubborn, willfull nor full of contention; nor to contrary and
overthwart men after a spiteful sort.

Not to be a babbler, brawler or chatter, nor lavish of his tongue.

Not to be given to vanity and lightness, nor to have a fantastical head.

No liar.

No fond flatterer.

To be well spoken and fair languaged.

To be wise and well seen in discourses upon states.

To have a judgment to frame himself to the manners of the country wherever he cometh.

To be able to allege good and probable reasons upon every matter.

10 To be seen in tongues, and especially in Italian, French, and Spanish.

To direct all things to a good end.

To procure wherever he goeth that men may first conceive a good opinion of him before he cometh there.

To fellowship himself for the most part with men of the best sort and of
most estimation, and with his equals, so he be also beloved of his inferiors.

To play for his pastime at dice and cards, not wholly for money's sake,
nor fume and chafe in his loss.

To be meanly seen in the play at chess, and not overcunning.

20 To be pleasantly disposed in common matters and in good company.

To speak and write the language that is most in use among the common people, without inventing new words, inkhorn terms, or strange
phrases, and such as be grown out of use by long time.

To be handsome and cleanly in his apparel.

To make his garments after the fashion of the most, and those to be
black, or of some darkish and sad color, not garish.

To get him an especial and hearty friend to company withal.

Not to be ill tongued, especially against his betters.

Not to use any fond sauciness or presumption.

30 To be no envious or malicious person.

To be an honest, a fair conditioned man, and of an upright conscience.

To have the virtues of the mind, as justice, manliness, wisdom, temperance, staidness, noble courage, sober mood, etc.

To be more than indifferently well seen in learning, in the Latin and
Greek tongues.

Not to be rash, nor persuade himself to know the thing that he knoweth
not.

To confess his ignorance, when he seeth time and place thereto, in such
qualities as he knoweth himself to have no manner skill in.

40 To be brought to show his feats and qualities at the desire and request of
others, and not rashly press to it of himself.

To speak always of matters likely, lest he be counted a liar in reporting of
wonders and strange miracles.

To have the feat of drawing and painting.

To dance well without over nimble footings or too busy tricks.

To sing well upon the book.

To play upon the lute, and sing to it with the ditty.

To play upon the viol, and all other instruments with frets.

To delight and refresh the hearers' minds in being pleasant, feat conceited, and a merry talker, applied to time and place.

Not to use sluttish and ruffianlike pranks with any man.

Not to become a jester or scoffer to put any man out of countenance.

To consider whom he doth taunt and where, for he ought not to mock 10 poor silly souls, nor men of authority, nor common ribalds and persons given to mischief, which deserve punishment.

To be skilful in all kind of martial feats both on horseback and afoot, and well practised in them; which is his chief profession, though his understanding be the less in all other things.

To play well at fence upon all kind of weapons.

To be nimble and quick at the play at tennis.

To hunt and hawk.

To ride and manage well his horse.

To be a good horseman for every saddle. 20

To swim well.
To leap well.
To run well.
To vault well.
To wrestle well.
To cast the stone well.
To cast the bar well.

Seldom in open sight of the people but privily with himself alone, or among his friends and familiars.

To run well at tilt, and at ring. 30
To tourney.
To fight at barriers.
To keep a passage or straight.
To play at *jogo di canne*.
To run at bull.
To fling a spear or dart.

These things in open sight to delight the common people withal.

Not to run, wrestle, leap, nor cast the stone or bar with men of the country, except he be sure to get the victory. 40

To set out himself in feats of chivalry in open shows well provided of horse and harness, well trapped and armed, so that he may show himself nimble on horseback.

Never to be of the last that appear in the lists at jousts, or in any open shows.

To have in triumphs comely armor, bases, scarves, trappings, liveries, and such other things of sightly and merry colors, and rich to behold, with witty poesies and pleasant devices to allure unto him chiefly the eyes of the people.

To disguise himself in maskery either on horseback or afoot, and to take the shape upon him that shall be contrary to the feat that he mindeth to work.

10 To undertake his bold feats and courageous enterprises in war out of company, and in the sight of the most noble personages in the camp, and (if it be possible) before his Prince's eyes.

Not to hazard himself in foraging and spoiling or in enterprises of great danger and small estimation, though he be sure to gain by it.

Not to wait upon or serve a wicked and naughty person.

Not to seek to come up by any naughty or subtle practise.

Not to commit any mischievous or wicked fact at the will and commandment of his Lord or Prince.

Not to follow his own fancy, or alter the express words in any point of

20 his commission from his Prince or Lord, unless he be assured that the profit will be more, in case it have good success, than the damage, if it succeed ill.

To use evermore toward his Prince or Lord the respect that becometh the servant toward his master.

To endeavor himself to love, please, and obey his Prince in honesty.

Not to covet to press into the Chamber or other secret part where his Prince is withdrawn at any time.

Never to be sad, melancholy, or sullen before his Prince.

Seldom or never to sue to his Lord for anything for himself.

30 His suit to be honest and reasonable when he sueth for others.

To reason of pleasant and merry matters when he is withdrawn with him into private and secret places, always doing him to understand the truth without dissimulation or flattery.

Not to love promotions so, that a man should think he could not live without them; nor unshamefastly to beg any office.

To refuse them after such a comely sort, that the Prince offering him them may have a cause to offer them with a more instance.

Not to press to his Prince wherever he be, to hold him with a vain tale, that others should think him in favor with him.

40 To consider well what it is that he doeth or speaketh, where, in presence of whom, what time, why, his age, his profession, the end, and the means.

The final end of a courtier, whereto all his good conditions and honest qualities tend, is to become an instructor and teacher of his Prince or Lord, inclining him to virtuous practises; and to be frank and free with him, after he is once in favor, in matters touching his honor and estimation, always putting him in mind to follow virtue and to flee vice, opening unto him the commodities of the one and inconveniences of the other; and to shut his ear against flatterers, which are the first beginning of self-seeking and all ignorance.

His conversation with women to be always gentle, sober, meek, lowly, modest, serviceable, comely, merry; not biting or slandering with jests, nips, frumps, or railings, the honesty of any.

His love toward women not to be sensual or fleshly, but honest and godly, and more ruled with reason than appetite; and to love better the beauty of the mind than of the body.

Not to withdraw his mistress' good will from his fellow lover with reviling or railing at him, but with virtuous deeds, and honest conditions, and with deserving more than he at her hands for honest affection's sake.

Of the chief conditions and qualities in a waiting gentlewoman.

To be well born and of a good house.

To flee affectation or curiosity.

To have a good grace in all her doings.

To be of good conditions and well brought up.

To be witty and foreseeing, not heady and of a running wit.

Not to be haughty, envious, ill-tongued, light, contentious, nor untowardly.

To win and keep her in her Lady's favor and all others'.

To do the exercises meet for women, comely and with a good grace.

To take heed that she give none occasion to be ill reported of.

To commit no vice, nor yet to be had in suspicion of any vice.

To have the virtues of the mind, as wisdom, justice, nobleness of courage, temperance, strength of the mind, continency, sober mood, etc.

To be good and discreet.

To have the understanding, being married, how to order her husband's substance, her house and children, and to play the good housewife.

To have a sweetness in language and a good utterance to entertain all kind of men with communication worth the hearing, honest, applied to time and place, and to the degree and disposition of the person which is her principal profession.

To accompany sober and quiet manners and honesty with a lively quickness of wit.

To be esteemed no less chaste, wise and courteous, than pleasant, feat conceited, and sober.

Not to make wise to abhor company and talk, though somewhat of the wantonest, to arise and forsake them for it.

To give the hearing of such kind of talk with blushing and bashfulness.

Not to speak words of dishonesty and bawdry to show herself pleasant, free, and a good fellow.

Not to use over much familiarity without measure and bridle.

10 Not willingly to give ear to such as report ill of other women.

To be heedful in her talk that she offend not where she meant it not.

To beware of praising herself indiscreetly, and of being too tedious and noisome in her talk.

Not to mingle with grave and sad matters, merry jests and laughing matters; nor with mirth, matters of gravity.

To be circumspect that she offend no man in her jesting and taunting, to appear thereby of a ready wit.

Not to make wise to know the thing that she knoweth not, but with soberness get her estimation with that she knoweth.

20 Not to come on loft nor use too swift measures in her dancing.

Not to use in singing or playing upon instruments too much division and busy points, that declare more cunning than sweetness.

To come to dance, or to show her music, with suffering herself to be first prayed somewhat and drawn to it.

To apparel herself so that she seem not fond and fantastical.

To set out her beauty and disposition of person with meet garments that shall best become her, but as feigningly as she can, making semblant to bestow no labor about it, nor yet to mind it.

To have an understanding in all things belonging to the Courtier, that

30 she may give her judgment to commend and to make of gentlemen according to their worthiness and deserts.

To be learned.

To be seen in the most necessary languages.

To draw and paint.

To dance.

To devise sports and pastimes.

Not to be light of credit that she is beloved, though a man commune familiarly with her of love.

To shape him that is oversaucy with her, or that hath small respect in

40 his talk, such an answer that he may well understand she is offended with him.

To take the loving communication of a sober gentleman in an other signification, seeking to stray from that purpose.

To acknowledge the praises which he giveth her as the gentleman's courtesy, in case she cannot dissemble the understanding of them, debasing
her own deserts.

To be heedful and remember that men may with less jeopardy show to be
in love than women.

To give her lover nothing but her mind, when either the hatred of her
husband or the love that he beareth to others inclineth her to love.

To love one that she may marry withal, being a maiden and minding to
love.

To show such a one all signs and tokens of love, saving such as may put
him in any dishonest hope.

To use a somewhat more familiar conversation with men well grown in
years than with young men.

To make herself beloved for her deserts, amiableness, and good grace,
not with any uncomely or dishonest behavior, or flickering enticement
with wanton looks, but with virtue and honest conditions.

The final end whereto the Courtier applieth all his good conditions, properties, feats and qualities, serveth also for a waiting gentlewoman to
grow in favor with her Lady, and by that means so to instruct her and
train her to virtue, that she may both refrain from vice and from committing any dishonest matter, and also abhor flatterers and give herself
to understand the full troth in every thing, without entering into self-
seeking and ignorance, either of other outward things, or yet of her
own self.

JOHN FOXE

The Introduction and Notes are at page 1310

FROM *Actes and Monuments,* 1563

*The history of Master John Rogers, most constantly suffer-
ing for the testimony of the truth.*

· · ·

JOHN ROGERS, brought up in the University of Cambridge, where he
profitably travailed in good learning, at the length was chosen and called
by the Merchants Adventurers to be their chaplain at Antwerp in Brabant,
where he served them to their good contentation many years. It chanced

him there to fall in company with that worthy martyr of God, William
Tyndale, and with Miles Coverdale (which both for the hatred they bare
to popish idolatry and for the love they bare toward true religion had forsaken their native country). In conferring with them on the Scriptures,
he came to great knowledge in the Gospel of God, in so much that he
cast off the heavy yoke of popery, perceiving it to be impure and filthy
idolatry, and joined himself with them two in that painful and most profitable labor of translating the Bible into the English tongue, which is entitled *The Translation of Thomas Matthew.*

10

*   *   *   *   *

After that John Rogers, as ye have heard, had been long and straitly
imprisoned, lodged in Newgate amongst thieves, often examined and very
uncharitably entreated, and at the length unjustly and most cruelly, by
wicked Winchester, condemned the fourth of February, in the year of
Our Lord 1554, being Monday, in the morning he was warned suddenly
by the wife of Newgate to prepare himself to the fire: who, then being
sound asleep, scarce with much shogging could be awaked. At length
being raised and awaked and bid to make haste, then saith he, "If it be
20 so, I need not tie my points." And so was had down, first to Bonner to
be disgraded. That done, he craved of Bonner but one petition. Bonner
asking what that should be, Nothing, saith he, but that he might talk a
few words with his wife before his burning. What, that could not be obtained of him? Then saith he, "You declare your charity, what it is."
And so he was brought into Smithfield by Master Chester and Master
Wodrose, then sheriffs of London, there to be burnt, where he shewed
most constant patiency, not using many words, for he could not be permitted, but only exhorting the people constantly to remain in that faith
and true doctrine which he before had taught and they had learned, and,
30 for the confirmation whereof, he was not only content patiently to suffer
and bear all such bitterness and cruelty as had been shewed him, but also
most gladly to resign up his life, and to give his flesh to the consuming
fire for the testimony of the same.

After these few words, the fire was put unto him, and when it had
taken hold both upon his legs and shoulders, he, as one feeling no smart,
washed his hands in the flame as though it had been in cold water. And
after lifting up his hands unto heaven, not removing the same until such
time as the devouring fire had consumed them, most mildly this happy
martyr yielded up his spirit into the hands of his Heavenly Father.

40

*   *   *   *

*The life, condemnation, and death of the reverend father in
Christ, Dr. Thomas Cranmer, archbishop of Canterbury,
which was burned at Oxford for the confession of true doctrine, under Queen Mary. Anno Domini 1556, the 21 of
March.*

THOMAS CRANMER, archbishop of Canterbury, born in Nottinghamshire
in the year of Our Lord 1489, the second day of July, had to his father
Thomas Cranmer, being of the same name, descended of a worshipful
stock whose ancestors were worthy esquires. His mother also was a gentlewoman named Agnes Hatfield, descending of like family and flourishing
in like virtue. In his childhood, so soon as by the capacity of his age he
was ready to take learning, he had the parish clerk of Aslocton town for
his first teacher. Under whom, not being very well instructed, when he
had spent some time in the first rudiments of grammar and seemed to be
well entered, being fourteen year old he was sent of his mother to Cambridge to be further instructed in high learning.

It was in that time when all good authors and fine writers being neglected, filthy barbarousness was embraced in all schools and universities.
The names and numbers of liberal arts did only remain; the arts themselves were clean lost. Logic was gone out of kind into sophistical trifles.
Philosophy, both moral and natural, was miserably defaced with infinite
questions and subtleties. The use of tongues and eloquent learning was
either small or none at all. Yea, and divinity itself was fallen into the state
that, being laden with articles and distinctions, it served rather for the
gain of a few than for the edification of many. Unluckily, therefore, so
good a wit, falling into these unhappy times, is constrained to spend a
great part of his youth (worthy of better instruction) in the peevish questions of Duns, and other masters of the same sort, until he was 20 year
old. At the length, after so long darkness of barbarism, the tongues and
other good learning began by little and little to spring up again, and the
books of Faber and Erasmus began to be much occupied and had in good
estimation with a number of good authors beside. In whom the same
Cranmer, taking no small pleasure, did daily rub away his old rustiness on
them, as upon a whetstone, until at the length, when Martin Luther was
risen up, the more bright and happy day of God's knowledge did waken
men's minds to the clear light of the truth.

At which time, when he was about 30 year old, omitting all other
studies, he gave his whole mind to discuss matters of religion on both parts.
And because he saw that he could not judge of these matters unless he
first considered and beheld the very fountains thereof, before he would

addict his mind to any opinion he spent whole three years in overreading
the books of Holy Scriptures. After he had laid this foundation, no less
wisely than happily, when he thought himself sufficiently prepared, and
being now instructed with more ripeness of judgment, like a greedy
merchant of all good things, he gave his mind to read all kind of authors.
In the meanwhile, being addict to no part or age, but as a considering beholder or scholar of Pythagoras, he weighed all men's opinions with secret
judgment. He read the old writers, so as he despised not the new, and
all this while, in handling and conferring writers' judgments, he was a
10 slow reader but an earnest marker. He never came to any writer's book
without pen and ink, but yet so that he exercised his memory no less than
his pen. Whatsoever controversy came, he gathered every author's sentence briefly and the diversity of their judgments into commonplaces,
which he had prepared for that purpose. Or else, if the matter were too
long to write out, he noted the place of the author and the number of
the leaf, whereby he might have the more help for his memory. And thus
with great diligence he followeth this order of study until he was 35 year
old, and then he obtained that degree which in the school of divinity is
highest, and maketh of scholars teachers, and so was made Doctor of
20 Divinity.

About this time, the controversy of King Henry the Eighth's marriage
with Katherine, daughter of Ferdinand, king of Spain, was in question,
which, when she had been first married to Arthur, his brother, the question arose in the schools of divines and universities whether she that had
married the one brother and had been carnally known of him might lawfully marry with the other. Concerning which matter we have at large
discoursed before in the time and history of King Henry the Eighth, page
455, column 2. Therefore, when the king was persuaded by Longland,
bishop of Lincoln, that the marriage was unlawful and contrary to the
30 laws of God, it was decreed that six of the best learned should be chosen
out of either the universities of Cambridge and Oxford to decise this
matter, whether they thought it lawful that he might be married with
her that had been before his brother's wife. Among these twelve was
Cranmer one: but because at that time he was abroad from the university,
another was put in his stead which should supply his room while he was
absent. After long debating to and fro, the twelve agreed on this sentence,
that, though the marriage were unlawful of itself, yet, by dispensation of
the pope, it might be permitted. Not long after, when Dr. Cranmer, returning to the university, was demanded his sentence of that matter, he
40 so contended in arguments, disputing with the doctors, and prevailing in
the cause, that by good learning he pervinced and turned five of them
to his side and sentence; so that by and by upon that, through all Cam-

bridge, in meetings, in talkings, in drinkings, in the schools, and in private
houses, this was a common matter and question in every man's mouth,
whether the pope had authority to release God's law that one brother
might marry another brother's wife. And it came to this point, that most
judged against the pope's authority.

. . . Wherefore Cranmer, being sent for home by the king, was not
long after sent to Rome, ambassador to the pope: where he behaved himself with no less diligence than before, and contended a long time, till
the pope's chief divines in his university of rota, compelled by arguments,
did of necessity grant that this marriage was against the law of God, but 10
yet, by the dispensation of the bishop of Rome, it might be made lawful. On the contrary side, Cranmer contended that it could not be so. In
the meantime, William Warham, Archbishop of Canterbury, departed;
in whose place Cranmer succeeded. And not long after, as one occasion
bringeth in another, so upon this question of the marriage riseth another
question of the pope's authority, in so much that in the Parliament it was
doubted of the primacy of the Church of Rome. And here the new archbishop was not a little helped by his old collections and notes which he used
in studying. For all the weight of the business was chiefly laid on his shoulders; he therefore alone received, answered, and confuted all the objec- 20
tions of all the papists. And where the saying is: not Hercules against two,
he alone encountered with so many ensigns and armies of divines, he alone
sustained all the force of all his adversaries. He opened from the very
foundations abundantly and readily what was to be judged and determined
of the bishop of Rome and all his authority. He shewed that the pope's
lordship was brought in by no authority of the Scripture, but by affected
and ambitious tyranny of men, and that the chiefest power in earth belonged to the emperor, to kings, and other potentates, to whom the
bishops, priests, popes, and cardinals, by God's commandment were no
less subject than other men of the commonwealth. And therefore there 30
was no cause why the bishop of Rome should excel other bishops in authority, who should be subject to their own magistrates, and of them be
kept in order.

*   *   *   *   *

. . . To be short, a little before the day that the queen had appointed
for Cranmer's death, she called for D[r]. Cole, and gave him secretly
in commandment that against the 21 of March he should prepare a funeral
sermon for Cranmer, that should be burned, and, being instructed orderly
and diligently of her will and pleasure in that sermon, sendeth him away. 40
Soon after, the Lord Williams of Tame, and the Lord Chandois, Sir
Thomas Bridges, and Sir John Brown were sent for, with other worship-

ful men and justices, and commanded in the queen's name to be at Oxford at the same day, with their servants and retinue, lest Cranmer's death
should raise any tumult. Cole the Doctor, having his lesson given him before, and charged by her commandment, returned ready to play his part,
which, when the day of execution drew near at hand, even the day before,
came into the prison to Cranmer, to try whether he abode in the catholic
faith that he left him in or not. To whom, when Cranmer had answered,
that by God's grace he would daily be more confirmed in the catholic
faith: Cole prepared his colter's sermon against the next day, worthy to
be noted with a black coal (as the proverb saith), giving no signification
to him of his death that was prepared.

And therefore the next day, which was the 21 of March, appointed
for Cranmer's execution, the said Cole came to him in the morning, asking him if he had any money; to whom when he answered that he had
none, he delivered him 15 crowns, to give to poor men to whom he would.
And then Cole, exhorting him as much as he could to constancy in faith,
departed thence about his business, as to his sermon appertained. By this
partly and other like arguments, the Archbishop began more and more to
surmise what they went about. Then, because the day was not far past,
and the lords and knights that were looked for were not yet come, there
came to him the Spanish friar, witness of his recantation, bringing a paper
with articles which Cranmer should openly profess in his recantation before the people, earnestly desiring that he would write the said instrument with the articles with his own hand, and sign it with his name; which,
when he had done, the said friar desired him that he would write another
copy thereof, which should remain with him, and that he did also. But
yet the Archb[ishop], being not ignorant whereunto the secret causes
of their devises tended, and thinking that time was at hand in which he
could no longer dissemble the profession of his faith with Christ's people,
he put secretly in his bosom his paper with his exhortation, written on
another paper, which he meant to recite to the people before he should
make the last profession of his faith, fearing lest if they had heard that
confession of his faith first, they would not afterward have suffered him
to exhort the people.

Soon after about 9 of the clock the Lord Williams, Sir Thomas Bridges,
Sir John Brown, and the other justices with certain other noblemen that
were sent of the queen's council, came to Oxford with a great train of
waiting men. Also of the other multitude on every side (as is wont in
such a matter) was made a great concourse and greater expectation. For
first of all, they that were of the pope's side were in great hope that day
to hear something of Cranmer that should stablish the vanity of their
opinion; the other side, which were endued with a better mind, could not

yet doubt that he which by continual study and labor for so many years
had set forth the doctrine of the gospel, other would or could now in the
last act of his life forsake his part. Briefly, as every man's will inclined,
either to this part or to that, so, according to the diversity of their desires,
every man wished and hoped for. And yet because in an uncertain thing
the certainty could be known of none, what would be the end, all their
minds were waiting and hanging between hope and doubt. So that the
greater the expectation was in so doubtful a matter, the more was the
multitude that were gathered thither to hear and behold.

In this so great frequence and expectation, Cranmer at length cometh 10
from the prison Bocardo unto St. Mary's church (because it was a foul
and a rainy day), the chief church in the university, in this order. The
Mayor went before; next him the Aldermen, in their place and degree;
after them was Cranmer brought, between two friars, which, mumbling
to and fro certain psalms in the streets, answered one another until they
came to the church door; and there they began the song of Symeon *Nunc
dimittis*, and entering into the church, the psalmsaying friars brought him
to his standing, and there left him.

There was a stage set up over against the pulpit, of a mean height from
the ground, where Cranmer had his standing, waiting until Cole made 20
him ready to his sermon. The lamentable case and sight of that man gave
a sorrowful spectacle to all Christian eyes that beheld him. He that of late
was archbishop, metropolitan, primate of all England, and the king's privy
counselor, being now in a bare and ragged gown, and ill-favoredly
clothed with an old square cap, exposed to the contempt of all men, did
not seem so much to admonish men of his calamity as of their own state
and fortune. For who would not pity his case, and bewail his fortune, and
fear his own chance, to see so noble a prelate, so grave a counselor, of so
long-continued honor, after so many dignities, in his old years to be deprived of his estate, adjudged to die, and in so painful a death to end his 30
life, and now presently from such fresh ornaments to descend to such vile
and ragged a gown and despicable apparel. And yet with a Christian
judgment if we behold the matter, we shall see the said archbishop never
before more gloriously, or more like a true archbishop invested in all his
pontifical array, as now he standeth in this seely poor weed. For then true
humility (as is wont to be in that state), sincere patience, ardent crying to
God, deep sighing in spirit, joined with perfect contempt of things present
(which as I think are the truest ornaments of bishops) did worthily
furnish and adorn his mind, erected unto Christ.

In this habit when he had stood a good while upon the stage, turning 40
to a pillar next unto the stage, and kneeling, and lifting up his hands to
heaven, he prayed unto God once or twice. And then Cole not long after,

coming into the pulpit, began his sermon, taking his argument of Tobias
and Zachary, whom after he had praised in the beginning of his oration for
their perseverance in that true worshipping of God, he divided his whole
sermon into three parts (according to the solemn customs of the schools),
intending to speak first of the mercy of God, secondly of his justice to be
shewed, and last of all how the prince's secrets are not to be opened. And
proceeding a little from the beginning, he took occasion by and by to turn
his tale to Cranmer, and with many hot words reproved him, that once he
being endued with the favor and feeling of wholesome and catholic
10 doctrine, he fell into the contrary opinion of pernicious error, which he
had not only defended by writings and all his power, but also allured other
men to do the like, with great liberality of gifts, as it were, appointing rewards for error; and after he had allured them, by all means did cherish
them. It were too long to repeat all things, that in long order were then
pronounced. The sum of this tripartite declamation was that he said, God's
mercy was so tempered with his justice, that he did not altogether require
punishment according to the merits of offenders, nor yet sometimes suffered the same altogether to go unpunished, yea though they had repented.

20   *   *   *   *

   But Cranmer, in the meantime, with how great sorrow and perturbation of mind he was affected all the sermon while, the outward signs of
his body and his countenance did better express than any man could declare. One while lifting up his hands and eyes unto heaven, and then again,
for shame, letting them down to the earth, a man might have seen in him
the very image and shape of sorrow and sadness lively expressed. More
than twenty several times the tears, being shed abundantly, dropped down
marvelously from his fatherly face. They which were present do testify
that they never saw in any child more tears than brast out from him at
30 that time, all the sermon while; but specially when he recited his prayer
before the people. It is marvelous how great commiseration and pity
moved all men's hearts that beheld so heavy a countenance and such abundance of tears in an old man of so reverend dignity.

   Cole, after he had ended his sermon, called back the people that were
ready to depart, to prayers. "Brethren," saith he, "lest any man should
doubt of this man's earnest conversion and repentance, you shall hear
him speak before you. And therefore I pray you, Mr. Cranmer, that you
will now perform that you promised not long ago; namely, that you would
openly express the true and undoubted profession of your faith, that you
40 may take away all suspicion from men, and that all men may understand
that you are a Catholic indeed."

   "I will do it," said the archbishop, "and with a good will." Which by and by rising up and putting off his cap, began to speak thus to the people: "I desire you, well-beloved brethren in the Lord, that you will pray to God for me to forgive me my sins which, above all men both in number and greatness, I have committed. But, among all the rest, there is one offense which of all at this time doth vex and trouble me, whereof, in process of my talk, you shall hear more in his proper place and then, putting his hand into his bosom, he drew forth his prayer, which he recited to the people in this sense. . . .

"And now, for as much as I am come to the last end of my life, where-upon hangeth all my life past and all my life to come, either to live with my master Christ forever in joy, or else to be in pain forever with wicked devils in hell, and I see before mine eyes presently either heaven ready to receive me or else hell ready to swallow me up, I shall therefore declare unto you my very faith: how I believe, without any color or dissimulation; for now is no time to dissemble whatsoever I have said or written in time past.

"First, I believe in God, the Father Almighty, Maker of heaven and earth, etc. And I believe every article of the Catholic faith, every word and sentence taught by Our Saviour, Jesus Christ, His apostles and proph-ets, in the New and Old Testament. And now I come to the great thing that so much troubled my conscience, more than anything that ever I did or said in my whole life, and that is the setting abroad of a writing contrary to the truth, which now here I renounce and refuse as things written with my hand contrary to the truth which I thought in my heart, and written for fear of death and to save my life, if it might be; and that is, all such bills and papers which I have written or signed with my hand since my degradation, wherein I have written many things untrue. And forasmuch as my hand offended, writing contrary to my heart, my hand shall first be punished therefor. For, may I come to the fire, it shall be first burned. And as for the pope, I refuse him as Christ's enemy and Antichrist, with all his false doctrine. And as for the sacrament, I believe as I have taught in my book against the Bishop of Winchester, the which my book teacheth so true a doctrine of the sacrament that it shall stand at the last day be-fore the judgment of God, where the papistical doctrine contrary thereto shall be ashamed to shew her face."

Here the standers-by were all astonied, did marvel, were amazed, did look one upon another, whose expectation he had so notably deceived. Some began to admonish him of his recantation and to accuse him of falsehood. Briefly, it was a world to see the doctors beguiled of so great an hope. I think there was never cruelty more notably or better in time deluded and deceived. For it is not to be doubted but they looked for a faithful victory and a perpetual triumph of glory by this man's recantation, which, as soon as they heard these things, began to let down their ears, to fret and be grievously angry. And so much the more grievously that they could not revenge their grief; for they could now no longer threaten or hurt him. For to the most miserable man in the world this one thing is granted, that he can die but once. And whereas of necessity he must needs die that day, though the papists had been never so well pleased, now that they were most offended he could not be twice killed of them. Then they, when they could do nothing else, lest they should say nothing, ceased not to object unto him the vice of falsehood and dissimulation.

10   Unto which accusation he answered: "Ah, my masters," quod he, "do not you take it so. Always since I lived hitherto, I have been a hater of falsehood and a lover of simplicity, and never before this time have I dissembled." And, in saying this, all the tears that remained in his body appeared in his eyes. And when he began to speak more of the sacrament and of the papacy, some of them began to cry out, yelp, and bawl, and specially Cole cried to stop the heretic's mouth and to take him away.

And then Cranmer, being pulled down from the seat, was led to the fire, accompanied with those friars, vexing, troubling, and threatening him most cruelly. What madness (say they) hath brought thee again into
20 this error, by which thou wilt draw innumerable souls with thee into hell? To whom he answered nothing, but directed all his talk to the people, saving that to one troubling him in the way, he spake and exhorted him to get him home to his study and apply his book diligently, saying if he did diligently call upon God, by reading more he should get knowledge. But the other Spanish barker, raging and foaming, was almost out of his wits, always having this in his mouth, *Non fecisti?* Didst thou it not?

But when he came to the place where the holy bishops and martyrs of God, Hugh Latimer and Ridley, were burnt before him for the confession of the truth, kneeling down, he prayed to God, and, not long tarrying in
30 his prayers, putting off his garments to his shirt, he prepared himself to death. His shirt was made long down to his feet. His feet were bare; likewise his head, when both his caps were off, was shewed bare, on which was not seen one hair; his beard was long and thick, covering his face with marvelous gravity. Such a countenance of gravity struck the affection both of his friends and of his enemies. Then the Spanish friars, John and Richard, of whom mention hath been made before, began to exhort him afresh, but with vain and lost labor. Cranmer, with steadfast purpose abiding in the profession of his doctrine, gave his hand to certain old men and others that stood by, bidding them farewell. And when he had thought
40 to have done so likewise to Ely, the said Ely drew back his hand and refused, saying it was not lawful to salute heretics, and specially such a one as falsely returned into the opinions that he had forsworn. And if he had

known before that he would have done so, he would never have used his
company so familiarly, and chid those sergeants and citizens which had
not refused to give him their hands. This Ely was a priest lately made,
and student in divinity, being then one of the fellows of Brasenose.

Then was an iron chain tied about Cranmer, whom when they perceived to be more steadfast than that he could be moved from his sentence,
they commanded the fire to be set unto him. And when the wood was
kindled and the fire began to burn near him, stretching out his arm, he
put his right hand in the flame, which he held so steadfast and immovable
(saving that once with the same hand he wiped his face) that all men
might see his hand burned before his body was touched. His body did so
abide the burning of the flames with such constancy and steadfastness
that, standing always in one place without moving of his members, he
seemed to move no more than the stake to which he was bound. His eyes
were lifted up into heaven, and oftentimes he repeated his unworthy
right hand, so long as his voice would suffer him: and, using often the
words of Stephen, "Lord Jesus, receive my spirit," in the greatness of
the flames he gave up the ghost.

SIR THOMAS NORTH

The Introduction and Notes are at page 1311

FROM *The Diall of Princes*, 1557, NORTH's translation of ANTONIO
DE GUEVARA's *El relox de principes*, 1529

The Dial of Princes

THE XX. CHAPTER

*The emperor persuadeth those that are old to give no more credit to
the world nor to any of his flatteries.*

THAT which I have spoken now tendeth more to advertise the young
than to teach the old. For you others have now passed the prime time of
childhood, the summer of youth, and the harvest of adolescency, and are
in the winter of age, where it seemeth an uncomely thing that those your
hoary hairs should be accompanied with such vain follies. Sithence young
men know not that they have to end their youth, it is no marvel that they
follow the world; but the old men, which see themselves fall into this
guile, why will they run after vices again? O world, for that thou art the
world, so small is our force, and so great our debility that thou willing it,

and we not resisting it, thou dost swallow us up in the most perilous gulf,
and in the thorns most sharp thou dost prick us; by the priviest ways thou
leadest us, and by the most stony ways thou carriest us. I mean that thou
bringest us to the highest favors, to the end that afterwards with a push
of thy pick thou might overthrow us. O world, wherein all is worldly,
52 years have passed since in thee I was first born, during the which time
thou never toldst me one truth; but I have taken thee with 10 thousand
lies. I never demanded the thing but thou didst promise it me, and yet it is
nothing at all that ever thou didst perform. I never put my trust in thee,
10 but ever thou beguiledst me. I never came to thee but thou didst undo me;
finally, never saw I aught in thee whereby thou deservedst love, but always hatred. This presupposed, I know not what is in the world or what
we worldlings want, for if thou hatest us we cannot hate thee; if thou dost
us injury, we cannot dissemble it; if thou strikest us with thy feet, we will
suffer it; if thou beatest us with a staff, we will hold our peace; also,
though thou persecutest us, we will not complain; though thou takest
ours, we will not demand it of thee; though thou dost beguile us, we will
not call ourselves beguiled; and the worst of all is that thou dost chase us
from the house, yet we will not from thence depart. I know not what this
20 meaneth, I know not from whence this cometh, I wot not who ought to
praise this same, that we covet to follow the world which will hate us,
and hate the gods which love us. Oftimes I make account of my years
past; sometimes also I turn and toss my books to see what I have read;
and another time I desire my friends to give me good counsel; and for no
otherwise I do it than to attain to that I have spoken, and to know that I
will say.

I reading rhetoric in Rhodes, Adrian, my lord, maintaining me there,
knowing that I was 32 years of age, it happened that in the springtime I
found myself solitarily; and solitariness with liberty smelled the world;
30 and smelling it, I knew it; and knowing it, I followed it; and following it,
I attained unto it; and attaining unto it, thereunto I joined myself; and
joining myself therewith, I proved it; and in proving it, I tasted it; and
in tasting it methought it bitter; and in finding it bitter, I hated it; and
hating it, I left it; and leaving it, it is returned; and returning it, I received it again; finally, the world inviting me, and I not resisting it, 52
years we did eat our bread togethers, and in one house we have always
remained. Wilt thou know after what sort the world and I do live in
one house togethers, or better to say in one heart remain? Hearken then,
and in one word I will tell it thee. When I saw the world brave, I served
40 him; when he saw me sad, he flattered me; when I saw him wealthy, I
asked him; when he saw me merry, he beguiled me; when I desired anything, he help me to attain to it; and afterwards when the same I best

enjoyed, then he took it from me; when he saw me not pleased, he visited me; when he saw me, he forgot me; when he saw me overthrown, he gave me his hand to relieve me; when he saw me exalted, he tripped me again to overthrow me. Finally, when I think that I have somewhat in the world, I find that all that I have is a burden.

If this which I have spoken of the world be anything, more is that a great deal which yet of myself I will say, which is, that without doubt my folly is greater than his malice, since I am beguiled so oft, and yet always I follow the deceiver. O world, world, thou hast such moods and fashions in thy proceeding that thou leadest us all to perdition. Of one thing I 10 marvel much, whereof I cannot be satisfied. Which is, since that we may go upon the bridge, and yet, without any gain, that we wade through the water; and whereas the shallow is sure, we seek to run into the gulf; and where the way is dry, we go into the plash; where we may eat healthsome meats to nourish the life, we receive poison to hasten death; we seek to destroy ourselves, whereas we may be without danger. Finally I say, without profit we commit a fault, though we see with our eyes the pain to follow. Wise men ought circumspectly to see what they do, to examine that they speak, to prove that they take in hand, to beware whose company they use, and, above all, to know whom they trust. For our judgment is 20 so corrupt that to beguile us, one sufficeth; and to make us not to be deceived, 10 thousand would not suffice. They have so great care of us, I mean the world, to beguile us, and the flesh to flatter us, that the highway being as it is narrow, the pathway dangerous and full of pricks, the journey is long, and the life short; our bodies are never but loden with vices, and our hearts but full of cares.

I have wondered at divers things in this world, but that which astonisheth me most is that those that be good, we make them believe they are evil; and those which are evil, we persuade others to believe that they are good; so that we shoot at the white of virtues, and hit the butt of vices. I 30 will confess one thing, the which, being disclosed, I know that infamy will follow me, but peradventure some virtuous man will marvel at it; that is, that in these two and fifty years of my life I have proved all the vices of this world for no other intent but for to prove if there be anything wherein man's malice might be satisfied. And afterwards, all well considered, all examined, and all proved, I find that the more I eat, the more I die for hunger; the more I drink, the greater thirst I have; the more I rest, the more I am broken; the more I sleep, the more drowsier I am; the more I have, the more I covet; the more I desire, the more I am tormented; the more I procure, the less I attain. Finally, I never had so great 40 pain through want, but afterward I had more trouble with excess. It is a great folly to think that as long as a man liveth in this flesh, that he can satisfy the flesh; for at the last cast, she may take from us our life, but we others cannot take from her her disordinate covetousness.

If men did speak with the gods, or the gods were conversant with men, the first thing that I would ask them should be why they have appointed an end to our woeful days, and will not give us an end of our wicked desires? O cruel gods, what is it you do? or what do you suffer us? It is certain that we shall not pass one good day of life only, but in tasting this, and that, life consumeth. O intolerable life of man, wherein there are such malices, from the which we ought to beware, and such perils to fall
10 in, and also so many things to consider, that then both she, and we, do end to know ourselves when the hour of death approacheth. Now those that know not that the world taketh our will, and we others like ignorants cannot deny him, and afterwards, having power of our will, doth constrain us to that which we would not, so that many times we would do virtuous works, and, for that we are now put into the world's hands, we dare not do it. The world useth another subtlety with us, that, to the end we should not strive with it, it praiseth the times past, because we should live according to the time present. And the world saith further that, if we others employ our forces in his vices, he giveth us license that we have
20 a good desire of virtue. O would to God in my days I might see that the care which the world hath to preserve us, the worldlings would take it to withdraw them from his vices. I swear that the gods should then have more servants, and the world and the flesh should not have so many slaves.

*   *   *   *   *

FROM *The Lives of the Noble Grecians and Romanes*, 1579, NORTH's
translation of PLUTARCH's *Parallel Lives*

The Life of Julius Caesar

30   *   *   *   *   *

. . . And for the war he made in Alexandria, some say he needed not have done it, but that he willingly did it for the love of Cleopatra: wherein he won little honor and besides did put his person in great danger. Others do lay the fault upon the king of Egypt's ministers, but specially on Pothinus the Eunuch who, bearing the greatest sway of all the king's servants, after he had caused Pompey to be slain and driven Cleopatra from the court, secretly laid wait all the ways he could, how he might likewise kill Caesar. Wherefore Caesar, hearing an inkling of it, began
40 thenceforth to spend all the night long in feasting and banqueting, that his person might be in the better safety. But besides all this, Pothinus the Eunuch spake many things openly, not to be borne, only to shame Caesar

and to stir up the people to envy him. For he made his soldiers have the worst and oldest wheat that could be gotten; then, if they did complain of it, he told them they must be contented, seeing they eat at another man's cost. And he would serve them also at the table in treen and earthen dishes, saying that Caesar had away all their gold and silver for a debt that the king's father (that then reigned) did owe unto him; which was a thousand seven hundred and fifty myriads, whereof Caesar had before forgiven seven hundred and fifty thousand unto his children. Howbeit, then he asked a million to pay his soldiers withal. Thereto Pothinus answered him that, at that time, he should do better to follow his other causes of greater importance, and afterwards that he should at more leisure recover his debt with the king's good will and favor.

Caesar replied unto him and said that he would not ask counsel of the Egyptians for his affairs, but would be paid; and thereupon secretly sent for Cleopatra, which was in the country, to come unto him. She only taking Apollodorus Sicilian, of all her friends, took a little boat and went away with him in it in the night, and came and landed hard by the foot of the castle. Then, having no other mean to come into the court without being known, she laid herself down upon a mattress or flockbed, which Apollodorus, her friend, tied and bound up together like a bundle with a great leather thong, and so took her upon his back, and brought her thus hampered in this fardle unto Caesar in at the castle gate. This was the first occasion (as it is reported) that made Caesar to love her; but afterwards, when he saw her sweet conversation and pleasant entertainment, he fell then in further liking with her, and did reconcile her again unto her brother, the king, with condition that they two jointly should reign together.

Upon this new reconciliation, a great feast being prepared, a slave of Caesar's, that was his barber, the fearfullest wretch that lived, still busily prying and listening abroad in every corner, being mistrustful by nature: found that Pothinus and Achillas did lie in wait to kill his master Caesar. This being proved unto Caesar, he did set such sure watch about the hall where the feast was made that, in fine, he slew the eunuch Pothinus himself. Achillas, on th'other side, saved himself and fled unto the king's camp, where he raised a marvelous dangerous and difficult war for Caesar; because he having then but a few men about him as he had, he was to fight against a great and strong city.

The first danger he fell into was for the lack of water he had, for that his enemies had stopped the mouth of the pipes, the which conveyed the water unto the castle. The second danger he had was that, seeing his enemies came to take his ships from him, he was driven to repulse that danger with fire, the which burnt the arsenal where the ships lay, and that notable

library of Alexandria withal. The third danger was in the battle by sea,
that was fought by the tower of Phar, where, meaning to help his men
that fought by sea, he leapt from the pier into a boat. Then the Egyptians
made towards him with their oars on every side; but he, leaping into the
sea, with great hazard saved himself by swimming. It is said that then
holding divers books in his hand, he did never let them go, but kept them
always upon his head above water and swam with the other hand, notwithstanding that they shot marvelously at him, and was driven sometime
to duck into the water. Howbeit the boat was drowned presently. In fine,
10 the king coming to his men that made war with Caesar, he went against
him and gave him battle, and won it with great slaughter and effusion of
blood. But for the king, no man could ever tell what became of him after.
Thereupon Caesar made Cleopatra his sister queen of Egypt, who, being
great with child by him, was shortly brought to bed of a son, whom the
Alexandrians named Caesarion.

From thence he went into Syria, and so going into Asia, there it was
told him that Domitius was overthrown in battle by Pharnaces, the son of
King Mithridates, and was fled out of the realm of Ponte with a few men
with him; and that this King Pharnaces, greedily following his victory,
20 was not contented with the winning of Bithynia and Cappadocia, but
further would needs attempt to win Armenia the less, procuring all those
kings, princes, and governors of the provinces thereabouts to rebel against
the Romans. Thereupon Caesar went thither straight with three legions
and fought a great battle with King Pharnaces by the city of Zela, where
he slew his army and drave him out of all the realm of Ponte. And because
he would advertise one of his friends of the suddenness of this victory, he
only wrote three words unto Anitius at Rome: *Veni, vidi, vici;* to wit, I
came, I saw, I overcame. These three words, ending all with like sound
and letters in the Latin, have a certain short grace, more pleasant to the
30 ear than can be well expressed in any other tongue.

*   *   *   *   *

But the ordinance of the calendar and reformation of the year to take
away all confusion of time, being exactly calculated by the mathematicians
and brought to perfection, was a great commodity unto all men. For the
Romans, using then the ancient computation of the year, had not only
such incertainty and alteration of the month and times that the sacrifices
and yearly feasts came, by little and little, to seasons contrary for the purpose they were ordained; but also in the revolution of the sun (which is
40 called *annus solaris*) no other nation agreed with them in account; and
of the Romans themselves, only the priests understood it. And therefore
when they listed, they suddenly (no man being able to control them)

did thrust in a month above their ordinary number, which they called in old time Mercedonius. Some say that Numa Pompilius was the first that devised this way to put a month between; but it was a weak remedy and did little help the correction of the errors that were made in the account of the year, to frame them to perfection. But Caesar, committing this matter unto the philosophers and best expert mathematicians at that time, did set forth an excellent and perfect calendar, more exactly calculated than any other that was before; the which the Romans do use until this present day, and do nothing err as others in the difference of time. But his enemies, notwithstanding, that envied his greatness, did not stick to find fault withal. As Cicero the Orator, when one said, "To-morrow the star Lyra will rise": "Yea," said he, "at the commandment of Caesar"; as if men were compelled so to say and think by Caesar's edict.

But the chiefest cause that made him mortally hated was the covetous desire he had to be called king; which first gave the people just cause, and next his secret enemies honest color, to bear him ill will. This notwithstanding, they that procured him this honor and dignity gave it out among the people that it was written in the Sibylline prophecies how the Romans might overcome the Parthians if they made war with them and were led by a king, but otherwise that they were unconquerable. And furthermore they were so bold besides that Caesar, returning to Rome from the city of Alba, when they came to salute him they called him king. But the people being offended and Caesar also angry, he said he was not called king, but Caesar. Then every man keeping silence, he went his way heavy and sorrowful. When they had decreed divers honors for him in the senate, the consuls and praetors, accompanied with the whole assembly of the senate, went unto him in the market-place, where he was set by the pulpit for orations, to tell him what honors they had decreed for him in his absence. But he, sitting still in his majesty, disdaining to rise up unto them when they came in, as if they had been private men, answered them: that his honors had more need to be cut off than enlarged. This did not only offend the senate, but the common people also, to see that he should so lightly esteem of the magistrates of the commonwealth; insomuch as every man that might lawfully go his way departed thence very sorrowfully. Thereupon also Caesar, rising, departed home to his house, and tearing open his doublet collar, making his neck bare, he cried out aloud to his friends that his throat was ready to offer to any man that would come and cut it.

Notwithstanding, it is reported that afterwards, to excuse this folly, he imputed it to his disease, saying that their wits are not perfect which have this disease of the falling evil, when, standing of their feet, they speak to the common people, but are soon troubled with a trembling of their body and a sudden dimness and giddiness. But that was not true. For he would have risen up to the senate, but Cornelius Balbus, one of his friends (but rather a flatterer), would not let him, saying: "What, do you not remember that you are Caesar, and will you not let them reverence you and do their duties?"

Besides these occasions and offenses, there followed also his shame and reproach, abusing the tribunes of the people in this sort. At that time, the feast Lupercalia was celebrated, the which, in old time, men say was the feast of shepherds or herdmen, and is much like unto the feast of the
10 Lycaeians in Arcadia. But howsoever it is, that day there are divers noblemen's sons, young men (and some of them magistrates themselves that govern then), which run naked through the city, striking in sport them they meet in their way, with leather thongs, hair and all on, to make them give place. And many noblewomen and gentlewomen also go of purpose to stand in their way, and do put forth their hands to be stricken, as scholars hold them out to their schoolmaster to be stricken with the ferula, persuading themselves that, being with child, they shall have good delivery and also, being barren, that it will make them to conceive with child. Caesar sate to behold that sport upon the pulpit for orations, in a chair of
20 gold, apparelled in triumphing manner. Antonius, who was consul at that time, was one of them that ran this holy course. So when he came into the market-place, the people made a lane for him to run at liberty, and he came to Caesar and presented him a diadem wreathed about with laurel. Whereupon there rose a certain cry of rejoicing, not very great, done only by a few appointed for the purpose. But when Caesar refused the diadem, then all the people together made an outcry of joy. Then Antonius offering it him again, there was a second shout of joy, but yet of a few. But when Caesar refused it again the second time, then all the whole people shouted. Caesar having made this proof, found that the people did
30 not like of it, and thereupon rose out of his chair and commanded the crown to be carried unto Jupiter in the Capitol.

After that, there were set up images of Caesar in the city, with diadems upon their heads like kings. Those the two tribunes Flavius and Marullus went and pulled down; and furthermore, meeting with them that first saluted Caesar as king, they committed them to prison. The people followed them, rejoicing at it, and called them "Brutes," because of Brutus, who had, in old time, driven the kings out of Rome, and that brought the kingdom of one person unto the government of the senate and people. Caesar was so offended withal that he deprived Marullus and Flavius of
40 their tribuneships, and, accusing them, he spake also against the people and called them *bruti* and *cumani*, to wit, beasts and fools.

Hereupon the people went straight unto Marcus Brutus, who, from his father, came of the first Brutus, and, by his mother, of the house of the Servilians, a noble house as any was in Rome, and was also nephew and son-in-law of Marcus Cato. Notwithstanding, the great honors and favor Caesar shewed unto him kept him back that, of himself alone, he did not conspire nor consent to depose him of his kingdom. For Caesar did not only save his life after the battle of Pharsalia, when Pompey fled, and did, at his request, also save many moe of his friends besides; but furthermore he put a marvelous confidence in him. For he had already preferred him to the praetorship for that year, and furthermore was appointed to be consul the fourth year after that, having through Caesar's friendship 10 obtained it before Cassius, who likewise made suit for the same. And Caesar also, as it is reported, said in this contention, "Indeed Cassius hath alleged best reason, but yet shall he not be chosen before Brutus." Some-one accusing Brutus while he practised this conspiracy, Caesar would not hear of it, but, clapping his hand on his body, told them, Brutus will look for this skin, meaning thereby that Brutus, for his virtue, deserved to rule after him, but yet that for ambition's sake he would not shew himself unthankful nor dishonorable.

Now they that desired change and wished Brutus only their prince and governor above all other: they durst not come to him themselves to 20 tell him what they would have him to do, but, in the night, did cast sundry papers into the praetor's seat where he gave audience, and the most of them to this effect: "Thou sleepest, Brutus, and art not Brutus indeed."

Cassius, finding Brutus' ambition stirred up the more by these seditious bills, did prick him forward and egg him on the more for a private quarrel he had conceived against Caesar, the circumstance whereof we have set down more at large in Brutus' life. Caesar also had Cassius in great jeal-ousy, and suspected him much; whereupon he said on a time to his friends, "What will Cassius do, think ye? I like not his pale looks." Another time, when Caesar's friends complained unto him of Antonius and Dolabella 30 that they pretended some mischief towards him, he answered them again, "As for those fat men and smooth-combed heads," quoth he, "I never reckon of them; but these pale-visaged and carrion-lean people, I fear them most," meaning Brutus and Cassius.

Certainly destiny may easier be foreseen than avoided, considering the strange and wonderful signs that were said to be seen before Caesar's death. For, touching the fires in the element, and spirits running up and down in the night, and also these solitary birds to be seen at noondays sitting in the great market-place—are not all these signs perhaps worth the noting in such a wonderful chance as happened? But Strabo the philoso- 40 pher writeth that divers men were seen going up and down in fire; and, furthermore, that there was a slave of the soldiers that did cast a marvelous burning flame out of his hand, insomuch as they that saw it thought he had been burnt, but, when the fire was out, it was found he had no hurt. Caesar self also doing sacrifice unto the gods, found that one of the beasts which was sacrificed had no heart; and that was a strange thing in nature, how a beast could live without a heart. Furthermore, there was a certain soothsayer that had given Caesar warning long time afore to take heed of the day of the ides of March (which is the fifteenth of the month), for on that day he should be in great danger.

That day being come, Caesar, going unto the senate house and speaking
10 merrily unto the soothsayer, told him, "The ides of March be come."

"So be they," softly answered the soothsayer, "but yet are they not past."

And the very day before, Caesar, supping with Marcus Lepidus, sealed certain letters, as he was wont to do at the board. So, talk falling out amongst them, reasoning what death was best, he, preventing their opinions, cried out aloud, "Death unlooked for."

Then going to bed the same night as his manner was, and lying with his wife Calpurnia, all the windows and doors of his chamber flying open, the noise awoke him and made him afraid when he saw such light; but
20 more when he heard his wife Calpurnia, being fast asleep, weep and sigh, and put forth many fumbling, lamentable speeches. For she dreamed that Caesar was slain, and that she had him in her arms. Others also do deny that she had any such dream, as, amongst other, Titus Livius writeth that it was in this sort. The senate having set upon the top of Caesar's house for an ornament and setting forth of the same a certain pinnacle, Calpurnia dreamed that she saw it broken down, and that she thought she lamented and wept for it. Insomuch that Caesar rising in the morning, she prayed him, if it were possible, not to go out of the doors that day, but to adjourn the session of the senate until another day. And, if that he made
30 no reckoning of her dream, yet that he would search further of the soothsayers, by their sacrifices to know what should happen him that day. Thereby it seemed that Caesar likewise did fear and suspect somewhat, because his wife Calpurnia until that time was never given to any fear or superstition, and then for that he saw her so troubled in mind with this dream she had. But much more afterwards when the soothsayers, having sacrificed many beasts one after another, told him that none did like them. Then he determined to send Antonius to adjourn the session of the senate.

But in the meantime came Decius Brutus, surnamed Albinus, in whom Caesar put such confidence that in his last will and testament he had ap-
40 pointed him to be his next heir, and yet was of the conspiracy with Cassius and Brutus; he, fearing that if Caesar did adjourn the session that day, the conspiracy would out, laughed the soothsayers to scorn, and reproved

Caesar, saying that he gave the senate occasion to mislike with him, and that they might think he mocked them, considering that by his commandment they were assembled; and that they were ready willingly to grant him all things, and to proclaim him king of all the provinces of the empire of Rome out of Italy; and that he should wear his diadem in all other places, both by sea and land. And, furthermore, that if any man should tell them from him they should depart for that present time and return again when Calpurnia should have better dreams, what would his enemies and ill-willers say, and how could they like of his friends' words? And who could persuade them otherwise but that they would think his do- 10 minion a slavery unto them and tyrannical in himself? "And yet, if it be so," said he, "that you utterly mislike of this day, it is better that you go yourself in person, and, saluting the senate, to dismiss them till another time." Therewithal he took Caesar by the hand and brought him out of his house.

Caesar was not gone far from his house but a bondman, a stranger, did what he could to speak with him; and when he saw he was put back by the great press and multitude of people that followed him, he went straight into his house, and put himself into Calpurnia's hands to be kept till Caesar came back again, telling her that he had great matters to impart unto 20 him. And one Artemidorus, also born in the isle of Gnidos, a doctor of rhetoric in the Greek tongue who, by means of his profession, was very familiar with certain of Brutus' confederates and therefore knew the most part of all their practises against Caesar, came and brought him a little bill, written with his own hand, of all that he meant to tell him. He, marking how Caesar received all the supplications that were offered him, and that he gave them straight to his men that were about him, pressed nearer to him and said: "Caesar, read this memorial to yourself, and that quickly, for they be matters of great weight and touch you nearly."

Caesar took it of him, but could never read it, though he many times 30 attempted it, for the number of people that did salute him; but holding it still in his hand, keeping it to himself, went on withal into the senate house. Howbeit, other are of opinion that it was some man else that gave him that memorial, and not Artemidorus, who did what he could all the way as he went to give it to Caesar, but he was always repulsed by the people.

For these things, they may seem to come by chance; but the place where the murder was prepared, and where the senate were assembled, and where also there stood up an image of Pompey dedicated by himself amongst other ornaments which he gave unto the theater—all these were manifest proofs that it was the ordinance of some god that made this 40 treason to be executed, specially in that very place. It is also reported that Cassius (though otherwise he did favor the doctrine of Epicurus), beholding the image of Pompey before they entered into the action of their traitorous enterprise, he did softly call upon it to aid him. But the instant danger of the present time, taking away his former reason, did suddenly put him into a furious passion and made him like a man half beside himself.

Now Antonius, that was a faithful friend to Caesar and a valiant man besides, of his hands, him Decius Brutus Albinus entertained out of the senate house, having begun a long tale of set purpose. So Caesar coming into the house, all the senate stood up on their feet to do him honor. Then part of Brutus' company and confederates stood round about Caesar's
10 chair, and part of them also came towards him, as though they made suit with Metellus Cimber to call home his brother again from banishment; and thus prosecuting still their suit, they followed Caesar till he was set in his chair. Who, denying their petitions and being offended with them one after another because, the more they were denied, the more they pressed upon him and were the earnester with him, Metellus at length, taking his gown with both his hands, pulled it over his neck, which was the sign given the confederates to set upon him. Then Casca behind him strake him in the neck with his sword; howbeit the wound was not great nor mortal because it seemed the fear of such a devilish attempt did amaze
20 him and take his strength from him, that he killed him not at the first blow. But Caesar, turning straight unto him, caught hold of his sword, and held it hard; and they both cried out, Caesar in Latin: "O vile traitor, Casca, what dost thou?" And Casca in Greek to his brother, "Brother, help me!"

At the beginning of this stir, they that were present, not knowing of the conspiracy, were so amazed with the horrible sight they saw, they had no power to fly, neither to help him, not so much as once to make any outcry. They on the other side that had conspired his death, compassed him in on every side with their swords drawn in their hands, that Caesar turned him
30 nowhere but he was stricken at by some, and still had naked swords in his face, and was hacked and mangled among them as a wild beast taken of hunters. For it was agreed among them that every man should give him a wound because all their parts should be in this murder. And then Brutus himself gave him one wound about his privities. Men report also that Caesar did still defend himself against the rest, running every way with his body, but when he saw Brutus with his sword drawn in his hand, then he pulled his gown over his head and made no more resistance, and was driven, either casually, or purposedly by the counsel of the conspirators, against the base whereupon Pompey's image stood, which ran all of a
40 gore blood, till he was slain. Thus it seemed that the image took just revenge of Pompey's enemy, being thrown down on the ground at his feet and yielding up his ghost there for the number of wounds he had upon

him. For it is reported that he had three and twenty wounds upon his body; and divers of the conspirators did hurt themselves, striking one body with so many blows.

When Caesar was slain, the senate (though Brutus stood in the midst amongst them, as though he would have said somewhat touching this fact) presently ran out of the house, and, flying, filled all the city with marvelous fear and tumult. Insomuch as some did shut to their doors, others forsook their shops and warehouses, and others ran to the place to see what the matter was, and others also that had seen it ran home to their houses again. But Antonius and Lepidus, which were two of Caesar's 10 chiefest friends, secretly conveying themselves away, fled into other men's houses and forsook their own. Brutus and his confederates, on th'other side, being yet hot with this murder they had committed, having their swords drawn in their hands, came all in a troop together out of the senate and went into the market-place, not as men that made countenance to fly, but otherwise boldly holding up their heads like men of courage, and called to the people to defend their liberty, and stayed to speak with every great personage whom they met in their way. Of them, some followed this troupe and went amongst them as if they had been of the conspiracy, and falsely challenged part of the honor with them; amongst them was 20 Caius Octavius and Lentulus Spinther. But both of them were afterwards put to death for their vain covetousness of honor by Antonius and Octavius Caesar the younger, and yet had no part of that honor for the which they were put to death; neither did any man believe that they were any of the confederates or of counsel with them. For they that did put them to death took revenge rather of the will they had to offend than of any fact they had committed.

The next morning Brutus and his confederates came into the market-place to speak unto the people, who gave them such audience that it seemed they neither greatly reproved nor allowed the fact; for, by their 30 silence, they showed that they were sorry for Caesar's death, and also that they did reverence Brutus. Now the senate granted general pardon for all that was past, and, to pacify every man, ordained besides that Caesar's funerals should be honored as a god, and established all things that he had done; and gave certain provinces also and convenient honors unto Brutus and his confederates, whereby every man thought all things were brought to good peace and quietness again.

But when they had opened Caesar's testament and found a liberal legacy of money bequeathed unto every citizen of Rome, and that they saw his body (which was brought into the market-place) all bemangled 40 with gashes of swords, then there was no order to keep the multitude and common people quiet; but they plucked up forms, tables, and stools and laid them all about the body and, setting them afire, burnt the corpse. Then when the fire was well kindled, they took the firebrands and went unto their houses that had slain Caesar to set them afire. Other also ran up and down the city to see if they could meet with any of them to cut them in pieces; howbeit, they could meet with never a man of them, because they had locked themselves up safely in their houses. There was one of Caesar's friends called Cinna that had a marvelous strange and terrible dream the night before. He dreamed that Caesar bade him to supper, and that he refused and would not go; then that Caesar took him by the hand 10 and led him against his will. Now Cinna, hearing at that time that they burnt Caesar's body in the market-place, notwithstanding that he feared his dream and had an ague on him besides, he went into the market-place to honor his funerals. When he came thither, one of the mean sort asked what his name was. He was straight called by his name. The first man told it to another, and that other unto another, so that it ran straight through them all that he was one of them that murdered Caesar (for indeed one of the traitors to Caesar was also called Cinna, as himself); wherefore, taking him for Cinna the murderer, they fell upon him with such fury that they presently dispatched him in 20 the market-place.

This stir and fury made Brutus and Cassius more afraid than of all that was past; and therefore, within few days after, they departed out of Rome. And touching their doings afterwards and what calamity they suffered till their deaths, we have written at large in the life of Brutus.

Caesar died at six and fifty years of age; and Pompey also lived not passing four years more than he. So he reaped no other fruit of all his reign and dominion, which he had so vehemently desired all his life and pursued with such extreme danger, but a vain name only and a superficial glory that procured him the envy and hatred of his country. But his great 30 prosperity and good fortune that favored him all his lifetime did continue afterwards in the revenge of his death, pursuing the murderers both by sea and land till they had not left a man more to be executed of all them that were actors or counselors in the conspiracy of his death. Furthermore, of all the chances that happen unto men upon the earth, that which came to Cassius above all other is most to be wondered at. For he, being overcome in battle at the journey of Philippes, slew himself with the same sword with the which he strake Caesar. Again, of signs in the element, the great comet which seven nights together was seen very bright after Caesar's death, the eighth night after was never seen more. Also the 40 brightness of the sun was darkened, the which all that year through rose very pale and shined not out, whereby it gave but small heat; therefore, the air being very cloudy and dark by the weakness of the heat that could not come forth, did cause the earth to bring forth but raw and unripe fruit, which rotted before it could ripe.

But, above all, the ghost that appeared unto Brutus shewed plainly that the gods were offended with the murder of Caesar. The vision was thus. Brutus, being ready to pass over his army from the city of Abydos to the other coast lying directly against it, slept every night (as his manner was) in his tent; and, being yet awake thinking of his affairs (for by report he was as careful a captain and lived with as little sleep as ever man did), he thought he heard a noise at his tent door, and, looking towards the light of the lamp that waxed very dim, he saw a horrible vision of a man of a wonderful greatness and dreadful look, which at the first made him marvelously afraid. But when he saw that it did him no hurt, but stood by his bedside and said nothing, at length he asked him what he was. The image answered him: "I am thy ill angel, Brutus, and thou shalt see me by the city of Phillipes."

Then Brutus replied again and said: "Well, I shall see thee then."

Therewithal the spirit presently vanished from him. After that time Brutus, being in battle near unto the city of Phillippes against Antonius and Octavius Caesar, at the first battle he won the victory and, overthrowing all them that withstood him, he drave them into young Caesar's camp, which he took. The second battle being at hand, this spirit appeared again unto him, but spake never a word. Thereupon Brutus, knowing he should die, put himself to all hazard in battle, but yet fighting could not be slain. So, seeing his men put to flight and overthrown, he ran unto a little rock not far off, and there, setting his sword's point to his breast, fell upon it and slew himself; but yet, as it is reported, with the help of his friend that dispatched him.

The end of Caesar's life.

JOHN LYLY

The Introduction and Notes are at page 1313
FROM *Euphues: The Anatomy of Wit*, 1579; the 2nd edition; the 1st edition appeared in 1578

Euphues. The Anatomy of Wit
To the Gentlemen Readers

I WAS driven into a quandary, Gentlemen, whether I might send this my pamphlet to the printer or to the pedlar. I thought it too bad for the press and too good for the pack. But seeing my folly in writing to be as great

as others', I was willing my fortune should be as ill as any's. We commonly see the book that at Christmas lieth bound on the stationer's stall, at Easter to be broken in the haberdasher's shop; which, sith it is the order of proceeding, I am content this winter to have my doings read for a toy, that in summer they may be ready for trash. It is not strange, whenas the greatest wonder lasteth but nine days, that a new work should not endure but three months. Gentlemen use books as gentlewomen handle their flowers, who in the morning stick them in their heads and at night strew them at their heels. Cherries be fulsome when they be
10 through ripe because they be plenty, and books be stale when they be printed in that they be common. In my mind printers and tailors are bound chiefly to pray for gentlemen: the one hath so many fantasies to print, the other such divers fashions to make, that the pressing-iron of the one is never out of the fire nor the printing-press of the other any time lieth still. But a fashion is but a day's wearing and a book but an hour's reading; which seeing it is so, I am of the shoemaker's mind, who careth not so the shoe hold the plucking on, nor I so my labours last the running over. He that cometh in print because he would be known is like the fool that cometh into the market because he would be seen. I am not he that
20 seeketh praise for his labour, but pardon for his offence; neither do I set this forth for any devotion in print, but for duty which I owe to my patron. If one write never so well he cannot please all, and write he never so ill he shall please some. Fine heads will pick a quarrel with me if all be not curious, and flatterers a thank if anything be current. But this is my mind, let him that findeth fault amend it and him that liketh it use it. Envy braggeth but draweth no blood, the malicious have more mind to grip than might to cut. I submit myself to the judgment of the wise and I little esteem the censure of fools. The one will be satisfied with reason, the other are to be answered with silence. I know gentlemen will find no fault
30 without cause, and bear with those that deserve blame; as for others I care not for their jests, for I never meant to make them my judges.

Farewell.

JOHN LYLY

There dwelt in Athens a young gentleman of great patrimony and of so comely a personage that it was doubted whether he were more bound to Nature for the lineaments of his person or to Fortune for the increase of his possessions. But Nature, impatient of comparisons, and, as it were, disdaining a companion or copartner in her working, added to this comeliness of his body such a sharp capacity of mind that not only she proved Fortune
40 counterfeit, but was half of that opinion that she herself was only current.

This young gallant, of more wit than wealth, and yet of more wealth than wisdom, seeing himself inferior to none in pleasant conceits, thought

himself superior to all in honest conditions, insomuch that he thought
himself so apt to all things that he gave himself almost to nothing; but
practising of those things commonly which are incident to these sharp
wits: fine phrases, smooth quips, merry taunts, using jesting without mean
and abusing mirth without measure. As, therefore, the sweetest rose hath
his prickle, the finest velvet his brack, the fairest flour his bran, so the
sharpest wit hath his wanton will, and the holiest head his wicked way.
And true it is that some men write and most men believe that, in all perfect shapes, a blemish bringeth rather a liking every way to the eyes than
a loathing any way to the mind. Venus had her mole in her cheek, which 10
made her more amiable; Helen her scar in her chin, which Paris called
cos amoris, the whetstone of love; Aristippus his wart; Lycurgus his wen.
So likewise, in the disposition of the mind, either virtue is overshadowed
with some vice, or vice overcast with some virtue. Alexander valiant in
war, yet given to wine. Tully eloquent in his glosses, yet vainglorious.
Solomon wise, yet too, too wanton. David holy, but yet an homicide.
None more witty than Euphues, yet at the first none more wicked. The
freshest colors soonest fade, the teenest razor soonest turneth his edge,
the finest cloth is soonest eaten with moths, and the cambric sooner stained
than the coarse canvas: which appeared well in this Euphues, whose wit, 20
being like wax, apt to receive any impression, and bearing the head in
his own hand, either to use the rein or the spur, disdaining counsel, leaving his country, loathing his old acquaintance, thought either by wit to
obtain some conquest, or by shame to abide some conflict; who, preferring fancy before friends and his present humor before honor to come,
laid reason in water, being too salt for his taste, and followed unbridled
affection, most pleasant for his tooth. When parents have more care how
to leave their children wealthy than wise and are more desirous to have
them maintain the name than the nature of a gentleman; when they put
gold into the hands of youth, where they should put a rod under their gir- 30
dle; when, instead of awe, they make them past grace and leave them
rich executors of goods and poor executors of godliness; then is it no marvel that the son, being left rich by his father's will, become reckless by his
own will.

But it hath been an old said saw, and not of less truth than antiquity,
that wit is the better if it be the dearer bought; as in the sequel of this
history shall most manifestly appear. It happened this young imp to arrive
at Naples (a place of more pleasure than profit, and yet of more profit than
piety), the very walls and windows whereof shewed it rather to be the
tabernacle of Venus than the temple of Vesta. There was all things nec- 40
essary and in readiness that might either allure the mind to lust or entice
the heart to folly: a court more meet for an atheist than for one of Athens;

for Ovid than for Aristotle; for a graceless lover than for a godly liver; more fitter for Paris than Hector, and meeter for Flora than Diana.

Here my youth (whether for weariness he could not, or for wantonness would not, go any further) determined to make his abode; whereby it is evidently seen that the fleetest fish swalloweth the delicatest bait, that the highest soaring hawk traineth to the lure, and that the wittiest brain is inveigled with the sudden view of alluring vanities. Here he wanted no companions which courted him continually with sundry kinds of devices, whereby they might either soak his purse to reap commodity or
10 soothe his person to win credit; for he had guests and companions of all sorts.

There frequented to his lodging, as well the spider to suck poison of his fine wit, as the bee to gather honey; as well the drone as the dove; the fox as the lamb; as well Damocles to betray him as Damon to be true to him. Yet he behaved himself so warily that he singled his game wisely. He could easily discern Apollo's music from Pan his pipe, and Venus' beauty from Juno's bravery, and the faith of Laelius from the flattery of Aristippus. He welcomed all, trusted none; he was merry but yet so wary that neither the flatterer could take advantage to entrap him in his
20 talk nor the wisest any assurance of his friendship. Who, being demanded of one what countryman he was, he answered, "What countryman am I not? If I be in Crete, I can lie; if in Greece, I can shift; if in Italy, I can court it. If thou ask whose son I am also, I ask thee whose son I am not. I can carouse with Alexander, abstain with Romulus, eat with the epicure, fast with the stoic, sleep with Endymion, watch with Chrysippus," using these speeches and other like. An old gentleman in Naples seeing his pregnant wit, his eloquent tongue somewhat taunting, yet with delight; his mirth without measure, yet not without wit; his sayings vainglorious, yet pithy: began to bewail his nurture and to muse at his nature, being
30 incensed against the one as most pernicious, and inflamed with the other as most precious. For he well knew that so rare a wit would in time either breed an intolerable trouble or bring an incomparable treasure to the commonweal; at the one he greatly pitied, at the other he rejoiced.

Having therefore gotten opportunity to communicate with him his mind, with watery eyes, as one lamenting his wantonness, and smiling face, as one loving his wittiness, encountered him on this manner.

"Young gentleman, although my acquaintance be small to entreat you, and my authority less to command you, yet my good will in giving you good counsel should induce you to believe me, and my hoary hairs (am-
40 bassadors of experience) enforce you to follow me; for by how much the more I am a stranger to you, by so much the more you are beholding to me; having, therefore, opportunity to utter my mind, I mean to be im-

portunate with you to follow my meaning. As thy birth doth shew the express and lively image of gentle blood, so thy bringing up seemeth to me to be a great blot to the lineage of so noble a brute; so that I am enforced to think that either thou didst want one to give thee good instructions, or that thy parents made thee a wanton with too much cockering; either they were too foolish in using no discipline, or thou too froward in rejecting their doctrine; either they willing to have thee idle, or thou wilful to be ill employed. Did they not remember that which no man ought to forget, that the tender youth of a child is like the tempering of new wax, apt to receive any form? He that will carry a bull with Milo must use to 10 carry him a calf also; he that coveteth to have a straight tree must not bow him being a twig. The potter fashioneth his clay when it is soft, and the sparrow is taught to come when he is young. As, therefore, the iron being hot receiveth any form with the stroke of the hammer, and keepeth it, being cold, forever, so the tender wit of a child, if with diligence it be instructed in youth, will with industry use those qualities in his age.

"They might also have taken example of the wise husbandmen, who, in their fattest and most fertile ground, sow hemp before wheat, a grain that drieth up the superfluous moisture and maketh the soil more apt for corn; or of good gardeners, who, in their curious knots, mix hyssop with 20 thyme, as aiders, the one to the growth of the other, the one being dry, the other moist; or of cunning painters, who, for the whitest work, cast the blackest ground, to make the picture more amiable. If, therefore, thy father had been as wise an husbandman as he was a fortunate husband, or thy mother as good a housewife as she was a happy wife; if they had been both as good gardeners to keep their knot as they were grafters to bring forth such fruit; or as cunning painters as they were happy parents, no doubt they had sowed hemp before wheat, that is, discipline before affection; they had set hyssop with thyme, that is, manners with wit, the one to aid the other; and to make thy dexterity more, they had cast a black 30 ground for their white work, that is, they had mixed threats with fair looks. But things past are past calling again; it is too late to shut the stable door when the steed is stolen; the Troyans repented too late when their town was spoiled; yet the remembrance of thy former follies might breed in thee a remorse of conscience and be a remedy against further concupiscence. But now to thy present time. The Lacedemonians were wont to shew their children drunken men and other wicked men that, by seeing their filth, they might shun the like fault and avoid the like vices when they were at the like state. The Persians, to make their youth abhor gluttony, would paint an epicure sleeping with meat in his mouth and most 40 horribly overladen with wine, that by the view of such monstrous sights they might eschew the means of the like excess. The Parthians, to cause

their youth to loathe the alluring trains of women's wiles and deceitful enticements, had most curiously carved in their houses a young man blind,
besides whom was adjoined a woman so exquisite that, in some men's
judgment, Pygmalion's image was not half so excellent, having one hand
in his pocket, as noting her theft, and holding a knife in the other hand to
cut his throat. If the sight of such ugly shapes caused a loathing of the like
sins, then, my good Euphues, consider their plight and beware of thine
own peril.

"Thou art here in Naples a young sojourner, I an old senior; thou a
10 stranger, I a citizen; thou secure, doubting no mishap, I sorrowful, dreading thy misfortune. Here mayest thou see that which I sigh to see: drunken
sots wallowing in every house, in every chamber, yea, in every channel;
here mayest thou behold that which I cannot without blushing behold, nor
without blubbering utter: those whose bellies be their gods, who offer their
goods as sacrifice to their guts; who sleep with meat in their mouths, with
sin in their hearts, and with shame in their houses. Here, yea, here,
Euphues, mayest thou see not the carved vizard of a lewd woman, but
the incarnate visage of a lascivious wanton; not the shadow of love, but
the substance of lust. My heart melteth in drops of blood to see an harlot
20 with the one hand rob so many coffers, and with the other to rip so many
corses. Thou art here amidst the pikes between Scylla and Charybdis,
ready, if thou shun Syrtis, to sink into Semphlegades. Let the Lacede-
monian, the Persian, the Parthian, yea, the Neapolitan, cause thee rather
to detest such villany, at the sight and view of their vanity.

"Is it not far better to abhor sins by the remembrance of others' faults
than by repentance of thine own follies? Is not he accounted most wise
whom other men's harms do make most wary? But thou wilt haply say
that, although there be many things in Naples to be justly condemned,
yet are there some things of necessity to be commended; and as thy will
30 doth lean unto the one, so thy wit would also embrace the other. Alas,
Euphues, by how much the more I love the high climbing of thy capacity,
by so much the more I fear thy fall. The fine crystal is sooner crazed than
the hard marble; the greenest beech burneth faster than the dryest oak;
the fairest silk is soonest soiled; and the sweetest wine turneth to the
sharpest vinegar. The pestilence doth most rifest infect the clearest complexion, and the caterpillar cleaveth unto the ripest fruit; the most delicate
wit is allured with small enticement unto vice, and most subject to yield
unto vanity. If, therefore, thou do but hearken to the sirens, thou wilt be
enamored; if thou haunt their houses and places, thou shalt be enchanted.
40 One drop of poison infecteth the whole tun of wine; one leaf of *coloquintida* marreth and spoileth the whole pot of porridge; one iron mole defaceth the whole piece of lawn. Descend into thine own conscience and

consider with thyself the great difference between staring and stark blind,
wit and wisdom, love and lust. Be merry, but with modesty; be sober, but
not too sullen; be valiant, but not too venturous. Let thy attire be comely,
but not costly; thy diet wholesome, but not excessive; use pastime as the
word importeth, to pass the time in honest recreation. Mistrust no man
without cause, neither be thou credulous without proof; be not light to
follow every man's opinion, nor obstinate to stand in thine own conceit.
Serve God, love God, fear God, and God will so bless thee as either heart
can wish or thy friends desire. And so I end my counsel, beseeching thee
to begin to follow it."   10

This old gentleman having finished his discourse, Euphues began to
shape him an answer in this sort: "Father and friend (your age sheweth
the one, your honesty the other), I am neither so suspicious to mistrust
your good will, nor so sottish to mislike your good counsel; as I am therefore to thank you for the first, so it stands me upon to think better on the
latter. I mean not to cavil with you, as one loving sophistry; neither to
control you, as one having superiority; the one would bring my talk into
the suspicion of fraud, the other convince me of folly. Whereas you argue,
I know not upon what probabilities, but sure I am upon no proof, that my
bringing up should be a blemish to my birth, I answer, and swear too,   20
that you were not therein a little overshot; either you gave too much credit
to the report of others or too much liberty to your own judgment. You
convince my parents of peevishness in making me a wanton, and me of
lewdness in rejecting correction. But so many men, so many minds; that
may seem in your eye odious which in another's eye may be gracious.
Aristippus a philosopher, yet who more courtly? Diogenes a philosopher,
yet who more carterly? Who more popular than Plato, retaining always
good company? Who more envious than Timon, denouncing all human
society? Who so severe as the stoics, which, like stocks, were moved with
no melody? Who so secure as the epicures, which wallowed in all kind   30
of licentiousness? Though all men be made of one metal, yet they be not
cast all in one mold; there is framed of the self-same clay as well the tile
to keep out water as the pot to contain liquor; the sun doth harden the
dirt and melt the wax; fire maketh the gold to shine and the straw to
smother; perfumes doth refresh the dove and kill the beetle, and the nature of the man disposeth that consent of the manners. Now, whereas you
seem to love my nature and loathe my nurture, you bewray your own
weakness in thinking that nature may any ways be altered by education,
and as you have ensamples to confirm your pretense, so I have most evident and infallible arguments to serve for my purpose. It is natural for   40
the vine to spread; the more you seek by art to alter it, the more, in the
end, you shall augment it. It is proper for the palm tree to mount; the

heavier you load it, the higher it sprouteth. Though iron be made soft with
fire, it returneth to his hardness; though the falcon be reclaimed to the
fist, she retireth to her haggardness; the whelp of a mastiff will never
be taught to retrieve the partridge; education can have no shew where
the excellency of Nature doth bear sway. The silly mouse will by no
manner of means be tamed; the subtle fox may well be beaten, but never
broken from stealing his prey. If you pound spices, they smell the sweeter;
season the wood never so well, the wine will taste of the cask; plant and
translate the crabtree where and whensoever it please you, and it will
never bear sweet apple, unless you graft it by art, which nothing toucheth
Nature.

"Infinite and innumerable were the examples I could allege and declare
to confirm the force of Nature, and confute these your vain and false
forgeries, were not the repetition of them needless, having shewed sufficient, or bootless, seeing those alleged will not persuade you. And can you
be so unnatural whom Dame Nature hath nourished and brought up so
many years, to repine, as it were, against Nature?

"The similitude you rehearse of the wax argueth your waxing and
melting brain, and your example of the hot and hard iron sheweth in
you but cold and weak disposition. Do you not know that which all men
do affirm and know, that black will take no other color? That the stone
abeston, being once made hot, will never be made cold? That fire cannot
be forced downward? That Nature will have course after kind? That
everything will dispose itself according to Nature? Can the Æthiope
change or alter his skin? or the leopard his hue? Is it possible to gather
grapes of thorns, or figs of thistles, or to cause anything to strive against
Nature? But why go I about to praise Nature, the which as yet was never
any imp so wicked and barbarous, any Turk so vile and brutish, any
beast so dull and senseless, that could, or would, or durst dispraise or
contemn? Doth not Cicero conclude and allow that if we follow and
obey Nature we shall never err? Doth not Aristotle allege and confirm
that Nature frameth or maketh nothing in any point rude, vain, or unperfect.

"Nature was had in such estimation and admiration among the heathen
people that she was reputed for the only goddess in heaven. If Nature,
then, have largely and bountifully endued me with her gifts, why deem
you me so untoward and graceless? If she have dealt hardly with me, why
extol you so much my birth? If Nature bear no sway, why use you this
adulation? If Nature work the effect, what booteth any education? If
Nature be of strength or force, what availeth discipline or nurture? If
of none, what helpeth Nature? But let these sayings pass as known evi-

dently and granted to be true, which none can or may deny unless he be false, or that he be an enemy to humanity.

"As touching my residence and abiding here in Naples, my youthly affections, my sports and pleasures, my pastimes, my common dalliance, my delights, my resort and company, and companions which daily use to visit me, although to you they breed more sorrow and care than solace and comfort, because of your crabbed age, yet to me they bring more comfort and joy than care and grief, more bliss than bale, more happiness than heaviness, because of my youthful gentleness. Either you would have all men old, as you are, or else you have quite forgotten that you yourself were young or ever knew young days; either in your youth you were a very vicious and ungodly man or now, being aged, very superstitious and devout above measure.

"Put you no difference between the young flourishing bay tree and the old withered beech? No kind of distinction between the waxing and the waning of the moon, and between the rising and the setting of the sun? Do you measure the hot assaults of youth by the cold skirmishes of age, whose years are subject to more infirmities than our youth? We merry, you melancholy; we zealous in affection, you jealous in all your doings; you testy without cause, we hasty for no quarrel; you careful, we careless; we bold, you fearful; we, in all points, contrary unto you, and ye in all points unlike unto us. Seeing, therefore, we be repugnant each to the other in nature, would you have us alike in qualities? Would you have one potion ministered to the burning fever and to the cold palsy? one plaster to an old issue and a fresh wound? one salve for all sores? one sauce for all meats? No, no, Eubulus, but I will yield to more than either I am bound to grant, either thou able to prove. Suppose that which I never will believe, that Naples is a cankered storehouse of all strife, a common stews for all strumpets, the sink of shame, and the very nurse of all sin; shall it, therefore, follow of necessity that all that are wooed of love should be wedded to lust? Will you conclude, as it were *ex consequenti*, that whosoever arriveth here shall be enticed to folly, and, being enticed, of force shall be entangled? No, no, it is the disposition of the thought that altereth the nature of the thing. The sun shineth upon the dunghill and is not corrupted; the diamond lieth in the fire and is not consumed; the crystal toucheth the toad and is not poisoned; the bird *trochilus* liveth by the mouth of the crocodile and is not spoiled; a perfect wit is never bewitched with lewdness, neither enticed with lasciviousness.

"Is it not common that the holm tree springeth amidst the beech? that the ivy spreadeth upon the hard stones? that the soft featherbed breaketh the hard blade? If experience have not taught you this, you have lived long and learned little; or if your moist brain have forgot it, you have learned much and profited nothing. But it may be that you measure my affections by your own fancies, and, knowing yourself either too simple to raise the siege of policy or too weak to resist the assault by prowess, you deem me of as little wit as yourself or of less force; either of small capacity or of no courage. In my judgment, Eubulus, you shall as soon catch a hare with a tabor as you shall persuade youth, with your aged and overworn eloquence, to such severity of life, which, as yet, there was never stoic so strict, nor Jesuit so superstitious, neither votary so devout, but 10 would rather allow it in words than follow it in works, rather talk of it than try it. Neither were you such a saint in your youth that, abandoning all pleasures, all pastimes, and delights, you would choose rather to sacrifice the first fruits of your life to vain holiness than to youthly affections. But as to the stomach quatted with dainties, all delicates seem queasy, and as he that surfeiteth with wine useth afterward to allay with water, so these old huddles, having overcharged their gorges with fancy, accompt all honest recreation mere folly, and, having taken a surfeit of delight, seem now to savor it with despite. Seeing, therefore, it is labor lost for me to persuade you, and wind vainly wasted for you to exhort me, here I found 20 you and here I leave you, having neither bought nor sold with you, but changed ware for ware; if you have taken little pleasure in my reply, sure I am that, by your counsel, I have reaped less profit. They that use to steal honey burn hemlock to smoke the bees from their hives, and it may be that, to get some advantage of me, you have used these smoky arguments, thinking thereby to smother me with the conceit of strong imagination. But as the chameleon though he have most guts draweth least breath, or as the elder tree though he be fullest of pith is farthest from strength, so, though your reasons seem inwardly to yourself somewhat substantial and your persuasions pithy in your own conceit, yet, being well weighed with- 30 out, they be shadows without substance, and weak without force. The bird *taurus* hath a great voice, but a small body; the thunder a great clap, yet but a little stone; the empty vessel giveth a greater sound than the full barrel. I mean not to apply it, but look into yourself and you shall certainly find it, and thus I leave you seeking it; but were it not that my company stay my coming, I would surely help you to look it, but I am called hence by my acquaintance."

Euphues, having thus ended his talk, departed, leaving this old gentleman in a great quandary; who, perceiving that he was more inclined to wantonness than to wisdom, with a deep sigh, the tears trickling down his 40 cheeks, said: "Seeing thou wilt not buy counsel at the first hand good cheap, thou shalt buy repentance at the second hand at such an inreasonable rate that thou wilt curse thy hard pennyworth and ban thy hard heart.

Ah, Euphues, little dost thou know that if thy wealth waste, thy wit will give but small warmth, and if thy wit incline to wilfulness, that thy wealth will do thee no great good. If the one had been employed to thrift, the other to learning, it had been hard to conjecture whether thou shouldst have been more fortunate by riches or happy by wisdom, whether more esteemed in the commonweal for wealth to maintain war or for counsel to conclude peace. But, alas, why do I pity that in thee which thou seemest to praise in thyself?" And so saying, he immediately went to his own house, heavily bewailing the young man's unhappiness.

Here ye may behold, gentlemen, how lewdly wit standeth in his own 10 light, how he deemeth no penny good silver but his own, preferring the blossom before the fruit, the bud before the flower, the green blade before the ripe ear of corn, his own wit before all men's wisdoms. Neither is that geason, seeing, for the most part, it is proper to all those of sharp capacity to esteem of themselves as most proper. If one be hard in conceiving, they pronounce him a dolt; if given to study, they proclaim him a dunce; if merry, a jester; if sad, a saint; if full of words, a sot; if without speech, a cipher. If one argue with them boldly, then is he impudent; if coldly, an innocent; if there be reasoning of divinity, they cry, *Quae supra nos, nihil ad nos;* if of humanity, *Sententias loquitur carnifex.* Hereof cometh such 20 great familiarity between the ripest wits when they shall see the disposition the one of the other, the *sympathia* of affections, and, as it were, but a pair of shears to go between their natures; one flattereth another in his own folly, and layeth cushions under the elbow of his fellow when he seeth him take a nap with fancy; and as their wit wresteth them to vice, so it forgeth them some feat excuse to cloak their vanity.

Too much study doth intoxicate their brains, for (say they), although iron, the more it is used the brighter it is, yet silver, with much wearing, doth waste to nothing; though the cammock, the more it is bowed the better it serveth, yet the bow, the more it is bent and occupied, the weaker 30 it waxeth; though the camomile, the more it is trodden and pressed down, the more it spreadeth, yet the violet, the oftener it is handled and touched, the sooner it withereth and decayeth. Besides this, a fine wit, a sharp sense, a quick understanding is able to attain to more in a moment or a very little space than a dull and blockish head in a month. The scythe cutteth far better and smoother than the saw, the wax yieldeth better and sooner to the seal than the steel to the stamp; the smooth and plain beech is easier to be carved than the knotty box. For neither is there anything but that hath his contraries.

Such is the nature of these novices that think to have learning without 40 labor, and treasure without travail; either not understanding or else not remembering that the finest edge is made with the blunt whetstone and

the fairest jewel fashioned with the hard hammer. I go not about, gentlemen, to inveigh against wit, for then I were witless, but frankly to confess
mine own little wit. I have ever thought so superstitiously of wit that I fear
I have committed idolatry against wisdom, and, if Nature had dealt so
beneficially with me, to have given me any wit, I should have been readier
in the defense of it to have made an apology than any way to turn to
apostasy. But this I note, that, for the most part, they stand so on their
pantofles that they be secure of perils, obstinate in their own opinions, impatient of labor, apt to conceive wrong, credulous to believe the worst,
10 ready to shake off their old acquaintance without cause, and to condemn
them without color. All which humors are by so much the more easier to
be purged by how much the less they have festered the sinews. But return
we again to Euphues.

Euphues having sojourned by the space of two months in Naples,
whether he were moved by the courtesy of a young gentleman named
Philautus, or enforced by destiny; whether his pregnant wit, or his pleasant conceits wrought the greater liking in the mind of Euphues I know
not for certainty. But Euphues shewed such entire love towards him
that he seemed to make small account of any others, determining to enter
20 into such an inviolable league of friendship with him as neither time by
piecemeal should impair, neither fancy utterly desolve, nor any suspicion
infringe. "I have read," saith he, "and well I believe it, that a friend is
in prosperity a pleasure, a solace in adversity, in grief a comfort, in joy a
merry companion, at all times an other I, in all places the express Image of mine own person; insomuch that I cannot tell whether the immortal Gods have bestowed any gift upon mortal men either more noble,
or more necessary, than friendship. Is there anything in the world to be
reputed (I will not say compared) to friendship? Can any treasure in this
transitory pilgrimage be of more value than a friend? In whose bosom
30 thou mayst sleep secure without fear, whom thou mayst make partner
of all thy secrets without suspicion of fraud, and partaker of all thy misfortune without mistrust of fleeting, who will account thy bale his bane,
thy mishap his misery, the pricking of thy finger, the piercing of his heart.
But whither am I carried? Have I not also learned that one should eat a
bushel of salt with him whom he meaneth to make his friend? that trial
maketh trust? that there is falsehood in fellowship? and what then? Doth
not the sympathy of manners make the conjunction of minds? Is it not
a byword, like will to like? Not so common as commendable it is, to see
young gentlemen choose them such friends with whom they may seem,
40 being absent, to be present; being asunder, to be conversant; being dead,
to be alive. I will therefore have Philautus for my fere, and by so much

the more I make myself sure to have Philautus, by how much the more I view in him the lively image of Euphues."

Although there be none so ignorant that doth not know, neither any so impudent that will not confess friendship to be the jewel of human joy, yet whosoever shall see this amity grounded upon a little affection will soon conjecture that it will be dissolved upon a light occasion; as in the sequel of Euphues and Philautus you shall see, whose hot love waxed soon cold. For as the best wine doth make the sharpest vinegar, so the deepest love turneth to the deadliest hate. Who deserved the most blame, in mine opinion, it is doubtful, and so difficult that I dare not presume to give ver- 10 dict. For love being the cause for which so many mischiefs have been attempted, I am not yet persuaded whether of them was most to be blamed, but certainly neither of them was blameless. I appeal to your judgment, gentlemen, not that I think any of you of the like disposition able to decide the question, but being of deeper discretion than I am, are more fit to debate the quarrel. Though the discourse of their friendship and falling out be somewhat long, yet, being somewhat strange, I hope the delightfulness of the one will attenuate the tediousness of the other.

Euphues had continual access to the place of Philautus and no little familiarity with him, and, finding him at convenient leisure, in these 20 short terms unfolded his mind unto him.

"Gentleman and friend, the trial I have had of thy manners cutteth off divers terms which to another I would have used in the like matter. And sithens a long discourse argueth folly, and delicate words incur the suspicion of flattery, I am determined to use neither of them, knowing either of them to breed offence. Weighing with myself the force of friendship by the effects, I studied ever since my first coming to Naples to enter league with such a one as might direct my steps, being a stranger, and resemble my manners, being a scholar; the which two qualities as I find in you able to satisfy my desire, so I hope I shall find a heart in you willing 30 to accomplish my request. Which if I may obtain, assure yourself that Damon to his Pythias, Pylades to his Orestes, Titus to his Gysippus, Theseus to his Pyrothus, Scipio to his Lælius, was never found more faithful than Euphues will be to his Philautus."

Philautus by how much the less he looked for this discourse, by so much the more he liked it, for he saw all qualities both of body and mind in Euphues, unto whom he replied as followeth:

"Friend Euphues (for so your talk warranteth me to term you), I dare neither use a long process, neither loving speech, lest unwittingly I should cause you to convince me of those things which you have already con- 40 demned. And verily I am bold to presume upon your courtesy, since you

yourself have used so little curiosity, persuading myself that my short answer will work as great an effect in you as your few words did in me. And seeing we resemble (as you say) each other in qualities, it cannot be that the one should differ from the other in courtesy, seeing the sincere affection of the mind cannot be expressed by the mouth, and that no art can unfold the entire love of the heart, I am earnestly to beseech you not to measure the firmness of my faith by the fewness of my words, but rather think that the overflowing waves of good will leave no passage for many words. Trial shall prove trust. Here is my hand; my heart, my
10 lands, and my life at thy commandment. Thou mayst well perceive that I did believe thee, that so soon I did love thee, and I hope thou wilt the rather love me in that I did believe thee." Either Euphues and Philautus stood in need of friendship, or were ordained to be friends; upon so short warning, to make so soon a conclusion might seem in mine opinion, if it continued, miraculous, if shaken off, ridiculous.

But after many embracings and protestations one to an other, they walked to dinner, where they wanted neither meat, neither music, neither any other pastime; and having banqueted, to digest their sweet confections they danced all that afternoon. They used not only one board, but one
20 bed, one book (if so be it they thought not one too many). Their friendship augmented every day, insomuch that the one could not refrain the company of the other one minute. All things went in common between them, which all men accounted commendable.

Philautus being a town born child, both for his own countenance and the great countenance which his father had while he lived, crept into credit with Don Ferardo, one of the chief governors of the city, who, although he had a courtly crew of gentlewomen sojourning in his palace, yet his daughter, heiress to his whole revenues, stained the beauty of them all; whose modest bashfulness caused the other to look wan for
30 envy, whose lily cheeks dyed with a vermilion red made the rest to blush for shame. For as the finest ruby staineth the color of the rest that be in place, or as the sun dimmeth the moon that she cannot be discerned, so this gallant girl, more fair than fortunate, and yet more fortunate than faithful, eclipsed the beauty of them all, and changed their colors. Unto her had Philautus access, who won her by right of love, and should have won her by right of law, had not Euphues by strange destiny broken the bonds of marriage, and forbidden the banns of matrimony.

It happened that Don Ferardo had occasion to go to Venice about certain his own affairs, leaving his daughter the only steward of his house-
40 hold, who spared not to feast Philautus her friend, with all kinds of delights and delicates, reserving only her honesty as the chief stay of her honor. Her father being gone, she sent for her friend to supper, who

came not as he was accustomed solitarily alone, but accompanied with
his friend Euphues. The gentlewoman, whether it were for niceness or
for niggardness of courtesy, gave him such a cold welcome that he repented that he was come.

Euphues, though he knew himself worthy every way to have a good
countenance, yet could he not perceive her willing any way to lend him
a friendly look. Yet lest he should seem to want gestures, or to be dashed
out of conceit with her coy countenance, he addressed him to a gentlewoman called Livia, unto whom he uttered this speech:

"Fair lady, if it be the guise of Italy to welcome strangers with strange- 10
ness, I must needs say the custom is strange and the country barbarous;
if the manner of ladies to salute gentlemen with coyness, then I am enforced to think the women without courtesy to use such welcome, and
the men past shame that will come. But hereafter I will either bring a
stool on mine arm for an unbidden guest, or a vizard on my face for a
shameless gossip."

Livia replied: "Sir, our country is civil and our gentlewomen are courteous, but in Naples it is counted a jest at every word to say, 'In faith you
are welcome.'"

As she was yet talking, supper was set on the board. Then Philautus 20
spake thus unto Lucilla: "Yet gentlewoman, I was the bolder to bring
my shadow with me (meaning Euphues), knowing that he should be the
better welcome for my sake."

Unto whom the gentlewoman replied: "Sir, as I never when I saw you
thought that you came without your shadow, so now I cannot a little
marvel to see you so overshot in bringing a new shadow with you."

Euphues, though he perceived her coy nip, seemed not to care for it, but
taking her by the hand said: "Fair lady, seeing the shade doth often shield
your beauty from the parching sun, I hope you will the better esteem of
the shadow; and by so much the less it ought to be offensive by how much 30
the less it is able to offend you, and by so much the more you ought to like
it by how much the more you use to lie in it."

"Well, gentleman," answered Lucilla, "in arguing of the shadow, we
forego the substance. Pleaseth it you therefore to sit down to supper."

And so they all sat down, but Euphues fed of one dish which ever stood
before him, the beauty of Lucilla. Here Euphues at the first sight was so
kindled with desire that almost he was like to burn to coals.

Supper being ended, the order was in Naples that the gentlewomen
would desire to hear some discourse, either concerning love or learning.
And although Philautus was requested, yet he posted it over to Euphues, 40
whom he knew most fit for that purpose. Euphues being thus tied to the
stake by their importunate entreaty, began as followeth:

"He that worst may, is always enforced to hold the candle; the weakest must still to the wall; where none will, the devil himself must bear the cross. But were it not, gentlewomen, that your lust stands for law, I would borrow so much leave as to resign my office to one of you, whose experience in love hath made you learned, and whose learning hath made you so lovely; for me to entreat of the one, being a novice, or to discourse of the other, being a truant, I may well make you weary but never the wiser, and give you occasion rather to laugh at my rashness than to like my reasons. Yet I care the less to excuse my boldness to you who were the
10 cause of my blindness. And since I am at my own choice either to talk of love or of learning, I had rather for this time be deemed an unthrift in rejecting profit than a Stoic in renouncing pleasure.

"It hath been a question often disputed, but never determined, whether the qualities of the mind or the composition of the man cause women most to like, or whether beauty or wit move men most to love. Certainly by how much the more the mind is to be preferred before the body, by so much the more the graces of the one are to be preferred before the gifts of the other; which if it be so that the contemplation of the inward quality ought to be respected more than the view of the outward beauty, then
20 doubtless women either do or should love those best whose virtue is best, not measuring the deformed man with the reformed mind. The foul toad hath a fair stone in his head, the fine gold is found in the filthy earth, the sweet kernel lyeth in the hard shell. Virtue is harbored in the heart of him that most men esteem misshapen. Contrariwise, if we respect more the outward shape than the inward habit, good God into how many mischiefs do we fall? into what blindness are we led? Do we not commonly see that in painted pots is hidden the deadliest poison? that in the greenest grass is the greatest serpent? in the clearest water the ugliest toad? Doth not experience teach us that in the most curious sepulchre are enclosed rotten
30 bones? That the cypress tree beareth a fair leaf but no fruit? That the estridge carrieth fair feathers but rank flesh? How frantic are those lovers which are carried away with the gay glistering of the fine face? the beauty whereof is parched with the summer's blaze and chipped with the winter's blast, which is of so short continuance that it fadeth before one perceive it flourish, of so small profit that it poisoneth those that possess it, of so little value with the wise that they account it a delicate bait with a deadly hook, a sweet panther with a devouring paunch, a sour poison in a silver pot.

"Here I could enter into discourse of such fine dames as being in love with their own looks make such coarse account of their passionate lovers;
40 for commonly, if they be adorned with beauty, they be so straight laced, and made so high in the instep, that they disdain them most that most desire them. It is a world to see the doting of their lovers, and their dealing

with them, the revealing of whose subtle trains would cause me to shed tears, and you, gentlewomen, to shut your modest ears. Pardon me, gentlewomen, if I unfold every wile and shew every wrinkle of women's dispositions. Two things do they cause their servants to vow unto them, secrecy and sovereignty: the one to conceal their enticing sleights, by the other to assure themselves of their only service. Again—but ho there! If I should have waded any further and sounded the depth of their deceit, I should either have procured your displeasure or incurred the suspicion of fraud, either armed you to practice the like subtlety or accused myself of perjury. But I mean not to offend your chaste minds with the rehearsal 10 of their unchaste manners, whose ears I perceive to glow and hearts to be grieved at that which I have already uttered, not that amongst you there be any such, but that in your sex there should be any such.

"Let not gentlewomen therefore make too much of their painted sheath, let them not be so curious in their own conceit, or so currish to their loyal lovers. When the black crow's foot shall appear in their eye or the black ox tread on their foot, when their beauty shall be like the blasted rose, their wealth wasted, their bodies worn, their faces wrinkled, their fingers crooked, who will like of them in their age who loved none in their youth? If you will be cherished when you be old, be courteous while 20 you be young; if you look for comfort in your hoary hairs, be not coy when you have your golden locks; if you would be embraced in the vaining of your bravery, be not squeamish in the waxing of your beauty; if you desire to be kept like the roses when they have lost their color, smell sweet as the rose doth in the bud; if you would be tasted for old wine, be in the mouth a pleasant grape—so shall you be cherished for your courtesy, comforted for your honesty, embraced for your amity; so shall you be preserved with the sweet rose, and drunk with the pleasant wine. Thus far I am bold, gentlewomen, to counsel those that be coy that they weave not the web of their own woe, nor spin the thread of their own thralldom 30 by their own overthwartness. And seeing we are even in the bowels of love, it shall not be amiss to examine whether man or woman be soonest allured; whether be most constant the male or the female. And in this point I mean not to be my own carver, lest I should seem either to pick a thank with men, or a quarrel with women. If therefore it might stand with your pleasure, Mistress Lucilla, to give your censure, I would take the contrary; for sure I am though your judgment be sound, yet affection will shadow it."

Lucilla, seeing his pretence, thought to take advantage of his large proffer, unto whom she said: "Gentleman, in my opinion women are to 40 be won with every wind, in whose sex there is neither force to withstand the assaults of love, neither constancy to remain faithful. And because your discourse hath hitherto bred delight, I am loath to hinder you in the sequel of your devices."

Euphues, perceiving himself to be taken napping, answered as followeth: "Mistress Lucilla, if you speak as you think, these gentlewomen present have little cause to thank you; if you cause me to commend women, my tale will be accounted a mere trifle and your words the plain truth. Yet, knowing promise to be debt, I will pay it with performance. And I would the gentlemen here present were as ready to credit my proof as the gentlewomen are willing to hear their own praises, or I as able to 10 overcome as Mistress Lucilla would be content to be overthrown. Howsoever the matter shall fall out, I am of the surer side; for if my reasons be weak, then is our sex strong; if forcible, then your judgment feeble; if I find truth on my side, I hope I shall for my wages win the good will of women; if I want proof, then gentlewomen of necessity you must yield to men. But to the matter.

"Touching the yielding to love, allbeit their hearts seem tender, yet they harden them like the stone of Sicilia, the which the more it is beaten, the harder it is; for, being framed as it were of the perfection of men, they be free from all such cogitations as may any way provoke them to un-20 cleanness, insomuch as they abhor the light love of youth which is grounded upon lust and dissolved upon every light occasion. When they see the folly of men turn to fury, their delight to doting, their affection to frenzy; when they see them as it were pine in pleasure and to wax pale through their own peevishness, their suits, their service, their letters, their labors, their loves, their lives seem to them so odious that they harden their hearts against such concupiscence to the end they might convert them from rashness to reason, from such lewd disposition to honest discretion. Hereof it cometh that men accuse women of cruelty because they themselves want civility, they account them full of wiles in not yielding to their wickedness, faith-30 less for resisting their filthiness. But I had almost forgot myself—you shall pardon me, Mistress Lucilla, for this time, if thus abruptly I finish my discourse. It is neither for want of good will or lack of proof, but that I feel in myself such alteration, that I can scarcely utter one word. Ah Euphues, Euphues!"

The gentlewomen were struck into such a quandary with this sudden change that they all changed color. But Euphues, taking Philautus by the hand and giving the gentlewomen thanks for their patience and his repast, bade them all farewell, and went immediately to his chamber.

But Lucilla, who now began to fry in the flames of love, all the com-40 pany being departed to their lodgings, entered into these terms and contrarieties:

"Ah wretched wench Lucilla, how art thou perplexed! What a doubtful fight dost thou feel betwixt faith and fancy, hope and fear, conscience and concupiscence! O my Euphues, little dost thou know the sudden sorrow that I sustain for thy sweet sake, whose wit hath bewitched me, whose rare qualities have deprived me of mine old quality, whose courteous behavior without curiosity, whose comely feature without fault, whose filed speech without fraud, hath wrapped me in this misfortune. And canst thou, Lucilla, be so light of love in forsaking Philautus to fly to Euphues? Canst thou prefer a stranger before thy countryman? A starter before thy companion? Why Euphues doth perhaps desire my love, but Philautus hath deserved it. Why Euphues' feature is worthy as good as I, but 10 Philautus his faith is worthy a better. Aye, but the latter love is most fervent. Aye, but the first ought to be most faithful. Aye, but Euphues hath greater perfection. Aye, but Philautus hath deeper affection.

"Ah fond wench, dost thou think Euphues will deem thee constant to him, when thou hast been unconstant to his friend? Weenest thou that he will have no mistrust of thy faithfulness, when he hath had trial of thy fickleness? Will he have no doubt of thine honor, when thou thyself callest thine honesty in question? Yes, yes, Lucilla, well doth he know that the glass once crazed will with the least clap be cracked, that the cloth which staineth with milk will soon lose his color with vinegar, that the eagle's 20 wing will waste the feather as well of the phoenix as of the pheasant, that she that hath been faithless to one will never be faithful to any. But can Euphues convince me of fleeting, seeing for his sake I break my fidelity? Can he condemn me of disloyalty, when he is the only cause of my disliking? May he justly condemn me of treachery, who hath this testimony as trial of my good will? Doth not he remember that the broken bone, once set together, is stronger than ever it was? That the greatest blot is taken off with the pumice? That though the spider poison the fly, she cannot infect the bee? That although I have been light to Philautus, yet I may be lovely to Euphues? It is not my desire but his deserts that moveth 30 my mind to this choice, neither the want of the like good will in Philautus but the lack of the like good qualities that removeth my fancy from the one to the other.

"For, as the bee that gathereth honey out of the weed, when she spyeth the fair flower flyeth to the sweetest; or as the kind spaniel, though he hunt after birds, yet forsakes them to retrieve the partridge; or as we commonly feed on beef hungrily at the first, yet seeing the quail more dainty, change our diet; so I, although I loved Philautus for his good properties, yet seeing Euphues to excell him, I ought by Nature to like him better. By so much the more, therefore, my change is to be excused, by how much 40 the more my choice is excellent; and by so much the less I am to be condemned, by how much the more Euphues is to be commended. Is not the

diamond of more value than the ruby because he is of more virtue? Is not
the emerald preferred before the sapphire for his wonderful property?
Is not Euphues more praiseworthy than Philautus, being more witty?

"But fie, Lucilla, why dost thou flatter thyself in thine own folly?
Canst thou fain Euphues thy friend, whom by thine own words thou
hast made thy foe? Didst not thou accuse women of inconstancy? Didst
not thou account them easy to be won? Didst not thou condemn them of
weakness? What sounder argument can he have against thee than thine
own answer? What better proof than thine own speech? What greater
10 trial than thine own talk? If thou hast belied women, he will judge thee
unkind; if thou have revealed the truth, he must needs think thee unconstant; if he perceive thee to be won with a nut, he will imagine that thou
wilt be lost with an apple; if he find thee wanton before thou be wooed,
he will guess thou wilt be wavering when thou art wedded.

"But suppose that Euphues love thee, that Philautus leave thee, will
thy father, thinkest thou, give thee liberty to live after thine own lust?
Will he esteem him worthy to inherit his possessions whom he accounteth
unworthy to enjoy thy person? Is it like that he will match thee in marriage
with a stranger, with a Grecian, with a mean man? Aye, but what know-
20 eth my father whether he be wealthy, whether his revenues be able to
countervail my father's lands, whether his birth be noble, yea, or no?
Can anyone make doubt of his gentle blood that seeth his gentle conditions? Can his honor be called into question whose honesty is so great?
Is he to be thought thriftless, who in all qualities of the mind is peerless?
No, no, the tree is known by his fruit, the gold by his touch, the son by the
sire. And as the soft wax receiveth whatsoever print be in the seal, and
sheweth no other impression, so the tender babe, being sealed with his
father's gifts, representeth his Image most lively. But were I once certain of Euphues' good will I would not so superstitiously account of my
30 father's ill will. Time hath weaned me from my mother's teat, and age
rid me from my father's correction; when children are in their swath-
clouts, then are they subject to the whip, and ought to be careful of the
rigor of their parents. As for me, seeing I am not fed with their pap, I
am not to be led by their persuasions. Let my father use what speeches
he list, I will follow mine own lust. Lust, Lucilla? What sayst thou? No,
no, mine own love I should have said, for I am as far from lust as I am
from reason, and as near to love as I am to folly. Then stick to thy determination, and shew thyself what love can do, what love dares do,
what love hath done. Albeit I can no way quench the coals of desire with
40 forgetfulness, yet will I rake them up in the ashes of modesty; seeing I
dare not discover my love for maidenly shamefastness, I will dissemble it
till time I have opportunity. And I hope so to behave myself as Euphues

shall think me his own, and Philautus persuade himself I am none but his. But I would to God Euphues would repair hither, that the sight of him might mitigate some part of my martyrdom."

She having thus discoursed with herself her own miseries, cast herself on the bed. And there let her lie, and return we to Euphues, who was so caught in the gin of folly that he neither could comfort himself nor durst ask counsel of his friend, suspecting that which indeed was true, that Philautus was co-rival with him and cock-mate with Lucilla. Amidst therefore these his extremities between hope and fear, he uttered these or the like speeches: 10

"What is he, Euphues, that knowing thy wit, and seeing thy folly, but will rather punish thy lewdness than pity thy haughtiness? Was there ever any so fickle so soon to be allured? Any ever so faithless to deceive his friend? Ever any so foolish to bathe himself in his own misfortune? Too true it is that as the sea crab swimmeth always against the stream, so wit always striveth against wisdom. And as the bee is oftentimes hurt with her own honey, so is wit not seldom plagued with his own conceit.

"O ye gods, have ye ordained for every malady a medicine, for every sore a salve, for every pain a plaster, leaving only love remediless? Did ye deem no man so mad to be entangled with desire, or thought ye them 20 worthy to be tormented that were so misled? Have ye dealt more favorably with brute beasts than with reasonable creatures. The filthy sow when she is sick eateth the sea crab and is immediately recured; the tortoise, having tasted the viper, sucketh *Origanum* and is quickly revived; the bear, ready to pine, licketh up the ants and is recovered; the dog having surfeited, to procure his vomit eateth grass, and findeth remedy; the hart being pierced with the dart, runneth out of hand to the herb *Dictanum*, and is healed. And can men by no herb, by no art, by no way, procure a remedy for the impatient disease of love? Ah well I perceive that love is not unlike the fig tree, whose fruit is sweet, whose root is more bitter 30 than the claw of a bitter; or like the apple in Persia, whose blossom savoreth like honey, whose bud is more sour than gall.

"But O impiety! O broad blasphemy against the heavens! Wilt thou be so impudent, Euphues, to accuse the gods of iniquity? No fond fool, no! Neither is it forbidden us by the gods to love, by whose divine providence we are permitted to live; neither do we want remedies to recure our maladies, but reason to use the means. But why go I about to hinder the course of love with the discourse of law? Hast thou not read, Euphues, that he that loppeth the vine causeth it to spread fairer? That he that stoppeth the stream forceth it to swell higher? That he that casteth water 40 on the fire in the smith's forge maketh it to flame fiercer? Even so he that seeketh by counsel to moderate his overlashing affections increaseth his

own misfortune. Ah my Lucilla, would thou were either less fair or I more
fortunate, either I wiser or thou milder; either would I were out of this
mad mood, either I would we were both of one mind. But how should
she be persuaded of my loyalty, that yet had never one simple proof of
my love? Will she not rather imagine me to be entangled with her beauty
than with her virtue. That my fancy being so lewdly chained at the first,
will be as lightly changed at the last; that nothing violent can be permanent. Yes, yes, she must needs conjecture so, although it be nothing
so, for by how much the more my affection cometh on the sudden, by so
much the less will she think it certain. The rattling thunderbolt hath but
his clap, the lightning but his flash, and as they both come in a moment,
so do they both end in a minute.

"Aye, but Euphues, hath she not heard also that the dry touchwood is
kindled with lime, that the greatest mushroom groweth in one night?
That the fire quickly burneth the flax? That love easily entreth into the
sharp wit without resistance, and is harbored there without repentance?
If therefore the Gods have endowed her with as much bounty as beauty;
if she have no less wit than she hath comeliness, certes she will neither
conceive sinisterly of my sudden suit, neither be coy to receive me into
her service, neither suspect me of lightness in yielding so lightly, neither
reject me disdainfully, for loving so hastily. Shall I not then hazard my
life to obtain my love? And deceive Philautus to receive Lucilla? Yes
Euphues, where love beareth sway, friendship can have no show. As
Philautus brought me for his shadow the last supper, so will I use him
for my shadow till I have gained his saint. And canst thou, wretch, be
false to him that is faithful to thee? Shall his courtesy be cause of thy
cruelty? Wilt thou violate the league of faith to inherit the land of folly?
Shall affection be of more force than friendship, love than law, lust than
loyalty? Knowest thou not that he that loseth his honesty hath nothing
else to lose?

"Tush, the case is light where reason taketh place; to love and to live
well is not granted to Jupiter. Who so is blinded with the caul of beauty
discerneth no color of honesty. Did not Gyges cut Candaules a coat by
his own measure? Did not Paris, though he were a welcome guest to
Menelaus, serve his host a slippery prank? If Philautus had loved Lucilla,
he would never have suffered Euphues to have seen her. Is it not the prey
that enticeth the thief to rifle? Is it not the pleasant bait that causeth the
fleetest fish to bite? Is it not a byword amongst us that gold maketh an
honest man an ill man? Did Philautus account Euphues too simple to
decipher beauty, or superstitious not to desire it? Did he deem him a saint
in rejecting fancy, or a sot in not discerning? Thought he him a Stoic
that he would not be moved, or a stock that he could not?

"Well, well, seeing the wound that bleedeth inward is most dangerous, that the fire kept close burneth most furious, that the oven dammed up baketh soonest, that sores having no vent fester secretly, it is high time to unfold my secret love to my secrete friend. Let Philautus behave himself never so craftily, he shall know that it must be a wily mouse that shall breed in the cat's ear, and because I resemble him in wit I mean a little to dissemble with him in wiles. But O my Lucilla, if thy heart be made of that stone which may be mollified only with blood, would I had sipped of that river in Caria which turneth those that drink of it to stones. If thine ears be anointed with the oil of Syria that bereaveth hearing, would mine eyes had been rubbed with the syrup of the cedar tree which taketh away sight. If Lucilla be so proud to disdain poor Euphues, would Euphues were so happy to deny Lucilla; or if Lucilla be so mortified to live without love, would Euphues were so fortunate to live in hate. Aye, but my cold welcome foretelleth my cold suit. Aye, but her privy glances signify some good fortune. Fie, fond fool Euphues, why goest thou about to allege those things to cut off thy hope which she perhaps would never have found, or to comfort thyself with those reasons which she never meaneth to propose.

"Tush, it were no love if it were certain, and a small conquest it is to overthrow those that never resisteth. In battles there ought to be a doubtful fight, and a desperate end; in pleading a difficult entrance, and a diffused determination; in love a life without hope, and a death without fear. Fire cometh out of the hardest flint with the steel; oil out of the driest jet by the fire; love out of the stoniest heart by faith, by trust, by time. Had Tarquinius used his love with colors of continuance, Lucretia would either with some pity have answered his desire, or with some persuasion have stayed her death. It was the heat of his lust that made her haste to end her life; wherefore love in neither respect is to be condemned, but he of rashness to attempt a lady furiously, and she of rigor to punish his folly in her own flesh, a fact (in mine opinion) more worthy the name of cruelty than chastity, and fitter for a monster in the deserts than a matron of Rome. Penelope, no less constant than she, yet more wise, would be weary to unweave that in the night she spun in the day, if Ulysses had not come home the sooner. There is no woman, Euphues, but she will yield in time; be not therefore dismayed either with high looks or froward words."

Euphues having thus talked with himself, Philautus entered the chamber, and finding him so worn and wasted with continual mourning, neither joying in his meat nor rejoicing in his friend, with watery eyes uttered this speech:

"Friend and fellow, as I am not ignorant of thy present weakness,

so I am not privy of the cause, and although I suspect many things, yet can I assure myself of no one thing. Therefore, my good Euphues, for these doubts and dumps of mine, either remove the cause or reveal it. Thou hast hitherto found me a cheerful companion in thy mirth, and now shalt thou find me as careful with thee in thy moan. If altogether thou mayst not be cured, yet mayst thou be comforted. If there be anything that either by my friends may be procured, or by my life attained, that may either heal thee in part or help thee in all, I protest to thee, by the name of a friend, that it shall rather be gotten with the loss of my
10 body than lost by getting a kingdom. Thou hast tried me, therefore trust me. Thou hast trusted me in many things, therefore try me in this one thing. I never yet failed, and now I will not faint. Be bold to speak and blush not; thy sore is not so angry but I can salve it, the wound not so deep but I can search it, thy grief not so great but I can ease it. If it be ripe it shall be lanced, if it be broken it shall be tainted, be it never so desperate it shall be cured. Rise, therefore, Euphues, and take heart at grace; younger thou shalt never be; pluck up thy stomach; if love itself have stung thee it shall not stifle thee. Though thou be enamored of some lady thou shalt not be enchanted. They that begin to pine of a consump-
20 tion, without delay preserve themselves upon cullises; he that feeleth his stomach enflamed with heat cooleth it eftsoons with conserves; delays breed dangers; nothing so perilous as procrastination.

Euphues, hearing this comfort and friendly counsel, dissembled his sorrowing heart with a smiling face, answering him forthwith as followeth:

"True it is, Philautus, that he which toucheth the nettle tenderly is soonest stung, that the fly which playeth with the fire is singed in the flame, that he that dallieth with women is drawn to his woe. And as the adamant draweth the heavy iron, the harp the fleet dolphin, so beauty
30 allureth the chaste mind to love, and the wisest wit to lust. The example whereof, I would it were no less profitable than the experience to me is like to be perilous. The vine watered with wine is soon withered, the blossom in the fattest ground is quickly blasted, the goat the fatter she is the less fertile she is; yea, man the more witty he is, the less happy he is. So it is, Philautus (for why should I conceal it from thee, of whom I am to take counsel), that since my last and first being with thee at the house of Ferardo, I have felt such a furious battle in mine own body, as if it be not speedily repressed by policy, it will carry my mind (the grand captain in this fight) into endless captivity.

40 "Ah Livia, Livia! Thy courtly grace without coyness, thy blazing beauty without blemish, thy courteous demeanor without curiosity, thy sweet speech savored with wit, thy comely mirth tempered with modesty,

thy chaste looks yet lovely, thy sharp taunts yet pleasant have given me such a check that sure I am, at the next view of thy virtues, I shall take thee mate. And taking it not of a pawn, but of a prince, the loss is to be accounted the less. And though they be commonly in a great choler that receive the mate, yet would I willingly take every minute ten mates, to enjoy Livia for my loving mate. Doubtless if ever she herself have been scorched with the flames of desire, she will be ready to quench the coals with courtesy in another; if ever she have been attached of love, she will rescue him that is drenched in desire; if ever she have been taken with the fever of fancy, she will help his ague, who by a quotidian fit is con- ¹⁰ verted into frenzy. Neither can there be under so delicate a hue lodged deceit, neither in so beautiful a mold a malicious mind. True it is that the disposition of the mind followeth the composition of the body. How then can she be in mind any way imperfect, who in body is perfect every way? I know my success will be good, but I know not how to have access to my goddess; neither do I want courage to discover my love to my friend, but some color to cloak my coming to the house of Ferardo; for if they be in Naples as jealous as they be in the other parts of Italy, then it behooveth me to walk circumspectly, and to forge some cause for mine often coming. ²⁰

"If therefore, Philautus, you canst set but this feather to mine arrow, you shalt see me shoot so near that thou wilt account me for a cunning archer. And verily if I had not loved thee well, I would have swallowed mine own sorrow in silence, knowing that in love nothing is so dangerous as to participate the means thereof to an other, and that two may keep counsel if one be away. I am therefore enforced perforce to challenge that courtesy at thy hands which first thou didst promise with thy heart, the performance whereof shall bind me to Philautus, and prove thee faithful to Euphues. Now if thy cunning be answerable to thy good will, practice some pleasant conceit upon thy poor patient: one dram of Ovid's ³⁰ art, some of Tibullus' drugs, one of Propertius' pills, which may cause me either to purge my new disease or recover my hoped desire. But I fear me where so strange a sickness is to be recured of so unskillful a physician, that either thou wilt be too bold to practice, or my body too weak to purge. But seeing a desperate disease is to be committed to a desperate doctor, I will follow thy counsel and become thy cure, desiring thee to be as wise in ministring thy physic as I have been willing to put my life into thy hands."

Philautus, thinking all to be gold that glistered, and all to be gospel that Euphues uttered, answered his forged glose with this friendly close: ⁴⁰

"In that thou hast made my privy to thy purpose, I will not conceal my practice; in that thou cravest my aid, assure thyself I will be the finger next the thumb, insomuch as thou shalt never repent thee of the one or the other. For persuade thyself that thou shalt find Philautus during life ready to comfort thee in thy misfortunes, and succor thee in thy necessity. Concerning Livia, though she be fair, yet is she not so amiable as my Lucilla, whose servant I have been the term of three years; but lest comparisons should seem odious, chiefly where both the parties be without comparison, I will omit that; and seeing that we had both rather be talking with them than tattling of them, we will immediately go to them.

"And truly, Euphues, I am not a little glad that I shall have thee not
10 only a comfort in my life, but also a companion in my love. As thou hast been wise in thy choice, so I hope thou shalt be fortunate in thy chance. Livia is a wench of more wit than beauty, Lucilla of more beauty than wit; both of more honesty than honor, and yet both of such honor as in all Naples there is not one in birth to be compared with any of them both. How much therefore have we to rejoice in our choice? Touching our access, be thou secure. I will flap Ferardo in the mouth with some conceit, and fill his old head so full of new fables that thou shalt rather be earnestly entreated to repair to his house than evil-entreated to leave it. As old men are very suspicious to mistrust everything, so are they very credulous to
20 believe anything; the blind man doth eat many a fly."

"Yea, but," said Euphues, "take heed, my Philautus, that thou thyself swallow not a gudgeon."

Which word Philautus did not mark, until he had almost digested it. "But," said Philautus, "let us go devoutly to the shrine of our saints, there to offer our devotion. For my books teach me that such a wound must be healed where it was first hurt; and for this disease we will use a common remedy, but yet comfortable. The eye that blinded thee shall make thee see; the scorpion that stung thee shall heal thee; a sharp sore hath a short cure. Let us go." To the which Euphues consented willingly,
30 smiling to himself to see how he had brought Philautus into a fool's Paradise.

Here you may see, gentlemen, the falsehood in fellowship, the fraud in friendship, the painted sheath with the leaden dagger, the fair words that make fools fain; but I will not trouble you with superfluous addition, unto whom I fear me I have been tedious, with the bare discourse of this rude history.

Philautus and Euphues repaired to the house of Ferardo, where they found Mistress Lucilla and Livia accompanied with other gentlewomen, neither being idle nor well employed, but playing at cards. But when
40 Lucilla beheld Euphues she could scarcely contain herself from embracing him, had not womanly shamefastness, and Philautus his presence, stayed her wisdom.

Euphues on the other side was fallen into such a trance that he had not the power either to succor himself, or salute the gentlewomen. At the last Lucilla began as one that best might be bold, on this manner:

"Gentlemen, although your long absence gave me occasion to think that you disliked your late entertainment, yet your coming at the last hath cut off my former suspicion. And by so much the more you are welcome by how much the more you were wished for. But you, gentleman (taking Euphues by the hand), were the rather wished for, for that your discourse, being left unperfect, caused us all to long (as women are wont for things that like them) to have an end thereof."

Unto whom Philautus replied as followeth: "Mistress Lucilla, though your courtesy made us nothing to doubt of our welcome, yet modesty caused us to pinch courtesy who should first come. As for my friend, I think he was never wished for here so earnestly of any as of himself; whether it might be to renew his talk or to recant his sayings, I cannot tell."

Euphues, taking the tale out of Philautus' mouth, answered: "Mistress Lucilla, to recant verities were heresy, and renew the praises of women flattery. The only cause I wished myself here was to give thanks for so good entertainment, the which I could no ways deserve, and to breed a greater acquaintance, if it might be to make amends."

Lucilla, enflamed with his presence, said, "Nay, Euphues, you shall not escape so. For if my courtesy, as you say, were the cause of your coming, let it also be the occasion of the ending your former discourse; otherwise I shall think your proof naked, and you shall find my reward nothing."

Euphues, now as willing to obey as she to command, addressed himself to a farther conclusion; who, seeing all the gentlewomen ready to give him the hearing, proceeded as followeth: "I have not yet forgotten that my last talk with these gentlewomen tended to their praises, and therefore the end must tie up the just proof; otherwise I should set down Venus' shadow without the lively substance.

"As there is no one thing which can be reckoned either concerning love or loyalty wherein women do not excell men, yet in fervency, above all others, they so far exceed that men are liker to marvel at them than to imitate them, and readier to laugh at their virtues than emulate them. For as they be hard to be won without trial of great faith, so are they hard to be lost without great cause of fickleness. It is long before the cold water seethe, yet being once hot, it is long before it be cooled; it is long before salt come to his saltness, but, being once seasoned, it never looseth his savor.

"I for mine own part am brought into a Paradise by the only imagina-

tion of women's virtues; and were I persuaded that all the devils in hell were women, I would never live devoutly to inherit heaven; or that they were all Saints in heaven, I would live more strictly for fear of hell. What could Adam have done in his Paradise before his fall without a woman, or how would he have rise again after his fall without a woman? Artificers are wont in their last works to excell themselves; yea, God when he had made all things, at the last made man as most perfect, thinking nothing could be framed more excellent; yet after him he created a woman, the express image of eternity, the lively picture of nature, the only steel glass
10 for man to behold his infirmities by comparing them with women's perfections. Are they not more gentle, more witty, more beautiful than men? Are not men so bewitched with their qualities that they become mad for love, and women so wise that they detest lust.

"I am entered into so large a field, that I shall sooner want time than proof, and so cloy you with variety of praises that I fear me I am like to infect women with pride, which yet they have not, and men with spite, which yet I would not. For as the horse, if he knew his own strength, were no ways to be bridled; or the unicorn his own virtue, were never to be caught; so women, if they knew what excellency were in them, I fear
20 me men should never win them to their wills, or wean them from their mind."

Lucilla began to smile, saying, "In faith, Euphues, I would have you stay there; for as the sun when he is at the highest beginneth to go down, so when the praises of women are at the best, if you leave not, they will begin to fail."

But Euphues (being rapt with the sight of his saint) answered, "No, no, Lucilla."

But whilst he was yet speaking, Ferardo entered, whom they all dutifully welcomed home; who, rounding Philautus in the ear, desired him
30 to accompany him immediately without farther pausing, protesting it should be as well for his preferment as for his own profit. Philautus consenting, Ferardo said unto his daughter:

"Lucilla, the urgent affairs I have in hand will scarce suffer me to tarry with you one hour; yet my return I hope will be so short that my absence shall not breed thy sorrow. In the mean season I commit all things into thy custody, wishing thee to use thy accustomable courtesy. And seeing I must take Philautus with me, I will be so bold to crave you gentleman (his friend) to supply his room, desiring you to take this hasty warning for a hearty welcome, and so to spend this time of mine absence in
40 honest mirth. And thus I leave you."

Philautus knew well the cause of this sudden departure, which was to redeem certain lands that were mortgaged in his father's time to the use of Ferardo, who on that condition had before time promised him his daughter in marriage. But return we to Euphues.

Euphues was surprised with such incredible joy at this strange event that he had almost sounded; for seeing his co-rival to be departed, and Ferardo to give him so friendly entertainment, doubted not in time to get the good will of Lucilla. Whom finding in place convenient without company, with a bold courage and comely gesture, he began to assay her in this sort:

"Gentlewoman, my acquaintance being so little, I am afraid my credit will be less, for that they commonly are soonest believed that are best be- 10 loved, and they liked best whom we have known longest; nevertheless, the noble mind suspecteth no guile without cause, neither condemneth any wight without proof; having therefore notice of your heroical heart, I am the better persuaded of my good hap. So it is Lucilla, that coming to Naples but to fetch fire, as the byword is, not to make my place of abode, I have found such flames that I can neither quench them with the water of free will, neither cool them with wisdom. For as the hop, the pole being never so high, groweth to the end; or as the dry beech kindled at the root, never leaveth until it come to the top; or as one drop of poison disperseth itself into every vein; so affection, having caught hold of my 20 heart, and the sparkles of love kindled my liver, will suddenly, though secretly, flame up into my head, and spread itself into every sinew. It is your beauty (pardon my abrupt boldness), Lady, that hath taken every part of me prisoner, and brought me unto this deep distress; but seeing women, when one praiseth them for their deserts, deem that he flattereth them to obtain his desire, I am here present to yield myself to such trial as your courtesy in this behalf shall require. Yet will you commonly ob-ject this to such as serve you and strive to win your good will, that hot love is soon cold; that the faggot, though it burn bright, is but a blaze; that scalding water, if it stand a while, turneth almost to ice; that pepper, 30 though it be hot in the mouth, is cold in the maw; that the faith of men, though it fry in their words, it freezeth in their works. Which things, Lucilla, albeit they be sufficient to reprove the lightness of some one, yet can they not convince every one of lewdness; neither ought the constancy of all to be brought in question through the subtlety of a few. For al-though the worm entereth almost into every wood, yet he eateth not the cedar tree. Though the stone cylindrus, at every thunder clap, roll from the hill, yet the pure sleek stone mounteth at the noise; though the rust fret the hardest steel, yet doth it not eat into the emerald; though Poly-pus change his hue, yet the salamander keepeth his color, though Proteus 40 transform himself into every shape, yet Pygmalion retaineth his old form; though Aeneas were too fickle to Dido, yet Troilus was too faithful to

Cressid; though others seem counterfeit in their deeds, yet, Lucilla, persuade yourself that Euphues will be always current in his dealings. But as the true gold is tried by the touch, the pure flint by the stroke of the iron, so the loyal heart of the faithful lover is known by the trial of his Lady. Of the which trial, Lucilla, if you shall account Euphues worthy, assure yourself he will be as ready to offer himself a sacrifice for your sweet sake as yourself shall be willing to employ him in your service. Neither doth he desire to be trusted any way, until he shall be tried every way; neither doth he crave credit at the first, but a good countenance till time
10 his desire shall be made manifest by his deserts. Thus not blinded by light affection, but dazzled with your rare perfection, and boldened by your exceeding courtesy, I have unfolded mine entire love, desiring you, having so good leisure, to give so friendly an answer as I may receive comfort, and you commendation."

　　Lucilla, although she were contented to hear this desired discourse, yet did she seem to be somewhat displeased. And truly I know not whether it be peculiar to that sex to dissemble with those whom they most desire, or whether by craft they have learned outwardly to loathe that which
20 inwardly they most love; yet wisely did she cast this in her head: that if she should yield at the first assault he would think her a light housewife; if she should reject him scornfully, a very haggard; minding therefore that he should neither take hold of her promise, neither unkindness of her preciseness, she fed him indifferently with hope and despair, reason and affection, life and death. Yet in the end, arguing wittily upon certain questions, they fell to such agreement as poor Philautus would not have agreed unto if he had been present; yet always keeping the body undefiled. And thus she replied:

　　"Gentleman, as you may suspect me of idleness in giving ear to your
30 talk, so may you convince me of lightness in answering such toys; certes, as you have made mine ears glow at the rehearsal of your love, so have you galled my heart with the remembrance of your folly. Though you came to Naples as a stranger, yet were you welcome to my father's house as a friend. And can you then so much transgress the bonds of honor (I will not say of honesty) as to solicit a suit more sharp to me than death? I have hitherto, God be thanked, lived without suspicion of lewdness; and shall I now incur the danger of sensual liberty? What hope can you have to obtain my love, seeing yet I could never afford you a good look? Do you therefore think me easily enticed to the bent of your bow, because
40 I was easily entreated to listen to your late discourse? Or seeing me (as finely you glose) to excell all other in beauty, did you deem that I would exceed all other in beastliness? But yet I am not angry, Euphues, but in an agony; for who is she that will fret or fume with one that loveth her,

if this love to delude me be not dissembled. It is that which causeth me most to fear; not that my beauty is unknown to myself, but that commonly we poor wenches are deluded through light belief, and ye men are naturally inclined craftily to lead your life. When the fox preacheth the geese perish. The crocodile shroudeth greatest treason under most pitiful tears; in a kissing mouth there lieth a galling mind. You have made so large proffer of your service, and so fair promises of fidelity, that were I not over chary of mine honesty you would inveigle me to shake hands with chastity. But certes I will either lead a virgin's life in earth (though I lead apes in hell) or else follow thee rather than thy gifts; yet am I 10 neither so precise to refuse the proffer, neither so peevish to disdain thy good will; so excellent always are the gifts which are made acceptable by the virtue of the giver. I did at the first entrance discern thy love but yet dissemble it. Thy wanton glances, thy scalding sighs, thy loving signs, caused me to blush for shame, and to look wan for fear, lest they should be perceived of any. These subtle shifts, these painted practices (if I were to be won) would soon wean me from the teat of Vesta to the toys of Venus. Besides this, thy comely grace, thy rare qualities, thy exquisite perfection, were able to move a mind half mortified to transgress the bonds of maidenly modesty. But God shield Lucilla, that thou shouldest be so 20 careless of thine honor as to commit the state thereof to a stranger. Learn thou by me, Euphues, to despise things that be amiable, to forego delightful practices; believe me it is piety to abstain from pleasure.

"Thou art not the first that hath solicited this suit, but the first that goeth about to seduce me; neither discernest thou more than other, but darest more than any; neither hast thou more art to discover thy meaning, but more heart to open thy mind. But thou preferrest me before thy lands, thy livings, thy life; thou offerest thyself a sacrifice for my security; thou profferest me the whole and only sovereignty of thy service. Truly I were very cruel and hard-hearted if I should not love thee; hard-hearted 30 albeit I am not, but truly love thee I cannot, whom I doubt to be my lover.

"Moreover, I have not been used to the court of Cupid, wherein there be more slights than there be hares in Athon, than bees in Hybla, than stars in heaven. Besides this, the common people here in Naples are not only both very suspicious of other men's matters and manners, but also very jealous over other men's children and maidens; either therefore dissemble thy fancy, or desist from thy folly.

"But why shouldest thou desist from the one, seeing thou canst cunningly dissemble the other. My father is now gone to Venice, and as I 40 am uncertain of his return, so am I not privy to the cause of his travel. But yet is he so from hence that he seeth me in his absence. Knowest thou not, Euphues, that kings have long arms and rulers large reaches? Neither

let this comfort thee, that at his departure he deputed thee in Philautus' place. Although my face cause him to mistrust my loyalty, yet my faith enforceth him to give me this liberty; though he be suspicious of my fair hue, yet is he secure of my firm honesty. But alas, Euphues, what truth can there be found in a traveller? what stay in a stranger? whose words and bodies both watch but for a wind, whose feet are ever fleeting, whose faith plighted on the shore is turned to perjury when they hoist sail. Who more traitorous to Phyllis than Demophoon? yet he a traveller. Who more perjured to Dido than Aeneas? and he a stranger: both these queens,
10 both they caitifs. Who more false to Ariadne than Theseus? yet he a sailor. Who more fickle to Medea than Jason? yet he a starter: both these daughters to great princes, both they unfaithful of their promises. Is it then likely that Euphues will be faithful to Lucilla, being in Naples but a sojourner? I have not yet forgotten the invective (I can no otherwise term it) which thou madest against beauty, saying it was a deceitful bait with a deadly hook, and a sweet poison in a painted pot. Canst thou then be so unwise to swallow the bait which will breed thy bane? To swill the drink that will expire thy date? To desire the wight that will work thy death? But it may be that with the scorpion thou canst feed on the earth;
20 or with the quail and roebuck, be fat with poison; or with beauty live in all bravery. I fear me thou hast the stone Continens about thee, which is named of the contrary; that though thou pretend faith in thy words, thou devisest fraud in thy heart; that though thou seem to prefer love, thou art inflamed with lust. And what for that? Though thou have eaten the seeds of rocket, which breed incontinency, yet have I chewed the leaf cress, which maintaineth modesty. Though thou bear in thy bosom the herb *araxa*, most noisome to virginity, yet have I the stone that groweth in the mount Tmolus, the upholder of chastity.

"You may, gentleman, account me for a cold prophet, thus hastily to
30 divine of your disposition; pardon me, Euphues, if in love I cast beyond the moon, which bringeth us women to endless moan. Although I myself were never burnt, whereby I should dread the fire, yet the scorching of others in the flames of fancy warneth me to beware. Though I as yet never tried any faithless, whereby I should be fearful, yet have I read of many that have been perjured, which causeth me to be careful; though I am able to convince none by proof, yet am I enforced to suspect one upon probabilities. Alas, we silly souls which have neither wit to decipher the wiles of men nor wisdom to dissemble our affection, neither craft to train in young lovers, neither courage to withstand their encounters,
40 neither discretion to discern their doubling, neither hard hearts to reject their complaints—we, I say, are soon enticed, being by nature simple and easily entangled, being apt to receive the impression of love. But alas it

is both common and lamentable, to behold simplicity entrapped by subtlety, and those that have most might to be infected with most malice. The spider weaveth a fine web to hang the fly, the wolf wearest a fair face to devour the lamb, the merlin striketh at the partridge, the eagle often snappeth at the fly, men are always laying baits for women, which are the weaker vessels; but as yet I could never hear man by such snares to entrap man. For true it is that men themselves have by use observed that it must be a hard winter when one wolf eateth an other. I have read that the bull, being tied to the fig-tree, loseth his strength; that the whole herd of deer stand at the gaze, if they smell a sweet apple; that the dolphin 10 by the sound of music is brought to the shore. And then no marvel it is that if the fierce bull be tamed with the fig-tree; if that women, being as weak as sheep, be overcome with a fig; if the wild deer be caught with an apple, that the tame damsel is won with a blossom; if the fleet dolphin be allured with harmony, that women be entangled with the melody of men's speech, fair promises, and solemn protestations.

"But folly it were for me to mark their mischiefs, since I am neither able, neither they willing, to amend their manners; it becometh me rather to show what our sex should do than to open what yours doth. And seeing I cannot by reason restrain your importunate suit, I will by rigor done 20 on myself cause you to refrain the means. I would to God Ferardo were in this point like to Lysander, which would not suffer his daughters to wear gorgeous apparel, saying it would rather make them common than comely. I would it were in Naples a law, which was a custom in Egypt, that women should always go barefoot, to the intent they might keep themselves always at home; that they should be ever like to the snail, which hath ever his house on his head. I mean so to mortify myself that instead of silks I will wear sackcloth; for owches and bracelets, leere and caddis; for the lute use the distaff; for the pen, the needle; for lovers' sonnets, David's Psalms. But yet I am not so senseless altogether to 30 reject your service, which if I were certainly assured to proceed of a simple mind, it should not receive so simple a reward. And what greater trial can I have of thy simplicity and truth than thine own request which desireth a trial. Aye, but in the coldest flint there is hot fire, the bee that hath honey in her mouth hath a sting in her tail, the tree that beareth the sweetest fruit hath a sour sap, yea the words of men, though they seem smooth as oil, yet their hearts are as crooked as the stalk of ivy. I would not, Euphues, that thou shouldest condemn me of rigor, in that I seek to assuage thy folly by reason, but take this by the way; that although as yet I am disposed to like of none, yet whensoever I shall love any I will not 40 forget thee. In the mean season, account me thy friend, for thy foe I will never be."

Euphues was brought into a great quandary, and as it were a cold shivering, to hear this new kind of kindness—such sweet meat, such sour sauce, such fair words, such faint promises, such hot love, such cold desire, such certain hope, such sudden change—and stood like one that had looked on Medusa's head, and so had been turned into a stone.

Lucilla, seeing him in this pitiful plight and fearing he would take stand if the lure were not cast out, took him by the hand and wringing him softly with a smiling countenance, began thus to comfort him:

"Methinks, Euphues, changing so your color upon the sudden, you 10 will soon change your copy. Is your mind on your meat? A penny for your thought."

"Mistress," quoth he, "if you would buy all my thoughts at that price, I should never be weary of thinking; but seeing it is too dear, read it, and take it for nothing."

"It seems to me," said she, "that you are in some brown study, what colors you might best wear for your Lady."

"Indeed, Lucilla, you level shrewdly at my thought by the aim of your own imagination, for you have given unto me a true love's knot wrought of changeable silk, and you deem that I am devising how I might have 20 my colors changeable also, that they might agree. But let this, with such toys and devices, pass. If it please you to command me any service, I am here ready to attend your leisure."

"No service, Euphues, but that you keep silence until I have uttered my mind; and secrecy when I have unfolded my meaning."

"If I should offend in the one I were too bold, if in the other too beastly."

"Well then, Euphues," said she, "so it is that for the hope that I conceive of thy loyalty and the happy success that is like to ensue of this our love, I am content to yield thee the place in my heart which thou desirest 30 and deservest above all other; which consent in me, if it may any ways breed thy contentation, sure I am that it will every way work my comfort. But as either thou tenderest mine honor or thine own safety, use such secrecy in this matter that my father have no inkling hereof before I have framed his mind fit for our purpose. And though women have small force to overcome men by reason, yet have they good fortune to undermine them by policy. The soft drops of rain pierce the hard marble, many strokes overthrow the tallest oak, a silly woman in time may make such a breach into a man's heart as her tears may enter without resistance; then doubt not but I will so undermine mine old father, as quickly I will enjoy 40 my new friend. Tush, Philautus was liked for fashion sake, but never loved for fancy sake; and this I vow by the faith of a virgin and by the love I bear thee (for greater bands to confirm my vow I have not), that my father shall sooner martyr me in the fire than marry me to Philautus. No, no, Euphues, thou only hast won me by love, and shalt only wear me by law. I force not Philautus his fury, so I may have Euphues his friendship; neither will I prefer his possessions before thy person, neither esteem better of his lands than of thy love. Ferardo shall sooner disherit me of my patrimony than dishonor me in breaking my promise. It is not his great manors, but thy good manners, that shall make my marriage. In token of which my sincere affection, I give thee my hand in pawn and my heart for ever to be thy Lucilla."

Unto whom Euphues answered in this manner: 10

"If my tongue were able to utter the joys that my heart hath conceived, I fear me though I be well beloved, yet I should hardly be believed. Ah my Lucilla, how much am I bound to thee, which preferrest mine unworthiness before thy Father's wrath, my happiness before thine own misfortune, my love before thine own life! How might I excell thee in courtesy, whom no mortal creature can exceed in constancy! I find it now for a settled truth, which before I accounted for a vain talk, that the purple dye will never stain, that the pure civet will never lose his savor, that the green laurel will never change his color, that beauty can never be blotted with discourtesy. As touching secrecy in this behalf, 20 assure thyself that I will not so much as tell it to myself. Command Euphues to run, to ride, to undertake any exploit be it never so dangerous, to hazard himself in any enterprise be it never so desperate."

As they were thus pleasantly conferring the one with the other, Livia (whom Euphues made his pretext) entered into the parlor, unto whom Lucilla spake in these terms:

"Dost thou not laugh, Livia, to see my ghostly father keep me here so long at shrift?"

"Truly," answered Livia, "methinks that you smile at some pleasant shift; either he is slow in enquiring of your faults, or you slack in answering 30 of his questions."

And thus being supper time, they all sat down, Lucilla well pleased; no man better content than Euphues, who after his repast having no opportunity to confer with his lover, had small lust to continue with the gentlewomen any longer. Seeing therefore he could frame no means to work his delight, he coined an excuse to hasten his departure, promising the next morning to trouble them again as a guest more bold than welcome, although indeed he thought himself to be the better welcome in saying that he would come.

But as Ferardo went in post, so he returned in haste, having concluded 40 with Philautus that the marriage should immediately be consummated; which wrought such a content in Philautus that he was almost in an ecstasy through the extremity of his passions. Such is the fullness and force of pleasure, that there is nothing so dangerous as the fruition; yet knowing that delays bring dangers, although he nothing doubted of Lucilla, whom he loved, yet feared he the fickleness of old men, which is always to be mistrusted. He urged therefore Ferardo to break with his daughter, who being willing to have the match made, was content incontinently to procure the means; finding therefore his daughter at leisure, and having knowledge of her former love, spake to her as followeth:

"Dear daughter, as thou hast long time lived a maiden, so now thou 10 must learn to be a Mother, and as I have been careful to bring thee up a virgin, so am I now desirous to make thee a wife. Neither ought I in this matter to use any persuasions, for that maidens commonly nowadays are no sooner born but they begin to bride it; neither to offer any great portions, for that thou knowest thou shalt inherit all my possessions. Mine only care hath been hitherto to match thee with such an one as should be of good wealth able to maintain thee, of great worship able to compare with thee in birth, of honest conditions to deserve thy love, and an Italian born to enjoy my lands. At the last I have found one answerable to my desire, a gentleman of great revenues, of a noble progeny, of honest be-20 havior, of comely personage, born and brought up in Naples. Philautus (thy friend as I guess) thy husband Lucilla, if thou like it; neither canst thou dislike him, who wanteth nothing that should cause thy liking, neither hath anything that should breed thy loathing. And surely I rejoice the more, that thou shalt be linked to him in marriage whom thou hast loved as I hear being a maiden; neither can there any jars kindle between them, where the minds be so united; neither any jealousy arise, where love hath so long been settled. Therefore, Lucilla, to the end the desire of either of you may now be accomplished to the delight of you both, I am here come to finish the contract by giving hands, which you have already begun be-30 tween yourselves by joining of hearts, that as God doth witness the one in your consciences, so the world may testify the other by your conversations. And therefore, Lucilla, make such answer to my request as may like me, and satisfy thy friend."

Lucilla, abashed with this sudden speech of her father, yet boldened by the love of her friend, with a comely bashfulness answered him in this manner:

"Reverend Sir, the sweetness that I have found in the undefiled estate of virginity, causeth me to loathe the sour sauce which is mixed with matrimony; and the quiet life which I have tried being a maiden, maketh me 40 to shun the cares that are always incident to a mother; neither am I so wedded to the world that I should be moved with great possessions; neither so bewitched with wantonness that I should be enticed with any man's proportion; neither if I were so disposed would I be so proud to desire one of noble progeny, or so precise to choose one only in mine own country, for that commonly these things happen always to the contrary. Do we not see the noble to match with the base, the rich with the poor, the Italian oftentimes with the Portingale? As love knoweth no laws, so it regardeth no conditions; as the lover maketh no pause where he liketh, so he maketh no conscience of these idle ceremonies. In that Philautus is the man that threateneth such kindness at my hands, and such courtesy at yours, that he should account me his wife before he woo me, certainly he is like for me to make his reckoning twice, because he reckoneth without 10 his hostess. And in this Philautus would either show himself of great wisdom to persuade, or me of great lightness to be allured; although the loadstone draw iron, yet it cannot move gold; though the jet gather up the light straw, yet can it not take up the pure steel. Although Philautus think himself of virtue sufficient to win his lover, yet shall he not obtain Lucilla. I cannot but smile to hear that a marriage should be solemnized, where never was any mention of assuring, and that the wooing should be a day after the wedding. Certes, if when I looked merrily on Philautus, he deemed it in the way of marriage; or if seeing me disposed to jest, he took me in good earnest; then sure he might gather some presumption of 20 my love, but no promise. But me thinks it is good reason that I should be at mine own bridal, and not given in the Church before I know the bridegroom. Therefore, dear father, in mine opinion, as there can be no bargain where both be not agreed, neither any indentures sealed where the one will not consent, so can there be no contract where both be not content, no banns asked lawfully where one of the parties forbiddeth them, no marriage made where no match was meant. But I will hereafter frame myself to be coy, seeing I am claimed for a wife because I have been courteous; and give myself to melancholy, seeing I am accounted won in that I have been merry. And if every gentleman be made of the metal that Philautus 30 is, then I fear I shall be challenged of as many as I have used to company with, and be a common wife to all those that have commonly resorted hither.

"My duty therefore ever reserved, I here on my knees foreswear Philautus for my husband, although I accept him for my friend; and seeing I shall hardly be induced ever to match with any, I beseech you, if by your fatherly love I shall be compelled, that I may match with such a one as both I may love, and you may like."

Ferardo, being a grave and wise gentleman, although he were thoroughly angry, yet he dissembled his fury, to the end he might by craft dis- 40 cover her fancy, and whispering Philautus in the ear (who stood as though he had a flea in his ear), desired him to keep silence until he had under-

mined her by subtlety; which Philautus having granted, Ferardo began
to sift his daughter with this device.

"Lucilla, thy color showeth thee to be in a great choler, and thy hot
words bewray thy heavy wrath; but be patient. Seeing all my talk was
only to try thee, I am neither so unnatural to wrest thee against thine
own will, neither so malicious to wed thee to any against thine own
liking; for well I know what jars, what jealousy, what strife, what storms
ensue, where the match is made rather by the compulsion of the parents
than by the consent of the parties; neither do I like thee the less, in that
10 thou likest Philautus so little; neither can Philautus love thee the worse,
in that thou lovest thyself so well, wishing rather to stand to thy chance
than to the choice of any other. But this grieveth me most, that thou art
almost vowed to the vain order of the vestal virgins, despising, or at the
least not desiring the sacred bands of Juno her bed. If thy mother had
been of that mind when she was a maiden, thou haddest not now been
born to be of this mind to be a virgin. Weigh with thyself what slender
profit they bring to the commonwealth, what slight pleasure to themselves,
what great grief to their parents which joy most in their offspring, and
desire most to enjoy the noble and blessed name of a grandfather.

20 "Thou knowest that the tallest ash is cut down for fuel, because it
beareth no good fruit, that the cow that gives no milk is brought to the
slaughter, that the drone that gathereth no honey is contemned, that the
woman that maketh herself barren by not marrying is accounted among
the Grecian ladies worse than a carrion, as Homer reporteth. Therefore,
Lucilla, if thou have any care to be a comfort to my hoary hairs, or a commodity to thy common weal, frame thyself to that honorable estate of
matrimony, which was sanctified in Paradise, allowed of the patriarchs,
hallowed of the old prophets, and commended of all persons. If thou like
any, be not ashamed to tell it me, which only am to exhort thee—yea, and
30 as much as in me lieth to command thee—to love one. If he be base, thy
blood will make him noble; if beggarly, thy goods shall make him wealthy;
if a stranger, thy freedom may enfranchise him. If he be young, he is the
more fitter to be thy fellow; if he be old, the liker to thine aged father. For
I had rather thou shouldest lead a life to thine own liking in earth than to
thy great torments lead apes in Hell. Be bold, therefore, to make me
partner of thy desire, which will be partaker of thy disease—yea, and a
furtherer of thy delights, as far as either my friends, or my lands, or my
life will stretch."

Lucilla, perceiving the drift of the old fox her father, weighed with
40 herself what was the best to be done; at the last, not weighing her father's
ill will, but encouraged by love, shaped him an answer which pleased

Ferardo but little, and pinched Philautus on the parson's side on this manner:

"Dear father Ferardo, although I see the bait you lay to catch me, yet I am content to swallow the hook; neither are you more desirous to take me napping, than I willing to confess my meaning. So it is that love hath as well inveigled me as others, which make it as strange as I. Neither do I love him so meanly that I should be ashamed of his name, neither is his personage so mean that I should love him shamefully. It is Euphues, that lately arrived here at Naples, that hath battered the bulwark of my breast, and shall shortly enter as conqueror into my bosom. What his wealth is I 10 neither know it nor weigh it, what his wit is all Naples doth know it, and wonder at it; neither have I been curious to enquire of his progenitors, for that I know so noble a mind could take no original but from a noble man; for as no bird can look against the sun but those that be bred of the eagle, neither any hawk soar so high as the brood of the hobby, so no wight can have such excellent qualities except he descend of a noble race; neither be of so high capacity, unless he issue of a high progeny. And I hope Philautus will not be my foe, seeing I have chosen his dear friend; neither you, father, be displeased in that Philautus is displaced. You need not muse that I should so suddenly be entangled; love gives no reason of choice, 20 neither will it suffer any repulse. Myrrha was enamored of her natural father, Biblis of her brother, Phaedra of her son-in-law. If nature can no way resist the fury of affection, how should it be stayed by wisdom?"

Ferardo, interrupting her in the middle of her discourse, although he were moved with inward grudge, yet he wisely repressed his anger, knowing that sharp words would but sharpen her froward will, and thus answered her briefly:

"Lucilla, as I am not presently to grant my good will, so mean I not to reprehend thy choice; yet wisdom willeth me to pause until I have called what may happen to my remembrance, and warneth thee to be circum- 30 spect, lest thy rash conceit bring a sharp repentance. As for you Philautus I would not have you despair, seeing a woman doth oftentimes change her desire."

Unto whom Philautus in few words made answer, "Certainly, Ferardo, I take the less grief in that I see her so greedy after Euphues, and by so much the more I am content to leave my suit, by how much the more she seemeth to disdain my service; but as for hope, because I would not by any means taste one dram thereof, I will abjure all places of her abode and loathe her company, whose countenance I have so much loved. As for Euphues"—and there staying his speech, he flang out of the doors, and 40 repairing to his lodging, uttered these words:

"Ah, most dissembling wretch Euphues! O counterfeit companion! Couldest thou under the show of a steadfast friend cloak the malice of a mortal foe? under the color of simplicity shrowd the image of deceit? Is thy Livia turned to my Lucilla, thy love to my lover, thy devotion to my saint? Is this the courtesy of Athens, the cavilling of scholars, the craft of Grecians? Couldest thou not remember, Philautus, that Greece is never without some wily Ulysses, never void of some Synon, never to seek of some deceitful shifter? Is it not commonly said of Grecians that craft cometh to them by kind, that they learn to deceive in their cradle? Why
10 then did his pretended courtesy bewitch thee with such credulity? Shall my good will be the cause of his ill will? Because I was content to be his friend, thought he me meet to be made his fool? I see now that as the fish scolopidus in the flood Araris at the waxing of the moon is as white as the driven snow, and at the waning as black as the burnt coal, so Euphues, which at the first increasing of our familiarity was very zealous, is now at the last cast become most faithless. But why rather exclaim I not against Lucilla, whose wanton looks caused Euphues to violate his plighted faith? Ah, wretched wench, canst thou be so light of love as to change with every wind? so unconstant as to prefer a new lover before thine old friend? Ah,
20 well I wot that a new broom sweepeth clean, and a new garment maketh thee leave off the old though it be fitter, and new wine causeth thee to forsake the old though it be better; much like to the men in the island Scyrum, which pull up the old tree when they see the young begin to spring, and not unlike unto the widow of Lesbos, which changed all her old gold for new glass, have I served thee three years faithfully, and am I served so unkindly? Shall the fruit of my desire be turned to disdain? But unless Euphues had inveigled thee thou haddest yet been constant. Yea, but if Euphues had not seen thee willing to be won, he would never have wooed thee. But had not Euphues enticed thee with fair words, thou
30 wouldst never have loved him. But haddest thou not given him fair looks, he would never have liked thee. Aye, but Euphues gave the onset. Aye, but Lucilla gave the occasion. Aye, but Euphues first break his mind. Aye, but Lucilla first bewrayed her meaning. Tush, why go I about to excuse any of them, seeing I have just cause to accuse them both? Neither ought I to dispute which of them hath proffered me the greatest villany, since that either of them hath committed perjury. Yet although they have found me dull in perceiving their falsehood, they shall not find me slack in revenging their folly. As for Lucilla, seeing I mean altogether to forget her, I mean also to forgive her, lest in seeking means to be revenged mine old
40 desire be renewed."

Philautus having thus discoursed with himself, began to write to Euphues as followeth:

"Although hitherto, Euphues, I have shrined thee in my heart for a
trusty friend, I will shun thee hereafter as a trothless foe; and although
I cannot see in thee less wit than I was wont, yet do I find less honesty. I
perceive at the last (although being deceived, it be too late) that musk,
though it be sweet in the smell, is sour in the smack; that the leaf of the
cedar tree, though it be fair to be seen, yet the syrup depriveth sight; that
friendship, though it be plighted by shaking the hand, yet it is shaken off
by fraud of the heart. But thou hast not much to boast of, for as thou hast
won a fickle lady, so hast thou lost a faithful friend. How canst thou be
secure of her constancy when thou hast had such trial of her lightness? 10
How canst thou assure thyself that she will be faithful to thee, which hath
been faithless to me? Ah Euphues, let not my credulity be an occasion
hereafter for thee to practise the like cruelty. Remember this, that yet
there hath never been any faithless to his friend that hath not also been
fruitless to his God. But I weigh the treachery the less, in that it cometh
from a Grecian in whom is no truth. Though I be too weak to wrestle for
a revenge, yet God, who permitteth no guile to be guiltless, will shortly
requite this injury; though Philautus have no policy to undermine thee,
yet thine own practises will be sufficient to overthrow thee.

"Couldest thou, Euphues, for the love of a fruitless pleasure, violate 20
the league of faithful friendship? Diddest thou weigh more the enticing
looks of a lewd wench than the entire love of a loyal friend? If thou
diddest determine with thyself at the first to be false, why diddest thou
swear to be true? If to be true, why art thou false? If thou wast minded
both falsely and forgedly to deceive me, why diddest thou flatter and dissemble with me at the first? If to love me, why dost thou flinch at the last?
If the sacred bands of amity did delight thee, why diddest thou break
them? if dislike thee, why diddest thou praise them? Dost thou not know
that a perfect friend should be like the glazeworm, which shineth most
bright in the dark? or like the pure frankincense, which smelleth most 30
sweet when it is in the fire? or at the least not unlike to the damask rose,
which is sweeter in the still than on the stalk? But thou, Euphues, dost
rather resemble the swallow which in the summer creepeth under the
eves of every house, and in the winter leaveth nothing but dirt behind her;
or the humble bee, which having sucked honey out of the fair flower, doth
leave it and loathe it; or the spider, which in the finest web doth hang the
fairest fly. Dost thou think, Euphues, that thy craft in betraying me shall
any whit cool my courage in revenging thy villany? or that a gentleman
of Naples will put up such an injury at the hands of a scholar? And if I
do, it is not for want of strength to maintain my just quarrel, but of will, 40
which thinketh scorn to get so vain a conquest. I know that Menelaus for
his ten years' war endured ten years' woe; that after all his strife he won

but a strumpet; that for all his travail he reduced (I cannot say reclaimed) but a straggler; which was as much in my judgment as to strive
for a broken glass which is good for nothing. I wish thee rather Menelaus' care than myself his conquest, that thou, being deluded by Lucilla,
mayst rather know what it is to be deceived, than I, having conquered
thee, should prove what it were to bring back a dissembler. Seeing therefore there can no greater revenge light upon thee than that as thou hast
reaped where another hath sown, so another may thresh that which thou
hast reaped. I will pray that thou mayst be measured unto with the like
measure that thou hast meted unto others; that as thou hast thought it no
conscience to betray me, so others may deem it no dishonesty to deceive
thee; that as Lucilla made it a light matter to foreswear her old friend
Philautus, so she may make it a mock to forsake her new fellow Euphues.
Which if it come to pass, as it is like by my compass, then shalt thou see the
troubles and feel the torments which thou hast already thrown into the
hearts and eyes of others. Thus hoping shortly to see thee as hopeless as
myself is hapless, I wish my wish were as effectually ended as it is heartily
looked for. And so I leave thee.

Thine once
PHILAUTUS."

Philautus, dispatching a messenger with this letter speedily to Euphues,
went into the fields to walk there, either to digest his choler or chew upon
his melancholy. But Euphues, having read the contents, was well content,
setting his talk at naught and answering his taunts in these gibing terms:

"I remember, Philautus, how valiantly Ajax boasted in the feats of
arms, yet Ulysses bore away the armor; and it may be that though thou
crake of thine own courage, thou mayst easily lose the conquest. Dost
thou think Euphues such a dastard that he is not able to withstand thy
courage, or such a dullard that he cannot descry thy craft. Alas, good soul!
It fareth with thee as with the hen, which when the puttock hath caught
her chicken beginneth to cackle; and thou, having lost thy lover, begin-
nest to prattle. Tush, Philautus, I am in this point of Euripides his mind,
who thinks it lawful for the desire of a kingdom to transgress the bounds
of honesty and for the love of a lady to violate and break the bands of
amity.

"The friendship between man and man, as it is common, so is it of
course; between man and woman, as it is seldom, so is it sincere; the one
proceedeth of the similitude of manners, the other of the sincerity of the
heart. If thou haddest learned the first point of hawking thou wouldst
have learned to have held fast, or the first note of descant thou wouldest
have kept thy *sol. fa.* to thyself.

"But thou canst blame me no more of folly in leaving thee to love Lucilla, than thou mayst reprove him of foolishness that, having a sparrow in his hand, letteth her go to catch the pheasant; or him of unskillfulness that seeing the heron, leaveth to level his shoot at the stock dove; or that woman of coyness that, having a dead rose in her bosom, throweth it away to gather the fresh violet. Love knoweth no laws. Did not Jupiter transform himself into the shape of Amphitrio to embrace Alcmæna? into the form of a swan to enjoy Læda? into a bull to beguile Ió? Into a shower of gold to win Danaë? Did not Neptune change himself into a heifer, a ram, a flood, a dolphin, only for the love of those he lusted after? 10 Did not Apollo convert himself into a shepherd, into a bird, into a lion, for the desire he had to heal his disease? If the Gods thought no scorn to become beasts to obtain their best beloved, shall Euphues be so nice in changing his copy to gain his lady? No, no! He that cannot dissemble in love is not worthy to live. I am of this mind, that both might and malice, deceit and treachery, all perjury, any impiety may lawfully be committed in love, which is lawless. In that thou arguest Lucilla of lightness, thy will hangs in the light of thy wit. Dost thou not know that the weak stomach, if it be cloyed with one diet, doth soon surfeit? That the clown's garlik cannot ease the courtier's disease so well as the pure treacle? That 20 far fetched and dear bought is good for ladies? That Euphues, being a more dainty morsel than Philautus, ought better to be accepted? Tush, Philautus, set thy heart at rest, for thy hap willeth thee to give over all hope both of my friendship and her love. As for revenge, thou art not so able to lend a blow as I to ward it, neither more venturous to challenge the combat than I valiant to answer the quarrel. As Lucilla was caught by fraud, so shall she be kept by force; and as thou wast too simple to espy my craft, so I think thou wilt be too weak to withstand my courage; but if thy revenge stand only upon thy wish, thou shalt never live to see my woe, or to have thy will. And so farewell. 30

EUPHUES."

This letter being dispatched, Euphues sent it and Philautus read it; who, disdaining those proud terms, disdained also to answer them, being ready to ride with Ferardo.

Euphues, having for a space absented himself from the house of Ferardo because he was at home, longed sore to see Lucilla; which now opportunity offered unto him, Ferardo being gone again to Venice with Philautus. But in this his absence one Curio, a gentleman of Naples of little wealth and less wit, haunted Lucilla her company, and so enchanted her 40 that Euphues was also cast off with Philautus. Which thing being unknown to Euphues, caused him the sooner to make his repair to the presence of his lady, whom he finding in her muses began pleasantly to salute in this manner:

"Mistress Lucilla, although my long absence might breed your just anger (for that lovers desire nothing so much as often meeting), yet I hope my presence will dissolve your choler (for that lovers are soon pleased when of their wishes they be fully possessed). My absence is the rather to be excused in that your father hath been always at home, whose frowns seemed to threaten my ill fortune, and my presence at this present the better to be accepted in that I have made such speedy repair to your pres-
10 ence."

Unto whom Lucilla answered with this taunt: "Truly, Euphues, you have missed the cushion, for I was neither angry with your long absence, neither am I well pleased at your presence; the one gave me rather a good hope hereafter never to see you, the other giveth me a greater occasion to abhor you."

Euphues being nipped on the head, with a pale countenance, as though his soul had forsaken his body, replied as followeth: "If this sudden change, Lucilla, proceed of any desert of mine, I am here not only to answer the fact, but also to make amends for my fault; if of any new mo-
20 tion or mind to forsake your new friend, I am rather to lament your inconstancy than revenge it; but I hope that such hot love cannot be so soon cold, neither such sure faith be rewarded with so sudden forgetfulness."

Lucilla, not ashamed to confess her folly, answered him with this frump: "Sir, whether your deserts or my desire have wrought this change, it will boot you little to know; neither do I crave amends, neither fear revenge. As for fervent love, you know there is no fire so hot but it is quenched with water, neither affection so strong but is weakened with reason. Let this suffice thee, that thou know I care not for thee."

30 "Indeed," said Euphues, "to know the cause of your alteration would boot me little, seeing the effect taketh such force. I have heard that women either love entirely or hate deadly, and seeing you have put me out of doubt of the one, I must needs persuade myself of the other. This change will cause Philautus to laugh me to scorn, and double thy lightness in turning so often. Such was the hope that I conceived of thy constancy, that I spared not in all places to blaze thy loyalty; but now my rash conceit will prove me a liar, and thee a light housewife."

"Nay," said Lucilla, "now shalt thou not laugh Philautus to scorn, seeing you have both drunk of one cup; in misery, Euphues it is great
40 comfort to have a companion. I doubt not but that you will both conspire against me to work some mischief, although I nothing fear your malice; whosoever accounteth you a liar for praising me, may also deem you a

lecher for being enamored of me; and whosoever judgeth me light in forsaking of you, may think thee as lewd in loving of me; for thou that thoughtest it lawful to deceive thy friend, must take no scorn to be deceived of thy foe."

"Then I perceive, Lucilla," said he, "that I was made thy stale, and Philautus thy laughing stock; whose friendship (I must confess indeed) I have refused to obtain thy favor. And since another hath won that we both have lost, I am content for my part; neither ought I to be grieved, seeing thou art fickle."

"Certes, Euphues," said Lucilla, "you spend your wind in waste, for your welcome is but small, and your cheer is like to be less. Fancy giveth no reason of his change, neither will be controlled for any choice. This is therefore to warn you, that from henceforth you neither solicit this suit, neither offer any way your service. I have chosen one (I must needs confess) neither to be compared to Philautus in wealth, nor to thee in wit; neither in birth to the worst of you both. I think God gave it me for a just plague, for renouncing Philautus, and choosing thee; and since I am an example to all women of lightness, I am like also to be a mirror to them all of unhappiness; which ill luck I must take by so much the more patiently, by how much the more I acknowledge myself to have deserved it worthily."

"Well, Lucilla," answered Euphues, "this case breedeth my sorrow the more, in that it is so sudden; and by so much the more I lament it, by how much the less I looked for it. In that my welcome is so cold and my cheer so simple, it nothing toucheth me, seeing your fury is so hot, and my misfortune so great, that I am neither willing to receive it, nor you to bestow it. If tract of time or want of trial had caused this metamorphosis, my grief had been more tolerable, and your fleeting more excusable; but coming in a moment undeserved, unlooked for, unthought of, it increaseth my sorrow and thy shame."

"Euphues," quoth she, "you make a long harvest for a little corn, and angle for the fish that is already caught. Curio, yea, Curio is he that hath my love at his pleasure, and shall also have my life at his commandment; and although you deem him unworthy to enjoy that which before you accounted no wight worthy to embrace, yet seeing I esteem him more worth than any, he is to be reputed as chief. The wolf chooseth him for her make that hath or doth endure most travail for her sake. Venus was content to take the blacksmith with his powlt foot. Cornelia here in Naples disdained not to love a rude miller. As for changing, did not Helen, that pearl of Greece, thy countrywoman, first take Menelaus, then Theseus, and last of all Paris? If brute beasts give us examples that those are most to be liked of whom we are best beloved, or if the princess of beauty,

Venus, and her heirs Helen and Cornelia, show that our affection standeth on our free will, then am I rather to be excused than accused. Therefore, good Euphues, be as merry as you may be, for time may so turn
that once again you may be."

"Nay, Lucilla," said he, "my harvest shall cease, seeing others have
reaped my corn; as for angling for the fish that is already caught, that
were but mere folly. But in my mind, if you be a fish you are either an
eel, which as soon as one hath hold on her tail will slip out of his hand, or
else a minnow, which will be nibbling at every bait but never biting. But
what fish soever you be, you have made both me and Philautus to swallow
a gudgeon. If Curio be the person, I would neither wish thee a greater
plague, nor him a deadlier poison. I for my part think him worthy of thee,
and thou unworthy of him; for although he be in body deformed, in mind
foolish, an innocent born, a beggar by misfortune, yet doth he deserve a
better than thyself, whose corrupt manners have stained thy heavenly
hue, whose light behavior hath dimmed the lights of thy beauty, whose
unconstant mind hath betrayed the innocence of so many a gentleman.
And in that you bring in the example of a beast to confirm your folly, you
show therein your beastly disposition, which is ready to follow such beastliness. But Venus played false; and what for that? Seeing her lightness
serveth for an example, I would wish thou mightest try her punishment
for a reward, that being openly taken in an iron net all the world might
judge whether thou be fish or flesh. And certes in my mind no angle will
hold thee; it must be a net. Cornelia loved a miller, and thou a miser; can
her folly excuse thy fault? Helen of Greece, my countrywoman born,
but thine by profession, changed and rechanged at her pleasure, I grant.
Shall the lewdness of others animate thee in thy lightness? Why then dost
thou not haunt the stews because Laïs frequented them? why dost thou
not love a bull, seeing Pasiphaë loved one? why art thou not enamored of
thy father, knowing that Myrrha was so incensed? These are set down
that we, viewing their incontinency, should fly the like impudence, not
follow the like excess; neither can they excuse thee of any inconstancy.
Merry I will be as I may, but if I may hereafter as thou meanest, I will
not. And therefore farewell, Lucilla, the most inconstant that ever was
nursed in Naples! Farewell Naples, the most cursed town in all Italy!
And women all, farewell!"

Euphues having thus given her his last farewell, yet being solitary, began
afresh to recount his sorrow on this manner:

"Ah, Euphues, into what misfortune art thou brought? in what sudden
misery art thou wrapped? It is like to fare with thee as with the eagle,
which dieth neither for age, nor with sickness, but with famine; for although thy stomach hunger, yet thy heart will not suffer thee to eat. And

why shouldest thou torment thyself for one in whom is neither faith nor fervency? O the counterfeit love of women! Oh inconstant sex! I have lost Philautus, I have lost Lucilla, I have lost that which I shall hardly find again, a faithful friend! Ah, foolish Euphues, why diddest thou leave Athens, the nurse of wisdom, to inhabit Naples, the nourisher of wantonness? Had it not been better for thee to have eaten salt with the philosophers in Greece, than sugar with the courtiers of Italy? But behold the course of youth, which always inclineth to pleasure! I forsook mine old companions to search for new friends; I rejected the grave and fatherly counsel of Eubulus, to follow the brainsick humor of mine own will. I addicted myself wholly to the service of women, to spend my life in the laps of ladies, my lands in maintenance of bravery, my wit in the vanities of idle sonnets. I had thought that women had been as we men; that is, true, faithfull, zealous, constant; but I perceive they be rather woe unto men, by their falsehood, jealousy, inconstancy. I was half persuaded that they were made of the perfection of men, and would be comforters; but now I see they have tasted of the infection of the serpent, and will be corrosives. The physician saith it is dangerous to minister physic unto the patient that hath a cold stomach and a hot liver, lest in giving warmth to the one he inflame the other; so verily it is hard to deal with a woman whose words seem fervent, whose heart is congealed into hard ice, lest trusting their outward talk, he be betrayed with their inward treachery. I will to Athens, there to toss my books; no more in Naples to live with fair looks. I will so frame myself as all youth hereafter shall rather rejoice to see mine amendment than be animated to follow my former life. Philosophy, Physic, Divinity, shall be my study. O the hidden secrets of Nature, the express image of moral virtues, the equal balance of Justice, the medicines to heal all diseases, how they begin to delight me! The *Axiomaes* of Aristotle, the *Maxims* of Justinian, the *Aphorisms* of Galen have suddenly made such a breach into my mind that I seem only to desire them, which did only before detest them. If wit be employed in the honest study of learning, what thing so precious as wit? if in the idle trade of love, what thing more pestilent than wit? The proof of late hath been verified in me, whom nature hath endued with a little wit, which I have abused with an obstinate will. Most true it is that the thing, the better it is the greater is the abuse; and that there is nothing but through the malice of man may be abused.

"Doth not the fire (an element so necessary that without it man cannot live) as well burn the house as burn in the house, if it be abused? Doth not treacle as well poison as help if it be taken out of time? Doth not wine, if it be immoderately taken, kill the stomach, inflame the liver, mischief the drunken? Doth not physic destroy if it be not well tempered? Doth

not law accuse if it be not rightly interpreted? Doth not divinity condemn
if it be not faithfully construed? Is not poison taken out of the honeysuckle by the spider, venom out of the rose by the canker, dung out of the
maple tree by the scorpion? Even so the greatest wickedness is drawn out
of the greatest wit, if it be abused by will, or entangled with the world, or
inveigled with women.

"But seeing I see mine own impiety, I will endeavor myself to amend
all that is past, and to be a mirror of godliness hereafter. The rose, though
a little it be eaten with the canker, yet being distilled yieldeth sweet water;
10 the iron, though fretted with the rust, yet being burnt in the fire shineth
brighter; and wit, although it hath been eaten with the canker of his own
conceit, and fretted with the rust of vain love, yet being purified in the
still of wisdom, and tried in the fire of zeal, will shine bright and smell
sweet in the nostrils of all young novices.

"As therefore I gave a farewell to Lucilla, a farewell to Naples, a farewell to women, so now do I give a farewell to the world; meaning rather
to macerate myself with melancholy than pine in folly, rather choosing
to die in my study amidst my books than to court it in Italy in the company
of ladies."

20 Euphues having thus debated with himself, went to his bed, there either
with sleep to deceive his fancy, or with musing to renew his ill fortune or
recant his old follies.

But it happened immediately Ferardo to return home, who hearing
this strange event was not a little amazed, and was now more ready to
exhort Lucilla from the love of Curio than before to the liking of Philautus.
Therefore, in all haste, with watery eyes and a woeful heart, began on
this manner to reason with his daughter:

"Lucilla (daughter I am ashamed to call thee, seeing thou hast neither
care of thy father's tender affection, nor of thine own credit), what sprite
30 hath enchanted thy spirit that every minute thou alterest thy mind? I had
thought that my hoary hairs should have found comfort by thy golden
locks, and my rotten age great ease by thy ripe years. But alas, I see in
thee neither wit to order thy doings, neither will to frame thyself to discretion, neither the nature of a child, neither the nurture of a maiden,
neither (I cannot without tears speak it) any regard of thine honor, neither
any care of thine honesty.

"I am now enforced to remember thy mother's death, who I think was
a prophetess in her life, for oftentimes she would say that thou haddest
more beauty than was convenient for one that should be honest, and more
40 cockering than was meet for one that should be a matron.

"Would I had never lived to be so old or thou to be so obstinate; either
would I had died in my youth in the court, or thou in thy cradle! I would

to God that either I had never been born, or thou never bred! Is this the comfort that the parent reapeth for all his care? Is obstinacy paid for obedience, stubbornness rendered for duty, malicious desperateness for filial fear? I perceive now that the wise painter saw more than the foolish parent can, who painted love going downward, saying it might well descend, but ascend it could never. Danaus, whom they report to be the father of fifty children, had among them all but one that disobeyed him in a thing most dishonest; but I that am father to one more than I would be, although one be all, have that one most disobedient to me in a request lawful and reasonable. If Danaus, seeing but one of his daughters without 10 awe, became himself without mercy, what shall Ferardo do in this case, who hath one and all most unnatural to him in a most just cause? Shall Curio enjoy the fruit of my travails, possess the benefit of my labors, inherit the patrimony of mine ancestors, who hath neither wisdom to increase them, nor wit to keep them? Wilt thou, Lucilla, bestow thyself on such an one as hath neither comeliness in his body, nor knowledge in his mind, nor credit in his country? Oh, I would thou haddest either been ever faithful to Philautus, or never faithless to Euphues; or would thou wouldest be most fickle to Curio! As thy beauty hath made thee the blaze of Italy, so will thy lightness make thee the byword of the world. 20 O Lucilla, Lucilla, would thou wert less fair or more fortunate, either of less honor or greater honesty! either better minded, or soon buried! Shall thine old father live to see thee match with a young fool? shall my kind heart be rewarded with such unkind hate? Ah Lucilla, thou knowest not the care of a father, nor the duty of a child, and as far art thou from piety as I from cruelty.

"Nature will not permit me to disherit my daughter, and yet it will suffer thee to dishonor thy father. Affection causeth me to wish thy life, and shall it entice thee to procure my death? It is mine only comfort to see thee flourish in thy youth, and is it thine to see me fade in mine age? To 30 conclude, I desire to live to see thee prosper, and thou to see me perish. But why cast I the effect of this unnaturalness in thy teeth, seeing I myself was the cause? I made thee a wanton and thou hast made me a fool; I brought thee up like a cockney, and thou hast handled me like a cockscomb (I speak it to mine own shame). I made more of thee than became a father, and thou less of me than beseemed a child. And shall my loving care be cause of thy wicked cruelty? Yea, yea, I am not the first that hath been too careful, nor the last that shall be handled so unkindly! It is common to see fathers too fond, and children too froward. Well Lucilla, the tears which thou seest trickle down my cheeks and my drops of blood 40 (which thou canst not see) that fall from my heart, enforce me to make an end of my talk; and if thou have any duty of a child, or care of a friend,

or courtesy of a stranger, or feeling of a Christian, or humanity of a reasonable creature, then release thy father of grief, and acquit thyself of ungratefulness. Otherwise thou shalt but hasten my death, and increase
thine own defame; which if thou do, the gain is mine, and the loss thine,
and both infinite."

Lucilla, either so bewitched that she could not relent or so wicked that
she would not yield to her Father's request, answered him on this manner:

"Dear father, as you would have me to show the duty of a child, so
ought you to show the care of a parent, for as the one standeth in obedi-
10 ence, so the other is grounded upon reason. You would have me, as I owe
duty to you, to leave Curio; and I desire you, as you owe me any love,
that you suffer me to enjoy him. If you accuse me of unnaturalness in
that I yield not to your request, I am also to condemn you of unkindness,
in that you grant not my petition. You object I know not what to Curio,
but it is the eye of the master that fatteth the horse, and the love of the
woman that maketh the man. To give reason for fancy were to weigh the
fire, and measure the wind. If therefore my delight be the cause of your
death, I think my sorrow would be an occasion of your solace. And if you
be angry because I am pleased, certes I deem you would be content if I
20 were deceased; which if it be so, that my pleasure breed your pain, and
mine annoy your joy, I may well say that you are an unkind father and
I an unfortunate child. But, good father, either content yourself with my
choice, or let me stand to the main chance; otherwise the grief will be
mine, and the fault yours, and both untolerable."

Ferardo seeing his daughter to have neither regard of her own honor
nor his request, conceived such an inward grief that in short space he died,
leaving Lucilla the only heir of his lands, and Curio to possess them. But
what end came of her, seeing it is nothing incident to the history of
Euphues, it were superfluous to insert it, and so incredible that all women
30 would rather wonder at it than believe it. Which event being so strange,
I had rather leave them in a muse what it should be, than in a maze in
telling what it was.

Philautus having intelligence of Euphues his success, and the falsehood
of Lucilla, although he began to rejoice at the misery of his fellow, yet
seeing her fickleness, could not but lament her folly, and pity his friend's
misfortune, thinking that the lightness of Lucilla enticed Euphues to so
great liking.

Euphues and Philautus having conference between themselves, casting discourtesy in the teeth each of the other, but chiefly noting disloyalty
40 in the demeanor of Lucilla, after much talk renewed their old friendship,
both abandoning Lucilla as most abominable. Philautus was earnest to
have Euphues tarry in Naples, and Euphues desirous to have Philautus to

Athens, but the one was so addicted to the court, the other so wedded to
the university, that each refused the offer of the other; yet this they agreed
between themselves: that though their bodies were by distance of place
severed, yet the conjunction of their minds should neither be separated
by the length of time, nor alienated by change of soil. "I for my part,"
said Euphues, "to confirm this league give thee my hand and my heart."
And so likewise did Philautus; and so shaking hands, they bid each other
farewell.

Euphues, to the intent he might bridle the overlashing affections of
Philautus, conveyed into his study a certain pamphlet which he termed a 10
cooling card for Philautus, yet generally to be applied to all lovers; which
I have inserted as followeth.

*   *   *   *   *

To my very good friends, the gentlemen scholars of Oxford.

THERE is no privilege that needeth a pardon, neither is there any remission to be asked where a commission is granted. I speak this, gentlemen,
not to excuse the offense which is taken, but to offer a defense where I was
mistaken. A clear conscience is a sure card; truth hath the prerogative to 20
speak with plainness and the modesty to bear with patience. It was reported by some, and believed of many, that in the education of Ephoebus,
where mention is made of universities, that Oxford was too much defaced
or defamed. I know not what the envious have picked out by malice, or
the curious by wit, or the guilty by their own galled consciences, but this
I say: that I was as far from thinking ill as I find them from judging well.
But if I should now go about to make amends, I were then faulty in somewhat amiss, and should show myself like Apelles' prentice, who coveting
to mend the nose, marred the cheek; and not unlike the foolish dyer, who
never thought his cloth black until it was burned. If any fault be com- 30
mitted, impute it to Euphues, who knew you not, not to Lyly, who hates
you not.

Yet may I of all the rest most condemn Oxford of unkindness—of vice
I cannot—, who seemed to wean me before she brought me forth, and
to give me bones to gnaw before I could get the teat to suck. Wherein
she played the nice mother in sending me into the country to nurse, where
I tired at a dry breast three years, and was at the last enforced to wean
myself. But it was destiny, for if I had not been gathered from the tree
in the bud, I should, being blown, have proved a blast; and as good it is
to be an addle egg as an idle bird.   40

Euphues at his arrival, I am assured, will view Oxford, where he will
either recant his sayings or renew his complaints. He is now on the seas,

and how he hath been tossed I know not, but whereas I thought to receive him at Dover, I must meet him at Hampton. Nothing can hinder his coming but death, neither anything hasten his departure but unkindness.

Concerning myself, I have always thought so reverently of Oxford, of the scholars, of the manners, that I seemed to be rather an idolater than a blasphemer. They that invented this toy were unwise, and they that reported it unkind; and yet none of them can prove me unhonest.

But suppose I glanced at some abuses: did not Jupiter's egg bring forth as well Helen a light housewife in earth, as Castor a light star in 10 heaven? The estrich that taketh the greatest pride in her feathers picketh some of the worst out and burneth them; there is no tree but hath some blast, no countenance but hath some blemish; and shall Oxford then be blameless? I wish it were so, yet I cannot think it is so. But, as it is, it may be better, and were it badder, it is not the worst.

I think there are few universities that have less faults than Oxford, many that have more, none but have some.

But I commit my cause to the consciences of those that either know what I am or can guess what I should be; the one will answer themselves in construing friendly, the other, if I knew them, I would satisfy reasonably. 20 Thus loath to incur the suspicion of unkindness in not telling my mind, and not willing to make any excuse where there need no amends, I can neither crave pardon, lest I should confess a fault, nor conceal my meaning, lest I should be thought a fool. And so I end, yours assured to use.

JOHN LYLY.

STEPHEN GOSSON

The Introduction and Notes are at page 1316

FROM *The Schoole of Abuse*, 1579

The School of Abuse

THE SYRACUSANS used such variety of dishes in their banquets that when they were set and their boards furnished they were many times in doubt which they should touch first or taste last. And, in my opinion, the world giveth every writer so large a field to walk in that, before he set pen to the book, he shall find himself feasted at Syracusa, uncertain where to begin or when to end. This caused Pindarus to question with his muse 40 whether he were better with his art to decipher the life of the nymph Melia, or Cadmus' encounter with the dragon, or the wars of Hercules at the walls of Thebes, or Bacchus' cups, or Venus' juggling? He saw so many turnings laid open to his feet that he knew not which way to bend his pace.

Therefore, as I cannot but commend his wisdom which, in banqueting, feeds most upon that that doth nourish best; so must I dispraise his method in writing which, following the course of amorous poets, dwelleth longest in those points that profit least, and, like a wanton whelp, leaveth the game to run riot. The *scarab* flies over many a sweet flower, and lights in a cowshard; it is the custom of the fly to leave the sound places of the horse and suck at the botch; the nature of *coloquintida* to draw the worst humors to itself; the manner of swine to forsake the fair fields and wallow 10 in the mire; and the whole practise of poets, either with fables to shew their abuses or with plain terms to unfold their mischief, discover their shame, discredit themselves, and disperse their poison through the world. Virgil sweats in describing his gnat; Ovid bestirreth him to paint out his flea; the one shews his art in the lust of Dido; the other his cunning in the incest of Myrrha, and that trumpet of bawdry, the craft of love.

I must confess that poets are the whetstones of wit, notwithstanding that wit is dearly bought; where honey and gall are mixed, it will be hard to sever the one from the other. The deceitful physician giveth sweet syrups to make his poison go down the smoother; the juggler casteth a 20 mist to work the closer; the sirens' song is the sailor's wrack; the fowler's whistle the bird's death; the wholesome bait the fish's bane; the harpies have virgins' faces and vultures' talons; hyena speaks like a friend and devours like a foe; the calmest seas hide dangerous rocks; the wolf jets in wether's fells; many good sentences are spoken by Davus to shadow his knavery, and written by poets as ornaments to beautify their works and set their trumpery to sale without suspect.

But if you look well to Epaeus' horse, you shall find in his bowels the destruction of Troy; open the sepulchre of Semiramis, whose title promiseth such wealth to the kings of Persia, you shall see nothing but dead 30 bones; rip up the golden ball that Nero consecrated to Jupiter Capitolinus, you shall have it stuffed with the shavings of his beard; pull off the vizard that poets mask in, you shall disclose their reproach, bewray their vanity, loathe their wantonness, lament their folly, and perceive their sharp sayings to be placed as pearls in dunghills, fresh pictures on rotten walls, chaste matrons' apparel on common courtesans. These are the cups of Circe that turn reasonable creatures into brute beasts, the balls of Hippomenes that hinder the course of Atalanta, and the blocks of the devil that are cast in our ways to cut off the race of toward wits. No marvel though Plato shut them out of his school, and banished them quite from his com- 40 monwealth as effeminate writers, unprofitable members, and utter enemies to virtue.

The Romans were very desirous to imitate the Greeks, and yet very loath to receive their poets; insomuch that Cato layeth it in the dish of Marcus the noble as a foul reproach that, in the time of his consulship, he brought Ennius the poet into his province. Tully accustomed to read them with great diligence in his youth, but when he waxed graver in study, elder in years, riper in judgment, he accompted them the fathers of lies, pipes of vanity, and schools of abuse. Maximus Tyrius taketh upon him to defend the discipline of these doctors under the name of Homer, wresting the rashness of Ajax to valor; the cowardice of Ulysses to policy; the dotage of Nestor to grave counsel; and the battle of Troy to the wonderful conflict of the four elements, where Juno, which is counted the air, sets in her foot to take up the strife and steps boldly betwixt them to part the fray. It is a pageant worth the sight to behold how he labors with mountains to bring forth mice, much like to some of those players that come to the scaffold with drum and trumpet to proffer skirmish, and, when they have sounded alarm, off go the pieces to encounter a shadow or conquer a paper monster. You will smile, I am sure, if you read it, to see how this moral philosopher toils to draw the lion's skin upon Æsop's ass, Hercules' shoes on a child's feet, amplifying that which the more it is stirred, the more it stinks; the less it is talked of, the better it is liked; and as wayward children, the more they be flattered, the worse they are; or as cursed sores with often touching wax angry and run the longer without healing. He attributeth the beginning of virtue to Minerva, of friendship to Venus, and the root of all handicrafts to Vulcan; but if he had broke his arm as well as his leg, when he fell out of heaven into Lemnos, either Apollo must have played the bonesetter or every occupation been laid awater.

* * * * *

. . . Were the Argives and Pythagoras now alive and saw how many frets, how many strings, how many stops, how many keys, how many clefs, how many moods, how many flats, how many sharps, how many rules, how many spaces, how many notes, how many rests, how many quirks, how many corners, what chopping, what changing, what tossing, what turning, what wresting and wringing is among our musicians, I believe verily that they would cry out with the countryman, *Heu, quòd tam pingui macer est mihi taurus in arvo.* Alas, here is fat feeding and lean beasts! Or, as one said at the shearing of hogs, great cry and little wool; much ado and small help. To shew the abuses of these unthrifty scholars that despise the good rules of their ancient masters and run to the shop of their own devices, defacing old stamps, forging new prints, and coining strange precepts, Phaerecrates, a comical poet, bringeth in Music and

Justice upon the stage: Music with her clothes tattered, her flesh torn, her face deformed, her whole body mangled and dismembered; Justice, viewing her well and pitying her case, questioneth with her how she came in that plight. To whom Music replies that Melanippides, Phrynis, Timotheus, and such fantastical heads had so disfigured her looks, defaced her beauty, so hacked her and hewed her, and with many strings given her so many wounds that she is stricken to death, in danger to perish, and present in place the least part of herself. When the Sicilians and Dores forsook the plain-song that they had learned of their ancestors in the mountains and practised long among their herds, they found out such descant in Sybaris' instruments that, by dancing and skipping, they fell into lewdness of life. Neither stayed those abuses in the compass of that country; but, like to ill weeds, in time spread so far that they choked the good grain in every place.

For as poetry and piping are cousin germans, so piping and playing are of great affinity, and all three chained in links of abuse.

*   *   *   *   *

. . . But the exercise that is now among us is banqueting, playing, piping, and dancing, and all such delights as may win us to pleasure or rock us in sleep. *Quantum mutatus ab illo?* Oh, what a wonderful change is this? Our wrestling at arms is turned to wallowing in ladies' laps, our courage to cowardice, our running to riot, our bows into bowls, and our darts to dishes. We have robbed Greece of gluttony, Italy of wantonness, Spain of pride, France of deceit, and Dutchland of quaffing. Compare London to Rome and England to Italy, you shall find the theaters of the one, the abuses of the other, to be rife among us. *Experto crede,* I have seen somewhat, and therefore I think I may say the more. In Rome, when plays or pageants are shewn, Ovid chargeth his pilgrims to creep close to the saints whom they serve, and shew their double diligence to lift the gentlewomen's robes from the ground for soiling in the dust, to sweep motes from their kirtles, to keep their fingers in ure, to lay their hands at their backs for an easy stay, to look upon those whom they behold, to praise that which they commend, to like everything that pleaseth them, to present them pomegranates to pick as they sit, and, when all is done, to wait on them mannerly to their houses. In our assemblies at plays in London you shall see such heaving and shoving, such itching and shouldering to sit by women; such care for their garments that they be not trod on; such eyes to their laps that no chips light in them; such pillows to their backs that they take no hurt; such masking in their ears, I know not what; such giving them pippins to pass the time; such playing at foot-saunt without cards; such ticking, such toying, such smiling, such winking, and such

manning them home when the sports are ended that it is a right comedy
to mark their behavior, to watch their conceits, as the cat for the mouse,
and as good as a course at the game itself to dog them a little, or follow
aloof by the print of their feet, and so discover by slot where the deer
taketh soil.

If this were as well noted as ill seen, or as openly punished as secretly
practised, I have no doubt but the cause would be seared to dry up the
effect, and these pretty rabbits very cunningly ferreted from their burrows. For they that lack customers all the week, either because their
10 haunt is unknown or the constables and officers of their parish watch them
so narrowly that they dare not quetch, to celebrate the Sabbath flock to
theaters, and there keep a general market of bawdry. Not that any filthiness, indeed, is committed within the compass of that ground, as was once
done in Rome, but that every wanton and [h]is paramour, every man and
his mistress, every John and his Joan, every knave and his quean are there
first acquainted, and cheapen the merchandise in that place, which they
pay for elsewhere as they can agree. These worms, when they dare not
nestle in the peascod at home, find refuge abroad and are hid in the ears
of other men's corn.

20 Every vauter in one blind tavern or other is tenant at will, to which she
tolleth resort, and plays the stale to utter their victuals and help them to
empty their musty casks. There is she so entreated with words and received with courtesy that every back room in the house is at her commandment. Some that have neither land to maintain them nor good occupation to get their bread, desirous to strut it with the best yet disdaining to
live by the sweat of their brows, have found out this cast of legerdemain
to play fast and loose among their neighbors.

If any part of music have suffered shipwreck and arrived by fortune at
their fingers' ends, with shew of gentility they take up fair houses, receive
30 lusty lasses at a price for boards, and pipe from morning till evening for
wood and coal. By the brothers, cousins, uncles, great grandsires, and
such like acquaintance of their guests, they drink of the best, they sit rent
free, they have their own table spread to their hands without wearing the
strings of their purse, or anything else but household and honesty. When
resort so increaseth that they grow in suspicion, and the pots which are sent
so often to the tavern get such a knock before they come home that they
return their master a crack to his credit, though he be called in question of
his life, he hath shifts enough to avoid the blank. If their houses be searched,
some instrument of music is laid in sight to dazzle the eyes of every officer,
40 and all that are lodged in the house by night, or frequent it by day, come
thither as pupils to be well schooled. Other there are which, being so
known that they are the byword of every man's mouth and pointed at

commonly as they pass the streets, either couch themselves in alleys or blind lanes or take sanctuary in friaries or live a mile from the city, like Venus' nuns in a cloister of Newington, Ratliffe, Islington, Hogsdon, or some such place, where, like penitents, they deny the world and spend their days in double devotion. And when they are weary of contemplation, to consort themselves and renne their acquaintance, they visit theaters, where they make full accompt of a prey before they depart.

Solon made no law for parricides, because he feared that he should rather put men in mind to commit such offenses than, by any strange punishment, give them a bit to keep them under; and I intend not to shew you all that I see, nor half that I hear of these abuses, lest you judge me more wilful to teach them than willing to forbid them. I look still when players should cast me their gauntlets and challenge a combat for entering so far into their possessions, as though I made them lords of this misrule or the very schoolmasters of these abuses; though the best clerks be of that opinion, they hear not me say so. There are more houses than parish churches, more maids than Malkin, more ways to the wood than one, and more causes in nature than efficients. The carpenter raiseth not his frame without tools, nor the devil his work without instruments; were not players the mean to make these assemblies, such multitudes would hardly be drawn in so narrow room. They seek not to hurt, but desire to please; they have purged their comedies of wanton speeches, yet the corn which they sell is full of cockle, and the drink that they draw overcharged with dregs. There is more in them than we perceive, the devil stands at our elbow when we see not, speaks when we hear him not, strikes when we feel not, and woundeth sore when he raseth no skin nor rends the flesh. In those things that we least mistrust the greatest danger doth often lurk; the countryman is more afeared of the serpent that is hid in the grass than the wild beast that openly feeds upon the mountains; the mariner is more endangered by privy shelves than known rocks; the soldier is sooner killed with a little bullet than a long sword. There is more peril in close fistulas than outward sores, in secret ambush than main battles, in undermining than plain assaulting, in friends than foes, in civil discord than foreign wars. Small are the abuses, and slight are the faults that now in theaters escape the poet's pen; but tall cedars from little grains shoot high; great oaks from slender roots spread wide; large streams from narrow springs run far; one little spark fires a whole city; one dram of *hellebore* ransacks every vein; the fish *remora* hath a small body and great force to stay ships against wind and tide; *ichneumon*, a little worm, overcomes the elephant; the viper slays the bull; the weasel, the cockatrice; and the weakest wasp stingeth the stoutest man of war. The height of heaven is taken by the staff, the bottom of the sea sounded with lead, the farthest coast discovered by compass, the secrets of nature searched by wit, the anatomy of man set out by experience, but the abuses of plays cannot be shown because they pass the degrees of the instrument, reach of the plummet, sight of the mind, and for trial are never brought to the touchstone. Therefore, he that will avoid the open shame of privy sin, the common plague of private offenses, the great wracks of little rocks, the sure disease of uncertain causes must set hand to the stern and eye to his steps to shun the occasion as near as he can, neither running to bushes for rending his clothes, nor rend his clothes for impairing his thrift, nor walk upon ice for taking of a fall, nor take a fall for bruising himself, nor go to theaters for being allured, nor once be allured for fear of abuse.

Bunduica, a notable woman and a queen of England that time that Nero was emperor of Rome, having some of the Romans in garrison here against her, in an oration which she made to her subjects seemed utterly to contemn their force and laugh at their folly. For she accounted them unworthy the name of men or title of soldiers because they were smoothly appareled, soft lodged, daintily feasted, bathed in warm waters, rubbed with sweet ointments, strewed with fine powders, wine swillers, singers, dancers, and players.

God hath now blessed England with a queen, in virtue excellent, in power mighty, in glory renowned, in government politic, in possession rich, breaking her foes with the bent of her brow, ruling her subjects with shaking her hand, removing debate by diligent foresight, filling her chests with the fruits of peace, ministering justice by order of law, reforming abuses with great regard, and bearing her sword so even that neither the poor are trod under foot nor the rich suffered to look too high: nor Rome, nor France, nor tyrant, nor Turk dare, for their lives, to enter the list. But we, unworthy servants of so mild a mistress, degenerate children of so good a mother, unthankful subjects of so loving a prince, wound her sweet heart with abusing her lenity and stir Jupiter to anger to send us a stork that shall devour us. How often hath Her Majesty, with the grave advice of her whole council, set down the limits of apparel to every degree? And how soon again hath the pride of our hearts overflown the channel? How many times hath access to theaters been restrained, and how boldly again have we re-entered? Overlashing in apparel is so common a fault that the very hirelings of some of our players, which stand at reversion of six shillings by the week, jet under gentlemen's noses in suits of silk, exercising themselves to prating on the stage and common scoffing when they come abroad, where they look askance over the shoulder at every man of whom the Sunday before they begged an alms. I speak not this as though every one that professeth the quality so abused himself, for it is well known that some of them are sober, discreet, properly learned, honest householders, and citizens well thought on among their neighbors at home, though the pride of their shadows (I mean those hang-bys whom they succor with stipend) cause them to be somewhat ill talked of abroad.

And as some of the players are far from abuse, so some of their plays are without rebuke; which are easily remembered as quickly reckoned. The two prose books played at the Belsavage, where you shall find never a word without wit, never a line without pith, never a letter placed in vain. The Jew and Ptolemy, shown at the Bull: the one representing the greediness of worldly choosers and bloody minds of usurers; the other very lively describing how seditious estates with their own devices, false friends with their own swords, and rebellious commons in their own snares are overthrown; neither with amorous gesture wounding the eye, nor with slovenly talk hurting the ears of the chaste hearers. The Blacksmith's Daughter and Catiline's Conspiracies, usually brought in at The Theater: the first containing the treachery of Turks, the honorable bounty of a noble mind, and the shining of virtue in distress; the last, because it is known to be a pig of mine own sow, I will speak the less of it, only giving you to understand that the whole mark which I shot at in that work was to show the reward of traitors in Catiline, and the necessary government of learned men in the person of Cicero, which foresees every danger that is likely to happen and forestalls it continually ere it take effect. Therefore, I give these plays the commendation that Maximus Tyrius gave to Homer's works—καλά μὲν γὰρ τὰ Ὁμήρου ἔπη, καὶ ἔπων τὰ κάλλιστα, καὶ φανώτατα, καὶ ἄδεσθαι μουσαῖς πρέποντα ἀλλα οὐ πᾶσι καλά, οὐδὲ ἀεὶ καλά.

These plays are good plays and sweet plays, and of all plays the best plays, and most to be liked, worthy to be sung of the Muses, or set out with the cunning of Roscius himself, yet are they not fit for every man's diet: neither ought they commonly to be shown. Now, if any man ask me why myself have penned comedies in time past, and inveigh so eagerly against them here, let him know that *Semel insanivimus omnes:* I have sinned, and am sorry for my fault; he runs far that never turns; better late than never. I gave myself to that exercise in hope to thrive, but I burnt one candle to seek another, and lost both my time and my travail when I had done.

* * * *

Notwithstanding, it behooveth us in the mean season not to stick in the mire and gape for succor without using some ordinary way ourselves; or to lie wallowing like lubbers in the ship of the commonwealth, crying, Lord, Lord, when we see the vessel toil, but jointly lay our hands and heads and helps together to avoid the danger and save that which must

be the surety of us all. For as to the body there are many members serving
to several uses, the eye to see, the ear to hear, the nose to smell, the tongue
to taste, the hand to touch, the feet to bear the whole burden of the rest,
and every one dischargeth his duty without grudging, so should the whole
body of the commonwealth consist of fellow laborers, all generally serving
one head and particularly following their trade without repining. From
the head to the foot, from top to the toe, there should nothing be vain,
no body idle. Jupiter himself shall stand for example, who is ever in work,
still moving and turning about the heavens; if he should pull his hand
10 from the frame it were impossible for the world to endure. All would be
day or all night; all spring or all autumn; all summer or all winter; all
heat or all cold; all moisture or all drought; no time to till, no time to sow,
no time to plant, no time to reap, the earth barren, the rivers stopped, the
seas stayed, the seasons changed, and the whole course of nature overthrown. The mean must labor to serve the mighty, the mighty must study
to defend the mean. The subjects must sweat in obedience to their prince,
the prince must have a care over his poor vassals. If it be the duty of every
man in a commonwealth one way or other to bestir his stumps, I cannot
but blame those lither contemplators very much which sit concluding of
20 syllogisms in a corner, within a close study in the university coop themselves up forty years together studying all things and profess nothing. The
bell is known by his sound, the bird by her voice, the lion by his roar, the
tree by the fruit, a man by his works. To continue so long without moving,
to read so much without teaching, what differeth it from a dumb picture
or a dead body? No man is born to seek private profit—part for his country, part for his friends, part for himself. The fool that comes into a fair
garden likes the beauty of flowers and sticks them in his cap; the physician
considereth their nature and puts them in the pot. In the one they wither
without profit; in the other they serve to the health of the body. He that
30 readeth good writers and picks out their flowers for his own nose is like a
fool; he that preferreth their virtue before their sweet smell is a good
physician.

* * * * *

. . . I will content myself to shew you no more abuses in my school
than myself have seen, nor so many by hundreds as I have heard of. Lions
fold up their nails when they are in their dens, for wearing them in the
earth and need not; eagles draw in their talons as they sit in their nests,
for blunting them there among dross; and I will cast anchor in these
40 abuses, rest my bark in this simple road, for grating my wits upon needless
shelves. And because I accuse other for treading awry, which since I was
born never went right; because I find so many faults abroad, which have

at home more spots on my body than the leopard, more stains on my coat than the wicked Nessus, more holes in my life than the open sieve, more sins in my soul than hairs on my head: if I have been tedious in my lecture, or yourselves be weary of your lesson, hearken no longer for the clock, shut up the school, and get you home.

FINIS.

SIR PHILIP SIDNEY

The Introduction and Notes are at page 1318
From *The Defence of Poesie*, 1595 [written about 1582–83].

The Defence of Poesy

WHEN the right virtuous E[dward] W[otton] and I were at the Emperor's court together, we gave ourselves to learn horsemanship of Jon Pietro Pugliano, one that, with great commendation, had the place of an esquire in his stable; and he, according to the fertileness of the Italian wit, 20 did not only afford us the demonstration of his practise, but sought to enrich our minds with the contemplations therein, which he thought most precious. But with none, I remember, mine ears were at any time more loaden than when (either angered with slow payment, or moved with our learner-like admiration) he exercised his speech in the praise of his faculty.

He said soldiers were the noblest estate of mankind, and horsemen the noblest of soldiers. He said they were the masters of war and ornaments of peace, speedy goers and strong abiders, triumphers both in camps and courts; nay, to so unbelieved a point he proceeded, as that no earthly thing 30 bred such wonder to a prince as to be a good horseman. Skill of government was but a *pedanteria* in comparison. Then would he add certain praises by telling what a peerless beast the horse was, the only serviceable courtier, without flattery, the beast of most beauty, faithfulness, courage, and such more, that if I had not been a piece of a logician before I came to him, I think he would have persuaded me to have wished myself a horse. But thus much, at least, with his no few words he drave into me, that self love is better than any gilding to make that seem gorgeous wherein ourselves be parties.

Wherein, if Pugliano's strong affection and weak arguments will not 40 satisfy you, I will give you a nearer example of myself, who, I know not by what mischance, in these my not old years and idlest times, having slipped into the title of a poet, am provoked to say something unto you in the defence of that my unelected vocation; which if I handle with more good will than good reasons, bear with me, since the scholar is to be pardoned that followeth the steps of his master.

And yet I must say, that as I have more just cause to make a pitiful defence of poor poetry, which from almost the highest estimation of learning is fallen to be the laughing-stock of children, so have I need to bring some more available proofs, since the former is by no man barred of his deserved credit, the silly latter hath had even the names of philosophers
10 used to the defacing of it, with great danger of civil war among the Muses.

At first, truly, to all them that professing learning inveigh against poetry, may justly be objected, that they go very near to ungratefulness to seek to deface that which, in the noblest nations and languages that are known, hath been the first light-giver to ignorance, and first nurse, whose milk [by] little and little enabled them to feed afterwards of tougher knowledges. And will you play the hedgehog, that being received into the den, drave out his host? or rather the vipers, that with their birth kill their parents?

Let learned Greece, in any of his manifold sciences, be able to show me
20 one book before Musaeus, Homer, and Hesiod, all three nothing else but poets. Nay, let any history be brought that can say any writers were there before them, if they were not men of the same skill, as Orpheus, Linus, and some other are named, who, having been the first of that country that made pens deliverers of their knowledge to the posterity, may justly challenge to be called their fathers in learning. For not only in time they had this priority (although in itself antiquity be venerable), but went before them as causes to draw with their charming sweetness the wild untamed wits to an admiration of knowledge. So as Amphion was said to move stones with his poetry to build Thebes, and Orpheus to be listened to by
30 beasts, indeed stony and beastly people. So among the Romans were Livius Andronicus, and Ennius; so in the Italian language, the first that made it aspire to be a treasurehouse of science were the poets Dante, Bocace, and Petrarch; so in our English were Gower and Chaucer; after whom, encouraged and delighted with their excellent foregoing, others have followed to beautify our mother tongue, as well in the same kind as other arts.

This did so notably show itself that the philosophers of Greece durst not a long time appear to the world but under the masks of poets; so Thales, Empedocles, and Parmenides sang their natural philosophy in
40 verses; so did Pythagoras and Phocylides their moral counsels; so did Tyrtaeus in war matters; and Solon in matters of policy; or rather they, being poets, did exercise their delightful vein in those points of highest

knowledge, which before them lay hidden to the world; for that wise Solon was directly a poet it is manifest, having written in verse the notable fable of the Atlantic Island, which was continued by Plato. And truly, even Plato, whosoever well considereth shall find that in the body of his work, though the inside and strength were philosophy, the skin, as it were, and beauty depended most of poetry. For all stands upon dialogues, wherein he feigns many honest burgesses of Athens speak of such matters that if they had been set on the rack they would never have confessed them; besides, his poetical describing the circumstances of their meetings, as the well-ordering of a banquet, the delicacy of a walk, with interlacing 10 mere tales, as Gyges's Ring, and others; which who knows not to be flowers of poetry did never walk into Apollo's garden.

And even historiographers, although their lips sound of things done, and verity be written in their foreheads, have been glad to borrow both fashion and, perchance, weight of the poets. So Herodotus entitled his history by the name of the nine Muses; and both he, and all the rest that followed him, either stole or usurped of poetry their passionate describing of passions, the many particularities of battles which no man could affirm; or, if that be denied me, long orations, put in the mouths of great kings and captains, which it is certain they never pronounced. 20

So that truly neither philosopher nor historiographer could, at the first, have entered into the gates of popular judgments if they had not taken a great passport of poetry; which in all nations, at this day, where learning flourisheth not, is plain to be seen; in all which they have some feeling of poetry. In Turkey, besides their lawgiving divines they have no other writers but poets. In our neighbor-country Ireland, where truly learning goes very bare, yet are their poets held in a devout reverence. Even among the most barbarous and simple Indians, where no writing is, yet have they their poets who make and sing songs, which they call *areytos*, both of their ancestors' deeds and praises of their gods. A sufficient probability that if 30 ever learning come among them, it must be by having their hard dull wits softened and sharpened with the sweet delights of poetry; for until they find a pleasure in the exercise of the mind, great promises of much knowledge will little persuade them that know not the fruits of knowledge. In Wales, the true remnant of the ancient Britons, as there are good authorities to show the long time they had poets, which they called bards, so through all the conquests of Romans, Saxons, Danes, and Normans, some of whom did seek to ruin all memory of learning from among them, yet do their poets, even to this day, last; so as it is not more notable in the soon beginning than in long continuing. 40

But since the authors of most of our sciences were the Romans, and before them the Greeks, let us, a little, stand upon their authorities, but even so far as to see what names they have given unto this now scorned skill. Among the Romans a poet was called *vates*, which is as much as a diviner, foreseer, or prophet, as by his conjoined words *vaticinium*, and *vaticinari*, is manifest; so heavenly a title did that excellent people bestow upon this heart-ravishing knowledge! And so far were they carried into the admiration thereof, that they thought in the chanceable hitting upon any of such verses, great foretokens of their following fortunes were placed. Whereupon grew the word of *sortes Virgilianae*, when, by sudden opening Virgil's book, they lighted upon some verse of his, as it is reported by many. Whereof the histories of the Emperors' lives are full. As of Albinus, the governor of our island, who in his childhood met with this verse,

Arma amens capio, nec sat rationis in armis;

and in his age performed it, although it were a very vain and godless superstition. As also it was to think spirits were commanded by such verses; whereupon this word "charms," derived of "carmina," cometh; so yet serveth it to show the great reverence those wits were held in; and altogether not without ground, since both the oracles of Delphos and Sibylla's prophecies were wholly delivered in verses; for that same exquisite observing of number and measure in the words, and that high-flying liberty of conceit proper to the poet, did seem to have some divine force in it.

And may not I presume a little farther to show the reasonableness of this word *vates*, and say that the holy David's Psalms are a divine poem? If I do, I shall not do it without the testimony of great learned men, both ancient and modern. But even the name of "Psalms" will speak for me, which, being interpreted, is nothing but "Songs"; then, that it is fully written in metre, as all learned Hebricians agree, although the rules be not yet fully found. Lastly, and principally, his handling his prophecy, which is merely poetical. For what else is the awaking his musical instruments; the often and free changing of persons; his notable *prosopopoeias*, when he maketh you, as it were, see God coming in his majesty; his telling of the beasts' joyfulness, and hills leaping, but a heavenly poesy, wherein almost he showeth himself a passionate lover of that unspeakable and everlasting beauty to be seen by the eyes of the mind only, cleared by faith? But truly, now, having named him, I fear I seem to profane that holy name, applying it to poetry, which is among us thrown down to so ridiculous an estimation. But they that with quiet judgments will look a little deeper into it shall find the end and working of it such as, being rightly applied, deserveth not to be scourged out of the Church of God.

But now let us see how the Greeks have named it, and how they deemed of it. The Greeks named him ποιητήν which name hath, as the most excellent, gone through other languages; it cometh of this word ποιεῖν, which is to make; wherein, I know not whether by luck or wisdom, we Englishmen have met with the Greeks in calling him "a maker"; which name how high and incomparable a title it is, I had rather were known by marking the scope of other sciences than by any partial allegation.

There is no art delivered unto mankind that hath not the works of nature for his principal object, without which they could not consist, and on which they so depend as they become actors and players, as it were, of what nature will have set forth. So doth the astronomer look upon the stars, and by that he seeth set down what order nature hath taken therein 10 So doth the geometrician and arithmetician, in their diverse sorts of quantities. So doth the musicians, in times, tell you which by nature agree, which not. The natural philosopher thereon hath his name; and the moral philosopher standeth upon the natural virtues, vices, or passions of man; and follow nature, saith he, therein, and thou shalt not err. The lawyer saith what men have determined, the historian, what men have done. The grammarian speaketh only of the rules of speech; and the rhetorician and logician, considering what in nature will soonest prove and persuade, thereon give artificial rules, which still are compassed within the circle of a question, according to the proposed matter. The physician weigheth 20 the nature of man's body, and the nature of things helpful and hurtful unto it. And the metaphysic, though it be in the second and abstract notions, and therefore be counted supernatural, yet doth he, indeed, build upon the depth of nature. Only the poet, disdaining to be tied to any such subjection, lifted up with the vigor of his own invention, doth grow, in effect, into another nature, in making things either better than nature bringeth forth, or quite anew—forms such as never were in nature, as the heroes, demi-gods, cyclops, chimeras, furies, and such like—; so as he goeth hand in hand with Nature, not enclosed within the narrow warrant of her gifts, but freely ranging within the zodiac of his own wit 30 Nature never set forth the earth in so rich tapestry as divers poets have done; neither with so pleasant rivers, fruitful trees, sweet-smelling flowers, nor whatsoever else may make the too-much-loved earth more lovely; her world is brazen, the poets only deliver a golden.

But let those things alone, and go to man, for whom as the other things are, so it seemeth in him her uttermost cunning is employed; and know, whether she have brought forth so true a lover as Theagenes; so constant a friend as Pylades; so valiant a man as Orlando; so right a prince as Xenophon's Cyrus; so excellent man every way as Virgil's Aeneas? Neither let this be jestingly conceived, because the works of the one be 40 essential, the other in imitation or fiction; for every understanding knoweth the skill of each artificer standeth in that idea, or foreconceit of the

work, and not in the work itself. And that the poet hath that idea is manifest by delivering them forth in such excellency as he had imagined them;
which delivering forth, also, is not wholly imaginative, as we are wont to
say by them that build castles in the air; but so far substantially it worketh,
not only to make a Cyrus, which had been but a particular excellency, as
Nature might have done; but to bestow a Cyrus upon the world to make
many Cyruses, if they will learn aright why, and how, that maker made
him. Neither let it be deemed too saucy a comparison to balance the highest point of man's wit with the efficacy of nature; but rather give right
honor to the heavenly Maker of that maker, who, having made man to
his own likeness, set him beyond and over all the works of that second
nature; which in nothing he showeth so much as in poetry, when, with
the force of a divine breath, he bringeth things forth surpassing her doings,
with no small arguments to the incredulous of that first accursed fall of
Adam; since our erected wit maketh us know what perfection is, and yet
our infected will keepeth us from reaching unto it. But these arguments
will by few be understood, and by fewer granted; thus much I hope will
be given me, that the Greeks, with some probability of reason, gave him
the name above all names of learning.

Now let us go to a more ordinary opening of him, that the truth may
be the more palpable; and so, I hope, though we get not so unmatched a
praise as the etymology of his names will grant, yet his very description,
which no man will deny, shall not justly be barred from a principal commendation.

Poesy, therefore, is an art of imitation; for so Aristotle termeth it in
the word μίμησις, that is to say, a representing, counterfeiting, or figuring
forth: to speak metaphorically, a speaking picture, with this end, to teach
and delight.

Of this have been three general kinds: the chief, both in antiquity and
excellency, were they that did imitate the unconceivable excellencies of
God. Such were David in his *Psalms;* Salomon in his *Song of Songs,* in
his *Ecclesiastes,* and *Proverbs;* Moses and Deborah in their hymns; and
the writer of Job; which, beside other, the learned Emanuel Tremellius
and F[ranciscus] Junius do entitle the poetical part of the scripture;
against these none will speak that hath the Holy Ghost in due holy reverence. In this kind, though in a full wrong divinity, were Orpheus, Amphion, Homer in his hymns, and many other, both Greeks and Romans.
And this poesy must be used by whosoever will follow St. Paul's counsel,
in singing psalms when they are merry; and I know is used with the fruit
of comfort by some, when, in sorrowful pangs of their death-bringing sins,
they find the consolation of the never-leaving goodness.

The second kind is of them that deal with matters philosophical; either moral, as Tyrtaeus, Phocylides, Cato; or natural, as Lucretius, and Virgil's Georgics; or astronomical, as Manilius and Pontanus; or historical, as Lucan; which who mislike, the fault is in their judgment, quite out of taste, and not in the sweet food of sweetly uttered knowledge.

But because this second sort is wrapped within the fold of the proposed subject, and takes not the free course of his own invention; whether they properly be poets or no, let grammarians dispute, and go to the third, indeed right poets, of whom chiefly this question ariseth; betwixt whom and these second is such a kind of difference as betwixt the meaner sort of painters, who counterfeit only such faces as are set before them, and 10 the more excellent, who having no law but wit, bestow that in colors upon you which is fittest for the eye to see; as the constant though lamenting look of Lucretia, when she punished in herself another's fault; wherein he painteth not Lucretia, whom he never saw, but painteth the outward beauty of such a virtue. For these third be they which most properly do imitate to teach and delight; and to imitate, borrow nothing of what is, hath been, or shall be; but range, only reined with learned discretion, into the divine consideration of what may be, and should be. These be they that, as the first and most noble sort, may justly be termed *vates;* so these are waited on in the excellentest languages and best understand 20 ings, with the foredescribed name of poets. For these, indeed, do merely make to imitate, and imitate both to delight and teach, and delight to move men to take that goodness in hand which, without delight, they would fly as from a stranger; and teach to make them know that goodness whereunto they are moved; which being the noblest scope to which ever any learning was directed, yet want there not idle tongues to bark at them.

These be subdivided into sundry more special denominations; the most notable be the heroic, lyric, tragic, comic, satiric, iambic, elegiac, pastoral, and certain others; some of these being termed according to the matter they deal with, some by the sort of verse they like best to write in; for, 30 indeed, the greatest part of poets have appareled their poetical inventions in that numbrous kind of writing which is called verse. Indeed but appareled; verse being but an ornament, and no cause to poetry, since there have been many most excellent poets that never versified, and now swarm many versifiers that need never answer to the name of poets. For Xenophon, who did imitate so excellently as to give us *effigiem justi imperii*, the portraiture of a just empire, under the name of Cyrus, as Cicero saith of him, made therein an absolute heroical poem. So did Heliodorus, in his sugared invention of that picture of love in Theagenes and Chariclea; and yet both these wrote in prose; which I speak to show that it is not rhyming 40 and versing that maketh a poet (no more than a long gown maketh an advocate, who, though he pleaded in armor, should be an advocate and no soldier); but it is that feigning notable images of virtues, vices, or what else, with that delightful teaching, which must be the right describing note to know a poet by. Although, indeed, the senate of poets hath chosen verse as their fittest raiment, meaning as in matter they passed all in all, so in manner to go beyond them; not speaking table-talk fashion, or like men in a dream, words as they chanceably fall from the mouth, but piecing each syllable of each word by just proportion, according to the dignity of the subject.

Now, therefore, it shall not be amiss, first, to weigh this latter sort of poetry by his works, and then by his parts; and if in neither of these anatomies he be condemnable, I hope we shall obtain a more favorable sentence. This purifying of wit, this enriching of memory, enabling of judgment, and enlarging of conceit, which commonly we call learning, under what name soever it come forth, or to what immediate end soever it be directed, the final end is, to lead and draw us to as high a perfection as our degenerate souls, made worse by their clay lodgings, can be capable of. This, according to the inclination of man, bred many formed impressions; for some that thought this felicity principally to be gotten by knowledge, and no knowledge to be so high or heavenly as to be acquainted with the stars, gave themselves to astronomy; others, persuading themselves to be demigods if they knew the causes of things, became natural and supernatural philosophers. Some an admirable delight drew to music, and some the certainty of demonstration to the mathematics; but all, one and other, having this scope—to know, and by knowledge to lift up the mind from the dungeon of the body to the enjoying his own divine essence. But when, by the balance of experience, it was found that the astronomer, looking to the stars, might fall in a ditch; that the inquiring philosopher might be blind in himself; and the mathematician might draw forth a straight line with a crooked heart; then lo! did proof, the overruler of opinions, make manifest that all these are but serving sciences, which, as they have a private end in themselves, so yet are they all directed to the highest end of the mistress knowledge, by the Greeks called ἀρχιτεκτονική, which stands, as I think, in the knowledge of a man's self, in the ethic and politic consideration, with the end of well doing, and not of well knowing only; even as the saddler's next end is to make a good saddle, but his further end to serve a nobler faculty, which is horsemanship; so the horseman's to soldiery; and the soldier not only to have the skill, but to perform the practise of a soldier. So that the ending end of all earthly learning being virtuous action, those skills that most serve to bring forth that, have a most just title to be princes over all the rest; wherein, if we can show, the poet is worthy to have it before any other competitors.

Among whom principally to challenge it, step forth the moral philosophers; whom, methinks, I see coming towards me with a sullen gravity, as though they could not abide vice by daylight, rudely clothed, for to witness outwardly their contempt of outward things; with books in their hands against glory, whereto they set their names; sophistically speaking against subtilty, and angry with any man in whom they see the foul fault of anger. These men, casting largess as they go of definitions, divisions, and distinctions, with a scornful interrogative do soberly ask whether it be possible to find any path so ready to lead a man to virtue as that which teacheth what virtue is; and teacheth it not only by delivering forth his very being, his causes and effects, but also by making known his enemy, vice, which must be destroyed, and his cumbersome servant, passion, which must be mastered; by showing the generalities that contain it, and the specialities that are derived from it; lastly, by plain setting down how it extends itself out of the limits of a man's own little world, to the government of families, and maintaining of public societies.

The historian scarcely gives leisure to the moralist to say so much, but that he (laden with old mouse-eaten records, authorizing himself for the most part upon other histories, whose greatest authorities are built upon the notable foundation [of] hearsay, having much ado to accord differing writers, and to pick truth out of partiality; better acquainted with a thousand years ago than with the present age, and yet better knowing how this world goes than how his own wit runs; curious for antiquities, and inquisitive of novelties, a wonder to young folks, and a tyrant in table-talk) denieth, in a great chafe, that any man for teaching of virtue and virtuous actions is comparable to him. "I am *Testis temporum, lux veritatis, vita memoriae, magistra vitae, nuntia vetustatis.* The philosopher," saith he, "teacheth a disputative virtue, but I do an active; his virtue is excellent in the dangerless Academy of Plato, but mine showeth forth her honorable face in the battles of Marathon, Pharsalia, Poictiers, and Agincourt; he teacheth virtue by certain abstract considerations, but I only bid you follow the footing of them that have gone before you. Old-aged experience goeth beyond the fine-witted philosopher; but I give the experience of many ages. Lastly, if he make the song book, I put the learner's hand to the lute; and if he be the guide, I am the light." Then would he allege you innumerable examples, confirming story by stories, how much the wisest senators and princes have been directed by the credit of history, as Brutus, Alphonsus of Aragon, and who not, if need be. At length, the long line of their disputation makes a point in this, that the one giveth the precept, and the other the example.

Now whom shall we find, since the question standeth for the highest form in the school of learning, to be moderator? Truly, as me seemeth, the poet; and if not a moderator, even the man that ought to carry the title from them both, and much more from all other serving sciences. Therefore compare we the poet with the historian, and with the moral philosopher; and if he go beyond them both, no other human skill can match him; for as for the divine, with all reverence, it is ever to be excepted, not only for having his scope as far beyond any of these as eternity exceedeth a moment, but even for passing each of these in themselves; and for the lawyer, though *Jus* be the daughter of Justice, the chief of virtues, yet because he seeks to make men good rather *formidine poenae* than *virtutis amore*, or, to say righter, doth not endeavor to make men good, but that their evil hurt not others, having no care, so he be a good citizen, how bad a man he be. Therefore, as our wickedness maketh him necessary, and necessity maketh him honorable, so is he not in the deepest truth to stand in rank with these, who all endeavor to take naughtiness away, and plant goodness even in the secretest cabinet of our souls. And these four are all that any way deal in the consideration of men's manners, which being the supreme knowledge, they that best breed it deserve the best commendation.

The philosopher, therefore, and the historian are they which would win the goal, the one by precept, the other by example; but both, not having both, do both halt. For the philosopher, setting down with thorny arguments the bare rule, is so hard of utterance, and so misty to be conceived, that one that hath no other guide but him shall wade in him until he be old, before he shall find sufficient cause to be honest. For his knowledge standeth so upon the abstract and general that happy is that man who may understand him, and more happy that can apply what he doth understand. On the other side the historian, wanting the precept, is so tied, not to what should be, but to what is; to the particular truth of things, and not to the general reason of things; that his example draweth no necessary consequence, and therefore a less fruitful doctrine.

Now doth the peerless poet perform both; for whatsoever the philosopher saith should be done, he giveth a perfect picture of it, by some one by whom he pre-supposeth it was done, so as he coupleth the general notion with the particular example. A perfect picture, I say; for he yieldeth to the powers of the mind an image of that whereof the philosopher bestoweth but a wordish description, which doth neither strike, pierce, nor possess the sight of the soul so much as that other doth. For as in outward things, to a man that had never seen an elephant, or a rhinoceros, who should tell him most exquisitely all their shape, color, bigness, and particular marks; or of a gorgeous palace, an architecture, who, declaring the full beauties, might well make the hearer able to repeat, as it were by rote, all he had heard, yet should never satisfy his inward conceit with being witness to itself of a true lively knowledge; but the same man, as soon as he might see those beasts well painted, or that house well in model, should straightway grow, without need of any description, to a judicial comprehending of them; so, no doubt, the philosopher, with his learned definitions, be it of virtues or vices, matters of public policy or private government, replenisheth the memory with many infallible grounds of wisdom, which, notwithstanding, lie dark before the imaginative and judging power, if they be not illuminated or figured forth by the speaking picture of poesy.

Tully taketh much pains, and many times not without poetical helps, to make us know the force love of our country hath in us. Let us but hear old Anchises speaking in the midst of Troy's flames, or see Ulysses, in the 10 fulness of all Calypso's delights, bewail his absence from barren and beggarly Ithaca. Anger, the Stoics said, was a short madness; let but Sophocles bring you Ajax on a stage, killing and whipping sheep and oxen, thinking them the army of the Greeks, with their chieftains Agamemnon and Menelaus, and tell me if you have not a more familiar insight into anger than finding in the schoolmen his genus and difference. See whether wisdom and temperance in Ulysses and Diomedes, valor in Achilles, friendship in Nisus and Euryalus, even to an ignorant man carry not an apparent shining; and, contrarily, the remorse of conscience in Oedipus; the soon-repenting pride in Agamemnon; the self-devouring cruelty in 20 his father Atreus; the violence of ambition in the two Theban brothers; the sour sweetness of revenge in Medea; and, to fall lower, the Terentian Gnatho, and our Chaucer's Pandar, so expressed that we now use their names to signify their trades; and finally, all virtues, vices, and passions so in their own natural states laid to the view, that we seem not to hear of them but clearly to see through them.

But even in the most excellent determination of goodness, what philosopher's counsel can so readily direct a prince as the feigned Cyrus in Xenophon? or a virtuous man in all fortunes as Aeneas in Virgil? or a whole commonwealth as the way of Sir Thomas More's *Utopia?* I say the way, 30 because where Sir Thomas More erred, it was the fault of the man, and not of the poet; for that way of patterning a commonwealth was most absolute, though he, perchance, hath not so absolutely performed it. For the question is, whether the feigned image of poetry or the regular instruction of philosophy hath the more force in teaching. Wherein if the philosophers have more rightly showed themselves philosophers than the poets have attained to the high top of their profession, (as in truth,

Mediocribus esse poëtis
Non Di, non homines, non concessere columnae,
40

it is, I say again, not the fault of the art, but that by few men that art can be accomplished. Certainly, even our Savior Christ could as well have

given the moral commonplaces of uncharitableness and humbleness as
the divine narration of Dives and Lazarus; or of disobedience and mercy
as that heavenly discourse of the lost child and the gracious father; but
that his through-searching wisdom knew the estate of Dives burning in
hell, and of Lazarus in Abraham's bosom, would more constantly, as it
were, inhabit both the memory and judgment. Truly, for myself (me
seems), I see before mine eyes the lost child's disdainful prodigality turned
to envy a swine's dinner; which, by the learned divines, are thought not
historical acts, but instructing parables.

10   For conclusion, I say the philosopher teacheth, but he teacheth obscurely, so as the learned only can understand him; that is to say, he
teacheth them that are already taught. But the poet is the food for the
tenderest stomachs; the poet is, indeed, the right popular philosopher.
Whereof Aesop's tales give good proof; whose pretty allegories, stealing
under the formal tales of beasts, makes many, more beastly than beasts,
begin to hear the sound of virtue from those dumb speakers.

But now may it be alleged, that if this imagining of matters be so fit for
the imagination, then must the historian needs surpass, who brings you
images of true matters, such as indeed were done, and not such as fan-
20 tastically or falsely may be suggested to have been done. Truly, Aristotle
himself, in his discourse of Poesy, plainly determineth this question, saying that poetry is φιλοσοφώτερον and σπουδαιότερον that is to say, it is more
philosophical and more [studiously serious] than history. His reason is,
because poesy dealeth with καθόλου that is to say, with the universal consideration, and the history καθ'ἕκαστον, the particular. "Now," saith he,
"the universal weighs what is fit to be said or done, either in likelihood or
necessity; which the poesy considereth in his imposed names, and the particular only marketh, whether Alcibiades did or suffered this or that."
Thus far Aristotle. Which reason of his, as all his, is most full of reason.
30 For, indeed, if the question were whether it were better to have a particular
act truly or falsely set down, there is no doubt which is to be chosen, no
more than whether you had rather have Vespasian's picture right as he
was, or, at the painter's pleasure, nothing resembling. But if the question
be, for your own use and learning, whether it be better to have it set down
as it should be, or as it was, then, certainly, is more doctrinable the feigned
Cyrus in Xenophon than the true Cyrus in Justin; and the feigned Aeneas
in Virgil than the right Aeneas in Dares Phrygius; as to a lady that desired
to fashion her countenance to the best grace, a painter should more benefit her to portrait a most sweet face, writing Canidia upon it, than to paint
40 Canidia as she was, who, Horace sweareth, was full ill-favored. If the
poet do his part aright, he will show you in Tantalus, Atreus, and such
like, nothing that is not to be shunned; in Cyrus, Aeneas, Ulysses, each

thing to be followed; where the historian, bound to tell things as things were, cannot be liberal—without he will be poetical—of a perfect pattern; but, as in Alexander, or Scipio himself, show doings, some to be liked, some to be misliked; and then how will you discern what to follow, but by your own discretion, which you had without reading Q[uintus] Curtius? And whereas a man may say, though in universal consideration of doctrine the poet prevaileth, yet that the history, in his saying such a thing was done, doth warrant a man more in that he shall follow; the answer is manifest: that if he stand upon that *was*, as if he should argue, because it rained yesterday therefore it should rain to-day; then, indeed, hath it some advantage to a gross conceit. But if he know an example only enforms a conjectured likelihood, and so go by reason, the poet doth so far exceed him, as he is to frame his example to that which is most reasonable, be it in warlike, politic, or private matters; where the historian in his bare *was* hath many times that which we call fortune to overrule the best wisdom. Many times he must tell events whereof he can yield no cause; or if he do, it must be poetically.

For, that a feigned example hath as much force to teach as a true example (for as for to move, it is clear, since the feigned may be tuned to the highest key of passion), let us take one example wherein an historian and a poet did concur. Herodotus and Justin do both testify that Zopyrus, King Darius's faithful servant, seeing his master long resisted by the rebellious Babylonians, feigned himself in extreme disgrace of his king; for verifying of which he caused his own nose and ears to be cut off, and so flying to the Babylonians, was received; and, for his known valor, so far credited that he did find means to deliver them over to Darius. Muchlike matter doth Livy record of Tarquinius and his son. Xenophon excellently feigneth such another stratagem, performed by Abradates in Cyrus's behalf. Now would I fain know, if occasion be presented unto you to serve your prince by such an honest dissimulation, why do you not as well learn it of Xenophon's fiction as of the other's verity? And, truly, so much the better, as you shall save your nose by the bargain; for Abradates did not counterfeit so far. So, then, the best of the historian is subject to the poet; for, whatsoever action or faction, whatsoever counsel, policy, or war stratagem the historian is bound to recite, that may the poet, if he list, with his imitation make his own, beautifying it both for further teaching and more delighting, as it please him; having all, from Dante his heaven to his hell, under the authority of his pen. Which if I be asked, what poets have done so; as I might well name some, so yet, say I, and say again, I speak of the art, and not of the artificer.

Now, to that which commonly is attributed to the praise of history, in respect of the notable learning, is got by marking the success, as though therein a man should see virtue exalted, and vice punished: truly, that commendation is peculiar to poetry, and far off from history. For, indeed, poetry ever sets virtue so out in her best colors, making fortune her well-waiting handmaid, that one must needs be enamored of her. Well may you see Ulysses in a storm, and in other hard plights; but they are but exercises of patience and magnanimity, to make them shine the more in the near following prosperity. And of the contrary part, if evil men come to the stage, they ever go out (as the tragedy writer answered to one that misliked the show of such persons) so manacled as they little animate folks to follow them. But the history, being captived to the truth of a foolish world, is many times a terror from well-doing and an encouragement to unbridled wickedness. For see we not valiant Miltiades rot in his fetters? the just Phocion and the accomplished Socrates put to death like traitors? the cruel Severus live prosperously? the excellent Severus miserably murdered? Sylla and Marius dying in their beds? Pompey and Cicero slain then when they would have thought exile a happiness? See we not virtuous Cato driven to kill himself, and rebel Caesar so advanced that his name yet, after sixteen hundred years, lasteth in the highest honor? And mark but even Caesar's own words of the forenamed Sylla (who in that only did honestly, to put down his dishonest tyranny), *literas nescivit;* as if want of learning caused him to do well. He meant it not by poetry, which, not content with earthly plagues, deviseth new punishments in hell for tyrants; nor yet by philosophy, which teacheth *occidendos esse;* but, no doubt, by skill in history; for that, indeed, can afford you Cypselus, Periander, Phalaris, Dionysius, and I know not how many more of the same kennel, that speed well enough in their abominable injustice or usurpation.

I conclude, therefore, that he excelleth history, not only in furnishing the mind with knowledge, but in setting it forward to that which deserves to be called and accounted good: which setting forward, and moving to well-doing, indeed, setteth the laurel crown upon the poets as victorious, not only of the historian, but over the philosopher, howsoever in teaching it may be questionable. For suppose it be granted, that which I suppose with great reason may be denied, that the philosopher in respect of his methodical proceeding teach more perfectly than the poet, yet do I think that no man is so much φιλοφιλόσοφος as to compare the philosopher in moving with the poet. And that moving is of a higher degree than teaching, it may by this appear, that it is well nigh both the cause and effect of teaching; for who will be taught, if he be not moved with desire to be taught? And what so much good doth that teaching bring forth (I speak still of moral doctrine) as that it moveth one to do that which it doth teach? For, as Aristotle saith, it is not γνῶσις but πρᾶξις must be the fruit;

and how πρᾶξις can be without being moved to practise, it is no hard matter to consider. The philosopher showeth you the way, he informeth you of the particularities, as well of the tediousness of the way and of the pleasant lodging you shall have when your journey is ended, as of the many by-turnings that may divert you from your way; but this is to no man but to him that will read him, and read him with attentive, studious painfulness; which constant desire whosoever hath in him hath already passed half the hardness of the way, and therefore is beholding to the philosopher but for the other half. Nay, truly, learned men have learnedly thought that where once reason hath so much overmastered passion as that the mind hath a free desire to do well, the inward light each mind hath in itself is as good as a philosopher's book; since in nature we know it is well to do well, and what is well and what is evil, although not in the words of art which philosophers bestow upon us; for out of natural conceit the philosophers drew it. But to be moved to do that which we know, or to be moved with desire to know, *hoc opus, hic labor est*.

Now therein of all sciences (I speak still of human, and according to the human conceit), is our poet the monarch. For he doth not only show the way, but giveth so sweet a prospect into the way as will entice any man to enter into it; nay, he doth, as if your journey should lie through a fair vineyard, at the very first give you a cluster of grapes, that full of that taste you may long to pass further. He beginneth not with obscure defini-tions, which must blur the margent with interpretations and load the memory with doubtfulness, but he cometh to you with words set in de-lightful proportion, either accompanied with, or prepared for, the well-enchanting skill of music; and with a tale, forsooth, he cometh unto you, with a tale which holdeth children from play and old men from the chimney-corner; and, pretending no more, doth intend the winning of the mind from wickedness to virtue; even as the child is often brought to take most wholesome things by hiding them in such other as have a pleas-ant taste; which, if one should begin to tell them the nature of the aloes or rhubarbarum they should receive, would sooner take their physic at their ears than at their mouth. So is it in men (most of which are childish in the best things till they be cradled in their graves); glad they will be to hear the tales of Hercules, Achilles, Cyrus, Aeneas; and, hearing them, must needs hear the right description of wisdom, valor, and justice; which, if they had been barely (that is to say, philosophically) set out, they would swear they be brought to school again.

That imitation whereof poetry is, hath the most conveniency to nature of all other; insomuch that, as Aristotle saith, those things which in them-selves are horrible, as cruel battles, unnatural monsters, are made, in poetical imitation, delightful. Truly, I have known men that even with reading Amadis de Gaule, which, God knoweth, wanteth much of a perfect poesy, have found their hearts moved to the exercise of courtesy, liberality, and especially courage. Who readeth Aeneas carrying old Anchises on his back, that wisheth not it were his fortune to perform so excellent an act? Whom doth not those words of Turnus move (the tale of Turnus having planted his image in the imagination)

> ———*fugientem haec terra videbit?*
> *Usque adeone mori miserum est?*

10 Where the philosophers, as they think scorn to delight, so must they be content little to move, saving wrangling whether *virtus* be the chief or the only good; whether the contemplative or the active life do excel; which Plato and Boethius well knew, and therefore made mistress Philosophy very often borrow the masking raiment of poesy. For even those hard-hearted evil men who think virtue a school-name, and know no other good but *indulgere genio,* and therefore despise the austere admonitions of the philosopher and feel not the inward reason they stand upon, yet will be content to be delighted, which is all the good-fellow poet seems to promise; and so steal to see the form of goodness, which seen, they
20 cannot but love, ere themselves be aware, as if they took a medicine of cherries.

Infinite proofs of the strange effects of this poetical invention might be alleged: only two shall serve, which are so often remembered as I think all men know them. The one of Menenius Agrippa, who, when the whole people of Rome had resolutely divided themselves from the senate, with apparent show of utter ruin, though he were, for that time, an excellent orator, came not among them upon trust either of figurative speeches or cunning insinuations, and much less with far-fet maxims of philosophy, which, especially if they were Platonic, they must have learned
30 geometry before they could well have conceived; but, forsooth, he behaveth himself like a homely and familiar poet. He telleth them a tale, that there was a time when all the parts of the body made a mutinous conspiracy against the belly, which they thought devoured the fruits of each other's labor; they concluded they would let so unprofitable a spender starve. In the end, to be short (for the tale is notorious, and as notorious that it was a tale), with punishing the belly they plagued themselves. This, applied by him, wrought such effect in the people as I never read that only words brought forth but then so sudden and so good an alteration, for upon reasonable conditions a perfect reconcilement ensued.

40 The other is of Nathan the prophet, who, when the holy David had so far forsaken God as to confirm adultery with murther, when he was to

do the tenderest office of a friend, in laying his own shame before his eyes, sent by God to call again so chosen a servant, how doth he it? But by telling of a man whose beloved lamb was ungratefully taken from his bosom. The application most divinely true, but the discourse itself feigned; which made David (I speak of the second and instrumental cause) as in a glass see his own filthiness, as that heavenly Psalm of Mercy well testifieth.

By these, therefore, examples and reasons, I think it may be manifest that the poet, with that same hand of delight, doth draw the mind more effectually than any other art doth. And so a conclusion not unfitly en- 10 sueth: that as virtue is the most excellent resting-place for all worldly learning to make his end of, so poetry, being the most familiar to teach it, and most princely to move towards it, in the most excellent work is the most excellent workman.

But I am content not only to decipher him by his works (although works in commendation and dispraise must ever hold a high authority), but more narrowly will examine his parts; so that, as in a man, though all together may carry a presence full of majesty and beauty, perchance in some one defectuous piece we may find blemish.

Now, in his parts, kinds, or species, as you list to term them, it is to be 20 noted that some poesies have coupled together two or three kinds; as the tragical and comical, whereupon is risen the tragi-comical; some, in the manner, have mingled prose and verse, as Sannazzaro and Boethius; some have mingled matters heroical and pastoral; but that cometh all to one in this question, for, if severed they be good, the conjunction cannot be hurtful. Therefore, perchance forgetting some, and leaving some as needless to be remembered, it shall not be amiss in a word to cite the special kinds, to see what faults may be found in the right use of them.

Is it, then, the pastoral poem which is misliked? For, perchance, where the hedge is lowest, they will soonest leap over. Is the poor pipe disdained, 30 which sometimes, out of Melibaeus's mouth, can show the misery of people under hard lords and ravening soldiers? And again, by Tityrus, what blessedness is derived to them that lie lowest, from the goodness of them that sit highest? sometimes, under the pretty tales of wolves and sheep, can include the whole considerations of wrong doing and patience; sometimes show that contentions for trifles can get but a trifling victory; where, perchance, a man may see that even Alexander and Darius, when they strave who should be cock of this world's dunghill, the benefit they got was, that the after-livers may say,

Haec memini, et victum frustra contendere Thyrsim. 40
Ex illo Corydon, Corydon est tempore nobis.

Or is it the lamenting elegiac, which, in a kind heart, would move rather pity than blame; who bewaileth with the great philosopher Heraclitus the weakness of mankind, and the wretchedness of the world; who, surely, is to be praised, either for compassionately accompanying just causes of lamentations, or for rightly painting out how weak be the passions of woefulness?

Is it the bitter but wholesome iambic, who rubs the galled mind, in making shame the trumpet of villainy, with bold and open crying out against naughtiness?

Or the satiric? who,

Omne vafer vitium ridenti tangit amico;

who sportingly never leaveth till he make a man laugh at folly, and, at length, ashamed to laugh at himself, which he cannot avoid without avoiding the folly; who, while circum praecordia ludit, giveth us to feel how many headaches a passionate life bringeth us to; how when all is done,

Est Ulubris, animus si nos non deficit aequus.

No, perchance, it is the comic, whom naughty play-makers and stage-keepers have justly made odious. To the arguments of abuse I will after answer; only thus much now is to be said, that the comedy is an imitation of the common errors of our life, which he representeth in the most ridiculous and scornful sort that may be; so as it is impossible that any beholder can be content to be such a one. Now as in geometry the oblique must be known as well as the right, and in arithmetic the odd as well as the even; so in the actions of our life, who seeth not the filthiness of evil wanteth a great foil to perceive the beauty of virtue. This doth the comedy handle so, in our private and domestical matters, as with hearing it we get, as it were, an experience of what is to be looked for of a niggardly Demea, of a crafty Davus, of a flattering Gnatho, of a vain-glorious Thraso; and not only to know what effects are to be expected, but to know who be such, by the signifying badge given them by the comedian. And little reason hath any man to say that men learn the evil by seeing it so set out; since, as I said before, there is no man living but by the force truth hath in nature, no sooner seeth these men play their parts but wisheth them in pistrinum; although, perchance, the sack of his own faults lie so behind his back that he seeth not himself to dance in the same measure, whereto yet nothing can more open his eyes than to see his own actions contemptibly set forth. So that the right use of comedy will, I think, by nobody be blamed.

And much less of the high and excellent tragedy, that openeth the greatest wounds, and showeth forth the ulcers that are covered with tissue; that maketh kings fear to be tyrants, and tyrants manifest their tyrannical humours; that with stirring the effects of admiration and commiseration teacheth the uncertainty of this world, and upon how weak foundations gilden roofs are builded; that maketh us know,

Qui sceptra saevus duro imperio regit,
Timet timentes, metus in authorem redit.

But how much it can move, Plutarch yieldeth a notable testimony of the 10 abominable tyrant Alexander Pheraeus; from whose eyes a tragedy, well made and represented, drew abundance of tears, who without all pity had murthered infinite numbers, and some of his own blood; so as he that was not ashamed to make matters for tragedies yet could not resist the sweet violence of a tragedy. And if it wrought no further good in him, it was that he in despite of himself withdrew himself from hearkening to that which might mollify his hardened heart. But it is not the tragedy they do mislike, for it were too absurd to cast out so excellent a representation of whatsoever is most worthy to be learned.

Is it the lyric that most displeaseth, who with his tuned lyre and well- 20 accorded voice giveth praise, the reward of virtue, to virtuous acts? who giveth moral precepts and natural problems? who sometime raiseth up his voice to the height of the heavens, in singing the lauds of the immortal God? Certainly I must confess mine own barbarousness; I never heard the old song of Percy and Douglas that I found not my heart moved more than with a trumpet; and yet it is sung but by some blind crowder, with no rougher voice than rude style; which being so evil appareled in the dust and cobwebs of that uncivil age, what would it work trimmed in the gorgeous eloquence of Pindar? In Hungary I have seen it the manner at all feasts, and other such-like meetings, to have songs of their ancestors' 30 valor, which that right soldier-like nation think one of the chiefest kindlers of brave courage. The incomparable Lacedaemonians did not only carry that kind of music ever with them to the field, but even at home, as such songs were made, so were they all content to be singers of them; when the lusty men were to tell what they did, the old men what they had done, and the young what they would do. And where a man may say that Pindar many times praiseth highly victories of small moment, rather matters of sport than virtue; as it may be answered, it was the fault of the poet, and not of the poetry, so, indeed, the chief fault was in the time and custom of the Greeks, who set those toys at so high a price that Philip of Macedon 40 reckoned a horse-race won at Olympus among his three fearful felicities.

But as the unimitable Pindar often did, so is that kind most capable, and most fit, to awake the thoughts from the sleep of idleness, to embrace honorable enterprises.

There rests the heroical, whose very name, I think, should daunt all backbiters. For by what conceit can a tongue be directed to speak evil of that which draweth with him no less champions than Achilles, Cyrus, Aeneas, Turnus, Tydeus, Rinaldo? who doth not only teach and move to truth, but teacheth and moveth to the most high and excellent truth; who maketh magnanimity and justice shine through all misty fearfulness and foggy desires; who, if the saying of Plato and Tully be true, that who could see virtue would be wonderfully ravished with the love of her beauty, this man setteth her out to make her more lovely, in her holiday apparel, to the eye of any that will deign not to disdain until they understand. But if anything be already said in the defence of sweet poetry, all concurreth to the maintaining the heroical, which is not only a kind, but the best and most accomplished kind, of poetry. For, as the image of each action stirreth and instructeth the mind, so the lofty image of such worthies most inflameth the mind with desire to be worthy, and informs with counsel how to be worthy. Only let Aeneas be worn in the tablet of your memory, how he governeth himself in the ruin of his country; in the preserving his old father, and carrying away his religious ceremonies; in obeying God's commandment to leave Dido, though not only passionate kindness, but even the human consideration of virtuous gratefulness, would have craved other of him; how in storms, how in sports, how in war, how in peace, how a fugitive, how victorious, how besieged, how besieging, how to strangers, how to allies, how to enemies, how to his own; lastly, how in his inward self, and how in his outward government; and I think, in a mind most prejudiced with a prejudicating humour, he will be found in excellency fruitful. Yea, as Horace saith, *Melius Chry-sippo et Crantore:* but, truly, I imagine it falleth out with these poet-whippers as with some good women who often are sick, but in faith they cannot tell where. So the name of poetry is odious to them, but neither his cause nor effects, neither the sum that contains him, nor the particularities descending from him, give any fast handle to their carping dispraise.

Since, then, poetry is of all human learnings the most ancient, and of most fatherly antiquity, as from whence other learnings have taken their beginnings; since it is so universal that no learned nation doth despise it, nor barbarous nation is without it; since both Roman and Greek gave such divine names unto it, the one of prophesying, the other of making, and that indeed that name of making is fit for him, considering that where all other arts retain themselves within their subject, and receive, as it were, their being from it, the poet only, only bringeth his own stuff, and doth not learn a conceit out of a matter, but maketh matter for a conceit; since neither his description nor end containeth any evil, the thing described cannot be evil; since his effects be so good as to teach goodness, and delight the learners of it; since therein (namely in moral doctrine, the chief of all knowledges) he doth not only far pass the historian, but, for instructing, is well nigh comparable to the philosopher, for moving, leaveth him behind him; since the Holy Scripture (wherein there is no uncleanness) hath whole parts in it poetical, and that even our Savior Christ vouchsafed to use the flowers of it; since all his kinds are not only in their united forms but in their severed dissections fully commendable; I think, and think I think rightly, the laurel crown appointed for triumphant captains doth worthily, of all other learnings, honor the poet's triumph.

But because we have ears as well as tongues, and that the lightest reasons that may be, will seem to weigh greatly if nothing be put in the counterbalance, let us hear, and, as well as we can, ponder, what objections be made against this art, which may be worthy either of yielding or answering.

First, truly, I note, not only in these μισομούσοι, poet-haters, but in all that kind of people who seek a praise by dispraising others, that they do prodigally spend a great many wandering words in quips and scoffs, carping and taunting at each thing which, by stirring the spleen, may stay the brain from a thorough beholding the worthiness of the subject. Those kind of objections, as they are full of a very idle easiness (since there is nothing of so sacred a majesty but that an itching tongue may rub itself upon it), so deserve they no other answer but, instead of laughing at the jest, to laugh at the jester. We know a playing wit can praise the discretion of an ass, the comfortableness of being in debt, and the jolly commodities of being sick of the plague; so, of the contrary side, if we will turn Ovid's verse,

Ut lateat virtus proximitate mali.

"That good lie hid in nearness of the evil," Agrippa will be as merry in showing the vanity of science, as Erasmus was in the commending of folly; neither shall any man or matter escape some touch of these smiling railers. But for Erasmus and Agrippa, they had another foundation than the superficial part would promise. Marry, these other pleasant fault-finders, who will correct the verb before they understand the noun, and confute others' knowledge before they confirm their own, I would have them only remember that scoffing cometh not of wisdom; so as the best title in true English they get with their merriments is to be called good fools; for so have our grave forefathers ever termed that humourous kind of jesters.

But that which giveth greatest scope to their scorning humour is rhyming and versing. It is already said, and, as I think, truly said, it is not rhyming and versing that maketh poesy; one may be a poet without versing, and a versifier without poetry. But yet, presuppose it were inseparable, as indeed it seemeth Scaliger judgeth, truly it were an inseparable commendation; for if *oratio* next to *ratio,* speech next to reason, be the greatest gift bestowed upon mortality, that cannot be praiseless which doth most polish that blessing of speech—which considereth each word, not only as a man may say by his forcible quality, but by his best measured
10 quantity, carrying even in themselves a harmony—without, perchance, number, measure, order, proportion be in our time grown odious.

But lay aside the just praise it hath, by being the only fit speech for music—music, I say, the most divine striker of the senses—thus much is undoubtedly true, that if reading be foolish without remembering, memory being the only treasure of knowledge, those words which are fittest for memory are likewise most convenient for knowledge. Now, that verse far exceedeth prose in the knitting up of the memory, the reason is manifest; the words, besides their delight, which hath a great affinity to memory, being so set as one cannot be lost but the whole work fails; which
20 accusing itself calleth the remembrance back to itself, and so most strongly confirmeth it. Besides, one word so, as it were, begetting another, as, be it in rhyme or measured verse, by the former a man shall have a near guess to the follower. Lastly, even they that have taught the art of memory have showed nothing so apt for it as a certain room divided into many places, well and thoroughly known; now that hath the verse in effect perfectly, every word having his natural seat, which seat must needs make the word remembered. But what needs more in a thing so known to all men? Who is it that ever was scholar that doth not carry away some verses of Virgil, Horace, or Cato, which in his youth he learned, and even to his
30 old age serve him for hourly lessons? as,

Percontatorem fugito: nam garrulus idem est.
Dum sibi quisque placet credula turba sumus.

But the fitness it hath for memory is notably proved by all delivery of arts, wherein, for the most part, from grammar to logic, mathematics, physic, and the rest, the rules chiefly necessary to be borne away are compiled in verses. So that verse being in itself sweet and orderly, and being best for memory, the only handle of knowledge, it must be in jest that any man can speak against it.
40 Now then go we to the most important imputations laid to the poor poets; for aught I can yet learn, they are these:

First, that there being many other more fruitful knowledges, a man might better spend his time in them than in this.

Secondly, that it is the mother of lies.

Thirdly, that it is the nurse of abuse, infecting us with many pestilent desires, with a siren's sweetness drawing the mind to the serpent's tail of sinful fancies; and herein, especially, comedies give the largest field to ear, as Chaucer saith; how, both in other nations and ours, before poets did soften us, we were full of courage, given to martial exercises, the pillars of manlike liberty, and not lulled asleep in shady idleness with poets' pastimes.

And lastly and chiefly, they cry out with open mouth, as if they had overshot Robin Hood, that Plato banished them out of his commonwealth. Truly this is much, if there be much truth in it.

First, to the first, that a man might better spend his time is a reason indeed; but it doth, as they say, but *petere principium*. For if it be, as I affirm, that no learning is so good as that which teacheth and moveth to virtue, and that none can both teach and move thereto so much as poesy, then is the conclusion manifest, that ink and paper cannot be to a more profitable purpose employed. And certainly, though a man should grant their first assumption, it should follow, methinks, very unwillingly, that good is not good because better is better. But I still and utterly deny that there is sprung out of earth a more fruitful knowledge.

To the second, therefore, that they should be the principal liars, I answer paradoxically, but truly, I think truly, that of all writers under the sun, the poet is the least liar; and though he would, as a poet can scarcely be a liar. The astronomer, with his cousin the geometrician, can hardly escape when they take upon them to measure the height of the stars. How often, think you, do the physicians lie, when they aver things good for sicknesses which afterwards send Charon a great number of souls drowned in a potion before they come to his ferry? And no less of the rest which take upon them to affirm. Now for the poet, he nothing affirmeth, and therefore never lieth; for, as I take it, to lie is to affirm that to be true which is false; so as the other artists, and especially the historian, affirming many things, can, in the cloudy knowledge of mankind, hardly escape from many lies. But the poet, as I said before, never affirmeth; the poet never maketh any circles about your imagination, to conjure you to believe for true what he writeth; he citeth not authorities of other histories, but even for his entry calleth the sweet Muses to inspire into him a good invention; in truth, not laboring to tell you what is or is not, but what should or should not be. And, therefore, though he recount things not true, yet because he telleth them not for true, he lieth not; without we will say

that Nathan lied in his speech, before alleged, to David; which, as a
wicked man durst scarce say, so think I none so simple would say that
Aesop lied in the tales of his beasts; for who thinketh that Aesop wrote it
for actually true were well worthy to have his name chronicled among
the beasts he writeth of. What child is there that cometh to a play, and
seeing Thebes written in great letters upon an old door, doth believe that
it is Thebes? If then a man can arrive to the child's age, to know that the
poet's persons and doings are but pictures what should be, and not stories
what have been, they will never give the lie to things not affirmatively, but
10 allegorically and figuratively written; and therefore, as in history, looking for truth, they may go away full fraught with falsehood, so in poesy,
looking but for fiction, they shall use the narration but as an imaginative
ground-plot of a profitable invention.

But hereto is replied, that the poets give names to men they write of,
which argueth a conceit of an actual truth, and so, not being true, proveth
a falsehood. And doth the lawyer lie then, when, under the names of John
of the Stile, and John of the Nokes, he putteth his case? But that is easily
answered, their naming of men is but to make their picture the more lively,
and not to build any history. Painting men, they cannot leave men name-
20 less; we see we cannot play at chess but that we must give names to our
chess-men; and yet, methinks, he were a very partial champion of truth
that would say we lied for giving a piece of wood the reverend title of a
bishop. The poet nameth Cyrus and Aeneas no other way than to show
what men of their fames, fortunes, and estates should do.

Their third is, how much it abuseth men's wit, training it to wanton
sinfulness and lustful love. For, indeed, that is the principal if not only
abuse I can hear alleged. They say the comedies rather teach than reprehend amorous conceits; they say the lyric is larded with passionate sonnets;
the elegiac weeps the want of his mistress; and that even to the heroical
30 Cupid hath ambitiously climbed. Alas! Love, I would thou couldst as well
defend thyself as thou canst offend others! I would those on whom thou
dost attend could either put thee away or yield good reason why they keep
thee! But grant love of beauty to be a beastly fault, although it be very
hard, since only man, and no beast, hath that gift to discern beauty; grant
that lovely name of love to deserve all hateful reproaches, although even
some of my masters the philosophers spent a good deal of their lamp-oil in
setting forth the excellency of it; grant, I say, what they will have granted,
that not only love, but lust, but vanity, but, if they list, scurrility, possess
many leaves of the poets' books; yet, think I, when this is granted, they
40 will find their sentence may, with good manners, put the last words foremost; and not say that poetry abuseth poetry. For I will not deny but that
man's wit may make poesy, which should be εἰκαστική, which some learned

have defined, figuring forth good things, to be φανταστική, which doth
contrariwise infect the fancy with unworthy objects; as the painter, [that]
should give to the eye either some excellent perspective, or some fine picture fit for building or fortification, or containing in it some notable example, as Abraham sacrificing his son Isaac, Judith killing Holofernes,
David fighting with Goliath, may leave those, and please an illpleased
eye with wanton shows of better-hidden matters.

But, what! Shall the abuse of a thing make the right use odious? Nay,
truly, though I yield that poesy may not only be abused, but that being
abused, by the reason of his sweet charming force it can do more hurt than 10
any other army of words, yet shall it be so far from concluding that the
abuse should give reproach to the abused, that, contrariwise, it is a good
reason that whatsoever being abused doth most harm, being rightly used
(and upon the right use each thing receives his title) doth most good. Do
we not see skill of physic, the best rampire to our often-assaulted bodies,
being abused, teach poison, the most violent destroyer? Doth not knowledge of law, whose end is to even and right all things, being abused, grow
the crooked fosterer of horrible injuries? Doth not (to go to the highest)
God's word abused breed heresy, and his name abused become blasphemy?
Truly, a needle cannot do much hurt, and as truly (with leave of ladies 20
be it spoken) it cannot do much good. With a sword thou mayst kill thy
father, and with a sword thou mayst defend thy prince and country; so
that, as in their calling poets fathers of lies they said nothing, so in this
their argument of abuse, they prove the commendation.

They allege herewith, that before poets began to be in price, our nation
had set their heart's delight upon action, and not imagination; rather doing things worthy to be written, than writing things fit to be done. What
that before-time was, I think scarcely Sphinx can tell; since no memory
is so ancient that gives not the precedence to poetry. And certain it is that,
in our plainest homeliness, yet never was the Albion nation without poetry. 30
Marry, this argument, though it be leveled against poetry, yet it is indeed
a chain-shot against all learning—or bookishness, as they commonly term
it. Of such mind were certain Goths, of whom it is written that having
in the spoil of a famous city taken a fair library, one hangman, belike fit to
execute the fruits of their wits, who had murthered a great number of
bodies, would have set fire in it. "No," said another, very gravely, "take
heed what you do, for while they are busy about those toys we shall with
more leisure conquer their countries."

This, indeed, is the ordinary doctrine of ignorance, and many words
sometimes I have heard spent in it; but because this reason is generally 40
against all learning, as well as poetry, or rather all learning but poetry;
because it were too large a digression to handle it, or at least too super-

fluous, since it is manifest that all government of action is to be gotten by
knowledge, and knowledge best by gathering many knowledges, which
is reading; I only say with Horace, to him that is of that opinion,

Jubeo stultum esse libenter;

for as for poetry itself, it is the freest from this objection, for poetry is the
companion of camps. I dare undertake *Orlando Furioso* or honest King
Arthur will never displease a soldier: but the quiddity of *ens* and *prima
materia* will hardly agree with a corselet. And, therefore, as I said in the
10 beginning, even Turks and Tartars are delighted with poets. Homer, a
Greek, flourished before Greece flourished; and if to a slight conjecture a
conjecture may be opposed, truly it may seem, that as by him their learned
men took almost their first light of knowledge, so their active men received their first motions of courage. Only Alexander's example may
serve, who by Plutarch is accounted of such virtue that fortune was not
his guide but his footstool; whose acts speak for him, though Plutarch did
not; indeed, the phoenix of warlike princes. This Alexander left his schoolmaster, living Aristotle, behind him, but took dead Homer with him. He
put the philosopher Callisthenes to death for his seeming philosophical, in-
20 deed mutinous, stubbornness; but the chief thing he was ever heard to wish
for was that Homer had been alive. He well found he received more
bravery of mind by the pattern of Achilles than by hearing the definition
of fortitude. And therefore, if Cato misliked Fulvius for carrying Ennius
with him to the field, it may be answered that if Cato misliked it the noble
Fulvius liked it, or else he had not done it; for it was not the excellent
Cato Uticensis, whose authority I would much more have reverenced,
but it was the former, in truth a bitter punisher of faults, but else a man
that had never sacrificed to the Graces. He misliked and cried out against
all Greek learning, and yet, being fourscore years old, began to learn it,
30 belike fearing that Pluto understood not Latin. Indeed, the Roman laws
allowed no person to be carried to the wars but he that was in the soldiers'
roll. And therefore, though Cato misliked his unmustered person, he misliked not his work. And if he had, Scipio Nasica (judged by common consent the best Roman) loved him; both the other Scipio brothers, who had
by their virtues no less surnames than of Asia and Afric, so loved him that
they caused his body to be buried in their sepulture. So as Cato's authority
being but against his person, and that answered with so far greater than
himself, is herein of no validity.

But now, indeed, my burthen is great, that Plato his name is laid upon
40 me, whom, I must confess, of all philosophers I have ever esteemed most
worthy of reverence; and with good reason, since of all philosophers he
is the most poetical; yet if he will defile the fountain out of which his

flowing streams have proceeded, let us boldly examine with what reasons he did it.

First, truly, a man might maliciously object that Plato, being a philosopher, was a natural enemy of poets. For, indeed, after the philosophers had picked out of the sweet mysteries of poetry the right discerning of true points of knowledge, they forthwith, putting it in method, and making a school-art of that which the poets did only teach by a divine delightfulness, beginning to spurn at their guides, like ungrateful apprentices were not content to set up shop for themselves, but sought by all means to discredit their masters; which, by the force of delight being barred them, the less they could overthrow them the more they hated them. For, indeed, they found for Homer seven cities strave who should have him for their citizen, where many cities banished philosophers as not fit members to live among them. For only repeating certain of Euripides' verses many Athenians had their lives saved of the Syracusans, where the Athenians themselves thought many philosophers unworthy to live. Certain poets, as Simonides and Pindarus, had so prevailed with Hiero the First, that of a tyrant they made him a just king; where Plato could do so little with Dionysius that he himself of a philosopher was made a slave. But who should do thus, I confess, should requite the objections raised against poets with like cavillations against philosophers; as likewise one should do, that should bid one read *Phaedrus* or *Symposium* in Plato, or the discourse of Love in Plutarch, and see whether any poet do authorize abominable filthiness as they do.

Again, a man might ask, out of what commonwealth Plato doth banish them? In sooth, thence where he himself alloweth community of women. So as belike this banishment grew not for effeminate wantonness, since little should poetical sonnets be hurtful when a man might have what woman he listed. But I honor philosophical instructions, and bless the wits which bred them, so as they be not abused, which is likewise stretched to poetry. Saint Paul himself sets a watchword upon philosophy, indeed upon the abuse. So doth Plato upon the abuse, not upon poetry. Plato found fault that the poets of his time filled the world with wrong opinions of the gods, making light tales of that unspotted essence, and therefore would not have the youth depraved with such opinions. Herein may much be said; let this suffice: the poets did not induce such opinions, but did imitate those opinions already induced. For all the Greek stories can well testify that the very religion of that time stood upon many and many-fashioned gods; not taught so by poets, but followed according to their nature of imitation. Who list may read in Plutarch the discourses of Isis and Osiris, of the cause why oracles ceased, of the divine providence, and see whether the theology of that nation stood not upon such dreams, which the poets in-

deed superstitiously observed; and truly, since they had not the light of
Christ, did much better in it than the philosophers, who, shaking off superstition, brought in atheism.

    Plato, therefore, whose authority I had much rather justly construe
than unjustly resist, meant not in general of poets, in those words of which
Julius Scaliger saith, *Qua authoritate barbari quidam atque hispidi abuti
velint ad poetas e republica exigendos;* but only meant to drive out those
wrong opinions of the Deity, whereof now, without farther law, Christianity hath taken away all the hurtful belief, perchance, as he thought,
10 nourished by the then esteemed poets. And a man need go no further
than to Plato himself to know his meaning; who, in his dialogue called
Ion, giveth high and rightly divine commendation unto poetry. So as Plato,
banishing the abuse not the thing, not banishing it, but giving due honor
to it, shall be our patron and not our adversary. For indeed, I had much
rather, since truly I may do it, show their mistaking of Plato, under whose
lion's skin they would make an ass-like braying against poesy, than go
about to overthrow his authority; whom, the wiser a man is, the more
just cause he shall find to have in admiration; especially since he attributeth unto poesy more than myself do, namely to be a very inspiring of a
20 divine force, far above man's wit, as in the forenamed dialogue is apparent.

    Of the other side, who would show the honors have been by the best
sort of judgments granted them, a whole sea of examples would present
themselves; Alexander's, Caesar's, Scipio's, all favorers of poets; Laelius,
called the Roman Socrates, himself a poet; so as part of *Heautontimerou-
menos,* in Terence, was supposed to be made by him. And even the Greek
Socrates, whom Apollo confirmed to be the only wise man, is said to have
spent part of his old time in putting Aesop's fables into verses; and, therefore, full evil should it become his scholar Plato to put such words in his
master's mouth against poets. But what needs more? Aristotle writes the
30 *Art of Poesy;* and why, if it should not be written? Plutarch teacheth the
use to be gathered of them; and how, if they should not be read? And who
reads Plutarch's either history or philosophy, shall find he trimmeth both
their garments with guards of poesy.

    But I list not to defend poesy with the help of his underling histori-
ography. Let it suffice to have showed it is a fit soil for praise to dwell upon;
and what dispraise may be set upon it is either easily overcome, or transformed into just commendation. So that since the excellences of it may
be so easily and so justly confirmed, and the low creeping objections so
soon trodden down; it is not being an art of lies, but of true doctrine; not
40 of effeminateness, but of notable stirring of courage; not of abusing man's
wit, but of strengthening man's wit; not banished, but honored by Plato;
let us rather plant more laurels for to ingarland the poets' heads (which

honor of being laureate, as besides them only triumphant captains were, is a sufficient authority to show the price they ought to be held in) than suffer the ill-savored breath of such wrong speakers once to blow upon the clear springs of poesy.

But since I have run so long a career in this matter, methinks, before I give my pen a full stop, it shall be but a little more lost time to inquire why England, the mother of excellent minds, should be grown so hard a step-mother to poets, who certainly in wit ought to pass all others, since all only proceeds from their wit, being, indeed, makers of themselves, not takers of others. How can I but exclaim, 10

Musa, mihi causas memora, quo numine laeso?

Sweet poesy! that hath anciently had kings, emperors, senators, great captains, such as, besides a thousand others, David, Adrian, Sophocles, Germanicus, not only to favor poets, but to be poets; and of our nearer times can present for her patrons, a Robert, King of Sicily; the great King Francis of France; King James of Scotland; such cardinals as Bembus and Bibiena; such famous preachers and teachers as Beza and Melanchthon; so learned philosophers as Fracastorius and Scaliger; so great orators as Pontanus and Muretus; so piercing wits as George Buchanan; so grave 20 counselors as, besides many, but before all, that Hospital of France, than whom, I think that realm never brought forth a more accomplished judgment more firmly builded upon virtue; I say these, with numbers of others, not only to read others' poesies, but to poetize for others' reading; that poesy, thus embraced in all other places, should only find in our time a hard welcome in England, I think the very earth laments it, and therefore decks our soil with fewer laurels than it was accustomed. For heretofore poets have in England also flourished; and, which is to be noted, even in those times when the trumpet of Mars did sound loudest. And now that an over-faint quietness should seem to strew the house for poets 30 they are almost in as good reputation as the mountebanks at Venice. Truly, even that, as of the one side it giveth great praise to poesy, which, like Venus (but to better purpose), had rather be troubled in the net with Mars than enjoy the homely quiet of Vulcan; so serveth it for a piece of a reason why they are less grateful to idle England, which now can scarce endure the pain of a pen. Upon this necessarily followeth that base men with servile wits undertake it, who think it enough if they can be rewarded of the printer; and so as Epaminondas is said with the honor of his virtue to have made an office, by his exercising it, which before was contemptible to become highly respected; so these men, no more but 40 setting their names to it, by their own disgracefulness disgrace the most graceful poesy. For now, as if all the Muses were got with child to bring forth bastard poets, without any commission they do post over the banks of Helicon, until they make their readers more weary than post-horses; while, in the meantime, they,

Queis meliore luto finxit praecordia Titan,

are better content to suppress the outflowings of their wit than by publishing them to be accounted knights of the same order.

But I, that before ever I durst aspire unto the dignity am admitted into the company of the paper-blurrers, do find the very true cause of our 10 wanting estimation is want of desert, taking upon us to be poets in despite of Pallas. Now, wherein we want desert were a thankworthy labor to express. But if I knew, I should have mended myself; but as I never desired the title so have I neglected the means to come by it; only, overmastered by some thoughts, I yielded an inky tribute unto them. Marry, they that delight in poesy itself should seek to know what they do, and how they do; and especially look themselves in an unflattering glass of reason, if they be inclinable unto it.

For poesy must not be drawn by the ears, it must be gently led, or rather it must lead; which was partly the cause that made the ancient learned 20 affirm it was a divine gift, and no human skill, since all other knowledges lie ready for any that have strength of wit: a poet no industry can make, if his own genius be not carried into it. And therefore is an old proverb, *Orator fit, poeta nascitur.* Yet confess I always, that as the fertilest ground must be manured, so must the highest flying wit have a Daedalus to guide him. That Daedalus, they say, both in this and in other, hath three wings to bear itself up into the air of due commendation; that is art, imitation, and exercise. But these neither artificial rules nor imitative patterns we much cumber ourselves withal. Exercise, indeed, we do, but that very forebackwardly; for where we should exercise to know, we 30 exercise as having known; and so is our brain delivered of much matter which never was begotten by knowledge. For there being two principal parts, matter to be expressed by words, and words to express the matter, in neither we use art or imitation rightly. Our matter is *quodlibet*, indeed, though wrongly performing Ovid's verse,

Quicquid conabor dicere, versus erit;

never marshalling it into any assured rank, that almost the readers cannot tell where to find themselves.

Chaucer undoubtedly did excellently in his *Troilus and Cresseid;* of 40 whom, truly, I know not whether to marvel more, either that he in that misty time could see so clearly, or that we in this clear age go so stumblingly after him. Yet had he great wants, fit to be forgiven in so reverend an antiquity. I account the *Mirror of Magistrates* meetly furnished of beautiful parts. And in the Earl of Surrey's lyrics, many things tasting of a noble birth, and worthy of a noble mind. The *Shepherds' Calender* hath much poesy in his eclogues, indeed, worthy the reading, if I be not deceived. That same framing of his style to an old rustic language, I dare not allow, since neither Theocritus in Greek, Virgil in Latin, nor Sannazzaro in Italian, did affect it. Besides these, I do not remember to have seen but few (to speak boldly) printed that have poetical sinews in them. For proof whereof, let but most of the verses be put in prose, and then ask the meaning, and it will be found that one verse did but beget another, without ordering at the first what should be at the last; which becomes a confused mass of words, with a tinkling sound of rhyme, barely accompanied with reason.

Our tragedies and comedies, not without cause cried out against, observing rules neither of honest civility nor skilful poetry. Excepting *Gorboduc* (again I say of those that I have seen), which notwithstanding as it is full of stately speeches and well-sounding phrases, climbing to the height of Seneca his style, and as full of notable morality, which it doeth most delightfully teach, and so obtain the very end of poesy; yet, in truth, it is very defective in the circumstances, which grieves me, because it might not remain as an exact model of all tragedies. For it is faulty both in place and time, the two necessary companions of all corporal actions. For where the stage should always represent but one place, and the uttermost time presupposed in it should be, both by Aristotle's precept and common reason, but one day; there is both many days and many places inartificially imagined.

But if it be so in *Gorboduc*, how much more in all the rest? Where you shall have Asia of the one side, and Afric of the other, and so many other under kingdoms, that the player, when he comes in, must ever begin with telling where he is, or else the tale will not be conceived. Now shall you have three ladies walk to gather flowers, and then we must believe the stage to be a garden. By and by, we hear news of shipwreck in the same place, then we are to blame if we accept it not for a rock. Upon the back of that comes out a hideous monster with fire and smoke, and then the miserable beholders are bound to take it for a cave; while, in the meantime, two armies fly in, represented with four swords and bucklers, and then what hard heart will not receive it for a pitched field?

Now of time they are much more liberal; for ordinary it is, that two young princes fall in love; after many traverses she is got with child, delivered of a fair boy, he is lost, groweth a man, falleth in love, and is ready to get another child; and all this in two hours' space; which, how absurd it is in sense, even sense may imagine; and art hath taught, and all ancient

examples justified, and at this day the ordinary players in Italy will not err
in. Yet will some bring in an example of *Eunuchus* in Terence, that containeth matter of two days, yet far short of twenty years. True it is, and
so was it to be played in two days, and so fitted to the time it set forth. And
though Plautus have in one place done amiss, let us hit it with him, and
not miss with him. But they will say, how then shall we set forth a story
which contains both many places and many times? And do they not know
that a tragedy is tied to the laws of poesy, and not of history; not bound
to follow the story, but having liberty either to feign a quite new matter
or to frame the history to the most tragical conveniency? Again, many
things may be told which cannot be showed—if they know the difference
betwixt reporting and representing. As for example, I may speak, though
I am here, of Peru, and in speech digress from that to the description of
Calicut; but in action I cannot represent it without Pacolet's horse. And
so was the manner the ancients took, by some *Nuntius* to recount things
done in former time, or other place.

Lastly, if they will represent an history they must not (as Horace saith)
begin *ab ovo*, but they must come to the principal point of that one action
which they will represent. By example this will be best expressed. I have
a story of young Polydorus, delivered, for safety's sake, with great riches,
by his father Priamus to Polymnestor, King of Thrace, in the Trojan war
time. He, after some years, hearing of the overthrow of Priamus, for to
make the treasure his own, murthereth the child; the body of the child is
taken up by Hecuba; she, the same day, findeth a sleight to be revenged
most cruelly of the tyrant. Where, now, would one of our tragedy-writers
begin, but with the delivery of the child? Then should he sail over into
Thrace, and so spend I know not how many years, and travel numbers
of places. But where doth Euripides? Even with the finding of the body;
leaving the rest to be told by the spirit of Polydorus. This needs no further
to be enlarged; the dullest wit may conceive it.

But, besides these gross absurdities, how all their plays be neither right
tragedies nor right comedies, mingling kings and clowns, not because
the matter so carrieth it, but thrust in the clown by head and shoulders
to play a part in majestical matters, with neither decency nor discretion;
so as neither the admiration and commiseration, nor the right sportfulness,
is by their mongrel tragi-comedy obtained. I know Apuleius did somewhat
so, but that is a thing recounted with space of time, not represented in one
moment; and I know the ancients have one or two examples of tragi-
comedies as Plautus hath *Amphytrio*. But, if we mark them well, we shall
find that they never, or very daintily, match hornpipes and funerals. So
falleth it out, that having indeed no right comedy in that comical part of
our tragedy, we have nothing but scurrility, unworthy of any chaste ears;

or some extreme show of doltishness, indeed fit to lift up a loud laughter, and nothing else; where the whole tract of a comedy should be full of delight, as the tragedy should be still maintained in a well-raised admiration.

But our comedians think there is no delight without laughter, which is very wrong; for though laughter may come with delight, yet cometh it not of delight, as though delight should be the cause of laughter. But well may one thing breed both together. Nay, rather in themselves they have, as it were, a kind of contrariety. For delight we scarcely do, but in things that have a conveniency to ourselves, or to the general nature; laughter almost ever cometh of things most disproportioned to ourselves and nature. Delight hath a joy in it either permanent or present; laughter hath only a scornful tickling. For example, we are ravished with delight to see a fair woman, and yet are far from being moved to laughter. We laugh at deformed creatures, wherein certainly we cannot delight. We delight in good chances; we laugh at mischances. We delight to hear the happiness of our friends and country, at which he were worthy to be laughed at that would laugh; we shall, contrarily, sometimes laugh to find a matter quite mistaken, and go down the hill against the bias, in the mouth of some such men as, for the respect of them, one shall be heartily sorry he cannot choose but laugh, and so is rather pained than delighted with laughter. Yet deny I not but that they may go well together; for as in Alexander's picture well set out we delight without laughter, and in twenty mad antics we laugh without delight. So in Hercules painted, with his great beard and furious countenance, in a woman's attire, spinning at Omphale's commandment, it breeds both delight and laughter; for the representing of so strange a power in love procures delight, and the scornfulness of the action stirreth laughter.

But I speak to this purpose, that all the end of the comical part be not upon such scornful matters as stir laughter only, but mix with it that delightful teaching which is the end of poesy. And the great fault, even in that point of laughter, and forbidden plainly by Aristotle, is, that they stir laughter in sinful things, which are rather execrable than ridiculous; or in miserable, which are rather to be pitied than scorned. For what is it to make folks gape at a wretched beggar, and a beggarly clown; or against law of hospitality, to jest at strangers because they speak not English so well as we do? What do we learn? Since it is certain,

> *Nil habet infelix paupertas durius in se,*
> *Quam quod ridiculos homines facit.*

But rather a busy loving courtier, and a heartless threatening Thraso; a self-wise-seeming schoolmaster; a wry-transformed traveler—these, if we saw walk in stage-names, which we play naturally, therein were de-

lightful laughter, and teaching delightfulness; as in the other, the tragedies
of Buchanan do justly bring forth a divine admiration.

But I have lavished out too many words of this play matter; I do it
because, as they are excelling parts of poesy, so is there none so much
used in England, and none can be more pitifully abused; which, like an
unmannerly daughter, showing a bad education, causeth her mother
Poesy's honesty to be called in question.

Other sorts of poetry, almost, have we none, but that lyrical kind of
songs and sonnets, which, Lord if he gave us so good minds, how well it
10 might be employed, and with how heavenly fruits, both private and public,
in singing the praises of the immortal beauty, the immortal goodness of
that God who giveth us hands to write and wits to conceive! of which we
might well want words, but never matter; of which we could turn our
eyes to nothing but we should ever have new-budding occasions.

But, truly, many of such writings as come under the banner of un-
resistible love, if I were a mistress, would never persuade me they were
in love; so coldly they apply fiery speeches, as men that had rather read
lover's writings, and so caught up certain swelling phrases—which hang
together like a man that once told me the wind was at northwest and by
20 south, because he would be sure to name winds enough—than that in
truth they feel those passions, which easily, as I think, may be bewrayed
by that same forcibleness, or "energia" (as the Greeks call it) of the
writer. But let this be a sufficient, though short note, that we miss the right
use of the material point of poesy.

Now for the outside of it, which is words, or (as I may term it) diction,
it is even well worse; so is it that honey-flowing matron Eloquence, appareled, or rather disguised, in a courtesan-like painted affectation; one
time with so far-fet words, that many seem monsters, but must seem
strangers, to any poor Englishman; another time with coursing of a letter,
30 as if they were bound to follow the method of a dictionary; another time
with figures and flowers, extremely winter-starved.

But I would this fault were only peculiar to versifiers, and had not as
large possession among prose-printers; and, which is to be marveled,
among many scholars, and, which is to be pitied, among some preachers.
Truly, I could wish (if at least I might be so bold to wish, in a thing beyond the reach of my capacity) the diligent imitators of Tully and
Demosthenes (most worthy to be imitated) did not so much keep Nizolian
paperbooks of their figures and phrases, as, by attentive translation, as it
were devour them whole and make them wholly theirs. For now they cast
40 sugar and spice upon every dish that is served at the table; like those Indians, not content to wear ear-rings at the fit and natural place of the
ears, but they will thrust jewels through their nose and lips, because they

will be sure to be fine. Tully, when he was to drive out Catiline, as it were with a thunderbolt of eloquence, often useth the figure of repetition, as *Vivit et vincit, imo in senatum venit, imo in senatum venit*, &c. Indeed, inflamed with a well-grounded rage, he would have his words, as it were, double out of his mouth; and so do that artificially which we see men in choler do naturally. And we, having noted the grace of those words, hale them in sometimes to a familiar epistle, when it were too much choler to be choleric.

How well store of *similiter cadenses* doth sound with the gravity of the pulpit, I would but invoke Demosthenes' soul to tell, who with a rare daintiness useth them. Truly, they have made me think of the sophister, that with too much subtilty would prove two eggs three, and though he may be counted a sophister, had none for his labor. So these men, bringing in such a kind of eloquence, well may they obtain an opinion of a seeming fineness, but persuade few, which should be the end of their fineness.

Now for similitudes in certain printed discourses, I think all herbarists, all stories of beasts, fowls, and fishes, are rifled up, that they may come in multitudes to wait upon any of our conceits, which certainly is as absurd a surfeit to the ears as is possible. For the force of a similitude not being to prove anything to a contrary disputer but only to explain to a willing hearer, when that is done, the rest is a most tedious prattling, rather overswaying the memory from the purpose whereto they were applied, than any whit informing the judgment, already either satisfied, or by similitudes not to be satisfied.

For my part, I do not doubt, when Antonius and Crassus, the great forefathers of Cicero in eloquence, the one (as Cicero testifieth of them) pretended not to know art, the other not to set by it, because with a plain sensibleness they might win credit of popular ears, which credit is the nearest step to persuasion (which persuasion is the chief mark of oratory) —I do not doubt, I say, but that they used these knacks very sparingly; which who doth generally use, any man may see doth dance to his own music; and so to be noted by the audience, more careful to speak curiously than truly. Undoubtedly (at least to my opinion undoubtedly) I have found in divers small-learned courtiers a more sound style than in some professors of learning; of which I can guess no other cause but that the courtier, following that which by practise he findeth fittest to nature, therein (though he know it not) doth according to art, though not by art: where the other, using art to show art, and not hide art (as in these cases he should do), flieth from nature, and indeed abuseth art.

But what! Methinks I deserve to be pounded for straying from poetry to oratory; but both have such an affinity in the wordish consideration, that I think this digression will make my meaning receive the fuller under-

standing: which is not to take upon me to teach poets how they should do, but only finding myself sick among the rest, to show some one or two spots of the common infection grown among the most part of writers; that, acknowledging ourselves somewhat awry, we may bend to the right use both of matter and manner; whereto our language giveth us great occasion, being, indeed, capable of any excellent exercising of it. I know some will say, it is a mingled language. And why not so much the better, taking the best of both the other? Another will say, it wanteth grammar. Nay, truly, it hath that praise, that it wants not grammar; for grammar
10 it might have, but it needs it not, being so easy in itself, and so void of those cumbersome differences of cases, genders, moods, and tenses; which, I think, was a piece of the tower of Babylon's curse, that a man should be put to school to learn his mother tongue. But for the uttering sweetly and properly the conceit of the mind, which is the end of speech, that hath it equally with any other tongue in the world; and is particularly happy in compositions of two or three words together, near the Greek, far beyond the Latin; which is one of the greatest beauties can be in a language.

Now, of versifying there are two sorts, the one ancient, the other mod-
20 ern. The ancient marked the quantity of each syllable, and according to that framed his verse; the modern, observing only number, with some regard of the accent, the chief life of it standeth in that like sounding of the words, which we call rhyme. Whether of these be the more excellent would bear many speeches; the ancient no doubt more fit for music, both words and tune observing quantity; and more fit lively to express divers passions, by the low or lofty sound of the well-weighed syllable. The latter, likewise, with his rhyme striketh a certain music to the ear; and, in fine, since it doth delight, though by another way, it obtaineth the same purpose, there being in either, sweetness, and wanting in neither, majesty.
30 Truly the English, before any vulgar language I know, is fit for both sorts; for, for the ancient, the Italian is so full of vowels that it must ever be cumbered with elisions; the Dutch so, of the other side, with consonants that they cannot yield the sweet sliding fit for a verse. The French, in his whole language, hath not one word that hath his accent in the last syllable saving two, called antepenultima; and little more hath the Spanish; and therefore very gracelessly may they use dactyls. The English is subject to none of these defects.

Now for rhyme, though we do not observe quantity, we observe the accent very precisely, which other languages either cannot do, or will not
40 do so absolutely. That caesura, or breathing-place in the midst of the verse, neither Italian nor Spanish have; the French and we never almost fail of. Lastly, even the very rhyme itself the Italian cannot put it in the last

syllable, by the French named the masculine rhyme, but still in the next to the last, which the French call the female; or the next before that, which the Italians term *sdrucciola*. The example of the former is, *"buono," "suono"*; of the *sdrucciola* is, *"femina," "semina."* The French, of the other side, hath both the male, as *"bon," "son,"* and the female, as *"plaise," "taise"*; but the *sdrucciola* he hath not. Where the English hath all three, as "due," "true," "father," "rather," "motion," "potion"; with much more which might be said, but that already I find the trifling-ness of this discourse is much too much enlarged.

So that since the ever praiseworthy poesy is full of virtue-breeding de- 10 lightfulness, and void of no gift that ought to be in the noble name of learning; since the blames laid against it are either false or feeble; since the cause why it is not esteemed in England is the fault of poet-apes, not poets; since, lastly, our tongue is most fit to honor poesy, and to be hon-ored by poesy; I conjure you all that have had the evil luck to read this ink-wasting toy of mine, even in the name of the Nine Muses, no more to scorn the sacred mysteries of poesy; no more to laugh at the name of poets, as though they were next inheritors to fools; no more to jest at the reverend title of "a rhymer"; but to believe, with Aristotle, that they were the ancient treasurers of the Grecians' divinity; to believe, with 20 Bembus, that they were the first bringers in of all civility; to believe, with Scaliger, that no philosopher's precepts can sooner make you an honest man than the reading of Virgil; to believe, with Clauserus, the translator of Cornutus, that it pleased the heavenly deity by Hesiod and Homer, under the veil of fables, to give us all knowledge, logic, rhetoric, philosophy natural and moral, and *quid non;* to believe, with me, that there are many mysteries contained in poetry, which of purpose were written darkly, lest by profane wits it should be abused; to believe, with Landin, that they are so beloved of the gods that whatsoever they write proceeds of a divine fury. Lastly, to believe themselves, when they tell you they will make 30 you immortal by their verses.

Thus doing, your name shall flourish in the printers' shops. Thus doing, you shall be of kin to many a poetical preface. Thus doing, you shall be most fair, most rich, most wise, most all; you shall dwell upon superla-tives. Thus doing, though you be *Libertino patre natus,* you shall suddenly grow *Herculea proles, Si quid mea Carmina possunt.* Thus doing, your soul shall be placed with Dante's Beatrix, or Virgil's Anchises.

But if (fie of such a but!) you be born so near the dull-making cata-ract of Nilus that you cannot hear the planet-like music of poetry; if you have so earth-creeping a mind that it cannot lift itself up to look to the 40 sky of poetry, or rather, by a certain rustical disdain, will become such a mome as to be a Momus of poetry, then, though I will not wish unto you the ass's ears of Midas, nor to be driven by a poet's verse, as Bubonax was, to hang himself, nor to be rhymed to death, as is said to be done in Ireland; yet thus much curse I must send you in the behalf of all poets: that while you live, you live in love, and never get favor for lacking skill of a sonnet; and when you die, your memory die from the earth for want of an epitaph.

FROM *The Countesse of Pembrokes Arcadia,* 1590

The Countess of Pembroke's Arcadia

To my dear lady and sister, the Countess of Pembroke.

HERE now have you (most dear, and most worthy to be most dear, lady) this idle work of mine, which I fear (like the spider's web) will be thought fitter to be swept away than worn to any other purpose. For my part, in very truth (as the cruel fathers among the Greeks were wont to do to the babes they would not foster), I could well find in my heart to cast out in some desert of forgetfulness this child which I am loath to father. But you desired me to do it, and your desire to my heart is an absolute command-
20 ment. Now it is done only for you, only to you; if you keep it to yourself, or to such friends who will weigh errors in the balance of good will, I hope, for the father's sake, it will be pardoned, perchance made much of, though in itself it have deformities. For indeed, for severer eyes it is not, being but a trifle, and that triflingly handled. Your dear self can best wit-ness the manner, being done in loose sheets of paper, most of it in your presence, the rest by sheets sent unto you as fast as they were done. In sum, a young head, not so well stayed as I would it were (and shall be when God will), having many, many fancies begotten in it, if it had not been in some way delivered would have grown a monster, and more sorry
30 might I be that they came in than that they gat out. But his chief safety shall be the not walking abroad; and his chief protection, the bearing the livery of your name; which (if much, much good will do not deceive me) is worthy to be a sanctuary for a greater offender. This say I because I know the virtue so; and this say I because it may be ever so; or, to say better, because it will be ever so. Read it then at your idle times, and the follies your good judgment will find in it blame not, but laugh at. And so, looking for no better stuff than, as in an haberdasher's shop, glasses or feathers, you will continue to love the writer, who doth exceedingly love you; and most, most heartily prays you may long live, to be a princi-
40 pal ornament to the family of the Sidneys.

Your loving brother,

PHILIP SIDNEY.

The division and summing of the chapters was not of Sir Philip Sidney's doing, but adventured by the overseer of the print, for the more ease of the readers. He therefore submits himself to their judgment, and if his labor answer not the worthiness of the book, desireth pardon for it. As also if any defect be found in the Eclogues, which although they were of Sir Philip Sidney's writing, yet were they not perused by him, but left till the work had been finished, that then choice should have been made which should have been taken and in what manner brought in. At this time they have been chosen and disposed as the overseer thought best.

THE FIRST BOOK

CHAP. I.

[1] *The shepherdish complaints of the absented lovers, Strephon and Claius.* [2]*The second shipwreck of Pyrocles and Musidorus. Their strange saving,* [3]*interview, and* [4]*parting.*

[1] IT WAS in the time that the earth begins to put on her new apparel against the approach of her lover, and that the sun, running a most even course, becomes an indifferent arbiter between the night and the day when the hopeless shepherd Strephon was come to the sands which lie against the island of Cithera; where, viewing the place with a heavy kind of delight, and sometimes casting his eyes to the isleward, he called his friendly rival the pastor Claius unto him, and setting first down in his darkened countenance a doleful copy of what he would speak, "O my Claius," said he, "hither we are now come to pay the rent for which we are so called unto by over-busy Remembrance, Remembrance, restless Remembrance, which claims not only this duty of us, but for it will have us forget ourselves. I pray you, when we were amid our flock, and that, of other shepherds, some were running after their sheep strayed beyond their bounds, some delighting their eyes with seeing them nibble upon the short and sweet grass, some medicining their sick ewes, some setting a bell for an ensign of a sheepish squadron, some with more leisure inventing new games of exercising their bodies and sporting their wits: did Remembrance grant us any holiday, either for pastime or devotion, nay, either for necessary food or natural rest? but that still it forced our thoughts to work upon this place where we last (alas that the word last should so long last) did graze our eyes upon her ever-flourishing beauty? Did it not still cry within us, 'Ah, you base-minded wretches, are your thoughts so deeply bemired in the trade of ordinary worldlings, as for respect of gain some paltry wool may yield you to let so much time pass without knowing perfectly her estate, especially in so troublesome a season? to leave that

shore unsaluted from whence you may see to the island where she dwelleth? to leave those steps unkissed wherein Urania printed the farewell
of all beauty?'

"Well then, Remembrance commanded, we obeyed, and here we find
that as our remembrance came ever clothed unto us in the form of this
place, so this place gives new heat to the fever of our languishing remembrance. Yonder, my Claius, Urania lighted, the very horse (methought)
bewailed to be so disburdened; and as for thee, poor Claius, when thou
wentest to help her down, I saw reverence and desire so divide thee that
10 thou didst at one instant both blush and quake, and, instead of bearing
her, wert ready to fall down thyself. There she sate, vouchsafing my
cloak (then most gorgeous) under her; at yonder rising of the ground,
she turned herself, looking back toward her wonted abode, and, because
of her parting, bearing much sorrow in her eyes, the lightsomeness whereof
had yet so natural a cheerfulness as it made even sorrow seem to smile;
at that turning she spake unto us all, opening the cherry of her lips, and
Lord how greedily mine ears did feed upon the sweet words she uttered!
And here she laid her hand over thine eyes when she saw the tears springing in them, as if she would conceal them from other, and yet herself feel
20 some of thy sorrow. But woe is me; yonder, yonder, did she put her foot
into the boat, at that instant, as it were, dividing her heavenly beauty between the earth and the sea. But when she was embarked, did you not
mark how the winds whistled and the seas danced for joy, how the sails
did swell with pride, and all because they had Urania? O Urania, blessed
be thou Urania, the sweetest fairness and fairest sweetness."

With that word his voice brake so with sobbing that he could say no
further; and Claius thus answered: "Alas, my Strephon," said he, "what
needs this score to reckon up only our losses? What doubt is there but that
the light of this place doth call our thoughts to appear at the court of af-
30 fection, held by that racking steward, Remembrance? As well may sheep
forget to fear when they spy wolves as we can miss such fancies when we
see any place made happy by her treading. Who can choose, that saw her,
but think where she stayed, where she walked, where she turned, where
she spoke? But what is all this? Truly no more but as this place served
us to think of those things, so those things serve as places to call to memory
more excellent matters. No, no, let us think with consideration, and consider with acknowledging, and acknowledge with admiration, and admire
with love, and love with joy in the midst of all woes: let us in such sort
think, I say, that our poor eyes were so enriched as to behold, and our low
40 hearts so exalted as to love a maid who is such that, as the greatest thing
the world can shew is her beauty, so the least thing that may be praised in
her, is her beauty. Certainly as her eye-lids are more pleasant to behold

than two white kids climbing up a fair tree and browsing on his tenderest branches, and yet are nothing compared to the day-shining stars contained in them; and as her breath is more sweet than a gentle southwest wind which comes creeping over flowery fields and shadowed waters in the extreme heat of summer, and yet is nothing compared to the honey-flowing speech that breath doth carry; no more all that our eyes can see of her (though when they have seen her, what else they shall ever see is but dry stubble after clovers grass) is to be matched with the flock of unspeakable virtues laid up delightfully in that best-builded fold. But, indeed, as we can better consider the sun's beauty by marking how he gilds these waters and mountains than by looking upon his own face, too glorious for our weak eyes; so it may be our conceits (not able to bear her sun-staining excellency) will better weigh it by her works upon some meaner subject employed. And, alas, who can better witness that than we, whose experience is grounded upon feeling? Hath not the only love of her made us (being silly, ignorant shepherds) raise up our thoughts above the ordinary level of the world so as great clerks do not disdain our conference? Hath not the desire to seem worthy in her eyes made us, when others were sleeping, to sit viewing the course of heavens? when others were running at base, to run over learned writings? when other mark their sheep, we to mark ourselves? Hath not she thrown reason upon our desires and, as it were, given eyes unto Cupid? Hath in any, but in her, love-fellowship maintained friendship between rivals, and beauty taught the beholders chastity?"

He was going on with his praises, but Strephon bade him stay and look; and so they both perceived a thing which floated, drawing nearer and nearer to the bank, but rather by the favorable working of the sea than by any self-industry. They doubted a while what it should be, till it was cast up even hard before them; at which time they fully saw that it was a man. Whereupon running, for pity sake, unto him, they found his hands (as it should appear, constanter friends to his life than his memory) fast gripping upon the edge of a square, small coffer, which lay all under his breast; else in himself no shew of life, so as the board seemed to be but a bier to carry him aland to his sepulchre. So drew they up a young man of so goodly shape and well-pleasing favor that one would think death had in him a lovely countenance; and that, though he were naked, nakedness was to him an apparel. That sight increased their compassion, and their compassion called up their care; so that, lifting his feet above his head, making a great deal of salt water to come out of his mouth, they laid him upon some of their garments and fell to rub and chafe him till they brought him to recover both breath, the servant, and warmth, the companion, of living. At length, opening his eyes, he gave a great groan (a doleful note

but a pleasant ditty), for by that they found not only life but strength of
life in him.

They therefore continued on their charitable office until (his spirits
being well returned) he (without so much as thanking them for their
pains) gat up and, looking round about to the uttermost limits of his sight
and crying upon the name of Pyrocles, nor seeing nor hearing cause of
comfort: "What," said he, "and shall Musidorus live after Pyrocles?"

Therewithal he offered wilfully to cast destruction and himself again
into the sea—a strange sight to the shepherds, to whom it seemed that
10 before, being in appearance dead, had yet saved his life, and now, coming
to his life, should be a cause to procure his death; but they ran unto him
and, pulling him back (then too feeble for them), by force stickled that
unnatural fray. "I pray you," said he, "honest men, what such right have
you in me as not to suffer me to do with myself what I list? And what
policy have you to bestow a benefit where it is counted an injury?"

They, hearing him speak in Greek (which was their natural language),
became the more tender-hearted towards him; and considering by his
calling and looking that the loss of some dear friend was great cause of
his sorrow, told him they were poor men that were bound by course of
20 humanity to prevent so great a mischief; and that they wished him, if
opinion of somebody's perishing bred such desperate anguish in him, that
he should be comforted by his own proof, who had lately escaped as apparent danger as any might be. "No, no," said he, "it is not for me to
attend so high a blissfulness; but, since you take care of me, I pray you
find means that some bark may be provided that will go out of the haven,
that, if it be possible, we may find the body, far, far too precious a food
for fishes. And for the hire," said he, "I have within this casket of value
sufficient to content them."

Claius presently went to a fisherman and, having agreed with him and
30 provided some apparel for the naked stranger, he embarked, and the shepherds with him: and were no sooner gone beyond the mouth of the haven
but that, some way into the sea, they might discern (as it were) a stain
of the water's color, and by times some sparks and smoke mounting there-
out. But the young man no sooner saw it but that, beating his breast, he
cried that there was the beginning of his ruin, entreating them to bend
their course as near unto it as they could, telling how that smoke was but
a small relic of a great fire which had driven both him and his friend rather
to commit themselves to the cold mercy of the sea than to abide the hot
cruelty of the fire; and that therefore, though they both had abandoned
40 the ship, that he was (if anywhere) in that course to be met withal. They
steered, therefore, as near thitherward as they could; but when they came
so near as their eyes were full masters of the object, they saw a sight full

of piteous strangeness: a ship, or rather the carcass of the ship, or rather some few bones of the carcass, hulling there, part broken, part burned, part drowned: death having used more than one dart to that destruction. About it floated great store of very rich things and many chests which might promise no less. And amidst the precious things were a number of dead bodies, which likewise did not only testify both elements' violence, but that the chief violence was grown of human inhumanity; for their bodies were full of grisly wounds, and their blood had (as it were) filled the wrinkles of the sea's visage, which it seemed the sea would not wash away, that it might witness it is not always his fault when we condemn his 10 cruelty; in sum, a defeat where the conquered kept both field and spoil; a shipwreck without storm or ill-footing; and a waste of fire in the midst of water.

[3]   But a little way off they saw the mast, whose proud height now lay along, like a widow having lost her mate of whom she held her honor; but upon the mast they saw a young man (at least if he were a man) bearing shew of about 18 years of age, who sate (as on horseback) having nothing upon him but his shirt, which, being wrought with blue silk and gold, had a kind of resemblance to the sea: on which the sun (then near his western home) did shoot some of his beams. His hair (which the 20 young men of Greece used to wear very long) was stirred up and down with the wind, which seemed to have a sport to play with it, as the sea had to kiss his feet; himself full of admirable beauty set forth by the strangeness both of his seat and gesture; for, holding his head up full of unmoved majesty, he held a sword aloft with his fair arm, which often he waved about his crown as though he would threaten the world in that extremity. But the fishermen, when they came so near him that it was time to throw out a rope by which hold they might draw him, their simplicity bred such amazement and their amazement such a superstition that (assuredly thinking it was some god begotten between Neptune and 30 Venus that had made all this terrible slaughter) as they went under sail by him, held up their hands and made their prayers. Which when Musidorus saw, though he were almost as much ravished with joy as they with astonishment, he leapt to the mariner and took the rope out of his hand and (saying, "Dost thou live, and art well?" who answered, "Thou canst tell best, since most of my well-being stands in thee") threw it out, but already the ship was passed beyond Pyrocles. And therefore Musidorus could do no more but persuade the mariners to cast about again, assuring them that he was but a man, although of most divine excellencies, and promising great rewards for their pain.   40

[4]   And now they were already come upon the stays, when one of the sailors descried a galley which came with sails and oars directly in the

chase of them, and straight perceived it was a well-known pirate who hunted not only for goods but for bodies of men, which he employed either to be his galley slaves or to sell at the best market. Which, when the master understood, he commanded forthwith to set on all the canvas they could and fly homeward, leaving in that sort poor Pyrocles so near to be rescued. But what did not Musidorus say? What did he not offer to persuade them to venture the fight? But fear standing at the gates of their ears put back all persuasions, so that he had nothing to accompany Pyrocles but his eyes, nor to succor him but his wishes. Therefore, praying for him and casting 10 a long look that way, he saw the galley leave the pursuit of them and turn to take up the spoils of the other wreck; and lastly he might well see them lift up the young man; and, alas (said he to himself), dear Pyrocles, shall that body of thine be enchained? Shall those victorious hands of thine be commanded to base offices? Shall virtue become a slave to those that be slaves to viciousness? Alas, better had it been thou hadst ended nobly thy noble days: what death is so evil as unworthy servitude?

But that opinion soon ceased when he saw the galley setting upon another ship, which held long and strong fight with her: for then he began afresh to fear the life of his friend and to wish well to the pirates, whom 20 before he hated, lest in their ruin he might perish. But the fishermen made such speed into the haven that they absented his eyes from beholding the issue; where being entered, he could procure neither them nor any other as then to put themselves into the sea. So that being as full of sorrow for being unable to do anything as void of counsel how to do anything, besides that sickness grew something upon him, the honest shepherds, Strephon and Claius (who being themselves true friends did the more perfectly judge the justness of his sorrow) advise him that he should mitigate somewhat of his woe, since he had gotten an amendment in fortune, being come from assured persuasion of his death to have no cause to de-30 spair of his life: as one that had lamented the death of his sheep should after know they were but strayed, would receive pleasure though readily he knew not where to find them.

CHAP. II.

[1]*The pastors' comforts to the wrecked Musidorus.* [2]*His passage into Arcadia. The descriptions of* [3]*Laconia,* [4]*Arcadia, Kalander's* [5]*person,* [6]*house, and* [7]*entertainment to Musidorus, now called Palladius. His* [8]*sickness, recovery,* [9]*and perfections.*

40 [I] "Now, sir," said they, "thus for ourselves it is. We are in profession but shepherds, and in this country of Laconia little better than strangers,

and therefore neither in skill nor ability of power greatly to stead you. But what we can present unto you is this: Arcadia, of which country we are, is but a little way hence, and even upon the next confines.

[5]   There dwelleth a gentleman, by name Kalander, who vouchsafeth much favor unto us. A man who for his hospitality is so much haunted that no news stir but come to his ears; for his upright dealing so beloved of his neighbors that he hath many ever ready to do him their uttermost service, and, by the great good will our prince bears him, may soon obtain the use of his name and credit, which hath a principal sway not only in his own Arcadia but in all these countries of Peloponnesus; and (which is worth all) all these things give him not so much power as his nature gives him will to benefit; so that it seems no music is so sweet to his ear as deserved thanks. To him we will bring you, and there you may recover again your health, without which you cannot be able to make any diligent search for your friend, and therefore but in that respect you must labor for it. Besides we are sure the comfort of courtesy and ease of wise counsel shall not be wanting.

[2]   Musidorus (who, besides he was merely unacquainted in the country, had his wits astonished with sorrow) gave easy consent to that from which he saw no reason to disagree; and therefore (defraying the mariners with a ring bestowed upon them), they took their journey together through Laconia; Claius and Strephon by course carrying his chest for him, Musidorus only bearing in his countenance evident marks of a sorrowful mind supported with a weak body, which they perceiving, and knowing that the violence of sorrow is not at the first to be striven withal (being like a mighty beast, sooner tamed with following than overthrown by withstanding), they gave way unto it for that day and the next, never troubling him, either with asking questions or finding fault with his melancholy, but rather fitting to his dolor dolorous discourses of their own and other folks' misfortunes. Which speeches, though they had not a lively entrance to his senses shut up in sorrow, yet, like one half asleep, he took hold of much of the matters spoken unto him, so as a man may say, ere sorrow was aware, they made his thoughts bear away something else beside his own sorrow, which wrought so in him that at length he grew content to mark their speeches, then to marvel at such wit in shepherds, after to like their company, and lastly to vouchsafe conference. So that the third day after, in the time that the morning did strow roses and violets in the heavenly floor against the coming of the sun, the nightingales (striving one with the other which could in most dainty variety recount their wrong-caused sorrow) made them put off their sleep, and rising from under a tree (which that night had been their pavilion), they went on their

journey, which by and by welcomed Musidorus' eyes (wearied with the
wasted soil of Laconia) with delightful prospects. [4]   There were hills
which garnished their proud heights with stately trees; humble valleys,
whose base estate seemed comforted with refreshing of silver rivers;
meadows enameled with all sorts of eye-pleasing flowers; thickets which,
being lined with most pleasant shade, were witnessed so too by the cheerful deposition of many well-tuned birds; each pasture stored with sheep
feeding with sober security while the pretty lambs with bleating oratory
craved the dam's comfort; here a shepherd's boy piping as though he
10 should never be old; there a young shepherdess knitting, and withal singing, and it seemed that her voice comforted her hands to work and her
hands kept time to her voice's music. As for the houses of the country (for
many houses came under their eye), they were all scattered, no two being
one by th'other, and yet not so far off as that it barred mutual succor; a
shew, as it were, of an accompanable solitariness and of a civil wildness.
"I pray you," said Musidorus, then first unsealing his long-silent lips,
"what countries be these we pass through, which are so diverse in shew,
the one wanting no store, th'other having no store but of want."

[3]   "The country," answered Claius, "where you were cast ashore and
20 now are passed through is Laconia, not so poor by the barrenness of the
soil (though in itself not passing fertile) as by a civil war, which being
these two years within the bowels of that estate between the gentlemen
and the peasants (by them named Helots) hath in this sort, as it were,
disfigured the face of nature and made it so unhospitable as now you have
found it, the towns neither of the one side nor the other willingly opening their gates to strangers, nor strangers willingly entering for fear of
being mistaken.

[4]   "But this country (where now you set your foot) is Arcadia; and
even hard by is the house of Kalander, whither we lead you, this country
30 being thus decked with peace and (the child of peace) good husbandry.
These houses you see so scattered are of men, as we two are, that live
upon the commodity of their sheep; and therefore in the division of the
Arcadian estate are termed shepherds; a happy people, wanting little
because they desire not much."

"What cause then," said Musidorus, "made you venture to leave this
sweet life and put yourself in yonder unpleasant and dangerous realm?"

"Guarded with poverty," answered Strephon, "and guided with
love."

"But now," said Claius, "since it hath pleased you to ask anything of us
40 whose baseness is such as the very knowledge is darkness, give us leave to
know something of you and of the young man you so much lament, that

at least we may be the better instructed to inform Kalander, and he the better know how to proportion his entertainment."

Musidorus (according to the agreement between Pyrocles and him to alter their names) answered that he called himself Palladius and his friend Daiphantus. "But till I have him again," said he, "I am indeed nothing; and therefore my story is of nothing, his entertainment (since so good a man he is) cannot be so low as I account my estate; and, in sum, the sum of all his courtesy may be to help me by some means to seek my friend."

[6] They perceived he was not willing to open himself further, and therefore, without further questioning, brought him to the house, about which they might see (with fit consideration both of the air, the prospect, and the nature of the ground) all such necessary additions to a great house as might well shew Kalander knew that provision is the foundation of hospitality, and thrift the fuel of magnificence. The house itself was built of fair and strong stone, not affecting so much any extraordinary kind of fineness as an honorable representing of a firm stateliness. The lights, doors, and stairs rather directed to the use of the guest than to the eye of the artificer; and yet as the one chiefly heeded so the other not neglected; each place handsome without curiosity, and homely without loathsome- ness; not so dainty as not to be trod on, nor yet slubbered up with good fellowship; all more lasting than beautiful, but that the consideration of the exceeding lastingness made the eye believe it was exceeding beautiful. The servants not so many in number as cleanly in apparel and serviceable in behavior, testifying even in their countenances that their master took as well care to be served as of them that did serve. One of them was forth- with ready to welcome the shepherds as men who, though they were poor, their master greatly favored; and understanding by them that the young man with them was to be much accounted of, for that they had seen tokens of more than common greatness, howsoever now eclipsed with fortune, he ran to his master; who came presently forth, and pleasantly welcom- ing the shepherds, but especially applying him to Musidorus, Strephon privately told him all what he knew of him and particularly that he found this stranger was loath to be known.

[7] "No," said Kalander (speaking aloud), "I am no herald to inquire of men's pedigrees, it sufficeth me if I know their virtues: which (if this young man's face be not a false witness) do better apparel his mind than you have done his body."

While he was speaking, there came a boy in shew like a merchant's prentice, who, taking Strephon by the sleeve, delivered him a letter written jointly both to him and Claius, from Urania; which they no sooner had

read but that, with short leave-taking of Kalander (who quickly guessed and smiled at the matter), and once again (though hastily) recommending the young man unto him, they went away, leaving Musidorus even loath to part with them, for the good conversation he had of them and obligation he accounted himself tied in unto them. And therefore, they delivering his chest unto him, he opened it and would have presented them with two very rich jewels, but they absolutely refused them, telling him they were more than enough rewarded in the knowing of him, and, without hearkening unto a reply (like men whose hearts disdained all
10 desires but one) gat speedily away, as if the letter had brought wings to make them fly. But by that sight Kalander soon judged that his guest was of no mean calling; and therefore the more respectfully entertaining him, Musidorus found his sickness (which the fight, the sea, and late travel had laid upon him) grow greatly; so that, fearing some sudden accident, he delivered the chest to Kalander, which was full of most precious stones, gorgeously and cunningly set in divers manners, desiring him he would keep those trifles and, if he died, he would bestow so much of it as was needful to find out and redeem a young man naming himself Daiphantus, as then in the hands of Laconia pirates.
20 [8]   But Kalander, seeing him faint more and more, with careful speed conveyed him to the most commodious lodging in his house; where, being possessed with an extreme burning fever, he continued some while with no great hope of life. But youth at length got the victory of sickness, so that in six weeks the excellency of his returned beauty was a credible ambassador of his health, to the great joy of Kalander: who, as in this time he had by certain friends of his that dwelt near the sea in Messenia set forth a ship and a galley to seek and succor Daiphantus, so at home did he omit nothing which he thought might either profit or gratify Palladius.
30 [9]   For having found in him (besides his bodily gifts beyond the degree of admiration) by daily discourses, which he delighted himself to have with him, a mind of most excellent composition (a piercing wit quite void of ostentation, high-erected thoughts seated in a heart of courtesy, an eloquence as sweet in the uttering as slow to come to the uttering, a behavior so noble as gave a majesty to adversity: and all in a man whose age could not be above one and twenty years), the good old man was even enamored with a fatherly love towards him; or rather became his servant by the bonds such virtue laid upon him; once he acknowledged himself so to be, by the badge of diligent attendance.

CHAP. III.

The ¹pictures of Kalander's dainty garden-house. His narration of the ²Arcadian estate, ³the king, ⁴the queen, ⁵their two daughters, and ⁶their guardians, with their qualities, which is the ground of all this story.

But Palladius having gotten his health and only staying there to be in place where he might hear answer of the ships set forth, Kalander one afternoon led him abroad to a well-arrayed ground he had behind his house, which he thought to shew him before his going as the place himself more than in any other delighted. The back side of the house was neither field, garden, nor orchard; or rather it was both field, garden, and orchard; for, as soon as the descending of the stairs had delivered them down, they came into a place cunningly set with trees of the most taste-pleasing fruits. But scarcely they had taken that into their consideration but that they were suddenly stepped into a delicate green, of each side of the green a thicket bend, behind the thickets again new beds of flowers, which, being under the trees, the trees were to them a pavilion, and they to the trees a mosaical floor; so that it seemed that art therein would needs be delightful by counterfeiting his enemy error, and making order in confusion.

[1] In the midst of all the place was a fair pond whose shaking crystal was a perfect mirror to all the other beauties, so that it bare shew of two gardens; one in deed, the other in shadows; and in one of the thickets was a fine fountain made thus. A naked Venus of white marble, wherein the graver had used such cunning that the natural blue veins of the marble were framed in fit places to set forth the beautiful veins of her body. At her breast she had her babe Æneas, who seemed (having begun to suck) to leave that to look upon her fair eyes, which smiled at the babe's folly, the meanwhile the breast running. Hard by was a house of pleasure built for a summer retiring-place, whither Kalander leading him, he found a square room full of delightful pictures made by the most excellent workman of Greece. There was Diana when Actaeon saw her bathing, in whose cheeks the painter had set such a color as was mixed between shame and disdain; and one of her foolish nymphs, who weeping and withal louring, one might see the workman meant to set forth tears of anger. In another table was Atalanta, the posture of whose limbs was so lively expressed that, if the eyes were the only judges as they be the only seers, one would have sworn the very picture had run. Besides many mo, as of Helena, Omphale, Iole, but in none of them all beauty seemed to speak so much as in a large table which contained a comely old man,

with a lady of middle age, but of excellent beauty, and more excellent would have been deemed but that there stood between them a young maid whose wonderfulness took away all beauty from her but that which it might seem she gave her back again by her very shadow. And such difference, being known that it did indeed counterfeit a person living, was there between her and all the other, though goddesses, that it seemed the skill of the painter bestowed on the other new beauty, but that the beauty of her bestowed new skill of the painter.

Though he thought inquisitiveness an uncomely guest, he could not
10 choose but ask who she was that, bearing shew of one being indeed, could with natural gifts go beyond the reach of invention. Kalander answered that it was made by Philoclea, the younger daughter of his prince, who also with his wife were contained in that table, the painter meaning to represent the present condition of the young lady, who stood watched by an overcurious eye of her parents; and that he would also have drawn her eldest sister, esteemed her match for beauty, in her shepherdish attire, but that the rude clown, her guardian, would not suffer it; neither durst he ask leave of the prince for fear of suspicion. Palladius perceived that the matter was wrapped up in some secrecy, and therefore would for
20 modesty demand no further; but yet his countenance could not but with dumb eloquence desire it. Which Kalander perceiving, "Well," said he, "my dear guest, I know your mind, and I will satisfy it. Neither will I do it like a niggardly answerer, going no further than the bounds of the question, but I will discover unto you as well that wherein my knowledge is common with others as that which by extraordinary means is delivered unto me, knowing so much in you, though not long acquainted, that I shall find your ears faithful treasurers."

So then, sitting down in two chairs, and sometimes casting his eye to the picture, he thus spake:
30 [2] "This country Arcadia, among all the provinces of Greece, hath ever been had in singular reputation, partly for the sweetness of the air and other natural benefits, but principally for the well-tempered minds of the people, who (finding that the shining title of glory so much affected by other nations doth indeed help little to the happiness of life) are the only people which, as by their justice and providence, give neither cause nor hope to their neighbors to annoy them; so are they not stirred with false praise to trouble others' quiet, thinking it a small reward for the wasting of their own lives in ravening that their posterity should long after say they had done so. Even the muses seem to approve their good
40 determination by choosing this country for their chief repairing-place, and by bestowing their perfections so largely here that the very shepherds have their fancies lifted to so high conceits as the learned of other nations

are content both to borrow their names and imitate their cunning.
[3]   "Here dwelleth and reigneth this prince (whose picture you see),
by name Basilius, a prince of sufficient skill to govern so quiet a country,
where the good minds of the former princes had set down good laws,
and the well-bringing up of the people doth serve as a most sure bond to
hold them. But to be plain with you, he excels in nothing so much as in
the zealous love of his people, wherein he doth not only pass all his own
foregoers but, as I think, all the princes living. Whereof the cause is that,
though he exceed not in the virtues which get admiration, as depth of
wisdom, height of courage, and largeness of magnificence, yet is he 10
notable in those which stir affection, as truth of word, meekness, courtesy,
mercifulness, and liberality.
[4]   "He, being already well stricken in years, married a young princess
named Gynecia, daughter to the king of Cyprus, of notable beauty, as by
her picture you see; a woman of great wit, and in truth of more princely
virtues than her husband; of most unspotted chastity, but of so working
a mind and so vehement spirits as a man may say it was happy she took a
good course, for otherwise it would have been terrible.
[5]   "Of these two are brought to the world two daughters, so beyond
measure excellent in all the gifts allotted to reasonable creatures that we 20
may think they were born to shew that Nature is no stepmother to that
sex, how much soever some men (sharp-witted only in evil speaking) have
sought to disgrace them. The elder is named Pamela, by many men not
deemed inferior to her sister. For my part, when I marked them both,
methought there was (if at least such perfections may receive the word
of more) more sweetness in Philoclea, but more majesty in Pamela; methought love played in Philoclea's eyes, and threatened in Pamela's;
methought Philoclea's beauty only persuaded, but so persuaded as all
hearts must yield; Pamela's beauty used violence, and such violence as
no heart could resist. And it seems that such proportion is between their 30
minds: Philoclea so bashful as though her excellencies had stolen into
her before she was aware; so humble that she will put all pride out of
countenance; in sum, such proceeding as will stir hope, but teach hope
good manners. Pamela of high thoughts, who avoids not pride with not
knowing her excellencies, but by making that one of her excellencies to
be void of pride; her mother's wisdom, greatness, nobility, but (if I can
guess aright) knit with a more constant temper. Now then, our Basilius
being so publicly happy as to be a prince, and so happy in that happiness
as to be a beloved prince, and so in his private blessed as to have so excellent
a wife and so over-excellent children, hath of late taken a course which 40
yet makes him more spoken of than all these blessings. For having made
a journey to Delphos and safely returned, within short space he brake

up his court and retired himself, his wife, and children into a certain
forest hereby, which he calleth his desert, wherein (besides a house appointed for stables and lodgings for certain persons of mean calling, who
do all household services), he hath builded two fine lodges. In the one
of them himself remains with his younger daughter Philoclea, which was
the cause they three were matched together in this picture, without having
any other creature living in that lodge with him.

[6] "Which though it be strange, yet not so strange as the course he
hath taken with the Princess Pamela, whom he hath placed in the other
lodge; but how think you accompanied? Truly with none other but one
Dametas, the most arrant, doltish clown that I think ever was without
the privilege of a bauble, with his wife Miso and daughter Mopsa, in
whom no wit can devise anything wherein they may pleasure her but to
exercise her patience and to serve for a foil of her perfections. This loutish
clown is such that you never saw so ill-favored a vizor; his behavior such
that he is beyond the degree of ridiculous; and for his apparel, even as I
would wish him. Miso his wife, so handsome a beldame that only her
face and her splayfoot have made her accused for a witch; only one good
point she hath: that she observes decorum, having a froward mind in a
wretched body. Between these two personages (who never agreed in
any humor but in disagreeing) is issued forth Mistress Mopsa, a fit woman
to participate of both their perfections; but because a pleasant fellow of
my acquaintance set forth her praises in verse, I will only repeat them,
are these, which I have so often caused to be sung that I have them without book.
and spare mine own tongue, since she goes for a woman. These verses

What length of verse can serve, brave Mopsa's good to show?
Whose virtues strange, and beauties such, as no man them may know,
Thus shrewdly burdened then, how can my muse escape?
The gods must help, and precious things must serve, to shew her shape.
Like great god Saturn fair, and like fair Venus chaste:
As smooth as Pan, as Juno mild, like goddess Iris faced.
With Cupid she foresees, and goes god Vulcan's pace:
And for a taste of all these gifts, she steals god Momus' grace.
Her forehead jacinth-like, her cheeks of opal hue,
Her twinkling eyes bedecked with pearl, her lips as sapphire blue;
Her hair like crapal-stone; her mouth, oh heavenly wide:
Her skin like burnished gold, her hands like silver ore untried.
As for her parts unknown, which hidden sure are best:
Happy be they which well believe, and never seek the rest.

"Now truly having made these descriptions unto you, methinks you
should imagine that I rather feign some pleasant device than recount a

truth that a prince (not banished from his own wits) could possibly make so unworthy a choice. But truly (dear guest) so it is that princes (whose doings have been often soothed with good success) think nothing so absurd, which they cannot make honorable. The beginning of his credit was by the prince's straying out of the way one time he hunted, where, meeting this fellow and asking him the way, and so, falling into other questions, he found some of his answers (as a dog, sure, if he could speak, had wit enough to describe his kennel) not unsensible, and all uttered with such rudeness, which he interpreted plainness (though there be great difference between them), that Basilius, conceiving a sudden delight, took him to his court with apparent shew of his good opinion; where the flattering courtier had no sooner taken the prince's mind but that there were straight reasons to confirm the prince's doing, and shadows of virtues found for Dametas. His silence grew wit, his bluntness integrity, his beastly ignorance virtuous simplicity; and the prince (according to the nature of great persons, in love with that he had done himself) fancied that his weakness with his presence would much be mended. And so, like a creature of his own making, he liked him more and more, and thus, having first given him the office of principal herdman, lastly, since he took this strange determination, he hath in a manner put the life of himself and his children into his hands. Which authority (like too great a sail for so small a boat) doth so oversway poor Dametas that, if before he were a good fool in a chamber, he might be allowed it now in a comedy. So as I doubt me (I fear me, indeed), my master will in the end (with his cost) find that his office is not to make men, but to use men as men are; no more than a horse will be taught to hunt, or an ass to manage. But, in sooth, I am afraid I have given your ears too great a surfeit with the gross discourses of that heavy piece of flesh. But the zealous grief I conceive to see so great an error in my lord hath made me bestow more words than I confess so base a subject deserveth."

* * * * *

THE SECOND BOOK

CHAP. VII

[1]*The education of Pyrocles and Musidorus.* [2]*Their friendship,*
[3]*navigation,* [4]*and first shipwreck.* [5]*The strange gratitude of two*
brothers to them, upon their liberality to those two brothers.

[1] "But the mother of Pyrocles (shortly after her childbirth) dying was cause that Euarchus recommended the care of his only son to his sister; doing it the rather because the war continued in cruel heat betwixt him and those evil neighbors of his. In which meantime, those young princes (the only comforters of that virtuous widow) grew on so that Pyrocles taught admiration to the hardest conceits; Musidorus (perchance because among his subjects) exceedingly beloved: and by the good order of Euarchus (well performed by his sister) they were so brought up that all the sparks of virtue which nature had kindled in them were so blown to give forth their uttermost heat that justly it may be affirmed they inflamed the affections of all that knew them. For almost before they could perfectly speak, they began to receive conceits not unworthy of the best speakers: excellent devices being used to make even their sports profitable; images of battles and fortifications being then delivered to their memory, which after, their stronger judgments might dispense; the delight of tales being converted to the knowledge of all the stories of worthy princes, both to move them to do nobly and teach them how to do nobly; the beauty of virtue still being set before their eyes, and that taught them with far more diligent care than grammatical rules; their bodies exercised in all abilities, both of doing and suffering, and their minds acquainted by degrees with dangers; and, in sum, all bent to the making up of princely minds: no servile fear used towards them, nor any other violent restraint, but still as to princes; so that a habit of commanding was naturalized in them, and therefore the farther from tyranny, nature having done so much for them in nothing as that it made them lords of truth, whereon all the other goods were builded.

[2]   "Among which I nothing so much delight to recount as the memorable friendship that grew betwixt the two princes, such as made them more like than the likeness of all other virtues, and made them more near one to the other than the nearness of their blood could aspire unto; which I think grew the faster, and the faster was tied between them, by reason that Musidorus being elder by three or four years, it was neither so great a difference in age as did take away the delight in society, and yet, by the difference, there was taken away the occasion of childish contentions till they had both passed over the humor of such contentions. For Pyrocles bare reverence full of love to Musidorus, and Musidorus had a delight full of love in Pyrocles. Musidorus, what he had learned either for body or mind, would teach it to Pyrocles; and Pyrocles was so glad to learn of none as of Musidorus; till Pyrocles, being come to sixteen years of age, he seemed so to overrun his age in growth, strength, and all things following it that not Musidorus, no, nor any man living (I think), could perform any action, either on horse or foot, more strongly, or deliver that strength more nimbly, or become the delivery more grace-

fully, or employ all more virtuously. Which may well seem wonderful, but wonders are no wonders in a wonderful subject.

[3] "At which time, understanding that the King Euarchus, after so many years' war and the conquest of all Pannonia and almost Thrace, had now brought the conclusion of all to the siege of Byzantium (to the raising of which siege great forces were made), they would needs fall to the practise of those virtues which they before learned. And therefore the mother of Musidorus, nobly yielding over her own affects to her children's good (for a mother she was, in effect, to them both), the rather that they might help her beloved brother, they brake off all de- 10 lays; which Musidorus, for his part, thought already had devoured too much of his good time, but that he had once granted a boon (before he knew what it was) to his dear friend Pyrocles: that he would never seek the adventures of arms until he might go with him; which, having fast bound his heart (a true slave to faith), he had bid a tedious delay of following his own humor for his friend's sake, till, now finding him able every way to go through with that kind of life, he was as desirous for his sake as for his own to enter into it. So, therefore preparing a navy that they might go like themselves, and not only bring the comfort of their presence, but of their power, to their dear parent Euarchus, they recom- 20 mended themselves to the sea, leaving the shore of Thessalia full of tears and vows; and were received thereon with so smooth and smiling a face as if Neptune had as then learned falsely to fawn on princes. The wind was like a servant, waiting behind them so just that they might fill the sails as they listed; and the best sailors, shewing themselves less covetous of his liberality, so tempered it that they all kept together like a beautiful flock which so well could obey their master's pipe; without sometimes, to delight the princes' eyes, some two or three of them would strive who could (either by the cunning of well spending the wind's breath, or by the advantageous building of their moving houses) leave their fellows 30 behind them in the honor of speed: while the two princes had leisure to see the practise of that which before they had learned by books; to consider the art of catching the wind prisoner, to no other end but to run away with it; to see how beauty and use can so well agree together, that of all the trinkets wherewith they are attired, there is not one but serves to some necessary purpose. And (O Lord) to see the admirable power and noble effects of love, whereby the seeming insensible loadstone, with a secret beauty (holding the spirit of iron in it) can draw that hard-hearted thing unto it, and (like a virtuous mistress) not only make it bow itself but with it make it aspire to so high a love as of the heavenly 40 poles, and thereby to bring forth the noblest deeds that the children of

the earth can boast of. And so the princes, delighting their conceits with confirming their knowledge, seeing wherein the sea-discipline differed from land-service, they had for a day and almost a whole night as pleasing entertainment as the falsest heart could give to him he means worst to.

[4] "But by that the next morning began a little to make a gilden shew of a good meaning, there arose even with the sun a veil of dark clouds before his face, which shortly (like ink poured into water) had blacked over all the face of heaven, preparing (as it were) a mournful stage for a tragedy to be played on. For forthwith the winds began to
10 speak louder, and, as in a tumultuous kingdom, to think themselves fittest instruments of commandment; and, blowing whole storms of hail and rain upon them, they were sooner in danger than they could almost bethink themselves of change. For then the traitorous sea began to swell in pride against the afflicted navy, under which (while the heaven favored them) it had lain so calmly, making mountains of itself over which the tossed and tottering ship should climb, to be straight carried down again to a pit of hellish darkness; with such cruel blows against the sides of the ship (that which way soever it went was still in his malice) that there was left neither power to stay nor way of escape. And shortly had it so
20 dissevered the loving company which the day before had tarried together that most of them never met again, but were swallowed up in his never-satisfied mouth. Some indeed (as since was known), after long wandering, returned into Thessalia; other recovered Byzantium and served Euarchus in his war. But in the ship wherein the princes were (now left as much alone as proud lords be when fortune fails them), though they employed all industry to save themselves, yet what they did was rather for duty to nature than hope to escape. So ugly a darkness, as if it would prevent the night's coming, usurped the day's right; which (accompanied sometimes with thunders, always with horrible noises of the chafing
30 winds) made the masters and pilots so astonished that they knew not how to direct, and, if they knew, they could scarcely (when they directed) hear their own whistle. For the sea strave with the winds which should be louder, and the shrouds of the ship, with a ghastful noise to them that were in it, witnessed that their ruin was the wager of the others' contention, and the heaven roaring out thunders the more amazed them, as having those powers for enemies. Certainly there is no danger carries with it more horror than that which grows in those flowing kingdoms. For that dwelling-place is unnatural to mankind, and then the terribleness of the continual motion, the desolation of the far-being from comfort,
40 the eye and the ear having ugly images ever before it, doth still vex the mind, even when it is best armed against it. But thus the day passed (if that might be called a day), while the cunningest mariners were so con-

quered by the storm as they thought it best with striking sails to yield to
be governed by it: the valiantest feeling inward dismayedness, and yet the
fearfullest ashamed fully to shew it, seeing that the princes (who were
to part from the greatest fortunes) did in their countenances accuse no
point of fear, but, encouraging them to do what might be done (putting
their hands to every most painful office) taught them at one instant to
promise themselves the best and yet not to despise the worst. But so were
they carried by the tyranny of the wind and the treason of the sea all
that night, which the elder it was the more wayward it shewed itself
towards them, till the next morning (known to be a morning better by 10
the hour-glass than by the day clearness), having run fortune as blindly
as itself ever was painted, lest the conclusion should not answer to the
rest of the play, they were driven upon a rock: which, hidden with those
outrageous waves, did, as it were, closely dissemble his cruel mind, till,
with an unbelieved violence (but to them that have tried it), the ship
ran upon it; and, seeming willinger to perish than to have her course
stayed, redoubled her blows, till she had broken herself in pieces; and, as
it were, tearing out her own bowels to feed the sea's greediness, left
nothing within it but despair of safety and expectation of a loathsome
end. There was to be seen the divers manner of minds in distress: some 20
sate upon the top of the poop weeping and wailing, till the sea swallowed
them; some one, more able to abide death than fear of death, cut his own
throat to prevent drowning; some prayed, and there wanted not of them
which cursed, as if the heavens could not be more angry than they were.
But a monstrous cry begotten of many roaring vows was able to infect
with fear a mind that had not prevented it with the power of reason.
[5] "But the princes, using the passions of fearing evil, and desiring to
escape only to serve the rule of virtue, not to abandon one's self, leapt to
a rib of the ship which, broken from his fellows, floated, with more likelihood to do service than any other limb of that ruinous body; upon which 30
there had gotten already two brethren, well-known servants of theirs;
and straight they four were carried out of sight, in that huge rising of
the sea, from the rest of the ship. But the piece they were on sinking by
little and little under them, not able to support the weight of so many,
the brethren (the elder whereof was Leucippus, the younger Nelsus)
shewed themselves right faithful and grateful servants unto them; grateful (I say) for this cause: those two gentlemen had been taken prisoners
in the great war the king of Phrygia made upon Thessalia in the time of
Musidorus his infancy, and having been sold into another country (though
peace fell after between these realms) could not be delivered, because 40
of their valor known, but for a far greater sum than either all their friends
were able, or the dowager willing, to make, in respect of the great ex-

penses herself and people had been put to in those wars. And so had they remained in prison about thirteen years when the two young princes (hearing speeches of their good deserts) found means, both by selling all the jewels they had of great price and by giving under their hands great estates when they should come to be kings (which promises their virtue promised for them should be kept), to get so much treasure as redeemed them from captivity. This remembered, and kindly remembered by these two brothers, perchance helped by a natural duty to their princes' blood, they willingly left hold of the board, committing themselves to the sea's
10 rage, and, even when they went to die, themselves praying for the princes' lives. It is true that neither the pain nor danger so moved the princes' hearts as the tenderness of that loving part, far from glory, having so few lookers on; far from hope of reward, since themselves were sure to perish.

CHAP. VIII

[1]*Pyrocles, cast on the shore of Phyrgia,* [2]*led prisoner to the king.*
[3]*That suspicious tyrant naturalized.* [4]*His intent to kill Pyrocles.*
[5]*Musidorus his escape from sea, and offer to die for his friend.*
20 [6]*Their contention for death.* [7]*Preparation for Musidorus' execu-*
tion. [8]*His strange delivery by Pyrocles,* [9]*and a sudden mutiny.*
[10]*Their killing the bad king,* [11]*and creating a better.*

"But now, of all the royal navy, they had left but one piece of one ship, whereon they kept themselves in all truth, having interchanged their cares while either cared for other, each comforting and counseling how to labor for the better and to abide the worse. But so fell it out that, as they were carried by the tide (which there, seconded by the storm, ran exceedingly swiftly), Musidorus seeing (as he thought) Pyrocles not
30 well upon the board, as he would with his right hand have helped him on better, he had no sooner unfastened his hold but that a wave forcibly spoiled his weaker hand of hold; and so for a time parted those friends, each crying to the other, but the noise of the sea drowned their farewell. But Pyrocles (then careless of death, if it had come by any means but his own) was shortly brought out of the sea's fury to the land's comfort; when (in my conscience I know) that comfort was but bitter unto him. And bitter indeed it fell out, even in itself, to be unto him.

[2] "For being cast on land much bruised and beaten both with the sea's hard farewell and the shore's rude welcome; and even almost deadly
40 tired with the length of his uncomfortable labor, as he was walking up to discover somebody to whom he might go for relief, there came straight running unto him certain who (as it was after known) by appointment

watched (with many others) in divers places along the coast; who laid hands of him, and, without either questioning with him or shewing will to hear him (like men fearful to appear curious), or, which was worse, having no regard to the hard plight he was in (being so wet and weak), they carried him some miles thence to a house of a principal officer of that country. Who with no more civility (though with much more business than those under-fellows had shewed) began, in captious manner, to put interrogatories unto him. To which he (unused to such entertainment) did shortly and plainly answer what he was and how he came thither.

"But that no sooner known, with numbers of armed men to guard him 10 (for mischief, not from mischief), he was sent to the king's court, which as then was not above a day's journey off, with letters from that officer containing his own serviceable diligence in discovering so great a person-age; adding withal more than was true of his conjectures, because he would endear his own service.

[3] "This country whereon he fell was Phrygia, and it was to the king thereof to whom he was sent, a prince of a melancholy constitution both of body and mind; wickedly sad, ever musing of horrible matters; suspect-ing, or rather condemning, all men of evil because his mind had no eye to espy goodness; and therefore accusing sycophants, of all men, did best 20 sort to his nature; but therefore, not seeming sycophants, because of no evil they said, they could bring any new or doubtful thing unto him, but such as already he had been apt to determine; so as they came but as proofs of his wisdom: fearful and never secure; while the fear he had figured in his mind had any possibility of event. A toad-like retiredness and closeness of mind, nature teaching the odiousness of poison and the danger of odiousness. Yet while youth lasted in him, the exercises of that age and his humor (not yet fully discovered) made him something the more frequentable and less dangerous. But after that years began to come on with some, though more seldom, shews of a bloody nature, and that 30 the prophecy of Musidorus' destiny came to his ears (delivered unto him and received of him with the hardest interpretation, as though his sub-jects did delight in the hearing thereof). Then gave he himself, indeed, to the full current of his disposition, especially after the war of Thessalia, wherein (though in truth wrongly) he deemed his unsuccessings pro-ceeded of their unwillingness to have him prosper; and then, thinking himself contemned (knowing no countermine against contempt but ter-ror), began to let nothing pass which might bear the color of a fault without sharp punishment. And when he wanted faults, excellency grew a fault; and it was sufficient to make one guilty that he had power to be 40 guilty. And as there is no honor to which impudent poverty cannot make itself serviceable, so were there enough of those desperate ambitious who

would build their houses upon others' ruins, which after should fall by
like practises. So as servitude came mainly upon that poor people, whose
deeds were not only punished but words corrected, and even thoughts, by
some mean or other, pulled out of them: while suspicion bred the mind of
cruelty and the effects of cruelty stirred a new cause of suspicion. And in
this plight (full of watchful fearfulness) did the storm deliver sweet
Pyrocles to the stormy mind of that tyrant, all men that did such wrong
to so rare a stranger (whose countenance deserved both pity and admiration) condemning themselves as much in their hearts as they did brag in
10 their forces.

[4]   "But when this bloody king knew what he was and in what order
he and his cousin Musidorus (so much of him feared) were come out
of Thessalia, assuredly thinking (because ever thinking the worst) that
those forces were provided against him; glad of the perishing (as he
thought) of Musidorus, determined in public sort to put Pyrocles to
death. For having quite lost the way of nobleness, he strave to climb to
the height of terribleness; and thinking to make all men adread, to make
such one an enemy who would not spare, nor fear, to kill so great a
prince; and, lastly, having nothing in him why to make him his friend,
20 thought he would make him away for being his enemy. The day was
appointed, and all things appointed for that cruel blow, in so solemn an
order as if they would set forth tyranny in most gorgeous decking. The
princely youth, of invincible valor, yet so unjustly subjected to such outrageous wrong, carrying himself in all his demeanor so constantly, abiding extremity, that one might see it was the cutting away of the greatest
hope of the world and destroying virtue in his sweetest growth.

[5]   "But so it fell out that his death was prevented by a rare example
of friendship in Musidorus, who, being almost drowned, had been taken
up by a fisherman belonging to the kingdom of Pontus; and being there
30 and understanding the full discourse (as fame was very prodigal of so
notable an accident) in what case Pyrocles was, learning withal that
his hate was far more to him than to Pyrocles, he found means to acquaint himself with a nobleman of that country, to whom largely discovering what he was, he found him a most fit instrument to effectuate
his desire. For this nobleman had been one who in many wars had served
Euarchus, and had been so mind-stricken by the beauty of virtue in that
noble king that (though not born his subject) he even professed himself his servant. His desire, therefore, to him was to keep Musidorus in a
strong castle of his, and then to make the king of Phrygia understand that
40 if he would deliver Pyrocles, Musidorus would willingly put himself into
his hands, knowing well that, how thirsty soever he was of Pyrocles'
blood, he would rather drink that of Musidorus.

"The nobleman was loath to preserve one by the loss of another, but time urging resolution, the importunity of Musidorus (who shewed a mind not to overlive Pyrocles), with the affection he bare to Euarchus, so prevailed that he carried this strange offer of Musidorus; which by that tyrant was greedily accepted.

[6] "And so upon security of both sides, they were interchanged. Where I may not omit that work of friendship in Pyrocles, who both in speech and countenance to Musidorus well shewed that he thought himself injured and not relieved by him, asking him what he had ever seen in him, why he could not bear the extremities of mortal accidents as well as any man? and why he should envy him the glory of suffering death for his friend's cause, and (as it were) rob him of his own possession? But in this notable contention (where the conquest must be the conqueror's destruction, and safety the punishment of the conquered), Musidorus prevailed because he was a more welcome prize to the unjust king, that wished none well, to them worse than others, and to him worst of all; and as cheerfully going towards, as Pyrocles went frowardly fromward, his death, he was delivered to the king, who could not be enough sure of him without he fed his own eyes upon one whom he had begun to fear as soon as the other began to be.

[7] "Yet because he would in one act both make ostentation of his own felicity (into whose hands his most feared enemy was fallen) and withal cut off such hopes from his suspected subjects (when they should know certainly he was dead), with much more skilful cruelty and horrible solemnity he caused each thing to be prepared for his triumph of tyranny. And so the day being come, he was led forth by many armed men (who often had been the fortifiers of wickedness) to the place of execution: where, coming with a mind comforted in that he had done such service to Pyrocles, this strange encounter he had.

[8] "The excelling Pyrocles was no sooner delivered by the king's servants to a place of liberty than he bent his wit and courage (and what would not they bring to pass?) how either to deliver Musidorus or to perish with him. And (finding he could get in that country no forces sufficient by force to rescue him) to bring himself to die with him (little hoping of better event), he put himself in poor raiment, and, by the help of some few crowns he took of that nobleman (who, full of sorrow, though not knowing the secret of his intent, suffered him to go in such order from him) he (even he, born to the greatest expectation and of the greatest blood that any prince might be) submitted himself to be servant to the executioner that should put to death Musidorus—a far notabler proof of his friendship, considering the height of his mind, than any death could be. That bad officer, not suspecting him, being arrayed fit for such

an estate and having his beauty hidden by many foul spots he artificially put upon his face, gave him leave not only to wear a sword himself but to bear his sword, prepared for the justified murder. And so Pyrocles taking his time, when Musidorus was upon the scaffold (separated somewhat from the rest, as allowed to say something), he stepped unto him; and putting the sword into his hand not bound (a point of civility the officers used towards him because they doubted no such enterprise), 'Musidorus,' said he, 'die nobly.' In truth, never man between joy, before knowledge what to be glad of, and fear after considering his case, had
10 such a confusion of thoughts as I had when I saw Pyrocles so near me."

But with that Dorus blushed and Pamela smiled; and Dorus the more blushed at her smiling, and she the more smiled at his blushing; because he had (with the remembrance of that plight he was in) forgotten, in speaking of himself, to use the third person. But Musidorus turned again her thoughts from his cheeks to his tongue in this sort: "But," said he, "when they were with swords in hands, not turning backs one to the other (for there they knew was no place of defense), but making that a preservation in not hoping to be preserved, and now acknowledging themselves subject to death, meaning only to do honor to their princely
20 birth, they flew amongst them all (for all were enemies), and had quickly, either with flight or death, left none upon the scaffold to annoy them. Wherein Pyrocles (the excellent Pyrocles) did such wonders beyond belief as was able to lead Musidorus to courage, though he had been born a coward. But, indeed, just rage and desperate virtue did such effects that the popular sort of the beholders began to be almost superstitiously amazed, as at effects beyond mortal power. But the king, with angry threatenings from out a window (where he was not ashamed the world should behold him a beholder), commanded his guard and the rest of his soldiers to hasten their death. But many of them lost their bodies to lose
30 their souls, when the princes grew almost so weary as they were ready to be conquered with conquering.

[9] "But as they were still fighting with weak arms and strong hearts, it happened that one of the soldiers (commanded to go up after his fellows against the princes), having received a light hurt, more wounded in his heart, went back with as much diligence as he came up with modesty; which another of his fellows seeing, to pick a thank of the king, strake him upon the face, reviling him that, so accompanied, he would run away from so few. But he (as many times it falls out), only valiant when he was angry, in revenge thrust him through; which, with his death, was
40 straight revenged by a brother of his, and that again requited by a fellow of the other's. There began to be a great tumult amongst the soldiers; which seen and not understood by the people (used to fears but not used

to be bold in them), some began to cry 'Treason!' And that voice straight multiplying itself, the king (oh, the cowardice of a guilty conscience), before any man set upon him, fled away. Wherewith a bruit (either by art of some well-meaning men or by such chance as such things often fall out by) ran from one to the other that the king was slain; wherewith certain young men of the bravest minds cried with loud voice, 'Liberty!' and, encouraging the other citizens to follow them, set upon the guard and soldiers as chief instruments of tyranny, and quickly aided by the princes, they had left none of them alive, nor any other in the city who they thought had, in any sort, set his hand to the work of their servi- tude, and (God knows), by the blindness of rage killing many guiltless persons, either for affinity to the tyrant or enmity to the tyrant-killers. But some of the wisest (seeing that a popular license is indeed the many-headed tyranny) prevailed with the rest to make Musidorus their chief, choosing one of them (because princes) to defend them, and him because elder and most hated of the tyrant, and by him to be ruled. Whom forthwith they lifted up, Fortune (I think) smiling at her work therein, that a scaffold of execution should grow a scaffold of coronation.

[10] "But by and by there came news of more certain truth that the king was not dead, but fled to a strong castle of his, near hand, where he was gathering forces in all speed possible to suppress this mutiny. But now they had run themselves too far out of breath to go back again the same career; and too well they knew the sharpness of his memory to forget such an injury; therefore, learning virtue of necessity, they continued resolute to obey Musidorus. Who, seeing what forces were in the city, with them issued against the tyrant while they were in this heat, before practises might be used to dissever them; and with them met the king, who likewise hoping little to prevail by time (knowing and finding his people's hate) met him with little delay in the field; where himself was slain by Musidorus, after he had seen his only son (a prince of great courage and beauty, but fostered in blood by his naughty father) slain by the hand of Pyrocles. This victory obtained with great, and truly not undeserved, honor to the two princes, the whole estates of the country, with one consent, gave the crown and all other marks of sovereignty to Musidorus, desiring nothing more than to live under such a government as they promised themselves of him.

[11] "But he, thinking it a greater greatness to give a kingdom than get a kingdom, understanding that there was left of the blood royal, and next to the succession, an aged gentleman of approved goodness (who had gotten nothing by his cousin's power but danger from him and odiousness for him), having passed his time in modest secrecy and as much from intermeddling in matters of government as the greatness of his blood would suffer him, did (after having received the full power to his own hands)

resign all to the nobleman; but with such conditions, and cautions of the conditions, as might assure the people (with as much assurance as worldly matters bear) that not only that governor, of whom indeed they looked for all good, but the nature of the government, should be no way apt to decline to tyranny."

* * * * *

10 **THE THIRD BOOK**

CHAP. VI.

* * * * *

Pamela's prayer

. . . Pamela did walk up and down, full of deep (though patient) thoughts. For her look and countenance was settled, her pace soft, and almost still of one measure, without any passionate gesture or violent motion; till at length (as it were) awaking and strengthening herself, 20 "Well," said she, "yet this is the best, and of this I am sure, that howsoever they wrong me, they cannot overmaster God. No darkness blinds His eyes, no jail bars Him out. To whom then else should I fly but to Him for succor?"

And therewith kneeling down, even in the same place where she stood, she thus said: "O all-seeing Light and eternal Life of all things, to whom nothing is either so great that it may resist, or so small that it is contemned, look upon my misery with Thine eye of mercy, and let Thine infinite power vouchsafe to limit out some proportion of deliverance unto me, as to Thee shall seem most convenient. Let not injury, O Lord, triumph over 30 me, and let my faults by Thy hands be corrected, and make not mine unjust enemy the minister of Thy justice. But yet, my God, if in Thy wisdom this be the aptest chastisement for my inexcusable folly; if this low bondage be fittest for my over-high desires; if the pride of my not enough humble heart be thus to be broken, O Lord, I yield unto Thy will, and joyfully embrace what sorrow Thou wilt have me suffer. Only thus much let me crave of Thee (let my craving, O Lord, be accepted of Thee, since even that proceeds from Thee), let me crave, even by the noblest title which in my greatest affliction I may give myself, that I am Thy creature, and by Thy goodness (which is Thyself), that Thou wilt suffer some beam 40 of Thy majesty so to shine into my mind that it may still depend confidently upon Thee. Let calamity be the exercise, but not the overthrow, of my virtue; let their power prevail, but prevail not to destruction; let

my greatness be their prey; let my pain be the sweetness of their revenge;
let them (if so it seem good unto Thee) vex me with more and more punishment. But, O Lord, let never their wickeness have such a hand but that
I may carry a pure mind in a pure body."

(And pausing a while) "And, O most gracious Lord," said she, "whatever become of me, preserve the virtuous Musidorus."

THOMAS LODGE

The Introduction and Notes are at page 1322

FROM *Rosalynde, Euphues golden legacie,* 1590

Rosalynde: Euphues' Golden Legacy

To the Right Honorable and his most esteemed Lord, the
Lord of Hunsdon, Lord Chamberlain of Her Majesty's
household, and Governor of her Town of Berwick: T. L.,
G., wisheth increase of all honorable virtues.

SUCH ROMANS (Right Honorable) as delighted in martial exploits attempted their actions in the honor of Augustus, because he was a patron
of soldiers; and Virgil, dignified him with his poems as a Maecenas of
scholars; both jointly advancing his royalty as a prince warlike and
learned. Such as sacrifice to Pallas present her with bays as she is wise, and
with armor as she is valiant; observing herein that excellent τὸ πρέπον,
which dedicateth honors according to the perfection of the person. When
I entered (Right Honorable) with a deep insight into the consideration
of these premises, seeing Your Lordship to be a patron of all martial men
and a Maecenas of such as apply themselves to study, wearing with Pallas
both the lance and the bay, and aiming with Augustus at the favor of all
by the honorable virtues of your mind; being myself first a student, and
afterwards falling from books to arms, even vowed in all my thoughts
dutifully to affect Your Lordship. Having with Captain Clarke made a
voyage to the islands of Terceras and the Canaries, to beguile the time
with labor I writ this book; rough, as hatched in the storms of the ocean,
and feathered in the surges of many perilous seas. But as it is the work of
a soldier and a scholar, I presumed to shroud it under Your Honor's
patronage, as one that is the fautor and favorer of all virtuous actions, and
whose honorable loves, grown from the general applause of the whole
commonwealth for your higher deserts, may keep it from the malice of
every bitter tongue. Other reasons more particular (Right Honorable)

challenge in me a special affection to Your Lordship, as being a scholar with your two noble sons, Master Edmund Carew and Master Robert Carew (two scions worthy of so honorable a tree, and a tree glorious in such honorable fruit), as also being scholar in the University under that learned and virtuous knight Sir Edward Hoby, when he was bachelor in arts, a man as well lettered as well born, and, after the etymology of his name, soaring as high as the wings of knowledge can mount him, happy every way, and the more fortunate as blessed in the honor of so virtuous a Lady. Thus (Right Honorable) the duty that I owe to the sons chargeth 10 me that all my affection be placed on the father; for, where the branches are so precious, the tree of force must be most excellent. Commanded and emboldened thus with the consideration of these forepast reasons to present my book to Your Lordship, I humbly entreat Your Honor will vouch of my labors, and favor a soldier's and a scholar's pen with your gracious acceptance; who answers in affection what he wants in eloquence; so devoted to Your Honor as his only desire is to end his life under the favor of so martial and learned a patron. Resting thus in hope of Your Lordship's courtesy in deigning the patronage of my work, I cease, wishing you as many honorable fortunes as Your Lordship can desire, or I 20 imagine.

> Your Honor's soldier
> humbly affectionate:
> THOMAS LODGE

To the Gentlemen Readers

Gentlemen, look not here to find any sprigs of Pallas' bay tree, nor to hear the humor of any amorous laureate, nor the pleasing vein of any eloquent orator. *Nolo altum sapere*, they be matters above my capacity; the cobbler's check shall never light on my head, *Ne sutor ultra crepidam*, 30 I will go no further than the latchet, and then all is well. Here you may perhaps find some leaves of Venus' myrtle, but hewn down by a soldier with his curtal-axe, not bought with the allurement of a filed tongue. To be brief, gentlemen, room for a soldier and a sailor, that gives you the fruits of his labors that be wrote in the ocean, when every line was wet with a surge, and every humorous passion counterchecked with a storm. If you like it, so; and yet I will be yours in duty, if you be mine in favor. But if Momus or any squint-eyed ass that hath mighty ears to conceive with Midas, and yet little reason to judge; if he come aboard our bark to find fault with the tackling when he knows not the shrouds, I'll down 40 into the hold and fetch out a rusty pole-axe, that saw no sun this seven year, and either will bebaste him, or heave the cockscomb overboard to feed cods. But courteous gentlemen that favor most, backbite none, and pardon what is overslipped, let such come and welcome; I'll into the steward's room and fetch them a can of our best beverage. Well, gentlemen, you have *Euphues' Legacy*, I fetched it as far as the islands of Terceras, and therefore read it; censure with favor, and farewell.

Yours T. L.

THERE dwelled adjoining to the city of Bordeaux a knight of most honorable parentage, whom fortune had graced with many favors, and nature honored with sundry exquisite qualities, so beautified with the excellency of both as it was a question whether fortune or nature were more prodigal in deciphering the riches of their bounties. Wise he was, as holding in his head a supreme conceit of policy, reaching with Nestor into the depth of all civil government; and to make his wisdom more gracious, he had that *salem ingenii* and pleasant eloquence that was so highly commended in Ulysses. His valor was no less than his wit, nor the stroke of his lance no less forcible than the sweetness of his tongue was persuasive; for he was, for his courage, chosen the principal of all the Knights of Malta. This hardy knight thus enriched with virtue and honor, surnamed Sir John of Bordeaux, having passed the prime of his youth in sundry battles against the Turks, at last (as the date of time hath his course) grew aged. His hairs were silver-hued, and the map of his age was figured on his forehead; honor sat in the furrows of his face, and many years were portrayed in his wrinkled lineaments, that all men might perceive his glass was run, and that nature of necessity challenged her due. Sir John (that with the phoenix knew the term of his life was now expired, and could with the swan discover his end by her songs) having three sons by his wife Lynida, the very pride of all his forepast years, thought now (seeing death by constraint would compel him to leave them) to bestow upon them such a legacy as might bewray his love and increase their ensuing amity. Calling therefore these young gentlemen before him in the presence of all his fellow Knights of Malta, he resolved to leave them a memorial of all his fatherly care in setting down a method of their brotherly duties. Having, therefore, death in his looks to move them to pity, and tears in his eyes to paint out the depth of his passions, taking his eldest son by the hand, he began thus.

Sir John of Bordeaux's legacy he gave to his sons

O my sons, you see that fate hath set a period of my years, and destinies have determined the final end of my days; the palm tree waxeth away-ward, for he stoopeth in his height, and my plumes are full of sick feathers touched with age. I must to my grave, that dischargeth all cares, and leave you to the world that increaseth many sorrows. My silver hairs containeth

great experience, and in the number of my years are penned down the subtleties of fortune. Therefore, as I leave you some fading pelf to counter-check poverty, so I will bequeath you infallible precepts that shall lead you unto virtue. First, therefore, unto thee, Saladyne, the eldest, and there-fore the chiefest pillar of my house, wherein should be engraved as well the excellency of thy father's qualities as the essential form of his propor-tion, to thee I give fourteen plowlands, with all my manor houses and richest plate. Next, unto Fernandyne I bequeath twelve plowlands. But unto Rosader, the youngest, I give my horse, my armor, and my lance,
10 with sixteen plowlands; for, if the inward thoughts be discovered by out-ward shadows, Rosader will exceed you all in bounty and honor.

Thus (my sons) have I parted in your portions the substance of my wealth, wherein, if you be as prodigal to spend as I have been careful to get, your friends will grieve to see you more wasteful than I was bounti-ful, and your foes smile that my fall did begin in your excess. Let mine honor be the glass of your actions, and the fame of my virtues the loadstar to direct the course of your pilgrimage. Aim your deeds by my honorable endeavors, and shew yourselves scions worthy of so flourishing a tree; lest, as the birds *halcyones,* which exceed in whiteness, I hatch young ones that
20 surpass in blackness. Climb not, my sons; aspiring pride is a vapor that ascendeth high, but soon turneth to a smoke; they which stare at the stars stumble upon the stones; and such as gaze at the sun (unless they be eagle-eyed) fall blind. Soar not with the hobby, lest you fall with the lark; nor attempt not with Phaëton, lest you drown with Icarus. Fortune, when she wills you to fly, tempers your plumes with wax, and therefore either sit still and make no wing, or else beware the sun, and hold Dedalus' axiom authentical (*Medium tenere tutissimum.*) Low shrubs have deep roots, and poor cottages great patience. Fortune looks ever upward, and envy aspireth to nestle with dignity. Take heed, my sons, the mean is sweetest
30 melody; where strings high stretched either soon crack or quickly grow out of tune. Let your country's care be your hearts' content, and think that you are not born for yourselves, but to level your thoughts to be loyal to your prince, careful for the commonweal and faithful to your friends; so shall France say, these men are as excellent in virtues as they be ex-quisite in features.

O my sons, a friend is a precious jewel, within whose bosom you may unload your sorrows and unfold your secrets, and he either will relieve with counsel or persuade with reason. But take heed in the choice; the outward shew makes not the inward man, nor are the dimples in the face
40 the calendars of truth. When the licorice leaf looketh most dry, then it is most wet. When the shores of Lepanthus are most quiet, then they fore-point a storm. The baaran leaf, the more fair it looks, the more infectious

it is, and in the sweetest words is oft hid most treachery. Therefore, my sons, choose a friend as the *Hyperborei* do the metals; sever them from the ore with fire, and let them not bide the stamp before they be current; so try, and then trust; let time be the touchstone of friendship, and then friends faithful lay them up for jewels. Be valiant, my sons, for cowardice is the enemy to honor; but not too rash, for that is an extreme. Fortitude is the mean, and that is limited within bonds and prescribed with circumstance. But, above all, and with that he fetched a deep sigh, beware of love, for it is far more perilous than pleasant, and yet I tell you it allureth as ill as the sirens. O my sons, fancy is a fickle thing, and beauty's paint- 10 ings are tricked up with time's colors, which, being set to dry in the sun, perish with the same. Venus is a wanton, and though her laws pretend liberty, yet there is nothing but loss and glistering misery. Cupid's wings are plumed with the feathers of vanity, and his arrows, where they pierce, enforce nothing but deadly desires; a woman's eye, as it is precious to behold, so is it prejudicial to gaze upon; for, as it affordeth delight, so it snareth unto death. Trust not their fawning favors, for their loves are like the breath of a man upon steel, which no sooner lighteth on but it leapeth off; and their passions are as momentary as the colors of a polyp, which changeth at the sight of every object. 20

My breath waxeth short, and mine eyes dim; the hour is come, and I must away; therefore, let this suffice: women are wantons, and yet men cannot want one. And therefore, if you love, choose her that hath eyes of adamant, that will turn only to one point; her heart of a diamond that will receive but one form; her tongue of a sethin leaf, that never wags but with a southeast wind. And yet, my sons, if she have all these qualities, to be chaste, obedient, and silent; yet, for that she is a woman, shalt thou find in her sufficient vanities to countervail her virtues. Oh now, my sons, even now, take these my last words as my latest legacy; for my thread is spun, and my foot is in the grave. Keep my precepts as memorials of your 30 father's counsels, and let them be lodged in the secret of your hearts; for wisdom is better than wealth, and a golden sentence worth a world of treasure. In my fall, see and mark, my sons, the folly of man, that, being dust, climbeth with Biares to reach at the heavens; and ready every minute to die, yet hopeth for an age of pleasures. Oh, man's life is like lightning, that is but a flash; and the longest date of his years but as a bavin's blaze. Seeing then man is so mortal, be careful that thy life be virtuous, that thy death may be full of admirable honors. So shalt thou challenge fame to be thy fautor, and put oblivion to exile with thine honorable actions. But, my sons, lest you should forget your father's axioms, take this 40 scroll, wherein read what your father, dying, wills you to execute, living. At this he shrunk down in his bed, and gave up the ghost.

John of Bordeaux, being thus dead, was greatly lamented of his sons, and bewailed of his friends; especially of his fellow Knights of Malta, who attended on his funerals, which were performed with great solemnity. His obsequies done, Saladyne caused, next his epitaph, the contents of the scroll to be portrayed out, which were to this effect.

The contents of the schedule which Sir John of Bordeaux gave to his sons

My sons, behold what portion I do give;
I leave you goods, but they are quickly lost;
I leave advice, to school you how to live;
I leave you wit, but won with little cost.
But keep it well; for counsel still is one,
When father, friends, and worldly goods are gone.

In choice of thrift, let honor be thy gain,
Win it by virtue, and by manly might;
In doing good, esteem thy toil no pain;
Protect the fatherless and widow's right;
Fight for thy faith, thy country and thy king.
For why? This thrift will prove a blessed thing.

In choice of wife, prefer the modest-chaste,
Lilies are fair in show, but foul in smell;
The sweetest looks by age are soon defaced;
Then choose thy wife by wit, and living well.
Who brings thee wealth, and many faults withal,
Presents thee honey mixed with bitter gall.

In choice of friends, beware of light belief,
A painted tongue may shroud a subtle heart;
The siren's tears do threaten mickle grief,
Foresee, my sons, for fear of sudden smart.
Choose in thy wants, and he that friends thee then,
When richer grown, befriend him thou again.

Learn of the ant in summer to provide;
Drive with the bee the drone from out the hive;
Build like the swallow in the summertide;
Spare not too much (my son), but sparing thrive.
Be poor in folly, rich in all but sin;
So by thy death, thy glory shall begin.

Saladyne having thus set up the schedule and hanged about his father's hearse many passionate poems, that France might suppose him to be passing sorrowful, he clad himself and his brothers all in black, and in such sable suits discoursed his grief. But as the hyena when she mourns is then most guileful, so Saladyne, under the shew of grief shadowed a heart full of contented thoughts. The tiger, though he hide his claws, will at last discover his rapine; the lion's looks are not the maps of his meaning, nor a man's phys[iog]nomy is not the display of his secrets. Fire cannot be hid in straw, nor the nature of man so concealed but at last it will have his course. Nurture and art may do much, but that *Natura naturans* which by propagation is engrafted in the heart will be at last perforce predominant, according to the old verse:

Naturam expellas furca licet, tamen usque recurret.

So fares it with Saladyne, for, after a month's mourning was past, he fell to consideration of his father's testament, how he had bequeathed more to his younger brothers than to himself; that Rosader was his father's darling, but now under his tuition; that as yet they were not come to years, and he, being their guardian, might (if not defraud them of their due) yet make such havoc of their legacies and lands as they should be a great deal the lighter. Whereupon he began thus to meditate with himself.

Saladyne's meditation with himself

Saladyne, how art thou disquieted in thy thoughts and perplexed with a world of restless passions, having thy mind troubled with the tenor of thy father's testament and thy heart fired with the hope of present preferment? By the one, thou art counselled to content thee with thy fortunes; by the other persuaded to aspire to higher wealth. Riches (Saladyne) is a great royalty, and there is no sweeter physic than store. Avicen, like a fool, forgot in his aphorisms to say that gold was the most precious restorative, and that treasure was the most excellent medicine of the mind. O Saladyne, what, were thy father's precepts breathed into the wind? Hast thou so soon forgotten his principles? Did he not warn thee from coveting without honor and climbing without virtue? Did he not forbid thee to aim at any action that should not be honorable? And what will be more prejudicial to thy credit than the careless ruin of thy brothers' welfare? Why, shouldst not thou be the pillar of thy brothers' prosperity; and wilt thou become the subversion of their fortunes? Is there any sweeter thing than concord, or a more precious jewel than amity? Are you not sons of one father, scions of one tree, birds of one nest? And wilt thou become so unnatural as to rob them whom thou shouldst relieve? No, Saladyne, entreat them with favors and entertain them with love; so shalt thou have thy conscience clear and thy renown excellent.

Tush, what words are these, base fool; far unfit (if thou be wise) for thy humor. What though thy father at his death talked of many frivolous matters, as one that doteth for age and raved in his sickness; shall his words be axioms and his talk be so authentical that thou wilt (to observe

them) prejudice thyself? No, no, Saladyne, sick men's wills that are
parole, and have neither hand nor seal, are like the laws of a city written
in dust, which are broken with the blast of every wind. What, man, thy
father is dead, and he can neither help thy fortunes nor measure thy actions! Therefore bury his words with his carcass, and be wise for thyself.
What, 'tis not so old as true: *Non sapit, qui sibi non sapit!* Thy brother
is young; keep him now in awe, make him not checkmate with thyself;
for,

Nimia familiaritas contemptum parit.

Let him know little, so shall he not be able to execute much; suppress his
wits with a base estate, and, though he be a gentleman by nature, yet form
him anew and make him a peasant by nurture. So shalt thou keep him as
a slave, and reign thyself sole lord over all thy father's possessions. As for
Fernandyne thy middle brother, he is a scholar, and hath no mind but on
Aristotle. Let him read on Galen while thou riflest with gold, and pore on
his book till thou dost purchase lands. Wit is great wealth; if he have learning, it is enough; and so let all rest.

In this humor was Saladyne making his brother Rosader his footboy
for the space of two or three years, keeping him in such servile subjection
as if he had been the son of any country vassal. The young gentleman bare
all with patience, till on a day, walking in the garden by himself, he began
to consider how he was the son of John of Bordeaux, a knight renowned
for many victories and a gentleman famoused for his virtues; how, contrary to the testament of his father, he was not only kept from his land
and entreated as a servant, but smothered in such secret slavery as he might
not attain to any honorable actions. Ah, quoth he to himself (nature working these effectual passions), why should I, that am a gentleman born,
pass my time in such unnatural drudgery? Were it not better either in
Paris to become a scholar, or in the court a courtier, or in the field a soldier, than to live a footboy to my own brother? Nature hath lent me wit
to conceive, but my brother denied me art to contemplate. I have strength
to perform any honorable exploit, but no liberty to accomplish my virtuous endeavors. Those good parts that God hath bestowed upon me, the
envy of my brother doth smother in obscurity; the harder is my fortune,
and the more his frowardness.

With that, casting up his hand, he felt hair on his face, and, perceiving
his beard to bud, for choler he began to blush, and swore to himself he
would be no more subject to such slavery. As thus he was ruminating of
his melancholy passions, in came Saladyne with his men, and, seeing his

brother in a brown study and to forget his wonted reverence, thought to shake him out of his dumps thus. Sirrah (quoth he), is your heart on your halfpenny; or are you saying a dirge for your father's soul? What, is my dinner ready?

At this question, Rosader, turning his head askance and bending his brows as if anger there had plowed the furrows of her wrath, with his eyes full of fire he made this reply. Dost thou ask me (Saladyne) for thy cates? Ask some of thy churls who are fit for such an office. I am thy equal by nature, though not by birth; and, though thou hast more cards in the bunch, I have as many trumps in my hands as thyself. Let me ques- 10 tion with thee why thou hast felled my woods, spoiled my manor houses, and made havoc of such utensils as my father bequeathed unto me? I tell thee, Saladyne, either answer me as a brother or I will trouble thee as an enemy.

At this reply of Rosader's, Saladyne smiled as laughing at his presumption, and frowned as checking his folly. He therefore took him up thus shortly. What, sirrah! Well I see, early pricks the tree that will prove a thorn. Hath my familiar conversing with you made you coy, or my good looks drawn you to be thus contemptuous? I can quickly remedy such a fault, and I will bend the tree while it is a wand. In faith (sir boy), I have 20 a snaffle for such a headstrong colt. You, sirs, lay hold on him and bind him, and then I will give him a cooling card for his choler.

This made Rosader half mad, that, stepping to a great rake that stood in the garden, he laid such load upon his brother's men that he hurt some of them and made the rest of them run away. Saladyne, seeing Rosader so resolute, and with his resolution so valiant, thought his heels his best safety, and took him to a loft adjoining to the garden, whither Rosader pursued him hotly. Saladyne, afraid of his brother's fury, cried out to him thus. Rosader, be not so rash; I am thy brother and thine elder, and if I have done thee wrong, I'll make thee amends. Revenge not anger in blood, for 30 so shalt thou stain the virtue of old Sir John of Bordeaux. Say wherein thou art discontent, and thou shalt be satisfied. Brothers' frowns ought not to be periods of wrath. What, man, look not so sourly! I know we shall be friends, and better friends than we have been. For, *Amantium ira amoris redintegratio est.*

These words appeased the choler of Rosader (for he was of a mild and courteous nature), so that he laid down his weapons, and, upon the faith of a gentleman, assured his brother he would offer him no prejudice. Whereupon Saladyne came down, and, after a little parley, they embraced each other and became friends; and Saladyne promising Rosader the 40 restitution of all his lands, and what favor else (quoth he) any ways my

ability or the nature of a brother may perform. Upon these sugared rec-
onciliations, they went into the house arm in arm together, to the great
content of all the old servants of Sir John of Bordeaux.

Thus continued the pad hidden in the straw, till it chanced that Torismond, King of France, had appointed for his pleasure a day of wrestling
and of tournament to busy his commons' heads, lest, being idle, their
thoughts should run upon more serious matters, and call to remembrance
their old banished king. A champion there was to stand against all comers,
a Norman, a man of tall stature and of great strength, so valiant that in
10 many such conflicts he always bare away the victory, not only overthrowing them which he encountered, but often with the weight of his body
killing them outright. Saladyne hearing of this, thinking now not to let
the ball fall to the ground but to take opportunity by the forehead, first by
secret means convented with the Norman, and procured him with rich
rewards to swear that if Rosader came within his claws he should never
more return to quarrel with Saladyne for his possessions. The Norman,
desirous of pelf, as (*Quis nisi mentis inops oblatum respuit aurum*), taking
great gifts for little gods, took the crowns of Saladyne to perform the
stratagem.

20   Having thus the champion tied to his villainous determination by oath,
he prosecuted the intent of his purpose thus. He went to young Rosader
(who, in all his thoughts, reached at honor, and gazed no lower than
virtue commanded), and began to tell him of this tournament and wrestling, how the king should be there, and all the chief peers of France,
with all the beautiful damosels of the country. Now, brother (quoth he),
for the honor of Sir John of Bordeaux, our renowned father, to famous
that house that never hath been found without men approved in chivalry,
shew thy resolution to be peremptory. For myself, thou knowest, though
I am eldest by birth, yet never having attempted any deeds of arms, I am
30 youngest to perform any martial exploits, knowing better how to survey
my lands than to charge my lance. My brother Fernandyne, he is at Paris
poring on a few papers, having more insight into sophistry and principles
of philosophy than any warlike endeavors. But thou, Rosader, the youngest in years but the eldest in valor, art a man of strength, and darest do
what honor allows thee. Take thou my father's lance, his sword, and his
horse, and hie thee to the tournament; and either there valiantly crack a
spear, or try with the Norman for the palm of activity.

The words of Saladyne were but spurs to a free horse; for he had
scarce uttered them ere Rosader took him in his arms, taking his proffer so
40 kindly that he promised in what he might to requite his courtesy.

The next morrow was the day of the tournament, and Rosader was so
desirous to shew his heroical thoughts that he passed the night with little

sleep; but, as soon as Phoebus had vailed the curtain of the night and made Aurora blush with giving her the *bezo les labres* in her silver couch, he gat him up, and, taking his leave of his brother, mounted himself towards the place appointed, thinking every mile ten leagues till he came there.

But leaving him so desirous of the journey, to Torismond, the King of France, who, having by force banished Gerismond, their lawful king, that lived as an outlaw in the Forest of Arden, sought now by all means to keep the French busied with all sports that might breed their content. Amongst the rest, he had appointed this solemn tournament; whereunto he in most solemn manner resorted, accompanied with the twelve peers 10 of France, who, rather for fear than love, graced him with the shew of their dutiful favors. To feed their eyes, and to make the beholders pleased with the sight of most rare and glistering objects, he had appointed his own daughter Alinda to be there, and the fair Rosalynde, daughter unto Gerismond, with all the beautiful damosels that were famous for their features in all France.

Thus in that place did love and war triumph in a sympathy; for such as were martial might use their lance to be renowned for the excellency of their chivalry; and such as were amorous might glut themselves with gazing on the beauties of most heavenly creatures. As every man's eye 20 had his several survey, and fancy was partial in their looks, yet all in general applauded the admirable riches that nature bestowed on the face of Rosalynde; for upon her cheeks there seemed a battle between the Graces, who should bestow most favors to make her excellent. The blush that gloried Luna when she kissed the shepherd of the hills of Latmos was not tainted with such a pleasant dye as the vermilion flourished on the silver hue of Rosalynde's countenance. Her eyes were like those lamps that make the wealthy covert of the heavens more gorgeous, sparkling favor and disdain; courteous and yet coy, as if in them Venus had placed all her amorets, and Diana all her chastity. The trammels of her hair, folded in 30 a caul of gold, so far surpassed the burnished glister of the metal as the sun doth the meanest star in brightness. The tresses that folds in the brows of Apollo were not half so rich to the sight; for in her hairs it seemed love had laid herself in ambush, to entrap the proudest eye that durst gaze upon their excellence. What should I need to decipher her particular beauties when, by the censure of all, she was the paragon of all earthly perfection?

This Rosalynde sat, I say, with Alinda as a beholder of these sports, and made the cavaliers crack their lances with more courage. Many deeds of knighthood that day were performed, and many prizes were given ac- 40 cording to their several deserts. At last, when the tournament ceased, the wrestling began; and the Norman presented himself as a challenger

against all comers. But he looked like Hercules when he advanced himself against Acheloüs; so that the fury of his countenance amazed all that durst attempt to encounter with him in any deed of activity, till at last a lusty franklin of the country came with two tall men that were his sons, of good lineaments and comely personage. The eldest of these, doing obeisance to the king, entered the list, and presented himself to the Norman, who straight coped with him, and, as a man that would triumph in the glory of his strength, roused himself with such fury that not only he gave him the fall but killed him with the weight of his corpulent personage.
10 Which the younger brother seeing, leapt presently into the place and, thirsty after the revenge, assailed the Norman with such valor that, at the first encounter, he brought him to his knees. Which repulsed so the Norman that, recovering himself, fear of disgrace doubling his strength, he stepped so earnestly to the young franklin that, taking him up in his arms, he threw him against the ground so violently that he broke his neck, and so ended his days with his brother. At this unlooked-for massacre, the people murmured and were all in a deep passion of pity; but the franklin, father unto these, never changed his countenance; but, as a man of a courageous resolution, took up the bodies of his sons without shew of out-
20 ward discontent.

All this while stood Rosader and saw this tragedy; who, noting the undoubted virtue of the franklin's mind, alighted off from his horse and presently sate down on the grass, and commanded his boy to pull off his boots, making him ready to try the strength of this champion. Being furnished as he would, he clapped the franklin on the shoulder and said thus: Bold yeoman, whose sons have ended the term of their years with honor, for that I see thou scornest fortune with patience, and thwartest the injury of fate with content, in brooking the death of thy sons; stand a while, and either see me make a third in their tragedy, or else revenge
30 their fall with an honorable triumph.

The franklin, seeing so goodly a gentleman to give him such courteous comfort, gave him hearty thanks, with promise to pray for his happy success. With that, Rosader vailed bonnet to the king and lightly leapt within the lists, where, noting more the company than the combatant, he cast his eye upon the troop of ladies that glistered there like the stars of heaven. But at last love, willing to make him as amorous as he was valiant, presented him with the sight of Rosalynde, whose admirable beauty so inveigled the eye of Rosader that, forgetting himself, he stood and fed his looks on the favor of Rosalynde's face, which she perceiving, blushed. Which was such
40 a doubling of her beauteous excellency that the bashful red of Aurora, at the sight of unacquainted Phaëton, was not half so glorious.

The Norman, seeing this young gentleman fettered in the looks of the ladies, drave him out of his *memento* with a shake by the shoulder. Rosader, looking back with an angry frown, as if he had been wakened from some pleasant dream, discovered to all by the fury of his countenance that he was a man of some high thoughts. But when they all noted his youth and the sweetness of his visage, with a general applause of favors, they grieved that so goodly a young man should venture in so base an action; but seeing it were to his dishonor to hinder him from his enterprise, they wished him to be graced with the palm of victory. After Rosader was thus called out of his *memento* by the Norman, he roughly clapped him with so fierce an encounter that they both fell on the ground, and with the violence of the fall were forced to breathe. In which space the Norman called to mind by all tokens that this was he whom Saladyne had appointed him to kill; which conjecture made him stretch every limb and try every sinew, that, working his death, he might recover the gold which so bountifully was promised him. On the contrary part, Rosader, while he breathed, was not idle, but still cast his eye upon Rosalynde; who, to encourage him with a favor, lent him such an amorous look as might have made the most coward desperate. Which glance of Rosalynde so stirred the passionate desires of Rosader that, turning to the Norman, he ran upon him and braved him with a strong encounter; the Norman received him as valiantly, that there was a sore combat, hard to judge on whose side fortune would be prodigal. At last Rosader, calling to mind the beauty of his new mistress, the fame of his father's honors, and the disgrace that should fall to his house by his misfortune, roused himself and threw the Norman against the ground, falling upon his chest with so willing a weight that the Norman yielded nature her due, and Rosader the victory. The death of this champion, as it highly contented the franklin, as a man satisfied with revenge, so it drew the king and all the peers into a great admiration that so young years and so beautiful a personage should contain such martial excellence. But when they knew him to be the youngest son of Sir John of Bordeaux, the king rose from his seat and embraced him, and the peers entreated him with all favorable courtesy, commending both his valor and his virtues, wishing him to go forward in such haughty deeds that he might attain to the glory of his father's honorable fortunes.

As the king and lords graced him with embracing, so the ladies favored him with their looks; especially Rosalynde, whom the beauty and valor of Rosader had already touched. But she accounted love a toy, and fancy a momentary passion, that, as it was taken in with a gaze, might be shaken off with a wink; and therefore feared not to dally in the flame, and, to make Rosader know she affected him, took from her neck a jewel and sent it by a page to the young gentleman. The prize that Venus gave to Paris was not half so pleasing to the Trojan as this gem was to Rosader;

for, if fortune had sworn to make himself sole monarch of the world, he would rather have refused such dignity than have lost the jewel sent him by Rosalynde. To return her with the like he was unfurnished; and yet, that he might more than in his looks discover his affection, he stepped into a tent and, taking pen and paper, writ this fancy:

Two suns at once from one fair heaven there shined,
Ten branches from two boughs tipped all with roses,
Pure locks more golden than is gold refined,
Two pearled rows that Nature's pride encloses;
10   Two mounts fair marble-white, down-soft and dainty,
A snow-dyed orb, where love increased by pleasure
Full woeful makes my heart and body fainty.
Her fair (my woe) exceeds all thought and measure.

In lines confused my luckless harm appeareth,
Whom sorrow clouds, whom pleasant smiling cleareth.

This sonnet he sent to Rosalynde; which when she read, she blushed, but with a sweet content in that she perceived love had allotted her so amorous a servant. Leaving her to her new-entertained fancies, again to 20 Rosader; who, triumphing in the glory of this conquest, accompanied with a troop of young gentlemen that were desirous to be his familiars, went home to his brother Saladyne's, who was walking before the gates to hear what success his brother Rosader should have, assuring himself of his death and devising how, with dissimuled sorrow, to celebrate his funerals. As he was in this thought, he cast up his eye and saw where Rosader returned with the garland on his head, as having won the prize, accompanied with a crew of boon companions. Grieved at this, he stepped in and shut the gate. Rosader seeing this, and not looking for such unkind entertainment, blushed at the disgrace, and yet smothering his grief with 30 a smile, he turned to the gentlemen and desired them to hold his brother excused, for he did not this upon any malicious intent or niggardize, but, being brought up in the country, he absented himself as not finding his nature fit for such youthful company.

Thus he sought to shadow abuses proffered him by his brother; but in vain, for he could by no means be suffered to enter. Whereupon he ran his foot against the door and brake it open, drawing his sword and entering boldly into the hall, where he found none (for all were fled) but one Adam Spencer, an Englishman who had been an old and trusty serv-ant to Sir John of Bordeaux. He, for the love he bare to his deceased 40 master, favored the part of Rosader, and gave him and his such enter-tainment as he could. Rosader gave him thanks, and looking about, seeing the hall empty, said: Gentlemen, you are welcome; frolic and be merry;

you shall be sure to have wine enough, whatsoever your fare be. I tell
you, cavaliers, my brother hath in his house five tun of wine, and, as long
as that lasteth, I beshrew him that spares his liquor. With that, he burst
open the buttery door and, with the help of Adam Spencer, covered the
tables and set down whatsoever he could find in the house. But what they
wanted in meat, Rosader supplied with drink. Yet had they royal cheer,
and withal such hearty welcome as would have made the coarsest meats
seem delicates.

After they had feasted and frolicked it twice or thrice with an upsy
friese, they all took their leaves of Rosader and departed. As soon as they 10
were gone, Rosader, growing impatient of the abuse, drew his sword and
swore to be revenged on the discourteous Saladyne; yet by the means of
Adam Spencer, who sought to continue friendship and amity betwixt the
brethren, and through the flattering submission of Saladyne, they were
once again reconciled and put up all forepast injuries with a peaceable
agreement, living together for a good space in such brotherly love as did
not only rejoice the servants but made all the gentlemen and bordering
neighbors glad of such friendly concord. Saladyne, hiding fire in the
straw and concealing a poisoned hate in a peaceable countenance, yet
deferring the intent of his wrath till fitter opportunity, he shewed himself 20
a great favorer of his brother's virtuous endeavors. Where, leaving them
in this happy league, let us return to Rosalynde.

Rosalynde, returning home from the triumph, after she waxed solitary,
love presented her with the *idea* of Rosader's perfection and, taking her
at discovert, struck her so deep as she felt herself grow passing passionate.
She began to call to mind the comeliness of his person, the honor of his
parents, and the virtues that, excelling both, made him so gracious in the
eyes of every one. Sucking in thus the honey of love, by imprinting in her
thoughts his rare qualities, she began to surfeit with the contemplation of
his virtuous conditions; but when she called to remembrance her present 30
estate and the hardness of her fortunes, desire began to shrink and fancy
to vail bonnet, that between a chaos of confused thoughts she began to
debate with herself in this manner.

Rosalynde's passion

Infortunate Rosalynde, whose misfortunes are more than thy years,
and whose passions are greater than thy patience. The blossoms of thy
youth are mixed with the frosts of envy; and the hope of thy ensuing fruits
perish in the bud. Thy father is by Torismond banished from the crown,
and thou, the unhappy daughter of a king, detained captive, living as dis- 40
quieted in thy thoughts as thy father discontented in his exile. Ah, Rosalynde, what cares wait upon a crown! What griefs are incident to dignity!

What sorrows haunt royal palaces! The greatest seas have the sorest storms, the highest birth subject to the most bale, and of all trees the cedars soonest shake with the wind; small currents are ever calm, low valleys not scorched in any lightnings, nor base men tied to any baleful prejudice. Fortune flies, and if she touch poverty, it is with her heel, rather disdaining their want with a frown than envying their wealth with disparagement. O Rosalynde, hadst thou been born low, thou hadst not fallen so high; and yet, being great of blood, thine honor is more if thou brookest misfortune with patience. Suppose I contrary fortune with content, yet
10 Fates, unwilling to have me any ways happy, have forced love to set my thoughts on fire with fancy.

Love, Rosalynde? Becometh it women in distress to think on love? Tush, desire hath no respect of persons! Cupid is blind and shooteth at random, as soon hitting a rag as a robe, and piercing as soon the bosom of a captive as the breast of a libertine. Thou speakest it, poor Rosalynde, by experience; for, being every way distressed, surcharged with cares, and overgrown with sorrows, yet, amidst the heap of all mishaps, love hath lodged in thy heart the perfection of young Rosader, a man every way absolute as well for his inward life as for his outward lineaments,
20 able to content the eye with beauty and the ear with the report of his virtue. But consider, Rosalynde, his fortunes and thy present estate; thou art poor and without patrimony and yet the daughter of a prince; he a younger brother and void of such possessions as either might maintain thy dignities or revenge thy father's injuries. And hast thou not learned this of other ladies, that lovers cannot live by looks; that women's ears are sooner content with a dram of *give me* than a pound of *hear me*; that gold is sweeter than eloquence; that love is a fire and wealth is the fuel; that Venus' coffers should be ever full. Then, Rosalynde, seeing Rosader is poor, think him less beautiful because he is in want, and account his vir-
30 tues but qualities of course, for that he is not endued with wealth. Doth not Horace tell thee what method is to be used in love,

Quaerenda pecunia primum, post nummos virtus.

Tush, Rosalynde, be not over rash; leap not before thou look; either love such a one as may with his lands purchase thy liberty or else love not at all. Choose not a fair face with an empty purse, but say as most women use to say, *Si nihil attuleris, ibis Homere foras.*

Why, Rosalynde, can such base thoughts harbor in such high beauties? Can the degree of a princess, the daughter of Gerismond, harbor such
40 servile conceits as to prize gold more than honor, or to measure a gentleman by his wealth, not by his virtues. No, Rosalynde, blush at thy base resolution and say, if thou lovest, either Rosader or none. And why? Be-

cause Rosader is both beautiful and virtuous. Smiling to herself to think
of her new-entertained passions, taking up her lute that lay by her, she
warbled out this ditty.

Rosalynde's Madrigal

Love in my bosom like a bee
  doth suck his sweet;
Now with his wings, he plays with me,
  now with his feet.
Within mine eyes he makes his nest,
His bed amidst my tender breast,   10
My kisses are his daily feast;
And yet he robs me of my rest.
  Ah, wanton, will ye?

And if I sleep, then percheth he
  with pretty flight,
And makes his pillow of my knee
  the livelong night.
Strike I my lute, he tunes the string,
He music plays if so I sing,
He lends me every lovely thing;   20
Yet cruel he my heart doth sting.
  Whist, wanton, still ye!

Else I with roses every day
  will whip you hence;
And bind you when you long to play,
  for your offense.
I'll shut my eyes to keep you in,
I'll make you fast it for your sin,
I'll count your power not worth a pin;
Alas, what hereby shall I win,   30
  If he gainsay me?

What if I beat the wanton boy
  with many a rod?
He will repay me with annoy,
  because a god.
Then sit thou safely on my knee,
And let thy bower my bosom be;
Lurk in mine eyes, I like of thee.
O Cupid, so thou pity me,
  Spare not, but play thee.   40

Scarce had Rosalynde ended her madrigal before Torismond came in
with his daughter Alinda and many of the peers of France, who were

enamored at her beauty. Which Torismond perceiving, fearing lest her
perfection might be the beginning of his prejudice, and the hope of his
fruit end in the beginning of her blossoms, he thought to banish her from
the court; for, quoth he to himself, her face is so full of favor that it pleads
pity in the eye of every man; her beauty is so heavenly and divine that
she will prove to me as Helen did to Priam. Some one of the peers will
aim at her love, end the marriage, and then in his wife's right attempt
the kingdom. To prevent, therefore, *had I wist* in all these actions, she
tarries not about the court, but shall (as an exile) either wander to her
10 father or else seek other fortunes.

   In this humor, with a stern countenance full of wrath, he breathed out
this censure unto her before the peers, that charged her that that night she
were not seen about the court. For (quoth he) I have heard of thy aspiring
speeches and intended treasons. This doom was strange unto Rosalynde,
and presently, covered with the shield of her innocence, she boldly brake
out in reverent terms to have cleared herself. But Torismond would admit
of no reason, nor durst his lords plead for Rosalynde, although her beauty
had made some of them passionate, seeing the figure of wrath portrayed
in his brow. Standing thus all mute, and Rosalynde amazed, Alinda, who
20 loved her more than herself, with grief in heart and tears in her eyes, falling down on her knees, began to entreat her father thus.

                    *   *   *   *   *

   Cheerily, woman, as we have been bedfellows in royalty, we will be
fellowmates in poverty. I will ever be thy Alinda and thou shalt ever rest
to me Rosalynde. So shall the world canonize our friendship, and speak
of Rosalynde and Alinda as they did of Pylades and Orestes. And if ever
fortune smile and we return to our former honor, then, folding ourselves
in the sweet of our friendship, we shall merrily say (calling to mind our
30 forepast miseries):

                    Olim haec meminisse juvabit.

   At this Rosalynde began to comfort her; and, after she had wept a few
kind tears in the bosom of her Alinda, she gave her hearty thanks; and
then they sat them down to consult how they should travel. Alinda
grieved at nothing but that they might have no man in their company,
saying it would be their greatest prejudice in that two women went
wandering without either guide or attendant. Tush (quoth Rosalynde),
art thou a woman and hast not a sudden shift to prevent a misfortune? I
40 (thou seest) am of a tall stature and would very well become the person
and apparel of a page. Thou shalt be my mistress, and I will play the man

so properly that (trust me) in what company soever I come I will not be discovered. I will buy me a suit, and have my rapier very handsomely at my side, and if any knave offer wrong, your page will shew him the point of his weapon.

At this Alinda smiled, and upon this they agreed, and presently gathered up all their jewels, which they trussed up in a casket, and Rosalynde in all haste provided her of robes, and Alinda (from her royal weeds) put herself in more homely attire. Thus fitted to the purpose, away go these two friends, having now changed their names, Alinda being called Aliena, and Rosalynde, Ganimede. They traveled among the vineyards and by by 10 many by-ways; at last got to the forest side, where they traveled by the space of two or three days without seeing any creature, being often in danger of wild beasts and pained with many passionate sorrows. Now the black ox began to tread on their feet, and Alinda thought of her wonted royalty; but when she cast her eyes on her Rosalynde, she thought every danger a step to honor.

Passing thus on along, about midday they came to a fountain, compassed with a grove of cypress trees, so cunningly and curiously planted as if some goddess had entreated nature in that place to make her an arbor. By this fountain sat Aliena and her Ganimede, and forth they 20 pulled such victuals as they had, and fed as merrily as if they had been in Paris with all the king's delicates, Aliena only grieving that they could not so much as meet with a shepherd to discourse them the way to some place where they might make their abode. At last Ganimede, casting up his eye, espied where on a tree was engraven certain verses; which as soon as he espied, he cried out: Be of good cheer, mistress, I spy the figures of men; for here in these trees be engraven certain verses of shepherds, or some other swains that inhabit hereabout. With that Aliena start up joyful to hear these news, and looked, where they found carved in the bark of a pine tree this passion. 30

Montanus' passion

Hadst thou been born whereas perpetual cold
Makes Tanaïs hard, and mountains silver old;
Had I complained unto a marble stone,
Or to the floods bewrayed my bitter moan,
   I then could bear the burden of my grief.
But even the pride of countries at thy birth,
Whilst heavens did smile, did new array the earth
              with flowers chief.
Yet thou, the flower of beauty, blessed born, 40
Hast pretty looks, but all attired in scorn.

Had I the power to weep sweet Mirrha's tears,
Or by my plaints to pierce repining ears;
Hadst thou the heart to smile at my complaint,
To scorn the woes that doth my heart attaint,
    I then could bear the burden of my grief.
But not my tears, but truth with thee prevails,
And seeming sour my sorrows thee assails;
                                            yet small relief.
For if thou wilt, thou art of marble hard;
And if thou please, my suit shall soon be heard.

No doubt (quoth Aliena) this poesy is the passion of some perplexed
shepherd that, being enamored of some fair and beautiful shepherdess,
suffered some sharp repulse, and therefore complained of the cruelty of
his mistress.

You may see (quoth Ganimede) what mad cattle you women be,
whose hearts sometimes are made of adamant, that will touch with no
impression, and sometime of wax, that is fit for every form. They delight
to be courted, and then they glory to seem coy, and, when they are most
desired, then they freeze with disdain; and this fault is so common to the
sex that you see it painted out in the shepherd's passions, who found his
mistress as froward as he was enamored.

And I pray you (quoth Aliena) if your robes were off, what mettle are
you made of that you are so satirical against women? Is it not a foul bird
defiles the own nest? Beware (Ganimede) that Rosader hear you not;
if he do, perchance you will make him leap so far from love that he will
anger every vein in your heart.

Thus (quoth Ganimede) I keep decorum; I speak now as I am Aliena's
page, not as I am Gerismond's daughter; for, put me but into a petticoat
and I will stand in defiance to the uttermost that women are courteous,
constant, virtuous, and what not.

Stay there (quoth Aliena), and no more words; for yonder be characters graven upon the bark of a beech tree.

Let us see (quoth Ganimede). And with that they read a fancy written
to this effect.

First shall the heavens want starry light,
The seas be robbèd of their waves,
The day want sun, and sun want bright,
The night want shade, the dead men graves;
    The April, flowers and leaf and tree,
    Before I false my faith to thee.

First shall the tops of highest hills
By humble plains be overpried,
And poets scorn the muses' quills,
And fish forsake the water glide;
    And Iris lose her colored weed,
    Before I fail thee at thy need.

First direful hate shall turn to peace,
And love relent in deep disdain,
And death his fatal stroke shall cease,
And envy pity every pain,
    And pleasure mourn, and sorrow smile,   10
    Before I talk of any guile.

First time shall stay his stayless race,
And winter bless his brows with corn,
And snow bemoisten July's face,
And winter spring, and summer mourn,
    Before my pen, by help of fame,
    Cease to recite thy sacred name.
                 Montanus.

No doubt (quoth Ganimede) this protestation grew from one full of 20 passions.

I am of that mind too (quoth Aliena); but see, I pray, when poor women seek to keep themselves chaste, how men woo them with many feigned promises, alluring with sweet words as the sirens, and after proving as trothless as Æneas.

      *   *   *   *   *

. . . As thus they chatted, the sun being ready to set and they not having folded their sheep, Coridon requested she would sit there with her 30 page till Montanus and he lodged their sheep for that night. You shall go, quoth Aliena, but first I will entreat Montanus to sing some amorous sonnet that he made when he hath been deeply passionate.

That I will, quoth Montanus. And with that he began thus.

Montanus' Sonnet

Phoebe sate,
Sweet she sate,
    Sweet sate Phoebe when I saw her;
White her brow,
Coy her eye;
    Brow and eye how much you please me!   40

Words I spent,
Sighs I sent;
    Sighs and words could never draw her.
O my love,
Thou art lost;
    Since no sight could ever ease thee.

Phoebe sat
By a fount;
    Sitting by a fount I spied her;
Sweet her touch,
Rare her voice;
    Touch and voice what may distain you?
As she sung,
I did sigh,
    And by sighs whilst that I tried her,
O mine eyes,
You did lose
    Her first sight whose want did pain you.

Phoebe's flocks
White as wool,
    Yet were Phoebe's looks more whiter.
Phoebe's eyes
Dovelike mild;
    Dovelike eyes, both mild and cruel,
Montan swears
In your lamps
    He will die for to delight her.
Phoebe, yield,
Or I die;
    Shall true hearts be fancy's fuel?

Montanus had no sooner ended his sonnet but Coridon, with a low
curtsey, rose up and went with his fellow and shut their sheep in the
folds; and, after returning to Aliena and Ganimede, conducted them
home weary to his poor cottage. . . .

The next morn they lay long in bed, as wearied with the toil of unac-
customed travel; but, as soon as they got up, Aliena resolved there to set
up their rest, and, by the help of Coridon, swapped a bargain with his
landlord, and so became mistress of the farm and the flock, herself putting
on the attire of a shepherdess and Ganimede of a young swain, every day
leading forth her flocks with such delight that she held her exile happy,
and thought no content to the bliss of a country cottage. Leaving her thus
famous amongst the shepherds of Arden, again to Saladyne.

When Saladyne had a long while concealed a secret resolution of revenge, and could no longer hide fire in the flax nor oil in the flame (for envy is like lightning, that will appear in the darkest fog), it chanced in a morning very early he called up certain of his servants and went with them to the chamber of Rosader. Which being open, he entered with his crew, and surprised his brother when he was asleep and bound him in fetters, and, in the midst of his hall, chained him to a post. Rosader, amazed at this strange chance, began to reason with his brother about the cause of this sudden extremity, wherein he had wronged? and what fault he had committed worthy so sharp a penance? Saladyne answered him only with a look of disdain and went his way, leaving poor Rosader in a deep perplexity. Who (thus abused) fell into sundry passions, but no means of relief could be had; whereupon (for anger) he grew into a discontented melancholy. In which humor he continued two or three days without meat; insomuch that, seeing his brother would give him no food, he fell into despair of his life. Which Adam Spencer the old servant of Sir John of Bordeaux seeing, touched with the duty and love he ought to his old master, felt a remorse in his conscience of his son's mishap; and therefore, although Saladyne hath given a general charge to his servants that none of them, upon pain of death, should give either meat or drink to Rosader, yet Adam Spencer in the night rose secretly and brought him such victuals as he could provide, and unlocked him and set him at liberty.

After Rosader had well feasted himself and felt he was loose, straight his thoughts aimed at revenge, and now (all being asleep) he would have quit Saladyne with the method of his own mischief. But Adam Spencer did persuade him to the contrary with these reasons: Sir, quoth he, be content, for this night go again into your old fetters, so shall you try the faith of friends and save the life of an old servant. Tomorrow hath your brother invited all your kindred and allies to a solemn breakfast, only to see you, telling them all that you are mad, and fain to be tied to a post. As soon as they come, complain to them of the abuse proffered you by Saladyne. If they redress you, why so. But if they pass over your plaints *sicco pede*, and hold with the violence of your brother before your innocence, then thus I will leave you unlocked, that you may break out at your pleasure, and at the end of the hall shall you see stand a couple of good poleaxes, one for you and another for me. When I give you a wink, shake off your chains, and let us play the men and make havoc amongst them, drive them out of the house and maintain possession by force of arms till the king hath made a redress of your abuses.

These words of Adam Spencer so persuaded Rosader that he went to the place of his punishment, and stood there while the next morning. About the time appointed came all the guests bidden by Saladyne, whom

he entreated with courteous and curious entertainment as they all perceived their welcome to be great. The tables in the hall where Rosader
was tied were covered, and Saladyne, bringing in his guests together,
shewed them where his brother was bound and was enchained as a man
lunatic. Rosader made reply and, with some invectives, made complaints
of the wrongs proffered him by Saladyne, desiring they would in pity seek
some means for his relief. But in vain. They had stopped their ears with
Ulysses, that, were his words never so forcible, he breathed only his passions into the wind. They, careless, sate down with Saladyne to dinner,
10 being very frolic and pleasant, washing their heads well with wine. At last,
when the fume of the grape had entered pell-mell into their brains, they
began in satirical speeches to rail against Rosader; which Adam Spencer
no longer brooking, gave the sign, and Rosader, shaking off his chains,
got a poleax in his hand and flew amongst them with such violence and
fury that he hurt many, slew some, and drave his brother and all the rest
quite out of the house.

Seeing the coast clear, he shut the doors, and, being sore anhungered
and seeing such good victuals, he sate him down with Adam Spencer and
such good fellows as he knew were honest men, and there feasted them-
20 selves with such provision as Saladyne had prepared for his friends. After
they had taken their repast, Rosader rampired up the house, lest upon a
sudden his brother should raise some crew of his tenants and surprise them
unawares. But Saladyne took a contrary course and went to the sheriff of
the shire and made complaint of Rosader, who, giving credit to Saladyne,
in a determined resolution to revenge the gentleman's wrongs, took with
him five and twenty tall men, and made a vow either to break into the
house and take Rosader or else to coop him in till he made him yield by
famine. In this determination, gathering a crew together, he went forward to set Saladyne in his former estate.

30 News of this was brought unto Rosader, who, smiling at the cowardice
of his brother, brooked all the injuries of fortune with patience, expecting the coming of the sheriff. As he walked upon the battlements of the
house, he descried where Saladyne and he drew near with a troop of lusty
gallants. At this he smiled and called up Adam Spencer, and shewed him
the envious treachery of his brother and the folly of the sheriff to be so
credulous. Now Adam, quoth he, what shall I do? It rests for me either to
yield up the house to my brother and seek a reconcilement, or else issue
out and break through the company with courage, for cooped in like a
coward I will not be. If I submit (ah, Adam), I dishonor myself, and that
40 is worse than death; for by such open disgraces the fame of men grows
odious. If I issue out amongst them, fortune may favor me, and I may

escape with life. But suppose the worst. If I be slain, then my death shall be honorable to me, and so unequal a revenge infamous to Saladyne.

Why then, master, forward and fear not! Out amongst them! They be but faint-hearted losels. And for Adam Spencer, if he die not at your foot, say he is a dastard.

These words cheered up so the heart of young Rosader that he thought himself sufficient for them all, and therefore prepared weapons for him and Adam Spencer, and were ready to entertain the sheriff. For no sooner came Saladyne and he to the gates but Rosader, unlooked for, leapt out and assailed them, wounded many of them, and caused the rest to give 10 back, so that Adam and he broke through the press in despite of them all, and took their way towards the forest of Arden.

This repulse so set the sheriff's heart on fire to revenge that he straight raised all the country and made hue and cry after them. But Rosader and Adam, knowing full well the secret ways that led through the vineyards, stole away privily through the province of Bordeaux, and escaped safe to the forest of Arden. Being come thither, they were glad they had so good a harbor; but fortune (who is like the chameleon), variable with every object, and constant in nothing but inconstancy, thought to make them mirrors of her mutability, and therefore still crossed them thus contrarily. 20 Thinking still to pass on by the byways to get to Lyons, they chanced on a path that led into the thick of the forest, where they wandered five or six days without meat, that they were almost famished, finding neither shepherd nor cottage to relieve them. And hunger growing on so extreme, Adam Spencer (being old) began to faint, and, sitting him down on a hill and looking about him, espied where Rosader lay as feeble and as ill perplexed. Which sight made him shed tears, and to fall into these bitter terms:

Adam Spencer's speech

30

Oh, how the life of man may well be compared to the state of the ocean seas, that for every calm hath a thousand storms; resembling the rose tree that, for a few flowers, hath a multitude of sharp prickles; all our pleasures end in pain, and our highest delights are crossed with deepest discontents. The joys of man, as they are few, so are they momentary, scarce ripe before they are rotten; and withering in the blossom, either parched with the heat of envy or fortune. Fortune, O inconstant friend, that in all thy deeds art froward and fickle, delighting, in the poverty of the lowest, and the overthrow of the highest, to decipher thy inconstancy. Thou standest upon a globe, and thy wings are plumed with time's feathers, that thou 40 mayest ever be restless; thou art double-faced like Janus, carrying frowns in the one to threaten, and smiles in the other to betray; thou profferest an eel and performest a scorpion; and where thy greatest favors be, there is the fear of the extremest misfortunes, so variable are all thy actions.

But why, Adam, dost thou exclaim against Fortune? She laughs at the plaints of the distressed; and there is nothing more pleasing unto her than to hear fools boast in her fading allurements, or sorrowful men to discover the sour of their passions. Glut her not, Adam, then with content, but thwart her with brooking all mishaps with patience. For there is no greater check to the pride of Fortune than, with a resolute courage, to
10 pass over her crosses without care. Thou art old, Adam, and thy hairs wax white; the palm tree is already full of blooms, and in the furrows of thy face appears the calendars of death! Wert thou blessed by Fortune, thy years could not be many, nor the date of thy life long. Then, sith nature must have her due, what is it for thee to resign her debt a little before the day? Ah, it is not this which grieveth me, nor do I care what mishaps fortune can wage against me, but the sight of Rosader, that galleth unto the quick. When I remember the worships of his house, the honor of his fathers, and the virtues of himself, then do I say that fortune and fates are most injurious to censure so hard extremes against a youth
20 of so great hope. O Rosader, thou art in the flower of thine age and in the pride of thy years, buxom and full of May. Nature hath prodigally enriched thee with her favors, and virtue made thee the mirror of her excellence. And now, through the decree of the unjust stars, to have all these good parts nipped in the blade and blemished by the inconstancy of fortune. Ah, Rosader! Could I help thee, my grief were the less, and happy should my death be if it might be the beginning of thy relief; but seeing we perish both in one extreme, it is a double sorrow. What shall I do? Prevent the sight of his further misfortune with a present despatch of mine own life? Ah, despair is a merciless sin!

30

As he was ready to go forward in his passion, he looked earnestly on Rosader, and, seeing him change color, he rise up and went to him and, holding his temples, said: What cheer, master? Though all fail, let not the heart faint; the courage of a man is shewed in the resolution of his death.

At these words, Rosader lifted up his eye and, looking on Adam Spencer, began to weep. Ah, Adam, quoth he, I sorrow not to die, but I grieve at the manner of my death. Might I with my lance encounter the enemy, and so die in the field, it were honor, and content; might I
40 (Adam) combat with some wild beast and perish as his prey, I were satisfied. But to die with hunger! O Adam, it is the extremest of all extremes.

Master (quoth he), you see we are both in one predicament, and long I cannot live without meat; seeing, therefore, we can find no food, let the death of the one preserve the life of the other. I am old and overworn with age; you are young and are the hope of many honors. Let me then die. I will presently cut my veins, and, master, with the warm blood relieve your fainting spirits. Suck on that till I end, and you be comforted.

With that Adam Spencer was ready to pull out his knife when Rosader, full of courage (though very faint) rose up, and wished Adam Spencer to sit there till his return. For my mind gives me, quoth he, I shall bring thee meat. With that, like a madman, he rose up and ranged up and 10 down the woods, seeking to encounter some wild beast with his rapier, that either he might carry his friend Adam food, or else pledge his life in pawn for his loyalty.

It chanced that day that Gerismond, the lawful king of France, banished by Torismond, who, with a lusty crew of outlaws, lived in that forest, that day in honor of his birth made a feast to all his bold yeomen, and frolicked it with store of wine and venison, sitting all at a long table under the shadow of lemon trees. To that place by chance Fortune conducted Rosader, who, seeing such a crew of brave men having store of that for want of which he and Adam perished, he stepped boldly to the board's end and saluted the company thus.

Whatsoever thou be that art master of these lusty squires, I salute thee as graciously as a man in extreme distress may. Know that I and a fellow friend of mine are here famished in the forest for want of food; perish we must unless relieved by thy favors. Therefore, if thou be a gentleman, give meat to men, and to such as are every way worthy of life. Let the proudest squire that sits at thy table rise and encounter with me in any honorable point of activity whatsoever, and if he and thou prove me not a man, send me away comfortless. If thou refuse this, as a niggard of thy cates, I will have amongst you with my sword; for rather will I die 30 valiantly than perish with so cowardly an extreme.

Gerismond, looking him earnestly in the face, and seeing so proper a gentleman in so bitter a passion, was moved with so great pity that, rising from the table, he took him by the hand and bade him welcome, willing him to sit down in his place, and in his room not only to eat his fill but be lord of the feast.

Gramercy, sir (quoth Rosader) but I have a feeble friend that lies hereby famished almost for food; aged and therefore less able to abide the extremity of hunger than myself, and dishonor it were for me to taste one crumb before I made him partner of my fortunes; therefore will I 40 run and fetch him, and then I will gratefully accept of your proffer.

Away hies Rosader to Adam Spencer, and tells him the news; who was

glad of so happy fortune but so feeble he was that he could not go. Whereupon Rosader got him up on his back and brought him to the place. Which,
when Gerismond and his men saw, they greatly applauded their league of
friendship; and Rosader having Gerismond's place assigned him, would
not sit there himself, but set down Adam Spencer. Well, to be short,
those hungry squires fell to their victuals and feasted themselves with
good delicates and great store of wine.

As soon as they had taken their repast, Gerismond (desirous to hear
what hard fortune drave them into those bitter extremities) requested
10 Rosader to discourse (if it were not any way prejudicial unto him) the
cause of his travel. Rosader (desirous any way to satisfy the courtesy of
his favorable host, first beginning his *exordium* with a volley of sighs and
a few lukewarm tears) prosecuted his discourse, and told him from point
to point all his fortunes; how he was the youngest son of Sir John of
Bordeaux, his name Rosader; how his brother sundry times had wronged
him; and, lastly, how for beating the sheriff and hurting his men he fled.
And this old man (quoth he) whom I so much love and honor is surnamed Adam Spencer, an old servant of my father's, and one (that for
his love) never failed me in all my misfortunes.

20 When Gerismond heard this, he fell on the neck of Rosader; and next
discoursing unto him how he was Gerismond, their lawful king, exiled
by Torismond; what familiarity had ever been betwixt his father, Sir
John of Bordeaux, and him; how faithful a subject he lived, and how
honorably he died; promising (for his sake) to give both him and his
friend such courteous entertainment as his present estate could minister;
and upon this made him one of his foresters. Rosader, seeing it was the
king, craved pardon for his boldness, in that he did not do him due reverence, and humbly gave him thanks for his favorable courtesy. Gerismond,
not satisfied yet with news, began to inquire if he had been lately in the
30 court of Torismond, and whether he had seen his daughter Rosalynde or
no? At this, Rosader fetched a great sigh and, shedding many tears, could
not answer. Yet at last, gathering his spirits together, he revealed to the
king how Rosalynde was banished, and how there was such a sympathy
of affections betwixt Alinda and her that she chose rather to be partaker
of her exile than to part fellowship. Whereupon the unnatural king
banished them both; and now they are wandered none knows
whither, neither could any learn since their departure the place of their
abode.

This news drave the king into a great melancholy, that presently he
40 arose from all the company and went into his privy chamber, so secret as
the harbor of the woods would allow him. The company was all dashed

at these tidings, and Rosader and Adam Spencer, having such opportunity, went to take their rest.

*   *   *   *   *

Rosader, being thus preferred to the place of a forester by Gerismond, rooted out the remembrance of his brother's unkindness by continual exercise, traversing the groves and wild forests, partly to hear the melody of the sweet birds which recorded, and partly to shew his diligent endeavor in his master's behalf. Yet whatsoever he did or howsoever he walked, the lively image of Rosalynde remained in memory. On her sweet per- 10 fections he fed his thoughts, proving himself, like the eagle, a true-born bird, since that the one is known by beholding the sun, so was he by regarding excellent beauty. One day among the rest, finding a fit opportunity and place convenient, desirous to discover his woes in the woods, he engraved with his knife on the bark of a myrtle tree, to this pretty estimate of his mistress' perfection.

Sonetto

Of all chaste birds the phoenix doth excel,
Of all strong beasts the lion bears the bell, 20
Of all sweet flowers the rose doth sweetest smell,
Of all fair maids my Rosalynde is fairest.

Of all pure metals gold is only purest,
Of all high trees the pine hath highest crest,
Of all soft sweets I like my mistress' breast,
Of all chaste thoughts my mistress' thoughts are rarest.

Of all proud birds the eagle pleaseth Jove,
Of pretty fowls kind Venus likes the dove,
Of trees Minerva doth the olive love,
Of all sweet nymphs I honor Rosalynde. 30

Of all her gifts her wisdom pleaseth most,
Of all her graces virtue she doth boast;
For all these gifts my life and joy is lost,
If Rosalynde prove cruel and unkind.

In these and such like passions, Rosader did every day eternize the name of his Rosalynde. And this day especially, when Aliena and Ganimede (enforced by the heat of the sun to seek for shelter) by good fortune arrived in that place where this amorous forester registered his melancholy passions, they saw the sudden change of his looks, his folded arms, his pas- 40 sionate sighs; they heard him often abruptly call on Rosalynde. Who (poor soul) was as hotly burned as himself, but that she shrouded her pains in the cinders of honorable modesty. Whereupon (guessing him to be in love, and, according to the nature of their sex, being pitiful in that behalf) they suddenly brake off his melancholy by their approach, and Ganimede shook him out of his dumps thus.

What news, forester? Hast thou wounded some deer and lost him in the fall? Care not, man, for so small a loss; thy fees was but the skin, the shoulder, and the horns. 'Tis hunter's luck to aim fair and miss, and a woodman's fortune to strike and yet go without the game.

Thou art beyond the mark, Ganimede (quoth Aliena). His passions are greater, and his sighs discover more loss; perhaps in traversing these thickets he hath seen some beautiful nymph and is grown amorous.

It may be so (quoth Ganimede) for here he hath newly engraven some sonnet. Come and see the discourse of the forester's poems. Reading the sonnet over and hearing him name Rosalynde, Aliena looked on Ganimede and laughed, and Ganimede, looking back on the forester and seeing it was Rosader, blushed. Yet thinking to shroud all under her page's apparel, she boldly returned to Rosader, and began thus.

I pray thee tell me, forester, what is this Rosalynde for whom thou pinest away in such passions? Is she some nymph that waits upon Diana's train whose chastity thou hast deciphered in such epithets? Or is she some shepherdess that haunts these plains whose beauty hath so bewitched thy fancy, whose name thou shadowest in covert under the figure of Rosalynde, as Ovid did Julia under the name of Corinna? Or say me forsooth, is it that Rosalynde of whom we shepherds have heard talk; she, forester, that is the daughter of Gerismond, that once was king, and now an outlaw in this forest of Arden?

At this Rosader fetched a deep sigh, and said, It is she, O gentle swain, it is she. That saint it is whom I serve, that goddess at whose shrine I do bend all my devotions; the most fairest of all fairs, the phoenix of all that sex, and the purity of all earthly perfection.

And why (gentle forester), if she be so beautiful and thou so amorous, is there such a disagreement in thy thoughts? Happily she resembleth the rose, that is sweet but full of prickles? or the serpent *Regius*, that hath scales as glorious as the sun and a breath as infectious as the *Aconitum* is deadly? So thy Rosalynde may be most amiable and yet unkind; full of favor and yet froward; coy without wit, and disdainful without reason.

O shepherd (quoth Rosader) knewest thou her personage graced with the excellence of all perfection, being a harbor wherein the graces shroud their virtues, thou wouldst not breathe out such blasphemy against the beauteous Rosalynde. She is a diamond, bright but not hard, yet of most chaste operation; a pearl, so orient that it can be stained with no blemish;

a rose without prickles, and a princess absolute as well in beauty as in virtue. But I, unhappy I, have let mine eye soar with the eagle against so bright a sun that I am quite blind; I have, with Apollo, enamored myself of a Daphne, not (as she) disdainful, but far more chaste than Daphne; I have, with Ixion, laid my love on Juno, and shall (I fear) embrace naught but a cloud. Ah, shepherd, I have reached at a star; my desires have mounted above my degree, and my thoughts above my fortunes. I, being a peasant, have ventured to gaze on a princess whose honors are too high to vouchsafe such base loves.

Why, forester (quoth Ganimede) comfort thyself. Be blithe and frolic, 10 man. Love souseth as low as she soareth high, Cupid shoots at a rag as soon as at a robe, and Venus' eye that was so curious sparkled favor on pole-footed Vulcan. Fear not, man! Women's looks are not tied to dignity's feathers, nor make they curious esteem where the stone is found, but what is the virtue. Fear not, forester! Faint heart never won fair lady. But where lives Rosalynde now; at the court?

Oh no (quoth Rosader) she lives I know not where, and that is my sorrow; banished by Torismond, and that is my hell. For might I but find her sacred personage, and plead before the bar of her pity the plaint of my passions, hope tells me she would grace me with some favor; and 20 that would suffice as recompense of all my former miseries.

Much have I heard of thy mistress' excellence; and I know, forester, thou canst describe her at the full, as one that hast surveyed all her parts with a curious eye. Then do me that favor, to tell me what her perfections be.

That I will (quoth Rosader) for I glory to make all ears wonder at my mistress' excellence. And with that he pulled a paper forth his bosom, wherein he read this.

Rosalynde's description

30

Like to the clear in highest sphere
Where all imperial glory shines,
Of selfsame color is her hair,
Whether unfolded or in twines:
    Heigh ho, fair Rosalynde.
Her eyes are sapphires set in snow,
Refining heaven by every wink;
The gods do fear whenas they glow,
And I do tremble when I think:
    Heigh ho, would she were mine.

40

Her cheeks are like the blushing cloud
That beautifies Aurora's face,

Or like the silver crimson shroud
That Phoebus' smiling looks doth grace:
    Heigh ho, fair Rosalynde:
Her lips are like two budded roses,
Whom ranks of lilies neighbor nigh,
Within which bounds she balm encloses,
    Apt to entice a deity:
    Heigh ho, would she were mine.

Her neck like to a stately tower,
Where love himself imprisoned lies
To watch for glances every hour
    From her divine and sacred eyes:
    Heigh ho, fair Rosalynde.
Her paps are centers of delight,
Her paps are orbs of heavenly frame,
Where nature molds the dew of light
    To feed perfection with the same:
    Heigh ho, would she were mine.

With orient pearl, with ruby red,
With marble white, with sapphire blue,
Her body every way is fed;
    Yet soft in touch, and sweet in view:
    Heigh ho, fair Rosalynde.
Nature herself her shape admires,
The gods are wounded in her sight,
And love forsakes his heavenly fires,
    And at her eyes his brand doth light:
    Heigh ho, would she were mine.

Then muse not, nymphs, though I bemoan
The absence of fair Rosalynde;
Since for her fair there is fairer none,
    Nor for her virtues so divine:
    Heigh ho, fair Rosalynde;
    Heigh ho, my heart, would God that she were mine.
        Periit, quia deperibat.

    Believe me (quoth Ganimede) either the forester is an exquisite painter
or Rosalynde far above wonder; so it makes me blush to hear how women
should be so excellent and pages so unperfect.

    Rosader, beholding her earnestly, answered thus. Truly, gentle page,
thou hast cause to complain thee, wert thou the substance; but resembling
the shadow, content thyself, for it is excellence enough to be like the excellence of nature.

He hath answered you, Ganimede (quoth Aliena). It is enough for pages to wait on beautiful ladies, and not to be beautiful themselves.

O mistress (quoth Ganimede) hold you your peace, for you are partial. Who knows not but that all women have desire to tie sovereignty to their petticoats and ascribe beauty to themselves, where, if boys might put on their garments, perhaps they would prove as comely; if not as comely, it may be more courteous. But tell me, forester (and with that she turned to Rosader) under whom maintainest thou thy walk?

Gentle swain, under the king of outlaws, said he, the unfortunate Gerismond; who, having lost his kingdom, crowneth his thoughts with content, accounting it better to govern among poor men in peace than great men in danger.

But hast thou not, said she (having so melancholy opportunities as the forest affordeth thee) written more sonnets in commendations of thy mistress?

I have, gentle swain, quoth he, but they be not about me. Tomorrow by dawn of day, if your flocks feed in these pastures, I will bring them you, wherein you shall read my passions whiles I feel them; judge my patience when you read it. Till when, I bid farewell.

So giving both Ganimede and Aliena a gentle good-night, he resorted to his lodge, leaving Aliena and Ganimede to their prittle-prattle. So, Ganimede (said Aliena, the forester being gone) you are mightily beloved; men make ditties in your praise, spend sighs for your sake, make an idol of your beauty. Surely it grieves me not a little to see the poor man so pensive, and you so pitiless.

*   *   *   *   *

. . . Ganimede, pitying her Rosader, thinking to drive him out of this amorous melancholy, said that now the sun was in his meridional heat and that it was high noon; therefore we shepherds say 'tis time to go to dinner. For the sun and our stomachs are shepherds' dials. Therefore, forester, if thou wilt take such fare as comes out of our homely scrips, welcome shall answer whatsoever thou wantest in delicates. Aliena took the entertainment by the end, and told Rosader he should be her guest. He thanked them heartily, and sate with them down to dinner, where they had such cates as country state did allow them, sauced with such content and such sweet prattle as it seemed far more sweet than all their courtly junkets.

As soon as they had taken their repast, Rosader, giving them thanks for his good cheer, would have been gone. But Ganimede, that was loath to let him pass out of her presence, began thus: Nay, forester, quoth he, if thy business be not the greater, seeing thou sayest thou art so deeply in love, let me see how thou canst woo. I will represent Rosalynde, and thou shalt be as thou art, Rosader. See in some amorous eclogue how if Rosalynde were present, how thou couldst court her. And while we sing of love Aliena shall tune her pipe and play us melody.

Content, quoth Rosader. And Aliena, she to shew her willingness, drew forth a recorder and began to wind it. Then the loving forester began thus.

10   *The wooing eclogue betwixt Rosalynde and Rosader*

ROSADER

I pray thee, nymph, by all the working words,
By all the tears and sighs that lovers know,
Or what or thoughts or faltering tongue affords,
I crave for mine in ripping up my woe.
Sweet Rosalynde, my love (would God, my love),
My life (would God, my life), aye pity me;
Thy lips are kind, and humble like the dove,
And but with beauty pity will not be.
Look on mine eyes, made red with rueful tears,

20 From whence the rain of true remorse descendeth,
All pale in looks, and I though young in years,
And naught but love or death my days befriendeth.
Oh let no stormy rigor knit thy brows,
Which love appointed for his mercy seat,
The tallest tree by Boreas' breath it bows,
The iron yields with hammer, and to heat.
    O Rosalynde, then be thou pitiful,
    For Rosalynde is only beautiful.

ROSALYNDE

30 Love's wantons arm their trait'rous suits with tears,
With vows, with oaths, with looks, with showers of gold;
But when the fruit of their affects appears,
The simple heart by subtle sleights is sold.
Thus sucks the yielding ear the poisoned bait,
Thus feeds the heart upon his endless harms,
Thus glut the thoughts themselves on self-deceit,
Thus blind the eyes their sight by subtle charms.
The lovely looks, the sighs that storm so sore,
The dew of deep-dissembled doubleness—
These may attempt, but are of power no more,
40 Where beauty leans to wit and soothfastness.
    O Rosader, then be thou wittiful,
    For Rosalynde scorns foolish pitiful.

ROSADER

I pray thee, Rosalynde, by those sweet eyes
That stain the sun in shine, the morn in clear,
By those sweet cheeks where love encamped lies
To kiss the roses of the springing year.
I tempt thee, Rosalynde, by ruthful plaints,
Not seasoned with deceit of fraudful guile,
But firm in pain, far more than tongue depaints,
Sweet nymph, be kind, and grace me with a smile.
So may the heavens preserve from hurtful food
Thy harmless flocks, so may the summer yield   10
The pride of all her riches and her good
To fat thy sheep (the citizens of field).
Oh, leave to arm thy lovely brows with scorn;
The birds their beak, the lion hath his tail,
And lovers naught but sighs and bitter mourn,
The spotless sort of fancy to assail.
  O Rosalynde, then be thou pitiful,
  For Rosalynde is only beautiful.

ROSALYNDE

The hardened steel by fire is brought in frame;   20

ROSADER

And Rosalynde, my love, than any wool more softer,
And shall not sighs her tender heart inflame?

ROSALYNDE

Were lovers true, maids would believe them ofter.

ROSADER

Truth, and regard, and honor guide my love.

ROSALYNDE

Fain would I trust, but yet I dare not try.   30

ROSADER

Oh pity me, sweet nymph, and do but prove.

ROSALYNDE

I would resist, but yet I know not why.

ROSADER

O Rosalynde be kind, for times will change,
Thy looks aye nill be fair as now they be;
Thine age from beauty may thy looks estrange;
Ah, yield in time, sweet nymph, and pity me.

ROSALYNDE

O Rosalynde, thou must be pitiful,   40
For Rosader is young and beautiful.

ROSADER

O gain more great than kingdoms or a crown.

ROSALYNDE

O trust betrayed if Rosader abuse me.

ROSADER

First let the heavens conspire to pull me down,
And heaven and earth as abject quite refuse me.
Let sorrows stream about my hateful bower,
And retchless horror hatch within my breast,
Let beauty's eye afflict me with a lour,
Let deep despair pursue me without rest,
Ere Rosalynde my loyalty disprove;
Ere Rosalynde accuse me for unkind.

ROSALYNDE

Then Rosalynde will grace thee with her love;
Then Rosalynde will have thee still in mind.

ROSADER

Then let me triumph more than Tithon's dear,
Sith Rosalynde will Rosader respect;
Then let my face exile his sorry cheer,
And frolic in the comfort of affect,
    And say that Rosalynde is only pitiful,
    Sith Rosalynde is only beautiful.

When thus they had finished their courting eclogue in such a familiar
clause, Ganimede, as augur of some good fortunes to light upon their
affections, began to be thus pleasant. How now, forester, have I not
fitted your turn? Have I not played the woman handsomely, and shewed
myself as coy in grants as courteous in desires, and been as full of suspicion
as men of flattery? And yet, to salve all, jumped I not all up with the sweet
union of love? Did not Rosalynde content her Rosader?

The forester, at this smiling, shook his head and, folding his arms, made
this merry reply.

Truth, gentle swain, Rosader hath his Rosalynde but as Ixion had Juno,
who, thinking to possess a goddess, only embraced a cloud. In these imaginary fruitions of fancy, I resemble the birds that fed themselves with
Zeuxis' painted grapes; but they grew so lean with pecking at shadows
that they were glad, with Æsop's cock, to scrape for a barley cornel. So
fareth it with me, who, to feed myself with the hope of my mistress'
favors, soothe myself in thy suits, and only in conceit reap a wished-for
content. But if my food be no better than such amorous dreams, Venus,
at the year's end, shall find me but a lean lover. Yet do I take these follies
for high fortunes, and hope these feigned affections do divine some unfeigned end of ensuing fancies.

And thereupon (quoth Aliena) I'll play the priest; from this day forth Ganimede shall call thee husband, and thou shalt call Ganimede wife, and so we'll have a marriage.

Content (quoth Rosader), and laughed.

Content (quoth Ganimede), and changed as red as a rose. And so, with a smile and blush, they made up this jesting match, that after proved to a marriage in earnest, Rosader full little thinking he had wooed and won his Rosalynde.

*   *   *   *   *

... As soon as they had taken their repast and well dined, Rosader took his brother Saladyne by the hand and shewed him the pleasures of the forest, and what content they enjoyed in that mean estate. Thus for two or three days he walked up and down with his brother, to shew him all the commodities that belonged to his walk. In which time he was missed of his Ganimede, who mused greatly (with Aliena) what should become of their forester. Some while they thought he had taken some word unkindly, and had taken the pet; then they imagined some new love had withdrawn his fancy; or haply he was sick, or detained by some great business of Gerismond's, or that he had made a reconcilement with his brother, and so returned to Bordeaux.

These conjectures did they cast in their heads, but especially Ganimede: who, having love in her heart, proved restless, and half without patience that Rosader wronged her with so long absence. For love measures every minute, and thinks hours to be days, and days to be months, till they feed their eyes with the sight of their desired object. Thus perplexed lived poor Ganimede, while on a day sitting with Aliena in a great dump, she cast up her eye and saw where Rosader came pacing towards them with his forest bill on his neck. At that sight her color changed, and she said to Aliena: See, mistress, where our jolly forester comes.

And you are not a little glad thereof (quoth Aliena). Your nose bewrays what porridge you love; the wind cannot be tied within his quarter, the sun shadowed with a veil, oil hidden in water, nor love kept out of a woman's looks. But no more of that, *Lupus est in fabula.*

As soon as Rosader was come within the reach of her tongue's end, Aliena began thus. Why, how now, gentle forester, what wind hath kept you from hence? that, being so newly married, you have no more care of your Rosalynde but to absent yourself so many days? Are these the passions you painted out so in your sonnets and roundelays? I see well hot love is soon cold, and that the fancy of men is like to a loose feather that wandereth in the air with the blast of every wind.

You are deceived, mistress, quoth Rosader; 'twas a copy of unkindness that kept me hence, in that, I being married, you carried away the bride.

But if I have given any occasion of offense by absenting myself these three days, I humbly sue for pardon; which you must grant of course in that the fault is so friendly confessed with penance. But to tell you the truth (fair mistress, and my good Rosalynde) my eldest brother, by the injury of Torismond, is banished from Bordeaux, and by chance he and I met in the forest. And here Rosader discoursed unto them what had happened betwixt them; which reconcilement made them glad, especially Ganimede. But Aliena, hearing of the tyranny of her father, grieved inwardly, and yet smothered all things with such secrecy that the concealing was more sorrow than the conceit. Yet that her estate might be hid still, she made fair weather of it and so let all pass.

Fortune, that saw how these parties valued not her deity, but held her power in scorn, thought to have a bout with them, and brought the matter to pass thus. Certain rascals that lived by prowling in a forest, who, for fear of the provost marshal, had caves in the groves and thickets to shroud themselves from his trains, hearing of the beauty of this fair shepherdess Aliena, thought to steal her away and give her to the king for a present; hoping, because the king was a great lecher, by such a gift to purchase all their pardons, and therefore came to take her and her page away. Thus resolved, while Aliena and Ganimede were in sad talk, they came rushing in and laid violent hands upon Aliena and her page; which made them cry out to Rosader. Who, having the valor of his father stamped in his heart, thought rather to die in defense of his friends than any way be touched with the least blemish of dishonor; and therefore dealt such blows amongst them with his weapon as he did witness well upon their carcasses that he was no coward. But as *Ne Hercules quidem contra duos*, so Rosader could not resist a multitude, having none to back him; so that he was not only rebated but sore wounded, and Aliena and Ganimede had been quite carried away by these rascals had not Fortune (that meant to turn her frown into a favor) brought Saladyne that way by chance, who, wandering to find out his brother's walk, encountered this crew. And seeing not only a shepherdess and her boy forced but his brother wounded, he heaved up a forest bill he had on his neck, and the first he struck had never after more need of the physician; redoubling his blows with such courage that the slaves were amazed at his valor.

Rosader, espying his brother so fortunately arrived and seeing how valiantly he behaved himself, though sore wounded, rushed amongst them, and laid on such load that some of the crew were slain and the rest fled, leaving Aliena and Ganimede in the possession of Rosader and Saladyne.

Aliena, after she had breathed a while and was come to herself from this fear, looked about her, and saw where Ganimede was busy dressing up the wounds of the forester. But she cast her eye upon this courteous champion that had made so hot a rescue, and that with such affection as she began to measure every part of him with favor, and in herself to commend his personage and his virtue, holding him for a resolute man that durst assail such a troupe of unbridled villains. At last, gathering her spirits together, she returned him these thanks.

Gentle sir, whatsoever you be that have adventured your flesh to relieve our fortunes, as we hold you valiant so we esteem you courteous, and to have as many hidden virtues as you have manifest resolutions. We poor shepherds have no wealth but our flocks, and therefore can we not make requital with any great treasures; but our recompense is thanks, 10 and our rewards to our friends without feigning. For ransom, therefore, of this our rescue, you must content yourself to take such a kind gramercy as a poor shepherdess and her page may give, with promise (in what we may) never to prove ingrateful. For this gentleman that is hurt, young Rosader, he is our good neighbor and familiar acquaintance; we'll pay him with smiles and feed him with love-looks. And though he be never the fatter at the year's end, yet we'll so hamper him that he shall hold himself satisfied.

Saladyne, hearing this shepherdess speak so wisely, began more narrowly to pry into her perfection and to survey all her lineaments with a 20 curious insight, so long dallying in the flame of her beauty that to his cost he found her to be most excellent. For love, that lurked in all these broils to have a blow or two, seeing the parties at the gaze, encountered them both with such a veny that the stroke pierced to the heart so deep as it could never after be rased out. At last, after he had looked so long till Aliena waxed red, he returned her this answer.

Fair shepherdess, if fortune graced me with such good hap as to do you any favor, I hold myself as contented as if I had gotten a great conquest; for the relief of distressed women is the special point that gentlemen are tied unto by honor. Seeing, then, my hazard to rescue your harms was 30 rather duty than courtesy, thanks is more than belongs to the requital of such a favor. But lest I might seem either too coy or too careless of a gentlewoman's proffer, I will take your kind gramercy for a recompense.

All this while that he spake, Ganimede looked earnestly upon him and said: Truly, Rosader, this gentleman favors you much in the feature of your face.

No marvel (quoth he) gentle swain, for 'tis my eldest brother Saladyne.

Your brother? quoth Aliena (and with that she blushed). He is the more welcome, and I hold myself the more his debtor. And for that he 40 hath in our behalf done such a piece of service, if it please him to do me that honor, I will call him servant and he shall call me mistress.

Content, sweet mistress, quoth Saladyne, and when I forget to call you so, I will be unmindful of mine own self.

Away with these quirks and quiddities of love, quoth Rosader, and give me some drink, for I am passing thirsty! And then will I home, for my wounds bleed sore, and I will have them dressed. Ganimede had tears in her eyes and passions in her heart to see her Rosader so pained, and therefore stepped hastily to the bottle and, filling out some wine in a mazer, she spiced it with such comfortable drugs as she had about her and gave it him; which did comfort Rosader, that rising (with the help of his brother) he took his leave of them and went to his lodge.

Ganimede, as soon as they were out of sight, led his flock down to a vale and there, under the shadow of a beech tree, sate down and began to mourn the misfortunes of her sweetheart. And Aliena (as a woman passing discontent) severing herself from her Ganimede, sitting under a lemon tree, began to sigh out the passions of her new love and to meditate with herself on this manner.

* * * * *

With this, Ganimede start up, made her ready, and went into the fields with Aliena, where, unfolding their flocks, they sate them down under an olive tree, both of them amorous, and yet diversely affected; Aliena joying in the excellence of Saladyne, and Ganimede sorrowing for the wounds of her Rosader, not quiet in thought till she might hear of his health. As thus both of them sate in their dumps, they might espy where Coridon came running towards them (almost out of breath with his haste). What news with you (quoth Aliena) that you come in such post?

Oh mistress (quoth Coridon) you have a long time desired to see Phoebe, the fair shepherdess whom Montanus loves; so now, if it please you and Ganimede but to walk with me to yonder thicket, there shall you see Montanus and her sitting by a fountain, he courting her with his country ditties, and she as coy as if she held love in disdain.

The news were so welcome to the two lovers that up they rose and went with Coridon. As soon as they drew nigh the thicket, they might espy where Phoebe sate (the fairest shepherdess in all Arden, and he the frolickest swain in the whole forest), she in a petticoat of scarlet, covered with a green mantle; and to shroud her from the sun, a chaplet of roses, from under which appeared a face full of nature's excellence, and two such eyes as might have amated a greater man than Montanus. At gaze upon this gorgeous nymph sate the shepherd, feeding his eyes with her favors, wooing with such piteous looks, and courting with such deep-strained sighs as would have made Diana herself to have been compassion-

ate, at last fixing his looks on the riches of her face, his head on his hand,
and his elbow on his knee, he sung this mournful ditty.

Montanus' sonnet

A turtle sate upon a leafless tree,
  Mourning her absent fere
  With sad and sorry cheer;
  About her wond'ring stood
  The citizens of wood,
  And whilst her plumes she rents
  And for her love laments,   10
  The stately trees complain them,
  The birds with sorrow pain them.
  Each one that doth her view,
  Her pain and sorrows rue.
  But were the sorrows known
  That me hath overthrown,
Oh how would Phoebe sigh, if she did look on me!

The lovesick Polypheme that could not see,
  Who on the barren shore
  His fortunes did deplore,   20
  And melteth all in moan
  For Galatea gone;
  And with his piteous cries
  Afflicts both earth and skies;
  And to his woe betook,
  Doth break both pipe and hook;
  For whom complains the morn,
  For whom the sea-nymphs mourn;
  Alas, his pain is naught.
  For were my woe but thought,
Oh how would Phoebe sigh, if she did look on me! 30

  Beyond compare my pain,
    Yet glad am I,
  If gentle Phoebe deign
    To see her Montan die.

After this Montanus felt his passions so extreme that he fell into this
exclamation against the injustice of love:

  Hélas, tirant, plein de rigueur,
  Modère un peu ta violence,   40
  Que te sert si grande despense?

> C'est trop de flammes pour un coeur.
> Espargnez en une étincelle,
> Puis fais ton effort d'esmouvoir
> La fière qui ne veut point voir,
> En quel feu je brusle pour elle.
> Exécute, Amour, ce dessein,
> Et rabaisse un peu son audace,
> Son coeur ne doit estre de glace,
> Bien que elle ait de neige le sein.

10 Montanus ended his sonnet with such a volley of sighs and such a stream of tears as might have moved any but Phoebe to have granted him favor. But she, measuring all his passions with a coy disdain, and triumphing in the poor shepherd's pathetical humors, smiling at his martyrdom as though love had been no malady, scornfully warbled out this sonnet.

Phoebe's sonnet, a reply to Montanus' passion

> *Down a down,*
>   Thus Phyllis sung,
>   by fancy once distressed;
20 Whoso by foolish love are stung
>   are worthily oppressed.
>   And so sing I, *with a down, down, etc.*

> When love was first begot,
> And by the mover's will
> Did fall to human lot
> His solace to fulfil;
> Devoid of all deceit,
> A chaste and holy fire
> Did quicken man's conceit,
30 And women's breast inspire.
> The gods that saw the good
> That mortals did approve,
> With kind and holy mood
> Began to talk of love.
>   *Down a down,*
>   Thus Phyllis sung,
>   by fancy once distressed, *etc.*

> But during this accord,
> A wonder strange to hear,
> Whilst love in deed and word,
40 Most faithful did appear,
> False semblance came in place,

By jealousy attended,
And with a double face,
Both love and fancy blended.
Which make the gods forsake,
And men from fancy fly,
And maidens scorn a make;
Forsooth, and so will I.
                Down a down,
        Thus Phyllis sung,
                by fancy once distressed:
    Whoso by foolish love are stung   10
        are worthily oppressed.
    And so sing I, *with down, a down, a down, a down, a.*

* * * * *

Ganimede, overhearing all these passions of Montanus, could not brook the cruelty of Phoebe, but, starting from behind the bush, said: And if, damsel, you fled from me, I would transform you as Daphne to a bay, and then in contempt trample your branches under my feet.

Phoebe at this sudden reply was amazed, especially when she saw so fair a swain as Ganimede; blushing, therefore, she would have been gone, 20 but that he held her by the hand and prosecuted his reply thus. What, shepherdess, so fair and so cruel? Disdain beseems not cottages, nor coyness maids; for either they be condemned to be too proud or too froward. Take heed (fair nymph) that, in despising love, you be not overreached with love and, in shaking off all, shape yourself to your own shadow, and so, with Narcissus, prove passionate and yet unpitied. Oft have I heard, and sometimes have I seen, high disdain turned to hot desires. Because thou art beautiful, be not so coy; as there is nothing more fair, so is there nothing more fading; as momentary as the shadows which grows from a cloudy sun. Such (my fair shepherdess) as disdain in youth desire in 30 age, and then are they hated in the winter that might have been loved in the prime. A wrinkled maid is like to a parched rose, that is cast up in coffers to please the smell, not worn in the hand to content the eye. There is no folly in love to *Had I wist!* And therefore be ruled by me. Love while thou art young, lest thou be disdained when thou art old. Beauty nor time cannot be recalled; and, if thou love, like of Montanus; for, as his desires are many, so his deserts are great.

Phoebe all this while gazed on the perfection of Ganimede, as deeply enamored on his perfection as Montanus inveigled with hers. For her eye made survey of his excellent feature, which she found so rare that she 40 thought the ghost of Adonis had been leapt from Elysium in the shape of a swain. When she blushed at her own folly to look so long on a stranger, she mildly made answer to Ganimede thus. I cannot deny, sir, but I have heard of love, though I never felt love; and have read of such a goddess as Venus, though I never saw any but her picture; and perhaps—

And with that she waxed red and bashful and withal silent. Which Ganimede perceiving, commended in herself the bashfulness of the maid, and desired her to go forward. And perhaps, sir (quoth she) mine eyes hath been more prodigal today than ever before.

And with that she stayed again, as one greatly passionate and perplexed. Aliena, seeing the hare through the maze, bade her forward with her prattle. But in vain, for, at this abrupt period, she brake off and, with her eyes full of tears and her face covered with a vermilion dye, she sate down and sighed. Whereupon Aliena and Ganimede, seeing the shepherdess in such a strange plight, left Phoebe with her Montanus, wishing her friendly that she would be more pliant to love, lest in penance Venus joined her to some sharp repentance. Phoebe made no reply, but fetched such a sigh that Echo made relation of her plaint, giving Ganimede such an adieu with a piercing glance that the amorous girl-boy perceived Phoebe was pinched by the heel.

But leaving Phoebe to the follies of her new fancy and Montanus to attend upon her, to Saladyne, who all this last night could not rest for the remembrance of Aliena; insomuch that he framed a sweet-conceited sonnet to content his humor, which he put in his bosom, being requested by his brother Rosader to go to Aliena and Ganimede to signify unto them that his wounds were not dangerous. A more happy message could not happen to Saladyne, that, taking his forest bill on his neck, he trudged in all haste towards the plains where Aliena's flocks did feed, coming just to the place when they returned from Montanus and Phoebe. Fortune so conducted this jolly forester that he encountered them and Coridon, whom he presently saluted in this manner.

Fair shepherdess, and too fair, unless your beauty be tempered with courtesy and the lineaments of the face graced with the lowliness of mind; as many good fortunes to you and your page as yourselves can desire, or I imagine. My brother Rosader (in the grief of his green wounds) still mindful of his friends, hath sent me to you with a kind salute, to shew that he brooks his pains with the more patience in that he holds the parties precious in whose defense he received the prejudice. The report of your welfare will be a great comfort to his distempered body and distressed thoughts, and therefore he sent me with a strict charge to visit you.

And you (quoth Aliena) are the more welcome in that you are messenger from so kind a gentleman, whose pains we compassionate with as great sorrow as he brooks them with grief; and his wounds breeds in us as many passions as in him extremities, so that what disquiet he feels in body, we partake in heart, wishing (if we might) that our mishap might salve his malady. But seeing our wills yields him little ease, our orisons are never idle to the gods for his recovery.

I pray you (quoth Ganimede with tears in his eyes), when the surgeon searched him, held he his wounds dangerous?

Dangerous (quoth Saladyne) but not mortal; and the sooner to be cured in that his patient is not impatient of any pains. Whereupon my brother hopes within these ten days to walk abroad and visit you himself.

In the meantime (quoth Ganimede) say his Rosalynde commends her to him, and bids him be of good cheer. 10

I know not (quoth Saladyne) who that Rosalynde is, but, whatsoever she is, her name is never out of his mouth; but, amidst the deepest of his passions, he useth Rosalynde as a charm to appease all sorrows with patience. Insomuch that I conjecture my brother is in love, and she some paragon that holds his heart perplexed, whose name he oft records with sighs, sometimes with tears; straight with joy, then with smiles; as if in one person love had lodged a chaos of confused passions. Wherein I have noted the variable disposition of fancy that, like the *polyp* in colors, so it changeth into sundry humors; being, as it should seem, a combat mixed with disquiet, and a bitter pleasure wrapped in a sweet prejudice, like to 20 the *sinople* tree, whose blossoms delight the smell and whose fruit infects the taste.

By my faith (quoth Aliena) sir, you are deep read in love; or grows your insight into affection by experience? Howsoever, you are a great philosopher in Venus' principles, else could you not discover her secret aphorisms. But, sir, our country amours are not like your courtly fancies, nor is our wooing like your suing; for poor shepherds never plain them till love pain them, where the courtier's eyes is full of passions when his heart is most free from affections. They court to discover their eloquence, we woo to ease our sorrows; every fair face with them must have a new 30 fancy sealed with a forefinger kiss, and a far-fetched sigh, we here love one and live to that one so long as life can maintain love, using few ceremonies because we know few subtleties, and little eloquence for that we lightly account of flattery. Only faith and troth, that's shepherd's wooing.

*   *   *   *   *

At the word marriage, Aliena stood in a maze what to answer, fearing that if she were too coy, to drive him away with her disdain; and, if she were too courteous, to discover the heat of her desires. In a dilemma thus what to do, at last this she said. Saladyne, ever since I saw thee, I favored 40 thee. I cannot dissemble my desires because I see thou dost faithfully manifest thy thoughts, and, in liking thee, I love thee so far as mine honor holds fancy still in suspense; but if I knew thee as virtuous as thy father, or as well qualified as thy brother Rosader, the doubt should be quickly decided. But, for this time to give thee an answer, assure thyself thus: I will either marry with Saladyne or still live a virgin.

And with this they strained one another's hand. Which Ganimede espying, thinking he had had his mistress long enough at shrift, said: What, a match or no?

A match (quoth Aliena), or else it were in ill market.

I am glad (quoth Ganimede). I would Rosader were well here to
10 make up the mess.

Well remembered (quoth Saladyne). I forgot I left my brother Rosader alone; and therefore, lest, being solitary, he should increase his sorrows, I will haste me to him. May it please you then to command me any service to him, I am ready to be a dutiful messenger.

Only at this time commend me to him (quoth Aliena) and tell him though we cannot pleasure him, we pray for him.

And forget not, quoth Ganimede, my commendations; but say to him that Rosalynde sheds as many tears from her heart as he drops of blood from his wounds, for the sorrow of his misfortunes; feathering all her
20 thoughts with disquiet till his welfare procure her content. Say thus (good Saladyne), and so farewell.

He, having his message, gave a courteous adieu to them both, especially to Aliena; and so, playing loath to depart, went to his brother.

But Aliena, she perplexed and yet joyful, passed away the day pleasantly, still praising the perfection of Saladyne, not ceasing to chat of her new love till evening drew on; and then they, folding their sheep, went home to bed. Where we leave them and return to Phoebe.

Phoebe, fired with the uncouth flame of love, returned to her father's house so galled with restless passions as now she began to acknowledge
30 that there was no flower so fresh but might be parched with the sun, no tree so strong but might be shaken with a storm; so there was no thought so chaste but time, armed with love, could make amorous. For she that held Diana for the goddess of her devotion was now fain to fly to the altar of Venus, as suppliant now with prayers as she was froward afore with disdain.

*   *   *   *   *

With that, Montanus took them and perused them, but with such sorrow in his looks as they bewrayed source of confused passions in his heart;
40 at every line his color changed, and every sentence was ended with a period of sighs.

At last, noting Phoebe's extreme desire towards Ganimede and her disdain towards him, giving Ganimede the letter, the shepherd stood as though he had neither won nor lost. Which Ganimede perceiving, wakened him out of his dream thus: Now, Montanus, dost thou see thou vowest great service and obtainest but little reward; but, in lieu of thy loyalty she maketh thee, as Bellerophon, carry thine own bane. Then drink not willingly of that potion wherein thou knowest is poison; creep not to her that cares not for thee. What, Montanus, there are many as fair as Phoebe, but most of all more courteous than Phoebe! I tell thee, shepherd, favor is love's fuel; then, since thou canst not get that, let the flame vanish into smoke, and rather sorrow for a while than repent thee 10 forever.

I tell thee, Ganimede (quoth Montanus) as they which are stung with the scorpion cannot be recovered but by the scorpion, nor he that was wounded with Achilles' lance be cured but with the same truncheon, so Apollo was fain to cry out that love was only eased with love, and fancy healed by no medicine but favor. Phoebus had herbs to heal all hurts but this passion; Circe had charms for all chances but for affection; and Mercury subtle reasons to refel all griefs but love. Persuasions are bootless, reason lends no remedy, counsel no comfort to such whom fancy hath made resolute; and therefore, though Phoebe loves Ganimede, yet Montanus 20 must honor none but Phoebe.

Then, quoth Ganimede, may I rightly term thee a despairing lover that livest without joy and lovest without hope. But what shall I do, Montanus, to pleasure thee? Shall I despise Phoebe as she disdains thee?

Oh (quoth Montanus) that were to renew my griefs and double my sorrows; for the sight of her discontent were the censure of my death. Alas, Ganimede, though I perish in my thoughts, let not her die in her desires. Of all passions, love is most impatient; then let not so fair a creature as Phoebe sink under the burden of so deep a distress. Being lovesick, she is proved heartsick, and all for the beauty of Ganimede. Thy pro- 30 portion hath entangled her affection, and she is snared in the beauty of thy excellence. Then, sith she loves thee so dear, mislike not her deadly. Be thou paramour to such a paragon; she hath beauty to content thine eye and flocks to enrich thy store. Thou canst not wish for more than thou shalt win by her; for she is beautiful, virtuous, and wealthy—three deep persuasions to make love frolic.

Aliena, seeing Montanus cut it against the hair and plead that Ganimede ought to love Phoebe, when his only life was the love of Phoebe, answered him thus. Why, Montanus, dost thou further this motion? seeing if Ganimede marry Phoebe, thy market is clean marred. 40

Ah, mistress (quoth he), so hath love taught me to honor Phoebe that I would prejudice my life to pleasure her, and die in despair rather than she should perish for want. It shall suffice me to see him contented and to feed mine eye on her favor. If she marry, though it be my martyrdom, yet, if she be pleased, I will brook it with patience, and triumph in mine own stars to see her desires satisfied. Therefore, if Ganimede be as courteous as he is beautiful, let him shew his virtues in redressing Phoebe's miseries.

And this Montanus pronounced with such an assured countenance that it amazed Aliena and Ganimede to see the resolution of his loves; so that they pitied his passions and commended his patience, devising how they 10 might, by any subtlety, get Montanus the favor of Phoebe. Straight (as women's heads are full of wiles) Ganimede had a fetch to force Phoebe to fancy the shepherd, *malgrado* the resolution of her mind. He prosecuted his policy thus. Montanus (quoth he) seeing Phoebe is so forlorn, lest I might be counted unkind in not salving so fair a creature, I will go with thee to Phoebe, and there hear herself in word utter that which she hath discoursed with her pen, and then, as love wills me, I will set down my censure. I will home to our house and send Coridon to accompany Aliena. Montanus seemed glad of his determination, and away they go toward the house of Phoebe.

20 When they drew nigh to the cottage, Montanus ran afore, and went in and told Phoebe that Ganimede was at the door. This word Ganimede, sounding in the ears of Phoebe, drove her into such an ecstasy for joy that, rising up in her bed, she was half revived, and her wan color began to wax red. And with that came Ganimede in, who saluted Phoebe with such a courteous look that it was half a salve to her sorrows. Sitting him down by her bedside, he questioned about her disease and where the pain chiefly held her. Phoebe, looking as lovely as Venus in her nightgear, tainting her face with as ruddy a blush as Clytia did when she bewrayed her loves to Phoebus, taking Ganimede by the hand, began thus. Fair 30 shepherd, if love were not more strong than nature, or fancy the sharpest extreme, my immodesty were the more, and my virtues the less. For nature hath framed women's eyes bashful, their hearts full of fear, and their tongues full of silence. But love, that imperious love, where his power is predominant, then he perverts all and wresteth the wealth of nature to his own will. An instance in myself, fair Ganimede, for such a fire hath he kindled in my thoughts that, to find ease for the flame, I was forced to pass the bounds of modesty and seek a salve at thy hands for my secret harms. Blame me not if I be overbold, for it is thy beauty; and, if I be too forward, it is fancy and the deep insight into thy virtues that 40 makes me thus fond. For let me say in a word what may be contained in a volume, Phoebe loves Ganimede.

At this she held down her head and wept, and Ganimede rose as one that would suffer no fish to hang on his fingers, made this reply. Water not thy plants, Phoebe, for I do pity thy plaints; nor seek not to discover thy loves in tears, for I conjecture thy truth by thy passions. Sorrow is no salve for loves, nor sighs no remedy for affection. Therefore frolic, Phoebe, for if Ganimede can cure thee, doubt not of recovery. Yet this let me say without offense, that it grieves me to thwart Montanus in his fancies, seeing his desires have been so resolute and his thoughts so loyal. But thou allegest that thou art forced from him by fate; so I tell thee, Phoebe, either some star, or else some destiny, fits my mind rather with Adonis to die in chase than be counted a wanton on Venus' knee. Al- 10 though I pity thy martyrdom, yet I can grant no marriage; for though I held thee fair, yet mine eye is not fettered. Love grows not like the herb *spattanna* to his perfection in one night, but creeps with the snail, and yet at last attains to the top. *Festina lente*, especially in love; for momentary fancies are oft times the fruits of follies. If, Phoebe, I should like thee as the *Hyperborei* do their dates, which banquet with them in the morning and throw them away at night, my folly should be great, and thy repentance more. Therefore I will have time to turn my thoughts, and my loves shall grow up as the watercresses, slowly, but with a deep root. Thus, Phoebe, thou mayest see I disdain not, though I desire not, remaining 20 indifferent till time and love makes me resolute. Therefore, Phoebe, seek not to suppress affection, and with the love of Montanus quench the remembrance of Ganimede; strive thou to hate me as I seek to like of thee, and ever have the duties of Montanus in thy mind; for I promise thee, thou mayest have one more wealthy, but not more loyal.

These words were corrosives to the perplexed Phoebe, that, sobbing out sighs and straining out tears, she blubbered out these words.

And shall I, then, have no salve of Ganimede but suspense, no hope but a doubtful hazard, no comfort but be posted off to the will of time? Justly have the gods balanced my fortunes, who, being cruel to Montanus, 30 found Ganimede as unkind to myself; so, in forcing him perish for love, I shall die myself with overmuch love.

I am glad (quoth Ganimede) you look into your own faults and see where your shoe wrings you, measuring now the pains of Montanus by your own passions.

Truth, quoth Phoebe, and so deeply I repent me of my frowardness towards the shepherd that, could I cease to love Ganimede, I would resolve to like Montanus.

What if I can with reason persuade Phoebe to mislike of Ganimede, will she then favor Montanus?
40

When reason (quoth she) doth quench that love that I owe to thee, then will I fancy him; conditionally, that if my love can be suppressed with no reason, as being without reason, Ganimede will only wed himself to Phoebe.

I grant it, fair shepherdess, quoth he; and, to feed thee with the sweetness of hope, this resolve on: I will never marry myself to woman but to thyself.

And with that Ganimede gave Phoebe a fruitless kiss and such words of comfort that, before Ganimede departed, she arose out of her bed and made him and Montanus such cheer as could be found in such a country cottage, Ganimede, in the midst of their banquet, rehearsing the promises 10 of either in Montanus' favor, which highly pleased the shepherd. Thus, all three content and soothed up in hope, Ganimede took his leave of Phoebe and departed, leaving her a contented woman, and Montanus highly pleased.

But poor Ganimede, who had her thoughts on Rosader, when she called to remembrance his wounds, filled her eyes full of tears and her heart full of sorrows, plodded to find Aliena at the folds, thinking with her presence to drive away her passions. As she came on the plains, she might espy where Rosader and Saladyne sate with Aliena under the shade; which sight was a salve to her grief and such a cordial unto her 20 heart that she tripped alongst the lawns full of joy.

At last Coridon, who was with them, spied Ganimede, and with that the clown rose and, running to meet him, cried, O sirrah, a match, a match! Our mistress shall be married on Sunday! Thus the poor peasant frolicked it before Ganimede, who, coming to the crew, saluted them all, and especially Rosader, saying that he was glad to see him so well recovered of his wounds.

I had not gone abroad so soon, quoth Rosader, but that I am bidden to a marriage, which on Sunday next must be solemnized, between my brother and Aliena. I see well, where love leads, delay is loathsome, and 30 that small wooing serves where both the parties are willing.

Truth, quoth Ganimede, but what a happy day should it be if Rosader that day might be married to Rosalynde!

Ah, good Ganimede (quoth he) by naming Rosalynde renew not my sorrows; for the thought of her perfections is the thrall of my miseries.

Tush, be of good cheer, man! quoth Ganimede. I have a friend that is deeply experienced in necromancy and magic; what art can do shall be acted for thine advantage. I will cause him to bring in Rosalynde, if either France or any bordering nation harbor her; and upon that take the faith of a young shepherd.

40 Aliena smiled to see how Rosader frowned, thinking that Ganimede had jested with him. But breaking off from those matters, the page (somewhat pleasant) began to discourse unto them what had passed between

him and Phoebe; which, as they laughed, so they wondered at, all confessing that there is none so chaste but love will change. Thus they passed away the day in chat, and, when the sun began to set, they took their leaves and departed, Aliena providing for their marriage day such solemn cheer and handsome robes as fitted their country state, and yet somewhat the better, in that Rosader had promised to bring Gerismond thither as a guest. Ganimede (who then meant to discover herself before her father) had made her a gown of green and a kirtle of the finest sendal, in such sort that she seemed some heavenly nymph harbored in country attire.

Saladyne was not behind in care to set out the nuptials, nor Rosader 10 unmindful to bid guests, who invited Gerismond and all his followers to the feast, who willingly granted; so that there was nothing but the day wanting to this marriage. In the meanwhile, Phoebe, being a bidden guest, made herself as gorgeous as might please the eye of Ganimede; and Montanus suited himself with the cost of many of his flocks to be gallant against that day; for then was Ganimede to give Phoebe an answer of her loves, and Montanus either to hear the doom of his misery or the censure of his happiness. But while this gear was abrewing, Phoebe passed not one day without visiting her Ganimede, so far was she wrapped in the beauties of this lovely swain. Much prattle they had, and discourse 20 of many passions, Phoebe wishing for the day (as she thought) of her welfare, and Ganimede smiling to think what unexpected events would fall out at the wedding. In these humors, the week went away, that at last Sunday came.

No sooner did Phoebus' henchman appear in the sky, to give warning that his master's horses should be trapped in his glorious coach, but Coridon, in his holiday suit marvelous seemly, in a russet jacket welted with the same, and faced with red worsted, having a pair of blue chamlet sleeves bound at the wrists with four yellow laces, closed afore very richly with a dozen of pewter buttons. His hose was of grey kersey, with a large 30 slop, barred overthwart the pocket holes with three fair guards stitched of either side with red thread; his stock was of the own, sewed close to his breech, and, for to beautify his hose, he had trussed himself round with a dozen of newthreaden points of medley color; his bonnet was green, whereon stood a copper brooch with the picture of St. Denis; and, to want nothing that might make him amorous in his old days, he had a fair shirtband of fine lockram, whipped over with Coventry blue of no small cost. Thus attired, Coridon bestirred himself as chief stickler in these actions, and had strowed all the house with flowers, that it seemed rather some of Flora's choice bowers than any country cottage. 40

Thither repaired Phoebe with all the maids of the forest to set out the bride in most seemliest sort that might be; but howsoever she helped to prank out Aliena, yet her eye was still on Ganimede, who was so neat in a suit of grey that he seemed Endymion when he won Luna with his looks, or Paris when he played the swain to get the beauty of the nymph Oenone. Ganimede, like a pretty page, waited on his mistress Aliena, and overlooked that all was in readiness against the bridegroom should come. Who, attired in a forester's suit, came accompanied with Gerismond and his brother Rosader early in the morning; where arrived, they were solemnly entertained by Aliena and the rest of the country swains, Gerismond very highly commending the fortunate choice of Saladyne in that 10 he had chosen a shepherdess whose virtues appeared in her outward beauties, being no less fair than seeming modest.

Ganimede, coming in and seeing her father, began to blush, nature working affects by her secret effects. Scarce could she abstain from tears to see her father in so low fortunes; he that was wont to sit in his royal palace attended on by twelve noble peers, now to be contented with a simple cottage, and a troop of reveling woodmen for his train. The consideration of his fall made Ganimede full of sorrows; yet, that she might triumph over fortune with patience and not any way dash that merry day with her dumps, she smothered her melancholy with a shadow of mirth, 20 and very reverently welcomed the king, not according to his former degree, but to his present estate, with such diligence as Gerismond began to commend the page for his exquisite person and excellent qualities.

As thus the king with his foresters frolicked it among the shepherds, Coridon came in with a fair mazer full of cider and presented it to Gerismond with such a clownish salute that he began to smile, and took it of the old shepherd very kindly, drinking to Aliena and the rest of her fair maids, amongst whom Phoebe was the foremost. Aliena pledged the king and drank to Rosader; so the carouse went round from him to Phoebe, etc. As they were thus drinking and ready to go to church, came in 30 Montanus, apparelled all in tawny, to signify that he was forsaken; on his head he wore a garland of willow, his bottle hanged by his side, whereon was painted despair, and on his sheep-hook hung two sonnets, as labels of his loves and fortunes.

*   *   *   *   *

Gerismond, desirous to prosecute the end of these passions, called in Ganimede; who, knowing the case, came in graced with such a blush as beautified the crystal of his face with a ruddy brightness. The king, noting well the phys[iog]nomy of Ganimede, began by his favors to call to mind 40 the face of his Rosalynde, and with that fetched a deep sigh. Rosader, that was passing familiar with Gerismond, demanded of him why he sighed so sore? Because, Rosader (quoth he) the favor of Ganimede put me in mind of Rosalynde.

At this word, Rosader sighed as deeply as though his heart would have burst. And what's the matter (quoth Gerismond) that you quite me with such a sigh?

Pardon me, sir (quoth Rosader); because I love none but Rosalynde. And upon that condition (quoth Gerismond) that Rosalynde were here, I would this day make up a marriage betwixt her and thee.

At this, Aliena turned her head and smiled upon Ganimede, and she could scarce keep countenance. Yet she salved all with secrecy; and 10 Gerismond, to drive away such dumps, questioned with Ganimede what the reason was he regarded not Phoebe's love, seeing she was as fair as the wanton that brought Troy to ruin.

Ganimede mildly answered, If I should affect the fair Phoebe, I should offer poor Montanus great wrong to win that from him in a moment that he hath labored for so many months. Yet have I promised to the beautiful shepherdess to wed myself never to woman except unto her; but with this promise, that if I can by reason suppress Phoebe's love towards me, she shall like of none but of Montanus.

To that, quoth Phoebe, I stand; for my love is so far beyond reason 20 as it will admit no persuasion of reason.

For justice, quoth he, I appeal to Gerismond.

And to his censure will I stand, quoth Phoebe.

And in your victory, quoth Montanus, stands the hazard of my fortunes; for if Ganimede go away with the conquest, Montanus is in conceit love's monarch; if Phoebe win, then am I in effect most miserable.

We will see this controversy, quoth Gerismond, and then we will to church; therefore, Ganimede, let us hear your argument.

Nay, pardon my absence a while (quoth she) and you shall see one in store.

30

In went Ganimede and dressed herself in woman's attire, having on a gown of green with a kirtle of rich sendal, so quaint that she seemed Diana triumphing in the forest; upon her head she wore a chaplet of roses, which gave her such a grace that she looked like Flora perked in the pride of all her flowers. Thus attired came Rosalynde in, and presented herself at her father's feet, with her eyes full of tears, craving his blessing, and discoursing unto him all her fortunes, how she was banished by Torismond, and how ever since she lived in that country disguised.

Gerismond, seeing his daughter, rose from his seat and fell upon her neck, uttering the passions of his joy in watery plaints, driven into such 40 an ecstasy of content that he could not utter one word. At this sight, if

Rosader was both amazed and joyful, I refer myself to the judgment of such as have experience in love, seeing his Rosalynde before his face, whom so long and so deeply he had affected.

At last Gerismond recovered his spirits, and in most fatherly terms entertained his daughter Rosalynde, after many questions demanding of her what had passed between her and Rosader.

So much, sir (quoth she) as there wants nothing but Your Grace to make up the marriage.

Why, then (quoth Gerismond) Rosader, take her; she is thine. And let this day solemnize both thy brother's and thy nuptials.

Rosader, beyond measure content, humbly thanked the king, and embraced his Rosalynde; who, turning towards Phoebe, demanded if she had shewn sufficient reason to suppress the force of her loves.

Yea, quoth Phoebe, and so great a persuasive that, if it please you, madam, and Aliena to give us leave, Montanus and I will make this day the third couple in marriage.

She had no sooner spake this word but Montanus threw away his garland of willow, his bottle, where was painted despair, and cast his sonnets in the fire, shewing himself as frolic as Paris when he hanseled his love with Helena. At this, Gerismond and the rest smiled, and concluded that Montanus and Phoebe should keep their wedding with the two brethren. Aliena, seeing Saladyne stand in a dump, to wake him from his dream began thus. Why, how now, my Saladyne, all amort! what, melancholy, man, at the day of marriage? Perchance thou art sorrowful to think on thy brother's high fortunes and thine own base desires to choose so mean a shepherdess. Cheer up thy heart, man, for this day thou shalt be married to the daughter of a king! For know, Saladyne, I am not Aliena, but Alinda, the daughter of thy mortal enemy Torismond.

At this, all the company was amazed, especially Gerismond, who, rising up, took Alinda in his arms, and said to Rosalynde: Is this that fair Alinda, famous for so many virtues, that forsook her father's court to live with thee, exiled in the country?

The same, quoth Rosalynde.

Then, quoth Gerismond, turning to Saladyne, jolly forester, be frolic; for thy fortunes are great and thy desires excellent. Thou hast got a princess as famous for her perfection as exceeding in proportion.

And she hath, with her beauty, won, quoth Saladyne, an humble servant, as full of faith as she of amiable favor.

While every one was amazed at these comical events, Coridon came skipping in, and told them that the priest was at church, and tarried their coming. With that, Gerismond led the way, and the rest followed; where, to the admiration of the country swains in Arden, their marriages were solemnly solemnized.

As soon as the priest had finished, home they went with Alinda, where Coridon had made all things in readiness. Dinner was provided, and the tables being spread and the brides set down by Gerismond. Rosader, Saladyne, and Montanus that day were servitors. Homely cheer they had, such as their country could afford; but to mend their fare they had mickle good chat and many discourses of their loves and fortunes. About mid-dinner, to make them merry, Coridon came in with an old crowd, and played them a fit of mirth, to which he sung this pleasant song. 10

Coridon's song

A blithe and bonny country lass,
    heigh ho, the bonny lass,
Sate sighing on the tender grass,
    and weeping said, Will none come woo her.
A smicker boy, a lither swain,
    heigh ho, a smicker swain,
That in his love was wanton fain,
    with smiling looks straight came unto her. 20

Whenas the wanton wench espied,
    heigh ho, when she espied,
The means to make herself a bride,
    she simpered smooth like Bonnybell.
The swain that saw her squint-eyed kind,
    heigh ho, squint-eyed kind,
His arms about her body twined,
    and said, "Fair lass, how fare ye; well?"

The country kit said, "Well, forsooth"; 30
    heigh ho, well, forsooth,
"But that I have a longing tooth,
    a longing tooth that makes me cry."
"Alas," said he, "what gars thy grief?"
    heigh ho, what gars thy grief;
"A wound," quoth she, "without relief;
    I fear a maid that I shall die."

"If that be all," the shepherd said,
    heigh ho, the shepherd said,
"I'll make thee wive it, gentle maid,
    and so recure thy malady." 40
Hereon they kissed with many a oath,

> heigh ho, with many a oath,
> And fore god Pan did plight their troth,
> and to the church they hied them fast.

> And God send every pretty peat
> heigh ho, the pretty peat
> That fears to die of this conceit,
> so kind a friend to help at last.

Coridon, having thus made them merry, as they were in the midst of their jollity, word was brought in to Saladyne and Rosader that a brother of theirs, one Fernandyne, was arrived and desired to speak with them. Gerismond, overhearing this news, demanded who it was?

It is, sir (quoth Rosader) our middle brother, that lives a scholar in Paris; but what fortune hath driven him to seek us out I know not.

With that, Saladyne went and met his brother, whom he welcomed with all courtesy, and Rosader gave him no less friendly entertainment. Brought he was by his two brothers into the parlor where they all sate at dinner. Fernandyne, as one that knew as many manners as he could points of sophistry, and was as well brought up as well lettered, saluted them all. But when he espied Gerismond, kneeling on his knee, he did him what reverence belonged to his estate, and with that burst forth into these speeches.

Although (right mighty Prince) this day of my brothers' marriage be a day of mirth, yet time craves another course; and therefore, from dainty cates rise to sharp weapons. And you, the sons of Sir John of Bordeaux, leave off your amours and fall to arms; change your loves into lances, and now this day shew yourselves valiant, as hitherto you have been passionate. For know, Gerismond, that hard by at the edge of this forest the twelve peers of France are up in arms to recover thy right; and Torismond, trooped with a crew of desperate runagates, is ready to bid them battle. The armies are ready to join; therefore, shew thyself in the field to encourage thy subjects. And you, Saladyne and Rosader, mount you and shew yourselves as hardy soldiers as you have been hearty lovers. So shall you, for the benefit of your country, discover the *idea* of your father's virtues to be stamped in your thoughts, and prove children worthy of so honorable a parent.

At this alarum given him by Fernandyne, Gerismond leapt from the board, and Saladyne and Rosader betook themselves to their weapons. Nay, quoth Gerismond, go with me. I have horse and armor for us all; and then, being well mounted, let us shew that we carry revenge and honor at our falchions' points.

Thus they leave the brides full of sorrow, especially Alinda, who desired Gerismond to be good to her father. He not returning a word because his haste was great, hied him home to his lodge, where he delivered Saladyne and Rosader horse and armor; and himself, armed royally, led the way, not having ridden two leagues before they discovered where, in a valley, both the battles were joined. Gerismond, seeing the wing wherein the peers fought, thrust in there, and cried, Saint Denis, Gerismond laying on such load upon his enemies that he shewed how highly he did estimate of a crown.

When the peers perceived that their lawful king was there, they grew more eager; and Saladyne and Rosader so behaved themselves that none durst stand in their way nor abide the fury of their weapons. To be short, the peers were conquerors, Torismond's army put to flight, and himself slain in battle. The peers then gathered themselves together and saluting their king, conducted him royally into Paris, where he was received with great joy of all the citizens.

As soon as all was quiet and he had received again the crown, he sent for Alinda and Rosalynde to the court, Alinda being very passionate for the death of her father, yet brooking it with the more patience in that she was contented with the welfare of her Saladyne. Well, as soon as they were come to Paris, Gerismond made a royal feast for the peers and the lords of his land, which continued thirty days, in which time summoning a parliament, by the consent of his nobles he created Rosader heir apparent to the kingdom. He restored Saladyne to all his father's land, and gave him the dukedom of Nameurs; he made Fernandyne principal secretary to himself; and, that fortune might every way seem frolic, made Montanus lord over all the forest of Arden, Adam Spencer captain of the king's guard, and Coridon master of Alinda's flocks.

Here, gentlemen, may you see in *Euphues' Golden Legacy* that such as neglect their fathers' precepts incur much prejudice; that division in nature, as it is a blemish in nurture, so 'tis a breach of good fortunes; that virtue is not measured by birth but by action; that younger brethren, though inferior in years, yet may be superior to honors; that concord is the sweetest conclusion; and amity betwixt brothers more forceable than fortune. If you gather any fruit by this *Legacy,* speak well of Euphues for writing it, and me for fetching it. If you grace me with that favor, you encourage me to be more forward; and, as soon as I have overlooked my labors, expect the *Sailor's Calendar.*

T. LODGE.

RICHARD HAKLUYT AND THE VOYAGERS

The Introduction and Notes are at page 1325

From George Best's *A True Discourse of the late Voyages of discouerie*, 1578

¹⁰ *The first book of the first voyage of Martin Frobisher Esquire, Captain General for the discovery of the passage to Cataya and the East India, by the Northwest, first attempted in Anno Dom. 1576, the 15 of May.*

MAN is born not only to serve his own turn (as Tully sayeth) but his kinsfolk, friends, and the commonwealth especially, look for some furtherance at his hands and some fruits of his labor. Whereupon sundry men, finding themselves as it were tied by this bond and duty of human society, have willingly endeavoured sundry ways to show themselves
20 profitable members of their common weal. Some men by study of the mind have employed themselves to give out good laws and ordinances for government, as Solon, Lycurgus, and others. Some have spent their time in devising arts and sciences for the better sharpening of man's wit, and the easier expressing his conceits, as in time past Aristotle for Logic and Philosophy, Cicero and Demosthenes for Rhetoric, Euclid and others for Arithmetic and Geometry. Others again, by long and diligent observation, have found out the motion and courses of the celestial orbs, that thereby man might have the distinction of times and seasons, the better to direct his doings, both for taking pains and rest, as occasion and
30 circumstance doth require. Some delight in feats of arms, thereby to be better able to defend their countries from the force of the enemy, and rightfully (when occasion is) to enlarge their dominions.

And many others in sundry faculties and sciences have both heretofore, and especially now in these later days, do so bestow and employ their time that rightly they may be said to have deserved the name of profitable members in the commonwealth; so that now, by continual practice and exercising of good wits, the world is waxed finer and grown to more perfection, not only in all the speculative arts and sciences, but also in the practical application of the same to man's use, whereof as the one doth ex-
40 ceedingly delight the inward mind, in seeing the sequel of things by art and reason, so the other in the mechanical and practical application (which of late years, more than ever heretofore hath been used) doth so pleasure

and profit the world that this time only may rightly be called the liberal and flourishing age.

For when was there ever heard of such abundance of gold and silver (which no doubt, being well used, is the great benefit and good blessing of God to mankind) as in these our days? No, Solomon himself, with all the precious metal of Ophir, which he (one only King) had in that only place, can not be comparable to the great store of gold and all other metals which daily are digged out of the bowels of the earth almost in all parts of the world, and now lately in the supposed hard and congealed frozen lands, almost under the poles. Yea, now every private man can witness 10 this with me, that he is no more contented with the wealth and riches that his ancestors had, but thinks himself base minded if by his industry he increase not his private wealth proportionally, as the whole world increaseth in common wealth. And not only of gold and silver is such great increase, but also of all other things serving as well for pleasure and delights of the mind as for the necessary uses of man's life.

For as we are placed in these lower Elements, first to know and acknowledge the high Creator, and then thankfully to take the fruition of things for our maintenance, which are especially two; that is, meat and drink to sustain the body, and coverture to defend the same from the 20 rigor of heat and cold, and so thereby to glorify God in his works. What age hath been ever heretofore that hath so abounded with store not only of necessary meats, but also of pleasant and delectable confections to delight man withal? For whatsoever sundry sort of corn, grain, and meats former years have had, we not only have all the same in far greater abundance, but thereunto are added thousands of new things simple and compound never heretofore seen or heard of. And as for coverture to defend the body, the matter is grown to such excellency of architecture and building, to such fineness of cloth and silks of all sorts and colors, that man studieth no more to multiply the increase thereof, so much as to devise 30 fashions to make it serve more for ornament than for necessary uses.

And the chiefest cause of all these effects (next after the divine Providence) is the searching wit of man, which being more curious and inquisitive of new and strange devices than heretofore, bringeth out daily more strange inventions, and causeth others through emulation to do the like, not only in providing the necessary things aforesaid, but also a continual care and constancy to find out other new arts, occupations, and faculties. For to remember one or two inventions for all, found out of late years. The use and benefit of Printing Books, a device so commodious and necessary, saving within these few years in respect hath lain utterly hid 40 and unknown. The Art of War is now grown to that excellency that if Achilles, Alexander the Great, Julius Caesar, and other should come in

these later days, they themselves would more admire and wonder at the
courages of our men, their engines, their policies in war, than the ignorant and barbarous multitude in their days did to them in celebrating their
solemnities with all the honor that might be.

But to draw near to my purposed scope, that is, to discourse of inventions by way of discoveries, I say that one of the excellentest arts that ever
hath been devised is the Art of Navigation, which in times past was so
raw and unknown that no man durst travel by sea, saving only alongst the
shore; and if by wind, current, or tempest, he were driven against his will
10 so far from the land that he lost the sight thereof, he made no other account but to be cast away, his vessel was so rude, and his skill so little.

In those days they knew not the singular use and benefit of the Loadstone, called in Latin *Magnes,* which besides the property of drawing iron
unto it, it directeth and with opposite points sheweth two principal parts of
the world, the North and the South, and that more distinctly than the
rising of the sun doth show East and West (except it be only in the days
of *Aequinoctium,* which is but twice a year). Which rare property of the
Loadstone if any man desire at large to see, let him put the said stone into
a round dish, and they both so together in some vessel of water wherein
20 they might swim at pleasure voluntarily; which dish, when it standeth still,
then do the two principal and opposite points of the stone firmly and constantly point out North and South. And if before the quarters of North and
South were known, by this experience he may find out the two principal
points of the stone, so that the one being known, the other can not be
wanting. And that a man may be the better persuaded of this effect, let
him remove or turn round the dish after it hath once stood still, and he
shall ever find it to return constantly to the same point again. Also, a pillar
or piece of steel, being but touched with the foresaid *Magnes,* playing
Aequilibra upon some pyramid or point, receiveth such virtue that it
30 produceth like effect. Whereunto, if wood or paper in circular form
divided into 32 equal parts be handsomely compacted, it will distinguish
and point out all parts of the horizon, and direct into all coasts of the world,
and that only by the influent spirit of the two principal points, respecting
ever North and South.

This excellent property and benefit of the Loadstone I the rather remember at large because some Seamen which know this rare and miraculous effect as well as I do not sufficiently admire the same, because it is now
so commonly known, and yet indeed is to be preferred before all precious
stones in the world, which only tend to ornament and have no other
40 virtue, whereas this serveth to so necessary use. The virtue of this stone,
as it is not long since it was first found, so in these days it is like to receive

his perfection concerning his Northeasting and Northwesting to be brought in rule, and particularly in this noble voyage of our worthy Captain Martin Frobisher, who, as you shall after understand in the discourse, hath diligently observed the variation of the needle. And such observations of skillful pilots is the only way to bring it in rule, for it passeth the reach of Natural Philosophy.

The making and pricking of cards, the shifting of sun and moon, the use of the compass, the hour glass for observing time, instruments of astronomy to take longitudes and latitudes of countries, and many other helps are so commonly known of every mariner nowadays that he that 10 hath been twice at sea is ashamed to come home if he be not able to render account of all these particularities. By which skill in navigation is brought to pass that the people of Europe can as easily and far more easilier make long voyages by sea than by land. Whereby hath come to pass that within the memory of man, within these four score years, there hath been more new countries and regions discovered than in five thousand years before; yea, more than half the world hath been discovered by men that are yet (or might very well for their age be) alive. When I name the world in this sense, I mean the uppermost face and superficies of the Earth and Sea, which unite together, make one globe or sphere. And this face of the 20 Earth, which Almighty God hath given man as most convenient place to inhabit in, through the negligence of man hath, until of late days, lain so hid and unknown that he hath lost the fruition and benefit of more than half the earth.

A marvellous thing that man, who hath always abhorred so much thraldom and restraint, and so greedily desired liberty, could be contented so many thousand years to be shut up in so narrow bounds. For it is to be thought, that only such countries in times past have been known as either did bound and hang together, or else were separated by very narrow seas, as are Europe, Africa, and Asia, out of which, from either to other, a man 30 may travel by land, or else shall find in some places very narrow seas separating them, and so might sail from the one to the other only by land marks, without the art of navigation, because the one was within a ken of the other.

For even the great strength and stoutness of Hercules himself, when out of Græcia westward he had travelled and conquered all the regions and countries, coming to the strait between Spain and Barbarie, made account to have been at the west end of the world, and therefore there erected two pillars as a perpetual monument of his fame; which to this day are called *Herculeæ Columnæ,* the Pillars of Hercules, the one stand- 40 ing in Spain of Europe, the other in Africa; and called the strait *Fretum*

Herculeum, and now commonly is named the straits of Malega, or Gibraltar. And having come so far westward, contented himself and said: *Non plus ultra,* no further.

Likewise Alexander Magnus out of Macedonia in Greece, passing through Armenia, Persia, and India, coming to the great River Ganges, and conquering all these countries (although he was persuaded that Asia extended somewhat further into the east and northeast), yet knowing them not to be very great countries and thinking them to be of small moment, erected there certain altars which are yet called *Aræ Alexandrinæ,* 10 as beyond which no man else in those days had passed, or need to pass, more eastward. And this was accounted, as it were, a bounder of the east side of the world, although indeed Asia doth extend further 20 degrees, and is environed with *Mare Eoum,* and the strait Anian, which our Captain Frobisher pretendeth to find out.

Touching the south parts of the world towards Africa, Ptolomeus King of Egypt, a famous Cosmographer, who was more solicit and curious in describing all the face of the Earth, than any king before him or after (except of late days), delivered in plat described and known only 16 degrees beyond the Equinoctial to the southwards or Pole Antarctic, and 20 that bounder was called *Montes Lunae,* out of which the great river Nilus is supposed to have his beginning and spring. And as for the known land on the north parts of the world, Thyle, being one of the islands of Orcades (more probably than Iceland), was so long pronounced and continued Ultima that it was esteemed a great error for any man to imagine any land more north than that.

Thus have I briefly named the four principal bounders of the world, which was only known from the beginning of the world (as some think) until within these 80 last years. That is the straits of Gibraltar or Malega, westward; the east part of Asia beyond *Aræ Alexandrinæ,* eastward; 30 Ultima Thyle by Scotland, northward; and 16 grades beyond the Equinoctial, southward. But these 16 degrees of South Latitude are to be understood only in the continent of Africa, which extendeth not passing 70 degrees in longitude. Therefore, whatsoever countries or regions have since been discovered and known beyond 180 degrees in longitude, 60 degrees in North Latitude, and 16 degrees in South Latitude, all the commendation, honor, renown, glory, and fame thereof must be attributed to the Englishmen, Spaniards, Portingales, Frenchmen, and Italians, whose valiant courage and high minds be such that either they already have, or shortly will discover and search out every narrow corner of the 40 world. By these men's valors and industries the known regions of the world, which before were divided into three parts, that is, Europe, Africa, and Asia, are now made six by addition of other three. For like as the

whole massy frame of the world, being first divided into two principal
regions, the one Elemental, the other Heavenly, the Elemental containeth
four parts, that is, the four Elements, the Earth, the Water, the Air, and
the Fire; the Heavenly region, although one, yet for diversity of motion
may be counted two, that is, Primum Mobile, moving only upon the
poles Arctic and Antarctic, and all the rest of Orbs and Planets, moving
upon the poles of the Zodiac, are by this difference of motion imagined
two. Whereby ariseth the number of six substantial parts of the world,
that is, the four Elements and the two varieties of Orbs. So likewise the
inferior world, I mean the superficies of the earth, is also divided into six 10
parts; that is Europe, Africa, Asia, Terra Septentrionalis, America, and
Terra Austrialis, whose bounders, because this division seemeth somewhat strange, I thought good for the more particularity, here briefly to
repeat.

* * * * *

Upon the bounds and description of this part of the earth [Terra Sep-
tentrionalis] I have the longer stayed because I find it discovered only by
the English nation. And although the greatest part hereof was made 20
known 200 and odd years past, yet some bounders thereof were described
and set out by the travel of Sir Hugh Willoby Knight, an Englishman,
who ventured and lost his life in the cause, and so died an honorable death;
and with him Richard Chancellor, chief pilot in that voyage, in Anno
1554; who discovered and found out that Norway and Lapland, etc.
conjoined not to Groneland or any part of the Northern Regions, as one
firm and continent, but that by sea a man might travel to the country of
Moscovia and a great way more eastward, as far as the great river Obby.
Also our worthy General Captain Frobisher, in his three last voyages,
whereof we are briefly to entreat in these three books, hath discovered 30
and described a great part of the southwest bounds thereof, and meaneth
(God willing) not only to describe the one half thereof in going to Cataia
by the Northwest, but also to put in trial whether he may return into
England by the Northeast, and so also to describe the other part. Which
to do is one of the weightiest matters of the world, and a thing that will
cause other Princes to admire the fortunate state and the great valor of
the English nation. But to return again to the bounding of the other parts
of the world.

America, an island, is included on the east side with the Sea Atlantique;
on the west side with *Mare del Sur*, or *Mare Pacificum*; on the south side 40
it is bounded with the strait of Magellanus; and on the north with
Frobisher's straits.

Terra Australis seemeth to be a great firm land, lying under and about the South Pole, being in many places a fruitful soil; and is not yet thoroughly discovered, but only seen and touched on the north edge thereof by the travail of the Portingales and Spaniards in their voyages to their East and West Indies. . . .

Thus I have briefly butted and bounded out all the parts of the Earth, according unto this latter division into six parts. Which, that it might be more apparent and sensible to every man's understanding, I have hereunto adjoined an universal map, wherein my mind was to make known to
10 the eye what countries have been discovered of late years, and what before of old time. The old known parts have their bounds traced and drawn with whole lines, the new discovered Countries have their bounds drawn with points or broken lines. . . .

By this discourse and map is to be seen the valiant courages of men in this later age, within these 80 years, that have so much enlarged the bounds of the world that now we have twice and thrice so much scope for our earthly peregrination as we have had in times past; so that now men need no more contentiously to strive for room to build an house on, or for a little turf of ground of one acre or two, when great countries, and whole
20 worlds, offer and reach out themselves to them that will first vouchsafe to possess, inhabit, and till them. Yea, there are countries yet remaining without masters and possessors, which are fertile to bring forth all manner of corn and grain, infinite sorts of land cattle, as horse, elephants, kine, sheep; great variety of flying fowls of the air, as pheasants, partridge, quail, popingeys, ostriches, etc.; infinite kind of fruits, as almonds, dates, quinces, pomegranates, oranges, etc., wholesome, medicinable, and delectable. Great variety of flowers continually springing, winter and summer, beautiful for color, odoriferous, and comfortable. Abundance of fair hills and valleys, furnished with all manner woods and pleasant rivers.
30 Millions of new fashions, and strange beasts and fishes, both in sea and fresh waters. Mountains bringing forth all manner of metals, as gold, silver, iron, etc. All sorts of precious stones and spices, in all which land wanteth nothing that may be desired, either for pleasure, profit, or necessary uses. Which sundry countries to possess and obtain, as it is an easy thing, so would I not have our English Nation to be slack therein, lest perhaps again they overshoot themselves, in refusing occasion offered, as it was in the time of King Henry the seventh, when all the West Indies were first proffered to the Englishmen, to be given into their hands; which they little regarding, was afterward offered to the Spaniards, who pres-
40 ently accepted the occasion and now enjoy the infinite treasure and commodity thereof. I would not wish Englishmen to be now unlike them-

selves, for in all the later discoveries the English nation hath been as forward, as any other.

*   *   *   *   *

Also the valor of the Englishmen did first of all discover and find out all that part of America which now is called Baccalaos; for Sebastian Cabot, an Englishman born in Bristol, was by commandment of King Henry the Seventh, in Anno 1508 furnished with shipping, munition, and men, and sailed along all that tract, pretending to discover the passage to Cataya, and went aland in many places, and brought home sundry of the people, and many other things of that country in token of possession, being (I say) the first Christians that ever there set foot on land.

Also, the said Englishman Cabot did first discover, at the procurement of the King of Spain, all that other part of America adjoining next beyond Brazil, lying about the famous river called Rio de la Plata.

Also, the Englishmen have made sundry voyages to Guinea and Benin, although the Spaniards and Portugalles, because of their near dwelling thereunto, get thither the first start of them, and there prevented them in building towns and castles, whereby appeareth that the English nation, by their long and dangerous navigations, have diligently and painfully searched out by sea, the temperature of all the Zones, whether they were burning, frozen, hot, cold, or indifferent, even from the Pole Arctic, to the Equinoctial; and crossing it also, passed beyond the Tropic of Capricorn and returned again.

And therefore, as we are inferior to no other nation in making great and long voyages by sea, so know I no nation comparable unto us in taking in hand long travels and voyages by land. For what nation is it that hath ever had such a long trade by land as is the Englishmen's into Persia, which besides two months' sailing by sea along the west and northern coasts of Norway and Lapland, by Wardhouse, unto the Bay of Saint Nicholas, it remaineth more in voyage by land and fresh rivers about three thousand English miles. For from the Merchants' house at Saint Nicholas, by the River Dvina and Sughana, to the City Volugda, is counted seven hundred English miles; from thence to the City Yearuslave, standing upon the great River Volga, travelling by only land, is reckoned about 140 miles; where the merchants, making new shipping for the fresh River Volga, go eastward about seven hundred miles; then the said river turning again south by many windings, at the last by the great City Astracan delivereth itself into the south side of the Sea Caspium, that tract being above nine hundred miles. Then after, in two or three days, with a good wind crossing the Caspium Sea, they arrive at a port named Bilbill; where after, by land journeying with camels, in one and twenty days, being almost 600 miles, they come to the famous city of Tauris or Teuris, being the greatest city of Persia for trade of merchandise. This long and painful voyage by land was taken in hand by a worthy Gentleman, Master Anthony Jenkinson, who made thereof a plat, with the first particular description that I have seen of the whole country of Moscovia, which is yet extant. And therefore the Englishmen are to be preferred before all other nations in making long voyages by land.

The Spaniards and Portugalles undoubtedly are worthy immortal
10 fame and glory for their great enterprises, and good successes they have therein; yet have they never seen nor heard such strange and extraordinary accidents of the Sphere as hath happened unto the Englishmen. For neither Spaniard nor Portugal ever saw, in all their long voyages, the sun and the moon to make whole and perfect revolutions above the horizon, as our men yearly do see in their voyage to Moscovia, where, when they abide any time at Wardehouse, they see the sun go continually above ground the space of above two months together; where if they take not great heed, they shall not know what day of the month it is after the order of our calendar, for that they have no nights. But yet because once
20 every 24 hours the sun draweth near to the horizon in the north parts, it is there commonly shadowed with vapors and thick fogs, which usually rise from the earth, and seem a little to shadow the body of the sun. And that lowest approaching of the sun to the Earthward they count night, and so make good enough reckoning of the days of the month according to our usual fashion.

But one inconvenience there is, that dismayeth and deterreth most men (though they be of valiant courage) from taking in hand long voyages, either by sea or by land, and that is the new and uncustomed elements, and the extreme airs of hot and cold, whereby (as some think) if they
30 travel far northward they shall be frozen to death in the hard congealed and frozen sea. And again, if they travel far toward the south, they fear they should be parched and broiled to death with the extreme heat of the middle burning Zone; or else, if perhaps they escape alive, yet at least they should be burned as black as a coal, as the Indians or Black Moors there are; and this to believe they are partly persuaded by the sight of those Indians, and partly by the persuasions of certain philosophers who went about with reasons to prove that between the two Tropics was no dwelling or being, for the extreme heat, the sun beating on them continually; neither near either Pole, for the extreme frosts, cold, and snow, which
40 continually hath there (from the beginning of the world as some think) increased, the sun being so far distant from them. Which opinion of some, because it importeth very much, I thought good here to do my endeavor

to refel, both because I know the contrary by my own experience, and
also for that I find the course of the sun in Zodiac (which God hath ordained to give light and life to all things) can induce no such kind of extremity; and so lastly to confirm all parts of the world to be habitable.

FROM RICHARD HAKLUYT'S *The Principall Navigations, Voiages,
and Discoveries of the English Nation,* 1589

To The Right Honorable Sir Francis Walsingham, Knight, 10
Principal Secretary to Her Majesty, Chancellor of the
Duchy of Lancaster, and One of Her Majesty's Most
Honorable Privy Council.

RIGHT Honorable, I do remember that, being a youth, and one of Her
Majesty's scholars at Westminster, that fruitful nursery, it was my hap
to visit the chamber of Mr. Richard Hakluyt, my cousin, a gentleman of
the Middle Temple well known unto you, at a time when I found lying
open upon his board certain books of cosmography, with an universal map.
He seeing me somewhat curious in the view thereof, began to instruct my
ignorance by shewing me the division of the earth into three parts, after 20
the old account, and then according to the latter and better distribution
into more. He pointed with his wand to all the known seas, gulfs, bays,
straits, capes, rivers, empires, kingdoms, dukedoms, and territories of
each part, with declaration also of their special commodities and particular wants which by the benefit of traffic and intercourse of merchants are
plentifully supplied. From the map he brought me to the Bible, and turning to the 107 Psalm, directed me to the 23 and 24 verses, where I read
that they which go down to the sea in ships and occupy by the great waters,
they see the works of the Lord and His wonders in the deep, etc. Which
words of the prophet, together with my cousin's discourse (things of high 30
and rare delight to my young nature) took in me so deep an impression
that I constantly resolved if ever I were preferred to the university, where
better time and more convenient place might be ministered for these
studies, I would, by God's assistance, prosecute that knowledge and kind
of literature, the doors whereof (after a sort) were so happily opened
before me.

According to which my resolution, when, not long after, I was removed
to Christ Church in Oxford, my exercises of duty first performed, I fell
to my intended course and by degrees read over whatsoever printed or
written discoveries and voyages I found extant either in the Greek, Latin, 40
Italian, Spanish, Portugal, French, or English languages, and in my public lectures was the first that produced and shewed both the old, imper-

fectly composed, and the new, lately reformed, maps, globes, spheres, and
other instruments of this art for demonstration in the common schools,
to the singular pleasure and general contentment of my auditory. In
continuance of time, and by reason principally of my insight in this study,
I grew familiarly acquainted with the chiefest captains at sea, the greatest
merchants, and the best mariners of our nation. By which means, having
gotten somewhat more than common knowledge, I passed at length the
narrow seas into France with Sir Edward Stafford, Her Majesty's careful and discreet lieger, where, during my five years abroad with him in
10 his dangerous and chargeable residency in Her Highness' service, I both
heard in speech and read in books other nations miraculously extolled for
their discoveries and notable enterprises by sea, but the English, of all
others, for their sluggish security and continual neglect of the like attempts,
especially in so long and happy a time of peace, either ignominiously reported or exceedingly condemned. Which singular opportunity, if some
other people our neighbors had been blessed with, their protestations are
often and vehement they would far otherwise have used. And that the
truth and evidence hereof may better appear, these are the very words of
Popilinière in his book called *L'Admiral de France*, and printed at Paris.
20 Fol. 73, pag. I, 2. The occasion of his speech is the commendation of the
Rhodians, who being (as we are) islanders, were excellent in navigation,
whereupon he wondereth much that the English should not surpass in
that quality, in this sort: *Ce qui m'a fait autresfois rechercher les occasions,
qui empeschent, que les Anglois, qui ont d'esprit, de moyens, et valeur
assez, pour s'aquerir un grand honneur parmi tous les Chrestiens, ne se
font plus valoir sur l'element qui leur est, et doit estre plus naturel qu'à
autres peuples: qui leur doivent ceder en la structure, accommodement et
police de navires: comme i' ay veu en plusieurs endroits parmi eux.* Thus
both hearing and reading the obloquy of our nation, and finding few or
30 none of our own men able to reply herein: and further, not seeing any man
to have care to recommend to the world the industrious labors and painful
travails of our countrymen: for stopping the mouths of the reproachers,
myself being the last winter returned from France with the honorable
the Lady Sheffield, for her passing good behavior highly esteemed in all
the French court, determined, notwithstanding all difficulties, to undertake the burden of that work wherein all others pretended either ignorance, or lack of leisure, or want of sufficient argument, whereas (to speak
truly) the huge toil and the small profit to ensue were the chief causes
of the refusal. I call the work a burden in consideration that these voyages
40 lay so dispersed, scattered, and hidden in several hucksters' hands, that I
now wonder at myself, to see how I was able to endure the delays, curi-

osity, and backwardness of many from whom I was to receive my originals. . . .

Now whereas I have always noted your wisdom to have had a special
care of the honor of Her Majesty, the good reputation of our country,
and the advancing of navigation, the very walls of this our island, as the
oracle is reported to have spoken of the sea forces of Athens; and whereas
I acknowledge in all dutiful sort how honorably, both by your letter and
speech, I have been animated in this and other my travails, I see myself
bound to make presentment of this work to yourself, as the fruits of your
own encouragements and the manifestation both of my unfeigned service 10
to my prince and country and of my particular duty to your honor: which
I have done with the less suspicion either of not satisfying the world or of
not answering your own expectation, in that, according to your order, it
hath passed the sight, and partly also the censure, of the learned physician,
Master Doctor James, a man many ways very notably qualified.

And thus beseeching God, the giver of all true honor and wisdom, to
increase both these blessings in you, with continuance of health, strength,
happiness, and whatsoever good thing else yourself can wish, I humbly take
my leave. London the 17 of November.

Your Honor's most humble always to be 20
commanded, RICHARD HAKLUYT.

*   *   *   *   *

The voyage passed by sea into Egypt by John Evesham, Gentleman,
Anno 1586.

The 5 of December, 1586, we departed from Gravesend in the Tiger,
of London, wherein was master under God for the voyage Robert Rick-
man, and the 21 day at night we came to the Isle of Wight. Departing
from thence in the morning following, we had a fair wind, so that on 30
the 27 day we came in sight of the rock of Lisbon, and so sailing along
we came in sight of the South Cape the 29 of the same; and on the morrow, with a westerly wind, we entered the Straits; and the 2 of January,
we being as high as Cape de Gate, we departed from our fleet towards
Argier. And the 4 day we arrived at the port of Argier aforesaid, where
we stayed till the first of March. At which time we set sail towards a place
called Tunis, to the eastward of Argier 100 leagues, where we arrived
the 8 of the same. This Tunis is a small city up 12 miles from the sea, and
at the port or road where shipping do ride is a castle or fort called the
Goletta, sometimes in the hands of the Christians, but now in the Turks'. 40
At which place we remained till the third of April; at which time we set

sail towards Alexandria, and having sometime fair winds, sometime contrary, we passed on the 12 day between Sicilia and Malta (where near adjoining hath been the fort and hold of the Knights of the Rhodes), and so the 19 day we fell with the isle of Candie, and from thence to Alexandria, where we arrived the 27 of April, and there continued till the 5 of October.

The said city of Alexandria is an old thing, decayed or ruinated, having been a fair and great city near two miles in length, being all vaulted underneath for provision of fresh water, which water cometh thither but once
10 every year out of one of the four rivers of paradise (as it is termed) called Nilus, which in September floweth near eighteen foot upright higher than his accustomed manner; and so the bank being cut as it were a sluice, about thirty miles from Alexandria at a town called Rocetto, it doth so come to the said city with such abundance that barks of twelve ton do come upon the same water, which water doth fill all the vaults, cisterns, and wells in the said city with very good water, and doth so continue good till the next year following. For they have there very little rain, or none at all; yet have they exceeding great dews. Also they have very good corn, and very plentiful. All the country is very hot, especially in the months of
20 August, September, and October. Also, within the said city, there is a pillar of marble, called by the Turks King Pharaoh's Needle, and it is foursquare, every square is twelve foot, and it is in height 90 foot. Also there is without the walls of the said city, about twenty score paces, another marble pillar, being round, called Pompey his Pillar. This pillar standeth upon a great square stone, every square is fifteen foot, and the same stone is fifteen foot high, and the compass of the pillar is 27 foot, and the height of it is 101 feet, which is a wonder to think how ever it was possible to set the said pillar upon the said square stone.

The port of the said city is strongly fortified with two strong castles,
30 and one other castle within the city, being all very well planted with munition. And there is to the eastward of this city, about three days' journey, the city of Grand Cairo, otherwise called Memphis. It hath in it, by report of the register's books which we did see, to the number of 2400 churches, and is wonderfully populous, and is one day's journey about the walls; which was journeyed by one of our mariners for trial thereof. Also, near to the said city, there is a place called the pyramids, being, as I may well term it, one of the nine wonders of the world; that is, seven several places of flint and marble stone, foursquare, the walls thereof are seven yards thick in those places that we did see. The squareness
40 is in length about twenty score every square, being built, as it were, a pointed diamond, broad at the foot and small or narrow at the top; the height of them, to our judgment, doth surmount twice the height of

Paul's steeple. Within the said pyramids no man doth know what there is, for that they have no entrance, but in one of them there is a hole where the wall is broken; and so we went in there, having torchlight with us, for that it hath no light to it, and within the same is, as it were, a great hall, in the which there is a costly tomb, which tomb, they say, was made for King Pharaoh in his lifetime, but he was not buried there, being drowned in the Red Sea. Also there are certain vaults or dungeons which go down very deep under those pyramids, with fair stairs, but no man dare venture to go down into them by reason that they can carry no light with them, for the damp of the earth doth put out the light. The Red Sea is but three days' journey from this place, and Jerusalem about seven days' journey from thence. But to return to Cairo.

There is a castle wherein is the house that Pharaoh's wives were kept in, and in the palace or court thereof standeth 55 marble pillars in such order as our Exchange standeth in London. The said pillars are in height 60 foot, and in compass 14 foot. Also in the said city is the castle where Joseph was in prison, where to this day they put in rich men when the king would have any sum of money of them. There are seven gates to the said prison, and it goeth near 50 yards downright. Also the water that serveth this castle cometh out of the foresaid river of Nilus, upon a wall made with arches, five miles long, and it is twelve foot thick. Also there are in old Cairo two monasteries, the one called St. George's, the other St. Mary's; and in the courts where the churches be was the house of King Pharaoh. In this city is great store of merchandise, especially pepper and nutmegs, which come thither by land out of the East India. And it is very plentiful of all manner of victuals, especially of bread, roots, and herbs. To the eastwards of Cairo there is a well, five miles off, called Matria, and, as they say, when the Virgin Mary fled from Bethlehem and came into Egypt, and, being there, had neither water nor any other thing to sustain them, by reason of the providence of God an angel came from heaven and strake the ground with his wings, where presently issued out a fountain of water; and the wall did open, where the Israelites did hide themselves; which fountain or well is walled foursquare to this day.

Also we were at an old city, all ruinated and destroyed, called in old time the great city of Carthage, where Hannibal and Queen Dido dwelt. This city was but narrow, but was very long; for there was, and is yet, to be seen one street three mile long; to which city fresh water was brought upon arches (as afore) above 25 miles, of which arches some are standing to this day. Also we were at divers other places on the coast as we came from Cairo, but of other antiquities we saw but few.

The town of Argier, which was our first and last port within the straits, standeth upon the side of an hill, close upon the seashore. It is very strong, both by sea and land, and it is very well victualled with all manner of fruits, bread, and fish, good store and very cheap. It is inhabited with Turks, Moors, and Jews, and so are Alexandria and Cairo. In this town are a great number of Christian captives, whereof there are of Englishmen only 15. From which port we set sail towards England the seventh of January, anno 1587, and the 30 day of the said month we arrived at Dartmouth, on the coast of England.

*　　*　　*　　*　　*

10 The opinion of Master William Burrough sent to a friend, requiring his judgment for the fittest time of the departure of our ships towards St. Nicholas in Russia.

Whereas you request me to persuade the company not to send their ships from hence before the fine of May, I do not think the same so good a course for them to observe; for you know that the sooner we send them hence, the sooner we may look for their return. If we send them in the beginning of May, then may they be at St. Nicholas by the fine of the same month; and by that time the greatest part of your lading of necessity 20 must be come down, especially the flax. But if it should fall out so lateward a breaking up of the river of Dvina, that by the end of May the goods cannot be brought to St. Nicholas, yet this is always to be accounted for certain: that before our ships can come thither, the goods may be brought down to that place. And if through ice the ships be kept back any time, the loss and charge of that time toucheth not the company at all, but the owners of the ships; and yet will the owners put that in adventure rather than tarry longer time before their going hence.

Now seeing by sending our ships hence in the beginning of May, their arrival at St. Nicholas may be at the end of the same month, and remaining 30 thirty days there, they may be laden and come thence by the last of June, and return home hither by the 10 of August with commodities to serve the market then, it cannot be denied but we should reap thereby great commodity.

But it may be objected, that if all our ships be sent then to return as aforesaid, you shall not be able to send us in so much cordage, wax, and oils as otherwise you should do if they remained a month longer, neither could you by that time perfect your accounts to be sent in them as you would do.

For answer thereunto this is my meaning: though I wish the greatest 40 part of our shipping to go as aforesaid, yet would I have one good ship, or two at the most, well furnished in all points, that should depart always from hence between the beginning and the 10 of June; and the same to be conditioned withal to remain at St. Nicholas from the first arrival there until the midst of August, or to be dispatched thence sooner, at the will and liking of our factors for the same. By this order these commodities following may ensue:

1. You may have our commodities there timely to send up the river before it wax shallow, to be dispersed in the country at your pleasure.

2. The greatest part of our goods may be returned hither timely to serve the first markets.

3. Our late ships remaining so long here may serve to good purpose for returning answer of such letters as may be sent over land, and received here before their departure.

4. Their remaining so late with you shall satisfy your desire for perfecting your accounts, and may bring such cordage, wax, oil, and other commodities as you can provide before that time; and chiefly may serve us in stead to bring home our goods that may be sent us from Persia.

Now seeing it may be so many ways commodious to the company to observe this order, without any charge unto them, I wish that you put to your helping hand to further the same.

*　*　*　*　*

The first voyage of Master John Davis, undertaken in June 1585, for the discovery of the Northwest Passage. Written by John Janes, Merchant, sometimes servant to the worshipful Master William Sanderson.

*　*　*　*　*

The next morning being the 30 of July, there came 37 Canoas rowing by our ships, calling to us to come on shore. We not making any great haste unto them, one of them went up to the top of the rock and leapt and danced as they had done the day before, showing us a seal's skin and another thing made like a timbrel, which he did beat upon with a stick, making a noise like a small drum. Whereupon we manned our boats and came to them, they all staying in their Canoas. We came to the water side where they were; and after we had sworn by the sun, after their fashion, they did trust us. So I shook hands with one of them, and he kissed my hand, and we were very familiar with them. We were in so great credit with them upon this single acquaintance, that we could have any thing they had. We bought five Canoas of them; we bought their clothes from their backs, which were all made of seals' skins and birds' skins; their buskins, their hose, their gloves, all being commonly sewed and well dressed, so that we were fully persuaded that they have divers artificers among them. We had a pair of buskins of them full of fine wool like beaver. Their apparel for heat was made of birds' skins with their feathers

on them. We saw among them leather dressed like glovers' leather, and thick thongs like white leather of a good length. We had of their darts and ores, and found in them that they would by no means displease us, but would give us whatsoever we asked of them, and would be satisfied with whatsoever we gave them. They took great care one of another; for when we had bought their boats, then two other would come and carry him away between them that had sold us his. They are very tractable people, void of craft or double dealing, and easy to be brought to any civility or good order. But we judge them to be idolaters and to worship
10 the sun.

During the time of our abode among these islands we found reasonable quantity of wood, both fir, spruce, and juniper; which whether it came floating any great distance to these places where we found it, or whether it grew in some great islands near the same place by us not yet discovered, we know not; but we judge that it groweth there further into the land then we were, because the people had great store of darts and ores which they made none account of, but gave them to us for small trifles, as points and pieces of paper. We saw about this coast marvelous great abundance of seals skulling together like skulls of small fish. We found no fresh
20 water among these islands, but only snow water, whereof we found great pools. The cliffs were all of such ore as M. Frobisher brought from Meta Incognita. We had divers shows of study or muscovy glass shining not altogether unlike to crystal. We found an herb growing upon the rocks, whose fruit was sweet, full of red juice; and the ripe ones were like corinths. We found also birch and willow growing like shrubs low to the ground. These people have great store of furs, as we judge. They made shows unto us the 30 of this present, which was the second time of our being with them, after they perceived we would have skins and furs, that they would go into the country and come again the next day with such
30 things as they had. But this night the wind coming fair, the captain and the master would by no means detract the purpose of our discovery. And so the last of this month about four of the clock in the morning in God's name we set sail, and were all that day becalmed upon the coast.

The first of August we had a fair wind, and so proceeded towards the Northwest for our discovery.

ROBERT GREENE

The Introduction and Notes are at page 1327

FROM *A Notable Discouery of Coosenage*, 1591

A Notable Discovery of Cozenage

To The Young Gentlemen, Merchants, Apprentices, Farmers, and plain Countrymen Health

DIOGENES, gentlemen, from a counterfeit coiner of money, became a current corrector of manners, as absolute in the one as dissolute in the other. Time refineth men's affects, and their humors grow different by the distinction of age. Poor Ovid, that amorously writ in his youth the art of love, complained in his exile amongst the Getes of his wanton follies. And Socrates' age was virtuous though his prime was licentious. So, gentlemen, my younger years had uncertain thoughts, but now my ripe days calls on to repentant deeds, and I sorrow as much to see others willful as I delighted once to be wanton. The odd mad-caps I have been 20 mate to, not as a companion but as a spy to have an insight into their knaveries, that seeing their trains I might eschew their snares; those mad fellows I learned at last to loathe, by their own graceless villanies, and what I saw in them to their confusion I can forewarn in others to my country's commodity. None could decipher Tyranism better than Aristippus; not that his nature was cruel, but that he was nurtured with Dionisius. The simple swain that cuts the Lapidary's stones can distinguish a ruby from a diamond only by his labor. Though I have not practised their deceits, yet conversing by fortune and talking upon purpose with such copes-mates hath given me light into their conceits; and I can de- 30 cipher their qualities, though I utterly mislike of their practises.

To be brief, gentlemen, I have seen the world and rounded it, though not with travel yet with experience, and I cry out with Solomon, *Omnia sub sole vanitas*. I have smiled with the Italian, and worn the viper's head in my hand, and yet stopped his venom. I have eaten Spanish *Mirabolanes*, and yet am nothing the more metamorphosed. France, Germany, Poland, Denmark, I know them all, yet not affected to any in the form of my life; only I am English born, and I have English thoughts; not a devil incarnate because I am Italianate, but hating the pride of Italy, because I know their peevishness. Yet in all these countries where I have travelled 40 I have not seen more excess of vanity than we Englishmen practise through vain glory; for as our wits be as ripe as any, so our wills are more

ready than they all to put in effect any of their licentious abuses. Yet
amongst the rest, letting ordinary sins pass because custom hath almost
made them a law, I will only speak of two such notable abuses, which
the practitioners of them shadow with the name of Arts, as never have
been heard of in any age before. The first and chief is called the Art of
Conny catching; the second, the Art of Crosbiting; two such pestilent
and prejudicial practises as of late have been the ruin of infinite persons,
and the subversion and overthrow of many merchants, farmers, and
honest-minded yeomen.

10   The first is a deceit at Cards, which growing by enormity into a cozenage, is able to draw (by the subtle show thereof) a man of great judgment
to consent to his own confusion. Yet, gentlemen, when you shall read this
book, written faithfully to discover these cozening practises, think I go
not about to disprove or disallow the most ancient and honest pastime or
recreation of Cardplay, for thus much I know by reading. When the city
of Thebes was besieged by them of Lacedemonia, being girt within strong
fenced walls, and having men enough, and able to rebate the enemy, they
found no inconvenience of force to breed their ensuing bane but famine,
in that when victuals waxed scant, hunger would either make them yield
20 by a fainting composition or a miserable death. Whereupon, to weary the
foe with wintering at the siege, the Thebans devised this policy: they
found out the Method of Cards and Dice, and so busied their brains with
the pleasantness of that new invention, passing away the time with strange
recreations and pastimes, beguiling hunger with the delight of the new
sports, and eating but every third day, and playing two; so their frugal
sparing of victuals kept them from famine, the city from sacking, and
raised the foe from a mortal siege. Thus was the use of Cards and Dice
first invented, and since amongst Princes highly esteemed, and allowed
in all commonwealths as a necessary recreation for the mind. But as time
30 and malice of man's nature hatcheth abuse, so good things by ill wits are
wrested to the worse; and so in Cards: for from an honest recreation it
is grown to a prejudicial practise and most high degree of cozenage, as
shall be discovered in my Art of Conny-catching, for not only simple
swains whose wits is in their hands, but young gentlemen, and merchants,
are all caught like Connies in the hay, and so led like lambs to their confusion.

The poor man that cometh to the Term to try his right, and layeth his
land to mortgage to get some crowns in his purse to see his lawyer, is drawn
in by these devilish Conny-catchers, that at one cut at Cards loseth all his
40 money; by which means, he, his wife and children, is brought to utter
ruin and misery. The poor prentice, whose honest mind aimeth only at
his master's profits, by these pestilent vipers of the commonwealth is

smoothly enticed to the hazard of this game at Cards, and robbed of his master's money; which forceth him oft times either to run away, or bankrupt all, to the overthrow of some honest and wealthy citizen. Seeing then such a dangerous enormity groweth by them, to the discredit of the estate of England, I would wish the Justices appointed as severe Censors of such fatal mischiefs, to show themselves *patres patriæ* by weeding out such worms as eat away the sap of the tree, and rooting this base degree of cozeners out of so peaceable and prosperous a country; for of all devilish practises this is the most prejudicial. The high lawyer that challengeth a purse by the high wayside, the foist, the nip, the stale, the snap, I mean the pick-pockets and cut-purses, are nothing so dangerous to meet withal as these Cozening Conny-Catchers. The Cheaters that with their false dice make a hand, and strike in at Hazard or Passage with their dice of advantage, are nothing so dangerous as these base minded caterpillars. For they have their vies and their revies upon the poor Conny's back till they so ferret beat him that they leave him neither hair on his skin, nor hole to harbor in.

There was before this many years ago a practise put in use by such shifting companions, which was called the Barnard's Law, wherein as in the Art of Conny-catching, four persons were required to perform their cozening commodity: the Taker-up, the Verser, the Barnard, and the Rutter; and the manner of it indeed was thus. The Taker-up seemeth a skillful man in all things, who hath by long travel learned without book a thousand policies to insinuate himself into a man's acquaintance. Talk of matters in law, he hath plenty of cases at his fingers' ends, and he hath seen, and tried, and ruled in the King's Courts. Speak of grazing and husbandry, no man knoweth more shires than he, nor better which way to raise a gainful commodity, and how the abuses and overture of prices might be redressed. Finally, enter into what discourse they list, were it into a Broomeman's faculty, he knoweth what gains they have for old boots and shoes. Yea, and it shall scape him hardly, but that before your talk break off he will be your countryman at least, and peradventure either of kin, ally, or some stale sib to you, if your reach far surmount not his.

In case he bring to pass that you be glad of his acquaintance, then doth he carry you to the taverns, and with him goes the Verser, a man of more worship than the Taker-up, and he hath the countenance of a landed man. As they are set, comes in the Barnard stumbling into your company, like some aged farmer of the country, a stranger unto you all, that had been at some market town thereabout, buying and selling, and there tippled so much malmesy that he had never a ready word in his mouth, and is so careless of his money that out he throweth some forty angels on the board's end, and standing somewhat aloof, calleth for a pint of wine, and saith:

"Masters, I am somewhat bold with you; I pray you be not grieved if I drink my drink by you"; and thus ministers such idle drunken talk that the Verser, who counterfeited the landed man, comes and draws more near to the plain honest dealing man and prayeth him to call the Barnard more near to laugh at his folly.

Between them two the matter shall be so workmanly conveyed and finely argued that out cometh an old pair of Cards, whereat the Barnard teacheth the Verser a new game that he says cost him for the learning two pots of ale not two hours ago. The first wager is drink, the next two
10 pence or a groat; and lastly, to be brief, they use the matter so that he that were an hundred years old, and never played in his life for a penny, cannot refuse to be the Verser's half; and consequently at one game at Cards he looseth all they play for, be it a hundred pound. And if perhaps when the money is lost (to use their word of Art) the poor country man begin to smoke them, and swears the drunken knave shall not get his money so, then standeth the Rutter at the door and draweth his sword and picketh a quarrel at his own shadow, if he lack an ostler or a tapster or some other to brabble with, that while the street and company gather to the fray, as the manner is, the Barnard steals away with all the coin, and
20 gets him to one blind tavern or other, where these cozeners had appointed to meet.

Thus, gentlemen, I have glanced at the Barnard's Law, which though you may perceive it to be a prejudicial insinuating cozenage, yet is the Art of Conny-catching so far beyond it in subtlety as the devil is more dishonest than the holiest angel. For so unlikely is it for the poor Conny to lose, that, might he pawn his stake to a pound, he would lay it that he cannot be crossbitten in the cut at Cards, as you shall perceive by my present discovery. Yet, gentlemen, am I sore threatened by the hacksters of that filthy faculty, that if I set their practises in print they will cut off
30 that hand that writes the pamphlet; but how I fear their bravadoes you shall perceive by my plain painting out of them. Yea, so little do I esteem such base-minded braggarts that were it not I hope of their amendment I would in a schedule set down the names of such cozening Conny-catchers.

Well, leaving them and their course of life to the honorable and the worshipful of the land, to be censors of with Justice, have about for a blow at the Art of Cross-biting. I mean not Cross-biters at dice, when the Cheater with a langret cut contrary to the vantage will cross-bite a bard cater tray. Nor I mean not when a broking knave cross-biteth a
40 gentleman with a bad commodity; nor when the Foist (the pick-pocket's sir reverence I mean) is cross-bitten by the Snap, and so smoked for his purchase; nor when the Nip, which the common people call a cut-purse,

hath a cross-bite by some bribing officer, who, threatening to carry him to prison, takes away all the money and lets him slip without any punishment. But I mean a more dishonorable Art, when a base rogue either keepeth a whore as his friend, or marries one to be his maintainer, and with her not only cross-bites men of good calling, but especially poor ignorant country farmers, who God wot be by them led like sheep to the slaughter. Thus, gentle readers, have I given you a light in brief, what I mean to prosecute at large; and so with an humble suit to all Justices that they will seek to root out these two roguish Arts, I commit you to the Almighty.

Yours ROB. GREENE.

The Art of Conny-catching

There be requisite effectually to act the Art of Conny-catching three several parties: the Setter, the Verser, and the Barnacle. The nature of the Setter is to draw any person familiarly to drink with him, which person they call the Conny, and their method is according to the man they aim at; if a gentleman, merchant, or apprentice, the Conny is the more easily caught in that they are soon induced to play, and therefore I omit the circumstance which they use in catching of them. And for because the poor country farmer or yeoman is the mark which they most shoot at, who they know comes not empty to the Term, I will discover the means they put in practise to bring in some honest, simple and ignorant men to their purpose. The Conny-catchers, apparelled like honest civil gentlemen, or good fellows, with a smooth face, as if butter would not melt in their mouths, after dinner when the clients are come from Westminster Hall and are at leisure to walk up and down Paul's, Fleet-street, Holborne, the Strand, and such common hunted places where these cozening companions attend only to spy out a prey: who as soon as they see a plain country fellow well and cleanly apparelled, either in a coat of homespun russet or of frieze, as the time requires, and a side pouch at his side, "There is a Conny," saith one.

At that word out flies the Setter, and overtaking the man, begins to salute him thus: "Sir, God save you, you are welcome to London. How doth all our good friends in the country; I hope they be all in health?"

The countryman, seeing a man so courteous he knows not, half in a brown study at this strange salutation, perhaps makes him this answer: "Sir, all our friends in the country are well, thanks be to God; but truly I know you not, you must pardon me."

"Why sir," saith the setter, guessing by his tongue what countryman he is, "are you not a Yorkshire man, or such a country man?"

If he say yes, then he creeps upon him closely; if he say no, then straight the setter comes over him thus: "In good sooth, sir, I know you by your face and have been in your company before. I pray you (if without offence) let me crave your name, and the place of your abode."

The simple man straight tells him where he dwells, his name, and who be his next neighbors, and what Gentlemen dwell about him. After he hath learned all of him, then he comes over his fallows kindly: "Sir, though I have been somewhat bold to be inquisitive of your name, yet hold me excused, for I took you for a friend of mine; but since by mistaking I have made you slack your business, we'll drink a quart of wine or a pot of ale together."

If the fool be so ready as to go, then the Conny is caught; but if he smack the Setter, and smells a rat by his clawing, and will not drink with him, then away goes the Setter, and discourseth to the Verser the name of the man, the parish he dwells in, and what gentlemen are his near neighbors. With that, away goes he, and crossing the man at some turning, meets him full in the face, and greets him thus:

"What, good man Barton, how fare all our friends about you? You are well met. I have the wine for you; you are welcome to town."

The poor countryman, hearing himself named by a man he knows not, marvels, and answers that he knows him not, and craves pardon. "Not me, good man Barton? Have you forgot me? Why, I am such a man's kinsman, your neighbor not far off. How doth this or that good gentleman, my friend? Good Lord that I should be out of your remembrance; I have been at your house divers times."

"Indeed, sir," saith the farmer, "are you such a man's kinsman? Surely, sir, if you had not challenged acquaintance of me, I should never have known you. I have clean forgot you, but I know the good gentleman your cousin well. He is my very good neighbor."

"And for his sake," saith the Verser, "we'll drink afore we part."

Haply the man thanks him, and to the wine or ale they go; then, before they part, they make him a Conny, and so ferret-claw him at cards that they leave him as bare of money as an ape of a tail.

Thus have the filthy fellows their subtle fetches to draw on poor men to fall into their cozening practises; thus, like consuming moths of the commonwealth, they prey upon the ignorance of such plain souls as measure all by their own honesty, not regarding either conscience or the fatal revenge that is threatened for such idle and licentious persons; but do employ all their wits to the overthrow of such as with their handy thrift satisfy their hearty thirst, they preferring cozenage before labor, and choosing an idle practise before any honest form of good living.

Well, to the method again of taking up their Connies. If the poor countryman smoke them still, and will not stoop unto either of their lures, then one, either the Verser, or the Setter, or some of their crew (for there is a general fraternity betwixt them) steppeth before the Conny as he goeth, and letteth drop twelvepence in the highway, that of force the Conny must see it. The countryman, spying the shilling, maketh not dainty (for *quis nisi mentis inops oblatum respuit aurum*), but stoopeth very mannerly and taketh it up. Then one of the Conny-catchers behind crieth half part, and so challengeth half of his finding. The countryman content, offereth to change the money. "Nay, faith friend," saith the Verser, " 'tis ill luck to keep found money; we'll go spend it in a pottle of wine"; or in a breakfast, dinner, or supper, as the time of day requires. ₁₀ If the Conny say he will not, then answers the Verser, "Spend my part." If still the Conny refuse, he taketh half away.

If they spy the countryman to be of a having and covetous humor, then have they a further policy to draw him on. Another that knoweth the place of his abode, meeteth him and saith, "Sir, well met. I have run hastily to overtake you. I pray you, dwell you not in Darbishire, in such a village?"

"Yes marry do I, friend," saith the Conny. Then replies the Verser, "Truly, sir, I have a suit to you. I am going out of town, and must send a letter to the parson of your parish. You shall not refuse to do a stranger ₂₀ such a favor as to carry it him? Haply, as men may in time meet, it may lie in my lot to do you as good a turn, and for your pains I will give you twelve pence."

The poor Conny, in mere simplicity, saith, "Sir, I'll do so much for you with all my heart; where is your letter?"

"I have it not, good sir, ready written; but may I entreat you to step into some tavern or alehouse. We'll drink the while, and I will write but a line or two."

At this the Conny stoops, and for greediness of the money, and upon kind courtesy goes with the Setter unto the tavern. As they walk they ₃₀ meet the Verser, and then they all three go into the tavern together.

See, Gentlemen, what great logicians these Conny-catchers be, that have such rhetorical persuasions to induce the poor countryman to his confusion; and what variety of villany they have to strip the poor farmer of his money.

Well, imagine the Conny is in the tavern. Then sits down the Verser, and saith to the Setter, "What, sirra, wilt thou give me a quart of wine, or shall I give thee one?"

"We'll drink a pint," saith the Setter, "but we'll play a game at cards for it, respecting more the sport than the loss." ₄₀

"Content," saith the Verser. "Go call for a pair."

And while he is gone to fetch them, he saith to the Conny, "You shall see me fetch over my young master for a quart of wine finely, but this you must do for me. When I cut the cards, as I will not cut above five off, mark then of all the great pack which is undermost, and when I bid you call a card for me, name that, and you shall see we'll make him pay for a quart of wine straight."

"Truly," saith the Conny, "I am no great player at cards, and I do not well understand your meaning."

"Why," saith he, "it is thus: I will play at mum-chance, or decoy, that he shall shuffle the cards, and I will cut. Now either of us must call a card. 10 You shall call for me, and he for himself; and whose card comes first wins. Therefore, when I have cut the cards, then mark the nethermost of the greatest heap, that I set upon the cards which I cut off, and always call that for me."

"O now," saith the Conny, "I understand you. Let me alone; I warrant I'll fit your turn."

With that, in comes the Setter with his cards, and asketh at what game they shall play. "Why," saith the Verser, "at a new game called mumchance, that hath no policy nor knavery, but plain as a pikestaff. You shall shuffle and I'll cut; you shall call a card, and this honest man, a 20 stranger almost to us both, shall call another for me, and which of our cards comes first, shall win."

"Content," saith the Setter; "for that's but mere hazard." And so he shuffles the cards, and the Verser cuts off some four cards, and then taking up the heap to set upon them, giveth the Conny a glance of the bottom card of that heap, and saith, "Now sir, call for me."

The Conny, to blind the Setter's eyes, asketh as though he were not made privy to the game, "What shall I cut?"

"What card?" saith the Verser. "Why what you will, either heart, spade, club, or diamond, coat-card or other."

30 "O, is it so?" saith the Conny. "Why then you shall have the four of hearts," which was the card he had a glance of.

And saith the Setter (holding the cards in his hand, and turning up the uppermost card, as if he knew not well the game), "I'll have the knave of trumps."

"Nay," saith the Verser, "there is no trump. You may call what card you will."

Then saith he, "I'll have the ten of spades."

With that he draws, and the four of hearts comes first. "Well," saith the Setter, " 'tis but hazard; mine might have come as well as yours. Five 40 is up; I fear not the set."

So they shuffle and cut, but the Verser wins. "Well," saith the Setter. "no butter will cleave on my bread. What, not one draught among five?

Drawer, a fresh pint! I'll have another bout with you. But sir, I believe," saith he to the Conny, "you see some card, that it goes so cross on my side."

"I?" saith the Conny. "Nay, I hope you think not so of me; 'tis but hazard and chance, for I am but a mere stranger unto the game. As I am an honest man, I never saw it before."

Thus this simple Conny closeth up smoothly to take the Verser's part, only for greediness to have him win the wine. "Well," answers the Setter, "then I'll have one cast more." And to it they go, but he loseth all, and beginneth to chafe in this manner: "Were it not," quoth he, "that I 10 care not for a quart of wine, I could swear as many oaths for anger as there be hairs on my head, why should not my luck be as good as yours, and fortune favor me as well as you? What, not one called card in ten cuts! I'll foreswear the game for ever!"

"What, chafe not, man," saith the Verser. "Seeing we have your quart of wine, I'll show you the game"; and with that discourseth all to him, as if he knew it not.

The Setter, as simply as if the knave were ignorant, saith, "Aye, marry, I think so. You must needs win, when he knows what card to call. I might have played long enough before I had got a set!" 20

"Truly," says the Conny, " 'tis a pretty game, for 'tis not possible for him to lose that cuts the cards. I warrant the other that shuffles may lose Saint Peter's cope if he had it. Well, I'll carry this home with me into the country, and win many a pot of ale with it."

"A fresh pint," saith the Verser, "and then we'll away. But seeing, sir, you are going homeward, I'll learn you a trick worth the noting, that you shall win many a pot with in the winter nights."

With that he culls out the four knaves, and pricks one in the top, one in the midst, and one in the bottom. "Now, sir," said he, "you see these three knaves apparently. Thrust them down with your hand, and cut 30 where you will; and though they be so far asunder, I'll make them all come together."

"I pray you, let's see that trick," saith the Conny. "Methinks it should be impossible."

So the Verser draws, and all the three knaves comes in one heap. This he doth once or twice, that the Conny wonders at it, and offers him a pint of wine to teach it him. "Nay," saith the Verser, "I'll do it for thanks; and therefore mark me where you have taken out the four knaves. Lay two together above, and draw up one of them that it may be seen; then prick the other in the midst, and the third in the bottom; so, when any 40 cuts, cut he never so warily, three knaves must of force come together; for the bottom knave is cut to lie upon both the upper knaves."

"Aye, marry," saith the Setter, "but then the three knaves you showed come not together."

"Truth," saith the Verser; "but one among a thousand marks not that. It requires a quick eye, a sharp wit, and a reaching head to spy at the first."

"Now gramercy, sir, for this trick," saith the Conny. "I'll domineer with this amongst my neighbors."

Thus doth the verser and the setter feign friendship to the Conny, offering him no show of cozenage, nor once to draw him in for a pint of wine, the more to shadow their villany.

But now begins the sport. As thus they sit tippling, comes the Barnacle and thrusts open the door, looking into the room where they are, and, as one bashful, steps back again, and very mannerly saith, "I cry you mercy, gentlemen. I thought a friend of mine had been here. Pardon my boldness."

"No harm," saith the Verser. "I pray you drink a cup of wine with us and welcome."

So in comes the Barnacle, and taking the cup, drinks to the Conny, and then saith, "What, at cards, gentlemen? Were it not I should be offensive to the company, I would play for a pint till my friend come that I look for."

"Why, sir," saith the Verser, "if you will sit down you shall be taken up for a quart of wine."

"With all my heart," saith the Barnacle. "What will you play at? At Primero, Primo visto, Sant, one and thirty, new cut, or what shall be the game?"

"Sir," saith the Verser, "I am but an ignorant man at cards, and I see you have them at your fingers' end. I will play with you at a game wherein can be no deceit. It is called mum-chance at cards; and it is thus: you shall shuffle the cards, and I will cut; you shall call one, and this plain honest country yeoman shall call a card for me, and which of our cards comes first shall win. Here you see is no deceit, and at this I'll play."

"No, truly," saith the Conny; "methinks there can be no great craft in this."

"Well," saith the Barnacle, "for a pint of wine, have at you."

So they play as before, five up, and the Verser wins. "This is hard luck," saith the Barnacle, "and I believe the honest man spies some card in the bottom, and therefore I'll make this: always to prick the bottom card."

"Content," saith the Verser.

And the Conny, to cloak the matter, saith: "Sir, you offer me injury to think that I can see a card, when I neither touch them, shuffle, cut, nor draw them."

"Ah sir," saith the Barnacle, "give losers leave to speak."

Well, to it they go again; and then the Barnacle, knowing the game better than they all, by chopping a card, wins two of the five, but lets the Verser win the set. Then in a chafe he sweareth 'tis but his ill luck, and he can see no deceit in it; and therefore he will play twelve pence a cut. The Verser is content, and wins two or three shillings of the Barnacle; whereat he chafes, and saith, "I came hither in an ill hour; but I will win my money again, or lose all in my purse."

With that he draws out a purse with some three or four pound, and claps it on the board. The Verser asketh the Conny secretly by signs if he will be his half. He says aye, and straight feels for his purse. Well, the Barnacle shuffles the cards throughly, and the Verser cuts as before. The Barnacle, when he hath drawn one card, saith, "I'll either win something or lose something; therefore I'll vie and revie every card at my pleasure, till either yours or mine come out; and therefore twelve pence upon this card. My card comes first for twelve pence."

"No," saith the Verser.

"Aye," saith the Conny, "and I durst hold twelve pence more."

"Why, I hold you," saith the Barnacle.

And so they vie and revie till some ten shillings be on the stake. And then next comes forth the Verser's card, that the Conny called; and so the Barnacle loseth.

Well, this flesheth the Conny; the sweetness of gain maketh him frolic, and no man is more ready to vie and revie than he. Thus for three or four times the Barnacle loseth. At last, to whet on the Conny, he striketh his chopped card, and winneth a good stake. "Away with the witch!" cries the Barnacle. "I hope the cards will turn at last."

"Aye, much," thinketh the Conny; "'twas but a chance that you asked so right, to ask one of the five that was cut off. I am sure there was forty to one on my side, and I'll have you on the lurch anon."

So still they vie and revie, and for once that the Barnacle wins, the Conny gets five. At last, when they mean to shave the Conny clean of all his coin, the Barnacle chafeth, and upon a pawn borroweth some money of the tapster, and swears he will vie it to the uttermost. Then thus he chops his card to cross-bite the Conny. He first looks on the bottom card, and shuffles often, but still keeping that bottom card, which he knows, to be uppermost. Then sets he down the cards, and the Verser, to encourage the Conny, cuts off but three cards, whereof the Barnacle's card must needs be the uppermost. Then shows he the bottom card of the other heap cut off to the Conny, and sets it upon the Barnacle's card which he knows, so that of force the card that was laid uppermost must come forth first. And then the Barnacle calls that card. They draw a card,

and then the Barnacle vies, and the countryman vies upon him; for this is the law: as often as one vies or revies, the other must see it, else he loseth the stake. Well, at last the Barnacle plies it so, that perhaps he vies more money than the Conny hath in his purse. The Conny upon this, knowing his card is the third or fourth card, and that he hath forty to one against the Barnacle, pawns his rings if he hath any, his sword, his cloak, or else what he hath about him, to maintain the vie. And when he laughs in his sleeve, thinking he hath fleeced the Barnacle of all, then the Barnacle's card comes forth, and strikes such a cold humor unto his heart that he
10 sits as a man in a trance, not knowing what to do, and sighing while his heart is ready to break, thinking on the money that he hath lost.

Perhaps the man is very simple and patient, and whatsoever he thinks, for fear goes his way quiet with his loss, while the Conny-catchers laugh and divide the spoil. And being out of doors, poor man, goeth to his lodging with a heavy heart and watery eyes, pensive and sorrowful, but too late; for perhaps the man's state did depend on that money, and so he, his wife, his children, and his family are brought to extreme misery. Another perhaps, more hardy and subtle, smokes the Conny-catchers, and smelleth cozenage, and says they shall not have his money so; but they
20 answer him with braves, and though he bring them before an officer, yet the knaves are so favored that the man never recovers his money, and yet he is let slip without punishment. Thus are the poor Connies robbed by these base-minded caterpillars. Thus are serving men oft enticed to play, and lose all. Thus are prentices induced to be Connies, and so are cozened of their master's money. Yea, young gentlemen, merchants, and others, are fetched in by these damnable rakehells, a plague as ill as hell, which is present loss of money, and ensuing misery. A lamentable case in England, when such vipers are suffered to breed and are not cut off with the sword of Justice.

30

* * * *

From *The Third and last part of Conny-catching*, 1592

A pleasant tale how an honest substantial Citizen was made
a Conny, and simply entertained a knave that carried away
his goods very politicly.

WHAT LAWS are used among this hellish crew, what words and terms
40 they give themselves and their copesmates, are at large set down in the former two books. Let it suffice ye, then, in this, to read the simple true discourses of such as have by extraordinary cunning and treachery been

deceived; and remembering their subtle means there, and sly practises here, be prepared against the reaches of any such companions.

Not long since, a crew of Conny-catchers meeting together, and in conference laying down such courses as they severally should take to shun suspect and return a common benefit among them, the Carders received their charge, the Dicers theirs, the hangers about the court theirs, the followers of sermons theirs, and so the rest to their offices. But one of them especially, who at their wonted meetings, when report was made how every purchase was gotten, and by what policy each one prevailed, this fellow, in a kind of priding scorn, would usually say: 10

"In faith, Masters, these things are prettily done; common sleights, expressing no deep reach of wit, and I wonder men are so simple to be so beguiled. I would fain see some rare artificial feat indeed, that some admiration and frame might ensue the doing thereof. I promise ye, I disdain these base and petty paltries, and may my fortune jump with my resolution, ye shall hear, my boys, within a day or two, that I will accomplish a rare stratagem indeed, of more value than forty of yours; and when it is done shall carry some credit with it." They, wondering at his words, desired to see the success of them; and so dispersing themselves as they were accustomed, left this frolic fellow pondering on his affairs. 20

A citizen's house in London, which he had diligently eyed and aimed at for a fortnight's space, was the place wherein he must perform this exploit. And having learned one of the servant maids' name of the house, as also where she was born and her kindred, upon a Sunday in the afternoon, when it was her turn to attend on her master and mistress to the garden in Finsbury fields to regard the children while they sported about, this crafty mate, having duly watched their coming forth, and seeing that they intended to go down St. Lawrence Lane, stepped before them, ever casting an eye back, lest they should turn some contrary way. But their following still fitting his own desire, near unto the Conduit in Alderman- 30 bury he crossed the way and came unto the maid, and kissing her said: "Cousin Margaret, I am very glad to see you well. My uncle your father, and all your friends in the country are in good health, God be praised."

The maid, hearing herself named and not knowing the man, modestly blushed; which he perceiving, held way on with her amongst her fellow apprentices, and thus began again: "I see Cousin, you know me not, and I do not greatly blame you, it is so long since you came forth of the country. But I am such a one's son"; naming her uncle right, and his son's name, which she very well remembered, but had not seen him in eleven years. Then taking forth a bowed groat, and an old penny bowed, he gave it 40 her as being sent from her uncle and aunt, whom he termed to be his father and mother: "Withall," quoth he, "I have a gammon of bacon

and a cheese from my uncle your father, which are sent to your master
and mistress, which I received of the carrier, because my uncle enjoined
me to deliver them; when I must entreat your mistress that at Whitsuntide
next she will give you leave to come down into the country."

The maid, thinking simply all he said was true, and as they so far from
their parents are not only glad to hear of their welfare, but also rejoice
to see any of their kindred, so this poor maid, well knowing her uncle had
a son so named as he called himself, and thinking from a boy (as he was
at her leaving the country), he was now grown such a proper handsome
10 young man, was not a little joyful to see him. Beside, she seemed proud
that her kinsman was so neat a youth; and so she held on questioning with
him about her friends, he soothing each matter so cunningly, as the maid
was confidently persuaded of him.

In this time, one of the children stepped to her mother and said, "Our
Marget, mother, have a fine cousin come out of the country, and he hath
a cheese for my father and you." Whereon she looking back, said: "Maid,
is that your kinsman?"

"Yea forsooth, mistress," quoth she, "my uncle's son, whom I left a
little one when I came forth of the country."

20 The wily treacher, being master of his trade, would not let slip this
opportunity, but courteously stepping to the Mistress (who loving her
maid well, because indeed she had been a very good servant, and from her
first coming to London had dwelt with her, told her husband thereof),
coined such a smooth tale unto them both, fronting it with the gammon
of bacon and the cheese sent from their maid's father, and hoping they
would give her leave at Whitsuntide to visit the country, as they with very
kind words entertained him, inviting him the next night to supper, when
he promised to bring with him the gammon of bacon and the cheese. Then,
framing an excuse of certain business in the town, for that time he took his
30 leave of the master and mistress, and his new Cousin Margaret, who gave
many a look after him (poor wench) as he went, joying in her thoughts
to have such a kinsman.

On the morrow he prepared a good gammon of bacon, which he closed
up in a soiled linen cloth, and sewed an old card upon it, whereon he wrote
a superscription unto the master of the maid, and at what sign it was to
be delivered, and afterward scraped some of the letters half out, that it
might seem they had been rubbed out in the carriage. A good cheese he
prepared likewise, with inscription accordingly on it, that it could not be
discerned but that some unskillful writer in the country had done it, both
40 by the gross proportion of the letters, as also the bad orthography, which
amongst plain husbandmen is very common, in that they have no better
instruction. So, hiring a porter to carry them, between five and six in the

evening he comes to the citizen's house, and entering the shop, receives
them of the porter, whom the honest meaning citizen would have paid
for his pains, but this his maid's new-found cousin said he was satisfied
already, and so straining courtesy would not permit him. Well, up are
carried the bacon and the cheese, where, God knows, Margaret was not
a little busy to have all things fine and neat against her cousin's coming up;
her mistress likewise (as one well affecting her servant), had provided
very good cheer, set all her plate on the cupboard for show, and beautified
the house with cushions, carpets, stools, and other devices of needle work,
as at such times divers will do to have the better report made of their 10
credit amongst their servant's friends in the country, albeit at this time
(God wot) it turned to their own after-sorrowing.

The master of the house, to delay the time while supper was ready, he
likewise shows this dissembler his shop, who, seeing things fadge so pat to
his purpose, could question of this sort and that well enough I warrant
you, to discern the best from the worst and their appointed places, purposing a further reach than the honest citizen dreamed of. And to be plain
with ye, such was this occupier's trade, as though I may not name it, yet
thus much I dare utter, that the worst thing he could carry away was above
twenty nobles, because he dealt altogether in whole and great sale; which 20
made this companion forge this kindred and acquaintance, for an hundred pound or twain was the very least he aimed at.

At length the mistress sends word supper is on the table; whereupon, up
he conducts his guest, and after divers welcomes, as also thanks for the
cheese and bacon, to the table they sit. Where let it suffice he wanted
no ordinary good fare, wine, and other knacks, beside much talk of the
country, how much his friends were beholding for his Cousin Margaret,
to whom by her mistress' leave he drank twice or thrice, and she, poor
soul, doing the like again to him with remembrance of her father and other
kindred, which he still smoothed very cunningly. Countenance of talk 30
made them careless of the time, which slipped from them faster than they
were aware of. Nor did the deceiver hasten his departing, because he expected what indeed followed; which was that, being past ten of the clock,
and he feigning his lodging to be at Saint Giles in the Field, was entreated
both by the good man and his wife to take a bed there for that night. For
fashion sake (though very glad of this offer) he said he would not trouble
them, but giving them many thanks, would to his lodging though it were
further. But wonderful it was to see how earnest the honest citizen and
his wife labored to persuade him, that was more willing to stay than they
could be to bid him, and what dissembled willingness of departure he used 40
on the other side, to cover the secret villany intended.

Well, at the length, with much ado, he is contented to stay. When

Margaret and her mistress presently stirred to make ready his bed, which
the more to the honest man's hardhap, but all the better for this artificial
Conny-catcher, was in the same room where they supped, being commonly called their hall. And there indeed stood a very fair bed, as in such
sightly rooms it may easily be thought citizens use not to have anything
mean or simple. The mistress, lest her guest should imagine she disturbed
him, suffered all the plate to stand still on the cupboard; and when she
perceived his bed was warmed, and everything else according to her mind,
she and her husband, bidding him good night, took themselves to their
10 chamber, which was on the same floor, but inward, having another chamber between them and the hall, where the maids and children had their
lodging. So, desiring him to call for anything he wanted, and charging
Margaret to look it should be so, to bed are they gone. When the apprentices having brought up the keys of the street door and left them in
their master's chamber as they were want to do, after they had said prayers,
their evening exercise, to bed go they likewise, which was in a garret backward over their master's chamber. None are now up but poor Margaret
and her counterfeit cousin, whom she, loath to offend with long talk because it waxed late, after some few more speeches about their parents and
20 friends in the country, she seeing him laid in bed, and all such things by
him as she deemed needful, with a low curtsey I warrant ye, commits
him to his quiet, and so went to bed to her fellows, the maidservants.

Well did this hypocrite perceive the keys of the doors carried into the
good man's chamber, whereof he being not a little glad, thought now
they would imagine all things sure, and therefore doubtless sleep the
sounder. As for the keys, he needed no help of them, because such as he
go never unprovided of instruments fitting their trade, and so at this time
was this notable treacher. In the dead time of the night, when sound sleep
makes the ear unapt to hear the very least noise, he forsaketh his bed, and
30 having gotten all the plate bound up together in his cloak, goeth down into
the shop, where, well remembering both the place and parcels, maketh up
his pack with some twenty-pounds-worth of goods more. Then settling
to his engine, he getteth the door off the hinges; and being forth, lifteth
close to again, and so departs, meeting within a dozen paces three or four
of his companions that lurked thereabouts for the purpose. Their word for
knowing each other, as is said, was "Quest," and this villain's comfortable
news to them was "Twag," signifying he had sped. Each takes a fleece
for easier carriage, and so away to "Bell brow," which, as I have heard
is as they interpret it, the house of a thief receiver, without which they can
40 do nothing. And this house, with an apt porter to it, stands ready for
them all hours of the night. Too many such are there in London, the
masters whereof bear countenance of honest substantial men, but all their

living is gotten in this order; the end of such (though they scape awhile) will be sailing westward in a cart to Tyburn. Imagine these villains there in their jollity, the one reporting point by point his cunning deceit, and the other (fitting his humor) extolling the deed with no mean commendations.

But returning to the honest citizen, who finding in the morning how dearly he paid for a gammon of bacon and a cheese, and how his kind courtesy was thus treacherously requited, blames the poor maid, as innocent herein as himself, and imprisoning her, thinking so to regain his own. Grief, with ill cherishing there, shortens her life. And thus ensueth one hard hap upon another, to the great grief both of master and mistress, when the truth was known, that they so wronged their honest servant. How it may forewarn others, I leave to your own opinions, that see what extraordinary devices are nowadays, to beguile the simple and honest liberal minded.

FROM *Greenes Groats-worth of witte*, 1592

* * * * *

To those gentleman, his quondam acquaintance, that spend their wits in making plays, R.G. wisheth a better exercise, and wisdom to prevent his extremities.

If woeful experience may move you (gentlemen) to beware, or unheard of wretchedness entreat you to take heed, I doubt not but you will look back with sorrow on your time past and endeavor with repentance to spend that which is to come. Wonder not (for with thee will I first begin), thou famous gracer of tragedians, that Greene, who hath said with thee (like the fool in his heart) "There is no God," should now give glory unto His greatness. For penetrating is His power; His hand lies heavy upon me, He hath spoken unto me with a voice of thunder, and I have felt He is a God that can punish enemies. Why should thy excellent wit, His gift, be so blinded that thou shouldst give no glory to the giver? Is it pestilent Machiavellian policy that thou hast studied? Oh, peevish folly! What are his rules but mere confused mockeries, able to extirpate in small time the generation of mankind. For if *Sic volo, sic jubeo* hold in those that are able to command; and if it be lawful *fas et nefas* to do anything that is beneficial; only tyrants should possess the earth, and they, striving to exceed in tyranny, should each to other be a slaughterman; till the mightiest outliving all, one stroke were left for death, that in one age man's life should end. The broacher of this diabolical atheism is dead, and in his life had never the felicity he aimed at; but as he began in craft,

lived in fear, and ended in despair. *Quàm inscrutabilia sunt Dei judicia!*
This murderer of many brethren had his conscience seared like Cain;
this betrayer of Him that gave His life for him inherited the portion of
Judas: this apostate perished as ill as Julian; and wilt thou, my friend, be
his disciple? Look unto me, by him persuaded to that liberty, and thou
shalt find it an infernal bondage. I know the least of my demerits merit
this miserable death, but wilful striving against known truth exceedeth
all the terrors of my soul. Defer not (with me) till this last point of extremity; for little knowest thou how in the end thou shalt be visited.

10   With thee I join young Juvenal, that biting satirist, that lastly with me
together writ a comedy. Sweet boy, might I advise thee, be advised; and
get not many enemies by bitter words; inveigh against vain men, for
thou canst do it, no man better, no man so well; thou hast a liberty to
reprove all and name none; for one being spoken to, all are offended;
none being blamed, no man is injured. Stop shallow water still running,
it will rage; or tread on a worm, and it will turn. Then blame not scholars
vexed with sharp lines, if they reprove thy too much liberty of reproof.

And thou, no less deserving than the other two, in some things rarer,
in nothing inferior; driven (as myself) to extreme shifts; a little have I
20   to say to thee. And were it not an idolatrous oath, I would swear by sweet
Saint George thou art unworthy better hap, sith thou dependest on so
mean a stay. Base-minded men, all three of you, if, by my misery, ye be
not warned; for unto none of you (like me) sought those burrs to cleave;
those Puppets (I mean) that spake from our mouths, those Antics garnished in our colors. Is it not strange that I, to whom they all have been
beholding; is it not like that you, to whom they all have been beholding,
shall (were ye in that case as I am now) be both at once of them forsaken?
Yes, trust them not; for there is an upstart crow, beautified with our
feathers, that, with his *tiger's heart wrapped in a player's hide,* supposes
30   he is as well able to bombast out a blank verse as the best of you; and, being
an absolute *Johannes fac totum,* is, in his own conceit, the only Shake-
scene in a country. O, that I might entreat your rare wits to be employed
in more profitable courses; and let those Apes imitate your past excellence
and nevermore acquaint them with your admired inventions. I know the
best husband of you all will never prove an usurer, and the kindest of
them all will never prove a kind nurse. Yet, whilst you may, seek you
better masters; for it is pity men of such rare wits should be subject to the
pleasures of such rude grooms.

In this I might insert two more, that both have writ against these
40   buckram gentlemen; but let their own works serve to witness against
their own wickedness, if they persevere to maintain any more such peasants. For other newcomers, I leave them to the mercy of these painted

monsters, who (I doubt not) will drive the best-minded to despise them; for the rest, it skills not though they make a jest at them.

But now return I again to you three, knowing my misery is to you no news; and let me heartily entreat you to be warned by my harms. Delight not (as I have done) in irreligious oaths; for from the blasphemer's house a curse shall not depart. Despise drunkenness, which wasteth the wit and maketh men all equal unto beasts. Fly lust as the deathsman of the soul, and defile not the temple of the Holy Ghost. Abhor those epicures whose loose life hath made religion loathsome to your ears; and when they soothe you with terms of Mastership, remember Robert Greene, 10 whom they have often so flattered, perishes now for want of comfort. Remember, gentlemen, your lives are like so many lighted tapers that are with care delivered to all of you to maintain; these with wind-puffed wrath may be extinguished, which drunkenness put out, which negligence let fall; for man's time is not of itself so short but it is more shortened by sin. The fire of my light is now at the last snuff, and for want of wherewith to sustain it, there is no substance left for life to feed on. Trust not, then (I beseech ye), to such weak stays; for they are as changeable in mind as in many attires. Well, my hand is tired and I am forced to leave where I would begin; for a whole book cannot contain their wrongs, 20 which I am forced to knit up in some few lines of words.

Desirous that you should live though himself be dying:

ROBERT GREENE.

THOMAS NASHE

The Introduction and Notes are at page 1329

From Nashe's preface to Robert Greene's *Menaphon: Camillas   30 alarum to slumbering Euphues*, 1589

To the Gentlemen Students of both Universities.

Courteous and wise, whose judgements (not entangled with envy) enlarge the deserts of the learned by your liberal censures; vouchsafe to welcome your scholar-like shepherd with such university entertainment, as either the nature of your bounty, or the custome of your common civility may afford. To you he appeals that knew him *ab extreme pueritia*, whose *placet* he accounts the *plaudite* of his pains; thinking his day labor 40 was not altogether lavished *sine linea*, if there be any thing of all in it that doth *olere atticum* in your estimate. I am not ignorant how eloquent our

gowned age is grown of late; so that every mechanical mate abhors the
English he was born to, and plucks, with a solemn periphrasis, his *ut vales*
from the inkhorn: which I impute not so much to the perfection of arts,
as to the servile imitation of vain-glorious tragedians, who contend not so
seriously to excel in action as to embowel the clouds in a speech of comparison, thinking themselves more than initiated in poets' immortality if
they but once get Boreas by the beard, and the heavenly Bull by the dew-
lap. But herein I cannot so fully bequeath them to folly as their idiot art-
masters, that intrude themselves to our ears as the alchemists of eloquence,
10 who (mounted on the stage of arrogance) think to outbrave better pens
with the swelling bombast of a bragging blank verse. Indeed it may be
the ingrafted overflow of some kilcow conceit, that overcloyeth their
imagination with a more than drunken resolution, being not extemporal
in the invention of any other means to vent their manhood, commits the
disgestion of their choleric incumbrances to the spacious volubility of a
drumming decasillabon. Mongst this kind of men that repose eternity in
the mouth of a player, I can but engross some deep-read grammarians
who, having no more learning in their skull than will serve to take up a
commodity, nor art in their brain than was nourished in a serving man's
20 idleness, will take upon them to be the ironical censors of all, when God
and Poetry doth know they are the simplest of all.

To leave these to the mercy of their mother tongue, that feed on
nought but the crumbs that fall from the translator's trencher, I come
(sweet friend) to thy Arcadian *Menaphon*, whose attire though not so
stately, yet comely, doth entitle thee above all other to that *temperatum
dicendi genus* which Tully in his *Orator* termeth true eloquence. Let
other men (as they please) praise the mountain that in seven years brings
forth a mouse, or the Italianate pen, that of a packet of pilfries affordeth
the press a pamphlet or two in an age, and then in disguised array vaunts
30 Ovid's and Plutarch's plumes as their own; but give me the man whose
extemporal vein in any humor will excel our greatest art-masters' deliberate thoughts; whose invention, quicker than his eye, will challenge the
proudest Rhetorician to the contention of like perfection with like expedition.

What is he amongst students so simple that cannot bring forth (*tandem
aliquando*) some or other thing singular, sleeping betwixt every sentence?
Was it not Maro's twelve years' toil that so famed his xii *Aeneidos?* Or
Peter Ramus' sixteen years' pains that so praised his petty *Logic?* How
is it, then, our drooping wits should so wonder at an exquisite line, that
40 was his masters' day labor? Indeed I must needs say, the descending
years from the philosophers of Athens, have not been supplied with such
present orators as were able in any English vein to be eloquent of their

own, but either they must borrow invention of Ariosto and his countrymen, take up choice of words by exchange in Tully's *Tusculane* and the
Latin historiographers' storehouses; similitudes, nay whole sheets and
tractates *verbatim*, from the plenty of Plutarch and Pliny; and to conclude, their whole method of writing from the liberty of comical fictions
that have succeeded to our Rhetoricians by a second imitation; so that,
well may the adage, *Nil dictum quod non dictum prius*, be the most judicial estimate of our latter writers.

But the hunger of our unsatiate humorists being such as it is, ready to
swallow all draff without indifference that insinuates itself to their senses 10
under the name of delight, employs oft-times many threadbare wits to
empty their invention of their apish devices, and talk most superficially of
policy, as those that never wore gown in the university; wherein they
revive the old said adage, *Sus Minervam* and cause the wiser to quip them
with *Asinus ad lyram*. Would gentlemen and riper judgments admit my
motion of moderation in a matter of folly, I would persuade them to
physic their faculties of seeing and hearing, as the Sabeans do their dulled
senses with smelling; who (as Strabo reporteth) overcloyed with such
odoriferous savors as the natural increase of their country (Balsamum,
Amomum, with Myrrh and Frankincense) sends forth, refresh their 20
nostrils with the unsavory scent of the pitchy slime that Euphrates casts
up, and the contagious fumes of goats' beards burnt; so would I have
them, being surfeited unawares with the sweet satiety of eloquence, which
the lavish of our copious language may procure, to use the remedy of contraries; and recreate their rebated wits, not, as they did, with the scenting
of slime or goats' beards burnt, but with the overseeing of that *sublime
dicendi genus* which walks abroad for waste paper in each serving man's
pocket, and the otherwhile perusing of our Gothamists' barbarism; so
should the opposite comparison of purity expel the infection of absurdity,
and their overracked rhetoric be the ironical recreation of the reader. 30

But so far discrepant is the idle usage of our unexperienced punies from
this prescription, that a tale of John a Brainford's will, and *The Unlucky
Furmenty* will be as soon entertained into their libraries as the best poem
that ever Tasso eternisht; which, being the effect of an undiscerning
judgment, makes dross as valuable as gold, and loss as welcome as gain;
the glowworm mentioned in Aesop's fables, namely the ape's folly, to be
mistaken for fire, when as God wot, poor souls, they have nought but
their toil for their heat, their pains for their sweat, and (to bring it to
our English proverb) their labor for their travail. Wherein I can but resemble them to the panther, who is so greedy of men's excrements that 40
if they be hanged up in a vessel higher than his reach, he sooner killeth
himself with the overstretching of his windless body than he will cease

from his intended enterprise. Oft have I observed what I now set down:
a secular wit that hath lived all days of his life by "What do you lack?"
to be more judicial in matters of conceit than our quadrant crepundios,
that spit *ergo* in the mouth of every one they meet. Yet those and these
are so affectionate to dogged detracting, as the most poisonous Pasquil
any dirty mouthed Martin or Momus ever composed is gathered up with
greediness before it fall to the ground and bought at the dearest, though
they smell of the fripler's lavender half a year after. For I know not how
the mind of the meanest is fed with this folly: that they impute singularity
to him that slanders privily, and count it a great piece of art in an ink-
horne man, in any tapsterly terms whatsoever, to oppose his superiors to
envy. I will not deny but in scholar-like matters of controversy, a quicker
style may pass as commendable; and that a quip to an ass is as good as a
goad to an ox; but when an irregular idiot, that was up to the ears in
divinity before ever he met with *probabile* in the University, shall leave
pro et contra before he can scarcely pronounce it, and come to correct
commonweales, that never heard of the name of Magistrate before he
came to Cambridge, it is no marvel if every alehouse vaunt the table of
the world turned upside down, since the child beats his father, and the
ass whips his master.

But lest I might seem with these night crows, *Nimis curiosus in aliena
republica,* I will turn back to my first text, of studies of delight, and talk
a little in friendship with a few of our trivial translators. It is a common
practice nowadays amongst a sort of shifting companions, that run through
every art and thrive by none, to leave the trade of *Noverint,* whereto they
were born, and busy themselves with the endeavors of art, that could
scarcely latinize their neck-verse if they should have need; yet English
Seneca read by candlelight yields many good sentences, as "Blood is a
beggar," and so forth; and if you entreat him fair in a frosty morning, he
will afford you whole *Hamlets,* I should say handfuls, of tragical speeches.
But O grief! *tempus edax rerum,* what's that will last always? The sea
exhaled by drops will in continuance be dry, and Seneca let blood line by
line and page by page, at length must needs die to our stage; which makes
his famished followers to imitate the Kidde in Aesop, who enamored with
the Fox's new fangles, forsook all hopes of life to leap into a new occupation; and these men renouncing all possibilities of credit or estimation to
intermeddle with Italian translations. Wherein how poorly they have
plodded (as those that are neither provenzal men, nor are able to distinguish of articles), let all indifferent gentlemen that have travailed in
that tongue discern by their twopenny pamphlets. And no marvel though
their home-born mediocrity be such in this matter; for what can be hoped
of those that thrust Elisium into hell, and have not learned, so long as

they have lived in the spheres, the just measure of the horizon without an hexameter. Sufficeth them to bodge up a blank verse with ifs and ands; and other while for recreation after their candle stuff, having starched their beards most curiously, to make a peripatetical path into the inner parts of the city, and spend two or three hours in turning over French *Doudie*, where they attract more infection in one minute than they can do eloquence all days of their life by conversing with any authors of like argument.

But lest in this declamatory vein I should condemn all and commend none, I will propound to your learned imitation those men of import that 10 have labored with credit in this laudable kind of translation; in the forefront of whom I cannot but place that aged father Erasmus that invested most of our Greek writers in the robes of the ancient Romans; in whose traces Philip Melancthon, Sadolet, Plantin, and many other reverent Germans insisting, have re-edified the ruins of our decayed libraries, and marvellously enriched the Latin tongue with the expense of their toil. Not long after, their emulation being transported into England, every private scholar, William Turner, and who not, began to vaunt their smattering of Latin in English impressions. But amongst others in that age, Sir Thomas Elyot's elegance did sever itself from all equals, although Sir 20 Thomas More, with his comical wit, at that instant was not altogether idle. Yet was not knowledge fully confirmed in her monarchy amongst us till that most famous and fortunate nurse of all learning, Saint Johns in Cambridge, that at that time was as an university within itself, shining so far above all other houses, halls, and hospitals whatsoever, that no college in the town was able to compare with the tithe of her students; having (as I have heard grave men of credit report) more candles' light in it every winter morning before four of the clock than the four of clock bell gave strokes; till she (I say) as a pitying mother, put to her helping hand and sent, from her fruitful womb, sufficient scholars both to support 30 her own weal as also to supply all other inferior foundations' defects; and namely that royal erection of Trinity College, which the University Orator, in an Epistle to the Duke of Somerset, aptly termed *Colonia diducta* from the suburbs of Saint Johns. In which extraordinary conception, *uno partu in rempublicam prodiere*, the Exchequer of eloquence Sir John Cheke, a man of men, supernaturally traded in all tongues, Sir John Mason, Doctor Watson, Redman, Ascham, Grindal, Lever, Pilkington; all which have, either by their private readings or public works, repurged the errors of Art expelled from their purity, and set before our eyes a more perfect method of study. 40

But how ill their precepts have prospered with our idle age, that leave the fountains of sciences to follow the rivers of knowledge, their overfraught studies with trifling compendiaries may testify. For I know not how it comes to pass, by the doting practice of our Divinity dunces that strive to make their pupils pulpit men before they are reconciled to Priscian, but those years, which should be employed in Aristotle, are expired in Epitomes; and well, too, they may have so much Catechism vacation to rake up a little refuse philosophy.

And here could I enter into a large field of invective against our abject abbreviations of Arts, were it not grown to a new fashion amongst our nation to vaunt the pride of contraction in every manuary action; insomuch that the *Pater noster*, which was wont to fill a sheet of paper, is written in the compass of a penny; whereupon one merrily affirmed that proverb to be derived, "No pennie, no *pater noster*." Which their nice curtailing puts me in mind of the custom of the Scythians, who if they be at any time distressed with famine, take in their girdles shorter, and swaddle themselves straighter, to the intent no vacuum being left in their entrails, hunger should not so much tyrannize over their stomachs; even so, these men, oppressed with a greater penury of Art, do pound their capacity in barren compendiums, and bound their base humors in the beggarly straits of a hungry *Analysis*, lest longing after that *infinitum* which the poverty of their conceit cannot compass, they sooner yield up their youth to destiny than their heart to understanding.

How is it, then, such bungling practitioners in principles should ever profit the Commonwealth by their negligent pains, who have no more cunning in Logic or dialogue Latin than appertains to the literal construction of either? Nevertheless, it is daily apparent to our domesticall eyes that there is none so forward to publish their imperfections, either in the trade of gloss or translations, as those that are more unlearned than ignorance, and less conceiving than infants. Yet dare I not impute absurdity to all of that society, though some of them have set their names to their simplicity. Whoever my private opinion condemneth as faulty, Master Gascoigne is not to be abridged of his deserved esteem, who first beat the path to that perfection which our best poets have aspired to since his departure; whereto he did ascend by comparing the Italian with the English, as Tully did *Graeca cum Latinis*. Neither was Master Turbervile the worst of his time, although in translating he attributed too much to the necessity of rime. And in this page of praise, I cannot omit aged Arthur Golding for his industrious toil in Englishing Ovid's *Metamorphoses*, besides many other exquisite editions of Divinity turned by him out of the French tongue into our own. Master Phaer likewise is not to be forgot in regard of his famous Virgil, whose heavenly verse, had it not been blemished by his haughty thoughts, England might have long insulted in his wit, and *corrigat qui potest* have been subscribed to his works.

But Fortune, the mistress of change, with a pitying compassion respecting Master Stanihurst's praise, would that Phaer should fall that he might rise, whose heroical poetry infired—I should say inspired—with an hexameter fury, recalled to life whatever hissed barbarism hath been buried this hundred year; and revived by his ragged quill such carterly variety as no hodge plowman in a country but would have held as the extremity of clownery; a pattern whereof I will propound to your judgments, as near as I can, being part of one of his descriptions of a tempest, which is thus,

> Then did he make heavens vault to rebound, with rounce robble hobble   10
> Of ruffe raffe roaring, with thwick thwack thurlery bouncing.

Which strange language of the firmament, never subject before to our common phrase, makes us that are not used to terminate heaven's movings in the accents of any voice, esteem of their triobulare interpreter as of some Thrasonical huffe-snuffe, for so terrible was his style to all mild ears as would have affrighted our peaceable poets from intermiddling hereafter with that quarrelling kind of verse, had not sweet Master Fraunce, by his excellent translation of Master Thomas Watson's sugared *Amintas*, animated their dulled spirits to such high-witted endeavours. 20 But I know not how, their over-timorous cowardice hath stood in awe of envy, that no man since him durst imitate any of the worst of those Roman wonders in English; which makes me think that either the lovers of mediocrity are very many or that the number of good poets are very small; but in truth (Master Watson except, whom I mentioned before), I know not almost any of late days that hath shewed himself singular in any special Latin poem; whose *Amintas* and translated *Antigone* may march in equipage of honour with any of our ancient poets. I will not say but we had a Haddon, whose pen would have challenged the laurel from Homer, together with Carr, that came as near 30 him as Virgil to Theocritus. But Thomas Newton with his Leland, and Gabriel Harvey, with two or three other, is almost all the store that is left us at this hour.

Epitaphers and position poets have we more than a good many, that swarm like crows to a dead carcass, but fly like swallows in the winter from an continuate subject of wit. The efficient whereof I imagine to issue from the upstart discipline of our reformatory churchmen, who account wit vanity, and poetry impiety; whose error, although the necessity of philosophy might confute, which lies couched most closely under dark fables' profundity, yet I had rather refer it as a disputative plea to divines 40 than set it down as a determinate position, in my unexperienced opinion. But however their dissentious judgments should decree in their afternoon sessions of *an sit*, the private truth of my discovered creed in this controversy is this: that as that beast was thought scarce worthy to be sacrificed to the Egyptian Epaphus who had not some or other black spot on his skin, so I deem him far unworthy of the name of a scholar, and so consequently to sacrifice his endeavours to art, that is not a poet, either in whole or in a part.

And here, peradventure, some desperate quipper will canvas my proposed comparison *plus ultra*, reconciling the allusion of the black spot to the black pot; which makes our poets' undermeal muses so mutinous, as every stanza they pen after dinner is full-pointed with a stab. Which their dagger drunkenness, although it might be excused with *Tam Marti quàm Mercurio*, yet will I cover it as well as I may with that proverbial *faecundi calices* that might well have been doorkeeper to the can of Silenus, when nodding on his ass trapt with ivy, he made his moist nosecloth the pausing intermedium twixt every nap. Let frugal scholars and fine fingered novices take their drink by the ounce, and their wine by the half-penny-worths, but it is for a poet to examine the pottle pots and gage the bottom of whole gallons; *qui bene vult* ποίειν, *debet ante* πίνειν. A pot of blue burning ale with a fiery flaming toast, is as good as Pallas with the nine muses on Parnassus top; without the which in vain may they cry, "O thou, my muse, inspire me with some pen," when they want certain liquid sacrifice to rouse her forth her den.

Pardon me, gentlemen, though somewhat merrily I glance at their immoderate folly, who affirm that no man can write with conceit except he take counsel of the cup; nor would I have you think that, *Theonino dente*, I arm my style against all, since I do know the moderation of many gentlemen of that study to be so far from infamy as their verse from equality; whose sufficiency, were it as well seen into by those of higher place as it wanders abroad unrewarded in the mouths of ungrateful monsters, no doubt but the remembrance of Maecenas' liberality extended to Maro, and men of like quality, would have left no memory to that proverb of poverty, *Si nihil attuleris, ibis Homere foras*. Tut, says our English Italians, the finest wits our climate sends forth are but dry-brained dolts in comparison of other countries; whom if you interrupt with *redde rationem*, they will tell you of Petrarch, Tasso, Celiano, with an infinite number of others, to whom if I should oppose Chaucer, Lyd-gate, Gower, with such like that lived under the tyranny of ignorance, I do think their best lovers would be much discontented with the collation of contraries if I should write over all their heads "Hail fellow, well met!" One thing I am sure of, that each of these three have vaunted their meters with as much admiration in English as ever the proudest Ariosto did his verse in Italian.

What should I come to our court, where the otherwhile vacations of our graver nobility are prodigal of more pompous wit and choice of words than ever tragic Tasso could attain to? But as for pastoral poems, I will not make the comparison, lest our countrymen's credit should be discountenanced by the contention; who, although they cannot fare with such inferior facility, yet I know would carry the bucklers full easily from all foreign bravers if their *subjectum circa quod* should savor of anything haughty. And should the challenge of deep conceit be intruded by any foreigner to bring our English wits to the touchstone of Art, I would prefer divine Master Spenser, the miracle of wit, to bandy line for line 10 for my life, in the honor of England against Spain, France, Italy, and all the world. Neither is he the only swallow of our summer (although Apollo, if his *Tripos* were up again, would pronounce him his Socrates), but he being forborne, there are extant about London many most able men to revive poetry, though it were executed ten thousand times, as in Plato's, so in Puritans' commonwealth; as for example, Mathew Roydon, Thomas Atchelow, and George Peele; the first of whom, as hath shewed himself singular in the immortal Epitaph of his beloved Astrophel, besides many other most absolute comic inventions (made more public by every man's praise than they can be by my speech), so the second hath 20 more than once or twice manifested his deep witted scholarship in places of credit. And for the last, though not the least of them all, I dare commend him to all that know him as the chief supporter of pleasance now living, the Atlas of poetry, and *primus verborum artifex;* whose first increase, *The Arraignment of Paris,* might plead to your opinions his pregnant dexterity of wit, and manifold variety of invention, wherein (*me judice*) he goeth a step beyond all that write. Sundry other sweet gentlemen I know, that have vaunted their pens in private devices and tricked up a company of taffeta fools with their feathers, whose beauty if our poets had not picked with the supply of their periwigs, they might have 30 antickt it until this time up and down the country with the King of Fairies, and dined every day at the pease-porridge ordinary with Delphrigus.

But Tolossa hath forgot that it was sometime sacked, and beggars that ever they carried their fardles on footback; and in truth no marvel, when as the deserved reputation of one Roscius is of force to enrich a rabble of counterfeits. Yet let subjects, for all their insolence, dedicate a *De profundis* every morning to the preservation of their Caesar, lest their increasing indignities return them ere long to their juggling to mediocrity, and they bewail in weeping blanks the wane of their monarchy.

As poetry hath been honoured in those her forenamed professors, so 40 it hath not been any wit disparaged by William Warner's absolute *Albions.* And here authority hath made a full point; in whose reverence insisting, I cease to oppose to your sport the picture of those pamphleteers and poets that make a patrimony of *In speech* and more than a younger brother's inheritance of their *Abcie*. Read favourably, to encourage me in the firstlings of my folly, and persuade yourselves I will persecute those idiots and their heirs unto the third generation that have made Art bankrupt of her ornaments and sent Poetry abegging up and down the country. It may be my *Anatomie of Absurdities* may acquaint you ere long with my skill in surgery, wherein the diseases of Art more merrily discovered may make our maimed poets put together their blanks to the 10 building of an hospital.

If you chance to meet it in Paul's, shaped in a new suit of similitudes, as if, like the eloquent apprentice of Plutarch, it were popped at seven years old in double apparel, think his master hath fulfilled covenants, and only cancelled the indentures of duty. If I please, I'll think my ignorance indebted to you that applaud it; if not, what rests but that I be excluded from your courtesy, like *Apocrypha* from your Bibles?

However, yours ever,

THOMAS NASH.

20

FROM *The Unfortunate Traveller,* 1594

The Unfortunate Traveler

ABOUT that time that the terror of the world and fever quartan of the French, Henry the Eighth (the only true subject of chronicles), advanced his standard against the two hundred and fifty towers of Turney and Turwin, and had the emperor and all the nobility of Flanders, Holland, and Brabant as mercenary attendants on his full-sailed fortune, I, Jack Wilton (a gentleman at least), was a certain kind of an appendix 30 or page, belonging or appertaining in or unto the confines of the English court, where what my credit was, a number of my creditors that I cozened can testify, *Coelum petimus stultitia,* which of us all is not a sinner. Be it known to as many as will pay money enough to peruse my story that I followed the camp or the court, or the court and the camp, when Turwin lost her maidenhead, and opened her gates to more than Jane Trosse did. There did I (soft, let me drink before I go any further) reign sole king of the cans and black-jacks, prince of the pygmies, county palatine of clean straw and provant, and, to conclude, lord high regent of rashers of the coals and red herring cobs. *Paulô maiora canamus.*

40 Well, to the purpose. What stratagemical acts and monuments do you think an ingenious infant of my age might enact? You will say it were sufficient if he slur a die, pawn his master to the utmost penny, and minis-

ter the oath of the pantofle artificially. These are signs of good education, I must confess, and arguments of, "In grace and virtue to proceed." Oh, but *Aliquid latet quod non patet*, there's a farther path I must trace. Examples confirm; list, lordings, to my proceedings.

Whosoever is acquainted with the state of a camp understands that in it be many quarters, and yet not so many as on London Bridge. In those quarters are many companies: much company, much knavery, as true as that old adage, Much courtesy, much subtlety. Those companies, like a great deal of corn, do yield some chaff; the corn are cormorants, the chaff are good fellows, which are quickly blown to nothing with bearing 10 a light heart in a light purse. Amongst this chaff was I winnowing my wits to live merrily, and, by my troth, so I did; the prince could but command men spend their blood in his service, I could make them spend all the money they had for my pleasure. But poverty in the end parts friends; though I was prince of their purses and exacted of my unthrift subjects as much liquid allegiance as any kaiser in the world could do, yet where it is not to be had the king must lose his right; want cannot be withstood, men can do no more than they can do; what remained, then, but the fox's case must help when the lion's skin is out at the elbows.

There was a lord in the camp, let him be a lord of misrule, if you will, 20 for he kept a plain alehouse without welt or guard of any ivy bush, and sold cider and cheese by pint and by pound to all that came (at that very name of cider, I can but sigh, there is so much of it in Rhenish wine nowadays). Well, *tendit ad sydera virtus*, there's great virtue belongs (I can tell you) to a cup of cider, and very good men have sold it, and at sea it is *aqua coelestis*; but that's neither here nor there; if it had no other patron but this peer of quart pots to authorize it, it were sufficient. This great lord, this worthy lord, this noble lord, thought no scorn (Lord have mercy upon us) to have his great velvet breeches larded with the droppings of this dainty liquor, and yet he was an old servitor, a cavalier of an 30 ancient house, as it might appear by the arms of his ancestry, drawn very amiably in chalk on the inside of his tent door.

He and no other was the man I chose out to damn with a lewd, moneyless device; for coming to him on a day, as he was counting his barrels and setting the price in chalk on the head of every one of them, I did my duty very devoutly and told his *aley* honor I had matters of some secrecy to impart unto him, if it pleased him to grant me private audience.

"With me, young Wilton," quoth he, "marry and shalt; bring us a pint of cider of a fresh tap into the Three Cups here; wash the pot." So into a back room he led me, where, after he had spit on his finger and 40 picked off two or three motes of his old, moth-eaten velvet cap, and sponged and wrung all the rheumatic drivel from his ill-favored goat's

beard, he bade me declare my mind, and thereupon he drank to me on
the same. I up with a long circumstance, alias, a cunning shift of the
seventeens, and discoursed unto him what entire affection I had borne
him time out of mind, partly for the high descent and lineage from whence
he sprung, and partly for the tender care and provident respect he had of
poor soldiers, that whereas the vastity of that place (which afforded them
no indifferent supply of drink or of victuals) might humble them to some
extremity, and so weaken their hands, he vouchsafed in his own person
to be a victualler to the camp (a rare example of magnificence and hon-
10 orable courtesy) and diligently provided that, without far travel, every
man might for his money have cider and cheese his bellyful; nor did he
sell his cheese by the way only, or his cider by the great, but abased himself with his own hands to take a shoemaker's knife (a homely instrument for such a high personage to touch) and cut it out equally like a true
justiciary, in little pennyworths, that it would do a man good for to look
upon. So likewise of his cider, the poor man might have his moderate
draught of it (as there is a moderation in all things) as well for his doit
or his dandiprat as the rich man for his half-sous or his denier. "Not so
much," quoth I, "but this tapster's linen apron which you wear before
20 you to protect your apparel from the imperfections of the spigot, most
amply bewrays your lowly mind. I speak it with tears, too few such
humble-spirited noble men have we that will draw drink in linen aprons.
Why, you are every child's fellow; any man that comes under the name
of a soldier and a good fellow, you will sit and bear company to the last
pot, yea, and you take in as good part the homely phrase of 'Mine host,
here's to you,' as if one saluted you by all the titles of your barony. These
considerations, I say, which the world suffers to slip by in the channel of
carelessness, have moved me, in ardent zeal of your welfare, to forewarn you of some dangers that have beset you and your barrels."
30 At the name of dangers, he start up, and bounced with his fist on the
board so hard that his tapster, overhearing him, cried, "Anon, anon, sir,
by and by"; and came and made a low leg and asked him what he lacked.
He was ready to have stricken his tapster for interrupting him in attention of this, his so much desired relation, but, for fear of displeasing me, he
moderated his fury, and, only sending him for the other fresh pint, willed
him look to the bar, and come when he is called, with a devil's name.
Well, at his earnest importunity, after I had moistened my lips to make
my lie run glib to his journey's end, forward I went as followeth. "It
chanced me the other night, amongst other pages, to attend where the
40 king with his lords and many chief leaders sat in counsel. There amongst
sundry serious matters that were debated and intelligences from the
enemy given up, it was privily informed (no villains to these privy in-

formers) that you, even you that I now speak to, had——would I had no tongue to tell the rest; by this drink it grieves me so I am not able to repeat it."

Now was my drunken lord ready to hang himself for the end of the full point, and over my neck he throws himself very lubberly, and entreated me, as I was a proper young gentleman and ever looked for pleasure at his hands, soon to rid him out of this hell of suspense and resolve him of the rest; then fell he on his knees, wrung his hands, and I think, on my conscience, wept out all the cider that he had drunk in a week before. To move me to have pity on him, he rose and put his rusty 10 ring on my finger, gave me his greasy purse with that single money that was in it, promised to make me his heir, and a thousand more favors, if I would expire the misery of his unspeakable tormenting uncertainty. I, being by nature inclined to Mercy (for indeed I knew two or three good wenches of that name), bade him harden his ears and not make his eyes abortive before their time, and he should have the inside of my breast turned outward, hear such a tale as would tempt the utmost strength of life to attend it and not die in the midst of it. "Why," quoth I, "myself, that am but a poor, childish well-willer of yours, with the very thought that a man of your desert and state, by a number of peasants and varlets 20 should be so injuriously abused in hugger-mugger, have wept all my urine upward. The wheel under our city bridge carries not so much water over the city as my brain hath welled forth gushing streams of sorrow. I have wept so immoderately and lavishly that I thought verily my pallet had been turned to Pissing Conduit in London. My eyes have been drunk, outrageously drunk, with giving but ordinary intercourse through their sea-circled islands to my distilling dreariment. What shall I say? That which malice hath said is the mere overthrow and murder of your days. Change not your color, none can slander a clear conscience to itself; receive all your fraught of misfortune in at once. 30

"It is buzzed in the king's head that you are a secret friend to the enemy, and, under pretense of getting a license to furnish the camp with cider and such like provant, you have furnished the enemy, and in empty barrels sent letters of discovery and corn innumerable."

I might well have left here, for by this time his white liver had mixed itself with the white of his eye, and both were turned upwards, as if they had offered themselves a fair white for death to shoot at. The truth was, I was very loath mine host and I should part with dry lips; wherefore the best means that I could imagine to wake him out of his trance was to cry loud in his ear, "Ho, host, What's to pay? will no man look to the reckon- 40 ing here?" And, in plain verity, it took expected effect, for with the noise he started and bustled, like a man that had been scared with fire out of his sleep, and ran hastily to his tapster, and all to-belabored him about the ears for letting gentlemen call so long and not look in to them. Presently he remembered himself, and had like to have fallen into his memento again, but that I met him half ways, and asked his lordship what he meant to slip his neck out of the collar so suddenly, and, being revived, strike his tapster so rashly.

"Oh," quoth he, "I am bought and sold for doing my country such good service as I have done. They are afraid of me because my good deeds have brought me into such estimation with the commonalty. I see,
10 I see, it is not for the lamb to live with the wolf."

The world is well amended, thought I, with your cidership; such another forty years' nap as Epimenides had would make you a perfect wise man. "Answer me," quoth he, "my wise young Wilton; is it true that I am thus underhand dead and buried by these bad tongues?"

"Nay," quoth I, "you shall pardon me, for I have spoken too much already; no definitive sentence of death shall march out of my well-meaning lips; they have but lately sucked milk, and shall they so suddenly change their food and seek after blood?"

"Oh, but," quoth he, "a man's friend is his friend—fill the other pint.
20 tapster. What said the king? did he believe it when he heard it? I pray thee, say. I swear to thee by my nobility, none in the world shall ever be made privy that I received any light of this matter from thee."

"That firm affiance," quoth I, "had I in you before, or else I would never have gone so far over the shoes to pluck you out of the mire. Not to make many words (since you will needs know) the king says flatly, you are a miser and a snudge, and he never hoped better of you."

"Nay then," quoth he, "questionless some planet that loves not cider hath conspired against me."

"Moreover, which is worse, the king hath vowed to give Turwin one
30 hot breakfast only with the bungs that he will pluck out of your barrels. I cannot stay at this time to report each circumstance that passed, but the only counsel that my long-cherished, kind inclination can possibly contrive is now in your old days to be liberal; such victuals or provision as you have, presently distribute it frankly amongst poor soldiers; I would let them burst their bellies with cider, and bathe in it, before I would run into my prince's ill opinion for a whole sea of it. The hunter pursuing the beaver for his stones, he bites them off, and leaves them behind for him to gather up, whereby he lives quiet. If greedy hunters and hungry tell-tales pursue you, it is for a little pelf which you have. Cast it behind
40 you, neglect it, let them have it, lest it breed a further inconvenience. Credit my advice; you shall find it prophetical; and thus I have discharged the part of a poor friend."

With some few like phrases of ceremony, "Your honor's suppliant," and so forth, and "Farewell, my good youth, I thank thee and will remember thee," we parted.

But the next day I think we had a dole of cider, cider in bowls, in scuppets, in helmets, and, to conclude, if a man would have filled his boots full, there he might have had it. Provant thrust itself into poor soldiers' pockets whether they would or no. We made five peals of shot into the town together, of nothing but spigots and faucets of discarded empty barrels; every underfoot soldier had a distenanted tun, as Diogenes had his tub to sleep in. I myself got as many confiscated tapsters' aprons as 10 made me a tent as big as any ordinary commander's in the field. But, in conclusion, my well-beloved baron of double beer got him humbly on his marybones to the king, and complained he was old and stricken in years, and had ne'er an heir to cast at a dog; wherefore if it might please His Majesty to take his lands into his hands, and allow him some reasonable pension to live on, he should be marvelous well pleased: as for the wars, he was weary of them, and yet as long as Highness should venture his own person, he would not flinch a foot, but make his withered body a buckler, to bear off any blow that should be advanced against him.

The king, marveling at this strange alteration of his great merchant of 20 cider (for so he would often pleasantly term him), with a little further talk bolted out the whole complotment. Then was I pitifully whipped for my holiday lie, although they made themselves merry with it many a fair winter's evening after.

Yet, notwithstanding, his good ass-headed honor, mine host, persevered in his former simple request to the king to accept of the surrender of his lands and allow him a beadsmanry or out-brothership of brachet, which at length, through his vehement instancy, took effect, and the king jestingly said, since he would needs have it so, he would distrain on part of his land for impost of cider, which he was behindhand with him and never 30 paid.

This was one of my famous achievements, insomuch as I never light upon the like famous fool; but I have done a thousand better jests if they had been booked in order as they were begotten. It is pity posterity should be deprived of such precious records, and yet there is no remedy; and yet there is too, for, when all fails, well fare a good memory. Gentle readers (look you be gentle now since I have called you so), as freely as my knavery was mine own, it shall be yours to use in the way of honesty.

* * * * *

40

Dismissing this fruitless annotation *pro et contra*, towards Venice we progressed, and took Rotterdam in our way, that was clean out of our way.

There we met with aged learning's chief ornament, that abundant and superingenious clerk Erasmus, as also with merry Sir Thomas More, our countryman, who was come purposely over a little before us to visit the said grave father Erasmus. What talk, what conference we had then, it were here superfluous to rehearse; but this I can assure you, Erasmus in all his speeches seemed so much to mislike the indiscretion of princes in preferring of parasites and fools that he decreed with himself to swim with the stream, and write a book forthwith in commendation of folly. Quick-witted Sir Thomas More traveled in a clean contrary province, for he, seeing most commonwealths corrupted by ill custom, and that principalities were nothing but great piracies which, gotten by violence and murder, were maintained by private undermining and bloodshed; that in the chiefest flourishing kingdoms there was no equal or well-divided weal one with another, but a manifest conspiracy of rich men against poor men, procuring their own unlawful commodities under the name and interest of the commonwealth: he concluded with himself to lay down a perfect plot of a commonwealth or government, which he would entitle his *Utopia*.

So left we them to prosecute their discontented studies, and made our next journey to Wittenberg.

At the very point of our entrance into Wittenberg, we were spectators of a very solemn scholastical entertainment of the Duke of Saxony thither. Whom, because he was the chief patron of their university, and had took Luther's part in banishing the mass and all like papal jurisdiction out of their town, they crouched unto extremely. The chief ceremonies of their entertainment were these. First, the heads of their university (they were great heads of certainty) met him in their hooded hypocrisy and doctorly accoutrements, *secundum formam statuti*, where, by the orator of the university, whose pickedevant was very plentifully be-sprinkled with rose water, a very learned or rather ruthful oration was delivered (for it rained all the while) signifying thus much: that it was all by patch and by piecemeal stolen out of Tully, and he must pardon them, though in emptying their phrase books, the air emptied his entrails, for they did it not in any ostentation of wit (which they had not), but to shew the extraordinary good will they bare the duke (to have him stand in the rain till he was thorough wet); a thousand *quemadmodums* and *quaprupters* he came over him with, every sentence he concluded with *Esse posse videatur;* through all the nine worthies he ran with praising and comparing him; Nestor's years he assured him of under the broad seal of their supplications, and, with the crow-trodden verse in Virgil, *Dum juga montis aper*, he packed up his pipes, and cried *dixi*.

That pageant overpast, there rushed upon him a miserable rabblement

of junior graduates, that all cried out upon him mightily in their gibberish
like a company of beggars, "God save Your Grace, God save Your Grace,
Jesus preserve Your Highness, though it be but for an hour."

Some three half-pennyworth of Latin here also had he thrown at his
face, but it was choice stuff, I can tell you, as there is a choice even
amongst rags gathered up from the dunghill. At the town's end met him
the burghers and dunsticall incorporationers of Wittenberg in their distinguished liveries; their distinguished livery faces, I mean, for they were
most of them hot-livered drunkards, and had all the coat colors of sanguine, purple, crimson, copper, carnation that were to be had, in their ₁₀
countenances. Filthy knaves, no cost had they bestowed on the town for
his welcome, saving new painted their houghs and boozing houses, which
commonly are fairer than their churches; and over their gates set the
town arms carousing a whole health to the Duke's arms, which sounded
gulping after this sort, *Vanhotten, slotten, irk bloshen glotten gelderslike.*
Whatever the words were, the sense was this, Good drink is a medicine
for all diseases.

A bursten-belly inkhorn orator called Vanderhulke they picked out
to present him with an oration, one that had a sulphurous big swollen large
face, like a Saracen, eyes like two Kentish oysters, a mouth that opened ₂₀
as wide every time he spake as one of those old knit trap doors, a beard
as though it had been made of a bird's nest plucked in pieces, which consisteth of straw, hair, and dirt mixed together. He was apparelled in
black leather new licourd, and a short gown without any gathering in the
back, faced before and behind with a boisterous bear skin, and a red night-
cap on his head. To this purport and effect was this broccing double-beer
oration.

"Right noble Duke (*ideo nobilis quasi no bilis,* for you have no bile or
choler in you), know that our present incorporation of Wittenberg, by
me the tongue-man of their thankfulness, a townsman by birth, a free ₃₀
German by nature, an orator by art, and a scrivener by education, in all
obedience and chastity, most bountifully bid you welcome to Wittenberg.
Welcome, said I? O orificial rhetoric, wipe thy everlasting mouth, and
afford me a more Indian metaphor than that, for the brave princely
blood of a Saxon. Oratory, uncask the barred hutch of thy compliments,
and with the triumphantest troop in thy treasury do trewage unto him.
What impotent speech with his eight parts may not specify, this unestimable
gift, holding his peace, shall as it were (with tears I speak it) do whereby
as it may seem or appear to manifest or declare, and yet it is, and yet it
is not, and yet it may be a diminitive oblation meritorious to your high ₄₀
pusillanimity and indignity. Why should I go gadding and fizgigging after
firking flantado amphibologies? wit is wit, and good will is good will.

With all the wit I have, I here, according to the premises, offer up unto you the city's general good will, which is a gilded Can, in manner and form following, for you and the heirs of your body lawfully begotten to drink healths in. The scholastical squitter-books clout you up canopies and foot-clothes of verses. We that are good fellows, and live as merry as cup and can, will not verse upon you as they do, but must do as we can, and entertain you if it be but with a plain empty Can. He hath learning enough that hath learned to drink to his first man.

"Gentle Duke, without paradox be it spoken, thy horses at our own proper costs and charges shall kneed up to the knees all the while thou art here in spruce beer and Lübeck liquor. Not a dog thou bringest with thee but shall be banquetted with rhenish wine and sturgeon. On our shoulders we wear no lamb-skin or miniver like these academics, yet we can drink to the confusion of all thy enemies. Good lambs-wool have we for their lamb-skins, and for their miniver, large minerals in our coffers. Mechanical men they call us, and not amiss, for most of us being *Mœchi*, that is, cuckolds and whoremasters, fetch our antiquity from the temple of Mæcha, where Mahomet was hung up. Three parts of the world, America, Afric, and Asia, are of this our mechanic religion. Nero, when he cried, *O quantus artifex pereo,* professed himself of our freedom, insomuch as *Artifex* is a citizen or craftsman, as well as *Carnifex* a scholar or hangman. Pass on by leave into the precincts of our abomination. Bonny Duke, frolic in our bower, and persuade thy self that even as garlick hath three properties, to make a man wink, drink, and stink, so we will wink on thy imperfections, drink to thy favorites, and all thy foes shall stink before us. So be it. Farewell."

The Duke laughed not a little at this ridiculous oration, but that very night as great an ironical occasion was ministered, for he was bidden to one of the chief schools to a Comedy handled by scholars. *Acolastus, the Prodigal Child* was the name of it, which was so filthily acted, so leathernly set forth, as would have moved laughter in Heraclitus. One, as if he had been planing a clay floor, stampingly trod the stage so hard with his feet that I thought verily he had resolved to do the carpenter that set it up some utter shame. Another flung his arms like cudgels at a pear tree, insomuch as it was mightily dreaded that he would strike the candles that hung above their heads out of their sockets, and leave them all dark. Another did nothing but wink and make faces. There was a parasite and he, with clapping his hands and thripping his fingers, seemed to dance an antic to and fro. The only thing they did well was the prodigal child's hunger, most of their scholars being hungrily kept; and surely you would have said they had been brought up in hogs' academy to learn to eat acorns, if you had seen how sedulously they fell to them. Not a jest had they to keep their auditors from sleeping but of swill and draff; yes, now and then the servant put his hand into the dish before his master, and almost choked himself, eating slovenly and ravenously to cause sport.

The next day they had solemn disputations, where Luther and Carolostadius scolded level coil. A mass of words I wot well they heaped up against the mass and the pope, but farther particulars of their disputations I remember not. I thought verily they would have worried one another with words, they were so earnest and vehement. Luther had the louder voice, Carolostadius went beyond him in beating and bouncing with his fists, *Quae supra nos nihil ad nos.* They uttered nothing to make a man laugh; therefore I will leave them. Marry, their outward gestures now and then would afford a man a morsel of mirth—of those two I mean not so much as of all the other train of opponents and respondents. One pecked like a crane with his forefinger at every half syllable he brought forth, and nodded with his nose like an old singing-man teaching a young chorister to keep time. Another would be sure to wipe his mouth with his handkerchief at the end of every full point. And ever when he thought he had cast a figure so curiously as he dived over head and ears into his auditors' admiration, he would take occasion to stroke up his hair and twine up his mustachios twice or thrice over, while they might have leisure to applaud him. A third wavered and waggled his head, like a proud horse playing with his bridle, or as I have seen some fantastical swimmer, at every stroke, train his chin side-long over his left shoulder. A fourth sweat and foamed at the mouth for very anger his adversary had denied that part of his syllogism which he was not prepared to answer. A fifth spread his arms like an usher that goes before to make room, and thripped with his finger and his thumb when he thought he had tickled it with a conclusion. A sixth hung down his countenance like a sheep, and stutted and slavered very pitifully when his invention was stepped aside out of the way. A seventh gasped and gaped for wind, and groaned in his pronunciation as if he were hard bound with some bad argument. Gross plodders they were all, that had some learning and reading, but no wit to make use of it. They imagined the duke took the greatest pleasure and contentment under heaven to hear them speak Latin, and, as long as they talked nothing but Tully, he was bound to attend them. A most vain thing it is in many universities at this day that they count him excellent eloquent who stealeth not whole phrases but whole pages out of Tully. If of a number of shreds of his sentences he can shape an oration, from all the world he carries it away, although in truth it be no more than a fool's coat of many colors. No invention or matter have they of their own, but tack up a style of his stale gallimaufries. The leaden-headed Germans first began this, and we Englishmen have surfeited of their absurd imitation. I pity Nizolius that had nothing to do but pick threads' ends out of an old, overworn garment. . . .

* * * * *

FROM *Nashes Lenten Stuffe, Containing . . . the praise of the Red Herring,* 1599

. . . To recount *ab ovo,* or from the church-book of his birth, how the herring first came to be a fish, and then how he came to be king of
10 fishes, and, gradionately, how from white to red he changed, would require as massy a tome as Holinshed; but, in half a pennyworth of paper, I will epitomize them. Let me see, hath anybody in Yarmouth heard of Leander and Hero, of whom divine Musaeus sung, and a diviner muse than him, Kit Marlowe?

Two faithful lovers they were, as every apprentice in Paul's Churchyard will tell you for your love, and sell you for your money; the one dwelt at Abydos in Asia, which was Leander; the other, which was Hero, his mistress or Delia, at Sestos in Europe, and she was a pretty pinkany and Venus' priest; and but an arm of the sea divided them. It divided
20 them and it divided them not, for over that arm of the sea could be made a long arm. In their parents the most division rested, and their towns that, like Yarmouth and Leystoffe, were still at wrig-wrag and sucked from their mothers' teats serpentine hatred one against each other. Which drove Leander, when he durst not deal above board or be seen aboard any ship to sail to his lady dear, to play the didapper and ducking water spaniel to swim to her; nor that in the day, but by owl-light.

What will not blind night do for blind Cupid? And what will not blind Cupid do in the night, which is his blindman's holiday? By the seaside on the other side stood Hero's tower, such another tower as one of
30 our Irish castles, that is not so wide as a belfry and a cobbler cannot jert out his elbows in; a cage or pigeon-house, roomthsome enough to comprehend her and the toothless trot, her nurse, who was her only chatmate and chambermaid; consultively by her parents being so encloistered from resort that she might live chaste, vestal priest to Venus, the queen of unchastity. She would none of that, she thanked them, for she was better provided; and that which they thought served their turn best of sequestering her from company, served her turn best to embrace the company she desired. Fate is a spaniel that you cannot beat from you; the more you think to cross it, the more you bless it and further it.
40 Neither her father nor mother vowed chastity when she was begot; therefore, she thought they begat her not to live chaste, and either she must prove herself a bastard or shew herself like them. Of Leander you

may write upon, and it is written upon, she liked well; and for all he was a naked man and clean despoiled to the skin when he sprawled through the brackish suds to scale her tower, all the strength of it could not hold him out. Oh, ware a naked man! Cytherea's nuns have no power to resist him; and some such quality is ascribed to the lion. Were he never so naked when he came to her, because he should not scare her, she found a means to cover him in her bed; and for he might not take cold after his swimming, she lay close by him to keep him warm. This scuffling or bo-peep in the dark they had a while without wem or brack; and the old nurse (as there be three things seldom in their right kind till they be old: a bawd, a witch, and a midwife) executed the huckstering office of her years very charily and circumspectly till their sliding stars revolted from them. And then, for seven days together, the wind and the Hellespont contended which should howl louder; the waves dashed up to the clouds, and the clouds, on the other side, spit and drivelled upon them as fast.

Hero wept as trickling as the heavens, to think that heaven should so divorce them. Leander stormed worse than the storms, that by them he should be so restrained from his Cynthia. At Sestos was his soul, and he could not abide to tarry in Abydos. Rain, snow, hail, or blow it how it could, into the pitchy Hellespont he leapt when the moon and all her torchbearers were afraid to peep out their heads; but he was peppered for it; he had as good have took meat, drink, and leisure. For the churlish, frampold waves gave him his bellyful of fish-broth ere out of their laundry or wash-house they would grant him his coquet or *transire*; and not only that, but they sealed him his *quietus est* for curvetting any more to the maiden tower, and tossed his dead carcass, well bathed or parboiled, to the sandy threshold of his leman or orange for a disjune or morning breakfast. All that livelong night could she not sleep, she was so troubled with the rheum, which was a sign she should hear of some drowning. Yet towards cock-crowing she caught a little slumber; and then she dreamed that Leander and she were playing at checkstone with pearls in the bottom of the sea.

You may see dreams are not so vain as they are preached of, though not in vain preachers inveigh against them and bend themselves out of the people's minds to exhale their foolish superstition. The rheum is the students' disease, and who study most dream most. The laboring men's hands glow and blister after their day's work; the glowing and blistering of our brains after our day-laboring cogitations are dreams, and those dreams are reeking vapors of no impression if our mateless couches be not half empty. Hero hoped, and therefore she dreamed (as all hope is but a dream) her hope was where her heart was; and her heart winding and turning with the wind, that might wind her heart of gold to her, or else turn him from her. Hope and fear both combatted in her, and both these are wakeful; which made her, at break of day (what an old crone is the day, that is so long abreaking) to unloop her luket or casement, to look whence the blasts came or what gate or pace the sea kept; when forthwith her eyes bred her eyesore, the first white whereon their transpiercing arrows stuck being the breathless corpse of Leander. With the sudden contemplation of this piteous spectacle of her love, sodden to haddock's meat, her sorrow could not choose but be indefinite, if her delight 10 in him were but indifferent; and there is no woman but delights in sorrow, or she would not use it so lightly for everything.

Down she ran in her loose nightgown, and her hair about her ears (even as Semiramis ran out with her lye-pot in her hand and her black dangling tresses about her shoulders, with her ivory comb ensnarled in them, when she heard that Babylon was taken) and thought to have kissed his dead corse alive again; but, as on his blue-jellied sturgeon lips she was about to clap one of those warm plasters, boisterous woolpacks of ridged tides came rolling in and raught him from her (with a mind belike to carry him back to Abydos). At that she became a frantic bacchanal 20 outright, and made no more bones but sprang after him, and so resigned up her priesthood and left work for Musaeus and Kit Marlowe. The gods, and gods and goddesses all on a row, bread and crow, from Ops to Pomona the first apple-wife, were so dumped with this miserable wrack that they began to abhor all moisture for the sea's sake; and Jupiter could not endure Ganimede his cupbearer to come in his presence, both for the dislike he bore to Neptune's baneful liquor, as also that he was so like to Leander. The sun was so in his mumps upon it, that it was almost noon before he could go to cart that day, and then with so ill a will he went that he had thought to have toppled his burning car, or hurry-curry, into 30 the sea (as Phaeton did) to scorch it and dry it up; and at night, when he was begrimed with dust and sweat of his journey, he would not descend, as he was wont, to wash him in the ocean, but under a tree laid him down to rest in his clothes all night. And so did the scowling moon under another, fast by him; which, of that, are behighted the trees of the sun and moon, and are the same that Sir John Mandeville tells us he spoke with, and that spoke to Alexander. Venus, for Hero was her priest, and Juno Lucina, the midwife's goddess, for she was now quickened, and cast away by the cruelty of Æolus, took bread and salt and eat it, that they would be smartly revenged on that truculent windy jailer; and they 40 forgot it not, for Venus made his son and his daughter to commit incest together. Lucina, that there might be some lasting characters of his shame, helped to bring her to bed of a goodly boy, and Æolus, bolting out all this, heaped murder upon murder.

The dint of destiny could not be repealed in the reviving of Hero and
Leander, but their heavenly hoods in their synod thus decreed: that for
they were, either of them, seaborderers and drowned in the sea, still to
the sea they must belong, and be divided in habitation after death as they
were in their lifetime. Leander, for that in a cold, dark, testy night he
had his passport to Charon, they terminated to the unquiet, cold coast of
Iceland, where half the year is nothing but mirk night, and to that fish
translated him which of us is termed Ling. Hero, for that she was paggled
and tympanized, and sustained two losses under one, they foot-balled
their heads together and protested to make the stem of her loins, of all 10
fishes, the slanting Fabyan or Palmerin of England, which is Cadwalader
herring. And as their meetings were but seldom, and not so oft as welcome, so but seldom should they meet in the heel of the week at the best
men's tables upon Fridays and Saturdays, the holy time of Lent exempted;
and then they might be at meat and meal for seven weeks together.

* * * * *

THOMAS DELONEY

The Introduction and Notes are at page 1333

FROM *Thomas of Reading*, [about 1599; the earliest extant edition, the
fourth, was printed in 1612]

Thomas of Reading

The pleasant history of the six worthy yeoman of the West.

IN THE days of King Henry the First, who was the first king that in- 30
stituted the High Court of Parliament, there lived nine men which for
the trade of Clothing were famous throughout all England. Which Art
in those days was held in high reputation, both in respect of the great riches
that thereby was gotten, as also of the benefit it brought to the whole
commonwealth; the younger sons of knights and gentlemen, to whom
their fathers would leave no lands, were most commonly preferred to
learn this trade, to the end that thereby they might live in good estate and
drive forth their days in prosperity.

Among all Crafts this was the only chief, for that it was the greatest
merchandise by the which our country became famous through all nations. 40
And it was verily thought that the one-half of the people in the land lived
in those days thereby, and in such good sort that in the commonwealth
there were few or no beggars at all. Poor people, whom God lightly

blesseth with most children, did by means of this occupation so order them that by the time that they were come to be six or seven years of age they were able to get their own bread. Idleness was then banished our coast, so that it was a rare thing to hear of a thief on those days. Therefore it was not without cause that Clothiers were then both honored and loved; among these, nine persons in this king's days were of great credit; viz., Thomas Cole of Reading, Gray of Gloucester, Sutton of Salisbury, Fitzallen of Worcester (commonly called William of Worcester), Tom Dove of Excester, and Simon of Southampton, alias Supbroth; who were by the king called "The six worthy husbands of the West." Then there were three living in the North; that is to say, Cutbert of Kendall, Hodgekins of Halifax, and Martin Byram of Manchester. Every one of these kept a great number of servants at work—spinners, carders, weavers, fullers, dyers, sheermen, and rowers—to the great admiration of all those that came into their houses to behold them.

Now you shall understand these gallant Clothiers, by reason of their dwelling places, separated themselves in three several companies: Gray of Gloucester, William of Worcester, and Thomas of Reading, because their journey to London was all one way, they conversed commonly together. And Dove of Excester, Sutton of Salisbury, and Simon of Southampton, they in like sort kept company the one with the other, meeting ever all together at Basingstoke. And the three northern clothiers did the like, who commonly did not meet till they came to Bosom's Inn in London.

Moreover, for the love and delight that these western men had in each other's company, they did so provide that their wains and themselves would ever meet upon one day in London at Jarrat's Hall, surnamed the Giant, for that he surpassed all other men of that age both in stature and strength; whose merriments and memorable deeds I will set down unto you in this following discourse.

* * * * *

CHAPTER 2.

How William of Worcester, Gray of Gloucester, and old Cole of Reading met all together at Reading, and of their communication by the way as they rode to London.

* * * * *

Now when they came to London, they were welcome to the host Jarrat the Giant, and as soon as they were alighted, they were saluted by the Merchants, who waited their coming thither, and always prepared for them a costly supper, where they commonly made their bargain; and upon every bargain made, they still used to send some tokens to the Clothiers' wives. The next morning they went to the hall, where they met the Northern clothiers, who greeted one another in this sort.

What, my Masters of the West, well met: what cheer? what cheer?

Even the best cheer our Merchants could make us: (quoth Gray).

Then you could not choose but fare well (quoth Hodgekins).

And you be weary of our company, adieu (quoth Sutton).

Not so, said Martin, but shall we not have a game ere we go?

Yes faith for an hundred pounds.

Well said, old Cole (said they), and with that Cole and Gray went to the dice with Martin and Hodgekins; and the dice running on Hodgekins' side, Cole's money began to waste.

Now by the Mass (quoth Cole) my money shrinks as bad as Northern cloth.

When they had played long, Gray stepped to it, and recovered again the money that Cole had lost. But while they were thus playing, the rest being delighted in contrary matters, every man satisfied his own humor.

Tom Dove called for music, William of Worcester for wine, Sutton set his delight in hearing merry tales, Simon of Southampton got him into the kitchen, and to the pottage pot he goes, for he esteemed more of a mess of pottage than of a venison pasty. Now sir, Cutbert of Kendall was of another mind, for no meat pleased him so well as mutton, such as was laced in a red petticoat. And you shall understand that always when they went to dice, they got into Bosom's Inn, which was so called of his name that kept it; who being a foul sloven, went always with his nose in his bosom, and one hand in his pocket, the other on his staff, figuring forth a description of cold winter, for he always wore two coats, two caps, two or three pair of stockings, and a high pair of shoes, over the which he drew on a great pair of lined slippers; and yet would oft complain of cold, wherefore of all men generally he was called Old Bosom, and his house Bosom's Inn.

This lump of cold ice had lately married a young wife, who was as wily as she was wanton, and in her company did Cutbert only delight; and the better to make passage to his love, he would often thus commune with her: I muse good wife (quoth he).

Good wife (quoth she)? Verily sir, in mine opinion, there is none good but God, and therefore call me Mistress.

Then said Cutbert, Fair Mistress, I have often mused that you, being a proper woman, could find in your heart for to match with such a greasy Carl as this, an evil-mannered mate, a foul lump of kitchen stuff, and such a one as is, indeed, a scorn of men; how can you like him that all women mislike? or love such a loathsome creature? methinks verily it should grieve you to lend him a kiss, much more to lie with him.

Indeed sir, quoth she, I had but hard fortune in this respect, but my friends would have it so, and truly my liking and my love toward him are alike; he never had the one, nor never shall get the other; yet I may say to you, before I married him there were divers proper young men that were suitors unto me, who loved me as their lives, and glad was he that could get my company. Those were my golden days, wherein my pleasure abounded, but these are my years of care and grief, wherein my sorrows exceed. Now no man regards me, no man cares for me; and albeit in secret they might bear me good will, yet who dares shew it? And this is a double grief, he carries over me so jealous a mind that I cannot look at a man but presently he accuseth me of inconstancy, although (I protest) without cause.

And in troth (quoth Cutb.) he should have cause to complain for somewhat, were I as you.

As sure as I live, and so he shall, quoth she, if he do not change his bias.

Cutb. hearing her say so, began to grow further in requesting her favor, wishing he might be her servant and secret friend; and the better to obtain his desire, he gave her divers gifts, insomuch that she began something to listen unto him. And albeit she liked well of his speeches, yet would she blame him, and take him up very short sometimes for the same; till in the end, Cutbert shewed himself to be desperate, saying he would drown himself rather than live in her disdain.

O my sweetheart not so, qd. she, God forbid I should be the death of any man. Comfort thyself, kind Cutbert, and take this kiss in token of further kindness, and if thou wilt have my favor, thou must be wise and circumspect, and in my husband's sight I would always have thee to find fault with my doings, blame my bad housewifery, dispraise my person, and take exceptions at everything; whereby he will be as well pleased as Simon of Southampton with a mess of pottage.

Dear Mistress, quoth he, I will fulfil your charge to the uttermost, so that you will not take my jest in earnest.

She answered, Thy foulest speeches I will esteem the fairest and take every dispraise to be a praise from thee, turning each word to the contrary. And so for this time adieu, good Cutb., for supper time draws near, and it is meet for me to look for my meat.

With that down comes old Bosom, calling his wife, saying, Ho Winifred, is supper ready? they have done playing above; therefore let the Chamberlain cover the table.

By and by husband, qd. she, it shall be done straight way.

How now, my Masters, who wins, qd. Cutb.

Our money walks to the West, qd. Martin; Cole hath won forty pound of me, and Gray hath gotten well.

The best is, qd. Hodgekins, they will pay for our supper.

Then let us have good store of sack, qd. Sutton.

Content, said Cole, for I promise you, I strive not to grow rich by dice-playing; therefore call for what you will, I will pay for all.

Yea, said Simon! Chamberlain, I pray thee bring a whole bottle of pottage for me.

Now Tom Dove had all the fiddlers at a beck of his finger, which 10 follow him up and down the city, as diligent as little chickens after a hen, and made a vow that there should want no music. And at that time there lived in London a musician of great reputation, named Reior, who kept his servants in such costly garments that they might seem to come before any Prince. Their coats were all of one color; and it is said, that afterward the nobility of this land, noting it for a seemly sight, used in like manner to keep their men all in one livery. This Reior was the most skillfulest musician that lived at that time, whose wealth was very great, so that all the instruments whereon his servants played were richly gar- nished with studs of silver, and some gold; the bows belonging to their 20 Violins were all likewise of pure silver. He was also for his wisdom called to great office in the city; who also builded (at his own cost) the priory and hospital of Saint Bartholomew in Smithfield. His servants, being the best consorts in the city, were by Tom Dove appointed to play before the young Princes.

Then supper being brought to the board, they all sat down, and by and by after comes up their host, who took his place among them; and anon after, the good-wife in a red petticoat and a waistcoat, comes among them as white as a Lily, saying, My Masters, you are welcome, I pray you be merry. 30

Thus falling close to their meat, when they had well fed, they found leisure to talk one with another: at what time Cutb. began thus to find fault, Ywis, my host, quoth he, you have a wise housewife to your wife; here is meat dressed of a new fashion; God sends meat, and the devil sends cooks.

Why what ails the meat, quoth she, serves it not your turn? Better men than yourself are content withal, but a paltry companion is ever worst to please.

Away, you sluttish thing, qd. Cutb., your husband hath a sweet jewel of you. I marvel such a grave ancient man would match himself with 40 such a young giglot, that hath as much handsomeness in her as good housewifery, which is just nothing at all.

Well sir, said she, in regard of my husband's presence I am loth to aggravate anger; otherwise I would tell thee thy own.

Go to, what need all this, quoth the company? In good faith, Cutb., you are to blame; you find fault where none is.

Tush, I must speak my mind, quoth Cutbert, I cannot dissemble; I trust the good man thinks never the worse of me; so I have his good will, what the foul evil care I for his wife's.

Enough, quoth Tom Dove, let us with music remove these brabbles; we mean to be merry, and not melancholy.

Then said old Cole, Now trust me, Cutbert, we will have your hostess and you friends ere we part. Here, woman, I drink to you, and regard not his words, for he is babbling wheresoever he comes.

Quoth the woman, nothing grieves me so much as that he should thus openly check me; if he had found anything amiss, he might have spied a better time to tell me of it than now; ywis, he need not thrust my bad housewifery into my husband's head; I live not so quietly with him, God wot. And with that she wept.

Come Cutb., quoth they, drink to her, and shake hands and be friends.

Come on, you puling baggage, quoth he, I drink to you; here, will you pledge me and shake hands?

No (quoth she) I will see thee choked first. Shake hands with thee! I will shake hands with the devil as soon.

Go to, said her husband, you shall shake hands with him then. If you will not shake hands, I'll shake you. What, you young housewife!

Well husband, said she, it becomes a woman to obey her husband; in regard whereof, I drink to him.

That's well said, quoth the company. And so she took her leave and went down.

And within a while after, they paid the shot, and departed thence to Jarrat's Hall, where they went to their lodging. And the next day they took their way homeward all together; and coming to Colebrook, they took up their lodging. And it was Cole's custom to deliver his money to the good-wife of the house to keep it till morning, which in the end turned to his utter destruction, as hereafter shall be shewed.

CHAPTER 3.

How Gray's wife of Gloucester, with one or two more of her neigh-bors, went to the Fair, where servants came to be hired, and how she took the Earl of Shrewsbury's Daughter into her service.

It was wont to be an old custom in Gloucestershire, that at a certain time in the year all such young men and maidens as were out of service resorted to a fair that was kept near Gloucester, there to be ready for any that would come to hire them; the young men stood all on a row on the one side, and the maidens on the other. It came to pass that the Earl of Shrewsbury's daughter, whose father was lately banished, being driven into great distress, and weary with travail, as one whose delicate life was never used to such toil, sat her down upon the highway side, making this lamentation.

O false and deceitful world, qd. she! Who is in thee that wishes not to be rid of thee, for thy extremities are great? Thou are deceitful to all, and trusty to none. Fortune is thy treasurer, who is like thyself, wavering 10 and unconstant; she setteth up tyrants, beateth down Kings; giveth shame to some, and renown to others. Fortune giveth these evils, and we see it not; with her hands she toucheth us, and we feel it not; she treads us under foot, and we know it not; she speaks in our ears, and we hear her not; she cries aloud, and we understand her not. And why? Because we know her not until misery doth make her manifest.

Ah my dear father, well mayest thou do! Of all misfortunes it is most unhappy to be fortunate; and by this misfortune came my fall. Was ever good Lady brought to this extremity? What is become of my rare Jewels, my rich array, my sumptuous fare, my waiting servants, my many friends, 20 and all my vain pleasures? My pleasure is banished by displeasure, my friends fled like foes, my servants gone, my feasting turned to fasting, my rich array consumed to rags, and my jewels deck out my chiefest enemies. Therefore of all things the meanest state is best, poverty with surety is better than honor mixed with fear; seeing God hath allotted me to this misery of life, I will frame my heart to embrace humility, and carry a mind answerable to my misfortunes. Fie on this vain title of Ladyship! how little doth it avail the distressed? No, no, I must therefore forget my birth and parentage, and think no more on my father's house, where I was wont to be served; now will I learn to serve, and plain 30 Meg shall be my name. Good Lord grant I may get a good service; nay, any service shall serve, where I may have meat, drink, and apparel.

She had no sooner spoke these words, but she spied a couple of maidens more coming toward her, who were going to the fair; and bidding her good morrow, asked her if she went to the fair.

Yea marry, qd. she, I am a poor man's child that is out of service, and I hear that at the Statute folks do come of purpose to hire servants.

True it is, said the maidens, and thither go we for the same purpose, and would be glad of your company.

With a good will, and I am right glad of yours, said she, beseeching 40 you, good maidens, you will do me the favor to tell me what service were best for me; for the more to blame my parents, they would never put me forth to know anything.

Why what can you do (quoth the maidens) can you brew and bake, make butter and cheese, and reap corn well?

No verily, said Margaret, but I would be right glad to learn to do anything whatsoever it be.

If you could spin or card, said another, you might do excellent well with a clothier, for they are the best services that I know; there you shall be sure to fare well, and to live merrily.

10 Then Margaret wept, saying alas, what shall I do? I was never brought up to these things.

What, can you do nothing, quoth they?

No truly (quoth she) that is good for anything, but I can read and write, and sew; some skill I have in my needle, and a little on my Lute; but this, I see, will profit me nothing.

Good Lord, quoth they, are you bookish? We did never hear of a maid before that could read and write. And although you can do no other thing, yet possibly you may get a service, if you can behave yourself mannerly.

20 I pray you, qd. another, seeing you are bookish, will you do so much as to read a love-letter that is sent me, for I was at a friend's of mine with it, and he was not at home; and so I know not what is in it.

I pray you let me see it, quoth Margaret, and I will shew you.

Whereupon she readeth as followeth.

O Jenny my joy, I die for thy love,
And now I hear say that thou dost remove;
And therefore, Jenny, I pray thee recite,
Where I shall meet thee soon at night.

30 For why, with my Master no more will I stay,
But for thy love I will run away;
O Jenny, Jenny, thou putst me to pain,
That thou no longer wilt here remain.

I will wear out my shoes of Neats Leather,
But thou and I will meet together,
And in spite of Fortune, Rat, or Mouse,
We will dwell together in one house.

For who doth not esteem of thee
Shall have no service done of me;
40 Therefore good Jenny have a care
To meet poor Fragment at the fair.

Now alas, good soul (quoth Jenny) I think he be the kindest young man in the world.

The rest answered, that he seemed no less.

And surely it appeareth that he is a pretty witty fellow, quoth one of them, how finely he hath written his letter in rhyme; trust me, I will give you a good thing, and let me have a copy of it to send to my sweetheart.

That you shall with all my heart. And so coming to the fair, they took up their standing.

Within a while after, goodwife Gray of Gloucester came thither to store herself of divers commodities; and when she had bought what she would, she told her neighbor she had great need of a maidservant or twain. Therefore qd. she, good neighbor go with me, and let me have your opinion.

With a good will, said her neighbor, and together they went, and looking and viewing the maidens over, she took special notice of Margaret.

Believe me, quoth she, there stands a very proper maiden, and one of a modest and comely countenance.

Verily, said her neighbor, so she is, as ever I looked upon.

The maiden seeing them to view her so well, was so abashed that a scarlet color overspread her lily cheeks, which the woman perceiving came unto her and asked if she were willing to serve.

The maid with a low curtsey, and a most gentle speech, answered it was the only cause of her coming.

Can you spin or card, said goodwife Gray?

Truly Dame, said she, though my cunning therein be but small, my goodwill to learn is great, and I trust my diligence shall content you.

What wages will you take, quoth goodwife Gray?

I will refer that, said Margaret, to your conscience and courtesy, desiring no more than what I shall deserve. Then asking what country woman she was, the maiden wept, saying, Ah good Dame, I was untimely born in Shropshire, of poor parents, and yet not so needy as unfortunate; but death having ended their sorrows, hath left me to the cruelty of these envious times, to finish my parents' tragedy with my troubles.

What Maiden! qd. her dame, have you a care to do your business, and to live in God's fear, and you shall have no care to regard Fortune's frowns. And so they went home together.

Now, so soon as the goodman saw her, he asked his wife where she had that maiden. She said, at the fair.

Why then, quoth he, thou hast brought all the fair away, and I doubt it were better for us to send the fair to another Town than to keep the fair here.

Why man, quoth she, what mean you by that?

Woman, I mean this, that she will prove a Loadstone, to draw the hearts of all my men after her; and so we shall have wise service done of all sides.

Then said his wife, I hope, husband, Margaret will have a better care both to her own credit and our commodity than so; and so let her alone to look to such matters.

Is thy name Margaret (quoth her Master)? Proper is thy name to thy person, for thou art a pearl indeed, orient, and rich in beauty.

His wife hearing him say so, began to change her opinion. What husband (quoth she) is the wind at that door? Begin you to like your maid so well? I doubt I had most need to look to yourself. Before God, I had rather than an angel I had chosen some other. But hear you, maid; you shall pack hence; I will not nourish a snake in my bosom; and therefore get you gone; I will none of you; provide a service where you may.

The maiden hearing her say so, fell down on her knees and besought her, saying, O sweet dame, be not so cruel to me, to turn me out of doors now. Alas, I know not where to go, or what to do, if you forsake me. O let not the fading beauty of my face despoil me of your favor; for rather than that shall hinder my service, this my knife shall soon disfigure my face, and I will banish beauty as my greatest enemy. And with that her abundant tears stopped her speech, that she could not utter one word more.

The woman, seeing this, could not harbor anger longer, nor could her master stay in the room for weeping.

Well, Margaret, said her dame (little knowing that a Lady kneeled before her) using thyself well, I will keep thee; and thou shalt have my good will, if thou govern thyself with wisdom. And so she sent her about her business.

Her husband, coming to supper, said: How now wife, art thou so doubtful of me that thou hast put away thy maiden?

I wis (qd. she) you are a wise man, to stand praising of a maid's beauty before her face.

And you a wise woman (qd. he) to grow jealous without a cause.

So to supper they went, and because Margaret shewed herself of finest behavior above the rest, she was appointed to wait on the table. And it is to be understood that Gray did never eat his meat alone, but still had some of his neighbors with him, before whom he called his maid, saying, Margaret, come hither. Now because there was another of the same name in the house, she made answer.

I call not you, maiden, quoth he, but Margaret with the lily white hand.

After which time she was ever called so.

* * * * *

CHAPTER 5.

How the Clothiers had provided a sumptuous feast for the King's sons, Prince William and Prince Richard, at Jarrat's Hall, shewing 10 *also what chance befell Cutbert of Kendall at that same instant.*

* * * * *

It is to be remembered, that while this preparation was in hand, that Cutbert of Kendall had not forgot his kindness to his hostess of Bosom's Inn. Therefore, finding time convenient when her husband was over-seeing his haymakers, he greeted her in this sort, Sweet hostess, though I were the last time I was in town over bold with you, yet I hope it was not so offensive to you as you made shew for.

Bold, my Cut, quoth she? thou hast vowed thyself my servant; and so 20 being, you are not to be blamed for doing what I willed you. By my honesty, I could not choose but smile to myself, so soon as I was out of their sight, to think how prettily you began to brabble.

But now, quoth he, we will change our chidings to kissings, and it vexeth me that these cherry lips should be subject to such a Lobcock as thy husband.

Subject to him, quoth she! In faith sir, no. I will have my lips at as much liberty as my tongue; the one to say what I list, and the other to touch whom I like. In troth, shall I tell thee, Cutbert, the churl's breath smells so strong that I care as much for kissing of him as for looking on 30 him; 'tis such a misshapen miser, and such a bundle of beastliness, that I can never think on him without spitting. Fie upon him! I would my friends had carried me to my grave, when they went with me to the Church to make him my husband. And so shedding a few dissembling tears, she stopped.

What my sweet Mistress (quoth he) weep you? Nay, sit down by my side, and I will sing thee one of my country Jigs to make thee merry.

Wilt thou in faith (quoth she)?

Yes verily, said Cutbert.

And in troth, quoth she, if you fall a-singing I will sing with you. 40

That is well; you can so suddenly change your notes, quoth Cut. Then have at it.

MAN.　Long have I lov'd this bonny Lass,
　　　　　Yet durst not shew the same.
WOM.　There in you prove yourself an Ass.
MAN.　　I was the more to blame.
　　　　　Yet still will I remain to thee,
　　　　　Trang dilly do, trang dilly:
　　　　　Thy friend and lover secretly.
WOM.　Thou art my own sweet bully.

MAN.　But when shall I enjoy thee,
　　　　　delight of thy fair love?
WOM.　Even when thou seest that fortune doth,
　　　　　all manner lets remove.
MAN.　O, I will fold thee in my arms,
　　　　　Trang dilly do, trang dilly,
　　　　　And keep thee so from sudden harms,
WOM.　Thou art my own sweet bully.

WOM.　My husband he is gone from home,
　　　　　You know it very well.
MAN.　But when will he return again?
WOM.　　In troth I cannot tell.
　　　　　If long he keep him out of sight,
　　　　　Trang dilly do, trang dilly,
　　　　　Be sure thou shalt have thy delight.
MAN.　Thou art my bonny lassie.

While they were singing this song, her husband being on a sudden
come home, stood secretly in a corner and heard all, and blessing himself
with both his hands, said, O abhominable dissimulation, monstrous hypocrisy, and are you in this humor? can you brawl together and sing together? Well, quoth he, I will let them alone, to see a little more of
their knavery. Never did Cat watch Mouse so narrowly as I will watch
them. And so going into the Kitchen, he asked his wife if it were not
dinner time.

Even by and by, husband (quoth she) the meat will be ready.

Presently after comes in Hodgekins and Martin, who straight asked
for Cutbert of Kendall. Answer was made, that he was in his Chamber.
So when they had called him, they went to dinner. Then they requested
that their host and hostess would sit with them.

Husband (said she) you may go if you please; but as for me, I will desire pardon.

Nay, good wife, go up, said her husband. What woman, you must
bear with your guests.

Why husband, qd. she, do you think that any can bear the flirts and frumps which that Northern tike gave me the last time he was in town? Now God forgive me, I had as lief see the devil as to see him. Therefore, good husband, go up yourself, and let me alone, for in faith I shall never abide that Jack while I live.

Upon these words away went her husband, and though he said little, he thought more. Now when he came up, his guests bade him welcome.

I pray you sit down, good mine host, quoth they, where is your wife? what will not she sit with us?

No verily, said he, the foolish woman hath taken such a displeasure against Cutbert that she swears she will never come in his company. 10

Is it so, said the other? then trust me we are well agreed. And I swear by my father's soul, quoth he, that were it not more for good will to you than love to her, I would never come to your house more.

I believe it well, said old Bosom. And so with other communication they drove out the time, till Dinner was ended.

After they were risen, Martin and Hodgekins got them forth about their affairs, but Cut. took his host by the hand, saying, My host, I'll go talk with your wife; for my part I thought we had been friends; but seeing her stomach is so big, and her heart so great, I will see what she will say to me. And with that he stepped into the kitchen, saying, God 20 speed you hostess.

It must be when you away then, said she.

What is your reason, said the other?

Because God never comes where knaves are present.

Gip gooddy draggletail, qd. he, had I such a wife I would present her tallow-face to the devil for a candle.

With that she bent her brows, and like a fury of hell began to fly at him, saying, Why you gag-tooth Jack, you blinking companion, get thee out of my Kitchen quickly, or with my powdered Beef broth I will make your pate as bald as a Friar's. 30

Get me gone, quoth he? thou shalt not bid me twice. Out, you dirty heels, you will make your husband's hair grow through his hood I doubt.

And with that he got him into the Hall, and sat him down on the bench by his host, to whom he said: Tis pity, my Host, that your aged years that loves quietness should be troubled with such a scolding quean.

Aye, God help me, God help me, quoth the old man, and so went towards the Stable; which his wife watching, suddenly stepped out and gave Cutbert a kiss.

Within an hour after, the old man craftily called for his Nag to ride to field; but as soon as he was gone, Cutbert and his Hostess were such 40 good friends that they got into one of the Warehouses, and locked the door to them. But her husband having set a spy for the purpose, suddenly turned back, and called for a capcase which lay in the Warehouse. The servant could not find the key by any means. Whereupon he called to have the lock broke open. Which they within hearing, opened the door of their own accord.

So soon as her husband spied her in that place, with admiration he said: O the passion of my heart, what do you here? what, you two that cannot abide one another? what make you so close together? is your chiding and railing, brabbling and brawling, come to this? O what dissemblers are these!

10 Why, my host, qd. Cutbert, what need you take the matter so hot? I gave a Cheese to my countryman Hodgekins, to lay up, and delivered it to your wife to be kept; and then is it not reason that she should come and seek me my Cheese?

O, qd. the old man, belike the door was locked because the cheese should not run away.

The door, said his wife, unknown to us clapped to itself, and having a spring lock was presently fast.

Well housewife, qd. he; I will give you as much credit as a Crocodile; but as for your companion, I will teach him to come hither to look cheeses.

20 And with that he caused his men to take him presently, and to bind him hand and foot. Which being done, they drew him up in a basket into the smoky louvre of the hall, and there they did let him hang all that night, even till the next day dinner time, when he should have been at the banquet with the princes; for neither Hodgekins nor Martin could entreat their inflamed host to let him down.

And in such a heat was he driven with drawing him up, that he was fain to cast off his gowns, his coats, and two pair of his stockings to cool himself, making a vow he should hang there seven years, except the king's sons came in person to beg his pardon, which most of all grieved

30 Cutbert. When Cole and the rest of the western yeomen heard hereof, they could not choose but laugh to think that he was so taken tardy.

The young princes having given promise to be with the Clothiers, kept their hour, but when all the rest went to give them entertainment, Simon was so busy in supping his pottage that he could not spare so much time. Which when the princes saw, with a smiling countenance they said, Sup Simon, there's good broth,

Or else beshrew our hostess: quoth he, never looking behind him to see who spake, till the Prince clapped him on the shoulder. But good Lord, how blank he was when he spied them, knowing not how to excuse the

40 matter.

Well, the princes having ended their banquet, Jarrat comes and with one of his hands took the table of sixteen foot long quite from the ground over their heads, from before the princes, and set it on the other side of the hall, to the great admiration of all them that beheld it.

The princes being then ready to depart, the Clothiers moved them in pleasant manner to be good to one of their company, that did neither sit, lie, nor stand.

Then he must needs hang, qd. the princes.

And so he doth, most excellent princes, qd. they; and therewithal told them the whole matter.

When they heard the story, down to Bosom's Inn they go, where looking up into the roof, spied poor Cutbert pinned up in a basket, and almost smoked to death; who, although he were greatly ashamed, yet most pitifully desired that they would get him released.

What is his trespass, said the prince?

Nothing, if it shall like your Grace, qd. he, but for looking for a cheese:

But he could not find it without my wife, said the goodman; the villain had lately dined with mutton, and could not digest his meat without cheese; for which cause I have made him to fast these twenty hours, to the end he may have a better stomach to eat his dinner than to use dalliance.

Let me entreat you, quoth the prince, to release him; and if ever hereafter you catch him in the corn, clap him in the pound.

Your Grace shall request or command anything at my hand, said the old man; and so Cutbert was let down unbound; but when he was loose, he vowed never to come within that house more.

And it is said the old man Bosom ordained that in remembrance of this deed, every year once all such as came thither to ask for cheeses should be so served; which thing is to this day kept.

*　　*　　*　　*　　*

CHAPTER 10.

How Duke Robert came a-wooing to Margaret with the white hand, and how he appointed to come and steal her away from her Masters.

The beautiful Margaret, who had now dwelt with her Dame the space of four years, was highly regarded and secretly beloved of many gallant Gentlemen of the country, but of two most especially, Duke Robert, and Sir William Ferris.

It chanced on a time that fair Margaret with many others of her Master's folks, went a hay-making attired in a red stammell petticoat, and a broad straw hat upon her head. She had also a hay fork, and in her lap she did carry her breakfast. As she went along, Duke Robert, with one or two of his keepers, met with her, whose amiable sight did now anew kindle the secret fire of love, which long lay smothering in his heart. Wherefore meeting her so happily, he saluted her thus friendly.

Fair maid, good morrow; are you walking so diligently to your labor? Needs must the weather be fair, where the sun shines so clear, and the hay wholesome that is dried with such splendant rays.

Renowned and most notable Duke (qd. she) poor harvest folks pray
10 for fair weather, and it is the laborers' comfort to see his work prosper; and the more happy may we count the day that is blessed with your princely presence.

But more happy, said the Duke, are they which are conversant in thy company. But let me entreat thee to turn back to thy master's with me, and commit thy fork to some that are fitter for such toil; trust me, methinks thy dame is too much ill advised in setting thee to such homely business. I muse thou canst endure this vile beseeming servitude, whose delicate limbs were never framed to prove such painful experiments.

Albeit, quoth she, it becometh not me to control your judicial thoughts,
20 yet were you not the Duke, I would say your opinion deceived you. Though your fair eyes seem clear, yet I deemed them unperfect, if they cast before your mind any shadow or spark of beauty in me. But I rather think, because it hath been an old saying, that women are proud to hear themselves praised, that you either speak this to drive away the time, or to wring me from my too apparent imperfections. But I humbly entreat pardon; too long have I foreslowed my business, and shewn myself over bold in your presence. And therewith, with a courtly grace, bending her knees to the courteous Duke, she went forward to the field, and the Duke to the town of Gloucester.

30 When he came thither, he made his keepers great cheer, entreating them they would give him respite to be awhile with old Gray; for we twain must have a game or two, quoth he. And for my safe return, I gage to you my princely word, that as I am a true Knight and a Gentleman, I will return safe to your charge again.

The Keepers being content, the Duke departed, and with old Gray goes to the field to peruse the workfolks, where while Gray found himself busy in many matters, he took opportunity to talk with Margaret. She who by his letters before was privy to his purpose, guessed beforehand the cause of his coming; to whom he spake to this effect:

40 Fair Maid, I did long since manifest my love to thee by my letter; tell me therefore, were it not better to be a Duchess than a drudge? a Lady of high reputation than a servant of simple degree? With me thou mightest

live in pleasure, where here thou drawest thy days forth in pain; by my love thou shouldst be made a Lady of great treasures; where now thou art poor and beggarly, all manner of delights should then attend on thee, and whatsoever thy heart desired thou shouldst have. Wherefore, seeing it lies in thy own choice, make thyself happy by consenting to my suit.

Sir (quoth she) I confess your love deserves a Lady's favor, your affection a faithful friend, such a one as could make but one heart and mind of two hearts and bodies; but far unfit it is that the Turtle should match with the Eagle; though her love be never so pure, her wings are unfit to mount so high. While Thales gazed on the stars, he stumbled in a pit. 10 And they that climb unadvisedly, catch a fall suddenly; what availeth high dignity in time of adversity? It neither helpeth the sorrow of the heart, nor removes the body's misery. As for wealth and treasure, what are they but fortune's baits to bring men in danger? good for nothing but to make people forget themselves. And whereas you allege poverty to be a hinderer of the heart's comfort, I find it in myself contrary, knowing more surety to rest under a simple habit than a royal robe. And verily there is none in the world poor, but they that think themselves poor; for such as are indued with content, are rich, having nothing else; but he that is possessed with riches, without content, is most wretched and miser- 20 able. Wherefore most noble Duke, albeit I account my life unworthy of your least favor, yet I would desire you to match your love to your like, and let me rest to my Rake, and use my Fork for my living.

Consider, fair Margaret (quoth he) that it lies not in man's power to place his love where he list, being the work of an high deity. A bird was never seen in Pontus, nor true love in a fleeting mind; never shall I remove the affection of my heart, which in nature resembleth the stone Abiston, whose fire can never be cooled. Wherefore, sweet maiden, give not obstinate denial, where gentle acceptance ought to be received.

Fair sir (quoth she) consider what high displeasure may rise by a rash 30 match, what danger a King's frowns may breed. My worthless matching with your royalty, may perhaps regain your liberty, and hazard my life; then call to mind how little you should enjoy your love, or I my wedded Lord.

The Duke at these words made this reply, that if she consented, she should not dread any danger. The thunder (quoth he) is driven away by ringing of bells, the Lion's wrath qualified by a yielding body; how much more a brother's anger with a brother's entreaty? By me he hath received many favors, and never yet did he requite any one of them; and who is ignorant that the princely crown which adorneth his head is my 40 right? All which I am content he shall still enjoy, so he requite my kindness. But if he should not, then would I be like those men (that eating of the tree Lotus) forget the country where they were born, and never more should this clime cover my head; but with thee would I live in a strange land, being better content with an egg in thy company than with all the delicates in England.

The maiden hearing this, who with many other words was long wooed, at last consented; where yielding to him her heart with her hand, he departed, appointing to certify her from Cardiff Castle what determination he would follow. So taking his leave of Gray, he went to his keepers, and with them posted to Cardiff.

10   Now it is to be remembered that Sir William Ferris within a day or two after came unto Gray's house, as it was his ordinary custom, but not so much I wis for Gray's company, as for the mind he had to Margaret his maid; who, although he were a married man and had a fair Lady to his wife, yet he laid hard siege to the fort of this maiden's chastity, having with many fair words sought to allure her, and by the offer of sundry rich gifts to tempt her. But when she saw that by a hundred denials she could not be rid of him, she now chanced on a sudden to give him such an answer as drove him from deceit into such a conceit as never after that time he troubled her.

20   Sir William Ferris being very importunate to have her grant his desire, and when after sundry assaults she gave him still the repulse, he would needs know the reason why she would not love him. Quoth he, If thou didst consider who he is that seeketh thy favor, what pleasure he may do thee by his purse, and what credit by his countenance, thou wouldst never stand on such nice points. If I be thy friend, who dareth be thy foe? and what is he that will once call thy name in question for any thing? Therefore, sweet girl, be better advised, and refuse not my offer, being so large.

Truly, Sir William (quoth she) though there be many reasons to make me deny your suit, yet is there one above the rest that causes me I 30 cannot love you.

Now I pray thee, my wench, let me know that, quoth he, and I will amend it whatsoever it be.

Pardon me, sir, said Margaret, if I should speak my mind, it would possibly offend you and do me no pleasure, because it is a defect in nature which no physic can cure.

Sir William hearing on her so, being abashed at her speech, said, Fair Margaret, let me (if I may obtain no more at thy hands) yet entreat thee to know what this defect should be, I am not wry-necked, crook-legged, stub-footed, lame-handed, nor bleary-eyed: what can make this 40 mislike? I never knew anybody that took exceptions at my person before.

And the more sorry am I, quoth she, that I was so malapert to speak it, but pardon my presumption, good Sir William, I would I had been like the stork, tongueless; then should I never have caused your disquiet.

Nay sweet Margaret, quoth he, tell me dear love. I commend thy singleness of heart; good Margaret, speak.

Good Sir William, let it rest, quoth she. I know you will not believe it when I have revealed it, neither is it a thing that you can help; and yet such is my foolishness, had it not been for that, I think verily I had granted your suit ere now. But seeing you urge me so much to know what it is, I will tell you. It is sir, your ill-favored great nose, that hangs sagging so loathsomely to your lips that I cannot find in my heart so much as to kiss you.

What, my nose, quoth he? Is my nose so great and I never knew it? Certainly I thought my nose to be as comely as any man's; but this it is, we are all apt to think well of ourselves, and a great deal better than we ought. But let me see? My nose! By the mass, 'tis true; I do now feel it myself. Good Lord, how was I blinded before!

Hereupon it is certain that the Knight was driven into such a conceit, as none could persuade him but his nose was so great indeed; his Lady, or any other that spake to the contrary, he would say they were flatterers, and that they lied; insomuch that he would be ready to strike some of them that commended and spake well of his nose. If they were men of worship, or any other that contraried him in his opinion, he would swear they flouted him, and be ready to challenge them the field. He became so ashamed of himself that after that day he would never go abroad; whereby Margaret was well rid of his company.

On a time, a wise and grave gentleman, seeing him grounded in his conceit so strongly, gave his Lady counsel not to contrary him therein, but rather say that she would seek out some cunning Physician to cure him; for, said he, as Sir William hath taken this conceit of himself, so is he like never to bear other opinion till his own conceit doth remove it, the which must be wisely wrought to bring it to pass.

Whereupon, the Lady having conferred with a Physician that bear a great name in the country, he undertook to remove this fond conceit by his skill. The day being appointed when the Physician should come, and the knight being told thereof, for very joy he would go forth to meet him, when a woman of the Town saw the Knight, having heard what rumor went because of his nose, she looked very steadfastly upon him. The knight casting his eye upon her, seeing her to gaze so wistly in his face, with an angry countenance said thus to her, Why, how now, good housewife, can you not get you about your business?

The woman being a shrewish quean, answered him cuttedly, No, Marry, can I not, qd. she.

No, you drab! What is the cause, said the knight?

Because, quoth she, your nose stands in my way. Wherewith the knight being very angry, and abashed, went back again to his house.

The Physician being come, he had filled a certain bladder with sheep's blood, and conveyed it into his sleeve, where at the issue of the bladder he had put in a piece of swan's quill, through the which the blood should run out of the bladder so close by his hand that he, holding the knight by the nose, it might not be perceived but that it issued thence. All things being prepared, he told the knight that by a foul corrupt blood wherewith the veins of his nose were overcharged his impediment did grow; there-
10 fore, qd. he, to have redress for this disease, you must have a vein opened in your nose, whence this foul corruption must be taken; whereupon it will follow that your nose will fall again to his natural proportion, and never shall you be troubled with this grief any more; and thereupon will I gage my life.

I pray you master doctor, said the Knight, is my nose so big as you make it?

With reverence I may speak it, said the physician, to tell the truth, and avoid flattery, I never saw a more misshapen nose so foul to sight.

Lo you now, Madam, quoth the knight, this is you that said my nose
20 was as well, as handsome, and as comely a nose as any man's.

Alas sir, quoth she, I spake it (God wot) because you should not grieve at it, nor take my words in ill part; neither did it indeed become me to mislike of your nose.

All this we will quickly remedy, said the physician, have no doubt. And with that, he very orderly pricked him in the nose, but not in any vein whereby he might bleed; and presently having a trick finely to unstop the quill, the blood ran into a basin in great abundance. And when the blad-der was empty, and the basin almost full, the Physician seemed to close the vein, and asked him how he felt his nose, shewing the great quantity
30 of filthy blood which from thence he had taken.

The knight beholding it with great wonder, said he thought that no man in the world had been troubled with such abundance of corrupt blood in his whole body, as lay in his misshapen nose; and therewithal he began to touch and handle his nose, saying that he felt it mightily assuaged. Im-mediately a glass was brought wherein he might behold himself.

Yea marry, qd. he, now I praise God, I see my nose is come into some reasonable proportion, and I feel myself very well eased of the burden thereof; but if it continue thus, that's all.

I will warrant your worship, said the physician, for ever being troubled
40 with the like again.

Whereupon the Knight received great joy, and the Doctor a high reward.

CHAPTER II.

*How Thomas of Reading was murdered at his host's house of Cole-
brook, who also had murdered many before him, [and] how their
wickedness was at length revealed.*

Thomas of Reading having many occasions to come to London, as
well about his own affairs as also the king's business, being in a great
office under his Majesty, it chanced on a time that his host and hostess of
Colebrook, who through covetousness had murdered many of his guests, 10
and having every time he came thither great store of his money to lay
up, appointed him to be the next fat pig that should be killed. For it is to
be understood, that when they plotted the murder of any man, this was
always their term, the man to his wife, and the woman to her husband:
Wife, there is now a fat pig to be had, if you want one.

Whereupon she would answer thus, I pray you put him in the hogsty
till tomorrow.

This was, when any man came thither alone without others in his
company, and they saw he had great store of money.

This man should be then laid in the chamber right over the kitchen, 20
which was a fair chamber, and better set out than any other in the house;
the best bedstead therein, though it were little and low, yet was it most
cunningly carved, and fair to the eye; the feet whereof were fast nailed
to the chamber floor, in such sort that it could not in any wise fall; the
bed that lay therein was fast sewed to the sides of the bedstead. Moreover,
that part of the chamber whereupon this bed and bedstead stood was made
in such sort that by the pulling out of two iron pins below in the kitchen,
it was to be let down and taken up by a drawbridge, or in manner of
a trapdoor. Moreover, in the kitchen, directly under the place where this
should fall, was a mighty great caldron, wherein they used to seethe their 30
liquor when they went to brewing. Now, the men appointed for the
slaughter were laid into this bed, and in the dead time of the night, when
they were sound asleep, by plucking out the foresaid iron pins, down would
the man fall out of his bed into the boiling caldron, and all the clothes
that were upon him; where being suddenly scalded and drowned, he was
never able to cry or speak one word.

Then had they a little ladder ever standing ready in the kitchen, by
the which they presently mounted into the said chamber, and there closely
take away the man's apparel, as also his money, in his male or capcase;
and then lifting up the said falling floor which hung by hinges, they made 40
it fast as before.

The dead body would they take presently out of the Caldron and throw it down the river, which ran near unto their house, whereby they escaped all danger.

Now if in the morning any of the rest of the guests that had talked with the murdered man over eve, chanced to ask for him as having occasion to ride the same way that he should have done, the goodman would answer, that he took horse a good while before day, and that he himself did set him forward. The horse the goodman would also take out of the stable, and convey him by a haybarn of his that stood from his house a mile or two; whereof himself did always keep the keys full charily, and when 10 any hay was to be brought from thence, with his own hands he would deliver it. Then, before the horse should go from thence, he would dismark him; as, if he wore a long tail, he would make him curtal; or else crop his ears, or cut his mane, or put out one of his eyes; and by this means he kept himself unknown.

Now Thomas of Reading, as I said before, being marked, and kept for a fat pig, he was laid in the same chamber of death; but by reason Gray of Gloucester chanced also to come that night, he escaped scalding.

The next time, he came, he was laid there again, but before he fell asleep, or was warm in his bed, one came riding through the town and 20 cried piteously that London was all on a fire, and that it had burned down Thomas Becket's house in Westcheape, and a great number more in the same street, and yet (quoth he) the fire is not quenched.

Which tidings when Thomas of Reading heard, he was very sorrowful, for of the same Becket that day he had received a great piece of money, and had left in his house many of his writings, and some that appertained to the king also. Therefore there was no nay but he would ride back again to London presently, to see how the matter stood; thereupon making himself ready, departed. This cross fortune caused his host to frown; nevertheless the next time (quoth he) will pay for all.

30 Notwithstanding God so wrought, that they were prevented then likewise, by reason of a great fray that happened in the house betwixt a couple that fell out at Dice, insomuch as the murderers themselves were enforced to call him up, being a man in great authority, that he might set the house in quietness; out of the which by means of this quarrel, they doubted to lose many things.

Another time when he should have been laid in the same place, he fell so sick that he requested to have somebody to watch with him, whereby also they could not bring their vile purpose to pass. But hard it is to escape the ill fortunes whereunto a man is allotted. For albeit that the next time 40 that he came to London, his horse stumbled and broke one of his legs as he should ride homeward, yet hired he another to hasten his own death; for there is no remedy but he should go to Colebrook that night. But by the way he was heavy asleep, that he could scant keep himself in the saddle; and when he came near unto the Town, his nose burst out suddenly ableeding.

Well, to his Inn he came, and so heavy was his heart that he could eat no meat. His host and hostess hearing he was so Melancholy, came up to cheer him, saying, Jesus, Master Cole, what ails you tonight? Never did we see you thus sad before; will it please you to have a quart of burned sack?

With a good will (quoth he) and would to God Thomas Dove were here; he would surely make me merry, and we should lack no music. But I am sorry for the man with all my heart, that he is come so far behind hand; but alas, so much can every man say, but what good doth it him? No no, it is not words can help a man in this case; the man had need of other relief than so. Let me see; I have but one child in the world and that is my daughter, and half that I have is hers, the other half my wife's. What then? Shall I be good to nobody but them? In conscience, my wealth is too much for a couple to possess, and what is our Religion without charity? And to whom is charity more to be shown than to decayed householders?

Good my host, lend me a pen and ink, and some paper, for I will write a letter unto the poor man straight; and something I will give him. That alms which a man bestows with his own hands, he shall be sure to have delivered, and God knows how long I shall live.

With that, his hostess dissemblingly answered, saying: Doubt not, Master Cole, you are like enough by the course of nature to live many years.

God knows (quoth he) I never found my heart so heavy before.

By this time pen, ink, and paper was brought, setting himself in writing as followeth.

In the name of God, Amen. I bequeath my soul to God, and my body to the ground, my goods equally between my wife Elenor, and Isabel, my daughter. Item I give to Thomas Dove of Exeter one hundred pounds, nay that is too little, I give to Thomas Dove two hundred pounds in money, to be paid unto him presently upon his demand thereof by my said wife and daughter.

Ha, how say you host (qd. he) is not this well? I pray you read it.

His host looking thereon, said, why Master Cole, what have you written here? You said you would write a letter, but methinks you have made a will; what need have you to do thus? Thanks be to God, you may live many fair years.

Tis true (quoth Cole) if it please God, and I trust this writing cannot shorten my days; but let me see, have I made a will? Now, I promise you, I did verily purpose to write a letter; notwithstanding I have written that that God put into my mind. But look once again my host, is it not written there, that Dove shall have two hundred pounds, to be paid when he comes to demand it?

Yes indeed, said his host.

Well then, all is well, said Cole, and it shall go as it is for me. I will not bestow the new writing thereof any more.

10 Then folding it up, he sealed it, desiring that his host would send it to Exeter. He promised that he would; notwithstanding Cole was not satisfied, but after some pause, he would needs hire one to carry it. And so sitting down sadly in his chair again, upon a sudden he burst forth aweeping; they demanding the cause thereof, he spake as followeth:

No cause of these tears I know: but it comes now into my mind (said Cole) when I set toward this my last journey to London, how my daughter took on, what a coil she kept to have me stay; and I could not be rid of the little baggage a long time, she did so hang about me. When her mother by violence took her away, she cried out most mainly, O my 20 father, my father, I shall never see him again.

Alas, pretty soul, said his hostess, this was but mere kindness in the girl, and it seemeth she is very fond of you. But alas, why should you grieve at this? You must consider that it was but childishness.

Aye, it is indeed, said Cole, and with that he began to nod.

Then they asked him if he would go to bed.

No, said he, although I am heavy, I have no mind to go to bed at all.

With that certain musicians of the town came to the chamber, and knowing Master Cole was there, drew out their instruments and very 30 solemnly began to play.

This music comes very well (said Cole) and when he had listened a while thereunto, he said, Methinks these instruments sound like the ring of St. Mary Overie's bells, but the base drowns all the rest; and in my ear it goes like a bell that rings a forenoon's knell. For God's sake let them leave off, and bear them this simple reward.

The musicians being gone, his host asked if now it would please him to go to bed; for (quoth he) it is well near eleven of the clock.

With that, Cole beholding his host and hostess earnestly, began to start back, saying, what ail you to look so like pale death? Good Lord, what have you done, that your hands are thus bloody?

40 What, my hands, said his host? Why, you may see they are neither bloody nor foul; either your eyes do greatly dazzle, or else fancies of a troubled mind do delude you.

Alas, my host, you may see, said he, how weak my wits are; I never had my head so idle before. Come, let me drink once more, and then I will to bed, and trouble you no longer.

With that he made himself unready, and his hostess was very diligent to warm a kerchief, and put it about his head.

Good Lord, said he, I am not sick, I praise God, but such an alteration I find in myself as I never did before.

With that the screech owl cried piteously, and anon after the night raven sat croaking hard by his window.

Jesu have mercy upon me, quoth he, what an ill-favored cry do yon- 10 der carrion birds make! And therewithal he laid him down in his bed, from whence he never rose again.

His host and hostess, that all this while noted his troubled mind, began to commune betwixt themselves thereof. And the man said he knew not what were best to be done. By my consent (quoth he) the matter should pass, for I think it is not best to meddle on him.

What man (quoth she) faint you now? Have you done so many, and do you shrink at this? Then showing him a great deal of gold which Cole had left with her, she said, Would it not grieve a body's heart to lose this? Hang the old churl, what should he do living any longer? He hath too 20 much, and we have too little. Tut, husband, let the thing be done, and then this is our own.

Her wicked counsel was followed, and when they had listened at his chamber door, they heard the man sound asleep. All is safe, quoth they, and down into the kitchen they go, their servants being all in bed, and pulling out the iron pins, down fell the bed, and the man dropped out into the boiling caldron. He being dead, they betwixt them cast his body into the river, his clothes they hid away, and made all things as it should be. But when he came to the stable to convey thence Cole's horse, the stable door being open, the horse had got loose, and, with a part of the 30 halter about his neck and straw trussed under his belly, as the ostlers had dressed him ore eve, he was gone out at the back side, which led into a great field adjoining to the house; and so leaping divers hedges, being a lusty stout horse, had got into a ground where a mare was grazing, with whom he kept such a coil that they got into the highway, where one of the town meeting them, knew the mare, and brought her and the horse to the man that owned her.

In the mean space, the Musicians had been at the Inn, and in requital of their evening's gift, they intended to give Cole some music in the morning. The goodman told them he took horse before day. Likewise 40 there was a guest in the house that would have bore him company to Reading; unto whom the host also answered, that he himself set him upon horseback, and that he went long ago. Anon came the man that owned the mare, inquiring up and down to know and if none of them missed a horse; who said no. At the last he came to the sign of the Crane where Cole lay; and calling the ostlers he demanded of them if they lacked none. They said no.

Why then, said the man, I perceive my mare is good for something; for if I send her to field single, she will come home double. Thus it passed on all that day and the night following.

But the next day after, Cole's wife musing that her husband came not
10 home, sent one of her men on horseback to see if he could meet him; and if (quoth she) you meet him not betwixt this and Colebrook, ask for him at the Crane; but if you find him not there, then ride to London; for I doubt he is either sick, or else some mischance hath fallen unto him.

The fellow did so; and asking for him at Colebrook, they answered, he went homeward from thence such a day. The servant musing what should be become of his Master, and making much inquiry in the town for him, at length one told him of a horse that was found on the highway, and no man knew whence he came. He going to see the horse, knew him presently, and to the Crane he goes with him. The host of the house per-
20 ceiving this, was blank; and that night fled secretly away. The fellow going unto the Justice, desired his help; presently after word was brought that Jarman of the Crane was gone, then all the men said he had sure made Cole away. And the musicians told what Jarman said to them, when they would have given Cole music. Then the woman being apprehended and examined, confessed the truth. Jarman soon after was taken in Windsor Forest. He and his wife were both hanged, after they had laid open all these things before expressed. Also he confessed that he, being a carpenter, made that false falling floor, and how his wife devised it. And how they had murdered by that means sixty persons. And yet notwith-
30 standing all the money which they had gotten thereby, they prospered not, but at their death were found very far in debt.

When the king heard of this murder, he was for the space of seven days so sorrowful and heavy as he would not hear any suit, giving also commandment that the house should quite be consumed with fire wherein Cole was murdered, and that no man should even build upon that cursed ground.

Cole's substance at his death was exceeding great; he had daily in his house an hundred menservants and forty maids; he maintained beside above two or three hundred people, spinners and carders, and a great
40 many other householders. His wife after never married; and at her death she bestowed a mighty sum of money toward the maintaining of the new-builded monastery. Her daughter was most richly married to a gentleman

of great worship, by whom she had many children. And some say that the river whereinto Cole was cast did ever since carry the name of Cole, being called The river of Cole, and the Town of Colebrook.

* * * * *

CHAPTER 13.

How Duke Robert deceived his keepers, and got from them; how he met fair Margaret, and in carrying her away was taken, for the which he had his eyes put out.

Duke Robert, having, as you heard, obtained the love of fair Margaret, did now cast in his mind how he might delude his keepers, and carry her away. In the end, he being absolutely resolved what to do, sent his letter unto her, wherein he requested that she would be ready to meet him in the forest, betwixt Cardiff and Gloucester.

The young Lady having secretly received his message, unknown to her master or dame, in a morning betime made her ready and got forth, walking to the appointed place where her love should meet her.

During her abode there, and thinking long ere her love came, she entered into divers passions, which indeed presaged some disaster fortune to follow.

O my dear Love, said she, how slack art thou in performing thy promise! Why do not thy deeds agree with thy inditing? See these are thy words, Come, my dear Margaret, and with Cupid's swift wings fly to thy friend; be now as nimble in thy footing as the Camels of Bactria, that run an hundred miles a day; I will wait and stay for thee, so I stay not too long. There is no country like Austria for ambling horses, and to carry thee I have got one.

O my Love (quoth she) here am I, but where art thou? O why dost thou play the truant with Time, who like the wind slides away unseen? An ambling jennet of Spain is too slow to serve our turns. A flying horse, for flying Lovers were most meet. And thus casting many looks through the Silvan shades up and down to espy him, she thought every minute an hour till she might see him; sometimes she would wish herself a bird, that she might fly through the air to meet him, or a pretty squirrel to climb the highest tree to descry his coming; but finding her wishes vain, she began thus to excuse him and persuaded herself, saying.

How much to blame am I, to find fault with my friend? Alas, men that lack their liberty must come when they can, not when they would; poor prisoners cannot do what they desire, and then why should I be so hasty? Therefore if safely I may lay me down I will beguile unquiet thoughts with quiet sleep; it is said that Galino breeds no Serpents, nor

doth England's forests nourish Bears or Lions; therefore without hurt I
hope I may rest awhile. Thus leaving fair Margaret in a sweet slumber,
we will return to Duke Robert, who had thus plotted his escape from his
keepers.

Having liberty of the King to hawk and hunt, he determined on a day,
as he should follow the chase, to leave the hounds to the Hart, and the
hunters to their horns, and being busy in their sport, himself would fly;
which he performed at that time when he appointed Margaret to meet
him. And so coming to the place, his horse all on a water, and himself in
a sweat, finding his love asleep, he awakened her with a kiss, saying, Arise,
fair Margaret, now comes the time wherein thou shalt be made a Queen.
And presently setting her on horseback, he posted away.

Now when the keepers saw they had lost his company, and that at the
killing of the game he was not present, they were among themselves in
such a mutiny that they were ready one to stab another.

It was thy fault, said one, that he thus escaped from us, that hadst more
mind of thy pleasure than of thy prisoner, and by this means we are all
undone.

The other said as much to him, that he had thought he had followed
him in the chase. But leaving at last this contention, the one posted up to
the King, while the others coasted up and down the country to search
for the Duke, who having killed his horse in travelling, was most unhappily
met on foot with fair Margaret ere he could come to any Town where
he might for money have another. But when he spied his Keepers come
to take him, he desired Margaret to make shift for herself, and to seek to
escape them. But she being of a contrary mind, said she would live and
die with him.

The Duke seeing himself ready to be surprised, drew out his sword, and
said he would buy his liberty with his life before he would yield to be any
more a prisoner; and thereupon began a great fight betwixt them, insomuch that the Duke had killed two of them; but himself being sore
wounded, and faint with overmuch bleeding, at length fell down, being
not able any longer to stand. And by this means the good Duke was
taken with his fair love, and both of them committed to prison.

But in the mean space, when Gray's wife had missed her maid, and
saw she was quite gone, she made great lamentation for her among her
neighbors; for she loved her as dearly as any child that ever she bore of
her own body. O Margaret (quoth she) what cause hadst thou thus to
leave me? If thou didst mislike of anything, why didst thou not tell me?
If thy wages were too little, I would have mended it; if thy apparel had
been too simple, thou shouldst have had better; if thy work had been too
great, I would have had help for thee.

Farewell my sweet Meg, the best servant that ever came in any man's house; many may I have of thy name, but never any of thy nature; thy diligence is much; in thy hands I laid the whole government of my house, and thereby eased myself of that care which now will cumber me.

Here she hath left me my keys unto my chests, but my comfort is gone with her presence; every gentle word that she was wont to speak comes now into my mind; her courteous behavior shall I never forget. With how sweet and modest a countenance would she qualify my over-hasty nature? It repents my heart that ever I spoke foul word unto her. O Meg, wert thou here again, I would never chide thee more. But I was an unworthy 10 dame for such a servant. What will become of me now, if I should chance to be sick, seeing she is gone, that was wont to be both my Apothecary and Physician?

Well, quoth her neighbors, there is no remedy now but to rest content; you shall one day hear of her, doubt you not; and think this, that she was not so good but you may get another as good, and therefore do not take it so heavily.

O neighbor, blame me not to grieve, seeing I have lost so great a jewel; and sure I am persuaded that scant in a body's lifetime they shall meet with the like. I protest, I would circuit England round about on my bare 20 feet to meet with her again. O, my Meg was surely stole away from me, else would she not have gone in such sort.

Her husband, on the other side, grieved as much, and rested not night nor day riding up and down to seek her; but she, poor soul, is fast locked in prison, and therefore cannot be met withal.

But when the King understood of his brother's escape, he was marvelous wroth, giving great charge and commandment when he was taken, that both his eyes should be put out and he kept in prison till his dying day; appointing also that the maid should lose her life for presumption of loving him. 30

This matter being rumored over all England, it came to the ears of Gray and his wife, who hearing that Margaret also was there in prison appointed to die, the good aged woman never rested till she came to the court, where kneeling before the King, with many tears she besought his Majesty to spare the maiden's life, saying, Most royal king, consider, I humbly beseech you, that the duke your brother was able to entice any woman to his love: much more a silly maiden, especially promising her marriage, to make her a Lady, a Duchess, or a Queen. Who would refuse such an offer, when at the instant they might get both a princely husband and a high dignity? If death be a Lover's guerdon, then what is due 40 to hatred? I am in my heart persuaded that had my poor Margaret thought it would have bred your highness' displeasure, she would never have bought his love so dear. Had your Grace made it known to your commons, that it was unlawful for any to marry the duke your brother, who would have attempted such an action? If she had wilfully disobeyed your Grace's commandment, she might have been thought worthy of death; but seeing ignorantly she offended, I beseech your Grace to recall the sentence, and let me still enjoy my servant, for never will I rise till your Majesty have granted my petition.

His Highness, who was of nature merciful, beholding the woman's abundant tears, took pity on her, and granted her suit; which being ob-
10 tained, she went home in all haste possible. And from thence, she with her husband taking their journey to Cardiff castle, they came at that very instant when the maiden was led toward her death; who went in most joyful sort to the same, saying that they were not worthy to be accounted true Lovers, that were not willing to die for love. And so with a smiling countenance she passed on, as if she had eaten *Apium Risus,* which causeth a man to die laughing. But her dame Gray seeing her, fell about her neck, and with many kisses embraced her, saying, Thou shalt not die, my wench, but go home with me; and for thy delivery, behold here the King's letters; and with that she delivered them up to the governor of the
20 Castle; who reading them, found these words written: We pardon the maid's life, and grant her liberty, but let her not pass till she see her lover's eyes put out, which we will have you do in such sort that not only the sight may perish, but the eye continue fair; for which cause I have sent down Doctor Piero, that he may execute the same.

The governor of the Castle having read the King's letter, said thus to the maiden: The King's Majesty hath pardoned thy life, and allowed thy liberty; but you must not pass before you see your lover's eyes put out.

O sir, said the maiden, mistake not yourself; they are my eyes that must be put out, and not the Duke's. As his offence grew by my means,
30 so I being guilty, ought to receive the punishment.

The king's commandment must be fulfilled, said the governor.

And therewithal D[uke] Robert was brought forth, who hearing that he must lose his eyes, said thus: The noble mind is never conquered by grief, nor overcome by mischance; but as the Hart reneweth his age by eating the serpent, so doth a man lengthen his life with devouring sorrow. My eyes have offended the King, and they must be punished; my heart is in as great fault, why is not that killed?

The King's Majesty, said the governor, spares your life of mere love, and only is content to satisfy the Law with the loss of your eyes; where-
40 fore take in good part this punishment, and think you have deserved greater than is granted.

With this Margaret cried out, saying, O my dear love, most gentle

Prince, well may you wish that I had never been born, who by seeing of me must lose your sight; but happy should I count myself, if it so please the King, that I might redeem thy eyes with my life: or else, that being an equal offender, I might receive equal punishment. Hadst thou sustained this smart for some Queen or Princess of high blood, it might with the more ease be borne, but to endure it for such a one as I, it must needs cause a treble grief to be increased.

Content thee, fair Margaret, said the duke, for honor ought to be given to virtue and not riches; for glory, honor, nobility, and riches without virtue are but cloaks of maliciousness. And now let me take my leave of 10 thy beauty, for never must I behold thy face. Notwithstanding, I account my eyes well lost, in that I do forego them for so peerless a paragon. Now fair heavens, farewell; the Sun, Moon, and Stars shall I in this world never behold again; and farewell also the fruitful earth; well may I feel thee, but those poor windows of my body are now denied to view thee any more. And though the world hath ever been my foe, yet will I bid it farewell too; and farewell all my friends; while I live here in this world, I must suppose to sleep, and wake when I come in heaven, where I hope to see you all again. Yet had it pleased the King, I had rather have lost my life than my eyes. Life, why, what is it but a flower, a bubble in the 20 water, a span long, and full of misery? Of such small account is life, that every soldier will sell it for six pence. And trust me, I do now detest life worse than a goat doth hate basil.

With that the Doctor prepared his instrument, and being ready to set to the Duke's eyes, he said, O stay, master doctor, till I have conveyed my love's countenance down into my heart. Come hither my sweet, and let me give thee my last kiss, while mine eyes may direct me to thy cherry lips. Then embracing her in his arms, he said, O that I might give thee a kiss of twenty years long, and to satisfy my greedy eyes with thy fair sight; yet it doth somewhat content me, because thou art present at my punishment, 30 that I may hold thee by the hand, to comfort my heart at the sudden prick of my eye.

This being said, the Doctor performed his duty, and so put out the crystal sight; at what time D[uke] Robert started up, and with a most manly courage said, I must thank his Majesty, that though he depriveth me of my sight, yet he leaveth me eyes to weep for my sins.

But so soon as Margaret beheld the deed, she fell down in a swoon, and much ado her dame had to recover her life; which when the duke understood, he was wondrous woe, groping for her with his bleeding eyes, saying, O where is my love? For God's sake have regard to her. And I pray 40 you most heartily, good goodwife Gray, let her have this favor for my sake, that she may be used kindly. And with that the Keepers led him into

the castle, and Margaret was carried away wondrous sick and ill. But her
dame was most tender over her, and would suffer her to lack nothing.
When she was somewhat well recovered, her dame Gray set her on horseback; and at her coming to Gloucester, there was no small joy.

CHAPTER 14.

How Thomas Dove being fallen to decay, was forsaken of his friends,
and despised of his servants: and how in the end he was raised again
through the liberality of the Clothiers.

10   Such as seek the pleasure of the world, follow a shadow wherein is no
substance; and as the adder Aspis tickleth a man to death, so doth vain
pleasure flatter us, till it makes us forget God and consume our substance,
as by Tom Dove it is apparent, who had through a free heart and a liberal
mind wasted his wealth; and look how his goods consumed, so his friends
fled from him. And albeit he had been of great ability, and thereby done
good unto many, yet no man regarded him in his poverty, but casting a
scornful countenance upon him, they passed by him with slender salutation; neither would any of his former acquaintance do him good, or
20 pleasure him the value of a farthing; his former friendship done to them
was quite forgot, and he made of as much account as Job when he sat on
the dunghill.

    Now, when his wicked servants saw him in this disgrace with the world,
they on the other side began to disdain him. Notwithstanding that he (to
his great cost) had long time brought them up, yet did they nothing regard it, but behind his back in most scornful sort derided him, and both
in their words and actions greatly abuse him; reverence they would do
none unto him, but when they spake, it was in such malapert sort as would
grieve an honest mind to hear it.

30   At last it came to pass, that breaking out into mere contempt, they said
they would stay no longer with him, and that it was a great discredit for
them to serve a person so beggarly; whereupon they thought it convenient to seek for their benefits elsewhere. When the distressed man
found the matter so plain, being in great grief, he spake thus unto them:

    Now do I find, to my sorrow, the small trust that is in this false world.
Why, my Masters (quoth he) have you so much forgotten my former
prosperity that you nothing regard my present necessity? In your wants
I forsook you not, in your sickness I left you not, nor despised you in your
great poverty. It is not unknown, though you do not consider it, that I
40 took some of you up in the highway, other some from your needy parents,
and brought the rest from mere beggary to a house of bounty; where from
paltry boys, I brought you up to man's state, and have, to my great cost,

taught you a trade whereby you may live like men. And in requital of all my courtesy, cost, and good will, will you now on a sudden forsake me? Is this the best recompence that you can find your hearts to yield me?

This is far from the minds of honest servants. The fierce Lion is kind to those that do him good; pluck but one thorn out of his foot, and for the same he will show manifold favors. The wild Bull will not overthrow his Dam; and the very Dragons are dutiful to their nourishers. Be better advised, and call to mind, I beseech you, that I have not plucked a thorn out of your feet, but drawn your whole bodies out of perils; and when you had no means to help yourselves, I only was your support, and he, that when all other forsook you, did comfort you in all your extremities.

And what of all this, quoth one of them? Because you took us up poor, doth it therefore follow that we must be your slaves? We are young men, and for our parts, we are no further to regard your profit than it may stand with our preferment. Why should we lose our benefit to pleasure you? If you taught us our trade, and brought us up from boys to men, you had our service for it, whereby you made no small benefit, if you had as well used it as we got it. But if you be poor, you may thank yourself, being a just scourge for your prodigality; and it is my opinion plain, that to stay with you is the next way to make us like you, neither able to help ourselves, nor our friends. Therefore, in brief, come pay me my wages, for I will not stay; let the rest do as they will, for I am resolved.

Well, said his Master, if needs thou wilt be gone, here is part of thy wages in hand, and the rest, so soon as God sends it thou shalt have it. And with that, turning to the rest, he said, Let me yet entreat you to stay, and leave me not altogether destitute of help; by your labors must I live, and without you I know not what to do. Consider therefore my need, and regard my great charge. And if for my sake you will do nothing, take compassion on my poor children; stay my sliding foot, and let me not utterly fall through your flying from me.

Tush (quoth they) what do you talk to us? We can have better wages, and serve a man of credit, where our fare shall be far better, and our gains greater; therefore the world might count us right coxcombs if we should forsake our profit to pleasure you. Therefore, adieu. God send you more money, for you are like to have no more men. And thus they departed.

When they were gone, within a while after they met one with another, saying, What cheer? Are you all come away?

In faith, aye; what should we do else (quoth they). But hear'st thou sirra, hast thou got thy wages?

Not yet, saith the other, but I shall have it; and that is as good; 'tis but ten shillings.

Sayest thou so (quoth he) now I see thou are one of God Almighty's idiots.

Why so, said the other?

Because (quoth he) thou wilt be fed with shales; but I'll tell thee one thing, 'twere better for thee quickly to arrest him, lest some other doing it before, there be nothing left to pay thy debt. Hold thy peace, fair words make fools fain, and it is an old saying, One bird in hand is worth two in bush; if thou dost not arrest him presently, I will not give thee two pence for thy ten shillings.

10 How shall I come by him (quoth the other)?

Give me but two pots of ale, and I'll betray him, saith he.

So they being agreed, this smooth-faced Judas comes to his late Master, and told him that a friend of his at the door would speak with him. The unmistrusting man, thinking no evil, went to the door where presently an Officer arrested him at his man's suit.

The poor man seeing this, being strucken into a sudden sorrow, in the grief of his heart spake to this effect: Ah, thou lewd fellow, are thou the first man that seeks to augment my misery? Have I thus long given thee bread, to breed my overthrow? and nourished thee in thy need, to work my

20 destruction? Full little did I think, when thou so often didest dip thy false fingers in my dish, that I gave food to my chiefest foe. But what booteth complaints in these extremes? Go, wife, quoth he, unto my neighbors, and see if thou canst get any of them to be my bail.

But in vain was her pains spent. Then he sent to his kinsfolks, and they denied him; to his brother, and he would not come at him; so that there was no shift, but to prison he must. But as he was going, a messenger met him with a letter from Master Cole, wherein as you heard, he had promised him two hundred pounds; which when the poor man read, he greatly rejoiced, and shewing the same to the officer, he was content to take his

30 own word. Whereupon Tom Dove went presently to Reading, where, at his coming, he found all the rest of the Clothiers, lamenting Cole's untimely death; where the woeful widow paid him the money, by which deed all the rest of the Clothiers were induced to do something for Dove. And thereupon one gave him ten pounds, another twenty, another thirty pounds, to begin the world anew. And by this means (together with the blessing of God) he grew into greater credit than ever he was before. And riches being thus come upon him, his former friends came fawning unto him; and when he had no need of them, then every one was ready to proffer him kindness. His wicked servants also, that disdained him in his

40 distress, were after glad to come creeping unto him, entreating with cap and knee for his favor and friendship. And albeit he seemed to forgive

their trespasses done against him, yet he would often say, he would never trust them for a straw.

And thus he ever after lived in great wealth and prosperity, doing much good to the poor, and at his death left to his children great lands.

*   *   *   *   *

ROBERT ASHLEY

The Introduction and Notes are at page 1335

FROM ASHLEY's translation of LOUIS LEROY, *Of The Interchangeable Course, or Variety of Things in the Whole World,* 1594

*   *   *   *   *

Whether it be true, or no, that there can be nothing said which hath not been said before; and that we must by our own inventions augment the doctrine of the ancients, not contenting ourselves only with translations, expositions, corrections, and abridgements of their writings.

The Twelfth and Last Book.

The beginnings of the arts have been small, and the greatest difficulty was in the first inventing of them; then by the industry of the learned, they were by little and little augmented, correcting such things as were evil observed, and supplying such as were omitted, but yet without making anything entirely absolute, whereunto there might nothing be added. Nothing is begun and ended at one time; but by succession of time things are increased, amended, and become better polished. Almost all the arts have been invented by use and experience; and afterwards gathered and made by observation and reason: and then consequently reduced into better form, and more certain, by divisions, definitions, argumentations, and demonstrations; by general precepts and rules drawn from nature, not from opinion and tending to the same end; not by staying and resting on that which men had formerly done, said, or written; nor by only imitating of them, after the manner of slothful and cowardly persons: but by the adding of somewhat of their own, by some that came after, according as the matters from time to time discovered and cleared themselves; the honor commonly remaining to the last comers, as the most exquisite and accomplished. By whose example we ought to travail courageously, with

hope to make ourselves better than them; aspiring continually to perfection, which as yet is not seen anywhere, considering that there remain
more things to be sought out than are already invented and found.

And let us not be so simple as to attribute so much unto the ancients
that we believe that they have known all and said all, without leaving anything to be said by those that should come after them. They have not been
so arrogant as to look that none should meddle or deal with those matters
which they had handled; but on the contrary, considering the difficulty of
knowledge, and the weakness of man's understanding, they have exhorted
10 others to travail therein; speaking rather to stir them up and provoke them
thereunto than to keep them back or stay them from writing. Let us
not think that nature hath given them all her good gifts that she might
be barren in time to come; but that as she hath in times past brought forth
certain notable personages who have manifested many of her secrets, so
she can again bring forth such as by the influence of heaven, and a singular inclination, by liveliness of understanding, and perseverance of labor,
shall attain thither; whither long experience, diligent observation, and
subtlety of reason have not pierced till this present. She is the same that
she was in the former famous ages. The world is such as it was before. The
20 heaven and the time keep the same order which they did. The sun and the
other planets have not changed their courses, and there is no star removed
out of his place. The elements have the same power. Men are made of
the same matter, and in the same sort disposed as they were in old time.
And were not the manner of living corrupted which we use, preferring
idleness before diligence, pleasure before profit, and riches before virtue,
nothing would let but this age might bring forth as eminent personages in
Philosophy as were Plato and Aristotle; in Physic as Hippocrates and
Galen; or in the Mathematics as Euclid, Archimedes, and Ptolemy. Considering the help which we receive of their books, the examples wherewith
30 antiquity hath instructed us, so many observations and inventions sithence
their time, and so long experience of all things: in such sort that (if we
consider it well) there was never age more happy for the advancement
of learning than this present; if, weighing the shortness of man's life, we
resolve to employ our whole endeavor and industry on the study of true
knowledge. Wisdom hath not fulfilled her work; much remaineth, and
will always remain; there will never be wanting occasion to add thereunto. Truth doth offer herself to all those that will seek her, and are of
capacity to receive her, albeit Democritus complaineth that she is hid in a
place as deep as a well, wherehence (in his opinion) it is not possible to
40 draw her forth. Whosoever giveth himself to it in good earnest shall find
alway somewhat to do therein.

All the mysteries of God and secrets of nature are not discovered at one time. The greatest things are difficult and long in coming. How many are there not yet reduced into art? How many have been first known and found out in this age? I say, new lands, new seas, new forms of men, manners, laws, and customs; new diseases, and new remedies; new ways of the heaven and of the ocean, never before found out; and new stars seen? yea, and how many remain to be known by our posterity? That which is now hidden, with time will come to light; and our successors will wonder that we were ignorant of them.

M. Varro witnesseth that in the space of a thousand years the arts were 10 invented and augmented, which yet until this time are not perfected and accomplished. But if the perfection of them hath not hitherto been found, it followeth not thereof that it cannot be found. For those things which at this day are held to be the greatest, and most admirable, had a time of beginning: and that which is now very good was not so at the first, but is increased by little and little, amending from time to time. Certainly, the excellency in all things is slow, difficult, and rare, seeing that there is scarcely found in many hundreds and thousands of years, amongst an infinite number of students, one man worthy of admiration, being learned and eloquent indeed; that with a good natural wit, liveliness and sharp- 20 ness of understanding, experience and use of things, hath the constancy and patience to persevere, which are requisite to such an enterprise. This notwithstanding, we ought not to faint, or to despair; for if there be but small hope to excel and go beyond the best; yet is it an honor to follow them; and if there be no means to reach them, yet it is commendable to be second or third unto them. It is therefore convenient to apply our industry to the searching out of the truth, as they have done; and to endeavor to augment the doctrine of the ancients, without so much subjecting ourselves to antiquity that we do nothing for our age, and have no care of our posterity. 30

Moreover, many things invented by the ancients are lost. The wisdom of the Egyptians, Persians, Indians, and Bactrians hath not come unto us; many good Greek and Latin authors are not found; and amongst those that remain there are few agreeable to the present manners and affairs. We do not build nowadays after the fashion of Vitruvius; neither till the ground nor plant according to Varro or Columella; nor take food or physic after the ordinance of Hippocrates and Galen. We judge not according to the civil law of the Romans; neither plead we as did Demosthenes and Cicero; or govern our commonwealths by the laws of Solon and Lycurgus, or following the politic precepts of Plato and Aristotle. 40 We sing not as did the ancients; neither war we according to Vegetius, the art military being changed, and all kind of arms, both offensive and defensive. Ptolemy in his cosmography doth advertise men to believe the latest travelers touching the longitude and latitude of places. Aristotle saith that the quadrature of the circle may be known; but that is not yet found out. Plato affirmeth that geometry was unperfect in his time and that stereometry and the cubic wanted. The calculations of the heavens are not all found true. Vesalius, curiously observing anatomy, hath found many points therein omitted by Aristotle and Galen. Pliny boasteth that he hath added in the *History of living creatures* that which Aristotle was ignorant of. Leonicenus reproveth Pliny of lies and errors in many places. Avenreis hath written against Galen; Galen against Aristotle; and Aristotle against Plato. There is no author so accomplished or perfected in whom one may not find somewhat wanting or worthy of reproof.

And that which is worse, there are some men so given and so affectionate to antiquity that they are ignorant or have very small knowledge of the country and time wherein they live. They know in every point how Athens, Lacedemon, Carthage, Persia, and Egypt were governed, not knowing the affairs of their own country, wherein they are strangers. As there are found many among us discoursing of the assembly of the *Ario-pagites,* and of the *Comices* of the Romans, understanding nothing of the council of France, the handling of the revenues, and the order of the parliaments. Is it not then an abusing of study and of learning to dwell continually among the ancients, and not to endeavor to bring forth new inventions, agreeable to the manners and affairs of this time? When will we leave taking of grass for corn; the flower for the fruit; and the rind for the wood; doing nothing but translate, correct, expound, or abridge, the books of the ancients? who, if they had been also of this mind, not setting themselves to write or to say anything but that which had been written or said before, no art should have been invented; or at least they had all remained in their beginnings, without receiving any increase. The perpetual imitators, or always translators or commentators, hiding themselves under the shadow of others, are very slaves, and have no generous courage in them, if they dare not once to do that which they have so long time learned. They always distrust themselves, and follow the first in those things wherein the latter have not agreed with the former; namely, in those which are not yet sought out, and will never be found if we content ourselves with that which is already invented without adding anything thereunto.

* * * * *

FROM *Ellesmere Ms. 1117,* [1596]

Of Honour

* * * * *

CHAPTER 7.

Of Honor as it consisteth in him which bestoweth it on an-
other, and of the duty and parts of him which giveth honor
to others. 10

I THINK we have already sufficiently entreated of honor as it is in the
party which is honored, having set down both what it is, and what manner
of thing, and also wherein it consisteth and of whom it is to be desired,
and lastly the parts thereof and the degrees of the same. Now it is requisite that we should see what he which giveth honor unto others is to do,
and to respect that he may discharge his duty; wherein we must especially
consider what it is that he doth which honoreth another, that he may no
less perceive what his duties are in giving of honor than the other in desiring or accepting of it. And although I have by the way somewhat 20
touched it heretofore as the place required, yet is it in this place to be repeated, unto which it especially belongeth.

He therefore which honoreth another doth this, that he maketh himself a judge and an allower of another man's virtue. For as it is the part
of the one without hope of praise to embrace virtue, so is it the part of
th'other beholding the same virtue to use his judgment therein and to
weigh the merits thereof; which, when he hath well (that is, without
perturbation of mind) considered, then let him add thereunto such ap-
probation as is worthy of his judgment and estimation; and that neither
greater than his virtue deserveth, nor less than it requireth. Therefore as 30
in the desire of honor we said that a mediocrity agreeable to reason was to
be respected, so also the same in giving of honor ought to be regarded;
because that in giving honor to anyone according to desert, the greatness
and weight of the thing is to be well examined, lest we seem either flatterers or detractors; for they are both contrary to justice, which willeth that
every one have his own and neither more nor less than befitteth him.

Wherefore they which are to honor others, let them think that they
take upon them the person of a good and upright judge and are therefore
to refrain their affections, as love, desire, hatred, envy, strife, and such
others, or rather (because they are altogether evil) even utterly root them 40
out, lest they bereave them of judgment and take away all power of dis-

cerning. For as he which is distempered with anger or drunkenness cannot easily perceive the truth because his mind is removed from his place of constancy, so whosoever is disturbed with envy, love, or hatred can never rightly discern who is worthy of honor or otherwise. For envy maketh you to hide and extenuate that virtue which you acknowledge in another, and hatred will not let you know it, for by reason of it you judge every thing in him to be evil and vicious; displeasure, either rising out of contention or some other cause, doth the like; and friendship maketh you to attribute more than his deserts do require.

10 What is then to be done in so great an alienation of mind but even as the Stoic would have it, to rid yourself of all affections that you may judge aright; that envy, hatred, and strife do not detract anything from desert, nor love add anything thereunto; and to think that you are not to judge the man himself which is to be honored, but of his virtue. To these I add also temerity, sprung up out of a conceived opinion, which doth no less distemper the mind than those affections which I have named; namely, when we commend or dispraise one, not that we have had knowledge of his deserts, but because we follow the opinion of the multitude, or because we have given consent to the opinion of others without judgment or de-
20 liberation. For which cause also, ambitious men do endeavor to please many and be well thought of, because they think by those means to prepare themselves a way unto honor, for that men commonly follow the concourse of the multitude. Therefore both this rash opinion, and those affections also, are to be laid aside, and we must judge with a quiet and clear mind. And the sharpness of our understanding is to be used herein, that we be not deceived; because it is a very difficult thing to be able to judge aright. For every one hath not either such sufficiency of wisdom, or such ability and sharpness of judgment, as to search so deeply into another's disposition and manners, and to examine them so narrowly; or if
30 they have, yet may they often be deceived, because the mind of man is prone to error.

But you will say peradventure, that if this be so, no man shall ever judge aright of another's virtue, and therefore shall not honor any, lest he go astray. I answer that he may if he carefully and curiously consider the appearance of virtue, which shineth sufficiently of itself; and if when he suspecteth his own judgment, he use the advice of others whom he knoweth to be expert and wise, and see what is their opinion. For so (as in other things also) the truth is easier found, and the judgment void of rashness and temerity. For we are not only to judge whether one be
40 worthy of honor or no, but also of how much, and of what kind of honor, that there be respect had of his deserts. You consider in buying of a horse his goodness, commodity and use, his shape and condition, his kind and

breeding, with many other things. And in conceiving an opinion of another man's virtue, will you not consider of what weight it is, lest you be
accompted unwise and of small judgment? Then are the husbandmen
wiser in knowing the goodness of a ground before they bestow seed
thereon than they which boast of sharpness of understanding, experience, and sincerity of judgment? Certainly it becometh not great and
grave men to judge amiss, neither to attribute more or less unto any than
his deserts shall require.

These things thus respected, it remaineth that as you esteem and reckon
the men, or rather their merits, as you find them, so you give every one 10
that honor which is fit for him; that is, the greatest unto such as are of
greatest excellency, less to the inferior sort, and least of all to the lowest,
and yet some unto all. For their opinion is good which think that we ought
to honor and reverence all, and to contemn no man. For it is the part of
civil courtesy and modest humanity to speak gently to all, to salute, embrace, and entertain them without difference, because nothing doth more
easily draw the good wills of men than this gracious and courteous kind
of behavior. Notwithstanding, it is also the part of a prudent man to respect the desert of every one's virtue and also the dignity of his person,
and whatsoever else is of moment toward th'attaining of honor. Where- 20
fore the first and chiefest respect of giving honor is virtue itself, which
we ought to honor in whomsoever we find it, be he never so base. The
second is knowledge and learning, which cometh near unto virtue. The
next is wit and towardness of disposition, with the rest of the good gifts
both of mind and body, which although they are much reckoned of by the
multitude, yet have they here their due place; because they are farthest
removed from virtue.

As therefore there is such distinction of good things made by us that
the greater are preferred before the less; so also in giving of honor there
must more respect be had of the greater good than of the lesser, and in 30
like sort of the rest. And because more good things are preferred before
fewer, there is also much greater cause of honor in a heap of many good
things than where there are but few. Therefore unto him who, besides
the virtue of the mind and other good gifts of the body hath lineage,
riches and wealth, power, office, and dignity, there is more honor to be
given than to him which excelleth but in one thing alone. Hence it cometh
to pass that unto princes, noblemen, and all such as are over others and
excel them in anything we give great honor, not because we think there
is greatest virtue in them, but because these things either be or should be
the ornaments of great virtues; and because that for the dignity and 40
order of the commonwealth there ought to be these degrees of honor,
lest the common people and the nobility, private men and magistrates, an

edile and a consul, a king and a captain should be all of one accompt.

Whereunto is to be added that it is many times requisite and necessary to honor some not for virtue only (which peradventure is wanting in them) but either for courtesy's sake, for show of some outward good, or else for fear of offence. Civility and courtesy (as we said before) must be used towards all, in saluting of them and speaking gently unto them, and in all other things which belong to the conversation of human society.

As also certain external good things, as wealth and riches, magnificence and ornament, and other of like sort (because they may be instruments of good things, though they be not good of themselves) are not to be contemned, especially being joined with virtue.

The fear also of offending any with our incivility and contempt is of great moment unto honor; because as nothing is more to be avoided than to have the evil will or hatred of any by our own procurement, so by all means ought we to labor that by our humanity and honest endeavor we may gain the good will and favor of all that have power to honor us.

But there are divers sorts of giving honor unto others which are peculiar and different according to the custom and diversity of nations. As some in rising from their seat, others in attending, following, and accompanying, others in uncovering their heads, and others in such other things do imagine honor to consist. All which, since they cannot be comprehended under any certain rule, must be observed towards every one according to that degree which they have amongst those where they are used. Neither shall that which is the sign of the greatest honor (as to worship on bended knees, or to do some such other thing) be fit to use to every private man; no, nor to every prince; neither yet to give unto a great man such honor as is used to an inferior person. Moreover, this caution is to be held amongst all men, that those which are but light signs of honor are to be used indifferently to all, but such as are tokens of greater honor to be used only to the worthiest, or else to those whom reason shall teach that they ought to be used with such kind of honor.

*   *   *   *   *

RICHARD HOOKER

The Introduction and Notes are at page 1336

FROM *Of the Lawes of Ecclesiaticall Politie,* [1593]

Of the Laws of Ecclesiastical Polity

The First Book

Concerning Laws, and their several kinds in general.

The matter contained in this first book.

1. The cause of writing this general discourse concerning laws.
2. Of that law which God from before the beginning hath set for himself to do all things by.
3. The law which natural agents observe, and their necessary manner of keeping it.
4. The law which the Angels of God obey.
5. The law whereby man is in his actions directed to the imitation of God.
6. Men's first beginning to understand that law.
7. Of man's will, which is the first thing that laws of action are made to guide.
8. Of the natural finding out of laws by the light of reason, to guide the will unto that which is good.
9. Of the benefit of keeping that law which reason teacheth.
10. How reason doth lead men unto the making of human laws, whereby politic societies are governed, and to agreement about laws whereby the fellowship or communion of independent societies standeth.
11. Wherefore God hath by Scripture further made known such supernatural laws as do serve for men's direction.
12. The cause why so many natural or rational laws are set down in Holy Scripture.
13. The benefit of having divine laws written.
14. The sufficiency of Scripture unto the end for which it was instituted.
15. Of laws positive contained in Scripture, the mutability of certain of them, and the general use of Scripture.
16. A conclusion, showing how all this belongeth to the cause in question.

I. He that goeth about to persuade a multitude that they are not so
well governed as they ought to be, shall never want attentive and favour-
able hearers; because they know the manifold defects whereunto every
kind of regiment is subject, but the secret lets and difficulties, which in
public proceedings are innumerable and inevitable, they have not ordinarily
the judgment to consider. And because such as openly reprove supposed
disorders of state are taken for principal friends to the common benefit
of all, and for men that carry singular freedom of mind; under this fair
and plausible colour whatsoever they utter passeth for good and current.
10 That which wanteth in the weight of their speech is supplied by the aptness
of men's minds to accept and believe it. Whereas on the other side, if we
maintain things that are established, we have not only to strive with a
number of heavy prejudices deeply rooted in the hearts of men, who think
that herein we serve the time, and speak in favour of the present state
because thereby we either hold or seek preferment; but also to bar such
exceptions as minds so averted beforehand usually take against that which
they are loth should be poured into them.

[2] Albeit therefore much of that we are to speak in this present cause
may seem to a number perhaps tedious, perhaps obscure, dark, and intri-
20 cate (for many talk of the truth which never sounded the depth from
whence it springeth, and therefore when they are led thereunto they are
soon weary, as men drawn from those beaten paths wherewith they have
been inured); yet this may not so far prevail as to cut off that which the
matter itself requireth, howsoever the nice humour of some be therewith
pleased or no. They unto whom we shall seem tedious are in no wise injured by us, because it is in their own hands to spare that labour which
they are not willing to endure. And if any complain of obscurity, they
must consider that in these matters it cometh no otherwise to pass than in
sundry the works both of art and also of nature, where that which hath
30 greatest force in the very things we see, is notwithstanding itself oftentimes
not seen. The stateliness of houses, the goodliness of trees, when we behold them delighteth the eye; but that foundation which beareth up the
one, that root which ministereth unto the other nourishment and life, is
in the bosom of the earth concealed; and if there be at any time occasion
to search into it, such labour is then more necessary than pleasant, both
to them which undertake it and for the lookers-on. In like manner, the
use and benefit of good laws all that live under them may enjoy with delight and comfort, albeit the grounds and first original causes from whence
they have sprung be unknown, as to the greatest part of men they are.
40 But when they who withdraw their obedience pretend that the laws which
they should obey are corrupt and vicious; for better examination of their
quality, it behoveth the very foundation and root, the highest well-spring

and fountain of them to be discovered. Which because we are not often-times accustomed to do, when we do it the pains we take are more needful a great deal than acceptable, and the matters which we handle seem, by reason of newness (till the mind grow better acquainted with them), dark, intricate, and unfamiliar. For as much help whereof as may be in this case, I have endeavoured throughout the body of this whole discourse, that every former part might give strength unto all that follow, and every later bring some light unto all before. So that if the judgments of men do but hold themselves in suspense as touching these first more general medi-tations, till in order they have perused the rest that ensue, what may seem 10 dark at the first will afterwards be found more plain, even as the later particular decisions will appear I doubt not more strong, when the other have been read before.

[3] The Laws of the Church, whereby for so many ages together we have been guided in the exercise of Christian religion and the service of the true God, our rites, customs, and orders of ecclesiastical government are called in question; we are accused as men that will not have Christ Jesus to rule over them, but have wilfully cast his statutes behind their backs, hating to be reformed and made subject unto the sceptre of his discipline. Behold therefore we offer the laws whereby we live unto the 20 general trial and judgment of the whole world, heartily beseeching Al-mighty God, whom we desire to serve according to his own will, that both we and others (all kind of partial affection being clean laid aside) may have eyes to see and hearts to embrace the things that in his sight are most acceptable.

And because the point about which we strive is the quality of our laws, our first entrance hereinto cannot better be made than with considera-tion of the nature of law in general, and of that law which giveth life unto all the rest which are commendable, just, and good; namely the law whereby the Eternal himself doth work. Proceeding from hence to 30 the law, first of Nature, then of Scripture, we shall have the easier access unto those things which come after to be debated, concerning the particu-lar cause and question which we have in hand.

II. All things that are, have some operation not violent or casual. Neither doth any thing ever begin to exercise the same without some fore-conceived end for which it worketh. And the end which it worketh for is not obtained, unless the work be also fit to obtain it by. For unto every end every operation will not serve. That which doth assign unto each thing the kind, that which doth moderate the force and power, that which doth appoint the form and measure of working, the same we term 40 a Law. So that no certain end could ever be attained, unless the actions whereby it is attained were regular; that is to say, made suitable, fit and correspondent unto their end, by some canon, rule, or law. Which thing doth first take place in the works even of God himself.

[2] All things therefore do work after a sort according to law: all other things according to a law whereof some superior, unto whom they are subject, is author; only the works and operations of God have Him both for their worker, and for the law whereby they are wrought. The being of God is a kind of law to his working: for that perfection which God is, giveth perfection to that he doth. Those natural, necessary, and internal operations of God—the generation of the Son, the proceeding of
10 the Spirit—are without the compass of my present intent; which is to touch only such operations as have their beginning and being by a voluntary purpose, wherewith God hath eternally decreed when and how they should be. Which eternal decree is that we term an eternal law.

Dangerous it were for the feeble brain of man to wade far into the doings of the Most High, whom although to know be life, and joy to make mention of his name; yet our soundest knowledge is to know that we know him not as indeed he is, neither can know him; and our safest eloquence concerning him is our silence, when we confess without confession that his glory is inexplicable, his greatness above our capacity and
20 reach. He is above, and we upon earth; therefore it behoveth our words to be wary and few.

Our God is one, or rather very Oneness, and mere unity, having nothing but itself in itself, and not consisting (as all things do besides God) of many things. In which essential Unity of God a Trinity personal nevertheless subsisteth, after a manner far exceeding the possibility of man's conceit. The works which outwardly are of God, they are in such sort of Him being one, that each Person hath in them somewhat peculiar and proper. For being Three, and they all subsisting in the essence of one Deity; from the Father, by the Son, through the Spirit, all things are.
30 That which the Son doth hear of the Father, and which the Spirit doth receive of the Father and the Son, the same we have at the hands of the Spirit as being the last, and therefore the nearest unto us in order, although in power the same with the second and the first.

[3] The wise and learned among the very heathens themselves have all acknowledged some first cause, whereupon originally the being of all things dependeth. Neither have they otherwise spoken of that cause than as an Agent, which knowing what and why it worketh, observeth in working a most exact order or law. Thus much is signified by that which Homer mentioneth, Διὸς δ' ἐτελείετο βουλή. Thus much acknowledged by
40 Mercurius Trismegistus, τὸν πάντα κόσμον ἐποίησεν ὁ δημιουργὸς οὐ χερσὶν ἀλλὰ λόγῳ. Thus much confest by Anaxagoras and Plato, terming the Maker of the world an Intellectual worker. Finally the Stoics, although

imagining the first cause of all things to be fire, held nevertheless that the same fire, having art, did ὁδῷ βαδίζειν ἐπὶ γενέσει κόσμου. They all confess therefore in the working of that first cause, that Counsel is used, Reason followed, a Way observed; that is to say, constant Order and Law is kept, whereof itself must needs be author unto itself. Otherwise it should have some worthier and higher to direct it, and so could not itself be the first. Being the first, it can have no other than itself to be the author of that law which it willingly worketh by.

God therefore is a law both to himself, and to all other things besides. To himself he is a law in all those things, whereof our Saviour speaketh, saying, "My Father worketh as yet, so I." God worketh nothing without cause. All those things which are done by him have some end for which they are done; and the end for which they are done is a reason of his will to do them. His will had not inclined to create woman, but that he saw it could not be well if she were not created. *Non est bonum*, "It is not good man should be alone; therefore let us make a helper for him." That and nothing else is done by God, which to leave undone were not so good.

If therefore it be demanded, why God having power and ability infinite, the effects notwithstanding of that power are all so limited as we see they are: the reason hereof is the end which he hath proposed, and the law whereby his wisdom hath stinted the effects of his power in such sort that it doth not work infinitely, but correspondently unto that end for which it worketh, even "all things χρηστῶς, in most decent and comely sort, all things in measure, number, and weight."

[4] The general end of God's external working is the exercise of his most glorious and most abundant virtue. Which abundance doth shew itself in variety, and for that cause this variety is oftentimes in Scripture exprest by the name of riches. "The Lord hath made all things for his own sake." Not that any thing is made to be beneficial unto him, but all things for him to shew beneficence and grace in them.

The particular drift of every act proceeding externally from God we are not able to discern, and therefore cannot always give the proper and certain reason of his works. Howbeit undoubtedly a proper and certain reason there is of every finite work of God, inasmuch as there is a law imposed upon it; which if there were not, it should be infinite, even as the worker himself is.

[5] They err therefore who think that of the will of God to do this or that there is no reason besides his will. Many times no reason known to us; but that there is no reason thereof I judge it most unreasonable to imagine, inasmuch as he worketh all things κατὰ τὴν βουλὴν τοῦ θελήματος αὐτοῦ, not only according to his own will, but "the counsel of his own will." And whatsoever is done with counsel or wise resolution hath of necessity

some reason why it should be done, albeit that reason be to us in some things so secret, that it forceth the wit of man to stand, as the blessed Apostle himself doth, amazed thereat: "O the depth of the riches both of the wisdom and knowledge of God! how unsearchable are his judgments," &c. That law eternal which God himself hath made to himself, and thereby worketh all things whereof he is the cause and author; that law in the admirable frame whereof shineth with most perfect beauty the countenance of that wisdom which hath testified concerning herself, "The Lord possessed me in the beginning of his way, even before his works of old, I was set up"; that law, which hath been the pattern to make, and is the card to guide the world by; that law which hath been of God and with God everlastingly; that law, the author and observer whereof is one only God to be blessed for ever: how should either men or angels be able perfectly to behold? The book of this law we are neither able nor worthy to open and look into. That little thereof which we darkly apprehend we admire, the rest with religious ignorance we humbly and meekly adore.

[6] Seeing therefore that according to this law He worketh, "of whom, through whom, and for whom, are all things," although there seem unto us confusion and disorder in the affairs of this present world: *Tamen quoniam bonus mundum rector temperat, recte fieri cuncta ne dubites:* "let no man doubt but that every thing is well done, because the world is ruled by so good a guide," as transgresseth not His own law, than which nothing can be more absolute, perfect, and just.

The law whereby He worketh is eternal, and therefore can have no show or colour of mutability; for which cause, a part of that law being opened in the promises which God hath made (because his promises are nothing else but declarations what God will do for the good of men) touching those promises the Apostle hath witnessed that God may as possibly "deny himself" and not be God, as fail to perform them. And concerning the counsel of God, he termeth it likewise a thing "unchangeable"; the counsel of God, and that law of God whereof now we speak, being one.

Nor is the freedom of the will of God any whit abated, let, or hindered by means of this; because the imposition of this law upon himself is his own free and voluntary act.

This law therefore we may name eternal, being "that order which God before all ages hath set down with himself, for himself to do all things by."

III. I am not ignorant that by "law eternal" the learned for the most part do understand the order, not which God hath eternally purposed himself in all his works to observe, but rather that which with himself he hath set down as expedient to be kept by all his creatures, according to

the several condition wherewith he hath endued them. They who thus
are accustomed to speak apply the name of Law unto that only rule of
working which superior authority imposeth; whereas we somewhat more
enlarging the sense thereof, term any kind of rule or canon whereby actions are framed, a law. Now that law which, as it is laid up in the bosom
of God, they call Eternal, receiveth according unto the different kinds of
things which are subject unto it different and sundry kinds of names. That
part of it which ordereth natural agents we call usually Nature's law;
that which angels do clearly behold and without any swerving observe is
a law Celestial and heavenly; the law of Reason, that which bindeth 10
creatures reasonable in this world, and with which by reason they may most
plainly perceive themselves bound; that which bindeth them, and is not
known but by special revelation from God, Divine law; Human law, that
which out of the law either of reason or of God, men probably gathering
to be expedient, they make it a law. All things therefore, which are as they
ought to be, are conformed unto this second law eternal; and even those
things which to this eternal law are not conformable are notwithstanding
in some sort ordered by the first eternal law. For what good or evil is
there under the sun, what action correspondent or repugnant unto the
law which God hath imposed upon his creatures, but in or upon it God 20
doth work according to the law which himself hath eternally purposed to
keep; that is to say, the first law eternal? So that a twofold law eternal
being thus made, it is not hard to conceive how they both take place in
all things.

[2] Wherefore to come to the law of nature, albeit thereby we sometimes mean that manner of working which God hath set for each created
thing to keep, yet forasmuch as those things are termed most properly
Natural agents which keep the law of their kind unwittingly, as the
heavens and elements of the world, which can do no otherwise than they
do; and forasmuch as we give unto intellectual natures the name of Vol- 30
untary agents, that so we may distinguish them from the other, expedient
it will be that we sever the law of nature observed by the one from that
which the other is tied unto. Touching the former, their strict keeping of
one tenure, statute, and law, is spoken of by all, but hath in it more than
men have as yet attained to know, or perhaps ever shall attain, seeing the
travail of wading herein is given of God to the sons of men, that perceiving how much the least thing in the world hath in it more than the wisest
are able to reach unto, they may by this means learn humility. Moses, in
describing the work of creation, attributeth speech unto God: "God said,
Let there be light: let there be a firmament: let the waters under the 40
heaven be gathered together into one place: let the earth bring forth: let
there be lights in the firmament of heaven." Was this only the intent of

Moses, to signify the infinite greatness of God's power by the easiness of his accomplishing such effects, without travail, pain, or labour? Surely it seemeth that Moses had herein besides this a further purpose; namely, first to teach that God did not work as a necessary but a voluntary agent, intending beforehand and decreeing with himself that which did outwardly proceed from him; secondly, to shew that God did then institute a law natural to be observed by creatures, and therefore according to the manner of laws, the institution thereof is described as being established by solemn injunction. His commanding those things to be which are, and 10 to be in such sort as they are, to keep that tenure and course which they do, importeth the establishment of Nature's law. This world's first creation, and the preservation since of things created, what is it but only so far forth a manifestation by execution what the eternal law of God is concerning things natural? And as it cometh to pass in a kingdom rightly ordered, that after a law is once published, it presently takes effect far and wide, all states framing themselves thereunto; even so let us think it fareth in the natural course of the world: since the time that God did first proclaim the edicts of his law upon it, heaven and earth have hearkened unto his voice, and their labour hath been to do his will. He "made a law for the 20 rain"; He gave his "decree unto the sea, that the waters should not pass his commandment." Now if nature should intermit her course, and leave altogether though it were but for a while the observation of her own laws; if those principal and mother elements of the world, whereof all things in this lower world are made, should lose the qualities which now they have; if the frame of that heavenly arch erected over our heads should loosen and dissolve itself; if celestial spheres should forget their wonted motions, and by irregular volubility turn themselves any way as it might happen; if the prince of the lights of heaven, which now as a giant doth run his unwearied course, should as it were through a languishing faint- 30 ness begin to stand and to rest himself; if the moon should wander from her beaten way, the times and seasons of the year blend themselves by disordered and confused mixture, the winds breathe out their last gasp, the clouds yield no rain, the earth be defeated of heavenly influence, the fruits of the earth pine away as children at the withered breasts of their mother no longer able to yield them relief: what would become of man himself, whom these things now do all serve? See we not plainly that obedience of creatures unto the law of nature is the stay of the whole world?

[3] Notwithstanding, with nature it cometh sometimes to pass as with art. Let Phidias have rude and obstinate stuff to carve, though his art do 40 that it should, his work will lack that beauty which otherwise in fitter matter it might have had. He that striketh an instrument with skill may cause notwithstanding a very unpleasant sound, if the string whereon he

striketh chance to be uncapable of harmony. In the matter whereof things natural consist, that of Theophrastus taketh place, πολὺ τὸ οὐχ ὑπακοῦον οὐδὲ δεχόμενον τὸ εὖ. "Much of it is oftentimes such as will by no means yield to receive that impression which were best and most perfect." Which defect in the matter of things natural, they who gave themselves unto the contemplation of nature amongst the heathen observed often; but the true original cause thereof, divine malediction laid for the sin of man upon these creatures which God had made for the use of man, this being an article of that saving truth which God hath revealed unto his Church, was above the reach of their merely natural capacity and understanding. But 10 howsoever these swervings are now and then incident into the course of nature, nevertheless so constantly the laws of nature are by natural agents observed that no man denieth but those things which nature worketh are wrought, either always or for the most part, after one and the same manner.

[4] If here it be demanded what that is which keepeth nature in obedience to her own law, we must have recourse to that higher law whereof we have already spoken, and because all other laws do thereon depend, from thence we must borrow so much as shall need for brief resolution in this point. Although we are not of opinion, therefore, as 20 some are, that nature in working hath before her certain exemplary draughts or patterns, which subsisting in the bosom of the Highest, and being thence discovered, she fixeth her eye upon them, as travellers by sea upon the pole-star of the world, and that according thereunto she guideth her hand to work by imitation; although we rather embrace the oracle of Hippocrates, that "each thing both in small and in great fulfilleth the task which destiny hath set down"; and concerning the manner of executing and fulfilling the same, "what they do they know not, yet is it in show and appearance as though they did know what they do; and the truth is they do not discern the things which they look on": neverthe- 30 less, forasmuch as the works of nature are no less exact than if she did both behold and study how to express some absolute shape or mirror always present before her; yea, such her dexterity and skill appeareth, that no intellectual creature in the world were able by capacity to do that which nature doth without capacity and knowledge; it cannot be but nature hath some director of infinite knowledge to guide her in all her ways. Who the guide of nature, but only the God of nature? "In him we live, move, and are." Those things which nature is said to do, are by divine art performed, using nature as an instrument; nor is there any such art or knowledge divine in nature herself working, but in the Guide of nature's work. 40

Whereas therefore things natural which are not in the number of voluntary agents (for of such only we now speak, and of no other), do so necessarily observe their certain laws that as long as they keep those forms which give them their being, they cannot possibly be apt or inclinable to do otherwise than they do; seeing the kinds of their operations are both constantly and exactly framed according to the several ends for which they serve, they themselves in the meanwhile, though doing that which is fit, yet knowing neither what they do, nor why, it followeth that all which they do in this sort proceedeth originally from some such agent as knoweth, appointeth, holdeth up, and even actually frameth the same.

The manner of this divine efficiency, being far above us, we are no more able to conceive by our reason than creatures unreasonable by their sense are able to apprehend after what manner we dispose and order the course of our affairs. Only thus much is discerned, that the natural generation and process of all things receiveth order of proceeding from the settled stability of divine understanding. This appointeth unto them their kinds of working, the disposition whereof in the purity of God's own knowledge and will is rightly termed by the name of Providence. The same being referred unto the things themselves here disposed by it, was wont by the ancient to be called Natural Destiny. That law, the performance whereof we behold in things natural, is as it were an authentical or an original draught written in the bosom of God himself; whose Spirit being to execute the same useth every particular nature, every mere natural agent, only as an instrument created at the beginning, and ever since the beginning used, to work his own will and pleasure withal. Nature therefore is nothing else but God's instrument: in the course whereof Dionysius perceiving some sudden disturbance is said to have cried out, *Aut Deus naturae patitur, aut mundi machina dissolvetur:* "either God doth suffer impediment, and is by a greater than himself hindered; or if that be impossible, then hath he determined to make a present dissolution of the world; the execution of that law beginning now to stand still, without which the world cannot stand."

This workman whose servitor nature is, being in truth but only one, the heathens imagining to be moe, gave him in the sky the name of Jupiter, in the air the name of Juno, in the water the name of Neptune, in the earth the name of Vesta and sometimes of Ceres, the name of Apollo in the sun, in the moon the name of Diana, the name of Aeolus and divers other in the winds; and to conclude, even so many guides of nature they dreamed of, as they saw there were kinds of things natural in the world. These they honoured, as having power to work or cease accordingly as men deserved of them. But unto us there is one only Guide of all agents natural, and he both the Creator and the Worker of all in all, alone to be blessed, adored and honoured by all for ever.

[5] That which hitherto hath been spoken concerneth natural agents

considered in themselves. But we must further remember also (which thing to touch in a word shall suffice), that as in this respect they have their law, which law directeth them in the means whereby they tend to their own perfection; so likewise another law there is, which toucheth them as they are sociable parts united into one body; a law which bindeth them each to serve unto other's good, and all to prefer the good of the whole before whatsoever their own particular; as we plainly see they do when things natural in that regard forget their ordinary natural wont, that which is heavy mounting sometime upwards of it own accord and forsaking the centre of the earth which to itself is most natural, even as if it did ro hear itself commanded to let go the good it privately wisheth and to relieve the present distress of nature in common.

IV. But now that we may lift up our eyes (as it were) from the footstool to the throne of God, and leaving these natural, consider a little the state of heavenly and divine creatures; touching Angels, which are spirits immaterial and intellectual, the glorious inhabitants of those sacred palaces where nothing but light and blessed immortality, no shadow of matter for tears, discontentments, griefs, and uncomfortable passions to work upon, but all joy, tranquillity, and peace, even for ever and ever doth dwell; as in number and order they are huge, mighty, and royal armies, so likewise 2c in perfection of obedience unto that law which the Highest, whom they adore, love, and imitate, hath imposed upon them, such observants they are thereof, that our Saviour himself being to set down the perfect *idea* of that which we are to pray and wish for on earth, did not teach to pray or wish for more than only that here it might be with us, as with them it is in heaven. God which moveth mere natural agents as an efficient only, doth otherwise move intellectual creatures, and especially his holy angels. For beholding the face of God, in admiration of so great excellency they all adore him; and being rapt with the love of his beauty, they cleave inseparably for ever unto him. Desire to resemble him in goodness maketh 30 them unweariable and even unsatiable in their longing to do by all means all manner good unto all the creatures of God, but especially unto the children of men; in the countenance of whose nature, looking downward, they behold themselves beneath themselves; even as upward, in God, beneath whom themselves are, they see that character which is no where but in themselves and us resembled. Thus far even the paynims have approached; thus far they have seen into the doings of the angels of God; Orpheus confessing that "the fiery throne of God is attended on by those most industrious angels, careful how all things are performed amongst men"; and the Mirror of human wisdom plainly teaching that God 40 moveth angels, even as that thing doth stir man's heart which is thereunto presented amiable. Angelical actions may therefore be reduced unto these three general kinds: first, most delectable love arising from the visible apprehension of the purity, glory, and beauty of God, invisible saving only unto spirits that are pure; secondly, adoration grounded upon the evidence of the greatness of God, on whom they see how all things depend; thirdly, imitation bred by the presence of his exemplary goodness, who ceaseth not before them daily to fill heaven and earth with the rich treasures of most free and undeserved grace.

[2] Of angels, we are not to consider only what they are and do in regard of their own being, but that also which concerneth them as they are linked into a kind of corporation amongst themselves, and of society or fellowship with men. Consider angels each of them severally in himself, and their law is that which the prophet David mentioneth, "All ye his angels praise him." Consider the angels of God associated, and their law is that which disposeth them as an army, one in order and degree above another. Consider finally the angels as having with us that communion which the apostle to the Hebrews noteth, and in regard whereof angels have not disdained to profess themselves our "fellow-servants"; from hence there springeth up a third law, which bindeth them to works of ministerial employment. Every of which their several functions are by them performed with joy.

[3] A part of the angels of God notwithstanding (we know) have fallen, and that their fall hath been through the voluntary breach of that law which did require at their hands continuance in the exercise of their high and admirable virtue. Impossible it was that ever their will should change or incline to remit any part of their duty, without some object having force to avert their conceit from God, and to draw it another way; and that before they attained that high perfection of bliss, wherein now the elect angels are without possiblity of falling. Of any thing more than of God they could not by any means like, as long as whatsoever they knew besides God they apprehended it not in itself without dependency upon God; because so long God must needs seem infinitely better than any thing which they so could apprehend. Things beneath them could not in such sort be presented unto their eyes, but that therein they must needs see always how those things did depend on God. It seemeth therefore that there was no other way for angels to sin but by reflex of their understanding upon themselves; when being held with admiration of their own sublimity and honour, the memory of their subordination unto God and their dependency on him was drowned in this conceit; whereupon their adoration, love, and imitation of God could not choose but be also interrupted. The fall of angels therefore was pride. Since their fall, their practices have been the clean contrary unto those before mentioned. For being dispersed, some in the air, some on the earth, some in the water, some among the

minerals, dens, and caves that are under the earth, they have by all means laboured to effect an universal rebellion against the laws, and, as far as in them lieth, utter destruction of the works of God. These wicked spirits the heathens honoured instead of gods, both generally under the name of *Dü inferi,* "gods infernal"; and particularly, some in oracles, some in idols, some as household gods, some as nymphs—in a word, no foul and wicked spirit which was not one way or other honoured of men as God, till such time as light appeared in the world and dissolved the works of the devil. Thus much therefore may suffice for angels, the next unto whom in degree are men.   10

V. God alone excepted, who actually and everlastingly is whatsoever he may be, and which cannot hereafter be that which now he is not; all other things besides are somewhat in possibility, which as yet they are not in act. And for this cause there is in all things an appetite or desire, whereby they incline to something which they may be; and when they are it, they shall be perfecter than now they are. All which perfections are contained under the general name of Goodness. And because there is not in the world any thing whereby another may not some way be made the perfecter, therefore all things that are, are good.

[2] Again, sith there can be no goodness desired which proceedeth not 20 from God himself, as from the supreme cause of all things; and every effect doth after a sort contain, at leastwise resemble, the cause from which it proceedeth: all things in the world are said in some sort to seek the highest, and to covet more or less the participation of God himself. Yet this doth no where so much appear as it doth in man, because there are so many kinds of perfections which man seeketh. The first degree of goodness is that general perfection which all things do seek, in desiring the continuance of their being. All things therefore coveting as much as may be to be like unto God in being ever, that which cannot hereunto attain personally doth seek to continue itself another way, that is by offspring 30 and propagation. The next degree of goodness is that which each thing coveteth by affecting resemblance with God in the constancy and excellency of those operations which belong unto their kind. The immutability of God they strive unto, by working either always or for the most part after one and the same manner; his absolute exactness they imitate, by tending unto that which is most exquisite in every particular. Hence have risen a number of axioms in philosophy, showing how "the works of nature do always aim at that which cannot be bettered."

[3] These two kinds of goodness rehearsed are so nearly united to the things themselves which desire them that we scarcely perceive the 40 appetite to stir in reaching forth her hand towards them. But the desire of those perfections which grow externally is more apparent; especially

of such as are not expressly desired unless they be first known, or such as are not for any other cause than for knowledge itself desired. Concerning perfections in this kind, that by proceeding in the knowledge of truth, and by growing in the exercise of virtue, man amongst the creatures of this inferior world aspireth to the greatest conformity with God; this is not only known unto us, whom he himself hath so instructed, but even they do acknowledge who amongst men are not judged the nearest unto him. With Plato what one thing more usual than to excite men unto the love of wisdom, by shewing how much wise men are thereby exalted above
10 men; how knowledge doth raise them up into heaven; how it maketh them, though not gods, yet as gods, high, admirable, and divine? And Mercurius Trismegistus speaking of the virtues of a righteous soul, "Such spirits" (saith he) "are never cloyed with praising and speaking well of all men, with doing good unto every one by word and deed, because they study to frame themselves according to THE PATTERN of the Father of spirits."

VI. In the matter of knowledge, there is between the angels of God and the children of men this difference: angels already have full and complete knowledge in the highest degree that can be imparted unto them;
20 men, if we view them in their spring, are at the first without understanding or knowledge at all. Nevertheless, from this utter vacuity they grow by degrees, till they come at length to be even as the angels themselves are. That which agreeth to the one now, the other shall attain unto in the end; they are not so far disjoined and severed but that they come at length to meet. The soul of man being therefore at the first as a book, wherein nothing is and yet all things may be imprinted, we are to search by what steps and degrees it riseth unto perfection of knowledge.

[2] Unto that which hath been already set down concerning natural agents this we must add: that albeit therein we have comprised as well
30 creatures living as void of life, if they be in degree of nature beneath men; nevertheless a difference we must observe between those natural agents that work altogether unwittingly, and those which have though weak yet some understanding what they do, as fishes, fowls, and beasts have. Beasts are in sensible capacity as ripe even as men themselves, perhaps more ripe. For as stones, though in dignity of nature inferior unto plants, yet exceed them in firmness of strength or durability of being; and plants, though beneath the excellency of creatures endued with sense, yet exceed them in the faculty of vegetation and of fertility: so beasts, though otherwise behind men, may notwithstanding in actions of sense and fancy go beyond
40 them; because the endeavours of nature, when it hath a higher perfection to seek, are in lower the more remiss, not esteeming thereof so much as those things do which have no better proposed unto them.

[3] The soul of man, therefore, being capable of a more divine per-

fection, hath (besides the faculties of growing unto sensible knowledge which is common unto us with beasts) a further ability, whereof in them there is no show at all, the ability of reaching higher than unto sensible things. Till we grow to some ripeness of years, the soul of man doth only store itself with conceits of things of inferior and more open quality, which afterwards do serve as instruments unto that which is greater; in the meanwhile, above the reach of meaner creatures it ascendeth not. When once it comprehendeth any thing above this, as the differences of time, affirmations, negations, and contradictions in speech, we then count it to have some use of natural reason. Whereunto if afterwards there might be added the right helps of true art and learning (which helps, I must plainly confess, this age of the world, carrying the name of a learned age, doth neither much know nor greatly regard), there would undoubtedly be almost as great difference in maturity of judgment between men therewith inured, and that which now men are, as between men that are now, and innocents. Which speech if any condemn as being over-hyperbolical, let them consider but this one thing. No art is at the first finding out so perfect as industry may after make it. Yet the very first man that to any purpose knew the way we speak of and followed it, hath alone thereby performed more very near in all parts of natural knowledge than sithence in any one part thereof the whole world besides hath done.

[4] In the poverty of that other new devised aid two things there are notwithstanding singular. Of marvellous quick despatch it is, and doth shew them that have it as much almost in three days, as if it dwell threescore years with them. Again, because the curiosity of man's wit doth many times with peril wade farther in the search of things than were convenient; the same is thereby restrained unto such generalities as every where offering themselves are apparent unto men of the weakest conceit that need be. So as following the rules and precepts thereof, we may define it to be, an Art which teacheth the way of speedy discourse, and restraineth the mind of man that it may not wax over-wise.

[5] Education and instruction are the means, the one by use, the other by precept, to make our natural faculty of reason both the better and the sooner able to judge rightly between truth and error, good and evil. But at what time a man may be said to have attained so far forth the use of reason as sufficeth to make him capable of those Laws whereby he is then bound to guide his actions; this is a great deal more easy for common sense to discern, than for any man by skill and learning to determine; even as it is not in philosophers, who best know the nature both of fire and of gold, to teach what degree of the one will serve to purify the other, so well as the artisan, who doth this by fire, discerneth by sense when the fire hath that degree of heat which sufficeth for his purpose.

VII. By reason man attaineth unto the knowledge of things that are and are not sensible. It resteth therefore that we search how man attaineth unto the knowledge of such things unsensible as are to be known that they may be done. Seeing then that nothing can move unless there be some end, the desire whereof provoketh unto motion; how should that divine power of the soul, that "spirit of our mind," as the apostle termeth it, ever stir itself unto action, unless it have also the like spur? The end for which we are moved to work is sometimes the goodness which we conceive of the very working itself, without any further respect at all; and the cause that procureth action is the mere desire of action, no other good besides being 10 thereby intended. Of certain turbulent wits it is said, *Illis quieta movere magna merces videbatur:* they thought the very disturbance of things established an hire sufficient to set them on work. Sometimes that which we do is referred to a further end, without the desire whereof we would leave the same undone; as in their actions that gave alms to purchase thereby the praise of men.

[2] Man in perfection of nature being made according to the likeness of his Maker, resembleth him also in the manner of working; so that whatsoever we work as men, the same we do wittingly work and freely; neither are we according to the manner of natural agents any way so tied 20 but that it is in our power to leave the things we do undone. The good which either is gotten by doing, or which consisteth in the very doing itself, causeth not action, unless apprehending it as good we so like and desire it: that we do unto any such end, the same we choose and prefer before the leaving of it undone. Choice there is not, unless the thing which we take be so in our power that we might have refused and left it. If fire consume the stubble, it chooseth not so to do, because the nature thereof is such that it can do no other. To choose is to will one thing before another. And to will is to bend our souls to the having or doing of that which they see to be good. Goodness is seen with the eye of the understanding. And the 30 light of that eye, is Reason. So that two principal fountains there are of human action: Knowledge and Will; which Will, in things tending towards any end, is termed Choice. Concerning Knowledge, "Behold," saith Moses, "I have set before you this day good and evil, life and death." Concerning Will, he addeth immediately, "Choose life"; that is to say, the things that tend unto life, them choose.

[3] But of one thing we must have special care, as being a matter of no small moment; and that is, how the Will, properly and strictly taken, as it is of things which are referred unto the end that man desireth, differeth greatly from that inferior natural desire which we call Appetite. 40 The object of Appetite is whatsoever sensible good may be wished for; the object of Will is that good which Reason doth lead us to seek. Affections, as joy, and grief, and fear, and anger, with such like, being as it

were the sundry fashions and forms of Appetite, can neither rise at the conceit of a thing indifferent, nor yet choose but rise at the sight of some things. Wherefore it is not altogether in our power whether we will be stirred with affections or no; whereas actions which issue from the disposition of the Will are in the power thereof to be performed or stayed. Finally, Appetite is the Will's solicitor, and the Will is Appetite's controller; what we covet according to the one by the other we often reject; neither is any other desire termed properly Will, but that where Reason and Understanding, or the show of Reason, prescribeth the thing desired.

It may be therefore a question, whether those operations of men are to be counted voluntary wherein that good which is sensible provoketh Appetite, and Appetite causeth action, Reason being never called to counsel; as when we eat or drink, and betake ourselves unto rest, and such like. The truth is, that such actions in men having attained to the use of Reason are voluntary. For as the authority of higher powers hath force even in those things which are done without their privity, and are of so mean reckoning that to acquaint them therewith it needeth not; in like sort, voluntarily we are said to do that also, which the Will if it listed might hinder from being done, although about the doing thereof we do not expressly use our Reason or understanding, and so immediately apply our Wills thereunto. In cases therefore of such facility, the Will doth yield her assent as it were with a kind of silence, by not dissenting; in which respect her force is not so apparent as in express mandates or prohibitions, especially upon advice and consultation going before.

[4] Where understanding therefore needeth, in those things Reason is the director of man's Will by discovering in action what is good. For the Laws of well-doing are the dictates of right Reason. Children, which are not as yet come unto those years whereat they may have; again, innocents, which are excluded by natural defect from ever having; thirdly, madmen, which for the present cannot possibly have the use of right Reason to guide themselves, have for their guide the Reason that guideth other men, which are tutors over them to seek and to procure their good for them. In the rest there is that light of Reason, whereby good may be known from evil, and which discovering the same rightly is termed right.

[5] The Will notwithstanding doth not incline to have or do that which Reason teacheth to be good, unless the same do also teach it to be possible. For albeit the Appetite, being more general, may wish any thing which seemeth good, be it never so impossible; yet for such things the reasonable Will of man doth never seek. Let Reason teach impossibility in any thing, and the Will of man doth let it go; a thing impossible it doth not affect, the impossibility thereof being manifest.

[6] There is in the Will of man naturally that freedom whereby it is

apt to take or refuse any particular object whatsoever being presented unto
it. Whereupon it followeth, that there is no particular object so good, but
it may have the shew of some difficulty or unpleasant quality annexed to
it, in respect whereof the Will may shrink and decline it; contrariwise
(for so things are blended) there is no particular evil which hath not some
appearance of goodness whereby to insinuate itself. For evil as evil cannot
be desired; if that be desired which is evil, the cause is the goodness which
is, or seemeth to be, joined with it. Goodness doth not move by being, but
by being apparent; and therefore many things are neglected which are
10 most precious, only because the value of them lieth hid. Sensible Goodness
is most apparent, near, and present; which causeth the Appetite to be
therewith strongly provoked. Now pursuit and refusal in the Will do follow, the one the affirmation the other the negation of goodness, which
the understanding apprehendeth, grounding itself upon sense, unless some
higher Reason do chance to teach the contrary. And if Reason have taught
it rightly to be good, yet not so apparently that the mind receiveth it with
utter impossibility of being otherwise, still there is place left for the Will
to take or leave. Whereas therefore amongst so many things as are to be
done, there are so few the goodness whereof Reason in such sort doth
20 or easily can discover, we are not to marvel at the choice of evil even
then when the contrary is probably known. Hereby it cometh to pass that
custom inuring the mind by long practice, and so leaving there a sensible
impression, prevaileth more than reasonable persuasion what way soever.
Reason therefore may rightly discern the thing which is good, and yet the
Will of man not incline itself thereunto, as oft as the prejudice of sensible
experience doth oversway.

[7] Nor let any man think that this doth make any thing for the just
excuse of iniquity. For there was never sin committed, wherein a less
good was not preferred before a greater, and that wilfully; which cannot
30 be done without the singular disgrace of Nature, and the utter disturbance
of that divine order whereby the preëminence of chiefest acceptation is
by the best things worthily challenged. There is not that good which concerneth us, but it hath evidence enough for itself, if Reason were diligent
to search it out. Through neglect thereof, abused we are with the show
of that which is not; sometimes the subtilty of Satan inveigling us as it
did Eve, sometimes the hastiness of our Wills preventing the more con-
siderate advice of sound Reason, as in the Apostles, when they no sooner
saw what they liked not, but they forthwith were desirous of fire from
heaven; sometimes the very custom of evil making the heart obdurate
40 against whatsoever instructions to the contrary, as in them over whom our
Saviour spake weeping, "O Jerusalem, how often, and thou wouldest

not!" Still therefore that wherewith we stand blameable, and can no way
excuse it, is, In doing evil, we prefer a less good before a greater, the
greatness whereof is by Reason investigable and may be known. The
search of knowledge is a thing painful; and the painfulness of knowledge
is that which maketh the Will so hardly inclinable thereunto. The root
hereof, divine malediction; whereby the instruments being weakened
wherewithal the soul (especially in reasoning) doth work, it preferreth
rest in ignorance before wearisome labour to know. For a spur of diligence,
therefore, we have a natural thirst after knowledge ingrafted in us. But
by reason of that original weakness in the instruments, without which the 10
understanding part is not able in this world by discourse to work, the very
conceit of painfulness is as a bridle to stay us. For which cause the Apostle,
who knew right well that the weariness of the flesh is an heavy clog to
the Will, striketh mightily upon this key, "Awake thou that sleepest; Cast
off all which presseth down; Watch; Labour; Strive to go forward, and
to grow in knowledge."

VIII. Wherefore to return to our former intent of discovering the
natural way whereby rules have been found out concerning that goodness
wherewith the Will of man ought to be moved in human actions; as every
thing naturally and necessarily doth desire the utmost good and greatest 20
perfection whereof Nature hath made it capable, even so man. Our felicity
therefore being the object and accomplishment of our desire, we cannot
choose but wish and covet it. All particular things which are subject unto
action, the Will doth so far forth incline unto as Reason judgeth them the
better for us, and consequently the more available to our bliss. If Reason
err, we fall into evil, and are so far forth deprived of the general perfection we seek. Seeing therefore that for the framing of men's actions the
knowledge of good from evil is necessary, it only resteth that we search
how this may be had. Neither must we suppose that there needeth one rule
to know the good and another the evil by. For he that knoweth what is 30
straight doth even thereby discern what is crooked, because the absence
of straightness in bodies capable thereof is crookedness. Goodness in actions is like unto straightness; wherefore that which is done well we term
"right." For as the straight way is most acceptable to him that travelleth,
because by it he cometh soonest to his journey's end; so in action, that
which doth lie the evenest between us and the end we desire must needs
be the fittest for our use. Besides which fitness for use, there is also in
rectitude, beauty; as contrariwise in obliquity, deformity. And that which
is good in the actions of men doth not only delight as profitable, but as
amiable also. In which consideration the Grecians most divinely have 40
given to the active perfection of men a name expressing both beauty and

goodness, because goodness in ordinary speech is for the most part applied only to that which is beneficial. But we in the name of goodness do here imply both.

[2] And of discerning goodness there are but these two ways: the one the knowledge of the causes whereby it is made such; the other the observation of those signs and tokens, which being annexed always unto goodness, argue that where they are found, there also goodness is, although we know not the cause by force whereof it is there. The former of these is the most sure and infallible way, but so hard that all shun it, and
10 had rather walk as men do in the dark by haphazard than tread so long and intricate mazes for knowledge' sake. As therefore physicians are many times forced to leave such methods of curing as themselves know to be the fittest, and being overruled by their patients' impatiency are fain to try the best they can, in taking that way of cure which the cured will yield unto; in like sort, considering how the case doth stand with this present age full of tongue and weak of brain, behold we yield to the stream thereof; into the causes of goodness we will not make any curious or deep inquiry; to touch them now and then it shall be sufficient, when they are so near at hand that easily they may be conceived without any far-removed
20 discourse. That way we are contented to prove, which being the worse in itself, is not withstanding now by reason of common imbecility the fitter and likelier to be brooked.

[3] Signs and tokens to know good by are of sundry kinds; some more certain and some less. The most certain token of evident goodness is, if the general persuasion of all men do so account it. And therefore a common received error is never utterly overthrown till such time as we go from signs unto causes, and shew some manifest root or fountain thereof common unto all, whereby it may clearly appear how it hath come to pass that so many have been overseen. In which case surmises and slight proba-
30 bilities will not serve, because the universal consent of men is the perfectest and strongest in this kind which comprehendeth only the signs and tokens of goodness. Things casual do vary, and that which a man doth but chance to think well of cannot still have the like hap. Wherefore, although we know not the cause, yet thus much we may know; that some necessary cause there is, whensoever the judgments of all men generally or for the most part run one and the same way, especially in matters of natural discourse. For of things necessarily and naturally done there is no more affirmed but this, "they keep either always or for the most part one tenure." The general and perpetual voice of men is as the sentence of God himself.
40 For that which all men have at all times learned, Nature herself must needs have taught; and God being the author of Nature, her voice is but his instrument. By her from Him we receive whatsoever in such sort we

learn. Infinite duties there are, the goodness whereof is by this rule suffi-ciently manifested, although we had no other warrant besides to approve them. The Apostle St. Paul having speech concerning the heathen saith of them, "They are a law unto themselves." His meaning is, that by force of the light of Reason, wherewith God illuminateth every one which cometh into the world, men being enabled to know truth from falsehood, and good from evil, do thereby learn in many things what the will of God is; which will himself not revealing by any extraordinary means unto them, but they by natural discourse attaining the knowledge thereof, seem the makers of those Laws which indeed are his, and they but only the finders of them out.

[4] A law, therefore, generally taken, is a directive rule unto goodness of operation. The rule of divine operations outward, is the definitive ap-pointment of God's own wisdom set down within himself. The rule of natural agents that work by simple necessity is the determination of the wisdom of God, known to God himself, the principal director of them, but not unto them that are directed to execute the same. The rule of natu-ral agents which work after a sort of their own accord, as the beasts do, is the judgment of common sense or fancy concerning the sensible good-ness of those objects wherewith they are moved. The rule of ghostly or immaterial natures, as spirits and angels, is their intuitive intellectual judg-ment concerning the amiable beauty and high goodness of that object, which with unspeakable joy and delight doth set them on work. The rule of voluntary agents on earth is the sentence that Reason giveth concern-ing the goodness of those things which they are to do. And the sentences which Reason giveth are some more, some less general, before it come to define in particular actions what is good.

[5] The main principles of Reason are in themselves apparent. For to make nothing evident of itself unto man's understanding were to take away all possibility of knowing any thing. And herein that of Theophrastus is true, "They that seek a reason of all things do utterly overthrow Rea-son." In every kind of knowledge some such grounds there are as that, being proposed, the mind doth presently embrace them as free from all possibility of error, clear and manifest without proof. In which kind axioms or principles more general are such as this, "that the greater good is to be chosen before the less." If therefore it should be demanded what reason there is, why the Will of man, which doth necessarily shun harm and covet whatsoever is pleasant and sweet, should be commanded to count the pleasures of sin gall, and notwithstanding the bitter accidents where-with virtuous actions are compassed, yet still to rejoice and delight in them: surely this could never stand with Reason, but that wisdom, thus prescrib-ing, groundeth her laws upon an infallible rule of comparison, which is,

that small difficulties, when exceeding great good is sure to ensue, and on
the other side momentany benefits, when the hurt which they draw after
them is unspeakable, are not at all to be respected. This rule is the ground
whereupon the wisdom of the Apostle buildeth a law, enjoining patience
unto himself: "The present lightness of our affliction worketh unto us
even with abundance upon abundance an eternal weight of glory; while
we look not on the things which are seen, but on the things which are not
seen. For the things which are seen are temporal, but the things which
are not seen are eternal"; therefore Christianity to be embraced, whatso-
10 ever calamities in those times it was accompanied withal. Upon the same
ground our Saviour proveth the law most reasonable that doth forbid
those crimes which men for gain's sake fall into. "For a man to win the
world if it be with the loss of his soul, what benefit or good is it?" Axioms
less general, yet so manifest that they need no further proof, are such as
these, "God to be worshipped"; "parents to be honoured"; "others to be
used by us as we ourselves would by them." Such things, as soon as they
are alleged. all men acknowledge to be good; they require no proof or
further discourse to be assured of their goodness.

Notwithstanding whatsoever such principle there is, it was at the first
20 found out by discourse, and drawn from out of the very bowels of heaven
and earth. For we are to note that things in the world are to us discernible,
not only so far forth as serveth for our vital preservation, but further also
in a twofold higher respect. For first, if all other uses were utterly taken
away, yet the mind of man being by nature speculative and delighted
with contemplation in itself, they were to be known even for mere knowledge and understanding's sake. Yea further besides this, the knowledge
of every the least thing in the whole world hath in it a second peculiar
benefit unto us, inasmuch as it serveth to minister rules, canons, and laws,
for men to direct those actions by, which we properly term human. This
30 did the very heathens themselves obscurely insinuate, by making Themis,
which we call *Jus*, or Right, to be the daughter of heaven and earth.

[6] We know things either as they are in themselves, or as they are in
mutual relation one to another. The knowledge of that which man is in
reference unto himself, and other things in relation unto man, I may justly
term the mother of all those principles which are as it were edicts, statutes,
and decrees, in that Law of Nature whereby human actions are framed.
First, therefore, having observed that the best things, where they are not
hindered, do still produce the best operations (for which cause, where
many things are to concur unto one effect, the best is in all congruity of
40 reason to guide the residue, that it prevailing most, the work principally
done by it may have greatest perfection); when hereupon we come to
observe in ourselves, of what excellency our souls are in comparison of

our bodies, and the diviner part in relation unto the baser of our souls; seeing that all these concur in producing human actions, it cannot be well unless the chiefest do command and direct the rest. The soul then ought to conduct the body, and the spirit of our minds the soul. This is therefore the first Law, whereby the highest power of the mind requireth general obedience at the hands of all the rest concurring with it unto action.

[7] Touching the several grand mandates which, being imposed by the understanding faculty of the mind, must be obeyed by the Will of man, they are by the same method found out, whether they import our duty towards God or towards man.   10

Touching the one, I may not here stand to open by what degrees of discourse the minds even of mere natural men have attained to know, not only that there is a God, but also what power, force, wisdom, and other properties that God hath, and how all things depend on him. This being therefore presupposed, from that known relation which God hath unto us as unto children, and unto all good things as unto effects whereof himself is the principal cause, these axioms and laws natural concerning our duty have arisen: "that in all things we go about his aid is by prayer to be craved"; "that he cannot have sufficient honour done unto him, but the utmost of that we can do to honour him we must"; which is in 20 effect the same that we read, "Thou shalt love the Lord thy God with all thy heart, with all thy soul, and with all thy mind," which Law our Saviour doth term the "first and the great commandment."

Touching the next, which as our Saviour addeth is "like unto this" (he meaneth in amplitude and largeness, inasmuch as it is the root out of which all Laws of duty to men-ward have grown, as out of the former all offices of religion towards God), the like natural inducement hath brought men to know that it is their duty no less to love others than themselves. For seeing those things which are equal must needs all have one measure, if I cannot but wish to receive all good, even as much at every man's hand 30 as any man can wish unto his own soul, how should I look to have any part of my desire herein satisfied, unless myself be careful to satisfy the like desire which is undoubtedly in other men, we all being of one and the same nature? To have any thing offered them repugnant to this desire must needs in all respects grieve them as much as me, so that if I do harm I must look to suffer; there being no reason that others should shew greater measure of love to me than they have by me shewed unto them. My desire therefore to be loved of my equals in nature as much as possible may be, imposeth upon me a natural duty of bearing to them-ward fully the like affection. From which relation of equality between ourselves and 40 them that are as ourselves, what several rules and canons natural Reason hath drawn for direction of life no man is ignorant; as namely, "That because we would take no harm, we must therefore do none"; "That sith we would not be in any thing extremely dealt with, we must ourselves avoid all extremity in our dealings"; "That from all violence and wrong we are utterly to abstain"; with such like; which further to wade in would be tedious, and to our present purpose not altogether so necessary, seeing that on these two general heads already mentioned all other specialities are dependent.

[8] Wherefore the natural measure whereby to judge our doings, is the sentence of Reason, determining and setting down what is good to be 10 done. Which sentence is either mandatory, shewing what must be done; or else permissive, declaring only what may be done; or thirdly admonitory, opening what is the most convenient for us to do. The first taketh place where the comparison doth stand altogether between doing and not doing of one thing which in itself is absolutely good or evil; as it had been for Joseph to yield or not to yield to the impotent desire of his lewd mistress, the one evil, the other good simply. The second is when, of divers things evil, all being not evitable, we are permitted to take one; which one, saving only in case of so great urgency, were not otherwise to be taken; as in the matter of divorce amongst the Jews. The last when, of divers 20 things good, one is principal and most eminent; as in their act who sold their possessions and laid the price at the Apostles' feet, which possessions they might have retained unto themselves without sin. Again, in the Apostle St. Paul's own choice to maintain himself by his own labour; whereas in living by the Church's maintenance, as others did, there had been no offence committed. In Goodness, therefore, there is a latitude or extent, whereby it cometh to pass that even of good actions some are better than other some; whereas otherwise one man could not excel another, but all should be either absolutely good, as hitting jump that indivisible point or centre wherein goodness consisteth; or else, missing it, they 30 should be excluded out of the number of well-doers. Degrees of well-doing there could be none, except perhaps in the seldomness and oftenness of doing well. But the nature of Goodness being thus ample, a Law is properly that which Reason in such sort defineth to be good that it must be done. And the Law of Reason or human nature is that which men by discourse of natural Reason have rightly found out themselves to be all for ever bound unto in their actions.

[9] Laws of Reason have these marks to be known by. Such as keep them resemble most lively in their voluntary actions that very manner of working which Nature herself doth necessarily observe in the course 40 of the whole world. The works of Nature are all behooveful, beautiful, without superfluity or defect; even so theirs, if they be framed according to that which the Law of Reason teacheth. Secondly those Laws are in-

vestigable by Reason, without the help of Revelation supernatural and divine. Finally, in such sort they are investigable, that the knowledge of them is general, the world hath always been acquainted with them; according to that which one in Sophocles observeth concerning a branch of this Law, "It is no child of to-day's or yesterday's birth, but hath been no man knoweth how long sithence." It is not agreed upon by one, or two, or few, but by all. Which we may not so understand, as if every particular man in the whole world did know and confess whatsoever the Law of Reason doth contain; but this Law is such that, being proposed, no man can reject it as unreasonable and unjust. Again, there is nothing in it but any man (having natural perfection of wit and ripeness of judgment) may by labour and travail find out. And to conclude, the general principles thereof are such, as it is not easy to find men ignorant of them. Law rational therefore, which men commonly use to call the Law of Nature, meaning thereby the Law which human Nature knoweth itself in reason universally bound unto, which also for that cause may be termed most fitly the Law of Reason: this Law, I say, comprehendeth all those things which men by the light of their natural understanding evidently know, or at leastwise may know, to be beseeming or unbeseeming, virtuous or vicious, good or evil for them to do.

[10] Now although it be true, which some have said, that "whatsoever is done amiss, the Law of Nature and Reason thereby is transgressed," because even those offences which are by their special qualities breaches of supernatural laws do also, for that they are generally evil, violate in general that principle of Reason which willeth universally to fly from evil; yet do we not therefore so far extend the Law of Reason as to contain in it all manner laws whereunto reasonable creatures are bound, but (as hath been shewed) we restrain it to those only duties which all men by force of natural wit either do or might understand to be such duties as concern all men. "Certain half-waking men there are" (as Saint Augustine noteth), "who neither altogether asleep in folly, nor yet throughly awake in the light of true understanding, have thought that there is not at all any thing just and righteous in itself; but look wherewith nations are inured, the same they take to be right and just. Whereupon their conclusion is, that seeing each sort of people hath a different kind of right from other, and that which is right of its own nature must be everywhere one and the same, therefore in itself there is nothing right. These good folk," saith he, "(that I may not trouble their wits with rehearsal of too many things) have not looked so far into the world as to perceive that 'Do as thou wouldest be done unto' is a sentence which all nations under heaven are agreed upon. Refer this sentence to the love of God, and it extinguisheth all heinous crimes; refer it to the love of

thy neighbour, and all grievous wrongs it banisheth out of the world."
Wherefore as touching the Law of Reason, this was (it seemeth) Saint
Augustine's judgment: namely, that there are in it some things which
stand as principles universally agreed upon; and that out of those principles, which are in themselves evident, the greatest moral duties we owe
towards God or man may without any great difficulty be concluded.

[11] If then it be here demanded, by what means it should come to
pass (the greatest part of the Law moral being so easy for all men to know)
that so many thousands of men notwithstanding have been ignorant even
10 of principal moral duties, not imagining the breach of them to be sin: I
deny not but lewd and wicked custom, beginning perhaps at the first
amongst few, afterwards spreading into greater multitudes, and so continuing from time to time, may be of force even in plain things to smother
the light of natural understanding; because men will not bend their wits
to examine whether things wherewith they have been accustomed be
good or evil. For example's sake, that grosser kind of heathenish idolatry,
whereby they worshipped the very works of their own hands, was an
absurdity to Reason so palpable, that the Prophet David, comparing idols
and idolaters together, maketh almost no odds between them, but the one
20 in a manner as much without wit and sense as the other. "They that
make them are like unto them, and so are all that trust in them." That
wherein an idolater doth seem so absurd and foolish is by the Wise Man
thus exprest, "He is not ashamed to speak unto that which hath no life;
he calleth on him that is weak for health; he prayeth for life unto him
which is dead; of him which hath no experience he requireth help; for
his journey he sueth to him which is not able to go; for gain and work and
success in his affairs he seeketh furtherance of him that hath no manner of
power." The cause of which senseless stupidity is afterwards imputed to
custom. "When a father mourned grievously for his son that was taken
30 away suddenly, he made an image for him that was once dead, whom
now he worshippeth as a god, ordaining to his servants ceremonies and
sacrifices. Thus by process of time this wicked custom prevailed, and was
kept as a law"; the authority of rulers, the ambition of craftsmen, and
such like means thrusting forward the ignorant, and increasing their
superstition.

Unto this which the Wise Man hath spoken somewhat besides may be
added. For whatsoever we have hitherto taught, or shall hereafter, concerning the force of man's natural understanding, this we always desire
withal to be understood: that there is no kind of faculty or power in man
40 or any other creature which can rightly perform the functions allotted to
it, without perpetual aid and concurrence of that Supreme Cause of all
things. The benefit whereof as oft as we cause God in his justice to with-

draw, there can no other thing follow than that which the Apostle noteth, even men endued with the light of reason to walk notwithstanding "in the vanity of their mind, having their cogitations darkened, and being strangers from the life of God through the ignorance which is in them, because of the hardness of their hearts." And this cause is mentioned by the prophet Esay, speaking of the ignorance of idolaters, who see not how the manifest Law of Reason condemneth their gross iniquity and sin. "They have not in them," saith he, "so much wit as to think, 'Shall I bow to the stock of a tree?' All knowledge and understanding is taken from them; for God hath shut their eyes that they cannot see." 10

That which we say in this case of idolatry serveth for all other things wherein the like kind of general blindness hath prevailed against the manifest Laws of Reason. Within the compass of which laws we do not only comprehend whatsoever may be easily known to belong to the duty of all men, but even whatsoever may possibly be known to be of that quality, so that the same be by necessary consequence deduced out of clear and manifest principles. For if once we descend unto probable collections what is convenient for men, we are then in the territory where free and arbitrary determinations, the territory where human laws take place; which laws are after to be considered. 20

IX. Now the due observation of this law which reason teacheth us, cannot but be effectual unto their great good that observe the same. For we see the whole world and each part thereof so compacted that as long as each thing performeth only that work which is natural unto it, it thereby preserveth both other things, and also itself. Contrariwise, let any principal thing, as the Sun, the Moon, any one of the heavens or elements, but once cease or fail, or swerve, and who doth not easily conceive that the sequel thereof would be ruin both to itself and whatsoever dependeth on it? And is it possible that man, being not only the noblest creature in the world but even a very world in himself, his transgressing the law of his 30 nature should draw no manner of harm after it? Yes, "tribulation and anguish unto every soul that doth evil." Good doth follow unto all things by observing the course of their nature, and on the contrary side, evil by not observing it; but not unto natural agents that good which we call "Reward," not that evil which we properly term "Punishment." The reason whereof is, because amongst creatures in this world, only man's observation of the law of his nature is "Righteousness," only man's transgression "Sin." And the reason of this is the difference in his manner of observing or transgressing the law of his nature. He doth not otherwise than voluntarily the one or the other. What we do against our wills, or 40 constrainedly, we are not properly said to do it; because the motive cause of doing it is not in ourselves, but carrieth us as if the wind should drive

a feather in the air, we no whit furthering that whereby we are driven. In such cases, therefore, the evil which is done moveth compassion; men are pitied for it, as being rather miserable in such respect than culpable. Some things are likewise done by man, though not through outward force and impulsion, though not against, yet without their wills; as in aliena- tion of mind, or any the like inevitable utter absence of wit and judgment. For which cause, no man did ever think the hurtful actions of furious men and innocents to be punishable. Again, some things we do neither against nor without, and yet not simply and merely with our wills, but with our
10 wills in such sort moved that, albeit there be no impossibility but that we might, nevertheless we are not so easily able to do otherwise. In this con- sideration one evil deed is made more pardonable than another. Finally, that which we do being evil, is notwithstanding by so much more pardon- able, by how much the exigence of so doing, or the difficulty of doing otherwise, is greater; unless this necessity or difficulty have originally risen from ourselves. It is no excuse therefore unto him who, being drunk, committeth incest, and allegeth that his wits were not his own, in as much as himself might have chosen whether his wits should by that mean have been taken from him. Now rewards and punishments do always presuppose
20 some thing willingly done well or ill; without which respect, though we may sometimes receive good or harm, yet then the one is only a benefit, and not a reward; the other simply an hurt, not a punishment. From the sundry dispositions of man's will, which is the root of all his actions, there groweth variety in the sequel of rewards and punishments, which are by these and the like rules measured: "Take away the will, and all acts are equal. That which we do not, and would do, is commonly accepted as done." By these and the like rules men's actions are determined of and judged, whether they be in their own nature rewardable or punishable.

[2] Rewards and punishments are not received but at the hands of
30 such as being above us, have power to examine and judge our deeds. How men have come to have this authority one over another in external ac- tions we shall more diligently examine in that which followeth. But for this present, so much all do acknowledge, that since every man's heart and conscience doth in good or evil, even secretly committed and known to none but itself, either like or disallow itself, and accordingly either re- joice—very nature exulting (as it were) in certain hope of reward—, or else grieve (as it were) in a sense of future punishment, neither of which can in this case be looked for from any other saving only from Him who discerneth and judgeth the very secrets of all hearts; therefore He is the
40 only rewarder and revenger of all such actions, although not of such actions only, but of all whereby the law of nature is broken, whereof Him- self is author. For which cause the Roman laws called the Laws of the

Twelve Tables, requiring offices of inward affection which the eye of man cannot reach unto, threaten the neglecters of them with none but divine punishment.

*   *   *   *   *

THE BIBLE

The Introduction and Notes are at page 1339

FROM *The Holy Bible . . . Newly Translated,* 1611 [the King James Version]

The Translators to the Reader

ZEAL to promote the common good, whether it be by devising anything ourselves, or revising that which hath been laboured by others, deserveth certainly much respect and esteem, but yet findeth but cold entertainment in the world. It is welcomed with suspicion instead of love, and with emulation instead of thanks: and if there be any hole left for cavil to 20 enter (and cavil, if it do not find a hole, will make one), it is sure to be misconstrued, and in danger to be condemned. This will easily be granted by as many as know story, or have any experience. For, was there ever anything projected, that savoured any way of newness or renewing, but the same endured many a storm of gainsaying, or opposition? A man would think that Civility, wholesome Laws, learning and eloquence, Synods, and Church-maintenance (that we speak of no more things of this kind), should be as safe as a Sanctuary, and out of shot, as they say, that no man would lift up the heel, no, nor dog move his tongue against the motioners of them. For by the first, we are distinguished from brute- 30 breasts led with sensuality: By the second, we are bridled and restrained from outrageous behaviour, and from doing of injuries, whether by fraud or by violence: By the third, we are enabled to inform and reform others, by the light and feeling that we have attained unto ourselves: Briefly, by the fourth being brought together to a parle face to face, we sooner compose our differences than by writings, which are endless: And lastly, that the Church be sufficiently provided for, is so agreeable to good reason and conscience, that those mothers are holden to be less cruel, that kill their children as soon as they are born, than those nursing fathers and mothers (wheresoever they be) that withdraw from them who hang upon their 40 breasts (and upon whose breasts again themselves do hang to receive the Spiritual and sincere milk of the word) livelihood and support fit for their estates. Thus it is apparent, that these things which we speak of, are of most necessary use, and therefore, that none, either without absurdity can speak against them, or without note of wickedness can spurn against them.

Yet for all that, the learned know that certain worthy men have been brought to untimely death for none other fault, but for seeking to reduce their Countrymen to good order and discipline: and that in some Commonweals it was made a capital crime, once to motion the making of a new Law for the abrogating of an old, though the same were most perni-
10 cious: And that certain, which would be counted pillars of the State, and paterns of Virtue and Prudence, could not be brought for a long time to give way to good Letters and refined speech, but bare themselves as averse from them, as from rocks or boxes of poison: And fourthly, that he was no babe, but a great clerk, that gave forth (and in writing to remain to posterity) in passion peradventure, but yet he gave forth, that he had not seen any profit to come by any Synod, or meeting of the Clergy, but rather the contrary: And lastly, against Church-maintenance and allowance, in such sort, as the Embassadors and messengers of the great King of Kings should be furnished, it is not unknown what a fiction or fable (so it is
20 esteemed, and for no better by the reporter himself, though superstitious) was devised; Namely, that at such time as the professors and teachers of Christianity in the Church of Rome, then a true Church, were liberally endowed, a voice forsooth was heard from heaven, saying; Now is poison poured down into the Church, &c. Thus not only as oft as we speak, as one saith, but also as oft as we do anything of note or consequence, we subject ourselves to everyone's censure, and happy is he that is least tossed upon tongues; for utterly to escape the snatch of them it is impossible. If any man conceit that this is the lot and portion of the meaner sort only, and that Princes are privileged by their high estate, he is deceived.

30   *   *   *   *   *

This, and more to this purpose, His Majesty that now reigneth (and long, and long may he reign, and his offspring forever, *Himself and children, and children's children always*) knew full well, according to the singular wisdom given unto him by God, and the rare learning and experience that he hath attained unto; namely that whosoever attempteth anything for the public (specially if it pertain to Religion, and to the opening and clearing of the word of God) the same setteth himself upon a stage to be glouted upon by every evil eye, yea, he casteth himself headlong upon
40 pikes, to be gored by every sharp tongue. For he that medleth with men's Religion in any part, medleth with their custom, nay, with their freehold; and though they find no content in that which they have, yet they cannot

abide to hear of altering. Notwithstanding his Royal heart was not daunted or discouraged for this or that colour, but stood resolute, *as a statue immoveable, and an anvil not easy to be beaten into plates,* as one saith; he knew who had chosen him to be a Soldier, or rather a Captain, and being assured that the course which he intended made much for the glory of God, and the building up of his Church, he would not suffer it to be broken off for whatsoever speeches or practises. It doth certainly belong unto Kings, yea, it doth specially belong unto them, to have care of Religion, yea, to know it aright, yea, to profess it zealously, yea to promote it to the uttermost of their power. This is their glory before all nations which mean 10 well, and this will bring unto them a far most excellent weight of glory in the day of the Lord Jesus. For the Scripture saith not in vain, *Them that honor me, I will honor,* neither was it a vain word that *Eusebius* delivered long ago, that piety towards God was the weapon, and the only weapon that both preserved *Constantine's* person, and avenged him of his enemies.

But now what piety without truth? what truth (what saving truth) without the word of God? what word of God (whereof we may be sure) without the Scripture?

* * * * * 20

But how shall men meditate in that, which they cannot understand? How shall they understand that which is kept close in an unknown tongue? . . . Translation it is that openeth the window, to let in the light; that breaketh the shell, that we may eat the kernel; that putteth aside the curtain, that we may look into the most Holy place; that removeth the cover of the well, that we may come by the water, even as *Jacob* rolled away the stone from the mouth of the well, by which means the flocks of *Laban* were watered. Indeed without translation into the vulgar tongue, the unlearned are but like children at *Jacob's* well (which was deep) without a 30 bucket or some thing to draw with: or as that person mentioned by *Esay,* to whom when a sealed book was delivered, with this motion, *Read this, I pray thee,* he was fain to make this answer, *I cannot, for it is sealed.*

While God would be known only in *Jacob,* and have his Name great in *Israel,* and in none other place, while the dew lay on *Gideon's* fleece only, and all the earth besides was dry; then for one and the same people, which spake all of them the language of *Canaan,* that is, *Hebrew,* one and the same original in *Hebrew* was sufficient. But when the fulness of time drew near, that the Sun of righteousness, the Son of God should come into the world, whom God ordained to be a reconciliation through faith in his 40 blood, not of the *Jew* only, but also of the *Greek,* yea, of all them that were scattered abroad; then lo, it pleased the Lord to stir up the spirit of a *Greek*

Prince (*Greek* for descent and language) even of *Ptolome Philadelph* King of *Egypt*, to procure the translating of the Book of God out of *Hebrew* into *Greek*. This is the translation of the *Seventy* Interpreters, commonly so called, which prepared the way for our Saviour among the Gentiles by written preaching, as Saint *John* Baptist did among the *Jews* by vocal. For the *Grecians* being desirous of learning, were not wont to suffer books of worth to lie moulding in Kings' Libraries, but had many of their servants, ready scribes, to copy them out, and so they were dispersed and made common. Again, the *Greek* tongue was well known and 10 made familiar to most inhabitants in *Asia*, by reason of the conquest that there the *Grecians* had made, as also by the Colonies, which thither they had sent. For the same causes also it was well understood in many places of *Europe*, yea, and of *Affrike*, too. Therefore the word of God being set forth in *Greek*, becometh hereby like a candle set upon a candelstick, which giveth light to all that are in the house, or like a proclamation sounded forth in the market place, which most men presently take knowledge of; and therefore that language was fittest to contain the Scriptures, both for the first Preachers of the Gospel to appeal unto for witness, and for the learners also of those times to make search and trial by. It is cer- 20 tain, that that Translation was not so sound and so perfect, but that it needed in many places correction; and who had been so sufficient for this work as the Apostles or Apostolike men? Yet it seemed good to the holy Ghost and to them, to take that which they found, (the same being for the greatest part true and sufficient) rather than by making a new, in that new world and green age of the Church, to expose themselves to many exceptions and cavilations, as though they made a Translation to serve their own turn, and therefore bearing witness to themselves, their witness not to be regarded. This may be supposed to be some cause, why the Translation of the *Seventy* was allowed to pass for current. Notwithstanding, though 30 it was commended generally, yet it did not fully content the learned, no not of the *Jews*. For not long after *Christ*, *Aquila* fell in hand with a new Translation, and after him *Theodotion*, and after him *Symmachus*: yea, there was a fift and sixt edition, the Authours whereof were not known. These with the *Seventy* made up the *Hexapla*, and were worthily and to great purpose compiled together by *Origen*. Howbeit the Edition of the *Seventy* went away with the credit, and therefore not only was placed in the midst by *Origen* (for the worth and excellency thereof above the rest, as Epiphanius gathered) but also was used by the *Greek* fathers for the ground and foundation of their Commentaries. Yea, *Epiphanius* above 40 named doth attribute so much unto it, that he holdeth the Authors thereof not only for Interpreters, but also for Prophets in some respect: and *Justinian* the Emperour enjoining the *Jews* his subjects to use specially the Translation of the *Seventy*, rendreth this reason thereof, because they were as it were enlightened with prophetical grace. Yet for all that, as the *Egyptians* are said of the Prophet to be men and not God, and their horses flesh and not spirit: so it is evident (and Saint *Hierome* affirmeth as much) that the *Seventy* were Interpreters, they were not Prophets; they did many things well, as learned men; but yet as men they stumbled and fell, one while through oversight, another while through ignorance, yea, sometimes they may be noted to add to the Original, and sometimes to take from it; which made the Apostles to leave them many times, when they left the *Hebrew*, and to deliver the sence thereof according to the truth of the word, as the spirit gave them utterance. This may suffice touching the *Greek* Translations of the old Testament.

There were also within a few hundreth years after CHRIST, translations many into the Latin tongue: for this tongue also was very fit to convey the Law and the Gospel by, because in those times very many Countries of the West, yea of the South, East and North, spake or understood Latin, being made Provinces to the *Romanes*. But now the Latin Translations were too many to be all good, for they were infinite (*Latini Interpretes nullo modo numerari possunt*, saith S. *Augustine*.) Again they were not out of the *Hebrew* fountain (we speak of the *Latin* Translations of the Old Testament) but out of the *Greek* stream, therefore the *Greek* being not altogether clear, the *Latin* derived from it must needs be muddie. This moved S. *Hierome* a most learned father, and the best linguist without controversy, of his age, or of any that went before him, to undertake the translating of the Old Testament, out of the very fountains themselves; which he performed with that evidence of great learning, judgment, industry and faithfulness, that he hath forever bound the Church unto him, in a debt of special remembrance and thankfulness.

Now though the Church were thus furnished with *Greek* and *Latin* Translations, even before the faith of CHRIST was generally embraced in the Empire: (for the learned know that even in S. *Hierom's* time, the Consul of *Rome* and his wife were both Ethnicks, and about the same time the greatest part of the Senate also) yet for all that the godly-learned were not content to have the Scriptures in the Language which themselves understood, *Greek* and *Latin*, (as the good Lepers were not content to fare well themselves, but acquainted their neighbours with the store that God had sent, that they also might provide for themselves) but also for the behoof and edifying of the unlearned which hungred and thirsted after Righteousness, and had souls to be saved as well as they, they provided Translations into the vulgar for their Countrymen, insomuch that most nations under heaven did shortly after their conversion, hear CHRIST speaking unto them in their mother tongue, not by the voice of their Minister only, but also by the written word translated. If any doubt hereof, he may be satisfied by examples enough, if enough will serve the turn.

*   *   *   *   *

Now the Church of Rome would seem at the length to bear a motherly affection towards her children, and to allow them the Scriptures in their mother tongue: but indeed it is a gift, not deserving to be called a gift, an unprofitable gift: they must first get a Licence in writing before they may use them, and to get that, they must approve themselves to their Confessor, that is, to be such as are, if not frozen in the dregs, yet soured with the leaven of their superstition. Howbeit, it seemed too much to *Clement the 8.* that there should be any Licence granted to have them in the vulgar tongue, and therefore he overruleth and frustrateth the grant of *Pius* the fourth. So much are they afraid of the light of the Scripture, (*Lucifugae Scripturarum*, as *Tertullian* speaketh) that they will not trust the people with it, no not as it is set forth by their own sworn men, no not with the License of their own Bishops and Inquisitors. Yea, so unwilling they are to communicate the Scriptures to the people's understanding in any sort, that they are not ashamed to confess, that we forced them to translate it into English against their wills. This seemeth to argue a bad cause, or a bad conscience, or both. Sure we are, that it is not he that hath good gold, that is afraid to bring it to the touch-stone, but he that hath the counterfeit; neither is it the true man that shunneth the light, but the malefactour, lest his deeds should be reproved: neither is it the plain dealing merchant that is unwilling to have the weights, or the meteyard brought in place, but he that useth deceit. But we will let them alone for this fault, and return to translation.

*   *   *   *   *

. . . . How many books of profane learning have been gone over again and again, by the same translators, by others? Of one and the same book of Aristotle's Ethikes, there are extant not so few as six or seven several translations. Now if this cost may be bestowed upon the goord, which affordeth us a little shade, and which today flourisheth, but tomorrow is cut down; what may we bestow, nay what ought we not to bestow upon the Vine, the fruit whereof maketh glad the conscience of man, and the stem whereof abideth forever? And this is the word of God, which we translate. *What is the chaff to the wheat, saith the Lord? Tanti vitreum, quanti verum margaritum* (saith *Tertullian*,) if a toy of glass be of that reckoning with us, how ought we to value the true pearl? Therefore let no man's eye be evil, because his Majesty's is good; neither let any be grieved, that we have a Prince that seeketh the increase of the spiritual wealth of Israel (let *Sanballats* and *Tobiahs* do so, which therefore do bear their just reproof) but let us rather bless God from the ground of our heart, for working this religious care in him, to have the translations of the Bible maturely considered of and examined. For by this means it cometh to pass, that whatsoever is sound already (and all is sound for substance, in one or other of our editions, and the worst of ours far better than their authentic vulgar) the same will shine as gold more brightly, being rubbed and polished; also, if anything be halting, or superfluous, or not so agreeable to the original, the same may be corrected, and the truth set in place. And what can the King command to be done, that will bring him more true honour than this? and wherein could they that have been set a work, approve their duty to the King, yea their obedience to God, and love to his Saints more, than by yielding their service, and all that is within them, for the furnishing of the work? But besides all this, they were the principal motives of it, and therefore ought least to quarel it: for the very Historical truth is, that upon the importunate petitions of the Puritans, at his Majesty's coming to this Crown, the Conference at Hampton Court having been appointed for hearing their complaints: when by force of reason they were put from all other grounds, they had recourse at the last, to this shift, that they could not with good conscience subscribe to the Communion book, since it maintained the Bible as it was there translated, which was as they said, a most corrupted translation. And although this was judged to be but a very poor and empty shift; yet even hereupon did his Majesty begin to bethink himself of the good that might ensue by a new translation, and presently after gave order for this Translation which is now presented unto thee. Thus much to satisfy our scrupulous Brethren.

Now to the later we answer; that we do not deny, nay we affirm and avow, that the very meanest translation of the Bible in English, set forth by men of our profession (for we have seen none of theirs of the whole Bible as yet) containeth the word of God, nay, is the word of God. As the King's Speech which he uttered in Parliament, being translated in *French*, *Dutch*, *Italian* and *Latin*, is still the King's speech, though it be not interpreted by every Translator with the like grace, nor peradventure so fitly for phrase, nor so expressly for sense, everywhere. For it is confessed, that things are to take their denomination of the greater part; and a natural man could say, *Verùm ubi multa nitent in carmine, non ego paucis offendor maculis, &c.* A man may be counted a virtuous man, though he have made many slips in his life (else, there were none virtuous, for *in many things we offend all*), also a comely man and lovely, though he have some warts upon his hand, yea, not only freckles upon his face, but also scars. No cause therefore why the word translated should be denied to be the word, or forbidden to be current, not withstanding that some imperfections and blemishes may be noted in the setting forth of it. For whatever was perfect under the Sun, where Apostles or Apostle-like men, that is, men imbued with an extraordinary measure of God's spirit, and privileged with the privilege of infallibility, had not their hand? The Romanists therefore in refusing to hear, and daring to burn the Word translated, did no less than despite the spirit of grace, from whom originally it proceeded, and whose sense and meaning, as well as man's 10 weakness would enable, it did express.

* * * * *

Yet before we end, we must answer a third cavil and objection of theirs against us, for altering and amending our Translations so oft; wherein truly they deal hardly, and strangely with us. For to whom ever was it imputed for a fault (by such as were wise) to go over that which he had done, and to amend it where he saw cause? Saint *Augustine* was not afraid to exhort S. *Hierome* to a *Palinodia* or recantation; the same S. *Augustine* was not ashamed to retractate, we might say revoke, many things that 20 had passed him, and doth even glory that he seeth his infirmities. If we will be sons of the Truth, we must consider what it speaketh, and trample upon our own credit, yea, and upon other men's too, if either be any way an hinderance to it. This to the cause: then to the persons we say, that of all men they ought to be most silent in this case. For what varieties have they, and what alterations have they made, not only of their Service books, Portesses, and Breviaries, but also of their *Latin* Translation?

* * * * *

But it is high time to leave them, and to shew in brief what we proposed 30 to ourselves, and what course we held in this our perusal and survey of the Bible. Truly (good Christian Reader) we never thought from the beginning, that we should need to make a new Translation, nor yet to make of a bad one a good one (for then the imputation of *Sixtus* had been true in some sort, that our people had been fed with gall of Dragons instead of wine, with whey instead of milk); but to make a good one better, or out of many good ones, one principal good one, not justly to be excepted against; that hath been our endeavour, that our mark. To that purpose there were many chosen, that were greater in other mens' eyes than in their own, and that sought the truth rather than their own praise. . 40 In this confidence, and with this devotion did they assemble together; not too many, lest one should trouble another; and yet many, lest many things haply might escape them. If you ask what they had before them, truly it was the *Hebrew* text of the Old Testament, the Greek of the New. These are two golden pipes, or rather conduits, where-through the olive branches empty themselves into the gold. Saint *Augustine* calleth them precedent, or original tongues; Saint *Hierome*, fountains. The same Saint *Hierome* affirmeth, and *Gratian* hath not spared to put it into his Decree, That *as the credit of the old Books* (he meaneth of the Old Testament) *is to be tried by the Hebrew Volumes, so of the New by the Greek tongue,* he meaneth by the original *Greek.* If truth be to be tried by these tongues, then whence should a Translation be made, but out of them? These tongues therefore, the Scriptures we say in those tongues, we set 10 before us to translate, being the tongues wherein God was pleased to speak to his Church by his Prophets and Apostles. Neither did we run over the work with that posting haste that the *Septuagint* did, if that be true which is reported of them, that they finished it in 72 days; neither were we barred or hindered from going over it again, having once done it, like S. *Hierome,* if that be true which himself reporteth, that he could no sooner write anything, but presently it was caught from him, and published, and he could not have leave to mend it: neither, to be short, were we the first that fell in hand with translating the Scripture into English, and consequently destitute of former helps, as it is written of *Origen,* that he was the first 20 in a manner, that put his hand to write Commentaries upon the Scriptures, and therefore no marvel, if he overshot himself many times. None of these things: the work hath not been huddled up in 72 days, but hath cost the workmen, as light as it seemeth, the pains of twice seven times seventy-two days and more: matters of such weight and consequence are to be speeded with maturity: for in a business of moment a man feareth not the blame of convenient slackness. Neither did we think much to consult the Translators or Commentators, *Chaldee, Hebrew, Syrian, Greek, or Latin,* or nor the *Spanish, French, Italian,* or *Dutch;* neither did we disdain to revise that which we had done, and to bring back to the anvil that which 30 we had hammered: but having and using as great helps as were needful, and fearing no reproach for slowness, nor coveting praise for expedition, we have at the length, through the good hand of the Lord upon us, brought the work to that pass that you see.

Some peradventure would have no variety of senses to be set in the margin, lest the authority of the Scriptures for deciding of controversies by that shew of uncertainty, should somewhat be shaken. But we hold their judgment not to be so sound in this point. For though, *whatsoever things are necessary are manifest,* as S. *Chrysostome* saith, and as S. *Augustine, In those things that are plainly set down in the Scriptures,* 40 *all such matters are found that concern Faith, hope, and Charity.* Yet for all that it cannot be dissembled, that partly to exercise and whet our wits, partly to wean the curious from loathing of them for their every-where-plainness, partly also to stir up our devotion to crave the assistance of God's spirit by prayer, and lastly, that we might be forward to seek aid of our brethren by conference, and never scorn those that be not in all respects so complete as they should be, being to seek in many things our-selves, it hath pleased God in his divine providence, here and there to scatter words and sentences of that difficulty and doubtfulness, not in doctrinal points that concern salvation (for in such it hath been vouched that the Scriptures are plain), but in matters of less moment, that fear-fulness would better beseem us than confidence, and if we will resolve, to resolve upon modesty with S. *Augustine*, (though not in this same case altogether, yet upon the same ground) *Melius est dubitare de occultis, quàm litigare de incertis*, it is better to make doubt of those things which are secret, than to strive about those things that are uncertain. There be many words in the Scriptures, which be never found there but once (hav-ing neither brother nor neighbour, as the *Hebrews* speak) so that we cannot be holpen by conferences of places. Again, there be many rare names of certain birds, beasts and precious stones, &c. concerning which the *Hebrews* themselves are so divided among themselves for judgment, that they may seem to have defined this or that, rather because they would say something, than because they were sure of that which they said, as S. *Hierome* somewhere saith of the *Septuagint*. Now in such a case, doth not a margin do well to admonish the Reader to seek further, and not to conclude or dogmatize upon this or that peremptorily? For as it is a fault of incredulity, to doubt of those things that are evident: so to determine of such things as the Spirit of God hath left (even in the judgment of the judicious) questionable, can be no less than presumption. Therefore as S. *Augustine* saith, that variety of Translations is profitable for the finding out of the sense of the Scriptures: so diversity of signification and sense in the margin, where the text is not so clear, must needs do good, yea, is necessary, as we are persuaded. We know that *Sixtus Quintus* expressly forbiddeth, that any variety of readings of their vulgar edition, should be put in the margin (which though it be not altogether the same thing to that we have in hand, yet it looketh that way), but we think he hath not all of his own side his favourers, for this conceit. They that are wise, had rather have their judgments at liberty in differences of readings, than to be captivated to one, when it may be the other. If they were sure that their high Priest had all laws shut up in his breast, as *Paul* the second bragged, and that he were as free from errour by special privilege, as the Dictators of *Rome* were made by law inviolable, it were another matter; then his word were an Oracle, his opinion a decision. But the eyes of the world are now open, God be thanked, and have been a great while, they find that he is subject to the same affections and infirmities that others be, that his skin is penetrable, and therefore so much as he proveth, not as much as he claimeth, they grant and embrace.

Another thing we think good to admonish thee of (gentle Reader) that we have not tied ourselves to an uniformity of phrasing or to an identity of words, as some peradventure would wish that we had done, because they observe, that some learned men somewhere, have been as exact as they could that way. Truly, that we might not vary from the sense of that which we had translated before, if the word signified the same thing in both places (for there be some words that be not of the same 10 sense everywhere) we were especially careful, and made a conscience, according to our duty. But, that we should express the same notion in the same particular word; as for example, if we translate the *Hebrew* or *Greek* word once by *Purpose*, never to call it *Intent*; if one where *Journeying*, never *Traveiling*; if one where *Think*, never *Suppose*; if one where *Pain*, never *Ache*; if one where *Joy*, never *Gladness*, &c. Thus to mince the matter, we thought to savour more of curiosity than wisdom, and that rather it would breed scorn in the Atheist, than bring profit to the godly Reader. For is the kingdom of God become words or syllables? why should we be in bondage to them if we may be free, use one precisely 20 when we may use another no less fit, as commodiously? A godly Father in the Primitive time shewed himself greatly moved, that one of newfangleness called κράββατον, σκίμπους, though the difference be little or none; and another reporteth, that he was much abused for turning *Cucurbita* (to which reading the people had been used) into *Hedera*. Now if this happen in better times, and upon so small occasions, we might justly fear hard censure, if generally we should make verbal and unnecessary changings. We might also be charged (by scoffers) with some unequal dealing towards a great number of good English words. For as it is written of a certain great Philosopher, that he should say, that those logs were happy 30 that were made images to be worshipped; for their fellows, as good as they, lay for blocks behind the fire: so if we should say, as it were, unto certain words, Stand up higher, have a place in the Bible always, and to others of like quality, Get ye hence, be banished forever, we might be taxed peradventure with S. *James* his words, namely, *To be partial in ourselves and judges of evil thoughts.* Add hereunto, that niceness in words was always counted the next step to trifling, and so was to be curious about names too: also that we cannot follow a better pattern for elocution than God himself; therefore he using divers words, in his holy writ, and indifferently for one thing in nature: we, if we will not be super- 40 stitious, may use the same liberty in our English versions out of *Hebrew* & *Greek*, for that copy or store that he hath given us. Lastly, we have on

the one side avoided the scrupulosity of the Puritans, who leave the old Ecclesiastical words, and betake them to other, as when they put *washing* for *Baptism*, and *Congregation* instead of *Church:* as also on the other side we have shunned the obscurity of the Papists, in their *Azimes, Tunike, Rational, Holocausts, Praepuce, Pasche,* and a number of such like, whereof their late Translation is full, and that of purpose to darken the sense, that since they must needs translate the Bible, yet by the language thereof, it may be kept from being understood. But we desire that the Scripture may speak like itself, as in the language of *Canaan,* that it may
10 be understood even of the very vulgar.

Many other things we might give thee warning of (gentle Reader) if we had not exceeded the measure of a Preface already. It remaineth, that we commend thee to God, and to the Spirit of his grace, which is able to build further than we can ask or think. He removeth the scales from our eyes, the veil from our hearts, opening our wits that we may understand his word, enlarging our hearts, yea correcting our affections, that we may love it above gold and silver, yea that we may love it to the end. Ye are brought unto fountains of living water which ye digged not; do not cast earth into them with the Philistines, neither prefer broken pits
20 before them with the wicked Jews. Others have laboured, and you may enter into their labours; O receive not so great things in vain, O despise not so great salvation! Be not like swine to tread under foot so precious things, neither yet like dogs to tear and abuse holy things. Say not to our Saviour with the *Gergesites,* Depart out of our coasts; neither yet with *Esau* sell your birthright for a mess of potage. If light be come into the world, love not darkness more than light; if food, if clothing be offered, go not naked, starve not yourselves. Remember the advice of *Nazianzene, It is a grievous thing* (or dangerous) *to neglect a great fair, and to seek to make markets afterwards:* also the encouragement of S. *Chrysostome,*
30 *It is altogether impossible, that he that is sober* (and watchful) *should at any time be neglected:* Lastly, the admonition and menacing of S. *Augustine, They that despise God's will inviting them, shall feel God's will taking vengeance of them.* It is a fearful thing to fall into the hands of the living God; but a blessed thing it is, and will bring us to everlasting blessedness in the end, when God speaketh unto us, to hearken; when he setteth his word before us, to read it; when he stretcheth out his hand and calleth, to answer, Here am I; here we are to do thy will, O God. The Lord work a care and conscience in us to know him and serve him, that we may be acknowledged of him at the appearing of our Lord Jesus Christ, to whom
40 with the holy Ghost, be all praise and thanksgiving. Amen.

The Sermon on the Mount (*Matthew, Chapter 5*)

The King James Version compared with Five Sixteenth-Century Versions

FROM (1) *The Holy Bible . . . Newly Translated,* 1611: KING JAMES

    (2) *The newe Testament, dylygently corrected and compared with the Greke by Willyam Tindale,* 1534: TYNDALE

    (3) *The Byble in Englyshe,* 1539: GREAT BIBLE

    (4) *The Bible and Holy Scriptures,* 1560: GENEVA BIBLE

    (5) *The holie Byble,* 1572: BISHOPS' BIBLE (revised)

    (6) *The New Testament of Iesus Christ,* 1582: RHEIMS BIBLE

(1) KING JAMES, 1611

CHAP. V

Christ beginneth his Sermon in the Mount: 3 declaring who are blessed, 13 who are the salt of the earth, 14 the light of the world, the city on an hill, 15 the candle: 17 that he came to fulfill the Law: 21 what it is to kill, 27 to commit adultery, 33 to swear: 38 Exhorteth to suffer wrong, 44 to love even our enemies, 48 and to labour after perfectness.

1 And seeing the multitudes, he went up into a mountain: and when he was set, his disciples came unto him.

2 And he opened his mouth, and taught them, saying,

3 Blessed *are* the poor in spirit: for theirs is the kingdom of heaven.

(2) TYNDALE'S NEW TESTAMENT, 1534

THE V. CHAPTER

When he saw the people, he went up into a mountain, and when he was set, his disciples came to him;

and he opened his mouth and taught them, saying:

Blessed are the povre in sprete: for theirs is the kingdom of heaven.

(3) GREAT BIBLE, 1539

THE V. CHAPTER

In thys Chapter and in the two nexte followynge is conteyned the moste excellent & loving Sermon of Christ in the mount: which sermon, is the very keye that openeth the understandyng into the lawe. In this fyfth Chapter, specially he preacheth of the viii beatitudes or blessynges, of manslaughter, wrath, and anger: of advoutry, of sweringe, of sufferynge wronge, and of love, even towarde a mans enemyes.

When he saw the people, he went up into a mountain, & when he was set his disciples came to him: and after that he had opened his

mouth, he taught them, saying blessed are the poor in sprete: for theirs is the kingdom of heaven.

(4) GENEVA, 1560

CHAP. V.

3 Christ teacheth who are blessed. 13 The salt of the earth & light of the world. 16 Good works. 17 Christ came to fulfil the Law. 21 What is meant by killing. 23 Reconciliation. 27 Adulterie. 29 Offences. 31 Divorcement. 33 Not to sweare. 39 To suffer wrong. 43 To love our enemies. 48 Perfection.

1 And when he saw the multitude, he went up into a mountain: and when he was set, his disciples came to him.

2 And he opened his mouth and taught them, saying,

3 Blessed *are* the poor in spirit, for theirs is the kingdom of heaven.

(5) BISHOPS' BIBLE, 1572

THE V. CHAPTER

In this Chapter, and in the two next following, is contained the most excellent and loving sermon of Christ, in the mount. Which sermon, is the very key, that openeth the understanding into the lawe. In this fifth Chapter specially, 3. he preacheth of the eight beatitudes or blessings, 21. of manslaughter, 22. wrath, and anger, 27. of adultery, 33. of swearing, 39. of suffering wrong. 44. and of love, even toward a mans enemy.

1 When he saw the multitude, he went up into a mountain: and when he was set, his disciples came to him.

2 And when he had opened his mouth, he taught them, saying,

3 Blessed (*are*) the poor in spirit: for theirs is the kingdom of heaven.

(6) RHEIMS NEW TESTAMENT, 1582

CHAP. V.

First, 3 he promiseth rewards, 13 and he layeth before the Apostles their office. 17 Secondly, he protesteth unto us that We must keep the commandments, and that more exactly than the Scribes and Pharisees, whose justice was counted most perfite: but yet that it was unsufficient, he sheweth in the precepts of 21 Murder, 27 Advoutrie, 31 Divorce, 33 Swearing, 38 Revenge, 42 Usurie, 43 Enemies.

1 And seeing the multitudes, he went up into a mountain:

2 and when he was set, his Disciples came unto him, and

opening his mouth he taught them, saying,

3 Blessed are the poor in Spirit: for theirs is the Kingdom of

(1) KING JAMES, 1611

CHAP. V (continued)

4 Blessed *are* they that mourn: for they shall be comforted.

5 Blessed *are* the meek: for they shall inherit the earth.

6 Blessed *are* they which do hunger and thirst after righteousness: for they shall be filled.

7 Blessed *are* the merciful: for they shall obtain mercy.

8 Blessed *are* the pure in heart: for they shall see God.

9 Blessed *are* the peacemakers: for they shall be called the children of God.

10 Blessed *are* they which are persecuted for righteousness' sake: for theirs is the kingdom of heaven.

11 Blessed *are* ye, when men shall revile you, and persecute you, and shall say all manner of evil against you falsely for my sake.

(2) TYNDALE'S NEW TESTAMENT, 1534

THE V. CHAPTER (continued)

Blessed are they that mourn: for they shall be conforted.

Blessed are the meek: for they shall inherit the earth.

Blessed are they which hunger and thirst for rightewesnes: for they shall be filled.

Blessed are the merciful: for they shall obtain mercy.

Blessed are the pure in heart: for they shall see God.

Blessed are the peacemakers: for they shall be called the children of God.

Blessed are they which suffer persecution for rightewesnes sake: for theirs is the kingdom of heaven.

Blessed are ye when men revile you, and persecute you, and shall falsely say all manner of evil sayings against you for my sake.

(3) GREAT BIBLE, 1539

THE V. CHAPTER (continued)

Blessed are they that mourn: for they shall receive comfort.

Blessed are the meek: for they shall receive the inheritance of the earth.

Blessed are they which hunger and thirst after rightwesnes: for they shall be satisfied.

Blessed are the merciful: for they shall obtain mercy.

Blessed are the pure in heart: for they shall see God.

Blessed are the peacemakers: for they shall be called the children of God.

Blessed are they which suffer persecution for rightwesnes sake: for theirs is the kingdom of heaven.

Blessed are ye, when men revile you, and persecute you, and shall falsely say all manner of evil sayings against you, for my sake.

(4) GENEVA, 1560
CHAP. V. (*continued*)

4 Blessed *are* they that mourn: for they shall be comforted.

5 Blessed *are* the meek: for they shall inherit the earth.

6 Blessed *are* they which hunger and thirst for righteousness: for they shall be filled.

7 Blessed *are* the merciful: for they shall obtain mercy.

8 Blessed *are* the pure in heart: for they shall see God.

9 Blessed *are* the peacemakers: for they shall be called the children of God.

10 Blessed *are* they which suffer persecution for righteousness sake: for theirs is the kingdom of heaven.

11 Blessed *are* ye when men revile you, and persecute *you,* and say all manner of evil against you for my sake, falsely.

(5) BISHOPS' BIBLE, 1572
THE V. CHAPTER (*continued*)

4 Blessed (*are*) they that mourn: for they shall be comforted.

5 Blessed (*are*) the meek: for they shall inherit the earth.

6 Blessed (*are*) they which do hunger and thirst (*after*) righteousness: for they shall be satisfied.

7 Blessed (*are*) the merciful: for they shall obtain mercy.

8 Blessed (*are*) the pure in heart: for they shall see God.

9 Blessed (*are*) the peacemakers: for they shall be called the children of God.

10 Blessed (*are*) they which have been persecuted for righteousness' sake: for theirs is the kingdom of heaven.

11 Blessed are ye, when (*men*) shall revile you, and persecute (*you*), and lying, shall say all manner of evil saying against you, for my sake.

(6) RHEIMS NEW TESTAMENT, 1582
CHAP. V. (*continued*)

4 heaven. Blessed are the meek: for they shall possess the land.

5 Blessed are they that mourn: for they shall be comforted.

6 Blessed are they that hunger & thirst after justice: for they

7 shall have their fill. Blessed are the merciful: for they shall ob-

8 tain mercy. Blessed are the clean of heart: for they shall

9 see God. Blessed are the peacemakers: for they shall be called

10 the children of God. Blessed are they that suffer persecution for justice: for theirs is the

11 Kingdom of heaven. Blessed are ye when they shall revile you, and persecute you, and speak all that naught is against

12 you, untruly, for my sake: be

(1) KING JAMES, 1611
CHAP. V (*continued*)

12 Rejoice, and be exceeding glad: for great is your reward in heaven: For so persecuted they the Prophets which were before you.

13 Ye are the salt of the earth: But if the salt have lost his savour, wherewith shall it be salted? It is thenceforth good for nothing, but to be cast out, and to be trodden under foot of men.

14 Ye are the light of the world. A city that is set on an hill cannot be hid.

15 Neither do men light a candle, and put it under a bushel: but on a candlestick, and it giveth light unto all that are in the house.

16 Let your light so shine before men, that they may see your good works, and glorify your father which is in heaven.

(2) TYNDALE'S NEW TESTAMENT, 1534
THE V. CHAPTER (*continued*)

Rejoice and be glad, for great is your reward in heaven. For so persecuted they the Prophets which were before your days.

Ye are the salt of the earth: but and if the salt have lost her saltness, what can be salted therewith? It is thenceforth good for nothing, but to be cast out, and to be trodden under foot of men.

Ye are the light of the world. A city that is set on an hill, cannot be hid,

neither do men light a candle and put it under a bushel, but on a candle-stick, and it lighteth all that are in the house.

Let your light so shine before men, that they may see your good works, and glorify your father which is in heaven.

(3) GREAT BIBLE, 1539
THE V. CHAPTER (*continued*)

Rejoice and be glad, for great is your reward in heaven. For so persecuted they the Prophets, which were before you.

Ye are the salt of the earth: But if the salt have lost the saltness, what shall be seasoned therewith? It is thenceforth good for nothing, but to be cast out, and to be trodden down of men.

Ye are the light of the world. A city that is set on an hill cannot be hid,

neither do men light a candle, and put it under a bushel, but on a candle-stick, and it giveth light unto all that are in the house.

Let your light so shine before men That they may see your good works and glorify your father which is in heaven.

(4) GENEVA, 1560

CHAP. V. (*continued*)

12 Rejoice and be glad, for great is your reward in heaven: for so persecuted they the Prophets which were before you.

13 Ye are the salt of the earth: but if the salt have lost his savour, wherewith shall it be salted? It is thenceforth good for nothing, but to be cast out, & to be trodden under foot of men.

14 Ye are the light of the world. A city that is set on an hill, cannot be hid.

15 Neither do men light a candle, and put it under a bushel, but on a candlestick, & it giveth light unto all that are in the house.

16 Let your light so shine before men, that they may see your good works, & glorify your Father which is in heaven.

(5) BISHOPS' BIBLE, 1572

THE V. CHAPTER (*continued*)

12 Rejoice ye and be glad, for great is your reward in heaven. For so persecuted they the prophets, which were before you.

13 Ye are the salt of the earth: but if the salt become unsavory, wherein shall it be salted? It is thenceforth good for nothing, but to be cast out, and to be trodden under foot of men.

14 Ye are the light of the world. A city that is set on an hill cannot be hid.

15 Neither do men light a candle, and put it under a bushel: but on a candlestick, and it giveth light unto all that are in the house.

16 Let your light so shine before men, that they may see your good works, and glorify your father, which is in heaven.

(6) RHEIMS NEW TESTAMENT, 1582

CHAP. V. (*continued*)

glad & rejoice, for your reward is very great in heaven. For so they persecuted the Prophets that were before you.

13 You are the salt of the earth.

14 But if the salt leese his virtue, wherewith shall it be salted? It is good for nothing any more but to be cast forth, and to be

15 trodden of men. You are the light of the world. A city can-

not be hid, situated on a moun-

16 tain. Neither do men light a candle and put it under a bushel, but upon a candlestick, that it may shine to all that are

17 in the house. So let your light shine before men: that they may see your good works, and glorify your father which is in heaven.

(1) KING JAMES, 1611

CHAP. V (*continued*)

17 Think not that I am come to destroy the law or the Prophets. I am not come to destroy, but to fulfil.

18 For verily I say unto you, Till heaven and earth pass, one jot or one tittle, shall in no wise pass from the law, till all be fulfilled.

19 Whosoever therefore shall break of these least commandments, and shall teach men so, he shall be called the least in the kingdom of heaven: but whosoever shall do and teach *them*, the same shall be called great in the kingdom of heaven.

20 For I say unto you, that except your righteousness shall exceed the righteousness of the Scribes and Pharisees, ye shall in no case enter into the kingdom of heaven.

(2) TYNDALE'S NEW TESTAMENT, 1534

THE V. CHAPTER (*continued*)

Think not that I am come to destroy the law or the Prophets: no, I am not come to destroy them, but to fulfil them.

For truly I say unto you, till heaven and earth perish, one jot or one tittle of the law shall not 'scape, till all be fulfilled.

Whosoever breaketh one of these least commandments, and teacheth men so, he shall be called the least in the kingdom of heaven. But whosoever observeth & teacheth, the same shall be called great in the kingdom of heaven.

(3) GREAT BIBLE, 1539

THE V. CHAPTER (*continued*)

Think not that I am come to destroy the law, or the Prophets: no, I am not come to destroy, but to fulfill.

For truly I say unto you, till heaven and earth pass, one jot or one tittle of the law shall not 'scape, till all be fulfilled.

Whosoever therefore breaketh one of these least commandments, and teacheth men so, he shall be called the least in the kingdom of heaven. But whosoever doeth and teacheth, the same shall be called great in the kingdom of heaven.

For I say unto you, except your rightewesness exceed the rightewesness of the Scribes and Pharisees, ye cannot enter into the kingdom of heaven.

(4) GENEVA, 1560

CHAP. V. (*continued*)

17 Think not that I am come to destroy the Law, or the Prophets. I am not come to destroy them, but to fulfil them.

18 For truly I say unto you, Till heaven, and earth perish, one jot, or one tittle of the Law shall not 'scape, till all things be fulfilled.

19 Whosoever therefore shall break one of these least commandments, & teach men so, he shall be called the least in the kingdom of heaven: but whosoever shall observe and teach *them*, the same shall be called great in the kingdom of heaven.

20 For I say unto you, except your righteousness exceed the *righteousness* of the Scribes and Pharisees, ye shall not enter into the kingdom of heaven.

(5) BISHOPS' BIBLE, 1572

THE V. CHAPTER (*continued*)

17 Think not that I am come to destroy the law or the prophets. I am not come to destroy, but to fulfil.

18 For truly I say unto you, Till heaven & earth pass, one jot or one tittle of the law shall not 'scape, till all be fulfilled.

19 Whosoever therefore shall break one of these least commandments, and shall teach men so, he shall be called the least in the kingdom of heaven: but whosoever shall do and teach (*so*), the same shall be called great in the kingdom of heaven.

(6) RHEIMS NEW TESTAMENT, 1582

CHAP. V. (*continued*)

18 Do not think that I am come to break the Law or the Prophets. I am not come to break:
19 but to fulfil. For assuredly I say unto you, till heaven and earth pass, one jot or one tittle shall not pass of the Law; till all be 20 fulfilled. He therefore that shall break one of these least commandments, & shall so teach men: shall be called the least in the Kingdom of heaven. But he that shall do and teach: he shall be called great in the kingdom of heaven.

(1) KING JAMES, 1611
CHAP. V (*continued*)

21 Ye have heard that it was said by them of old time, Thou shalt not kill: and whosoever shall kill, shall be in danger of the judgment.

22 But I say unto you, that whosoever is angry with his brother without a cause, shall be in danger of the Judgment: and whosoever shall say to his brother, Racha, shall be in danger of the council: but whosoever shall say, *Thou* fool, shall be in danger of hell fire.

23 Therefore if thou bring thy gift to the altar, and there remembrest that thy brother hath aught against thee:

(2) TYNDALE'S NEW TESTAMENT, 1534
THE V. CHAPTER (*continued*)

For I say unto you, except your rightewesness exceed the righteweseness of the Scribes and Pharisees, ye cannot enter into the kingdom of heaven.

Ye have heard how it was said unto them of the old time: Thou shalt not kill. For whosoever killeth shall be in danger of judgment. But I say unto you, whosoever is angry with his brother shall be in danger of judgment. Whosoever sayeth unto his brother Racha, shall be in danger of a council. But whosoever sayeth thou fool, shall be in danger of hell fire.

Therefore when thou offerest thy gift at the altar, and there remembrest that thy brother hath aught against thee:

(3) GREAT BIBLE, 1539
THE V. CHAPTER (*continued*)

Ye have heard that it was said unto them of the old time: Thou shalt not kill: whosoever killeth, shall be in danger of judgment. But I say unto you: that whosoever is angry with his brother (unadvisedly) shall be in danger of judgment. And whosoever say unto his brother, Racha, shall be in danger of a council. But whosoever sayeth, Thou fool, shall be in danger of hell fire.

Therefore, if thou offrest thy gift at the altar, and there remembrest that thy brother hath aught against thee:

(4) GENEVA, 1560

CHAP. V. (*continued*)

21 Ye have heard that it was said unto them of the old time, Thou shalt not kill: for whosoever killeth, shall be culpable of judgment.

22 But I say unto you, whosoever is angry with his brother unadvisedly shall be culpable of judgment. And whosoever sayeth unto his brother, Raca, shall be worthy to be punished by the council; and whosoever shall say, Fool, shall be worthy to be punished with hell fire.

23 If then thou bring thy gift to the altar, & there remembrest that thy brother hath aught against thee,

(5) BISHOPS' BIBLE, 1572

THE V. CHAPTER (*continued*)

20 For I say unto you, Except your righteousness shall exceed the righteousness of the Scribes and Pharisees, ye shall in no case enter into the kingdom of heaven.

21 Ye have heard, that it was said to them of old time, Thou shalt not kill: whosoever killeth, shall be in danger of judgment.

22 But I say unto you, that whosoever is angry with his brother, unadvisedly, shall be in danger of judgment: and whosoever shall say unto his brother *Racha* shall be in danger of a council: but whosoever shall say (*thou*) fool, shall be in danger of hell fire.

23 Therefore if thou bring thy gift to the altar, & there remembrest that thy brother hath aught against thee:

(6) RHEIMS NEW TESTAMENT, 1582

CHAP. V. (*continued*)

21 For I tell you, that unless your justice abound more than that of the Scribes and Pharisees, you shall not enter into the Kingdom of heaven.

22 You have heard that it was said to them of old. Thou shalt not kill, and whoso killeth, shall be in danger of judgment. But I say to you, that whosoever is angry with his brother, shall be in danger of judgment. And whosoever shall say to his brother, Raca: shall be in danger of a council. And whosoever shall say, Thou fool: shall be guilty of the hell of fire.

(1) KING JAMES, 1611
CHAP. V (*continued*)

24 Leave there thy gift before the altar, and go thy way, first be reconciled to thy brother, and then come and offer thy gift.

25 Agree with thine adversary quickly, whiles thou art in the way with him: lest at any time the adversary deliver thee to the judge, and the judge deliver thee to the officer, and thou be cast into prison.

26 Verily I say unto thee, thou shalt by no means come out thence, till thou hast paid the uttermost farthing.

27 Ye have heard that it was said by them of old time, Thou shalt not commit adultery.

28 But I say unto you, that whosoever looketh on a woman to lust after her, hath committed adultery with her already in his heart.

(2) TYNDALE'S NEW TESTAMENT, 1534
THE V. CHAPTER (*continued*)

leave there thine offering before the altar, and go thy way first and be reconciled to thy brother, and then come and offer thy gift.

Agree with thine adversary quickly, whiles thou art in the way with him, lest that adversary deliver thee to the judge, and the judge deliver thee to the minister, & then thou be cast into prison.

I say unto thee verily: thou shalt not come out thence till thou have paid the utmost farthing.

Ye have heard how it was said to them of old time: Thou shalt not commit advoutry.

But I say unto you, that whosoever looketh on a wife, lusting after her, hath committed advoutry with her already in his heart.

(3) GREAT BIBLE, 1539
THE V. CHAPTER (*continued*)

leave there thine offering before the altar & go thy way first, and be reconciled to thy brother, and then come and offer thy gift.

Agree with thine adversary quickly, whiles thou art in the way with him, lest at any time the adversary deliver thee to the judge, and the judge deliver thee to the minister, and then thou be cast into prison.

Verily I say unto thee: thou shalt not come out thence till thou have paid the utmost farthing.

Ye have heard that it was said to them of old time: Thou shall not commit advoutry.

But I say unto you that whosoever looketh on another man's wife to lust after her, hath committed advoutry with her already in his heart.

(4) GENEVA, 1560

CHAP. V. (*continued*)

24 Leave there thine offering before the altar, and go thy way: first be reconciled to thy brother, & then come & offer thy gift.

25 Agree with thine adversary quickly, whiles thou are in the way with him, lest thine adversary deliver thee to the judge, and the judge deliver thee to the sergeant, and thou be cast into prison.

26 Verily I say unto thee, thou shalt not come out thence, till thou hast paid the utmost farthing.

27 Ye have heard that it was said to them of old time, Thou shalt not commit adultery.

28 But I say unto you, that whosoever looketh on a woman to lust after her, hath committed adultery with her already in his heart.

(5) BISHOPS' BIBLE, 1572

THE V. CHAPTER (*continued*)

24 Leave there thy gift before the altar, and go thy way, first be reconciled to thy brother: and then come and offer thy gift.

25 Agree with thine adversary quickly, whiles thou art in the way with him: lest at any time the adversary deliver thee to the judge, and the judge deliver thee to the minister, and then thou be cast into prison.

26 Verily I say unto thee, thou shalt by no means come out thence, till thou hast paid the uttermost farthing.

27 Ye have heard that it was said unto them of time, Thou shalt not commit adultery.

28 But I say unto you, that whosoever looketh on a woman to lust after her, hath committed adultery with her already in his heart.

(6) RHEIMS NEW TESTAMENT, 1582

CHAP. V. (*continued*)

24 If therefore thou offer thy gift at the altar, and there thou re-member that thy brother hath
25 aught against thee: leave there thy offering before the altar, and go first to be reconciled to thy brother; and then coming
26 thou shalt offer thy gift. Be at agreement with thy adversary betimes whiles thou art in the

way with him: lest perhaps the adversary deliver thee to the judge, and the judge deliver thee to the officer, and thou be
27 cast into prison. Amen I say to thee, thou shalt not go out from thence till thou repay the last farthing.
28 You have heard that it was said to them of old, Thou shall

(1) KING JAMES, 1611
CHAP. V (*continued*)

29 And if thy right eye offend thee, pluck it out, and cast it from thee. For it is profitable for thee that one of thy members should perish, and not that thy whole body should be cast into hell.

30 And if thy right hand offend thee, cut it off, and cast it from thee. For it is profitable for thee that one of thy members should perish, and not that thy whole body should be cast into hell.

31 It hath been said, Whosoever shall put away his wife, let him give her a writing of divorcement.

32 But I say unto you, that whosoever shall put away his wife, saving for the cause of fornication, causeth her to commit adultery: and whosoever shall marry her that is divorced, committeth adultery.

(2) TYNDALE'S NEW TESTAMENT, 1534
THE V. CHAPTER (*continued*)

Wherefore if thy right eye offend thee, pluck him out, and cast him from thee. Better it is for thee that one of thy members perish, than that thy whole body should be cast into hell. Also if thy right hand offend thee, cut him off and cast him from thee. Better it is that one of thy members perish, than that all thy body should be cast into hell.

It is said, whosoever put away his wife, let him give her a testimonial also of the divorcement. But I say unto you: whosoever put away his wife (except it be for fornication) causeth her to break matrimony. And whosoever marrieth her that is divorced breaketh wedlock.

(3) GREAT BIBLE, 1539
THE V. CHAPTER (*continued*)

If thy right eye hinder thee, pluck him out, & cast him from thee. For better it is unto thee, that one of thy members perish, than that thy whole body should be cast into hell. And if thy right hand hinder thee, cut him off, and cast him from thee. For better it is unto thee, that one of thy members perish, than

that all thy body should be cast into hell.

It is said, whosoever putteth away his wife let him give her a letter of the divorcement. But I say unto you: that whosoever doth put away his wife (except it be for fornication) causeth her to break matrimony. And whosoever marrieth her that is divorced, committeth advoutry.

(4) GENEVA, 1560

CHAP. V. (continued)

29 Wherefore if thy right eye cause thee to offend, pluck it out, and cast it from thee: for better it is for thee that one of thy members perish, than that thy whole body should be cast into hell.

30 Also if thy right hand make thee to offend, cut it off, and cast it from thee: for better it is for thee that one of thy members perish, than that thy whole body should be cast into hell.

31 It hath been said also, Whosoever shall put away his wife, let him give her a testimonial of divorcement.

32 But I say unto you, whosoever shall put away his wife (except it be for fornication) causeth her to commit adultery: and whosoever shall marry her that is divorced, committeth adultery.

(5) BISHOPS' BIBLE, 1572

THE V. CHAPTER (continued)

29 If thy right eye offend thee, pluck it out, and cast it from thee: for it is profitable for thee, that one of thy members should perish, and not that thy whole body should be cast into hell.

30 And if thy right hand offend thee, cut it off, and cast it from thee: for it is profitable for thee, that one of thy members should

perish, and not that all thy body should be cast into hell.

31 It hath been said, Whosoever will put away his wife, let him give her a writing of divorcement.

32 But I say unto you, that whosoever doth put away his wife, except it be for fornication, causeth her to commit adultery: and whosoever marrieth her that is divorced, committeth adultery.

(6) RHEIMS NEW TESTAMENT, 1582

CHAP. V. (continued)

29 not commit advoutry. But I say to you, that whosoever shall see a woman to lust after her, hath already committed advoutry

30 with her in his heart. And if thy right eye scandalize thee, pluck it out, & cast it from thee; for it is expedient for thee that one of thy limbs perish, rather than thy whole body be cast

31 into hell. And if thy right hand scandalize thee, cut it off, and cast it from thee: for it is expedient for thee that one of thy limbs perish, rather than that thy whole body go into hell.

32 It was said also, whosoever shall dimiss his wife, let him give her a bill of divorcement.

(1) KING JAMES, 1611
CHAP. V (continued)

33 Again, ye have heard that it hath been said by them of old time, Thou shalt not forswear thyself, but shalt perform unto the Lord thine oaths.

34 But I say unto you, Swear not at all, neither by heaven, for it is God's throne:

35 Nor by the earth, for it is his foot-stool: neither by Hierusalem, for it is the city of the great king.

36 Neither shalt thou swear by thy head, because thou canst not make one hair white or black.

37 But let your communication be Yea, yea: Nay, nay: For whatsoever is more than these, cometh of evil.

(2) TYNDALE'S NEW TESTAMENT, 1534
THE V. CHAPTER (continued)

Again ye have heard how it was said to them of old time, thou shalt not forswear thyself, but shalt perform thine oath to God.
But I say unto you, swear not at all: neither by heaven, for it is God's seat:
nor yet by the earth, for it is his footstool: neither by Jerusalem, for it is the city of that great king: neither shalt thou sware by thy head, because thou canst not make one white hair, or black:
But your communication shall be, yea, yea: nay, nay. For whatsoever is more than that, cometh of evil.

(3) GREAT BIBLE, 1539
THE V. CHAPTER (continued)

Again, ye have heard how it was said to them of old time: thou shalt not forswear thyself, but shall perform unto the lord those things that thou swearest.
But I say unto you, swear not at all: neither by heaven, for it is God's seat,
nor by the earth, for it is his footstool: neither by Jerusalem: for it is the city of the great king:
neither shalt thou swear by thy head, because thou canst not make one hair white or black.
But your communication shall be yea, yea: nay, nay. For whatsoever is added more than these, it cometh of evil.

(4) GENEVA, 1560

CHAP. V. (*continued*)

33 Again, ye have heard that it was said to them of old time, Thou shalt not forswear thyself, but shalt perform thine oaths to the Lord.

34 But I say unto you, Swear not at all, neither by heaven, for it is the throne of God:

35 Nor yet by the earth: for it is his foot-stool: neither by Jerusa-lem: for it is the city of the great King.

36 Neither shalt thou swear by thine head, because thou canst not make one hair white or black.

37 But let your communication be, Yea, yea: Nay, nay. For whatsoever *is* more than these, cometh of evil.

(5) BISHOPS' BIBLE, 1572

THE V. CHAPTER (*continued*)

33 Again, ye have heard that it hath been said unto them of old time, Thou shalt not forswear thee self, but shalt perform unto the Lord thine oaths.

34 But I say unto you, Swear not at all, neither by heaven, for it is God's seat:

35 Nor by the earth, for it is his foot-stool: neither by Hierusalem, for it is the city of the great king.

36 Neither shalt thou swear by thy head, because thou canst not make one hair white or black.

37 But let your communication be yea, yea: nay, nay: for whatsoever is more than these, cometh of evil.

(6) RHEIMS NEW TESTAMENT, 1582

CHAP. V. (*continued*)

33 But I say to you, whosoever shall dimiss his wife, excepting the cause of fornication, maketh her to commit advoutry: and he that shall marry her that is dimissed, committeth advoutry.

34 Again you have heard that it was said to them of old, Thou shalt not commit perjury; but thou shalt perform thy oaths to

35 our Lord. But I say to you not to swear at all: neither by heaven, because it is the throne of God: neither by the earth, because it is the foot-stool of his feet: neither by Hierusalem, because it is the city of the great

36 King. Neither shalt thou swear by thy head, because thou canst not make one hair white or

37 black. Let your talk be yea, yea: no, no: and that which is over and above these is of evil.

(1) KING JAMES, 1611

CHAP. V (*continued*)

38 Ye have heard that it hath been said, An eye for an eye, and a tooth for a tooth.

39 But I say unto you, that ye resist not evil: but whosoever shall smite thee on thy right cheek, turn to him the other also.

40 And if any man will sue thee at the law, and take away thy coat, let him have thy cloak also.

41 And whosoever shall compel thee to go a mile, go with him twain.

42 Give to him that asketh thee: and from him that would borrow of thee, turn not thou away.

43 Ye have heard that it hath been said, Thou shalt love thy neighbor, and hate thine enemy:

(2) TYNDALE'S NEW TESTAMENT, 1534

THE V. CHAPTER (*continued*)

Ye have heard how it is said, an eye for an eye: a tooth for a tooth. But I say to you, that ye resist not wrong. But whosoever give thee a blow on thy right cheek, turn to him the other.
And if any man will sue thee at the law, and take away thy coat. let him have thy cloak also.

And whosoever will compel thee to go a mile, go with him twain. Give to him that axeth, and from him that would borrow turn not away.
Ye have heard how it is said: thou shalt love thine neighbor, and hate thine enemy.

(3) GREAT BIBLE, 1539

THE V. CHAPTER (*continued*)

Ye have heard that it is said: an eye for an eye: and a tooth for a tooth.
But I say unto you, that ye resist not evil. But whosoever give thee a blow on the right cheek, turn to him the other also.
And if any man will sue thee at the law, & take away thy coat, let him have thy cloak also.

And whosoever will compel thee to go a mile, go with him twain.
Give to him that asketh thee: and from him that would borrow, turn not thou away.
Ye have heard that it is said thou shalt love thine neighbor, and hate thine enemy.

(4) GENEVA, 1560

CHAP. V. (continued)

38 Ye have heard that it hath been said, An eye for an eye, & a tooth for a tooth.

39 But I say unto you, Resist not evil: but whosoever shall smite thee on thy right cheek, turn to him the other also.

40 And if any man will sue thee at the law, and take away thy coat, let him have thy cloak also.

41 And whosoever will compel thee *to go* a mile, go with him twain.

42 Give to him that asketh, and from him that would borrow of thee, turn not away.

(5) BISHOPS' BIBLE, 1572

THE V. CHAPTER (continued)

38 Ye have heard that it hath been said, An eye for an eye, and a tooth for a tooth.

39 But I say unto you, that ye resist not evil: but whosoever will give thee a blow on thy right cheek, turn to him the other also.

40 And if any man will sue thee at the law, and take away thy coat, let him have thy cloak also.

41 And whosoever will compel thee to go a mile, go with him twain.

42 Give to him that asketh thee: and from him that would borrow of thee, turn not thou away.

43 Ye have heard that it hath been said, Thou shalt love thy neighbor, and hate thine enemy.

(6) RHEIMS NEW TESTAMENT, 1582

CHAP. V. (continued)

38 You have heard that it was said, An eye for an eye, and a
39 tooth for a tooth. But I say to you not to resist evil: but if one strike thee on thy right cheek,
40 turn to him also the other: and to him that will contend with thee in judgment, and take away thy coat, let go thy cloak

41 also unto him. And whosoever will force thee one mile, go
42 with him other twain. He that asketh of thee, give to him: and to him that would borrow of thee, turn not away.

43 You have heard that it was said, Thou shalt love thy neigh-

(1) KING JAMES, 1611
CHAP. V (*continued*)

44 But I say unto you, Love your enemies, bless them that curse you, do good to them that hate you, and pray for them which despitefully use you, and persecute you:

45 That ye may be the children of your father which is in heaven: for he maketh his sun to rise on the evil and on the good, and sendeth rain on the just, and on the unjust.

46 For if ye love them which love you, what reward have ye? Do not even the Publicans the same?

47 And if ye salute your brethren only, what do you more *than others?* Do not even the Publicans so?

48 Be ye therefore perfect, even as your father, which is in heaven, is perfect.

(2) TYNDALE'S NEW TESTAMENT, 1534
THE V. CHAPTER (*continued*)

But I say unto you, love your enemies. Bless them that curse you. Do good to them that hate you. Pray for them which do you wrong and persecute you,

that ye may be the children of your father that is in heaven: for he maketh his sun to arise on the evil, and on the good, and sendeth his rain on the just and unjust.

For if ye love them, which love you, what reward shall ye have? Do not the Publicans even so? And if ye be friendly to your brethren only: what singular thing do ye? Do not the Publicans likewise?

Ye shall therefore be perfect, even as your father which is in heaven, is perfect.

(3) GREAT BIBLE, 1539
THE V. CHAPTER (*continued*)

But I say unto you, love your enemies. Bless them that curse you. Do good to them that hate you. Pray for them which hurt you and persecute you,

that ye may be the children of your father which is in heaven: for he maketh his sun to arise on the evil, & on the good, & sendeth rain on the just & unjust.

For if ye love them, which love you: what reward have ye? Do not the publicans also even the same? And if ye make much of your brethren only, what singular thing do ye? Do not also the Publicans likewise?

Ye shall therefore be perfect, even as your father which is in heaven, is perfect.

(4) GENEVA, 1560

CHAP. V. (*continued*)

43 Ye have heard that it hath been said, Thou shalt love thy neighbor, and hate thine enemy.

44 But I say unto you, Love your enemies: bless them that curse you: do good to them that hate you, and pray for them which hurt you, and persecute you,

45 That ye may be the children of your Father that is in heaven: for he maketh his sun to arise on the evil, and the good, and sendeth rain on the just, & unjust.

46 For if ye love them, which love you, what reward shall you have? Do not the Publicans even the same?

47 And if ye be friendly to your brethren only, what singular thing do ye? Do not even the Publicans likewise?

48 Ye shall therefore be perfit, as your Father which is in heaven, is perfit.

(5) BISHOPS' BIBLE, 1572

THE V. CHAPTER (*continued*)

44 But I say unto you, Love your enemies, bless them that curse you, do good to them that hate you, pray for them which hurt you, and persecute you:

45 That ye may be the children of your father which is in heaven: for he maketh his sun to rise on the evil and on the good, and sendeth rain on the just and on the unjust.

46 For if ye love them which love you, what reward have ye? Do not the Publicans even the same?

47 And if ye salute your brethren only, what singular thing do ye? Do not also the Publicans likewise?

48 Ye shall therefore be perfect, even as your father which is in heaven is perfect.

(6) RHEIMS NEW TESTAMENT, 1582

CHAP. V. (*continued*)

44 bor, and hate thine enemy. But I say to you, love your enemies, do good to them that hate you: and pray for them that per-

45 secute and abuse you: that you may be the children of your father which is in heaven, who maketh his sun to rise upon good & bad, and raineth upon

46 just & unjust. For if you love them that love you, what reward shall you have? do not

47 also the Publicans this? And if you salute your brethren only, what do you more? do not also

48 the heathen this? Be you perfect therefore, as also your heavenly father is perfect.

THOMAS DEKKER

The Introduction and Notes are at page 1342

FROM *The Wonderfull yeare,* 1603

The Wonderful Year

* * * * *

HERE would I fain make a full point, because posterity should not be frighted with those miserable tragedies, which now my muse (as Chorus) stands ready to present. Time, would thou hadst never been made wretched by bringing them forth! Oblivion, would in all the graves and sepulchers, whose rank jaws thou hast already closed up or shalt yet hereafter burst open, thou couldst likewise bury them for ever!

A stiff and freezing horror sucks up the rivers of my blood. My hair stands an end with the panting of my brains. Mine eye-balls are ready to start out, being beaten with the billows of my tears. Out of my weeping pen does the ink mournfully and more bitterly than gall drop on the pale-faced paper, even when I do but think how the bowels of my sick country have been torn. Apollo, therefore, and you bewitching silvertongued Muses, get you gone! I invocate none of your names. Sorrow and Truth, sit you on each side of me, whilst I am delivered of this deadly burden. Prompt me that I may utter ruthfull and passionate condolement. Arm my trembling hand, that it may boldly rip up and anatomize the ulcerous body of this anthropophagized plague. Lend me art (without any counterfeit shadowing) to paint and delineate to the life the whole story of this mortal and pestiferous battle. And you, the ghosts of those more (by many) than 40,000, that with the virulent poison of infection have been driven out of your earthly dwellings; you desolate hand-wringing widows, that beat your bosoms over your departing husbands; you woefully distracted mothers that with disheveled hair are fallen into swounds, whilst you lie kissing the insensible cold lips of your breathless infants; you out-cast and down-trodden orphans, that shall many a year hence remember more freshly to mourn, when your mourning garments shall look old and be forgotten; and you, the Genii of all those emptied families, whose habitations are now among the antipodes; join all your hands together, and with your bodies cast a ring about me. Let me behold your ghastly visages, that my paper may receive their true pictures. Echo forth your groans through the hollow trunk of my pen, and rain down your gummy tears into mine ink, that even marble bosoms may be shaken with terror, and hearts of adamant melt into compassion.

What an unmatchable torment were it for a man to be barred up every night in a vast silent charnel-house? hung (to make it more hideous) with lamps dimly and slowly burning, in hollow and glimmering corners; where all the pavement should, in stead of green rushes, be strewd with blasted rosemary, withered hyacinths, fatal cypress and ewe, thickly mingled with heaps of dead men's bones; the bare ribs of a father that begat him, lying there; here the chapless hollow skull of a mother that bore him; round about him a thousand corses, some standing bolt upright in their knotted winding sheets, others half molded in rotten coffins, that should suddenly yawn wide open, filling his nostrils with noisome stench, and his eyes with the sight of nothing but crawling worms. And to keep such a poor wretch waking, he should hear no noise but of toads croaking, screech-owls howling, mandrakes shrieking; were not this an infernal prison? Would not the strongest-hearted man (beset with such a ghastly horror) look wild? and run mad? and die? And even such a formidable shape did the diseased city appear in. For he that durst (in the dead hour of gloomy midnight) have been so valiant as to have walked through the still and melancholy streets, what think you should have been his music? Surely the loud groans of raving sick men, the struggling pangs of souls departing; in every house grief striking up an allarum, servants crying out for masters, wives for husbands, parents for children, children for their mothers. Here he should have met some franticly running to knock up sextons; there, others fearfully sweating with coffins, to steal forth dead bodies, lest the fatal hand-writing of death should seal up their doors. And to make this dismal consort more full, round about him bells heavily tolling in one place, and ringing out in another. The dreadfulness of such an hour is inutterable. Let us go further.

If some poor man, suddenly starting out of a sweet and golden slumber, should behold his house flaming about his ears, all his family destroyed in their sleeps by the merciless fire, himself in the very midst of it, woefully and like a madman calling for help, would not the misery of such a distressed soul appear the greater, if the rich usurer dwelling next door to him should not stir (though he felt part of the danger), but suffer him to perish, when the thrusting out of an arm might have saved him? O how many thousands of wretched people have acted this poor man's part! How often hath the amazed husband waking, found the comfort of his bed lying breathless by his side! his children at the same instant gasping for life! and his servants mortally wounded at the heart by sickness! The distracted creature beats at death's doors, exclaims at windows; his cries are sharp enough to pierce heaven, but on earth no ear is opened to receive them.

*   *   *   *   *

. . . But thou art gotten safe (out of the civil city calamity) to thy parks and palaces in the country. Lading thy asses and thy mules with thy gold (thy god), thy plate, and thy jewels; and the fruits of thy womb thriftily growing up but in one only son (the young landlord of all thy careful labors), him also hast thou rescued from the arrows of
10 infection. Now is thy soul jocund, and thy senses merry. But open thine eyes, thou fool! and behold that darling of thine eye (thy son) turned suddenly into a lump of clay; the hand of pestilence hath smote him even under thy wing. Now dost thou rend thine hair, blaspheme thy Creator, cursest thy creation, and basely descendest into brutish and unmanly passions, threatening, in despite of death and his plague, to maintain the memory of thy child in the everlasting breast of Marble. A tomb must now defend him from tempests. And for that purpose, the sweaty hind (that digs the rent he pays thee out of the entrails of the earth) he is sent for, to convey forth that burden of thy sorrow. But note how thy
20 pride is disdained. That weather-beaten sun-burnt drudge, that not a month since fawned upon thy worship like a spaniel, and like a bond-slave would have stooped lower than thy feet, does now stop his nose at thy presence, and is ready to set his mastiff as high as thy throat, to drive thee from his door. All thy gold and silver cannot hire one of those (whom before thou didst scorn) to carry the dead body to his last home. The country round about thee shun thee as a basilisk; and therefore to London (from whose arms thou cowardly fledst away) post upon post must be gallping, to fetch from thence those that may perform that funeral office. But there are they so full of grave-matters of their own that they have
30 no leisure to attend thine. Doth not this cut thy very heart-strings in sunder? If that do not, the shutting up of this tragical act, I am sure, will; for thou must be enforced with thine own hands to wind up that blasted flower of youth in the last linen that ever he shall wear. Upon thine own shoulders must thou bear part of him, thy amazed servant the other; with thine own hands must thou dig his grave, not in the church or common place of burial (thou hast not favor, for all thy riches, to be so happy), but in thine orchard, or in the proud walks of thy garden, wringing thy palsy-shaken hands in stead of bells (most miserable father), must thou search him out a sepulcher.
40 My spirit grows faint with rowing in this Stygian ferry; it can no longer endure the transportation of souls in this doleful manner. Let us therefore shift a point of our compass, and (since there is no remedy but

that we must still be tossed up and down in this *Mare mortuum*) hoist up all our sails, and on the merry wings of a lustier wind seek to arrive on some prosperous shore.

Imagine, then, that all this while Death (like a Spanish Leaguer, or rather like stalking Tamburlaine) hath pitched his tents (being nothing but a heap of winding sheets tacked together) in the sinfully-polluted suburbs; the plague is muster-master and marshall of the field; burning fevers, boils, blains, and carbuncles, the leaders, lieutenants, sergeants, and corporals; the main army consisting (like Dunkirk) of a mingle-mangle; viz., dumpish mourners, merry sextons, hungry coffin-sellers, scrubbing bearers, and nasty grave-makers. But indeed they are the pioneers of the camp that are employed only (like moles) in casting up of earth and digging of trenches; Fear and Trembling (the two catch-polls of Death) arrest every one. No parley will be granted, no composition stood upon, but the allarum is struck up, the toxin rings out for life, and no voice heard but *Tue, Tue, Kill, Kill;* the little bells only (like small shot) do yet go off, and make no great work for worms; a hundred or two lost in every skirmish, or so. But alas that's nothing. Yet by these desperate sallies, what by open setting upon them by day, and secret ambuscadoes by night, the skirts of London were pitifully pared off, by little and little. Which they within the gates perceiving, it was no boot to bid them take their heels, for away they trudge thick and three-fold, some riding, some on foot, some without boots, some in their slippers, by water, by land, in shoales swam they westward; marry, to Graves-end none went unless they were driven, for whosoever landed there never came back again. Hacknies, waterman and wagons were not so terribly employed many a year; so that within a short time there was not a good horse in Smithfield, nor a coach to be set eye on. For after the world had once run upon the wheels of the pest-cart, neither coach nor caroche durst appear in his likeness.

* * * * *

Never let any man ask me what became of our physicians in this massacre; they hid their synodical heads as well as the proudest. And I cannot blame them, for their phlebotomies, losenges, and electuaries, with their diacatholicons, diacodions, amulets, and antidotes, had not so much strength to hold life and soul together as a pot of Pindar's ale and a nutmeg. Their drugs turned to dirt, their simples were simple things; Galen could do no more good than Sir Giles Goosecap; Hipocrates, Avicen, Paracelsus, Rasis, Fernelius, with all their succeeding rabble of doctors and watercasters, were at their wits' end, or I think rather at the world's end, for not one of them durst peep abroad; or if any one did take upon him to play the venturous knight, the plague put him to his *Nonplus;* in such strange, and such changeable shapes did this cameleon-like sickness appear, that they could not (with all the cunning in their budgets) make pursenets to take him napping.

Only a band of Desper-vewes, some few empirical madcaps (for they could never be worth velvet caps) turned themselves into bees (or more properly into drones) and went humming up and down, with honey-brags in their mouths, sucking the sweetness of silver (and now and then of *aurum potabile*) out of the poison of blains and carbuncles. And these 10 jolly mountebanks clapped up their bills upon every post (like a fencer's challenge) threatening to canvas the plague, and to fight with him at all his own several weapons. I know not how they sped, but some they sped I am sure; for I have heard them banned for the heavens, because they sent those thither that were wished to tarry longer upon earth.

*   *   *   *   *

It is plain, therefore, by the evidence of these two witnesses, that death, like a thief, sets upon men in the highway, dogs them into their own houses, breaks into their bed-chambers by night, assaults them by day, 20 and yet no law can take hold of him. He devours man and wife: offers violence to their fair daughters; kills their youthful sons, and deceives them of their servants. Yea, so full of treachery is he grown (since this plague took his part) that no lovers dare trust him, nor by their good wills would come near him; for he works their downfall even when their delights are at the highest.

Too ripe a proof have we of this in a pair of lovers. The maid was in the pride of fresh blood and beauty. She was that which to be now is a wonder, young and yet chaste. The gifts of her mind were great, yet those which fortune bestowed upon her (as being well descended) were 30 not much inferior. On this lovely creature did a young man so stead-fastly fix his eye that her looks kindled in his bosom a desire, whose flames burnt the more brightly, because they were fed with sweet and modest thoughts. Hymen was the God to whom he prayed day and night that he might marry her. His prayers were received, and at length (after many tempests of her denial and the frowns of kinsfolk) the element grew clear, and he saw the happy landing-place where he had long sought to arrive. The prize of her youth was made his own, and the solemn day appointed when it should be delivered to him. Glad of which blessedness (for to a lover it is a blessedness) he wrought by all the possible art he 40 could use to shorten the expected hour, and bring it nearer. For whether he feared the interception of parents, or that his own soul (with excess of joy) was drowned in strange passions, he would often, with sighs mingled with kisses and kisses half sinking in tears, prophetically tell her, that sure he should never live to enjoy her. To discredit which opinion of his, behold, the sun has made haste and wakened the bridal morning.

Now does he call his heart traitor, that did so falsely conspire against him. Lively blood leaps into his cheeks. He's got up, and gaily attired to play the bridegroom; she likewise does as cunningly turn herself into a bride; kindred and friends are met together; sops and muscadine run sweating up and down till they drop again, to comfort their hearts; and because so many coffins pestered London churches that there was no room left for weddings, coaches are provided, and away rides all the train into the country. On a Monday morning are these lusty lovers on their journey, and before noon are they alighted, entering (in stead of an inn) for more State into a church, where they no sooner appeared but the priest fell to his business, the holy knot was a tying, but he that should fasten it, coming to this, "In sickness and in health," there he stopped; for suddenly the bride took hold of, "in sickness," for "in health" all that stood by were in fear she should never be kept. The maiden-blush into which her cheeks were lately dyed, now began to lose color. Her voice (like a coward) would have shrunk away, but that her lover reaching her a hand, which he brought thither to give her (for he was not yet made a full husband), did with that touch somewhat revive her. On went they again so far till they met with "For better, for worse"; there was she worse than before, and had not the holy officer made haste, the ground on which she stood to be married might easily have been broken up for her burial.

All ceremonies being finished, she was led between two, not like a bride, but like a corse, to her bed. *That;* must now be the table on which the wedding dinner is to be served up (being at this time nothing but tears and sighs and lamentation), and Death is chief waiter; yet at length her weak heart, wrestling with the pangs, gave them a fall, so that up she stood again, and in the fatal funeral coach that carried her forth, was she brought back (as upon a bier) to the city. But see the malice of her enemy that had her in chase; upon the Wednesday following being overtaken, was her life overcome; Death rudely lay with her, and spoiled her of a maidenhead in spite of her husband.

Oh the sorrow that did round beset him! Now was his divination true; she was a wife, yet continued a maid. He was a husband and a widower, yet never knew his wife. She was his own, yet he had her not; she had him, yet never enjoyed him. Here is a strange alteration, for the rosemary that was washed in sweet water to set out the bridal is now wet in tears to furnish her burial. The music that was heard to sound forth dances cannot now be heard for the ringing of bells; all the comfort that happened to either side being this, that he lost her before she had time to be an ill wife, and she left him ere he was able to be a bad husband.

* * * * *

A merrier bargain than the poor sexton's did a tinker meet withal in a country town; through which a citizen of London being driven (to keep himself under the lee-shore in this tempestuous contagion) and casting up his eye for some harbor, spied a bush at the end of a pole (the ancient badge of a country ale-house). Into which as good luck was
10 (without any resistance of the barbarians, that all this year used to keep such landing places), vailing his bonnet, he struck in. The host had been a mad Greek (marry, he could now speak nothing but English); a goodly fat burgher he was, with a belly arching out like a beer-barrell, which made his legs (that were thick and short like two piles driven under London-bridge) to straddle half as wide as the top of Paul's, which upon my knowledge hath been burnt twice or thrice. A leathern pouch hung at his side, that opened and shut with a snap hance, and was indeed a flask for gunpowder when King Henry went to Boulogne. An antiquary might have picked rare matter out of his nose, but that it was worm-
20 eaten (yet that proved it to be an ancient nose). In some corners of it there were bluish holes that shone like shells of mother of pearl, and to do his nose right, pearls had been gathered out of them. Other were richly garnished with rubies, chrysolites and carbuncles, which glistered so oriently that the Hamburgers offered I know not how many dollars for his company in an East-Indian voyage, to have stood a nights in the poop of their Admiral, only to save the charges of candles.

In conclusion, he was an host to be led before an emperor, and though he were one of the greatest men in all the shire, his bigness made him not proud, but he humbled himself to speak the base language of a
30 tapster, and upon the Londoner's first arrival, cried "Welcome, a cloth for this gentleman." The linen was spread, and furnished presently with a new cake and a can; the room voided, and the guest left (like a French Lord) attended by nobody. Who, drinking half a can (in conceit) to the health of his best friend the city, which lay extreme sick, and had never more need of health, I know not what qualms came over his stomach, but immediately he fell down without uttering any more words, and never rose again.

Anon (as it was his fashion) enters my puffing host, to relieve (with a fresh supply out of his cellar) the shrinking can, if he perceived it stood
40 in danger to be overthrown. But seeing the chief leader dropped at his feet, and imagining at first he was but wounded a little in the head, held up his gouty golls and blessed himself that a Londoner (who had wont

to be the most valiant [of] rob-pots) should now be struck down only with two hoops; and thereupon jogged him, fumbling out these comfortable words of a soldier, If thou art a man, stand a thy legs! He stirred not for all this. Whereupon the maids, being raised (as it had been with a hue and cry) came hobbling into the room, like a flock of geese, and having upon search of the body given up this verdict, that the man was dead, and murthered by the plague; oh daggers to all their hearts that heard it! Away trudge the wenches, and one of them having had a freckled face all her life time, was persuaded presently that now they were the tokens, and had liked to have turned up her heels upon it. My gorbelly host, that in many a year could not without grunting crawl over a threshhold but two foot broad, leaped half a yard from the corse (it was measured by a carpenter's rule) as nimbly as if his guts had been taken out by the hangman. Out of the house he wallowed presently, being followed with two or three dozen of napkins to dry up the lard that ran so fast down his heels, that all the way he went was more greasy than a kitchen-stuff-wife's basket. You would have sworn it had been a barrel of pitch on fire, if you had looked upon him, for such a smoky cloud (by reason of his own fatty hot steam) compassed him round that, but for his voice, he had quite been lost in that stinking mist. Hanged himself he had, without all question (in this pitiful taking), but that he feared the weight of his intolerable paunch would have burst the rope, and so he should be put to a double death.

At length the town was raised, the country came down upon him, and yet not upon him neither, for after they understood the tragedy, every man gave ground, knowing my pursy ale-cunner could not follow them. What is to be done in this strange allarum? The whole village is in danger to lie at the mercy of God, and shall be bound to curse none but him for it. They should do well, therefore, to set fire on his house before the plague scape out of it, lest it forage higher into the country, and knock them down, man, woman, and child, like oxen, whose blood (they all swear) shall be required at his hands.

At these speeches my tender-hearted host fell down on his maribones, meaning indeed to entreat his audience to be good to him; but they, fearing he had been peppered too, as well as the Londoner, tumbled one over another, and were ready to break their necks for haste to be gone. Yet some of them (being more valiant than the rest because they heard him roar out for some help) very desperately stepped back, and with rakes and pitch-forks lifted the gulch from the ground; concluding (after they had laid their hogsheads together to draw out some wholesome counsel) that whosoever would venture upon the dead man and bury him, should have forty shillings (out of the common town-purse, though it would

be a great cut to it) with the love of the churchwardens and sidemen
during the term of life. This was proclaimed, but none darst appear to
undertake the dreadful execution. They loved money well; marry, the
plague hanging over any man's head that should meddle with it in that
sort, they all vowed to die beggars before it should be chronicled they
killed themselves for forty shillings. And in that brave resolution, everyone with bag and baggage marched home, barricadoing their doors and
windows with firbushes, fern, and bundles of straw to keep out the pestilence at the stave's end.

10   At last a tinker came sounding through the town, mine host's house
being the ancient watering place where he did use to cast anchor. You
must understand he was none of those base rascally tinkers that with a
bandog and a drab at their tails, and a pikestaff on their necks, will take
a purse sooner than stop a kettle. No, this was a devout tinker, he did
honor God Pan; a musical tinker, that upon his kettle-drum could play
any country dance you called for, and upon holidays had earned money
by it, when no fiddler could be heard of. He was only feared when he
stalked through some towns where bees were, for he struck so sweetly on
the bottom of his copper instrument that he would empty whole hives,
20 and lead the swarms after him only by the sound.

This excellent egregious tinker calls for his draught (being a double
jug). It was filled for him, but before it came to his nose the lamentable
tale of the Londoner was told; the chamber-door (where he lay) being
thrust open with a long pole (because none durst touch it with their
hands), and the tinker bidden (if he had the heart) to go in and see if he
knew him. The tinker, being not to learn what virtue the medicine had
which he held at his lips, poured it down his throat merrily, and crying
trillill, he feared no plagues, in he stepped, tossing the dead body to and
fro, and was sorry he knew him not. Mine host, that with grief began to
30 fall away villanously, looking very ruefully on the tinker, and thinking
him a fit instrument to be played upon, offered a crown out of his own
purse if he would bury the party. A crown was a shrewd temptation to a
tinker; many a hole might he stop before he could pick a crown of it;
yet, being a subtle tinker (and to make all sextons pray for him, because
he would raise their fees) an angel he wanted to be his guide, and under
ten shillings (by his ten bones) he would not put his finger in the fire.

The whole parish had warning of this presently. Thirty shillings was
saved by the bargain, and the town likely to be saved too; therefore ten
shillings was levied out of hand, put into a rag, which was tied to the end
40 of a long pole and delivered (in sight of all the parish, who stood aloof
stopping their noses) by the Headborough's own self in proper person to
the tinker, who with one hand received the money, and with the other

struck the board, crying, hey, a fresh double-pot. Which armor of proof being fitted to his body, up he hoists the Londoner on his back (like a schoolboy), a shovel and pick-axe standing ready for him. And thus furnished, into a field some good distance from the town he bears his deadly load, and there throws it down, falling roundly to his tools; upon which the strong beer having set an edge, they quickly cut out a lodging in the earth for the citizen. But the tinker, knowing that worms needed no apparel, saving only sheets, stripped him stark naked; but first dived nimbly into his pockets, to see what linings they had, assuring himself that a Londoner would not wander so far without silver. His hopes were of the right stamp, for from one of his pockets he drew a leathern bag with seven pounds in it. This music made the tinker's heart dance; he quickly tumbled his man into the grave, hid him over head and ears in dust, bound up his clothes in a bundle, and carrying that at the end of his staff on his shoulder, with the purse of seven pounds in his hand, back again comes he through the town, crying aloud, Have ye any more Londoners to bury, hey downe a downe derry, have ye any more Londoners to bury? the hobbinolls running away from him as if he had been the dead citizen's ghost, and he marching away from them in all the haste he could, with that song still in his mouth.

You see, therefore, how dreadful a fellow Death is, making fools even of wise men, and cowards of the most valiant; yea, in such a base slavery hath it bound men's senses that they have no power to look higher than their own roofs, but seem by their Turkish and barbarous actions to believe that there is no felicity after this life, and that (like beasts) their souls shall perish with their bodies. How many upon sight only of a letter (sent from London) have started back, and durst have laid their salvation upon it that the plague might be folded in that empty paper, believing verily that the arm of omnipotence could never reach them, unless it were with some weapon drawn out of the infected city; in so much that even the western pugs receiving money here, have tied it in a bag at the end of their barge, and so trailed it through the Thames, lest plague-sores sticking upon shillings, they should be nailed up for counterfeits when they were brought home.

JOHN STOW

The Introduction and Notes are at page 1343

FROM *A Survey of London*, 1598

The City of Westminster, with the Antiquities, Bounds, and Liberties thereof.

10   *   *   *   *   *

AND NOW to pass to the famous monastery of Westminster. At the very entrance of the close thereof is a lane that leadeth toward the west, called Thieving Lane, for that thieves were led that way to the gatehouse while the sanctuary continued in force.

This monastery was founded and builded by Sebert, king of the East Saxons, upon the persuasion of Ethelbert, king of Kent, who, having embraced Christianity, and being baptized by Melitus, Bishop of London, immediately (to shew himself a Christian indeed) built a church to the
20 honor of God and Saint Peter on the west side of the city of London, in a place (which because it was overgrown with thorns and environed with water) the Saxons called Thorney, and now of the monastery and west situation thereof is called Westminster.

In this place (saith Fulcardus) long before was a temple of Apollo, which being overthrown, King Lucius built therein a church of Christianity.

Sebert was buried in this church with his wife Athelgoda; whose bodies many years after, to wit, in the reign of Richard the Second (saith Walsingham) were translated from the old church to the new and there
30 interred.

Edgar, king of the West Saxons, repaired this monastery about the year of Christ 958. Edward the Confessor built it of new, whereupon T. Clifford writeth thus.

Without the walls of London (saith he), upon the river of Thames, there was, in times past, a little monastery, builded to the honor of God and Saint Peter, with a few Benedict monks in it under an abbot, serving Christ. Very poor they were, and little was given them for their relief. Here the king intended (for that it was near to the famous city of London and the river of Thames, that brought in all kind of merchandises from
40 all parts of the world) to make his sepulcher; he commanded, therefore, that, of the tenths of all his rents, the work should be begun in such sort as should become the Prince of the Apostles.

At this his commandment the work is nobly begun, even from the foundation, and happily proceedeth till the same was finished; the charges bestowed, or to be bestowed, are not regarded. He granted to this church great privileges, above all the churches in this land, as partly appear by this his charter.*

Edweard cyng graet Willm biscope & Leofstane & Alfsie port gerefen & ealle minre burhthegn on Lunden freondlice: And ic cythe eow thaet ic haebbe seo gifta gyfen and unnam Christ and S. Peter tham haligan Apostel into Westminster: fulra freodome ofer ealle tha land the longath into thaere haligan stow, &c.   10

Edward, king, greets William, bishop, and Leofstan and Alfsie, port-reeves, and all my burgesses of London, friendly, and I tell you that I have this gift given and granted to Christ and St. Peter the holy apostle at Westminster, full freedom over all the land that belongeth to that holy place, *etc.*

He also caused the parish church of St. Margaret to be newly builded without the abbey church of Westminster, for the ease and commodity of the monks, because before that time the parish church stood within the old abbey church in the south aisle, somewhat to their annoyance. This church of St. Margaret (which that King Edward builded) continued 20 till the days of King Edward the First, at what time the staple of wools was at Westminster, and then the parishioners and Merchants of the Staple builded it all of new (the great chancel excepted, which was done by the abbots of Westminster, as is afore shewed).

King Henry the Third, in the year of Christ 1220, began the new work of Our Lady's Chapel, and, in the year 1245, the walls and steeple of the old church (builded by King Edward) were taken down, and, enlarging the same church, caused them to be made more comely; for the furtherance whereof, in the year 1246, the same king (devising how to extort money from the citizens of London towards the charges) ap- 30 pointed a mart to be kept at Westminster, the same to last fifteen days, and, in the mean space, all trade of merchandise to cease in the city, which thing the citizens were fain to redeem with two thousand pound of silver.

The work of this church, with the houses of office, was finished to the end of the choir in the year 1285, the 14 of Edward the First. All which labor of 66 years was, in the year 1299, defaced by a fire kindled in the lesser hall of the king's palace at Westminster. The same, with many other houses adjoining, and with the queen's chamber, were all con-sumed, the flame thereof also (being driven with the wind) fired the monastery, which was also with the palace consumed.   40

Then was this monastery again repaired by the abbots of that church,

* The charter that follows is printed in Old English characters.

King Edward the First and his successors putting to their helping hands.

Edward the Second appropriated unto this church the patronages of the churches of Kelveden and Sabritsworth in Essex, in the diocese of London.

Simon Langham, abbot (having been a great builder there in the year 1362) gave 400 pounds to the building of the body of the church; but (amongst others) Abbot Islip was in his time a great builder there, as may appear in the stone work and glass windows of the church.

Since whose decease that work hath stayed as he left it, unperfected, 10 the church and steeple being all of one height.

King Henry the Seventh, about the year of Christ 1502, caused the chapel of Our Lady, builded by Henry the Third, with a tavern also, called the White Rose near adjoining, to be taken down. In which plot of ground, on the 24 of January, the first stone of the new chapel was laid by the hands of Abbot Islip, Sir Reginald Bray, Knight of the Garter, Dr. Barnes, Master of the Rolls, Dr. Wall, chaplain to the king, Master Hugh Aldham, chaplain to the Countess of Derby and Richmond (the king's mother), Sir Edward Stanhope, knight, and divers other; upon the which stone was engraven the same day and year, etc.

20   *   *   *   *   *

This church hath had great privilege of sanctuary within the precinct thereof, to wit, the church, churchyard, and close, etc., from whence it hath not been lawful for any prince or other to take any person that fled thither for any cause. Which privilege was first granted by Sebert, King of the East Saxons, since increased by Edgar, king of the West Saxons, renewed and confirmed by King Edward the Confessor, as appeareth by this his charter following:

Edward, by the grace of God, King of Englishmen: I make it to be 30 known to all generations of the world after me that, by special commandment of our holy father, Pope Leo, I have renewed and honored the holy church of the blessed apostle St. Peter of Westminster, and I order and establish forever that what person, of what condition or estate soever he be, from whence soever he come, or for what offense or cause it be, either for his refuge into the said holy place, he be assured of his life, liberty, and limbs. And over this, I forbid, under the pain of everlasting damnation, that no minister of mine, or of my successors, intermeddle them with any the goods, lands, or possessions of the said persons taking the said sanctuary; for I have taken their goods and livelihood into my special 40 protection, and therefore I grant to every each of them, inasmuch as my terrestrial power may suffice, all manner freedom of joyous liberty. And whosoever presumes or doth contrary to this my grant, I will he lose his name, worship, dignity, and power, and that, with the great traitor Judas that betrayed Our Saviour, he be in the everlasting fire of hell; and I will and ordain that this my grant endure as long as there remaineth in England either love or dread of Christian name.

*　　*　　*　　*　　*

Now since that I have given you an outward view of this city, it shall not be impertinent to let you take an insight also of the same, such as a Londoner born discoursed above twenty years agone, for answer (as it seemeth) to some objections that then were made against the growing 10 greatness thereof. The author gave it me, and therefore howsoever I conceal his name (which itself pretendeth not), I think I may without his offense impart it to others, that they may take pleasure in the reading, as I doubt not but he did in the writing. Long may they (that list) envy, and long may we and our posterity enjoy the good estate of this city.

*　　*　　*　　*　　*

And whereas commonwealths and kingdoms cannot have (next after God) any surer foundation than the love and good will of one man towards another, that also is closely bred and maintained in cities, where 20 men by mutual society and companying together do grow to alliances, communalties, and corporations.

The liberal sciences and learnings of all sorts, which be *lumina reipublicae* do flourish only in peopled towns, without the which a realm is in no better case than a man that lacketh both his eyes.

Manual arts or handicrafts, as they have for the most part been invented in towns and cities, so they cannot any where else be either maintained or amended. The like is to be said of merchandise, under which name I comprehend all manner of buying, selling, bartering, exchanging, communicating of things that men need, to and fro. Wealth and riches 30 (which are truly called *subsidia belli, et ornamenta pacis*) are increased chiefly in towns and cities, both to the prince and people.

The necessity of the poor and needy is in such places both sooner to be espied, and hath means to be more charitably relieved.

The places themselves be surer refuges in all extremities of foreign invasion, and the inhabitants be a ready hand and strength of men with munition to oppress intestine sedition.

Moreover, for as much as the force of the wars of our time consisteth chiefly in shot (all other soldiers being either horsemen or footmen armed on land, or mariners at the sea) it seemeth to me that citizens and towns- 40 men be as fit to be employed in any of these services (that on horseback only excepted) as the inhabitants that be drawn out of the country.

Furthermore, even as these societies and assemblies of men in cities and great towns are a continual bridle against tyranny, which was the cause that Tarquin, Nero, Dionisius, and such others have always sought to weaken them. So (being well tempered) they are a strong fort and bulwark not only in the Aristocracy, but also in the lawful kingdom or just royalty.

At once the propagation of religion, the execution of good policy, the exercise of charity, and the defence of the country is best performed by towns and cities; and this civil life approacheth nearest to the shape of that mystical body whereof Christ is the head, and men be the members. Whereupon both at the first that man of God, Moses, in the commonwealth of the Israelites, and the governors of all countries in all ages sithence have continually maintained the same. And to change it were nothing else but to *metamorphose* the world, and to make wild beasts of reasonable men. To stand longer upon this it were, *in re non dubia, uti oratione non necessaria;* and therefore I will come to London.

The singularities of the City of London

Whatsoever is said of cities generally, maketh also for London specially. Howbeit, these things are particularly for our purpose to be considered in it: the situation; the former estimation that it hath had; the service that it hath done; the present estate and government of it; and such benefits as do grow to the realm by the maintenance thereof.

This realm hath only three principal rivers whereon a royal city may well be situated: Trent in the north, Severne in the southwest, and Thames in the southeast. Of the which, Thames, both for the straight course in length reachest furthest into the belly of the land, and for the breadth and stillness of the water is most navigable up and down the stream; by reason whereof London (standing almost in the middle of that course) is more commodiously served with provision of necessaries than any town standing upon any of the other two rivers can be, and doth also more easily communicate to the rest of the realm the commodities of her own intercourse and traffic.

This river openeth indifferently upon France and Flanders, our mightiest neighbours, to whose doings we ought to have a bent eye, and special regard. And this city standeth thereon in such convenient distance from the sea, as it is not only near enough for intelligence of the affairs of those princes and for the resistance of their attempts, but also sufficiently removed from the fear of any sudden dangers that may be offered by them; whereas for the Prince of this realm to dwell upon Trent were to turn his back, or blind side, to his most dangerous borderers; and for him to rest and dwell upon Severne were to be shut up in a cumbersome corner which openeth but upon Ireland only, a place of much less importance.

Neither could London be pitched so commodiously upon any other part of the same river of Thames, as where it now standeth. For if it were removed more to the west, it should lose the benefit of the ebbing and flowing; and if it were seated more towards the east, it should be nearer to danger of the enemy, and further both from the good air and from doing good to the inner parts of the realm. Neither may I omit that none other place is so plentifully watered with springs as London is.

*   *   *   *   *   10

. . . This, shortly as I could, is the historical and outward estate of London. Now come I to the inward pith and substance.

The estate of this city is to be examined by the quantity, and by the quality.

The quantity therefore consisteth in the number of the citizens, which is very great, and far exceedeth the proportion of Hippodamus, which appointed 10,000, and of others which have set down other numbers as meet stints, in their opinions, to be well governed. But yet, seeing both reason and experience have freed us from the law of any definite number, so that other things be observed, let that be admitted. Neither is Lon- 20 don, I fear me, so great as populous; for well saith one, *Non idem est magna Civitas & frequens, magna est enim quae multos habet qui arma ferre possunt.* Whatsoever the number be, it breedeth no fear of sedition; for as much as the same consisteth not in the extremes, but in a very mediocrity of wealth and riches, as it shall better appear anon. And if the causes of English rebellions be searched out, they shall be found in effect to be these twain, *ambition* and *covetousness;* of which the first reigneth in the minds of high and noble personages, or of such others as seek to be gracious and popular, and have robbed the hearts of the multitude; whereas in London, if any where in the world, *honos vere onus est,* and 30 every man rather shunneth than seeketh the mayoralty which is the best mark amongst them. Neither hath there been any strong faction, nor any man more popular than the rest, forasmuch as the government is by a pattern (as it were) and always the same, how often soever they change their magistrate. *Covetousness* (that other sire of sedition) possesseth the miserable and needy sort, and such as be naughty packs, unthrifts (which although it cannot be chosen but that in a frequent city as London is, there shall be found many); yet bear they not any great sway, seeing the multitude and most part there is of a competent wealth, and earnestly bent to honest labour. I confess that London is a mighty arm and instru- 40 ment to bring any great desire to effect, if it may be won to a man's devotion; whereof also there want not examples in the English history. But forasmuch as the same is by the like reason serviceable and meet to impeach any disloyal attempt, let it rather be well governed than evil liked therefore; for it shall appear anon that as London has adhered to some rebellions, so hath it resisted many, and was never the author of any one.

The quality of this city consisteth either in the law and government thereof, or in the degrees and condition of the citizens, or in their strength and riches.

It is besides the purpose to dispute, whether the estate of the government here be a *Democracy* or *Aristocracy;* for whatsoever it be, being
10 considered in it self, certain it is that in respect of the whole realm, London is but a citizen, and no city, a subject, and no free estate, an obedienciary, and no place endowed with any distinct or absolute power. For it is governed by the same law that the rest of the realm is, both in causes criminal and civil, a few customs only excepted, which also are to be adjudged or forjudged by the common law. And in the assembly of the estates of our realm (which we call Parliament) they are but a member of the Comminaltie, and send two Burgesses for their city, as every poor borough doth, and two knights for their county as every other shire doth, and are as straightly bound by such laws as any part of the realm is; for
20 if contribution in subsidy of money to the Prince be decreed, the Londoners have none exemption, no not so much as to assess themselves, for the prince doth appoint the Commissioners.

*　　　*　　　*　　　*

The wealth and warlike furniture of London is either public or private, and no doubt the common treasure cannot be much there, seeing that the revenue which they have hardly sufficeth to maintain their bridge and conduits, and to pay their officers and servants. Their toll doth not any
30 more than pay their fee-farm, that they pay to the Prince. Their issues for default of appearances be never levied, and the profits of their courts of justice do go to particular men's hands. Arguments hereof be these two: one, that they can do nothing of extraordinary charge without a general contribution; another, that they have suffered such as have borne the chief office amongst them, and were become bankrupt, to depart the city without relief, which I think they neither would nor could have done if the common treasure had sufficed to cover their shame. Hereof, therefore, we need not be afraid. The public armour and munition of this city remaineth in the halls of the companies, as it doth throughout the whole realm for a great part in the parish churches. Neither is that kept together
40 but only for obedience to the law which commandeth it, and therefore if that threaten danger to the estate it may by another law be taken from them, and committed to a more safe armoury.

The private riches of London resteth chiefly in the hands of the merchants and retailers, for artificers have not much to spare, and labourers have need that it were given unto them. Now how necessary and serviceable the estate of merchandise is to this realm, it may partly appear by the practise of that peaceable, politic and rich Prince, King Henry the Seventh, of whom Polydore (writing his life) sayeth thus: *Mercatores ille saepenumero pecunia multa data gratuito juvabat, ut mercatura (ars una omnium cunctis aequé mortalibus tum commoda, tum necessaria) in suo regno copiosior esset.* But chiefly by the inestimable commodities that grow thereby; for who knoweth not that we have extreme need of many things whereof foreign countries have great store, and that we may spare many things whereof they have need? Or who is ignorant of this, that we have no mines of silver or gold within our realm? So that the increase of our coin and bullion cometh from else where, and yet nevertheless we be both fed, clad, and otherwise served with foreign commodities and delights as plentiful as with our domestical. Which thing cometh to pass by the mean of merchandise only, which importeth necessaries from other countries, and exporteth the superfluities of our own. For seeing we have no way to increase our treasure by mines of gold or silver at home, and can have nothing without money or ware from other countries abroad, it followeth necessarily that if we follow the counsel of that good old husband Marcus Cato, saying, *oportet patrem familias vendacem esse, non emacem*, and do carry more commodities in value over the seas than we bring hither from thence, that then the realm shall receive that overplus in money. But if we bring from beyond the seas merchandise of more value than that which we do send over may countervail, then the realm payeth for that overplus in ready money, and consequently is a loser by that ill husbandry. And therefore, in this part, great and heedful regard must be had that *symmetria* and due proportion be kept, lest otherwise either the realm be defrauded of her treasure, or the subjects corrupted in vanity by excessive importation of superfluous and needless merchandise, or else that we feel penury, even in our greatest plenty and store, by immoderate exportation of our own needful commodities.

Other the benefits that merchandise bringeth shall hereafter appear in the general recital of the commodities that come by London; and therefore it resteth that I speak a word of retailers, and finally show that much good groweth by them both. The chief part of retailing is but a handmaid to merchandise, dispersing by piecemeal that which the merchant bringeth in gross. Of which trade be mercers, grocers, vintners, haberdashers, ironmongers, milliners, and all such as sell wares growing or made beyond the seas; and therefore so long as merchandise it self shall be profitable, and such proportion kept as neither we lose our treasure

thereby nor be cloyed with unnecessary foreign wares, this kind of retailing is to be retained also.

Now that merchants and retailers of London be very rich and great,
it is so far from any harm that it is a thing both praiseworthy and profitable.
For *Mercatura* (sayeth Cicero) *si tenuis est, sordida putanda est, sin
magna est et copiosa, non est vituperanda.* And truly merchants and retailers do not altogether *intus canere,* and profit themselves only, for the
prince and realm both are enriched by their riches. The realm winneth
treasure, if their trade be so moderated by authority that it break not
10 proportion; and they besides bear a good fleece, which the prince may
shear when she seeth good.

But here, before I conclude this part, I have shortly to answer the
accusation of those men which charge London with the loss and decay
of many or most of the ancient cities, corporate towns, and markets within
this realm, by drawing from them to her self alone, say they, both all
trade of traffic by sea, and the retailing of wares and exercise of manual
arts also. Touching navigation, which I must confess is apparently decayed in many port towns, and flourisheth only or chiefly at London, I
impute that partly to the fall of the staple, the which being long since a
20 great trade, and bestowed sometimes at one town and sometimes at another within the realm, did much enrich the place where it was; and being
now not only diminished in force, but also translated over the seas, cannot
but bring some decay with it, partly to the impairing of havens, which in
many places have impoverished those towns whose estate doth ebb and
flow with them, and partly to the dissolution of religious houses, by whose
wealth and haunt many of those places were chiefly fed and nourished. I
mean not to rehearse particular examples of every sort; for the thing it
self speaketh, and I haste to an end.

As for retailers therefore, and handicrafts men, it is no marvel if they
30 abandon country towns and resort to London. For not only the Court
(which is now a days much greater and more gallant than in former
times, and which was wont to be contented to remain with a small company, sometimes at an abbey or priory, sometimes at a Bishop's house,
and sometimes at some mean manor of the king's own) is now for the
most part either abiding at London, or else so near unto it, that the provision of things most fit for it may easily be fetched from thence; but also
by occasion thereof, the gentlemen of all shires do fly and flock to this
city, the younger sort of them to see and shew vanity, and the elder to
save the cost and charge of hospitality and house keeping. For hereby it
40 cometh to pass that the gentlemen being either for a good portion of the
year out of the country, or playing the farmers, graziers, brewers or
such like, more than gentlemen were wont to do within the country,

retailers and artificers, at the least of such things as pertain to the back or belly, do leave the country towns where there is no vent, and do fly to London, where they be sure to find ready and quick market. And yet I wish that, even as many towns in the Low Countries of King Philip do stand, some by one handy art, and some by an other, so also that it might be provided here, that the making of some things might by discreet dispensation be allotted to some special towns, to the end that although the daintiness of men cannot be restrained, which will needs seek those things at London, yet other places also might be relieved, at the least by the workmanship of them.   10

Thus much, then, of the estate of London, in the government thereof, in the condition of the citizens, and in their power and riches. Now follow the enumeration of such benefits as redound to the Prince and this realm by this city. In which doing I profess not to rehearse all, but only to recite and run over the chief and principal of them.

Besides the commodities of the furtherance of religion and justice, the propagation of learning, the maintenance of arts, the increase of riches, and the defence of countries (all which are before shewed to grow generally by cities, and be common to London with them), London bringeth singularly these good things following: 20

By advantage of the situation it disperseth foreign wares (as the stomach doth meat) to all the members most commodiously.

By the benefit of the river of Thames, and great trade of merchandise, it is the chief maker of mariners, and nurse of our navy; and ships (as men know) be the wooden walls for defence of our realm.

It maintaineth, in flourishing estate, the countries of Norfolk, Suffolk, Essex, Kent, and Sussex, which, as they lie in the face of our most puissant neighbor, so ought they (above others) to be conserved in the greatest strength and riches; and these, as it is well known, stand not so much by the benefit of their own soil as by the neighborhood and nearness which 30 they have to London.

It relieveth plentifully, and with good policy, not only her own poor people (a thing which scarcely any other town or shire doth) but also the poor that from each quarter of the realm doth flock unto it, and it imparteth liberally to the necessity of the Universities besides.

It is an ornament to the realm by the beauty thereof, and a terror to other countries by reason of the great wealth and frequency.

It spreadeth the honor of our country far abroad by her long navigations, and maketh our power feared, even of barbarous Princes.

It only is stored with rich merchants, which sort only is tolerable; for 40 beggarly merchants do bite too near, and will do more harm than good to the realm.

It only of any place in this realm is able to furnish the sudden necessity with a strong army. It availeth the prince in tonnage, poundage, and other her customs, much more than all the rest of the realm.

It yieldeth a greater subsidy than any one part of the realm. I mean not for the proportion of the value of the goods only, but also for the faithful service there used in making the assess; for no where else be men taxed so near to their just value as in London. Yea, many are found there that for their countenance and credit sake refuse not to be rated above their ability, which thing never happeneth abroad in the country. 10 I omit that in ancient time the inhabitants of London and other cities were accustomably taxed after the tenth of their goods, when the country was assessed at the fifteenth; and rated at the eighth when the country was set at the twelfth, for that were to awake a sleeping dog, and I should be thought *dicenda, tacenda, locutus,* as the poet said.

It only doth and is able to make the Prince a ready prest, or loan of money.

It only is found fit and able to entertain strangers honorably, and to receive the Prince of the Realm worthily.

Almighty God (*qui nisi custodiat ciuitatem, frustra vigilat custos*), 20 grant that her Majesty evermore rightly esteem and rule this city, and he give grace that the citizens may answer duty, as well towards God and her Majesty as towards this whole realm and country, *Amen.*

JOHN FLORIO

The Introduction and Notes are at page 1345

30 FROM *The Essayes, or Morall, Politike and Militarie Discourses of Lo: Michaell de Montaigne,* 1603 [translated by FLORIO from the French edition of 1595; the first edition of MONTAIGNE's *Essais* was published in 1580]

The Essays of Montaigne

THE NINETEENTH CHAPTER.

That to philosophi[z]e is to learn how to die.

Cicero saith that "to philosophi[z]e is no other thing than for a man 40 to prepare himself to death." Which is the reason that study and contemplation doth, in some sort, withdraw our soul from us and severally employ it from the body, which is a kind of apprenticeage and resemblance of death; or else it is that all the wisdom and discourse of the world doth in the end resolve upon this point, to teach us not to fear to die. Truly either reason mocks us or it only aimeth at our contentment and, in fine, bends all her travail to make us live well, and, as the Holy Scripture saith, "at our ease." All the opinions of the world conclude that pleasure is our end, howbeit they take divers means unto and for it, else would men reject them at their first coming.

*   *   *   *

The end of our career is death; it is the necessary object of our aim. If it affright us, how is it possible we should step one foot further without an ague? The remedy of the vulgar sort is not to think on it. But from what brutal stupidity may so gross a blindness come upon him? He must be made to bridle his ass by the tail,

> *Qui capite ipse suo instituit vestigia retro.*
> Who doth a course contrary run
> With his head to his course begun.

It is no marvel if he be so often taken tripping. Some do no sooner hear the name of death spoken of but they are afraid, yea, the most part will cross themselves as if they heard the devil named. And because mention is made of it in men's wills and testaments, I warrant you there is none will set his hand to them till the physician have given his last doom and utterly forsaken him. And God knows, being then between such pain and fear, with what sound judgment they endure him. Forsomuch as this syllable sounded so unpleasantly in their ears and this voice seemed so ill-boding and unlucky, the Romans had learned to allay and dilate the same by a periphrasis. In lieu of saying, "He is dead," or, "He hath ended his days," they would say, "He hath lived." So it be life, be it past or no, they are comforted.

*   *   *   *

. . . They come, they go, they trot, they dance: but no speech of death. All that is good sport. But if she be once come and, on a sudden and openly, surprise either them, their wives, their children, or their friends, what torments, what outcries, what rage, and what despair doth then overwhelm them? Saw you ever anything so drooping, so changed, and so distracted? A man must look to it and, in better times, foresee it. . . .

Let us learn to stand and combat her with a resolute mind. And [to] begin to take the greatest advantage she hath upon us from her, let us take a clean contrary way from the common. Let us remove her strange-

ness from her; let us converse, frequent and acquaint ourselves with her; let us have nothing so much in mind as death; let us at all times and seasons, and in the ugliest manner that may be, yea, with all faces, shapen and represent the same unto our imagination. At the stumbling of a horse, at the fall of a stone, at the least prick with a pin, let us presently ruminate and say with ourselves, What if it were death itself? And thereupon let us take heart of grace and call our wits together to confront her. Amidst our banquets, feasts, and pleasures, let us ever have this restraint or object before us, that is, the remembrance of our condition, and let not pleasure
10 so much mislead or transport us that we altogether neglect or forget how many ways our joys or our feastings be subject unto death, and by how many hold-fasts she threatens us and them. So did the Ægyptians, who, in the midst of their banquetings and in the full of their greatest cheer, caused the anatomy of a dead man to be brought before them as a memorandum and warning to their guests.

> *Omnem crede diem tibi diluxisse supremum,*
> *Grata superveniet, quae non sperabitur hora.*
> Think every day shines on thee as thy last,
> Welcome it will come, whereof hope was past.

20 It is uncertain where death looks for us; let us expect her everywhere. The premeditation of death is a forethinking of liberty. He who hath learned to die hath unlearned to serve. There is no evil in life for him that hath well conceived how the privation of life is no evil. To know how to die doth free us from all subjection and constraint.

* * * * *

Our religion hath had no surer human foundation than the contempt of life. Discourse of reason doth not only call and summon us unto it (for
30 why should we fear to lose a thing which, being lost, cannot be moaned?), but also, since we are threatened by so many kinds of death, there is no more inconvenience to fear them all than to endure one. What matter is it when it cometh, since it is unavoidable? Socrates answered one that told him, "The Thirty Tyrants have condemned thee to death"; "And nature them," said he. What fondness is it to cark and care so much at that instant and passage from all exemption of pain and care? As our birth brought us the birth of all things, so shall our death the end of all things. Therefore, is it as great folly to weep we shall not live a hundred years hence as to wail we lived not a hundred years ago. "Death is the
40 beginning of another life." So wept we, and so much did it cost us to enter into this life; and so did we spoil us of our ancient veil in entering into it. Nothing can be grievous that is but once. Is it reason so long to fear a

thing of so short time? Long life or short life is made all one by death. For long or short is not in things that are no more. Aristotle saith there are certain little beasts alongst the River Hispanis that live but one day; she which dieth at 8 o'clock in the morning dies in her youth, and she that dies at 5 in the afternoon dies in her decrepitude. Who of us doth not laugh when we shall see this short moment of continuance to be had in consideration of good or ill fortune? The most and the least in ours, if we compare it with eternity, or equal it to the lasting of mountains, rivers, stars, and trees, or any other living creature is no less ridiculous.

But nature compels us to it. "Depart," saith she, "out of this world, even as you came into it. The same way you came from death, to death return, without passion or amazement, from life to death. Your death is but a piece of the world's order and but a parcel of the world's life." . . .

All the time you live, you steal it from death. It is at her charge. The continual work of your life is to contrive death; you are in death during the time you continue in life. For you are after death when you are no longer living. Or if you had rather have it so, you are dead after life: but during life you are still dying; and death doth more rudely touch the dying than the dead, and more lively and essentially. If you have profited by life, you have also been fed thereby; depart then satisfied.

> *Cur non ut plenus vitae conviva recedis?*
> Why, like a full-fed guest,
> Depart you not to rest?

If you have not known how to make use of it; if it were unprofitable to you, what need you care to have lost it? To what end would you enjoy it longer?

> ————————*cur amplius addere quaeris*
> *Rursum quod pereat male, et ingratum occidat omne?*
> Why seek you more to gain, what must again
> All perish ill, and pass with grief or pain?

Life in itself is neither good nor evil; it is the place of good or evil, according as you prepare it for them. And if you have lived one day, you have seen all; one day is equal to all other days. There is no other light, there is no other night. This sun, this moon, these stars, and this disposition, is the very same which your forefathers enjoyed and which shall also entertain your posterity.

> *Non alium videre patres: aliumve nepotes*
> *Aspicient.*
> No other saw our sires of old,
> No other shall their sons behold.

And if the worst happen, the distribution and variety of all the acts of my comedy is performed in one year. If you have observed the course of my four seasons, they contain the infancy, the youth, the virility, and the old age of the world. . . .

Death is less to be feared than nothing, if there were anything less than nothing.

> *——multo mortem minus ad nos esse putandum,*
> *Si minus esse potest quàm quod nihil esse videmus.*
> Death is much less to us, we ought esteem,
> If less may be, than what doth nothing seem.

Nor alive, nor dead, it doth concern you nothing. Alive, because you are; dead, because you are no more. Moreover, no man dies before his hour. The time you leave behind was no more yours than that which was before your birth, and concerneth you no more.

> *Respice enim quam nil ad nos anteacta vetustas*
> *Temporis aeterni fuerit,*
> For mark how all antiquity foregone
> Of all time ere we were, to us was none.

Wheresoever your life endeth, there is it all. The profit of life consists not in the space but rather in the use. Some man hath lived long that hath had a short life. Follow it whilst you have time. It consists not in number of years, but in your will that you have lived long enough. Did you think you should never come to the place where you were still going? There is no way but hath an end. And if company may solace you, doth not the whole world walk the same path? . . .

. . . I have oftentimes bethought myself whence it proceedeth that in times of war the visage of death (whether we see it in us or in others) seemeth, without all comparison, much less dreadful and terrible unto us than in our houses or in our beds (otherwise it should be an army of physicians and whiners); and she ever being one, there must needs be much more assurance amongst country people and of base condition than in others. I verily believe these fearful looks and astonishing countenances wherewith we encompass it are those that more amaze and terrify us than death. A new form of life; the outcries of mothers; the wailing of women and children; the visitation of dismayed and swooning friends; the assistance of a number of pale-looking, distracted, and whining servants; a dark chamber, tapers burning round about; our couch beset round with physicians and preachers; and, to conclude, nothing but horror and astonishment on every side of us—are we not already dead and buried? The very children are afraid of their friends when they see them masked;

and so are we. The mask must as well be taken from things as from men. Which, being removed, we shall find nothing hid under it but the very same death that a sely varlet or a simple maidservant did lately suffer without amazement or fear. Happy is that death which takes all leisure from the preparations of such an equipage.

* * * * *

THE FIVE AND TWENTIETH CHAPTER   10

Of The Institution and Education of Children: To the Lady
Diana of Foix, Countess of Gurson

I never knew father, how crooked and deformed soever his son were, that would either altogether cast him off, or not acknowledge him for his own; and yet (unless he be merely besotted or blinded in his affection) it may not be said but he plainly perceiveth his defects, and hath a feeling of his imperfections. But so it is, he is his own. So it is in myself. I see better than any man else, that what I have set down is nought but the fond imaginations of him who in his youth hath tasted nothing but the paring, and seen but the superficies of true learning; whereof he hath 20 retained but a general and shapeless form: a smack of every thing in general, but nothing to the purpose in particular, after the French manner. To be short, I know there is an art of Physic; a course of Laws; four parts of the Mathematics; and I am not altogether ignorant what they tend unto. And perhaps I also know the scope and drift of Sciences in general to be for the service of our life. But to wade further, or that ever I tired myself with plodding upon Aristotle (the monarch of our modern doctrine) or obstinately continued in search of any one science—I confess I never did it. Nor is there any one art whereof I am able so much as to draw the first lineaments. And there is no scholar (be he of the 30 lowest form) that may not repute himself wiser than I, who am not able to oppose him in his first lesson; and if I be forced to it, I am constrained very impertinently to draw in matter from some general discourse, whereby I examine and give a guess at his natural judgment—a lesson as much unknown to them as theirs is to me. I have not dealt or had commerce with any excellent book, except Plutarch or Seneca, from whom (as the Danaïdes) I draw my water, uncessantly filling, and as fast emptying. Some thing whereof I fasten to this paper, but to myself nothing at all.

And touching books, History is my chief study, Poesy my only delight, 40 to which I am particularly affected; for as Cleanthes said, that as the voice being forcibly pent in the narrow gullet of a trumpet, at last issueth forth more strong and shriller, so, meseems, that a sentence cunningly and closely couched in measure-keeping Poesie darts it self forth more furiously, and wounds me even to the quick. And concerning the natural faculties that are in me (whereof behold here an essay), I perceive them to faint under their own burthen; my conceits, and my judgment march but uncertain, and as it were groping, staggering, and stumbling at every rush. And when I have gone as far as I can, I have no whit pleased myself; for the further I sail the more land I descry, and that so dimmed with fogs and overcast with clouds that my sight is so weakened I cannot 10 distinguish the same. And then undertaking to speak indifferently of all that presents itself unto my fantasy, and having nothing but mine own natural means to employ therein, if it be my hap (as commonly it is) among good authors to light upon those very places which I have undertaken to treat of, as even now I did in Plutarch, reading his discourse of the power of imagination, wherein, in regard of those wise men, I acknowledge myself so weak and so poor, so dull and gross-headed, as I am forced both to pity and disdain myself. Yet am I pleased with this, that my opinions have often the grace to jump with theirs, and that I follow them aloof-off, and thereby possess at least that which all other men 20 have not; which is, that I know the utmost difference between them and myself. All which notwithstanding, I suffer my inventions to run abroad as weak and faint as I have produced them, without bungling and botching the faults which this comparison hath discovered to me in them. A man had need have a strong back to undertake to march foot to foot with these kind of men. The indiscreet writers of our age, amidst their trivial compositions, intermingle and wrest in whole sentences taken from ancient authors, supposing by such filching theft to purchase honor and reputation to themselves, do clean contrary. For this infinite variety and dissemblance of lustres makes a face so wan, so ill-favored, and so ugly in 30 respect of theirs, that they lose much more than gain thereby. . . .

I have no authority to purchase belief, neither do I desire it; knowing well that I am not sufficiently taught to instruct others. Some having read my precedent Chapter, told me not long since in mine own house, I should somewhat more have extended myself in the discourse concerning the institution of children. Now (Madam) if there were any sufficiency in me touching that subject, I could not better employ the same than to bestow it as a present upon that little lad which ere long threateneth to make a happy issue from out your honorable womb: for (Madame) you are too generous to begin with other than a man child. And 40 having had so great a part in the conduct of your successful marriage, I may challenge some right and interest in the greatness and prosperity of all that shall proceed from it. Moreover, the ancient and rightful possession which you from time to time have ever had, and still have, over my service, urgeth me with more than ordinary respects to wish all honor, welfare, and advantage to whatsoever may in any sort concern you and yours. And truly, my meaning is but to shew that the greatest difficulty and importing [of] all human knowledge seemeth to be in this point where the nurture and institutions of young children is in question. For as in matters of husbandry, the labor that must be used before sowing, setting, and planting, yea in planting itself, is most certain and easy; but when that which was sowen, set, and planted cometh to take life, before it come to ripeness, much ado, and great variety of proceeding belongeth to it. So in men, it is no great matter to get them; but being born, what continual cares, what diligent attendance, what doubts and fears do daily wait to their parents and tutors before they can be nurtured and brought to any good? The fore-shew of their inclination whilest they are young is so uncertain, their humours so variable, their promises so changing, their hopes so false, and their proceedings so doubtful, that it is very hard (yea for the wisest) to ground any certain judgment, or assured success upon them. Behold Cymon, view Themistocles, and a thousand others, how they have differed, and fallen to better from themselves, and deceive the expectation of such as knew them. The young whelps both of dogs and bears at first sight shew their natural disposition, but men headlong embracing this custom or fashion, following that humor or opinion, admitting this or that passion, allowing of that or this law, are easily changed, and soon disguised. Yet it is hard to force the natural propension or readiness of the mind, whereby it followeth that, for want of heedy fore-sight in those that could not guide their course well, they often employ much time in vain, to address young children in those matters whereunto they are not naturally addicted. All which difficulties notwithstanding, mine opinion is to bring them up in the best and profitablest studies, and that a man should slightly pass over those fond presages, and deceiving prognostics, which we over precisely gather in their infancy. And (without offence be it said) me thinks that Plato in his *Commonwealth* allowed them too-too much authority.

Madame, Learning joined with true knowledge is an especial and graceful ornament, and an implement of wonderful use and consequence; namely, in persons raised to that degree of fortune wherein you are. And in good truth, learning hath not her own true form, nor can she make shew of her beauteous lineaments, if she fall into the hands of base and vile persons. . . .

To a gentleman born of noble parentage, and heir of a house, that aimeth at true learning and in it would be disciplined, not so much for gain or commodity to himself (because so abject an end is far unworthy

the grace and favour of the Muses, and besides hath a regard or dependencie of others), nor for external shew and ornament, but to adorn and enrich his inward mind, desiring rather to shape and institute an able and sufficient man, than a bare learned man; my desire is, therefore, that the parents or overseers of such a gentleman be very circumspect and careful in choosing his director, whom I would rather commend for having a well composed and temperate brain than a full-stuffed head, yet both will do well. And I would rather prefer wisdom, judgment, civil customs, and modest behavior than bare and mere literal learning; and
10 that in his charge he hold a new course. . . .

I would have him make his scholar narrowly to sift all things with discretion, and harbour nothing in his head by mere authority, or upon trust. Aristotle's principles shall be no more axioms unto him than the Stoic's or Epicurians'. Let this diversity of judgments be proposed unto him. If he can, he shall be able to distinguish the truth from falsehood; if not, he will remain doubtful.

> *Che non men che saper dubbiar m'aggrada.*
> No less it pleaseth me,
> To doubt, than wise to be.

20
For if by his own discourse he embrace the opinions of Xenophon, or of Plato, they shall be no longer theirs, but his. He that merely followeth another, traceth nothing, and seeketh nothing: *Non sumus sub rege, sibi quisque se vindicet:* "We are not under a King's command; every one may challenge himself, for let him at least know that he knoweth." It is requisite he endeavor as much to feed himself with their conceits, as labour to learn their precepts; which, so he know how to apply, let him hardily forget where or whence he had them. Truth and reason are common to all, and are no more proper unto him that spake them heretofore than
30 unto him that shall speak them hereafter. And it is no more according to Plato's opinion than to mine, since both he and I understand and see alike. The bees do here and there suck this and cull that flower, but afterward they produce the honey, which is peculiarly their own; then is it no more thyme or marjoram. So of pieces borrowed of others, he may lawfully alter, transform, and confound them, to shape out of them a perfect piece of work, altogether his own; always provided his judgment, his travel, study, and institution tend to nothing but to frame the same perfect.

*   *   *   *   *

40
There is a marvelous clearness, or as I may term it an enlightening of man's judgment drawn from the commerce of men, and by frequenting

abroad in the world; we are all so contrived and compact in our selves, that our sight is made shorter by the length of our nose. When Socrates was demanded whence he was, he answered, not "of Athens," but "of the world"; for he, who had his imagination more full and farther stretching, embraced all the world for his native city, and extended his acquaintance, his society, and affections to all man-kind, and not as we do, that look no further than our feet. If the frost chance to nip the vines about my village, my Priest doth presently argue that the wrath of God hangs over our head, and threateneth all mankind, and judgeth that the pip is already fallen upon the cannibals.   10

In viewing these intestine and civil broils of ours, who doth not exclaim that this world's vast frame is near unto a dissolution, and that the day of judgment is ready to fall on us? never remembering that many worse revolutions have been seen, and what whilst we are plunged in grief, and overwhelmed in sorrow, a thousand other parts of the world besides are blessed with all happiness, and wallow in pleasures, and never think on us? Whereas, when I behold our lives, our license, and impunity, I wonder to see them so mild and easy. He on whose head it haileth, thinks all the hemisphere besides to be in a storm and tempest. And as that dull-pated Savoyard said, that if the seely King of France could cunningly 20 have managed his fortune, he might very well have made himself chief steward of his Lord's household; whose imagination conceived of no other greatness than his Master's; we are all insensible of this kind of error—an error of great consequence and prejudice.

*   *   *   *   *

But touching philosophy, namely, in that point where it treateth of man, and of his duties and offices, it hath been the common judgment of the wisest that in regard of the pleasantness of her conversation, she ought not to be rejected, neither at banquets nor at sports. And Plato hav- 30 ing invited her to his solemn feast, we see how kindly she entertaineth the company with a mild behaviour, fitly suiting her self to time and place, notwithstanding it be one of his learned'st and profitable discourses.

> Æquè pauperibus prodest, locupletibus aequè,
> Et neglecta aequè pueris senibusque nocebit.

> Poor men alike, alike rich men it easeth,
> Alike it, scorned, old and young displeaseth.

So doubtless he shall less be idle than others; for even as the paces we bestow walking in a gallery, although they be twice as many more, weary 40 us not so much as those we spend in going a set journey; so our lesson being past over, as it were, by chance or way of encounter, without strict

observance of time or place, being applied to all our actions, shall be digested and never felt. All sports and exercises shall be a part of his study:
running, wrestling, music, dancing, hunting, and managing of arms and
horses. I would have the exterior demeanor or decency, and the disposition
of his person to be fashioned together with his mind. For, it is not a mind,
it is not a body that we erect, but it is a man, and we must not make
two parts of him. And as Plato saith, "They must not be erected one
without another, but equally be directed, no otherwise than a couple of
horses matched to draw in one self-same team."

10
*   *   *   *   *

Yet can no man say but that to speak well is most gracious and commendable, but not so excellent as some make it; and I am grieved to see
how we employ most part of our time about that only. I would first know
mine own tongue perfectly; then my neighbor's with whom I have most
commerce. I must needs acknowledge that the Greek and Latin tongues
are great ornaments in a gentleman, but they are purchased at over-
high a rate. Use it who list, I will tell you how they may be gotten better
cheap, and much sooner than is ordinarily used; which was tried in my-
20 self. My late father, having, by all the means and industry that is possible
for man, sought amongst the wisest and men of best understanding to find
a most exquisite and ready way of teaching, being advised of the inconveniences then in use, was given to understand that the lingering while and
best part of our youth that we employ in learning the tongues which cost
them nothing, is the only cause we can never attain to that absolute perfection of skill and knowledge of the Greeks and Romans. I do not believe
that to be the only cause. But so it is, the expedient my father found out
was this; that being yet at nurse, and before the first loosing of my tongue,
I was delivered to a German (who died since, a most excellent physician
30 in France) he being then altogether ignorant of the French tongue, but
exquisitely ready and skilful in the Latin. This man, whom my father had
sent for of purpose, and to whom he gave very great entertainment, had
me continually in his arms, and was mine only overseer. There was also
joined unto him two of his countrymen, but not so learned, whose charge
was to attend, and now and then to play with me. And all these together
did never entertain me with other than the Latin tongue. As for others of
his household, it was an inviolable rule that neither himself, nor my mother,
nor man, nor maid-servant, were suffered to speak one word in my company, except such Latin words as every one had learned to chat and prattle
40 with me. It were strange to tell how every one in the house profited
therein. My father and my mother learned so much Latin that for a need
they could understand it when they heard it spoken; even so did all the

household servants, namely such as were nearest and most about me. To be short, we were all so Latinized that the towns round about us had their share of it, insomuch as even at this day many Latin names both of workmen and of their tools are yet in use amongst them. And as for myself, I was above six years old, and could understand no more French or Perigordine than Arabic; and that without art, without books, rules, or grammar, without whipping or whining, I had gotten as pure a Latin tongue as my master could speak, the rather because I could neither mingle or confound the same with other tongues. If for an essay they would give me a theme, whereas the fashion in colleges is to give it in French, I had it in bad Latin, 10 to reduce the same into good. And Nicholas Grouchy, who hath written *De comitiis Romanorum;* William Guerente, who hath commented Aristotle; George Buchanan, that famous Scottish poet; and Marc Antoine Muret, whom (while he lived) both France and Italy to this day, acknowledge to have been the best orator—all which have been my familiar tutors—have often told me that in mine infancy I had the Latin tongue so ready and so perfect that themselves feared to take me in hand. And Buchanan, who afterward I saw attending on the Marshall of Brissac, told me he was about to write a treatise of the institution of children, and that he took the model and pattern from mine. For at that time he had the 20 charge and bringing up of the young Earl of Brissac, whom since we have seen prove so worthy and so valiant a Captain.

* * * * *

The first taste or feeling I had of books, was of the pleasure I took in reading the fables of Ovid's *Metamorphoses;* for, being but seven or eight years old, I would steal and sequester my self from all other delights, only to read them; forsomuch as the tongue wherein they were written was to me natural, and it was the easiest book I knew, and by reason of the matter therein contained most agreeing with my young age. For of King Arthur, 30 of Lancelot du Lake, of Amadis, of Huon of Bordeaux, and such idle, time-consuming and wit-besotting trash of books wherein youth doth commonly amuse itself, I was not so much as acquainted with their names, and to this day know not their bodies, nor what they contain, so exact was my discipline. Whereby I became more careless to study my other prescript lessons. And well did it fall out for my purpose, that I had to deal with a very discreet master, who out of his judgment could with such dexterity wink at and second my untowardliness, and such other faults that were in me. For by that means I read over Virgil's *Æneados,* Terence, Plautus, and other Italian comedies, allured thereunto by the pleasantness of their 40 several subjects. Had he been so foolishly-severe, or so severely froward as to cross this course of mine, I think verily I had never brought any thing from the college but the hate and contempt of books, as doth the greatest part of our nobility. Such was his discretion, and so warily did he behave himself, that he saw and would not see; he would foster and increase my longing, suffering me but by stealth and by snatches to glut my self with those books, holding ever a gentle hand over me concerning other regular studies. For, the chiefest thing my father required at their hands (unto whose charge he had committed me) was a kind of well conditioned mildness and facility of complexion. And, to say truth, mine had no other fault but a certain dull languishing and heavy slothfulness. The danger was not, 10 I should do ill, but that I should do nothing.

*   *   *   *   *

And I have ever accused them of impertinency that condemn and disallow such kinds of recreations, and blame those of injustice that refuse good and honest comedians, or (as we call them) players, to enter our good towns, and grudge the common people such public sports. Politic and well ordered commonwealths endeavor rather carefully to unite and assemble their citizens together; as in serious offices of devotion, so in honest exercises of recreation. Common society and loving friendship is 20 thereby cherished and increased. And besides, they cannot have more formal and regular pastimes allowed them than such as are acted and represented in open view of all, and in the presence of the magistrates themselves. And if I might bear sway, I would think it reasonable that Princes should sometimes, at their proper charges, gratify the common people with them, as an argument of a fatherly affection and loving goodness towards them. And that in populous and frequented cities, there should be theatres and places appointed for such spectacles, as a diverting of worse inconveniences, and secret actions.

But to come to my intended purpose, there is no better way to allure 30 the affection, and to entice the appetite; otherwise a man shall breed but asses laden with books. With jerks of rods they have their satchels full of learning given them to keep; which to do well, one must not only harbor in himself, but wed and marry the same with his mind.

EDWARD GRIMESTON

The Introduction and Notes are at page 1347

FROM GRIMESTON's translation of Nicholas Coeffeteau's *A Table of Humane Passions*, 1621 [the French edition was published in 1615]

Of Human Passions

The Preface

As PROVIDENT Nature hath prescribed certain ends to all the creatures of this universe, whom she hath clothed with certain qualities and allurements fit to inflame them with their love; so there is not anyone in this world but doth endeavor by all means to attaine unto those ends which are propounded. As the sun, having been placed in the firmament to contribute to the birth and preservation of beasts and plants, runs continually from one hemisphere to the other, to pour out the beams of his influence and light over all; so, after his example, there is not any other cause in all this great world but is careful to seek and pursue her end, according to the motions which Nature hath engrafted. But to make them capable, it was necessary that the same Nature which hath prescribed them their ends, should also give them as it were two wings to raise them up. That is to say, it was needful she should impart unto them the knowledge, and engraft in them the inclination and desire to pursue them. Desire alone were not sufficient, for that is fashioned in the Appetite, which is a blind power, and requires some light to guide and conduct it in its motions; even as they say the whale, which hath a weak and heavy sight, hath need of a guide to conduct it through the waves of the sea, lest that this great and weighty mass which she draws after her should strike against some rock and be crushed in pieces. Neither were Knowledge alone sufficient, for that it proceeds from a faculty which, being born to give light, doth necessarily presuppose another power which doth receive the beams of her light, and, as we may say, suffers itself to be guided by that light. As for example, to cause the king (being incited by the glory of his ancestors, or induced by the greatness of his courage) to undertake the sack of Constantinople, or to replant the cross in Palestine, it were not sufficient that he knew where Constantinople stood, or in what part of the world Palestine were; but besides all this it were needful that with this knowledge the heat and ardor to carry him to so glorious a conquest should breed a desire. As in old time to thrust on Alexander to undertake the voyage of Persia, or of the Indies, it was not only requisite this prince should have some knowledge of that stately empire and of those rich provinces; but it was also necessary his generosity should beget in him a passion and will to conquer them. So as no man embraceth any design whatsoever, until that knowledge be united with desire, and desire joined unto knowledge.

In this manner, then, if things knew their ends and did not desire them, or if they desired them without the knowledge, they could not be drawn to endeavor to get them; for as much as, through the want of those helps,
10 they should be in danger to labor in vain, and to lose all the pains of their pursuits. So as to effect it they had need of Knowledge and Desire. The proofs hereof are seen in all the creatures which make a part of this universal world. For leaving apart the angels of heaven, whose actions show sufficiently that their substance is indued with an understanding full of knowledge, and a will capable to frame divers desires, if we will fix our eyes upon visible nature, we shall find that there is not any creature, not only among those that have life, but even among those that have no souls, in the motions and course of whose actions this truth doth not appear and demonstrate itself plainly.
20 It is true, that in things which are insensible and without life, it is not necessary that the knowledge of their ends should remain in themselves, as the desires and inclinations to attain unto them do reside; but it sufficeth that they be guided and conducted by a cause conjoined to their actions. And to return to our last example, as it was necessary (to draw Alexander to undertake the voyage of Asia and the Indies) he should have knowledge of the provinces, yet he might borrow this knowledge from those which had seen them and observed them. Even as blind men, who, led by their guides, go where their affairs do call them; even so, although that natural things which of themselves are not indued with any knowledge besides
30 the inclination which they have unto their end, have yet some need to know it, to the end they may affect it and seek it; yet having a desire, it imports not whether the knowledge be precisely in themselves, or that some other cause supplies this defect and insinuates itself into this action to guide it. The reason whereof is, that although they be deprived of knowledge, yet it hinders not the force of their motions; for that they are united to that great Intelligence which knoweth all things, and cannot err in her knowledge, but guides all the natural causes to their ends by her wise providence.

But these things have always need of Knowledge and Desire to put
40 them into action, although that in regard of knowledge it is not absolutely necessary it reside in them, but it sufficeth that it be imparted unto them by the influence and assistance of a more eminent cause. As for those which

have life, it may be plainly observed in the course of their lives. But we must remember that the soul, being the form of living things, and natural forms having this in particular, that the more noble contains the perfection of that which is less noble; as a quadrangle comprehends with a certain eminency all that enters into the composition of a triangle; and as the forms of beasts contain the forms of the Elements; it follows that there being three degrees of souls; that is to say, that which gives life, which is the less perfect; that which gives sense, which is the second rank; and the Reasonable, which is the noblest of all; this Reasonable soul, which is peculiar only to man, contains all the powers and perfections of the other, and can effect as much as all the rest together. By reason whereof man hath a Vegetative soul, which is common with plants; he hath the Sensitive, which he hath common with brute beasts; but he alone is in possession of the Reasonable soul, whereby he hath nothing common with the rest of the creatures.

After this, either of these souls hath a number of powers befitting the operations which must arise. The powers of the Vegetative soul are principally those which nourish, which contribute to the growing and increase, and which serve to generation. And those have other powers for instruments to their actions, as the power to draw, the power to retain, the power to expell the excrements, the power to digest the nourishment, and others which philosophers assign unto them.

Moreover, there is a power which is as it were the queen of all the rest, to whose command and conduct they refer all their actions. And that is the power of the Natural Appetite, the which (as we have said) is one of those two things necessary to accomplish the actions of Nature. According unto these laws, we see that the power we call Attractive draws the nourishment unto her, for that the Natural Appetite doth press and command her; and in like manner the power which they call Expulsive, doth cast forth and expel those things which the same Natural Appetite doth abhor; and so of the other powers which are ordained to diverse ends. But for that the Appetite, which is blind and void of all Knowledge, is not sufficient in Vegetative things to exercise their action, but withal it is requisite that they be accompanied with Knowledge; it therefore happens that the Vegetative soul, being not so noble that among all her powers there is not any one indued with Knowledge, the universal Nature, which provides for all, supplies this defect, and conducts by her light the inclination of Vegetative substances to their ends, and by the same means guides all the other powers which follow her motions in their actions. So as Nature, knowing the substance fitting and proper for the nourishment, shews it and instructs the Natural Appetite, and ordains that it shall be drawn and digested, and converted into nourishment for the preserva-

tion of the Vegetable Individue; and the like may be said of the other actions; wherein doubtless living things differ not much from those that have no life. And we must not object that plants seem to be indued with Knowledge, for that they can distinguish a juice which is proper for them from that which is pernicious, the which seems to be a mark of Knowledge. For although there were Philosophers which did attribute unto plants a feeling of things, which they said was less pure and less active than that of creatures, yet it is most certain that the nature of the Vegetative soul is too earthly to be fit for the functions of the senses, which re-
10 quire other organs than those of the plants. And therefore, although they draw unto them good juice, and reject the bad, it proceeds not from any Knowledge wherewith they are indued, but from their Natural virtues, and properties, guided by that sovereign Intelligence which disperseth her care over all the creatures how base and abject soever. And it is also by her motion that the same plants fly their contraries, as the vine shuns the bay tree; and that they shew such grace and beauty in their works, as we see in the springtime; so as all these things bind us not to believe that they are indued with Knowledge.

But let us return to our discourse, and (leaving the Vegetative soul)
20 ascend a degree higher, and come to the Sensitive. This as the more noble hath in herself the possession of Knowledge and hath no need to borrow it, like unto the Vegetative soul and things without life. Moreover, she hath three kinds of powers; that is to say, the faculty to know, the faculty to desire, and the moving power. By the moving power I understand that which executes the motion from one place to another, as it is commanded and ordained by the faculty where the Desire is framed, after that it is enlightened and guided by Knowledge.

The Knowing powers are of two sorts; that is to say, the exterior and the interior. The exterior are the five senses of Nature, as seeing, hearing,
30 smelling, tasting, and touching, the which as messengers carry to the interior powers indued with Knowledge whatsoever we can comprehend and desire. These exterior powers of the senses answer in some sort to the bodies of the universe, whereof they comprehend the colors, the sounds, the smells, the savors, the cold, the heat, and the other natural qualities wherewith they are clothed. The interior powers capable of Knowledge are three; whereof the first is the Common sense, the which is called by that name for that it is, as it were, the center to which do flow the forms which are sent unto it from the other senses. So as from the eyes it receives the forms of colors which they have seen; from the hear-
40 ing the forms of sounds which have touched the ear; from smelling the forms of savors which it hath scented; from the tongue, the form of sweetness or bitterness which it hath tasted; and from the body the forms

of those things which fall under the sense of touching. And it not only receives the forms which the other senses send unto it, but it also compares them, discerns them, and judgeth of them; the which the particular senses cannot do, for that they are limited and tied to their particular objects, and never exceed the bounds thereof.

For the eyes are only employed to judge of the difference of colors, as betwixt white and black, and never seek to meddle with that which concerns the sound, smelling, or the other qualities which have nothing common with colors. The Common sense, then, is necessary to judge thus generally of all the objects of the other senses, that by means thereof the creature may distinguish that which is healthful from that is hurtful.

But to the end the knowledge which this sense doth gather from the objects whose forms are presented unto it by the exterior senses be not lost by their absence, it sends all it hath gathered, compared and distinguished, to another power merely Knowing, which is called the Imaginative, as that wherein are graven the forms of things which are offered unto it by the Common sense, to the end the Knowledge may remain after they are vanished away. Besides this Imaginative, there is another power proper to perform things, which is the Memory, the which, although it be not directly ordained to judge but rather to serve as a storehouse and treasury to shut up and to preserve the forms of things which are imprinted in her; yet for that she doth continually represent unto the Common sense the forms which are consigned unto her, she may well be said also to help to Knowledge.

These, then, are the three interior powers capable of Knowledge; to the which, although that some add others, yet I will hold with their opinion who not willing to multiply the powers without necessity, reject them as superfluous, seeing the Imaginative power sufficeth to do all the offices which are attributed unto them. There are then in the Sensitive soul eight Knowing faculties; five external, and three internal, as we have shewed.

As for the Appetitive powers where the desires are formed, there are but two; that is to say, the Concupiscible or desiring power, and the Irascible or angry power; the one of which without the other sufficeth not for the health of the creatures. For if the lion had no other inclination, nor any other spur of desire than to run after meat fit for his nourishment, doubtless the least difficulty and obstacle he should encounter would hinder the pursuit of his prey; for that he should be without any desire to surmount this difficulty, and so he should not be able to preserve his life for want of nourishment.

In like manner men would be daunted for the least crosses they should find in the pursuit of any good thing, or in the avoiding of evil; and al-

though the danger were not great nor urgent, yet would they not dare
to oppose themselves and encounter it. And so they would yield to these
difficulties, and not pursue the objects of their desires, how great soever
their inclination were to seek them. Wherefore provident Nature, to
prevent this inconvenience, besides the other powers hath given unto the
Sensitive soul two Appetites; that is to say, the Concupiscible and the
Irascible; whereof this last, when as any difficulty ariseth and opposeth
itself to the desire of the Concupiscible, comes presently to succour it;
and inflaming the blood, excites choler, hope, courage, or some other
10 like passion destined and ordained to make him surmount the difficulties
which cross the contentment of the soul. For that which concerns the
powers of the Sensitive soul, there remains none but the faculty moving
from one place to another, which is dispersed and resides in the sinews,
muscles and ligaments, and which is dispersed over all the members of
the creature. This power, being commanded by the Appetite, doth presently exercise his office, serving for an instrument to that part of the
blood which for the great subtlety and pureness thereof hath gotten the
name of Spirit.

   To come now to the Reasonable soul, it hath two principal powers;
20 the one indued with Knowledge, which is the Understanding; and the
other capable of Desire, which is the Will; the which being blind as all
the Appetites are naturally, she followeth in the pursuit of her objects the
light of the Understanding, by reason whereof she is termed the Intellectual Appetite, but more properly the Will. The office of our Understanding, particularly of that which we call possible, is to receive, and in
receiving to know, and in knowing to offer unto the Will those kinds or
forms which are sent unto it from the Imagination. It is true that, being
a more noble power than the Sensitive, it cannot receive those images
and forms so material, gross, and sensible as they are of themselves in
30 their particular being, for that they are not proportionable to the purity
and excellency of her condition. By reason whereof the philosophers have
placed in our souls another power wonderfully noble, whose office is to
purge and to clothe as it were with a new lustre all the images or forms
which are found in the Imagination or fantasy; and by the means of this
light, to cause those forms which were material, sensible, and singular to
become so purified from these earthly conditions as they seem universal,
and so well proportioned to the pureness of our Understanding as they
easily receive the impression.

   Thus, then, the powers of all the three souls concur in man in regard
40 of the Rational, the which as more noble than the Sensitive or Vegetative,
comprehends all their powers, and withal adds many things to their perfection. In the mean time, we must consider that man hath no kind of

command, neither over the powers of the Vegetative soul, whose actions are merely natural; nor over those of the Sensitive soul, which are destined to Knowledge, as the interior and exterior senses, unless it be by accident, when as by a resolution of his Will, he denies these powers the means which are necessary to put them in action. But he may well have power over those of the Sensitive Appetite, which are proper to obey the discourse of Reason, and the command of the Will, as over the Irascible and Concupiscible.

To the end, then, that amidst the bond of the Intellectual powers with the Sensitive, and the communication and correspondency which is betwixt them for the exercise of their functions, we may the better see how the less noble obey and serve the more noble, and execute their offices, we must here represent the form. As soon as the exterior senses, busied about the objects which are proper for them, have gathered the forms of things which come from without, they carry them to the Common sense; the which receives them, judgeth of them, and distinguisheth them, and then to preserve them in the absence of their objects, presents them to the Imagination; which, having gathered them together, to the end she may represent them whensoever need shall require, she delivers them to the custody of the Memory; from whence retiring them when occasion requires, she propounds them unto the Appetite, under the appearance of things that are pleasing or troublesome, that is to say, under the form of good and evil; and at the same instant the same forms, enlightened with the light of the Understanding, and purged from the Sensible and singular conditions which they retain in the Imagination, and instead of that which they represented of particular things, representing them general, they become capable to be embraced by the Understanding; the which, under the appearance of things which are profitable or hurtful, that is to say, under the form of good and evil, represents them unto the Will; the which, being blind, refers itself to that which the Understanding proposeth unto it. And then, as queen of the powers of the soul, she ordains what they shall embrace and what they shall fly as it pleaseth her; whereunto the Sensitive Appetite, yielding a prompt obedience to execute her command, from the which it never strays so long as it contains itself within the bounds and order prescribed by Nature, quickeneth all the powers and passions over which she commands, and sets to work those which are necessary to that action, and by their means commands the moving power, dispersed over all the members, to follow or fly, to approach or to recoil, or to do any other motion which it requireth. And she obeying suddenly, if she be not hindered, moves the whole body with the organs which reside in the parts, and induceth them to fly or embrace things according to the command which she hath received.

After this manner man proceeds in his free operations, if he will observe the order which he ought. The which I say, for that oftentimes he
overthrows and perverts this order, either by bad education, or by custom,
or the organs being unsound, or for that his Will hath bad inclination, so
as reason cannot enjoy her power and subject the Sensual Appetite unto
her; but contrariwise he abandons himself in prey unto this disordered
Appetite, and suffers himself to be transported by his furious motions.
So as suddenly whenas Fantasy offers to the Appetite the forms which
she receives from the senses under the show of good or evil, he without
10 stay to have them judged by the discourse of Understanding and chosen
by the Will, commands of himself the moving power, and makes it to
act according to his pleasure. And herein consists the disorder which the
passions cause in the life of man, which divert him many times from the
laws of Reason. But we have spoken enough hereof. Let us now enter the
subject, and begin by the definition of passions to know their nature and
essence.

SIR WALTER RALEGH

The Introduction and Notes are at page 1347

From *The History of the World*, 1614

The History of the World

The Preface

How UNFIT and how unworthy a choice I have made of myself to undertake a work of this mixture, mine own reason, though exceeding weak,
30 hath sufficiently resolved me. For had it been begotten then with my
first dawn of day, when the light of common knowledge began to open
itself to my younger years, and before any wound received, either from
fortune or time, I might yet well have doubted that the darkness of age
and death would have covered over both it and me long before the performance. For, beginning with the creation, I have proceeded with the
history of the world, and lastly purposed (some few sallies excepted) to
confine my discourse within this, our renowned island of Great Britain.
I confess that it had better sorted with my disability, the better part of
whose times are run out in other travails, to have set together (as I could)
40 the unjointed and scattered frame of our English affairs than of the universal; in whom, had there been no other defect (who am all defect)
than the time of the day, it were enough; the day of a tempestuous life

drawn on to the very evening ere I began. But those inmost and soul-piercing wounds which are ever aching while uncured, with the desire to satisfy those few friends which I have tried by the fire of adversity—the former enforcing, the latter persuading—have caused me to make my thoughts legible, and myself the subject of every opinion, wise or weak.

* * * * *

To me it belongs in the first part of this preface, following the common and approved custom of those who have left the memories of time past to other ages, to give, as near as I can, the same right to History which they have done. Yet, seeing therein I should but borrow other men's words, I will not trouble the reader with the repetition. True it is that, among many other benefits for which it hath been honored, in this one it triumpheth over all human knowledge: That it hath given us life in our understanding, since the world itself had life and beginning, even to this day; yea, it hath triumphed over time, which, besides it, nothing but eternity hath triumphed over. For it hath carried our knowledge over the vast and devouring space of so many thousands of years, and given so fair and piercing eyes to our mind, that we plainly behold, living now, as if we had lived then, that great world, *Magni Dei sapiens opus,* "The wise work" (saith Hermes) "of a great GOD," as it was then, when but new to itself. By it, I say it is, that we live in the very time when it was created. We behold how it was governed; how it was covered with waters, and again re-peopled; how kings and kingdoms have flourished and fallen; and for what virtue and piety GOD made prosperous, and for what vice and deformity he made wretched, both the one and the other. And it is not the least debt which we owe unto History that it hath made us acquainted with our dead ancestors, and, out of the depth and darkness of the earth, delivered us their memory and fame. In a word, we may gather out of History a policy no less wise than eternal, by the comparison and application of other men's forepast miseries with our own like errors and ill deservings.

But it is neither of examples the most lively instructions, nor the words of the wisest men, nor the terror of future torments that hath yet so wrought in our blind and stupefied minds as to make us remember that the infinite eye and wisdom of GOD doth pierce through all our pretenses; as to make us remember that the justice of GOD doth require none other accuser than our own consciences, which neither the false beauty of our apparent actions, nor all the formality which (to pacify the opinions of men) we put on, can in any, or the least, kind cover from his knowledge. And so much did that heathen wisdom confess, no way as yet qualified by the knowledge of a true GOD. "If any" (saith Euripides), "having in

his life committed wickedness, think he can hide it from the everlasting
gods, he thinks not well."

*   *   *   *

To Edward the Fourth succeeded Richard the Third, the greatest
master in mischief of all that forewent him. Who, although for the necessity of his tragedy he had more parts to play and more to perform in his
own person than all the rest, yet he so well fitted every affection that played
with him as if each of them had but acted his own interest. For he wrought
10 so cunningly upon the affections of Hastings and Buckingham, enemies
to the Queen and to all her kindred, as he easily allured them to con-
descend that Rivers and Grey, the king's maternal uncle and half-brother,
should (for the first) be severed from him. Secondly, he wrought their
consent to have them imprisoned, and lastly (for the avoiding of future
inconvenience) to have their heads severed from their bodies. And having
now brought those, his chief instruments, to exercise that common precept
which the devil hath written on every post, namely, To depress those
whom they had grieved, and to destroy those whom they had depressed;
he urged that argument so far and so forcibly, as nothing but the death of
20 the young king himself and of his brother could fashion the conclusion. For
he caused it to be hammered into Buckingham's head that whensoever
the king or his brother should have able years to exercise their power, they
would take a most severe revenge of that cureless wrong offered to their
uncle and brother, Rivers and Grey.

But this was not his manner of reasoning with Hastings, whose fidelity
to his master's sons was without suspect; and yet the devil, who never dis-
suades by impossibility, taught him to try him. And so he did. But when
he found by Catesby, who sounded him, that he was not fordable, he first
resolved to kill him sitting in council; wherein, having failed with his
30 sword, he set the hangman upon him with a weapon of more weight. And,
because nothing else could move his appetite, he caused his head to be
stricken off before he eat his dinner. A greater judgment of GOD than
this upon Hastings I have never observed in any story. For the self-same
day that the Earl Rivers, Grey, and others were (without trial of law or
offense given) by Hastings' advice executed at Pomfret, I say Hastings
himself, in the same day, and (as I take it) in the same hour, in the same
lawless manner, had his head stricken off in the Tower of London. But
Buckingham lived a while longer, and with an eloquent oration persuaded
the Londoners to elect Richard for their king. And having received the
40 earldom of Hereford for reward, besides the high hope of marrying his
daughter to the king's only son, after many grievous vexations of mind
and unfortunate attempts, being in the end betrayed and delivered up by

his trustiest servant, he had his head severed from his body as Salisbury, without the trouble of any of his peers. And what success had Richard himself after all these mischiefs and murders, policies, and counter-policies to Christian religion, and after such time as, with a most merciless hand, he had pressed out the breath of his nephews and natural lords, other than the prosperity of so short a life, as it took end ere himself could well look over and discern it? the great outcry of innocent blood obtaining at GOD'S hands the effusion of his; who became a spectacle of shame and dishonor both to his friends and enemies.

This cruel king, Henry the Seventh cut off; and was therein (no doubt) the immediate instrument of GOD'S justice. A politic prince he was, if ever there were any, and who, by the engine of his wisdom, beat down and overturned as many strong oppositions, both before and after he ware the crown, as ever king of England did. I say by his wisdom, because, as he ever left the reins of his affections in the hands of his profit, so he always weighed his undertakings by his abilities, leaving nothing more to hazard than so much as cannot be denied it in all human actions. He had well observed the proceedings of Louis the Eleventh, whom he followed in all that was royal or royal-like, but he was far more just, and begun not their processes whom he hated or feared by the execution, as Louis did.

* * * * *

But it is now time to sound a retreat, and to desire to be excused of this long pursuit; and withal, that the good intent which hath moved me to draw the picture of time past (which we call history) in so large a table, may also be accepted in place of a better reason.

The examples of divine Providence everywhere found (the first divine histories being nothing else but a continuation of such examples) have persuaded me to fetch my beginning from the beginning of all things; to wit, Creation. For though these two glorious actions of the Almighty be so near, and, as it were, linked together, that the one necessarily implieth the other: Creation inferring Providence (for what father forsaketh the child that he hath begotten?), and Providence presupposing Creation; yet many of those that have seemed to excel in worldly wisdom have gone about to disjoin this coherence, the Epicure denying both Creation and Providence, but granting that the world had a beginning; the Aristotelian granting Providence, but denying both the Creation and the beginning.

Now although this doctrine of faith, touching the creation in time (for "by faith we understand that the world was made by the word of God") be too weighty a work for Aristotle's rotten ground to bear up, upon which he hath (notwithstanding) founded the defences and fortresses of

all his verbal doctrine; yet that the necessity of infinite power, and the world's beginning, and the impossibility of the contrary, even in the judgment of natural reason, wherein he believed, had not better informed him, it is greatly to be marvelled at. And it is no less strange, that those men which are desirous of knowledge (seeing Aristotle hath failed in this main point, and taught little other than terms in the rest) have so retrenched their minds from the following and overtaking of truth, and so absolutely subjected themselves to the law of those philosophical principles, as all contrary kind of teaching, in the search of causes, they have condemned either
10 for fantastical or curious. But doth it follow, that the positions of heathen philosophers are undoubted grounds and principles indeed because so called? or that *ipsi dixerunt* doth make them to be such? Certainly no. But this is true, that where natural reason hath built any thing so strong against itself as the same reason can hardly assail it, much less batter it down, the same, in every question of nature, and finite power, may be approved for a fundamental law of human knowledge. For saith Charron, in his book *Of Wisdom, Toute proposition humaine a autant d'authorité que l'autre, si la raison n'on fait la différence:* "Every human proposition hath equal authority, if reason make not the difference," the rest being but
20 the fables of principles. But hereof how shall the upright and unpartial judgment of man give a sentence, where opposition and examination are not admitted to give in evidence? And to this purpose it was well said of Lactantius, *Sapientiam sibi adimunt, qui sine ullo judicio inventa majorum probant, et ab aliis pecudum more ducuntur:* "They neglect their own wisdom, who, without any judgment, approve the invention of those that forewent them; and suffer themselves, after the manner of beasts, to be led by them." By the advantage of which sloth and dullness, ignorance is now become so powerful a tyrant as it hath set true philosophy, physic, and divinity, in a pillory; and written over the first, *Contra negantem prin-*
30 *cipia;* over the second *Virtus specifica;* and over the third, *Ecclesia Romana.*

But for myself, I shall never be persuaded that GOD hath shut up all light of learning within the lantern of Aristotle's brains; or that it was ever said unto him, as unto Esdras, *Accendam in corde tuo lucernam intellectus;* that God hath given invention but to the heathen, and that they only have invaded Nature, and found the strength and bottom thereof; the same Nature having consumed all her store, and left nothing of price to after-ages. That these and these be the causes of these and these effects, time hath taught us, and not reason; and so hath experience, without art.
40 The cheese-wife knoweth it as well as the philosopher that sour runnet doth coagulate her milk into a curd. But if we ask a reason of this cause, why the sourness doth it? whereby it doth it? and the manner how? I

think that there is nothing to be found in vulgar philosophy to satisfy this and many other like vulgar questions. But man, to cover his ignorance in the least things, who cannot give a true reason for the grass under his feet, why it should be green rather than red or of any other colour; that could never yet discover the way and reason of Nature's working in those which are far less noble creatures than himself, who is far more noble than the heavens themselves; "man," saith Salomon, "that can hardly discern the things that are upon the earth, and with great labour find out the things that are before us"; that hath so short a time in the world as he no sooner begins to learn than to die; that hath in his memory but borrowed 10 knowledge; in his understanding, nothing truly; that is ignorant of the essence of his own soul, and which the wisest of the naturalists (if Aristotle be he) could never so much as define but by the action and effect, telling us what it works (which all men know as well as he), but not what it is, which neither he nor any else doth know but GOD that created it ("For though I were perfect, yet I know not my soul," saith Job)—man, I say, that is but an idiot in the next cause of his own life, and in the cause of all the actions of his life, will, notwithstanding, examine the art of GOD in creating the world; of God, who, saith Job, "is so excellent as we know him not"; and examine the beginning of the work which had end before 20 mankind had a beginning of being. He will disable God's power to make a world without matter to make it of. He will rather give the motes of the air for a cause; cast the work on necessity or chance; bestow the honour thereof on Nature; make two powers, the one to be the author of the matter, the other of the form; and lastly, for want of a workman, have it eternal. Which latter opinion Aristotle, to make himself the author of a new doctrine, brought into the world.

* * * *

For the rest, I do also account it not the meanest, but an impiety mon- 30 strous, to confound God and Nature, be it but in terms. For it is God that only disposeth of all things according to his own will, and maketh of one earth "vessels of honour and dishonour"; it is Nature that can dispose of nothing, but according to the will of the matter wherein it worketh. It is God that commandeth all; it is Nature that is obedient to all. It is God that doth good unto all, knowing and loving the good he doth; it is Nature that secondarily doth also good, but it neither knoweth nor loveth the good it doth. It is God that hath all things in himself; Nature nothing in itself. It is God which is the Father, and hath begotten all things; it is Nature which is begotten by all things, in which it liveth and laboureth, for by 40 itself it existeth not. For shall we say that it is out of affection to the earth that heavy things fall towards it? Shall we call it reason which doth conduct every river into the salt sea? Shall we term it knowledge in fire, that makes it to consume combustible matter? If it be affection, reason, and knowledge in these, by the same affection, reason, and knowledge it is that Nature worketh. And therefore, seeing all things work as they do (call it by form, by Nature, or by what you please), yet because they work by an impulsion which they cannot resist, or by a faculty infused by the supremest power, we are neither to wonder at nor to worship the faculty that worketh, nor the creature wherein it worketh. But herein lies the wonder, and to Him is the worship due, who hath created such a Nature

10 in things, and such a faculty, as, neither knowing itself the matter wherein it worketh, nor the virtue and power which it hath, doth yet work all things to their last and uttermost perfection. And therefore every reasonable man, taking to himself for a ground that which is granted by all antiquity, and by all men truly learned that ever the world had, to wit, that there is a power infinite and eternal (which also necessity doth prove unto us, without the help of faith; and reason, without the force of authority), all things do as easily follow which have been delivered by divine letters as the waters of a running river do successively pursue each other from the first fountains.

20   * * * * *

 For I protest before the majesty of GOD that I malice no man under the sun. Impossible I know it is to please all, seeing few or none are so pleased with themselves or so assured of themselves by reason of their subjection to their private passions, but that they seem divers persons in one and the same day. Seneca hath said it and so do I, *Unus mihi pro populo erat;* and to the same effect Epicurus, *Hoc ego non multis sed tibi;* or (as it hath since lamentably fallen out) I may borrow the resolution of an ancient philosopher, *Satis est unus, satis est nullus.* For it was for

30 the service of that inestimable Prince Henry, the successive hope and one of the greatest of the Christian world, that I undertook this work. It pleased him to peruse some part thereof and to pardon what was amiss. It is now left to the world without a master; from which all that is presented hath received both blows and thanks. *Eadem probamus, eadem reprehendimus: hic exitus est omnis judicii, in quo lis secundum plures datur.*

 But these discourses are idle. I know that as the charitable will judge charitably; so against those *qui gloriantur in malitia,* my present adversity hath disarmed me. I am on the ground already, and therefore have not far to fall; and for rising again, as in the natural privation there is no

40 recession to habit, so is it seldom seen in the privation politic. I do therefore forbear to style my readers "gentle," "courteous," and "friendly," thereby to beg their good opinions, or to promise a second and third volume (which

I also intend) if the first receive grace and good acceptance. For that which is already done may be thought enough; and too much. And it is certain, let us claw the reader with never so many courteous phrases, yet shall we evermore be thought fools that write foolishly. For conclusion, all the hope I have lies in this, That I have already found more ungentle and uncourteous readers of my love towards them, and well-deserving of them, than ever I shall do again. For had it been otherwise, I should hardly have had this leisure to have made myself a fool in print.

* * * * *   10

BOOK I, CHAP. IX, SECT. 2

Of the three commendable sorts of government, with their opposites:
and of the degrees of human society.

What other policy was exercised or state founded after such time as mankind was greatly multiplied before the flood, it cannot be certainly known, though it seem by probable conjecture that the same was not without kings in that first age, it being possible that many princes of the Egyptians (remembered among their antiquities) were before the general 20 flood; and very likely that the cruel oppressions in that age proceeded from some tyranny in government, or from some rougher form of rule than the paternal.

Berosus ascribeth the rule of the world in those days to the giants of Libanus, who mastered (saith he) all nations from the sunrising to the sunset. But in the second age of the world, and after such time as the rule of eldership failed, three several sorts of government were in several times established among men, according to the divers natures of places and people.

The first, the most ancient, most general, and most approved was the 30 government of one, ruling by just laws, called *monarchy*; to which *tyranny* is opposed, being also a sole and absolute rule, exercised according to the will of the commander, without respect or observation of the laws of God or men. For a lawful prince or magistrate (saith Aristotle) is the keeper of right and equity; and of this condition ought every magistrate to be, according to the rule of God's word. "Judges and officers shalt thou make thee in thy cities: and these shall judge the people with righteous judgment."

The second government is of divers principal persons established by order, and ruling by laws, called *aristocracy*, or *optimatum potestas*; to 40 which *oligarchia* (or the particular faction and usurpation of a few great ones) is opposed; as the *decemviri* or *triumviri,* and the like.

The third is a state popular (or government of the people) called *democratia*, to which is opposed *ochlocratia*, or the turbulent, unjust ruling of the confused multitude, seditiously swaying the state, contrary to their own laws and ordinances. These three kinds of government are briefly expressed by Tholosanus: *unius, paucorum, et multorum*: "of one, of few, of many."

*　　*　　*　　*　　*

BOOK III, CHAP. XII, SECT. 7

So died Epaminondas, the worthiest man that ever was bred in that nation of Greece, and hardly to be matched in any age or country; for he equalled all others in the several virtues which in each of them were singular. His justice and sincerity, his temperance, wisdom, and high magnanimity were no way inferior to his military virtue; in every part whereof he so excelled, that he could not [im]properly be called a wary, a valiant, a politic, a bountiful, or an industrious and a provident captain; all these titles, and many other, being due unto him, which, with his notable discipline and good conduct, made a perfect composition of an heroic general. Neither was his private conversation unanswerable to those high parts which gave him praise abroad. For he was grave, and yet very affable and courteous; resolute in public business, but in his own particular easy, and of much mildness; a lover of his people, bearing with men's infirmities, witty and pleasant in speech, far from insolence, master of his own affections, and furnished with all qualities that might win and keep love. To these graces were added great ability of body, much eloquence, and very deep knowledge in all parts of philosophy and learning, wherewith his mind being enlightened, rested not in the sweetness of contemplation, but brake forth into such effects as gave unto Thebes, which had evermore been an underling, a dreadful reputation among all people adjoining, and the highest command in Greece.

*　　*　　*　　*　　*

BOOK V, CHAP. I, SECT. 9

And to say the truth, it is impossible for any maritime country, not having the coasts admirably fortified, to defend itself against a powerful enemy that is master of the sea. Hereof I had rather that Spain than England should be an example. Let it therefore be supposed, that king Philip the Second had fully resolved to hinder Sir John Norris in the year 1589 from presenting Don Antonio, king of Portugal, before the gates of

Lisbon; and that he would have kept off the English by power of his land-forces, as being too weak at sea, through the great overthrow of his mighty Armada by the fleet of queen Elizabeth in the year foregoing. Surely it had not been hard for him to prepare an army that should be able to resist our eleven thousand. But where should this his army have been bestowed? if about Lisbon, then would it have been easy unto the English to take, ransack, and burn the town of Groin, and to waste the country round about it. For the great and threatening preparations of the Earl of Al-temira, the marquis of Seralba, and others, did not hinder them from per-forming all this. Neither did the hasty levy of eight thousand, under the 10 Earl of Andrada, serve to more effect than the increase of honour to Sir John Norris and his associates; considering that the English charged these at Puente de Burgos, and passing the great bridge behind which they lay, that was flanked with shot and barricadoed at the further end, routed them, took their camp, took their general's standard with the king's arms, and pursued them over all the country, which they fired. If a royal army, and not (as this was) a company of private adventurers, had thus begun the war in Galicia, I think it would have made the Spaniards to quit the guard of Portugal, and make haste to the defence of their St. Iago, whose temple was not far from the danger. But, had they held their first resolu- 20 tion, as knowing that Sir John Norris's main intent was to bring Don Antonio, with an army, into his kingdom, whither coming strong, he ex-pected to be readily and joyfully welcomed; could they have hindered his landing in Portugal? Did not he land at Penicha, and march over the country to Lisbon, six days' journey? Did not he (when all Don Antonio his promises failed) pass along by the river of Lisbon to Cascaliz, and there, having won the fort, quietly embark his men, and depart? But these, though no more than an handful, yet were they Englishmen.

Let us consider of the matter itself; what another nation might do, even against England, in landing an army by advantage of a fleet, if we had 30 none. This question, *Whether an invading army may be resisted at their landing upon the coast of England, were there no fleet of ours at the sea to impeach it?* is already handled by a learned gentleman of our nation, in his observations upon Caesar's *Commentaries,* that maintains the affirma-tive. This he holds only upon supposition, *in absence of our shipping;* and comparatively, as, that it is a more safe and easy course to defend all the coast of England, than to suffer an enemy to land, and afterwards to fight with him. Surely I hold, with him, that it is the best way to keep our enemy from treading upon our ground; wherein, if we fail, then must we seek to make him wish that he had stayed at his own home. In such a case, if it 40 should happen, our judgments are to weigh many particular circumstances that belong not unto this discourse. But making the question general and positive, *Whether England, without help of her fleet, be able to debar an enemy from landing,* I hold that it is unable so to do; and therefore I think it most dangerous to make the adventure. For the encouragement of a first victory to an enemy, and the discouragement of being beaten to the invaded, may draw after it a most perilous consequence.

It is true, that the marshal Monluc, in his *Commentaries,* doth greatly complain that, by his wanting forces wherewith to have kept the frontier of Guienne, they of the Protestant religion, after the battle of Moncounter, entered that country, and gathered great strength and relief thence; for
10 if the king (saith he) would have given me but reasonable means, *J'eusse bien gardé à monsieur l'admiral de faire boire ses chevaux en la Garonne:* "I would have kept the admiral from watering his horses in the river of Garonne." Monsieur de Langey, on the contrary side, prefers the not fighting upon a frontier with an invading enemy, and commends the delay; which course the constable of France held against the emperor Charles when he invaded Provençe. Great difference I know there is, and a diverse consideration to be had between such a country as France is, strengthened with many fortified places; and this of ours, where our ramparts are but of the bodies of men. And it was of invasions upon firm land
20 that these great captains spake, whose entrances cannot be uncertain.

But our question is, of an army to be transported over sea, and to be landed again in an enemy's country, and the place left to the choice of the invader. Hereunto I say, that such an army cannot be resisted on the coast of England without a fleet to impeach it; no, nor on the coast of France, or any other country, except every creek, port, or sandy bay, had a powerful army in each of them to make opposition. For let his whole supposition be granted: that Kent is able to furnish twelve thousand foot, and that those twelve thousand be laid in the three best landing places within that county, to wit, three thousand at Margate, three thousand at
30 the Ness, and six thousand at Folkstone, that is somewhat equally distant from them both; as also, that two of these troops (unless some other order be thought more fit) be directed to strengthen the third, when they shall see the enemy's fleet to bend towards it; I say that, notwithstanding this provision, if the enemy, setting sail from the Isle of Wight, in the first watch of the night, and towing their long boats at their sterns, shall arrive by dawn of day at the Ness, and thrust their army on shore there, it will be hard for those three thousand that are at Margate (twenty and four long miles from thence) to come time enough to reinforce their fellows at the Ness. Nay, how shall they at Folkstone be able to do it, who are nearer
40 by more than half the way? seeing that the enemy, at his first arrival, will either make his entrance by force, with three or four hundred shot of great artillery, and quickly put the first three thousand, that were entrenched at

the Ness, to run; or else give them so much to do, that they shall be glad to send for help to Folkstone, and perhaps to Margate, whereby those places will be left bare. Now let us suppose that all the twelve thousand Kentish soldiers arrive at the Ness ere the enemy can be ready to disembark his army, so that he shall find it unsafe to land in the face of so many prepared to withstand him; yet must we believe that he will play the best of his own game, and (having liberty to go which way he list) under covert of the night, set sail towards the east, where what shall hinder him to take ground, either at Margate, the Downs, or elsewhere, before they at the Ness can be well aware of his departure? Certainly there is nothing more 10 easy than to do it. Yea, the like may be said of Weymouth, Purbeck, Pool, and of all landing places on the south coast. For there is no man ignorant that ships, without putting themselves out of breath, will easily outrun the soldiers that coast them. *Les armées ne volent poynt en poste:* "Armies neither fly, nor run post," saith a marshal of France. And I know it to be true, that a fleet of ships may be seen at sunset, and after it, at the Lizard; yet by the next morning they may recover Portland; whereas an army of foot shall not be able to march it in six days. Again, when those troops, lodged on the sea-shores, shall be forced to run from place to place in vain after a fleet of ships, they will at length sit down in the midway, 20 and leave all at adventure. But say it were otherwise; that the invading enemy will offer to land in some such place where there shall be an army of ours ready to receive him; yet it cannot be doubted but that, when the choice of all our trained bands, and the choice of our commanders and captains, shall be drawn together (as they were at Tilbury in the year 1588) to attend the person of the prince, and for the defence of the city of London, they that remain to guard the coast can be of no such force as to encounter an army like unto that wherewith it was intended that the prince of Parma should have landed in England.

The isle of Tercera hath taught us by experience what to think in such 30 a case. There are not many islands in the world better fenced by nature and strengthened by art; it being everywhere hard of access, having no good harbour wherein to shelter a navy of friends, and upon every cove or watering-place a fort erected to forbid the approach of an enemy's boat. Yet when Emanuel de Sylva and Monsieur de Chattes, that held it to the use of Don Antonio with five or six thousand men, thought to have kept the Marquis of Santa Cruz from setting foot on ground therein, the Marquis, having shewed himself in the road of Angra, did set sail ere any was aware of it and arrived at the Port des Moles, far distant from thence, where he won a fort, and landed, ere Monsieur de Chattes, running 40 thither in vain, could come to hinder him. The example of Philip Strossie, slain the year before, without all regard of his worth, and of three hundred

French prisoners murdered in cold blood, had instructed de Chattes and his followers what they might expect at that marquis's hands; therefore it is not like that they were slow in carrying relief to Port des Moles. Whether our English would be persuaded to make such diligent haste from Margate to the Ness, and back again, it may be doubted. Sure I am that it were a greater march than all the length of Tercera, whereof the Frenchmen had not measured the one half when they found themselves prevented by the more nimble ships of Spain.

This may suffice to prove that a strong army, in a good fleet, which neither foot nor horse is able to follow, cannot be denied to land where it list in England, France, or elsewhere, unless it be hindered, encountered, and shuffled together by a fleet of equal or answerable strength.

The difficult landing of our English at Fayal, in the year 1597, is alleged against this; which example moves me no way to think that a large coast may be defended against a strong fleet. I landed those English in Fayal myself, and therefore ought to take notice of this instance. For whereas I find an action of mine cited with omission of my name, I may by a civil interpretation think that there was no purpose to defraud me of any honour, but rather an opinion that the enterprise was such, or so ill managed, as that no honour could be due unto it. There were indeed some which were in that voyage who advised me not to undertake it; and I hearkened unto them somewhat longer than was requisite, especially whilst they desired me to reserve the title of such an exploit (though it were not great) for a greater person. But when they began to tell me of difficulty, I gave them to understand the same which I now maintain, that it was more difficult to defend a coast than to invade it. The truth is, that I could have landed my men with more ease than I did, yea, without finding any resistance, if I would have rowed to another place; yea, even there where I landed, if I would have taken more company to help me. But, without fearing any imputation of rashness, I may say that I had more regard of reputation in that business than of safety. For I thought it to belong unto the honour of our prince and nation that a few islanders should not think any advantage great enough against a fleet set forth by Queen Elizabeth; and further, I was unwilling that some Low-Country captains, and others not of mine own squadron, whose assistance I had refused, should please themselves with a sweet conceit (though it would have been short, when I had landed in some other place) that for want of their help I was driven to turn tail. Therefore I took with me none but men assured, commanders of mine own squadron, with some of their followers, and a few other gentlemen, voluntaries, whom I could not refuse; as Sir William Brooke, Sir William Harvey, Sir Arthur Gorges, Sir John Skot, Sir Thomas Ridgeway, Sir Henry Thinne, Sir Charles Morgan, Sir Walter Chute,

Marcellus Throckmorton, Captain Laurence Kemis, Captain William Morgan, and others, such as well understood themselves and the enemy; by whose help, with God's favour, I made good the enterprise I undertook. As for the working of the sea, the steepness of the cliffs, and other troubles, that were not new to us; we overcame them well enough. And these (notwithstanding) made five or six companies of the enemy's, that sought to impeach our landing, abandon the wall whereon their musketeers lay on the rest for us, and won the place of them without any great loss. This I could have done with less danger, so that it should not have served for example of a rule that failed even in this example; but the rea- 10 sons before alleged (together with other reasons well known to some of the gentlemen above named, though more private than to be here laid down) made me rather follow the way of bravery and take the shorter course, having it still in mine own power to fall off when I should think it meet. It is easily said that "the enemy was more than a coward" (which yet was more than we knew); neither will I magnify such a small piece of service by seeking to prove him better; whom, had I thought equal to mine own followers, I would otherwise have dealt with. But for so much as concerns the proposition in hand, he that beheld this may well remember that the same enemy troubled us more in our march towards Fayal 20 than in our taking the shore; that he sought how to stop us in place of his advantage; that many of our men were slain or hurt by him, among whom Sir Arthur Gorges was shot in that march; and that such as, thinking all danger to be past when we had won good footing, would needs follow us to the town, were driven by him to forsake the pace of a man of war, and betake themselves to an hasty trot.

For end of this disgression, I hope that this question shall never come to trial; his majesty's many moveable forts will forbid the experience. And although the English will no less disdain, than any nation under heaven can do, to be beaten upon their own ground, or elsewhere, by a foreign 30 enemy, yet to entertain those that shall assail us with their own beef in their bellies, and before they eat of our Kentish capons, I take to be the wisest way. To do which, his majesty, after God, will employ his good ships on the sea, and not trust to any entrenchment upon the shore.

*   *   *   *   *

BOOK V, CHAP. III, SECT. 15

. . . But there lived at that time in Syracuse Archimedes the noble 40 mathematician, who at the request of Hiero the late king, that was his kinsman, had framed such engines of war, as being in this extremity put

in use, did more mischief to the Romans than could have been wrought by the cannon, or any instruments of gunpowder, had they in that age been known. This Archimedes, discoursing once with Hiero, maintained that it were possible to remove the whole earth out of the place wherein it is, if there were some other earth, or place of sure footing, whereon a man might stand. For proof of this bold assertion, he performed some strange works, which made the king entreat him to convert his study unto things of use, that might preserve the city from danger of enemies. To such mechanical works Archimedes, and the philosophers of those
10 times, had little affection. They held it an injury done unto the liberal sciences to submit learned propositions unto the workmanship and gain of base handicraftsmen. And of this opinion Plato was an author, who greatly blamed some geometricians that seemed unto him to profane their science by making it vulgar. Neither must we rashly task a man so wise as Plato with the imputation of supercilious austerity, or affected singularity in his reprehension. For it hath been the unhappy fate of great inventions to be vilified as idle fancies, or dreams, before they were published; and, being once made known, to be undervalued, as falling within compass of the meanest wit, and things that every one could well have
20 performed.

Hereof (to omit that memorable example of Columbus his discovery, with the much different sorts of neglect which he underwent before and after it), in a familiar and most homely example, we may see most apparent proof. He that looks upon our English brewers, and their servants that are daily exercised in the trade, will think it ridiculous to hear one say, that the making of malt was an invention proceeding from some of an extraordinary knowledge in natural philosophy. Yet is not the skill of the inventors any whit the less, for that the labour of workmanship grows to be the trade of ignorant men. The like may be said of many handicrafts;
30 and particularly in the printing of books, which being devised and bettered by great scholars and wise men, grew afterward corrupted by those to whom the practice fell; that is, by such as could slubber things easily over, and feed their workmen at the cheapest rate. In this respect therefore the alchemists, and all others that have or would seem to have any secret skill whereof the publication might do good unto mankind, are not without excuse of their close concealing. For it is a kind of injustice that the long travails of an understanding brain, beside the loss of time and other expense, should be cast away upon men of no worth; or yield less benefit unto the author of a great work than to mere strangers, and perhaps his
40 enemies. And surely, if the passion of envy have in it any thing allowable and natural, as have anger, fear, and other the like affections, it is in

some such case as this, and serveth against those which would usurp the knowledge wherewith God hath denied to endue them.

Nevertheless, if we have regard unto common charity, and the great affection that every one ought to bear unto the generality of mankind, after the example of Him that "suffereth his sun to shine upon the just and unjust," it will appear more commendable in wise men to enlarge themselves, and to publish unto the world those good things that lie buried in their own bosoms. This ought specially to be done when a profitable knowledge hath not annexed to it some dangerous cunning that may be perverted by evil men to a mischievous use. For if the secret of any rare 10 antidote contained in it the skill of giving some deadly and irrecoverable poison, better it were that such a jewel remain close in the hands of a wise and honest man than, being made common, bind all men to use the remedy by teaching the worst men how to do mischief.

But the works which Archimedes published were such as tended to very commendable ends. They were engines serving unto the defence of Syracuse, not fit for the Syracusians to carry abroad, to the hurt and op-pression of others. Neither did he altogether publish the knowledge how to use them, but reserved so much to his own direction that after his death more of the same kind were not made, nor those of his own making were 20 employed by the Romans. It sufficed unto this worthy man that he had approved, even unto the vulgar, the dignity of his science, and done es-pecial benefit unto his country. For to enrich a mechanical trade, or teach the art of murdering men, it was besides his purpose.

Marcellus had caused certain of his quinquereme galleys to be fastened together, and towers erected on them, to beat the defendants from the wall. Against these, Archimedes had sundry devices, of which any one sort might have repelled the assailants; but all of them together shewed the multiplicity of his great wit. He shot heavy stones and long pieces of timber, like unto the yards of ships, which brake some of the galleys by 30 their force and weight. These afflicted such as lay far off. They that were come nearer the walls lay open to a continual volley of shot, which they could not endure. Some with an iron grapple were taken by the prow and hoisted up, shaking out all the men, and afterward falling down into the water. Some by strange engines were lifted up into the air, where, turning round a while, they were broken against the walls, or cast upon the rocks; and all of them were so beaten that they durst never come to any second assault. In like sort was the land army handled. Stones and timber, falling upon it like hail, did not only overwhelm the men, but brake down the Roman engines of battery, and forced Marcellus to give over the assault. 40 For remedy hereof it was conceived that if the Romans could early before day get near unto the walls, they should be (as it were) under the point-blank, and receive no hurt by these terrible instruments, which were wound up hard to shoot a great compass. But this vain hope cost many of the assailants' lives; for the shot came down right upon them, and beating them from all parts of the wall, made a great slaughter of them all the way as they fled (for they were unable to stay by it), even till they were gotten very far off. This did so terrify the Romans that, if they perceived any piece of timber or a rope's end upon the walls, they ran away, crying out that Archimedes's engines were ready to discharge.

10   Neither knew Marcellus how to overcome these difficulties, or to take away from his men that fear, against the cause whereof he knew no remedy. If the engines had stood upon the walls, subject to firing, or any such annoyance from without, he might have holpen it by some device to make them unserviceable; but all, or the most of them, were out of sight, being erected in the streets behind the walls, where Archimedes gave directions how to use them. Wherefore the Roman had none other way left than to cut off from the town all provision of victuals, both by land and by sea. This was a desperate piece of work; for the enemies having so goodly an haven, the sea in a manner free, and the Carthaginians, that 20 were strong by sea, willing to supply them, were not likely so soon to be consumed with famine as the besiegers to be wearied out by lying in leaguer before so strong a city, having no probability to carry it. Yet, for want of better counsel to follow, this was thought the best and most honourable course.

*   *   *   *   *

BOOK V, CHAP. VI, SECT. 12

For the rest, if we seek a reason of the succession and continuance of 30 this boundless ambition in mortal men, we may add to that which hath been already said, that the kings and princes of the world have always laid before them the actions, but not the ends, of those great ones which preceded them. They are always transported with the glory of the one, but they never mind the misery of the other till they find the experience in themselves. They neglect the advice of God while they enjoy life, or hope it; but they follow the counsel of Death upon his first approach. It is he that puts into man all the wisdom of the world, without speaking a word, which God, with all the words of his law, promises, or threats, doth not infuse. Death, which hateth and destroyeth man, is believed; God, which 40 hath made him and loves him, is always deferred. "I have considered," saith Solomon, "all the works that are under the sun, and, behold, all is vanity and vexation of spirit; but who believes it till Death tells it us? It was Death which, opening the conscience of Charles the Fifth, made him enjoin his son Philip to restore Navarre; and King Francis the First of France to command that justice should be done upon the murderers of the Protestants in Merindol and Cabrières, which till then he neglected. It is therefore Death alone that can suddenly make man to know himself. He tells the proud and insolent that they are but abjects, and humbles them at the instant; makes them cry, complain, and repent, yea, even to hate their forepast happiness. He takes the account of the rich, and proves him a beggar, a naked beggar, which hath interest in nothing but in the gravel that fills his mouth. He holds a glass before the eyes of the most beautiful, and makes them see therein their deformity and rottenness, and they acknowledge it.

O eloquent, just, and mighty Death! whom none could advise, thou hast persuaded; what none hath dared, thou hast done; and whom all the world hath flattered, thou only hast cast out of the world and despised; thou has drawn together all the far-stretched greatness, all the pride, cruelty, and ambition of man, and covered it all over with these two narrow words, *Hic jacet!*

FROM *Sloane Ms. 3520*

The Copy of a Letter written by Sir Walter Ralegh to his wife

YOU SHALL now receive, dear wife, my last words in these my last lines. My love I send you, that you may keep it when I am dead; and my counsel, that you may remember it when I am no more. I would not, by my will, present you with sorrows, dear Besse. Let them go to the grave with me, and be buried in the dust. And, seeing it is not the will of God that ever I shall see you any more in this life, bear it patiently and with a heart like thy self.

First, I send you all the thanks which my heart can conceive, or my words can express, for your many travails and cares taken for me, which —though they have not taken effect as you wished—yet my debt to you is not the less; but pay it I never shall in this world.

Secondly, I beseech you, for the love you bare me living, do not hide yourself many days after my death, but by your travails seek to help your miserable fortunes, and the right of your poor child. Your mourning cannot avail me; I am but dust.

You shall understand that my land was conveyed *bona fide* to my child. The writings were drawn at midsummer twelvemonths. My honest cousin Brett can testify so much, and Dalberie, too, can remember somewhat therein. And I trust my blood will quench the malice that

have thus cruelly murdered me; and that they will not seek also to kill
thee and thine with extreme poverty.

To what friend to direct thee I know not, for all mine have left me
in the true time of trial; and I plainly perceive that my death was determined from the first day. Most sorry I am (God knows) that, being
thus surprised with death, I can leave you in no better estate. God is my
witness I meant you all my office of wines, or all that I could have purchased by selling it; half my stuff, and all my jewels; but some on't for
the boy. But God hath prevented all my resolutions; even that great
God that ruleth all in all. If you can live free from want, care for no
more; the rest is but vanity.

Love God, and begin betimes to repose yourself on Him; therein shall
you find true and lasting riches, and endless comfort. For the rest, when
you have travailed and wearied all your thoughts over all sorts of worldly
cogitations, you shall sit down by Sorrow in the end. Teach your son also
to love and fear God, while he is yet young, that the fear of God may
grow up with him. And the same God will be a husband unto you, and
a father unto him; a husband and a father which can not be taken from
you.

Bayly oweth me two hundred pounds, and Adrian Gilbert six hundred pounds. In Jersey I have also much money owing me. Besides, the
arrearages of the wines will pay my debts. And, howsoever you do, for
my soul's sake, pay all poor men.

When I am gone, no doubt you shall be sought by many, for the
world thinks that I was very rich; but take heed of the pretences of men
and of their affections; for they last not but in honest and worthy men.
And no greater misery can befall you in this life than to become a prey,
and afterwards to be despised. I speak not this (God knows) to dissuade
you from marriage—for it will be best for you, both in respect of the world
and of God. As for me, I am no more yours, nor you mine. Death hath
cut us asunder; and God hath divided me from the world, and you from
me.

Remember your poor child for his father's sake, who chose you and
loved you in his happiest times. Get those letters (if it be possible) which
I writ to the Lords, wherein I sued for my life. God is my witness, it was
for you and yours that I desired life. But it is true that I disdain myself
for begging it. For know it (dear wife) that your son is the son of a true
man, and one who, in his own respect, despiseth Death, and all his misshapen and ugly shapes.

I cannot write much. God he knows how hardly I steal this time,
while others sleep; and it is also high time that I should separate my
thoughts from the world. Beg my dead body, which living was denied

thee; and either lay it at Sherborne, if the land continue, or in Exeter
church, by my father and mother. I can say no more. Time and Death
call me away.

The everlasting, powerful, infinite and omnipotent God, that almighty God who is goodness itself, the true life and true light, keep thee
and thine; and have mercy on me, and teach me to forgive my perse-
cutors and accusers; and send us to meet in His glorious kingdom. My
dear wife, farewell. Bless my poor boy; pray for me; and let my good
God hold you both in His arms.

Written with the dying hand of sometime thy husband, but now 10
(alas!) overthrown.

Wa. Raleigh

Yours that was; but now not my own,

W. R.

SIR FRANCIS BACON

The Introduction and Notes are at page 1349

Essays

FROM *Essayes, Religious Meditations, Places of perswasion and dis-
swasion,* 1597

To M. Anthony Bacon, his dear brother.

LOVING and beloved brother, I do now like some that have an orchard
ill-neighbored, that gather their fruit before it is ripe, to prevent stealing.
These fragments of my conceits were going to print; to labor the stay
of them had been troublesome and subject to interpretation; to let them
pass had been to adventure the wrong they might receive by untrue 30
copies, or by some garnishment which it might please any that should set
them forth to bestow upon them. Therefore I held it best discretion to
publish them myself, as they passed long ago from my pen, without any
further disgrace than the weakness of the author. And, as I did ever hold,
there might be as great a vanity in retiring and withdrawing men's conceits (except they be of some nature) from the world as in obtruding
them; so, in these particulars, I have played myself the inquisitor, and find
nothing, to my understanding, in them contrary or infectious to the state
of religion or manners, but rather (as I suppose) medicinable. Only I
disliked now to put them out because they will be like the late new half- 40
pence, which, though the silver were good, yet the pieces were small. But
since they would not stay with their master, but would needs travel abroad,

I have preferred them to you that are next myself, dedicating them, such as they are, to our love, in the depth whereof (I assure you) I sometimes wish your infirmities translated upon myself, that Her Majesty might have the service of so active and able a mind, and I might be with excuse confined to these contemplations and studies for which I am fittest. So commend I you to the preservation of the Divine Majesty. From my chamber at Gray's Inn this 30 of January, 1597.

Your entire loving brother,
FRAN. BACON.

10

Of regiment of
health

There is a wisdom in this beyond the rules of physic. A man's own observation, what he finds good of, and what he finds hurt of, is the best physic to preserve health. But it is a safer conclusion to say, "This agreeth well with me; therefore I will continue it," than this, "I find no offense of this; therefore, I may use it." For strength of nature in youth passeth over many excesses which are owing a man till his age.

Discern of the coming on of years, and think not to do the same things 20 still.

Beware of any sudden change in any great point of diet, and, if necessity enforce it, fit the rest to it.

To be free-minded, and cheerfully disposed at hours of meat and of sleep and of exercise, is the best precept of long lasting.

If you fly physic in health altogether, it will be too strange to your body when you shall need it; if you make it too familiar, it will work no extraordinary effect when sickness cometh.

Despise no new accident in the body, but ask opinion of it.

In sickness, respect health principally; and in health, action. For those 30 that put their bodies to endure in health may, in most sicknesses which are not very sharp, be cured only with diet and tendering.

Physicians are, some of them, so pleasing and conformable to the humors of the patient as they press not the true cure of the disease; and some other are so regular in proceeding according to art for the disease as they respect not sufficiently the condition of the patient. Take one of a middle temper, or, if it may not be found in one man, compound two of both sorts, and forget not to call as well the best acquainted with your body as the best reputed of for his faculty.

Of Studies
40

Studies serve for pastimes, for ornaments, and for abilities. Their chief use for pastime is in privateness and retiring; for ornament is in discourse;

and for ability is in judgment. For expert men can execute, but learned men are fittest to judge or censure.

To spend too much time in them is sloth; to use them too much for ornament is affectation; to make judgment wholly by their rules is the humor of a scholar.

They perfect Nature, and are perfected by experience.

Crafty men contemn them, simple men admire them, wise men use them; for they teach not their own use, but that is a wisdom without them and above them, won by observation.

Read not to contradict nor to believe, but to weigh and consider. 10

Some books are to be tasted, others to be swallowed, and some few to be chewed and disgested: that is, some books are to be read only in parts; others to be read, but cursorily; and some few to be read wholly, and with diligence and attention.

Reading maketh a full man, conference a ready man, and writing an exact man. And therefore if a man write little, he had need have a great memory; if he confer little, he had need have a present wit; and if he read little, he had need have much cunning, to seem to know that he doth not.

Histories make men wise; poets, witty; the mathematics, subtle; 20 natural philosophy, deep; moral, grave; logic and rhetoric, able to contend.

FROM *The Essayes or Counsels, Civill and Morall,* 1625

Of Studies

STUDIES serve for delight, for ornament, and for ability. Their chief use for delight is in privateness and retiring; for ornament is in discourse; and for ability is in the judgment and disposition of business. For expert men can execute, and perhaps judge of particulars, one by one; but the gen- 30 eral counsels, and the plots and marshalling of affairs, come best from those that are learned. To spend too much time in studies is sloth; to use them too much for ornament is affectation; to make judgment wholly by their rules is the humour of a scholar. They perfect nature, and are perfected by experience; for natural abilities are like natural plants, that need pruning by study; and studies themselves do give forth directions too much at large, except they be bounded in by experience. Crafty men contemn studies, simple men admire them, and wise men use them; for they teach not their own use; but that is a wisdom without them, and above them, won by observation. 40

Read not to contradict and confute, nor to believe and take for granted, nor to find talk and discourse, but to weigh and consider. Some books are

to be tasted, others to be swallowed, and some few to be chewed and digested; that is, some books are to be read only in parts; others to be read, but not curiously; and some few to be read wholly, and with diligence and attention. Some books also may be read by deputy, and extracts made of them by others; but that would be only in the less important arguments, and the meaner sort of books; else distilled books are like common distilled waters, flashy things. Reading maketh a full man, conference a ready man, and writing an exact man. And therefore, if a man write little, he had need have a great memory; if he confer little, he had need have a
10 present wit: and if he read little, he had need have much cunning, to seem to know that he doth not. Histories make men wise; poets, witty; the mathematics, subtle; natural philosophy, deep; moral, grave; logic and rhetoric, able to contend. *Abeunt studia in mores.* Nay, there is no stand or impediment in the wit, but may be wrought out by fit studies; like as diseases of the body may have appropriate exercises. Bowling is good for the stone and reins; shooting for the lungs and breast; gentle walking for the stomach; riding for the head; and the like. So if a man's wit be wandering, let him study the mathematics; for in demonstrations, if his wit be called away never so little, he must begin again. If his wit be not apt to
20 distinguish or find differences, let him study the schoolmen; for they are *cymini sectores.* If he be not apt to beat over matters, and to call up one thing to prove and illustrate another, let him study the lawyers' cases. So every defect of the mind may have a special receipt.

Of Friendship

It had been hard for him that spake it to have put more truth and untruth together in few words than in that speech, "Whosoever is delighted in solitude is either a wild beast or a god." For it is most true that a natural and secret hatred and aversation towards society in any man hath some-
30 what of the savage beast; but it is most untrue that it should have any character at all of the divine nature except it proceed, not out of a pleasure in solitude, but out of a love and desire to sequester a man's self for a higher conversation, such as is found to have been falsely and feignedly in some of the heathen; as Epimenides the Candian, Numa the Roman, Empedocles the Sicilian, and Apollonius of Tyana; and truly and really in divers of the ancient hermits and Holy Fathers of the Church. But little do men perceive what solitude is, and how far it extendeth. For a crowd is not company, and faces are but a gallery of pictures, and talk but a tinkling cymbal, where there is no love. The Latin adage meeteth
40 with it a little: *Magna civitas, magna solitudo* [a great town is a great solitude]; because in a great town friends are scattered, so that there is not that fellowship, for the most part, which is in less neighbourhoods. But

we may go further, and affirm most truly, that it is a mere and miserable solitude to want true friends, without which the world is but a wilderness. And even in this sense also of solitude, whosoever in the frame of his nature and affections is unfit for friendship, he taketh it of the beast, and not from humanity.

A principal fruit of friendship is the ease and discharge of the fulness and swellings of the heart, which passions of all kinds do cause and induce. We know diseases of stoppings and suffocations are the most dangerous in the body, and it is not much otherwise in the mind. You may take sarza to open the liver, steel to open the spleen, flower of sulphur for the lungs, castoreum for the brain; but no receipt openeth the heart but a true friend, to whom you may impart griefs, joys, fears, hopes, suspicions, counsels, and whatsoever lieth upon the heart to oppress it, in a kind of civil shrift or confession.

It is a strange thing to observe how high a rate great kings and monarchs do set upon this fruit of friendship whereof we speak; so great, as they purchase it many times at the hazard of their own safety and greatness. For princes, in regard of the distance of their fortune from that of their subjects and servants, cannot gather this fruit, except (to make themselves capable thereof) they raise some persons to be as it were companions and almost equals to themselves, which many times sorteth to inconvenience. The modern languages give unto such persons the name of favourites, or privadoes, as if it were matter of grace or conversation. But the Roman name attaineth the true use and cause thereof, naming them *participes curarum;* for it is that which tieth the knot. And we see plainly that this hath been done, not by weak and passionate princes only, but by the wisest and most politic that ever reigned; who have oftentimes joined to themselves some of their servants; whom both themselves have called friends, and allowed others likewise to call them in the same manner, using the word which is received between private men.

L[ucius] Sulla, when he commanded Rome, raised Pompey (after surnamed the Great) to that height that Pompey vaunted himself for Sulla's over-match. For when he had carried the consulship for a friend of his against the pursuit of Sulla, and that Sulla did a little resent thereat, and began to speak great, Pompey turned upon him again, and in effect bade him be quiet, "for that more men adored the sun rising than the sun setting." With Julius Caesar, Decimus Brutus had obtained that interest, as he set him down in his testament for heir in remainder after his nephew. And this was the man that had power with him to draw him forth to his death. For when Caesar would have discharged the senate, in regard of some ill presages and especially a dream of Calpurnia, this man lifted him gently by the arm out of his chair, telling him he hoped he would not dis-

miss the senate till his wife had dreamt a better dream. And it seemeth his favour was so great, as Antonius, in a letter which is recited verbatim in one of Cicero's *Philippics*, calleth him *venefica*, witch; as if he had enchanted Caesar. Augustus raised Agrippa (though of mean birth) to that height as when he consulted with Maecenas about the marriage of his daughter Julia, Maecenas took the liberty to tell him that he must either marry his daughter to Agrippa, or take away his life; there was no third way, he had made him so great. With Tiberius Caesar, Sejanus had ascended to that height as they two were termed and reckoned as a pair of friends.
10 Tiberius in a letter to him saith, *haec pro amicitiâ nostrâ non occultavi* [these things, as our friendship required, I have not concealed from you]; and the whole senate dedicated an altar to Friendship as to a goddess, in respect of the great dearness of friendship between them two. The like or more was between Septimius Severus and Plautianus. For he forced his eldest son to marry the daughter of Plautianus; and would often maintain Plautianus in doing affronts to his son; and did write also in a letter to the senate, by these words: "I love the man so well, as I wish he may over-live me." Now if these princes had been as a Trajan or a Marcus Aurelius, a man might have thought that this had proceeded of an abun-
20 dant goodness of nature; but being men so wise, of such strength and severity of mind, and so extreme lovers of themselves as all of these were, it proveth most plainly that they found their own felicity (though as great as ever happened to mortal men) but as an half piece, except they mought have a friend to make it entire. And yet, which is more, they were princes that had wives, sons, nephews; and yet all these could not supply the comfort of friendship.

It is not to be forgotten what Comineus observeth of his first master, Duke Charles the Hardy; namely, that he would communicate his secrets with none, and least of all, those secrets which troubled him most.
30 Whereupon he goeth on and saith that towards his latter time that closeness did impair and a little perish his understanding. Surely Comineus mought have made the same judgment also, if it had pleased him, of his second master Lewis the Eleventh, whose closeness was indeed his tormentor. The parable of Pythagoras is dark, but true: *Cor ne edito:* "Eat not the heart." Certainly, if a man would give it a hard phrase, those that want friends to open themselves unto are cannibals of their own hearts. But one thing is most admirable (wherewith I will conclude this first fruit of friendship), which is, that this communicating of a man's self to his friend works two contrary effects; for it redoubleth joys, and cutteth
40 griefs in halfs. For there is no man that imparteth his joys to his friend but he joyeth the more; and no man that imparteth his griefs to his friend but he grieveth the less. So that it is, in truth of operation upon a man's mind,

of like virtue as the alchemists use to attribute to their stone for man's body; that it worketh all contrary effects, but still to the good and benefit of nature. But yet without praying in aid of alchemists, there is a manifest image of this in the ordinary course of nature. For in bodies, union strengtheneth and cherisheth any natural action; and, on the other side, weakeneth and dulleth any violent impression. And even so it is of minds.

The second fruit of friendship is healthful and sovereign for the understanding, as the first is for the affections. For friendship maketh indeed a fair day in the affections, from storm and tempests; but it maketh daylight in the understanding, out of darkness and confusion of thoughts. 10 Neither is this to be understood only of faithful counsel which a man receiveth from his friend; but before you come to that, certain it is that whosoever hath his mind fraught with many thoughts, his wits and understanding do clarify and break up, in the communicating and discoursing with another. He tosseth his thoughts more easily; he marshalleth them more orderly; he seeth how they look when they are turned into words; finally, he waxeth wiser than himself, and that more by an hour's discourse than by a day's meditation. It was well said by Themistocles to the king of Persia, That speech was like cloth of Arras, opened and put abroad; whereby the imagery doth appear in figure, whereas in thought 20 they lie but as in packs. Neither is this second fruit of friendship, in opening the understanding, restrained only to such friends as are able to give a man counsel (they indeed are best); but even without that, a man learneth of himself, and bringeth his own thoughts to light, and whetteth his wits as against a stone which itself cuts not. In a word, a man were better relate himself to a statua or picture than to suffer his thoughts to pass in smother.

Add now, to make this second fruit of friendship complete, that other point which lieth more open and falleth within vulgar observation; which is faithful counsel from a friend. Heraclitus saith well in one of his enigmas, "Dry light is ever the best." And certain it is that the light that a man 30 receiveth by counsel from another is drier and purer than that which cometh from his own understanding and judgment, which is ever infused and drenched in his affections and customs. So as there is as much difference between the counsel that a friend giveth, and that a man giveth himself, as there is between the counsel of a friend and of a flatterer. For there is no such flatterer as is a man's self; and there is no such remedy against flattery of a man's self as the liberty of a friend.

Counsel is of two sorts; the one concerning manners, the other concerning business. For the first, the best preservative to keep the mind in health is the faithful admonition of a friend. The calling of a man's self 40 to a strict account is a medicine, sometime, too piercing and corrosive. Reading good books of morality is a little flat and dead. Observing our faults in others is sometimes unproper for our case. But the best receipt (best, I say, to work, and best to take) is the admonition of a friend. It is a strange thing to behold what gross errors and extreme absurdities many (especially of the greater sort) do commit for want of a friend to tell them of them, to the great damage both of their fame and fortune. For, as St. James saith, they are as men that look sometimes into a glass, and presently forget their own shape and favour.

As for business, a man may think, if he will, that two eyes see no more than one; or that a gamester seeth always more than a looker-on; or that 10 a man in anger is as wise as he that hath said over the four and twenty letters; or that a musket may be shot off as well upon the arm as upon a rest; and such other fond and high imaginations, to think himself all in all. But when all is done, the help of good counsel is that which setteth business straight. And if any man think that he will take counsel, but it shall be by pieces, asking counsel in one business of one man, and in another business of another man, it is well (that is to say, better perhaps than if he asked none at all); but he runneth two dangers; one, that he shall not be faithfully counselled, for it is a rare thing, except it be from a perfect and entire friend, to have counsel given but such as shall be 20 bowed and crooked to some ends which he hath that giveth it. The other, that he shall have counsel given, hurtful and unsafe (though with good meaning), and mixed partly of mischief and partly of remedy; even as if you would call a physician that is thought good for the cure of the disease you complain of, but is unacquainted with your body; and therefore may put you in way for a present cure, but overthroweth your health in some other kind, and so cure the disease and kill the patient. But a friend that is wholly acquainted with a man's estate will beware, by furthering any present business, how he dasheth upon other inconvenience. And there- fore, rest not upon scattered counsels; they will rather distract and mis- 30 lead than settle and direct.

After these two noble fruits of friendship (peace in the affections, and support of the judgment), followeth the last fruit; which is like the pome- granate, full of many kernels; I mean aid, and bearing a part in all ac- tions and occasions. Here the best way to represent to life the manifold use of friendship is to cast and see how many things there are which a man cannot do himself; and then it will appear that it was a sparing speech of the ancients to say that a friend is another himself, for that a friend is far more than himself. Men have their time, and die many times in desire of some things which they principally take to heart—the bestow- 40 ing of a child, the finishing of a work, or the like. If a man have a true friend he may rest almost secure that the care of those things will continue after him. So that a man hath, as it were, two lives in his desires. A man hath a body, and that body is confined to a place; but where friendship is, all offices of life are as it were granted to him and his deputy. For he may exercise them by his friend. How many things are there which a man cannot, with any face or comeliness, say or do himself? A man can scarce allege his own merits with modesty, much less extol them; a man cannot sometimes brook to supplicate or beg; and a number of the like. But all these things are graceful in a friend's mouth, which are blushing in a man's own. So again, a man's person hath many proper relations which he cannot put off. A man cannot speak to his son but as a father; to his wife but as a husband; to his enemy but upon terms; whereas a friend may speak as the case requires, and not as it sorteth with the person. But to enumerate these things were endless. I have given the rule, where a man cannot fitly play his own part; if he have not a friend, he may quit the stage.

From *Ms. Sloane 4259*

The draft of a dedication to Prince Henry, intended for the 1612 edition of the Essayes [Prince Henry died 6 November, 1612]

To the most high and excellent Prince Henry, Prince of Wales, Duke of Cornwall and Earl of Chester
It may please your Highness

HAVING divided my life into the contemplative and active part, I am desirous to give His Majesty and Your Highness of the fruits of both, simple though they be. To write just treatises requireth leisure in the writer, and leisure in the reader, and therefore are not so fit, either in regard of Your Highness's princely affairs, nor in regard of my continual services. Which is the cause that hath made me choose to write certain brief notes, set down rather significantly than curiously, which I have called *Essays*. The word is late, but the thing is ancient. For Seneca's *Epistles to Lucilius*, if one mark them well, are but essays—that is, dispersed meditations, though conveyed in the form of epistles.

These labors of mine I know cannot be worthy of Your Highness—for what can be worthy of you? But my hope is they may be as grains of salt, that will rather give you an appetite than offend you with satiety. And although they handle those things wherein both men's lives and their pens be most conversant, yet (what I have attained I know not) but I have endeavored to make them not vulgar; but of a nature whereof a man shall find much in experience, little in books; so as they are neither repetitions nor fancies. But howsoever, I shall most humbly desire Your

Highness to accept them in gracious part, and to conceive that if I cannot rest, but must shew my dutiful and devoted affection to Your Highness in these things which proceed from myself, I shall be much more ready to do it in performance of any your princely commandments. And so, wishing Your Highness all princely felicity, I rest

Your Highness's most humble servant.

FROM *The Twoo Bookes of Francis Bacon Of the proficience and advancement of Learning*, 1605

The Proficience and Advancement of Learning

THE FIRST BOOK

To the King.

THERE were under the Law (excellent King) both daily sacrifices and free will offerings; the one proceeding upon ordinary observance, the other upon a devout cheerfulness. In like manner there belongeth to kings from their servants both tribute of duty and presents of affection. In the former of these, I hope I shall not live to be wanting according to my most humble duty and the good pleasure of Your Majesty's employments; for the latter, I thought it more respective to make choice of some oblation which might rather refer to the propriety and excellency of your individual person than to the business of your crown and state.

Wherefore, representing Your Majesty many times unto my mind, and beholding you not with the inquisitive eye of presumption, to discover that which the Scripture telleth me is inscrutable; but with the observant eye of duty and admiration; leaving aside the other parts of your virtue and fortune, I have been touched, yea, and possessed with an extreme wonder at those your virtues and faculties which the philosophers call intellectual: the largeness of your capacity, the faithfulness of your memory, the swiftness of your apprehension, the penetration of your judgment, and the facility and order of your elocution. And I have often thought that, of all the persons living that I have known, Your Majesty were the best instance to make a man of Plato's opinion that all knowledge is but remembrance, and that the mind of man by nature knoweth all things, and hath but her own native and original motions (which, by the strangeness and darkness of this tabernacle of the body are sequestered) again revived and restored. Such a light of nature I have observed in Your Majesty, and such a readiness to take flame and blaze from the least occasion presented or the least spark of another's knowledge delivered. And as the Scripture saith of the wisest King: that his heart was as the

sands of the sea, which, though it be one of the largest bodies, yet it consisteth of the smallest and finest portions; so hath God given Your Majesty
a composition of understanding admirable, being able to compass and
comprehend the greatest matters, and nevertheless to touch and apprehend the least; whereas it should seem an impossibility in nature for the
same instrument to make itself fit for great and small works. And for
your gift of speech, I call to mind what Cornelius Tacitus saith of Augustus Caesar: *Augusto profluens et quae principem deceret, eloquentia
fuit* [that his style of speech was flowing and prince-like]. For, if we note
it well, speech that is uttered with labor and difficulty, or speech that 10
savoreth of the affectation of art and precepts, or speech that is framed
after the imitation of some pattern of eloquence, though never so excellent
—all this hath somewhat servile, and holding of the subject. But Your
Majesty's manner of speech is indeed princelike, flowing as from a fountain, and yet streaming and branching itself into nature's order, full of
facility and felicity, imitating none and inimitable by any. And as in your
civil estate there appeareth to be an emulation and contention of Your
Majesty's virtue with your fortune; a virtuous disposition with a fortunate regiment; a virtuous expectation (when time was) of your greater
fortune, with a prosperous possession thereof in the due time; a virtuous 20
observation of the laws of marriage, with most blessed and happy fruit of
marriage; a virtuous and most Christian desire of peace, with a fortunate
inclination in your neighbor princes thereunto; so, likewise, in these intellectual matters, there seemeth to be no less contention between the
excellency of Your Majesty's gifts of nature and the universality and
perfection of your learning. For I am well assured that this which I shall
say is no amplification at all, but a positive and measured truth; which is
that there hath not been, since Christ's time, any king or temporal monarch which hath been so learned in all literature and erudition, divine and
human. For let a man seriously and diligently revolve and peruse the 30
succession of the emperors of Rome, of which Caesar the Dictator, who
lived some years before Christ, and Marcus Antoninus were the best
learned; and so descend to the emperors of Grecia, or of the West, and
then to the lines of France, Spain, England, Scotland, and the rest, and
he shall find this judgment is truly made. For it seemeth much in a king
if, by the compendious extractions of other men's wits and labors, he
can take hold of any superficial ornaments and shews of learning, or if
he countenance and prefer learning and learned men. But to drink indeed
of the true fountains of learning, nay, to have such a fountain of learning
in himself, in a king, and in a king born, is almost a miracle. And the 40
more because there is met in Your Majesty a rare conjunction as well of
divine and sacred literature as of profane and human; so as Your Majesty

standeth invested of that triplicity which, in great veneration, was ascribed to the ancient Hermes: the power and fortune of a king; the knowledge and illumination of a priest; and the learning and universality of a philosopher. This propriety inherent and individual attribute in Your Majesty deserveth to be expressed, not only in the fame and admiration of the present time, nor in the history or tradition of the ages succeeding, but also in some solid work, fixed memorial, and immortal monument bearing a character or signature both of the power of a king and the difference and perfection of such a king.

10   Therefore, I did conclude with myself that I could not make unto Your Majesty a better oblation than of some treatise tending to that end; whereof the sum will consist of these two parts: the former concerning the excellency of learning and knowledge, and the excellency of the merit and true glory in the augmentation and propagation thereof; the latter, what the particular acts and works are which have been embraced and undertaken for the advancement of learning, and again what defects and undervalues I find in such particular acts; to the end that, though I cannot positively or affirmatively advise Your Majesty, or propound unto you framed particulars, yet I may excite your princely cogitations to visit
20 the excellent treasure of your own mind, and thence to extract particulars for this purpose agreeable to your magnanimity and wisdom.

In the entrance to the former of these, to clear the way, and as it were to make silence to have the true testimonies concerning the dignity of learning to be better heard without the interruption of tacit objections, I think good to deliver it from the discredits and disgraces which it hath received; all from ignorance, but ignorance severally disguised, appearing sometimes in the zeal and jealousy of divines, sometimes in the severity and arrogancy of politics, and sometimes in the errors and imperfections of learned men themselves.

30

*   *   *   *   *

Now, therefore, we come to that third sort of discredit, or diminution of credit, that groweth unto learning from learned men themselves, which commonly cleaveth fastest. It is either from their fortune, or from their manners, or from the nature of their studies; for the first, it is not in their power; and the second is accidental; the third only is proper to be handled. But because we are not in hand with true measure, but with popular estimation and conceit, it is not amiss to speak somewhat of the two former. The derogations, therefore, which grow to learning from
40 the fortune or condition of learned men are either in respect of scarcity of means, or in respect of privateness of life and meanness of employments.

*   *   *   *   *

Not that I can tax or condemn the morigeration or application of learned men to men in fortune. For the answer was good that Diogenes made to one that asked him in mockery, How it came to pass that philosophers were the followers of rich men, and not rich men of philosophers? He answered soberly, and yet sharply, Because the one sort knew what they had need of, and the other did not. And of the like nature was the answer which Aristippus made, when having a petition to Dionysius and no ear given to him, he fell down at his feet; whereupon Dionysius stayed and gave him the hearing and granted it; and afterward some person tender on the behalf of philosophy reproved Aristippus that he would 10 offer the profession of philosophy such an indignity, as for a private suit to fall at a tyrant's feet; but he answered it was not his fault, but it was the fault of Dionysius, that had his ears in his feet. Neither was it accounted weakness, but discretion, in him that would not dispute his best with Adrianus Caesar; excusing himself, that it was reason to yield to him that commanded thirty legions. These and the like applications and stooping to points of necessity and convenience cannot be disallowed; for though they may have some outward baseness, yet in a judgment truly made they are to be accounted submissions to the occasion and not to the person. 20

Now I proceed to those errors and vanities which have intervened amongst the studies themselves of the learned; which is that which is principal and proper to the present argument, wherein my purpose is not to make a justification of the errors, but, by a censure and separation of the errors, to make a justification of that which is good and sound, and to deliver that from the aspersion of the other. For we see that it is the manner of men to scandalize and deprave that which retaineth the state and virtue, by taking advantage upon that which is corrupt and degenerate; as the Heathens in the primitive church used to blemish and taint the Christians with the faults and corruptions of heretics. But never- 30 theless I have no meaning at this time to make any exact animadversion of the errors and impediments in matters of learning which are more secret and remote from vulgar opinion, but only to speak unto such as do fall under, or near unto, a popular observation.

There be, therefore, chiefly three vanities in studies whereby learning hath been most traduced. For those things we do esteem vain which are either false or frivolous, those which either have no truth or no use; and those persons we esteem vain which are either credulous or curious; and curiosity is either in matter or words. So that in reason as well as in experience there fall out these three distempers (as I may term them) of 40 learning: the first, fantastical learning; the second, contentious learning; and the last, delicate learning—vain imaginations, vain altercations, and vain affectations. And with the last I will begin.

Martin Luther, conducted (no doubt) by an higher Providence, but in discourse of reason finding what a province he had undertaken against the bishop of Rome and the degenerate traditions of the church, and finding his own solitude being no ways aided by the opinions of his own time, was enforced to awake all antiquity, and to call former times to his succors to make a party against the present time; so that the ancient authors, both in divinity and in humanity, which had long time slept in libraries, began generally to be read and revolved. This, by consequence, did draw on a necessity of a more exquisite travail in the languages original wherein
10 those authors did write, for the better understanding of those authors and the better advantage of pressing and applying their words. And thereof grew again a delight in their manner of style and phrase and an admiration of that kind of writing; which was much furthered and precipitated by the enmity and opposition that the propounders of those (primitive, but seeming-new) opinions had against the schoolmen, who were generally of the contrary part; and whose writings were altogether in a differing style and form, taking liberty to coin and frame new terms of art to express their own sense, and to avoid circuit of speech, without regard to the pureness, pleasantness, and (as I may call it) lawfulness of the phrase
20 or word. And again, because the great labor that then was with the people (of whom the Pharisees were wont to say: *Execrabilis ista turba quae non novit legem* [the wretched crowd that has not known the law]) for the winning and persuading of them, there grew of necessity in chief price and request eloquence and variety of discourse, as the fittest and forciblest access into the capacity of the vulgar sort: so that these four causes concurring—the admiration of ancient authors, the hate of the schoolmen, the exact study of languages, and the efficacy of preaching— did bring in an affectionate study of eloquence and copie of speech, which then began to flourish. This grew speedily to an excess; for men began to
30 hunt more after words than matter, and more after the choiceness of the phrase, and the round and clean composition of the sentence, and the sweet falling of the clauses, and the varying and illustration of their works with tropes and figures than after the weight of matter, worth of subject, soundness of argument, life of invention, or depth of judgment. Then grew the flowing and watery vein of Osorius, the Portugal bishop, to be in price; then did Sturmius spend such infinite and curious pains upon Cicero the orator and Hermogenes the rhetorician, besides his own books of periods, and imitation, and the like; then did Car of Cambridge and Ascham, with their lectures and writings, almost deify Cicero and
40 Demosthenes, and allure all young men that were studious unto that delicate and polished kind of learning. Then did Erasmus take occasion to make the scoffing echo; *Decem annos consumpsi in legendo Cicerone*

[I have spent ten years in reading Cicero]; and the echo answered in Greek, *One: asine*. Then grew the learning of the schoolmen to be utterly despised as barbarous. In sum, the whole inclination and bent of those times was rather towards copie than weight.

Here therefore [is] the first distemper of learning, when men study words and not matter; whereof, though I have represented an example of late times, yet it hath been and will be *secundum majus et minus* in all time. And how is it possible but this should have an operation to discredit learning, even with vulgar capacities, when they see learned men's works like the first letter of a patent or limned book, which, though it hath large 10 flourishes, yet it is but a letter? It seems to me that Pygmalion's frenzy is a good emblem or portraiture of this vanity; for words are but the images of matter, and except they have life of reason and invention, to fall in love with them is all one as to fall in love with a picture.

But yet notwithstanding, it is a thing not hastily to be condemned to clothe and adorn the obscurity even of philosophy itself with sensible and plausible elocution. For hereof we have great examples in Xenophon, Cicero, Seneca, Plutarch, and of Plato also in some degree; and hereof likewise there is great use. For surely, to the severe inquisition of truth and the deep progress into philosophy, it is some hindrance, because it is too 20 early satisfactory to the mind of man, and quencheth the desire of further search before we come to a just period; but then if a man be to have any use of such knowledge in civil occasions, of conference, counsel, persuasion, discourse, or the like, then shall he find it prepared to his hands in those authors which write in that manner. But the excess of this is so justly contemptible that as Hercules, when he saw the image of Adonis, Venus' minion, in a temple, said in disdain, *Nil sacri es* [you are no divinity]; so there is none of Hercules' followers in learning, that is, the more severe and laborious sort of inquirers into truth, but will despise 30 those delicacies and affectations as indeed capable of no divineness. And thus much of the first disease or distemper of learning.

The second, which followeth, is in nature worse than the former; for as substance of matter is better than beauty of words, so contrariwise vain matter is worse than vain words. Wherein it seemeth the reprehension of St. Paul was not only proper for those times, but prophetical for the times following; and not only respective to divinity, but extensive to all knowledge: *Devita profanas vocum novitates, et oppositiones falsi nominis scientiae* [shun profane novelties of terms and oppositions of science falsely so called]. For he assigneth two marks and badges of suspected 40 and falsified science; the one, the novelty of and strangeness of terms; the other, the strictness of positions, which of necessity doth induce oppositions, and so questions and altercations. Surely, like as many substances in nature which are solid do putrefy and corrupt into worms, so it is the property of good and sound knowledge to putrefy and dissolve into a number of subtile, idle, unwholesome, and (as I may term them) vermiculate questions, which have indeed a kind of quickness and life of spirit, but no soundness of matter or goodness of quality. This kind of degenerate learning did chiefly reign amongst the Schoolmen; who, having sharp and strong wits, and abundance of leisure, and small variety of reading, but their wits being shut up in the cells of a few authors (chiefly Aristotle their dictator) as their persons were shut up in the cells of monasteries and 10 colleges, and knowing little history, either of nature or time, did out of no great quantity of matter, and infinite agitation of wit, spin out unto us those laborious webs of learning which are extant in their books. For the wit and mind of man, if it work upon matter, which is the contemplation of the creatures of God, worketh according to the stuff, and is limited thereby; but if it work upon itself, as the spider worketh his web, then it is endless, and brings forth indeed cobwebs of learning, admirable for the fineness of thread and work, but of no substance or profit.

This same unprofitable subtility or curiosity is of two sorts; either in the subject itself that they handle, when it is a fruitless speculation or 20 controversy (whereof there are no small number both in divinity and philosophy), or in the manner or method of handling of a knowledge, which amongst them was this: upon every particular position or assertion to frame objections, and to those objections, solutions; which solutions were for the most part not confutations, but distinctions; whereas indeed the strength of all sciences is as the strength of the old man's faggot, in the bond. For the harmony of a science supporting each part the other is, and ought to be, the true and brief confutation and suppression of all the smaller sort of objections. But on the other side, if you take out every axiom, as the sticks of the faggot, one by one, you may quarrel with them 30 and bend them and break them at your pleasure; so that as was said of Seneca, *Verborum minutiis rerum frangit pondera* [that he broke up the weight and mass of the matter by verbal points and niceties]; so a man may truly say of the Schoolmen, *Quaestionum minutiis scientiarum frangunt soliditatem* [they broke up the solidity and coherency of the sciences by the minuteness and nicety of their questions]. For were it not better for a man in a fair room to set up one great light, or branching candlestick of lights, than to go about with a small watch candle into every corner? And such is their method, that rests not so much upon evidence of truth proved by arguments, authorities, similitudes, examples, as 40 upon particular confutations and solutions of every scruple, cavillation, and objection; breeding for the most part one question as fast it solveth another; even as in the former resemblance, when you carry the light into one corner, you darken the rest; so that the fable and fiction of Scylla seemeth to be a lively image of this kind of philosophy or knowledge, which was transformed into a comely virgin for the upper parts, but then *Candida succinctam latrantibus inguina monstris* [there were barking monsters all about her loins]. So the generalities of the Schoolmen are for a while good and proportionable; but then when you descend into their distinctions and decisions, instead of a fruitful womb for the use and benefit of man's life, they end in monstrous altercations and barking questions. So as it is not possible but this quality of knowledge must fall under popular contempt, the people being apt to contemn truth upon occasion of controversies and altercations, and to think they are all out of their way which never meet; and when they see such digladiation about subtilities and matter of no use nor moment, they easily fall upon that judgment of Dionysius of Syracusa, *Verba ista sunt senum otiosorum* [it is the talk of old men that have nothing to do].

Notwithstanding, certain it is that if those Schoolmen to their great thirst of truth and unwearied travail of wit had joined variety and universality of reading and contemplation, they had proved excellent lights, to the great advancement of all learning and knowledge. But as they are, they are great undertakers indeed, and fierce with dark keeping; but as in the inquiry of the divine truth their pride inclined to leave the oracle of God's word and to vanish in the mixture of their own inventions, so in the inquisition of nature they ever left the oracle of God's works and adored the deceiving and deformed images which the unequal mirror of their own minds or a few received authors or principles did represent unto them. And thus much for the second disease of learning.

For the third vice or disease of learning, which concerneth deceit or untruth, it is of all the rest the foulest; as that which doth destroy the essential form of knowledge, which is nothing but a representation of truth: for the truth of being and the truth of knowing are one, differing no more than the direct beam and the beam reflected. This vice therefore brancheth itself into two sorts: delight in deceiving, and aptness to be deceived; imposture and credulity; which, although they appear to be of a diverse nature, the one seeming to proceed of cunning and the other of simplicity, yet certainly they do for the most part concur. For as the verse noteth,

Percontatorem fugito, nam garrulus idem est,

an inquisitive man is a prattler, so upon the like reason a credulous man is a deceiver; as we see it in fame, that he that will easily believe rumours will as easily augment rumours and add somewhat to them of his own; which Tacitus wisely noteth, when he saith, *Fingunt simul creduntque* [they invented a tale, and credited their own lie], so great an affinity hath fiction and belief.

This facility of credit, and accepting or admitting things weakly authorized or warranted, is of two kinds, according to the subject. For it is either a belief of history (as the lawyers speak, matter of fact), or else of matter of art and opinion. As to the former, we see the experience and inconvenience of this error in ecclesiastical history, which hath too easily received and registered reports and narrations of miracles wrought by martyrs, hermits, or monks of the deserts, and other holy men, and 10 their relics, shrines, chapels, and images; which though they had a passage for a time, by the ignorance of the people, the superstitious simplicity of some, and the politic toleration of others, holding them but as divine poesies, yet after a period of time, when the mist began to clear up, they grew to be esteemed but as old wives' fables, impostures of the clergy, illusions of spirits, and badges of antichrist, to the great scandal and detriment of religion.

So in natural history, we see there hath not been that choice and judgment used as ought to have been; as may appear in the writings of Plinius, Cardanus, Albertus, and divers of the Arabians; being fraught with much 20 fabulous matter, a great part not only untried but notoriously untrue, to the great derogation of the credit of natural philosophy with the grave and sober kind of wits. Wherein the wisdom and integrity of Aristotle is worthy to be observed, that having made so diligent and exquisite a history of living creatures, hath mingled it sparingly with any vain or feigned matter; and yet on the other side hath cast all prodigious narrations which he thought worthy the recording into one book, excellently discerning that matter of manifest truth, such whereupon observation and rule was to be built, was not to be mingled or weakened with matter of doubtful credit; and yet again that rarities and reports that seem uncredible are 30 not to be suppressed or denied to the memory of men.

And as for the facility of credit which is yielded to arts and opinions, it is likewise of two kinds; either when too much belief is attributed to the arts themselves, or to certain authors in any art. The sciences themselves which have had better intelligence and confederacy with the imagination of man than with his reason are three in number: Astrology, Natural Magic, and Alchemy; of which sciences nevertheless the ends or pretences are noble. For astrology pretendeth to discover that correspondence or concatenation which is between the superior globe and the inferior; natural magic pretendeth to call and reduce natural philosophy from a 40 variety of speculations to the magnitude of works; and alchemy pretendeth to make separation of all the unlike parts of bodies which in mixtures of nature are incorporate. But the derivations and prosecutions to these ends, both in the theories and in the practices, are full of error and vanity, which the great professors themselves have sought to veil over and conceal by enigmatical writings, and referring themselves to auricular traditions, and such other devices to save the credit of impostures. And yet surely to alchemy this right is due, that it may be compared to the husbandman whereof Æsop makes the fable, that when he died told his sons that he had left unto them gold buried under ground in his vineyard; and they digged all over the ground, and gold they found none; but by reason of their stirring and digging the mould about the roots of their vines, they had a great vintage the year following. So assuredly the search and stir to make gold hath brought to light a great number of good and fruitful inventions and experiments, as well for the disclosing of nature as for the use of man's life.

And as for the overmuch credit that hath been given unto authors in sciences, in making them dictators that their words should stand, and not counsels to give advice, the damage is infinite that sciences have received thereby, as the principal cause that hath kept them low, at a stay without growth or advancement. For hence it hath comen that in arts mechanical the first deviser comes shortest, and time addeth and perfecteth; but in sciences the first author goeth furthest, and time leeseth and corrupteth. So we see artillery, sailing, printing, and the like, were grossly managed at the first, and by time accommodated and refined; but contrariwise the philosophies and sciences of Aristotle, Plato, Democritus, Hippocrates, Euclide, Archimedes, of most vigour at the first, and by time degenerate and imbased; whereof the reason is no other, but that in the former many wits and industries have contributed in one; and in the later many wits and industries have been spent about the wit of some one, whom many times they have rather depraved than illustrated. For as water will not ascend higher than the level of the first spring-head from whence it descendeth, so knowledge derived from Aristotle, and exempted from liberty of examination, will not rise again higher than the knowledge of Aristotle. And therefore, although the position be good, *Oportet discentum credere* [a man who is learning must be content to believe what he is told], yet it must be coupled with this, *Oportet edoctum judicare* [when he has learned it he must exercise his judgment and see whether it be worthy of belief]; for disciples do owe unto masters only a temporary belief and a suspension of their own judgment until they be fully instructed, and not an absolute resignation or perpetual captivity. And therefore to conclude this point, I will say no more but, So let great authors have their due, as time, which is the author of authors, be not deprived of his due, which is further and further to discover truth.

Thus have I gone over these three diseases of learning; besides the which, there are some other rather peccant humours than formed diseases, which nevertheless are not so secret and intrinsic but that they fall under a popular observation and traducement, and therefore are not to be passed over.

The first of these is the extreme affecting of two extremities; the one antiquity, the other novelty; wherein it seemeth the children of time do take after the nature and malice of the father. For as he devoureth his children, so one of them seeketh to devour and suppress the other; while antiquity envieth there should be new additions, and novelty cannot be 10 content to add but it must deface. Surely the advice of the prophet is the true direction in this matter, *State super vias antiquas, et videte quaenam sit via recta et bona, et ambulate in ea* [stand ye in the old ways, and see which is the good way, and walk therein]. Antiquity deserveth that reverence that men should make a stand thereupon, and discover what is the best way; but when the discovery is well taken, then to make progression. And to speak truly, *Antiquitas saeculi juventus mundi.* These times are the ancient times, when the world is ancient, and not those which we account ancient *ordine retrograde*, by a computation backward from ourselves.

20 Another error, induced by the former, is a distrust that any thing should be now to be found out which the world should have missed and passed over so long time; as if the same objection were to be made to time that Lucian maketh to Jupiter and other heathen gods, of which he wondereth that they begot so many children in old time and begot none in his time, and asketh whether they were become septuagenary, or whether the law Pappia, made against old men's marriages, had restrained them. So it seemeth men doubt lest time is become past children and generation; wherein contrariwise we see commonly the levity and unconstancy of men's judgments, which, till a matter be done, wonder 30 that it can be done; and as soon as it is done, wonder again that it was no sooner done; as we see in the expedition of Alexander into Asia, which at first was prejudged as a vast and impossible enterprise; and yet afterwards it pleaseth Livy to make no more of it than this, *Nil aliud quàm bene ausus vana contemnere* [it was but taking courage to despise vain apprehensions]. And the same happened to Columbus in the western navigation. But in intellectual matters it is much more common; as may be seen in most of the propositions of Euclid, which till they be demonstrate, they seem strange to our assent; but being demonstrate, our mind accepteth of them by a kind of relation (as the lawyers speak) as if we 40 had known them before.

Another error, that hath also some affinity with the former, is a conceit that of former opinions or sects, after variety and examination, the best hath still prevailed and suppressed the rest; so as if a man should begin the labour of a new search, he were but like to light upon somewhat formerly rejected, and by rejection brought into oblivion; as if the multitude, or the wisest for the multitude's sake, were not ready to give passage rather to that which is popular and superficial than to that which is substantial and profound. For the truth is, that time seemeth to be of the nature of a river or stream, which carrieth down to us that which is light and blown up, and sinketh and drowneth that which is weighty and solid.

Another error, of a diverse nature from all the former, is the over- 10 early and peremptory reduction of knowledge into arts and methods; from which time, commonly, sciences receive small or no augmentation. But as young men, when they knit and shape perfectly, do seldom grow to a further stature; so knowledge, while it is in aphorisms and observations, it is in growth; but when it once is comprehended in exact methods, it may perchance be further polished and illustrate, and accommodated for use and practice, but it increaseth no more in bulk and substance.

Another error, which doth succeed that which we last mentioned, is that after the distribution of particular arts and sciences, men have abandoned universality, or *philosophia prima;* which cannot but cease and 20 stop all progression. For no perfect discovery can be made upon a flat or a level. Neither is it possible to discover the more remote and deeper parts of any science, if you stand but upon the level of the same science, and ascend not to a higher science.

Another error hath proceeded from too great a reverence, and a kind of adoration of the mind and understanding of man; by means whereof men have withdrawn themselves too much from the contemplation of nature and the observations of experience, and have tumbled up and down in their own reason and conceits. Upon these intellectualists, which are notwithstanding commonly taken for the most sublime and divine 30 philosophers, Heraclitus gave a just censure, saying, "Men sought truth in their own little worlds, and not in the great and common world." For they disdain to spell and so by degrees to read in the volume of God's works; and contrariwise by continual meditation and agitation of wit do urge and as it were invocate their own spirits to divine and give oracles unto them, whereby they are deservedly deluded.

Another error that hath some connexion with this latter is, that men have used to infect their meditations, opinions, and doctrines, with some conceits which they have most admired, or some sciences which they have most applied, and given all things else a tincture according to them, 40 utterly untrue and unproper. So hath Plato intermingled his philosophy with theology, and Aristotle with logic, and the second school of Plato,

Proclus and the rest, with the mathematics. For these were the arts which
had a kind of primogeniture with them severally. So have the alchemists
made a philosophy out of a few experiments of the furnace; and Gilbertus,
our countryman, hath made a philosophy out of the observations of a
loadstone. So Cicero, when, reciting the several opinions of the nature of
the soul, he found a musician that held the soul was but a harmony, saith
pleasantly, *Hic ab arte sua non recessit*, etc. [he was constant to his own
art]. But of these conceits Aristotle speaketh seriously and wisely, when
he saith, *Qui respiciunt ad pauca de facili pronunciant* [they who take only
10 few points into account find it easy to pronounce judgment].

   Another error is an impatience of doubt, and haste to assertion without due and mature suspension of judgment. For the two ways of contemplation are not unlike the two ways of action commonly spoken of by
the ancients; the one plain and smooth in the beginning, and in the end
impassable; the other rough and troublesome in the entrance, but after a
while fair and even. So it is in contemplation; if a man will begin with
certainties, he shall end in doubts; but if he will be content to begin with
doubts, he shall end in certainties.

   Another error is in the manner of the tradition and delivery of knowl-
20 edge, which is for the most part magistral and peremptory, and not in-
genuous and faithful; in a sort as may be soonest believed, and not
easiliest examined. It is true that in compendious treatises for practice, that
form is not to be disallowed. But in the true handling of knowledge, men
ought not to fall either on the one side into the vein of Velleius the Epi-
curean, *Nil tam metuens, quàm ne dubitare aliqua de re videretur* [who
feared nothing so much as the seeming to be in doubt about anything],
nor on the other side into Socrates his ironical doubting of all things, but
to propound things sincerely, with more or less asseveration, as they stand
in a man's own judgment proved more or less.

30   Other errors there are in the scope that men propound to themselves,
whereunto they bend their endeavours; for whereas the more constant
and devote kind of professors of any science ought to propound to themselves to make some additions to their science, they convert their labours
to aspire to certain second prizes; as to be a profound interpreter or com-
menter, to be a sharp champion or defender, to be a methodical com-
pounder or abridger; and so the patrimony of knowledge cometh to be
sometimes improved, but seldom augmented.

   But the greatest error of all the rest is the mistaking or misplacing of
the last or furthest end of knowledge. For men have entered into a desire
40 of learning and knowledge, sometimes upon a natural curiosity and inquisitive appetite; sometimes to entertain their minds with variety and
delight; sometimes for ornament and reputation; and sometimes to enable

them to victory of wit and contradiction; and most times for lucre and profession; and seldom sincerely to give a true account of their gift of reason, to the benefit and use of men. As if there were sought in knowledge a couch, whereupon to rest a searching and restless spirit; or a terrace, for a wandering and variable mind to walk up and down with a fair prospect; or a tower of state, for a proud mind to raise itself upon; or a fort or commanding ground, for strife and contention; or a shop, for profit or sale; and not a rich storehouse, for the glory of the Creator and the relief of man's estate. But this is that which will indeed dignify and exalt knowledge, if contemplation and action may be more nearly and straitly conjoined and united together than they have been; a conjunction like unto that of the two highest planets, Saturn the planet of rest and contemplation, and Jupiter the planet of civil society and action. Howbeit, I do not mean, when I speak of use and action, that end before-mentioned of the applying of knowledge to lucre and profession. For I am not ignorant how much that diverteth and interrupteth the prosecution and advancement of knowledge; like unto the golden ball thrown before Atalanta, which while she goeth aside and stoopeth to take up, the race is hindered,

Declinat cursus, aurumque volubile tollit.

Neither is my meaning, as was spoken of Socrates, to call philosophy down from heaven to converse upon the earth; that is, to leave natural philosophy aside, and to apply knowledge only to manners and policy. But as both heaven and earth do conspire and contribute to the use and benefit of man, so the end ought to be, from both philosophies to separate and reject vain speculations and whatsoever is empty and void, and to preserve and augment whatsoever is solid and fruitful; that knowledge may not be as a courtesan, for pleasure and vanity only, or as a bond-woman, to acquire and gain to her master's use, but as a spouse, for generation, fruit, and comfort.

Thus have I described and opened, as by a kind of dissection, those peccant humours (the principal of them) which have not only given impediment to the proficience of learning but have given also occasion to the traducement thereof; wherein if I have been too plain, it must be remembered *Fidelia vulnera amantis, sed dolosa oscula malignantis* [faithful are the wounds of a friend, but the kisses of an enemy are deceitful]. This I think I have gained: that I ought to be the better believed in that which I shall say pertaining to commendation, because I have proceeded so freely in that which concerneth censure.

* * * * *

JOHN DONNE

The Introduction and Notes are at page 1352

FROM *Juvenilia: Or Certaine Paradoxes, and Problemes*, 1633

Paradoxes

I.

A Defence of Women's Inconstancy

THAT women are *inconstant*, I with any man confess, but that *inconstancy* is a bad quality, I against any man will maintain. For every thing, as it is one better than another, so is it fuller of change. The heavens themselves continually turn, the stars move, the moon changeth; fire whirleth, air flyeth, water ebbs and flows, the face of the earth altereth her looks, time stays not; the colour that is most light will take most dyes.
20 So in men, they that have the most reason are the most intolerable in their designs, and the darkest or most ignorant do seldomest change; therefore women changing more than men, have also more reason. They cannot be immutable like stocks, like stones, like the earth's dull center. Gold that lyeth still, rusteth; water, corrupteth; air that moveth not, poisoneth; then why should that which is the perfection of other things be imputed to women as greatest imperfection?

Because thereby they deceive men? Are not your wits pleased with those jests which cozen your expectation? You can call it pleasure to be beguiled in troubles, and in the most excellent toy in the world, you call it treachery.
30 I would you had your mistresses so constant—that they would never change—no, not so much as their smocks; then should you see what sluttish virtue constancy were. Inconstancy is a most commendable and cleanly quality, and women in this quality are far more absolute than the heavens, than the stars, moon, or any thing beneath it; for long observation hath picked certainty out of their mutability. The learned are so well acquainted with the stars, signs, and planets, that they make them but characters to read the meaning of the heaven in his own forehead. Every simple fellow can bespeak the change of the moon a great while beforehand; but I would fain have the learned man so skillful as to tell when the
40 simplest woman meaneth to vary. Learning affords no rules to know, much less knowledge to rule the mind of a woman. For as philosophy teacheth us that light things do always tend upwards and heavy things de-

cline downward, experience teacheth us otherwise, that the disposition of a light woman is to fall down, the nature of women being contrary to all art and nature. Women are like flies which feed among us at our table, or fleas sucking our very blood, who leave not our most retired places free from their familiarity; yet for all their fellowship will they never be tamed nor commanded by us. Women are like the sun, which is violently carried one way, yet hath a proper course contrary; so, though they, by the mastery of some over-ruling churlish husbands, are forced to his bias, yet have they a motion of their own, which their husbands never know of.

It is the nature of nice and fastidious minds to know things only to be weary of them. Women by their sly changeableness, and pleasing doubleness, prevent even the mislike of those, for they can never be so well known but that there is still more unknown. Every woman is a science; for he that plods upon a woman all his life long shall at length find himself short of the knowledge of her. They are born to take down the pride of wit and ambition of wisdom, making fools wise in the adventuring to win them, wise men fools in conceit of loving their labours, witty men stark mad being confounded with their uncertainties. Philosophers write against them for spite, not desert, that having attained to some knowledge in all other things, in them only they know nothing, but are merely ignorant. Active and experienced men rail against them, because they love in their liveless and decrepit age, when all goodness leaves them. These envious libellers ballad against them, because having nothing in themselves able to deserve their love, they maliciously discommend all they cannot obtain, thinking to make men believe they know much because they are able to dispraise much, and rage against inconstancy, when they were never admitted into so much favour as to be forsaken. In mine opinion such men are happy that women are inconstant, for so may they chance to be beloved of some excellent women (when it comes to their turn) out of their inconstancy and mutability though not out of their own desert.

And what reason is there to clog any woman with one man, be he never so singular. Women had rather, and it is far better and more judicial to enjoy all the virtues in several men, than but some of them in one; for otherwise they lose their taste, like diverse sorts of meat minced together in one dish; and to have all excellencies in one man (if it were possible) is confusion and diversity. Now who can deny but such as are obstinately bent to undervalue their worth are those that have not soul enough to comprehend their excellency, women being the most excellentest creatures, in that man is able to subject all things else and to grow wise in every thing, but still persists a fool in woman! The greatest scholar, if he once take a wife, is found so unlearned that he must begin his hornbook, and all is by inconstancy. To conclude, therefore, this name of *inconstancy*, which hath so much been poisoned with slanders, ought to be changed into *variety*, for the which the world is so delightful, and a woman for that, the most delightful thing in this world.

FROM *A Sermon . . . Preach'd to the Honourable Company of the Virginian Plantation, 13° Nouemb. 1622, 1622*

A Sermon

10   ACTS I. 8.

But ye shall receive power, after that the Holy Ghost is come upon you, and ye shall be witnesses unto me both in Jerusalem, and in all Judea, and in Samaria, and unto the uttermost part of the earth.

There are reckoned in this book 22 sermons of the Apostles; and yet the book is not called the Preaching but the Practise, not the Words but the Acts of the Apostles: and the Acts of the Apostles were to convey that name of Christ Jesus and to propagate His Gospel over all the world. Beloved, you are actors upon the same stage too. The uttermost part of the

20 earth are your scene. Act over the Acts of the Apostles; be you a light to the Gentiles, that sit in darkness; be you content to carry Him over these seas, who dried up one Red Sea for His first people, and hath poured out another Red Sea, His own blood, for them and us. When man was fallen, God clothed him; made him a leather garment; there God descended to one occupation. When the time of man's redemption was come, then God, as it were to house him, became a carpenter's son; there God descended to another occupation. Naturally, without doubt, man would have been his own tailor and his own carpenter; something in these two kinds man would have done of himself, though he had had no pattern from

30 God. But in preserving man, who was fallen, to this redemption by which he was to be raised, in preserving man from perishing in the flood, God descended to a third occupation, to be his shipwright, to give him the model of a ship, an ark, and so to be the author of that which man himself, in likelihood, would never have thought of, a means to pass from nation to nation. Now, as God taught us to make clothes, not only to clothe ourselves, but to clothe Him, in His poor and naked members here; as God taught us to build houses, not to house ourselves, but to house Him, in erecting churches to His glory; so God taught us to make ships, not to transport ourselves, but to transport Him, *That when we have received*

40 *power, after that the Holy Ghost is come upon us, we might be witnesses unto Him, both in Jerusalem, and in all Judea, and in Samaria, and unto the uttermost parts of the earth.*

As I speak now principally to them who are concerned in this Plantation of Virginia, yet there may be divers in this congregation who, though they have no interest in this Plantation, yet they may have benefit and edification by that which they hear me say; so Christ spoke the words of this text principally to the Apostles who were present and questioned Him at His ascension, but they are, in their just extension and due accommodation, appliable to our present occasion of meeting here. As Christ Himself is alpha and omega, so first, as that He is last too, so these words which He spoke in the East belong to us, who are to glorify Him in the West; *That we, having received power after that the Holy Ghost is come upon us,* 10 *might be witnesses unto Him, both in Jerusalem, and in all Judea, and in Samaria, and unto the uttermost parts of the earth.*

*　　*　　*　　*　　*

2. PART.

. . . . . . God says to you, No kingdom, not ease, not abundance; nay, nothing at all yet; the Plantation shall not discharge the charges, not defray itself yet; but yet already, now at first, it shall conduce to great uses. It shall redeem many a wretch from the jaws of death, from the hands of 20 the executioner, upon whom perchance a small fault, or perchance a first fault, or perchance a fault heartily and sincerely repented, perchance no fault, but malice, had otherwise cast a present and ignominious death. It shall sweep your streets and wash your doors from idle persons, and the children of idle persons, and employ them; and truly, if the whole country were but such a Bridewell to force idle persons to work, it had a good use. But it is already not only a spleen, to drain the ill humors of the body, but a liver, to breed good blood; already the employment breeds mariners; already the place gives essays, nay, freights, of merchantable commodities; already it is a mark for the envy and for the ambition of our enemies. I 30 speak but of our doctrinal, not national, enemies; as they are papists, they are sorry we have this country; and surely twenty lectures in matter of controversy do not so much vex them as one ship that goes and strengthens that Plantation. Neither can I recommend it to you by any better rhetoric than their malice. They would gladly have it, and therefore let us be glad to hold it.

*　　*　　*　　*　　*

Those of our profession that go, you, that send them who go, do all an apostolical function. What action soever hath in the first intention 40 thereof a purpose to propagate the Gospel of Christ Jesus, that is an apostolical action; before the end of the world come, before this mortality shall put on immortality, before the creature shall be delivered of the bondage of corruption under which it groans, before the martyrs under the altar shall be silenced, before all things shall be subdued to Christ, His kingdom perfected, and the last enemy, Death, destroyed, the Gospel must be preached to those men to whom ye send; to all men. Further and hasten you this blessed, this joyful, this glorious consummation of all, and happy reunion of all bodies to their souls, by preaching the Gospel to those men. Preach to them doctrinally, preach to them practically; enamor them with your justice, and (as far as may consist with your security) your civility; but inflame them with your godliness and your religion. Bring them to love and reverence the name of that King that sends men to teach them the ways of civility in this world, but to fear and adore the name of that King of Kings that sends men to teach them the ways of religion for the next world. Those amongst you that are old now shall pass out of this world with this great comfort, that you contributed to the beginning of that commonwealth and of that church, though they live not to see the growth thereof to perfection: Apollos watered, but Paul planted; he that begun the work was the greater man. And you that are young now may live to see the enemy as much impeached by that place, and your friends, yea, children, as well accommodated in that place as any other. You shall have made this island, which is but as the suburbs of the old world, a bridge, a gallery, to the new; to join all to that world that shall never grow old, the kingdom of heaven, you shall add persons to this kingdom, and to the kingdom of heaven, and add names to the Books of our Chronicles, and to the Book of Life.

To end all as the orators which declaimed in the presence of the Roman emperors, in their pangeyrics took that way to make those emperors see what they were bound to do, to say in those public orations that those emperors had done so (for that increased the love of the subject to the prince to be so told that he had done those great things, and then it conveyed a counsel into the prince to do them after). As their way was to procure things to be done by saying they were done, so, beloved, I have taken a contrary way. For when I, by way of exhortation, all this while have seemed to tell you what should be done by you, I have, indeed, but told the congregation what hath been done already. Neither do I speak to move a wheel that stood still, but to keep the wheel in due motion; nor persuade you to begin, but to continue, a good work; nor propose foreign, but your own, examples to do still as you have done hitherto. For, for that, that which is especially in my contemplation, the conversion of the people, as I have received, so I can give this testimony, that, of those persons who have sent in moneys and concealed their names, the greatest part, almost all, have limited their devotion and contribution upon that point, the propagation of religion and the conversion of the people; for the building and beautifying of the house of God and for the instruction and education of their young children. *Christ Jesus Himself is yesterday, and to-day, and the same forever.* In the advancing of His glory, be you so too, yesterday, and to-day, and the same forever, here; and hereafter, when time shall be no more, no more yesterday, no more to-day, yet forever and ever you shall enjoy that joy and that glory which no ill accident can attain to diminish or eclipse it.

Prayer

We return to thee again, O God, with praise and prayer; as for all Thy mercies from before minutes began, to this minute; from our election to this present beam of sanctification, which Thou hast shed upon us now. And more particularly that Thou hast afforded us that great dignity to be this way witnesses of Thy Son, Christ Jesus, and instruments of His glory. Look graciously, and look powerfully, upon this body, which Thou hast been now some years in building and compacting together, this Plantation. Look graciously upon the head of this body, our sovereign, and bless him with a good disposition to this work, and bless him for that disposition. Look graciously upon them who are as the brain of this body, those who by his power counsel, and advise, and assist in the government thereof. Bless them with disposition to unity and concord, and bless them for that disposition. Look graciously upon them who are as eyes of this body, those of the clergy who have any interest therein: bless them with a disposition to preach there, to pray here, to exhort everywhere for the advancement thereof, and bless them for that disposition. Bless them who are the feet of this body, who go thither; and the hands of this body, who labor there; and them who are the heart of this body, all that are heartily affected, and declare actually that heartiness to this action; bless them all with a cheerful disposition to that, and bless them for that disposition. Bless it so in this calm, that, when the tempest comes, it may ride it out safely; bless it so with friends now, that it may stand against enemies hereafter; prepare Thyself a glorious harvest there, and give us leave to be Thy laborers; that so the number of Thy saints being fulfilled, we may with better assurance join in that prayer, *Come, Lord Jesus, come quickly,* and so meet all in that kingdom which the Son of God hath purchased for us with the inestimable price of His incorruptible blood. To which glorious Son of GOD, etc.

Amen.

FROM *Devotions upon Emergent Occasions*, 1624
Devotions
I.

Insultas Morbi primus: The first alteration; the first grudging of the
sickness.

1. *Meditation*

VARIABLE, and therefore miserable condition of man; this minute I was
well, and am ill this minute. I am surpriz'd with a sudden change and
alteration to worse, and can impute it to no cause, nor call it by any name.
We study Health, and we deliberate upon our meats, and drink, and air,
and exercises, and we hew, and we polish every stone that goes to that
building; and so our Health is a long and a regular work. But in a minute
a cannon batters all, overthrows all, demolishes all; a sickness unprevented
for all our diligence, unsuspected for all our curiosity; nay, undeserved,
if we consider only disorder, summons us, seizes us, possesses us, destroys
us in an instant. O miserable condition of man, which was not imprinted
by God, who as he is immortal himself, had put a coal, a beam of immortality into us, which we might have blown into a flame, but blew it out
by our first sin; we beggared our selves by hearkning after false riches,
and infatuated our selves by hearkning after false knowledge. So that
now, we do not only die, but die upon the rack, die by the torment of sickness; nor that only, but are preafflicted, superafflicted with these jealousies,
and suspicions, and apprehensions of sickness before we can call it a sickness; we are not sure we are ill; one hand asks the other by the pulse, and
our eye asks our urine, how we do.

O multiplied misery! we die, and cannot enjoy death, because we die
in this torment of sickness; we are tormented with sickness, and cannot
stay till the torment come, but pre-apprehensions and presages prophesy
those torments which induce that death, before either come; and our dissolution is conceived in these first changes, quickened in the sickness itself,
and born in death, which bears date from these first changes. Is this the
honour which man hath by being a little world, that he hath these earth-
quakes in himself, sudden shakings; these lightnings, sudden flashes; these
thunders, sudden noises; these eclipses, sudden offuscations, and darknings
of his senses; these blazing stars, sudden fiery exhalations; these rivers of
blood, sudden red waters? Is he a world to himself only, therefore, that
he hath enough in himself, not only to destroy and execute himself, but to
presage that execution upon himself; to assist the sickness, to antedate the
sickness, to make sickness the more irremediable by sad apprehensions;

and, as if he would make a fire the more vehement by sprinkling water
upon the coals, so to wrap a hot fever in cold melancholy, lest the fever
alone should not destroy fast enough without this contribution, nor perfit
the work (which is destruction) except we joined an artificial sickness
of our own melancholy; to our natural, our unnatural fever. O perplex'd
discomposition, O ridling distemper, O miserable condition of man!

* * * * *

IV. *Medicusque vocatur: The Physician is sent for.*

4. Meditation

It is too little to call man a little world. Except God, man is a diminutive
to nothing. Man consists of more pieces, more parts, than the world; than
the world doeth, nay than the world is. And if those pieces were extended,
and stretched out in man, as they are in the world, man would be the
giant, and the world the dwarf, the world but the map, and the man the
world. If all the veins in our bodies were extended to rivers; and all the
sinews, to veins of mines; and all the muscles, that lie upon one another, 20
to hills; and all the bones to quarries of stones; and all the other pieces, to
the proportion of those which correspond to them in the world, the air
would be too little for this orb of man to move in, the firmament would
be but enough for this star; for, as the whole world hath nothing to which
something in man doth not answer, so hath man many pieces of which
the whole world hath no representation.

Enlarge this meditation upon this great world, man, so far as to consider the immensity of the creatures this world produces; our creatures are
our thoughts, creatures that are born giants; that reach from east to west,
from earth to heaven, that do not only bestride all the sea, and land, but 30
span the sun and firmament at once. My thoughts reach all, comprehend
all. Inexplicable mystery; I their creator am in a close prison, in a sick
bed, any where, and any one of my creatures, my thoughts, is with the
sun, and beyond the sun, overtakes the sun, and overgoes the sun in one
pace, one step, everywhere. And then as the other world produces serpents
and vipers, malignant and venomous creatures; and worms, and caterpillars, that endeavour to devour that world which produces them; and
monsters compiled and complicated of divers parents, and kinds; so this
world, our selves, produces all these in us, in producing diseases and sicknesses of all those sorts; venomous, and infectious diseases, feeding and 40
consuming diseases, and manifold and entangled diseases, made up of many
several ones. And can the other world name so many venomous, so many

consuming, so many monstrous creatures, as we can diseases of all these kinds? O miserable abundance! O beggarly riches!

How much do we lack of having remedies for every disease, when as yet we have not names for them? But we have a Hercules against these giants, these monsters; that is the physician; he musters up all the forces of the other world, to succour this; all nature to relieve man. We have the physician, but we are not the physician. Here we shrink in our proportion, sink in our dignity, in respect of very mean creatures who are physicians to themselves. The hart that is pursued and wounded, they say, 10 knows an herb which, being eaten, throws off the arrow. A strange kind of vomit. The dog that pursues it, though he be subject to sickness, even proverbially knows his grass that recovers him. And it may be true that the drugger is as near to man as to other creatures; it may be that obvious and present simples, easy to be had, would cure him; but the apothecary is not so near him, nor the physician so near him, as they two are to other creatures. Man hath not that innate instinct to apply these natural medicines to his present danger, as those inferior creatures have; he is not his own apothecary, his own physician, as they are. Call back therefore thy meditation again, and bring it down; what's become of man's great ex-20 tent and proportion, when himself shrinks himself, and consumes himself to a handful of dust; what's become of his soaring thoughts, his compassing thoughts, when himself brings himself to the ignorance, to the thoughtlessness of the grave? His diseases are his own, but the physician is not; he hath them at home, but he must send for the physician.

*   *   *   *   *

VI. *Metuit: The Physician is afraid.*

6. *Meditation*

30

I observe the physician with the same diligence as he the disease; I see he fears, and I fear with him. I overtake him, I overrun him in his fear, and I go the faster because he makes his pace slow. I fear the more, because he disguises his fear; and I see it with the more sharpness, because he would not have me see it. He knows that his fear shall not disorder the practise and exercise of his art, but he knows that my fear may disorder the effect and working of his practise.

As the ill affections of the spleen complicate, and mingle themselves with every infirmity of the body, so doth fear insinuate itself in every 40 action or passion of the mind; and as the wind in the body will counterfeit any disease, and seem the stone, and seem the gout, so fear will counterfeit any disease of the mind. It shall seem love, a love of having; and it is but a fear, a jealous and suspicious fear of losing. It shall seem valor in despising, and undervaluing danger; and it is but fear, in an overvaluing of opinion and estimation, and a fear of losing that. A man that is not afraid of a lion is afraid of a cat; not afraid of starving, and yet is afraid of some joint of meat at the table, presented to feed him; not afraid of the sound of drums, and trumpets, and shot, and those which they seek to drown, the last cries of men, and is afraid of some particular harmonious instrument; so much afraid, as that with any of these the enemy might drive this man, otherwise valiant enough, out of the field.

I know not what fear is, nor I know not what it is that I fear now; I fear not the hastening of my death, and yet I do fear the increase of the disease; I should belie nature if I should deny that I feared this, and if I should say that I feared death, I should belie God. My weakness is from nature, who hath but her measure; my strength is from God, who possesses, and distributes infinitely. As then every cold air is not a damp, every shivering is not a stupefaction, so every fear is not a fearfulness, every declination is not a running away, every debating is not a resolving, every wish that it were not thus, is not a murmuring, nor a dejection though it be thus; but as my physician's fear puts not him from his practise, neither doth mine put me, from receiving from God, and man, and myself, spiritual, and civil, and moral assistances, and consolations.

* * * *

11. *Expostulation*

My God, my God, all that thou askest of me, is my heart, "My Son, give me thy heart." Am I thy son as long as I have but my heart? Wilt thou give me an inheritance, a filiation, any thing for my heart? O thou, who saidst to Satan, "Has thou considered my servant Job, that there is none like him upon the earth"; shall my fear, shall my zeal, shall my jealousy, have leave to say to thee, "Hast thou considered my heart, that there is not so perverse a heart upon earth; and wouldst thou have that, and shall I be thy son, thy eternal son's coheir, for giving that?" "The heart is deceitful above all things, and desperately wicked; who can know it?" He that asks that question, makes the answer, "I the Lord search the heart." When didst thou search mine? Dost thou think to find it, as thou madest it in Adam? Thou has searched since, and found all these gradations in the ill of our hearts, "That every imagination, of the thoughts of our hearts, is only evil continually." Dost thou remember this, and wouldest thou have my heart?

O God of all light, I know thou knowest all; and it is Thou, that declarest unto man, what is his heart. Without thee, O sovereign goodness,

I could not know how ill my heart were. Thou hast declared unto me, in thy Word, that for all this deluge of evil that hath surrounded all hearts, yet thou soughtest and "foundest a man after thine own heart." "That thou couldest and wouldest give thy people Pastors according to thine own heart." And I can gather out of thy Word so good testimony of the hearts of men, as to find single hearts, docile and apprehensive hearts; hearts that can, hearts that have learnt; wise hearts, in one place, and in another, in a great degree, wise, perfect hearts; straight hearts, no perverseness without, and clean hearts, no foulness within. Such hearts I can
10 find in thy Word; and if my heart were such a heart, I would give thee my heart. But I find stony hearts too, and I have made mine such. I have found hearts that are snares, and I have conversed with such; hearts that burn like ovens, and the fuel of lust, and envy, and ambition, hath inflamed mine; hearts in which their masters trust, and "he that trusteth in his own heart, is a fool." His confidence in his own moral constancy and civil fortitude will betray him, when thou shalt cast a spiritual damp, a heaviness, and dejection of spirit upon him. I have found these hearts, and a worse than these, a heart into the which the Devil himself is entered, Judas heart.
20 The first kind of heart, alas, my God, I have not; the last are not hearts to be given to thee. What shall I do? Without that present I cannot be thy Son, and I have it not. To those of the first kind thou givest joyfulness of heart, and I have not that. To those of the other kind, thou givest faintness of heart. And blessed be thou, O God, for that forbearance, I have not that yet. There is then a middle kind of hearts, not so perfect as to be given, but that the very giving mends them; not so desperate, as not to be accepted, but that the very accepting dignifies them. This is a melting heart, and a troubled heart, and a wounded heart, and a broken heart, and a contrite heart; and by the powerful working of thy piercing Spirit,
30 such heart I have. Thy Samuel spake unto all the house of thy Israel, and said, "If you return to the Lord with all your hearts, prepare your hearts unto the Lord." If my heart be prepared, it is a returning heart; and if thou see it upon the way, thou wilt carry it home. Nay, the preparation is thine too; this melting, this wounding, this breaking, this contrition which I have now, is thy way to thy end; and those discomforts are, for all that, "the earnest of thy Spirit in my heart"; and where thou givest earnest, thou wilt perform the bargain. Naball was confident upon his wine, but "in the morning his heart died within him"; Thou, O Lord, hast given me wormwood, and I have had some diffidence upon that; and thou hast
40 cleared a morning to me again, and my heart is alive. "David's heart smote him when he cut off the skirt from Saul"; and "his heart smote him when he had numbered his people." My heart hath struck me, when I

come to number my sins; but that blow is not to death, because those sins
are not to death, but my heart lives in thee. But yet as long as I remain in
this great hospital, this sick, this diseaseful world, as long as I remain in
this leprous house, this flesh of mine, this heart, though thus prepared *for*
thee, prepared *by* thee, will still be subject to the invasion of malign and
pestilent vapours. But I have my cordials in thy promise; "when I shall
know the plague of my heart, and pray unto thee in thy house," thou wilt
preserve that heart from all mortal force of that infection. And the
"peace of God, which passeth all understanding, shall keep my heart and
mind through Christ Jesus."   10

*   *   *   *   *

XVII. *Nunc lento sonitu dicunt, Morieris: Now, this bell tolling
       softly for another, says to me, thou must die.*

17. Meditation

Perchance he for whom this bell tolls may be so ill as that he knows not
it tolls for him. And perchance I may think my self so much better than
I am, as that they who are about me, and see my state, may have caused 20
it to toll for me, and I know not that. The church is catholic, universal;
so are all her actions. All that she does, belongs to all. When she baptizes
a child, that action concerns me; for that child is thereby connected to
that head which is my head too, and engraffed into that body, whereof I
am a member. And when she buries a man, that action concerns me. All
mankind is of one author, and is one volume; when one man dies, one
chapter is not torn out of the book, but translated into a better language;
and every chapter must be so translated. God employs several translators;
some pieces are translated by age, some by sickness, some by war, some by
justice; but God's hand is in every translation; and his hand shall bind 30
up all our scattered leaves again for that library where every book shall
lie open to one another.

   As therefore the bell that rings to a sermon calls not upon the preacher
only, but upon the congregation to come; so this bell calls us all. But how
much more me, who am brought so near the door by this sickness. There
was a contention as far as a suit (in which both piety and dignity, religion
and estimation, were mingled), which of the religious orders should ring
to prayers first in the morning; and it was determined that they should
ring first that rose earliest. If we understand aright the dignity of this bell
that tolls for our evening prayer, we would be glad to make it ours by 40
rising early, in that application that it might be ours, as well as His, whose
indeed it is. The bell doth toll for him that thinks it doth; and though it

intermit again, yet from that minute that that occasion wrought upon him, he is united to God. Who casts not up his eye to the sun when it rises? but who takes off his eye from a comet when that breaks out? Who bends not his ear to any bell, which upon any occasion rings? but who can remove it from that bell which is passing a piece of himself out of this world? No man is an island, entire of itself; every man is a piece of the continent, a part of the main; if a clod be washed away by the sea, Europe is the less, as well as if a promontory were, as well as if a manor of thy friend's or of thine own were. Any man's death diminishes me, because I am involved 10 in mankind. And therefore never send to know for whom the bell tolls. It tolls for thee.

*   *   *   *   *

XXI. *Atque annuit ille, qui, per eos, clamat, linquas iam, Lazare, lectum: God prospers their practice, and he, by them, calls Lazarus out of his tomb, me out of my bed.*

21. Meditation

20   If man had been left alone in this world at first, shall I think that he would not have fallen? If there had been no woman, would not man have served to have been his own tempter? When I see him now, subject to infinite weaknesses, fall into infinite sin without any foreign temptations, shall I think he would have had none if he had been alone? God saw that man needed a helper, if he should be well; but to make woman ill, the Devil saw that there needed no third. When God and we were alone in Adam, that was not enough; when the Devil and we were alone in Eve, it was enough. O what a giant is man, when he fights against himself, and what a dwarf when he needs, or exercises his own assistance for himself? 30 I cannot rise out of my bed till the physician enable me; nay, I cannot tell that I am able to rise, till he tell me so. I do nothing, I know nothing of myself. How little, and how impotent a piece of the world, is any man alone? and how much less a piece of himself is that man? So little, as that when it falls out (as it falls out in some cases) that more misery, and more oppression, would be an ease to a man, he cannot give himself that miserable addition of more misery. A man that is pressed to death, and might be eased by more weights, cannot lay those more weights upon himself. He can sin alone, and suffer alone, but not repent, not be absolved without another. Another tells me, I may rise, and I do so. But is every raising a 40 preferment? or is every present preferment a station? I am readier to fall to the earth, now I am up, than I was when I lay in the bed.

    O perverse way, irregular motion of man; even rising itself is the way to ruin. How many men are raised, and then do not fill the place they are raised to? No corner of any place can be empty; there can be no vacuity. If that man do not fill the place, other men will; complaints of his insufficiency will fill it. Nay, such an abhorring is there in nature of vacuity, that if there be but an imagination of not filling in any man, that which is but imagination neither, will fill it; that is, rumor and voice; and it will be given out (upon no ground but imagination, and no man knows whose imagination) that he is corrupt in his place, or insufficient in his place, and another prepared to succeed him in his place. A man rises, sometimes, and stands not, because he doth not, or is not believed to fill his place; and sometimes he stands not because he overfills his place. He may bring so much virtue, so much justice, so much integrity to the place as shall spoil the place, burthen the place; his integrity may be a libel upon his predecessor, and cast an infamy upon him, and a burthen upon his successor to proceed by example, and to bring the place itself to an undervalue, and the market to an uncertainty.

I am up, and I seem to stand, and I go round; and I am a new argument of the new philosophy that the earth moves round; why may I not believe that the whole earth moves in a round motion, though that seem to me to stand, when as I seem to stand to my company, and yet am carried, in a giddy, and circular motion, as I stand? Man hath no center but misery; there, and only there, he is fixt, and sure to find himself. How little soever he be raised, he moves, and moves in a circle, giddily. And as in the heavens there are but a few circles that go about the whole world, but many epicycles, and other lesser circles, but yet circles; so of those men which are raised and put into circles, few of them move from place to place, and pass through many and beneficial places, but fall into little circles, and, within a step or two, are at their end; and not so well as they were in the center, from which they were raised. Every thing serves to exemplify, to illustrate man's misery. But I need go no farther, than myself. For a long time, I was not able to rise. At last, I must be raised by others; and now I am up, I am ready to sink lower than before.

NOTES TO TUDOR POETRY

NOTES TO TUDOR POETRY

INTRODUCTIONS AND NOTES

We have used the following abbreviations:

Bibl. Acc. = J. P. Collier, *Bibliographical and Critical Account of the rarest books in the English language,* two volumes, London, 1865.

D. N. B. = *Dictionary of National Biography,* sixty-three volumes, London, 1885–1900.

E. L. = Norman Ault, *Elizabethan Lyrics,* London, 1925.

J. E. G. P. = *Journal of English and Germanic Philology,* University of Illinois.

M. L. N. = *Modern Language Notes,* Johns Hopkins University.

M. L. Q. = *Modern Language Quarterly,* London.

M. L. R. = *The Modern Language Review,* Cambridge University Press.

M. P. = *Modern Philology,* University of Chicago Press.

O. E. D. = *A New English Dictionary,* ten volumes, Oxford, 1888 ff.

P. M. L. A. = *Publications* of the Modern Language Association of America.

R. E. S. = *The Review of English Studies,* London, Sidgwick and Jackson.

S. P. = *Studies in Philology,* University of North Carolina.

T. L. S. = 'Literary Supplement' of *The London Times.*

Tr. Roy. Hist. Soc. = *Transactions* of the Royal Historical Society, London.

In quoting from or referring to contemporary or early sources of information, we have economized space by giving only the author's name. The following list will identify the edition used:

Aubrey = *Brief Lives . . . by John Aubrey* (ed. by A. Clark), two volumes, Oxford, 1898.

Baker = Richard Baker, *A Chronicle of the Kings of England,* London, 1674.

Birch = Thomas Birch, *The Court and Times of James the First, containing a series of historical and confidential letters,* two volumes, London, 1849.

Chappell = W. Chappell, *Old English Popular Music* (ed. by H. E. Wooldridge), two volumes, London, 1893.

Clarendon = Edward Hyde, Earl of Clarendon, *The History of the Rebellion and Civil Wars in England* (ed. by W. D. Macray), six volumes, Oxford, 1888.

Dryden = *Essays of John Dryden* (ed. by W. P. Ker), two volumes, Oxford, 1900.

Evelyn = John Evelyn, *Diary* (ed. by A. Dobson), three volumes, London, 1906.

Fuller = Thomas Fuller, *The History of the Worthies of England,* London, 1662.

Howell = *Epistolæ Ho-Elianæ: The Familiar Letters of James Howell* (ed. by J. Jacobs), London, 1890.

Hunter = Joseph Hunter, *Chorus Vatum,* British Museum *Additional Mss.* 24487–92 (rotograph copy in the Newberry Library, Chicago).

Johnson = Samuel Johnson, *Lives of the English Poets* (ed. by G. B. Hill), three volumes, Oxford, 1905.

Langbaine = Gerard Langbaine, *An Account of the English Dramatic Poets,* Oxford, 1691.

Meres = Francis Meres, *Palladis Tamia* in G. Gregory Smith's *Elizabethan Critical Essays,* Vol. ii, Oxford, 1904.

Osborne = Francis Osborne, *Works,* London, 1682.

Phillips = Edward Phillips, *Theatrum Poetarum,* London, 1675.

Walton = Izaak Walton, *The Lives of John Donne, Sir Henry Wotton, Richard Hooker, George Herbert, and Robert Sanderson,* Oxford, 1927.

Winstanley = William Winstanley, *Lives of the most famous English poets,* London, 1687.

Wood = Anthony à Wood, *Athenæ Oxonienses* (ed. by P. Bliss), four volumes, London, 1813–20.

In the introductions to the various authors, under the heading 'Text,' we have given the location of the original copies from which our text is taken. The following list expands the abbreviated forms used.

Adams = Professor J. Q. Adams, Jr., Cornell University, Ithaca, New York.
Bodleian = The Bodleian Library, Oxford, England.
B. M. = The British Museum, London, England.
Cambridge = Cambridge University Library, Cambridge, England.
Chetham = Chetham's Library, Manchester, England.
Cornell = Cornell University Library, Ithaca, New York.
Harvard = Harvard College Library, Cambridge, Massachusetts.
Hebel = Professor J. W. Hebel, Cornell University, Ithaca, New York.
Hudson = Professor H. H. Hudson, Princeton University, Princeton, New Jersey.
Huntington = The Henry E. Huntington Library and Art Gallery, San Marino, California.
Mandel = Leon Mandel II, Chicago, Illinois.
New York = New York Public Library, New York City, New York.
Princeton = Princeton University Library, Princeton, New Jersey.
White = the late Mr. W. A. White, Brooklyn, New York.
Yale = Elizabethan Club, Yale University, New Haven, Connecticut.

In giving textual variants in the notes, we have cited the various editions by dates only. The edition may be identified by referring to the section 'Text' printed just above the notes to each author.

JOHN SKELTON

JOHN SKELTON (c. 1460–1529) stands as the most striking figure in English letters at the opening of the 16th century. He personifies the transition from the medieval England of the Plantagenets and the Wars of the Roses to the new national life which was beginning under Henry VII and Henry VIII. The poet seems to look back rather than forward, his work belonging with the tradition of Chaucer, Lydgate, Gower, and the medieval Latinists rather than with the fresh growth of poetry which, nourished by streams from Italy and the classics, came to flower and fruit in the seventy-five years after his death.

Skelton made a notable record as a student, evidently at Cambridge; by 1493 he had received from each University, and perhaps from the University of Louvain, the academic title of poet laureate. For a time he was tutor in the household of Henry VII, with the next Henry in his care. Although his temperament hardly fitted him for the duties of priesthood, he entered holy orders and became rector of Diss, a parish in Norfolk. He probably remained in residence very little, but kept up his connections with the court, where his plain speaking often made his hold upon favor a precarious one. Under Henry VIII Skelton seems at first to have flourished, receiving recognition practically equivalent to the modern laureateship. In 1522 he turned his satire upon Cardinal Wolsey, who had been to him something of a patron; the poems, *Why Come Ye Not to Court?* and *Speak, Parrot*, are the principal extant specimens of this personal satire. A few years later Wolsey's retaliatory movements forced Skelton to take sanctuary with the Abbot of Westminster; and there he remained, virtually a prisoner, until his death in 1529—four months before Wolsey's fall.

Skelton was a prolific writer, but many of the works which he lists as his own in *A Garland of Laurel* have not survived. Besides poems already mentioned or here represented, the most notable we have are *The Tunning of Elinor Rumming,* a realistic and jocular celebration of low life; *The Bowge of Court,* an allegorical satire upon life at court; *Ware the Hawk,* a diatribe against a curate who brought his hawk into the church at Diss; and *Magnificence,* the only one extant of three morality plays by the poet. Skelton's *Ballad of the Scottish King* (1513?) is usually accounted the first printed broadside. From the number of editions which appeared and from references made to him, it is plain that Skelton was considerably read throughout the 16th century; but that he was thought of as a rather crude jocular writer, admired more for his buffoonery and 'pith' than for any higher qualities. Modern readers have been attracted by his vigor and originality as well as by his occasionally eloquent lyricism. The succession of short 'breathless' lines, rhyming in no set order, which he came to adopt as his usual versification, has been termed 'Skeltonic meter' or 'Skeltoniads.' It was used by several minor satirists of the 16th century, and adapted by Drayton in his odes.

MODERN EDITIONS: *The Poetical Works* (ed. by A. Dyce), two volumes, London, 1843; *A Selection from the Poetical Works* (ed. by W. H. Williams), London, 1902; *Poems* (ed. by R. Hughes), London, 1924.

COMMENT: J. M. Berdan, *Early Tudor Poetry,* New York, 1920, Chaps. ii, iii.

TEXT: *Pithy, Pleasant, and Profitable Works of Master Skelton,* 1568 (22608), Bodleian.

3–5 *Philip Sparrow*] occasioned by the death of a pet sparrow belonging to a girl in the conventual school of the Black Nuns at Carow, near Norwich. This girl, Jane Scroupe (or Scrope), is presented as speaking throughout the poem. The passages here reprinted make up less than a fourth of the whole. *Philip Sparrow* was composed before 1508. 1 *Placebo*] the opening of the antiphon in the service of vespers for the dead. 3 *Dilexi*] another part of the same service. 12 beadrolls] prayer lists. 29 Worrowëd] worried; the original meaning of 'worry' was 'choke'; a later meaning was 'shake and tear with the teeth.' 34 stound] moment. 35 swound] 1568 reads 'sound'; but see *O.E.D.* 37 Unneth] hardly. 64 *Heu, etc.*] 'Alas, woe is me!' 66 *Ad Dominum, etc.*] *Psalms* cxx. 1. 69 marees] waters. 74 Alecto] with Megera (l. 78), one of the Erinyes, or Furies. 75 blo] blue-black, livid. 79 For] the reading of *c.* 1545; 1568 reads 'From'. 83 Proserpina's bower] Hades. 87 outray] vanquish. 89 From] the reading of *c.* 1545; 1568 reads 'For'. 100 keep his cut] 'A phrase of obscure origin, meaning something like: "To keep one's distance, be coy or reserved." Most of the later occurrences appear to refer to Skelton's *Phyllyp Sparrowe,* or at least, to have the same origin.' *O.E.D.* But see 'A bonny, bonny bird,' p. 407, l. 7. 109 propre] proper, handsome. prest] alert. 119 gressop] grasshopper.

123 slo] slay. 125 *Si iniquitates*] from the first antiphon in the burial service. 127 *De profundis clamavi*] *Psalms* cxxx. 1. 140 untwined] tore to pieces. 146 Lybany] Libya, the old name for Africa. 150 mantycors] fabled beasts having the face of a man, the body of a lion, and the tail of a scorpion. 152 Melanchates] one of Actæon's hounds. 163 Ind] India. gripes] griffins. 167 Lycaon] According to Ovid, King Lycaon of Arcadia was transformed into a wolf. 175 isles of Orchady] the Orkney islands; Skelton follows the Latin form *Orcadas.* 181 corage] heart, disposition.

5–7 *Colin Clout*] The selection here printed constitutes about one-eighth of the whole poem, supposed to contain one of Skelton's earliest attacks upon Wolsey, written about 1522. The name Colin Clout, here used to represent the speaker as a common man of the people, was adopted by Spenser for references to himself in pastoral poetry. 2 drive forth a snail] This, and making a sail of the tail of a herring, are chosen as types of futile actions. 15–37] These lines tell what people say of an author who attempts 'to teach or to preach.' 57 take] the reading of *c.* 1545; 1568 reads 'talke'. 66 blother] gabble. 69 in hudder-mudder] either in disorder or in secret. 77 seely] simple, harmless. 80 Unnethes] scarcely. 83 glomming] looking gloomy or stern mumming] disguising, playing a part; the word may also mean keeping silent, or mumbling. 89 catch] 1568 misprints 'cath'. forkëd cap] the mitre, emblem of the bishop's office. 90 lewd] base. 91 all beshrewed] altogether accursed. 98 appose] get near to. 99 crose] crozier, symbol of the bishop's office; 1568 reads 'crosse', but *c.* 1545 reads 'crose'. 103 simoniac] one who practises simony, the buying and selling of offices in the church. 104 harmoniac] a word of unknown antecedents and meaning; probably, a harmonizer. The whole expression may mean: 'One who practises simony is [to their way of thinking] merely helping maintain harmony.' 108 foresaid lay] the aforesaid laity. 110 anker] anchorite, hermit. 117 purple and pall] the rich saddle-cloth and trappings of the bishop's mule. Ostentation of wealth, throughout the 16th century, frequently took the form of luxurious trappings for the owner's mount. This passage probably pointed directly to Wolsey. 121 rotchets] a special kind of surplice. Raynes] linen manufactured at Rennes. 122 morrow's] morning's; *Harl. Ms.* reads 'marys', sometimes modernized as 'mare's.' 124 begarred] trimmed, faced; the reading of *c.* 1545; 1568 misprints 'begarded'. 128 Gil] like Jack of the Noke in the following line, a conventional name for a rustic. 136 fit] experience. Here Colin Clout turns from reporting what he has heard people say of the clergy, and addresses these directly. 142 ascry] cry out against, de-

nounce. 147 Poules] St. Paul's, the cathedral in London.

7 *To Mistress Isabel Pennell*] This and the following poem, *To Mistress Margaret Hussey*, are parts of the long work, *A Garland of Laurel* (in the edition of 1568 called *The Crown of Laurel*), 1600 lines in length. The whole was written in honor of the poet himself and of his works, which he lists. The two selections here given belong to a series of tributes to ladies whom Skelton presents as weaving for him a crown of laurel. 5 reflaring rosabell] fragrant fair rose. 6 flagrant] sometimes used in Skelton's time as the equivalent of 'fragrant.' camamell] camomile. 7 rosary] rose-tree. 10 nepte] mint. 11 jeloffer] gillyflower, one of the class which includes pinks and carnations. 13 Ennewëd] fresh, vivid.

7 *To Mistress Margaret Hussey* 3 gentil] The falcon was called 'gentil' or 'gentle' because of the careful breeding of the birds and because of the association of falconry with nobility and royalty. 4 hawk of the tower] a tower-hawk was one trained to soar and to fly high. 22 Isiphill] Hypsipyle, a beautiful woman of Lemnos, in classical legend; she appears in medieval romances. 23 Coliander] coriander, an aromatic herb. 24 pomander] a ball or bag containing perfumes, suspended from a cord about the neck or carried in the pocket. 25 Good] 1568 misprints 'Oood'. Cassaunder] Cassandra, daughter of Priam in the Trojan legend.

HENRY VIII

HENRY VIII (1491-1547) was early given a bent to letters and poetry by excellent tutors, among them John Skelton, who later boasted,

> The honor of England I learnëd to spell,
> In dignity royal that doth excel;
> Note and mark well this parcel:
> I gave him drink of the sugared well
> Of Helicon's waters crystalline,
> Acquainting him with the Muses nine.

The accession of Henry to the throne in 1509 lent encouragement to the literary men of the realm, and of all Europe; there can be no doubt that the advance of lyrical poetry in his reign received some impetus from the King himself. Henry's fondness for music led him to compose melodies and verses, all his extant poems having been written for singing. He played on the lute, the organ, and the harpsichord, and brought to court the best musicians he could find. One of his anthems, *O Lord, the Maker of all thing*, according to Pollard 'still remains a favorite in English cathedrals.'

MODERN EDITION: *Miscellaneous Writings*, Golden Cockerel Press, London, 1924.

TEXT: *Additional Ms. 31922, B. M.*

8 *Pastime with good company*] This song appears in two other mss., in one of which it is entitled *The King's ballad*. Latimer, in his second sermon preached before Edward VI, alludes to this song: 'Yet a king may take his pastime in hawking or hunting, or such like pleasures. But he must use them for recreation, when he is weary of weighty affairs, that he may return to them more lusty; and this is called *Pastime with good company.*' The music for this song is printed in Chappell, i. 42. 3 grutch] grouch, complain. lust] list. 5 pastance] pastime. 10 let] hinder.

SIR THOMAS MORE

SIR THOMAS MORE (1478–1535), humanist, statesman, and martyr, made his most important contribution to literature in his Latin *Utopia*, 1516. In common with other learned men of his time, however, he also tried his hand at verse, his best work in this kind being his large collection of Latin epigrams, in part translated from the Greek Anthology. In English verse he wrote a considerable series of poems upon Fortune and a jocular account 'how a sergeant would learn to play the friar.' His shorter English poems were written in his early youth, except for the two seven-line epigrams which he composed in prison during the last months of his life.

MODERN EDITION: *Selections from his English works* (ed. by P. S. and H. M. Allen), Oxford, 1924.

TEXT: *The Works of Sir T. More, Knight*, 1557 (18076), Cornell.

9 *Childhood*] This and the two poems following are taken from a series of nine, thus explained in *Works:* 'Master Thomas More in his youth devised in his father's house in London a goodly hanging of fine painted cloth, with nine pageants, and verses over every of those pageants; which verses expressed and declared what the images in those pageants represented.' Such poems may be classified as emblems, since they moralize a picture. 2 cockstele] a stick to throw at a cock, in the Shrovetide sport of cock-throwing. The game consisted in throwing sticks at a cock tied to a post, to try which player should succeed in knocking down or killing the fowl.

10 *Manhood* 6 swetter] sweeter.

10 *Two short ballettes . . .*] Fortune, her caprices, and the turning of her wheel, were often in More's thoughts at all periods of his life. In his youth he wrote in verse *The Book of the Fair Gentlewoman . . . Lady Fortune.*

10 *Lewis, the lost lover* 5–6] More seems to have in mind a Greek epigram which both he and his friend William Lily had translated into Latin years before. Lily's version, one that gained wide currency, follows:

Inveni portum, Spes et Fortuna valete,
  Nil mihi vobiscum, ludite nunc alios.

('Hope and Fortune, farewell: I have reached the harbor. I have nothing more to do with you; sport now with others.')
7 thy] Fortune's.

JOHN HEYWOOD

JOHN HEYWOOD (*c.*1497–*c.*1580), a friend of Sir Thomas More's (whose niece he married), was a court musician and entertainer under Henry VIII, Edward VI, and Queen Mary. Because of his Catholic faith he left England after the death of Mary. In literature he is best known for his interludes, written for court performance, and for his epigrams. He also published a verse-dialogue upon marriage, containing all of the English proverbs he could collect, and a satirical poem having to do with religion, *The Spider and the Fly*, 1556. A collection of his epigrams appeared in 1550, to be followed by similar collections throughout the following decade; six hundred epigrams are included in the popular *Works* (1562, 1576, 1587, 1598). In common with most of his other writings, his epigrams are broadly humorous and thoroughly English in tone, owing little or nothing to classical models.

MODERN EDITIONS: *The Proverbs and Epigrams*, Spenser Society, 1867; *Proverbs, Epigrams, and Miscellanies* (ed. by J. S. Farmer), London, 1906.
COMMENT: R. W. Bolwell, *Life and Works of John Heywood*, New York, 1921.
TEXT: *Songs and Sonnets*, 1557 (13860), Bodleian; *Works*, 1562 (13285), Harvard.

11 *A praise of his lady*] This is a shortened version of a poem in *Harl. Ms.* 1703, headed 'A Description of a Most Noble Lady advewed [viewed?] by John Heywood, presently who advertising her years as face saith of her thus, in much eloquent phrase.' Stanzas at the end (omitted from *Songs and Sonnets*) also claim authorship for Heywood and tell that the poem was written of Princess (later Queen) Mary, when she was eighteen; hence in 1534 or 1535. 49] Ms. reads, 'How might

we do to have a graff'. Bolwell suggests that the reading of *Songs and Sonnets* 'is more personal, for the anonymity of the subject and the author prevents embarrassment because of the indelicacy.'
12 *Of loving a dog*] Heywood wrote several hundred of these epigrams upon proverbs and his were imitated by some later epigrammatists, notably Davies of Hereford and Herrick. See also Sir John Harington's epigram upon treason, p. 522.

SIR THOMAS WYATT

SIR THOMAS WYATT (*c.* 1503–1542) experienced in his thirty-nine years a man's full share of adventures, of travel, of imprisonments, dangers, and escapes, of honors and disgraces, and of such pleasures as attend upon love and poetry. In the record of 16th-century literature he takes his place as a lyricist of considerable grace and strength, the first to rifle the stores of Italian poetry for the enrichment of English.

Born at his father's castle in Kent, Wyatt was at court as a boy, and entered St. John's College, Cambridge, in 1516, the year of its opening. He took the degree of M. A. about 1520; and within a year was married to Elizabeth, daughter of Lord Cobham. His abilities were soon recognized and utilized in various capacities by King Henry VIII. He went on missions to France and to Italy before he was twenty-five, and acted as Marshal of Calais from 1528 to 1532. Knighted in 1536, he was in the same year imprisoned because of a quarrel with the Duke of Suffolk at the time of the downfall of Anne Boleyn. The suspicion that he was a lover of this unfortunate lady attached to his name at the time and frequently since. Regaining favor he served as member of the Privy Council and ambassador to Spain, in which country he remained for more than a year. In 1541 he was suddenly thrown into prison, charged with dishonesty and treason during his Spanish residence; but he cleared himself by a notable speech, and was unconditionally pardoned. In 1542 he was in Parliament and was designed as Commander of the Fleet. On a hurried trip toward Falmouth to meet the Spanish ambassador, he fell ill and died at Sherborne in Dorset, where he was also buried.

Wyatt's trip to Italy, in 1527, takes on special importance because of its effects in English poetry. The young Englishman evidently was attracted by the works of Italian love-poets, especially by those of Petrarch (1304–1374) and Serafino dell' Aquila (1466–1500). Translating Petrarch, Wyatt produced the first group of sonnets in English. His *Seven Penitential Psalms* (published 1549) was written in close imitation of a work by Pietro Aretino (1492–1557). Wyatt also drew by translation upon French poetry, and wrote rondeaus, as well as other short poems imitative of the French *etrennes*, *huictains*, and *dizaines*. In his satires he reflects his reading of the satires of Luigi Alamanni, an exiled Florentine who was living in France.

A few of his poems were printed in a collection entitled *The Court of Venus* which survives in three fragments, each representing a different edition, the earliest of which may have been published before 1540. Ninety-seven pieces were included, with poems by Surrey and others, in Tottel's miscellany, *Songs and Sonnets*, 1557 (for which also see pages 1192–93). Whoever edited the manuscript from which Wyatt's poems were printed in Tottel's collection made many changes in the poet's text; he usually modernized the older forms of third-person verb endings (e.g., *holds* for *holdeth*)—Wyatt himself may frequently have elided the suffix and pronounced such words as one syllable. Furthermore, by his alterations the editor sought to reduce Wyatt's skilfully varied rhythms to regular iambic lines. Versions much closer than Tottel's to the poet's intentions are preserved in some sixteenth-century manuscripts—especially *Egerton Ms. 2711*, in which some poems are in Wyatt's hand and others show revisions in his autograph. The reputation of no English poet, except perhaps Donne's, has undergone in the past thirty years such vigorous reappraisal as Wyatt's. No longer does one think of him as inferior to his friend and more influential successor, Surrey. The latter may be metrically smoother, but Wyatt was at once more dramatic and versatile as a poet. In the dramatic structure and conversational movement of his best verse he anticipates Donne.

MODERN EDITIONS: *The Poems* (ed. by A. K. Foxwell), two volumes, London, 1913; *The Poetry of Sir Thomas Wyatt: A Selection and a Study* (ed. by E. M. W. Tillyard), London, 1929; *Some Poems of Sir Thomas Wyatt* (ed. by Alan Swallow), New York, 1949; *The Collected Poems of Sir Thomas Wyatt* (ed. by Kenneth Muir), London, 1949.

COMMENT: A. K. Foxwell, *A Study of Sir Thomas Wyatt's Poems*, London, 1911; E. K. Chambers, *Sir Thomas Wyatt and Some Collected Studies*, London, 1933; Hallett Smith, 'The Art of Sir Thomas Wyatt,' *H. L. Q.*, ix (1946), 323–55; D. W. Harding, 'The Rhythmical Intention in Wyatt's Poetry,' *Scrutiny*, xiv (1946), 90–102; E. D. Mackerness, 'The Transitional Nature of Wyatt's Poetry,' *English*, vii (1948), 120–24; Alan Swallow, 'The Pentameter Line in Skelton and Wyatt,' *M. P.*, xlviii (1950), 1–11.

TEXT: *Songs and Sonnets*, 1557 (13860), Bodleian; *Egerton MS.* 2711, B. M.; *Additional Ms.* 17492, B. M.; *Harleian Ms. 78*, B. M.

13 *The lover compareth his state* . . .] translated from Petrarch, *Sonetto in vita* clvi. (Our numbers for Petrarch's sonnets are those of the translation in Bohn's Library.) The comparison of a lover to a storm-tossed ship became a favorite with sonneteers. See pp. 221, 222. We have inserted, for ease of reference, the titles assigned to the different poems in Tottel's *Songs and Sonnets*, even when we have taken our text from one of the manuscripts. 2 Thorrough] through; Wyatt's spelling, here and elsewhere, indicates his pronunciation of this word. 3 enemy] love,

as is also 'my lord' in the next line.

13 *The lover's life compared to the Alps*] from Sannazaro, *Rime*, Part iii, *sonetto* 3.

13–14 *Description of the contrarious passions* . . .] from Petrarch, *In vita*, civ. In *The Art of English Poesy*, 1589, the first two lines of this sonnet are quoted as specimens of iambic verses made up of monosyllables. 4 season] seize; more strictly, of birds or beasts of prey, to 'flesh' the talons or claws. 9 eyen] eyes. 9 plain] complain.

14 *The lover for shamefastness* . . .] from Petrarch, *In vita*, cix. Compare

Surrey's translation of the same sonnet, p. 29.

14 *A renouncing of love* 3 Senec] Seneca. 8 lever] liefer, dearer.

15 *Whoso list to hunt*] from Petrarch's *In vita*, clvii. In spite of the Petrarchan source, several students of Wyatt have interpreted it as referring to Anne Boleyn; if such is the reference, l. 13 indicates that she already is queen, or at least claimed by the King. 13 *Noli me tangere*] 'Touch me not!'

15 *Divers doth use*] not printed in *Songs and Sonnets*. 3 lin] cease. 4 pease] appease. 13 of kind] natural.

15–16 *Of his return from Spain*] This and the six following poems may be classified as epigrams, though they are not so pointed as the English epigram, under Martialian influence, later became. 1 Tagus] the principal river of Spain. 4 Gainward] against. 5 Brutus] according to Geoffrey of Monmouth, London, and hence Britain, was founded by Brutus, a grandson of Æneas. 8 O mighty Jove] *Egerton MS.* Of mighty love the wings.'

16 *A description of such a one . . .*] The subject has not been identified; Miss Foxwell suggests Mary, Duchess of Richmond, sister of the Earl of Surrey. 7 tied] *Egerton MS.* 2711; 1557 'tried'.

16 *Description of a gun*] a riddle, translated from the Latin of Pandolphus.

16 *Wyatt being in prison, to Bryan*] addressed to Sir Francis Bryan (d. 1550), a fellow-poet; written during Wyatt's imprisonment from January 17 to March 21, 1541. Unfortunately none of Bryan's poetry can now be identified. He was among the anonymous contributors to Tottel's *Songs and Sonnets,* and for this reason was described by Meres as one of 'the most passionate among us to bewail and bemoan the perplexities of love.' 8 the scar . . . remain] Surrey quotes these words; see p. 33.

17 *Of his love called Anna*] usually supposed to have been written of Anne Boleyn.

17 *To a lady, to answer . . .*] imitated from a *douzaine* by Saint Gelais. In *Egerton Ms.* 2711 this is followed by a poem headed 'Answer,' generally ascribed to a lady. Her answer is 'Nay.' 3 bordes] jests.

17–18 *The lover to his bed . . .*] based on Petrarch's *In vita*, cxcviii, but expanded.

18–19 *Help me to seek*] In form the poem is a rondeau, an attempted reproduction in English of a pattern already long in use among French poets

5 appear] Ms. 'apere'; usually read as 'appair' (deteriorate, suffer harm). 'Appear' seems the better reading, the sense being, 'Convey my heart secretly; and to this end handle it gently or it will complain and make its presence known.' 8 lese] lose it . . . near] it concerns me deeply.

19 *And wilt thou leave me thus?* 4 grame] anger, scorn.

19–20 *Blame not my lute*] Like many of Wyatt's poems, and notably those with refrains, this was doubtless set to music and sung, with lute accompaniment. 20 quit] requite.

20–21 *Since you will needs* 7] Compare Surrey in his epitaph of Wyatt (p. 31), l. 6.

21 *Tangled I was*] imitated, but not translated, from Serafino's first *barzalletto.*

21 *Hate whom ye list*] The substitution for rhyme of repeating a single word or syllable was called 'like loose,' a term borrowed from archery. For a later example see p. 225.

21–24 *Of the mean and sure estate*] Of John Poyntz (d. 1544), to whom this and the following satire are addressed, little is known. 10 dight] decked. 53 stemming] steeming, gleaming. 64 seely] not the exact equivalent of modern 'silly.' Here the meaning is 'foolish' but usually, as in l. 27 of the next poem, 'seely' means 'simple' or 'innocent.' 81 lust] pleasure, in a general sense. 88 hay] snare. 94 affects] affections, passions; usually with an unfavorable connotation. 105 high] omitted in T.

24–26 *Of the courtier's life*] The poem follows closely the tenth satire of Luigi Alamanni, published in 1532. Tottel's text has been slightly revised by adopting a few superior readings from the MSS. 48–49] After a contest in music between Pan and Apollo, Midas awarded the prize to Pan; for his bad judgment Apollo transformed Midas' ears to those of an ass. 50–51 Sir Thopas . . . Knight told] In *Canterbury Tales*, see the *Tale of Thopas*. 67 favel] cunning, duplicity; from the favel, or fallow-colored horse, used as a type of cunning, as in the proverbial expression, 'to curry favel.' 69 change . . . place] Cruelty is often excused by the plea that in some times and places custom makes or has made it justifiable. 86 clog] Wyatt was not at perfect liberty but was confined to his father's estate. 94 Flanders' cheer] the strong liquor of Flanders. lets] prevents. 98 at Rome] Tottel alters to 'of some.'

HENRY HOWARD, EARL OF SURREY

HENRY HOWARD (1517?–1547) was of royal blood, his father having been descended from Edward the Confessor, and his mother, the daughter of Elinor Percy, from Edward III. The young Surrey received excellent schooling under his learned tutor, John Clerk; and was early grounded in Latin, Spanish, Italian, and French. When he was thirteen he became the companion of Henry Fitzroy, Duke of Richmond, the illegitimate son of Henry VIII, and with him enjoyed the advantages of that life at Windsor Palace which later he celebrated in poetry. In 1532 the two boys went to France in the train of the King, remaining there as guests of King Francis and companions of the young French princes. After the better part of a year spent in travel, the two were recalled to England that Richmond might be married to Surrey's sister, Mary Howard. Surrey had already been married to Lady Frances Vere, but because of their youth the couple did not live together until 1535.

During Surrey's brief career as a retainer of the King's, he aided his father in suppressing a rebellion, in overthrowing the power of Thomas Cromwell, and in subduing Scotland; he built a mansion, Mount Surrey, on St. Leonard's Hill near Norwich, designed to exemplify the beauties of Greek architecture; he took part in several military and naval campaigns against France, in two of which he was commander of large English forces; and he performed many other duties such as devolved upon one of the most prominent and most engaging members of the court. In December, 1546, Surrey was arrested and charged with treason. The charge grew out of the question of who should succeed Henry VIII, then in his last illness. Surrey, or his father, may have taken some steps toward promoting their family claims; at least, the quartering by young Surrey of the arms of Edward the Confessor with his own was maliciously interpreted. Several jealous noblemen brought evidence against him, with the result that on January 21, 1547, he was beheaded on Tower Hill. The King died just a week later.

That intolerable pride which seems to have been Surrey's birthright, and which was partly responsible for his death, never forsook him. In 1537 he struck a courtier who accused him of half-heartedness in suppressing the Yorkshire rebellion. Since the incident took place in the park of Hampton Court, Surrey's action incurred the penalty of loss of the right hand; but this was commuted to imprisonment at Windsor. Again, in 1542 he suffered confinement in Fleet prison for quarreling with a courtier. Early in the next year he was committed to the same prison for rioting in the streets and eating meat in Lent. In a record of 1539 he is described as 'the most foolish proud boy that is in England.'

Surrey's mother seems to have been interested in letters; it was at her house that John Skelton composed his *Garland of Laurel*. Doubtless the boy was set at tasks of making verse, either in Latin or in English translations, by his tutor, John Clerk. During his French residence he may have come into contact with polite French poets; but it is evident that acquaintance with Sir Thomas Wyatt and his imitations of Italian and French poetry strongly influenced Surrey in his writing of poems which were destined to become models for a whole school of minor English writers. Surrey's longer tribute to Wyatt (p. 31) was printed as *An Excellent Epitaph* (1542?), and in 1547 William Baldwin included his sixteen-line translation from Martial in *A Treatise of Moral Philosophy*. In 1557 Richard Tottel printed Surrey's translation of two books of Virgil's *Æneid* (an undated edition of the translation of Book Four may have appeared earlier), and also forty poems in the well-known miscellany of *Songs and Sonnets*. Surrey was the only author mentioned on the title-page of Tottel's miscellany.

He followed Wyatt in playing tunes learned from foreign poetry upon the new instrument of English; but in smoothness of versification he improved upon his older friend. His important innovation of blank verse, used in translating Virgil, was copied from similar work by Italian humanists, who seem consciously to have tried to find a rhymeless measure comparable to the classical hexameter. With less of originality and poetic energy than Wyatt, Surrey more adequately voiced for his own and the following generation the emotions proper to lyrical poetry.

MODERN EDITIONS: *The Poems* (ed. by F. M. Padelford), Seattle, 1920, and revised, 1928; *Poems* (ed. by J. Yeowell), London, 1894.

COMMENT: Edmond Bapst, *Deux gentilshommes-poètes de la cour de Henry VIII* (Surrey and Rochford), Paris, 1891; H. F. Fehse, *Henry Howard, Earl of Surrey*, Chemnitz, 1883.

TEXT: *Songs and Sonnets*, 1557 (13860), Bodleian; William Baldwin's *Treatise of Moral Philosophy*, 1547 (1253), B. M.; *Additional Ms.* 36529, B. M.; *Certain Books of Virgil's Æneis*, 1557 (24798), B. M.

27 *Description of spring* . . .] adapted from Petrarch's *Sonetto in morte* xlii. Surrey presents, by his choice of details, an English spring where Petrarch's picture was of an Italian one. **1** soote] sweet; the presence of this word in the first line of Chaucer's Prologue to the *Canterbury Tales* may have helped to keep it in use by poets. **4** make] mate. **6** pale] paling, fence; Surrey has in mind the deer kept in enclosures. **10**] This line follows closely Chaucer, *Parlement of Foules*, 353. **11** mings] mingles, produces by mixing (*O.E.D.* 'meng'); 'remembers, calls to mind' is a possible meaning.

27–28 *The frailty and hurtfulness of beauty*] assigned to Lord Vaux in *Additional Ms.* 28635, though printed as Surrey's in *Songs and Sonnets*. Padelford finds that 'the alliteration is unduly studied and the imagery common, and the primitive tendency to two strong beats in each half of the verse is much less pronounced than in any of Surrey's unquestioned poems.' **4** tickle] delicate. **8** geason] rare.

28 *Description and praise of his love Geraldine*] This sonnet helped to disseminate a most interesting and persistent legend concerning Surrey, to the effect that he was long the lover of Elizabeth Fitzgerald, daughter of the Irish Earl of Kildare, and that to her he addressed all of his love-poetry. Thomas Nashe's *The Unfortunate Traveler*, 1594, and Michael Drayton's *England's Heroical Epistles* (see p. 290) are the chief 16th-century sources for the legend. Modern scholars have pointed out that Elizabeth was nine years old when Surrey met her, his own age then being twenty, that he never was in Italy, and that the present sonnet is the only one of his poems necessarily referring to her. This poem is therefore read as a compliment turned to please a little girl who had for the moment caught the young poet's fancy. **1** Tuscan] The Fitzgeralds were supposed to be descended from the Geraldis of Florence. **3–4**] Elizabeth grew up in Ireland, which faces the cliffs of Wales. **6** princes' blood] 'Geraldine's' mother was grand-daughter of Edward IV's queen. **8** With king's child] She was attached to the household of Princess Mary. **9**] The meeting of Surrey and Elizabeth probably took place at Hunsdon in March, 1537, as Princess Mary is known to have been there at that time. **11** Hampton] Princess Mary, and presumably Elizabeth, were at Hampton Court in July, 1537. **12** Windsor] Surrey was confined in Windsor in July, 1537.

28 *A complaint by night* . . .] adapted from Petrarch's *In vita*, cxxxi. **4** chair] chariot.

29 *Complaint of a lover rebuked*] translated from Petrarch's *In vita*, cix; see Wyatt's translation, p. 14.

29 *Vow to love faithfully . . .*] translated from Petrarch's *In vita*, cxiii; for a later translation see p. 198.

29–30 *The lover comforteth himself . . .* 28 ure] originally, use; here, state of prevalence or existence.

31 *How no age is content . . .*] written in 'poulter's measure,' consisting of couplets made up of a line of twelve syllables followed by one of fourteen. If the lines are broken in two, each couplet yields a four-line stanza of what is known in the hymn-book as 'short measure'; see Lord Vaux's *The aged lover renounceth love*, p. 38. For a late use of poulter's measure see Fulke Greville's epitaph on Sidney, p. 125. 12 chop] trade. 16 jaws] 1557 'chewes'.

31–32 *Of the death of Sir T. W. the elder*] in 1557 headed *Of the same*, the second of two poems on the subject. Our title is that of the first. 6 Whose hammers] See Wyatt's *Since you will needs*, l. 7. 15 unparfited] unfinished. 21 affect] passion.

32–33 *Prisoned in Windsor . . .* 6 hove] linger. 11 rue] melt, awaken pity in. 13 palm play] old form of tennis, resembling modern hand-ball. despoiled] with impeding garments stripped off. 16 leads] either the leaden window-sills of the maidens' tower or small flat roofs whence the ladies watched the game. 21 silver drops] probably dew, in which case 'for ruth' later in the line is figurative. 30 avaled] slackened, lowered. 46 fere] companion.

33 *Exhortation to learn . . .*] addressed to Thomas Radcliffe, third Earl of Sussex, who as a lad of eighteen was with Surrey for military operations in France in 1544. 5 Solomon said] The reference is obscure; possibly *Prov.* xii.13 or xxiv.16. 6 Wyatt said] See p. 16.

34 *The things that cause a quiet life*] This translation of an epigram of Martial's (x. 47) was probably the second specimen of Surrey's work to be printed. In Baldwin's *Treatise* of 1547 no mention is made of Surrey's authorship, though in some later editions of the work there is such mention. The epigram which Surrey chose to translate was popular throughout the 16th and 17th centuries. Versions were also made by Kendall, Jonson, Thomas Heywood, Randolph, Cowley, Sherburne, and Stanley, among authors represented in this book. It may be doubted whether Surrey's translation was ever surpassed.

See Sherburne's rendering at p. 828. 8 continuance] permanence, stability.

34–35 *London, hast thou accusëd me?*] Surrey was committed to the Fleet in April, 1543, for having gone about in the night with some companions, breaking windows with a stonebow. The younger Sir Thomas Wyatt, son of the poet, was one of his fellows in this escapade. The satire occasioned by this imprisonment is more readily understood when we remember that the city officials were drawn largely from that stricter group within the church which later became the Puritan faction. Padelford suggests these Biblical sources for various passages in the poem: *Isaiah* xlvii. 11; *Jeremiah* l and li. 48, 49; *Revelations* xviii; *Ezekiel* v. 12–17, vi. 11–14. 3–17] Padelford paraphrases these lines as follows: 'Such was my indignation at the dissolute life within the city walls that fear of retribution could not keep me from forcibly rebuking it. Mere words, as the preachers well know, are of small avail, and so I resorted to this novel method of voicing my protest. My punishment of the city under cover of the night accords with your secret sins, and should teach you that justice seeks out every fault, and that no one is secure from it.' 28 pride] This is the first to be named of the seven deadly sins, which are treated in turn. 33 shapp] Padelford's explanation of this word as 'conceive, imagine,' based upon one meaning of 'shape,' does not seem satisfactory. Of course the 'hyer' of the manuscript could be read as 'hire'; but such a reading does not explain 'shapp.' The manuscript may allow the reading 'shalbe' (shall be) instead of 'shapp'; if so, this should be preferred. 61 thy] ms. 'they'.

35 *Certain Books of Virgil's Æneis*] Surrey left a translation of the second and fourth books, published by Richard Tottel in June, 1557, two weeks after the first edition of *Songs and Sonnets*. The fourth book was published separately, and probably earlier, by John Day. Surrey is supposed to have read Italian versions by Cardinal Hippolito de Medici or his secretary Molza (1539), Nicolo Liburnio (1534), and Bartolomeo Piccolomini (1541); and to have used blank verse in imitation of the meter of these. It is evident that he also had access to the rhymed Scottish translation by Gawain Douglas (d. 1524), not published until 1553 but existing in manuscript. Padelford argues that in translating the second book Surrey had before him a French version (1529) made by Saint Gelais.

35–38 *Book II*] The passage here printed translates ll. 1–56, 199–245. 1 whisted] grew silent. 10 Dolopes] Thessalian. 29 Tenedon] Tenedos. 35 fet] fetched, in the sense of reached by sailing. 40 pight] pitched. 43 Behight] pledged. 55 Laocoon] The spelling of this name varies in 1557; sometimes three syllables were intended, and sometimes two, but never four. 94 raught] rended. 104 altar] 1557 'haltar'. 115 blive] belive, quickly.

THOMAS, LORD VAUX

THOMAS, LORD VAUX (1510–1556), without being a distinguished figure among the courtiers of Henry and Edward, has always held a place with Wyatt and Surrey as principal among the 'courtly makers.' At least two of the poems in Tottel's miscellany are Vaux's; but the greater part of his identifiable work appeared in *The Paradise of Dainty Devices*, 1576. Some of his poems gained wide currency as songs. The author of *The Art of English Poesy*, 1589, makes several references to Vaux's work, in two of which he mistakenly speaks of the poet as Sir Nicholas Vaux; Sir Nicholas was Thomas's father. For a sonnet which has been attributed to Vaux, see *The frailty and hurtfulness of beauty* (p. 27), here printed as Surrey's.

MODERN EDITION: *Poems* in *Miscellanies of the Fuller Worthies' Library* (ed. by A. B. Grosart), Vol. iv, 1872.

TEXT: *Songs and Sonnets*, 1557 (13860), Bodleian; *Paradise of Dainty Devices*, 1576 (7516), Huntington.

38 *The aged lover renounceth love*] This poem was one of the most popular of all those printed in Tottel's miscellany. In 1563 it was licensed for publication as a broadside ballad; it was set to music and other lyrics were written to be sung to the same tune. Gascoigne in a prefatory letter to his *Posies*, 1575, mentions in ridicule the legend that Vaux wrote this poem on his death-bed. It exists in several early mss.; and three stanzas, quoted with intentional inaccuracy, were used by Shakespeare as the song of the First Gravedigger in *Hamlet* (V. i. 69 ff.). 10 crutch] 1557, first edition, reads 'cowche'; 1557, second edition, and later editions read 'crowch'. The gravedigger in *Hamlet* sings 'clutch', which perhaps is the best reading of all, since it makes perfect alliteration with 'clawed.'

39 *A lover, disdained, complaineth* 4 gaze] 'At gaze' is a technical term used to describe the moment when the deer or stag hears the dogs and gazes around in apprehension.

40 *No pleasure without some pain*] This poem is another of Vaux's which caught the popular fancy. Beside appearing in the numerous editions of *The Paradise of Dainty Devices*, it was printed as a song in William Barley's *New Book of Tablature*, 1596, and in another song-book of 1626. It was imitated by George Peele in his *Sir Clyomon and Sir Clamydes*, 1599. It is extant in four early mss. The music is given in Chappell, i. 72.

40 *Of a contented mind* 2 He] 1576 'The'.

MINOR 'COURTLY MAKERS' OF HENRY VIII'S REIGN

'IN the latter end of the same king's [Henry VIII's] reign,' wrote the author of *The Art of English Poesy*, 1589, 'sprung up a new company of courtly makers, of whom Sir Thomas Wyatt the elder and Henry, Earl of Surrey, were the chieftains. . . . In the same time, or not long after, was the Lord Nicholas [*i.e.* Thomas] Vaux, a man of much facility in vulgar makings.' When we have named these three authors, however, we find it difficult, because of ignorance, to proceed with the list of noble and courtly poets of the first half of the 16th century. The Renaissance ideal demanded that one bred as a gentleman should be able to make verses; and we may be sure that a great number of Henry's courtiers fulfilled the ideal in this respect. Henry himself, as we have seen, composed verses for singing. We know that the ill-fated George Boleyn, Viscount Rochford, was a poet; but the one poem ascribed to him in modern collections is doubtfully his. Sir Francis Bryan is mentioned in early accounts as a contributor to *Songs and Sonnets*, but no one has named his contributions. Sir Anthony St. Leger (1496?–1559) was author of a brief tribute to Wyatt; Henry Parker, Lord Morley, left a number of poems and translations; Sir Thomas Chaloner (1521–1565) published verses both in Latin and in English.

If we dispense with the necessity for attributions by name, however, we find God's plenty when we turn to that great miscellany of poems largely from Henry VIII's reign, *Songs and Sonnets*, issued from the print-shop of Richard Tottel on June 5, 1557, and again, completely reset, with omissions and additions, on July 31 of the same year. Besides forty poems by Surrey, ninety-seven by Wyatt, forty by Grimald, at least two by Vaux, two by J. Canand, one by John Heywood, one by St. Leger, and one by Chaucer, these two editions preserve one hundred and twenty-six poems by 'Uncertain authors,' among these being Sir Francis Bryan and Thomas Churchyard. The three hundred and ten poems collected are for the most part lyrics (including sonnets), with a sprinkling of epigrams, epitaphs, elegies, satires, and pastoral and narrative verse. Some are translations or imitations of classical favorites, and others translate then modern French, Italian, or Latin originals. Here are the first published English sonnets and perhaps the first published English blank verse. The historical importance suggested by these facts is heightened by our knowledge of the popularity of the collection. Beside the two editions already mentioned, there are copies extant from editions of 1559, 1565, 1567, 1574, 1585, and 1587, making a total of eight within thirty years. Printers and poets used the words 'songs and sonnets' on title-pages of other books, hoping to borrow some of the interest created by the miscellany. Shakespeare alludes to the book when he makes Slender say (*Merry Wives of Windsor*, I. i): 'I had rather than forty shillings I had my book of *Songs and Sonnets* here.'

Besides *Songs and Sonnets*, the recently discovered fragment of *A Boke of Balettes* (*T. L. S.*, July 5, 1928) indicates the existence of another collection of pre-Elizabethan work; it contained poems by Wyatt and others.

In the present section we have included some of the song-lyrics written by professional musicians such as Fairfax, Cooper, and Cornish. These men were 'courtly makers' only in the sense that they were hired by the King, and their work may be said to reflect the taste of the court.

MODERN EDITIONS: *Tottel's Miscellany* (ed. by H. E. Rollins), Cambridge (Mass.), 1928–1929; *Tottel's Miscellany* (ed. by E. Arber), London, 1870; *Early 16th Century Lyrics* (ed. by F. M. Padelford), Boston, 1907; *The Surrey and Wyatt Anthology* (ed. by H. Frowde), London, 1900; *Neuenglisches Lesebuch* (ed. by E. Flügel), Halle, 1895.

COMMENT: J. M. Berdan, *Early Tudor Poetry*, New York, 1920, Chaps. iv, v, vi; H. J. Byrom, 'Richard Tottel—his Life and Work,' *The Library*, viii. 199.

TEXT: *Additional Ms.* 5465, B. M.; *Christmas Carols*, 1521 (5204), Bodleian; *XX Songs*, 1530 (22924), B. M.; *Royal Ms. Appendix* 58, B. M.; *Additional Ms.* 31922, B. M.; *Harleian Ms.* 7578, B. M.; *Additional Ms.* 26737, B. M.; *Ashmole Ms.* 48, Bodleian; *Songs and Sonnets*, 1557 (13860), Bodleian; *Songs and Sonnets*, 1557, 2nd ed. (13861), B. M.

41 *That was my woe*] Robert Fairfax (*c.* 1466–1521), author of this song, was a musician, a Gentleman of the Chapel Royal in 1496 or earlier. Several of his songs, with music, are preserved. 3 sikerness] sureness, safety.

41 *A carol, bringing . . .*] Only a single leaf of *Christmas Carols*, in which this song appeared, is preserved. The colophon gives the name of Wynken de Worde as printer, and the date. The form of this song suggests that it may belong to the 15th century. 1–2] 'The head of the boar I bear, giving praises to the Lord.' 2 *laudes*] 1521 '*laudens*'. 6] 'You who are at the feast.' 9 fand] found. 10] 'Serve with singing.'

41 *XX Songs*] This book is usually referred to as *Bassus*, the name of the only singing-part which is preserved. The title-page reads: 'In this book are contained xx songs, ix of iiii pts. and xi of three pts.,' etc.

41–42 *In youth, in age*] Robert Cooper (or Cowper), author of this poem, was a composer and court musician in the reign of Henry VIII. He was born about 1474 and died after 1529. In 1507 he was given by Cambridge University the degree of Doctor of Music. Several of his songs are preserved in manuscript, besides three in this song-book of 1530. 3, 8, 13] 'My help (cometh) from the Lord.' 12 force] care for, attach importance to.

42 *Pleasure it is*] William Cornish (d. 1524?), author of this and the following poem, was a court musician under Henry VII and Henry VIII. In 1509 he became Master of the Children of the Chapel Royal. He wrote music for several of Skelton's poems; his setting of *Woefully arrayed* is extant. *Pleasure it is* also appears in *Additional Ms.* 31922. The music is printed in Chappell, i. 35.

43 *These women all*] accompanied in ms. by a musical setting. At the beginning is a refrain, 'Hey down,' many times repeated, and another such refrain appears after l. 18. After the stanzas here reprinted is another imperfect stanza, of corrupt text, which we have omitted.

43 *O death, rock me asleep*] Ritson and others after him assign this poem to George Boleyn, Viscount Rochford, brother of Queen Anne Boleyn, and suppose it to have been written between May 1 and May 17, 1536, while Rochford was in the Tower awaiting execution. John Bale recorded that Rochford was the author of 'most elegant poems of various kinds, in the English tongue'; and Holinshed, probably following Bale, says that he 'wrote diverse songs and sonnets.' However, from Gascoigne's prefatory epistle to his *Posies*, 1575, we know that a popular poem referred to as *Soul-knell* was written by Richard Edwards, supposedly 'in extremity of sickness.' Edwards was old enough to have written the present poem in the reign of Henry VIII, from which time the ms. copy comes. Except for the reference in the third stanza, indicating that the author was imprisoned, Edwards's claim would seem to be stronger than Rochford's. Shakespeare represents Pistol (2 *Henry IV*, II. iv. 211) as saying, 'Then death, rock me asleep! Abridge my doleful days!'

44 *To his posterity*] Henry Parker, eighth Baron Morley (1476–1556), was deeply interested in literature. He published a translation of Petrarch's *Trionfi* under the title. *Triumphs of Francis Petrarch* (*c.* 1550). Bale mentions 'many books of comedies and tragedies' among Morley's works. 1] This line translates part of a saying quoted by Cicero (*De Officiis*, iii. 1) from Scipio Africanus, who had recorded it as a saying of Cato. The whole is: *Numquam se minus otiosum esse quam otiosus, nec minus solum quam solus esset.* 16 they] ms. 'the'.

44 *The poor estate . . .*] This poem, because the first letters of its lines, taken with the last letter of the last line, form the name 'Edwarde Somerset,' is usually supposed to have been written by Edward Seymour, Duke of Somerset, who was Protector in the early years of Edward VI's reign. The poem moralizes upon the Protector's fall, and may well have been written by some other poet concerning the unfortunate Duke. Somerset was deposed from the Protectorate in January, 1550, imprisoned in the Tower, and on January 22, 1552, beheaded as a felon.

44–45 *The lover showeth . . .* 1 marlian's] merlin's. 2 yelden] wearied, or submissive; usually 'yolden.'

45 *Upon consideration of the state . . .*] This poem exemplifies one of the figures of repetition which were especially cultivated in the period between 1550 and 1590. *The Art of English Poesy* expounds such devices as necessary to the equipment of a poet. For another specimen, see p. 73.

45 *Of a new-married student*] one of the earliest specimens in English of the true epigram.

45-47 *Harpalus' complaint . . .*] reprinted in *England's Helicon*, 1600, ascribed to Surrey; but the ascription doubtless was based only upon the association of Surrey's name with *Songs and Sonnets*. In *England's Helicon* the poem is followed by *Another on the same subject, but made as it were in answer*, by 'Shepherd Tony' or Anthony Munday. **6** yfere] in company, together. **12** forced] cared about. **68**

makes] mates; 'makes' is the reading of the second and later editions; first edition reads 'face'.
47-48 *Totus mundus in maligno positus*] 'The whole world lying in evil.' The poem, while conventional in expression, may reflect the actual feeling of many Englishmen living in the late years of Henry VIII's reign, or in the reign of Mary. **14** shent] ruined.

NICHOLAS GRIMALD

NICHOLAS GRIMALD (1519?–1562?), scholar, preacher, and author, holds his place in English literature chiefly by his forty poems which appeared in the first edition of Tottel's miscellany of *Songs and Sonnets*. All but nine of these were omitted from subsequent editions of the miscellany, a circumstance which has given rise to various conjectures; one being that Grimald was the collector and editor of the miscellany, and another, more credible, that he had fallen into bad odor because of his treachery toward the Protestant cause during the troublous reign of Queen Mary. His career as Cambridge scholar, lecturer on rhetoric at Oxford, and chaplain to Bishop Ridley, need not be detailed. He published two notable Latin plays, and made a widely circulated translation of Cicero's *De Officiis*.

A fair share of the poems by Grimald in *Songs and Sonnets* are translations from Latin, the sources having been indicated in only a few cases. Two of his translations are in blank verse; and it is not impossible that one of them was composed as early as Surrey's *Æneid*. In his use of this metrical form there is no evidence that Grimald was following an Italian model. He shows in his poems a certain ingenuity in fitting language to meter, and occasional compression and incisiveness. The rhetorical discipline in which he was trained required the composition of verses as an exercise; it was considered incumbent upon an educated man to produce epitaphs, New Year's greetings, and such occasional poems; and Grimald, in his English work at least, is versifier rather than poet.

MODERN EDITION: *The Life and Poems* (by L. R. Merrill), New Haven, 1925.
COMMENT: J. M. Berdan, *Early Tudor Poetry*, New York, 1920, Chapter iv.
TEXT: *Songs and Sonnets*, 1557 (13860), Bodleian.

49-50 *A true love* **3** Ver] spring. **9** Or] ere, before. **14** imp] child, offspring.
50 *Man's life, after Posidonius or Crates*] translation from the Greek Anthology, where the poem is ascribed to Posidippus; in the Planudean Anthology Crates is named as alternative author. It is followed in the Anthology by a reply of equal length, by Metrodorus, also translated by Grimald. These twin epigrams have been favorites with English translators. Kendall reprinted Grimald's two renderings in his *Flowers of Epigrams*, 1577; H. C. translated the first of the pair in *The Forest of Fancy*, 1579; *The Art of English Poesy*, 1589,

included translations of both; Sir John Beaumont and Philip Ayres translated both; see also Bacon's *In vitam humanam*, p. 549. **2** bate] debate.
50 *Metrodorus' mind to the contrary* **3** beek] bask.
50 *Description of virtue*] translated closely from a Latin epigram by Theodore de Beze (Beza), a French poet and religious reformer (1519–1605).
50 *To his familiar friend*] imitated from a longer Latin epigram by Marc-Antoine Muret (Muretus); this poem is a New Year's greeting sent in lieu of a gift.
51-53 *A funeral song . . .*] Merrill points out that in the parish register of

Winwick, Huntingdonshire, there is a record of the death of Agnes Grymbold in 1555. 5 disprove] disapprove. 9 Martius] Cnæus Martius, later emperor, known as Coriolanus. For the incident referred to, see Plutarch. Shakespeare and James Thomson wrote tragedies utilizing this incident. 11 Sertorius] Quintus Sertorius, a Roman general. 13 Sicil brethren] Amphinomus and Anapis, youths of Catana, who bore their parents to safety during an eruption of Ætna. Statues of them were erected in their native village. 15 Tyndar's imps] Castor and Pollux, sons of Tyndareus and Leda. 16 Arge . . . yoke] The legend of Cleobis and Biton (or Bito) who assumed the oxen's yoke and drew their mother, Cydippe of Argos, to the temple of Hera, is told by Herodotus (i. 31). 19 Caiet] Caieta, nurse of Creusa and Ascanius, in Virgil's Æneid. The town and harbor of Gaeta, in Latium, were supposed to have been named after her. fire-flame] that of burning Troy. 21-22 Acca . . . heaped] Acca was wife of the shepherd Faustulus, and nursed Romulus and Remus. Some accounts make her a prostitute, hence lupa in one sense; the other sense comes from the legend that Romulus and Remus were previously nursed by a she-wolf, lupa. The feast of Larentalia, celebrated by Romans in December, was in honor of Acca, who had been given the addition of Larentia (mother of the Lares). 23 Capra] the nymph who fed young Jove with goat's milk; her name in the legend was Amalthea, but she was placed in the heavens under the name of Capra. 25-26 Hyades . . . face] The Hyades, nymphs who nursed the infant Bacchus, or Lyæus (here Lyai), were placed as stars in the constellation of the Bull. 26 prime-tide] springtime. 43 web] misprinted 'wed' in all editions. 47 Brownshold] probably the modern Leighton-Bromswold, in Huntingdonshire. 49 Granta] the river Cam, on which Cambridge is located. 53 fair ford] Oxford. 70 dart-thirling] piercing with a dart. 86 once appair] sometime decay. 90 Ene] Æneas.

53-54 Marcus Tullius Cicero's death] This poem in blank verse is closely translated from Beza's Latin Mors Ciceronis, which appeared in his Juvenilia, 1548. Grimald also made a longer blank-verse translation, The death of Zoroas, from Phillipus Gualtherius' Alexandreis. The present excerpt gives the latter half of Marcus Tullius Cicero's death. 2 doubt] fear. 30 Grayes] Greeks, a transliteration of Beza's Graiæ. 32 Pytho] the Pythian, or Delphic, Sibyl. 39 grisly sight] Popilius took the head of Cicero to Antony, to be set up at Rome.

ELIZABETH

QUEEN ELIZABETH (1533-1603) is thus accredited as poet by the author of *The Art of English Poesy*, 1589: 'But last in recital and first in degree is the Queen, our sovereign lady, whose learned, delicate, noble muse easily surmounteth all the rest that have written before her time or since, for sense, sweetness, and subtility, be it in ode, elegy, epigram, or any other kind of poem heroic or lyric wherein it shall please her Majesty to employ her pen, even by as much odds as her own excellent estate and degree exceedeth all the rest of her most humble vassals.' Of the royal verse here alluded to, we have only a few specimens and those, for the most part, imperfectly authenticated. If the clever lyric with the refrain, 'Importune me no more,' is indeed hers, then the critic's praise is not mere flattery.

TEXT: *Rawlinson Poetry Ms.* 85, Bodleian; *The Art of English Poesy*, 1589 (20519), B. M.

54 When I was fair . . .] 'Elysabethe reginæ' is written at the end, after 'Finis.' Grosart states that in a ms. which he does not identify, this poem is attributed to the Earl of Oxford.

55 The doubt of future foes] This appears in *The Art of English Poesy* (III. xx) as an example of the figure *Expolitio,* or ornamental amplification. The passage preceding the poem is as follows: 'I find none example that ever I could see so well maintaining this figure in English meter as that ditty of her Majesty's own making, passing sweet and harmonical. . . . And this was th'

action: our sovereign Lady, perceiving how by the Sc[ottish] Q[ueen's] residence within this realm, at so great liberty and ease as were scarce worthy of so great and dangerous a prisoner, bred secret factions among her people and made many of her nobility incline to favor her party, . . . writeth this ditty most sweet and sententious, not hiding from all such aspiring minds the danger of their ambition and disloyalty.'

JOHN HARINGTON, THE ELDER

JOHN HARINGTON, the elder (*fl.* 1550), father of Sir John Harington (see p. 521), was a confidential servant of Henry VIII and married that king's natural daughter, Ethelreda. In the royal household Harington devoted himself especially to the service of the Princess Elizabeth. His first wife having died, he married Isabella Markham, one of Elizabeth's ladies-in-waiting; and under Queen Mary he and his wife suffered imprisonment with Elizabeth. His services to the Princess at this time won for Harington and for his son the favor of Elizabeth when she came to the throne. Several of the poems of Harington celebrate Elizabeth or her attendants. Since he copied into his manuscripts poems by other hands, some of the work ascribed to Harington in *Nugæ Antiquæ* is not his. The poem in Tottel's miscellany, *Comparison of life and death,* often ascribed to Harington upon manuscript authority, was printed in all editions of *The Paradise of Dainty Devices* as by D. S.

MODERN EDITION: *Nugæ Antiquæ* (ed. by Thomas Park), two volumes, London, 1804.

TEXT: *Nugæ Antiquæ,* 1769, Cornell.

55 *A sonnet made . . .*] The editor of *Nugæ Antiquæ* notes: 'From a Ms. of John Harington, dated 1564.' In its smoothness of versification the poem seems to show 18th-century 'improvements.'

THOMAS SACKVILLE, EARL OF DORSET

THOMAS SACKVILLE (1536–1608) as a young member of the Inner Temple showed great interest in poetry; but after a brief period of authorship he allowed professional and public duties entirely to engross him. He became one of Elizabeth's most trusted counsellors, going from a seat in Parliament to ambassadorships and the Privy Council, finally to serve as Lord Treasurer. He was also for many years Chancellor of the University of Oxford. Elizabeth honored him with the titles of Baron Buckhurst and Earl of Dorset.

In or before 1561 he wrote the last two acts of the blank-verse *Tragedy of Gorboduc* (the first three acts are by Thomas Norton), a notable landmark in English dramatic history. In the same period he, with other authors under the leadership of William Baldwin, was at work upon a poem modeled upon Lydgate's *Fall of Princes,* with the title, *A Mirror for Magistrates.* The writers attempted to tell in verse the stories of all English kings or prominent noblemen and courtiers who had suffered tragic falls from high estate. Sackville contributed the account of Henry, Duke of Buckingham; but he preceded his contribution with an induction which has proved to be the most memorable portion of the whole voluminous work. The *Mirror* was a popular success, and was issued, with successive expansions, in numerous editions dating from 1559 to 1610. Sackville's contributions appeared first in the edition of 1563. His *Induction* is usually accounted the most considerable poem written in the period between Chaucer's *Canterbury Tales* and Spenser's *Fairy Queen*.

There is evidence that Sackville wrote other poems, but none has been certainly identified. Throughout his lifetime his early work was referred to with praise by critics and fellow-poets, notably by Spenser, who acknowledged his debt to the older writer. Near the end of Sackville's life Sir Francis Bacon in a letter reminded him of his poetry, alluding to it as his 'first love.'

MODERN EDITIONS: *Mirror for Magistrates* (ed. by J. Haslewood), three volumes, London, 1815; *The Works* (ed. by R. W. Sackville-West), London, 1859.

COMMENT: J. Davies, *A Mirror for Magistrates, considered with special reference to the sources of Sackville's contributions*, Leipzig, 1906.

TEXT: *A Mirror for Magistrates*, 1563 (1248), Huntington.

56–69 *The induction*] in some copies of 1563, *Master Sackville's induction*. In this edition Baldwin sets down an account of how he brought Sackville's work before his group of collaborators. The account ends thus: '"Hath he made a preface?" said one. "What meaneth he thereby, seeing none other hath used the like order?" "I will tell you the cause thereof," said I, "which is this: after that he understood that some of the Council would not suffer the book to be printed in such order as we had agreed and determined, he purposed to have gotten at my hands all the tragedies that were before the Duke of Buckingham's, which he would have preserved in one volume. And from that time backward, even to the time of William the Conqueror, he determined to continue and perfect the story himself. . . . And therefore to make a meet induction into the matter, he devised this poesy; which, in my judgment, is so well penned that I would not have any verse thereof left out of our volume."' 7 tapets] figured cloths, tapestries; here figurative for foliage. 30 prest] ready. 39 Erythius] relating to the island Erythia, one of the 'happy isles' in the west (actually in the bay of Cadiz); perhaps a western star. 48 chair] chariot, car. 57 leams] gleams, lights. 97 deule] dole, lamentation. 122 shright] shrieked. 125 eft] in turn. 141 sike] sigh; 1563 misprinted 'stike' but corrected in the errata. 285 throne] 1563 'trone'. 415 Treby] Trebia, a river in upper Italy, scene of Hannibal's victory over the Romans. 441 lin] cease. 464 spercled] sparkled. 504 peased] became still.

THOMAS TUSSER

THOMAS TUSSER (*c.* 1524–1580) holds no place, or only the humblest, among English poets, but his versified advice to farmers and housewives was circulated and read throughout the realm during his own lifetime and for several generations thereafter. As a boy Tusser was trained in music and became a member of the choir of St. Paul's Cathedral. Thence he went to Eton, where he was a pupil of Nicholas Udall, author of *Ralph Roister Doister*. He also attended Cambridge for a short time. Later, unhappy as a musician at court, he retired to Suffolk, married, and became a farmer. From his farm he sent to the press of Richard Tottel in 1557 his book, *A Hundreth Good Points of Husbandry*. This was soon reprinted in several editions, and by 1570 *A Hundreth Good Points of Huswifery*, which had appeared earlier as a separate publication, was combined with the book on husbandry. In 1573 the book became *Five hundreth points of good husbandry united to as many of good huswifery*. In spite of his funds of good advice, Tusser seems never to have thrived himself; and he died while in prison for debt.

Except for being versified throughout, Tusser's book resembles the 'Farmer's Almanac' of later periods; it is a mine of lore concerning crops, tillage, weather, gardens, and household economy. In its final form it also contained a few religious poems, moral maxims, and a versified autobiography.

MODERN EDITION: *Five Hundred Points of Good Husbandrie* (ed. by W. Payne and S. J. Herrtage), English Dialect Society, London, 1878.

TEXT: *Five Hundred Points of Good Husbandry*, 1580 (24380), B. M.

70 *A preface* . . .] Saintsbury (*Manual of English Prosody*, p. 314) points out that in the history of English metrics Tusser is 'important because at the very time when men like Gascoigne were doubting whether English had any foot but the iambic, he produced lolloping but perfectly metrical continuous anapæsts, and mixed measures of various kinds.' This poem and several of those below illustrate this remark. 3] in an earlier edition this line read, 'Of Surrey so famous that crave'.

70 *The praise of husbandry*] In 1580 this title stands in the margin; the poem is a riddle, with these words giving the answer. 9 champian] champaign, open country.

71 *A description of the properties of winds* . . . 5 noyer] annoyer. 10] The meaning of the line is obscure; possibly 'The East is not at all a forbearer,' i. e., not at all indulgent; or, reading 'forebearer,' 'The East (in contrast with the West) is a parent of nothing.'

71 *Christmas husbandly fare* **7** shred pies] minced-meat pies.

BARNABE GOOGE

BARNABE GOOGE (1540–1594) was one of the small army of translators who made it their duty, during the early years of Elizabeth's reign, to put into English what seemed to them the treasures of other literatures. Googe chose for translation works of morality and religion that are now forgotten. His volume of original poems, *Eclogues, Epitaphs, and Sonnets*, represents the poetical exercises of a bright student who had read Tottel's miscellany with delight. In addition to the eclogues which make up the greater part of the book, there are bits of love-poetry, addresses to friends, tributes to and epitaphs upon famous men. The eclogues deserve notice as being among the early specimens of pastoral poetry in English. Googe's work is fairly representative of the verbose, conventional, highly alliterative verse which tended to prevail in the period between the passing of Surrey and the advent of Spenser. His favorite verse-form is the 'fourteener' or the poulter's measure from which it was adapted. In his book all the lines, whether of ten, twelve, or fourteen syllables, were printed in two parts, the break representing the cæsura.

MODERN EDITION: *Eglogs, Epytaphes, & Sonettes* (ed. by E. Arber), London, 1871.

TEXT: *Eclogues, Epitaphs, and Sonnets*, 1563 (12048), Huntington.

72–73 *To the right worshipful* . . .] This dedicatory letter expresses an unwillingness to appear in print often affected by poets of the 16th century. As here, the poet was likely to place upon his friends the responsibility for the publication of his work. The social feeling against exposing one's compositions to sale and to public knowledge kept the poems of many authors, particularly of noblemen, out of circulation except in manuscript. Googe had been a member of Gray's Inn. The quotation from Martial may be translated, 'You could be safer at home.'

73 *Out of sight, out of mind*] For a poem of similar schematic construction, see p. 45. 18 depart] separate; as in the marriage service of the old Prayer-book.

74 *Once musing as I sat* 25–32] omitted in text of 1563, but printed under 'Faults escaped.'

74 *To Doctor Bale*] For John Bale, see p. 377 and note.

GEORGE TURBERVILLE

GEORGE TURBERVILLE (*c*.1540–*c*.1595) spent several years at New College, Oxford, but left in 1561 without taking a degree. He went to London and resided in one of the Inns of Court, where his ability as a versifier was appreciated and developed. By 1567 he had three books ready for the printers, two of them translations, *The Heroical Epistles of Ovid* and *Eclogues of Mantuan*, and the third a collection of original poems (interspersed, however, with translated pieces) entitled *Epitaphs, Epigrams, Songs and Sonnets*. As this title suggests, Turberville to some extent imitated Barnabe Googe. In 1568 he went to Russia as secretary to Thomas Randolph, the Queen's ambassador, and sent back to his friends verse-epistles and other poems relating to that country. His principal publication aside from those already mentioned was *Tragical Tales*, 1587, a verse-translation from Italian originals, at the end of which he added a section of 'epitaphs and sonnets.' Turberville outlived his literary fame, though to the end of his life he seems to have been held in high personal regard. Among the epigrams of Sir John Harington occurs this tribute 'in commendation of George Turberville':

> When times were yet but rude, thy pen endeavored
> To polish barbarism with purer style;
> When times were grown most old, thy heart persévered,
> Sincere and just, unstained with gifts or guile.

The verse of Turberville now and then rises above that facile alliterative sing-song which was the poetic vernacular of the decades in which he was writing. A certain delicacy, or fineness, of idea and sentiment (which does not, however, save him from infelicitous diction) is his principal charm. In several passages he expressed great modesty regarding his place as a poet, with more sincerity than is usually revealed in such disclaimers.

MODERN EDITIONS: *Epitaphs, Epigrams, Songs and Sonnets* (ed. by J. P. Collier), *c*. 1870, and in *English Poets* (ed. by A. Chalmers), London, 1810; *Tragical Tales*, Edinburgh, 1837; *The Heroical Epistles of Ovid* (ed. by F. S. Boas), London, 1928.

COMMENT: H. E. Rollins, 'New Facts about George Turbervile,' *M.P.* xv. 129.

TEXT: *Epitaphs, Epigrams, Songs and Sonnets*, 1567 (24326), Huntington; *Tragical Tales*, 1587 (24330), Huntington.

75–76 *Verse in praise of Lord Henry Howard* 5 in mew] in keeping, a term from falconry. 15 fright] freighted. 23–24] These lines may be paraphrased: 'To do justice to the benefits he conferred and to the generosity of his mind, which duty he seems to have laid upon those who come after him, I write, etc.'

76 *Of drunkenness*] This epigram goes back to the Greek Anthology, though Turberville may have known it through Sir Thomas More's Latin version.

76 *The lover to his lady* . . .] This

is the best of Turberville's several translations of epigrams from the Greek Anthology, where this poem is ascribed to Plato. See also *Sonnet*, 'Were I as base,' p. 207, and note.

76–77 *To a fair gentlewoman* . . . 2 graff] graft, tree.

77–78 *Unable by long and hard travel* . . . 11 Wight] swift. 15 Suchan] the modern Sukhona, a tributary of the Dvina.

78–79 *To his friend* . . . 10 *A per se*] 'A by itself,' first or highest of all; an expression corresponding to modern 'A number one.'

THOMAS HOWELL

THOMAS HOWELL (*fl.* 1568–1581), a member of the household of the Earl of Shrewsbury, and later of that of the Countess of Pembroke, holds his place as a minor poet, an imitator of Surrey. He published three small collections. His *Devices*, 1581, was written at Wilton and dedicated to Mary, Countess of Pembroke. One poem, *Written to a most excellent book, full of rare invention*, pays a tribute to Sidney's *Arcadia*, which Howell must have seen in manuscript in the course of its composition.

MODERN EDITIONS: *The Poems* (ed. by A. B. Grosart), Manchester, 1879; *Howell's Devises* (ed. by W. Raleigh), Oxford, 1906.

COMMENT: Sir Walter Raleigh, *Some Authors*, Oxford, 1923.

TEXT: *The Arbor of Amity*, 1568 (13874), Bodleian; *H. His Devices*, 1581 (13875), Bodleian.

79 *When he thought* . . . 15 ear'th] plows.

80 *Of misery* 5 laide] probably French *laid*, foul; if English, then 'lade,' for 'laden.' Elsewhere Howell writes, 'My limbs are lade, I cannot fly.'

80–81 *Jack shows* . . .] a dialect-song, written with scant sympathy for the rustic supposed to be the speaker. The principal characteristics of the dialect are the use of 'ich' (often shortened to ' 'ch') for 'I,' 'v' for 'f,' and 'z' for 's.' 13 'chwot] ich wot, I know. 14 courtnoles] courtiers (used contemptuously); usually 'cortnolls.' 22 Dountoone's round] a country dance. 26 veow cunnigare] few cunninger. 35 bait] meal. 36 chee vore the] 'I warn you.' Cf. *Lear* IV. vi. 246. 50 red ones] gold coins. 55 friscals vet] play tricks.

81–82 *Of the golden world* 19 Irus'] proverbial name for a beggar, from that of the beggar in Ulysses' house in Ithaca, according to Homer.

THOMAS CHURCHYARD

THOMAS CHURCHYARD (*c.* 1520–1604) probably began writing in the reign of Henry VIII; his earliest publication appeared under Edward VI; he continued to publish works in verse and prose throughout the reign of Elizabeth, and issued two books after James I came to the throne. In his boyhood a page to Henry Howard, Earl of Surrey, Churchyard cherished the memory of that poet throughout his long life; nor did he materially improve upon the literary manner which he acquired in the middle decades of the century. For several years he was a soldier, serving in Ireland, Scotland, the Low Countries, and France.

According to Churchyard's account of his own writings (in *Churchyard's Challenge*, 1593), he wrote 'many things in the book of *Songs and Sonnets*,' but none of these has been identified. An extended tribute to Skelton from his pen was printed before Marsh's collected edition of Skelton's poems, 1568. Churchyard is the author of at least one poem in *The Paradise of Dainty Devices*, and one in *A Gorgeous Gallery of Gallant Inventions*. Perhaps his best work is the legend of *Shore's Wife*, contributed to the *Mirror for Magistrates* of 1563. He also wrote the story of Cardinal Wolsey for the *Mirror* of 1587. He was fond of alliterative titles, and besides *Churchyard's Challenge* he issued *Churchyard's Chips*, *Churchyard's Chance*, and *Churchyard's Charge*. Thomas Nashe in *Four Letters Confuted*, 1593, expressed admiration for Churchyard's 'aged muse, that may well be grandmother to our grandiloquentest poets at this period.' Spenser refers to Churchyard, under the name of Palemon, in *Colin Clout's Come Home Again*.

MODERN EDITIONS: *Churchyard's Good Will* (ed. by Thomas Park), in *Heliconia*, Vol. iii, 1815; *First Part of Churchyard's Chips* (ed. by J. P. Collier), 1870?; *The Worthiness of Wales*, Spenser Society, 1876; *Wished Reformation of Wicked Rebellion* and *Tragedy of Shore's Wife* in *Illustrations of Old English Literature* (ed. by J. P. Collier), 1866; *The Siege of Guisnes* in *An English Garner* (ed. by E. Arber), London, 1903.

COMMENT: H. W. Adnitt in *Transactions of the Shropshire Archæological and Natural History Society*, Vol. iii, 1880, pp. 1–68.

TEXT: *The First Part of Churchyard's Chips*, 1575 (5232), Huntington; *A Gorgeous Gallery of Gallant Inventions*, 1578 (20402), Bodleian.

84 *The lover deceived . . .*] This poem is identified as Churchyard's by the | fact that the first two stanzas of it were included in *Churchyard's Charge*, 1580.

GEORGE GASCOIGNE

ESTABLISHED biographical details concerning George Gascoigne (1542?–1577) have been so substantially altered as a result of recent scholarship that only a new biographical introduction at this point will save students from being completely misled.

As a boy Gascoigne spent some time at Cambridge University, probably between 1547 and 1555; and in 1561 he married Elizabeth Breton, widow, thereby becoming step-father to the poet Nicholas Breton (see p. 163). The circumstance that Mrs. Breton at the time was claimed as wife by another gentleman gave rise to some litigation and at least one street riot. In 1566 Gascoigne seems to have resided at Gray's Inn; for there in that year were presented the plays *Jocasta* (translated by him and his friend Kinwelmarsh, not from Seneca, but from Lodovico Dolce's Italian version) and *Supposes* (which Gascoigne translated from Ariosto, using both the author's original prose and a later verse rendition). The imprudence which marked Gascoigne's career as soldier and adventurer provoked his father's disapproval. Nevertheless he received a considerable patrimony, and was not by any means disinherited, as the marginal note in George Whetstone's rhymed obituary notice might lead us to believe. In 1572 Gascoigne was returned as a Burgess for Midhurst in the county of Sussex (having sat earlier in Elizabeth's first Parliament), but he did not take his seat. A letter, undoubtedly written by his numerous creditors, was received by the Privy Council, charging the poet with indifference to his own indebtedness, manslaughter, slander of public figures, and atheism. Despite the protection from his creditors which parliamentary immunity would have afforded him, Gascoigne left England for Holland in March, 1572/73, perhaps fearing investigation of the other charges.

The plays already mentioned were printed, together with an interesting short prose novel, "The Adventures of Master F. J.," and one hundred of Gascoigne's poems, in a volume bearing the title of *A Hundreth Sundry Flowers* (1573). The author undoubtedly saw the book through the press, but left for Holland just before its actual publication date. Certain anonymous introductory letters to the volume, suggesting multiple authorship, have now been shown to have been written, or caused to have been written, by Gascoigne himself. In 1575 he published a new edition of the same work entitled *The Posies of George Gascoigne Esquire, Corrected, Perfected, and Augmented by the Author*, in which he removed several obscene prose passages and one indelicate lyric from "The Adventures of Master F. J.," now disguised as a translation from "Bartello." He also changed the posy (motto or emblem) of one poem, omitted three poems, and inserted another.

In 1575 Gascoigne also published *The Glass of Government*, 'a tragical comedy' of moralistic cast; and in 1576 he issued *The Steel Glass*, a satire, and *The Complaint of Philomene*, a long narrative poem. His series of reflective poems, or elegies, *The Grief of Joy*, he presented in manuscript to Queen Elizabeth as a New Year's gift in 1577. His other works are in prose.

Gascoigne's writings show remarkable originality and range. *Supposes* is the first prose comedy in English; *The Steel Glass* is very nearly the first true satire and, for its time, an excellent specimen of blank verse; *Certain Notes of Instruction* (published with *Posies*) is our earliest treatise on English prosody.

Two more of Gascoigne's poems from *A Hundreth Sundry Flowers* appear in the section, 'Elizabethan Miscellanies,' pp. 187, 188.

MODERN EDITIONS: *The Complete Works of George Gascoigne* (ed. by J. W. Cunliffe), two volumes, Cambridge, 1907–10; *A Hundreth Sundrie Flowers* (ed. by C. T. Prouty), *Univ. Missouri Studies*, xvii (No. 2), 1942.

COMMENT: F. T. Bowers, 'Notes on Gascoigne's "A Hundreth Sundrie Flowers" and "The Posies,"' *Harvard Studies and Notes*, xvi (1934), 13–35; 'Gascoigne and the Oxford Cipher,' *M.L.N.*, lii (1937), 183–86; C. T. Prouty, *George Gascoigne: Elizabethan Courtier, Soldier, and Poet*, New York, 1942.

TEXT: *A Hundreth Sundry Flowers*, [1573] (11635), White, *The Whole Works*, 1587 (11638), Huntington; *The Steel Glass*, [1576] (11645), White.

85–86 *Gascoigne's good morrow* 17 darksome storms] 1573; later printings alter to 'darksomeness', which satisfies the demand of rhyme. 40 than] old form of 'then.'

86–87 *Gascoigne's arraignment* 13 fitteth] 1575; 1573 'sitteth'.

87–88 *Gascoigne's lullaby* 24 eft] again.

88 *Gascoigne's De profundis*] This is a preface and a proem to a translation of *Psalm* cxxx, known as *De profundis*. The translation was printed in Gascoigne's *Posies* (1575).

88–89 *Inscription in his garden*] This is the second of a series of poems representing inscriptions in Gascoigne's garden. In 1573 it is headed, 'In that other end of his said close walk were written these toys in rhyme.'

89 *Deep Desire sung this song*] Deep Desire is a character in the allegorical mask which Gascoigne devised as part of the entertainment for Queen Elizabeth at Kenilworth in 1575. 8 counterpeise] counterbalance.

89–99 *The steel glass*] The passages here printed make up nearly one-half of the poem. 1] marginal note: 'Here the substance of the theme beginneth.' 6 surquedry] pride. 33 rue] fall. 41 at latter Lammas] at a time which will never come. 43 preach at Tyburn] beg; Tyburn Cross, in London, was a favorite stand for beggars. 60 Lucilius] a Roman satirist, d. 103 B.C. 94 Sir Simony's deceits] the practice of simony, buying and selling ecclesiastical places and honors. 100 Melchizedek] see *Hebrews* vii. 103 leese] lose. 120 pluralities] plural livings, the holding of many appointments at once. 144 beads] prayers. 218–219 some . . . in Flanders] These, and the group mentioned (l. 224) as being in Liegeland (another part of the Low Countries) are the members of the extreme Protestant and pietistic sects then flourishing on the Continent. 220 For why] because. 250 curious *quids*] subtle questions beginning with *quid*. 270 Erato] muse of love-poetry. 271 Calliope] muse of heroic poetry. 274–275] Scholars were loath to allow that English could have a grammar, since words in it are not declined, but relations are shown by prepositions and other particles—Gascoigne's *monosyllaba*. 289 Piers] This type-name for the plowman had been put into general use by the 14th-century poem, *Piers Plowman*. 306 earing up the balks] plowing up the strips of vacant land left as boundaries. 330 cockets] seals of the customs officers, indicating duty paid. 340 utt'ring] marketing. 349 firmentie] frumenty, a drink made of grain boiled in milk; Gascoigne appears to be objecting to liquor which is too weak or which is imperfectly malted. 350 Davie Diker] a type-name for a ditch-digger, or diker. 367 parchmenters] makers of parchment (*i. e., passement*) lace, or lace trimming. ferret silk] floss silk. 372 covin] deceit, collusion. 374 spy no pence] Officers searching ships were sometimes bought off. 376 strain] constrain, take up, as stray animals. 386 precious coals] an obsolete oath; sometimes 'God's precious coals!' 388 bob] either a rap or a taunt.

GEORGE WHETSTONE

GEORGE WHETSTONE (c. 1544–1587) was a friend of George Gascoigne and wrote his biography in verse. Usually Whetstone is named with Churchyard, as both were miscellaneous writers who lived by what they received from patrons and printers for pamphlets, translations, elegies, and other poems. Like Churchyard also he had experience as a soldier; in fact he made the acquaintance of Gascoigne and Churchyard while all three were serving in Holland. During a later term of service Whetstone was present at the battle of Zutphen, where Sir Philip Sidney was fatally wounded; and he was a member of Sir Humphrey Gilbert's expedition to Newfoundland, 1578–79.

He began publication with *The Rock of Regard*, 1576, a collection of verse-tales and miscellaneous poems. He wrote numerous encomiastic poems upon noblemen recently dead, one in 1586, for example, upon Sir Philip Sidney. His most notable production was his unacted play in two parts, *Promos and Cassandra*, 1578, in the preface to which he set down some interesting dramatic criticism. This play embodied the plot used by Shakespeare in *Measure for Measure*.

MODERN EDITIONS: *The Rock of Regard* (ed. by J. P. Collier), 1870?; *A Remembrance . . . of Sir Nicholas Bacon, A Remembrance of . . . Sir James Dyer, A Remembrance of . . . Thomas, late Earl of Sussex, Sir Philip Sidney, his Honorable Life, etc.*, in *Frondes Caducæ* (ed. by A. Boswell), Auchinleck, 1816; *A Mirror of True Honor and Christian Nobility*, in *Heliconia* (ed. by T. Park), Vol. ii, 1815; *A Remembrance of . . . George Gascoigne, Esquire*, in *English Poets* (ed. by A. Chalmers), Vol. ii, 1810.

TEXT: *The Rock of Regard*, 1576 (25348), Huntington.

99–100 *Description of cozeners*] In 1576 the title is *P. Plasino's description of cozeners*. 15 kit ne follows kind] proverbial, implying 'like breeds like.'

100 *Epilogus*] At the end of one part of the book, called 'Arbor of Virtue.'

HUMPHREY GIFFORD

HUMPHREY GIFFORD (*fl.* 1580) was the son of a gentleman of Devonshire. He evidently became an official of the Poultry Counter, a debtor's prison in London. Aside from such scanty associations with his name, we have a volume of his authorship entitled, *A Posy of Gillyflowers*, 'each differing from other in color and odor, yet all sweet,' made up of prose translations from Italian tales and a fair body of poems, imitative of Surrey and of his disciples. The titles, *A doleful dump*, *In praise of a contented mind*, and *Of the uncontented estate of lovers*, suggest Gifford's quality. In his poem *For soldiers* he escapes, with good effect, from the conventions within which for the most part he writes.

MODERN EDITIONS: *The Poems* in *Miscellanies of the Fuller Worthies' Library* (ed. by A. B. Grosart), 1870; *The Complete Poems and Translations in Prose* (ed. by A. B. Grosart), Occasional Issues, 1875.

TEXT: *A Posy of Gillyflowers*, 1580 (11872), B. M.

100–101 *For soldiers* 1 Brutus' land] According to legend, England had been founded by Brutus, of Trojan descent. 10 denounceth] announces.

101–102 *A delectable dream*] The selection is a song from the longer poem of this title. The author represents himself as falling asleep and hearing a harper play for dancing fairies. The harper sang the song here given, with the result that 'the fairies all on him did frown'; they called down curses on him that he might be a warning to such as would speak ill of womankind.

Although petrified by the fairies' curse, the harper by silent signs petitioned to the gods for the privilege of singing another song. Upon the granting of this permission, he sang,

Among all creatures bearing life,
A woman is the worthiest thing, etc.

The countenance of the fairies lightened; but just as the author was about to speak his own mind to the effect 'how some were good and some were bad,' a passing friend awakened him. 22 glozer's] deceiver's, flatterer's.

RICHARD STANYHURST

RICHARD STANYHURST (1547–1618) was an Irishman, born in Dublin, the son of a speaker of the Irish House of Commons. He took the degree of B.A. at Oxford in 1568 and went to study law at the Inns of Court. For Holinshed's *Chronicles* of 1577 he prepared the 'Description of Ireland' and a part of the 'History of Ireland.' After the death of his wife, in 1579, Stanyhurst went to the Low Countries, embraced the Catholic faith, and never returned to England. His sole volume of poetry, *The First Four Books of Virgil his Æneis translated into English heroical verse,* was printed in Leyden in 1582, and in London in 1583 and 1620. Besides the translation from Virgil the volume contains 'other poetical devices thereto annexed,' some of which are translations, from Sir Thomas More's Latin and other sources.

Stanyhurst continues to attract interest because of his experiments, largely unsuccessful, in reproducing classical meters in English. The use of such measures, encouraged by Ascham and attempted by Spenser, Sidney, Harvey, and others, reaches its nadir in the work of Stanyhurst. By his spelling he sought to indicate or to fix the quantities of syllables; furthermore, he employed unusual, dialectical, and unpoetical words; with the result that his verses make, for the most part, strange and difficult reading. He received few commendations for his painful poetry, but was liberally satirized. (See Hall's *Satire VI,* p. 365, and note.) For other specimens of quantitative measures see under Sidney, Greene, and Campion.

MODERN EDITION: *Translation of the First Four Books of the Æneis, etc.* (ed. by E. Arber), Westminster, 1895.

TEXT: *The First Four Books of Virgil,* 1582 (24806), Huntington.

102 *A prayer to the Trinity*] This specimen of sapphic verse is without doubt the best of Stanyhurst's quantitative poems. It was also printed in *Greene's Funerals,* 1594, as 'used by R[obert] G[reene] at the instant of his death.' An imitation appears in the same volume.

EDWARD DE VERE, EARL OF OXFORD

EDWARD DE VERE, seventeenth Earl of Oxford (1550–1604), was on his father's side nephew to Frances Vere, wife of Henry Howard, Earl of Surrey, and on his mother's side nephew to Arthur Golding, early translator of Ovid. Oxford throughout his youth and early manhood was one of Elizabeth's favorite courtiers. Usually described as capricious and foppish, he introduced novelties of toilet from Italy, and was probably the butt of Gabriel Harvey's brief satire upon the Italianate Englishman, *Speculum Tuscanismi,* though Harvey disclaimed any personal animus in the caricature and avowed a debt to Oxford's patronage. In 1579 Oxford insulted Sir Philip Sidney and was challenged; only the intervention of the Queen prevented a duel. Oxford seems to have been a generous patron of actors and of literary men. John Lyly, in the early years of his literary career, was Oxford's private secretary, and dedicated to his employer *Euphues and his England*, 1580. After running through the fortune brought him by his first wife, Anne Cecil (daughter of Lord Burghley), Oxford mended his estate by a second marriage. In 1601 he was one of the noblemen sitting on the trial of Essex for treason, and he acted as Lord Great Chamberlain (an office his by inheritance) at the coronation of James I.

Oxford may be read as the Elizabethan courtly poet *par excellence*. The judgment of contemporary critics placed him at the head of the group of noble and polite lyrists, though Sidney, Greville, and perhaps Ralegh must now be ranked above him. The conventions of the time prevented one of Oxford's rank from publishing a volume of his verse, and no one of his family or friends gave his manuscripts to printers after his death. Hence his poems must be gleaned, sometimes uncertainly, from miscellanies. B. M. Ward has made it appear that some of the poems in *A Hundreth Sundry Flowers*, 1573, are Oxford's, and is convinced that Oxford was editor of that collection. He also believes that this nobleman is the author of the songs in Lyly's plays and of some poems attributed to Watson and to other writers whom Oxford patronized. Plays by Oxford, praised by Meres, are either not extant or not identified. For another poem by Oxford, see pp. 195–196; for a poem ascribed to him by Ward, see *The lover declareth his affection*, p. 188.

MODERN EDITIONS: *Poems* in *Miscellanies of the Fuller Worthies' Library* (ed. by A. B. Grosart), 1872; *The Courtly Poets from Raleigh to Montrose* (ed. by J. Hannah), London, 1870.

COMMENT: B. M. Ward, *The Seventeenth Earl of Oxford*, London, 1928.

TEXT: *The Paradise of Dainty Devices*, 1576 (7516), Huntington; *Rawlinson Poetry Ms.* 85, Bodleian; *The Phœnix Nest*, 1593 (21516), White; *Breton's Bower of Delights*, 1591 (3633), Huntington.

102–103 *Of the mighty power of love*] 'Finis. E. O.' at the end in *P. D. D.* 4 rede] tell, relate.

103 *Who taught thee first . . .*] 'Finis Earll of Oxenforde' at the end in ms. This sonnet, slightly altered, and with the word 'love' printed at the ends of ll. 1–12, is *Sonnet 60* in Thomas Watson's *Tears of Fancy*, 1593.

103–104 *If women could be fair*] 'Finis quod Earll of Oxenforde' at the end in ms. This poem was set to music by Byrd, *Psalms, Sonnets, and Songs*, 1588.

104 *Of the birth and bringing up of Desire*] A few lines of this poem appeared, attributed to Oxford, in *The Art of English Poesy*, 1589. A lengthened version appeared in Thomas Deloney's *Garland of Goodwill*, probably first published in 1593.

104–105 *What cunning can express?*] Signed 'E. O.' in *P. N.* 1 cunning] 1593 'cunnig'.

SIR PHILIP SIDNEY

SIR PHILIP SIDNEY (1554–1586) in the scant thirty-two years of his life wrote himself high as poet, scholar, courtier, diplomat, and soldier, and highest as gentleman. He was born at Penshurst, his father's fine country place in Kent, and at the age of nine went to Shrewsbury School where on the first day of his attendance he met Fulke Greville, who became his lifelong friend and companion. From his thirteenth to his seventeenth year Sidney was in residence at Christ Church, Oxford, and briefly at Cambridge, but he took no degree. In 1572 he went to France in the train of an English ambassador. His first-hand experience of the religious dissensions which racked France at this time, culminating in the Massacre of St. Bartholomew, seems to have influenced Sidney in his later championship of the Protestant cause in Europe. On his first trip abroad he traveled in Germany, Hungary, Italy, and the Netherlands, returning to England in time to be present at the famous reception of Queen Elizabeth by the Earl of Leicester (Sidney's maternal uncle) at Kenilworth Castle, July 9–27, 1575. Sidney followed the Queen and court to Chartley Castle, the home of Lord Essex; and it is here that he is supposed to have made the acquaintance of Essex's daughter, Penelope Devereux, the Stella of *Astrophel and Stella*, then aged thirteen. The later engagement of the two young people was broken off for reasons which now are obscure, and Penelope became the wife of Lord Rich.

In 1577 Sidney went abroad a second time, as Ambassador to the Emperor of Germany and the Elector Palatine. In the following year he wrote a mask, *The Lady of May*, to be used as a part of the entertainment of the Queen and court at the Earl of Leicester's castle at Wanstead. At about this time Sidney's interest in literature seems to have been heightened by his companionship with Fulke Greville, Edward Dyer, and other congenial young men; the group, referred to by Spenser and Gabriel Harvey as the Areopagus (though not organized as a club), interested itself in the possibility of reproducing in English the quantitative meters of Greek and Latin verse. In August, 1579, a Puritanical writer named Stephen Gosson published *The School of Abuse*, attacking plays and poetry but dedicated to Sidney; Sidney's *Defence of Poesy*, though perhaps not written until 1583, replies, though not by name, to Gosson's attack. (For extracts, see p. 885.) In 1580 Sidney wrote an open letter to Queen Elizabeth, dissuading her from her projected marriage with the Duke of Anjou; and for his boldness he was practically banished from court. During his retirement, spent at Wilton House, the home of his sister who had become by marriage Countess of Pembroke, he wrote at least part of his long pastoral romance, *Arcadia*. He was knighted in 1583 and in the same year married Frances Walsingham, daughter of Sir Francis Walsingham. In 1585 he was projecting an expedition to America with Sir Francis Drake, but the Protestant cause, endangered by Spain's war with the Netherlands, and the Queen's need of his services, sent him instead to Holland as Governor of Flushing. In September of the following year Sidney was wounded in an unimportant engagement before the city of Zutphen. After twenty-six days of suffering, during which time he composed a song about his wound, entitled *La cuisse rompue*, and caused it to be sung to him, he died, to the grief of all England and a share of Europe.

None of Sidney's literary productions was printed during his lifetime. The sixth song from *Astrophel and Stella* appeared, with musical setting, in Byrd's *Psalms, Sonnets, and Songs* of 1588; and three stanzas of the tenth song were printed with music in Byrd's *Songs of Sundry Natures*, 1589. *The Countess of Pembroke's Arcadia* was published in 1590, in an incomplete form representing the revision Sidney had begun of his first draft, and again (the revision having been carried to completion by his sister) in 1593. His *Astrophel and Stella* was published in 1591 by a printer named Newman, without the consent of Sidney's family, from one of the several manuscripts then in circulation. Another printer, Lownes by name, at once reprinted Newman's edition, making slight changes. Still in 1591 Newman issued his second edition, apparently receiving in its preparation some aid from Sidney's family. Not until 1598 did the fully authorized edition appear; at that time all of Sidney's principal works were collected and printed in a folio volume, prepared for the printer by the Countess of Pembroke herself. The *Defence of Poesy* appeared in two separate editions in 1595.

The publication in 1591 of *Astrophel and Stella* had much to do with the remarkable outburst of sonnet-cycles which characterized English poetry in the 1590's. Though Sidney does not maintain that freedom from literary influences and fashions which he claims for himself in several sonnets, yet his is certainly among the most personal and least artificial of all the numerous Elizabethan cycles. In spite of borrowings from Petrarch, Ronsard, and du Bellay, *Astrophel and Stella* gives us a fairly intimate picture of Sidney's unhappy relations with Penelope Devereux. Sidney hardly won among poets a place as high as that which *The Defence of Poesy* gives him among critics and æstheticians; yet in scattered sonnets and passages he attains to a grave and musical eloquence which is the idiom only of the greatest. *The Art of English Poesy*, 1589, preserves this little song not found elsewhere in Sidney's works (though used as the basis of a sonnet in the *Arcadia*), which has become a favorite:

> My true love hath my heart and I have his,
> By just exchange one for another given;
> I hold his dear, and mine he cannot miss,
> There never was a better bargain driven.
> My true love hath my heart and I have his.
>
> My heart in me keeps him and me in one,
> My heart in him his thoughts and senses guides;
> He loves my heart, for once it was his own,
> I cherish his, because in me it bides.
> My true love hath my heart and I have his.

For other poems by Sidney, see pp. 196 and 1210.

MODERN EDITIONS: *Astrophel and Stella* (ed. by A. W. Pollard), London, 1888; *The Poems* (ed. by J. Drinkwater), Muses' Library, London, 1910; *The Complete Works* (ed. by A. Feuillerat), four volumes, Cambridge, 1922–1926.

COMMENT: M. W. Wallace, *The Life of Sir Philip Sidney*, Cambridge, 1915; J. A. Symonds, *Sir Philip Sidney*, London, 1886.

TEXT: *Sir P. S. His Astrophel and Stella*, 1591 (22536), B. M.; *The Countess of Pembroke's Arcadia*, 1598 (22541), White; *The Countess of Pembroke's Arcadia*, 1593 (22540), White; *A Poetical Rhapsody*, 1602 (6373), White.

106 *To the reader*] This is an extract from the prefatory address placed before the authorized edition of Sidney's works. 'H. S.' was Henry Sandford, the Earl of Pembroke's secretary.

106-118 *Astrophel and Stella*] The present selection constitutes about one-third of this sequence, which consisted of 108 sonnets and eleven songs. The whole grew out of Sidney's love for Penelope Devereux, daughter of the first Earl of Essex. 'Astrophel' (from Greek words, meaning star-lover) is Sidney; 'Stella' (Latin, star) is Penelope. She was about eight years younger than he, and was but a girl when he first met her. From 1576 he seems to have been a serious suitor for her hand. When Essex died, in that year, he expressed the wish that Sidney might marry his daughter. The marriage of Sidney's uncle, the Earl of Leicester, to Lady Essex (Penelope's mother) in 1577 may have affected unfavorably the chances of the union. Sidney saw Penelope at various times for several years; but in 1581 she was married to Robert, Lord Rich. Sidney's love appears to have been heightened by this marriage; and while Wallace, following Pollard, believes that the first thirty-two sonnets of *Astrophel and Stella* (here the first fourteen),with the exception of 'Rich fools there be,' were written before Penelope's marriage in a spirit of friendship and 'literary courtship,' the greater part of the sequence must relate to the period when a marriage between 'Astrophel' and 'Stella' had become out of the question.

106 *Loving in truth*] This, like some other sonnets in the sequence, is written in lines of twelve syllables.

106-107 *Not at the first sight* 1 dribbed] a term from archery, describing a weak, short, or widely inaccurate shot. 3 mine] used in a military sense. 13 me] 1598; 1591 'my'.

107 *Let dainty wits* 3 Pindar's apes] imitators of Pindar. 7-8] The allusion here is to the Euphuism made popular by Lyly. B. M. Ward, following Courthope, argues that Sidney and his friends constituted a 'romantic' school definitely opposed to the Earl of Oxford and his group (which included Lyly), the 'Euphuistic' school.

108 *Alas, have I not* 5 rhubarb] bitter, tart; with the suggestion, also, of 'medicinal.'

109 *Fly, fly, my friends* 6 so fair level] so well take aim.

109-110 *Rich fools there be*] one of several sonnets playing upon the name of Penelope's husband. 4 blest] 1591 'rich'.

110 *You that with allegory's* 7 slake] slack.

110 *Whether the Turkish*] This sonnet lists the subjects of general conversation at the time of its writing, evidently late in 1580 or early in 1581. 1-2] A Turkish alliance with Persia in 1580 suggested to western Europe a Moslem attack upon Christendom. 3-4] Bathori, newly elected king of Poland, invaded Russia in 1580 and again in 1581. 5 three parts] the three religious parties in France: extreme Catholics, Politiques or moderate Catholics, and Huguenots. 6-8] Poliard says that these lines 'appear to refer to the meetings of the States on the subject of the acceptance of the sovereignty of Elizabeth's suitor, the Duke of Anjou. Though the Prince of Orange was in favor of this, the Hollanders refused any other governor than himself, and the States were thus to be divided into two friendly confederations, of one of which Anjou accepted the sovereignty in January, 1581, the month in which it is probable this sonnet was written.' 9-10] Sir Henry Sidney had three times been Lord Deputy of Ireland,

most recently from 1575 to 1578. 11] referring to the turbulent scenes preceding the Raid of Ruthven, August, 1581.

111 *Come, let me write* 4 fights] indistinct in 1598, which may read 'sights'; but we have retained 'fights' in view of this passage in Sidney's *Defence of Poesy:* 'as Aristotle saith, those things which in themselves are horrible, as cruel battles, unnatural monsters, are made in poetical imitation delightful.'

112 *My mouth doth water*] not in editions of 1591. 5 toward Aurora's court] Rich's seat was in Essex.

112 *Come sleep! O sleep* 5 prease] press.

113 *Having this day*] The reference to a tournament attended by 'some sent' from France points to a period between April 15 and August 1, 1581, when a French embassage was attempting to arrange a marriage between Anjou and Elizabeth.

114 *O grammar-rules* 12 weigh] 1591; 1598 'nay'.

115-116 *No more, my dear* 12 wish] 1591; 1598 'with'.

116-117 *Fourth song*] The first stanza was set to music by Henry Youll, *Canzonets*, 1608.

118 *Eleventh song*] The indentation of the stanzas indicates the change of speakers. 40 there] 1621; 1598 'thee'.

119-120 *Certain sonnets*] Under this title the folio of 1598 grouped twenty-seven poems from Sidney's mss. Eight of these had appeared in Henry Constable's *Diana*, 1594, and one in the *Arcadia*, but the others were printed for the first time.

119 *The nightingale*] In 1598 the heading is 'To the same tune', referring to the heading of the precedent poem, 'To the tune of *Non credo gia che piu infelice amante.*' 8-9 Tereus . . . Philomela] The legend of Philomela was a favorite among 16th-century poets. This lady was the dupe of the Thracian king, Tereus, who violated her and represented to her that her sister Procne, Tereus' queen, was dead. When the fraud was discovered, the sisters fled together, and were metamorphosed by the gods, one into a swallow and the other into a nightingale.

119-120 *Ring out your bells*] reprinted in *England's Helicon*, 1600, as *Astrophel's Love is dead. Additional Ms. 28253* shows the poem to have been written by 1584.

120 *Thou blind man's mark*] This

and the sonnet following may be read as the epilogue to *Astrophel and Stella*. The ascent from carnal to spiritual love is in keeping with the Petrarchan convention; that fact, however, does not invalidate the sincerity of these poems.

120 *Splendidis longum . . .*] 'A long farewell to these glittering trifles!'

121–122 *O sweet woods*] This represents the poet's experimentation with classical meters. The particular meter here used is the asclepiad, named after its inventor, the Greek poet Asclepiades. In the *Arcadia* the poem is introduced thus: 'Dorus had long, he thought, kept silence from saying somewhat which might tend to the glory of her in whom all glory to his seem-

ing was included, but now he brake it, singing these verses called *Asclepiadics.*' Sidney uses the lesser (or shorter) asclepiad, which scans normally as follows:

$$- - \mid - \cup \cup - \mid - \cup \cup - \mid \cup -$$

Line 26, 'Here wrong's name is unheard, slander a monster is,' may be taken as a norm. A rhymed imitation of this poem was set to music by John Dowland, *Second Book of Songs and Airs*, 1600. 14 if 't] 1633; 1593 omits ''t'. 20 humorists'] faddists'. 34 safety] 1613; 1593 'safely'. 38 pretext] 1593 'prelext'; corrected in 1598.

122 *Two pastorals*] Only the first of the poems so headed is here reprinted. 9 prest] ready, prompt.

SIR EDWARD DYER

SIR EDWARD DYER (d. 1607) is commonly named with his more famous friends, Greville and Sidney. Only a few scattered pieces of Dyer's poetry have come down to us, though a number of early references indicate that he was well known as a poet. However, both Bolton and Drummond complain, early in the 17th century, that they do not know Dyer's poetry at first-hand. Throughout most of his mature life Dyer lived in comparative obscurity, a fact which may be set down as a gloss upon his most famous poem, *My mind to me a kingdom is.*

MODERN EDITIONS: *Poems* in *Miscellanies of the Fuller Worthies' Library* (ed. by A. B. Grosart), 1872–1876; *The Courtly Poets from Raleigh to Montrose* (ed. by J. Hannah), London, 1870.

TEXT: Byrd's *Psalms, Sonnets, and Songs*, 1588 (4253), White; *Rawlinson Poetry Ms.* 85, Bodleian; *The Countess of Pembroke's Arcadia*, 1598 (22541), White.

123 *My mind to me a kingdom is*] This poem became popular as a song; cf. Ben Jonson, *Every Man Out of His Humor*, I. i. 11–14. John Taylor in *The Praise . . . of Beggary*, 1621, wrote:

He in his own conceit may have this
    bliss,
And sing, *My mind to me a kingdom
    is.*

Dyer's poem was also published as a broadside ballad; see *Shirburn Ballads*, p. 113. In the song-book in which the poem first was printed there appeared a song of similar sentiments in four stanzas of the same pattern. These may also be by Dyer, and may have been written as a part of the same poem. One of the stanzas follows:

I joy not in no earthly bliss,
    I force not Crœsus' wealth a straw;
For care, I know not what it is,
    I fear not Fortune's fatal law.

My mind is such as may not move
For beauty bright, nor force of love.

The version of Dyer's poem generally printed is that found in *Rawlinson Poetry Ms.* 85, which adds two stanzas to Byrd's version.

123–124 *The man whose thoughts*] 'Finis Mr. Dier' at the end in ms. 3 mishap] Grosart emends to 'desire' for the sake of rhyme. 4 pain] Grosart emends to 'plaint'.

124 *Prometheus when first*] With this poem, when first printed, appeared a reply by Sidney, as follows:

A satyr once did run away for dread
    With sound of horn which he him-
        self did blow;
    Fearing and feared, thus from him-
        self he fled,
    Deeming strange evil in that he did
        not know.

Such causeless fears when coward minds
        do take,

It makes them fly that which they
fain would have;
As this poor beast, who did his rest
forsake,
Thinking not why, but how, himself
to save.

Even thus might I, for doubts which I
conceive
Of mine own words, my own good
hap betray;

And thus might I, for fear of maybe,
leave
The sweet pursuit of my desirèd prey.
Better like I thy satyr, dearest
Dyer,
Who burnt his lips to kiss fair
shining fire.

3 delight] Hannah gives, from *Harleian
Ms.* 6910, 'the light'; Grosart defends
the reading 'delight'. 6 Wood] mad.

FULKE GREVILLE

FULKE GREVILLE, Lord Brooke (1554–1628), can hardly be mentioned
except in conjunction with his greater friend, Sir Philip Sidney. 'Well, my
lord,' wrote Greville in a letter shortly after Sidney's death, 'divide me
not from him, but love his memory, and me in it.' Born the same year as
Sidney, he entered Shrewsbury School on the same day; but in 1567 the
two friends were divided when Greville went to Jesus College, Cambridge,
and Sidney to Oxford. By 1577 Greville had joined Sidney at court, where
he enjoyed favor with the Queen, lasting, with some brief interruptions,
until her death. In 1583 he was host, at his house in London, to Giordano
Bruno. As a servant of the Queen and later of King James, he held many
official positions, and in 1621 he was made first Baron Brooke. He acted
as patron to Camden, Daniel, and Davenant. His death came as the result of
a wound inflicted by a disaffected servant, who killed himself immediately
after attacking his master. The epitaph Greville made for himself was:
'Servant to Queen Elizabeth, councillor to King James, and friend to Sir
Philip Sidney.'

With Sidney and Dyer, Greville had undertaken the writing of poetry,
probably before 1580; and he continued to write till past middle life. In
1633 appeared his collected *Works*, which did not contain his *Life of Sir
Philip Sidney*, first printed in 1652. His voluminous manuscripts yielded
material for another volume of verse, *Poems of Monarchy and Religion*,
1670. Greville was not a great poet, but his eager philosophical intellect
shines out in many of his verses, while in his long poems he displays thor-
oughness and profundity of thinking which should place him among the
leading speculative writers of his time. It has been suggested that under the
name 'Cælica' Greville's amorous poems are addressed to Queen Elizabeth,
to whom a few of them indubitably refer. It seems plain that several mistresses are celebrated in this rather miscellaneous collection.

MODERN EDITIONS: *The Works* (ed. by A. B. Grosart), four volumes, Fuller
Worthies' Library, 1870; *Cælica* in *Elizabethan Sonnet-Cycles* (ed. by M. F.
Crow), London, 1898.

COMMENT: M. W. Croll, *The Works of Fulke Greville*, Philadelphia, 1903;
A. H. Bullen, *Elizabethans*, London, 1924.

TEXT: *The Phœnix Nest*, 1593 (21516), White; *England's Helicon*, 1600
(3191), White; *Mustapha*, 1609 (12362), White; *Certain Learned and Elegant
Works*, 1633 (12361), Cornell.

125-126 *An epitaph . . .*] entitled
in 1593 *Another of the same*, referring
to the preceding epitaph by Ralegh
(see p. 135). The ascription of this
poem to Greville was first made, upon

internal evidence alone, by Charles
Lamb in his 'Defence of the Sonnets
of Sir Philip Sidney,' *London Magazine*,
1823; the essay is reprinted in *Essays
of Elia* as 'Some Sonnets of Sir Philip

Sidney.' Shortly after Sidney's death Greville wrote in a letter: 'The only question I now study is whether weeping sorrow or speaking sorrow may most honor his memory.' Cf. ll. 1–4. **9 Place**] high place, rank. **25 parallels**] 1593 and *Colin Clout's Come Home Again*, 1595, read 'parables'. The sense, however, demands 'parallels' and the change is one easily explained by a printer's misreading of ms. **126** *Another, of his Cynthia*] anonymous in 1600; by 'Another' the title evidently means 'another poet.' The poem had been set to music in John Dowland's *First Book of Songs and Airs*, 1597, and was taken, with two other poems, from that source by the editors of *E. H.* The presence of the poem in Greville's *Works* establishes it as his. **8** either] 1633 'causeless'. **126–127** *Chorus sacerdotum*] 'Chorus of priests.' **21** still] instil. **127** *You little stars*] set to music by Martin Peerson, *Motets*, 1630. **129** *Cælica, I overnight*] Greg suggests that in some cases Greville intended the name to be pronounced in two syllables, 'Cæl'ca,' with the accent upon the second. **129** *Under a throne*] plainly written to Queen Elizabeth; set to music by Martin Peerson, *Motets*, 1630. **6** ambition's] 1633 reads 'ambitious', but the 'u' seems to be a turned 'n.'

ROBERT DEVEREUX, EARL OF ESSEX

ROBERT DEVEREUX, second Earl of Essex (1567–1601), the brilliant favorite of Elizabeth and brother of Sidney's Stella, gave some moments from his crowded and ill-fated career to the writing of verse. Sir Henry Wotton records that it was a 'common way' with Essex 'to evaporate his thoughts in a sonnet.' Wotton preserves for us two lines of a sonnet otherwise lost, lines interesting in that, like most of his extant verse, they concern his relation with Elizabeth:

> And if thou should'st by her be now forsaken,
> She made thy heart too strong for to be shaken.

Essex's poems are preserved in various manuscripts and song-books. One of Campion's songs (*There is none, oh, none but you*) was attributed to Essex, on oral evidence, by Aubrey. See also *What if a day*, p. 446, and note.

MODERN EDITIONS: *Poems* in *Miscellanies of the Fuller Worthies' Library* (ed. by A. B. Grosart), 1872–1876; *Courtly Poets from Raleigh to Montrose* (ed. by J. Hannah), London, 1870.

COMMENT: Lytton Strachey, *Elizabeth and Essex*, London, 1928.

TEXT: Robert Dowland, *A Musical Banquet*, 1610 (7099), Huntington; *Chetham Ms.* 8012, Chetham.

130–131 *Change thy mind*] also in *Rawlinson Poetry Ms.* 85, with several variant readings; reprinted in *Wit's Interpreter*, 1671. In 1610 it is headed, 'The Right Honorable Robert, Earl of Essex: Earl Marshal of England'. **131–132** *To plead my faith*] headed in 1610 as the preceding poem.

132 *A passion*] 'of my Lo: of Essex' is added in ms.; also in *Ashmole Ms.* 781, headed, 'Certain verses made by Lord Essex'; said to have been sent to Elizabeth from Ireland in 1599. **1 fate**] 'dayes' was first written in the ms. and crossed out. **10 robin**] a play on Essex's name.

SIR WALTER RALEGH

SIR WALTER RALEGH (*c.* 1552–1618) must stand with Sidney and Oxford as a leading courtly poet of Elizabeth's reign. In his poetry as in other of his varied activities he fulfilled to a remarkable degree the pattern set for a Renaissance courtier. Most of the poetry which was connected with Ralegh's name during his lifetime was doubtless composed in the years from 1579 to

1586 when the author was a prominent courtier, winning the personal esteem of his royal mistress. The periods when he was out of favor gave rise to laments and pleas. A few pieces can be referred to bitter experiences which he underwent in the years from 1592 (when he was imprisoned for his marriage) to 1603 (when he was imprisoned, tried, and sentenced to death for complicity in plots against James I). During his lifetime a few of his poems appeared in miscellanies or as prefatory verses, but much of his poetry remained in manuscript until discovered by scholars of the eighteenth and nineteenth centuries. There can be no doubt that more of the unsigned poems in Elizabethan miscellanies, particularly in *The Phœnix Nest*, than have been ascribed to Ralegh are really his; and it is perhaps equally true that some of the ascriptions to him on the evidence of manuscripts are mistaken.

Ralegh's most ambitious poem was one entitled *The Ocean to Cynthia* (or perhaps *Cynthia, the Lady of the Sea*) in which under the name of 'the Ocean' or 'the Shepherd of the Ocean' he addressed his praise and vows to Queen Elizabeth, or 'Cynthia.' This poem, or a portion of it, he read to Spenser in Ireland, probably in 1589; and an account of the poem appears in that author's *Colin Clout's Come Home Again*, 1595. The poem as known to Spenser is lost; but we have what seems to be a first draft, in Ralegh's own hand, of the eleventh book and a part of the twelfth. From internal evidence we may judge that these belong to a later period than the portions of the poem read to Spenser, probably having been written during Ralegh's imprisonment and banishment from court, 1592–93. The material in the *Cecil Papers* containing the extant portion of *Cynthia* (including also some other poetical fragments by Ralegh) was first printed by Archdeacon Hannah in 1870.

The vigorous and eager mind which made Ralegh the associate of leading scholars and scientists of his time and country animates his poetry and sets the best of it above the level of conventional courtly verse. He seldom utilized the 'lumber' of the Petrarchan tradition. Sincerity and vigor, unhampered by superfluous ornament, characterize much of his work. For poems possibly by Ralegh see *Sought by the world*, p. 198, and *As you came from the holy land*, p. 414.

MODERN EDITIONS: *Poems by Sir Henry Wotton, Sir Walter Raleigh, and others* (ed. by J. Hannah), London, 1845; *The Courtly Poets from Raleigh to Montrose* (ed. by J. Hannah), London, 1870, reissued as *Poems of Sir Walter Raleigh . . . and other courtly poets*, 1875, 1892.

COMMENT: E. Gosse, *Raleigh*, London, 1886; W. Stebbing, *Sir Walter Raleigh*, Oxford, 1891.

TEXT: *Rawlinson Poetry Ms.* 160, Bodleian; *The Phœnix Nest*, 1593 (21516), White; *The Fairy Queen*, 1590 (23081), White; *England's Helicon*, 1600 (3191), White; *Malone Ms.* 19, Bodleian; *Harleian Ms.* 6917, B. M.; *A Poetical Rhapsody*, 1608 (6374), White; *Courtly Poets from Raleigh to Montrose*, 1870; Anthony Scoloker, *Daiphantus*, 1604 (21853), Bodleian.

132–133 *To Queen Elizabeth*] In the ms. this is headed ('absurdly,' says Hannah) 'Sir Walter Ralegh to Queen Elizabeth'. 14 access] *Rawl. Poet. Ms.;* other mss. 'excess'.

133–134 *Praised be Diana's . . .*] doubtless written of the Queen; unsigned in *P. N.*, but one of a group, some poems of which are known to be Ralegh's; reprinted in *England's Heli-*con, signed with Ralegh's initials, though in some copies a slip with the word 'Ignoto' has been pasted over the initials; marked 'W. R.' in Francis Davison's manuscript catalogue of poems in *E. H., Harl. Ms.* 280.

134 *Like truthless dreams*] unsigned in *P. N.*, but certainly identified as Ralegh's by these lines in the eleventh book of *Cynthia*:

'Of all which passed the sorrow only stays.'
So wrote I once, and my mishap foretold. . . .

The present poem was printed in *Le Prince d'Amour*, 1660, signed 'W. R.' 4, 8, 12] With this line compare also the passage in the Preface to Ralegh's *History of the World*, where the author says that one looking back over his life 'shall find nothing remaining but those sorrows which grow up after our fast-springing youth.' Cf. also the *History*, I. ii. 5, 'We find by dear and lamentable experience, and by the loss which can never be repaired, that of all our vain passions and affections past the sorrow only abideth'; and our selection from *Cynthia*, l. 49, and note.

134 *Like to a hermit*] unsigned in *P. N.*, but standing just before *Like truthless dreams;* ascribed to Ralegh in *To-day a Man, To-morrow None*, a pamphlet of 1644. There seems to be a reference to this poem in Ralegh's *Cynthia* (our selection, l. 31). The poem appears without signature in *Harl. Ms.* 6910 and in *Rawl. Poet. Ms.* 85. Six lines were set to music by Alfonso Ferrabosco, *Airs*, 1609.

135 *A description of love*] unsigned in *P. N.*; reprinted in *England's Helicon*, changed to a dialogue, signed 'S. W. R.' but with 'Ignoto' pasted over in some copies; also in *A Poetical Rhapsody* as *The anatomy of love*, unsigned; ascribed to 'S. W. Rawly' in Davison's manuscript list. The poem was set to music by Robert Jones, *Second Book of Songs and Airs*, 1601. Two stanzas, altered, were used as a song in Thomas Heywood's *Rape of Lucrece*. 4 sauncing-bell] saunce-bell, or sanctus-bell.

135-137 *An epitaph upon . . . Sir Philip Sidney*] unsigned in *P. N.*, but ascribed to Ralegh upon evidence of Sir John Harington's notes in his *Orlando Furioso*, 1591, Book xvi, where he speaks of Sidney as 'our English Petrarch, or, as Sir Walter Ralegh in his epitaph worthily calleth him, the Scipio and the Petrarch of our time.' This poem also appeared with Spenser's *Astrophel* in *Colin Clout's Come Home Again*, 1595. 13 princely line] Sidney's great-grandfather married Anne Brandon, whose family traced their descent from William the Conqueror and from Alexander, King of Scotland. 17 king . . . name] Sidney was named after King Philip of Spain. 57 their

Hannibal] Count Hannibal Gonzago, on the Spanish side, was mortally wounded in the engagement at Zutphen.

137-138 *The nymph's reply . . .*]
For Marlowe's poem to which this responds, see p. 168. In *E. H.* this is signed 'Ignoto'. Izaak Walton reprinted it in *The Complete Angler*, 1653, as 'made by Sir Walter Ralegh in his younger days.' In the second edition of the *Angler* Walton inserted after the fifth stanza the following, apparently from a contemporary broadside (see *Roxburghe Ballads*, Ballad Society, ii. 3 ff.):

What should we talk of dainties, then,
  Or better meat than's fit for men?
These are but vain; that's only good
  Which God hath blessed and sent for food.

The first stanza of *The nymph's reply* appeared in *The Passionate Pilgrim*, 1599, with the caption 'Love's answer.'
138 *To his son*] headed in the ms. 'Sir Walter Rauleigh To his sonne.'
138-139 *Nature that washed . . .*]
headed in ms. 'A poem of Sr Walter Rawleigh's'. The Calendar assigns the ms. to the early part of the 17th century. This poem was first printed by A. H. Bullen in *Speculum Amantis*, 1889. 26 discolors] *Harl. Ms.* 6917 reads 'discovers'; emended from *Add. Ms.* 25707, where the poem also appears. 31-36] This stanza, slightly altered and with two lines added, was found in the author's Bible in the Gatehouse at Westminster, whence he went to his execution; it was printed, with mention of this circumstance, with Ralegh's *Prerogative of Parliaments*, 1628, in *To-day a Man, To-morrow None*, 1644, and in *Reliquiæ Wottonianæ*, 1651, where it was given the title, *Sir Walter Ralegh the night before his death*. The presence of the stanza in this lyric, where it plainly belongs, proves that it was not written on the eve of his execution. The added couplet, however, might have been written at that time:

But from this earth, this grave, this dust,
  My God shall raise me up, I trust.

139-140 *The lie*] This poem exists in many ms. copies, several of which ascribe it to Ralegh; at least two are supposed to be in Ralegh's own hand. The earliest ms. appears to date about 1593. No two of the mss. agree in text, some giving more stanzas than were printed in 1608. Hannah (Introduction, xxvi–xxviii) prints extracts from a number of early answers to *The lie*, several of which connect Ralegh with the poem. 2 arrant] errand. 16 affection] Some mss. read 'a faction'.

140–141 *The Ocean to Cynthia, Book XI*] The manuscript heading is 'The 11th and last book of the Ocean'. Hannah misread '21st' for '11th'. (See Agnes M. C. Latham, 'Sir Walter Ralegh's *Cynthia*,' *R. E. S.*, iv. 129; but see also J. P. Gilson, 'Sir Walter Ralegh's *Cynthia*,' *R. E. S.*, iv. 340.) The present excerpt is from the end of the book, which is about 520 lines in all. The numerous cases of incomplete stanzas and imperfect syntax indicate that the manuscript is an early draft. 31] cf. *Like to a hermit*, l. 10. brast] broken. 49] cf. with this line the refrain of *Like truthless dreams*, 'Of all which passed the sorrow only stays,' and also this line from Ralegh's *Poesy to prove affection is not love* (Hannah, p. 22): 'The life expires, the woe remains.'

142–143 *The passionate man's pilgrimage*] not ascribed to Ralegh in *Daiphantus;* in *Ashmole Ms.* 38 the poem is entitled, *Verses made by Sr. Walter Ralegh the night before he was beheaded;* printed in Ralegh's *Remains*, 1661. The poem was doubtless written after Ralegh had been tried and condemned to death in 1603. He was then expecting to be executed, but his life was spared. The passage concerning the trial (ll. 35–50) definitely glances at the unjust trial accorded him, and the denunciations of him by Sir Edward Coke, attorney-general. 1 scallop-shell] worn by pilgrims as a badge. 3 scrip] wallet. 7 balmer] embalmer. 25 suckets] candied fruits, sweetmeats. 42 angels] a pun, involving the use of the word for a gold coin, the angel-noble. 58] Some mss. and *Remains*, 1661, add the lines,

Of death and judgment, heaven and hell,
Who oft doth think must needs die well.

MARY HERBERT, COUNTESS OF PEMBROKE

MARY SIDNEY, later Mary Herbert, Countess of Pembroke (1561–1621), 'Sidney's sister, Pembroke's mother,' was a notable patron of poets, numbering among her beneficiaries Spenser, Daniel, Breton, Jonson, and Davies of Hereford. Besides editing her brother's literary remains, she completed his translation of the *Psalms*, and translated from the French of Phillipe de Mornay *A Discourse of Life and Death*, and from the French of Robert Garnier a tragedy in blank verse, *Antonius*. These two works were published together in 1592; her tragedy was given separate publication as *The Tragedy of Antony* in 1595. Daniel wrote his tragedy *Cleopatra* in 1593 as a companion-piece to *Antonius*. Her elegy upon her brother appeared with Spenser's *Astrophel*, 1595, as *The doleful lay of Clorinda*.

MODERN EDITION: *The Countess of Pembroke's Antonie* (ed. by A. Luce), Weimar, 1897.

TEXT: *Antonius*, 1592 (18138), White.

143–144 *Chorus*] This ends the third act of the tragedy; the chorus is made up of Egyptian soldiers. 20 our] 1592 'or'.

WILLIAM WARNER

WILLIAM WARNER (*c.* 1558–1609) was an attorney who won great contemporary fame by writing a versified history of England. Four books of his *Albion's England*, written in 'fourteeners,' appeared in 1586. A second edition of 1589, with two books added, brought the history down to the close of Henry VII's reign; and the third edition (1592), of nine books, concluded with the accession of Elizabeth. Later additions carried the story through Elizabeth's reign and into that of James. The early portions of

Albion's England, dealing with legend, contain some episodes of independent interest, invented or elaborated by Warner himself. Nashe in 1589 referred to Warner's poem as 'absolute' (or perfect), and the epithet was often repeated. Drayton, in his verse-epistle to Henry Reynolds (see p. 306) paid a warm tribute to his 'old friend.' The contemporary popularity of *Albion's England* must be referred to the wave of patriotic fervor which swept England throughout the period immediately before and after the defeat of the Armada.

MODERN EDITION: *Albion's England* in *English Poets* (ed. by A. Chalmers), Vol. iv, London, 1810.

TEXT: *Albion's England*, 1592 (25081), B. M.

144–146 *Chapter XXXVIII*] first printed in the edition of 1592. 7 foison] harvest. 8 Terwin . . . Tournay] Térouanne and Tournai were French cities taken by Henry's forces, 1513. 26 barded] caparisoned with plates of metal set with spikes or bosses. 53 elder daughter] Margaret, sister of Henry VII, had married James IV of Scotland. 60 coiture]

union. 83 Foxe] *Acts and Monuments*, 1563, by John Foxe, usually called 'Foxe's Book of Martyrs', was the standard contemporary account of the religious troubles of Mary's reign. 84 for why] because. sexamus] not in *O.E.D.*; apparently a nonce word meaning 'one who marries six times'; perhaps made up from *sex* (L.), six, and γάμος (Gr.), marriage.

THOMAS WATSON

THOMAS WATSON (*c.* 1557–1592), although he wrote little to which succeeding ages have turned with pleasure, is a poet of considerable historical significance. Pre-eminently in his generation did he make himself the channel through which flowed strong influences from classical and continental literatures. He probably received his education at Oxford, but took no degree. His first book, published in 1581, was a Latin translation of *Antigone*. The work most often connected with his name in his own time was *Amyntas*, 1585, a poem in Latin hexameters built around Tasso's pastoral, *Aminta*. Abraham Fraunce published in 1587 an English rendering of Watson's work, without acknowledging his source; and in this form *Amyntas* enjoyed great popularity. Watson's first English book, Ἑκατομπαθία, or *a Passionate Century of Love*, 1582, helped center the attention of literary England upon the Petrarchan sonnet. After his early death appeared his *Tears of Fancy*, 1593, a conventional sonnet-cycle, containing some eight sonnets adapted from poems by Gascoigne and one sonnet by the Earl of Oxford. Scattered poems of Watson's were printed in *The Phœnix Nest*, *England's Helicon*, and other miscellanies. He was acquainted with Sir Philip Sidney and intimate with the Earl of Oxford, Lyly, Peele, Nashe, and other literary men of the 1580's, by some of whom he was highly praised.

MODERN EDITIONS: *The Poems* (ed. by E. Arber), London, 1870; *The First Set of Italian Madrigals Englished* (ed. by F. I. Carpenter), *Journal of Germanic Philology*, ii. 323 ff.

COMMENT: W. W. Greg, 'English Versions of Watson's Latin Poems,' *M. L. Q.* vi. 125.

TEXT: *Hecatompathia*, [1582] (25118a), White; *First Set of Italian Madrigals Englished*, 1590 (25119), White; *Tears of Fancy*, 1593 (25122), Huntington.

146–147 *Some that report*] Ward, following Arber, has suggested that the prose introductions above the poems were written by the Earl of Oxford, to whom the volume was dedicated.

148 *My love is past* 1–2] These lines follow closely the Italian source printed just above.

148 *The First Set of Italian Madrigals Englished*] in part translated from

two books by Luca Marenzio: *Il Primo Libro de Madrigali* (Venice, 1580) and *Madrigali a Quattro Voci* (Venice, 1585).

148–149 *Vezzosi augelli*] The title, 'lovely birds,' is taken over from the Italian madrigal here translated.

149 *Questo di verde*] The title consists of the first three words of the

Italian madrigal, to the tune of which Watson writes his words; he does not translate the madrigal, and the phrase is an incomplete one.

150 *In clouds she shines* 1 clouds] 1593 'clownes'. 13 clew] 1593 'cleane'; but the 'n' is probably a turned 'u' as 'cleaue', or 'clew', seems plainly intended.

ROBERT GREENE

ROBERT GREENE (1558?–1592), generally known as a writer of romances, plays, and pamphlets, takes high rank in his generation as a lyrical poet. Born at Norwich, he attended St. John's College, Cambridge, where he proceeded B. A. in 1578 and M. A. in 1583. Before taking his master's degree he had traveled on the Continent and had begun writing for the press. Established in London about 1584, he became a leader of the Bohemian literary group, turning out numerous pamphlets and romances, and involving himself scandalously with rogues and pick-purses. His long hair and beard made him a marked figure in the streets. 'His only care,' according to Thomas Nashe, 'was to have a spell in his purse to conjure up a good cup of wine at all times.' Greene's desertion of his wife and child, his excesses, his repentances, and the sordid circumstances of his death, have become familiar literary tradition; all these, with other anecdotes, were recounted in contemporary pamphlets either by Greene himself or by others writing shortly after his death. He published no book of poems, but wrote a great number of lyrics scattered through the pages of his romances. *Menaphon*, 1589, contains his best work in this kind. His verse-forms are varied and graceful; his sentiments are conventional but often far from superficial.

MODERN EDITIONS: *The Complete Works* (ed. by A. B. Grosart), Huth Library, fifteen volumes, 1881–86; *The Plays and Poems* (ed. by J. Churton Collins), two volumes, Oxford, 1902.

TEXT: *Menaphon*, 1589 (12272), White; *Greene's Mourning Garment*, 1590 (12251), Cambridge; *Greene's Never Too Late*, 1621 (12257), White; *Greene's Farewell to Folly*, 1617 (12242), White; *Philomela, the Lady Fitzwater's Nightingale*, 1592 (12296), White; *Greene's Orpharion*, 1599 (12260), Huntington.

152–153 *The shepherd's wife's song*
28 affects] passions. 42 sithe] time.

153–154 *Hexametra Alexis . . .*] 'Hexameters of Alexis in praise of Rosamund'; an experiment in English dactylic hexameters. See notes to Richard Stanyhurst.

154 *Greene's Never Too Late*] Our text follows the edition of 1621.

154 *Greene's Farewell to Folly*] Our text follows the edition of 1617.

155–156 *Cupid abroad was lated*] This version of an ode by Anacreon, usually referred to as his 'Cupid belated,' has been accounted the earliest translation into English from that poet; but a brief one in Whitney's *Emblems*, 1586, preceded it.

THOMAS LODGE

THOMAS LODGE (*c.* 1558–1625), son of a knight of the same name who was for a time Lord Mayor of London, received an excellent literary training at the Merchant Tailors' School, London, and Trinity College, Oxford. He was admitted B.A. in 1577, and the next year became a law student at Lincoln's Inn. Like many other law students, however, he yielded to the attractions of the growing literary and theatrical circle of the metropolis; and he entered upon authorship by answering Stephen Gosson's *School of Abuse*, 1579, with a *Defence of Plays*, 1580. Aside from some time spent as a soldier and as a member of Cavendish's expedition to South America (1591), Lodge engaged in a busy literary career lasting about fifteen years. Then he turned to the study of medicine, taking the degree of M.D. at Avignon in 1600 and at Oxford in 1602. He practised for about twenty-five years as one of the reputable physicians of London, though his clientele was limited somewhat by the fact that he had, while abroad, embraced the Roman Catholic faith.

Lodge's efforts to write for the stage seem to have been unfortunate, but in the fields of romance, lyrical poetry, and verse-satire he was more successful. He wrote several Euphuistic tales interspersed with poems, among which *Rosalind*, 1590, has become well known as the source of Shakespeare's *As You Like It*. In 1589 Lodge published *Scilla's Metamorphosis*, a mythological narrative poem (forerunner of *Venus and Adonis*), and with it a satire and a number of lyrics. Many poems of his appeared in *The Phœnix Nest*, 1593, and in the same year he issued *Phillis*, a sonnet-cycle liberally swelled out with songs and odes. He helped usher in a notable period of verse-satire by publishing *A Fig for Momus*, 1595. After he had become a physician, he made and published translations of Josephus and Seneca.

Lodge's lyrical poetry is fresh and tuneful. He leaned heavily upon French and Italian originals, but he avoided, it would seem, all the dangers inherent in translation.

MODERN EDITIONS: *Complete Works*, four volumes, Hunterian Club, 1875–1883; *Glaucus and Silla, with other . . . Poems*, Chiswick Press, 1819; *A Fig for Momus* in *Frondes Caducæ* (ed. by A. Boswell), Auchinleck, 1817.

COMMENT: E. Gosse, *Seventeenth Century Studies*, London, 1883.

TEXT: *Scilla's Metamorphosis*, 1589 (16674), Huntington; *Rosalind*, 1592 (16665), B. M.; *The Life and Death of William Longbeard*, 1593 (16659), White; *The Phœnix Nest*, 1593 (21516), White; *Phillis*, 1593 (16662), Huntington, White.

156 *Sonnet*] translated from a poem by Desportes. In his *Margarite of America* Lodge wrote of this French poet: 'Few men are able to second the sweet conceits of Philip Desportes, whose poetical writings [are] for the most part englished, and ordinarily in everybody's hands.' 4 teen] trouble, or anger.

156 *Rosalind*, 1592] The edition of 1590 was inaccessible to us.

160 *O pleasing thoughts* 2 mithridates] antidotes.

161 *Love guides the roses* 11 tempt] attempt.

162–163 *An ode*] also printed in *The Phœnix Nest;* set to music by Thomas Ford, *Music of Sundry Kinds*, 1607. 33] *P. N.; Phillis* reads, 'Prime youth lusts not age still follow'.

NICHOLAS BRETON

NICHOLAS BRETON (1545?–1626?), one of the most popular and prolific of Elizabethan and Jacobean authors, was the son of an old and respectable house. The death of his father, who had built up a fortune as a London trader, in 1559, and his mother's marriage to George Gascoigne, the poet, had an unfavorable effect upon the son's worldly fortunes; but the second of these events may have turned his attention to poetry. Breton seems to have spent some time at Oxford; and in 1577 he published two books of poetry. In 1592 he again appeared as poet, under the patronage of the

Countess of Pembroke, and from this time until 1626 he issued a stream of publications both in verse and prose, about forty in all. He wrote moral and religious as well as lyrical poetry; in prose he produced the usual pamphlets, being at his best in his dialogues and characters.

The facility and haste with which Breton wrote appear to have prevented him from rising to great heights as poet. In the pastoral vein, however, he succeeded better than most of his contemporaries, and won a popularity which endured for a generation after his death. His best poems show Elizabethan lyricism in its most typical and delightful vein; they manifest a joy in the sound and repetition of well-matched words which readers still can share.

MODERN EDITIONS: *The Works in Verse and Prose* (ed. by A. B. Grosart), two volumes, Chertsey Worthies' Library, 1879; *A Bower of Delights* (selected and ed. by A. B. Grosart), London, n. d.

COMMENT: A. H. Bullen, *Elizabethans*, London, 1924.

TEXT: *The Arbor of Amorous Devices*, 1597 (3631), Huntington; *England's Helicon*, 1600 (3191), White; *Melancholic Humors*, 1600 (3666), Huntington; *The Passionate Shepherd*, 1604 (3682), White.

163 *A pastoral of Phillis and Coridon*] This poem was reprinted in *England's Helicon*, signed 'N. Breton'. 15 *ipsa quæ*] 'the very she,' or 'she herself.'

163–164 *A sweet lullaby*] doubtfully Breton's, as it was printed only in *A. A. D.*, which contained work by other poets.

164–165 *Say that I should say*] In *E. H.* this is headed *Another of the same* and is signed 'N. Breton'.

165 *Phillida and Coridon*] signed 'N. Breton'. This poem was written as a three-man's song to be sung in an entertainment given Queen Elizabeth by the Earl of Hertford at his seat in Hampshire; it was printed with the account of that entertainment, *The Honorable Entertainment . . . at Elvetham*,

1591. It was sung below the window of the Queen, to greet her on the third morning of her visit. According to the account, 'it pleased her Highness to command it again, and highly to grace it with her cheerful acceptance and commendation.' The song was printed with musical setting in Michael East's *Madrigals*, 1604, Henry Youll's *Canzonets*, 1608, and John Playford's *Select Musical Airs and Dialogues*, 1653.

165–166 *Song of Phillida and Coridon*] The full title in *E. H.* is *Astrophel's song of Phillida and Coridon;* the editor evidently was of the opinion that the poem was Sidney's and he printed 'S. Phil. Sidney' at the end, but inserted a slip correcting this to 'N. Breton'. 43 constants'] constantest.

CHRISTOPHER MARLOWE

CHRISTOPHER MARLOWE (1564–1593) stands as a brilliant and attractive figure, one among the number of English poets whose careers were interrupted by an early death. He grew up at Canterbury, where his father was a prosperous shoe-maker; and having been granted one of the scholarships founded by Archbishop Parker, he attended Corpus Christi College, Cambridge. He was graduated B.A. in March, 1584, and M.A. in July, 1587. Between these dates he evidently spent some time abroad in government service, to the prejudice of his academic standing. An entry in the Privy Council Register (June 29, 1587) praises his 'orderly and discreet' behavior, and recommends 'that he should be furthered in the degree he was to take this next Commencement; because it was not her Majesty's pleasure that any one employed as he had been in matters touching the benefit of his country should be defamed by those that are ignorant in th' affairs he went about.' Of Marlowe's scant six years in London as a 'University wit' writing for the actors, little is known except for the plays which can be attributed to his authorship. His reputation for atheism has been much dwelt upon and made the basis for legends. He met his death at the hands of Ingram Friser, apparently in a quarrel which took place in a tavern in Deptford.

Marlowe's three or four important plays have overshadowed his non-dramatic poetry. His brief *Passionate shepherd to his love* was and remains one of the most popular of Elizabethan lyrics; and among sustained narrative poems only Shakespeare's may dispute primacy with Marlowe's *Hero and Leander*. At the time of Marlowe's death this poem, an expanded paraphrase of a Greek work by Musæus, was incomplete; George Chapman wrote the four sestiads which complete it. *Hero and Leander* belongs to a literary fashion, which it helped to set, of erotic poems upon mythological subjects, exemplified also in Lodge's *Glaucus and Scilla*, Shakespeare's *Venus and Adonis*, Drayton's *Endymion and Phœbe*, and several written later than these. Beside the poems already mentioned as his, Marlowe left verse-translations of Ovid's *Amores* and of the first book of Lucan's *Pharsalia*, the latter in blank verse. The poetic manner of Marlowe is that of the true Elizabethans, rich and exuberant. In spite of faults which derive from the influences under which it was written, *Hero and Leander* is yet a poem of great beauty, an enduring legacy left by 'that pure elemental wit' at the height of his powers.

MODERN EDITIONS: *The Works* (ed. by C. F. Tucker Brooke), Oxford, 1910; *The Works* (ed. by A. H. Bullen), three volumes, London, 1885; *Hero and Leander* (Haslewood Reprint), London, 1924.

COMMENT: U. M. Ellis-Fermor, *Christopher Marlowe*, London, 1927; J. L. Hotson, *The Death of Christopher Marlowe*, London, 1925; J. H. Ingram, *Christopher Marlowe and his Associates*, London, 1904.

TEXT: *England's Helicon*, 1600 (3191), White; *Hero and Leander . . . for* E. Blunt, 1598 (17413), White.

168 *The passionate shepherd . . .*] For Ralegh's *Reply* see p. 137. Marlowe's poem first appeared, unsigned and with the fourth and sixth stanzas omitted, in *The Passionate Pilgrim*, a miscellany published by William Jaggard in 1599 as the work of Shakespeare. In *E. H.* it is signed 'Chr. Marlowe'. It is interesting to find in Marlowe's *Jew of Malta* (produced *c.* 1589) the lines (1815–16):

Thou in those groves, by Dis above,
Shalt live with me and be my love.

Ingram reprints Marlowe's and Ralegh's poems from a late 16th-century commonplace-book, apparently kept by Thornborough, chaplain to the Earl of Pembroke. Marlowe's was also reprinted in *Poems, written by Wil. Shakespeare*, 1640, and in Izaak Walton's *Complete Angler*, 1653. In the second edition (1655) Walton adds, evidently from a contemporary broadside (cf. *Roxburghe Ballads*, ii. 3 ff.), the following stanza after the fifth:

Thy silver dishes for thy meat,
As precious as the gods do eat,

Shall on an ivory table be
Prepared each day for thee and me.

Marlowe's popular lyric inspired many imitations; see Donne's *The bait* (p. 459) and Herrick's *To Phyllis, to love and live with him* (p. 656). 10 posies] 1600 'poesies'.

168 *To . . . Sir Thomas Walsingham*] a patron and perhaps employer of Marlowe; Chapman dedicated his portion of *Hero and Leander* to Lady Walsingham.

169 *Hero and Leander*] We have reprinted all of Marlowe's portion of the poem, as first separately published. In the same year a printer named Linley issued the whole poem, as completed by Chapman.

169–180 *First sestiad*] Blount's edition does not divide the poem into sestiads. This division was introduced by Chapman; but it is here followed for the sake of ease in reference. 3 seaborderers] 1598 'sea-borders'. 52 Musæus] a Greek grammarian of about the fifth century A. D., who left a poem upon Hero and Leander, consisting of 340 verses. Marlowe and his contemporaries confused him with a legendary

Greek poet of the same name, a contemporary of Orpheus. 56 Colchis] the country east of the Black Sea, legendary location of the Golden Fleece. 73–75] The reference is to Narcissus. 77 Hippolytus] son of Theseus and Hippolyte, an Amazon queen; he rejected the advances of his step-mother, Phædra. 107 pale and wat'ry star] the moon; Diana. 108 thirling] flying, whirling. 114 Ixion's shaggy-footed race] the Centaurs; so called because they were supposed to have been begotten by Ixion on a cloud. 154 lovely boy] Cyparissus; for his metamorphosis, see Ovid, *Met.* x. 121 ff. 158 turtles' blood] the blood of doves, Venus's birds. 169 course] race. 296 tralucent] clear, luminous. 336 thought] 1598 misprints 'rhought'. 388 Argus] he of the hundred eyes, set to watch Mercury. 475 Midas' brood] the phrase implies the wealthy and also those without good taste, since Midas gave the palm in singing to Pan over Apollo.

180–187 *Second sestiad* 12 train] entrain, attract. 26 affied] betrothed. 32 peised] balanced. 46 Salmacis] the nymph of a fountain which rendered effeminate all who drank of it; see

Ovid, *Met.* iv. 337, 347. 51 Æsop's cock] In the fable, the cock found a jewel in a dung-heap but did not know its use or value. 118 thrust from his sphere] out of its proper place in the Ptolemaic system of spheres. 120 Alcides like] Hercules, when raging, attacked the ocean. 123 in a diameter] with direct rays. 155 sapphire-visaged god] the blue-faced god is Neptune. 179 Helle's bracelet] Helle, after whom the Hellespont was named, had been drowned there while in flight from her step-mother. 250 swoom] swum. 279–290] In all early quartos these lines are out of their position as demanded by the story, and come between our l. 300 and l. 301; we follow the order of Tucker Brooke. 291–292 strife . . . made the world] One of the philosophical commonplaces, from Heraclitus, was that war, or contention, is the father of all things. 305 Erycine] Venus; from Eryx, a Sicilian mountain, seat of her temple. 319 hair] Bullen emends to 'air'; 1598 reads 'heare'. 320 glimpse] gleams. 326 Dis] Pluto, god of riches. 335 *Desunt nonnulla*] 'Something is lacking.'

ELIZABETHAN MISCELLANIES

THE PUBLISHING of miscellanies, or anthologies, seems to have grown out of the custom of keeping commonplace-books. So long as poets did not print their collections, it behooved a lover of poetry to copy into his notebook any poems that struck his fancy, as they came under his hand in manuscript. If a printer could secure the commonplace-book of a discriminating collector, he had only to put it into type in order to publish an excellent anthology. Doubtless in the case of some miscellanies the conscious aim of collecting for the press actuated those who brought together the poems from manuscript sources; but these collectors were merely exploiting a fashion which the scores of extant commonplace-books prove to have been general. We should note also that there was at hand a classical model for the miscellany in the Greek Anthology, a favorite book with scholars and poets from the beginning of the sixteenth century; and that poetical miscellanies already had appeared in Renaissance Italy.

An account has already been given (see p. 1193) of Tottel's miscellany of *Songs and Sonnets*, which gathered together the best lyrical and reflective poetry produced during the reigns of Henry VIII, Edward VI, and Queen Mary, and which kept its popularity throughout the reign of Elizabeth. Clement Robinson and Richard Edwards were the early Elizabethan collectors whose work was most fruitful. Robinson, to be sure, interested himself in broadside ballads rather than in lyrics; and his *Handful of Pleasant Delights*, 1584, scarcely belongs in the succession of true miscellanies. As Rollins shows, this book was a second and altered edition of *Pleasant Sonnets and Stories*, licensed as by Robinson in 1566, and extant only in a single leaf. While the earlier title and the running title of the *Handful*, 'Sonnets and histories,' suggest an imitation of *Songs and Sonnets*, Robinson's book merely collects broadside ballads which already had been printed separately. Extracts from it will be found under 'Broadside Ballads,' pp. 410–414.

Richard Edwards died in 1566, leaving a commonplace-book which ten years later was printed with additions as *The Paradise of Dainty Devices*; the printer Henry Disle in his dedicatory letter wrote: 'I am bold to present unto your honor this small volume, entitled *The Paradise of Dainty Devices*, being penned by divers learned gentlemen, and collected together through the travail of one of both worship and credit, for his private use.' Edwards's taste made the *Paradise* a book of graver cast than Tottel's miscellany, with a smaller proportion of love-poems. The collection was immensely popular, copies of nine editions being extant, all published within the generation from 1576 to 1606.

B. M. Ward (see under Gascoigne) has made it appear that *A Hundreth Sundry Flowers* (1573) is a miscellany, as its title-page and table of contents indicate, in spite of Gascoigne's assumption in his *Posies* of the authorship of most of its contents. What authors are represented in the collection is harder to ascertain; Ward suggests Gascoigne, Oxford, and Sir Christopher Hatton as the principal contributors.

Timothe Kendall's *Flowers of Epigrams*, 1577, is a miscellany, although the greater part of the book consists of translations made by Kendall. It is limited, though not strictly, to epigrams. Kendall reprints short pieces by Sir Thomas Eliot, Ascham, Surrey, Grimald, and Turberville. This compiler, we may be sure, had in mind to imitate the Greek Anthology.

In 1578 appeared *A Gorgeous Gallery of Gallant Inventions*; this title had been accepted by the printer, Richard Jones, in place of his earlier choices, 'A handful of hidden secrets' and 'Delicate dainties to sweeten lovers' lips withal.' Credit for the collection is given to Thomas Procter, himself then a printer's apprentice, who contributes a number of poems. Owen Roydon seems also to have had a hand in preparing the work. This miscellany falls short of the *Paradise* in quality, and it also fell short in popularity. It draws upon *Songs and Sonnets* and the *Paradise*, without introducing any new writers of consequence.

Whether *The Forest of Fancy*, 1579, is a miscellany or a collection of verse and prose by a single author has never been ascertained. No author's name appears in the book, but at the end stands the line, 'L'acquis abonde. Finis H. C.' J. P. Collier (*Bibl. Acc.*, ii. 31) says: 'Our notion is that the various poems were contributed by various hands, and that H. C. undertook the task of editorship, which may in part serve to explain the French motto.' However, the prefatory epistle seems to claim all the contents for a single author. Ault (*E. L.*, p. 78) follows Malone in assigning Henry Cheke as author of the whole book.

With *The Phœnix Nest*, 1593, a new group of lyricists enters the field; and the general advance in poetic excellence brought about by the labors of Spenser, Sidney, Watson, Breton, and Lodge, is manifest when comparison is made between this collection and any of its predecessors. 'R. S. of the Inner Temple,' who is credited with the compilation, remains unidentified. The preservation in this anthology of otherwise unprinted poems by Ralegh and Lodge, not to mention anonymous gems, more than justifies the production.

Late in the 1590's the printer William Jaggard evidently came into possession of a poetical album containing twenty choice poems, at least four of them by Shakespeare; and his volume made from these poems, *The Passionate Pilgrim*, 1599, though issued as 'By W. Shakespeare,' was really a miscellany. It contains poems by Barnfield, Marlowe, Griffin, and some other writers, besides those by Shakespeare. Comparable to this book are the two collections *Breton's Bower of Delights*, 1591 and 1597, and *The Arbor of Amorous Devices*, 1597, assigned by the printers to Nicholas Breton and containing work by him, but including poems by other poets as well. Although the printer of the *Arbor*, Richard Jones, sets the words 'By N. B. Gent.' on the title-page, his prefatory epistle describes the book as 'many men's works, excellent poets, and most not the meanest in estate and degree'; and he complains that *The Phœnix Nest* had used 'some of the best stuff' which he had hoped to include. In this miscellany appear two poems from among the anonymous contributions to the old *Songs and Sonnets*.

England's Parnassus and *Belvedere* (later called *The Garden of the Muses*), both published for the first time in 1600, were dictionaries of quotations or poetical phrase-books rather than miscellanies. The extracts included are in almost no case complete poems, and often consist of a single line. Their editors show wide reading in the poetry of the century then closed; and they have made it possible to assign authors to otherwise anonymous poems and books.

England's Helicon, also published in 1600, stands eminent among Elizabethan miscellanies, or indeed among English anthologies of any period whatever. The *Helicon* was projected, if not actually edited, by John Bodenham, who seems to have been responsible also for *Belvedere* and for two earlier quotation-books of prose. The actual editor may have been the A.B. who writes some of the prefatory notices, or Nicholas Ling, well-known as publisher. Whoever made the choices for inclusion showed wide reading and considerable taste. He went back to *Songs and Sonnets* for two selections, and to *The Phœnix Nest* for a half-dozen. He drew upon Spenser's *Shepherd's Calendar*, Watson's *Hecatompathia*, Sidney's *Astrophel and Stella*, Drayton's *Idea*, Lodge's *Phillis*, and Spenser's *Astrophel*; he recognized the exquisite lyrics that had appeared in printed plays and romances, and copied out songs from Greene's *Menaphon*, Lodge's *Rosalind*, Sidney's *Arcadia*, Peele's *Arraignment of Paris*, and Shakespeare's *Love's Labor's Lost*. He also took into account the excellent songs in the newly popular madrigal-books and song-books, and made a choice of these. Finally, he printed for the first time important poems by Henry Constable, Anthony Munday, Bartholomew Young, and others whose names we do not know.

A Poetical Rhapsody, 1602, is the last of the Elizabethan miscellanies, and the most copious. Its editor was Francis Davison, then a young man, who himself had written considerable verse but did not care to issue a volume of his work. He put with his own a number of poems written by his younger brother Walter, others by various authors, and a great many which he assigns to A. W. These initials may stand for the name of a writer yet unidentified, or they may merely mean 'Anonymous writers.' In his first preface Davison speaks of 'my dear friend *anomos*,' and in his second of 'my dear friends *Anonymoi.*' He drew upon the writings of Thomas Watson, Henry Constable, Sir Philip Sidney, Edmund Spenser, Thomas Campion, and others. The second edition of the *Rhapsody,* 1608, adds many more poems, including work by Sir John Davies, Sir Walter Ralegh, Charles Best, and others, which had not previously been printed. Third and fourth editions included more new material, but nothing of importance. *The Poetical Rhapsody* reflects the altered taste of its period in that it contains a much larger proportion of madrigals and epigrams than its predecessors. Mr. Bullen, while granting that its poetic merit falls below that of the *Helicon,* points out that the special value of Davison's work lies in the great amount of material which it published from manuscript and which otherwise might have been lost.

CROSS REFERENCES: Poems from Tottel's *Songs and Sonnets:* Heywood, p. 11; Wyatt, pp. 13–18, 21–27; Surrey, pp. 27–33; Vaux, p. 38; Minor Courtly Makers, pp. 44–49; Grimald, pp. 49–53.

Poems, not in this section, from Elizabethan miscellanies:—*Paradise of Dainty Devices:* Vaux, pp. 39–41; Oxford, p. 102.—*Gorgeous Gallery of Gallant Inventions:* Churchyard, p. 84.—*Breton's Bower of Delights,* 1591: Oxford, p. 104.— *Phœnix Nest:* Oxford, p. 104; Greville, p. 125; Ralegh, pp. 133–137; Lodge, pp. 158–160, *An ode,* p. 162.—*Passionate Pilgrim:* Marlowe, *The passionate shepherd,* p. 168; Barnfield, *Ode, The unknown shepherd's complaint,* p. 241.— *England's Helicon: Harpalus' Complaint,* p. 45; Sidney, *The nightingale, Ring out your bells,* p. 119; Greville, p. 126; Ralegh, p. 137; Greene, *Doron's description of Samela,* p. 150, *Doron's jig,* p. 151; Lodge, *Rosalind's madrigal,* p. 156, *Montanus' sonnet,* p. 157, 'My Phillis hath,' p. 161; Breton, *A pastoral of Phillis and Coridon,* p. 163, pp. 164–166; Marlowe, p. 168; Constable, pp. 232– 235; Barnfield, *An ode, The unknown shepherd's complaint,* p. 241; Drayton, *The ninth eclogue,* p. 299; *Coridon and Melampus' song,* p. 386.—*Poetical Rhapsody,* 1602: Sidney, p. 122; Greene, *Cupid abroad was lated,* p. 155; Campion, *When to her lute,* p. 447; Wotton, p. 550.—*Poetical Rhapsody,* 1608: Ralegh, p. 139.

MODERN EDITIONS: *A Hundreth Sundrie Flowres* (ed. by B. M. Ward), London, 1926; *The Paradise of Dainty Devices* (ed. by H. E. Rollins), Cambridge (Mass.), 1927; *A Gorgeous Gallery of Gallant Inventions* (ed. by H. E. Rollins), Cambridge (Mass.), 1926, and in *Heliconia* (ed. by T. Park), Vol. i, London, 1815; *The Dr. Farmer Chetham Ms.* (ed. by A. B. Grosart), Chetham Society, 1873; *The Phœnix Nest* (ed. by H. Macdonald), London, 1926, and in *Heliconia* (ed. by T. Park), Vol. ii, London, 1815; *The Arbor of Amorous Devices* in *The Works of Nicholas Breton* (ed. by A. B. Grosart), Vol. i, Chertsey Worthies' Library, 1879; *The Passionate Pilgrim* in many editions of Shakespeare's complete works; *England's Helicon* (ed. by A. H. Bullen), London, 1887, and (ed. by H. Macdonald), London, 1925; *Davison's Poetical Rhapsody* (ed. by A. H. Bullen), two volumes, London, 1890–91.

COMMENT: C. Crawford, Introduction to his edition of *England's Parnassus,* Oxford, 1913.

TEXT: *A Hundreth Sundry Flowers* [1573] (11635), White; *The Paradise of Dainty Devices,* 1576 (7516), Huntington; *A Gorgeous Gallery of Gallant Inventions,* 1578 (20402), Bodleian; *The Forest of Fancy,* 1579 (4271), White; *Chetham Ms.* 8012, Chetham; *Verses of Praise and Joy,* 1586 (7605), B. M.; *The Phœnix Nest,* 1593 (21516), White; *England's Helicon,* 1600 (3191), White; *A Poetical Rhapsody,* 1602 (6373), White; *A Poetical Rhapsody,* 1608 (6374), White.

187–188 *A strange passion . . .*] This poem, like the one following, is found in the section of *A Hundreth Sundry Flowers* which is headed 'The devices of sundry gentlemen'. It has usually been ascribed to Gascoigne, as it was reprinted in his *Posies,* 1575, and *Works,* 1587.

188 *The lover declareth . . .*] Upon

the evidence of the affixed motto, *Meritum petere, grave,* Ward assigns this poem to the Earl of Oxford; usually ascribed to Gascoigne. 16 So] 1575; 1573 'Go'.

188–189 *Amantium iræ . . .*] 1576 has *redintigratia* in the title; corrected in 1606. The title is translated in the refrain which ends each stanza. Rollins traces the saying to Terence, *Andria,* III. iii. 23. The poem was set to music, extant in *Add. Ms.* 30513. It is signed in *P. D. D.* For Richard Edwards, see L. Bradner, *The Life and Poems of Richard Edwards,* New Haven, 1927. For a poem possibly by Edwards, see *O death, rock me asleep,* p. 43. 3 sweet] 1578; 1576 'sore'. 8, 16, 24, 32, 40] Our reading of the refrain follows 1576; the one usually reprinted in modern times, 'The falling out of faithful friends renewing is of love,' appeared at the ends of the first three stanzas in editions of 1578 and 1580, and throughout in 1585 and later editions.

189–190 *M. Edwards' May*] signed in all editions after the first; set to music in John Forbes's *Cantus* (2nd ed., 1666). *P. D. D.* of 1578 contained *A reply to M. Edwards' May,* signed 'M. S.'; *P. D. D.* of 1585 contained *Master Edwards his I may not,* unsigned.

190–191 *Being importunate . . .*] signed in 1576, 'M. B.'; these initials represent 'Master Bew.' All editions after the first, however, give this poem to Edwards. 3 I] 1578; omitted in 1576.

191 *No pains comparable . . .*] For Hunnis see Mrs. C. C. Stopes, *William Hunnis and the Revels of the Chapel Royal,* Louvain, 1910. 9–10] 'No foot to spare' and 'No near' ('No nearer') are the answers of the man making soundings to the master's question of 'How?'

192–193 *Respice finem*] 'Consider the end.' The author of this poem and compiler of the miscellany in which it appeared, Thomas Procter, was a printer and miscellaneous author. 2 fine] end. 11 hutch] box, coffer. ruddocks] gold (red) coins.

193 *A proper sonnet . . .*] This poem stands between two signed as by Procter, but is not signed. Its poetical quality is higher than that of poems known to be by Procter.

193–194 *A true description of love*] Only two rhymes are used in this sonnet. 10 lay] law. 11 lean until our stay] 'lean' is misprinted 'leaue' in 1578; the phrase means 'lean upon our support.' Professor Kittredge (Rollins's edition, p. 173) is responsible for the improved reading. 14 denay] denial.

194 *The lover in the praise . . .* 5] Polyxena, daughter of Priam, was sacrificed at Achilles' grave by his son Pyrrhus. 7 wise] means.

194–195 *The lover exhorteth . . .*]

This is plainly a ballad. *Attend thee, go play thee* is one of the broadsides reprinted in *A Handful of Pleasant Delights,* 1584. 28 Camma] a woman who revenged the killing of her husband; the legend is told by Plutarch and by Castiglione in *The Courtier.* Rollins notes two ballads embodying the tale, registered 1569–1570.

195 *The strange pangs . . .* 11 joy] The sense seems to demand some such word as 'pain.'

195 *Chetham Ms.* 8012] This is a commonplace-book or manuscript miscellany; it contains entries of various dates and different handwritings, both in prose and poetry. Besides poems of unknown authorship, the ms. furnishes copies of works by Sir John Davies, Ralegh, Donne, Hoskins, Jonson, Dyer, and Daniel.

196 *Another of another mind* [1] 2 swad] clodhopper.

196 *Another of another mind* [2] 2 For] Grosart reads 'The'.

196 *Verses of Praise and Joy . . .*] This volume celebrates the discovery and overthrow of the Babington conspiracy against Queen Elizabeth. In September, 1586, seven of the conspirators met execution, including Chidiock Tichborne, then eighteen years of age. A letter which Tichborne wrote from the Tower to his wife is also preserved.

196–197 *Tichborne's elegy . . .*] One must admit the possibility that these verses were written by some other poet, rather than by the protagonist himself. The poem was very popular; it appears, set to music, in John Mundy's *Songs and Psalms,* 1594, Michael East's *Madrigals,* 1604, and Richard Alison's *An Hour's Recreation in Music,* 1606.

197–198 *O night, O jealous night* 1 pleasures] some editors emend to 'measures'.

198 *Set me where Phœbus' heat*] translated from Petrarch's sonnet *In vita,* cxiii; see Surrey's translation of the same sonnet, p. 29.

198–199 *Sought by the world*] The present editors suggest that upon evidence of style and content this poem might be assigned to Ralegh; in 1593 it stands with some poems known to be by Ralegh.

199 *A nymph's disdain of love*] signed 'Ignoto' in *E. H.*

199–201 *Phillida's love-call . . .*] signed 'Ignoto' in *E. H.*; set to music in *Rawlinson Poetry Ms.* 148. 28 say] silk. 42 my] The sense seems to demand 'her', *i. e.* Cynthia's. 55–60] The distribution of speeches follows 1614; 1600 gives 55–57 to Corydon and 58–60 to Phillida.

201 *The nymph Selvagia . . .*] This and the following poem, signed 'Bar. Young' in *E. H.*, were taken from Young's translation (1589) of Montemayor's *Diana*, p. 28 and p. 473.

202 *A palinode*] signed 'E. B.' in *E. H.* Three other poems in the miscellany are similarly signed, while one is signed 'Edmund Bolton'. Bolton was a Catholic poet and antiquarian, author of *Hypercritica*, an essay upon writers and literature.

202–203 *A canzon pastoral . . .*] signed 'Edmund Bolton'.

203 *To Colin Clout*] signed 'Shepherd Tony' in *E. H.*, as is one other poem. *To Colin Clout* appeared in a romance, *Primaleon of Greece*, 1619, (possibly in the newly-discovered *Second Book of Primaleon*, 1596), by Anthony Munday, who is therefore generally believed to have been 'Shepherd Tony.' Munday (1553–1633) was a voluminous author, principally of plays and pageants, but also of romances, translations, pamphlets, and ballads. Webbe's praise of Munday's pastoral poetry may well apply to the present lyric. This poem appears in three songbooks: Pilkington's *First Book of Songs or Airs*, 1605, Jones's *Ultimum Vale*, 1608, and Corkine's *Airs*, 1610. It was also reprinted in *Wit's Interpreter*, 1655.

203–204 *Ode*] Because of its presence in several mss. containing poems by Donne, and because of its character, this poem has been attributed to that poet. Grierson argues on the authority of a Hawthornden ms. (also taking into account style and sentiments) that the poem is by John Hoskins; see pp. 527, 528.

206–207 *A fiction . . .*] signed 'Anomos' in 1602; unsigned in later editions; attributed to A. W. in ms. list left by Francis Davison.

207 *Sonnet*] signed, as is another sonnet in the miscellany, 'I. S.' and upon this evidence usually ascribed to Joshua Sylvester (1563–1618), translator of Du Bartas. This sonnet is of higher poetic merit, however, than any other work by Sylvester. 5 high] 1602 reads 'hight'. 9–11] These lines translate an epigram from the Greek Anthology. See notes to Turberville.

208 *Commendation of her beauty*] This and the two poems following appear in a section of the *P. R.* headed 'Sonnets, Odes, Elegies, Madrigals, and Epigrams by Francis Davison and Walter Davison, Brethren'. The name of Francis Davison appears about halfway through the section, and the initials 'W. D.' at the end. The three poems here reprinted are from the first part.

208 *Upon the timorous silence . . .*] set to music by Robert Jones, *First set of Madrigals*, 1607.

208 *To Cupid*] first stanza set to music by Robert Jones, *First set of Madrigals*, 1607.

209 *The sound of thy sweet name*] This poem first appeared in the edition of 1608, in the section of poems evidently by Francis Davison. These stanzas were so printed as to appear to be a part of a preceding madrigal.

209 *A sonnet of the moon*] not in 1602; signed 'Ch. B.' in 1608, 'Chas. Best' in 1611. Practically nothing is known of this author. John Davies of Hereford addressed a complimentary epigram in *The Scourge of Folly* (*c.* 1611) to 'My kind friend, Mr. Charles Best.' 4 her] Ault (*E. L.*) prints, as from 1611, 'his'.

SONNET-SEQUENCES

THE EARLIEST 'true' sonnets written in English, those of Wyatt and of Surrey, remained for a considerable period without being widely imitated. Poets seized upon the word 'sonnet,' but applied it, in its etymological meaning of 'a little song,' to poems of varied lengths and measures. In Googe's *Eclogues, Epitaphs, and Sonnets*, 1563, are only two poems in sonnet-form; and these are printed in such a way as to disguise that form. In Turberville's *Epitaphs, Epigrams, Songs and Sonnets*, 1567, there are no sonnets in fourteen lines. These and other writers used the word 'sonnets' on their title-pages rather because of the popularity of the original *Songs and Sonnets*, 1557, than as an indication of the presence of a particular form of verse.

An exception to this rule is Gascoigne, who wrote: 'I can best allow to call those Sonnets which are of fourteen lines, every line containing ten syllables.' In *A Hundreth Sundry Flowers* (1573) there appear thirty sonnets, of which at least eleven are by Gascoigne himself. It is notable that in one of these (see p. 88) the author seems to be attempting to follow the strict Italian rhyme-scheme and manages to avoid the final couplet. It is also notable that seven of Gascoigne's sonnets form a sequence, linked together by the author's repeating the last line of one as first line of the next; and that there are two other sequences, of three sonnets each, in *A Hundreth Sundry Flowers*. In the *Posies* (1575, 1587) all but two of the thirty sonnets were reprinted and two new ones were added. The circulation of these works, together with that of Tottel's miscellany in its successive editions, served to keep the fourteen-line sonnet before the eyes of readers.

A considerable number of sonnets, though confusingly designated, appeared in *A Theater . . . [for] Voluptuous Worldlings*, 1569, translated from the French version of a Flemish book of emblems by Van der Noodt. From later publication of some of these it seems evident that the translator was Edmund Spenser, then a school-boy. The *Theater* contained six sonnets (though five of them end at twelve lines) called 'Epigrams'; these were translated and adapted from the stanzas of a canzone by Petrarch (through the French of Marot), and were published, filled out to sonnet-length, with Spenser's *Complaints*, 1591. After the 'epigrams' in the *Theater* appeared fifteen poems in fourteen lines each, called 'Sonnets,' but written in blank verse. These were translated from du Bellay and also appeared, re-written with rhymes, in the *Complaints*. The chief significance of the *Theater* lies in the fact that what sonnets it contains came, though indirectly, from such authentic masters of this form as Petrarch and du Bellay; and in the fact that Spenser was thus early dabbling with the sonnet-form.

The prosperity of the sonnet, however, waited upon a further development—its use in an extended sequence with love as theme. Thomas Watson, whose *Hecatompathia, or Passionate Century of Love* appeared in 1582, is usually given credit for introducing into England this mode, already prevalent in Italy and France. Watson was not yet writing true sonnets, for most of the English poems in this volume are eighteen lines in length; but like Wyatt and Surrey before him he had gone to Petrarch for models and materials, as well as to minor Italian, French, and Latin authors; and his work was a forerunner of the later cycles of true sonnets. Indeed, as an apprentice task, he had translated all of Petrarch's sonnets into Latin verse; and two of these translations, one of them in fourteen lines, appear in *Hecatompathia*. Watson's only true sonnet in English in this volume is called a 'quatorzain,' a name borrowed from the French and used by many later sonneteers. With Watson we must at once name Sir Philip Sidney, who doubtless had written a large part of *Astrophel and Stella* by 1580; the circulation of this work in manuscript probably had more influence than the publication of Watson's book. Sidney also drew upon Petrarch and upon contemporary or recent French writers. Besides writing his sonnets in fourteen lines, Sidney may be said to have produced a sequence, or cycle, more truly than his contemporary. Watson's 'passionate century of love' was patched together of poems unrelated except by their general theme. *Astrophel and*

Stella, like Petrarch's work, is the lyrical reflection of a definite love story. And it was this use of the sonnet that prevailed in the hey-day of that form, following the publication of Sidney's work.

Fulke Greville, friend of Sidney, must also have written sonnets in the years about 1580; but his collection, *Cælica*, awaited publication until 1633, and then it contained a deal of later work. Nor is it a true cycle, but rather a miscellaneous gathering of various kinds of lyrics. There appeared in 1584 *Pandora*, containing some of Ronsard's sonnets translated ('with an unsurpassable crudity,' says Sidney Lee) by John Soowthern; but it seems to have been without influence. Two sonnets were printed with musical notes by Byrd in his *Psalms, Sonnets, and Songs* of 1588; and six more appeared in the same composer's *Songs of Sundry Natures*, 1589. These eight sonnets are quite in the best vein and deserve to stand with the work of minor sonneteers published in the decade following. Spenser used the sonnet for a considerable body of dedicatory material placed before the first issue of *The Fairy Queen* in 1590; and Ralegh wrote for the same publication a complimentary sonnet which is a high-water mark in its kind (see p. 137).

But the tide of sonneteering began to swell only after the publication of *Astrophel and Stella* in its three editions of 1591 and 1592. Then we find the best poets of England turning to this form and producing cycles addressed to real or imaginary mistresses. Twenty-eight sonnets by Daniel had been placed by Newman at the end of that printer's unauthorized first edition of *Astrophel and Stella*. Daniel himself issued in the next year his sonnet-cycle *Delia*, containing most of those printed by Newman and some thirty others. In *Delia and Rosamond augmented*, 1594, the cycle consists of fifty-five sonnets and an ode. Drayton published a sequence of fifty-two sonnets in 1594, under the title of *Idea's Mirror*. This sequence in its final form, the *Idea* of 1619, contained sixty-three sonnets. Spenser followed with a cycle of eighty-eight sonnets published in *Amoretti and Epithalamion*, 1595. And there is good reason to believe that the greater number of Shakespeare's sonnets, though not printed until 1609, were written in the early and middle years of the 1590's.

In the meanwhile, minor poets were also at work. Constable's *Diana* appeared in 1592, and again, 'augmented with divers quatorzains of honorable and learned persons,' in 1594. Lodge published his *Phillis* in 1593; and from the same year we have Barnabe Barnes's *Parthenophe and Parthenophil* (a title plainly imitated from Sidney's), Giles Fletcher's *Licia*, and a second cycle by Watson, *The Tears of Fancy*. In 1594, besides some cycles already mentioned, come the anonymous *Zepheria* and Percy's *Cœlia*; in 1595, *Emaricdulfe* by E. C., and a short cycle addressed to a young man by Barnfield in his *Cynthia*; in 1596, *Diella* by Lynche, *Fidessa* by Griffin, and *Chloris* by Smith; and in 1597, *Laura* by Robert Tofte. The last-named sequence is made up of poems of ten and twelve lines; and if we include it with sonnet-cycles we ought also to mention the same author's *Alba* and J. C.'s *Alcilia, Philoparthen's Loving Folly*, which is a love-cycle having a six-line form as its unit. But sequences of love-poems, in miscellaneous stanza-forms, were too numerous for mention here.

As may be seen from the titles, the conventional sonnet-cycle was addressed to a lady, corresponding to Petrarch's Laura (or Sidney's Stella), who usually was given a classical name. Some of the names, as Delia, Phillis, Diana, and Idea, had already been used in titles of French cycles. In some sequences, as in Spenser's *Amoretti* and E. C.'s *Emaricdulfe*, a real woman is the subject, and details of her life and character appear. In others, as Fletcher's *Licia*, Lodge's *Phillis*, and both of Watson's collections, the reader is aware that he has only literary exercises and translations—though such might have served, to be sure, in some actual romances. The general Petrarchan conventions of the cruel mistress, golden-haired and with lilies and roses contending in her cheeks, and the faithful lover, alternately hoping and fearing, at once freezing and burning, are at the basis of most of the cycles, though transcended by the best writers. Some other specific conventional themes are: the lady walks or sits in the garden, she plays on a musical instrument, she sings, she falls sick; the lover compares himself to a ship tossed by the sea, he invokes sleep, he promises eternity of fame to the lady through his verses. There is a continual search for comparisons worthy of the lady's beauty and grace: the four seasons and the heavenly bodies are under frequent requisition; as are legendary heroes and ladies, gods and goddesses, kings and kingdoms, usages of the law court, and even the signs of the zodiac. Yet in spite of this conventional lumber, and even by the aid of it, some of the sonneteers wrote poems of exquisite grace and charm; while now and again a genuine expression of deep emotion vivifies a page in one of these collections.

The flood of sonnets met with a counter-current of satire. It must have been about 1595 that Sir John Harington wrote *A comfort for poor poets,*

> Poets henceforth for pensions need not care;
> Who call you beggars, you may call them liars:
> Verses are grown such merchantable ware
> That now for sonnets sellers are—and buyers.

John Davies at the same time was using the sonnet-form for many of his coarse and bitter epigrams; he singled out an unfortunate conceit in one of Drayton's sonnets for ridicule (*In Decium*, p. 332); and he composed for circulation among his friends a set of nine 'gulling sonnets' which parodied the passions of the sonneteers (see pp. 332–334). Shakespeare voiced his impatience with conventional notes in sonnets:

> My mistress' eyes are nothing like the sun;
> Coral is far more red than her lips' red, etc.

Again, we find Mercutio laughing at the sonnet-fashion when he says of Romeo (*R. and J.* II. iv. 40): 'Now is he for the numbers that Petrarch flowed in: Laura to his lady was but a kitchen-wench; marry, she had a better love to berhyme her.' The temper of the times about 1600, tending toward sophistication and cynicism, furthered the literary reaction against the oversweet sonnet, and brought it about that satires and epigrams replaced sonnets in popular favor. Earlier than this, too, many readers (and writers) of love-poetry must have turned with relief from the cold ladies of the Petrarchan convention to the passionate and pursuing heroines of the Ovidian tradition as represented in *Venus and Adonis, Hero and Leander,* and other poems.

Religious impulses also influenced sonnet-writing, and soon after the cycles began to appear the form was turned to devotional uses. As early as 1593 the uninspired Henry Lok issued *Sundry Christian Passions contained in two hundred sonnets.* Chapman's *Coronet for his Mistress Philosophy* of

1595, while not religious, claims the sonnet for higher uses than the praise of a lady-love,—a line of thought already suggested by Giles Fletcher in his preface to *Licia*. Barnes turned from praising Parthenophe and wrote his *Divine Century of Spiritual Sonnets*, 1595, 'an hundreth quatorzains in honor of the greatest Disposer of all great honors.' Constable wrote but did not publish (doubtless because of its Catholic sentiments) a short sequence entitled *Spiritual Sonnets*. In 1597 Lok's collection, considerably augmented, saw a second printing. Some of the excellent religious sonnets of Donne will be found with the poems of that author; and it will be seen that Drummond issued both secular and religious sequences in his *Poems* of 1616, as Davies of Hereford had done in *Wit's Pilgrimage*, 1610.

Nor must it be thought that the love-cycle was extinct by 1600; besides the later works by Davies and Drummond, just mentioned, and new editions of earlier cycles, we have *Aurora*, 1604, an extended sequence by Sir William Alexander; *Amorous Songs, Sonnets, and Elegies*, 1606, by another Scottish poet, Alexander Craig; and another *Songs and Sonnets*, this time by Patrick Hannay, published with *The Nightingale*, 1622.

CROSS REFERENCES: For sonnets not in this section and not mentioned in the foregoing account, see under: Minor Courtly Makers, Oxford, Essex, Elizabethan Miscellanies, Epigrams.

MODERN EDITIONS: *Elizabethan Sonnets* (ed. by S. Lee), two volumes, Westminster, 1904; *Elizabethan Sonnet-Cycles* (ed. by M. F. Crow), four volumes, London, 1896–98; *Parthenophil and Parthenophe* (ed. by A. B. Grosart), 1875; *Divine Century of Spiritual Sonnets* in *Heliconia* (ed. by T. Park), Vol. ii, London, 1815; *Emaricdulfe* in *A Lamport Garland* (ed. by C. Edmunds), The Roxburghe Club, 1881; *The Poetical Works of Alexander Craig*, Hunterian Club, 1873.

TEXT: *Licia*, [1593] (11055), Huntington; *Parthenophil and Parthenophe*, [1593], text from Sidney Lee; *Cælia*, 1594 (19618), Huntington; *Zepheria*, 1594 (26124), White; *Emaricdulfe*, 1595 (4268), Huntington; *Diella*, 1596 (17091), Huntington; *Chloris*, 1596 (22872), B. M.; *Fidessa*, 1596 (12367), Huntington; *Laura*, 1597 (24097), Huntington; *Sonnets of Christian Passions*, 1597 (16696), White; *Amorous Songs, Sonnets, and Elegies*, 1606 (5956), White.

209 *Licia*] Giles Fletcher (*c.* 1549–1611), known as 'the elder' to distinguish him from his son of the same name (see p. 599), was more famous as scholar and man of affairs than as poet. He studied at Eton and at King's College, Cambridge, where he proceeded B. A. in 1569, M. A. in 1573, and Doctor of Laws in 1581. He saw diplomatic service in Scotland, and later in Russia, where he suffered notorious illtreatment. A book about Russia which he wrote was suppressed. It seems to have been in a period of enforced idleness after this suppression (in 1591) that Fletcher turned to the new fashion of sonneteering and produced *Licia*, a sequence of fifty-two sonnets with a half-dozen of odes and elegies appended. His other works (several of them in Latin) were historical, political, and religious. The poems in *Licia* are admittedly imitative, though Fletcher turned to Neo-Latin rather than to Italian sources (cf. Janet Scott, 'The Sources of Giles Fletcher's *Licia*,' *M.L.R.* xx. 187).

211 *Seven are the lights* 14 her] Venus's.

212 *Like Memnon's rock* 3 done] 1593 'dunne'; 'dumb' seems demanded by the sense, and 'done' by the rhyme-scheme.

214 *Parthenophil and Parthenophe*] Barnabe Barnes (1570–1609) was at Brasenose College, Oxford, about 1586, but left without taking a degree. *Parthenophil and Parthenophe* contained one hundred and five sonnets, twenty-six madrigals, twenty-one elegies, twenty odes, five sestines, and three canzons, besides a version of the first idyl of Moschus, the story of 'runaway Cupid.' The printer's preface to *Parthenophil and Parthenophe* promises from the author 'some more excellent work hereafter'; Barnes's *Divine Century of Spiritual Sonnets* (1595) may have been printed to fulfil that promise. Aside from laying himself open to attack from Nashe, the poet seems to have had personal defects which made him fair game for ridicule, notably by Thomas Campion. Barnes drew heavily upon French poets for his inspiration; even his translation from Moschus was probably made from French rather than from Greek. A modern reader finds his work antiquated and quaint, though graceful and poetic within the conventional fashion of his decade. The unique copy of the first edition of this book is in the library of the Duke of Devonshire; our text from Lee's *Elizabethan Sonnets.*

216 *No more lewd lays* 3 sparrows' plumes] The sparrow was Venus's bird.

217 *Cœlia*] William Percy (1575–1648) was a younger son of Henry Percy, eighth Earl of Northumberland. His friendship with Barnabe Barnes may have begun in Yorkshire, the home of both, whence they both went to Oxford. In writing *Sonnets to the Fairest Cœlia* Percy appears to have been following the example set by Barnes. He published no other books, but left six plays in ms.

218 *Zepheria*] The author of this sequence has not been identified. That he was a member of one of the Inns of Court is suggested by the legal phraseology which he often employs and which subjected him to satirical parody by Sir John Davies (see p. 334).

218–219 *Alli veri figlioli delle Muse*] 'To the true sons of the Muse.' 10 father of delicious phrases] Petrarch (?). 15 Delian sonnetry] a term often applied to sonneteering, from Daniel's popular sequence, *Delia.* 20 Naso] Ovid. 28 Mnemosyne] The Muses were the daughters of Mnemosyne, or Memory. 31 lawful] 1594 'leyful'; 'lay' was a not uncommon form of 'law.'

219 *Proud in thy love*] lacking from the White copy; text from Lee.

220 *Emaricdulfe*] Edmunds suggests Edmund Carew as possibly author of the sequence. Lee says: ' "Emaricdulfe" is an anagram on the name of one Marie Cufeld, or Cufaud, of Cufaud Manor, near Basingstoke.' The sequence contains a number of circumstantial allusions to the lady.

220–221 *I am enchanted*] Sonnets presenting the lady as playing on a musical instrument are not uncommon in sequences; compare Shakespeare's sonnet 128.

221 *Diella*] The known publications of Lynche, or Linche, are *The Fountain of English Fiction,* 1599, and *An Historical Treatise of the Travels of Noah into Europe,* 1601, both translated from the Italian. In 1596 had appeared *Diella, certain sonnets, adjoined to the* *Amorous Poem of Dom Diego and Ginevra,* the latter poem also a translation from the Italian. This work is claimed by 'R. L., Gentleman.' Most students accept Richard Lynche as the author, who may also be the R. L. to whom Richard Barnfield addressed a sonnet (see p. 239).

222 *Chloris*] Little is known of William Smith except what can be gleaned from this volume, which appeared under his name. One of the sonnets in *Chloris* had previously appeared in *The Phœnix Nest,* 1593, and a poem from the collection was reprinted in *England's Helicon.*

222–223 *To . . . Colin Clout*] addressed to Spenser, using the name which that poet adopted for himself.

224 *Fidessa*] Of this poet there remains only this volume, issued under the name B. Griffin. Grosart identified him as Bartholomew Griffin of Coventry (d. 1602). A sonnet appearing in *Fidessa,* beginning 'Venus and young Adonis sitting by her,' was printed, with alterations, in *The Passionate Pilgrim* as Shakespeare's. Griffin echoes previous English sonneteers rather than French or Italian poets.

224 *Compare me to the child* 3 foolish boy] Icarus.

225 *Fly to her heart*] an example of the form known as 'like loose'; see Wyatt's *Hate whom ye list* (p. 21) and note.

227 *Laura*] Robert Tofte (d. 1620) left two books of original poetry and several translated volumes. He is known to have traveled much in Italy; and he published versions of several works by Ariosto and of *Orlando Inamorata* by Boiardo. The lady celebrated by Tofte, if we can judge from internal evidence, was named Caryll. Tofte himself had some acquaintance among the minor writers of his time, by whom he was nick-named 'Robin Redbreast.' The poems in *Laura* are never true sonnets, but are ten or twelve lines in length.

228 *Sonnets of Christian Passions*] Lok, or Lock (c. 1553–c. 1608), most pedestrian of sonneteers, wrote little but religious poetry. In 1593 he published *Sundry Christian Passions contained in Two Hundred Sonnets.* These poems were reprinted with the author's verse-paraphrase of *Ecclesiastes* in 1597, augmented by verse-translations of some *Psalms,* 102 'Sundry affectionate sonnets of a feeling conscience' and twenty-two sonnets called 'Peculiar prayers,'

Some copies also contain sixty or more secular sonnets, addressed to notable men and women of the time.
228 *Amorous Songs, Sonnets, and Elegies*] Alexander Craig (*c.* 1567–1627) was a cultured Scotchman who came to London in the train of King James. He published *Poetical Essays* in 1604, and having received a generous pension from James, retired to Scotland to make his home. He published also his *Poetical Recreations* (1609 and 1623).
228–229 *To Pandora* 11 thame] Scottish form of 'them'. 14 saunt] Scottish variant for 'saint'; 1606 reads 'sanct'.

HENRY CONSTABLE

HENRY CONSTABLE (1562–1613), born of a good family in Warwickshire and educated at Cambridge, as a young man embraced the Catholic faith, with the result that he spent the greater part of his remaining years abroad, though in touch with English affairs and often in England. When it became apparent that James VI of Scotland was to succeed Elizabeth, Constable tried to open negotiations toward removing the disabilities of Catholics, but without avail.

A sonnet of his had appeared in King James's *Poetical Exercises* of 1591. In the next year was published his *Diana*, a sonnet-sequence of only twenty-three poems; in 1594 this was re-issued, 'augmented with divers quatorzains of honorable and learned personages.' In this second form, the sequence contains seventy-six sonnets, including eight known to be by Sir Philip Sidney. None of the others has been assigned with definiteness to any author besides Constable. In 1595 four sonnets by Constable in praise of Sidney appeared in the first edition of *An Apology for Poetry*; and four pastoral poems by him were included in *England's Helicon*, 1600. His religious sonnets, left unprinted doubtless because of their strongly Catholic sentiments, were published from manuscript early in the nineteenth century.

Constable's poetry enjoyed a deserved popularity in its generation. In *The Return from Parnassus*, the Cambridge play of 1600, one student pays this tribute:

> Sweet Constable doth take the wand'ring ear
> And lays it up in willing prisonment.

MODERN EDITIONS: *Diana: the sonnets and other poems* (ed. by T. Park), London, 1859; *Spiritual Sonnets to the honor of God and His Saints, in Heliconia* (ed. by T. Park), Vol. ii, London, 1815; *The Poems and Sonnets* (ed by J. Gray), London, 1897; *Diana in Elizabethan Sonnet-Cycles* (ed. by M. F. Crow), London, 1896, and in *Elizabethan Sonnets* (ed. by S. Lee), Westminster, 1904.

TEXT: *Diana*, 1592 (5637), Huntington; *Diana*, [1594] (5638), Huntington; *The Harleian Miscellany*, Vol. ix, 1812; *Harleian Ms.* 7553, B. M.; *England's Helicon*, 1600 (3191), White.

230 *Whilst echo cries . . .* 5 play'st] 1594 'pay'st'.
231–232 *To his mistress . . .*] unprinted until its appearance in *The Harleian Miscellany;* unfortunately Park does not tell from what ms. he printed it, and it does not appear in the *Harleian Mss.* of Constable's authorship.
232–233 *Damelus' song . . .*] signed 'H. C.' in 1600; set to music by Francis Pilkington, *First Book of Songs or Airs*, 1605.

233–235 *The shepherd's song of Venus and Adonis*] signed 'H. C.' in 1600; the question of priority of composition between this poem and Shakespeare's on the same subject has not been settled. The legend occurs in Ovid's *Metamorphoses*, x. Both Constable and Shakespeare, however, differ from Ovid in making Adonis cold to Venus's advances. This treatment of the story is suggested in Spenser's *Fairy Queen* (III. i. xxxiv–xxxviii) and in Marlowe's *Hero and Leander* (ll. 12–14). 5 Vesta's beauty] Vesta is sometimes identified with Terra, the earth. 72 Myrrha] Adonis was the incestuous son of Myrrha and her father Cinyras, king in Assyria and Cyprus. 129 orpëd] fierce. 139 flower] the anemone, formerly called the adonium.

ROBERT SOUTHWELL

ROBERT SOUTHWELL (*c.* 1561–1595) was a Catholic poet, a member of the Society of Jesus. He was educated at Douai and Paris; and for some time was prefect of studies in the English College at Rome. In 1584, when he was ordained priest, he asked to be sent to England; although a law promulgated in the same year made it a treasonable offense for an English subject ordained as priest after 1557 to remain in England for more than forty days. Southwell returned while the Babington plot was being fomented, but he seems to have had no immediate connection with that plot. He went under the name of Cotton, and acquired a vocabulary of sporting terms (especially from falconry) in order to conceal his profession. In 1589 he became chaplain to the wife of the Earl of Arundel. A proclamation of 1591 called for a more rigorous enforcement of laws against Catholics; Southwell was arrested in 1592, and spent the remainder of his life in prison. He was thirteen times examined, several times tortured, and finally executed by hanging. There seems to have been little, if any, popular feeling against him. His books, which printers began to issue immediately after his death, were widely sold in several editions.

Besides his English poems he wrote much Latin verse and several devotional tracts in prose. His desire in writing poetry was to show that religious subjects were suitable for the poet; in two or three cases he wrote sacred redactions, or parodies, of popular love-poems.

MODERN EDITIONS: *Complete Poems* (ed. by A. B. Grosart), Fuller Worthies' Library, London, 1872; *The Book of Robert Southwell* (ed. by C. M. Hood), Oxford, 1926.

COMMENT: Mario Praz, '*St. Peter's Complaint* and its Italian Source,' *M. L. R.* xix. 273; J. A. Langford, *Prison Books and their Authors*, London, 1861.

TEXT: *Mœoniæ*, 1595 (22954), White; *St. Peter's Complaint . . . for J. Wolfe,* 1595 (22957), Huntington (Chew copy); *St. Peter's Complaint, newly augmented,* [*c.* 1605] (22961), Huntington.

235 *Upon the image of death* 3 names] In Simon Wastell's *Microbiblion,* 1629, where this poem is reprinted, the reading is 'qualms'. 20 hearse] a canopy of black, to be placed over a coffin.

RICHARD BARNFIELD

RICHARD BARNFIELD (1574–1627) is remembered for three brief books of poetry published before he reached the age of twenty-five. From the age of fifteen to that of eighteen he was at Oxford, where he received the degree of B.A. in 1592. Then he spent a few years in London among the numerous young poets and poetasters of the time, and afterward retired to his country home. His publications were *The Affectionate Shepherd,* 1594, dedicated to Lady Penelope Rich (Sidney's Stella), *Cynthia,* 1595, and *The Encomion of Lady Pecunia,* 1598. Barnfield is notable for his generous tributes to contemporary authors. He seems to have been a friend of Watson, Drayton, and Meres; and his greatest admiration went out to Sidney,

Spenser, and Shakespeare. While he is distinctly a minor poet, he caught a little of the music of the great singers whom he praised. Three of the poems here reprinted, *Ode*, *To his friend Master R. L.*, and *The unknown shepherd's complaint*, were included in *The Passionate Pilgrim* of 1599 as Shakespeare's; and the first two named were generally thought to be by Shakespeare until their presence in *Poems in Divers Humors* of 1598 was pointed out; the third is ascribed to Barnfield on slighter evidence. It is possible that the R. B. who wrote and compiled the poetical pamphlet in memory of Robert Greene, *Greene's Funerals*, 1594, was Richard Barnfield.

MODERN EDITIONS: *Poems* (ed. by E. Arber), Westminster, 1895, and in *Some Longer Elizabethan Poems* (ed. by A. H. Bullen), London, n. d.; *Complete Poems*, (ed. by A. B. Grosart), The Roxburghe Club, 1876.

TEXT: *Cynthia*, 1595 (1483), Bodleian; *Poems in Divers Humors*, 1598 (1488), Bodleian.

239 *To his mistress* 2 president] probably 'presiding genius' or 'guardian'; the same form, however, frequently represents the modern 'precedent.'

239–240 *To his friend Master R. L.*] perhaps addressed to the poet Richard Lynche. 5 Dowland] see p. 981.

240 *Against the dispraisers of poetry* 13 The King of Scots] King James.

240 *A remembrance of some English poets* 8 The White Rose and the Red] Daniel's *Civil Wars*, five books of which were published in 1595.

241 *An ode*] reprinted in a shortened version in *England's Helicon*. 23 King Pandion] in Greek legend, the father of Philomela and Procne, who were changed by the gods, in pity for their sorrows, into birds, one into a swallow and the other into a nightingale.

241–242 *The unknown shepherd's complaint*] first appeared in Thomas Weelkes's *Madrigals*, 1597, then in *The Passionate Pilgrim* of 1599, with the foregoing *Ode*. In *England's Helicon* the *Ode* follows this poem, with the heading, 'Another of the same shepherd's'; on this basis we have ascribed the present poem to Barnfield.

SAMUEL DANIEL

SAMUEL DANIEL (*c.* 1562–1619) was educated at Magdalen Hall, Oxford. After three years' residence, he left without a degree, finding himself, if we are to believe Wood, 'more prone to easier and smoother studies than in pecking and hewing at logic.' His first publication, in 1585, was a translation of *The Worthy Tract of Paulus Jovius*, an Italian work on impresas. The preface shows Daniel already a master of a remarkably clear and fluent prose style. Before 1592, he had traveled on the Continent, and while in Italy, with Sir Edward Dymmock, he had met Guarini. In England, too, he was fortunate in literary friendships; for as tutor to William Herbert he was admitted to the circle of the Countess of Pembroke at Wilton, which he spoke of as 'my best school.' Here he began to write sonnets, and twenty-eight of his composition appeared in the surreptitious edition of Sir Philip Sidney's *Astrophel and Stella* in 1591. In the next year he issued an authorized edition of his sonnets, and also published his *Complaint of Rosamond*, a tragical legend modeled on the legends of the still popular *Mirror for Magistrates*. Stimulated by the same patriotic impetus which produced the chronicle plays, he continued to write of historical subjects in his *Civil Wars*, 1595. In 1612 we have the final result of this interest in his prose *History of England*.

Daniel found it necessary to continue to earn his living by tutoring, and before 1599 he entered the service of the Countess of Cumberland as tutor to her daughter, Lady Anne Clifford. Later he lamented that he had been 'constrained to live with children' whilst he should have 'written the actions of men.' The poems he wrote during this period—*Musophilus*, and the verse epistles of dignified advice to various members of the nobility—do bear the mark of the teacher. In 1602 Campion's attack on rhyme and accentual verse stirred Daniel to write his excellent *Defence of Rhyme*, the only Elizabethan critical treatise worthy to rank with Sidney's *Defence of Poesy*.

At the accession of James, Daniel was preferred to the favor of Queen Anne by the Countess of Bedford and was commissioned to write the first mask for the new court, *The Vision of the Twelve Goddesses*, 1604. Although Jonson superseded him as the writer of masks, Daniel retained the Queen's favor and held various offices in her household. With the exception of some difficulty over his play *Philotas*, which was thought to touch too closely on the fate of the Earl of Essex, he lived quietly, in as much retirement as possible. He kept a farm at Beckington in Somerset, the county of his birth, to which he retired in 1618 when he was discharged from the Queen's service for visiting Sir Robert Floud, then in disgrace.

Daniel was commended by his contemporaries for the purity of his diction—'well-languaged Daniel' he was called by Browne. Others thought that his poetry was pitched in too low an emotional key and that his manner was 'fitter perhaps for prose,' or that he was 'too much historian in verse.' In the early 19th century, Coleridge found him an excellent example of 'that style which, as the neutral ground of prose and verse, is common to both,' and praised highly his language, 'just such as any very pure and manly writer of the present day—Wordsworth, for example—would use.' The annotations in Wordsworth's copy of Daniel, now at Dove Cottage, show that Wordsworth paid him the honor of careful study.

Daniel would undoubtedly have been pleased with the comment that he was an historian in verse, for his settled conviction was that poetic subjects should be found in true history rather than in fictitious tales. Perhaps for him this was a wise choice, for his chief merit is in his meditative reflections on life, which led Coleridge to write to Lamb, 'Thousands of educated men would become more sensible, fitter to be members of Parliament or Ministers, by reading Daniel.'

MODERN EDITIONS: *The Complete Works* (ed. by A. B. Grosart), five volumes, London, 1885–1896; *A Selection from the Poetry of Daniel and Drayton* (ed. by H. C. Beeching), London, 1899.

COMMENT: A. H. Bullen, *Elizabethans*, London, 1924; H. Sellars, 'Samuel Daniel: Additions to the Text' in *M. L. R.*, xi. 28.

TEXT: *Delia and Rosamond augmented*, 1594 (6254), Huntington; *The Whole Works*, 1623 (6238), Cornell; *Certain Small Poems*, 1605 (6239), White; *Tethys' Festival*, 1610 (13161), White.

242 *To the . . . Countess of Pembroke*] first appeared in the edition of 1594, and not reprinted in the definitive edition of 1623, from which we take the text of the other sonnets that we print It seems possible that by 'Delia' Daniel intended his patroness, the Countess of Pembroke, to whom he is paying the conventional compliments. The intimate tone of several of the sonnets makes this ascription doubtful, but one must remember that Daniel was not attempting to give a literal account of their relations and did not wish to speak so clearly that all would recognize his Delia. The river Avon, referred to in the sonnet, 'None other fame,' is not the Warwickshire Avon, but the Wiltshire Avon, which flows near to Wilton, the seat of the Countess of Pembroke.

243 *Why should I sing* 9 If] 1594; 1623 'I'.

244 *But love whilst* 7 thy] 1623 'thy thy'.

245 *Most fair and lovely maid* 9
Stretch] 1594; 1623 'Stretcht'.
247 *An ode*] set to music in John
Farmer's *First Set of English Madrigals,*
1599.
247-261 *The complaint of Rosamond*]
We print 539 of the 910 lines. 4 kind]
sex. 25 Shore's wife] The reference
is probably to Churchyard's *Shore's
Wife,* which appeared in the *Mirror for
Magistrates* of 1563. In 1593, the year
following the first publication of Daniel's *Rosamond,* Anthony Chute published his *Beauty Dishonored, written
under the title of Shore's Wife.* 'Shore's
wife' is Jane Shore, the mistress of
Edward IV. 36 Although] 1623 'Al-
thoug'. 43 Delia] here certainly the
Countess of Pembroke. 136 woman]
1623 'women'. 249 dome] a 16th-cen-
tury spelling of 'doom.' Possibly a play
is intended on 'dome' and 'doom.'
305 Which] 1623 'Whih'. 382 Except]
1623 'Ecept'. 452 a-cross] Daniel probably means 'in the fashion of a cross.'
533 vanished] the reading of the two
editions of 1592; 1594 reads 'vanquished', which reading is retained
by 1623. It is possible that the later
reading is Daniel's own change, but it

seems more probable that it is a printer's error.
251-264 *To the . . . Countess of
Cumberland* 8 wilds] 1623 'weilds'.
89-96] quoted by Wordsworth in *The
Excursion,* bk. iv, ll. 323-331. In a
note on the passage he further quotes
four stanzas, ll. 33-64, which, he says,
give 'an admirable picture of the state
of a wise man's mind in a time of
public commotion.' 90 this] 1623; 1602
'his'. 100 work] 1623 'wotke'.
264-266 *To the . . . Countess of
Bedford*] next to the Countess of Pembroke, the most important patroness of
poetry in late Elizabethan and in Jacobean days. Daniel, Drayton, Jonson,
Donne, and many less well-known men
of letters, were befriended by her.
266-280 *Musophilus*] first appeared
in *Poetical Essays,* 1599, dedicated to
Fulke Greville. We print the first 567
lines, and 30 lines from the closing passage, out of the total 983 lines. 43
better] 1623 'hetter'. 71 Strive] 1623
'Srive'. 118 titlers] those who pretend
or assert a legal title. 231 'fords] affords, supplies from his own resources.
281 unhallowed] 1623 'unhollowed'.
329 wondrous trophy] Stonehenge.
367 became] came. 502 kay] key.

MICHAEL DRAYTON

MICHAEL DRAYTON (1563-1631) is the most representative of the Elizabethan poets, and his work reflects all the changing poetical fashions of his
day. In the 1590's he wrote with the fatal facility of that exuberant time,
piling phrase on phrase and clause on clause. During the reign of James, he
developed a neater, more concise expression, particularly in his odes; and
in the reign of Charles he rivaled the younger Carolines in the lightness
of his touch. He tried all the popular poetic forms—Biblical paraphrase,
pastoral, legend, sonnet, mythological poem, historical narrative, verse letter,
play, ode, and the mock-heroic fairy tale.

Drayton was fortunate in being brought up as a page in the house of Sir
Henry Goodere at Polesworth. Here he was soon fired with enthusiasm for
poetry, perhaps by the ballad singing of John Hewes,

> Which oft at Polesworth by the fire
> Hath made us gravely merry.

With youthful enthusiasm he asked his tutor to make him a poet, and diligently applied himself to study. The training at Polesworth was the whole
of his formal education, for he did not attend either of the universities.
Anne, the younger daughter of Sir Henry Goodere, was much in Drayton's
mind when he commenced writing poetry. She is the 'Idea' of his sonnets,
and the frequent occurrence of 'Idea' in his early titles seems to be a
tribute to her. In 1595 she married Sir Henry Rainsford, but her friendship

with Drayton continued, and each summer he spent a month at her home in the country.

Like Daniel, Drayton was moved by the patriotic enthusiasm of the 1590's to spend much energy on poems of historical narrative. He achieved his greatest success with such material in *England's Heroical Epistles*, 1597, in form modeled on Ovid's *Heroides*. In that year, lack of money forced him to become one of Henslowe's hacks, and between then and 1602 he collaborated on at least twenty-three plays. This was for him a disagreeable task, and he abandoned it as soon as he found a patron in Sir Walter Aston. With leisure he commenced work on his topographical poem, the *Poly-Olbion*, which he had already planned by 1597 as the best means of expressing adequately the glory and beauty of England. The first eighteen songs were completed and published in 1612, and in 1622 he added a second part of twelve songs. During this period, he also wrote a number of shorter poems and revised carefully his earlier ones, printing what may be regarded as a definitive edition in 1619. Then, with the long weary task of the *Poly-Olbion* completed and his early poems satisfactorily revised, his lighter muse sprang to life again in his delightful *Nymphidia* of 1627, and in his charming *Muses' Elysium* of 1630. In his later years, Drayton was looked upon as a leader by the younger Spenserians, and he numbered among his good friends Browne, Wither, Drummond, and Alexander.

Among his contemporaries, Drayton was known for his upright, respectable life. Meres says that 'among scholars, soldiers, poets, and all sorts of people, [he] is held for a man of virtues and well-governed carriage, which is almost miraculous among good wits of this declining and corrupt time.' His solidity of character is reflected in his poetry, which seems to be addressed not only to the brilliant court circle, as with so many poets then, but also to the sound, substantial citizens. Among them, if we may judge from the number of collected editions of Drayton's poetry published during his lifetime, he gained a large audience.

MODERN EDITIONS: *Poems* (ed. by J. P. Collier), London, 1856; *The Complete Works* (ed. by R. Hooper; contains only the *Poly-Olbion* and *The Harmony of the Church*), three volumes, London, 1876; *Selections from the Poems* (ed. by A. H. Bullen), Chilworth, 1883; *The Barons' Wars and other Poems* (ed. by H. Morley), London, 1887; *Poems*, Spenser Society, 1888; *Poems, Lyric and Pastoral*, Spenser Society, 1891; *The Muses' Elisium*, Spenser Society, 1892; *The Battle of Agincourt* (ed. by R. Garnett), London, 1893; *A Selection from the Poetry of Daniel and Drayton* (ed. by H. C. Beeching), London, 1899; *Minor Poems* (ed. by C. Brett), Oxford, 1907; *Endimion and Phœbe* (ed. by J. W. Hebel), Stratford-upon-Avon, 1925.

COMMENT: O. Elton, *Michael Drayton, a Critical Study*, London, 1905.

TEXT: *Idea, the Shepherd's Garland*, 1593 (7202), B. M.; *Idea's Mirror*, 1594 (7203), White; *England's Heroical Epistles*, 1599 (7195), Bodleian; *Poems*, 1619 (7222), Cornell; *Poly-Olbion*, [1612] (7226), Cornell; *The Battle of Agincourt*, 1627 (7190), Adams; *The Muses' Elysium*, 1630 (7210), Cornell.

282 *Idea, the Shepherd's Garland*] a pastoral poem in nine eclogues, inspired by Spenser's *Shepherd's Calendar*.

282–283 *The eighth eclogue* 3 Isenbras] sometimes spelled Isumbras, the hero of the medieval romance, *Sir Isumbras*. 6 Sir Thopas] the hero of a tale told by Chaucer himself in *The Canterbury Tales*. 11 yconned] taught, caused to learn. lere] lore. 15 march-

pine] marchpane, marzipan, an almond confection. 28 Lemster] Leominster. 29 Peakish hull] 1593 'peakish Hull'. It seems most probable that Drayton was thinking of a hill (obsolete spelling, 'hull') in the Peak region in Derbyshire. 33 cetywall] setwall, valerian plant. 34 harlock] unidentified flower; perhaps charlock. 43 leared] guided. 56 loke] lock of wool. 58 bauzens'] badgers'. 59 cockers] casings for the leg; high laced boots or leggings. cordiwin] cordwain, cordovan. 60 meniveere] miniver, a fur used for lining and trimming. 61 lingel] waxed thread. 62 tar-box] used by shepherds to hold tar as a salve for sheep. 63 cointrie] Coventry blue, a thread manufactured in Coventry and frequently used in embroidery. 76 a good] so well. 91 vail] lower. 110 Colin] Spenser, who had paid poetical tribute to Rosalind, as yet unidentified, in his *Shepherd's Calendar.*

284 *Idea's Mirror*] Drayton's sonnets first appeared in this volume. They were frequently reprinted, with omissions and additions, and many variant readings. We have taken his definitive edition of 1619 as the base text for his sonnets, adding from the editions of 1594 and 1599 three sonnets which he omitted in 1619.

284 *To . . . Ma. Anthony Cooke*] to whom Drayton was probably preferred by the Gooderes, Cooke's daughter Margaret having married Sir Ralph Rowlet, a family connection of the Gooderes. Later, Sir John Davies dedicated his *Gulling Sonnets* to Cooke; see p. 332. 11 Portes'] Desportes, a French sonneteer, frequently paraphrased and imitated by the English poets. 14] quoted from Sidney's sonnet, 'I never drank,' p. 116.

286 *To nothing fitter* 2 penny-father] miser, niggard.

287–288. *Our floods' queen*] marginal note: 'To the river Anker'. Polesworth, the home of Anne Goodere, is on the Anker. 4 Avon's] the Avon flowing near the Countess of Pembroke's seat in Wiltshire; frequently mentioned by Daniel.

288 *Some misbelieving* 1] 1594 has an interesting variant reading: 'Some atheist or vile infidel in love'. See Donne's *Love's deity*, l. 22, p. 456.

288–289 *Some men there be* 4 humor] disposition, mood, style.

289 *In pride of wit* 6 circuit] the playhouse, frequently referred to as round.

290 *England's Heroical Epistles*] In the first edition of 1597 there were interchanges of letters between nine pairs of famous lovers. The number was brought up to twenty-four letters between twelve pairs of lovers by additions in the 1598 and 1599 editions. This poem was reprinted thirteen times during Drayton's life and retained its popularity, probably because of the closed couplets, until the middle of the 18th century.

290–296 *Henry Howard . . . to the Lady Geraldine*] This poem helped to popularize the story of Surrey's travels in Italy, first given currency by Nashe's *Unfortunate Traveler*, 1594. See notes to Surrey, p. 1190. 37 flaws] sudden puffs of wind. 54 soul-reviving clime] Florence. 64 By] nearby. 84 riveled] shriveled. 96 lion] Drayton annotates: 'The blazon of the Howards' honorable armor was gules between six crosselets fitchée, a bend argent; to which afterwards was added by achievement, in the canton point of the bend an escutcheon, or within the Scottish tressure, a demi-lion rampant, gules.' 98 Flodden field] where the English, led by the Earl of Surrey (father of the poet), defeated the Scotch in 1513. 110 daded] supported when learning to walk. 145 Stanhope] Drayton annotates: 'Of the beauty of that lady, he himself testifies in an elegy which he writ of her refusing to dance with him, which he seemeth to allegorize under a lion and a wolf.' 153 Bryan] See notes to Wyatt, p. 1188. 226 Æson's spring] Æson, father of Jason, was, according to Ovid, rejuvenated by Medea after the return of the Argonauts.

296 *To the Virginian voyage*] first published in 1606; probably inspired by the preparations for the voyage of 1607.

297 *The crier* 5 Oyes] 'Hear ye'; a call by the public crier or court officer, usually uttered thrice. 11 owe] own.

298–299 *To the Cambro-Britons . . . his ballad of Agincourt* 8 King Harry] Henry V. 50 vaward] vanward. 51 main] main body of troops. 53 Excester] Exeter. 76 weather] atmosphere, air. 97 Gloster] Humphrey, Duke of Gloucester, brother to Henry V, but not senior to Thomas, Duke of Clarence, as Drayton's lines indicate. 113 Saint Crispin's day] October 25, 1415.

299–300 *The ninth eclogue*] Drayton's *Eclogues*, ten in number, first published in 1606, were a revision and expansion of *Idea, the Shepherd's Garland*, 1593. 6 likes] suits, becomes. 45 Batt] 1619 misprints 'Gorbo'.

300 *Poly-Olbion*] Drayton published the first eighteen songs of his 'chorographical description of tracts, rivers, mountains, forests, and other parts of this renowned isle of Great Britain' in 1612. There was a second issue bearing the date 1613. In 1622 he re-issued these eighteen songs and added twelve more.

300–304 *The thirteenth song* 5 bear] marginal note: 'The ancient coat of that kingdom.' 20 Here] 1612 'Her'. 22 gripple] greedy. 58 woosell] ouzel. 62 merle] the European blackbird; marginal note: 'Of all birds, only the blackbird whistleth.' 71 set in parts] compose part-songs. 74 nope] bullfinch. 79 tydie] tidy; possibly the wren or blue titmouse. 80 hecco] woodpecker. 82 greaves] branches. 87 thicks] thickets. 91 rascals] lean, ill-conditioned deer. 100 twiring] peeping, winking; perhaps the shifting play of light in the glades. 128 maund] hand basket. 150 lady's] Anne Goodere's. 156 eleven thousand maids] St. Ursula and the 11,000 virgins were supposed to have been slain by the Huns near Cologne.

304–309 *To . . . Henry Reynolds, Of poets and poesy*] For two of Henry Reynolds's poems, see p. 443. 19 *Pueriles*] *Sententiæ Pueriles*, the Latin text used by the Elizabethan child before beginning the translation of specific authors. 20 Cato] Dionysius Cato's *Disticha de Moribus*, which had been edited by Erasmus, was almost universally used in the early training of the Elizabethan student in translating Latin. 22 Amongst] 1627 'Amonst'. 36 Mantuan] Baptista Spagnuoli Mantuanus, whose *Eclogues* were widely used as a text in the Elizabethan schools. 40 biclift] This is Drayton's form. It is impossible to tell whether he intended 'bi-cliffed' or 'bi-cleft.' Parnassus is often referred to as double-peaked. 42 Elderton] the best known ballad-writer of the 1570's and the 1580's. See p. 1251. 67 Bryan] See notes to Wyatt, p. 1188. 90 Lyly's writing] Euphuism. 151 Sylvester] see p. 207. His translation of Du Bartas's *Semaines*, a lengthy poem on the creation, made the poem more popular in England than it was in France. 174 Menstry] Sir William Alexander of Menstry. Hawthornden] Drummond of Hawthornden. 175 two Beaumonts] Sir John and Francis. 185 set on every post] referring to the habit of advertising books by posting

up the title-pages; cf. Jonson's *To my bookseller*, p. 494. 189 transcription] Because of the unwillingness of some men of birth to become professional writers by printing their poetry, many poems circulated for years in ms. copies, sometimes reaching the publisher only after the author's death. As a professional, Drayton was irked by these amateurs. This passage is possibly aimed at Donne. 200 circuits] playhouses.

309–321 *Nymphidia* 3 Dowsabell] Drayton is referring to his own ballad of Dowsabell in *Idea, the Shepherd's Garland*, see p. 282. 24 Jove] 1627 'Jone'. 55 Mare] a goblin, supposed to produce nightmare by sitting on the chest of the sleeper. 79 auf] oaf. 193 Tuscan poet] Ariosto, author of *Orlando Furioso*. 274 Quishott] Quixote. 276 Pancha] Panza. 305 lin] cease, leave off. 418 lubrican's] leprechaun, a pigmy sprite of Irish folk-lore.

321–323 *The Shepherd's Sirena* 137 Darwin] Derwent.

323 *The Muses' Elysium*] a pastoral poem consisting of an introductory description of Elysium and ten nymphals.

323–324 *The description of Elysium* 53 gyres] spiral turns, whirls. 69 clives] cliffs.

325–330 *The sixth nymphal* 16 tired] adorned with head-dress. 61 lyam's] leash's. 63 gaffle] a steel lever to bend the cross-bow. 70 earning] making prolonged cries. 75 sylvans] 1630 'Sylvians'. 82 matachines] matachins; sword dances in fantastic costumes. 143 weels] wicker traps for catching fish. 146 trammel] long, narrow fishing-net. 200 nine-holes] 'A game in which the players endeavor to roll small balls into nine holes made in the ground.' *O. E. D.* 201 dust-point] 'A boy's game in which "points" were laid in a heap of dust, and thrown at with a stone.' *O. E. D.* 210 chapman] merchant. 222 Whig] variously applied to sour milk, buttermilk, etc. 228 sleave] sleave-silk; silk which can be divided into smaller filaments for use in embroidery. 229 yeanëd] given birth to.

SIR JOHN DAVIES

SIR JOHN DAVIES (1569–1626) was born in Wiltshire and educated at Winchester School and Queen's College, Oxford. In 1588 he became a member of the Middle Temple, London, and there he evidently took advantage of opportunities for association with authors. In 1594 his *Orchestra* was entered in the Stationers' Registers, but the earliest edition bears the date 1596. In this same year, or thereabouts, was published Davies' collection of epigrams, bound with Marlowe's translations from Ovid, under the title *Epigrams and Elegies*. All editions of this book (sometimes called *Ovid's Elegies* or *All Ovid's Elegies*) purport to have been published at Middleburgh (Holland); but this notation was doubtless a printer's ruse in the issuance of a book which quite certainly could not have been licensed. From 1598 until 1601 Davies suffered from disbarment and loss of membership in the Middle Temple, on account of an assault made upon his one-time friend, Richard Martin. During this period he published *Hymns of Astræa*, 1599, a series of acrostic poems praising the Queen, and, in the same year, *Nosce Teipsum*, a long philosophical argument for the soul's immortality, written during retirement at Oxford. After his restoration to the bar he turned from writing poetry and began pushing himself forward in his profession. When King James made him solicitor-general for Ireland, Davies was energetic in discharging the duties of this difficult office. In 1613 he was elected speaker of the Irish Parliament, but was able to assume the chair only after a riot in which he was lifted and placed in the lap of a speaker chosen by the Catholic party. After years of public service, he was appointed Lord Chief Justice of England, but before he could assume office he died of apoplexy after a supper-party.

Besides the poems mentioned, Davies wrote a set of 'gulling sonnets' parodying the sonneteers of the '90's. These were left in manuscript until the 19th century. He also wrote a series of twelve epigrams called *Twelve Wonders of the World*, printed in Davison's *Poetical Rhapsody* of 1608 and again, set to music by John Maynard, in 1611. He is credited with the authorship of verse-translations of several *Psalms* and a number of miscellaneous poems first printed by Grosart, from an anonymous manuscript.

As suggested elsewhere (Introduction to 'Sonnet-Sequences'), Davies' work stands in opposition to the 'sugared' lyrical and erotic poetry which dominated the 1580's and 1590's. He belongs to the order represented also by Chapman, Jonson, Marston, Hall, Ralegh and Greville in their mature phase, and supremely by Donne. Energy and play of intellect, rather than grace and beauty, characterize his best work. In distinction from practically all of his contemporaries, no single lyric, in the strictest sense, is connected with his name. His short poems are epigrams or epigrammatic. Even his 'hymns' to Elizabeth proclaim, by their acrostics, the author's ingenuity. His long poems are essays or treatises in verse. *Nosce Teipsum* is one of the very few permanently readable philosophical poems in English. *Orchestra*, though unfinished, accomplishes its object of treating rhetorically and poetically the subject of dancing, and is not wholly lacking in grace and music consonant with its subject.

MODERN EDITIONS: *The Complete Poems* (ed. by A. B. Grosart), Fuller Worthies' Library, 1869; *Orchestra*, The Stanton Press, 1922; *Nosce Teipsum* and *Orchestra* in *Some Longer Elizabethan Poems* (ed. by A. H. Bullen), Westminster, 1903.

COMMENT: Margarete Seemann, *Sir John Davies, sein Leben und seine Werke*, Leipzig, 1913; E. H. Sneath, *Philosophy in Poetry*, New York, 1913; J. S. Harrison, *Platonism in English Poetry of the 16th and 17th Centuries*, New York, 1915.

TEXT: *Epigrams and Elegies* [*c.* 1595] (6350), Huntington; *Chetham Ms.* 8012, Chetham; *Orchestra*, 1596 (6360), Huntington; *Hymns of Astræa*, 1599 (6351), Huntington; *Nosce Teipsum*, 1599 (6355), Harvard.

331 *Of a gull*] The term 'gull,' as used by Davies and some others, seems | to mean more than 'simpleton' and to refer specifically to the fop or would-

be town-gallant of the period. Dekker's *Gull's Hornbook,* 1609, is the classic treatment of this subject. Davies' character of the gull was imitated and enlarged upon by Guilpin in *Skialetheia,* 1599, and by Rowlands in *The Knave of Clubs,* 1609.

331 *In Ciprium* 1 terse] spruce. 7 lock] a love-lock, trained to fall over the temple. 10 Gascoigne's] White's copy (undated, *c.* 1621?) reads 'George Gascoigne's'.

331 *In Haywodum* 1 Heywood] John Heywood; see p. 11.

332 *In Dacum* 2 silent eloquence] supposed to refer to Daniel's *Complaint of Rosamond* (see p. 251, ll. 128–129); but Daniel was not writing of 'his love's beauty.'

332 *In Titum*] reprinted, with alterations, in almost all 17th-century and 18th-century collections of epigrams. 3 Lord Chancellor's tomb] the elaborate tomb in Westminster Abbey of Sir Christopher Hatton, erected 1592. 4 new water-work] a pumping station built in 1594–95. elephant] then being exhibited in the city as a great curiosity. 6 Counter] a debtors' prison.

332 *In Decium*] directed against Drayton; Jonson, in his conversations with Drummond, mentioned this epigram, connecting it with one of Drayton's sonnets, *To the celestial numbers* (*Amour 8* in *Idea's Mirror*) wherein Drayton adds his mistress to the nine Worthies. 4 Worthy] Huntington copy reads 'woorthly'. 6 a giant for her wit] Jonson said that this refers to a saying of Dametas in Sidney's *Arcadia,* 'For wit his mistress might be a giant.' No such saying, however, is in any printed version of the *Arcadia.*

332–333 *To . . . Sir Anthony Cooke*] This is prefatory to the *Gulling sonnets* which follow; signed 'J. D.' in the manuscript. For Cooke, see Drayton's sonnet, p. 284, and note. 3 antic] clown. 7 whisking] rapid, quickly changing.

333 *Gulling sonnets*] The entire series in the ms. consists of nine sonnets; signed 'Mr. Davyes' at the end.

333–334 *The sacred muse* 8 points] tagged laces holding together doublet and hose. 9 hose] not stockings, but breeches or trunks. codpiece] 'a bagged appendage to the front of the close-fitting hose or breeches worn by men from the 15th to the 17th century.' *O. E. D.* 12 pantofles] in view of the 'pumps' of the next line, here perhaps overshoes.

334 *My case is this*] See *Zepheria*

(p. 218) and note. 11 shrieve] sheriff; ms. reads 'sheife'. 12 esloigned] usually 'eloigned'; removed out of the jurisdiction of the court or of the sheriff. 14 withernam] legal term representing the medieval Latin *vetitum nanium,* illegal or forbidden distraint; 'in an action of replevin, the reprisal of other goods in lieu of those taken by a first distress and eloigned.' *O. E. D.*

334–356 *Orchestra*] The title-page of the collected poems of 1622 lists *Orchestra* as 'not finished'. 1–2] Jonson told Drummond that 'a gentleman reading a poem that began with,

Where is that man that never yet did hear
Of fair Penelope, Ulysses' queen,

calling his cook asked if he had ever heard of her; who, answering "no," demonstrate[d] to him,

Lo, there the man that never yet did hear
Of fair Penelope, Ulysses' queen.'

46 Tethys] sea-goddess, wife of Oceanus. 270 leman's] mistress'. 325 tralucent] transparent. 340–347] cf. Coleridge, *Rime of the Ancient Mariner,* ll. 414–421. 353–355] The doctrines of Copernicus, though advanced in 1543, had not yet gained general acceptance. 370 wringling] writhing. 394 Jump] exactly. 437 wries] twists. 491 victorious twins] Castor and Pollux. 500 imply] interweave. 530 prince of Crete] Zeus was supposed to have been hidden in a cave in Crete by his mother, to avoid the voracity of his father. 548 Linus] son of Apollo and Terpsichore, who instructed Orpheus and Hercules. 549–550 he . . . tongue] Hercules. 568 Cæneus] daughter of Elatus, turned into a boy by Neptune; Ovid, *Met.* xii. 575 Tiresias] a blind soothsayer who was metamorphosed into a woman when he killed a female snake; seven years later, upon killing a male snake, he again became a man. 635–637 wise Thessalians . . . governance] the word *coryphæus* was applied to the leader in a *choragus* (dramatic chorus) and also to a civic official. 687–693] The references in this stanza are to the classical stories of Medea and Thyestes. 698 Tereus' mad wife] Procne, sister of Philomela; the son was Itys. 703 dolphins] 1596 'Dilphins'. 883–917] omitted in 1622; new stanzas were substituted. 892 man of Mantua's] Virgil's. 894 Geoffrey's] Chaucer's. 895 Colin's] Spenser's. 896 Delia's serv-

ant's] Daniel's. 897–98] Grosart suggests Guilpin (see p. 523), but his *Skialetheia, or a Shadow of Truth* did not appear until 1599; Chapman, whose *Shadow of Night* appeared in 1594, seems better to fit Davies' description. 899 fair Salve's sad lover] not identified. 900–901] Grosart suggests Charles Best, who contributed to Davison's *Poetical Rhapsody*, 1608, *A sonnet of the sun*, 'a jewel, being a sun shining upon the marigold closed in a heart of gold, sent to his mistress named Mary.' This identification does not explain why the poet should be called 'the bay.' 904 Astrophel] Sidney. 907–910] Grosart writes: 'Perhaps a play on his (then) friend's name of Martin.' The reference to Idæas suggests Drayton, but the personal relation revealed in the next stanza strengthens Grosart's identification.

356 *Hymns of Astræa*] All of the twenty-six poems of this volume are acrostics upon the words 'Elisabetha Regina.' Astræa was the mythical goddess of justice, who wandered upon earth during the Golden Age but later returned to heaven.

357–362 *Of human knowledge*] This poem serves as an introduction or a preface to the entire work of *Nosce Teipsum*. 43 rude satyr] See Dyer's *Prometheus when first from heaven*, p. 124. 46 Jove's guest] Ixion. 50 the youth] Phaethon. 51 boy's] Icarus'. 77 wisest] Socrates. 79 mocking master] Democritus, Fragment 117. 113 lady fair] Io. 142 threat] 1608; 1599 'thereat'. 153] Davies refers to his disbarment.

362 *That the soul is immortal . . .*] one of the many sub-sections of *Nosce Teipsum*.

363 *An acclamation*] The conclusion of the work.

JOSEPH HALL

JOSEPH HALL (1574–1656), Bishop of Norwich, wrote the satires which give him a place in English poetry as a young man, before he had taken holy orders. He was educated at Emmanuel College, Cambridge, where he took the degree of B. A. in 1592 and that of M. A. in 1596. He added the degrees of B. D. (1603) and D. D. (1612). His satires appeared in two parts: *Virgidemiarum . . . first three books of Toothless Satires* bore the date 1597, to be augmented in the following year by *Three last books of Biting Satires*. In the Prologue to the first part Hall wrote:

I first adventure, with foolhardy might,
To tread the steps of perilous despite.
I first adventure,—follow me who list
And be the second English satirist.

His bold claim was not well founded, for Wyatt, Gascoigne, Hake, and Lodge (not to mention Barclay and Skelton) had preceded him as English satirists; and some of Donne's satires were in manuscript. Hall perhaps hoped to build up a reputation solely for satire, and to be his country's Juvenal or Persius.

Virgidemiarum, itself possibly a contribution to the Harvey-Nashe controversy, was followed by an outburst of satirical writing in verse. In an order of June 1, 1599, Archbishop Whitgift directed that all copies of Hall's and Marston's satires, and of *Epigrams and Elegies* by Marlowe and Davies, should be burned; and that no more satires or epigrams should be printed. The suppression called for by this order did not prevail, however, for long. Edward Guilpin's *Skialetheia*, 1599, contained both epigrams and satires; and the list of satirists continued to grow steadily, adding the names of Samuel Rowlands, John Weever, Henry Parrot, Robert Anton, John Taylor, Robert Braithwaite, and others.

Hall's many theological works, published from 1605 forward, need not here be dwelt upon. He became, late in life, a controversial antagonist to Milton. His satires have had readers in every generation since his time. They are spirited, concise, and witty. Among writers of satire before Dryden, Hall stands with Donne as pre-eminent in the qualities which distinguish that form.

MODERN EDITIONS: *Die Satiren Halls* (ed. by K. Schulze), Berlin, 1910; *Virgidemiarum*, Edinburgh, 1824; *Satires by Joseph Hall* (ed. by T. Warton and S. W. Singer), Chiswick, 1824.

COMMENT: R. M. Alden, *The Rise of Formal Satire*, Philadelphia, 1899; Sandford M. Salyer, 'Hall's Satires and the Harvey-Nashe Controversy,' *S. P.* xxv. 149; E. A. Beckwith, 'On the Hall-Marston Controversy,' *J. E. G. P.* xxv. 84.

TEXT: *Virgidemiarum*, 1597 (12716), Harvard.

364–365 *Satire I* 4 Mahound . . . Termagaunt] common in romances of chivalry; Termagaunt, or Trivigante, was a Saracen female divinity, sometimes represented in old religious plays as a fierce and violent character. 6 blowess] a blowzy wench. 13 trencher-poetry] poetry written in the hope of food or entertainment from a patron. 23 albe] albeit. 27–32] No Muse, he says, will stay by the Granta (or Cam) since Spenser had attracted all the Muses to the Thames and Medway by his account of the wedding of those streams (*Fairy Queen*, IV. xi).

365 *Satire VI*] attacks the English writers of hexameters. See Introduction to Richard Stanyhurst. 5 Manhood and garboils] Stanyhurst wrote (*First book*, 5) 'Manhood and *garbroyls* I chaunt'. 13 areed] divine, determine.

besets] accords with. 16 Thwick thwack, and riff raff] quoted from a translation by Stanyhurst of a passage from the eighth book of the *Æneid*, published with his completed four books, thus (modernized):

Now do they raise ghastly lightnings, now grisly reboundings
Of ruff raff roaring, men's hearts with terror agrising,
With pell mell ramping, with thwick thwack sturdily thund'ring.

Thomas Nashe in his preface to Greene's *Menaphon*, 1589, parodied two of these lines, as follows:

Then did he make heaven's vault to rebound with rounce hobble hobble
Of ruff raff roaring, with thwick thwack thurley bouncing.

JOHN MARSTON

JOHN MARSTON (*c.* 1575–1634), like Joseph Hall, turned to the ministry after having entered upon a career as author. Little is known of his life previous to 1598, when he seems to have been stimulated to publication by the appearance of Hall's *Virgidemiarum*. His *Pygmalion's Image* of that year is an erotic poem of the fashion set by *Venus and Adonis* and *Hero and Leander*; though in his next book Marston claimed that he intended a burlesque of the fashion. With *Pygmalion's Image* he printed five satires which seem to have been hastily written in order to take advantage of the 'rising market' for such wares. In the same year he published *The Scourge of Villainy*, more carefully (and more maliciously) written than its predecessor; in 1599 it was republished with additions. Both of Marston's books, however, fell under Archbishop Whitgift's ban upon satires (June 1, 1599), and were suppressed. The author then devoted himself to writing for the stage. His quarrel with Jonson was the basis of the *poetomachia* of 1599–1601; later he and Jonson became reconciled. Just when Marston took holy orders is not known, but he held a country living in Hampshire from 1616 to 1631.

Marston's satires are obscure to modern readers, but his crabbed and bitter spirit is always apparent. He provides an excellent criticism of his own work, in the line, 'I am myself, so is my poesy.' A long manuscript poem (B. M. *Add. Mss.* 14824, 14825, 14826), *The New Metamorphosis* by J. M., Gent., sometimes is assigned to Marston; but J. H. H. Lyon (*A Study of The Newe Metamorphosis*, 1919) assigns it to Gervase (or Jervase) Markham.

MODERN EDITIONS: *The Works* (ed. by A. H. Bullen), three volumes, London, 1887; *The Scourge of Villanie* (ed. by G. B. Harrison), London, 1925.

COMMENT: Morse S. Allen, *The Satire of John Marston,* Columbus (Ohio), 1920.

TEXT: *The Scourge of Villainy,* 1598 (17485), Huntington; *The Dutch Courtezan,* 1605 (17475), White.

367–368 *Humors*] Jonson's first 'comedy of humors,' *Every Man in His Humor,* was probably the play of the moment when Marston wrote. The holding up to ridicule of humors (which may be interpreted here as more or less affected inclinations, caprices, or fads) appears both in dramatic and non-dramatic poetry for several years following the date of Marston's book. 1–8] The parallel between these lines and the opening of Milton's *L'Allegro* has been several times noted; cf. *P.M.L.A.,* xliii. 569. 24 capreal] capriole, caper. 27 *Orchestra*] the next

six lines satirize Davies' poem. 31 Kemp's jig] Will Kemp, popular comedian, danced from London to Norwich in nine days. 39 H'hath] 1598 reads 'H'ath'. 41 Curtain] the Curtain theater. plaudities] appeals for applause at the end of plays; epilogues. 49 gerning] grinning. 55 engrossëd] set down and memorized.

368–369 *To everlasting Oblivion*] This poem stands at the end of the book. It is said that on Marston's tomb in the Temple Church, London, was engraved *Oblivioni sacrum,* 'Consecrated to oblivion.'

GEORGE CHAPMAN

GEORGE CHAPMAN (1559?–1634), although a writer of unusual learning, appears never to have taken a university degree. His career as poet began with Σκιὰ νυκτός, *the Shadow of Night,* 1594, to be followed by *Ovid's Banquet of Sense,* 1595, with which he included his short sonnet-sequence, *A Coronet for his Mistress Philosophy.* In 1598 was printed *Hero and Leander,* made complete by Chapman's four sestiads added to Marlowe's two. In the same year Chapman published *Seven Books of the Iliads,* the first instalment of his translation of Homer. By 1616 he had seen through the press his completed *Iliad* and *Odyssey;* and in 1624 he added the *Batrachomyomachia* and the Homeric hymns and epigrams. From about 1595 forward he wrote for the stage, with notable success; Jonson praised his masks, of which only one is extant. Tradition describes Chapman as a man of great personal dignity, temperate and religious, an account to which his works lend credence. In learning he stands next to Jonson in his poetic generation; yet neither his learning nor his continuous labors for press and stage preserved him from the bane of poets, poverty.

The tributes of Lamb and Keats have kept his *Homer* in the eye of modern readers. In this work Chapman took the liberty of adding epithets, phrases, and whole lines; and so infused the whole with the spirit of his time that Coleridge pronounced it as truly an original poem as *The Fairy Queen.* Some critics have considered the 'fourteener' couplets of his *Iliad* a better medium for Chapman's vigorous translation than the rhymed pentameters of his *Odyssey.* Schoell has shown how closely Chapman followed as a pattern the monumental edition (1583) of Homer, with Latin translation, by Jean de Sponde (Spondanus). Throughout his work, and notably in his own poems apart from translations, Chapman manifests a 'high seriousness' which commands respect even when the reader is repelled by obscure and unmusical verse.

MODERN EDITIONS: *Poems and Minor Translations* (introduction by A. C. Swinburne), London, 1875; *Homer's Iliad and Odyssey* (ed. by R. H. Shepherd), London, 1903; *The Iliads of Homer* (ed. by R. Hooper) 3rd edition, London, 1898; *The Odysseys of Homer* (ed. by R. Hooper) 2nd edition, London, 1897.

COMMENT: F. L. Schoell, *Études sur l'Humanisme Continental en Angleterre*, Paris, 1926; Alfred Lohff, *George Chapman*, Berlin, 1903.

TEXT: Σκιὰ νυκτός, *the Shadow of Night*, 1594 (4990), White; *Ovid's Banquet of Sense*, 1595 (4985), White; *The Memorable Mask of the Middle Temple and Lincoln's Inn*, 1613 (4981), White; *The Whole Works of Homer*, [1616] (13624), White; *Homer's Odysseys* [1614?] (13636), White.

369–370 *Hymnus in Noctem*] We give the ending of the poem, which with another, *Hymnus in Cynthiam*, fills the volume. 8 humor] mood, or spirit; Chapman's verb 'steeped' calls for the older meaning of this word as the fluid determining the temperament of a body. 11 glassy strumpet's] Judging from other references in Chapman (see his *Descend, fair sun*, p. 371), Tethys, wife of Oceanus, seems intended. 12 Themis' daughters] Chapman's note, 1594: 'Themis' daughters are the three hours —*viz.*, Dice, Irene, and Eunomia, begotten by Jupiter. They are said to make ready the horse and chariot of the Sun every morning. . . .' 15 bride of brides] Night. 19 Cyprian star] Venus.

21 she] Night. 25 Is] 1594 'In'. Hyperion's . . . daughter] Diana, the moon.

370 *A coronet . . .*] This is the title of a series of ten sonnets, of which the one here given is the first. 7 dying figures] material bodies.

371–374 *Iliad, Book XVIII* 1 he] Vulcan, who has consented to make a shield for Achilles, at the request of Thetis, Achilles' mother. 2 Apposed] applied. 37 queen of martials] Athena. 48 neat] cattle. 53 well-piled] well-pointed. 60 new-eared] newly plowed. 61 Larged] spacious, broad. 83 quickset] a hedge.

374 *Odyssey, Book XII* 2 spleenless] not angry, favorable.

EDWARD FAIRFAX

EDWARD FAIRFAX (d. 1635) stands in the front rank of Elizabethan translators. Little is known of his life previous to the appearance of his *magnum opus, Godfrey of Bulloigne, or the Recovery of Jerusalem*, 1600. This was the first complete translation from the Italian of Torquato Tasso's *Gerusalemme Liberata*, 1581, usually known in English as 'Jerusalem Delivered.' Fairfax also wrote twelve eclogues, most of which are lost. He spent his years largely in study and retirement in his native county of Yorkshire.

Ben Jonson stands almost alone in calling Fairfax's work 'not well done.' Henry Morley points out that Fairfax could not reproduce the simplicity of his original, but 'translated into English verse after the manner of his own vigorous time, adorning, as he went, with interwoven figures of speech and bits of classical mythology.' This license perhaps offended Jonson. But Fairfax's rich vocabulary, smooth versification, and thoroughly Elizabethan spirit united to make his work a landmark in translation. 'Many beside myself,' wrote John Dryden, 'have heard our famous Waller own that he derived the harmony of his number from *Godfrey of Bulloigne*, which was turned into English by Mr. Fairfax.' Fairfax learned much from Spenser, who had been an appreciative reader of Fairfax's original, the poem of Tasso.

MODERN EDITIONS: *Jerusalem Delivered . . . translated by Edward Fairfax* (ed. by Henry Morley), New York, 1901; 'Fairfax Eighth Eclogue' (ed. by W. W. Greg), *M. L. Q.* iv. 85.

TEXT: *Godfrey of Bulloigne*, 1600 (23698), Huntington.

375-377 *Book XVI*] Spenser drew upon this portion of Tasso's poem for a number of passages in the Second Book of *The Fairy Queen*, Canto xii; compare stanzas 59, 60, 50, 51 of that canto with ll. 1–24 of the present excerpt, stanza 71 with ll. 25–32, and stanzas 74–76 with ll. 41–64. 36 leden] singing, warbling. 57 He . . . he] so in all issues of 1600, and in the second edition of 1624; the sense seems to demand 'she.'

SONGS FROM PLAYS

'THE LYRICAL tradition is an unbroken one,' writes Edward Bliss Reed of song in drama, 'from the tenth century trope, *Quem quæritis*, to the songs of Shakespeare, of Dryden, and of Sheridan.' In the amazing development of the drama in 16th-century England this kind of lyricism gained proportionately; and the more so because of the circumstances that many plays were written for presentation by choir-boys and that boy-actors who took women's parts were often trained singers. In addition to the wealth of extant songs, many others are called for by stage directions but are missing from manuscript or printed texts of the plays. From George Peele's *Famous Chronicle of King Edward I*, printed in 1593, seven songs are omitted. Thirteen songs are indicated in stage directions of John Marston's *Antonio's Revenge* and *Antonio and Mellida, Part I*, but printed versions preserve none of them. Although we usually give credit to the dramatist of the play for lyrics contained in it, known cases of interpolating another poet's song suggest that many of the songs may have been owed to others. This fact may account for the omission of song-texts from printed plays.

The number of songs, if any, in a play varied from one to a dozen. All the singing sometimes was assigned to a single character, doubtless played by an actor chosen for his voice. Seldom do we find more than three characters having songs to sing, though there are many which call for two or three voices; the song in dialogue is not uncommon.

A few excellent lyrists of our period, as Fletcher, Dekker, and Peele, wrote almost no poems except for use in dramatic performances. A golden book of songs could be compiled from Fletcher's plays alone; Nashe's best poetry lies in the one play of *Summer's Last Will and Testament*; James Shirley is now most widely known for a single song used in one of his plays; and Jonson's lyrical talent seems to have been developed in writing songs for plays and masks. Shakespeare wrote for his plays a half-dozen of the world's best lyrics.

Some of the songs given in this group are taken from masks or pageant-like entertainments given to honor royalty or nobility. The number of masks presented grew under James and Charles; and since shows of this kind depended much upon the musical element, poets were spurred to the writing of songs.

CROSS REFERENCES: For poems, not in this section, which appeared as songs in plays and masks, see: Gascoigne, *Deep Desire sung this song;* Greville, *Chorus sacerdotum;* Mary Herbert, *Chorus;* Breton, *Phillida and Coridon;* Daniel, *Love is a sickness, Are they shadows;* Marston, *O love, how strangely sweet;* Chapman, *Descend, fair sun, Now, sleep, bind fast;* Campion, *Night as well as brightest day;* Jonson, pp. 514–520; Thomas Heywood, *Song* 'With fair Ceres', *Come, list, and hark, Pack, clouds, away, Song* 'Hence with passion'; Randolph, *Slaves are they;* Cartwright, *The song;* Suckling, *Song* 'Why so pale,' *Song* 'No, no, fair heretic,' *A Song to a lute;* Habington, *His mistress flouted;* Davenant, *Night's first song, The philosopher and the lover, Song;* Denham, *Somnus, the humble God.*

MODERN EDITIONS: *Lyrics from the Dramatists of the Elizabethan Age* (ed. by A. H. Bullen), London, 1892; *Songs from the British Drama* (ed. by E. B. Reed), New Haven, 1925.

COMMENT: R. S. H. Noble, *Shakespeare's Use of Song*, London, 1923.

TEXT: *King John*, text from Bang's facsimile; *Lusty Juventus* [*c.* 1560] (25147), Huntington; *Gammer Gurton's Needle*, 1575 (23263), White; *Tom Tyler and his Wife*, 1661, text from Farmer, *Tudor Facsimile Text*, 1912; *Misogonus*, text from Bond; *Comedy of Patient and Meek Grissell*, [*c.* 1566] (19865), Yale; *Horestes*, 1567 (19917), B. M.; *Trial of Treasure*, 1567 (24271), White; *Marriage of Wit and Science*, [*c.* 1570], text from Farmer, *Tudor Facsimile Text*, 1909; *Common Conditions*, [*c.* 1576] (5592), Yale; *Fedele and Fortunio*, 1585 (19447), Huntington; *Six Court Comedies*, 1632 (17088), Harvard; *Arraignment of Paris*, 1584 (19530), Huntington; *Polyhymnia*, 1590 (19546), Huntington; *Hunting of Cupid*, not extant, text from *Collections*, Malone Society, 1911, and *England's Helicon*; *Old Wive's Tale*, 1595 (19545), Huntington; *Love of King David and Fair Bethsabe*, 1599 (19540), White; *Lamentable Tragedy of Locrine*, 1595, text from Farmer, *Tudor Facsimile Text*, 1911; *Maid's Metamorphosis*, 1600 (17188), White; *Wily Beguiled*, 1606 (25818), Huntington; *Thracian Wonder*, 1661, Huntington; *Summer's Last Will and Testament*, 1600 (18376), White; *Shoemaker's Holiday*, 1600 (6523), White; *Pleasant Comedy of Patient Grissil*, 1603 (6518), White; *London's Tempe*, [1629] (6509), Huntington; *Sun's Darling*, 1656, Harvard; *White Devil*, 1612 (25178), White; *Duchess of Malfi*, 1623 (25176), White; *Knight of the Burning Pestle*, 1613 (1674), White; *Maid's Tragedy*, 1619 (1676), White; *Maid's Tragedy*, 1622 (1678), White; *Faithful Shepherdess*, [*c.* 1610] (11068), White; *Bloody Brother*, 1639 (11064), Huntington; *Comedies and Tragedies*, 1647, White; *Comedies, Histories, and Tragedies*, 1623 (22273), Princeton; *Chaste Maid in Cheapside*, 1630 (17877), Huntington; *The Widow*, 1652, B. M.; *More Dissemblers Besides Women*, 1657, Harvard; *Emperor of the East*, 1632 (17636), White; *Amends for Ladies*, 1618 (10851), Huntington; *Technogamia*, 1618 (13617), White; *Rival Friends*, 1632 (12935), Adams; *Broken Heart*, 1633 (11156), Huntington; *Fuimus Troes*, 1633 (10886), Harvard; *Tragedy of Orestes*, 1633 (11982), Huntington; *Vow Breaker*, 1636 (21688), Huntington; *Adrasta*, 1635 (14721), Adams; *Tragedy of Cleopatra*, 1639 (17717), White; *Old Couple*, 1658, Harvard; *Hannibal and Scipio*, 1637 (18341), Harvard; *Triumph of Peace*, 1633 (22459), Huntington; *Triumph of Beauty*, 1646, Harvard; *Cupid and Death*, 1653, B. M.; *Contention of Ajax and Ulysses*, 1659, Harvard; *Martyred Soldier*, 1638 (22435), Huntington; *Northern Lass*, 1632 (3819), Huntington; *Jovial Crew*, 1652, White; *Lost Lady*, 1639 (1903), Harvard; *Swaggering Damsel*, 1640 (4946), Huntington; *King John and Matilda*, 1655, Harvard.

377 *King John*] John Bale (1495–1563), Bishop of Ossory, besides plays wrote *Illustrium Majoris Britanniæ Scriptorum Summarium*, 1548, the earliest history of English literature. For Googe's tribute to Bale, see p. 74.

377 *Wassail, wassail*] Text from W. Bang's facsimile of *Devonshire Ms., Materialen zur Kunde des älteren Englischen Dramas*, 1909. 4 rail] a small wading bird.

377–378 *In a herber green*] This song opens the interlude, preceded only by the prologue. 1 herber] arbor. 9 pight] determined.

378 *Gammer Gurton's Needle*] Though not published until 1575, this play was acted at Cambridge before 1560 and licensed for publication in 1563. The title-page attributes it to 'Mr. S., Mr. of Art'; modern research has practically established that the author was William Stevenson, a fellow

of Christ's College 1551–54 and 1559–61, twice mentioned in the records of the college as author of a play.

378 *Back and side, go bare*] Dyce printed (in his edition of Skelton, 1843) from ms. a longer version of this song. The age of the ms., taken with the variants found therein, suggests that the author of *Gammer Gurton's Needle* may here have used a song already current. 17 nutbrown toast] Browned bread was frequently dipped or floated in beverages. 19 crab] crab-apple. 30 troll] circulate, pass around.

378 *Tom Tyler and His Wife*] An interlude of unknown authorship, referred to as about one hundred years old when printed in 1661.

379 *Misogonus*] of unknown authorship; text from R. W. Bond's *Early Plays from the Italian*, 1911.

379–380 *A song to the tune . . .* 5 snudges] sneaking fellows; sometimes, misers. 38 haking] loitering, wandering about.

380 *Comedy of Patient and Meek Grissell*] undated, but printed by Thomas Colwell whose press ran from 1562 to 1571.

380 *Lulla by baby* 5 I fancy thee, I] so in original; 'I fancy thee aye', adopted by some modern editors, seems a less likely reading.

380–381 *Farewell, adieu* 9 cheats] booty.

382 *Lustily, lustily*] preceded by the stage direction, 'here ent'reth the mariners with a song.'

383 *Fedele and Fortunio*] translated from the Italian of Luigi Pasqualigo, and doubtfully attributed to Anthony Munday.

383 *Six Court Comedies*] John Lyly (*c.* 1554–1606), popular author of *Euphues* (1578) and of court comedies, probably did not write the excellent songs printed with his plays. Twenty-one of these songs first appeared in the collected edition of 1632, having been omitted from editions published during Lyly's lifetime. One song, *What bird so sings*, was included in an altered form in Ford and Dekker's *The Sun's Darling*, and though this play was not printed until 1656, J. R. Moore ('The Songs in Lyly's Plays,' *P.M.L.A.* xlii. 623) argues that the song was 'an original part' of it when acted in 1624. *Oh, for a bowl of fat Canary* (a song in *Alexander and Campaspe*) was printed in Middleton's *A Mad World, My Masters* (1640, acted 1608). It seems quite possible that Blount, the printer of 1632, who set up his text from the songless quartos, engaged some one to write songs which he inserted as called for by stage directions. Greg ('The Authorship of the Songs in Lyly's Plays,' *M.L.R.* i. 43) would attribute some or all to Dekker. In this connection compare *A song in making of the arrows* with Dekker's 'Brave iron! brave hammer!' (p. 392). Ward, following J. T. Looney, suggests that Lyly's patron and employer, the Earl of Oxford, wrote these songs, but the suggestion hardly seems credible when they are compared with Oxford's known work. For a defence of Lyly's authorship, see W. J. Lawrence, 'The Problem of Lyly's Songs,' *T. L. S.*, December 20, 1923.

384 *A song in making . . . 2* Lemnian] Vulcan's forge was supposed to be on the isle of Lemnos.

384 *Arraignment of Paris*] George Peele (*c.* 1558–*c.* 1597), author of six songs here given, was one of the 'University Wits,' having taken at Oxford the degree of B.A. in 1577 and that of M.A. in 1579. *The Arraignment of Paris* evidently was produced as early as 1581, played 'before the Queen's Majesty by the Children of her Chapel.'

385 *Polyhymnia*] This book consists for the most part of an account, in blank verse, of a tournament held before Queen Elizabeth; Sir Henry Lee (1530–1610) had made, in 1559, a vow of chivalry to maintain Elizabeth's honor against all challengers, and each year on her birthday he held a tournament. In 1590, finding himself too old to engage in the tilting, Sir Henry caused to be sung, at the end of the tournament, the present song, written by Peele for the occasion.

385 *The Hunting of Cupid*] This play of Peele's is lost, except for some fragments preserved by Drummond of Hawthornden in a commonplace-book. The play was licensed to be acted in 1591. Our text of the first song is from the Malone Society's *Collections, Parts IV and V*, 1911.

386 *Coridon and Melampus' song*] This song, which on the evidence of Drummond's manuscript we know to have been sung in *The Hunting of Cupid*, was printed in *England's Helicon*, 1600, whence we have reprinted it.

386 *Hot sun, cool fire*] sung by Bethsabe at the beginning of the play, as she bathes.

388 *The Thracian Wonder*] published as by John Webster and William Rowley, but their authorship has not been accepted. The story of the play follows that of Greene's *Menaphon*, 1589.

388 *Summer's Last Will and Testament*] Thomas Nashe (1567–1601) made the deepest impression upon his generation by his satirical prose pamphlets. The son of a minister, he took the degree of B.A. at Cambridge in 1586; by 1588 he was in London as one of the 'University Wits' who wrote for stage and press. His pamphlets directed against the Puritan authors of the Marprelate tracts and those against Gabriel Harvey made for him a lasting reputation. Dekker, in his *News from Hell* (1606) said that Nashe 'made the doctor [Harvey] a flat dunce, and beat him at his two sundry tall weapons, poetry and oratory.' In his picaresque tale, *The Unfortunate Traveler*, 1594, he included three poems represented as having been written by Surrey to Geraldine. He left in ms. an erotic poem, *The Choice of Valentines*.

388–389 *Adieu, farewell earth's bliss*] apparently written during a period when the plague raged; theaters were closed on account of the plague in the autumn of 1592, and again from early in 1593 until the summer of 1594.

390 *Autumn hath all* 2 Croydon's] a suburb of London. 10 want of term] Term-time, when the courts were sitting, brought throngs of people to London.

390 *Shoemaker's Holiday*] Thomas Dekker (*c.* 1570–*c.* 1632) was a prolific playwright and miscellaneous writer of the literary generation immediately following that of the 'University Wits.' He was several times imprisoned for debt, once for a term of three years. His long poem, *Canaan's Calamity, Jerusalem's Misery*, 1598, enjoyed some popularity. Some of his prose pamphlets, as *The Bellman of London*, 1608, and *The Gull's Hornbook*, 1609, are always readable; but his best works are his comedies. The songs in his plays reveal a genuine, though not rich, lyrical vein. For other songs possibly by Dekker, see those selected from Lyly's *Six Court Comedies* (pp. 383–384).

392 *Brave iron! brave hammer!* 28 sparrowbills] sparables, nails for shoes.

393 *White Devil*] John Webster (*c.* 1580–1634?), son of a London tailor and for a time himself an apprentice tailor, won a place near Shakespeare as a writer of tragedies. In non-dramatic poetry his principal compositions are a poem in honor of the accession of James and one mourning the death of Prince Henry.

394 *Knight of the Burning Pestle*] The authorship of songs in the plays written in collaboration is of course uncertain. Because of the numerous and excellent songs in plays written by Fletcher alone, readers are inclined to assign to him the songs which appear in plays written with Beaumont.

395 *Faithful Shepherdess*] In the assigning of plays to Fletcher we follow E. H. C. Oliphant, *The Plays of Beaumont and Fletcher*, New Haven, 1927. John Fletcher (1579–1625) was a son of Richard Fletcher, Bishop of London, nephew of Giles Fletcher (the elder), and hence cousin of Phineas and Giles Fletcher. His collaboration with Beaumont began about 1607 and ceased with Beaumont's death in 1616. He also collaborated with Shakespeare, Massinger,

and others. He was notably successful in the composition of lyrics, but appears to have written practically no poetry apart from that in his plays.

395–396 *The drinking song* 7 tisic] phthisic, consumption.

396 *Take, oh, take*] The first stanza of this song was sung in the fourth act of Shakespeare's *Measure for Measure*, and was printed as part of that play in the folio edition of 1623. There is no reason for supposing the first stanza not to be Shakespeare's, but Fletcher may have added the second stanza.

396 *Care-charming Sleep*] The text of this song, corrupt in 1647, has been corrected by the edition of 1679. 2 thyself] 1647 'thy life'. 5 his] 1647 'her'. sweet] Bullen emends to 'light' for the sake of the rhyme. 7 sing] 1647 'sings'. 9 prince] omitted in 1647.

396 *God Lyæus* 1 Lyæus] Bacchus; printed 'Lizus' in 1647, corrected in 1679.

397 *Cast our caps* 15 officers] 1679; 1647 'offices'. 16 by] of uncertain reference; perhaps 'by and by'; or the beginning of an unfinished oath, in which case it should be printed 'by—'. 18 cessed] taxed.

397 *Hence, all you vain*] supposed to have given suggestions to Milton for *Il Penseroso*.

398 *Let the bells ring* 19 enow] 1679 'enough'.

399 *Orpheus with his lute*] Because of Fletcher's large share in the writing of *King Henry VIII*, taken with the fact that in style this song does not particularly suggest Shakespeare, the poem may be doubtfully ascribed to Fletcher.

399–400 *Come, my dainty doxies* 1 doxies] wenches, sweethearts, in gipsy cant; 'dells' in the next line is an equivalent.

401 *Technogamia*] Barten Holiday became a prominent divine, and published a number of his sermons. His play was an academic allegory written for presentation by students; after it was acted at Oxford, the students insisted upon presenting it before King James when he was at Woodstock on a progress in 1618. Wood records that because it was 'too grave for the King and too scholar-like for the auditory (or, as some say, that the actors had too much wine before), his Majesty after two acts offered several times to withdraw.' He was persuaded to stay, 'much against his will.' James, an enemy of tobacco, may have been offended by the song here reprinted.

401 *Tobacco's a musician* 41 whiffler] mace-bearer, an officer who precedes a dignitary; by a derived meaning, a bully. 44 visor] Taking this word in the ordinary sense raises difficulties; perhaps it should be read as 'vizier,' i. e., 'he is the vizier that does drink [smoke], and tobacco is the whiffler that goes before him.' Nichols (*Progresses, James I*, iv. 714) reads 'wiser'.

404 *Tragedy of Orestes*] Thomas Goffe, or Gough (1591–1629), a divine with considerable reputation as scholar and orator, achieved success in his profession while a bachelor; he married a widow with several children, though warned by a friend, Thomas Thimble, that marriage would be the death of him. Within a comparatively short time he was brought to his death-bed, where he is said to have murmured, 'Oracle, oracle, Tom Thimble!'

404 *Vow Breaker*] William Sampson left a considerable body of poetry in ms. See J. F. Godfrey, *William Sampson, a Seventeenth Century Poet and Dramatist*, London, 1894.

404 *Tragedy of Cleopatra*] Thomas May (1595–1650), best known as translator and continuer of Lucan's *Pharsalia*, achieved considerable fame in his own day. Defective speech prevented his practising law, though he trained himself for that profession. He published translations of Virgil's *Georgics* and Martial's epigrams.

405 *Changes*] James Shirley (1596–1666), the last of the major dramatists who wrote before the suppression of the theater, took the degree of B.A. at Oxford about 1618. In that year he published a poem, *Echo, or the Infortunate Lovers*, closely imitating *Venus and Adonis*. He took the degree of M.A.

and entered holy orders about 1620, but after a few years became a Catholic and began teaching school. For a time he lived in Ireland, where some of his plays were written and produced. A collection of his poems appeared in 1646.

407 *Northern Lass*] Richard Brome owed his slight success as a writer for the stage to the circumstance that he was for a time servant to Ben Jonson, who gave some care to his education, and started him upon a literary career. The reference to 'my man' in l. 20 of Jonson's *Inviting a friend to supper* (p. 498) is probably to Brome.

407 *A bonny, bonny bird*] This poem owes much to Skelton's *Philip Sparrow* (p. 3), and to an intermediate poem on the same subject by Gascoigne. 7 Keep cut] see notes to *Philip Sparrow*, l. 100.

407 *Lost Lady*] Sir William Berkeley (c. 1605–1677) was an accomplished gentleman who in 1641 became Governor of Virginia. Although forced from this position by the Parliamentary power, he continued to reside in the colony and resumed the governorship after the Restoration. He wrote his one play before removing to America.

407 *Where did you borrow* 8] 1639 prints after this line the additional one, 'Another sigh, then, I may hope', with no punctuation after it. This may represent the first line of a second stanza, or may have been spoken by one of the characters. The scene is printed confusingly in other particulars.

407 *Swaggering Damsel*] Robert Chamberlain (1607–1660) enjoyed some vogue as a writer of epigrams and light verse. Two books of his poems are *Nocturnal Lucubrations*, 1638, and *Jocabella*, 1640. A patron sent Chamberlain to study at Oxford in 1637, when he was thirty years of age.

BROADSIDE BALLADS

THE SURVIVING broadside ballads represent the popular poetry of the street-corner in Tudor-Stuart England. The learned John Selden, an early collector of broadsides in the 17th century, justifies concisely his, and our, interest in them: 'More solid things do not show the complexion of the times so well as ballads and libels.' The traditional ballads of medieval times, composed by unknown authors and handed down by word of mouth, though sometimes printed in debased versions as broadsides, are beyond the scope of this volume. We are concerned only with broadside ballads proper, written by the 'base ballad-makers' and sold by ballad singers on the street corners. The broadside ballad was printed in blackletter on a single sheet of paper, with a rough woodcut to catch the eye of the prospective buyer and the name of the tune to which the ballad was to be sung. These broadsides were evidently regarded as decorative, for their purchasers often pasted them up on the walls of taverns and cottages.

Under the early Tudors the production of ballads was stimulated by the needs of religious propaganda, and prominent men, both Catholic and Protestant, employed ballad writers to influence public opinion. During the reign of Elizabeth, when the need for propaganda was not so great, 'ballating' fell to free-lance writers of little education. Their ballads covered a wide range of subjects—political and military events of the day, murders, executions of criminals, strange occurrences, monstrous births, together with sentimental romances, ditties of love, complaints of the married state, exhortations to repentance and godly living—thus filling for that time the place which the modern newspaper and its Sunday supplement occupies in 20th-century life. Indeed, as the news-book developed in the 17th century, some of the ballad writers became the first journalists.

About the lives of the professional ballad writers little is known, even the names of many of them being lost because of anonymous publication. The best known ones are: Gray of Reading, Protestant controversialist, patronized by Henry VIII and Protector Somerset; William Elderton of early Elizabethan days, lawyer and actor, who 'armed himself with ale when he ballated' and whose red nose was the subject of many a joke; Thomas Deloney of later Elizabethan days, 'the ballating silk-weaver' of Norwich, author also of delightful prose romances of the life of craftsmen; and Martin Parker, writer of many sentimental ballads and later during the Civil War known as the 'Prelates' Poet' from his support of the Royalist cause. By the more serious men of letters, the ballad writers were regarded with scorn and contempt. Drayton, recalling his youth, writes,

> I scorned your ballad then though it were done
> And had for finis William Elderton,

and Herrick in *His farewell unto poetry* curses

> the blind and lame
> Base ballad-mongers, who usurp thy name
> And foul thy altar.

As a class they are characterized by John Earle in his *Microcosmography* as pot-poets, inspired by thin drink to write ballads which 'go out in single sheets, and are chanted from market to market to a vile tune and a worse throat, whilst the poor country wench melts like her butter to hear them.'

The fullest account of the ballad singer is in Chettle's *Kind-heart's Dream*, 1592. The old minstrel is described as 'an odd old fellow. . . . His treble viol in his hand assured me of his profession, on which (by his continual sawing, having left but one string) after his best manner he gave me a hunt's-up.' Ben Jonson introduces in his *Bartholomew Fair* a ballad singer caroling out his wares, catching the attention of the crowd, while pick-pockets, his confederates, are at their work. Shakespeare, in *The Winter's Tale* (IV. iii), gives a more sympathetic picture of the country peddler, the rogue Autolycus, who among his wares carries ballads telling of strange wonders.

CROSS REFERENCES: Poems, not in this section, which also appeared as broadside ballads: John Heywood, *A praise of his lady;* Surrey, *The lover comforteth himself;* Vaux, *The aged lover renounceth love;* Minor Courtly Makers, *Harpalus' complaint;* Gascoigne, *Gascoigne's arraignment;* Dyer, *My mind to me a kingdom is;* Ralegh, *The nymph's reply to the shepherd;* Marlowe, *The passionate shepherd to his love;* Elizabethan Miscellanies, *The lover exhorteth his lady to be constant;* Campion, *What if a day.*

MODERN EDITIONS: *Roxburghe Ballads* (ed. by W. Chappell and J. W. Ebsworth), eight volumes and supplementary volume, London, 1871–99; *Bagford Ballads* (ed. by J. W. Ebsworth), two volumes, Hertford, 1878; *Ballads from Manuscripts* (ed. by F. J. Furnivall and W. R. Morfill), two volumes, London, 1868–73; *Old English Ballads, 1553–1625* (ed. by H. E. Rollins), Cambridge, 1920; *A Pepysian Garland* (ed. by H. E. Rollins), Cambridge, 1922; *Cavalier and Puritan* (ed. by H. E. Rollins), New York, 1923; *The Pack of Autolycus* (ed. by H. E. Rollins), Cambridge (Mass.), 1927; *An American Garland* (ed. by C. H. Firth), Oxford, 1915; *Naval Songs and Ballads* (ed. by C. H. Firth), London, 1908; *Gray of Reading* (ed. by E. W. Dormer), Reading, 1923; *Songs and Ballads chiefly of the reign of Philip and Mary* (ed. by T. Wright), Roxburghe Club, 1860; *Harleian Miscellany,* vol. x. 252–78, London, 1813; *Ancient Songs and Ballads* (ed. by J. Ritson), two volumes, London, 1829; *A Collection of Seventy-nine Black-letter Ballads and Broadsides, 1559–97* (ed. by J. Lilly), London, 1867; *Ballads and Broadsides chiefly of the Elizabethan Period . . . now in the Library at Britwell Court* (ed. by H. L. Collman), Roxburghe Club, 1912; *Old Ballads from Early Printed Copies* (ed. by J. P. Collier), Percy Society, 1840; *A Collection of Songs and Ballads relating to the London Prentices and Trades* (ed. by C. Mackay), Percy Society, 1841; Clement Robinson's *Handful of Pleasant Delights* (ed. by H. E. Rollins), Cambridge (Mass.), 1924; *The Works of Thomas Deloney* (ed. by F. O. Mann), Oxford, 1912; *The Shirburn Ballads, 1585–1616* (ed. by A. Clark), Oxford, 1907; Richard Johnson's *Crown Garland of Golden Roses,* 1612 (ed. by W. Chappell), Percy Society, 1842 and 1845; *Political Ballads published in England during the Commonwealth* (ed. by T. Wright), Percy Society, 1841; *Cavalier Songs and Ballads, 1642–84* (ed. by C. Mackay), 1863; *A Century of Broadside Elegies* (ed. by J. W. Draper), London, 1928. Many of the ballad tunes are printed in W. Chappell's *Old English Popular Music* (ed. by Wooldridge), two volumes, London, 1893.

COMMENT: C. H. Firth, 'Ballads and Broadsides' in *Shakespeare's England,* vol. ii, Oxford, 1916, and articles in *Tr. Roy. Hist. Soc.,* 3rd series, ii. 21, iii. 51, v. 21, vi. 19, and *The Scottish Historical Review,* iii. 257, vi. 113, ix. 363; H. E. Rollins, articles in *S. P.* xvii. 199, and *M. P.* xvi. 449; E. v. Schaubert, 'Zur Geschichte der Black-Letter Broadside Ballad' in *Anglia,* N. F., xxxviii. 1.

TEXT: *A Handful of Pleasant Delights,* 1584 (21106), B. M.; *The Garland of Good Will,* n. d. (6554), Bodleian. The other texts are not taken from the broadsides, but from secondary sources as indicated in the notes.

408 *The king's hunt is up*] text from Dormer's *Gray of Reading,* p. 65. This ballad, written late in the reign of Henry VIII, was entered in the Stationers' Registers in 1565–6. Its popularity is spoken of in *The Art of English Poesy,* 1589: 'And one Gray, what good estimation did he grow unto with the same King Henry [VIII], and afterward with the Duke of Somerset, Protector, for making certain merry ballads, whereof one chiefly was *The Hunt is up.*' The name 'hunt's-up,' first applied to the tune played on the horn under the windows of sportsmen to awaken them, came to be extended to any tune or song intended to arouse in the morning.

408–410 *A song between the Queen's Majesty and England*] text from *Harleian Miscellany,* x. 260; entered in the Stationers' Registers in 1558–9. The tune to which this ballad was sung is printed in Chappell, i. 121. 7 Methink] *Harl. Misc.* reads 'My think'. 24 depart] cf. *The Book of Common Prayer,* 1549, 'Matrimony': 'Till death us depart.' In 1662, 'depart' was altered to 'do part'. 48 terribly] broadside reads 'treably'. 56 bands] bonds.

410–411 *A proper song, entitled: Fain would I have a pretty thing*] text from B. M. copy of *A Handful of Pleasant Delights,* 1584. This ballad was written by 1566, for in that year a moralization, *Fain would I have a godly thing,* was entered in the Stationers' Registers. The tune, 'Lusty Gallant,' is printed in Chappell, i. 234. 17 geason] rare. 31 Cheap] Cheapside, the street of fine shops in Elizabethan London. 43 than] old spelling for 'then', here kept for the rhyme.

411–413 *A new courtly sonnet . . .*] text from the B. M. copy of *A Handful of Pleasant Delights*, 1584. In 1580 a moralization of this ballad was entered in the Stationers' Registers. *Lady Greensleeves* was twice referred to by Shakespeare in *Merry Wives of Windsor*, II. i and V. v. Tune in Chappell, i. 239. 21 well favoredly] handsomely. 30 sendal] thin silken material. 48 grossy] usually applied to vegetation, meaning green and vigorous. 54 aglets] pendants or spangles attached to a fringe.

413–414 *A proper new song . . .*] text from the B. M. copy of *A Handful of Pleasant Delights*, 1584. Thomas Richardson, whose name is signed to this ballad, was admitted to Gonville and Caius College in 1572. 36 overgrown] 1584 'overgrowde'. 39 areed] advise.

414–415 *As you came . . .*] text from the Bodleian copy of Deloney's *Garland of Good Will*, n. d. The *Garland* was probably first published in 1593, in which year it was entered in the Stationers' Registers. The first stanza, with its Catholic note, is almost certainly traditional, but the rest of the ballad may be by Deloney. A copy of the poem in the Bodleian *Rawlinson Poetry Ms.* 85 is signed 'Sr. W. R.', but there is no other evidence that it is from Ralegh's hand. The ballad was possibly sung to the tune printed by Chappell, i. 69.

415–417 *The valorous acts . . . [of] Mary Ambree*] text from *Bagford Ballads*, i. 311. *Mary Ambree* was not entered in the Stationers' Registers until 1629, but this entry must be for a reissue, for the ballad had been referred to in *The Return from Parnassus, c.* 1598, and had long been a favorite with Ben Jonson, who mentions it in *The Silent Woman*, IV. i, and *A Tale of a Tub*, I. ii, and quotes from it in *The Fortunate Isles*. Rollins (*S. P.* xvii. 236) tentatively assigns the ballad to William Elderton. Tune in Chappell, ii. 16. 2 Gaunt] Ghent; the Spaniards had captured Ghent in 1584, and it was probably some assault on the city by the Dutch, aided by English volunteers, which gave rise to this ballad. 15 striped] Percy's *Folio Ms.* reads 'slipped'. 19 hand] Percy's *Folio Ms.;* broadside 'side'.

417–419 *Lord Willoughby*] text from *Roxburghe Ballads*, iv. 8. Lord Willoughby died in 1601. None of his recorded exploits are like those recounted in the ballad. Firth thinks that the ballad was written between 1624 and 1628 to aid the recruiting sergeant (*Tr. Roy. Hist. Soc.*, 3rd series, iii. 110). Tune in Chappell, i. 152. 21 caliver] a light musket.

419–420 *A sonnet upon . . .*] text from J. O. Halliwell-Phillips's *Outlines of the Life of Shakespeare* (1907), i. 310, collated with E. K. Chambers's *Elizabethan Stage*, ii. 420. Two ballads on the burning of the Globe were entered in the Stationers' Registers on June 30, 1613. Neither ballad is extant in print. This ballad, printed by Halliwell-Phillips from an early 17th-century ms., is probably a copy of one of them. Chambers suggests that this is the one written by William Parrat. The Globe caught fire during the production of *Henry VIII* on June 29, 1613. 6 Was] Chambers conjectures 'But was'. 7 all this is true] From a letter written by Sir Henry Wotton on July 2, 1613, describing the burning of the Globe, it seems that the play, *Henry VIII*, was then known by a sub-title, *All is True*. 17 clew] ball of thread. 18 snag] projection. 25 Condye] Condell. 37] Halliwell-Phillips leaves this line incomplete. 41 thatched] Sir Henry Wotton wrote of the origin of the fire: 'Certain cannon being shot off at [Henry VIII's] entry, some of the paper, or other stuff, wherewith one of them was stopped, did light on the thatch, where being thought at first an idle smoke, and their eyes more attentive to the show, it kindled inwardly and ran round like a train, consuming within less than an hour the whole house to the very ground.'

420–421 *The shepherd's wooing Dulcina*] text from *Roxburghe Ballads*, vi. 166; entered in the Stationers' Registers in 1615, and later expanded by the addition of a second and inferior part, here omitted. Without evidence, this ballad has been ascribed to Ralegh. In Walton's *Complete Angler* it is among those named by the milkmaid's mother as she is trying to recall what song Piscator wishes sung. Tune in Chappell, i. 160. 26–30] The text of these lines is corrupt in the broadside ballad; following the editor of the *Roxburghe Ballads*, we give the reading of *The Westminster Drollery*. 34 could] the reading of *W. D.;* broadside reads 'to'. 41–44] the reading of *W. D.*

421–422 *Truth's integrity . . .*] text from *Roxburghe Ballads,* ii. 639; written before 1633, in which year an answer to the ballad was entered in the Stationers' Registers. Palgrave included the first five stanzas in *The Golden Treasury.* Tune in Chappell, i. 189. 43 Guy of Warwick] a legendary hero, whose marvellous adventures were recounted in the popular romance bearing his name. 50 Bevis] Sir Bevis of Hampton, another hero of medieval romance.

422–423 *The milkmaid's life*] text from *Roxburghe Ballads,* ii. 116; entered in the Stationers' Registers in 1634. Eight lines of this ballad are quoted, with some changes, by Walton in *The Complete Angler.*

423 *The four wonders*] text from *Roxburghe Ballads,* i. 354. The two surviving copies of this ballad date from the reign of Charles II. By the number of wonders packed in one ballad, it illustrates this popular type of ballad better than any of the earlier ones.

426–427 *Sailors for my money*] text from *Roxburghe Ballads,* vi. 797. There is a later altered version, called *Neptune's raging fury,* at p. 432 of the same volume. This ballad is the original of Thomas Campbell's famous song, *Ye Mariners of England.* 111 Though he'll] broadside reads 'th' eile'.

428–429 *When the King enjoys his own again*] text from *Roxburghe Ballads,* vii. 633. There is a later Restoration version at p. 682 of the same volume. Martin Parker wrote this ballad *c.* 1643–6 and it quickly became one of the most popular of the Cavalier songs. At the Restoration it was frequently reprinted, and according to Ritson survived as a Jacobite song throughout the 18th century. Tune in Chappell, i. 210. 1 Booker] John Booker (1603–1667), an astrologer and maker of almanacs. 9 dade] a wading bird.

LYRICS FROM SONG-BOOKS

SINGING SEEMS to have been almost universal in Elizabethan England. The countryside, the street corner, the cottage, and the tavern rang with ballads, rounds, catches, and three-man's songs. The craftsman's shop was 'a very bird-cage' says Dekker, and Deloney in his *Gentle Craft* writes that every journeyman shoemaker had to be able to 'sound the trumpet, or play upon the flute, and bear his part in a three-man's song, and readily reckon up his tools in rhyme.' Among the educated, singing was a necessary social accomplishment. The breeding of a man who could not join in the song after supper, reading his part at sight, was in question. This enthusiasm for singing gave English composers their opportunity. Countless lyrics, almost demanding song by their simple directness and melodic beauty, were being written, and the composers set them to madrigals and airs which are still among the chief glories of English music.

During Henry VIII's reign, ecclesiastical music dominated the efforts of the greatest composers, but in the court circle secular music was also cultivated, the King himself writing a few songs which have survived in manuscript. In 1530, the first secular English song-book was published by Wynkyn de Worde. The three-man's, corrupted into freeman's, song was the popular musical form of the day, and it continued in popularity among the lower classes long after the introduction of new forms for the fashionable. The development of secular music was interrupted by the Reformation and between 1530 and 1588 only one song-book was published, Thomas Whythorne's *Songs of three, four, and five voices,* 1571. Other music of this period of transition is preserved in various manuscripts, especially in the *Mulliner Ms.,* in which appears the famous setting of Richard Edwards's 'In going to my naked bed' (see p. 188).

With the more settled conditions of the later years of Elizabeth's reign, secular music came into its own. A new Italian form, the madrigal, pleased English singers. Nicholas Yonge, a lay-clerk of St. Paul's, imported music-books from Italy and gathered at his house 'a great number of gentlemen and merchants . . . for the exercise of music daily.' In 1588 he published *Musica Transalpina,* a collection of Italian madrigals, and in the same year, possibly a little earlier, Byrd published the first collection of English madrigals, his *Psalms, Sonnets, and Songs.* These started the great vogue of madrigal publication which lasted until about 1630. The madrigal was an unaccompanied song of from three to six voice parts, to be sung by a small group of friends sitting around a table in the home or in the tavern. It differs from our part-song, for it was polyphonic. No one voice carried the melody with the others subordinated as an accompaniment, but all parts were of equal interest, often of the same melodic material, and the voices entered successively rather than simultaneously. The poem was treated in phrases, each several times repeated, and commonly overlapping in the different voices. With this repetition the true madrigal seldom used more than one stanza of six to ten lines. Sometimes the stanzas of a longer poem were set as separate songs. To make clear the treatment of the poem, compare *Beauty is a lovely sweet,* p. 433, with these words which the Cantus, the highest voice, sang: 'Beauty is a lovely sweet, Where pure white and crimson meet, and crimson meet, where pure white and crimson meet, Joined with favor of the face, Chiefest flower of female race, chiefest flower, O chiefest flower of female race. But if virtue might be seen, but if virtue might be seen, might be seen, It would more, it would more delight the eyne, it would more, it would more delight the eyne.' The madrigals were printed in small quarto volumes, each volume containing the part for one voice only.

To supply the demand for the solo song there also developed in England the air, which although it had some precursors on the Continent, especially in Spain, was more of a native growth than the madrigal. In 1597, John Dowland, a celebrated lute player, published the first book of airs. Many composers, including Campion, followed with their books of airs, the last being published in 1622. The air was more melodic and rhythmic than the madrigal, and was harmonized on homophonic rather than polyphonic principles. It was printed so that it might be sung either as a solo by the highest voice accompanied by a lute, sometimes reinforced by a viol de gamba, or as a part song with the highest voice carrying the melody and the others accompanying. Longer poems could be set to airs as the same music was repeated for additional stanzas, a practice impossible with the madrigal.

The lyrics in the song-books were sufficiently well chosen that the volumes sometimes served the purpose of poetical miscellanies; at least so the sub-title, 'To the well-disposed to read, and to the merry disposed to sing,' of Weelkes's *Pammelia,* 1609, seems to indicate. The composers treated the lyrics kindly, striving to frame their music 'to the life of the words.' There are certain conventions in their settings, such as phrases of rapid notes for 'joy,' 'sing,' and 'fly,' and a short rest preceding 'sigh.' Most of the poems which the composers of madrigals and airs set to music remain anonymous, for the name of the poet was not given in the song-books. The only composer known to have written his own words is Campion, and although other composers may have written a few of the lyrics which they set to music (Symonds thought it most likely that Dowland and Jones did), their usual practice evidently was to draw on the great store of poetry already printed or circulating in manuscript.

The composition and publication of songs fell off markedly in the reign of Charles I, but during the Commonwealth, when ecclesiastical music was suppressed by the Puritans, secular music flourished. Henry and William Lawes, Wilson, Gamble, and others published a number of volumes, usually called *Airs and Dialogues*. Polyphony was abandoned and the words were set to a succession of notes chosen to make prominent the syllables necessary for the rhythm and sense of the poetry. It was a declamatory style, early traces of which may be seen in Dowland's later songs. Music suffered, but the poets were grateful to composers like Henry Lawes who

> First taught our English music how to span
> Words with just note and accent.

CROSS REFERENCES: Poems, not in this section, which also appeared set to music in song-books or mss. (see notes for exact references to settings): Henry VIII, all four poems; Vaux, *No pleasure without some pain;* Minor Courtly Makers, *That was my woe, A carol, bringing in the boar's head, In youth, in age, Pleasure it is, Ah, the sighs, Western wind, My little fool, England, be glad, O death, rock me asleep;* Gascoigne, *Gascoigne's good morrow, Gascoigne's lullaby;* Oxford, *If women could be fair, Epigram;* Sidney, *The nightingale, Fourth song, O sweet woods* (a rhymed imitation); Dyer, *My mind to me a kingdom is;* Greville, *Another, of his Cynthia, You little stars, Under a throne;* Essex, *Change thy mind, To plead my faith;* Ralegh, *Like to a hermit, A description of love;* Watson, *Vezzosi augelli, Questo di verde;* Lodge, *An ode;* Breton, *Phillida and Coridon;* Elizabethan Miscellanies, *Amantium iræ,* M. *Edwards' May, Tichborne's Elegy, To Colin Clout, Upon his timorous silence in her presence, To Cupid;* Constable, *Damelus' song to his Diaphenia;* Barnfield, *The unknown shepherd's complaint;* Daniel, *An ode;* Songs from Plays, the entire section; Broadside Ballads, the entire section; Campion, all except *Rose-cheeked Laura;* Donne, *Break of day;* Jonson, *Song, to Celia* [1], *Had those that dwell in error foul, Beauties, have ye seen, Though I am young;* Wotton, *On his mistress, the Queen of Bohemia;* Aytoun, *The forsaken mistress;* Strode, *On Chloris walking in the snow;* Townshend, *Victorious beauty, A dialogue betwixt Time and a Pilgrim;* Herrick, *To the virgins, to make much of time, To Anthea, who may command him anything, How lilies came white;* Carew, *A song, Mediocrity in love rejected, Ingrateful beauty threatened, To my inconstant mistress, Disdain returned;* Suckling, *Sonnet I, Sonnet II, Song* ('I prithee send'); Lovelace, *To Althea, from prison, The Vintage to the Dungeon, To Amarantha, that she would dishevel her hair, The scrutiny, To Lucasta. The rose, To Lucasta. Going to the wars, To Lucasta. Going beyond the seas;* Stanley, all six poems; Davenant, *Song;* Waller, *Song* ('Go, lovely rose'); Katherine Philips, *Friendship's mystery;* Stuart and Commonwealth Miscellanies, *Chloris, forbear a while.*

MODERN EDITIONS: E. Flügel, 'Liedersammlungen des xvi. Jahrhunderts, besonders aus der Zeit Heinrich's VIII' in *Anglia,* xii. 225 and 585; *Lyrics from the Song-Books of the Elizabethan Age* (ed. by A. H. Bullen), London, 1887; *More Lyrics from the Song-Books* (ed. by A. H. Bullen), London, 1888; *Lyrics from the Song-Books of the Elizabethan Age,* a selection from the two previous volumes (ed. by A. H. Bullen), London, 1913; *English Madrigal Verse* (ed. by E. H. Fellowes), Oxford, 1920; *Lyrics from the old Song Books* (ed. by E. Duncan) New York, 1927. The lyrics with the musical settings are being edited by E. H. Fellowes in two series—*The English Madrigal School,* thirty-six volumes, Stainer and Bell, London, 1913–1924, and *The English School of Lutenist Song-Writers,* first series, fifteen volumes, and second series in progress, Stainer and Bell, 1920 ff.

COMMENT: J. A. Symonds, 'Lyrics from Elizabethan Song-Books' in *In the Key of Blue,* London, 1896; W. Chappell, *Old English Popular Music* (ed. by Wooldridge), two volumes, London, 1893; W. H. Grattan Flood, *Early Tudor Composers,* Oxford, 1925; E. H. Fellowes, *The English Madrigal Composers,*

Oxford, 1921, *William Byrd*, Oxford, 1923, and *The English Madrigal*, Oxford, 1925; Peter Warlock, *The English Ayre*, Oxford, 1926; Frank Howes, *William Byrd*, London, 1928.

TEXT: *Psalms, Sonnets, and Songs*, 1588 (4253), Harvard; *Songs of Sundry Natures*, 1589 (4256), Huntington; *Canzonets*, 1593 (18121), Huntington; *Songs and Psalms*, 1594 (18284), B. M.; *Second Book of Songs or Airs*, 1600 (7095), Huntington; *Third and Last Book of Songs or Airs*, 1603 (7096), Huntington; *First Set of English Madrigals*, 1604 (1586), Harvard; *Musical Humors. The first part of Airs*, 1605 (13958), B. M.; Michael East, *Second Set of Madrigals*, 1606 (7461), Huntington; *Funeral Tears*, 1606 (5679), Huntington; *Poetical Music*, 1607 (13957), B. M.; *Ultimum Vale*, 1608, not accessible to us, text from Fellowes; *Airs or Fantastic Spirits*, 1608 (25202), Huntington; John Wilbye, *Second Set of Madrigals*, 1609 (25619a), Harvard; *Muses' Garden for Delights*, 1610 (14736), Huntington; *First Set of Madrigals and Motets*, 1612 (11826), Harvard; *A Pilgrim's Solace*, 1612 (7098), Huntington; Thomas Bateson, *Second Set of Madrigals*, 1618 (1587), B. M.; *Private Music*, 1620 (19553), Bodleian; *Songs of three, four, five, and six parts*, 1622 (24099), Huntington; *First Book of Airs*, 1622 (901), B. M.; *Christ Church Ms*. K3, not accessible to us, text from Bullen; Playford, *Select Musical Airs and Dialogues*, 1653, B. M.; Lawes, *Airs and Dialogues*, 1653, New York; Lawes, *Airs and Dialogues*, 1655, New York; Wilson, *Cheerful Airs or Ballads*, 1660, White.

429 *Reasons briefly set down* 20 *Omnis spiritus laudet Dominum*] 'Let every spirit praise the Lord.'

431 *Arise, get up, my dear* 11 firk] dance, jig, be lively.

432 *In midst of woods*] set as two songs by Mundy: the first stanza being number xxvii, and the last two stanzas number xxviii. 5 charm] singing. noise] in the obsolete meaning of melodious sound.

432 *Fine knacks for ladies* 13 lives] omitted in 1600; supplied by Fellowes.

434 *The soldier's song*] Captain Hume, a soldier by profession and an eccentric, requires of the lute the seemingly impossible task of imitating trumpets, drums, and 'great ordnance.' 13 Hark] repeated in the song; the repetition omitted here for rhythm.

435–436 *The hunting song* 10–11] Between stanzas there is the direction, 'The hounds are now a-hunting.'

436 *Think'st thou, Kate*] We have been unable to get access to a copy of *Ultimum Vale;* our text is from Fellowes's *English Madrigal Verse*.

437 *Ye that do live in pleasures* 8 breath] Cantus part reads 'birth'; other parts 'breath'.

438 *Once did my thoughts* 19 made out of wax] perfectly made; the phrase 'man of wax' was a common term of commendation.

438–439 *The silver swan* 4 her] 1612 misprints 'his'.

439 *Ah, dear heart*] This poem, with several textual variants and an additional stanza, was also set by Dowland in his *Pilgrim's Solace*, 1612. The stanza set by Gibbons is printed, with several variants, in the 1669 edition of Donne's poems as a first stanza of *Break of day*. Professor Grierson denies it to Donne and thinks it 'probably by John Dowland.' That the stanza does not really belong to Donne's poem seems clear from internal evidence, but there is no real evidence for assigning it to Dowland.

440 *I heard a noise* 9–10] Between lines 9 and 10, Fellowes has supplied a line, 'I saw the shadow of some worthy thing', not in the original. Fellowes does not give the source for this line.

441–442 *Yet if his majesty*] text from Bullen's *Lyrics from the Song-Books,* collated with Ault's *17th Century Lyrics*. 14 dais] Ault reads 'dazie'.

443 *Greedy lover, pause awhile*] Huth discovered a copy of this song in a manuscript miscellany, where it was signed 'Sir Albertus Morton' (*Inedited Poetical Miscellanies*, 1870, sig. U2 recto). Sir Albertus Morton was a nephew of Sir Henry Wotton. He spent some time in the service of Elizabeth, Queen of Bohemia. In 1624 he was appointed one of the Secretaries of State, but his death in the next year cut short his tenure of this office.

THOMAS CAMPION

THOMAS CAMPION (1567–1620) was both musician and poet, a fitting combination at a time when the relation between the two arts was so close. With his heart given to music and poetry, he seems to have had difficulty in deciding on a profession, for he studied at Peterhouse, Cambridge, 1581–4, left without taking a degree, and entered Gray's Inn for the study of law, but was not called to the bar. Later, probably at a Continental university, he took a degree in medicine. He had begun writing poetry as a young legal student and five of his poems, without his signature, appeared in Newman's surreptitious edition of Sidney's *Astrophel and Stella*, 1591, while others were circulating in manuscript. In 1595, he published a volume of Latin epigrams, and in 1601, in collaboration with Philip Rosseter, a musician, he issued *A Book of Airs*, for which he wrote all of the lyrics and the musical settings for the first half. This marks Campion's appearance as a composer of airs for solo songs with a lute accompaniment. In writing of Campion as a composer, Warlock says that he was 'at his best in half serious songs' of 'deliciously pretty tunes,' distinguished by 'neatness of workmanship,' but he notes the 'absence of any deeper quality than surface charm in the music.' In 1602 Campion published a prose treatise, *Observations in the Art of English Poesy*, in which, carrying on the Cambridge tradition in the old battle between quantitative and accentual meter, he protested against the use of rhyme and accent, and wished to restore to English poetry the dignity of the classical, unrhymed, quantitative verse— a strange position for one so facile in rhyme and accent as Campion. His confusion of the two systems and his failure to understand the true nature of accent partially account for this. He was effectively answered in the next year by Daniel, and Ben Jonson said of himself that he had written 'a discourse of poesy both against Campion and Daniel,' which unfortunately has not survived. In 1607 Campion wrote his first mask, and in 1613 three others. His dramatic power is not great and the merit of his masks is their lyric beauty. Campion published two more volumes for which he composed both words and music, *Two Books of Airs, c.* 1613, and *The Third and Fourth Books of Airs, c.* 1617.

If in reading Campion the variety of rhythms, changing from line to line, is sometimes perplexing, one should remember that the poems were written to music and that Campion 'chiefly aimed to couple my words and notes lovingly together.'

MODERN EDITIONS: *Works* (ed. by P. Vivian), Oxford, 1909; *The Works* (ed. by A. H. Bullen), London, 1889; *Thomas Campion* (ed. by A. H. Bullen, omits Latin poems), London, 1903; *Poetical Works in English* (ed. by P. Vivian), Muses' Library, London, n. d. Both words and music have been reprinted by E. H. Fellowes in his series 'The English School of Lutenist Song Writers,' *Thomas Campian. Songs from Rosseter's Book of Airs, 1601*, parts 1 and 2, and *Thomas Campian. First, Second, Third, and Fourth Books of Airs*, Stainer and Bell, London, 1922 and 1925.

COMMENT: T. MacDonagh, *Thomas Campion and the Art of English Poetry*, Dublin, 1913; Peter Warlock, *The English Ayre*, Oxford, 1926.

TEXT: *A Book of Airs*, 1601 (21332), Huntington; *Two Books of Airs*, [*c*. 1613] (4547), Huntington; *Observations in the Art of English Poesy*, 1602 (4543), B. M.; *The Late Royal Entertainment . . . at Cawsome House*, 1613 (4545), Huntington; *The Third and Fourth Book of Airs*, [*c*. 1617] (4548), Huntington; Robert Jones, *Second Book of Songs and Airs*, 1601 (14733), B. M.; Richard Alison, *An Hour's Recreation in Music*, 1606 (356), Huntington.

445 *My love bound me*] The first stanza of the song appeared in Sidney's *Astrophel and Stella*, 1591. It is not signed by Campion in either printing, but internal evidence and the close similarity with one of his Latin epigrams (see ed. Vivian, p. li) makes the ascription reasonably certain.

446 *What if a day*] The authorship of this song—one of the most popular of the time, appearing in many mss., in several books of songs, and as a broadside ballad—is in dispute. It is attributed to Campion in Alison's *An Hour's Recreation in Music*, 1606, and in Alexander Gil's *Logonomia Anglica*, 1619. It had appeared in a ms. as early as 1592, and in *Rawlinson Poetry Ms.* 112 it is attributed to the E[arl] of E[ssex]. A. E. H. Swaen, in an exhaustive account of the different versions of the song (*M. P.* iv. 397 and v. 383), having misdated a manuscript (cf. ed. Vivian, p. 378), thinks it too early for Campion. There can be little doubt that the two stanzas printed by Alison in 1606 are Campion's, but the song was probably extended by other hands. A version in five stanzas may be found in the *Shirburn Ballads*, p. 238, or in the *Roxburghe Ballads*, i. 348.

448 *The man of life upright*] attributed in two mss. to Bacon, but almost certainly Campion's.

448–449 *Hark, all you ladies*] first appeared in Sidney's *Astrophel and Stella*, 1591. 24 Dione's] Venus's. 35 Apes in Avernus] The idea was common that old maids were condemned after death to lead apes in hell.

449 *When thou must home* 4 Iope] Campion is probably referring to the Iope who was the daughter of Iphicles and one of the wives of Theseus.

449–450 *Rose-cheeked Laura*] the most beautiful of the songs by which Campion illustrated his principles of quantitative versification. His comment in the *Observations* on this poem follows: 'The second kind consists of dimeter, whose first foot may either be a spondee or trochee. The two verses following are both of them trochaical and consist of four feet, the first of either of them being a spondee or trochee, the other three only trochees. The fourth and last verse is made of two trochees. The number is voluble and fit to express any amorous conceit.' 6 concent] playing or singing together in harmony.

450–451 *Jack and Joan* 7 Lash out] lavish, squander. 19 tutties] nosegays.

451 *Give beauty all her right* 8 swelling] 1613 'smelling'.

452–453 *Now winter nights enlarge* 13–14 dispense With] grant dispensation to, excuse.

454 *There is a garden* 6 cherryripe] the call of the London street venders.

454–455 *Young and simple though I am* 9–12] supplied from Ferrabosco's *Airs*, 1609; 1617 repeats the last four lines of the first stanza.

JOHN DONNE

JOHN DONNE (1572–1631) illustrates, in his early poetry, the diversity of the 1590's. As the Petrarchan code of love and the smooth felicities of the Spenserian manner came to their fullest development and their greatest triumph, Donne, an 'infidel in love' with an ear for rugged rhythm, steeped in medieval scholasticism rather than Renaissance humanism, broke with the tradition and, 'the lazy seeds of servile imitation thrown away,' followed the realistic bent of his 'imperious wit.' For him, thinking was a passionate experience, and it was in the play of his intellect that he found poetry— not calm, peaceful reflective poetry, but poetry intensely emotional. His striking figures of speech—drawn from the wide range of his learning rather than from his sensuous experience, intellectualized yet suffused with emotion—express aptly his mode of thought. Because of this originality, the young poets of the first half of the 17th century looked upon Donne as

> a king that ruled as he thought fit
> The universal monarchy of wit.

Naturally they imitated him, but often their thought did not fit such unusual expression and the result at times was an absurd involution of commonplace ideas. His influence did, however, help to produce in 17th-century poetry a new note of individuality, a keener intellectual activity, and a deepened passion.

To describe this manner of writing, the word 'metaphysical' came to be used, possibly first by Drummond of Hawthornden (see 'Extracts from Critical Essays,' p. 906). This term has been most clearly defined by Dr. Johnson, in his life of Cowley: 'About the beginning of the 17th century appeared a race of writers that may be termed the metaphysical poets. . . . [Their] wit . . . may be . . . considered as a kind of *discordia concors;* a combination of dissimilar images, or discovery of occult resemblances in things apparently unlike. . . . If they frequently threw away their wit upon false conceits, they likewise sometimes struck out unexpected truth; if their conceits were far-fetched, they were often worth the carriage. To write on their plan it was at least necessary to read and think.'

Donne's early education, carefully supervised by his mother (in whom flowed the blood of the Mores, the Rastells, and the Heywoods), was Catholic. In 1584 he entered Hart Hall, Oxford, and three years later transferred to Cambridge. He does not seem to have taken a degree at either University at this time, probably because as a Catholic he could not take the required oaths. A tour of the Continent possibly followed his leaving Cambridge, though the date of the tour is uncertain and is placed later by Walton and Gosse. In 1592 Donne was admitted to Lincoln's Inn for the study of law, but, as he later wrote a friend, he was 'diverted by the worst voluptuousness, which is an hydroptic, immoderate desire of humane learning and languages.' Some time went to the writing of poetry and some to a survey 'of the body of divinity as it was then controverted betwixt the Reformed and the Roman Church.' The exact history of Donne's religious change cannot be traced. Coming to the opinion that 'all churches are beams of one sun,' he was ready in 1601 to disclaim any 'love of a corrupt religion,' though it is evident from his later religious poetry that he always remained a Catholic in temperament and was at least a little uneasy within the confines of Anglicanism. Donne was a volunteer with the Earl of Essex on the expedition to Cadiz in 1596, and to the Azores in 1597. On his return he entered the service of Sir Thomas Egerton, the Lord Keeper of the Great Seal. According to Richard Baker, in his *Chronicle of the Kings of England,* Donne came to be known about London as 'not dissolute but very neat; a great visitor of ladies, a great frequenter of plays, a great writer of conceited verses.' He fell in love with Egerton's niece, Anne More, and in 1601 married her without the consent of her father, who, angry at a secret marriage, secured Donne's dismissal from his post. One observer of the time, Francis Osborne, noted that the Lord Keeper was not loath to part with a secretary so clever that he was given to 'mend the copy.' Donne, with a rapidly growing family, unable to find other employment, spent the next years in poverty and misery. He aided Morton, later Bishop of Durham, in his controversy with the Catholics, and as early as 1607 was urged by Morton to take orders in the Anglican church. Donne was unwilling, however, and continued to seek for civil preferment, even contemplating emigration in 1609, when he applied for the secretaryship of the colony of Virginia. But the King wished Donne for the Church, and all other ways of preferment were closed to him. At last sincerely convinced of his fitness for the calling and of its fitness for him, he was ordained in 1615. Then begins the period of his holy life, commemorated by his devoted parishioner, Izaak Walton. The glowing rhetoric of his sermons found him quick advancement, and in 1621 he was made Dean of St. Paul's. It was decided in 1630 to advance him to a bishopric, but his sickness and death left this plan unfulfilled.

With the exception of several occasional poems, Donne did not publish his poetry. Even the publication of his *Anniversaries* he regretted: 'The fault which I acknowledge in myself is to have descended to print anything in verse, which though it have excuse, even in our times, by example of men which one would think should as little have done it as I, yet I confess I wonder how I declined to it, and do not pardon myself.' His poems, however, circulated widely in manuscripts, the fashionable mode at court, of which Drayton complains in 1612: 'Verses are wholly deduced to chambers, and nothing esteemed in this lunatic age but what is kept in cabinets, and must only pass by transcription.' In 1614, just before entering the ministry, Donne considered publishing his poems as a public acknowledgment of them, so that the early poems might not be brought out to his scandal after he was in orders. Since no copy of such an edition survives, it is always assumed that it did not appear. His poems were published in 1633, two years after his death, and proved so popular that they went to their seventh edition in 1669.

MODERN EDITIONS: *Poetical Works* (ed. by H. J. C. Grierson), two volumes, Oxford, 1912; *Complete Poetry and Selected Prose* (ed. by J. Hayward), Bloomsbury, 1929; *The Works* (ed. by H. Alford), six volumes, London, 1839; *Poems* (ed. by E. K. Chambers), two volumes, Muses' Library, London, n. d.; *Letters to Severall Persons of Honour* (ed. by C. E. Merrill, Jr.), New York, 1910; *Sermons, Selected Passages* (ed. by L. Pearsall Smith), Oxford, 1919; *Devotions* (ed. by J. Sparrow), Cambridge, 1923; *Paradoxes and Problems* (ed. by G. Keynes), London, 1923; *Ten Sermons* (ed. by G. Keynes), London, 1923.

COMMENT: E. Gosse, *The Life and Letters of John Donne*, two volumes, London, 1899; G. Keynes, *Bibliography of the Works of Dr. John Donne*, Cambridge, 1914; M. P. Ramsay, *Les Doctrines Médiévales chez Donne*, Oxford, 1916; E. M. Simpson, *A Study of the Prose Works of John Donne*, Oxford, 1924; H. I'A. Fausset, *John Donne, A Study in Discord*, London, 1924.

TEXT: *Poems*, 1633 (7045), Harvard; *Poems*, 1635 (7046), Harvard.

455 *Songs and Sonnets*] The group headings (*Songs and Sonnets, Epigrams, Elegies, Satires, Letters, Divine Poems*) were not used in the edition of 1633, but appeared in 1635.

455–456 *Love's deity* 26 I'am] The use, by Donne, of the apostrophe with no letter omitted is probably intended to indicate a speeding up in pronunciation without a complete elision.

456 *Song* 2 mandrake root] The root of the mandrake was supposed to resemble the human shape.

458 *The flea*] This poem evidently pleased 17th-century readers. After the first edition of Donne's poems in 1633, publishers placed it first in all subsequent 17th-century editions.

459 *The message*] no title in 1633; title from 1635. 11 Which] 1633; 1635 'But'.

459–460 *The bait*] no title in 1633; title from 1635; one of the many imitations of Marlowe's *Passionate shepherd to his love*, p. 168. 18 with] 1635; 1633 'which'. 23 sleave-silk] 1635; 1633 'sleeve-sick'.

460–461 *The will* 39 Bedlam] a contraction for Bethlehem Hospital, an asylum for the insane.

461–462 *The sun rising* 24 alchemy] From its claims to transmute baser metals into gold, alchemy had the figurative meaning of 'glittering dross.'

462 *Break of day*] In 1669 this poem was printed with an additional first stanza, most probably not by Donne. For this stanza, beginning 'Ah, dear heart', see 'Lyrics from Song-Books,' p. 439, where it is printed from the version set by Orlando Gibbons. See also note, p. 983. *Break of day* was set to music by William Corkine in his *Second Book of Airs*, 1612. It is to be noted that the speaker in the poem is feminine.

463 *Confined love*] no title in 1633; title from 1635. 16 with all] 1635; 1633 reads 'withall', which reading Grierson defends.

464–465 *A lecture upon the shadow*] not in 1633; text from 1635, where the poem is headed *Song;* title from 1650. 26 short] 1635; 'first', the reading of many mss., was adopted by Grierson as the better reading.

465–467 *The ecstasy* 9 entergraft] a word of Donne's own coinage to express vividly the reciprocal nature of the grafting, entwining, of hands. 32] Grierson explains this passage: 'We see now that we did not see before the true source of our love. What we thought was due to bodily beauty, we perceive now to have its source in the soul.' 42 Interinanimates] many mss.; 1633 'Interanimates'. 52 sphere] many mss.; 1633 'spheres'. 55 forces, sense] many mss.; 1633 'senses force'.

467–468 *The good-morrow* 4 seven sleepers'] Seven Christian youths, fleeing to escape martyrdom during the Decian persecution, found refuge in a cave, where they remained asleep for 230 years. 5 but] except.

468 *Air and angels* 23–24] According to medieval belief, inherited from the Neo-Platonists, the incorporeal angels assumed bodies of air. The air was 'pure,' but not so 'pure' as the incorporeality of the angels.

468–469 *The prohibition* 5 thee then what to me] 1635; 1633 'me then that which'. 22 stage] 1635; 1633 'stay'. Grierson punctuates the line, 'So shall I, live, thy Stage, not triumph be;', and paraphrases it thus: 'Alive, I shall continue to be the stage on which your victories are daily set forth; dead, I shall be but your triumph, a thing achieved once, never to be repeated.'

469 *The undertaking*] no title in 1633; title from 1635. 6 specular stone] semi-transparent substance formerly used as window glass or for ornament; probably used here with reference to the crystal gazing of the astrologer.

469–470 *Lovers' infiniteness*] Grierson suggests that the title 'possibly should be *Love's infiniteness.*' 20 it] 1635; 1633 'is'.

470–471 *Love's growth* 18] Grierson was the first to clear up the meaning of this line: 'The stars at sunrise are not really made larger, but they are made to seem larger.'

471 *The anniversary* 22 we] many mss.; 1633 'now'.

472–473 *The canonization* 7 stampèd face] on coins. 15 plaguy bill] the weekly list of those dead from the plague. 30 legend] 1635; 1633 'legends'. 45 your] 1669; 1633 'our'.

473 *A valediction of weeping* 8–9] Grierson paraphrases, 'For, as your image perishes in each tear that falls, so shall we perish, be nothing, when

between us rolls the "salt, estranging sea."'

474–475 *A valediction forbidding mourning*] quoted by Walton in connection with his account of Donne's visit to France in 1612, probably indicating that it was written by Donne to his wife at that time. 11 trepidation] according to the Ptolemaic astronomy, a slow, swinging motion of the ninth sphere which accounted for certain phenomena really due to the motion of the earth's axis. 16 elemented] composed.

475 *The funeral*] This, and the following poem, were possibly addressed to Mrs. Magdalen Herbert, the mother of George Herbert. 17 with] 1635; 1633 'by'.

475–476 *The relic* 27–28] the kiss of salutation and of parting customary in Renaissance England.

476–477 *Twicknam garden*] Twickenham, where the Countess of Bedford had a country house, which Donne visited. 17 groan] many mss.; 1633 'grow'. The mandrake was popularly supposed to shriek when pulled from the ground. 24 woman's] many mss.; 1633 'womens'.

477–478 *A nocturnal upon Saint Lucy's Day*] According to the old style of reckoning, St. Lucy's Day, December 13, was the shortest day of the year. This poem was probably written in 1612, when Lucy, Countess of Bedford, was seriously ill. 3 flasks] powder-flasks. squibs] fireworks. 21 limbec] alembic, still. 28–36] These lines play on the subtle distinction between degrees of nothingness. By her death Donne would become the quintessence of the first nothing—no longer a man, or he would be conscious of so being; nor a beast, for then (according to scholastic doctrine) he would be perceptive and moving, able to select ends and means; nor a plant or stone, for the vegetable kingdom is capable of detesting and loving; nor an ordinary nothing, such as a shadow, for to produce that a body and light are necessary. 29 elixir] quintessence. 39 Goat] the zodiacal sign, Capricorn; with reference to the supposed lust of goats.

478–479 *On his mistress*] not printed in 1633; text from 1635. 28 mind's] many mss.; 1635 'mind'. 34 spitals] hospitals, particularly for persons of low class, afflicted with foul diseases.

479–481 *The autumnal*] probably written to Mrs. Magdalen Herbert. 6

Affection . . . takes] many mss.; 1633
'Affections . . . take'. 16 anachorit]
anchorite, hermit. 20 progress] the
journey of state made by a royal personage.

481–483 *Satire III* 33 foes] 1635;
1633 'foe'. devil, whom] many mss.;
1633 'devil h'is, whom'. 44 here] 1635;
1633 'her'. 47 her] many mss.; 1633
'the'. 96 Philip . . . Gregory] Philip
II of Spain and one of the Popes
Gregory, probably XIII or XIV. 97
Harry . . . Martin] Henry VIII and
Martin Luther.

483–485 *The calm* 17 lanthorns]
lanterns; Grierson explains that 'the
reference is to the lanterns in the high
sterns of the ships, used to keep the
fleet together.' 17–18] Jonson told
Drummond that he knew these lines
by heart. 23 calenture] a delirium
said to afflict sailors in the tropics;
the victim fancies the sea to be a green
field and wishes to leap into it. 36
emperor's] Tiberius's; according to
Suetonius, as Tiberius was once about
to enter Rome, a snake, which he fed
with his own hand, was devoured by
ants. This was taken to be an omen
that Tiberius should beware the fury of
the mob, so he turned back and did
not enter the city. 37 gaols] jails;
1633 reads 'goals'. 38 pinnaces] 1635;
1633 'venices'.

485 *To Sir Henry Wotton*] In several mss., the poem is dated July 20,
1598. 2 Cales'] Cadiz. St. Michael's]
a name sometimes applied to the
Azores. Donne is referring to the Cadiz
expedition of 1596 and the Island Voyage of 1597, which had become old
stories. 24 chests] chess.

486 *An Anatomy of the World. The
first anniversary*] Elizabeth, the daughter of Sir Robert Drury, died in 1610
at the age of fifteen. Donne secured
the patronage of the wealthy Sir Robert
by writing a *Funeral Elegy*, 1610, and
the two *Anniversaries*, 1611 and 1612,
which are grossly extravagant in their
eulogy of the young girl. We print the
passages which show Donne's bewilder-
ment in the face of the new science of

his day, and a few lines of the extravagant eulogy. 20 She] Elizabeth
Drury. 34 single money] small change.
37, 38 know'st] 1611; 1633 'knowest'.

487–488 *Of the Progress of the Soul.
The second anniversary* 1 She] Elizabeth Drury. 2 electrum] an alloy of
gold and silver. 11] marginal note:
'Her [*i. e.*, the soul's] ignorance in this
life and knowledge in the next.'

438 *Show me, dear Christ*] not
printed in any of the 17th-century editions. It was first printed in Gosse's
Life from the *Westmoreland Ms.* Our
text is taken from Grierson. 8 seven]
the seven hills of Rome.

490 *At the round earth's* 6 dearth]
Westmoreland Ms.; 1633 'death'.

491 *Good Friday, 1613. Riding westward*] In *Additional Ms.* 25707 this
poem is headed: 'Mr. J. Donne, going
from Sir H[enry] G[oodere] on Good
Friday sent him back this meditation
on the way.' The heading of the poem
in *Harleian Ms.* 4955 gives the objec-
tive of the ride: 'Riding to Sir Edward
Herbert in Wales.'

492 *A hymn to Christ* 12 seas] other
17th-century editions read 'blood',
which explains Donne's meaning.

492 *A hymn to God the Father*] In
speaking of this poem, Walton says
that Donne 'caused it to be set to a
most grave and solemn tune and to be
often sung to the organ by the choristers
of St. Paul's church in his own hearing,
especially at the evening service; and
at his customary devotions in that place
did occasionally say to a friend, "The
words of this hymn have restored me
to the same thoughts of joy that possessed my soul in my sickness when I
composed it. . . ."'

493–494 *Hymn to God, my God, in
my sickness*] not printed in 1633; text
from 1635. Walton, in the 1670 edition
of his *Life of Donne*, quotes part of
the poem and dates it March 23, 1631,
eight days before the death of Donne.
Walton's dating is not accepted by
all scholars. 10 *Per fretum febris*]
'Through the raging of fever.' 18
Anyan] Bering Strait.

BEN JONSON

BEN JONSON (1572–1637), the posthumous son of a minister, received his
education at Westminster School under the learned Camden, of whose
instruction he always speaks with reverent praise. He did not proceed to

a university, but worked for a time at bricklaying, the trade of his step-father. Finding this distasteful he enlisted for a period of service in Flanders and on his return from the wars he married. Not long after, he became associated with a company of actors. By 1597 he was one of Henslowe's playwrights, well enough known by 1598 to be listed by the patriotic Meres as one of 'our best for tragedy.' In that year he killed in a duel one of Henslowe's actors, Gabriel Spencer, and escaped the gallows only by claiming right of clergy. During his time in prison he was converted to Catholicism, in which religion he continued for twelve years. Jonson was the leading figure in the playwrights' quarrel, sometimes called 'the war of the theaters,' and later he was often in trouble because of his blunt speech. As his reputation increased, he became the chief writer of masks for court production, and from 1616 was granted a pension by James I, later renewed and increased by Charles I, as the 'King's poet.' In 1616 he collected his plays, masks, and poems for publication in a folio volume, called his *Works*. This choice of a dignified title occasioned many gibes at his expense, one of which appears in *Wit's Recreations*, 1640:

> Pray tell me, Ben, where doth the mystery lurk,
> What others call a play you call a work.

In his last years, he suffered greatly from illness and at times from poverty.

According to Jonson's statement to Drummond, his method of poetic composition was to write out what he had to say in prose and then to versify it. The merits and the defects of his poetry are those which one might expect from such a method. In his work, the traces of medievalism surviving in Spenser and so many Elizabethans disappear. His epigrams, his odes, his verse-letters, and his carefully fashioned songs are completely classical in form and in spirit. Like Donne he set a new manner of writing before the young poets of the 17th century, which helped to win many of them away from Petrarchism and Spenserianism.

Jonson's conversation, however, probably exercised more influence than did his poetry. He was an excellent boon companion, and young men—scholars as well as poets, for Jonson was one of the learned men of his time—loved to gather with him in the London taverns. Fortunately we have a sample of his vivid and combative conversation in the notes which Drummond of Hawthornden took of Ben's talk during his visit to Scotland. We have also his *Discoveries*, a commonplace-book largely made up of extracts and paraphrases from his reading, which indicates the tenor of his discussion of literary principles, and may have furnished the ammunition for his controversies. We may be certain that the taverns rang with Jonson's vociferous battle for 'pure and neat language,' for polished literary form, and for the use of the classics as models.

The favorite meeting place of men of letters in the first two decades of the 17th century was the Mermaid Tavern. Tom Coryate, traveling in Asia Minor in 1615, addressed a letter to 'the right worshipful fraternity of sireniacal gentlemen, that meet the first Friday of every month, at the sign of the Mermaid in Bread street.' Shakespeare at times met with this group and engaged in wit combats with Jonson, who, as described by Fuller, was 'like a Spanish great galleon . . . built far higher in learning, solid but slow in his performances,' while Shakespeare, like an 'English man-of-war, lesser in bulk but lighter in sailing, could turn with all tides, tack about, and take advantage of all winds, by the quickness of his wit and invention.' That Jonson was early recognized as a leader in these gatherings is shown by the poem which Beaumont addressed to him, about 1606, describing an evening at the Mermaid. By 1620, the Apollo Room of the Devil and St. Dunstan Tavern had supplanted the Mermaid in popularity, and Jonson's *Leges Convivales* were painted over its fireplace in letters of gold (see p. 513). From about this time the group was known as the Tribe of Ben, and the young poets after being 'sealed of the Tribe' became 'sons of Ben.' The esteem in which Jonson was held by these companions is shown by the volume of elegies, *Jonsonus Virbius*, published in the year following his death.

MODERN EDITIONS: *Ben Jonson* (ed. by C. H. Herford and P. Simpson), three volumes (to be completed in ten volumes), Oxford, 1925–1927; *The Works* (ed. by F. Cunningham), three volumes, London, n. d., and nine volumes, London, 1875.

COMMENT: A. C. Swinburne, *A Study of Ben Jonson*, London, 1889; M. Castelain, *Ben Jonson, L'Homme et l'Œuvre*, Paris, 1907; G. Gregory Smith, *Ben Jonson*, London, 1919.

TEXT: *Works*, 1616 (14751), Harvard; *Works*, 1641, Cornell; *Mr. William Shakespeare's Comedies, Histories, and Tragedies*, 1623 (22273), Princeton; Alexander Brome, *Songs and Other Poems*, 1661, Harvard.

494–495 *To my bookseller* 7 title-leaf] Title-pages were posted up, and, as this passage indicates, placed in cleft-sticks to advertise new books. This custom explains the full descriptions given of books on Elizabethan title-pages. 9 termers] those who came to London in term-time, the session of the law courts. 12 Bucklersbury] a street inhabited by grocers and apothecaries where the book would be used as wrapping paper, a custom commented on by Herrick in an epigram, *To his book*.

495 *To my mere English censurer* 4 Davies] Sir John Davies; see p. 331. Weever] see p. 525.

495 *On something that walks somewhere* 5 Lord] Objection was beginning to be voiced to the English nobility, because they gathered at court for amusement and neglected the old duties and kindly charities to the tenants on their country estates.

495 *To William Camden*] a renowned antiquary, and master of Westminster School when Jonson was a student there. 3–4] referring to Camden's *Britannia*, first published in 1586. The epigram was probably written too early to refer to the *Annales*, published in 1615.

496 *To Francis Beaumont*] possibly written in answer to *Mr. Francis Beaumont's letter to Ben Jonson*, p. 539.

496 *To John Donne* 1 where] whether. 10 pui'nes'] The puisne was an inferior or junior judge in the superior courts of common law; an unskilled beginner.

496 *On Lucy, Countess of Bedford*] the favorite of Queen Anne, and next to Mary, Countess of Pembroke, the patroness most frequently celebrated by poets of the day. She acted in many of Jonson's masks. 15 rock] distaff.

497 *To Lucy, Countess of Bedford, with Mr. Donne's satires* 10 heard] 1616 reads 'hard'.

497–498 *Inviting a friend to supper* 19–20 godwit, gnat, rail] various birds. 20 ruff] perch-like fish. 36 polly] 1616 reads 'poolye'.

498 *On my first son*] born in 1596, and died during the plague in 1603. Jonson told Drummond of a vision he had at the time of the child's death: 'When the King came in England, at that time the pest was in London, he [Jonson] being in the country at Sir Robert Cotton's house with old Camden, he saw in a vision his eldest son (then a child and at London) appear unto him with the mark of a bloody cross on his forehead as if it had been cutted with a sword. At which amazed, he prayed unto God, and in the morning he came to Mr. Camden's chamber to tell him, who persuaded him it was but an apprehension of his fantasy, at which he should not be dejected. In the meantime comes there letters from his wife of the death of that boy in the plague. He appeared to him, he said, of a manly shape, and of that growth that he thinks he shall be at the resurrection.'

499 *An epitaph on Salathiel Pavy*] on one of the Children of the Chapel, who after three years of acting died in 1603, aged thirteen.

499 *Epitaph on Elizabeth, L. H.*] as yet unidentified.

500–502 *To Penshurst*] the seat of the Sidney family in Kent. 2 touch] touchstone, a fine-grained dark stone. 4 lantern] a small tower, or erection, on a roof or dome with the sides pierced to admit light. 14 his great birth] On the birth of Philip Sidney, an oak tree was planted which survived until 1768. 19 Gamage] Sir Robert Sidney, Viscount Lisle (the younger brother of Sir Philip), owner of Penshurst at the time Jonson is writing, had married Barbara Gamage. 66 yet dine away] Jonson told Drummond that 'being at the end of my Lord Salisbury's table . . . and demanded by my Lord why he was not glad: "My Lord," said he, "you promised me I should dine with you, but I do not," for he had none of his meat—he esteemed only that his meat which was of his own dish.' 69 call] 1641 'call for'.

502 *Song, to Celia* (1)] first printed in *Volpone*, 1607; set to music by Alfonso Ferrabosco in his *Airs*, 1609.

502 *Song, to Celia* (2)] paraphrased from various scattered passages in a collection of letters written by a late Greek rhetorician, Philostratus. Cf. J. A. Symonds in *The Academy*, xxvi. 377.

503 *Underwoods*] In his preface to the reader, Jonson explains that he entitles 'these lesser poems of later growth by this of Underwood, out of the analogy they hold to the Forest in my former book, and no otherwise.'

503 *A celebration of Charis*] conjectured by Simpson and Herford (i. 53) to be about the lady who played Venus in the mask usually called *The Hue and Cry after Cupid*, because the chariot of Venus described in the mask is like the chariot in *Her triumph*. If Charis is a real woman, she has the honor of inspiring Jonson's finest love poetry, written at intervals from 1608 to 1622.

503–504 *Her triumph* 11–30] These two stanzas also serve as a song in *The Devil is an Ass*.

504 *Begging another kiss . . .*] according to Drummond, Jonson frequently repeated this poem.

504–505 *An ode to himself* 6 and destroys] Various editors have inserted a monosyllable ('quite,' 'so,' or 'soon') between 'and' and 'destroys' to perfect the meter. 9 Clarius'] Apollo, so called from his temple and oracle at Clarus. 27–30] Prometheus, son of Japetus, with the aid of Minerva ('the issue of Jove's brain') stole fire from the sun and gave it to man.

505 *A fit of rhyme against rhyme* 10 syllabes] syllables.

506–509 *To the immortal memory . . .*] a Pindaric ode in which Jonson gives English names to the three divisions: the strophe is the turn, the antistrophe the counter-turn, and the epode the stand. This ode was occasioned by the death of Sir Henry Morison, about 1629. Sir Lucius Cary, better known by his later title, Lord Falkland, was the author of a few poems and a member of Ben Jonson's literary group. At his country place, Great Tew, near Oxford, he kept a hospitable home for the week-end discussions of poets, philosophers, and theologians. At the outbreak of the Civil War, he espoused, with some hesitation, the King's cause, and met an early death, desired by himself, at Newbury, 1643. The charm of his personality has been preserved in Clarendon's pages (ed. Macray, iii. 178–190). 1 Brave infant of Saguntum] After a long siege Saguntum, a Roman city in Spain, was taken by Hannibal, but the inhabitants destroyed themselves and their belongings by fire. According to Pliny, one infant about to be born returned to the mother's womb to escape the Carthaginians. 24 fact] deed. 68 bald] 1641 'bold'. 123 Friendship in deed] 1641 'Friendship, indeed'.

509–511 *An epistle answering . . .* 32 Valteline] a valley stretching from the Lake of Como to the Tyrolean mountains, which Spain had taken under her protection in 1620, for it offered the only way by which Spanish armies could pass between Italy and Germany. By 1623 France, Venice, and Savoy had formed a league for the recovery of the Valteline. 36 match from Spain] between Charles, Prince of Wales, and the Infanta of Spain. Prince Charles, impatient of diplomatic delays, had rushed off to Spain incognito, arriving on March 7, 1623, but the Pope continued to delay the dispensation. Finally the ardor of Prince Charles cooled and he sailed for England on September 18. The treaty for the marriage, which had always been unpopular in England, was then dropped. Jonson's phrase, 'My prince's safety,' indicates that the poem was written while Prince Charles was in Spain; and a reference in line 48 (see note below) shows that it could not have been written earlier than June. 40] Frederick, Elector Palatine, who had married the Princess Elizabeth (daughter of James I), had been elected King of Bohemia, but had been driven out of Bohemia and the Palatinate by the Catholic powers, headed by Spain. Many Englishmen wished to join in the war to restore him to his rights. 44 Brunsfield] Perhaps Jonson shows his lack of interest in political affairs by writing Brunsfield for Brunswick. Evidently he means to refer to Christian of Brunswick, the cousin and avowed champion of the Princess Elizabeth, now the exiled Queen of Bohemia. Mansfield] Ernest, Count of Mansfeld, in command of the army of Frederick, Elector Palatine and King of Bohemia. 48 late mystery of reception] plans being made early in June, 1623, for the reception of Prince Charles on his expected return from Spain with the Infanta as bride. Inigo Jones, with whom Jonson had earlier devised court masks but with whom he was now at odds, and Edward Alleyn, a celebrated actor, were called in to arrange the projected entertainments and masks. Evidently Jonson felt slighted that he was replaced by Alleyn and doubtless attributed it to the inimical influence of Inigo Jones. 50 guides the motions and directs the bears] Herford and Simpson (i. 90) interpret this as a reference to Inigo Jones, but Jonson must have had in mind Edward Alleyn, who was interested in bear-baiting and had from 1594 been part owner of the Bear Garden, sometimes called Paris Garden. From 1604 he was Master of the Game of Paris Garden. This identification is made more certain by a letter of June 5, 1623 (Birch, ii. 403), recounting the preparations to receive Prince Charles,

from which we learn that 'Alleyn, sometime a player, now squire of the bears, Inigo Jones, surveyor of the king's works, rode hence on Tuesday towards Winchester and Southampton, to take order for his majesty's entertainment.' 52–53] Jonson is thinking of his masks, usually produced at court during the Christmas season. 65–70] Jonson continues to draw his figures from the production of masks, and to express scorn for the flimsy, temporary scenery with which Inigo Jones decked them out.

511–513 *To . . . Shakespeare* 19–21] 35 him of Cordova dead] Seneca.

513 *Ben Jonson's Sociable Rules . . .*] On June 19, 1624, John Chamberlain wrote to Sir Dudley Carleton: 'I send here certain *leges conviviales* of Ben Jonson for a fair room or chamber, lately built at the Tavern or Sign of the Devil and St. Dunstan by Temple Bar.' The rules were engraved in Latin over the fireplace of the Apollo Room. Brome's translation is the earliest. 24 without reflection] extemporaneous.

514 *Slow, slow, fresh fount* 4 division] a rapid passage of musical notes.

514 *Queen and huntress* 1 Queen and huntress] Diana; intended as a compliment to Queen Elizabeth.

516 *Swell me a bowl* 2 Lyæus] Bacchus.

517 *Had those that dwell in error foul*] set to music by Alfonso Ferrabosco in his *Airs*, 1609. 2] marginal note: 'There hath been such a profane paradox published.' 6 world's soul, true harmony] marginal note: 'The Platonic opinion. See also Mac[robius], lib. 1 and 2, Som[nium] Scip[ionis].'

517 *Beauties, have ye seen*] set to music by Henry Lawes in *Airs and Dialogues*, 1655. The source of this poem is the first idyl of Moschus, usually called *The runaway Cupid*. Jonson's mask, from which this poem is taken, is frequently called *The Hue and Cry after Cupid*.

519 *Though I am young*] set to music by Lanier in Playford's *Select Airs*, 1653. 6 heat] 1641 'heart'.

EPIGRAMS

THE EPIGRAM ('a short poem ending in a witty or ingenious turn of thought, to which the rest of the composition is intended to lead up,' *O.E.D.*) had been written in great numbers by John Heywood in the middle decades of the 16th century. But his homespun, thoroughly English poems in this kind (see pp. 11–12) were not immediately imitated. Turberville trans-

lated epigrams from the Greek Anthology and from the Latin poet Ausonius;
Kendall gathered into *Flowers of Epigrams*, 1577, a great number of
translations, mostly his own, from Greek and Latin epigrams, the latter including those by classical authors and by recent writers such as Sir Thomas
More.

It was not until the influence of Martial plainly manifested itself that
the epigram may be said to have come into its own. Surrey had translated
one of Martial's epigrams (see p. 34); Kendall had translated more than
one hundred and sixty of them; but Sir John Harington and Sir John
Davies first successfully reproduced in English the true Martialian satire.
Many of Harington's witty trifles were written between 1580 and 1590,
and Davies did his best work in the early 1590's. After Davies had published (about 1595) there came a flood of epigram-books; the form seems
to have been extremely popular for some twenty years. In the period from
1598 to 1620 there were printed more than fifty collections, aside from
reprints and renewed editions. Usually to these collections were joined
satires or other poems to fill out the measure of a volume. Seven of the
books included in our number were in Latin, but written by English authors
of the time. Besides being published in collections, epigrams were scattered
about as space-fillers in many volumes; they were passed from hand to hand
in manuscript, and from mouth to mouth wherever gallants met.

Jonson referred to his *Epigrams* (published with his *Works* in 1616,
though licensed separately in 1612) as 'the ripest of my studies.' Donne
and Browne each wrote a very few excellent poems in this kind; while
Herrick included in his *Hesperides*, 1648, epigrams sufficient to have formed
an excellent independent collection. A choice of the best English epigrams
available was made by the editors of *Wit's Recreations*, 1640, who included,
without naming their authors, 660 of these short poems (in later editions increased to 900) and a great many epitaphs, both serious and jocular. The
influence of the epigram upon the madrigal may be seen in such a madrigal
as *The silver swan* (p. 438).

While the satirical use of the epigram predominated, there are also many
of them to be classified as moralistic, encomiastic, and sepulchral. The last-
named type is equivalent to the epitaph; and even these were sometimes
satirical. Often a humorous anecdote was versified. Practically all of the English
epigrammatists of our period drew upon Martial, many of them by direct translation.

CROSS REFERENCES: For epigrams not printed in this section, see under: Sir
Thomas More, John Heywood, Wyatt, Surrey, Minor Courtly Makers, Turberville, Elizabethan Miscellanies, Sir John Davies, Donne, and Jonson.

MODERN EDITIONS: Kendall's *Flowers of Epigrams*, Spenser Society, 1874;
Epigrams of Sir John Harington (ed. by N. E. McClure), Philadelphia, 1926;
Guilpin's *Skialetheia* (ed. by A. B. Grosart), Manchester, 1878; Bastard's *Poems*
(ed. by A. B. Grosart), Manchester, 1880, and *Chrestoleros*, Spenser Society, 1888;
Weever's *Epigrammes* (ed. by R. B. McKerrow), Stratford-upon-Avon, 1922;
Rowlands's *Complete Works*, Hunterian Club, 1874–1880.

COMMENT: T. K. Whipple, *Martial and the English Epigram from Sir Thomas
Wyatt to Ben Jonson*, Berkeley, 1925.

TEXT: *Flowers of Epigrams*, 1577 (14927), White; *The Most Elegant and
Witty Epigrams*, 1618 (12776), Harvard; *Additional Ms.* 12049, B. M.; *Skialetheia*,
1598 (12504), White; *Chrestoleros*, 1598 (1559), White; *Epigrams in the Oldest
Cut and Newest Fashion*, 1599 (25224), Bodleian; *The Letting of Humor's Blood*,
1600 (21393), B. M.; *Humor's Looking-Glass*, 1608 (21386), Huntington; *Chetham
Ms.* 8012, Chetham; *Reliquiæ Wottonianæ*, 1672, Cornell; *The Mouse-Trap*,

1606 (19334), B. M.; *Epigrams*, 1608 (19329), White; *Laquei Ridiculosi*, 1613 (19332), White; *The Mastive*, 1615 (19333), White; *Two Centuries of Epigrams*, 1610 (13018), White; *Rub and a Great Cast*, 1614 (11370), White; *Quodlibets*, 1628 (12974), B. M.; *Two Books of Epigrams and Epitaphs*, 1639 (1354), White.

520 *Flowers of Epigrams*] Aside from information which can be gleaned from this book, little or nothing is known of Kendall. He was educated at Eton and Magdalen Hall, Oxford, took no degree, and became a law-student at Staple Inn. *Flowers of Epigrams* is an anthology of translations, mostly by Kendall himself. He appended to the collection a section headed *Trifles*, purporting to be made up of his own poems, but depending heavily upon the *Nugæ*, 1533, of Nicolas Bourbon. Cf. J. Hutton, 'Timothy Kendall's "Trifles" and Nicolas Bourbon's *Nugæ*,' *M.L.N.* xliv. 19.

520 *To Sabidius*] from Martial, i. 32; see Weever's version, p. 525. The most familiar English version is, of course, that beginning 'I do not like thee, Dr. Fell'.

520 *To Fidentinus*] from Martial, i. 38.

520 *To a married couple . . .*] from Martial, viii. 35.

520 *Of Fuscus, a drunkard*] from a Latin epigram by Sir Thomas More.

521 *Of Alphus*] from a Latin epigram by Bishop John Parkhurst, whose *Ludicra sive Epigrammata Juvenilia* had appeared in 1573.

521 *To the reader*] Kendall's own apology, from his *Trifles*, but imitated from Martial.

521 *Elegant and Witty Epigrams*] Sir John Harington (c. 1561-1612), a charming and witty member of Queen Elizabeth's entourage, amused his sovereign (who was also his godmother) by his jests, but gained little lasting emolument from his association with her. Educated at Eton and at Cambridge, Harington was a competent Latin writer, with an unusual knowledge of general literature. His principal literary achievement was his translation of Ariosto's *Orlando Furioso*, 1591; the introduction and notes which he added are still of interest. His *Metamorphosis of Ajax*, a rather scurrilous book (with the serious purpose, however, of improving domestic sanitation) caused Harington's temporary banishment from court upon its appearance, without a printer's license, in 1596. The epigrams which he had been composing from his youth onward were not printed until after his death. Harington's virtues

as a writer are a certain cleverness in rhyming and an easy, jocose urbanity such as characterizes later masters of *vers de société*. See Sir Walter Raleigh's *Some Authors*, Oxford, 1923.

521 *Against writers . . .*] from Martial, ix. 81.

522 *To Mr. John Davies*] later Sir John Davies.

523 *Skialetheia*] published anonymously with the sub-title, *A Shadow of Truth in Certain Epigrams and Satires*. Lines quoted from this book in *England's Parnassus*, 1600, are assigned to Guilpin, who may also be the E. G. whom Marston addresses as his 'very friend' in the second edition of *The Scourge of Villainy*, and the E. G. to whom Donne addresses a short verse-letter. That Everard (sometimes called Edward) Guilpin was a Cambridge man can be established both from the internal evidence of *Skialetheia* and from the records of the University. He seems to have been influenced by Davies in his epigrams and by Marston and Donne in his satires. A genuine love of letters appears to inspire the passage about books in *Satyra quinta*.

523 *Of Cornelius* 5 cudgeled] heavily trimmed. 6 slop] a pair of loose breeches. 8 cad's-beard] caddis-beard; 'caddis' was a common word for cotton wool. 13 Bevis] a hero of romances.

523-524 *Satyra quinta*] 'Fifth satire.' 26 Fitzherbert . . . Dyer] the standard writers on English law. 28-29 Rose, Curtain] two of the London playhouses. 30 pathetic Spaniard's] Seneca's.

524 *Chrestoleros*] Thomas Bastard (1566-1618) was an unfortunate country preacher, whose early promise and genial spirits were blighted by poverty and ill-fortune. In 1598 he published an extensive collection of original epigrams under the title *Chrestoleros*. The book and its author were made the butt of many jokes by rival wits; but they were defended by Harington and Heath (see p. 530).

525 *Epigrams . . .*] John Weever (1576-1632), after devoting some early years to poetry, became an antiquary and made an exhaustive study of the tombs of England. When he was twenty-three, at the end of four years spent at Cambridge, he published this volume of epigrams, which reflected wide reading both in older and in contemporary authors. He followed it with the satirical poem *Faunus and Melliflora,* 1600, and a more serious work in verse, *The Mirror of Martyrs,* 1601. In at least the first and third of these volumes Weever reveals his high regard for the works of Shakespeare by praising them outright and by echoing them in several passages. His tributes in the *Epigrams* to Spenser, Drayton, Marston, Jonson, Warner, and Daniel are fairly discerning.

525 *Translat. ex Martial*] From Martial, i. 32; see Kendall's version, p. 520.

526 *In tumulum Abrahami Simple*] 'On the tomb of Abraham Simple.'

526 *Ad Gulielmum Shakespeare*] the earliest poetic address to Shakespeare; it is the only one of Weever's epigrams in sonnet-form. **13** They] the thousands of readers mentioned in the previous line.

526 *Letting of Humor's Blood*] 'in the Head Vein' completes the title in 1600. Samuel Rowlands (*c.* 1570–*c.* 1630) was a satirist and pamphleteer who 'pestered the press' almost continuously from 1598 to 1628. In 1600 copies of his books were ordered to be burned.

527 *An epitaph on a bellows-maker*] This and the three epigrams following are by 'the facetious John Hoskins' (1566–1638), a clever lawyer who made a considerable reputation as a wit. After completing studies for the M.A. at Oxford in 1592, he taught school and began to compile a Greek lexicon, which he abandoned at the letter M. He entered the Middle Temple for training in law. After his admission to the bar he was several times in Parliament, and in 1614 he was imprisoned for making, in the House of Commons, satirical reference to the new Scottish favorites. He was a literary associate of Sir John Davies, Donne, Daniel, and others. According to Wood, Hoskins left 'a book of poems neatly written, bigger than those of Dr. Donne, which were lent by his son Sir Benedict . . . to a certain person in 1653, but he could never retrieve it.' For a poem possibly by Hoskins, see pp. 203–204. The present epitaph is signed in the manuscript, 'Mr. Hoskynes', and the two following are signed 'per eundem'.

528 *John Hoskins to his little child . . .*] His son's name is elsewhere given as Bennet or Benedict.

528 *Mouse-Trap*] Henry Parrot (*fl.* 1606–1626) left no records of his life outside the half-dozen of books which are attributed to him. He seems to have been a man of some education, perhaps

a member of one of the Inns of Court. *The Mastive* contains satires as well as epigrams, and *VIII Cures for the Itch,* 1626, contains epitaphs and characters. Otherwise the books are made up entirely of epigrams, some of which, however are not Parrot's own. His books throw considerable light on life in London as it was lived among pleasure-seekers and gallants.

528 *Paulus a pamphlet*] The incident here retold was recorded of Sir Thomas More in Harington's introduction to his translation of *Orlando Furioso,* 1591.

529 *Magus would needs* 4 *The Fox*] Jonson's *Volpone, or The Fox,* printed in 1607; this reference shows it to have been on the stage in 1606.

529 *Ortus novus urbe Britannus*] 'The new Englishman sprung up in the city.' This epigram exemplifies satire commonly directed against actors.

529 *Impar impares odit*] 'The inferior hates inferiors.'

529 *Suum cuique pulchrum*] 'To each his own is beautiful.'

529 *Nuptiæ post nummos*] 'Money, then marriage.'

530 *Ebrius dissimulans*] 'The sly sot.'

530 *Two Centuries . . .*] John Heath (*fl.* 1615), an M.A. of Oxford, is known chiefly for this book. He also translated several books from French and from Spanish, and contributed verses to memorial volumes. According to Drummond's record, Jonson classed Heath's epigrams with the works of Taylor, the water poet, as popular trash.

530 *Ad modernos epigrammatistas*] 'To modern epigrammatists.' **1** Heywood] John Heywood; see p. 11.

530 *Ad Tho. Bastardum epigrammatistam*] 'To Thomas Bastard, epigrammatist.' See p. 524.

530 *In Beatricem præpropere defunctam*] 'Upon Beatrice, too early deceased.'

531 *Ad Collegium Wintoniensem*] 'To Winchester College.'

531 *Rub and a Great Cast*] Thomas Freeman (*fl.* 1614) took the degree of B.A. at Oxford in 1611 and then went to London to try his fortune as poet. His sole publication seems to have been his volume of epigrams published in 1614 in two parts, the first entitled *Rub and a Great Cast,* and the second, *Run and a Great Cast.* These titles are taken from the sport of bowling. The book deserves reprinting.

531 *Me quoque vatem*] 'I, too, am a poet.'

CHAMBERS, John Skelton, T.L.S. (Leading Article), June 20, 1929, p. 493; A.
Gordon, John Skelton, Poet Laureate, London, 1943; H. L. R. Edwards,
London, 1949; William Nelson, John Skelton, Laureate, New York, 1939; L.
J. Lloyd, John Skelton, a Sketch of His Life and Writings, Oxford, 1938; Robert
Kinsman, 'Philip Sparrow,' etc., Ph.D. (U.C.), viii (1950), 473–41; Alan Swallow

SUPPLEMENTARY NOTES TO TUDOR POETRY

The following general discussions and surveys of sixteenth-century English poetry will prove useful:

Douglas Bush, *Mythology and the Renaissance Tradition in English Poetry,* Minnesota, 1932; Yvor Winters, 'The Sixteenth-Century Lyric in England,' *Poetry: A Magazine of Verse,* in three parts: liii (1939), 258–72, 320–35; liv (1939), 35–51; Louis R. Zocca, *Elizabethan Narrative Poetry,* Rutgers, 1950; Hallett Smith, *Elizabethan Poetry,* Harvard, 1952; C. S. Lewis, *The Sixteenth Century* (Oxford History of English Literature), Oxford (forthcoming).

To the original list of abbreviations add the following:

E.S.E.A. = Essays and Studies by Members of the English Association.
E.L.H. = ELH: A Journal of English Literary History, Johns Hopkins University.
Harvard Studies and Notes = Harvard Studies and Notes on Philology and Literature, Harvard University Press, Cambridge, Mass.
H.L.B. = Huntington Library Bulletin.
H.L.Q. = Huntington Library Quarterly.
M.L.Q. = Modern Language Quarterly, University of Washington, Seattle.
N.&Q. = Notes and Queries, Oxford University Press.
P.Q. = Philological Quarterly, University of Iowa.
Univ. Missouri Studies = The University of Missouri Studies, Columbia, Missouri.
U.T.Q. = University of Toronto Quarterly.

JOHN SKELTON

ACTIVE research on Skelton and a number of manuscript discoveries during the last two decades have added substantially to our knowledge of the poet's life and in a number of respects altered our estimate of his general significance, both for our time and for his contemporaries. Among other things, he has been shown to have been educated at both Universities, since he was definitely in residence at Oxford in 1479. The tradition that Skelton was held in universal disrepute by fellow-churchmen for writing verses considered discreditable to the Church is at least modified by the discovery of an occasional poem addressed by Skelton to Stephen Gardiner, indicating that the two men were on intimate and pleasant terms. Finally, there is much to disprove the belief that Skelton was regarded by his contemporaries as an eccentric and unlearned versifier. In 1519 the English humanist schoolmaster and poet laureate, Robert Whittington, accorded written praise to Skelton personally and to the eloquent and moving qualities of his poetry. Twenty years earlier Erasmus had composed an ode to Skelton, ranking him with Homer and Virgil and declaring that even Orpheus must give place to the English poet. There seems, in short, no question of Skelton's eminent reputation in the eyes and minds of the sixteenth-century humanist world, whether English or continental. That he was able to write successful poems dealing with low life turns out to be rather a tribute to his versatility than an index to his character and taste as a whole.

MODERN EDITIONS: *The Complete Poems of John Skelton Laureate* (ed. by Philip Henderson), London, 1931; *John Skelton: A Selection from His Poems* (ed. by Vivian de Sola Pinto), London, 1950.

COMMENT: 'John Skelton,' *T.L.S.* (Leading Article), June 20, 1929, p. 921; I. A. Gordon, *John Skelton: Poet Laureate,* London, 1943; H. L. R. Edwards, *Skelton,* London, 1949; William Nelson, *John Skelton: Laureate,* New York, 1939; L. J. Lloyd, *John Skelton: A Sketch of His Life and Writings,* Oxford, 1938; Robert S. Kinsman, 'Phyllip Sparowe: Titulus,' *S.P.,* xlvii (1950), 473–84; Alan Swallow, 'The Pentameter Line in Skelton and Wyatt,' *M.P.,* xlviii (1950), 1–11.

SIR THOMAS MORE

MODERN EDITIONS: *The English Works of Sir Thomas More* (ed. by W. E. Campbell and A. W. Reed), Vol. I, London, 1931; *Recusant Poets* (ed. by Louise Imogen Guiney), New York, 1939.
COMMENT: R. W. Chambers, *The Place of St. Thomas More in English Literature and History,* London, 1937; Hoyt H. Hudson, *The Epigram in the English Renaissance,* Princeton, 1947. For other recent studies, see p. 1286.

JOHN HEYWOOD

MODERN EDITIONS: *Recusant Poets* (ed. by Louise Imogen Guiney), New York, 1939.
COMMENT: J. M. Berdan, *Early Tudor Poetry,* New York, 1920, pp. 102–16; R. de la Bere, *John Heywood: Entertainer,* London, 1937.

HENRY HOWARD, EARL OF SURREY

BORN heir to the eventual leadership of the most powerful and influential of all English noble families, Surrey may be said to have been almost predestined to pride. That he was 'foolish' as well now seems questionable. Many of his acts, for generations scorned as rash, may be interpreted as an attempt on Surrey's part to demonstrate as dramatically as possible the loyalty of the Howard family to the crown (especially since they occurred in a time when opposing groups were busy circulating rumors, e.g., vague accusations of treason, in an effort to make King Henry suspicious and thereby to weaken the power of the Howards).
MODERN EDITIONS: *Surrey's Fourth Boke of Virgill* (ed. by Herbert Hartman), New York, 1933; *Silver Poets of the Sixteenth Century* (ed. by Gerald Bullett), Everyman's Library, London, 1947.
COMMENT: Edwin Casady, *Henry Howard, Earl of Surrey,* New York, 1938.

THOMAS, LORD VAUX

MODERN EDITIONS: *Recusant Poets* (ed. by Louise Imogen Guiney), New York, 1939.

NICHOLAS GRIMALD

MODERN EDITIONS: *Recusant Poets* (ed. by Louise Imogen Guiney), New York, 1939.

ELIZABETH

COMMENT: B. B. Gamzue, 'Elizabeth and Literary Patronage,' *P.M.L.A.,* xlix (1934), 1041–49.

THOMAS SACKVILLE, EARL OF DORSET

MODERN EDITIONS: *The Complaint of Henry Duke of Buckingham* (ed. by Marguerite Hearsey), New Haven, 1936; *The Mirror for Magistrates* (ed. by Lily B. Campbell), Cambridge, 1938.
COMMENT: 'A Poet Turned Statesman. Sir Thomas Sackville in Court and Study,'

T.L.S. (Leading Article), Jan. 25, 1936, pp. 61–62; Fitzroy Pyle, 'Thomas Sackville and *A Mirror for Magistrates,' R.E.S.,* xiv (1938), 315–21; Lily B. Campbell, *Tudor Conceptions of History and Tragedy in A Mirror for Magistrates,* Berkeley, 1936; J. Swart, *Thomas Sackville: A Study in Sixteenth-Century Poetry* (Groningen Studies in English, I), Groningen, J. B. Wolters, 1949.

THOMAS TUSSER

MODERN EDITIONS: *Five Hundred Points of Good Husbandry, with an Introduction by Sir Walter Scott and a Benediction by Rudyard Kipling,* London, 1931; *Thomas Tusser: His Good Points of Husbandry* (ed. by Dorothy Hartley), London, 1931.

BARNABE GOOGE

COMMENT: H. H. Hudson, 'Sonnets by Barnabe Googe,' *P.M.L.A.,* xlviii (1933), 293–94.

GEORGE TURBERVILLE

MODERN EDITIONS: *Recusant Poets* (ed. by Louise Imogen Guiney), New York, 1939.
COMMENT: John Erskine Hankins, *The Life and Works of George Turberville,* Lawrence, Kansas, 1940.

GEORGE WHETSTONE

COMMENT: Thomas C. Izard, *George Whetstone, Mid-Elizabethan Gentleman of Letters,* New York, 1942.

RICHARD STANYHURST

MODERN EDITIONS: *Recusant Poets* (ed. by Louise Imogen Guiney), New York, 1939.
COMMENT: Sidney H. Atkins, 'Certain of Sir Thomas More's Epigrams Translated by Stanihurst,' *M.L.R.,* xxvi (1931), 338–40; D. Van der Haar, *Richard Stanyhurst's 'Aeneis,'* Amsterdam, 1933.

SIR PHILIP SIDNEY

MODERN EDITIONS: *Silver Poets of the Sixteenth Century* (ed. by Gerald Bullett), Everyman's Library, London, 1947.
COMMENT: Mona Wilson, *Sir Philip Sidney,* London, 1931; Theodore H. Banks, 'Sidney's "Astrophel and Stella" Reconsidered,' *P.M.L.A.,* l (1935), 403–12; Hoyt H. Hudson, 'Penelope Devereux as Sidney's Stella,' *H.L.B.,* No. 7 (April, 1935), pp. 89–129; K. O. Myrick, *Sir Philip Sidney as a Literary Craftsman,* Harvard Studies in English, xiv, 1935; W. G. Friedrich, 'The Stella of Astrophel,' *E.L.H.,* iii (1936), 114–39; Denver Ewing Baughan, 'Sir Philip Sidney and the Matchmakers,' *M.L.R.,* xxxiii (1938), 506–19; and 'The Question of Sidney's Love for his Wife,' *N. & Q.,* clxxvii (July–Dec., 1939), 383–85; A. H. Bill, *Astrophel,* New York, 1937; Theodore Spencer, 'The Poetry of Sir Philip Sidney,' *E.L.H.,* xii (1945), 251–78; E. C. Pettet, 'Sidney and the Cult of Romantic Love,' *English,* vi (1946–47), 232–40. For other recent studies, see pp. 1318–20.

106–107 *Not at the first sight* 1 | a weak or curving shot; hence 'indirect.' dribbled] a term from archery, describing |

SIR EDWARD DYER

COMMENT: Ralph M. Sargent, *At the Court of Queen Elizabeth: the Life and Lyrics of Sir Edward Dyer,* Oxford, 1935.

FULKE GREVILLE, LORD BROOKE

MODERN EDITIONS: *Caelica* (ed. by Una Ellis-Fermor), London, 1937; *Poems and Dramas of Fulke Greville, Lord Brooke* (ed. by Geoffrey Bullough), two volumes, London, 1939.

COMMENT: Geoffrey Bullough, 'Fulke Greville, First Lord Brooke,' *M.L.R.,* xxviii (1933), 1–20; William Frost, *Fulke Greville's 'Caelica'; an Evaluation,* Pleasant-ville, New York, 1942.

SIR WALTER RALEGH

MODERN EDITIONS: *The Poems of Sir Walter Ralegh* (ed. by A. M. C. Latham), London, 1929; 2nd ed., 1951. *Silver Poets of the Sixteenth Century* (ed. by Gerald Bullett), Everyman's Library, London, 1947.
COMMENT: H. W. Garrod, 'Walter Raleigh,' in *The Profession of Poetry and Other Lectures,* Oxford, 1929, pp. 266–70; Hyder E. Rollins, 'Sir Walter Raleigh and *The Phoenix Nest*,' *T.L.S.,* Dec. 12, 1929, p. 1058; E. K. Chambers, 'The Dis-enchantment of the Elizabethans,' in *Sir Thomas Wyatt and Some Collected Studies,* London, 1933; E. C. Dunn, 'Ralegh and the "New" Poetry,' in *The Literature of Shakespeare's England,* New York, 1936, pp. 140–63; M. C. Bradbrook, *The School of Night,* Cambridge, 1936; Fred Sorenson, 'Sir Walter Ralegh's Marriage,' *S.P.,* xxxiii (1936), 182–202; A. M. Buchan, 'Ralegh's *Cynthia*—Facts or Legends,' *M.L.Q.,* i (1940), 461–74; Hugh Ross Williamson, *Sir Walter Raleigh,* London, 1951, For further recent items, see p. 1349.

134 *Like to a hermit*] A close trans-lation of a sonnet by Desportes, who supplied models for at least two other poems in *The Phoenix Nest.* Lodge and Breton each wrote versions of the same sonnet.

139–140 *The Lie*] 78 thy] The sense requires emendation to 'the', inasmuch as the entire poem is addressed to the soul.

THOMAS WATSON

COMMENT: Mark Eccles, *Christopher Marlowe in London,* Harvard, 1934. See works by Janet Scott and L. C. John listed under 'Sonnet-Sequences.'

ROBERT GREENE

COMMENT: For recent general studies, see p. 1328.

THOMAS LODGE

MODERN EDITIONS: *Recusant Poets* (ed. by Louise Imogen Guiney), New York, 1939.
COMMENT: For recent general studies, see p. 1323.

NICHOLAS BRETON

CONSIDERABLE light has recently been thrown on the tangled family affairs of Nicholas Breton, his parents, and his step-father George Gascoigne. The poet's father, William Breton, may or may not have engaged early in trading; it is now clear that he made his incredible fortune in land-grabbing, i.e., in acquir-ing confiscated property from the crown and selling it immediately at a tidy profit. At the same time he must have kept enough lands to bequeath an ex-tensive estate to his two sons. His will, while leaving the administration of the estate to his widow until the children came of age, specifically required her to forfeit all rights should she remarry. What Elizabeth Breton did, however, upon her marriage to Gascoigne was to ignore the will completely, continuing her management of the older son's inheritance through her new husband. Gas-coigne, in turn, contrived to have himself appointed guardian to the older son, to whose name he somehow succeeded in having Nicholas' heritage transferred. The two partners in crime seem effectively to have stolen the poet's birthright.
MODERN EDITIONS: *Melancolike Humours* (ed. by G. B. Harrison), London, 1929; *Poems by Nicholas Breton* (ed. by Jean Robertson), Liverpool, 1952.

COMMENT: Mary Bradford Whiting, 'Nicholas Breton, Gentleman, A Tercentenary,' *Fortnightly Review*, cxxxi (1929), 618–32; Hyder E. Rollins, 'Nicholas Breton's "The Works of a Young Wit," ' *S.P.*, xxxiii (1936), 119–23; Fitzgerald Flournoy, 'William Breton, Nicholas Breton, and George Gascoigne,' *R.E.S.*, xvi (1940), 262–73.

CHRISTOPHER MARLOWE

MODERN EDITIONS: *Marlowe's Poems* (ed. by L. C. Martin), London, 1931.

COMMENT: John Bakeless, *The Tragicall History of Christopher Marlowe*, two volumes, Harvard, 1942; Douglas Bush, 'Marlowe: *Hero and Leander*,' *Mythology and the Renaissance Tradition in English Poetry*, Minnesota, 1932; F. S. Boas, *Marlowe and his Critics*, Oxford, 1929; and *Christopher Marlowe*, Oxford, 1940; F. C. Owlett, 'The Eulogy of Marlowe,' *Poetry Review*, xxvi (1935), 5–18, 127–38; P. H. Kocher, *Christopher Marlowe: A Study of His Thought, Learning, and Character*, Chapel Hill, 1946; T. S. Eliot, 'Notes on the Blank Verse of Christopher Marlowe,' *The Sacred Wood*, London, 1928; Tucker Brooke, 'Marlowe's Versification and Style,' *S.P.*, xix (1922), 186–205; Mark Eccles, *Christopher Marlowe in London*, Harvard 1934; Michel Poirier, *Christopher Marlowe*, London, 1951; Harry Levin, *The Overreacher*, Harvard, 1952.

ELIZABETHAN MISCELLANIES

IT HAS now been demonstrated that all of the poems in *A Hundreth Sundry Flowers* (1573) were written by George Gascoigne, as he himself claimed in his revision entitled *The Posies of George Gascoigne* (1575). See introduction to Gascoigne.

MODERN EDITIONS: Further editions by Hyder E. Rollins of the more important miscellanies, all published by the Harvard Press, are as follows: *Tottel's Miscellany*, two volumes (1928–29); *A Handful of Pleasant Delights* (1924); *The Phoenix Nest* (1931); *England's Helicon*, two volumes (1935); *A Poetical Rhapsody*, two volumes (1931–32). *Englands Helicon* (ed. by Hugh MacDonald), The Muses' Library, London, 1950.

COMMENT: William R. Parker, 'The Sonnets in Tottel's Miscellany,' *P.M.L.A.*, liv (1939), 669–77.

SONNET-SEQUENCES

COMMENT: Janet Scott, *Les sonnets élizabéthains: les sources et l'apport personnel*, Paris, 1929; L. C. John, *The Elizabethan Sonnet Sequences*, New York, 1938; L. E. Pearson, *Elizabethan Love Conventions*, Berkeley, 1938; Paul N. Siegel, 'The Petrarchan Sonneteers and Neo-Platonic Love,' *S.P.*, xlii (1945), 164–82.

HENRY CONSTABLE

MODERN EDITIONS: *Recusant Poets* (ed. by Louise Imogen Guiney), New York, 1939.

COMMENT: All works listed under 'Sonnet-Sequences.'

ROBERT SOUTHWELL

MODERN EDITIONS: *The Book of Robert Southwell, Priest, Poet, Prisoner* (ed. by Christobel M. Hood), Oxford, 1926; *Recusant Poets* (ed. by Louise Imogen Guiney), New York, 1939.

COMMENT: Pierre Janelle, *Robert Southwell, the Writer: A Study in Religious Inspiration*, New York, 1935.

SAMUEL DANIEL

MODERN EDITIONS: *Poems and 'A Defence of Ryme,'* (ed. by Arthur Colby Sprague), Harvard, 1930.

COMMENT: J. H. Roberts, 'A Note on Samuel Daniel's *Civile Wars,' M.L.N.*, xli (1926), 48–50; L. F. Ball, 'The Background of the Minor English Renaissance Epics,' *E.L.H.*, i (1934), 63–89; Martha Hale Shackford, 'Samuel Daniel's *Poetical Epistles,* Especially that to the Countess of Cumberland,' *S.P.*, xlv (1948), 180–95; L. C. John, *The Elizabethan Sonnet Sequences,* New York, 1938.

MICHAEL DRAYTON

MODERN EDITIONS: *The Works of Michael Drayton* (ed. by J. W. Hebel and others), five volumes, Oxford, 1931–41; *Poems* (ed. by John Buxton), two volumes, London, 1953.
COMMENT: L. F. Ball, 'Minor English Renaissance Epics,' *E.L.H.*, i (1934), 63–89; Russell Noyes, 'Drayton's Literary Vogue Since 1631,' *Indiana University Studies,* xxii (March, 1935); F. Y. St. Clair, 'Drayton's First Revision of His Sonnets,' *S.P.*, xxxvi (1939), 40–59; Geoffrey Tillotson, 'Contemporary Praise of *Polyolbion,' R.E.S.*, xvi (1940), 181–83; Bernard H. Newdigate, *Michael Drayton and His Circle,* London, 1941; L. E. Pearson, *Elizabethan Love Conventions,* Berkeley, 1938; L. C. John, *The Elizabethan Sonnet Sequences,* New York, 1938; Leah Jonas, *The Divine Science: The Aesthetic of Some Representative Seventeenth-Century English Poets,* New York, 1940; R. L. Sharp, *From Donne to Dryden: the Revolt against Metaphysical Poetry,* Chapel Hill, 1940; Douglas Bush, *English Literature in the Earlier Seventeenth Century,* Oxford, 1945, pp. 76–80; Mario Praz, 'Michael Drayton,' *English Studies,* xxviii (1947), 97–107.

SIR JOHN DAVIES

MODERN EDITIONS: *The Poems of Sir John Davies* (ed. by Clare Howard), New York, 1941; *Orchestra* (ed. by E. M. W. Tillyard), London, 1945; *Silver Poets of the Sixteenth Century* (ed. by Gerald Bullett) Everyman's Library, London, 1947.
COMMENT: Richard Perkinson, 'The Polemical Use of Davies' *Nosce Teipsum,' S.P.*, xxxvi (1939), 597–608; Charles D. Murphy, 'John Davies' Versification of Sidney's Prose,' *P.Q.*, xxi (1942), 410–14; E. M. W. Tillyard, *The Elizabethan World Picture,* London, 1943, pp. 96–101; and 'Sir John Davies: *Orchestra,* 1594' in *Five Poems, 1470–1870: An Elementary Essay on the Background of English Literature,* London, 1948.

JOSEPH HALL

MODERN EDITIONS: *The Collected Poems of Joseph Hall, Bishop of Exeter and Norwich* (ed. by Arnold Davenport), Liverpool, 1949.
COMMENT: Arnold Davenport, 'Some Notes on References to Joseph Hall in Marston's Satires,' *R.E.S.*, ix (1933), 192–96; and 'The Quarrel of the Satirists,' *M.L.R.*, xxxvii (1942), 123–30; Arnold Stein, 'The Second English Satirist,' *M.L.R.*, xxxviii (1943), 273–78; and 'Joseph Hall's Imitation of Juvenal,' *M.L.R.*, xlii (1948), 315–22.

JOHN MARSTON

COMMENT: Theodore Spencer, 'John Marston,' *Criterion,* xiii (1934), 581–99; R. E. Brettle, 'John Marston, Dramatist: Some New Facts about His Life,' *M.L.R.*, xxii (1927), 7–14; and 'John Marston at Oxford,' *R.E.S.*, iii (1927), 398–405; articles by Arnold Davenport under 'Joseph Hall'; Herschel Baker, 'The Literature of Disenchantment,' *The Wars of Truth,* Harvard, 1952, pp. 50–56.

GEORGE CHAPMAN

MODERN EDITIONS: *The Poems of George Chapman* (ed. by Phyllis B. Bartlett), New York, 1941.
COMMENT: Janet Spens, 'Chapman's Ethical Thought,' *E.S.E.A.*, xi (1925), 145–69; E. Holmes, *Aspects of Elizabethan Imagery,* Oxford, 1929; George Williamson, *The Donne Tradition,* Harvard, 1930; J. Smith, 'George Chapman,' *Scrutiny,* iii (1934–35), 339–50; iv (1935–36), 45–61; M. C. Bradbrook, *The School of Night,* Cambridge, 1936; Phyllis B. Bartlett, 'Stylistic Devices in Chapman's *Iliads,'*

P.M.L.A., lvii (1942), 661–75; and 'The Heroes of Chapman's Homer,' *R.E.S.*, xvii (1941), 257–80; H. B. Lathrop, *Translations from the Classics into English from Caxton to Chapman*, Madison, Wisconsin, 1933; 'George Chapman,' *T.L.S.* (Leading Article), May 10, 1934, pp. 329–30; Margaret Bottrall, 'George Chapman's Defence of Difficulty in Poetry,' *Criterion*, xvi (1936–37), 638–54; G. G. Loane, 'Chapman's Homer,' *Cornhill*, clvi (July–Dec., 1937), 637–44; Donald Smalley, 'The Ethical Bias of Chapman's Homer,' *S.P.*, xxxvi (1939), 169–91; Roy W. Battenhouse, 'Chapman's "The Shadow of Night": An Interpretation,' *S.P.*, xxxviii (1941), 584–608; 'Chapman and the Nature of Man,' *E.L.H.*, xii (1945), 87–107; H. C. Fay, 'Chapman's Materials for His Translation of Homer,' *R.E.S.*, New Series, ii (1951), 121–28; and 'Poetry, Pedantry, and Life in Chapman's *Iliads*,' *R.E.S.*, iv (1953), 13–25; Douglas Bush, *English Literature in the Earlier Seventeenth Century*, Oxford, 1945, pp. 60–63; 126–29.

EDWARD FAIRFAX

COMMENT: R. E. N. Dodge, 'The Text of the *Gerusalemme Liberata* in the Versions of Carew and Fairfax,' *P.M.L.A.*, xliv (1929), 681–95; Ruth C. Wallerstein, 'The Development of the Rhetoric and Metre of the Heroic Couplet, Especially in 1625–45,' *P.M.L.A.*, l (1935), 166–209; Charles C. Bell, 'Edward Fairfax, a Natural Son,' *M.L.N.*, lxii (1947), 24–27; 'A History of Fairfax Criticism,' *P.M.L.A.*, lxii (1947), 644–56.

SONGS FROM PLAYS

MODERN EDITIONS: *Songs and Lyrics from the English Playbooks* (ed. by Frederick S. Boas), London, 1945; *Songs and Lyrics from the English Masques and Light Operas* (ed. by Frederick S. Boas), London, 1949.

COMMENT: J. R. Moore, 'The Songs of the Public Theaters in the Time of Shakespeare,' *J.E.G.P.*, xxviii (1929), 166–202; E. S. Lindsey, 'The Music in Ben Jonson's Plays,' *M.L.N.*, xliv (1929), 86–92; Ernest Brennecke, Jr., 'Shakespeare's Musical Collaboration with Morley,' *P.M.L.A.*, liv (1939), 139–52; Willa M. Evans, 'Shakespeare's "Harke Harke Ye Larke," ' *P.M.L.A.*, lx (1945), 95–101.

BROADSIDE BALLADS

MODERN EDITIONS: *The Pepys Ballads* (ed. by H. E. Rollins), eight volumes, Harvard, 1929–32.

COMMENT: Herschel Baker, 'Classical Material in Broadside Ballads, 1550–1625,' *P.M.L.A.*, liv (1939), 981–89.

LYRICS FROM SONG-BOOKS

MODERN EDITIONS: *Brittons [Breton's] Bowre of Delights (1591)* (ed. by H. E. Rollins), Harvard, 1933; Thomas Morley, *A Plaine and Easie Introduction to Practical Musicke* (ed. by R. Alec Harman), London, 1952.

COMMENT: Bernard M. Wagner, 'New Songs of the Reign of Henry VIII,' *M.L.N.*, l (1935), 452–55; Charles R. Baskervill, *The Elizabethan Jig and Related Song Drama*, Chicago, 1929; E. H. Fellowes, *English Madrigal Verse*, Oxford, 1929; *The English Madrigal Composers*, 2nd ed., London, 1948; M. C. Boyd, *Elizabethan Music and Musical Criticism*, Philadelphia, 1940; Bruce Pattison, *Music and Poetry of the English Renaissance*, London, 1948, Herbert M. Schueller, 'The Renaissance Forerunner of the Neo-Classic Lyric,' *M.L.N.*, lxii (1947), 310–16; Catherine Ing, *Elizabethan Lyrics*, London, 1951; Willa M. Evans, *Ben Jonson and Elizabethan Music*, Lancaster, Pa., 1929; E. D. Mackerness, 'Morley's Musical Sensibility, *The Cambridge Journal*, ii (Oct. 1948–Sept. 1949), 301–8.

THOMAS CAMPION

COMMENT: Wilbur Lang Schramm, 'Campion, Horace, and Catullus,' *P.Q.*, xii (1933), 307–8; John B. Emperor, 'The Catullian Influence in English Lyric Poetry Circa 1600–50,' *Univ. Missouri Studies*, iii (1928), 21–28; M. M. Kastendieck, *England's Musical Poet, Thomas Campion*, Oxford, 1938; Ralph W. Berringer, 'Thomas

Campion's Share in A Booke of Ayres,' *P.M.L.A.*, lviii (1943), 938–48. Catharine W. Pelz, 'Thomas Campion, an Elizabethan Neo-Classicist,' *M.L.Q.*, xi (1950), 3–6; Catherine Ing, *Elizabethan Lyrics*, London, 1951.

JOHN DONNE

MODERN EDITIONS: *The Poems of John Donne* (ed. by Sir Herbert J. C. Grierson), new ed., Oxford, 1933; *John Donne: Complete Poetry and Selected Prose* (ed. by John Hayward), London, 1930; *The Complete Poems of John Donne* (ed. by R. E. Bennett), Chicago, 1942; *The Divine Poems* (ed. by Helen Gardner), Oxford, 1952.

COMMENT: George Williamson, *The Donne Tradition*, Harvard, 1929; Pierre Legouis, *Donne the Craftsman*, Oxford, 1928; *A Garland for John Donne* (ed. by Theodore Spencer), Harvard, 1931; R. C. Bald, *Donne's Influence in English Literature*, Morpeth, 1932; J. B. Leishman, *The Metaphysical Poets: Donne, Herbert, Vaughan, and Traherne*, Oxford, 1934; Joan Bennett, *Four Metaphysical Poets: Donne, Herbert, Vaughan, Crashaw*, Cambridge, 1934; Helen C. White, *The Metaphysical Poets: A Study in Religious Experience*, New York, 1936; Charles Monroe Coffin, *John Donne and the New Philosophy*, New York, 1937; John B. Douds, 'Donne's Technique of Dissonance,' *P.M.L.A.*, lii (1937), 1051–61; Milton A. Rugoff, *Donne's Imagery: A Study in Creative Sources*, New York, 1939; Allen R. Benham, 'The Myth of John Donne the Rake,' *P.Q.*, xx (1941), 465–73; Evelyn Hardy, *Donne: A Spirit in Conflict*, London, 1943; E. M. W. Tillyard, 'A Note on Donne's *Extasie*,' *R.E.S.*, xix (1943), 67–70; Arnold Stein, 'Donne and the Satiric Spirit,' *E.L.H.*, xi (1944), 266–82; 'Donne's Harshness and Elizabethan Tradition,' *S.P.*, xli (1944), 390–409; 'Donne's Obscurity and the Elizabethan Tradition,' *E.L.H.*, xiii (1946), 98–118; Douglas Bush, *English Literature in the Earlier Seventeenth Century*, Oxford, 1945, pp. 129–36; William Empson, 'Donne and the Rhetorical Tradition,' *Kenyon Review*, xi (1949), 571–87; S. Ernest Sprott, 'The Legend of Jack Donne the Libertine,' *U.T.Q.*, xix (1949–50), 335–53; D. W. Harding, 'Coherence of Theme in Donne's Poetry,' *Kenyon Review*, xiii (1951), 427–44; J. B. Leishman, *The Monarch of Wit: An Analytical and Comparative Study of John Donne*, London, 1951; J. E. V. Crofts, 'John Donne,' *E.S.E.A.*, xxii (1936), 128–53; essays in *Seventeenth-Century Studies Presented to Sir Herbert Grierson*, Oxford, 1938, as follows: C. S. Lewis, 'Donne and Love Poetry in the Seventeenth Century,' pp. 64–84; Joan Bennett, 'The Love Poetry of John Donne: A Reply to Mr. C. S. Lewis,' pp. 85–104; M. F. Moloney, 'Donne's Metrical Practice,' *P.M.L.A.*, lxv (1950), 232–39. For other recent studies, see p. 1354.

474–475 *A valediction forbidding mourning*] 9 Moving of th' earth] an earthquake, the oscillating motion of which is contrasted in line 11 with the far greater oscillation imagined to take place in the supposed astronomical phenomenon of trepidation of the spheres. 13 sublunary] in the astronomical meaning of 'constantly changing.'

BEN JONSON

MODERN EDITIONS: *Ben Jonson* (ed. by C. H. Herford and Percy Simpson), eleven volumes, Oxford, 1925–52, Vol. VIII; notes in Vol. XI; *The Poems of Ben Jonson* (ed. by Bernard H. Newdigate), Oxford, 1936; *Ben Jonson: Selected Works* (ed. by Harry Levin), New York, 1938.

COMMENT: Ralph S. Walker, 'Ben Jonson's Lyric Poetry,' *Criterion*, xiii (1933–34), 430–48; 'The Triumph of Ben Jonson: Tests of Poetic Magic,' Leading Article, *T.L.S.*, July 4, 1936, pp. 549–50; George Burke Johnston, *Ben Jonson: Poet*, New York, 1945; R. L. Sharp, *From Donne to Dryden, the Revolt against Metaphysical Poetry*, Chapel Hill, 1940; Leah Jonas, *The Divine Science: the Aesthetic of Some Representative Seventeenth-Century English Poets*, New York, 1940; John Palmer, *Ben Jonson*, New York, 1934; Willa M. Evans, *Ben Jonson and Elizabethan Music*, Lancaster, Pa., 1929; C. F. Wheeler, *Classical Mythology in the Plays, Masques, and Poems of Ben Jonson*, Princeton, 1938; E. W. Talbert, 'New Light on Ben Jonson's Workmanship,' *S.P.*, xl (1943), 154–85; Douglas Bush, *English Literature in the Earlier Seventeenth Century*, Oxford, 1945, pp. 104–11; L. J. Potts, 'Ben Jonson and the Seventeenth Century,' *E.S.E.A.*, xxxiii (1949), 7–24; Ralph S. Walker, 'Ben Jonson's *Discoveries: A New Analysis*,' *E.S.E.A.*, xxxvi (1952), 32–51.

499 *An epitaph on Salomon Pavy*] The traditional editorial expansion of the boy's first name to 'Salathiel' has been proved a purely fanciful conjecture (see G. E. Bentley, *T.L.S.*, May 30, 1942, p. 276).

EPIGRAMS

COMMENT: T. K. Whipple, *Martial and the English Epigram from Sir Thomas Wyatt to Ben Jonson*, Berkeley, 1925; Hoyt H. Hudson, *The Epigram in the English Renaissance*, Princeton, 1947.

NOTES TO TUDOR PROSE

NOTES TO TUDOR PROSE

INTRODUCTIONS AND NOTES

It is not our purpose to begin these introductions with a general essay upon the history of English prose during the Renaissance. Instead, we have preferred to utilize the pages that would be required for such an essay to supply the students and teachers using this anthology with additional examples of the prose writing of the period. We have therefore confined the introductions to short biographical notices of the various authors of the selections in this volume, supplementing these notices by brief lists of modern editions, and of the most important works of critical commentary upon the author and the book from which our selection has been taken. We have also indicated the early printed book or manuscript upon which our text has been based. In listing modern editions we have designated by an asterisk (*) those we consider the best; but, since these editions are often relatively expensive and sometimes unavailable, we have prefixed a dagger (†) to the relatively inexpensive, yet satisfactory editions currently in print. The notes have been restricted to the minimum we believe would be required by an advanced college student to enable him to comprehend the texts. They are not intended as a substitute for a good dictionary such as *Webster's Collegiate* or the *Concise Oxford*.

We have used the following abbreviations:

Am. Math. Monthly = *American Mathematical Monthly*, Providence, Rhode Island.
CQR = *Church Quarterly Review*.
Bull. Inst. Hist. Research = *Bulletin of the Institute of Historical Research*, London.
EHR = *English Historical Review*, London.
ELH = *ELH: A Journal of English Literary History*, Johns Hopkins University.
ESEA = *Essays and Studies by Members of the English Association*.
ESt = *Englische Studien*, Leipzig.
HLB = *Huntington Library Bulletin*.
HLQ = *Huntington Library Quarterly*.
JEGP = *Journal of English and Germanic Philology*, University of Illinois.
MLN = *Modern Language Notes*, Johns Hopkins University.
MLQ = *Modern Language Quarterly*, University of Washington, Seattle.
MLR = *Modern Language Review*, Cambridge University Press.
OBS = *Oxford Bibliographical Society, Proceedings and Papers*.
Proc. Brit. Acad. = *Proceedings of the British Academy*.
PMLA = *Publications of the Modern Language Association of America*.
PQ = *Philological Quarterly*, University of Iowa.
Rev. Angl.-Am. = *Revue Anglo-Americaine*, Paris.
RES = *Review of English Studies*, Oxford University Press.
SP = *Studies in Philology*, University of North Carolina Press.
TLS = *Times Literary Supplement*, London.
Univ. Calif. Publ. = *University of California Publications in English*.
Univ. Mich. Cont. = *University of Michigan Contributions in Modern Philology*, Ann Arbor.
Univ. Michigan Publ. = *University of Michigan Publications in Language and Literature*, Ann Arbor.
Univ. Texas Studies = *University of Texas Studies in English*.
Univ. Wash. Publ. = *University of Washington Publications, Language and Literature*, Seattle.
Univ. Wisconsin Stud. = *University of Wisconsin Studies in Language and Literature*, Madison, Wis.

In giving citations we have used small roman numerals for the number of a volume or of a book; Arabic numerals for the number of a chapter, and also for the section, line, or page (e.g.: vii. 27. 6. should be read as 'Book Seven, Chapter 27, Section 6.').

For commentary in addition to that listed in the separate introductions below, the pertinent volumes in the *Oxford History of English Literature* will be found useful. The volume by Douglas Bush, *English Literature in the Earlier Seventeenth Century, 1600–1660,* has already been published (Oxford, 1945); that by C. S. Lewis, *English Literature in the Sixteenth Century,* is forthcoming.

THOMAS MORE

SIR THOMAS MORE (1478–1535), since his sanctification by Pius XI in 1935, should properly be styled St. Thomas More. For convenience and simplicity merely, and with no lack of respect for one who deserved the highest of titles, we shall refer to him as Thomas More. Son of Sir John More, a judge in London, Thomas began his education at St. Antony's School, where his later friends John Colet and William Latimer had attended. At the suggestion of the Archbishop of Canterbury, John Morton, in whose household Thomas More lived as a boy, he entered Canterbury College, later consolidated with Christ Church College, Oxford. At the university he became friendly with two other early English humanists, Thomas Linacre, with whom he studied Greek, and William Grocyn. Leaving Oxford without a degree, he entered New Inn at London for the study of law, but transferred after a short time to Lincoln's Inn, where he became a bencher and a reader. A religious fervor possessed him at the time he was completing his legal studies, and he was torn between sacred and secular callings. Although he decided not to take orders, he led a pious and abstinent life and even wore a hair shirt from this early period until the time of his death. At the age of twenty-three More delivered, upon the invitation of Grocyn, a series of lectures upon St. Augustine's *De Civitate Dei.* He became successful in his profession of law, was elected to Parliament in 1504, and made an under-sheriff of London in 1510.

Erasmus became, on his successive visits, a familiar friend of More's, and helped to spread his fame upon the Continent. In 1515, with Cuthbert Tunstall, More was sent to Flanders to negotiate a commercial treaty. In Antwerp, where he met Peter Giles, a friend of Erasmus, he conceived the plan for his *Utopia.* Becoming better known to Henry VIII, in 1518 he was appointed to the Privy Council, and in 1520 he was with the king at the Field of the Cloth of Gold. At Calais, where he enjoyed a meeting with Erasmus, he was introduced to William Budaeus, a renowned Greek scholar. In 1523, through the patronage of Wolsey, he became Speaker of the House of Commons; and in 1526 he was appointed to the chancellorship of the Duchy of Lancaster. More had little sympathy with the Reformation; still less did he wish to become engaged in religious disputes; yet when Luther replied to King Henry's *Defensio Septem Sacramentorum,* itself an answer to Luther's *Babylonish Captivity,* More retaliated with a book defending papal authority, saying that though evil existed, the fault lay not in the office of pope but in some of its incumbents. In 1528 he published his *Dialogue concerning Heresies,* directed at William Tyndale, with whom he continued to dispute for several years. In 1529, upon the removal of Wolsey, More became Lord Chancellor, but, because of differences with the king resulting from the divorcing of Queen Catharine, he resigned in 1532. He also refused to take the oath vesting the succession in the issue of Anne Boleyn. Adjudged guilty of violating the Act of Supremacy which recognized Henry VIII as supreme head of the church, he was executed on Tower Hill in July, 1535, and his head was placed on London Bridge.

Thomas More embodied most of what we mean by the Renaissance, so far as it appeared in England. In addition to his great public services, he was a classical scholar, a father who personally saw to the liberal education of his children, a patron of learning, a poet of sorts. He spoke French, and he was interested in music, drama, painting, and popular jests. Yet the pure simplicity of his religious faith kept him from that love of magnificence and that complexity of motive which characterized typical men of the Renaissance, even in England.

The second book of the Latin *Utopia* was written first, in 1515; the first book, providing a dramatic framework for the account of the imagined commonwealth, and also setting against it the realities of contemporary England, was written in 1516. The whole was published in the same year at Louvain, with a second edition in 1517, and in 1518 Erasmus supervised the publication of the third edition, with some illustrations by Holbein, at the famous press of Froben in Basle. With this edition appeared More's book of Latin epigrams. *Utopia* was the first book by an Englishman of the Renaissance to win a reputation on the Continent, and for a century More was the English writer best known outside of England. The work was translated into French in 1550 and into English in 1551. Giving his work a dramatic setting similar to that in some of Plato's dialogues and drawing upon the current interest in tales of exploration, More sets forth the legal, social, religious, and cultural evils of the England of his day, and suggests remedies for them. To the ancestry of More as a political theorist belong, to mention only a few, Lycurgus, Plato, and St. Augustine; to the offspring belong Bacon, Hobbes, and Harrington. We probably do wrong to read the second book of the *Utopia* as representing More's highest ideal, in every regard, of human society and action. In fact, R. W. Chambers reads it as an argument *a fortiori*: if the heathen Utopians, with only the light of reason, did so well, how much better ought European Christians do! Professor Chambers also points out the many traces of More's sympathy with the Christian communism (as represented in brotherhoods, orders, chapters, and so on) of the Middle Ages.

In English prose, More made a translation of a brief *Life of John Picus, Earl of Mirandola* (published 1510), including a paraphrase in verse of 'Twelve Rules of a Christian Life' by the same Pico della Mirandola, a Christian Platonist whom he greatly admired. In the field of biography he also wrote the excellent *History of Richard the Third*, which has come down to us both in Latin and in English. His principal works of religious controversy are in English; besides the *Dialogue* already noted, he wrote *The Supplication of Souls* (1529) in answer to Fish, and *Confutation of Tyndale's Answer* (1532–33). His *Dialogue of Comfort against Tribulation*, a devotional and ethical work comparable to Boethius' *Consolations of Philosophy*, he wrote in the Tower during the last months of his life.

RALPH ROBINSON, the first translator of *Utopia* into English, was born in 1521 and educated at Oxford. He served as a clerk in the employ of his former schoolfellow, Sir William Cecil, who became Lord Burghley, Elizabeth's great Lord Treasurer. Robinson's translation, dedicated to Cecil, is a fairly faithful and clear rendering. It has been kept in active circulation in our own times, though other translations have been made by Gilbert Burnet (1684), Arthur Cayley (1808), Richards (1923), and others. The recent translation by

H. V. S. Ogden (New York: Appleton-Century-Crofts, 1949) is available in the inexpensive "Crofts Classics" series; the student can consult this edition for the sections (principally from the Second Book) omitted in this volume because of lack of space.

MODERN EDITIONS: [All except the last two print the English translation of Ralph Robinson] *The Utopia of Sir Thomas More (ed. by J. H. Lupton), Oxford, 1895 [Latin and English texts]; Utopia (ed. by E. Arber), English Reprints, Birmingham, 1869; Utopia (ed. by J. Churton Collins), Oxford, 1904; Utopia (ed. by Mgr. Philip E. Hallett), London, 1937; †Utopia, Everyman's Library, London, 1928; †Famous Utopias (ed. by F. R. White), University Classics, Chicago, 1946; Utopia (trans. G. C. Richards), Oxford, 1923; †Utopia (trans. H. V. S. Ogden), New York, 1949.

COMMENT: N. Harpsfield, The Life of More (ed. by E. V. Hitchcock, with an essay by R. W. Chambers), London, 1932; W. Roper, The Life (ed. by E. V. Hitchcock), London, 1935; E. M. G. Routh, Sir Thomas More and His Friends, Oxford, 1934; R. W. Chambers, Thomas More, London, 1935; A. Cecil, A Portrait of Thomas More, London, 1937; K. Kautsky, Thomas More und seine Utopia, 1890 (English trans. by H. J. Stenning), London, 1927; E. Dermenghem, Thomas Morus et les Utopistes de la Renaissance, Paris, 1927; W. E. Campbell, More's Utopia and His Social Teaching, London, 1930; J. O. Hertzler, The History of Utopian Thought, New York, 1923; H. W. Donner, Introduction to Utopia, Uppsala, 1945, and London, 1946; R. Ames, Citizen Thomas More and His Utopia, Princeton, 1948.

TEXT: Utopia, trans. by Ralph Robinson, 1551 (18094), Huntington.

535 Utopia] from οὐ and τοπος, not a place, nowhere. 19 King of Castile] Charles V. 22 Cuthbert Tunstall] (1474–1559); a scholar and friend of More, later Bishop of London (1522), and of Durham (1530). 36 George Temsice] Georgius a Tempseca, historian and native of Bruges.

536 4 Peter Giles] Petrus Aegidius (1486–1533), pupil and friend of Erasmus, to whom More dedicated Utopia. 21 Our Lady's Church] the Cathedral of Notre Dame at Antwerp, completed only a few years before. 24 divine] divine service. 26 homely] carelessly. 27 favor] face, appearance. 31 quod] quoth, said. 40 Palynure] pilot of Aeneas; see Aeneid, iii and v. 42 Hythloday] a name coined by More, from ὕθλος, 'babble,' or 'idle talk,' and δαίειν, 'to distribute,' or δάϊος, 'skilled in.'

537 8 Amerigo Vespucci] Robinson's translation reads 'Amerike vespuce.' 8–9 voyages . . . in print] a Latin translation of Vespucci's four voyages as described by himself was printed in 1507 as an appendix to a little book entitled Cosmographiae Introductio; More connects his imaginative tale with the fourth voyage. 14 left . . . fort] here and in line 22 below we have emended the translator's English text by consulting More's Latin text; we have, however, retained, enclosed in square brackets, Robinson's erroneous English rendition because it illustrates a curious mistranslation. The Latin reads 'in Castello,' 'in the fort or stockade'; the capital letter led Robinson

to assume that the word was a proper name, and in the dictionaries he discovered that Castellum was the Latin name for Jülich, a town near Cologne, Englished as Gulike. 23 Trapobane] Ceylon. 24 Calicut] a seaport town on the Malabar coast, where Vasco da Gama landed in 1498. 25 nothing less than looked for] quite unexpected by everyone. 30 hailsed] greeted. 36 Gulike] in the fort; see note to line 14 above. 39 occupied] traded. 42 mere] pure.

538 5 weal publics] republics, commonwealths. 6 line equinoctial] the equator. 28 loadstone] the magnet; the use of the magnetic needle in navigation was a recent discovery in More's time. 32 farther . . . jeopardy] freer from anxiety than from danger.

539 3 Scylla] the monster represented by Homer, Odyssey, xii. 3 Celaeno] chief of the Harpies; see Aeneid, iii.211. 4 Laestrygons] or Lestrygones; a savage tribe of man-eaters; see Odyssey, x. 29 pass not] care not.

540 40 have despite at] hold in contempt.

541 5 dizzards] blockheads. 19–20 insurrection . . . king] the rebellion in Cornwall was defeated at Blackheath in 1497. 22 John Morton] More was brought up in the household of John Morton (d. 1500), Archbishop of Canterbury.

542 32 Blackheath field] the place where the Cornish rebels were defeated. 39 dors] drones. 40 poll] clip, rob.

543 5 incontinent] immediately. 11

appaired] impaired. 17 jet] strut and swagger. 21 stouter stomachs] greater courage. 40 Sallust] Roman statesman and historian (86–35 B.C.); the quotation is from *Cataline*, xvi.

544 6 ured] worked, trained; cf. inured. 18 other] a common 16th-cent. form of 'either.' 26 not only the] not the only.

545 2 glebe-land] a portion of cultivated land assigned to a clergyman as part of his benefice. 15 abide the sale] await an advantageous time for selling. 31 murrain] cattle plague. 35 they lust] they wish to. 39 passeth for] cares for.

546 2 incommodity] inconvenience. 3 make dearth] raise the price. 5 store] supply. 8 the which thing] that is, hospitality. 18 queans] loose women. 21 tables] backgammon. 28 engross] buy up wholesale, and thus monopolize. 28 forestall] buy up beforehand. 42] Several pages are omitted here; they contain the rest of the discussion of the economic evils in England which grew out of the conversion of farm lands to sheep grazing. Then More urges Hythloday to join some Prince's court, so that with his wise counsel he can further the happiness of some commonwealth. Hythloday replies that a king would pay no attention to his good advice. The text resumes on p. 13 in the midst of Hythloday's answer.

547 19 dispense] to remit a penalty incurred by a breach of the law. 28 endanger] subject to his absolute control. 35 pick a thank] curry favor.

548 5 Crassus] a Roman famous for his enormous wealth; he joined with Pompey and Julius Caesar to form the first triumvirate. 23 wealthily] in a state of well-being. 32 bolder stomached] bolder in disposition. 41 Fabrice] Caius Fabricius Luscinus, elected consul at Rome in 282 B.C.; he was noted for his frugality and incorruptibility.

549 18 Macariens] another word coined by More from the Greek; in English its meaning would be 'the happy people.'

550 14 Plautus] T. Maccius Plautus (254–184 B.C.), Roman comic dramatist. 16 *Octavia*] Roman tragedy of uncertain authorship, traditionally attributed to Lucius Annaeus Seneca (*c.* 4 B.C.–65 A.D.), Roman philosopher, writer of tragedies, and tutor to the Emperor Nero. 19 gallimaufry] confused jumble or mixture. 36 wittily and handsomely] wisely and in a suitable manner.

551 8 several] separate. 20 in open houses] openly on the housetops. 27 sickerly] securely. 30 Mitio] or Micio, a character in the *Adelphi*, a comedy by the Roman dramatist Terence (195–159 B.C.). 40 occasion] opportunity.

552 2 laid in his neck] laid to his charge. 4 Plato] see Plato's *Republic*, vi.496. 13–14 beareth all the stroke] has the chief influence. 23 common] common property. 31 hold well with Plato] agree with Plato. 37 proper] his own. 40 riches] Robin on treats this word as singular; cf. *richesse*.

553 6 propriety] right of possession or ownership. 13 nother] neither. 36 reverend] the quality of commanding respect. 41 presently] personally.

554 25 empery] empire.

555 20] The general description of Utopia is modelled upon Plato's picture of Atlantis in the *Critias*. 27 surmounteth] mounts over the two corners and forms a bay.

556 1 translating] transferring. 6] The remainder of the description of the island of Utopia has been omitted; also the ensuing seven sections dealing with various aspects of the political organization and way of life in the Utopian commonwealth. 23] The omitted passage (about two pages) relates how, upon hearing that Christ had instituted all things in common, many Utopians decided to embrace Christianity and were baptised. 28 several parts] different sides.

557 8 truth of the own power] the force of truth by itself. 23 avaled] degraded. 31 of all sort] by all classes. 33 punishment] the Latin text makes it clear that More means physical punishment. 37 dispute in his opinion] discuss his opinion. 38 and that only] the meaning would be clearer if the translator had omitted these three words; the prohibition applies only to attempting to convert the common people to his opinion. 42] The remainder of the section on the religions of Utopia (about 15 pages) has been omitted; the text is resumed on page 24 with the concluding paragraph of the second book.

558 7 occupying] using. 15 communication] conversation. 18 once] at some future time.

JOHN BOURCHIER, LORD BERNERS

JOHN BOURCHIER, second LORD BERNERS (*c.* 1467–1533) has perpetuated his name in English history and literature as the translator of Froissart. He was, like his nephew by the half-blood, Henry Howard, Earl of Surrey, also a diplomat, traveler, linguist, and soldier; he was one of the noblemen who aided in the revival of learning at the end of the fifteenth century. His father, Humphrey Bourchier, was killed at the Battle of Barnet in 1471; from his grandfather, John Bourchier, first Lord Berners, he received his title and estates.

Lord Berners was educated at Oxford University, probably at Balliol College. In 1477 he was made a Knight of the Bath. During travel on the Continent he became proficient in French and Spanish, thus preparing himself for his later work as a translator. His name is listed among those who were unsuccessful in their premature attempt to place Henry, Duke of Richmond (later Henry VII), on the throne, and he was forced to flee to Brittany. After Henry's accession, however, his activities were more fortunate. In 1492 he contracted to serve in the wars overseas for a year; later he aided in suppressing the Cornish rebellion in support of Perkin Warbeck. Under Henry VIII, with whom he enjoyed close friendship, he distinguished himself at the capture of Terouenne, and he acted as marshal of the forces of the Earl of Surrey (father of the poet) at about the time of the battle of Flodden Field. In 1516 he was made chancellor at the exchequer; and in 1518 he attempted to negotiate an alliance between the kings of England and France. In 1520 he was with King Henry at the Field of the Cloth of Gold; and was appointed deputy of Calais, where, except for a few years when he lost his appointment, he remained for the rest of his life.

His most extensive and valuable work is the translation from the French of Jean Froissart's *Chronicles*, published by Richard Pynson, the first volume in 1524 and the second in 1525. The work was soon afterwards reprinted by William Middleton. Although he is somewhat lacking in historical judgment and is at fault in not correcting even some English names wrongly given by Froissart, Berners has a pleasing humility, admitting that he still is a student of the French language; he is thoroughly patriotic, and his translation is so spirited, idiomatic, and graphic that it has the cogency of an original work. Much more than Fabyan, Lord Berners helped to popularize history in England.

In the occasional tautology (as in his tiresome doubling and tripling of words) and balance of his writing in the Froissart, Berners gives hints of the style at which he arrived in his work called *The Golden Book of Marcus Aurelius* (1534), translating Berthault's French version of the Spaniard Guevara's *Libro del Emperador Marco Aurelio con el Relox de Principes*. This furnishes an early example of patterned prose in English, anticipating Sir Thomas North's translation (1557) of the same work, under the title, *The Dial of Princes.* Lord Berners' interest in historical romance appears also in his translation of *Huon of Bordeaux*, one of the most important of the Charlemagne romances, also published in 1534. He translated *Arthur of Little Britain* from the French and *The Castle of Love* from the Spanish of Diego de San Pedro.

JEAN FROISSART (*c.* 1338–*c.* 1410) became interested in the wars between England and France which occupied the last seventy-four years of the fourteenth century. Basing his account, as he tells us, upon the work of Jean le Bel, he traveled from court to court in Europe, always collecting materials, and his story takes light and color from his environment and from his personal acquaintance with many people of whom he writes. Being Flemish himself, he could sympathize with both France and England. As early as 1356 he visited England, and returned in 1361, becoming one of the secretaries of Queen Philippa, originally of Hainault, Froissart's native province. Although not a sound critical historian by modern standards, Froissart writes with spirit and reveals a genuine appreciation of chivalric actions and ideals.

MODERN EDITIONS: *The Chronicles* (ed. by G. C. Macaulay), 1895; *The Chronicles* (ed. by W. P. Ker), The Tudor Translations, 1901–03; *Chronicles,* Oxford, 1927–28.

COMMENT: W. P. Ker, Introduction to his edition, above; J. H. McDill, 'The Life of Lord Berners,' *TLS,* April 17, 1930. For Froissart, G. C. Coulton, *The Chronicler of European Chivalry,* London, 1930; H. Newbolt, *Froissart in Britain,* 1900; F. S. Shears, *Froissart,* London, 1930.

TEXT: *The chronicles,* 1523 [January, 1524, new style] (11396), Huntington.

559 3 gestes] or gests; exploits, deeds of adventure. 5 ensign] instruct, inform; cf. the Fr., *enseigner.* 14 complect] embrace. 27 Once] in the first place. 41 cause] usually emended to 'praise'; but 'cause,' loosely used in the sense of 'importance,' was probably intended.

560 6 Duke Theseus] legendary king of Athens; slew the Minotaur and defeated the Amazons. 10 custos] guardian, custodian. 19 poistereth] encumbers, fetters. 21–23 testimony . . . antiquity] this translates a passage in Cicero *De oratore,* ii.9; the formula was often used by historians and appears, somewhat altered, on the title-page of Ralegh's *History of the World.* 23 Phalerius] Demetrius Phalereus, adviser to Ptolemy and librarian at Alexandria. 24 King Ptolemy] Ptolemy I, called Soter, the Saviour (*c.* 367–285 B.C.), of Egypt, founder of the Alexandrian Library. 34 volved] turned over pages, considered. 36 Hainault] or Hainaut, a province in Belgium; formerly a province in France and Flanders. 38 sith] since. 38 parts] 1523 reads 'parties.'

561 8 sixteen] an error; should be 'twenty-six,' and the 74 years indicated in parentheses is correct. 12 in gree] in a kindly spirit, with favor. 14 sentence] sense, meaning; not the grammatical sentence. 31 Calais] King Edward III beseiged the town of Calais after the English victory at the battle of Crecy in 1346; the town fell in August 1347. 33 Sangate] Sangatte, about seven miles west of Calais; the army sent by King Philip of France to relieve Calais encamped on the nearby high ground, but finally gave up the effort to raise the siege. 38 Sir Gualtier de Manny] Sir Walter de Manny, or Mauny (d. 1372); Edward III's military commander in the siege of Calais.

562 16 sort] company. 42 quod] quoth; said.

563 4 incontinent] immediately. 20 gossip] friend.

564 30 nobles] English gold coins current till 1461 at the value of 6s. 8d.

SIMON FISH

SIMON FISH (died *c.* 1530), attorney and theological pamphleteer, after study at Oxford, went to London about 1525, where, as a student at Gray's Inn, he allied himself with the opposition against Cardinal Wolsey. John Foxe tells us in *Acts and Monuments* that because Fish acted in an interlude which offended Wolsey he fled overseas, where he became associated with William Tyndale. Upon his return to England, he became a sales agent for Tyndale's New Testament; but, because of fear of arrest for the sale of the banned work of Tyndale, he once more sought refuge in the Low Countries, where, between 1527 and 1529, he wrote *A Supplication for the Beggars.* Foxe tells conflicting stories of the attitude of Henry VIII toward Fish's work. He says, first, that about 1530 Fish returned to England and had an interview with the king while they hunted together, and that the king bade Fish go home, but that

Fish expressed fear of prosecution by Sir Thomas More, the chancellor who had
succeeded Wolsey; whereupon Henry gave Fish his signet ring to insure him
against harm from More. He says, second, that two merchants spoke to the
king of new religious works from beyond the seas and told him of the book
by Fish, which was read to him; the king then said, 'If a man should pull down
an old stone wall and begin at the lower part, the upper part thereof might
chance to fall upon his head,' by which he meant that any action against the
monastic institution would be dangerous until the royal supremacy had been
established. Opportunely, just before Parliament convened, the *Supplication*
was disseminated throughout London. Foxe says also that Wolsey, somewhat
earlier, went to the king to warn him of seditious books which had appeared
in London, whereupon the king reached into his bosom and delivered to
Wolsey a copy of the *Supplication*. The cardinal thereupon forbade the reading
of this book and of Tyndale's New Testament and other similar works. It is to
be noted, however, that, a short while before, Wolsey had suppressed the
monasteries in Oxford and some other places. By way of counter-attack upon
the *Supplication*, Sir Thomas More wrote *The Supplication of Souls*, in which
he refers to Fish as the 'beggars' proctor,' and represents souls in purgatory indicting Fish as an ass, a goose, a mad dog, and a heretic. More in his *Apology*
(1533) says that Fish repented and came into the Church again. Fish was,
none the less, suspected of heresy, and was not defended by Henry, who clearly
sympathized with his work. He died of the plague about 1530.

His *Supplication*, published late in 1528 or early in 1529, is an early bom-
bardment of the English Reformation. Its vigorous style set the fashion for
religious propaganda, as later represented by the Marprelate pamphlets, some
of Milton's prose, and Defoe's *Shortest Way with the Dissenters*. The work is
intentionally bigoted. With nice malice Fish complains that the begging friars
have robbed the secular beggars of their living; then deliberately he confuses
the friars and the clergy in general. Not without justification, however, is much
of the invective; celibacy, for example, had been difficult to enforce in the
Church, as indicated by the fact that Wolsey and several of the popes were
supposed to be fathers of families. *A Supplication for the Beggars* is important
in that it represents a protest of the laity against abuses among the clergy and
is a forerunner of the establishment of the royal supremacy in England. Controversial zeal sharpens its style and makes the prose a more adequate instrument than most writers of the time could wield. The only known copy of the
original edition is in the British Museum.

MODERN EDITIONS: *A Supplicacyon* (ed. by W. Maskell), 1845; *A Supplication*
(included in *Four Supplications,* ed. by F. J. Furnivall, Early English Text Society),
1871; *A Supplication* (in *Religious Pamphlets,* ed. by P. Dearmer, The Pamphlet
Library), 1898; *A Supplication* (in The English Scholar's Library, ed. by E. Arber),
1878; *A Supplication* (included in *Complaint and Reform in England,* ed. by W. H.
Dunham and S. Pargellis, New York, 1938).

TEXT: *A supplicacyon for the beggars,* [1529?] (10883), British Museum.

565 13 bedemen] beadsmen; a beadsman is one who prays for a benefactor,
but came to mean a licensed beggar,
and a king's beadsman was one who
received alms on the king's birthday.
25 herds] shepherds. 27 suffragans]
assistants; especially auxiliaries or coad-
jutors of bishops. 42 mortuaries] gifts
demanded by parish priests from estates
of deceased parishioners, or gifts by
dying persons to parish priests.

566 4 acciting] citing, summoning.
5 commissaries' courts] ecclesiastical
courts under jurisdiction of a bishop's
commissary or representative. 9 fifty-
two thousand parish churches] More, in
his reply, pointed out the inaccuracy of
this statement; Fish considered every

hamlet to be a parish. 12 five orders of friars] the four recognized mendicant orders were the Franciscans (Grey Friars), Dominicans (Black Friars), Carmelites (White Friars), and the Augustinians (Austin Friars); the fifth is possibly that of the Trinitarians (Crutched Friars, so named from the cross embroidered on the habit); see Father Cuthbert, *The Friars and How They Came to England* (St. Louis and New York, 1903). 16 angels] gold coins, valued at the time of about 8s. 26 polled] plundered. 29 fifteens] a tax: one tenth of the worth of movable property was imposed on residents of cities, boroughs, and ancient demesnes, and one-fifteenth upon other persons. 39 Lucius] fictional king of England mentioned by Bede, Nennius, and Geoffrey of Monmouth; 'Sir Lucius Iberius,' the 'Emperor of Rome,' appears in Malory's *Mort d'Arthure*, but Wyntoun says that Leo, not Lucius, demanded tribute of Arthur. 42 find] support, maintain.

567 5 third part] the monasteries are said to have owned a third of the lands and tithes of England. 23 King John] of England (1167–1216); an unfavorable reference to the Magna Carta. 26 Stephen] Stephen Langton was instrumental in exacting the Magna Carta from King John. 27 interdicted his land] Pope Innocent placed England under an interdict when King John attempted to remove Langton from his see.

568 16 let] hinder, retard. The opposition between this sentence and that which precedes was noted by More. 17 inhabitable] not habitable. 20 illected] enticed. 22 to be brent with] to catch an inflammatory disease from.

569 13 Caesar] Fish confuses the celebrated Roman jurist Gaius (2nd cent. A.D.), with the emperor Gaius Caesar (Caligula). 18 Acts of the Apostles] *Acts*, 4. 32–35. 37 or] ere, before. 40 warmoll quest] an inquest by the wardmote, or meeting of citizens of a ward, once a year to redress vice. 41 Richard Hunne] a citizen of London who, being haled into the ecclesiastical court for failure to give a mortuary to the priest in whose parish his infant had died, brought countersuit against the priest. Hunne was charged with heresy and imprisoned. Soon thereafter he was found hanged by his own girdle. Horsey, chancellor of the Bishop of London, was convicted of the murder of Hunne, but Wolsey secured his freedom through payment of a fine of £600. The Bishop of London prosecuted the charge of heresy against the dead body of Hunne, which was burned at Smithfield. 41 praemunire] a legal action, corresponding somewhat to the modern injunction, and originally used against papal encroachments.

570 4 the statute of mortmain] enacted 1279, to prevent additional lands from passing to the possession of the Church. 19 other] either. 24 goulafres] 'engulfers,' from Old Fr. *goulfre*, gulf or whirlpool. 32 literature] literary culture.

571 20 remission of sins are] Looseness of agreement in number between subject and verb is common in 16th-century writing. 39 Dr. Allen] John Allen, Chaplain to Wolsey. 41 long] belong. 42 Dr. Horsey] see note to p. 35 l. 41.

572 2 Hunne] see note to p. 35 l. 41.

573 1 loobies] lubbers, louts. 3 Gen. iii.] *Genesis*, 3.19: 'In the sweat of thy face shalt thou eat bread.' 20 *Domine . . . regem*] 'O Lord, save the King.'

SIR THOMAS ELYOT

Sir Thomas Elyot (*c.* 1490–1546), scholar, translator, lexicographer, public servant, and diplomat, was the son of Sir Richard Elyot, Serjeant-at-law, Justice of Assize on the Western Circuit, and attorney-general to the queen consort of King Henry VII. The place of Thomas Elyot's birth, and the details of his education are uncertain; the efforts of his early biographers to claim him as an alumnus of Oxford or of Cambridge are offset by the absence of any record of his having been a student at either university, and by his own statement, in the prefatory address to the first edition of his dictionary, that he received instruction at home. Moreover, other statements by Elyot in various books and letters imply that his proficiency in the learning of his age was due to the personal assistance and inspiration he received from other scholars who were actively promoting humanistic scholarship in England at the beginning of the sixteenth century; for men such as Thomas Linacre and Thomas More were among Elyot's friends and acquaintances. In the preface to *The Castel of Helth*, Sir Thomas Elyot tells us that before he was twenty years old 'a worshipful physician, and one of the most renowned at that time in England' [probably Linacre], perceiving him by nature inclined to knowledge, read unto him works of Galen and Hippocrates, and that later he continued his medical studies independently, by reading works of Celsus, Dioscorides, Avicenna, Averroës, and other authorities, both classical and Arabic. Drawn by a natural affinity to the group that came together at Sir Thomas More's to engage in common in enthusiastic study of the literature and learning of Greece and Rome, Elyot and his wife jointly pursued their classical studies as members of this circle.

Upon his father's death in 1522, Elyot inherited large landholdings near Woodstock, became a Justice of the Peace for Oxfordshire, and Sheriff for that county and Berkshire in 1527. In 1523, Wolsey appointed him clerk of the Privy Council; in that position he served six and one-half years without pay until, on Wolsey's death, the long-awaited letters patent confirming the grant of that office were called in and canceled. About the same time, Sir Thomas Elyot was knighted, and the next year, in dedicating to King Henry VIII his first published work, *The Governour*, he announces that his purpose was to discuss the education of those who 'hereafter may be deemed worthy to be governours of the public weal'; thus he places his best-known work among the long line of famous treatises dealing with the proper training of those destined to become rulers. In the autumn of 1531, the same year that saw the first publication of *The Governour*, Henry VIII sent Elyot as his ambassador to the court of Charles V, with instructions to obtain the Emperor's favor toward the divorce from Catherine of Aragon—a difficult mission, fraught with the peril of incurring King Henry's distrust, especially because Elyot's sympathies were probably with Catherine, and his intimacy with Sir Thomas More and his friends was well known.

When Elyot returned to England in 1532, More had retired; and Elyot, aware of the storm that was gathering about many of his friends, and of his own inability to moderate it, avoided further active participation in the conflicts of the time, and thenceforth devoted his energies to serving his countrymen by making available to them in published books the fruits of his scholarship. By these literary works Elyot retained King Henry's good will; whereas, had he continued to hold diplomatic or political offices under that monarch, he might well have incurred Henry's active and perhaps fatal displeasure, and have suffered a fate similar to that of Sir Thomas More and many others of his friends. During the last years of his life, however, Elyot's only important official positions were those of member of Parliament for Cambridge in 1542, and sheriff of Cambridgeshire and Huntingdonshire in 1544. He died in March 1546.

To Elyot belongs the primary credit for establishing among the English scholars of the sixteenth century a vigorous tradition that they had an obligation to make their superior knowledge available to others by opening fully to their countrymen the rich storehouse of wisdom enclosed in the writings of the ancients in the Greek and Latin tongues. This zeal to disseminate sound learning in the various branches of natural and moral philosophy was communicated to a long line of Elyot's successors, who followed his lead in adapting or translating into English the scientific and philosophical works of the past, and who continued his program of enriching the technical vocabulary of the English language with the aim of making it an adequate medium for the accurate transmission of complex ideas and precise knowledge.

This aim for his native tongue had inspired the most ambitious of Elyot's scholarly achievements—his Latin-English dictionary based upon classical rather than medieval authors. First published in 1538, it had a second edition during Elyot's lifetime. After being three times re-issued in editions successively improved and enlarged by Thomas Cooper between 1548 and 1559, its fourth revision by Cooper, under the title of *Thesaurus linguae Romanae & Britannicae*, became the standard reference work for the remainder of the century. Elyot's example also contributed to the vogue of casting works of popular instruction in the form of a dialogue. As dialogues Elyot indited his *Pasquil the Playne* (1532), *Of the Knowledge which maketh a Wise Man* (1533), and *The Defence of Good Women* (1545).

Elyot's importance as a translator was due in great measure to his casting aside of the methods of most of his predecessors and contemporaries, who crept jerkily from word to word in a literal phrase-for-phrase rendition of the original. Instead, he attempted to recapture the form and spirit of his original by adopting a method of free interpolation, and succeeded in writing a far more idiomatic English than one can find in the halting prose of most other translators before the 1540's. Among the works which illustrate his superiority are his version of Saint Cyprian's *Sermon of Mortalitie of Man*, published in 1534 with Pico della Mirandola's *Rules of a Christian Lyfe*, his English rendering of Plutarch' essay *The Education or bringing up of Children* (about 1535), and his translation of Isocrates' *Ad Nicoclem* under the title of *The Doctrinal of Princes* (after 1534?).

By the translation of these works of Plutarch and of Isocrates, Elyot exemplifies his special interest in the writings of classical antiquity that dealt with education and moral philosophy, particularly as applied to the training of leaders in the state. From works of this sort he derived most of the material he incorporated into his own book, *The Governour*, although he was also indebted to other humanist treatises written under similar inspiration, notably to Erasmus' *Institutio principis Christiani* (1516), and Francesco Patrizi's *De regno et regis institutione* (written in the late 15th century and printed at Paris in 1518). But *The Governour* owes its greatest debts to Quintilian's *Institutio Oratoria*, that treatise of the first century A.D. on Roman education, and to Aristotle's *Nichomachean Ethics*. By its close links with two of the classical works most universally admired by the scholars of the sixteenth century—the one for its precepts on education, the other for moral philosophy—Elyot's book becomes one of the most typical of the Renaissance, and highly valuable for the insight it gives us into the thought of the age.

MODERN EDITIONS: *The Gouernour (ed. by H. H. S. Croft), 2 vols., London, 1883; †The Governour, Everyman's Library, London, 1907.

COMMENT: S. S. Laurie, 'The Governour,' in *Studies in the History of Educational Opinion from the Renaissance*, London, 1903; L. K. Born, Introduction to his translation of Erasmus' *The Education of a Christian Prince*, New York, 1936; D. T. Starnes, 'Notes on Elyot's *The Governour* (1531),' *RES*, iii (1927), 37–36; D. T. Starnes, 'Shakespeare and Elyot's *Governour*,' *Univ. Texas Studies*, No. 7 (1927), 112–132; James Wortham, 'Sir Thomas Elyot and the Translation of Prose,' *HLQ*, iii (1948), 219–40; L. Warren, 'Patrizi's *De Regno et Regis Institutione* and the Plan of Elyot's *The Boke named the Governour*,' *JEGP*, xlix (1950), 67–77.

TEXT: *The boke named the Gouernour*, 1531 (7635), Huntington.

574 7 attemptate] from the Latin *attemptare;* typical of the words Elyot coined directly from the Latin; the form that came to be preferred even in the 16th cent. was 'attempt.' 13 Plato] see *Republic* iv.423E. 14 Solomon] see *Proverbs*, 11.14. 39 again] against; a common 16th-cent. form of the word.

575 7] The first three chapters of the first book have the following titles: (i) 'The signification of the Public Weal, and why it is called in Latin *Respublica*'; (ii) 'That one sovereign governor ought to be in a public weal. And what damage hath happened where a multitude hath had equal authority without any sovereign'; (iii) 'That in a public weal ought to be inferior governors called magistrates: which shall be appointed or chosen by the sovereign governor.' 30 propice] fit; cf. 'propitious.' 35 ancient writers] e.g. Cicero, in *Tusc. Quaest.,* iii.1.

576 2 tache] moral spot or blemish. 11 slips] tender shoots or branches. 17 faictes] actions. 17 provecte] more advanced; another of Elyot's coinages from the Latin. 32 ne] nor. 32 advaunt] push forward. 38 radicate] root. 39 cautel] caution, subtlety. 41] Chapter v. is entitled: 'The order of learning that a nobleman should be trained in before he come to the age of seven years.'

577 6 sad] trustworthy. 12 eschew] avoid. 20 Homer] see *Iliad*, ix.432 ff. 31 vice] Elyot derived the notion that Alexander had been corrupted by his tutor from Quintilian, *Institutio oratoria*, Book i, chap. 1, paragraph 9. Throughout Book i of *The Governour* Elyot draws heavily upon Book i of Quintilian.

578 15 fatigate] fatigued. 38 Quintilian] See *Institutio oratoria*, i.1.12. 41 uneth] not easily, scarcely. 42 understande] a late Middle English and Early Modern form of the past participle of the verb 'understandan'; modern 'understood.'

579 36 Copie] L. *Copia*, abundance; the command of a variety of words for expressing one's thoughts. 37 Lucian] ancient satirist (*c.* 115–*c.* 200 A.D.); author of many satiric dialogues. 41 Aristophanes] the greatest of the Greek authors of satiric comedies (*c.* 448– *c.* 380 B.C.).

580 20 Iliados] the *Iliad;* Elyot here, and also five lines below, transliterates the Greek forms of the titles of Homer's epic poems. 27 ensearch] inquire into. 37 *Eneidos*] *Æneid*

581 12 skosers] scorsers; horse dealers. 18 Aristaeus] see Virgil's *4th Georgic*. 18 Dido and Æneas] see *Æneid*, iv. 22 Eurealus] see *Æneid*, v. 24 Iopas] see *Æneid*, i. 24 Demodocus] see *Odyssey*, viii. 31 Sibyl] see *Æneid*, vi. 32 Cerberus, Gorgon, Megæra] all mentioned in Virgil's *Æneid;* Cerberus was the monstrous watchdog of Hades; the Gorgon's head turned into stone anything that met its gaze; Megera was one of the Furies. 34 Sisyphus] legendary king of Corinth whose punishment in Hades was perpetually to roll a stone to the top of a hill, which, on reaching the summit, would roll down again. 36 Elysius] Elysium.

582 3 *Metamorphosios*] *Metamorphoses.* 5 *De fastis*] the *Fasti*, 22 Silius] Tiberius Catius Asconius (26–101), Roman poet and imitator of Virgil in his epic, the *Punica*, a narrative of the Second Punic War between Rome and Carthage. 22 Lucane] M. A. Lucanus (39–65), Roman poet whose epic the *Pharsalia* recounts the defeat of Pompey by Julius Caesar. 31 illecebrous] enticing. 35 deprehendeth] perceiveth.

583 22 Agricola] Rudolph Agricola (1444–1485), German humanist whose introductory manual of logic *De Inventione Dialectica* was one of the most popular textbooks of the 16th century. 28 Hermogenes] Greek rhetorician of the second century, A.D., whose manual of twelve elementary exercises in rhetoric, the *Progymnasmata*, was popular with teachers of the Middle Ages and Renaissance. 32 Tully] Marcus Tullius Cicero, Roman statesman and orator. 35 Erasmus] his textbook *De duplici copia verborum ac rerum* was written in 1511 for the students of John Colet's newly founded St. Paul's School; its popularity as a textbook in English grammar schools lasted for two centuries. 38 Isocrates] Greek rhetorician and orator (436–338 B.C.).

584 1 Nicocles] Isocrates' oration to the young Nicocles on the duties and virtues of a sovereign was translated by Elyot shortly after he wrote *The Governour* and published with the title *The Doctrinal of Princes.* 13 Octavius] Augustus. 21 tables of Ptolemy] the system of maps in Ptolemy's *Geography*, the geographical textbook composed by Claudius Ptolemaeus, Alexandrian astronomer and geographer of the second century A.D. 40 covenable] convenient.

585 4 Demetrius Phalereus] Demetrius of Phalerum (*c.* 354–*c.* 283 B.C.), pupil of Theophrastus, governed Athens as viceroy for Cassander of Macedonia 317–307 B.C., and after 307 B.C. went into exile in Egypt; he was eminent in literature as well as in politics. 10–11 witness . . . antiquity.] see note to p. 26, lines 21–23. 17 Quintilian] *Inst. orat.*, x.1.32. 18 Titus Livius] the Roman historian Livy (59 B.C.–17 A.D.). 26 Xenophon] Athenian writer (*c.* 430 B.C.–*c.* 355 B.C.); his *Cyropaedia* is one of the earliest of the long line of treatises on the education of a ruler which are direct ancestors of Elyot's *Governour.* 40–42 two . . . virtue] the first two books of Aristotle's *Nicomachean Ethics.*

586 15 Salomon] this was the common Elizabethan spelling of Solomon. 21 Oza] Uzzah. 22 *Archa federis*] Ark of the Covenant; see *2 Samuel* 6.7. 22 Gaba] Gibeah. 25 Erasmus] his *Insti-*

tutio Principis Christiani was published in 1516, dedicated to prince Charles, later Emperor Charles V. 29 Scipio] Scipio Africanus Major (*c.* 235–*c.* 183 B.C.), Roman general who won the victory over Hannibal, leader of the forces of Carthage, in the Second Punic War. 39 Aulus Gellius] Roman writer of the 2nd cent. A.D., noted especially for his collection of essays, which he entitled *Noctis Atticae;* the reference here is to book iv. 42 Galen] the most famous physician of antiquity (2nd cent. A.D.); his authority in medical matters was not seriously impaired until the 16th century. The reference is to his *De sanitate tuenda*, book i.

587 2 humecteth] moistens, humidifies. 4 temperature] temperament or complexion; the hot and moist complexion or humour was the sanguine.

EDWARD HALLE

EDWARD HALLE, or HALL (the former spelling predominates in contemporary documents and printed texts) was born about the end of the fifteenth century and died in April 1547, three months after Henry VIII, the monarch who was the hero of the chronicle upon which rests Halle's principal claim to renown. A native of London, Halle received his early education at Eton College; after receiving the degree of bachelor of arts at King's College, Cambridge, in 1517–8, he became a student of the law at Gray's Inn, and during the remainder of his life held a variety of offices at Gray's Inn, and in the government of the City of London. At the former he was autumn reader in 1533 and Lent reader in 1540; in London, through the King's favor, he was constituted common serjeant in 1533, under sheriff in 1535, and later held a succession of other official positions.

In the important Reformation Parliament of 1529, Halle represented Wenlock and took an active part in its proceedings as an ardent partisan of the English Reformation and supporter of the policies of Henry VIII; he was a member of the later Parliament that had sessions in 1539 and 1540, and to the Parliament of 1542 he was returned for Bridgnorth.

In his will, proved 25 May, 1547, Halle bequeathed to the printer Richard Grafton the manuscript of his 'Cronycle late made trusting that he will sett it forward.' Grafton was prompt in discharging his obligation as Halle's literary executor to print the *Chronicle*, for the work in his shop progressed with sufficient rapidity so that by the end of November his printers had set up and printed off the text pages from the beginning of the book to the end of the account of the reign of Edward IV; from this point they continued until they reached the end of the volume, whereupon for some reason not yet explained, they proceeded to reprint the early section. It was this second printing of this first section that was bound with the original printing of the later section and the preliminaries when Halle's *Chronicle* was first issued by Grafton in the spring of 1548 with the title of *The Union of the two noble and illustre famelies of Lancastre & Yorke.*

The unusual procedure followed by Grafton in the printing of the first edition of Halle's book gave rise to one of the peculiarities that have led scholars of the last hundred years and more to propose conflicting theories concerning the date and authorship of the book known as Halle's *Chronicle;* the other singularity is the difference in style between its account of the earlier reigns and its story of the reign of Henry VIII. In the first part, the author, in his efforts to achieve 'eloquence' and an artificially elevated style, cultivates to excess the devices of contemporary rhetoric and introduces so many Latin neologisms that Ascham complained that Halle wrote 'indenture English'; when he comes to describe the events of Henry VIII's reign, he writes with simple directness in an English prose both graceful and vigorous. Critics such as Krapp and Robert M. Smith, unable to believe that the same person could have written both the earlier and the later sections of the *Chronicle,* have suggested that the account of the reign of Henry VIII should be credited to Richard Grafton.

Recent scholarship, by means of a bibliographical analysis of the various printings of Halle's *Chronicle,* has demonstrated that the alleged first edition of a part of Halle's work, said to have been published in 1542 by Thomas Berthelet, can be dismissed as a myth; and, through the discovery of further facts about Edward Halle, has enabled us also to dismiss the suspicion that the most important part of his chief literary work should be credited to someone else. Some uncertainty still remains about the precise nature and extent of Grafton's editorial contributions to the original edition he published in 1548; but—at least until a greatly needed scholarly edition of the *Chronicle* appears—the following tentative account of the genesis of the copy that was printed by Grafton will serve to reconcile the earlier evidence of the contemporary statements of Grafton, Foxe, and others, with the new facts revealed by modern scholars.

Inasmuch as the most eminent modern historian of the period of Henry VIII describes the account in the *Chronicle* of the Reformation Parliament of 1529 as 'in a sense a parliamentary journal,' and has proved that Edward Halle was a member and active participant in that Parliament, we may infer that Halle's resolution to become a chronicler of the events of his own time and of the fame of the monarch he ardently admired was taken not later than 1529, and from that time forward he kept careful notes and wrote up the scenes and events to which he had been an eyewitness before allowing much time to elapse. This would account for the extraordinary vividness and fullness of detail with which he reports the occurrences of the years just before and after 1530. Grafton is our authority that the manuscript left by Halle was 'perfected' down to the year 24 Henry VIII (22 April 1532 to 21 April 1533), and that for the later years Halle had left many notes and papers but not a manuscript fully revised and ready for the press. Grafton, from Halle's extensive papers, completed the manuscript for the last fourteen years of the reign of Henry VIII. For the account of the first twenty-four years, Halle's manuscript may have been completed as early as 1535, before he decided to enlarge the scope of his history by beginning with the reign of Henry IV and leading up to a climax in the glorious period of the English Reformation and the rule of Henry VIII. This more ambitious scheme must have had its inception sometime after 1534, for that was the year of publication of Polydore Vergil's *Anglica Historia,* his chief authority for the period from Henry IV to Henry VII.

The last years of Halle's increasingly busy life found him at work compiling a history in the customary manner of the time, putting together the accounts of previous historians, although he probably continued at the same time to add to his notes and papers for future use the records of contemporary events in which he participated as a keen and purposeful observer. The idea of later using these materials to continue his account of Henry VIII's reign was always present in his mind. In translating Polydore Vergil's Latin he forsook the simplicity and directness with which he reported at first hand the things which he had himself seen or heard, and in trying to be 'literary,' he fell, like so many others before and after him who have misguidedly sought stylistic eloquence, into the worst forms of the vices of awkwardness and ostentation.

Later English historians have rightly turned to Halle's *Chronicle* as the principal authority for the reign of Henry VIII. The second edition of Holinshed's *Chronicles* (1587) usually reprints Halle *verbatim* for the years from 1509 to 1546. In fact, all of the selections on pages 55 to 64 of this volume are followed almost word for word in the 1587 edition of Holinshed.

MODERN EDITIONS: *Chronicle* (ed. by Sir Henry Ellis), London, 1809; **Henry VIII* (ed. by Charles Whibley), 2 vols., London, 1904.

COMMENT: G. P. Krapp, *The Rise of English Literary Prose*, New York, 1915, pp. 397–401; Robert M. Smith, 'The Date and Authorship of Hall's Chronicle,' *JEGP*, xvii (1918), 252–66; A. F. Pollard, 'Edward Hall's Will and Chronicle,' *Bull. Inst. Hist. Research*, ix (1931–32), 171–77; Graham Pollard, 'The Bibliographical History of Hall's Chronicle,' *ibid.*, x (1932–33), 12–17; W. Gordon Zeeveld, 'The Influence of Hall on Shakespeare's English Historical Plays,' *ELH*, iii (1936), 317–53.

TEXT: *The Union*, 1548 (12722), Huntington.

587 31 Mercury] Hermes Trismegistus, the Greek name of the Egyptian god Thoth. 32 Cadmus] in Greek legend, supposed to have brought the Phoenician alphabet to Greece.

588 15 Gildas] early British historian who wrote in Latin, *c.* 547 a sketch of the history of Britain. 18 Geoffrey of Monmouth] historian (*c.* 1100–54) whose *Historia Regum Britanniae* was, until the 17th century, the most influential authority on the early history of Britain. 20 Brute] the legendary founder of the British race, grandson of Æneas. 30 Matthew of Paris] English chronicler (d. 1259). 40 Robert Fabyan] (d. 1513) the first of the citizen chroniclers of London.

589 1 butt] target. 11 godly matrimony] Henry VII, of the House of Lancaster, married Elizabeth, daughter of the Yorkist Edward IV. 39 bishop of London] Cuthbert Tunstall; see p. 1.

590 5 commoned] communed, talked. 35–6 like you] please you.

591 25 bachelors] candidates for knighthood. 25–6 wafter and a foist] light galleys propelled by sails and oars. 27–8 Simon and Jude] the day of Simon and Jude is October 28. 30 targets] shield-shaped ornaments. 38 Collars of Esses] chains or necklaces made of *S*'s strung on ribbon; worn by certain officials. 42 shalms] musical instruments similar to the oboe. 42 shagbushes] bass trumpets with slides.

592 6 wherries] light rowboats. 21 pensels] narrow flags. 30 white roses and red] white for York; red for Lancaster.

593 3 incontinent] immediately. 11 letting of barges] allowing barges to pass. 12 or] before.

594 19 ray] striped. 30 lettice] a grey-white fur. 33 garter] the Garter-King-of-Arms.

595 4 laps] flaps. 26 *Agnus*] music and prayer of the Mass, beginning *Agnus Dei*. 31 nonce] single occasion. 32 coronal] circlet.

596 30 say] silk. 40 chrysm] chrisom, a white robe thrown over the child at christening.

597 24 pounced] embossed.

598 37 beard . . . cut it] in other accounts More went on: 'It has not committed treason.'

HUGH LATIMER

HUGH LATIMER (*c.* 1485–1555), preacher to Henry VIII and Edward VI, and martyr under Queen Mary, played an important role in establishing the tenets of the Church of England. Born at Thurcaston in Leicestershire, son of a diligent and patriotic yeoman-farmer, he was admitted B.A. at Cambridge in 1510 and M.A. in 1514. Until he was thirty, Latimer was a violent adherent to Roman Catholicism; thereafter, he became an ardent reformer, condemning elaborate gifts to the church, pilgrimages, the mass, adoration of the saints, and eventually denying transubstantiation. His sermons as court preacher and as Bishop of Worcester are free from elaborate theological discussions; their fervor and the easy familiarity and simplicity of their style established Latimer as one of the earliest of the popular preachers. In many ways Latimer's career is an anomaly: charged with heresy, he was several times a member of commissions to destroy heresy; a bishop, he said the devil was the most assiduous bishop in London. Yet the course of King Henry VIII himself was equally contradictory: he permitted the Bible to be printed in English, removed images from the church, abolished the monasteries; on the other hand, through the Six Articles, he provided for masses, demanded clerical celibacy, and supported belief in transubstantiation. Because he could not support the Six Articles, Latimer resigned his bishopric in 1539. Later, upon the accession of Edward VI, he returned to public life as a licensed preacher, and his sermons soon won for him a position of greater importance than before. He was appointed in 1548, and again in the two subsequent years, to preach the Lenten sermons before the young king. Fearlessly outspoken in lashing the evils of society in his age, he was feared as one of the most dangerous of the Protestant reformers by the Catholic Queen Mary, and imprisoned shortly after she ascended the throne. In 1555, with Ridley, he was burned at the stake in Oxford. John Foxe, in his account of Latimer's martyrdom, has preserved for all time the courageous words of Latimer to his fellow-martyr as the fire was applied: 'Be of good comfort, Master Ridley, and play the man; we shall this day light such a candle by God's grace in England, as I trust shall never be put out.'

Latimer's *First Sermon* preached before Edward VI was published separately in 1549, and six more sermons were printed and added to the collection in the same year. Twenty-seven sermons were published in a collected edition in 1562, and a decade later those sermons not previously published were collected in a separate edition and printed in three parts, 1571–75. His sermons were many times reprinted throughout the next hundred years.

MODERN EDITIONS: *Sermons (ed. by G. E. Corrie), Parker Society, 2 vols., Cambridge, 1844–45; *Seven Sermons before Edward VI* (ed. by Edward Arber), English Reprints, London, 1869; *Sermons* (ed. by H. C. Beeching), Everyman's Library, London, 1906.

COMMENT: R. M. and A. J. Carlyle, *Hugh Latimer*, London, 1899; J. C. Ryle, *Bishops Latimer and Ridley*, London, 1925; Elizabeth T. Hastings, 'A Sixteenth Century Manuscript Translation of Latimer's *First Sermon Before Edward*,' *PMLA*, lx (1945), 959–1002.

TEXT: *The fyrste Sermon*, 1549 (15271), Huntington.

599 31 *Quaecunque .*] Latimer's text is Romans 15.4.

600 27 *Quecunque . . . facite*] Matthew 23.3.   34] four pages are omitted at this point.

601 11] about 12 pages are omitted at this point.   21 that dead is] King Henry VIII.

602 6 the pages omitted here concern advice on the choosing of a wife.   14 salve] healthy. 35 Chrysostom] Church Father (*c.* 347–407 A.D.); for his statement, see his *Epist. ad Hebraeos,* xiii. 41 Whether] in Old English and Early Modern English, used to introduce a question.

603 6 rent-raisers] rents at this time were being increased to three or four times their former rate. 40 yeomanry] men below rank of gentlemen owning and cultivating a small estate. 40 shavery] for sake of the play on words, a term modeled humorously on slavery, to mean, apparently, the state of being cheated financially.

604 4 appropriations] it had been cus-tomary for only a portion of the tithes collected by the parish priests to be re-tained by them, the remainder going to monastic institutions; with the dissolu-tion of the monasteries, the 'appropria-tions' went to the crown. 4 reforma-tions is] another example of the lack of agreement between subject and verb that is common in sixteenth-century English. 8 marks] the mark was worth 13s. 4d. 13 find] furnish. 16 Blackheath field] the Cornish rebels were defeated here in 1497. 18 nobles] the noble was worth 6s. 8d.

605 5 Surveyors] overseers and tax-collectors.

ROGER ASCHAM

ROGER ASCHAM (1515–1568), scholar, teacher, and tutor to Queen Elizabeth, belonged to the group of Englishmen who have frequently been called the 'second generation of English humanists,' to distinguish them from an earlier group, which included Thomas Linacre, William Grocyn, and John Colet, who had gone to Italy at the end of the fifteenth century to acquire their training in Greek and Latin literature and had returned to establish humanistic studies in England. Ascham's generation, although many of them, like Ascham, made journeys to Italy, laid the foundations of their scholarship at home, most of them at Cambridge University, and especially at St. John's College, during the two decades between 1530 and 1550. Sir John Cheke (1514–1557) and Sir Thomas Smith (1513–1577) were the leaders of this generation, which, besides Ascham, included most of the Englishmen who were to become eminent as scholars and statesmen under the three children of King Henry VIII. Born of an old yeoman family in Yorkshire, Roger Ascham entered St. John's Col-lege, Cambridge, in 1530, received his B.A. in 1533 and was elected fellow of the College. After receiving his M.A. in 1537 he continued at St. John's as a fellow and as a Reader in Greek. In 1541 he was appointed a lecturer in Mathematics, and in 1547, public orator at Cambridge. Ascham's first work, *Toxophilus,* a treatise on archery in English rather than Latin, was presented to Henry VIII in 1545. In form the book was a Ciceronian dialogue between Toxophilus, 'lover of the bow,' and Philologus, 'lover of the word'; the style was consciously shaped to be at once learned and popular. The author's ex-planation, in his dedication to the king, of the reasons prompting him to write this treatise in English, is typical of the arguments used by the scholars of Ascham's generation for justifying the writing in the vernacular of works of sound learning for the benefit of their countrymen.

Appointed tutor to Elizabeth in 1548, he served her first as Princess, and later as Queen.

He travelled on the Continent as secretary to Sir Richard Moryson, am-bassador to Charles V, from 1550 until the death of Edward VI in 1553 brought about Moryson's recall and Ascham's return to England. While he was in Germany Ascham had been appointed Latin secretary to Edward VI; Queen Mary retained him as Latin secretary and Elizabeth, on her accession, gave him the same post in her service.

The *Scholemaster* was first published posthumously by Ascham's wife in

1570. The first draft of the first book (intended to be complete in itself) had been written in the winter of 1563–64; by the time Ascham had finished it he planned to add a second book on the methods of teaching Latin in the grammar school. In revising his first draft some four years later (1567 to 1568), Ascham added the preface describing his talk with Sir Richard Sackville as the immediate cause of his writing the treatise, and also the Second Book he had planned.

MODERN EDITIONS: *The Whole Works* (ed. by J. A. Giles), 4 vols., London, 1865; *The Scholemaster* (ed. by J. E. B. Mayor), London, 1863 and 1895; *The Scholemaster* (ed. by Edward Arber), English Reprints, London, 1870 and 1923; *Toxophilus* (ed. by Edward Arber), English Reprints, Birmingham, 1868; *English Works* (ed. by William Aldis Wright), Cambridge, 1904.

COMMENT: Robert Henry Quick, *Essays on Educational Reformers,* London, 1868; Gerhard Weidemann, *Roger Ascham als pädagoge,* Berlin, 1900; Max Adolf Emkes, *Das erziehungsideal bei Sir Thomas More, Sir Thomas Elyot, Roger Ascham, und John Lyly,* Marburg, 1904; A. Katterfeld, *Roger Ascham. Sein Leben und Seine Werke,* Strasburg, 1879; L. B. Radford, 'Roger Ascham,' *Quarterly Review,* cclvi (1931), 96–111; George B. Parks, 'The First Draft of Ascham's *Scholemaster,*' *HLQ,* (1938), 313–27.

TEXT: *Toxophilus,* 1545 (837) Huntington; *The Scholemaster,* 1570 (832), Huntington.

606 17 victorious journey into France] Henry VIII, during his war with France, crossed the Channel in 1544 and was present at the capture of Boulogne. 41 Sir William Paget (1505–1563), became Secretary of State to Henry VIII in 1543.

607 29 Bias] one of the seven sages of Greece; flourished about 570 B.C. 29 Croesus] king of Lydia, 560–546 B.C., famed for his fabulous wealth. 38 fond] foolish.

608 3 long-bow] the hand-discharged bow, as distinguished from the cross-bow; the length of the long bow was usually the height of the archer. 41 honest] honorable.

609 17 communed] conversed. 21 malvesy] malvoisie, or malmsey; a strong, sweet wine from the Cyclades and the Malavisi province of Crete. 21 sack] a dry wine (Fr. *sec.*); a name applied to the dry, white wines of southern France or Spain.

610 1 pluckethdown a side] pulls down the score on his side. 29 fletcher] arrow maker.

611 20 William Cecil] (1520–1598), Queen Elizabeth's famous secretary of state 1558–1572; and, 1572–1598, Lord Treasurer; created Baron Burghley in 1571; studied at St. John's College, Cambridge, at the time that Ascham and Cheke were fellows of that College.

612 22–26 Sir William Peter . . . Nicasius] Most of this distinguished company were among the most eminent scholars and statesmen of the time; many had served in important posts in the preceding reigns of Edward VI and Mary; several had been Ascham's contemporaries at Cambridge.

613 8 schoolhouse] in Latin, the term *ludus* signified 'play' or 'diversion'; *ludus literarius* was the term for grammar school. 10 Plato] see the *Republic*, vii. 15 curst] vicious. 17 best schoolmaster of our time] Nichol Udall, Master at Eton 1534–41, and later at Westminster School; the author of *Ralph Roister Doister.* 20 best scholars] Walter Haddon (1516–1572), one of the group present, had been educated at Eton before entering King's College, Cambridge. 30 Sir Richard Sackville] d. 1566, father of Thomas Sackville (1536–1608), the author of the Induction to the second edition of the *Mirror for Magistrates* and co-author of *Gorboduc.*

614 3 lewd] unlearned, bungling. 6 Robert Sackville] (1561–1609), eldest son of Thomas Sackville. 8 son much of his age] Sturm Ascham, born 1562; named after the humanist John Sturm, Ascham's friend and correspondent. 32 Mr. Goodricke] Richard Goodrich (c. 1524–1562), attorney of the court of augmentations of which Sir Richard Sackville was chancellor. 34 Sir John Cheke] see the notes, p. 1306.

615 15 Sir Thomas Smith] (1513–1577), Greek scholar, statesman, political writer; succeeded William Cecil, Lord Burghley, as Secretary of State in 1572, when the latter was appointed Lord Treasurer. 16 Mr. Watson] Thomas Watson (1513–1584), one of the scholars who, with Cheke, Ascham, and Sir Thomas Smith, led the revival of Greek learning at Cambridge; later bishop of Lincoln. 18 Sturmius] John Sturm (1507–1589), humanist scholar and teacher at Strasbourg; friend of Ascham. 22 mo] a common Elizabethan form of 'more.' 22 lets] hindrances. 23 Westminster Hall] the seat of the Court of the King's Bench; the allusion is probably to litigation connected with Ascham's financial troubles. 39 goodness of one] i.e., Sir William Cecil.

616 4 ἔχω . . . βροτῶν] 'For all I have I owe to thee alone,' *Oedipus at Colonnus*, 1129.

617 26 Horman and Whittington] William Horman (d. 1535), Master of Eton from 1485; author of elementary Latin textbooks published at the beginning of the 16th cent.; he attacked the works on Latin grammar of his contemporary, Robert Whittinton, or Whittington, in *Antibossicon* (1521). Ascham is critical of both. 29 *Cicero de Oratore*] see *De Oratore*, i.34, for Cicero's description of the method of improving one's Latin style by translation from Greek to Latin. 37 three concordances] grammatical agreements in number, gender, and person.

618 9 Tully's] i.e. Cicero's. 20 *N.*] here the master would insert the child's name; the *N.* stands for the Latin, *nomen.*

619 16 Budaeus] Guillaume Budé (1467–1540), French humanist.

620 12 *proprium*] literal statement. 12 *translatum*] figurative statement. 13 *synonymum*] synonyms. 13 *diversum*] distinction of meaning; not precisely synonymous. 13 *contraria*] of opposite meaning; antonyms. 14 *phrases*] apt locutions; vivid idiomatic phrases.

622 25 nipping] censuring. 38 privy] private; secret.

623 25 *de Rep.*] Plato's *Republic*, iii. 398–9. 27 book of shooting] Ascham's *Toxophilus*. 32 staffish] unmanageable. 33 *otium . . . languidum*] a calm but not listless tranquility. 33 *negotium . . . periculo*] an occupation with hard work, not with risk.

624 34 St. James's tide] May 1. 35 sweeting] sweet-flavored variety of apple. 35 rennet] a dessert apple of French origin; from Rennes, in Normandy. 41 store] stock or supply for future use.

626 2 seven plain notes] Ascham's requirements were suggested by Book vii of Plato's *Republic*. 23 wearish] sickly-looking.

627 13 *Usus . . . memoria*] 'practice begot me, memory, my mother, bore me';

this fragment from Lucuis Afranius (*c.* 150 B.C.) is quoted by Aulus Gellius, *Noctes Atticae*, xiii.8. 22 Isocrates] (436–338 B.C.), Greek orator and rhetorician. 24 Halicarnassaeus] Dionysius of Halicarnassus (fl. 25 B.C.), Greek historian and literary critic. 26 Epeius] the builder of the Trojan horse.

629 10 Plato] the quotation is from the *Republic*, vii.

630 6 Strabo] Roman geographer. 16 Cuspinian] Johannes Cuspinian (1473–1529), German classical scholar and writer on Roman history. 37 namely] especially.

631 7 popinjays] parrots. 23 Xenophon] *Cyropaedia*, i. 30 Jane Grey] (1537–1554), cousin to King Edward VI, daughter of Henry Grey, Duke of Suffolk; married to Lord Guildford Dudley; proclaimed Queen in 1553 by the adversaries of Mary opposed to Catholicism; deposed after a nine-days' reign, when Mary established herself as queen. The visit mentioned by Ascham occurred in 1550. 33 *Phaedon Platonis*] the *Phaedo* of Plato. 34 Bocace] Giovanni Boccaccio (1313–1375), author of the *Decameron*.

632 8 bobs] blows. 10 Mr. Elmer] John Aylmer (1521–1594), educated at Cambridge, tutor to Lady Jane Grey; later bishop of London (1576–1594).

633 34 Xenophon] *Cyropaedia*, vii. 40 Samson] see *Judges*, 14.1 ff.

635 34 Cyrus] see *Cyropaedia*, i. 41 frayed] frightened.

636 3 Crassus] see Cicero, *De Oratore*, iii.24. 15 busking] doublet. 22 rishe] dialectical form of 'rush'; a trifle. 25 Smithfield] the common duelling section of Elizabethan London.

637 8 Getae] plural of Geta, a slave in Terence's *Phormio;* also in his *Adelphi.* 8 Davi] Davus, the slave in Terence's *Andria.* 8 Gnatos] Gnatho, the parasite attending Thraso in Terence's *Eunuchus.* 8 Phormios] Phormio, the parasite in Terence's *Phormio.* 10 Parmeno] slave of Phaedria in Terence's *Eunuchus.*

638 9 St. Chrysostom] Church Father (347–407); John Cheke published the six discourses 'On Fate and Providence' in a Latin version in 1545. 15 Julianus Apostata] the Emperor Julian the Apostate (331–363). 37 Isocrates] the quotation that follows is from his *Areopagiticus.*

640 25 Langaeus] Guillaume du Bellay, Seigneur de Langey (1491–1553), noted French scholar, diplomat and general. 25 Bellaeus] Jean du Bellay

(1492–1560), next younger brother of Guillaume du Bellay, Seigneur de Langey; scholar and Cardinal (1535). His cousin, Joachim du Bellay (1524–1560), the poet, served for a time as his secretary.

641 10 bankrouts] bankruptcies. 24 Chamloe] Sir Roger Cholmley (d. 1565), Chief Justice of the King's Bench. 35 Tyburn] the principal place of execution of criminals in London.

642 8 rascal] the inferior deer of a herd. 36 Pallas] Pallas Athena, the patron goddess of Athens.

643 3 aegida] the shield. 3 oliva] the olive branch. 21 School of Shooting] Toxophilus. 21 Cockpit] a treatise on cock-fighting, now lost. 39–42 Fortunam . . . , ineptè] 'I sing a noble war, and Priam's Fate'; and 'How much better the man who attempted nothing ineptly?' Horace de Arte Poetica, 137 and 140.

644 9 Castiglione] see pp. 681–717, and the notes thereto. 26 Duke of Suffolk] Henry Brandon, 2nd Duke of Suffolk, and his brother Charles both attended St. John's College, Cambridge, where they were students of great promise; both died at Cambridge in 1551. 26 Lord Henry Matrevers] Henry Fitzalan, precocious young nobleman who died in 1556 at the age of 19 while on an embassy to the King of Bohemia. 30 Dr. Readman] John Redman (1499–1551), churchman, classical scholar; a friend of Ascham's at St. John's College; and later the first master of Trinity College, Cambridge (1546–1551).

645 24 big one of this court] this notorious person and the 'common proverb of Birching Lane' have not been identified.

647 3–4 sive . . . praedicetur] a paraphrase of Philippians 1.18; the King James version translates it 'Notwithstanding, every way, whether in pretence or in truth, Christ is preached.'

648 30 Mr. Watson] see note to p. 615, l. 16.

649 40 Circe's court] in Greek mythology anyone who drank from the cup of Circe, the enchantress, was transformed into a beast; see Odyssey, ix.

650 36 Hieremy] Jeremiah.

651 17–19 Nolite . . . constringe] See Psalms 32.9; 'Be ye not as the horse or as the mule; which have no understanding: whose mouth must be held with bit and bridle.' 23 Diverte . . . bonum] 'Depart from evil and do good'; Psalms 34.14. 39–40 Englese . . . incarnato]

'An Italianate Englishman is a devil incarnate.'

652 30 Louvain] the chief center of the English Catholic refugees in the first years of Elizabeth's reign. 37 St. Paul saith] Galatians, 5.19.

653 6 bawdy books translated out of the Italian] Ascham refers to recently issued translations of Italian novelle, such as William Painter's Palace of Pleasure (1566), and Geoffrey Fenton's translation of Bandello's Tragical Discourses (1567). 8 sound] tend. 13 Morte Arthure] Thomas Malory's Morte d'Arthur.

654 14–15 abhominabiles . . . Deus] Psalms, 14.1: 'The fool hath said in his heart, there is no God. They are corrupt, and have done abhominable works.' 20 Petrarch] (1304–1374), the famous Italian poet; writer of sonnets and of the Trionfi, allegorical poems in praise of Love, Fame, Chastity, Death, etc. 21 Tully's Offices] Cicero's De officiis, a treatise on moral duties. 22 Bocace] Boccaccio; his Decameron had not yet been translated into English, but several of the stories therein had been translated by Painter in his collection The Palace of Pleasure. 28 whether] which. 38 ἄθεοι] atheists.

655 10 Credat Iudaeus Appella] Appella, the Jew, may believe it, [not I]. Horace, Satires, i.5.100. 21 Pygius] Albertus Pighius (1490–1542), scholar, theologian, astronomer, and mathematician; champion of Catholicism against Luther. 31 one city] Venice; Ascham probably visited Italy in 1551. 35 pantocle] a slipper; from Fr. pantoufle.

656 11 Bridewell] in Ascham's time a house of correction in London.

657 6 Guelph or Ghibelline] the two great parties in medieval Italian politics.

659 37–38 dissimilis . . . tractatio] handling unlike matter in a similar manner; and handling like matter in a different manner.

660 4 Menander] (late 4th cent. B.C.) Greek writer of 'new comedy'; many of his plays were adapted in Latin by Terence in the 2nd cent. B.C. 11 Macrobius] Roman writer about 400 A.D.; his Saturnalia, Books iii to vi, analyze Virgil's debt to Homer. 14 Eobanus Hessus] (1488–1540), German humanist scholar and poet; among his works is an annotated edition of Virgil's Eclogues.

662 5–6 Cur . . . Platonis] 'Crassus, why do we not imitate Socrates as he appears in the Phaedrus of Plato?' De Oratore, i.7.28. 7 obiter] incidentally. 11 Atticus] Ascham, in the quotation in the following paragraph from Cicero's letter to Atticus, prints the Latin text. For the reader's convenience we have inserted an English translation based on the Loeb Library edition.

663 3 Cortesius] Paolo Cortesi (1465–1510), Italian humanist; at the age of 25 he wrote *De hominibus doctis*, addressed to Politian. 3 Politian] Angelo Poliziano (1454–1494), Florentine humanist and poet. 4 Bembus] Pietro Bembo (1470–1547) Italian cardinal and humanist; his letter in reply to Pico

della Mirandola, defending the imitation of Cicero against the criticisms of Pico, was in the Renaissance frequently published together with the original letter of Pico. 17 Barthol. Riccius Ferrariensis] Bartolomeo Ricci of Ferrara, humanist scholar, published his *De imitatione libri tres* at Venice in 1545; the treatise had later editions at Paris and Lyons.

664 6 *praeponendo . . . postponendo*] placing before, placing between, or placing after.

ROBERT RECORDE

ROBERT RECORDE (1510?-1558), scholar, physician, public official, and the first important writer on the mathematical sciences in English, was born at Tenby, Pembrokeshire, educated at Oxford, and elected a Fellow of All Souls College in 1531. Some time later he removed to Cambridge, probably because that university was then taking the lead in Greek studies through the energy and inspiration of John Cheke, and Thomas Smith and their pupils, among whom were Roger Ascham, William Cecil, and others who were to become eminent in the service of the state under Edward VI, Mary, and Elizabeth. In 1545 he received the degree of M.D. from Cambridge; two years later he was practising as a physician in London, and is said to have been royal physician to King Edward VI, and later to Queen Mary. Recorde's career as a public servant began, like that of many of his Cambridge contemporaries, after the accession of Edward VI. He was appointed Controller of the Mint at Bristol, and in 1551, Surveyor of the Mines and Monies of Ireland; the latter post put him in charge of the mining operations in Ireland for which miners from Germany were imported. As a result of disputes between the English administration and the foreign workmen, the Privy Council received complaints concerning Recorde's conduct of the mines. In 1557, five years later, Recorde was imprisoned by the Court of the King's Bench for reasons as yet not definitely ascertained. It is possible that Recorde's Protestant sympathies were responsible for the reviving and acting upon the old charges. While still a prisoner, Recorde died.

Recorde has a place of primary importance in the history of science and scholarship in England. He was the immediate heir to the tradition established by Sir Thomas Elyot of writing in English, for the benefit of his less-learned countrymen, scientific textbooks based upon the best classical and contemporary sources. He wrote one popular medical treatise, *The Urinal of Physick* (1547), but the rest of his publications dealt with the mathematical sciences. His *Ground of Arts* (1542) became the standard textbook of arithmetic in English for more than a century; he published the first English textbook of geometry, *The Pathway to Knowledge*, in 1551; and also the first textbook of algebra, *The Whetstone of Wit*, in 1557. In the *Pathway* he attempted to create new words of English derivation for the Latin mathematical terms; in the *Whetstone* he frankly abandoned this practice, acknowledging that it had been a misguided venture. Recorde enlivened many of his textbooks by writing them in the form of a dialogue between Master and Pupil. This was done in the *Whetstone*, and also in his *Castle of Knowledge* (1556), the first important original textbook of astronomy in English, from which our selection is taken. The clear exposition that Recorde gives therein of the structure of the physical universe pictures the commonly accepted beliefs of the sixteenth century, although the author mentions the fact that a different system of the universe had recently been proposed by Copernicus, and has the Master suggest to his scholar that a more careful study of the mathematical evidence for the Copernican theory may force him to abandon his former notions.

MODERN EDITIONS: none.

COMMENT: D. E. Smith, 'New Information Respecting Robert Recorde,' *Am. Math. Monthly,* xxviii (1921), 296–300; F. M. Clarke, 'New Light on Robert Recorde,' *Isis,* viii (1926), 50–70; F. R. Johnson and S. V. Larkey, 'Robert Recorde's Mathematical Teaching and the Anti-Aristotelian Movement,' *HLB,* no. 7 (1935), 59–87; F. R. Johnson, *Astronomical Thought in Renaissance England,* Baltimore, 1937.

TEXT: *The Castle of Knowledge,* 1556 (20796), Huntington.

664 23 Proclus' *Sphere*] an elementary treatise on astronomy written in the 5th century A.D.; widely known in the Renaissance, both in the Greek of its author and in the Latin translation by Linacre. 23 Joannes de Sacrobosco] the 13th-century author of the *Sphaera mundi,* which was still, in the 16th century, the most widely used Latin manual of astronomy. 23 Orontius' *Cosmography*] The *De mundi sphaera sive cosmographia* (1542), an important exposition of pre-Copernican astronomy by Orontius Finaeus (Oronce Finé, Regius Professor of Mathematics at the Collège de France). 36 Axe] axel.

665 17 Aristotle] Recorde's practice is first to quote the Greek of his authority, then to give a Latin translation, and finally an English translation; here, and elsewhere, we have omitted the Greek and the Latin and retained only the English. 19 Cleomedes] a Greek astronomer whose treatises were published and studied in the Renaissance.

668 13 Aratus] Greek poet, born *c.* 315 B.C., the author of an astronomical poem entitled *Phainomena.* 29 Ringelbergh] 16th-century author of astronomical treatises; his collected works were first published in 1531.

669 8 diversity] in limiting the number of spheres to the eight which are perceptible, Recorde follows Orontius; the majority of 16th-century astronomers portrayed ten spheres.

GEORGE CAVENDISH

GEORGE CAVENDISH (*c.* 1500–*c.* 1561), the faithful servant and biographer of Wolsey, was the son of Thomas Cavendish and the husband of Margery Kemp, niece of Sir Thomas More. As gentleman-usher to Cardinal Wolsey for the last five years of the latter's life, he saw the splendor and arrogance of his master at the height of his glory and witnessed the pathos of his downfall. After the death of Wolsey, King Henry offered Cavendish the appointment of gentleman-usher in his own service, but Cavendish requested permission to return to his estate in the country, where he spent the rest of his life in retirement. His *Life of Wolsey,* written near the end of Queen Mary's reign, circulated in manuscript from the early years of Elizabeth's; but, because of its depiction of living persons and its author's censure of certain aspects of the Reformation, it was not printed. Yet the many manuscript copies made in the sixteenth century prove its popularity. Although Stow included extracts from the manuscript in his *Annals,* and Shakespeare had probably read Cavendish's work before writing *Henry VIII,* the first printed edition, called *The Negotiations of Thomas Wolsey,* did not appear until 1641, as part of the Puritan campaign attacking Archbishop Laud. The editor brazenly alters Cavendish's text to portray Wolsey's career as a warning against the dangerous ambitions of Laud; his interpolations, such as an entire paragraph from Bacon's essay 'Of Ambition,' have that purpose; also his careful suppression of all passages that reflected sympathy for Wolsey, including the account of Wolsey's death.

The other editions printed in the seventeenth century follow the mangled text of the first; therefore they give a completely false picture of the quality of Cavendish as a biographer—especially of his integrity in depicting his subject with scrupulous fairness, showing both the faults of Wolsey and his virtues. The pattern of Cavendish's *Life of Wolsey* is that of the medieval tragic narratives, telling of the rise of a great man to power and prosperity, and of his subsequent fall to death and misery; but the simplicity and human feeling with which the author recounts the events which he has himself witnessed make the *Life* much more expressive than the usual didactic stories of the falls of princes, and give it a place as one of the earliest artistic biographies in English.

It was not until 1761 that this work was rescued from the mangling to which it had been subjected by its seventeenth-century editors, and printed from a good sixteenth-century manuscript. The first carefully edited text, based on Cavendish's holograph manuscript, was issued by S. W. Singer in 1825. Our text follows the manuscript that Singer used, and corrects a few errors in transcription that occur in his edition.

MODERN EDITIONS: *The Life of Cardinal Wolsey* (ed. by S. W. Singer), 2 vols., London, 1825; *The Life and Death of Thomas Wolsey* (ed. by F. S. Ellis), The Temple Classics, London, 1899; *The Life and Death of Thomas Wolsey*, Boston, 1905.

COMMENT: A. F. Pollard, *Wolsey*, London, 1929; Paul L. Wiley, 'Renaissance Exploitation of Cavendish's *Life of Wolsey*,' *SP*, xliii (1946), 121–46.

TEXT: *Egerton Ms. 2402*, British Museum.

674 3 Lord Marquess Dorset] Thomas Grey (1451–1501), the first Marquis of Dorset. 13 ordinary] one who has of his own right immediate jurisdiction in ecclesiastical matters.

675 16 Master Kingston] Sir William Kingston, constable of the Tower and captain of the guard, who had been sent to convey Wolsey to the Tower. 21 Hardwick Hall] in Nottinghamshire; not to be confused with the more famous Hardwick Hall in Derbyshire.

676 9 Doctor Palmes] George Palmes, Wolsey's chaplain; in 1559 Queen Elizabeth displaced him as prebendary of York to give the office to Roger Ascham. 16] the omitted passage (two pages) relates Kingston's examination of Wolsey concerning money that he owed or was accountable for.

677 5 cullis] a strong broth. 8 St. Andrew's Eve] November 29. 20 flux] an early term for dysentery.

678 11 Lutherans] the nobles and landlords of Southern Germany blamed the Reformation and the teaching of Martin Luther for the rise of social unrest leading to the Peasant's Revolt (1524–26), although Luther himself finally turned against the revolutionaries and urged the rulers to put down the insurrection without pity. A century before, John Huss, a Bohemian, greatly influenced by the works of John Wycliffe (*c*. 1320–1384) in England, had led a movement for Church Reform and had been burned as a heretic in 1415. Yet the Hussites continued strong and aggressive in Bohemia, and one of the chief centers of the Peasant's Revolt was there; Ferdinand, King of Bohemia, ruthlessly suppressed the rising. 42 Richard the Second] the rising of 1381 in England occurred in the early years of Richard II's reign.

679 10 Sir John Oldcastle] a leader of the Lollards, as the followers of Wycliffe's opinions were called in the fifteenth century, who was declared a heretic and hanged and burned in 1417.

680 2 seen] skilled.

SIR JOHN CHEKE

SIR JOHN CHEKE (1514–1557), scholar, tutor to the prince who became Edward VI, and the most influential teacher of a generation of students at Cambridge who were later to hold important posts under Queen Elizabeth, was educated at St. John's College, Cambridge, and afterwards a tutor at that college, where among his students were Roger Ascham and William Cecil, later Lord Burghley. Cheke graduated B.A. in 1529–30, M.A. in 1533, and in 1540 was appointed professor of Greek at Cambridge. Under his instruction, Ascham tells us, Demosthenes became as familiar as Cicero. In fact, Ascham says Cheke laid the 'very foundation of learning' at St. John's. Rejecting the modern Greek and continental pronunciation of classical Greek, Cheke, on the basis of study of ancient authorities, introduced the 'Erasmian' method of pronunciation. In 1544 he was commanded to act as tutor to Prince Edward. At about this time he was incorporated M.A. at Oxford. An ardent Protestant, he was in 1549 appointed to aid in framing laws for the government of the church. In 1552 he was knighted, and in 1553 he was made one of the secretaries of state and a member of the Privy Council. During the brief reign of Lady Jane Grey he served as secretary of state. After the accession of Queen Mary he was imprisoned for having favored the cause of Lady Jane. Upon his release he traveled about Europe, and gave Greek lectures at Strassbourg. On his journey home to England, he was seized because of his support of Protestantism. Under the shadow of the stake, he recanted and returned to the Roman Church.

As a translator and imitator of the ancients and an ardent promoter of Greek studies, Cheke is one of the most vital forces in the English Renaissance. In addition to a number of homilies from the Greek, he translated the Gospel according to St. Matthew as well as a part of the first chapter of the Gospel according to St. Mark. A dislike for the excessive use of words of Greek and Latin origin in the previous translations of The Bible caused him to use as much as possible words of Anglo-Saxon origin: *crucified* becomes *crossed* and *centurion* becomes *hundreder* in his translation. Yet Cheke retained a larger proportion of words of Latin derivation than one would infer from the statements in most literary histories.

Cheke also advocated a reformation in English orthography: to show that *a* is long, he doubles the *a* and omits the final *e*, as in *maad* for *made;* he omits medial letters not pronounced, as in *dout* for *doubt.* The letter included in this text was published in Hoby's translation of Castiglione's *Il Cortegiano.* Because its spelling exemplifies Cheke's theories, we have not modernized it, but have adhered to the original orthography.

COMMENT: John Strype, *Life,* London, 1705; Walter Ludwig Nathan, *Sir John Cheke und der englische humanismus,* Bonn, 1928; Herbert D. Meritt, 'The Vocabulary of Sir John Cheke's Partial Version of the Gospels,' *JEGP,* xxxix (1940), 450–5.
TEXT: *The Courtyer,* 1561 (4778), Huntington.

680 36 denisoned] naturalized.
681 1 exhortacion] Cheke's use of this word of Latin origin would seem to be an exception to his theories; but it had come into English during the Middle English period, so that he probably considered it an 'old denisoned' word.

SIR THOMAS HOBY

SIR THOMAS HOBY (1530–1566), translator and diplomat, was educated at St. John's College, Cambridge, where he was a friend and student of Sir John Cheke and Roger Ascham. In 1547 he began his travels in Europe to prepare for statecraft; he lived at Strassbourg with the reformer, Martin Bucer, whose *Gratulation* he translated and published in 1549. Proceeding to Italy, he visited Venice, Mantua, and Ferrara, as well as Padua, where he studied Italian at the University. He then visited Florence, Siena, and Rome. After a brief return to England, he traveled in France. Throughout his travels he kept a diary which gives an excellent picture of the English traveler, student, and diplomat of those days. Under Edward VI he served on several diplomatic missions. Upon the accession of Queen Mary, Hoby went to Padua, where Sir Anthony Cooke and Sir John Cheke were in exile. In his diary for the spring of 1558, he says, 'I communed with Mrs. Elizabeth Cooke in the way of marriage.' The 'communion' was successful, for he was married to the daughter of Sir Anthony Cooke, and the future aunt of Sir Francis Bacon, in May 1558. He was knighted in 1565–66, and sent as ambassador to France in 1566, during which year he died.

The Courtyer of Count Baldessar Castilio, as Hoby styled his translation of Castiglione's *Il Cortegiano*, was completed several years before its publication, probably during Hoby's stay in Padua during Queen Mary's reign. Because of reflections upon Roman Catholic dignitaries, it did not appear until 1561, when Protestantism had been restored. The letter of Sir John Cheke on translation and a eulogistic sonnet by Thomas Sackville are included in this edition. The work was republished many times during Elizabeth's reign. Hoby's translation had a marked influence upon English life and customs, bringing, as it did, to England not only Italian classicism but Italian culture as well. Even Ascham, who had small regard for the morality of Italy, was impelled to praise this work, which joins 'learning with comely exercises.' Dr. Johnson calls it 'the best book that ever was written upon good breeding.' Although Hoby made many slips in his translation and syntax, and although he frequently prefers an awkward, imprecise term of native Saxon derivation to the Latin-derived word that would more exactly convey his author's meaning, in this respect following the ideas of Cheke, he is, nevertheless vigorous in a homely fashion. His style is unlike the studied, artificial writing of many of his contemporaries. Cicero and Quintilian, in setting forth the qualities of the orator, foreshadow Castiglione in his conception of the courtier. A contemporary work of similar nature, *Il Galateo*, by Bishop Giovanni della Casa, was translated by Robert Peterson of Lincoln's Inn, in 1576. Bembo's discourse on love in the fourth book of *The Courtier*, is of central importance to the understanding of Renaissance Platonism; the ideas there expressed are the ones that underlie Spenser's *Foure Hymnes* and many of the Elizabethan sonnets.

BALDASSARE CASTIGLIONE (1478–1529), poet and author of *Il Cortegiano*, after being educated at Milan under the inspiration of the modern Greek scholarship of Demetrius Chalchondylas and others, entered the service of Guidobaldo di Montefeltro, Duke of Urbino, in whose retinue his cousin, Cesare Gonzaga, was serving. Castiglione's mother belonged to the Gonzaga family, and was therefore a relative of the Duchess of Urbino. While residing at the palace of Urbino between 1504 and 1508, he conceived the plan of his great work. In 1506 he visited the court of Henry VII. In 1513, as ambassador to the court of Pope Leo X, the famous son of Lorenzo the Magnificent, he became familiar with Raphael and Michelangelo and other distinguished men of the day. In 1524 he was sent by Pope Clement VII as nuncio to the court of Charles V at Madrid. When, however, Rome was sacked, the pope questioned not only the ability but the loyalty of Castiglione. Yet when Castiglione died in 1529, Charles V, by whose dissimulation he had been deceived, said, 'I tell you that one of the finest gentlemen of the world is dead.' *Il Cortegiano* was written between 1508 and 1516, and was first published in Venice at the Aldine Press in 1528.

MODERN EDITIONS: [of Hoby's translation] *The Book of the Courtier* (ed. by Walter Raleigh), Tudor Translations, London, 1900; †*The Book of the Courtier*, Everyman's Library, London, 1928. [in Italian] *Il Cortegiano* (ed. by V. Cian), Florence, 1929; [the best modern English translation] *The Book of the Courtier* (trans. and ed. by L. E. Opdycke), New York, 1903.

COMMENT: M. A. Scott, 'The Book of the Courtyer,' *PMLA*, xvi (1901), 475–502; T. F. Crane, *Italian Social Customs of the Sixteenth Century*, New Haven, 1920; Julia Cartwright, *Baldassare Castiglione*, 2 vols., New York, 1908; Ruth Kelso, *The Doctrine of the English Gentleman in the Sixteenth Century*, Urbana, Illinois, 1929; F. O. Matthiessen, *Translation: An Elizabethan Art*, Cambridge, Mass., 1931; E. Bianco di San Secondo, *Baldassare Castiglione nella vita e negli scritti*, Verona, 1941; H. Adams, '*Il Cortegiano* and *Il Galateo*,' *MLR*, xlii (1947), 457–66.

TEXT: *The Courtyer*, 1561 (4778), Huntington.

681 18 Alphonsus Ariosto] (d. 1526), cousin of the poet Ludovico, and friend of Castiglione.

682 26 in England] Castiglione was visiting the court of Henry VII in 1507 when the discussions described in *The Courtier* were supposed to have taken place. 35 Urbin] Urbino, a town on the eastern slope of the Apennines, over 70 miles east of Florence.

683 5 Duke Frederick] Federico di Montefeltro (1422–1482), Duke of Urbino; he was a great patron of art and letters. 29 Guidubaldo] Guidobaldo di Montefeltro.

684 10 entertainment] service, employment. 11 Alphonsus] Alfonso II of Naples (1448–1495). 11 Ferdinand] Ferdinand II of Naples (1469–1496). 12 Pope Alexander the VI.] Roderigo Borgia (1431–1503), elected pope by bribery in 1492. 13 Julius the II.] Giuliano della Rovere (1443–1513), nephew of Pope Sixtus IV; made cardinal in 1471; Pope in 1503. 34 Lady Elizabeth Gonzaga] Elisabetta Gonzaga, daughter of the Marquess of Mantua, married Guidobaldo di Montefeltro in 1489. 35 Lady Emilia Pia] the widow (1503) of the natural half-brother of Duke Guidobaldo.

686 2 the lines that follow name the chief participants in the dialogue besides Elisabetta Gonzaga: THE DUCHESS (aged 46), and Emilia Pia: LADY EMILIA (aged 30), they are Ottaviano Fregoso: LORD OCTAVIAN

Federico Fregoso: SIR FREDERICK (aged 27)

Giuliano de' Medici: LORD JULIAN (aged 29)

Pietro Bembo: M[aster]. PETER (aged 37)

Cesare Gonzaga: LORD CESARE (aged 32)

Ludovico da Canossa: COUNT LEWIS (aged 31)

Gaspar Pallavicino: LORD GASPAR (aged 21)

Sigismondo Morello da Ortona: M[aster]. MORELLO

Bernardo Acolti: UNICO ARETINO

688 10 Pulia] Apulia, in southern Italy, where music was believed to cure the bite of the tarantula. 16 privy operation] hidden touch. 19 some] one person. 21 making antiques] inventing mimes. 22 moine] native quality. 35 Friar Marion] Fra Mariano Fetti, famous as a jester.

689 3 remit . . . another] assent to another's proposal. 8 which ghostly spirit] which with her divine virtue. 16 to disgrace . . . ass heads] So, to repress the many fools. 23 keepeth disputations] proposes a thesis. 40 for losing] not to lose.

690 40 seely] simple, ignorant. 40 unhappy, witty] a more correct translation of the Italian *un scelerato, prudente* would be: 'a knave, discreet.' 42 reasonable discourses] rational discussion.

691 30 out of kind] degenerate. 42 Hippolitus da Este] Ippolito d'Este (1479–1520), advanced with such rapidity in the church that he became a Cardinal before he reached the age of 24.

692 4 so grave an authority] such weight of character. 5 more . . . learn] fitter to teach than to be taught. 16 a hue] an air. 26 yesternight] the discussion of the previous night, recounted in Book iii, centered upon the topic of the qualities of the perfect gentlewoman of the court, the feminine counterpart of the perfect courtier, and of love between the two. The first part of Book iv has been concerned with the courtier as the servant and counsellor of his Prince. 32 well drawn] advanced. 35 preciseness] elegancies.

693 5 perfection . . . above] an added perfection. 7 Peter Bembo] Pietro Bembo (1470-1547), Venetian scholar and poet, was one of the most eminent humanists of the Italian Renaissance; later he was made Cardinal. 27 of good fellowship] cf. 'on your faith.' 31 ladies to think me old] Bembo was 36 at the time. 37 Lavinello] in Bembo's *Gli Asolani* (1505), iii, a hermit discourses to Lavinello on the beauty of mystical Christian love. Since Bembo is known to have revised *Il Cortegiano* before publication, one may assume he was content with the discourse on love here ascribed to him.

694 18 manner] kinds of. 21 reason] Italian *ragione;* the discursive reason. 21 understanding] this is Hoby's translation of *intelletto;* the intuitive reason. 36-37 heavenly bountifulness] It., *bontà divina,* the divine Good. 40-41 limits of lines] outlines.

695 35 unluckily] unhappily.

696 9 the beginning] i.e., 'the first notions.' 19 setting case] assuming. 22 natural burning . . . warmth] the natural heat begins to become tepid. 35 where] whereas, although.

697 9-10 But . . . once] But if, even after they are old. 17 whist] quiet.

698 18 passeth] careth. 27 Stesichorus] Greek lyric poet supposed to have been miraculously stricken blind after writing an attack on Helen of Troy.

699 8 engine] It., *machina.* 22 little world] man, the *microcosm,* or little world, had, in the science of the time, an intricate set of correspondences with the *macrocosm,* or great world of the physical universe.

700 6-7 this comely . . . everything] this gracious and sacred beauty gives highest ornament to every thing. 14 spoil] trophy. 24 otherwhile] occasionally.

701 2 dishonest flickerings] cf. 'un-

seemly blandishments.' 4 unshamefastness] immodesty. 38 hue] complexion, spirit; It. *il sangue suo.*

702 18 virtue of seeing] power of sight. 36-37 most beautiful conditions] fairest behavior.

703 18 Lord Julian hath made his] In Book iii Lord Julian had taken the lead in the discussion of the proper conduct between the young courtier and his lady when they are in love.

704 14 Solomon] *Song of Solomon,* 1.2. 34 those spirits] the 'animal spirits' in Renaissance physiology. 37 aghast] cf. 'trembles with awe.'

705 11 wode] mad. 32 take thought] cf. 'endure suffering.' 42 meddling] mixing.

706 4 made dim] bewildered. 5 not pass upon] not care for. 15 flush] fledged. 23 out of his wit] outside himself. 24 come into his wit] turn his thoughts inward. 30 occupy] use. 32 partened with] communicated to. 34-35 stirring virtues] motive forces. 35 withdrawn . . . beholding] absorbed in earnest contemplation. 39-40 waxeth . . . it] becomes almost frenzied with desire to unite herself to that beauty. 41 happy] beatific.

707 33 the high bounty] the supreme Good. 37 stirring] motion. 37 natural provocation] natural instinct.

708 2 Oeta] Hercules, according to one version of the Greek myth, tormented by the poisoned shirt sent him by Deianeira, threw himself on a burning pyre on Mount Oeta and was caught up to heaven in a cloud. 23 bountiful temper] cf. 'benignant sway.' 26-27 stirrest . . . life] movest Nature to produce—and that which is born, to the perpetuation of life.

709 1 relieve] cf. 'quicken.' 5 right bliss] true beatitude. 17 beholding] contemplation. 28 to be instant upon] to entreat urgently.

710 15 Saint Paul] see *2 Corinthians,* 12.2-4. 17 Saint Stephen] see *Acts,* 7.54-60. 20 Diotima] see Plato, *Symposium.* 23 Mary Magdalen] see *St. Luke,* 7.37-50. 35 plead] controversy.

711 6 Mount Catri] about 20 miles south of Urbino. 10 biting cold] cf. 'crisp coolness.' 15 Lord General] Francesco Maria della Rovere, nephew and adopted heir of Guidobaldo di Montefeltro; he was a nephew of Pope Julius II and Prefect of Rome. Although not taking a prominent part in the sections we have reprinted, he was one of the chief participants in the discussions recounted in *The Courtier.* 22 wavering starter] cf. 'shifty disputant.' 25 4 *brief rehearsal of the chief conditions and qualities in a Courtier*] this is an addition by Hoby, compiled by him as a summary of the qualities recommended in the discussions comprising the four books of Castiglione's *Il Cortegiano.* Hoby makes some typically English adaptations of the Italian doctrines. 30 portly] stately in bearing and appear-

ance. 33 crake] equivalent of modern colloquial meaning of 'to crow.' 35 slight] an air of indifference. 36 recklessness] nonchalance.

712 6 seen] versed. 26 sad] somber. **716** 3 make wise] pretend, act as though. 20 come on loft] become elated. 37 commune] converse. **717** 24 troth] truth.

JOHN FOXE

JOHN FOXE (1517–1587), ardent Protestant and martyrologist, whose book was to have an influence second only to that of the Bible on the history of the Church of England, was born in Lincolnshire and educated at Brasenose College, Oxford. A fellow of Magdalen College from 1538, he resigned in 1545 because his extreme Protestantism conflicted with the rules of the College. He became a tutor in the family of the Duke of Norfolk, having as pupils the children of Henry Howard, Earl of Surrey, after their father had been beheaded by King Henry VIII in 1547. He also began at this time to publish theological tracts in support of the Reformation and in 1550 was ordained deacon by Bishop Ridley, whose martyrdom he was later to chronicle. During the reign of Queen Mary he became an exile on the continent and the first draft, in Latin, of the first book of his *Actes and Monuments,* which had probably been nearing completion when Foxe fled from England, was in 1554 published at Strassbourg under the title of *Commentarii rerum in ecclesia gestarum.* This volume deals principally with the persecution of Wycliffe and his followers in England, although it includes a few foreign martyrs such as Huss and Savonarola. From a beginning in this small volume grew the huge tomes of Foxe's *Book of Martyrs,* as his great work was popularly called. As fresh news of the Marian persecutions reached Foxe at his retreat in Basel, he began to collect his materials for the stories of the Protestant martyrs under 'Bloody Mary.' With this material he carried the story nearly to the end of Mary's reign in a greatly expanded Latin edition which he published at Basel in 1559. With the accession of Queen Elizabeth, Foxe's friend in exile and colleague in collecting materials for *The Book of Martyrs,* Edmund Grindal, returned to England and was made Bishop of London. Foxe soon followed him, was ordained a priest by Grindal, settled in London and completed the English edition of his martyrology by expanding, translating, and revising the Latin version. The book was published in March, 1563, under the title of *Actes and Monuments;* a greatly enlarged second edition was printed in 1570 in two large folio volumes. In 1571 the convocation ordered that a copy of 'that full history entitled "Monuments of Martyrs"' should be installed in each cathedral church, so that all and sundry might come to read or to listen; and that every archbishop, bishop, archdeacon, dean, and resident canon should place a copy in the hall or dining-room of his house for the use even of servants and visitors. Moreover the influence of Foxe's book was even greater than such an official order would indicate, for almost every parish church also owned a copy. The steady market for these gigantic volumes continued through the seventeenth century. Two more editions, containing revisions by Foxe, were issued during his lifetime, one in 1576 and another in 1583. The fifth edition appeared in 1596, the ninth in 1684.

During the latter part of his life, while holding various offices in the Church of England, Foxe continued his labors on the revisions of the *Book of Martyrs,* and wrote various theological treatises against Roman Catholicism.

Foxe's accuracy and reliability as a historian were naturally attacked vigorously by his opponents in that period of violently partisan theological controversy during which his book had its greatest effect upon the Protestant imagination. Recent examination of the evidence by historians has usually vindicated Foxe; granted that he was an avowed propagandist in matters of religious opinion, he has the true spirit of an historian and the charge that he is consistently undependable on matters of fact has not been sustained.

MODERN EDITIONS: *Book of Martyrs* (ed. and abridged by Henry Wightman), Boston, 1840; *Acts and Monuments* (ed. by S. R. Cattley, with a life by Canon George Townsend), 8 vols., London, 1837–41.

COMMENT: J. F. Mozley, *John Foxe and his Book,* London, 1940.

TEXT: *Actes and Monuments,* 1563 (11222), Huntington.

718 15 Winchester] see note to p. 725 line 32. 18 shogging] shaking. 21 Bonner] Edmund Bonner (1500?–1569), bishop of London and leader of the Marian persecutions.

719 29 Duns] Duns Scotus (*c.* 1265– *c.* 1308), famous scholastic philosopher and opponent of Thomistic philosophy. 32 Faber] Jacques Le Fèvre D'Étaples (1450–1537), French scholar who wrote textbooks on astronomy, commentaries on Aristotle, and translated some of the books of the Bible into French.

720 13 Commonplaces] topical headings. 28 Longland] John Longland (1473–1547). 31 decise] decide.

721 9 rota] Sacra Romana Rota, the supreme court of the Roman Catholic Church. 13 departed] died. 36 the queen] Queen Mary. 37 Cole] Henry Cole (1500?–1580), one of the leaders of the Roman Catholic clergy under Queen Mary, Dean of St. Paul's (1556–59);

imprisoned by Elizabeth on her accession.

722 6 abode in the Catholic faith] Cranmer had temporarily recanted his Protestantism. 9 colter's] a colter is the iron blade fixed in front of the share in a plough; Foxe is making a forced pun.

723 16 *Nunc dimittis*] the first words of the Song of Simeon in *Luke,* 2.29; or the canticle in the church service beginning with these words. The English version: 'Now lettest thou thy servant depart in peace.'

725 32 book against the Bishop of Winchester] *An answer unto a crafty cavillation by S. Gardiner,* 1551. Stephen Gardiner was Bishop of Winchester (1531–51); upon Queen Mary's accession he was reinstated and made Lord Chancellor; he had tried to save Cranmer from the stake.

726 40 Ely] William Ely (d. 1609), Roman Catholic divine.

SIR THOMAS NORTH

SIR THOMAS NORTH (1535–*c.* 1603) was educated at Peterhouse, Cambridge, after which, in 1557, he entered Lincoln's Inn. Like many of the students of the law at this time, however, his interests were literary rather than legal and in the same year he published *The Dial of Princes,* a translation from a French version of a Spanish work by Antonio de Guevara, entitled *El relox de principes.* In 1570 he published *The Moral Philosophy of Doni,* a translation from the Italian. North went to France in 1574 with his brother, Roger, second Lord North, who had been appointed ambassador to the court of Henri III. In the year that England was threatened with invasion by Spain, and saved by the defeat of the Armada, North was captain of a company of three hundred men from the isle of Ely, in Cambridgeshire. About 1591 he was knighted, and in 1601 Elizabeth granted to him an annual pension of forty pounds as a reward for his military service in the Low Countries and in Ireland. North's military career occupied the last two decades of his life. Before beginning his service in Ireland he had, in 1579, published his greatest work, his translation from the French version of Jacques Amyot of Plutarch's *Lives*, a work which entitles North to one of highest places among Elizabethan translators; in fact Shakespeare paid North's prose style the supreme compliment of transferring whole passages, almost unaltered, to the lines of his Roman plays. A second edition of the *Lives* was published in 1595, and a third, with several additional lives, in 1603.

ANTONIO DE GUEVARA (*c.* 1480–1545), Spanish bishop and author, spent part of his early days at the court of Queen Isabella; later in life he travelled in the retinue of the Emperor Charles V. Among other secular and religious duties, he served as court historiographer and Bishop of Guadix. His *Libro del Emperador Marco Aurelio con el relox de principes*, 1525, a didactic work purporting to be an autobiography of Marcus Aurelius, became so popular that it was translated into many languages. The sixteenth-century English translations are those of Lord Berners, 1534, and Sir Thomas North, 1557. Guevara's Spanish style exhibits to a certain extent the antithetical structure and schematic parallelism in form and sound that we later find in a more obtrusive form in Lyly's *Euphues;* hence earlier scholars were inclined to find in Guevara and in his English translators a principal source of the Euphuistic style of Lyly. Recent scholarship, however, minimizes the theory that Guevara had any direct influence of importance in the creation of Lyly's distinctive style.

PLUTARCH (*c.* 46 A.D.–*c.* 120 A.D.), Greek philosopher and biographer, studied and taught philosophy at both Athens and Rome. In Rome he acted as tutor to the future emperor Hadrian. He died in his native Chaeronea, where he was building inspector, archon, and priest.

Plutarch's forty-six *Parallel Lives*, as the title indicates, was intended to be a comparative study of both Greek and Roman warriors, statesmen, and orators; each of the twenty-three pairs of biographies was followed by a section in which the two men were compared. The ethical quality of Plutarch's work naturally appealed to all Elizabethans as well as to Sir Thomas North, who translated these lives in 1579 as examples to his contemporaries.

MODERN EDITIONS: *The Dial of Princes* (ed. by K. N. Colvile), London, 1919; **North's Plutarch* (ed. by George Wyndham), Tudor Translations, 6 vols., London, 1895; *Plutarch's Lives Englished by Sir Thomas North* (ed. by W. H. D. Rouse), Temple Classics, 6 vols., London, 1898; *North's Plutarch*, 8 vols., Oxford, 1928; *North's Plutarch*, 5 vols., London, 1929.

COMMENT: K. N. Colvile, *Fame's Twilight*, London, 1923; C. H. Conley, *The First English Translators of the Classics*, New Haven, 1927; F. O. Matthiessen, *Translation: An Elizabethan Art*, Harvard, 1931; P. S. Allen, 'The Birth of Thomas North,' *EHR*, xxxvii (1922), 565–66; H. H. Davis, 'The Military Career of Thomas North,' *HLQ*, xii (1949), 315–21.

TEXTS: *The Diall of Princes*, 1557 (12427), Huntington; *The Lives*, 1579 (22065), Huntington.

727 38 Sithence] since.
728 2 priviest] most private or secret. 27 Adrian] the Roman Emperor Hadrian (76–138 A.D.). 36 togethers] together.
731 4 treen] wooden. 7 myriad] ten thousand drachmas; the sum owed was 17,500,000 drachmas. 19 flockbed] a mattress of tufts of wool or cotton. 22 fardle] bundle. 33 in fine] in the end.

732 2 tower of Phar] the lighthouse at Pharos. 18 Ponte] Pontus.
733 41 falling evil] epilepsy.
735 40 Strabo] Greek geographer (64 B.C.–19 A.D.).
736 23 Titus Livius] Livy, the Roman historian (59 B.C.–17 A.D.).
739 42 forms] benches.
740 25–6 not passing] not more than. 36 journey of Philippes] the day of (the battle at) Philippi.

JOHN LYLY

JOHN LYLY (*c.* 1554–1606), poet, dramatist, producer of court comedies, and author of one of the most popular of Elizabethan novels, was born in Kent, the son of the Registrar of Canterbury and grandson of William Lyly, the humanist friend of Colet and Erasmus who at their suggestion had written the standard Latin grammar used in the schools of sixteenth-century England. Educated at Magdalen College, Oxford, he received his B.A. there in 1573 and his M.A. in 1575; but, disappointed in his hopes of being elected a fellow in spite of a plea to Lord Burghley for intercession in his behalf, he left Oxford for a career in London in the service of Burghley, and more particularly the service of his son-in-law, the Earl of Oxford. Just before Christmas in 1578, his novel *Euphues: the Anatomy of Wit* appeared on the London bookstalls and instantly became a 'best seller.' A second edition incorporating a few additions and minor revisions was issued the following spring, and a third edition before the end of 1579. A sequel, *Euphues and his England* was published in 1580. From 1580 to 1590 new editions of both the first book and its sequel were called for every two years. During the next decade the full tide of the popularity of *Euphues* began to recede, but both books remained in print for the first four decades of the seventeenth century.

With the hope of appointment to the mastership of the revels, Lyly produced, as assistant master of the children's companies at the Chapel Royal and at St. Paul's, a series of classical plays for the child-actors, many of them allegorical and topical dramas paying graceful tribute to the queen or symbolizing, for those keen enough to perceive the allusions, recent events within the circle of those at the court. Upon his failure to receive the preferment at court he anticipated, Lyly wrote to Queen Elizabeth and asked her, if she thought him unworthy, to send him into a country where 'I may . . . write prayers instead of plays, prayers for your long, prosperous life, and a repentance that I have played the fool so long.'

When the extreme Puritans began to attack the bishops in a series of tracts signed with the pseudonym 'Martin Marprelate,' Lyly, with other literary men such as Greene and Nashe, was engaged to answer them. Lyly's contribution was the pamphlet *Pappe with an Hatchet* (1589). Between 1589 and his death in 1606, Lyly sat in four Parliaments. Although he remained hopeful to the end of receiving the office of Master of the Revels, he suffered the common disappointment of courtiers of waiting for a royal gift that never came.

Although Lyly's importance as a dramatist among Shakespeare's immediate predecessors is exceeded only by that of Marlowe and Kyd, Lyly's fame is more closely linked with the novel he published at the beginning of his career and which, in sophisticated circles at court, became the rage for several years, until the fad subsided and other writers, including Shakespeare, began increasingly to ridicule the manifest artificiality of its style. It is in some ways unfortunate that *Euphues* has become so closely associated with the style to which it lent its name that Lyly's book is read chiefly as an example of ostentatiously artificial prose, and little attention is paid to its merits as a work of fiction. Considering first the style, one must remember that although today the term 'euphuistic' is applied to any style that is over-ornate and employs the devices of rhetoric without due propriety, the style of *Euphues* is distinguished from that of any consciously rhetorical prose by Lyly's excessive use, to the point of 'abuse,' of certain specific figures described in the handbooks of rhetoric. These same figures are to be found in the prose of many other writers from ancient Greek times to the Renaissance, but generally used with more restraint and without the monotonous insistence that is the trade-mark of true Euphuism. The figures that establish the structure of Euphuistic prose are those that aim at symmetry and parallelism in sound and form—valuable and employed with discretion by all good writers when this parallelism emphasizes a similar parallelism of thought, but becoming an affected mannerism when the parallelism in form and sound is elaborated as a stylistic end in itself, regardless of the sense. Traditionally the Euphuistic *schemata* have in the histories of rhetoric been grouped under the term of 'figures of Gorgias,' after the ancient Greek teacher of rhetoric who made them the chief feature of his balanced and rhythmic prose. Lyly, in *Euphues*, surpassed Gorgias and his follower Isocrates in his insistent use of them. Beginning with the first, *isocolon*—having corresponding members (phrases, clauses, sentences) of equal length—, Lyly proceeds to emphasize this exact balance by making these members syntactically parallel, with each word in one member answering to a corresponding word in the other—the figure known as *parison*. Not content with this, he ostentatiously enforces this syntactical parallelism by employing various forms of the figure *paramoion*; such as making the corresponding words in the two members begin with the same sound, or letter (alliteration) or end with the same sound (*homoioteleuton*). Other types of word play based upon correspondences of sound are frequently added, but by themselves they would not be characteristic of Euphuism, since they are frequently found without the consistently symmetrical structure that is the prime mark of Lyly's style.

Besides its structural pattern, the other distinguishing characteristic of the style is its preference, among figures of amplification, for the heaping up of a series of examples or comparisons drawn not only from mythology and history but even more frequently from the pseudo-scientific lore of natural history.

Inasmuch as nearly all of the rhetorical devices of Euphuism can be found, employed with greater moderation and propriety, in the prose of classical writers such as Isocrates and Cicero, of contemporary foreign authors such as Guevara, and even of English writers such as Ascham, it is not surprising that critics have assigned many different sources for Lyly's style. Few of the 'precursors' of Euphuism have matched Lyly's excesses in his use of his favorite figures. Those who approach it most closely seem to have derived their excessive passion for sound patterns of schematic prose from the study of medieval Latin writers; and Lyly and others, such as Pettie, Gosson, and Lodge, who between 1576 and 1580 published works marked by a 'Euphuistic' style, may all have been influenced by the admiration for symmetrically patterned prose displayed in the popular Latin lectures on rhetoric by John Rainoldes, who was teaching at Oxford while they were students.

The example of Lyly's style, in spite of its excesses, taught English writers many lessons that proved valuable in the development of English prose. But *Euphues* had more attractions for Elizabethan readers than the artificial brilliance of its style. By means of a story, it welds together witty discussions of many subjects of paramount interest to the young men and women of that age, and, in some measure, of any age: the conflict between the egotistical recklessness of youth and the sober prudence of old age; the rival claims of friendship and love; the fickleness of women; faith versus doubt in religion; the shortcomings of a university education compared with experience in the world. As a work of prose fiction in which the chief interest lies in the psychological analysis of human emotions rather than in the mere relation of physical action and adventure, it marks the climax of a tradition in Elizabethan prose fiction.

Our text follows the second edition published in the spring of 1579, because Lyly himself revised his work with care for this new edition.

MODERN EDITIONS: *Euphues, The Anatomy of Wit* and *Euphues and His England* (ed. by Edward Arber), English Reprints, London, 1868; **Euphues, The Anatomy of Wit; and Euphues and His England* (ed. by M. W. Croll and H. Clemons), New York, 1916; **The Complete Works of John Lyly* (ed. by R. Warwick Bond), 3 vols., Oxford, 1902.

COMMENT: A. Feuillerat, *John Lyly,* Cambridge, 1910; Morris P. Tilley, *Elizabethan Proverb Lore in Lyly's 'Euphues' and in Pettie's 'Petite Palace,'* University of Michigan Publications, Language and Literature, Vol. ii, New York, 1926; Violet M. Jeffery, *John Lyly and the Italian Renaissance,* Paris, 1928; B. M. Ward, 'John Lyly and the Office of the Revels,' *RES,* v (1929), 57–8; Morris P. Tilley, 'Euphues and Ovid's *Heroical Epistles,*' *MLN,* xlv (1930), 301–8; William Ringler, 'The Immediate Source of Euphuism,' *PMLA,* liii (1938), 678–86; George B. Parks, 'Before Euphues,' in *Joseph Quincey Adams Memorial Studies,* Washington, D.C., 1948, pp. 475–93.

TEXT: *Euphues. The Anatomy of Wit,* [1579] (17052), Trinity College, Cambridge.

742 2 Christmas] the 2nd ed. reads 'Midsummer'; we have emended to restore the reading of the 1st ed., issued at Christmas-time, 1578. 3 Easter] 2nd ed.: 'Christmas.'

743 6 brack] flaw. 18 teenest] keenest.

745 5 cockering] pampering. 10 Milo] legendary Greek athlete, able to carry a bull because he had carried it every day as it grew up from a calf. 20 knots] gardens of intricate design.

746 41 iron mole] iron mold.

747 14 sottish] foolish.

748 22 abeston] asbestos; this bit of erroneous scientific lore Lyly did not derive from Pliny, but from Bartholomaeus Anglicus *De proprietatibus rerum,* xvi.12. 30 Cicero] see *De Finibus,* iii–v. 31 Aristotle] see *De Caelo,* ii.11; much of Lyly's parade of learning comes from his use of published commonplace books.

750 14 quatted] surfeited.

751 14 geason] rare. 19–20 *Quae . . . nos*] 'those things that are above us are nothing to us.' 20 *Sententias . . . carnifex*] 'Even a murderer utters moral maxims.' 29 cammock] the shepherd's crook. 31 camomile] cf. Falstaff's parody of Euphuism in *2 Henry IV,* ii.4.441.

752 41 fere] companion.

753 24 sithens] since. 32–33 Damon . . . Laelius] all are famous pairs of friends in mythology and history.

755 6 good countenance] favorable reception. 15 vizard] mask.

756 3 lust] pleasure, wish. 21–22 foul toad . . . head] this superstition is

found in many of the encyclopaedic works of the Middle Ages and Renaissance. 31 estridge] ostrich.

759 5 filed] smooth, polished.

762 32 caul] cap, net. 33 Gyges] see the 6th tale of vol. i of Painter's *Palace of Pleasure.*

763 4 secret . . . secrete] the different spelling may be due to Lyly's desire to emphasize a pun on different meanings of the word.

765 30 Ovid's art] the Roman poet Ovid (43 B.C.–18 A.D.), author of the *Art of Love,* an ironic poem on the art of seduction. 31 Tibullus] (60–19 B.C.), Roman poet whose principal theme was love; his principal collections of poems were known by the names of *Delia* and *Nemesis.* 31 Propertius] Roman lyric poet (*c.* 50–16 B.C.), author of passionate love poems. 40 glose] explanation; cf. 'gloss.'

766 16 flap in the mouth] tell a barefaced lie. 22 gudgeon] a fish; colloquially, a gullible person, one who will swallow anything.

769 4 sounded] swooned. 37 cylindrus] this bit of pseudo-scientific lore seems to be an entirely fictitious creation of Lyly; a cylindrical stone will of course roll down hill if once set in motion. 39 Polypus] a fish; its attributes are mentioned in Pliny, *Natural History,* ix.46; Lyly's source of information was probably a commonplace-book collection of examples and similitudes compiled from Erasmus' *Adagia.*

772 8–11 Phyllis . . . Jason] these four examples of infidelity are found mentioned together in George Pettie's

Pallace of Pleasure (1576). 21 stone
Continens] apparently another addition
by Lyly to the lore of pseudo-scientific
natural history.

773 28 owches] brooches. 28 leere]
tape. 29 caddis] cotton wool.

777 5 Portingale] Portuguese.

780 7 Synon] Greek warrior who persuaded the Trojans to take the Trojan
horse within their walls; see *Aeneid*,
ii.79.

782 26-27 Ajax . . . armor] see
Ovid, *Metamorphoses*, xiii.1 ff. 31 put-
tock] kite. 41 descant] a melody or
counterpoint, sung above the plain song
of the tenor.

784 25 frump] taunting speech. 37
housewife] 'hussy.'

785 37 make] mate.

786 24 Cornelia] the story is not from
classical mythology but probably from
an Italian *novella*.

787 28-30 *Axiomaes . . . Galen*] i.e.
Euphues will devote himself to the study
of philosophy, law, and medicine.

789 34 cockney] spoiled child.

791 12] The remainder of Lyly's
Euphues: The Anatomy of Wit consists
of the following: (1) the letter entitled
'A Cooling Card for Philautus and all
fond lovers,' adapted from Ovid's *Remedia amoris* and similar treatises; (2)
a short treatise on the education of youth
entitled 'Euphues and his Ephoebus,'
adapted from Plutarch's *De Educatione
puerorum;* (3) a treatise entitled 'Euphues and Atheos,' setting forth the
arguments of the Christian religion in
reply to the criticisms of the atheist;
(4) certain letters of Euphues to Philautus and others which recount the evil
end of the fickle jilt Lucilla. The volume
concludes with the promise of a sequel
which shall tell of Euphues' visit to
England. 15 To . . . the gentlemen
scholars of Oxford] this Address first
appeared as a special preface to the
second edition; it appeared at the end of
the third and later editions.

STEPHEN GOSSON

STEPHEN GOSSON (1554–1624), the son of a Canterbury joiner, studied at
Corpus Christi College, Oxford; but left about 1576 without completing the
exercises for a degree and went to London where he began writing plays and
possibly also acted on the professional stage. About that time the *Theater*, the
first building in England to be constructed solely for the showing of plays,
was erected outside the city walls. The financial profits to be gained from the
larger audiences thus made possible brought about an increase in dramatic activity, which disturbed the more serious London citizens, for many rowdy members of the populace flocked to the playing places and were frequently the cause
of serious disorder. In 1577 John Northbrooke wrote *A Treatise wherein
Dicing, Dancing, Vain Plays or Interludes with Other Idle Pastimes . . . Are
Reproved*, and ministers began to attack the stage in their sermons. Two years
later Gosson, who by his own admission had not thrived as a playwright, turned
against his companions on the boards and published *The School of Abuse, Containing a Pleasant Invective against Poets, Pipers, Players, Jesters, and Such
Like Caterpillers of a Commonwealth*. He would have us believe that his
defection was brought about by a sudden moral reformation; but there is other
evidence which suggests that he was hired to write by some group of London
citizens. Answers by persons friendly to the players and attacks by other opponents of the stage followed. The controversy thus begun made the Elizabethans examine more closely their ideas about the nature and aims of poetry
and the drama and resulted in the production of the first important body of
English literary criticism. Occasional references to the principles of their art
are found in the works of earlier poets, and scattered observations on literature
occur in books like Elyot's *Governour* and Ascham's *Scholemaster*; but it was
not until Gosson's time that any systematic and comprehensive attempts were
made to evaluate contemporary literature and to analyze its principles. Among
the answers to his attack are *A Reply to Gosson*, about 1579, by Thomas Lodge,

and *The Defence of Poesy*, written about 1580–82, but not published until 1595, by Sir Philip Sidney, to whom the *School of Abuse* had been dedicated. The attack on the stage was carried on by men like Anthony Munday in his *Second and Third Blast of Retreat from Plays and Theaters*, 1580, John Rainolds in his *Overthrow of Stage-Plays*, 1599, and William Prynne in his *Histriomastix*, 1633. Public opinion was finally so aroused that the theaters were closed by act of Parliament in 1642, and were not opened again until the Restoration.

In 1579 Gosson also published the *Ephemerides of Phialo*, a work of prose fiction similar in style and form to Lyly's *Euphues*, and the *Apology of the School of Abuse*, a reaffirmation of the arguments in his first book. In 1582 he issued *Plays Confuted in Five Actions*, an answer to Lodge's *Reply*, which contains interesting information about the contemporary drama. His own plays are not extant. He was beneficed in 1586 and spent the rest of his life as a minister in various country parishes and in London. Gosson's prose has many of the characteristics of Euphuism, a manner he had learned from the Latin lectures of John Rainolds at Oxford; but his style is also notable for racy, colloquial vigor and vivid, picturesque phrasing, which relates it to the homely but forceful style of Latimer, who wrote earlier in the century, and to that of the Marprelate controversialists, who wrote later. As a master of what his contemporaries called 'witty' invective, Gosson occupies a position only a little below Nashe, the greatest of the Elizabethan prose satirists.

MODERN EDITIONS: *The School of Abuse* (ed. by J. P. Collier), The Shakespeare Society, London, 1841; *The School of Abuse and A Short Apologie of the Schoole of Abuse* (ed. by Edward Arber), English Reprints, London, 1868 and 1869, Westminster, 1895.

COMMENT: William Ringler, *Stephen Gosson: A Biographical and Critical Study*, Princeton, 1941.

TEXT: *The Schoole of Abuse*, 1579 (12097), Huntington.

792 39 Pindarus] Pindar, Greek lyric poet; the anecdote is told by Plutarch, *Morals*, 348.

793 8 cowshard] cow dung. 9 botch] sore. 14–15 gnat . . . flea] mock-serious poems, *Culex* and *De Pulice*, attributed to Virgil and Ovid; cf. Spenser's *Virgil's Gnat*. 15 Dido] a reference to her love for Aeneas, *Aeneid*, Book iv. 16 Myrrha] had a child, Adonis, by her father Cinyras; Ovid, *Metamorphoses*, x.298 ff. 16 craft of love] Ovid's poem, *Ars Amatoria*, on the art of seduction. 24 jets] struts. 25 Davus] a scheming servant in Terence's *Andria*. 28 Epaeus] builder of the Trojan horse; *Aeneid*, ii.264. 29 Semiramis] queen of Babylon; see Plutarch, *Morals*, 173. 31 Nero] the story is from Dio Cassius, *Roman History*. 37 Hippomenes] see Ovid, *Metamorphoses*, x.560 ff. 40 Plato] recommended the expulsion of poets in his *Republic*, iii.

794 2 Cato] the anecdote is told by Cicero, *Tusculan Disputations*, i.3. 4 Tully] Cicero; the statement is reported by Seneca, *Epistles*, xlix. 5. 7 Maximus Tyrius] Greek Neo-Platonist of the second century A.D.; the reference is to his *Disputations*, chap. xvi. 24 Vulcan] Hephaestus, hurled from heaven by Zeus, *Iliad*, i.590–4; cf. Milton, *Paradise Lost*, i.740. 27 awater] in the water; i.e., no crafts would have been invented. 30 Pythagoras] Greek philosopher of 6th cent. B.C. who discovered the mathematical relationship between the length of strings and the musical notes they emitted when vibrating; cf. Plutarch's essay on music in the *Morals*. 36–37 Heu . . . arvo] 'Alas, how lean is my bull in the rich pasture'; Virgil, *Eclogues*, iii.100. 42 Phaerecrates] Greek comic dramatist; the episode referred to from his play is quoted by Plutarch in his essay on music.

795 8 Sicilians] the information comes from Maximus Tyrius, *Dissertations*, chap. iv. 21 Quantum . . . illo] 'How changed from what he once was'; *Aeneid*, ii.274. 27 Experto crede] 'Believe one who knows by experience'; *Aeneid*, xi.283. 29 Ovid] see *Ars Amatoria*, i.89 ff. 32 in ure] in use. 41 foot-saunt] a game of cards.

796 4 slot] the trail. 11 quetch] stir.

18 peascod] pea-pod; cf. codpiece. 20 vauter] courtesan. 21 tolleth resort] attracts customers. 21 stale] decoy. 21 utter] sell. 26 cast] trick. 30 boards] boarders. 38 avoid the blank] get rid of the charge; get away from the dangerous spot in the center of the target. **797** 3 Venus' nuns] prostitutes. 3 Newington . . . Hogsdon] suburbs of London. 14 lords of . . . misrule] leaders of revels. 17 Malkin] a wanton woman; the expression is proverbial. 26 raseth] cuts. 38 *remora*] Spenser, *Visions of the World's Vanity,* ix, has the same notion concerning this fish. 39 ichneumon] the mongoose. **798** 12 Bunduica] Boadicea (died A.D. 62), a British queen who resisted the invasions of the Romans; her speech is taken from Dio Cassius, *Roman History.* 20 queen] Elizabeth. 31 stork] Zeus sent cranes (storks) to war on the pigmies—*Iliad,* iii.3–6; cf. Milton, *Paradise Lost,* i.575. 32 limits of apparel] several sumptuary laws, specifying the kind of clothing to be worn by people of various trades and social classes, were passed during Elizabeth's reign. Elaborate display in dress was common, and was thought by some to be an extrava-gance dangerous to national morals. 34 access to theaters] in time of the plague, which raged intermittently during the sixteenth century, to prevent contagion, orders were issued by the government forbidding public assemblies; at these times the theaters were usually closed by edict. 35 overlashing] extravagance. 36 stand at reversion] receive as salary. **799** 2 hang-bys] hangers-on. 6 Belsavage] a London inn at which plays were given. 8 The Jew] a play, now lost, apparently similar in plot to the *Merchant of Venice.* 8 Pompey] a play. 8 Bull] another London inn used as a playhouse. 14 The Blacksmith's Daughter and Catiline's Conspiracies] these plays are not extant. 15 Theater] the playhouse in the fields, built in 1576. 22 Maximus Tyrius] the quotation, translated and expanded by Gosson's following sentence, is from the *Disputationes,* chap. vii. 31 *Semel . . . omnes*] 'We have all done a mad thing once'; Mantuan, *Eclogues,* i.118. **800** 25 No man . . . himself] see Cicero, *De officiis,* i.7; the statement was often cited by Renaissance writers. **801** 2 Nessus] centaur slain by Hercules; Ovid, *Metamorphoses,* ix.101 ff.

SIR PHILIP SIDNEY

Sir Philip Sidney (1554–1586) in the scant thirty-two years of his life wrote himself high as poet, scholar, courtier, diplomat, and soldier, and highest as gentleman. He was born at Penshurst, his father's fine country place in Kent, and at the age of nine went to Shrewsbury School where on the first day of his attendance he met Fulke Greville, who became his lifelong friend and companion. From his thirteenth to his seventeenth year Sidney was in residence at Christ Church, Oxford, and briefly at Cambridge, but he took no degree. In 1572 he went to France in the train of an English ambassador. His first-hand experience of the religious dissensions which racked France at this time, culminating in the Massacre of St. Bartholomew, seems to have influenced Sidney in his later championship of the Protestant cause in Europe. On his first trip abroad he traveled in Germany, Hungary, Italy, and the Netherlands, returning to England in time to be present at the famous reception of Queen Elizabeth by the Earl of Leicester (Sidney's maternal uncle) at Kenilworth Castle, July 9–27, 1575. Sidney followed the Queen and court to Chartley Castle, the home of Lord Essex; and it is here that he is supposed to have made the acquaintance of Essex's daughter, Penelope Devereux, the Stella of *Astrophel and Stella,* then aged thirteen. The later engagement of the two young people was broken off for reasons which now are obscure, and Penelope became the wife of Lord Rich.

In 1577 Sidney went abroad a second time, as Ambassador to the Emperor of Germany and the Elector Palatine. In the following year he wrote a mask, *The Lady of May,* to be used as part of the entertainment of the Queen and court at the Earl of Leicester's castle at Wanstead. At about this time Sidney's interest in literature seems to have been heightened by his companionship with Fulke Greville, Edward Dyer, and other congenial young men; the group, referred to by Spenser and Gabriel Harvey as the Areopagus (though not organized as a club), interested itself in the possibility of reproducing in English the quantitative meters of Greek and Latin verse. In August, 1579, a Puritanical writer named Stephen Gosson published *The School of Abuse*, attacking plays and poetry but dedicated to Sidney; Sidney's *Defence of Poesy*, though perhaps not written until 1583, replies, though not by name, to Gosson's attack. In 1580 Sidney wrote an open letter to Queen Elizabeth, dissuading her from her projected marriage with the Duke of Anjou; and for his boldness he was practically banished from court. During his retirement, spent at Wilton House, the home of his sister who had become by marriage Countess of Pembroke, he wrote at least part (probably the whole of the original version) of his long pastoral romance, *Arcadia*. He was knighted in 1583 and in the same year married Frances Walsingham, daughter of Sir Francis Walsingham. In 1585 he was projecting an expedition to America with Sir Francis Drake, but the Protestant cause, endangered by Spain's war with the Netherlands, and the Queen's need of his services, sent him instead to Holland as Governor of Flushing. In September of the following year Sidney was wounded in an unimportant engagement before the city of Zutphen. After twenty-six days of suffering, during which time he composed a song about his wound, entitled *La cuisse rompue*, and caused it to be sung to him, he died, to the grief of all England and a great part of Europe.

None of Sidney's literary productions was printed during his lifetime. The sixth song from *Astrophel and Stella* appeared, with musical setting, in Byrd's *Psalms, Sonnets, and Songs* of 1588; and three stanzas of the tenth song were printed with music in Byrd's *Songs of Sundry Natures*, 1589. *The Countess of Pembroke's Arcadia* was published in 1590, in an incomplete form representing the revision and expansion Sidney had begun of his first draft, and again (the story having been completed by his sister, who used the text of the first draft to piece out Sidney's incomplete revised version) in 1593. *Astrophel and Stella* was published in 1591 by the printer Thomas Newman, without the consent of Sidney's family, from one of the several manuscripts then in circulation. Not until 1598 did the fully authorized edition appear; at that time all of Sidney's principal works were collected and printed in a folio volume prepared for the printer under the supervision of Mary Sidney, the Countess of Pembroke. The *Defence of Poesy* first appeared in two separate editions in 1595; the one, with the title *An Apologie for Poetrie*, published by Henry Olney; the other, with the title *The Defence of Poesie*, published by William Ponsonby with the authorization of the Sidney family from what is on the whole a better manuscript. Our text follows the Ponsonby edition (P), with a few emendations from the Olney edition (O).

MODERN EDITIONS: *Complete Works* (ed. by A. Feuillerat), Cambridge Classics, 4 vols., Cambridge, 1912–26; *The Countess of Pembroke's Arcadia* (ed. by E. A. Baker), London, 1907; *The Defence of Poesy* (ed. by A. S. Cook), Boston, 1890; *An Apologie for Poetrie* (ed. by E. S. Shuckburgh), Cambridge, 1891; *An Apologie for Poetrie* (ed. by J. C. Collins), Oxford, 1907.

COMMENT: M. W. Wallace, *Life of Sir Philip Sidney*, Cambridge, 1915; E. A. Greenlaw, 'Sidney's *Arcadia* as an Example of Elizabethan Allegory,' in *Kittredge Anniversary Papers*, Boston, 1913; E. A. Greenlaw, 'The Captivity Episode in Sidney's *Arcadia*,' in *Manly Anniversary Papers*, Chicago, 1923; S. Harkness, 'The

Prose Style of Sir Philip Sidney,' *Univ. Wisconsin Stud.*, ii (1918), 57–76; R. W. Zandvoort, *Sidney's Arcadia: A Comparison between the Two Versions*, Amsterdam, 1929; Mona Wilson, *Sir Philip Sidney*, London, 1931; W. D. Briggs, 'Political Ideas in Sidney's *Arcadia*,' *SP*, xxviii (1931), 137–61, and 'Sidney's Political Ideas,' *SP*, xxix (1932), 534–42; M. S. Goldman, *Sir Philip Sidney and the Arcadia*, Urbana, Illinois, 1934; K. O. Myrick, *Sir Philip Sidney as a Literary Craftsman*, Harvard, 1935; K. T. Rowe, 'The Countess of Pembroke's Editorship of the *Arcadia*,' *PMLA*, liv (1939), 122–38; K. T. Rowe, 'Elizabethan Morality and the Folio Revisions of Sidney's *Arcadia*,' *MP*, xxxvii (1939), 151–72; K. T. Rowe, *Romantic Love and Parental Authority in Sidney's Arcadia*, Univ. Mich. Cont., Ann Arbor, 1947; A. P. Duhamel, 'Sidney's *Arcadia* and Elizabethan Rhetoric,' *SP*, xlv (1948), 134–50; M. Poirier, *Sir Philip Sidney: Le Chevalier Poète Élizabéthain*, Lille, 1949.

TEXT: *Arcadia*, 1590 (22539), Huntington; *Defence of Poesie*, 1595 (22535), Harvard.

801 32 *pedanteria*] Italian for pedantic school learning.

803 11 Gyges's Ring] Gyges had a ring which could make him invisible; see Plato, *Republic*, ii.359. 29 *areytos*] O.; P. reads *arentos: aréitos*, a West Indies term for dance songs.

804 10–11 Albinus] Roman commander in Britain (192–197 A.D.). 13 *Arma . . . armis*] *Aeneid*, ii.314; 'Madly I take up arms, though arms are senseless now.' 31 *prosopopoeias*] figures of speech by which an imaginary or absent person is represented as speaking or acting; more loosely, 'personifications.'

805 37 Theagenes] hero of the Greek prose romance by Heliodorus, the *Aethiopica; An Aethiopian History* was translated by Thomas Underdowne in 1587. 38 Pylades] faithful friend of Orestes. 38 Orlando] Roland of the Charlemagne legend; hero of Ariosto's *Orlando Furioso*. 39 Cyrus] in the *Cyropaedia* of Xenophon.

806 25 Aristotle] in the *Poetics*, 1.2. 31 Salomon] Solomon; this was the usual spelling. 33–34 Tremellius . . . Junius] two Protestant scholars of the 16th century who had recently published a Latin translation of the Bible.

807 1 Cato] the *Disticha de moribus* or *Moral Distichs* attributed to Dionysius Cato was a popular elementary textbook for the study of Latin in the Middle Ages and Renaissance. 38 Heliodorus] see note to p. 271, line 37.

808 10 anatomies] analyses.

809 19 of] supplied from O. 25–26 *Testis . . . vetustatis*] Cicero, *de Oratore*, ii.9.36.; 'the witness of the times, the light of truth, the life of memory, the guide to human existence, the messenger of antiquity.' The quotation was frequently cited in the Renaissance; it appears, slightly altered, on the engraved title-page of Ralegh's *History of the World*.

810 8 *formidine poenae*] fear of punishment. 9 *virtutis amore*] love of virtue.

811 18 Nisus and Euryalus] Nisus died avenging his friend Euryalus; *Aeneid*, ix. 38–39 *Mediocribus . . . columnae*] 'neither gods, nor men, nor book-stalls have admitted mediocrity in poets.'

812 20 Aristotle] in *Poetics*, 9.3. 23 studiously serious] from O.; omitted in P. 37 Dares Phrygius] Medieval and Renaissance scholars believed Dares was an eyewitness of the fall of Troy and accepted the purported Latin translation of his work as a true account, more accurate than Homer's; the fifth-century *de excidio Troiae historia* has, however, been proved a forgery.

813 5 Quintus Curtius] late Roman author of a history of Alexander the Great. 27 Livy] in i.53–54. 28 Abradates] actually Araspes in *Cyropaedia* vi.1.31 ff.

814 12 Miltiades] this and the following examples Sidney draws from Greek and Roman history. 15 Sylla] Sulla (138–78 B.C.) and Marius (157–86 B.C.), Roman generals who by their rivalry began the period of the domination of Rome by successful military leaders; Pompey succeeded to the leadership of the faction of Sulla, and Julius Caesar to that of Marius. 20 *literas nescivit*] he was ignorant of letters. 23 *occidendos esse*] that they are to be put to death. 36 φιλοφιλόσοφος] fond of philosophers. 42 Aristotle] in *Ethics*, i.1; 'the ultimate object is not knowledge but practise.'

815 16 *hoc . . . est*] 'this is a task, this is labor'; *Aeneid*, vi.129. 23 margent] margin. 31 aloes] aloin; a bitter drug used as a purgative.

816 7–8 *fugientem . . . est?*] 'Shall this ground see [Turnus] fleeing? Is it so hard to die?' *Aeneid*, xii.645–46. 13 Boethius] (d. 524); author of *The Consolation of Philosophy*, an extremely popular work throughout the Middle Ages; in it Boethius alternates passages in verse with prose passages. 16 *indulgere genio*] indulge one's own inclinations. 24 Menenius Agrippa] see Shakespeare's *Coriolanus* and Plutarch's life of Coriolanus. 40 Nathan] see *2 Samuel*, 12.1–7.

817 6 Psalm of Mercy] *Psalms*, 25. 23 Sannazzaro] Italian poet (1458–1530), author of the pastoral romance *Arcadia*, which suggested the title for Sidney's own pastoral romance. 31–2 Melibaeus, Tityrus] traditional names for shepherds in pastoral poems. 40–41 *Haec . . . nobis*] Virgil, *Eclogues*, vii. 69–70; 'These things I remember, how the vanquished Thyrsis struggled in vain. From that day on it has been Corydon, only Corydon with us.'

818 11 *Omne . . . amico*] 'manages to probe every fault while making his friend laugh'; from Persius, *Satires*, i.116. 15 *circum praecordia ludit*] 'he plays about the innermost feelings.' 18 *Est . . . aequus*] (What you seek) 'is at Ulubrae, if a calm mind does not fail you there'; Horace, *Epistles*, i.11.30 30–31 Demea . . . Thraso] stock characters in the comedies of Terence; i.e. the grave father, clever servant, parasite, and braggart. 37 *pistrinum*] the pounding mill, where slaves were punished.

819 7–8 *Qui . . . redit*] Seneca, *Oedipus*, 705–6: 'Who harshly wields the scepter with tyrannic sway, fears those who fear; terror recoils upon its author's head.' 10 Plutarch] see his *Life of Pelopidas*. 25 old song of Percy and Douglas] the old Scottish ballad of *Chevy Chase*, or *The Hunting of the Cheviot*, as it is entitled in the ancient versions; F. J. Child's No. 162. 26 crowder] fiddler. 29 Hungary] Sidney visited Hungary with Languet in 1572–73.

820 7 Tydeus] in the *Iliad*. 7 Rinaldo] in Tasso's *Gerusalemme liberata*. 29–30 *Melius . . . Crantore*] 'Better than Chrysippus and Crantor.' Horace, *Epistles*, i.2.4.

821 31 Ovid's verse] adapted by Sidney from *Ars amatoria*, ii.662. 33 Agrippa] Henry Cornelius Agrippa (1486–1535), German humanist, author of *The Vanity and Uncertainty of Artes and Sciences*. The Latin text was published in 1531; editions of the English translation by James Sanford appeared in 1569 and 1575. 34 Erasmus] author of *Moriae encomium* (*The Praise of Folly*), written in England (1509–11) and dedicated to Sir Thomas More.

822 5 Scaliger] Julius Caesar Scaliger (1484–1558), Italian literary critic; Sidney is indebted to his *Poetice*. 31 *Percontatorem . . . est*] 'Fly from the

inquisitive man, for he is likewise a tattler.' 32 *Dum . . . sumus*] 'While each one is satisfying himself, we are ever a credulous set.' Ovid, *Remedia Amoris*, 686.

823 15 *petere principium*] to beg the question.

824 16–17 John of the Stile, and John of the Noakes] fictitious names in a legal action; cf. 'John Doe and Richard Roe.'

825 2 that] supplied from O.

826 4 *Jubeo . . . libenter*] 'I bid him be fool to his heart's content.' 8 quiddity of *ens* and *prima materia*] terms of metaphysical philosophy: the nature of being and of the original material of the universe.

827 31 Saint Paul] in *Colossians*, 2.8.

828 6–7 *Qua . . . exigendos*] 'which authority certain barbarous and rude persons would wrest into meaning that poets were to be expelled from the state.' Scaliger, *Poetice* i.2.

829 11 *Musa . . . laeso?*] 'O Muse, call to my mind the causes of these things: what divinity was injured?' *Aeneid*, i.8. 21 that Hospital of France] Michel de l'Hospital (1504–1573), one time Chancellor of France, whose policy was aimed at toleration of the Huguenots.

830 4 *Queis . . . Titan*] 'whose hearts Titan had formed of better clay.' 23 *Orator . . . nascitur*] 'The orator is made, the poet is born.' 33 *quodlibet*] anything you please. 35 *Quicquid . . . erit*] 'Whatever I shall try to write will be poetry.'

832 14 Pacolet's horse] a magic horse in the romance *Valentine and Orson*. 15 *Nuntius*] messenger. 36 Apuleius] the author (2nd cent.) of the satirical romance *The Golden Ass*.

833 24 Omphale] see Ovid, *Heroides*, ix.75. 37–38 *Nil . . . facit*] 'Unhappy poverty has nothing in it harder than this: that it makes men ridiculous.'

834 29 coursing of a letter] use of excessive alliteration; Sidney probably has Lyly, Gosson, and other Euphuists specifically in mind. 31 figures and flowers] 'figures of speech and flowers of rhetoric' (ornate amplifications and descriptions). 37–38 Nizolian paper books] Marius Nizzoli (1498?–1576), Italian rhetorician and dogmatic Ciceronian, compiler of a thesaurus of Ciceronian phrases, advocated the keeping by schoolboys of notebooks in which they entered the choicest words, locutions, and metaphors they came across in their reading of Cicero. Cf. Ascham's similar method set forth on pages 620–21.

835 3 *Vivit . . . venit*] 'He lives and survives, nay more, comes into the Senate, nay more, comes into the Senate.' 9 *similiter cadenses*] like endings of words. The Latin name for the figure of speech or 'scheme' known as homoioteleuton. 16 similitudes] a reference to the heaping up of comparisons drawn from pseudo-scientific lore, which was a vice of the Euphuistic style.

837 26 *quid non*] what not. 28 Landin] Cristofero Landino (1424?–1504), Italian scholar, tutor to Lorenzo de Medici. 35 *Libertino patre natus*] born of a freed-man. 35 *Herculea proles*] a descendant of Hercules. 36 *Si . . . possunt*] if my songs are of any avail. 42 mome] stupid person.

839 2 overseer of the print] the editor and proofreader at the press. The analyses at the head of each chapter and the divisions are present only in the 1590 edition. 15 second shipwreck] for the account of the first see Book ii.7 (page 322). 20 indifferent] impartial. 24 pastor] shepherd. 33 ensign] standard bearer; used humorously.

840 30 racking] rent-racking; extortionate.

841 19–20 running at base] playing a children's game similar to modern 'prisoner's base.'

843 41 come upon the stays] having headed the ship to windward for purposes of tacking.

845 6 news] Sidney regards this word as plural; hence the plural verbs.

847 20 curiosity] careful and over-elaborate workmanship. 21 slubbered up] soiled; cf. 'slobber.'

852 12 privilege of a bauble] of being a court-jester or fool. 32 Iris] the goddess of the rainbow. 33 Cupid] Cupid, the god of love, was blind. 33 god Vulcan's pace] Vulcan was lame. 34 Momus] the personification of fault-finding.

853 36 Chap. VII] As this chapter opens Musidorus, in disguise under the assumed name of Dorus, having obtained employment with Pamela's custodian, Dametus, is in the midst of relating to Pamela the earlier life and adventures of Musidorus and Pyrocles. His narrative gives us the chronological beginning of the tale of Pyrocles and Musidorus. In Book i, chap. 1, Sidney, in the epic tradition, began in the middle of the story.

863 3 bruit] noise, clamor.

864 14 Pamela's prayer] at this point in the story Pamela is held in prison by Cecropia; her prayer acquired particular celebrity by appearing in the treatise *Eikon Basilike,* attributed to King Charles I and published shortly after his execution in 1649. Milton in his *Eikonoklastes* (1649), published as a reply to this treatise, makes much of the fact that the prayer therein purporting to have been composed by King Charles was really taken from the *Arcadia.*

THOMAS LODGE

Thomas Lodge (*c.* 1558–1625), son of a knight of the same name who was a prominent member of the Grocers' Company and for a time Lord Mayor of London, received an excellent literary training at the Merchant Taylors' School, London, and at Trinity College, Oxford. He was admitted B.A. in 1577, and the next year became a law student at Lincoln's Inn. Like many other law students, however, he yielded to the attractions of the growing literary and theatrical circle of the metropolis; he entered upon authorship by answering Stephen Gosson's *School of Abuse,* 1579, with a *Defence of Plays,* 1580. Aside from some time spent as a soldier and as a member of Cavendish's expedition to South America (1591), Lodge engaged in a busy literary career lasting about fifteen years. Then he turned to the study of medicine, taking the degree of M.D. at Avignon in 1600 and at Oxford in 1602. He practised for about twenty-five years as one of the reputable physicians of London, though his clientele was limited somewhat by the fact that he had, while abroad, embraced the Roman Catholic faith.

Lodge's efforts to write for the stage seem to have been unfortunate, but in the fields of romance, lyrical poetry, and verse-satire he was more successful. He wrote several Euphuistic tales interspersed with poems, among which *Rosalynde,* 1590, has become well known as the source of Shakespeare's *As You*

Like It. In 1589 Lodge published *Scilla's Metamorphosis,* a mythological narrative poem (forerunner of *Venus and Adonis*), and with it a satire and a number of lyrics. Many poems of his appeared in *The Phoenix Nest,* 1593, and in the same year he issued *Phillis,* a sonnet-cycle liberally swelled out with songs and odes. He helped usher in a notable period of verse-satire by publishing *A Fig for Momus,* 1595. After he had become a physician, he made and published translations of Josephus (1602) and Seneca (1614).

The pastoral romance, a type of prose fiction combining romantic narrative, idyllic rural setting, and pastoral poetry, achieved a special vogue during the Renaissance. Sannazzaro's *Arcadia* in Italian and Montemayor's *Diana Enamorada* in Spanish contributed to establishing the type; in England Lodge and Greene, in the last two decades of the sixteenth century, were the most important authors of the shorter romances which did not aim at the epic magnitude of Sidney's revised *Arcadia. Rosalynde,* which Lodge tells us was written to 'beguile the time' during a voyage with Captain Clark to the Azores and Canaries, proved the most popular of these pastoral romances, going through at least four editions between its first publication in 1590 and the time Shakespeare used it as a source for *As You Like It,* and seven more in the first four decades of the seventeenth century. Lodge derived the main plot of his novel from a fourteenth-century poem, the *Tale of Gamelyn,* but transformed that realistic medieval story of the revenge of a young man for the injuries received at the hands of a wicked elder brother by adding the romantic love story and other materials suggested by the English ballads of the Robin Hood cycle and by the pastoral poetry of the day.

We have followed the practice of the original text in the punctuation of the passages of direct conversation, instead of modernizing punctuation by the introduction of quotation marks.

MODERN EDITIONS: Thomas Lodge, *The Complete Works* (ed. by Edmund Gosse), The Hunterian Club, 4 vols., Glasgow, 1883; **Rosalynde* (ed. by W. W. Greg), London, 1907 and 1931.

COMMENT: N. B. Paradise, *Thomas Lodge: The History of an Elizabethan,* New Haven, 1931; C. J. Sisson, *Thomas Lodge and Other Elizabethans,* Harvard, 1933; Alice Walker, 'The Reading of An Elizabethan,' *RES,* viii (1932), 264–81; Alice Walker, 'The Life of Thomas Lodge,' *RES,* ix (1933), 410–32, and x (1934), 46–54; E. A. Tenney, *Thomas Lodge,* Ithaca, 1935.

TEXT: *Rosalynde,* 1590 (16664), Folger.

865 16 Lord of Hunsdon] Henry Carey, Lord Chamberlain of Queen Elizabeth's household; created Baron Hunsdon in 1559. 23 Maecenas] Roman statesman of the 1st century B.C.; chiefly noted as a wealthy and enlightened patron of literature. 26 τὸ πρέπον] propriety. 35 Terceras] the Azores; Terceira is one of the principal islands of the Azores. 39 fautor] supporter.

866 2 sons] Edmund Carey and Robert Carey, the second and third sons of Henry Carey, Lord Hunsdon, were fellow students of Lodge at Oxford. 5 Sir Edward Hoby] eldest son of Sir Thomas Hoby, the translator of Castiglione's *Courtier;* a contemporary of Lodge at Trinity College, Oxford; son-in-law of Lord Hunsdon. 6 etymology of his name] hobby is the term for a small falcon. 28 *Nolo altum sapere*] I do not wish to know matters profound. 29 *Ne . . . crepidum*] 'Let the cobbler stick to his last'; a proverb quoted by Erasmus. 32 curtal-axe] a heavy, slashing sword; cutlass. 37 Momus] in Greek mythology, the personification of criticism and fault-finding. 41 bebaste] thrash.

867 14 *salem ingenii*] shrewdness of wit.

868 19 *halcyones*] kingfishers. 27 *Medium tenere tutissimum*] 'to hold the middle course is safest.'

869 23 want one] do without one. 34 Biares] probably Briareus, son of Ouranos; a monster with 100 arms. 36 bavin] brushwood. 39 fautor] advocate.

870 6 *schedule*] a scroll or piece of paper containing writing.

871 5 *Natura naturans*] Nature causing nature. 8 *Naturam . . . recurret*] 'you may drive out Nature with a pitchfork, but she will always hurry back.'— Horace, *Epistles*, i.10.24.

872 6 *Non sapit . . . sapit*] he is not wise who does not know himself. 9 *Nimia . . . parit*] too much familiarity breeds contempt.

873 34-35 *Amantium . . . est*] 'The anger of lovers is the renewing of love.' Terence, *Andria*, iii.3.23. Cf. Richard Edward's poem with this title (1576), where it is inaccurately translated as 'the falling out of faithful friends renewing is of love.'

874 17 *Quis . . . aurum*] 'who in his senses refuses offered gold.'

875 2 *bezo les labres*] kiss on the lips.

877 1 *memento*] reverie. 41 prize] i.e., Helen of Troy.

879 9-10 upsy friese] a toast; carousal.

880 33 *Quaerenda . . . virtus*] 'Seek money first; after money, virtue.' Horace, *Epistles*, i.1.53-54. 37 *Si . . . foras*] 'If you have brought nothing, Homer, go away.' Ovid, *Ars amatoria*, ii.280.

882 22] the omitted passage consists of 'Alinda's oration to her father in defence of fair Rosalynde'; after which Torismond sentences both Alinda and Rosalynde to banishment. Thereafter Rosalynde was disconsolate but Alinda endeavors to encourage her. 32 *Olim . . . juvabit*] 'At some time it will be pleasant to recall these things.' Virgil, *Aeneid*, i.203.

883 14 black ox] misfortune; the expression is proverbial.

885 26] the omitted passages discuss further the unrequited passion of Montanus for Phoebe, and contain other pastoral poems of Montanus and Coridon.

887 17 ought] owed. 33 *sicco pede*] dry-shod.

888 21 rampired] barricaded.

889 4 losels] scoundrels. 11 press] crowd.

893 3] the omitted pages return to the story of Torismond's actions on hearing of the flight of Rosader; of his imprisonment of Saladyne in order to seize the lands of the late Sir John of Bordeaux; of Saladyne's repentant lament for his misdeeds; of Torismond's banishment of Saladyne; of Saladyne's departure into exile. We then return to the story of Rosader.

896 34 *Periit quia deperibat*] he has perished because he was desperately in love.

897 26] omitted are Rosalynde's passionate soliloquy and three of Rosader's love poems which he reads to 'Ganimede' (Rosalynde).

898 6 recorder] a wind instrument similar to the modern flute.

901 10] Aliena interrupts the lovers ('Ganimede' and Rosader) to remind them it is almost sundown; we then return to Saladyne, who, wandering in the Forest of Arden, lies down to sleep beside a thicket. A hungry lion comes upon the sleeping Saladyne and prepares to pounce upon him as soon as he moves. Rosader arrives at this moment, perceives the situation, recognizes his evil brother, and ponders whether to do nothing and thus be revenged, or to attempt to rescue Saladyne by killing the lion. He finally decides to save his brother, and after he has slain the lion, Saladyne awakes, but does not at first recognize Rosader. His discourse is full of repentance for his past misdeeds, so Rosader then makes himself known to Saladyne and presents him to Gerismond. 33 *Lupus est in fabula*] There is a wolf in the story; Cf. 'speak of the devil and he appears.'

902 26-27 *Ne Hercules . . . duos*] Not even Hercules could contend with two persons.

904 7 mazer] wooden cup. 18] 'Aliena' in her meditation reveals that she has fallen in love with Saladyne; she then rejoins 'Ganimede,' and tries to divert her mind from her worries for the injured Rosader; they then go home to supper with Coridon. Before they all go to bed, Coridon determines to ask Montanus to bring his Phoebe down the next day so that they may see her.

907 14] Montanus makes ardent protestations of his love for Phoebe, but she rebuffs him sharply.

909 35] Saladyne woos 'Aliena' and proposes marriage.

910 36] Phoebe, consumed with a passion for the page Ganimede, writes letters and sonnets to 'him,' which Ganimede (Rosalynde) shows to Montanus.

912 12 *malgrado*] It.: 'in spite of.'

913 1 suffer no fish . . . fingers] tolerate no delay. 14 *Festina lente*] make haste slowly.

915 8 sendal] thin silk. 28 chamlet] cloth of camel's hair or similar material. 30 kersey] heavy woolen cloth. 31 guards] ornamental stripes or bands of color; the mark of a servant's costume. 38 thus attired] Coridon's costume is an incongruous medley of garments, some appropriate only for a courtier, others only for a rustic.

916 34] Montanus reads his sonnets; Phoebe is brought before Gerismond, who demands why she rewards Montanus' love with so little regard; Phoebe then proclaims she is in love with the page Ganimede.

918 39 comical] the Elizabethan meaning of comedy was based upon the ending of a story—comedy, in success and happiness; tragedy, in death and misery.

919 9 crowd] fiddle.

921 25 Nameurs] Nemours. 38–39 overlooked my labors] revised my work. 39 *Sailor's Calendar*] a book promised but never published.

RICHARD HAKLUYT

RICHARD HAKLUYT (1553–1616), clergyman, cosmographer and assiduous collector of the accounts of voyages made by Englishmen to both the Old and the New Worlds was, while still a boy at Westminster School, first roused to an enthusiasm for travel by his cousin, also Richard Hakluyt, a student of the law at the Middle Temple, who showed to him geographies, a universal map, and Psalm 107, telling of those who 'go down to the sea in ships.' After studying at Christ Church, Oxford—he was graduated B.A. in 1574 and M.A. in 1577—, he continued reading accounts of travels in ancient and modern tongues and lecturing thereon. Both he and his cousin were ardent proponents for the expansion of English trade and colonization beyond the seas, and the knowledge they collected about the geography and economic resources of distant regions made them valuable allies and advisers of the London merchants interested in launching maritime enterprises. In fact, their contributions to the researches that collected the information preparatory to the launching of the Levant Company were among the most important. A year or more after the founding of the Levant Company Hakluyt took holy orders and the next five years, 1583–88, he spent chiefly in Paris as chaplain to the English ambassador to France, Sir Edward Stafford. Before leaving England he published and dedicated to Sir Philip Sidney his first major work, *Divers Voyages Touching the Discovery of America* (1582), a collection he had assembled with one of his lifelong goals in mind—the promotion of English colonization in the New World. While in France he improved the opportunity to obtain accounts of French explorations and to translate into English the books and manuscripts he had gathered; moreover he dispatched the information he collected to Sir Francis Walsingham, Queen Elizabeth's Secretary of State, and in July of 1584, while temporarily back in London, he gathered up his material into a tract called *The Discourse of Western Planting,* which was in effect a prospectus for the colonization of North America, by which he hoped to gain the support of Elizabeth for this venture. After some minor publications, he issued in 1589 *The Principal Navigations, Voyages, and Discoveries of the English Nation,* which he was provoked to write by having heard abroad 'other nations miraculously extolled for their discoveries and notable enterprises by sea, but the English, of all others, for their sluggish security and continual neglect of the like attainments, either ignominiously reported or exceedingly condemned.' This work formed the nucleus of an augmented edition, under a practically identical title, *The Principal Navigations, Voyages, Traffiques and Discoveries of the English Nation,* published 1598–1600. In the three large folio volumes of this augmented edition Hakluyt sought to assemble every account of travel to remote regions of the Old and New Worlds that he was able to discover—the ones that he had himself already published; additional voyages that he had written up from the reports of mariners; ones translated from foreign tongues, including a translation, from the Old English of King Alfred the Great, of the tale of the voyages of Ohthere and Wulfstan that Alfred inserted in his Anglo-Saxon version of Orosius' *History;* and, finally, books already in print were reprinted and inserted in the collection. George Best's account of the three voyages of Martin Frobisher in search of the North-West Passage, which had been published in 1578, was included in the third volume of Hakluyt's compilation, although Hakluyt omitted Best's introductory sections to the report of the first voyage, with their eloquent praise of the material progress and the increased geographical knowledge that the expansion of trade had brought about. We have therefore based that part of our text on Best's *A True Discourse of the late Voyages of discovery* (1578), rather than taking it from Hakluyt's abridged reprint.

GEORGE BEST (d. 1584?), servant to Sir Christopher Hatton, accompanied Martin Frobisher on the three voyages he made in 1576, 1577, and 1578. On his return he published his report, dedicating it to Hatton.

Richard Hakluyt's collection of *Voyages* is a monument to the intelligence and industry of their compiler and editor. Not a discoverer or explorer himself, he was content to be the inspirer and recorder of exploration; not a sailor himself, he made the success of voyages possible by the knowledge he placed in the hands of captains and navigators. As his ultimate goal, he would have maintained that the advancement of England's power and prosperity had no more prominence than the advancement of religion by the adding of new territories to the realms of Protestantism. At Hakluyt's death in 1616 his manuscripts passed to the Reverend Samuel Purchas, who carried on Hakluyt's work as a collector and editor and in 1625 published another huge collection of voyages entitled: *Purchas his Pilgrimes.*

MODERN EDITIONS: *Divers Voyages* (ed. by John W. Jones), Hakluyt Society Publications, London, 1850; *The Principal Navigations* (ed. by Edmund Goldsmid), 16 vols., Edinburgh, 1885–90; *The Principal Navigations,* 12 vols., Hakluyt Society, Glasgow, 1903–05; †*The Principal Navigations,* Everyman's Library, 8 vols., London and New York, 1907; *The Principal Navigations* (introduced by John Masefield), 10 vols., London and New York, 1927; *The Three Voyages of Martin Frobisher* (ed. by R. Collinson), Hakluyt Society, London, 1867; *The Three Voyages of Martin Frobisher* (ed. by V. Stefansson), London, 1938.

COMMENT: C. R. Markham, *Richard Hakluyt,* London, 1896; G. B. Parks, *Richard Hakluyt and the English Voyages,* New York, 1928; W. Raleigh, *The English Voyages of the Sixteenth Century,* Glasgow, 1906; *Voyages and Travels Mainly during The Sixteenth and Seventeenth Centuries* (ed. by C. R. Beazley), 2 vols., Westminster, 1903; E. G. R. Taylor, *The Original Writings and Correspondence of the Two Richard Hakluyts,* Hakluyt Society, 2 vols., London, 1935; R. R. Cawley, *The Voyages and Elizabethan Drama,* Boston, 1938; R. R. Cawley, *Unpathed Waters: Studies in the Influence of the Voyagers on Elizabethan Literature,* Princeton, 1940; S. C. Chew, *The Crescent and the Rose,* New York, 1937.

TEXT: George Best, *A True Discourse of the late voyages,* 1578 (1972), Huntington; Richard Hakluyt, *The Principall Navigations, Voiages and Discoveries,* 1589 (12625), Huntington.

922 15 Tully] Cicero, in *De officiis,* i.7.22.

923 6 only] single.

924 28–29 playing *Aequilibra*] balanced.

925 1 Northeasting and Northwesting] the variation of the magnetic needle from the true North; the scientists of the time were hopeful of finding some mathematical relationship between the amount of the variation of the compass and the longitude, and hence an easy means of determining longitude. 7 cards] nautical charts. 33 within a ken] within range of vision.

926 13 Anian] Medieval and Renaissance geographers believed that there was in the polar regions a strait of Anian which would provide a short route from western Europe to China. **15** Ptolomeus King of Egypt] Best confuses Claudius Ptolomey, the geographer of the 2nd cent. A.D., with the kings of Egypt. **22** Orcades] the Orkney Islands, north of Scotland.

927 11 Terra Septentrionalis] the northern or Arctic regions. **12** Terra Austrialis] a misprint for terra Australis, the southern or Antarctic regions. **26** Groneland] Greenland. **28** Obby] the river Ob in western Siberia, emptying into the Arctic.

928 4 Portingales] Portuguese. **25** popingeys] popinjay; parrot. **38** first proffered to the Englishmen] Columbus first sought aid from Henry VII for his projected voyage of discovery before successfully obtaining the support of Ferdinand and Isabella of Spain.

929 6 Baccalaos] Labrador. **10** Cataya] Cathay; China. **16** Guinea and Benin] the Gulf of Guinea and the Bight of Benin, on the west coast of Africa. **23** Equinoctial] Equator. **41** Bilbill] Baboul, at the southern end of the Caspian Sea.

930 2 Tauris] Tabriz. **16** Wardehouse] Vardöhuus, on the northeast coast of Norway, above 70° N. Latitude. **34** Black Moors] blackamoors; Negroes.

931 15 Westminster] Westminster School; established by Henry VIII and re-established by Queen Elizabeth.

932 4 In continuance of time] With the passing of time. **23–28** *Ce qui . . . eux*] 'This has in times past caused me to seek the reasons which prevent the English, who have sufficient wit, ability, and courage to acquire great repute among all Christians, from setting a higher value upon that element which is, and ought to be, more native to them than it is to other peoples: who ought to yield precedence to them in the building, fitting out, and maintaining of ships such as I have seen at various places among them.' **37** argument] evidence; subject-matter.

933 34 Gate] Gata. **35** Argier] Algiers.

934 4 Candie] Crete. **13** Rocetto] Rosetta.

936 10 William Burrough] William Borough (1536–1599), navigator; agent for the Muscovy company. **12** St. Nicholas] modern Archangel. **15** fine] end.

937 26 Canoas] canoes. **39** commonly] usually. **41** buskins] boots. **41** wool] fur.

938 17 points] laces or cords for attaching hose to the doublet. **19** skulls] schools. **21** Meta Incognita] the name Frobisher gave to Baffin Island; the ore which he brought back from his second voyage did not prove to be gold ore, as he believed. **22** muscovy glass] mica. **25** corinths] currants. **27** shows] signs. **31** detract] delay.

ROBERT GREENE

ROBERT GREENE (1558–1592), novelist, poet, dramatist, and journalist, was born of middle-class parents at Norwich, entered St. Johns College, Cambridge, in 1575, and was granted the B.A. in February, 1580. Between the time of his receiving the bachelor's degree and his being admitted M.A. from Clare Hall in July 1583, he traveled abroad, where, according to his later statements in his books, perhaps exaggerated for journalistic effect, he led the sort of debauched life that Ascham and other Elizabethan moralists inveighed against as the usual consequences to young Englishmen of travels in Italy, France, and Spain. Greene's first literary work was an imitation of Lyly's *Euphues: The Anatomy of Wit*, entitled *Mamillia: A Mirrour or looking-glass for The Ladies of England.* The book was entered in the Stationers' Register in October of 1580, so that Greene must either have turned the manuscript over to his printer immediately upon his return from several months of foreign travel, or just before his departure from England, for he describes himself as "Robert Greene, Graduate in Cambridge." In the second part of *Mamillia*, which was entered in September 1583, he becomes 'Maister of Arts, in Cambridge.' Always proud of his academic distinction, Greene usually subscribes himself on his title-pages as 'Master of Arts,' and after June 1588, when he was incorporated Master of Arts at Oxford, he frequently styles himself as 'Master of Arts in both Universities.' From the time of his receiving the M.A. from Cambridge, Greene devoted the remainder of his short life to trying to maintain a precarious existence with the meager funds he could acquire by selling to publishers and to theatrical companies the products of his facile pen. The most versatile and talented of the hack writers of the time, he adapted himself to every shift in the tastes and interests of the Elizabethan public, and wrote the type of literature that promised the readiest market at the moment. According to his own statement, he married, probably some time about 1584, 'a gentleman's daughter of good account' with whom he lived a while, but after their child was born, having squandered his dowry, he deserted her, and went to live in London. In London, from 1585 until his death, he became a leader of the Bohemian literary group, notorious for his dissipation and the promptness with which he squandered whatever money came to him from the publishers or theatrical companies to which he sold the products of his intermittent periods of feverish literary composition.

His varied literary output, besides stories in imitation of the literary success of the 1580's, Lyly's *Euphues*, included tales in manner of the Italian *novelle;* romances of adventure; and pastoral romances, such as *Pandosto* (1588), which Shakespeare was later to use as a source for *A Winter's Tale*, and *Menaphon* (1589), to which his erstwhile fellow-student at St. John's College in Cambridge, Thomas Nashe wrote a preface satirizing the literary fashions of the time (see pp. 423–32). By 1590 he had turned his talents to writing plays for the dramatic companies, and at the same time changed from the Euphuistic prose of his romances to the simple realistic prose of his pamphlets, some of moral exhortation and edification, describing his own riotous life as a warning to others, some of confession, expressing repentance for his misspent life, and one series, the 'conny-catching' pamphlets, beginning with *A Notable Discovery of Cosenage* (1591), purporting to be an exposé of the ingenious tricks of the card-sharpers, confidence men, cutpurses, and other disreputable characters of the underworld of Elizabethan England. Although, for journalistic verisimilitude, he pretends to be writing from first-hand knowledge, and claims that his life has been threatened by the criminals whose secrets he was proposing to reveal, Greene adapted much of his material from earlier accounts of the ways of Elizabethan rogues and vagabonds. These pamphlets were an instant success, each having at least two editions in the year of publication.

Greene died on September 3, 1592. The manuscript of his *Groatsworth of Wit*, which purports to have been written as he lay dying, was copied for the press by Henry Chettle, who a few months later, in the preface to his *Kind-Harts Dreame*, apologizes for not having deleted the famous attack on Shakespeare as the 'upstart crow, beautified with our feathers.'

MODERN EDITIONS: Robert Greene, *Life and Complete Works* (ed. by A. B. Grosart), The Huth Library, 15 vols., London, 1881–86; *A Notable Discovery of Coosnage* (ed. by G. B. Harrison), The Bodley Head Quartos, London, 1923; *The Third and last part of Conny-catching* (ed. by G. B. Harrison), The Bodley Head Quartos, London, 1923; *Greens Groats-worth of witte* (ed. by G. B. Harrison), The Bodley Head Quartos, London, 1923; A. V. Judges, *The Elizabethan Underworld*, London, 1930.

COMMENT: J. C. Jordan, *Robert Greene*, New York, 1915; S. L. Wolff, 'Robert Greene and the Italian Renaissance,' *Englische Studien*, xxxvii (1907), 321–74; H. Jenkins, 'On the Authenticity of *Greens Groatsworth of Wit* and *The Repentance of Robert Greene,' RES*, xi (1935), 28–41; D. C. Allen, 'Science and Invention in Greene's Prose,' *PMLA*, liii (1938), 1007–18; René Pruvost, *Robert Greene et ses romans*, Paris, 1938.

TEXT: *A Notable Discovery of Coosenage*, 1591 (12279), Huntington; *The Third and last part of Conny-catching*, 1592 (12283). Huntington; *Greens Groats-worth of witte*, 1592 (12245), Harvard.

939 16 Getes] *Getae*, inhabitants of the region about the mouth of the Danube on the shores of the Black Sea. 33–34 *Omnia . . . vanitas*] 'Everything under the sun is vanity.' 35 *Mirabolanes*] myrobalan; an astringent plum-like fruit.

940 6 Conny] or coney, a rabbit; in Elizabethan slang 'conny' was the equivalent of the 20th-cent. American term 'sucker' for a person easily the dupe of smooth-talking confidence men, or 'conny-catchers.' 17 rebate] repulse. 37 Term] the sessions of the courts of law.

941 6 *patres patriae*] fathers of their country. 16 ferret] a polecat kept for driving rabbits from their burrows. 30 Broomeman] an itinerant dealer in old clothes, etc. 35–6 more worship] higher social standing. 36 countenance] appearance.

942 7 pair of Cards] pack of cards. 10 groat] a coin valued at four pence. 12 half] partner. 15 smoke] suspect. 20 blind] secret. 27 crossbitten] cheated; swindled. 36 have about] Let us turn around. 38 langret] a kind of false die. 39 bard cater tray] a sure four and three; i.e. throw a 'seven' that is assured because of the loaded dice. 38 broking] fraudulent dealing.

943 26 Westminster Hall] the place of meeting of the courts of justice.

944 6 fallows] ploughed land; Greene's metaphor suggests that the conny has already been well cultivated and prepared for the yielding of a bounteous harvest. 15 he] i.e., the Verser.

945 5 *quis . . . aurum* 'who in his right mind will refuse money that is offered.' 14 policy] trick, stratagem. 18 Verser] Greene seems to intend 'Setter' here; cf. l. 30 below.

947 28 pricks] inserts.

949 3 chopping] changing. 14 vie] bid, wager.

950 22 he] i.e., the conny-catcher; Greene is characteristically inconsistent in failing to use the plural number when the sense demands it. 38 *politicly*] craftily. 40 copesmates] associates.

951 26 Finsbury fields] a favorite recreation ground in the northern suburbs of Elizabethan London.

953 14 fadge] fit. 18 occupier] dealer; merchant. 30 countenance] a variant of 'continuance.'

954 2 artificial] skilful. 33 engine] plot.

955 2 Tyburn] the gallows where criminals were hanged was at Tyburn, in the northwest suburbs of London. 28 gracer of tragedians] probably a reference to Christopher Marlowe. 36 *Sic . . . jubeo*] thus I wish, thus I command. 37 *fas et nefas*] whether just or unjust.

956 1 *Quam . . . judicia!*] How inscrutable are the judgments of God! 10 young Juvenal] the allusion is probably to Thomas Nashe, but no comedy that he wrote with Greene has survived. 18 thou] probably George Peele. 23–4 those burrs . . . those Puppets] the actors who performed the plays written by Greene and his friends. 24 Antics] puppets. 28 upstart crow] Shakespeare; originally an actor, he was now usurping the rôle of the playwright and acquiring fame also as a writer of plays. 29 tiger's heart . . . hide] a parody of *3 Henry VI*, i.4.137: 'O tiger's heart wrapp'd in a woman's hide!' 31 *Johannes fac totum*] Jack-of-all-trades. 31 Shake-scene] the pun on Shakespeare's name makes Greene's allusion obvious.

THOMAS NASHE

THOMAS NASHE (1567–1601), pamphleteer, novelist, and satirist, compared by Lodge to Aretino and by Meres to Juvenal, was educated at St. John's College, Cambridge, receiving his B.A. in March, 1586. He continued at the University, but not for the time required for the M.A. Instead he left for London in the autumn of 1588, joining the other young men from the universities who sought literary fame and employment in the metropolis. His first work, *The Anatomie of Absurdity*, entered in September, 1588, and published at the beginning of the next year, shows a tendency, later overcome, to imitate the style of *Euphues*. The satirical bent of Nashe, however, is manifest from the first, for, although the book itself contains little original matter, it begins with an attack on the female sex and later expands its ridicule to include such diverse groups as the Puritans, the writers on astrology, the ballad makers, and those who acquiesced in the luxury of the age. Nashe's satiric wit and his hatred of the Puritans made it natural that he should be among the writers employed by the bishops at this time to answer the tracts appearing under the pseudonym of Martin Marprelate; but, although it seems certain that Nashe played some rôle in the Marprelate controversy, we cannot be positive exactly what that rôle was, or which of the anti-Martinist pamphlets, if any, came from his pen. On the whole, the best evidence seems to point to Nashe as the author of *An Almond for a Parrot*, although he is commonly credited, without proof, with being the author of the 'Pasquil' tracts. At about this time Nashe wrote an essay critical of the literary fashions and the writers of the day, which he published as a preface to Greene's *Menaphon* (1589). This was to involve him in another pamphlet warfare—a controversy between Nashe and Greene on the one hand and Gabriel Harvey and his brothers on the other. The interchange of invective and insult in print between the antagonists continued from 1592 to 1597. In 1593, at the suggestion of his 'good friends,' Nashe tells us, he attempted a different kind of writing, a work of prose fiction, *The Unfortunate Traveller, or the Life of Jack Wilton*, published in 1594. Usually described as the first example of the picaresque novel in English, this designation would be misleading if we inferred that Nashe's tale was an imitation of *Lazarillo de Tormes*, the Spanish prototype of the picaresque romance. Nashe's novel has many characteristics not present in *Lazarillo*, and typical of Nashe's other works. The tale has, it is true, the unity that comes from having all the adventures befall a single person—the saucy, lively rogue Jack Wilton, page to the Earl of Surrey and companion of his travels— but the fictitious linking of these adventures to historical persons and places would justify our describing *The Unfortunate Traveller* as an early example of the historical novel. Moreover, most of the adventures are lighthearted parodies or burlesques of literary themes and modes of the sixteenth century: the popular jest-books, the realistic descriptions of the plague, the code of love animating the Petrarchan sonnets, the courtly tournament with its pageantry and elaborate and ingenious *imprese*, academic celebrations and orations, the revenge theme in the current 'tragedies of blood,' and the typical accounts of foreign travel. In short, Nashe's talent for satire and parody is as fully indulged as in his other works; it is merely set in a different frame.

Nashe also wrote for the stage; probably his most characteristic play, composed in collaboration with Ben Jonson, was *The Isle of Dogs*, an Aristophanic comedy, now lost, but produced (at least once) in 1597. Its pointed satire resulted in the revocation of Henslowe's license, in Ben Jonson's imprisonment, and Nashe's hasty flight to the eastern counties. While in virtual exile from London he spent several weeks at Yarmouth, a fishing town which he celebrated in his last important work, *Nashes Lenten Stuffe* (1599), a mock panegyric of red herring—one of his most delightful and imaginative satires.

In his most characteristic writing Nashe displays a prose style all his own, compounded of mock-erudition, racy invective, 'aureate rhetoric,' and terse colloquialism. He is said to have learned something from Aretino and more from Rabelais; but he probably also derived at least a trick or two from the Marprelate pamphlets.

MODERN EDITIONS: *The Works of Thomas Nashe (ed. by R. B. McKerrow), 5 vols., London, 1904–10; †Menaphon (ed. by G. B. Harrison), Oxford, 1927; The Unfortunate Traveller (ed. by S. C. Chew), New York, 1926; The Unfortunate Traveller (ed. by H. F. Brett-Smith), Oxford, 1927; †The Unfortunate Traveller, in Shorter Novels, Elizabethan and Jacobean (ed. by G. Saintsbury), Everyman's Library, London, 1928; The Unfortunate Traveller (ed. by M. Ayrton), London, 1948.

COMMENT: D. C. Allen, 'The Anatomie of Absurditie: A Study in Literary Apprenticeship,' SP, xxxii (1935), 170–76; D. J. McGinn, 'Nashe's Share in the Marprelate Controversy,' PMLA, lix (1944), 952–84; A. H. Sackton, 'Thomas Nashe as an Elizabethan Critic,' Univ. Texas Studies (1947), pp. 18–25; A. M. C. Latham, 'Satire on Literary Themes and Modes in Nashe's Unfortunate Traveller,' in English Studies 1948, New Ser. i, 85–100; A. K. Croston, 'The Use of Imagery in Nashe's The Unfortunate Traveller,' RES, xxiv (1948), 90–101; T. L. Summersgill, 'The Influence of The Marprelate Controversy on the Style of Thomas Nashe,' SP, xlviii (1951), 145–60.

TEXT: Menaphon, 1589 (12272), Folger; The Unfortunate Traveller, 1594 (18380), Harvard; Nashes Lenten Stuffe, 1599 (18370), Harvard.

957 39 ab extreme pueritia] from earliest youth. 40 placet] approval. 40 plaudite] applause. 41 sine linea] without bounds. 42 olere atticum] savor of the Attic; i.e. of literary merit.

958 12 kilcow] bragging. 16 drumming] a sidelong allusion to the drums that announced theatrical performances. 25–26 temperatum . . . genus] the 'middle style' of the three oratorical styles: high, middle, or plain. 37 Maro's] Virgil's. 37 xii Aeneidos] twelve books of the Aeneid. 38 Ramus] Pierre de la Ramée (1515–1572), whose system of logic set up as an improvement over Aristotle's had a great vogue in England and Europe (and in the American colonies) for a century. The Ramus-versus-Aristotle controversy at Cambridge was at its height during Nashe's time as a student there.

959 7 adage] 'nothing has been ever said that hasn't been said before.' 26–7 sublime dicendi genus] the grand style; the term is that employed by Quintilian for the high or grand style in rhetoric, in his Institutio oratoria, xi.1.3.

960 2 "What do you lack?"] the common greeting to customers of Elizabethan shopkeepers and their assistants. Nashe in this passage is contrasting the uneducated merchant class with the pretentious university scholars, to the detriment of the latter. 8 fripler] fripper; old-clothes dealer. 19 world turned upside down] Nashe suggests that this was a common alehouse sign. 21 Nemis . . . republica] too greatly concerned in the affairs of a country not my own. 25 Noverint] scrivener. 31 tempus . . rerum] time devouring all things. 34 Kidde] this paragraph has been taken to be an allusion to Thomas Kyd, the dramatist, and to imply that Kyd was the author of a pre-Shakespearian play

of Hamlet. It may be a jibe at the imitation of Senecan tragedy by contemporary playwrights in general, without any specific allusion to Kyd; however, the fact that Kyd was the son of a scrivener makes him the most likely object of Nashe's satire, though the passage falls short of being a proof of Kyd's authorship of the Ur-Hamlet.

961 5–6 French Doudie] the allusion has not been satisfactorily explained; it may be a term for a harlot, or the allusion may be literary and refer to some book in French, perhaps a collection of lascivious tales. 14 Melancthon, Sadolet] Philip Melanchthon (1497–1560), and Jacopo Sadoleto (1477–1547), both eminent humanist scholars of the early 16th cent. 14 Plantin] Christoffel Plantin (1514–1589), a leading printer of scholarly works at Antwerp. 18 William Turner] d. 1568, an English translator and author of many theological works; also compiler of an herbal in English. He was an extreme Protestant, and a refugee abroad during Queen Mary's reign. 33 University Orator] Roger Ascham. Nashe apparently has in mind a passage from the second book of Ascham's Scholemaster; see English Works (ed. by W. A. Wright), p. 280. 35 uno . . . prodiere] to disclose single progeny of that commonwealth.

962 3 Priscian] author of the elementary Latin grammar used in the schools of the Middle Ages. 11 compass of a penny] Peter Bales, famous writing master, presented to Queen Elizabeth in 1576 a ring in which was set a penny on which he had engraved the Lord's Prayer, etc.; the penny, of course, was of silver and about 9/16 inches in diameter. 34 Graeca cum Latinus] Cicero perfected his style by translating Demosthenes and other Greek orators from

Greek into Latin. See Quintilian *Institutio oratoria*, x.5.2. 41–2 insulted in] boasted of. 42 *corrigat qui potest*] Let whoever is able correct (or improve).

963 2 Stanihurst; Phaer] Richard Stanyhurst's attempts at English hexameters were constantly, and justly, derided by the Elizabethans; his translation of the first four books of Virgil's *Aeneid* into English hexameters was published in 1582. Thomas Phaer's translation of the first nine books of the *Aeneid* was published in 1562; the remaining books were translated by Thomas Twyne, and the Phaer-Twyne translation published in 1573 and again in 1584.

964 3 Epaphus] Osiris or Apis, the son of Jupiter and Io, or Isis; it was the sacred bull Apis, supposed to be an incarnation of the soul of Osiris, that was sacrificed. Nashe's mythology is somewhat inaccurate, but scholarly accuracy was a quality he derided, and one he did not seek. 9 undermeal] the time after the mid-day meal. 11 *Tam Marti quam Mercurio*] as much of Mars as of Mercury; i.e. as much a soldier as a poet; George Gascoigne employed this motto. 12–13 *faecundi calices*] eloquent wine goblets. 14 Silenus] a satyr, foster-father of Bacchus; represented as a fat, jolly, intoxicated old man, riding on an ass, crowned with flowers and ivy; symbolic of one besotted with drink 18 *qui . . . η［ινεīν］* Loosely translated: 'whoever wishes to write good poetry must first get drunk.' 25 *Thenino dente*] i.e., with a slanderous tongue; Theoninus was a writer of satires. 32 *Si . . . foras*] 'If you have brought nothing, Homer, you will be thrust outside.' Ovid, *Ars Amatoria*, ii.280. 35 *redde rationem*] 'give your reasons'; i.e. a demand for an explanation or citation of evidence.

965 17 Thomas Atchelow] several extracts from his poems are included in *England's Parnassus*, an anthology of Elizabethan poetry published in 1600 by the printer Robert Allot. 25 *Arraignment of Paris*] this pastoral pageant by George Peele was first performed by the Children of the Chapel Royal in 1584, and published in the same year. 33 Tolossa] ancient name of Toulouse, a city in southern France. 41–2 *Albions*] Warner's historical poem, *Albion's England*, was first published in 1586; it had several later editions.

966 2 *In speech*] the opening words of William Lily's *Short Introduction of Grammar*, the standard textbook for the teaching of Latin grammar in the schools of Elizabethan England; hence a synonym for knowledge of Latin. 3 *Abcie*] *ABC;* the children's primer for commencing the learning of Latin. 7 *Anatomie of Absurdities*] Nashe's first published work; it was issued in 1589/90 and it was probably being printed at the same time that *Menaphon* was first issued. 24 fever quartan] a disease characterized by a fever recurring every fourth day. 26–27 Turney and Turwin] Tournay and Térouanne were towns in France captured by Henry VIII in 1513. 29 appendix] attendant. 32 *Coelum . . . stultitia*] 'we in our foolishness try to scale the heavens'; see Horace *Odes*, i.3.38. 39 *Paulô . . . canamus*] 'Let us sing of somewhat nobler things.' Virgil, *Eclogues*, iv.1.

967 3 *Aliquid . . . patet*] something lies hidden which is not well known. 6 London Bridge] the quartering of the bodies of criminals and placing them on London Bridge was a common custom. 20 lord of misrule] master of the revels. 21 ivy bush] the sign of a tavern or alehouse; cf. the adage: 'good wine needs no bush.' 24 *tendit . . . virtus*] virtue reaches to the stars; a pun on *sidera* [stars] and 'cider-a.' 26 *aqua coelestis*] water of heaven; the name of a drug considered a powerful restorative. 39 Three Cups] it was usual to give distinctive names to the rooms of a tavern.

968 12 way] unit of weight for cheese; equals about 250 lbs. 12 great] gross. 17–18 doit . . . denier] Dutch and English coins of very small value.

970 12 Epimenides] a Cretan (7th cent. B.C.) said to have slept 40 or 57 years. 26 snudge] miser. 37 beaver] this bit of pseudo-scientific lore comes from Pliny *Natural History*, viii.47; many Renaissance writers mention it.

971 5 scuppet] a type of shovel. 39] In the omitted pages (about 20), Jack Wilton gives a facetious account of the Anabaptist uprising in Munster, and of the execution of John of Leyden, one of its leaders. Then his master, the Earl of Surrey, confides to Jack his love for the fair Geraldine, and of Geraldine's granting her consent for him to travel in Italy.

972 2 Sir Thomas More] Nashe, although pretending to describe actual happenings, as a writer of fiction plays fast and loose with chronology. The uprising in Munster was suppressed in 1535, the year of More's execution and the year before Erasmus' death. 36–37 *quemadmodums* and *quodpropters*] how's and wherefore's. 38 *Esse posse videatur*] a favorite ending of a sentence among the imitators of Cicero; their passion for the phrase far exceeded that of Cicero himself, and they were laughed at for the cultivation of this mannerism. The phrase may be translated as: 'It is apparent that it may be.' 40–41 *Dum . . . aper*] 'As long as the boar loves the heights of the mountain.' Virgil, *Eclogues*, v.76. 41 *dixi*] I have spoken.

973 7 incorporationers] members of the corporation. 33 orificial] high-sounding.

974 20 *O quantus artifex pareo*] O how excellent a workman I am! 29 *Acolastus*] a Latin comedy by the Dutch scholar Gnapheus, a dramatization of the parable of the prodigal son. Written in 1529, it was translated into English in 1540.

975 4 Carolostadius] Andreas Rudolf Bodenstein (1480–1541), an associate of Luther. 5 level coil] from the French phrase, *lever le cul*, in the sense of *lève-cul*, a boisterous Christmas game; Nashe apparently means that the disputation was noisy and tumultuous. 10 *Quae . . . nos*] Things which are above us concern us not at all.

976 2 Nizolius] see note to p. 834, line 37. 3] The remainder of *The Un-*

fortunate Traveler recounts Jack Wilton's adventures in Italy. 8 *ab ovo*| 'from the egg,' i.e. from the beginning. 14 Marlowe] Christopher Marlowe's *Hero and Leander* was completed by George Chapman and published in 1598. 18 pickany] darling, or pigesney. 25 didapper] fool. 30 jert] a variant of 'jerk.' 32 trot] a hag; old woman.

977 4 Cytherea's nuns] devotees of Venus; courtesans. 9 wem or brack] harm or quarrel. 24 frampold] cross. 25 croquet or *transire*] a warrant issued by custom-house officials permitting goods to pass. 28 leman or orange] Nashe puns on the words 'leman,' mistress; and 'lemon,' a citrus fruit. 28 disjune] cf. Fr. *desjeuner*. 30 the rheum] a cold.

978 22–23 Ops to Pomona] Ops was the goddess of plenty; Pomona, the goddess of fruit trees. 35 Sir John Mandeville] reputed author of a 14th-cent book of travels. 37 Juno Lucina] the goddess Juno in her rôle as the goddess presiding over childbirth.

979 8 paggled] pregnant. 9 tympanized] stretched like a drum. 11 Palmerin of England] the hero of a romance with that title, written in Spanish by Luis Hurtado; an English translation was published in 1596. 11 Cadwalader] British king (d. 664); Nashe, by the term 'Cadwalader herring,' probably jestingly means 'king of herring.'

THOMAS DELONEY

THOMAS DELONEY (*c.* 1543–*c.* 1600), silk-weaver, ballad-writer, pamphleteer, and novelist, gained at first-hand the intimate knowledge of the lives and manners of the artisan class that he describes in the three novels he wrote at the end of his career. Very little is known about Deloney. He may have received the education offered at the grammar school of one of the provincial towns, but which one is uncertain, for there is insufficient evidence to support the assertion that he came from Norwich. As a journeyman silk-weaver he probably worked at one time or another at the various centers of the textile industry in England. Our records of him as a journalist date from the 1580's; the defeat of the Spanish Armada in 1588 was celebrated by Deloney, among others, in broadside ballads that were the popular newspapers of the day.

Deloney's fame in Elizabethan literature rests entirely upon his three novels of middle-class life, each of which aims at glorifying the members of one of the craft guilds of sixteenth-century England. In *Jack of Newberie*, registered in May of 1597, it is the Clothiers whom Deloney honors; in *The Gentle Craft*, entered in October of the same year, the Shoemakers are celebrated. In his last novel, *Thomas of Reading*, Deloney again aims at augmenting the renown of his own guild, the Clothiers. His stories were loosely constructed, but their lively blend of romance with realistic pictures of every-day middle-class life, and their portraits of the success that lay open to any apprentice who dedicated himself to thrift and hard work won them a steady popularity with their readers. For each of them the earliest edition surviving is one issued several years after the first. The novels are for the most part written in the simple colloquial English spoken by the tradesmen whose adventures they record, although Deloney frequently embarks on imitations of Euphuistic prose when the speaker is supposed to be a member of the court, or one who is consciously attempting to speak like a noble lady or gentleman. In our text we have not attempted to modernize the punctuation of dialogue by inserting quotation marks, but have followed the punctuation of the earliest extant edition.

MODERN EDITIONS: *Works* (ed. by F. O. Mann), Oxford, 1912; *Thomas of Reading* in *Early English Prose Romances* (ed. by W. J. Thoms), vol. i, London, 1858.

COMMENT: A. Chevalley, *Thomas Deloney: le roman des métiers au temps de Shakespeare*, Paris, 1926; H. E. Rollins, 'Deloney's Sources for Euphuistic Learning,' *PMLA,* li (1936), 399–406.

TEXT: *Thomas of Reading,* 1612 (6569), Huntington.

979 30 Henry the First] the historical background that Deloney employs to give an air of verisimilitude to his tale is drawn from Holinshed's account of the reign of Henry I.

980 9 Excester] Exeter. 14 admiration] in the original sense of 'wonder.' 23 Bosom's Inn] there was an inn by that name (a corruption of Blossoms) in St. Laurence's Lane in the London of the 16th century; Deloney invents a character to explain the name. 25 wains] wagons. 26 Jarrat's Hall] Gerrard's Hall, an actual hostelry in Elizabethan London, at the end of Basing Lane near Bread Street.

981 21 pottage] soup; cf. Fr. *potage.* 41 Carl] churl.

982 15 Cutb.] such abbreviations were common in the printed texts of the time. 18 bias] the metaphor is from the game of bowls; bias refers to the lop-sided shape of a bowl, causing it to swerve in a particular way. 41 Chamberlain] an attendant at an inn. 42 By and by] at once.

983 13 Reior] Raier, one of Henry I's musicians; Deloney gets his information from Holinshed, and embroiders upon it. 24 consorts] bands of musicians. 41 giglot] a giddy, wanton woman.

984 29 the shot] the reckoning.

985 38 Statute] statue.

989 5] Chapter 4 is entitled: 'How the King's Majesty sent for the Clothiers, and of the sundry favors which he did them.'

990 8 bully] an Elizabethan term of endearment.

991 1 tike] tyke; a dialectal term for a cur or boor; derived from the Old Norse word for 'bitch.' 19 stomach] ill-will; anger. 28 gag-tooth] gag-toothed; having protruding teeth. 35 quean] a bold wench; a term of disparagement, sometimes the equivalent of 'harlot.'

992 1 capcase] traveling bag. 22 louvre] a domed turret-like structure on the hall-roof of a medieval building, with lateral openings for the passage of smoke and light. 26 he] i.e., the innkeeper, old Bosom. 31 taken tardy] 'caught napping.'

993 10 pinned] confined; shut up. 30] Chapter 6 is entitled: 'How Simon's wife of Southampton, being wholly bent to pride and pleasure, requested her husband to see London, etc.' Chapter 7: 'How the Clothiers sent the King aid into France, and how he overcame his brother Robert, etc.' Chapter 8: 'How Hodgekins of Halifax came to the Court, and complained to the King, etc.' Chapter 9: 'How the Bailiffs of London could get no man to be a Catch-pole, and how certain Flemings took that office upon them, etc.' 42 stammell] coarse woolen cloth.

994 30 his keepers] Duke Robert was a prisoner to his brother King Henry, and rather loosely guarded. 40] Duke Robert, as a courtier, is made by Deloney to speak in Euphuistic prose. Margaret replies in the same style.

996 41 malapert] presumptuous.

1000 21 Thomas Becket] Deloney has confounded the reigns of Henry I and Henry II; Thomas à Becket lived in the reign of Henry II; was Archbishop of Canterbury from 1162 until his murder in 1170.

1002 9 bestow . . . more] employ more time in writing it again. 17 coil] noisy disturbance; 'fuss.'

1003 4 made himself unready] un-dressed.   32 ore eve] the evening before.

1005 4] Chapter 12 is entitled: 'How divers of the Clothiers' wives went to the Churching of Sutton's wife of Salis-bury, and of their merriment.'   20 dis-aster] ill-starred; unlucky.

1008 15 *Apium Risus*] the anemone, a flower which, according to the herbalists,

if it be eaten or drunk, makes a man die with laughter.

1011 33 coxcombs] fools.

1012 4 shales] husks; nut-shells.

1013 5] The 15th and final chapter is entitled; 'How fair Margaret made her estate and high birth known to her Mas-ter and Dame . . . [and] became a Nun in the Abbey at Gloucester.'

ROBERT ASHLEY

ROBERT ASHLEY (1565–1641), lawyer, translator, and man of letters, after receiving his early education at home, was placed at the age of ten in the cele-brated school of Hadrian Saravia at Southampton, where he acquired a sound knowledge of languages. In 1580 he went up to Hart Hall, Oxford, later transferring first to Merton and then to Magdalen, where he received his B.A. in 1582 and became a fellow of Magdalen a year later. In 1587 he proceeded M.A. and was designated public professor of geometry. The next year he entered New Inn to prepare himself for the law and was admitted to the Middle Temple in October 1588. The following year he turned his atten-tion to foreign travel and the study of languages, especially of French. In 1593 he returned to the study of law at the Temple, and was called to the bar in 1595. The principal patrons to whom Ashley looked for advancement all died in the 1590's; with the death of Sir John Puckering in 1596, his hope of achieving a post of importance in political life was defeated. Except for various journeys abroad he spent the remainder of his long life as a resident of the Middle Temple.

Ashley's first publications were a translation of an anonymous French work comparing the English and the Spanish nations, and a translation into Latin hexameters of Du Bartas' *L'Uranie*. Five years later, in 1594, he dedicated to Sir John Puckering, Lord Chancellor, his translation from the French of Louis Le Roy's *De la vicissitude ou variété des choses en l'univers*. Shortly afterwards he composed his treatise *Of Honour*, which he apparently intended to present in manuscript to Sir John Puckering, but after the latter's death he chose a new patron for the presentation, Sir Thomas Egerton. There is no record of any other works or translations by Ashley until 1627 when he presented to King Charles I a treatise translated from the Spanish with the title of *Almansor the Learned and Victorious King*. The remainder of Ashley's life was spent in translating various works from the Italian. On his death he bequeathed his books and £300 to the Middle Temple and by this act of generosity became the founder of the Middle Temple Library.

LOUIS LE ROY, French humanist and professor of Greek at the Collège Royal from 1572 until his death in 1577, drew upon his reading in classical literature for the material which he brought together in his treatise *De la vicissitude ou variété des choses en l'univers* (1577). A part of his material was derived from Seneca's *Natural Questions*, and his French style betrays the influence of Seneca's Latin. Ashley's translation, in its turn, displays at an early date the Senecan qualities that were later to become more notable in the prose style of English writers such as Bacon and Hall.

MODERN EDITIONS: [of Le Roy's treatise] *De la vicissitude ou variété des choses* (selections ed. by B. W. Bates), Princeton, 1944; *Of Honour* (ed. by Virgil B. Helt-zel), San Marino, California, 1947.

COMMENT: K. Koller, 'Two Elizabethan Expressions of the Idea of Mutability,'

SP, xxxv (1938), 229–37; Virgil B. Heltzel, 'Robert Ashley: Elizabethan Man of Letters,' *HLQ*, x (1947), 349–63.

TEXTS: *Of the Interchangeable Course, or Variety of Things in the Whole World*, 1594 (15488), Harvard; *Ellesmere Ms. 1117*, [1596], Huntington.

1015 1] The ideas expressed by Le Roy in this and the preceding paragraph are largely an expansion upon Seneca, *Natural Questions*, vii.31. 10 Varro] Marcus Terentius Varro (116–27 B.C.), the most learned of the Romans, according to Quintilian, was a poet, satirist, antiquarian, geographer, grammarian, and scientist. 35 Vitruvius] Vitruvius Pollio (d. *c.* 26 B.C.), Roman architect, whose treatise *De Architectura* had a great influence in the Renaissance. 36 Columella] Roman writer on agriculture of the 1st cent. A.D. 41 Vegetius] Roman military writer of the 4th cent. A.D.

1016 4 quadrature of the circle] squaring the circle; i.e. constructing a square of the same area as a given circle. The problem was attempted unsuccessfully by generations of ancient mathematicians; it has been proved impossible of solution by means of the ruler and compass only. 7 Vesalius] Andreas Vesalius (1514–1564); his *De Corporis humani fabrica* (1543) is the foundation of modern anatomy. 10 Leonicenus] Nicholas Leonicenus (1428–1524), Professor of Medicine at Ferrara; his book on the errors in Pliny and other writers was first published at Ferrara in 1492. 11 Avenreis] Rhazes (d. 923–4 A.D.), Arab physician and physicist at Bagdad; the greatest clinician in the Islamic world during the Middle Ages. 20 Ariopagites] the council of the Areopagus in ancient Athens. 21 Comices] the different *comitia*, or popular assemblies of ancient Rome.

1017 39 refrain] restrain.

RICHARD HOOKER

RICHARD HOOKER (1554–1600), scholar, philosopher, theologian, and defender of the Church of England against the attacks of the Puritan advocates of a presbyterian form of church government, was a native of Exeter, and received his early education at the Exeter Grammar School. Through Bishop Jewel he was granted a clerkship at Corpus Christi College, Oxford, where he proceeded B.A. in 1574 and became M.A. and Fellow in 1577. His proficiency in Hebrew led to appointment as deputy to the professor of Hebrew. At Corpus Christi College he had as pupils Edwin Sandys, son of the Archbishop of York, George Cranmer, great-nephew of the Archbishop who had suffered martyrdom under Queen Mary, and William Churchman, son of John Churchman, a prominent member of the Merchant Taylor's Company in London. In 1581 Hooker took orders and was chosen to preach at Paul's Cross. At this time the attacks upon the Elizabethan religious compromise and upon the organization of the Church of England established by that compromise were a matter of increasing concern to Queen Elizabeth and to the responsible heads of the Church. The danger was not from Rome, but from within the Church of England itself, for there were many fanatic extremists intent on 'purifying' the Anglican Church by remodeling it according to the pattern of Calvinism, setting up a presbyterian form of church government. Thomas Cartwright, deprived of his professorship of divinity at Cambridge in 1570, was still, in his retirement on the Continent, the most effective spokesman of the Puritan faction. In England Walter Travers, a leading Presbyterian, follower of Cartwright, author of the book *De Disciplina Ecclesiastica* advocating the establishment of the Calvinistic church, was a popular preacher at the Temple where he was Reader and one of the candidates for the Mastership. The senior Edwin Sandys, Archbishop of York, and John Whitgift, who in 1583 became Archbishop of Canterbury, saw that in Richard Hooker, because of his thorough scholarship and calmly reasoned style in argument, they had a young man particularly fitted to present the case of the Church of England against the Calvinists seeking radical changes in church government. Through Archbishop Sandys' influence Hooker was appointed Master of the Temple. Hooker was in London from December, 1584, waiting for the confirmation of his appointment to the Mastership; at that time he seems to have become a resident in John Churchman's house in Watling Street, near St. Paul's Church. After he became Master of the Temple in February, 1585, he apparently remained as a permanent resident, and continued to live at the Churchmans after his marriage to Joan Churchman in 1588. It was under the Churchmans' roof that Hooker's *Of the Laws of Ecclesiastical Polity* was planned and at least the first four books were written. Hooker's aides in the task included the younger Edwin Sandys, who was a law-student in the Temple during Hooker's mastership, George Cranmer, and John Spenser, all of whom had been students at Corpus Christi College, Oxford. Sandys and Cranmer probably contributed to this group their special knowledge of the law, and Spenser and Hooker the knowledge of theology and church history. All met frequently at the Churchmans' for discussion of particular problems and Sandys also resided there for a considerable period as a guest. In 1591 Hooker resigned his mastership at the Temple to devote his full time to the composition of his great book; by his 'judicious' and happy marriage to Joan Churchman he had acquired the independent means to afford such an action. The first four books were ready for the press in January of 1593; the volume was entered to John Windet on 29 January 1593; Windet and Edwin Sandys had entered into an agreement whereby Sandys advanced the money to pay for the printing and was to receive 2s.6d. for each copy Windet sold. The printing was completed in about six weeks, and the volume, issued in March, 1593, appeared just in time to support the bill then before Parliament reaffirming the act enforcing conformity in religion, now widened in its wording to deal with dissenters as well as Catholics.

The plan of Hooker's work called for eight books; the fifth book appeared in 1597. Hooker, meanwhile, had in 1595 been presented with the living of Bishopsbourne, near Canterbury, and had moved there with his family. There he completed the fifth book, and the more or less finished drafts of the remaining three books, which were among his papers when he died in 1600. The subsequent history of Books VI to VIII of Hooker's great work, and the controversy over the authenticity of the printed editions that appeared many years later (Books vi and viii in 1648 and Book vii in 1662) were not resolved until Professor C. J. Sisson's book in 1940 presented the evidence that, on all important points, vindicated the authenticity of the printed texts of the last three books and dispelled the errors that stem from Izaak Walton's life of Hooker, first prefixed to the edition of 1666.

Hooker's *Of the Laws of Ecclesiasticall Polity* stands as a masterpiece of English prose by virtue of the balance and lucidity of Hooker's style; it is also a great contribution to theology and to political thought. Hooker rests his defense of the Anglican Church upon a judicious appeal to reason and first principles, not upon partisan polemics. Hence, to vindicate the necessity for authority, he turns first to an examination, in terms of the thought of his age, of the nature of all law, and of the nature of man as a rational being. The structure of his argument is carefully built up, step by step, always with an appeal directly to reason, rather than to emotion. His aim is to persuade intelligent and responsible men—not fanatics claiming the authority of a special revelation granted to them alone.

In our text we have used Roman numerals to mark the various sections; we have inserted in square brackets the paragraph divisions within each section, following the divisions made in the standard edition of Keble.

MODERN EDITIONS: *Works* (ed. by John Keble), Oxford, 1836; *Works (Keble's ed. revised by R. W. Church and F. Paget), 3 vols., Oxford, 1888; *Of the Laws of Ecclesiastical Polity, Book I* (ed. by R. W. Church), Oxford, 1876; †*Of the Laws of Ecclesiastical Polity, Books I to V*, Everyman's Library, London and New York. 1907.

COMMENT: L. S. Thornton, *Richard Hooker: A Study of His Theology*, London, 1924; A. P. D'Entreves, *The Mediaeval Contribution to Political Thought: Thomas Aquinas, Marsilius of Padua, Richard Hooker*, Oxford, 1939; C. J. Sisson, *The Judicious Marriage of Mr. Hooker and the Birth of 'The Laws of Ecclesiastical Polity,'* Cambridge, 1940; E. T. Davies, *The Political Ideas of Richard Hooker*, London, 1946; F. J. Shirley, *Richard Hooker and Contemporary Political Ideas*, London, 1949.

TEXT: *Of the Lawes of Ecclesiasticall Politie*, 1593 (13712), Harvard.

1022 4 regiment] rule.

1024 27 peculiar] belonging exclusively to itself. 29 proper] its own. 39 Διὸs . . . βουλή] God's counsel was accomplished. 40 τὸν . . . λόγῳ] The Creator made the whole world not with his hands but by reason.

1025 2 ὁδῷ . . . κόσμου] Proceeded by a certain and a set *Way* in the making of the world. 28–29 "The Lord . . . sake."] *Proverbs*, 16.4. 37 They] the Calvinists. 40–41 κατὰ . . . will."] see *Ephesians*, 1.11.

1026 3 Apostle] Paul; the quotation is from *Romans*, 11.33. 8 herself] Wisdom; see *Proverbs*, 8.22. 17–18 "Of . . . things"] *Romans*, 11.36. 20 *Tamen* . . .] from Boethius' *Consolation of Philosophy*, iv.5.

1028 16 states] classes of society. 19–20 "made . . . rain"] *Job*, 28.26. 20–21 "decree . . . commandment."] see *Jeremiah*, 5.22. 27 volubility] revolving. 39 Phidias] the Greek sculptor of the 5th cent. B.C.

1029 37–38 "In . . . are."] Cf. *Acts*, 17.28.

1030 1 forms] form in other creatures is analogous to the soul in living creatures; according to the diversity of their inward forms the things existing in the world are distinguished; but form is not tangible, being discerned only by its effects. Hooker uses the term in accordance with its signification in Aristotelian philosophy, with its distinction between *matter* and *form*.

1031 9 it] here used in the possessive case, where in modern English 'its' would appear. 22 observants] observers. 26 efficient] efficient cause; the four causes in Aristotelian philosophy are: material, formal, efficient, and final. (1) material: the matter—(2) formal: the form or essence—(3) efficient: the producing agency—(4) final: the pur-

pose or end of a thing caused. 36 paynims] pagans. 40 Mirror of human wisdom] Aristotle.

1032 12 David] in *Psalms*, 148.2. 35 reflex] turning back.

1035 16 innocents] young children; simpletons. 19 way we speak of] the demonstrations of Aristotelian logic. 22 new devised aid] the dialectic of Peter Ramus. The so-called reform of Aristotle's logic by Ramus was, in fact, primarily a simplification which sacrificed precision for the sake of a method of dichotomies that schematized logic and apparently made it easier to learn.

1036 5 apostle] Paul, in *Ephesians*, 4.23. 33 Moses] in *Deuteronomy*, 30. 19.

1037 16 privity] concurrence. 41 affect] desire.

1038 37 Apostles] James and John; see *Luke*, 9.54. 41 Saviour spake] see *Matthew*, 23.37.

1039 12 Apostle] Paul, in a number of his Epistles.

1040 29 overseen] deluded. 38 "they . . . tenure."] Aristotle, *Rhetoric*, i.10.

1042 4 apostle] Paul in *2 Corinthians*, 4.17–18. 12–13 "For . . . it?"] see *Matthew*, 16.26.

1043 11 stand] pause; stop. 21 read] in *Deuteronomy*, 6.5. 23 Saviour] in *Matthew*, 22.38. 24 next] 'Thou shalt love thy neighbor as thyself.'

1044 6 two general heads] 'On these two commandments hangeth all the law and the prophets.' *Matthew*, 22.40. 15 Joseph] see *Genesis*, 39.9. 28 hitting jump] hitting exactly. 40 behooveful] needful.

1045 4 Sophocles] in *Antigone*, 456–57. 28 Those only] only those. 31 Saint Augustine] in *De Doctrina Christiana*, iii.14.

1046 18 David] in *Psalms*, 135.18. 22 Wise Man] Solomon; see the apochryphal book *The Wisdom of Solomon,* 13.17, and 14.15–16.

1047 1 Apostle] Saint Paul, in *Ephesians,* 4.17–18. 6 Esay] *Isaiah,* 44.18–19.

1048 5–6 alienation of mind] insanity. 7 furious] mad.

1049 1 Twelve Tables] the ancient Roman code of law drawn up and published in 451–450 B.C.

THE BIBLE

THE KING JAMES (OR 'AUTHORIZED') VERSION OF THE BIBLE (1611) has been called 'the noblest monument of English prose.' It was a monument built not by one person, but by many; and not at one time, but over many generations. The edifice was completed by a board of fifty-four scholars appointed by King James I after the conference on ecclesiastical matters held at Hampton Court shortly after his accession had suggested the desirability of an official revision of the English translation of the Bible popularly known as the Bishops' Bible. The revisers were divided into six companies, each of them charged with the responsibility for certain books of the Bible; two companies met at Oxford, two at Cambridge, and two at Westminster. Their instructions called for basing their revision on 'the ordinary Bible read in the church, commonly called the Bishops' Bible,' but they were to use other English translations wherever they agreed better with the original text than did the Bishops' Bible. The translators appointed by King James began their labors in 1607 and the result of their efforts was first published in 1611, with an admirable preface of the translators to the reader, which sets forth the history and problems of Biblical translation and the translators' aims and methods in preparing their version. They state clearly that they never thought from the beginning that they should need to make a new translation, 'nor yet to make of a bad one a good one'; but 'to make a good one better, or out of many good ones, one principal good one.'

We have included on pages 1049 to 1060 selections from this preface, and on pages 1062 to 1081 we have paralleled the 'principal good' translation—the King James version—of Christ's Sermon on the Mount (*Matthew*, Chapter 5), with five of the preceding sixteenth-century translations, to indicate the fashion in which that 'noblest monument of English prose' was built, and the quality of the many stones that the builders had at hand.

Although there were translations of parts of the Bible into English during the Old English and Middle English periods, and a translation by John Wycliffe and his followers at the end of the fourteenth century, it is to the sixteenth-century versions that our English Bible traces its immediate ancestry. The sixteenth-century scholars, no longer content to follow only the Latin translation of St. Jerome, went back to the original Greek and Hebrew texts. The history of the King James version properly begins with William Tyndale's translation of the New Testament which was published in 1525 at Cologne. Tyndale translated direct from the Greek, availing himself of the helps afforded by Erasmus' Greek-Latin New Testament (1522), the Latin *Vulgate* of Jerome, and Luther's German New Testament (1522). In 1534 Tyndale issued a revision of the New Testament. Before his death in 1536 Tyndale had translated several books of the Old Testament. Meanwhile Miles Coverdale, translating, not from the original tongues, but from the Latin and the German, published in 1535 a translation of the whole Bible. John Rogers, Tyndale's literary executor, prepared a well-edited version of other men's translations which he printed in 1537 under the pseudonym of Thomas

Matthew. For the most part 'Matthew's Bible' consisted of Tyndale's work, except for the books of the Old Testament that Tyndale had not yet translated; for these Rogers reprinted Coverdale's version. Although King Henry VIII had been persuaded to grant a royal license to 'Matthew's Bible,' the realization that a large share of it was actually Tyndale's translation, which earlier had been condemned as heretical, led to the resolve to supersede it as quickly as possible by a new version, essentially based upon it, but omitting its polemical notes. This version, issued in 1539, came to be known as 'The Great Bible'; a royal order prescribed that copies of the large folio edition should be set up in churches where the public would be free to read it. 'The Great Bible' and its predecessor, the 'Matthew Bible,' thus established Tyndale and Coverdale as the principal translators of the English Bible.

During the reign of Queen Mary many of the English exiles gathered at Geneva, the center of Calvinism, and the Genevan scholars decided that the English version of the Scriptures should be perfected, 'with most profitable annotations in all hard places.' The New Testament translation published at Geneva in 1557 was chiefly the work of William Whittingham; it was followed in 1560 by a revision of the whole Bible, in which the New Testament portion was a revision of Whittingham's Testament of 1557. The Geneva Bible (often called the 'Breeches Bible' because of its rendering of *Genesis*, 3.7.) introduced many new features not present in the English Bibles that preceded it, but generally adopted in later translations, including the King James. First, it began the practice of breaking up the text into numbered verses. It also initiated the custom of distinguishing the actual text, by a difference in type, from the words that had been inserted to express the full sense of the original. It was printed in Roman type instead of the old black-letter type in which earlier versions had been set. All in all, much was done to make the Bible a convenient book for private reading—to furnish the English people with a cheaper, less unwieldy Bible than they had had before. Among the devout Bible-reading Puritans it quickly established itself as the favorite, not only because of its greater convenience and cheapness, but because its many annotations enforced interpretations of the text of the Bible that supported Calvinistic doctrines. The popularity of the Geneva Bible was naturally disquieting to the authorities of the Church of England, especially since the Genevan annotations bristled with scornful attacks upon the organization of the Anglican church. A revision of the 'Great Bible' was begun under Archbishop Matthew Parker, and four years later, in 1568, was handsomely published as the official translation of the Church of England. A revision of 'The Bishops' Bible,' as this version came to be called, was issued in 1572. Although it incorporated most of the attractive innovations of the Geneva Bible, except for the more extreme Calvinistic annotations, it never achieved the popularity of the Geneva Bible. It remained for the King James version to supersede, slowly, over several decades, the popular Geneva version.

One other translation of the sixteenth century calls for special mention— the English version of the Scriptures produced by the Roman Catholics. Like the Geneva Bible, and unlike the Bishops' Bible and the King James version, the Catholic Bible was fully supplied with annotations to emphasize the particular interpretation of Biblical texts that supported the doctrinal points of view of its sponsors. The Roman Catholic translation of the New Testament was first published at Rheims in 1582; the Old Testament at Douai in 1609. The Rheims New Testament was reprinted in 1610 at Douai, making the complete

Bible available in two volumes. The Rheims-Douai Bible was based primarily on the Latin *Vulgate*, and is not a direct ancestor of the King James version, although its translators also made use of previous English translations. The Roman Catholic translation therefore provides an interesting contrast to the Protestant translations that are the direct ancestors of the King James version.

In our text we have followed the spelling and the punctuation of the original except for a few minor typographical conventions of sixteenth-century printing. We have not included the marginal notes, or the annotations at the end of the chapter, but where the notes are of particular significance we have mentioned them in our own notes.

MODERN EDITIONS: Not all of the innumerable modern editions of the King James or 'Authorized Version' include the translators' preface. The edition in the Tudor Translations, 6 vols., London, 1903–4; and that by W. A. Wright, Cambridge English Classics, 5 vols., Cambridge, 1909, contain this important preface. For other versions see: S. Bagster, *The English Hexapla, Exhibiting Six Important English Translations of the New Testament Scriptures*, London, 1841.

COMMENT: B. J. Westcott, *A General View of the History of the English Bible* (3rd ed., rev. by W. A. Wright), London, 1905; A. S. Cook, *The Authorized Version of the Bible and Its Influence*, New York, 1910; H. Guppy, *Catalogue of an Exhibition Illustrating the History of the Transmission of the Bible*, Manchester, 1935; *The English Bible* (ed. by V. F. Storr), New York, 1938; *The Bible in Its Ancient and English Versions* (ed. by H. W. Robinson), Oxford, 1941; C. C. Butterworth, *The Literary Lineage of the King James Bible*, Philadelphia, 1941; D. Daiches, *The King James Version of the English Bible*, Chicago, 1941.

TEXTS: *The Holy Bible . . . Newly Translated*, 1611 (2216) [KING JAMES], Huntington; *The newe Testament*, 1534 (2826) [TYNDALE], Huntington; *The Byble in Englyshe*, 1539 (2068) [GREAT BIBLE], Huntington; *The Bible and Holy Scriptures*, 1560 (2093) [GENEVA], Huntington; *The holie Byble*, 1572 (2107) [BISHOPS' BIBLE (revised)], Harvard; *The New Testament of Iesus Christ*, 1582 (2884) [RHEIMS], Huntington.

1051 12 Scripture] 1 *Samuel*, 2.30. 13 Eusebius] bishop of Nicomedia, and later of Constantinople (d. 341); banished from Nicomedia because of refusal to sign the condemnation of Arius pronounced by Council of Nicea; restored through influence of the sister of Constantine. 27 *Jacob*] see *Genesis*, 29.10. 31 *Esay*] *Isaiah*, 29.11.

1052 1 *Ptolome Philadelph*] Ptolemy II, Philadelphus (285–247 B.C.). 3 *Seventy* Interpreters] the *Septuagint* Version was the first translation of the Hebrew Old Testament made into popular Greek before the Christian era; the name comes from the legend that it was the work of seventy-two translators. 31 *Aquila*] one of the Jewish companions of Saint Paul, confused by tradition with another Aquila (fl. 130 A.D.), a proselyte from Christianity who made a new translation of the Old Testament from a different Hebrew text from that used for the *Septuagint* version. 32 *Theodotion, Symmachus*] both flourished at the end of the second century A.D., but it is uncertain which had priority as a Biblical translator. 33 fift and sixt edition] both Aquila and Symmachus produced two editions, later referred to by St. Jerome. 34 *Hexapla*] the name given to

the edition by Origen (185–253) of the Old Testament in Hebrew and Greek; this edition gives six parallel texts: (1) the Hebrew text in Hebrew characters; (2) the Hebrew text in Greek characters; (3) the version of Aquila; (4) the version of Symmachus; (5) the *Septuagint* version; (6) the version of Theodotion. 39 *Epiphanius*] a translator of various Greek theological works into Latin in the sixth century A.D. 42 *Justinian*] (527–565), Roman Emperor.

1053 4 Saint *Hierome*] Saint Jerome (*c.* 340–420 A.D.), Christian theologian and scholar; translator of the Bible, whose Latin version incorporated the best scholarship of his time, and became the accepted version of the Roman Catholic Church. The *Vulgate*, as the official Latin Bible of the Catholic Church came to be called, is basically the product of Jerome's scholarship; later versions of the *Vulgate* are revisions of Jerome's work. 19 S. *Augustine*] in *De doctrina Christiana*, ii.11. 32 Ethnicks] pagans. 35 good Lepers] see 2 *Kings*, 7.9.

1054 12 *Clement the 8.*] Pope Clement VIII (1536–1605); he ordered a revised edition of the *Vulgate* in 1592. 26 meteyard] yard measure. 39 *What . . . Lord?*] *Jeremiah*, 23.28. 40 Tertullian] Church Father (150–230 A.D.).

1055 2 *Sanballat*] a Samaritan; the most hostile opponent of Nehemiah in his efforts to restore the city of Jerusalem and its walls. 2 *Tobiahs*] Tobias, son of Tobit, in the apochryphal *Book of Tobit.* 41 *in many . . . all*] James, 3.2.

1056 33 *Sixtus*] Pope Sixtus V (1521–1590).

1057 5 *Gratian*] The Decree of Gratian was issued about 1150 A.D. 35 variety of senses] Where the word in the original has more than one meaning, the translators of the King James version have put the alternative meanings in the margin. 39 S. *Chrysostome*] Saint John Chrysostom (347–407), a celebrated father of the Greek Church.

1058 17 conferences of places] concordances. 32 vulgar edition] the *Vulgate.* 38 *Paul* the second] Pope Paul II (1418–1471); pope, 1464–71.

1059 23 κράββατουν, σκίμπους] both words mean a couch or bed. 24 *Cucurbita*] a gourd. 25 *Hedera*] an ivy-vine. 42 copy] L. *copia;* abundance.

1060 1–2 old . . . other] the criticism is directed against the Geneva Bible. 5 late translation] the Rheims-Douai Bible (1609–10), the English translation of the Roman Catholics. 18–19 Ye . . . Philistines] see *Genesis,* 26.15 ff. 24 *Gergesites*] inhabitants of Gergesenes on the sea of Galilee; see *Matthew,* 8.28–34. 27 Nazianzene] Gregory Nazian-

zen (325–390), one of the fathers of the Eastern Church.

1062 The marginal notes in the King James version are confined to giving references to other scriptural passages, and to giving the variant meanings of certain words. In Tyndale's New Testament (1534), the notes in the margin give indications of the subjects treated in the adjacent verses, and also give references to corresponding passages of Scripture.

1063 The Geneva Bible has many marginal notes enforcing the Calvinist interpretation of the passage annotated. The notes in the Bishops' Bible merely cite concordances. The Rheims New Testament has marginal notes giving explanatory comment; e.g. opposite verse 3: 'The right Beatitudes which are a part of the Catechism.' At the end of each chapter there is a paragraph of annotations explaining doctrinal points and attacking the false interpretations of the 'heretics.'

1064 KING JAMES, verse 11: falsely] The marginal note gives: 'Gr. lying,' indicating the more literal translation.

1066 KING JAMES, verse 15: bushel] annotated in the margin: 'The word in the original signifieth a measure containing about a pint less than a peck.' These annotations indicating the more literal translation of the original Greek are preserved in most modern editions of the 'Authorized' or King James version.

THOMAS DEKKER

THOMAS DEKKER (*c.* 1572–1632), poet dramatist, and pamphleteer, lived, wrote, and died in London. As a dramatist Dekker wrote or collaborated in a great number of plays for Henslowe's company, the best known today being *The Shoemaker's Holiday,* acted in 1599—a play based on Thomas Deloney's novel *The Gentle Craft* (1598). His many pamphlets as a journalist covered a wide range; they may be conveniently grouped under such headings as social satire, tales dealing with the rogues and criminals of the Elizabethan underworld, and accounts of the recurring plagues that visited London; yet these three groups would not cover the full variety of Dekker's journalistic writings, for his *Four Birds of Noah's Ark* (1609) could be classed as devotional literature, and he had a hand in the compilation of various collections that belong to the popular category of jest-books. Among the best known of his pamphlets that might be put under the heading of social satire in his ironic book of etiquette, *The Gull's Hornbook* (1609); to the literature of roguery his principal contributions were *The Bellman of London* and *Lanthorn and Candlelight,* both of 1608 but many times reprinted; of his numerous plague-pamphlets *The Wonderful Yeare* (1603) represents some of Dekker's liveliest and most characteristic writing. The 'Wonderful year' was 1603, marked by three great events that would each have afforded unparalleled opportunities for the Elizabethan journalist: first, the sickness and death of Queen Elizabeth in March, and her burial at Westminster in April; second, the proclamation of James VI of Scotland as her successor and his peaceful accession as James I of England; and finally, the severe plague that London suffered throughout the summer, making 1603 one of the very worst of the plague years.

MODERN EDITIONS: *Non-Dramatic Works of Thomas Dekker* (ed. by A. B. Grosart), Huth Library, 5 vols., London, 1884–86; *The Wonderfull yeare* (ed. by G. B. Harrison), The Bodley Head Quartos, London, 1924; **The Plague Pamphlets of Thomas Dekker* (ed. by F. P. Wilson), Oxford, 1925; *The Guls Horne-booke* (ed. by R. B. McKerrow), London, 1904; *Foure Birds of Noahs Arke* (ed. by F. P. Wilson), Stratford-on-Avon, 1924.

COMMENT: The editors' introductions to the separate works listed above; and M. L. Hunt, *Thomas Dekker*, New York, 1911; K. L. Gregg, *Thomas Dekker: A Study in Economic and Social Backgrounds*, Univ. Wash. Publ., Vol. ii, No. 22, Seattle, 1924, pp. 55–112; for Dekker's 'Characters' see *The Overburian Characters* (ed. by W. J. Paylor), Oxford, 1936; P. Shaw, 'The Position of Thomas Dekker in Jacobean Prison Literature,' *PMLA*, lxii (1947), 366–91.

TEXT: *The Wonderfull yeare*, 1603 (6534*), Bodleian [Wood 616 (1)].

1082 10] The earlier part of Dekker's treatise has told of the death of Queen Elizabeth, and the proclamation of James as king; Dekker now turns to a description of the plague. 28 anthropophagized] the marginal note reads: 'Anthropophagi are Scythians that feed on men's flesh.' 31 40,000] Dekker's totals are not exaggerated; they are confirmed by the bills of mortality for the year 1603.

1083 16 mandrakes shrieking] The mandrake plant had a forked root and was thought to resemble the human form; it was fabled to emit a shriek when pulled up from the ground.

1085 1 *Mare mortuum*] sea of death. 9 Dunkirk] At this time Dunkirk was a nest of pirates who preyed on the ships of all nations. 11 scrubbing] scratching. 24 Gravesend] a town below London at the mouth of the Thames; Dekker's pun is obvious. 35 phlebotomies] bleedings. 35 electuaries] medicines. 36 diacatholicons] an old term for a laxative electuary. 36 diacodions] opiates. 39–40 Hippocrates . . . Fernelius] famous physicians from ancient Greek times to the 16th century; Jean Fernel (1497–1558) was a famous French physician.

1086 5 Desper-vewes] poor beggars; O. F. *despourveu*. 6 velvet caps] the distinctive garb of a physician. 9 *aurum potabile*] potable gold; supposed to be a sovereign remedy for all diseases; as usual, Dekker cannot let pass an opportunity for a pun. 11 canvas] to beat.

1088 12 mad Greek] merry fellow. 17 snap hance] spring fastening. 18 King Henry . . . Boulogne.] Henry VIII took Boulogne in 1544; hence the flask was a very old one. 24 oriently] brightly. 24 Hamburgers] citizens of Hamburg. 26 Admiral] flagship. 42 golls] a facetious term for 'hands.'

1089 10 tokens] signs of the plague. 26 ale-cunner] inspector of ale. 39 gulch] glutton.

1090 35 angel] a gold coin valued at 6s. 8d.; a crown was 5s.

1091 18 hobbinolls] rude countrymen. 30 western pugs] men who navigated barges down the Thames to London.

JOHN STOW

JOHN STOW (1525–1605), chronicler and antiquary, spent much of his early life as a tailor in London, where he was a member of the Merchant Taylors' Company. The beginning of his long career as a scholar and historian was marked by his editing of the collection of the works of Chaucer (in which he included a few non-Chaucerian poems) that was published by John Kingston in 1561. To the next collected edition of Chaucer, which Thomas Speght edited many years later in 1598, Stow contributed valuable notes. In 1565 Stow published his *A Summary of English Chronicles*, which initiated a long controversy between Stow and the printer Richard Grafton, who two years before had published his *Abridgement of the Chronicles of England* and was irked by the competition resulting from the appearance of Stow's *Summary*, which had both abridged and enlarged editions. Stow was a member of the old Society of Antiquaries formed by Archbishop Matthew Parker in 1572. His editorial work for Parker brought him into association with the printer Reginald Wolfe who was preparing, at the time of his death in 1573, to publish a universal History. Wolfe's design was carried out in 1577 on a more modest scale by Raphael Holinshed, to whom Stow, from his historical knowledge, gave a variety of assistance; he made still further contributions to the enlarged second edition of Holinshed's *Chronicles* in 1587. Stow's principal historical work was first published in 1580 as *The Chronicles of England from Brute unto this present year . . . 1580*. In later editions this work was revised and brought up to date, and from 1592 was given the new title of *The Annals of England*. After Stow's death it was continued, beginning in 1615, by Edmund Howes. Stow's intimate knowledge of the history and antiquities of his native city are manifest in his greatest work, *A Survey of London*, first published in 1598, and revised and augmented by Stow for another edition in 1603. Later editions were revised and enlarged by Anthony Munday and by Humphrey Dyson.

MODERN EDITIONS: **A Survey of London* (ed. by C. L. Kingsford), 2 vols., Oxford, 1908.

COMMENT: Kingsford's introduction to his edition, and his *Additional Notes to 'A Survey of London*,' Oxford, 1927.

TEXT: *A Survay of London*, 1598 (23341), Folger.

1092 24 Fulcardus] misprint for Sulcardus, a monk of Westminster about 1075, author of a treatise *De Constitutione Ecclesiae Westmonasteriensis*. 27 Sebert] first Christian king of the East Saxons (d. *c.* 616). 28–29 Walsingham] Thomas Walsingham (d. 1422?), monk and historian; chief contemporary authority for reigns of Richard II to Henry V. 33 T. Clifford] Thomas Clifford; possibly a friend who supplied Stow with information; the two citations Stow attributes to Clifford are from an anonymous contemporary life of Edward the Confessor (d. 1066), dedicated to his widow, Eadgyth.

1093 21 staple] a town or place appointed by royal authority in which a body of merchants had exclusive right of purchase and sale of a particular commodity for export.

1095 7 this city] London.

1096 15–16 *in re non . . . necessaria*] in truth not uncertain, just as in speech not necessary. 34 indifferently] equally.

1097 16 Hippodamus] of Miletus, the Greek architect and engineer who laid out the Piraeus, the harbor of ancient Athens. 21–23 *Non idem . . . possunt.*] The greatness of a city lies not in the size of its population but in the numbers of its citizens capable of bearing arms. 25 mediocrity] moderate degree. 30 *honos . . . est*] honors are in fact a burden. 36 naughty packs] worthless persons.

1098 17 Comminaltie] the governing body; i.e. the House of Commons. 29 fee-farm] the rent of a borough to be paid as a form of tax to the ruler of the state. 33 general contribution] the levy of a special tax upon the citizens for the purpose. 38 companies] the livery companies, or guilds, of the city of London.

1099 6 Polydore] Polydore Vergil the historian; see introduction and notes to Edward Halle. 6–9 *Mercatores . . . esset*] Merchants indeed were very often the free givers of a great deal of money, as trade (an art which all fair-minded mortals agree is both useful and necessary), in his reign was to be more abundant. 22–3 *oportet . . . emacem*] it behooves the head of a family to be eager to sell, not to buy.

1100 5–6 *Mercatura . . . vituperandi*] Trade, if it be meager, is esteemed sordid, but if it be great and abundant, is not censured. 7 *intus canere*] seek their own interest.

1101 40 only] alone.

1102 14 *dicenda . . . locutus*] to have expressed myself by speaking and by remaining silent. 19 *qui . . . custos*] who, unless He protects a state, the defender stands guard in vain.

JOHN FLORIO

John (or Giovanni) Florio (1553–1625), language teacher and translator, was born in London, the son of Michael Angelo Florio, an Italian Protestant refugee, teacher, minister, and member of the household of Sir William Cecil. After spending his youth abroad, he returned to England and became a teacher of Italian and the author of many lively textbooks. The first of these, *Florio His First Fruites*, consisting of an Italian grammar and forty-four dialogues, with the English and Italian in parallel columns, was published in 1578. Shortly thereafter Florio moved to Oxford, where language teaching continued to be his chief means of livelihood. At Oxford he made the acquaintance of Hakluyt, who employed him to make a translation of Ramusio's account of the voyages to North America of Jacques Cartier, which Hakluyt arranged to have published in 1580, and later included in his collection of *Divers Voyages* in 1582. Florio also made the acquaintance of the poet Samuel Daniel while at Oxford, and married Daniel's sister. On returning to London, Florio was employed from 1583 until about 1589 at the French embassy. When Giordano Bruno came to England in 1583, he and Florio were fellows for two years in the service of the French Ambassador. After Florio left the French embassy, Lord Burghley seems to have appointed him as Italian tutor to the young noblemen who were his wards: the Earls of Southampton, Rutland, and Bedford. It was chiefly to these three families that Florio looked for patronage in his later career. His Italian-English Dictionary *A Worlde of Wordes* (1598) was dedicated to the Earls of Southampton and Rutland and to Lucy Russell, the Countess of Bedford. The second edition, in 1611, was dedicated to Queen Anne, the wife of James I.

Florio's most important work is his translation of Montaigne's *Essays*, licensed in 1600 and printed in 1603 in three books, with an individual dedication to each book—the first to the Countess of Bedford and Lady Anne Harrington; the second to the Countess of Rutland and Lady Rich; the third to Lady Elizabeth Grey and Lady Mary Neville, two of his favorite pupils. Florio's translation of Montaigne displays both the virtues and the defects of most Elizabethan translations. It has the vigorous raciness, the picturesque metaphors, the delight in proverbs, the vivid amplifications of its original, and the lively colloquialism of style that characterize the other great translations of the age, and make most of the later, more literal, translations seem dull and anemic by comparison. Yet it has, in larger measure than most others, the common defects of frequent inaccuracy, a delight in amplification that often leads the translator to misrepresent the style and even the sense of his original, and a habit of incorporating the foreign word in the English text—a habit that may enrich the English language but is just as likely to produce only awkwardness and ambiguity. Florio was peculiarly susceptible to such defects, since neither French nor English was his native tongue. The number of neologisms which the *New English Dictionary* credits to Florio is extremely high. Moreover, Florio often misinterprets the meaning of Montaigne, or, failing to apprehend it clearly, puts it into English that is both clumsy and well-nigh meaningless. We can forgive Florio for his infelicities and praise him for his virtues, but we must recognize that we have before us not a faithful reproduction of Montaigne himself, but very definitely *Florio's* Montaigne.

Many of Florio's mistranslations in the first edition of 1603 he corrected in the second edition of 1613. We have based our text on the first edition, but have adopted the readings of the second whenever they are clearer and closer to Montaigne's French than those of the first.

MICHEL EYQUEM DE MONTAIGNE (1533-1592) was born at his father's château near Bordeaux. He received his early education at home, and he learned Latin before he knew his native tongue. He then spent seven years at the Collège de Guienne, where he perfected his knowledge of the classics. After studying t' law, he was appointed counsellor of the Bordeaux Parliament, where he became acquainted with Etienne de la Boétie, to whom he addressed his essay on friendship. The difference between Bacon and Montaigne is strikingly mirrored in their essays on this subject: in Bacon friendship is utilitarian; between Montaigne and Boétie, friendship existed 'because it was he, because it was myself.' Although he was twice elected mayor of Bordeaux, Montaigne spent most of his life in studious retirement: his favorite studies were Seneca, and Amyot's *Plutarch*. The first two books of his essays were published in 1580; the third book, containing essays about four times as long as those in the first two books, was published in 1588.

MODERN EDITIONS: *The Essayes* (ed. by George Saintsbury), Tudor Translations, 3 vols., London, 1892-93; *The Essayes* (ed. by A. R. Waller), The Temple Classics, 6 vols., London, 1897-1902; **The Essayes* (ed. by J. I. M. Stewart), 2 vols., Oxford, 1931; †*The Essayes*, Everyman's Library, 3 vols., London, 1915-21; †*The Essayes*, The World's Classics, 3 vols., Oxford, 1904-6. The best modern translation is *The Essays of Montaigne* (trans. by G. B. Ives), 4 vols., Harvard, 1925.

COMMENT: Frances A. Yates, *John Florio*, Cambridge, 1934; F. O. Matthiessen, *Translation: An Elizabethan Art*, Harvard, 1931; A. Kozul, 'L'Offrande d'un Traducteur,' *Rev. Ang.-Am.*, ix (1931-32), 287-304, 508-24.

TEXT: *The Essayes*, 1603 (18041), Folger [Harmsworth copy].

1102 35 THE NINETEENTH CHAPTER] This chapter was the twentieth in the first edition of Montaigne's *Essaies* (1580); in the 1595 edition the editors transposed chapter 14 to chapter 40, with a consequent change in the numbers of the later chapters. Most modern editions follow the numbering of the 1580 edition of the first book of the *Essaies;* hence this essay appears as chapter 20. 39 Cicero] in *Tusculan Disputations*, i.30, which is an imitation of Plato's *Phaedo*.
1103 15 *Qui . . . retro*] Lucretius, *On the Nature of Things*, iv. 472. Montaigne usually incorporates Latin verses in his text, without, in general, identifying them; he does not translate them into French. Florio translates the lines into awkward English couplets, and usually their source appears in the margin. A better translation of this line would be: 'Who places himself with his head where his feet should be.'
1104 16-17 *Omnem . . . hora*] Horace, *Epistles*, i.4.13.
1105 2 Aristotle] see Cicero, *Tusculan Disputations*, i.39.; the river is the Hypanis, in Scythia. Florio failed to read his text carefully. 21 *Cur . . . recedis?*] Lucretius, iii.938. 28-29 *cur . . . omne?*] Lucretius, iii.940-1. 35 disposition] arrangement of things. 39

Non alium . . . aspicient] Manilius, *Astronomicon*, i.522.
1106 7-8 *multo . . . videmus*] Lucretius, iii.926. 16-17 *Respice . . . fuerit*] Lucretius, iii.972. 32 she ever being one] death ever being the same.
1107 5 equipage] parade. 9 FIVE AND TWENTIETH CHAPTER] the 26th chapter in the 1580 edition of the *Essaies*, and in most modern editions. 24 four parts of the Mathematics] arithmetic, music, geometry, and astronomy; the medieval *quadrivium*. 37 Danaïdes] daughters of Danaus, who, for the murder of their husbands, were condemned in Hades forever to fill with water a jar with holes in the bottom. 41 as Cleanthes said] see Seneca, *Epistles*, 108.10.
1108 14 Plutarch] see his *Table Talk*, v.7. 33 precedent chapter] entitled: 'Of Pedantry.' 40 marriage] Montaigne was present as proxy for the father and mother of the groom at the signing of the marriage contract.
1109 4-5 greatest . . . importing] greatest and most important difficulty. 18 Cymon, Themistocles] see Plutarch's essay, *Why Divine Justice Sometimes Defers the Punishment of Evil-Doers*, 6. 19 differed . . . themselves] Florio's revision in the 1613 ed.; 1603 reads 'degenerated' instead of 'differed.' Montaigne's text: *combien ils sont discon-*

venuz à eux mesmes; 'how inconsistent they were with themselves.' 27 address . . . matters] 1603 reads 'sciences,' instead of 'matters.' Montaigne: *à dresser les enfants aux choses auxquelles ils ne peuvent prendre goust;* 'training children to things to which they can not take a liking.' 32 Commonwealth] *Republic,* books iii, v, and vii.

1110 17 *Che no . . . m'aggrada*] Dante, *Inferno,* xi.93; taken by Montaigne from Guazzo's *Civil Conversation.* 23–24 *Non sumus . . . vindicet*] see Seneca, *Epistles,* 33.11.

1111 10 the pip] 1613; 'rheum,' 1603. Montaigne: *pepie;* the pip is a disease of birds, but in English the term is colloquially applied to a variety of mild diseases in human beings; e.g., a cold, or slight indisposition. 34–35 *Æque . . . nocebit*] Horace, *Epistles,* i.1.25.

1112 29 a German] Dr. Horstanus, who later became professor in the Collège de Guienne.

1113 11 Grouchy] the persons mentioned in this and the following lines were eminent humanist scholars in the group connected with the Collège de Guienne in the early years of its history.

1114 32–33 which to do well . . . mind] which, if it is to do any good, should not only be lodged within us, but should be espoused.

EDWARD GRIMESTON

EDWARD GRIMESTON (?–1640), the translator, was the second son of the Edward Grimeston who was controller of Calais until its fall in 1557 and later, under Queen Elizabeth, held many diplomatic posts and served as a member of Parliament. There is no record of when he was born, but after some eight years in France he returned to England, received in 1610 the post of sergeant-at-arms to wait upon the Speaker of the House of Commons, and spent the rest of his life in the discharge of his not-too-arduous official duties, and in the literary activity of translation. Most of his translations were from the French; his efforts made available to English readers the contemporary works on the history of the other countries of Europe. A firm believer in the usefulness of history to his countrymen, he also saw the utility of a clear, concise treatise on the contemporary doctrines of human psychology. This prompted his translation of Bishop Nicholas Coeffeteau's *Tableau des passions humaines,* which was published in 1621. Grimestone's style is characterized by simplicity and lucidity; rhetorical ostentation is notably absent from his writing.

NICHOLAS COEFFETEAU (1574–1623), French theologian, philosopher and preacher, was a member of the Dominican order and noted for his brilliance as a student and interpreter of Aristotle and Thomas Aquinas. In the Church he rose to the position of Bishop of Dardania. His *Tableau des passions humaines* was first published at Paris in 1615, and had later editions in 1620 and 1623.

MODERN EDITIONS: None.

COMMENT: G. N. Clark, 'Edward Grimeston, the Translator,' *EHR,* xliii (1928), 585–98.

TEXT: *A Table of Humane Passions,* 1621 (5473), Folger.

1121 20 retiring] drawing them forth again; Fr. *retirer.*

SIR WALTER RALEGH

SIR WALTER RALEGH (*c.* 1552–1618), soldier, sailor, courtier, statesman, colonizer, scholar, patron of poets and scientists, and himself a poet and historian, was engaged at one time or another during his career in nearly all the multifarious activities we associate with the Elizabethan age. A recent biographer has termed him, not inappropriately, 'the last of the Elizabethans.' Even an epitome of his tumultuous life would require more space than is available here; the student must therefore refer to the biographies of Ralegh, while we confine

ourselves here to the details that are most closely related to Ralegh's prose writings and their historical background. From the time he returned to England in 1581, after a career as a soldier in Ireland, Ralegh rose quickly in royal favor, wealth, and power. His influence throughout the next two decades was consistently exerted in promoting discovery and colonization in the New World, and in advancing England's naval power; he was ever an ardent partisan of the theory that military advantage would ever be on the side of the nation that controlled the sea. In the years when England was threatened by the Spanish navy Ralegh's reports to the Privy Council balanced the influence of the Earl of Leicester, who was not as vigorous as Ralegh in championing sea power. After the dispersal of the Spanish Armada in 1588 had magnificently vindicated Ralegh's strategy and his naval tactics, and Leicester had died later in the same year, Ralegh and the young Earl of Essex became rivals for the topmost place at the court of Elizabeth. Ralegh was the mainspring inspiring the naval harassment of Spain during the ensuing years; and the expeditions in which Ralegh participated would have resulted in more decisive gains for England had his strategy been followed. Elizabeth herself was responsible for the military blunder of forcing a division of command between the two feuding parties of Essex and Ralegh. The attack on Cadiz in 1596 and the Island voyage in 1597, both proved, because of the lack of a unified command, to be no more than brilliant military exploits; the opportunity for a conclusive victory was not seized. Before the first of these expeditions Ralegh had made his first voyage to the Orinoco, and on his return had published an account of his discoveries and a plea for English colonization in that area because of its richness in natural resources and (what was of more interest) in gold, which his subordinate, Captain Keymis, was asserted to have found. The *Discovery of Guiana* (1596) was one of the three important prose works published by Ralegh before his death; the first was his *Report* (1591) of the last fight of Sir Richard Grenville when his ship, the *Revenge*, was cut off by a Spanish fleet in the Azores. His most important work is his *History of the World*, written while he was imprisoned in the Tower of London for alleged complicity in plots against James I. Cast into prison, tried, and sentenced to death in 1603, he was reprieved and spent the ensuing years of captivity, with the aid of friends who visited him and supplied him with books, in the composition of his *History*, in which he planned to show the working of God's Providence in the affairs of men and of nations from the Creation to recent times—but perhaps, for the sake of discretion, not too recent. In any event, the death in 1612 of his young patron, Henry Prince of Wales, led him to break off with the year 168 B.C., and to publish the book in 1614. Ralegh's *History*, although but a fragment of the vast design originally intended, remained popular with English readers as the standard universal history until the eighteenth century. Well over a dozen editions appeared before 1700.

Ralegh's petitions to James I for pardon and release from the Tower were finally granted only on condition that he make another voyage to Guiana and bring back the gold he claimed was to be found there. His last voyage proved financially disappointing to Ralegh's royal master, and aroused protests from Spain. To appease Spain, James I finally ordered Ralegh's execution, in spite of many intercessions on his behalf; he was beheaded on October 29, 1618.

MODERN EDITIONS: *Works* (ed. by W. Oldys), 8 vols., Oxford, 1829; *The Discovery of Guiana* (ed. by V. T. Harlow), London, 1928; *The last Fight of the Revenge* (ed. by E. Arber), English Reprints, 1871; *Selections from the Historie of the World, etc.* (ed. by G. E. Hadow), Oxford, 1917.

COMMENT: E. Edwards, *The Life of Sir Walter Ralegh*, 2 vols., London, 1868; W. Stebbing, *Sir Walter Ralegh*, Oxford, 1891 and 1899; M. A. S. Hume, *Sir Walter Raleigh*, London, 1897; C. H. Firth, *Sir Walter Raleigh's History of the World*, London, 1918 [From *Proc. Brit. Acad.*, vol. viii]; M. Waldman, *Sir Walter Raleigh*, New York, 1928; V. T. Harlow, *Sir Walter Raleigh's Last Voyage*, London, 1932; E. Thompson, *Sir Walter Ralegh: The Last of the Elizabethans*, London, 1935; C. F. Tucker Brooke, 'Sir Walter Ralegh as Poet and Philosopher,' *ELH*, v (1938), 93–112 [reprinted in *Essays on Shakespeare and Other Elizabethans*, New Haven, 1948]; E. Strathmann, *Sir Walter Ralegh: A Study in Elizabethan Skepticism*, New York, 1951.

TEXT: *The History of the World*, 1614 (20637), Folger.

1124 4] In the preceding paragraphs Ralegh has reviewed the history of the Kings of England from the Norman Conquest as exemplifications of God's justice and Providence.

1125 22] The omitted paragraphs cite other examples of God's justice, chiefly from modern French history and from ancient history. 39 creation in time] Aristotle's theory that the world had no beginning and would exist forever was the chief objection to his cosmology advanced by Christian theologians of the Middle Ages and Renaissance.

1126 16 Charron] Pierre Charron (1541–1603), noted French philosopher, whose *De la Sagesse* was published in 1601; translated into English in 1612. 29–30] the inscriptions may be loosely translated, 'contradicting of predecessors prohibited,' 'specific virtue,' 'the Roman Catholic Church.' Aristotelian physics was based on the doctrine that each substance was impressed with a specific power or virtue which impelled it to seek its natural place in the universe; e.g. the element of earth possessed the virtue of 'gravity,' which caused it to seek the center; fire, the virtue of 'levity,' which caused it to move from the center.

1127 3–4 grass . . . colour] a favorite example of the limits of human knowledge; cf. Donne's *The Second Anniversary*, p. 488. 29] the omitted passage continues the discussion of the opinions of ancient philosophers concerning the origin of the world.

1129 24 Berosus] Babylonian priest and historian (3rd cent. B.C.), author of a history of Babylonia in Greek. 34 Aristotle] in his *Politics*, iii.15. 36–38 "Judges . . . judgment."] see *Deuteronomy*, 16.18.

1131 7 Groin] Corunna. 19 St. Iago]

Santiago de Compostella in northwestern Spain. 33 learned gentleman] Sir Clement Edmondes; his *Observations upon Caesar's Commentaries* was published in 1600 and again in 1604.

1132 30 the Ness] Dungeness, on the Channel coast between Rye and New Romney.

1133 30 Tercera] Terceira, one of the principal islands of the Azores. The French in 1582 launched an offensive against the Spaniards in the Azores. 41 Strossie] Philip Strozzi, leader of a French naval force dispatched in 1581 to assist the Spanish pretender, Don Antonio of Portugal, at Terceira.

1134 13 Fayal] one of the islands of the Azores. Ralegh was a subordinate commander to the Earl of Essex in this expedition. 24 greater person] the Earl of Essex.

1137 25 Marcellus] Marcus Claudius Marcellus, the Roman general who captured Syracuse in 212 B.C. 25 quinquereme] having five banks of oars.

1139 18 *Hic jacet*] the common first words of Latin inscriptions on tombstones; literally: 'here lies [buried].' 21–22 *Copy of a Letter . . wife*] The designation in the manuscript continues: 'the night before he expected to be put to death at Winchester, 1603.' King James commuted Ralegh's sentence to execution and confined him to the Tower. 27 Besse] Ralegh had incurred Queen Elizabeth's displeasure in 1592 because of his affair with Elizabeth Throckmorton, one of her maids of honor. On Ralegh's release from the Tower they were married. 41 Brett] Sir Alexander Brett.

1141 1 if the land continue] if my estate at Sherborne continues in your possession.

SIR FRANCIS BACON

SIR FRANCIS BACON (1561–1626), younger son of Sir Nicholas Bacon, Queen Elizabeth's Lord Keeper, and nephew to William Cecil, Lord Burghley, had far too important a career in Elizabethan and Jacobean England for it to be summarized in a few lines. A student at Trinity College, Cambridge, and later at Gray's Inn, a member of Parliament in 1584, his ability and merits were slow at first in obtaining for him political advancement; but after unsuccessful attempts under Elizabeth to obtain the offices of Solicitor-General and of Attorney-General, his steady rise began under James I. Appointed Solicitor-General in 1607, he rose to the Lord Chancellorship in 1618, was created Baron Verulam the same year, and Viscount St. Albans in 1621. Accused of accepting gifts from litigants whose cases he was adjudicating, he plead guilty, was imprisoned, fined, and banished from the court. After his fall, upon the remission of his fine and his release from imprisonment, he retired to his estate of Gorhambury, where he carried on his studies and writing until his death in 1626.

Bacon was hailed by the next generation as the philosopher of modern science; his grandiose plan for the systematic improvement of scientific knowledge was to be elaborated in several parts, which, when published, were together to make up his *Instauratio Magna*. The sketch of the entire plan was published in 1620, with the *Novum Organum*, which was the fulfilment of the second part of the scheme. For the first part, that was still wanting, but which was to comprise the divisions of the sciences, Bacon informed his readers that they might find some account of the matter in the second book of his English treatise *Of the proficience and advancement of Learning* (1605). To supply the first part of his *Instauratio Magna*, Bacon had his earlier work translated and greatly enlarged in Latin as *De Dignitate et Augmentis Scientiarum*, published in 1623. Latin, therefore, was the language in which Bacon gave to the world his principal work, though the grand design of the *Instauratio Magna* was never completed.

Bacon's importance in the history of English prose, therefore, rests on the earlier *Advancement of Learning* (1605), upon his *History of the Raigne of King Henry the Seventh* (1622), upon his unfinished *The New Atlantis*, published posthumously in 1627, and, above all, upon his *Essays*. In the first edition of 1597 there were only ten short essays which fully justify Bacon's own later description of them, in the dedication to Prince Henry of the manuscript for a revised edition, as 'certain brief notes, set down rather significantly than curiously.' The structure of the essays in this first edition would lead one to conjecture that many of them had been transcribed directly from Bacon's commonplace-book, wherein he had set down, under the appropriate headings, collections of aphorisms or *sententiae*. The second printed edition of the *Essays*, in 1612, contained nine essays, much enlarged, from the 1597 edition, and twenty-nine new ones. The final edition, in 1625, contained fifty-eight essays. Although, in their final form the *Essays* still retain their aphoristic quality, Bacon has sought to remedy the abrupt discontinuity of his earlier commonplace-book models by inserting transitional phrases, adding illustrative examples and quotations, and paying greater attention to rhythm and cadence.

Inasmuch as Latin quotations are frequently embedded in Bacon's text, especially in *The Advancement of Learning*, we have, for the reader's convenience, inserted, in square brackets, the English translation immediately afterwards. In this practice we have followed Spedding's edition of Bacon's *Works*.

MODERN EDITIONS: *Works (ed. by J. Spedding, R. L. Ellis, and D. D. Heath), 7 vols., London, 1857–59; *Philosophical Works of Francis Bacon* (ed. by J. M. Robertson, from the edition of Ellis and Spedding), London, 1905; *Essayes (ed. by W. A. Wright), Cambridge, 1862, and London, 1885; *Bacon's Essays* (ed. by R. Whately), revised ed., London, 1867; *A Harmony of the Essays of Francis Bacon* (ed. by E. Arber), English Reprints, London, 1871; *Essays* (ed. by E. A. Abbott), 2 vols., London, 1879 and 1886; *The Advancement of Learning* (ed. by W. A. Wright), Oxford, 1869, 1891, and 1900; †*Bacon's Advancement of Learning and The New Atlantis* (ed. by T. Case), The World's Classics, Oxford, 1906; †*Essays, Advancement of Learning, New Atlantis and Other Pieces* (ed. by R. F. Jones), New York, 1937.

COMMENT: J. Spedding, *Letters and Life of Francis Bacon,* 7 vols., London, 1861–74; R. W. Church, *Bacon,* English Men of Letters, New York, 1884; E. A. Abbott, *Francis Bacon,* London, 1885; C. Williams, *Bacon,* New York, 1933; R. S. Crane, 'The Relation of Bacon's Essays to his Program for the Advancement of Learning,' and M. W. Croll, 'Attic Prose: Lipsius, Montaigne, Bacon,' both in *Schelling Anniversary Papers,* New York, 1923, pp. 87–105, and 117–50; J. Zeitlin, 'The Development of Bacon's Essays,' *JEGP,* xxvii (1928), 496–519; K. R. Wallace, *Francis Bacon on Communication and Rhetoric,* Chapel Hill, 1943; F. H. Anderson, *The Philosophy of Francis Bacon,* Chicago, 1948; B. Farrington, *Francis Bacon: Philosopher of Industrial Science,* New York, 1949.

TEXTS: *Essayes,* 1597 (1137), Huntington; *Essayes,* 1625 (1147), Harvard; *Ms. Sloane* 4259, [*c.* 1611], British Museum; *The Twoo Bookes . . . Of the proficience and aduancement of Learning,* 1605 (1164), Folger.

1142 11 *Of regiment of health*] this was the seventh essay in the 1597 ed.; it was greatly enlarged in 1612, and still more in 1625, where it appeared as No. 30. 17 offense of] harm in. 23 meat] meals. 28 ask opinion of] seek medical advice concerning. 39 *Of Studies*] this was the first essay in the 1597 ed.; in 1625 it was No. 50.

1143 8 without] outside of.

1144 13 *Abeunt . . . mores.*] Studies pass into manners. 16 reins] kidneys. 21 *cymini sectores*] hair-splitters. 25 *Of Friendship*] first added in 1612, and entirely rewritten for 1625. 26 him that spake it] Aristotle, *Politics,* i.1.

1145 9 sarza] sarsaparilla. 25 *participes curarum*] partners in care. 31 Pompey] Bacon derives his information, in the passage that follows, from Plutarch's lives of Pompey and Julius Caesar. Cf. Shakespeare's *Julius Caesar,* derived also from Plutarch's account.

1146 3 *Philippics*] 13.11. 10 Tiberius] see Tacitus, *Annals,* iv.40. 27 Comineus] Philippe de Comines, French historian of the 15th cent.; his history was published at Paris in 1524; an English translation appeared in 1596. 34 parable of Pythagoras] metaphor of Pythagoras, Greek philosopher of the 6th cent. B.C.

1147 3 praying an aid] becoming an advocate; (a legal term).

1150 16 Law] the law of the Hebrews proclaimed by the Lord to Moses; cf. *Leviticus,* 22.18, and *Numbers,* 28.2–3. 22 respective] appropriate. 42 wisest King] Solomon; see *1 Kings,* 4.29.

1152 2 Hermes] Hermes Trismegistus is identified with Thoth, the Egyptian god of wisdom. 4 propriety] quality belonging to an individual. 8 difference] distinguishing mark. 17 undervalues]

deficiencies in value. 28 politics] politicians. 30] The omitted paragraphs discuss the discredits of learning due to the ignorance of zealous divines and of politicians or statesmen. 36 accidental] the term is used in the sense in which it is employed in logic: a property not of the essence or specific nature of a thing. 37 not in hand with true measure] not concerned with true values. 42] the further discussion of the derogations of learning due to the fortunes and the manners of learned men is omitted.

1153 1 morigeration] obsequiousness. 7 Aristippus] the founder of the Cyrenaic school of philosophy; Dionysius was the king of Syracuse (4th cent. B.C.). 15 Adrianus] the Roman emperor Hadrian (2nd cent. A.D.); the philosopher was Favorinus. 27 deprave] depreciate. 38 curious] fastidious.

1154 28 copie] copiousness; abundance and variety. 35 Osorius] (d. 1580); his imitation of the style of Cicero led to his being called 'the Cicero of Portugal.' 36 Sturmius] John Sturm, schoolmaster at Strasbourg and friend of Roger Ascham (q.v.). 38 Car] Nicholas Carr (1523–1568), professor of Greek at Cambridge. 42 *Cicerone*] Erasmus' joke lies in the fact that the last three letters in *Cicerone* form the Greek word for 'ass'; from Erasmus' *Ciceronianus* (1528), a dialogue in which he attacked the educational theories of those of his contemporaries who prescribed the exclusive imitation of Cicero.

1155 7 *secundum . . . minus*] more or less. 22–23 be . . . use of] have any occasion to use.

1157 12 digladiation] wrangling. 36 verse] Horace, *Epistles,* i.18.69.

1158 10 had a passage] passed current; were believed. 19 Arabians] the Arabians transmitted the science of the Greeks to the Middle Ages.

1159 4 save the credit of impostures] make their impostures believed. 20 leeseth] loses.

1160 16 *Antiquitas . . . mundi*] The Antiquity of time is the youth of the world. 25 septuagenary] seventy years old. 26 law Pappia] a law passed in the reign of Augustus granting special political privileges to all who married under a certain age.

1161 31 Heraclitus] Greek philosopher (540–475 B.C.) who held that Fire was the element from which all things sprang. 42 second school of Plato] the ancient

neo-Platonists, a school of philosophy arising in the 3rd cent. A.D.; its chief exponent was Plotinus; the last important writer of this school was Proclus (5th cent. A.D.).

1162 3 Gilbertus] William Gilbert, whose principal work *De Magnete* was published in 1600. 20 magistral] dogmatic. 24 Velleius] a participant in the dialogue in Cicero's *Of the Nature of the Gods*.

1163 20 *Declinat . . . tollit*] 'She swerves from the course and picks up the golden ball.' Ovid, *Metamorphoses*, x. 667. 41] The remainder of the first book deals with the dignity of knowledge, citing both divine evidences and human proofs.

JOHN DONNE

JOHN DONNE (1571/2–1631) was born in London, the son of a successful business man whose death in 1574 left the boy's rearing and education entirely to his mother. She was the daughter of John Heywood, the epigrammatist, sister of Jasper Heywood, the translator of Seneca's tragedies, and a descendant of John Rastell, publisher and brother-in-law of Sir Thomas More. Unwilling to violate such a distinguished Catholic family tree, she saw to it that her son was brought up in the old faith. Donne left Oxford after three years without taking a degree; three years followed at Cambridge, to which he also bade farewell before finishing his course. Doubtless religious scruples prompted these departures, and in May of 1591 he was in London studying law at Thavies' Inn, a year later at Lincoln's Inn.

During these years Donne seems to have taken all available studies in the curriculum to be his province, especially science—'the new philosophy'—and foreign languages. Of the latter he could scarcely get enough, and he wrote to a friend of his excessive hunger for 'humane learning and languages' which threatened to starve out altogether his study of the law. It was while he was a law student that his brother Henry died of a fever in the prison to which he had been committed for harboring a seminary priest, and Donne must have reflected upon the cost of loyalty to an outlawed faith. A tour of the Continent may have preceded or followed the period at Thavies' and Lincoln's Inn. At any rate Donne volunteered for both of Essex's expeditions to Cadiz and the Azores in 1596 and 1597. He had already begun to write: the 1590's witnessed the production of nearly all of his satirical and amatory verse as well as the youthful prose *Paradoxes and Problems*. The latter, though of course not as well known as the poems, also reflect, both in tone and content, the kind of worldly, semi-libertine life about town that Donne seems to have led during these years.

An equally worldly professional career was shipwrecked almost as soon as it had set sail. In 1598 Donne was made secretary to Sir Thomas Egerton, the Lord Keeper, and in 1601 he probably served in Parliament. But he committed the tactical error of falling in love with the Lord Keeper's niece, Anne More, whose wrathful father promptly had Donne dismissed and imprisoned upon his discovery of their secret marriage. The next fourteen years were ones of material poverty and mental despair. Unemployed, refused aid by his wife's father (though Sir George relented somewhat by 1608), Donne was forced to depend upon the good will of various unofficial patrons as he sought to provide for his rapidly multiplying family. He had at least one good offer in 1607, that of clerical appointment, but whether through the pressure of his Catholic background or of lingering hopes for advancement at Court, or of both, Donne refused. It presently became clear, however, that the only kind of advancement he could ever hope for was within the Church, and in 1615 he was ordained. It is true that he resisted ordination until all of his secular hopes were exhausted, but there is no real reason for us to question his integrity when he finally accepted orders.

It was during this so-called 'middle period' of Donne's life that much of his important prose writing was done. In 1610 he published his *Pseudo-Martyr*, a defense of the oath of allegiance, which, according to Walton, was written at the request of King James. If that is true, the writing of the document is another example of the king's singleness of purpose when it came to Donne's future: ecclesiastical, or not at all. Another brief work was *Ignatius his Conclave* (1611), a return in some ways to Donne's earlier satiric vein in its lampooning of Loyola and the Jesuits. But by far the most interesting work of this period and the one of which Donne himself seems to have been particularly fond, though he did not publish it, was *Biathanatos* (1608?). It is usually cited for its qualified defense of suicide, but actually that subject is only a vehicle for Donne's anxious and almost angry questionings of the traditional verities of Christian rational theology. The law of nature, right reason, good and evil themselves are all 'found out,' shown to be relative, not absolute. For all of that, we are never seriously in doubt as to the direction or sureness of Donne's conversion, which, in part, this treatise records. *Biathanatos* shows plainly its author's Jesuit training and Scholastic influence generally. One perfectly normal consequence of that training is always a respect for, if not a worship of, authority. So it was with Donne. His skepticism, though superficially dramatic, is never very fundamental or philosophic. It is confined on the whole to his mistrust of man's ability to perceive truth, though Donne never questions God as the repository of truth—however unknowable that truth may be.

The last third of Donne's life can hardly be called serene, but it was extraordinarily successful. Actually its happiness was marred only by the death of his wife in 1617, to which he reacted with characteristic intensity, now religious, and became practically an ascetic recluse from that time until his own death. In 1616 he had been appointed Reader in Divinity to the benchers of Lincoln's Inn, his last alma mater, and in 1621 he was elevated to the deanship of St. Paul's by King James, where his now fully developed pulpit powers received their most eloquent expression. He was, in addition, vicar of St. Dunstan's from 1624 onwards, where Izaak Walton was one of his parishioners. In 1630 he was considered for a bishopric, but the religious soldier's failing health stood in the way, and in 1631 he died.

With the exception of *Devotions Upon Emergent Occasions* (1624), a packet of *Five Sermons* (1626), and scattered single sermons, the remaining prose works of John Donne, all of them sermons and totalling 160 in all, were published posthumously. The *Devotions* is a highly personal document, written during the course of a near-fatal illness. Another spectacular utterance was the last sermon Donne ever preached, *Death's Duel*, in which he literally set the stage for his own death. All of Donne's sermons are as personal as his poetry, early or late. They will never be studied for their contribution to theology, but they are one of the most honest and—if the term may still be used—uninhibited revelations we have of a single soul struggling with the omnipresent problems of individual sin and retribution. From the point of view of their relation to Donne's congregation (they are so charged with the presence of their author that we sometimes forget that they were preached to others), the best word to describe them is evangelical. Donne never really regarded human reason as a worthy partner of religious intuition; doctrine he always placed second to exhortation. His religious ideas, however encrusted his sermons may be with scholastic and patristic learning, are, as Douglas Bush has remarked, about as simple as General Booth's.

MODERN EDITIONS: *Works* (ed. by H. Alford), 6 vols., London, 1839; **Juvenilia, or Certaine Paradoxes and Problems* (ed. by G. Keynes), London, 1923; **Devotions upon Emergent Occasions* (ed. by J. Sparrow), Cambridge, 1923; *Devotions* (ed. by W. H. Draper), Abbey Classics, London, 1925; *†Complete Poetry and Selected Prose* (ed. by J. Hayward), London, 1930; *†Donne's Shorter Prose Works* (ed. by E. Simpson and R. E. Bennett), New York, 1948.

COMMENT: E. M. Simpson, *A Study of the Prose Works of John Donne*, Oxford 1924; 2nd ed., Oxford, 1948; L. I. Bredvold, 'The Religious Thought of Donne in Relation to Medieval and Later Traditions,' in *Studies in Shakespeare, Milton, and Donne, Univ. Michigan Publ.*, Ann Arbor, 1925; L. I. Bredvold, 'The Naturalism of Donne in Relation to some Renaissance Traditions,' *JEGP*, xxii (1923), 471–502; J. Sparrow, 'Donne and Contemporary Preachers,' *ESEA*, xvi (1931), 144–78; W. F. Mitchell, *English Pulpit Oratory from Andrews to Tillotson*, London, 1932; Itrat-Husain, *The Dogmatic and Mystical Theology of John Donne*, London, 1938; H. H. Umbach, 'The Rhetoric of Donne's Sermons,' *PMLA*, lii (1937), 354–58; M. F. Moloney, *John Donne: His Flight from Medievalism*, Urbana, Illinois, 1944; H. C. White, 'John Donne and the Psychology of Spiritual Effort,' in *The Seventeenth Century: Studies by Richard Foster Jones and Others Writing in His Honor*, Stanford, 1951, pp. 355–68.

TEXT: *Juvenilia*, 1633 (7043), Folger; *A Sermon . . . to the Company of the Virginian Plantation*, 1622 (7051), Folger; *Devotions upon Emergent Occasions*, 1624 (7033), Folger.

1164 41 philosophy . . .] Aristotelian physics postulated that substances had an essential quality of either 'levity' or 'gravity' that caused them to tend to rise or to fall.

1165 6–7 sun . . . contrary] see Recorde's description of the motions of the various celestial spheres, p. 670. 20 only] alone.

1166 7 Virginian Plantation] the colony at Jamestown, Virginia. 15 this book] *The Acts of the Apostles*.

1167 26 Bridewell] a house of correction in London.

1168 17 Apollos] an Alexandrian Jew who came to Ephesus about 49 A.D., where he was converted to Christianity, and became a follower of Saint Paul and an able leader among the early Christians. 19 impeached] impeded.

1170 3 *Devotions*] each of the 23 devotions in the volume is divided into three parts: (1) a meditation upon our human condition; (2) an expostulation; (3) a prayer. 5 first grudging] first symptom or slight trace of an illness. 17 curiosity] care.

1173 24 *Expostulation*] the title of the eleventh devotion is: 'They use Cordials, to keep the venom and Malignity of the disease from the Heart.' Throughout the Expostulation, Donne makes great use of a Biblical concordance and quotes, or alludes to, numerous passages in the Bible referring to the heart.

1174 30 Samuel] see *1 Samuel*, 7.3. 37 Naball] see *1 Samuel*, 25. 40 David] see *1 Samuel*, 24.5.

1175 16 *Meditation*] the seventeenth devotion is the one best known to modern readers because of Ernest Hemingway's novel *For Whom the Bell Tolls*.

1176 7 the main] the mainland.

1177 18 new philosophy] the new scientific theories, especially in physics and astronomy, that were supplanting the older Aristotelian physics; here the specific reference is to the Copernican theory, which placed the center of our universe in the sun, not the earth, with the earth revolving about the sun. 25 epicycles] in the mathematics of astronomy, a small revolving circle that moves around a larger circle so that its center lies constantly on the circumference of that larger circle, called the 'deferent.' This deferent might also be an 'eccentric' circle; i.e. its center might be located at a point other than the center of the universe.

INDEX TO POETRY

Authors' names are printed in small capitals, titles of poems in italics, and first lines of poems in roman.